SELECTED POEMS AND SONGS

ROBERT BURNS was born in 1759 in the village of Alloway in the Kyle district of Ayrshire in south-west Scotland. His father was a smallholder and gardener and then, from 1766, a tenant farmer. Robert and his brother Gilbert moved the family to a farm at Mossgiel, near the village of Mauchline, after their father's death in 1784. Burns, who had written love-songs since his teens, began to write poetry following models borrowed from verse in Scots by Allan Ramsay and Robert Fergusson, as well as from English poets such as Gray, Shenstone, and Goldsmith. Embedded in the alternative, secular networks of social club and masonic lodge, Burns was able to publish *Poems, Chiefly in the Scottish Dialect* at Kilmarnock in 1786. Its fame spread beyond Ayrshire: in 1787 Burns travelled to Edinburgh to arrange a second edition, and was feted on his arrival by the literary establishment there. The Edinburgh edition of *Poems* was a huge success. In 1788 Burns settled with his wife Jean Armour on the farm of Ellisland on the river Nith in Dumfriesshire, and was commissioned into a part-time post in the Excise service. In 1791 he abandoned the farm, moved to an apartment in Dumfries, and became a full-time exciseman. In this period Burns wrote one of his greatest poems, 'Tam o' Shanter', but devoted most of his creative energy to writing lyrics for popular songs: such is the extent of his contribution to James Johnson's *Scots Musical Museum* that it deserves to stand alongside the *Poems* as the other book by Burns. From late 1792, with war looming with the new French Republic, Burns's radical political opinions threatened his government job; but he kept his post and even continued to publish songs with obvious democratic sympathies. Long-standing health problems, the physical demands of his job, and a recurrence of depressive illness, all contributed to his death in 1796.

ROBERT P. IRVINE is Senior Lecturer in English Literature at the University of Edinburgh. His publications include *Enlightenment and Romance: Gender and Agency in Smollett and Scott* (2000) and *Jane Austen* (2005).

OXFORD WORLD'S CLASSICS

*For over 100 years Oxford World's Classics have brought
readers closer to the world's great literature. Now with over 700
titles—from the 4,000-year-old myths of Mesopotamia to the
twentieth century's greatest novels—the series makes available
lesser-known as well as celebrated writing.*

*The pocket-sized hardbacks of the early years contained
introductions by Virginia Woolf, T. S. Eliot, Graham Greene,
and other literary figures which enriched the experience of reading.
Today the series is recognized for its fine scholarship and
reliability in texts that span world literature, drama and poetry,
religion, philosophy, and politics. Each edition includes perceptive
commentary and essential background information to meet the
changing needs of readers.*

ROBERT BURNS

Selected Poems and Songs

Edited with an Introduction and Notes by
ROBERT P. IRVINE

OXFORD
UNIVERSITY PRESS

OXFORD
UNIVERSITY PRESS

Great Clarendon Street, Oxford OX2 6DP
United Kingdom

Oxford University Press is a department of the University of Oxford.
It furthers the University's objective of excellence in research, scholarship,
and education by publishing worldwide. Oxford is a registered trade mark of
Oxford University Press in the UK and in certain other countries

Selection, introduction, and editorial material © Robert P. Irvine 2013
The moral rights of the author have been asserted

First published 2013

First published as an Oxford World's Classics paperback 2014
Impression: 8

Published in the United States of America by Oxford University Press
198 Madison Avenue, New York, NY 10016, United States of America

British Library Cataloguing in Publication Data
Data available

Library of Congress Control Number: 2013943737

ISBN 978-0-19-968232-4

Printed in Great Britain by
Clays Ltd, Elcograf S.p.A.

ACKNOWLEDGEMENTS

As the notes will make clear, this selection owes an enormous if unsurprising debt to twentieth-century editors of Burns, in particular James Kinsley and also, more recently, Carol McGuirk. Any knowledge that this edition can add to theirs is due entirely to the ease with which eighteenth-century texts can now be found and read, and other sources of information traced, online. From my electronic study, across the centuries, a tip of the hat also to William Scott Douglas, whose editions in the 1870s provided an emboldening precedent for the model followed here.

The Beugo portrait from the Edinburgh edition, and the Alloway engraving from Grose's *Antiquities*, are reproduced by kind permission of the Trustees of the National Library of Scotland; gratitude is due to the staff of the NLS, Edinburgh University Library's Centre for Research Collections, and the Advocates Library for all their assistance. Thanks also to Dr Gerard Carruthers and Professor Nigel Leask of the University of Glasgow for their occasional advice and encouragement.

Particular thanks are due to Bob and Jill Elliott for their help with the music, and to Kirsty Law for her transcription of the scores within exacting and, from a purely musical point of view, perhaps eccentric parameters. Robert Burns, in his travails with Stephen Clarke, could have wished for such a collaborator.

CONTENTS

From *Poems, Chiefly in the Scottish Dialect* (Edinburgh, 1787)

Songs from *The Scots Musical Museum*

Songs from *A Select Collection of Original Scotish Airs, for the Voice* (1798–9)

Other poems and songs published in Burns's lifetime

Other poems and songs published posthumously

INTRODUCTION

FEW poets are held in such reverence by so many as Robert Burns, both in his homeland and around the world. The vernacular energy of his verse, the simple beauty of his songs, his anger at injustice and hypoc-risy; and, framing these, the story of his life, of a man of humble origins rising to fame in defiance of prejudice and persecution; these have won him a following since his death so consistent that it is sometimes referred to as a 'cult'. What follows is a brief survey of that life. Burns's own account of the early part of it can be found in his 1787 letter to John Moore included in Appendix 1 of this volume. Where relevant, the notes to individual poems also refer to the poet's biography. The purpose of this introduction, however, is not to ask how the life finds expression in the poetry: the poems themselves are sufficiently eloquent in that regard. Instead, it will outline the role of the poetry in the life: how his writing allowed Burns to build a certain kind of career out of the resources available to him. Burns was not a prodigy, spontaneously moved to song by untutored feeling; nor was he the passive victim of social and economic circumstance. His poetry does not only reflect his society, but was also his way of acting within it: building friendships, courting lovers, cultivating patrons, and cheering those who, in the dangerous days of the mid-1790s, dared to hope for a better one.

1. Early life

Robert Burns was born on 25 January 1759 in Alloway, a small village near the river Doon just south of the town of Ayr in south-west Scotland (see Map, p. 280). He was the first child of Agnes Broun, a local girl, and William Burnes, originally from Kincardineshire in north-east Scotland who had moved south to find work as a gardener after the failure of his father's farm there ('Burness' is the north-east version of the name). The two-room cottage in which Robert was born was built by William himself from stone, clay, and thatch, on his own smallhold-ing. Literate and devout, but theologically liberal by the standards of his adopted county, William decided not to send his sons to the parish school, but with a group of neighbouring families to hire a young teacher, John Murdoch. Under Murdoch Burns was introduced to English verse and prose from an anthology that included extracts from Shakespeare, Milton, Thomson, and *The Spectator*, to add to the prose of the King James Bible familiar from home. He was also taught how to write and speak in English, as opposed to the Scots used in everyday life. Later, Murdoch would give the Burns boys a volume of Pope's poetry, and get Robert started in French.

In 1766, at the age of 45, William left his cottage and his gardening work for a rented farm further inland called Mount Oliphant. Robert and his brother Gilbert continued to attend school for another two years, until Murdoch moved to take a job elsewhere. At that point the boys were put to work on the farm, although William continued to teach them in the evenings. The farm supported a large family (two daughters born in Alloway were followed by another three children at Mount Oliphant) but did not generate the cash that could have paid for hired labour to help work it. At the expiry of the lease in 1777 the family moved to a new farm, Lochlie (now Lochlea), further east again in the parish of Tarbolton, and William died here in 1784.

On these farms the Burns family did not suffer terrible poverty by the standard of the times. But the life was characterized by hard, unremitting labour for the ageing William and his teenage boys, and by chronic economic insecurity. The Ayrshire economy had suffered lasting damage from the collapse, in 1772–3, of the Ayr bank of Douglas, Heron and Co., in which a high proportion of the county's property-owning families had invested. The struggle to rebuild their capital base put pressure on tenant farmers like William Burnes. To encourage agricultural improvement (enclosure, drainage, fertilization, the introduction of new crops and breeds of stock), rents were set at a high level, proportionate to the income the land could generate once improved. But improvement took time to produce results, and the risk of borrowing money to carry it out usually fell on the tenant, not the landowner. At both Mount Oliphant and Lochlie, the ground proved very poor; William spent his last years in a protracted legal battle with his landlord and his landlord's creditors, which he won just weeks before he died. Robert and Gilbert then moved the family to a third farm, Mossgiel, near the small town of Mauchline.

A self-consciously modernizing society like eighteenth-century Scotland presented opportunities as well as pitfalls for men from this background. There were economic opportunities, and Burns was on the lookout for career-paths that could take him away from, or at least reduce his dependence on, the toil and anxiety of farming. In 1775 he had spent a happy summer studying surveying in his mother's home village of Kirkoswald, and in 1782 there was an ultimately disastrous foray into the flax industry of Irvine, Ayrshire's largest town, which precipitated the first of the depressive episodes that would recur throughout his life. The search for economic security eventually led to his obtaining, through local contacts, an offer of work as overseer on one of the many Scottish-owned slave-plantations in Jamaica, to which Burns planned to emigrate in 1786. There were also opportunities for personal improvement, for the cultivation of the self, rather than the soil, and Burns grasped most eagerly at these. At Tarbolton in 1780, he and his friends founded a 'Batchelor's Club' which was at once a social organization and a debating society, a means of facilitating mutual social and intellectual self-improvement independently of church or college. The following year Burns joined the local Masonic Lodge, which fulfilled a similar function and extended his range of acquaintance into more privileged classes than his own. And above all there was reading and writing. Burns read widely in modern English prose and verse: John Locke's *Essay concerning Human Understanding*, Adam Smith's *Theory of Moral Sentiments*, and the novels of Richardson, Smollett, Sterne, and Mackenzie, as well as Dryden, Pope, Thomson, Shenstone, Gray, Collins, and Macpherson's 'Works of Ossian'. Crucially, probably in 1783, Burns discovered poetry in Scots by Robert Fergusson. Burns had been writing poems and songs in English, the language of the library and the debating society, since his late teens. He had known Allan Ramsay's work in Scots, but the near-contemporary Fergusson demonstrated how Ramsay's language and verse-forms could be brought to bear on the modern Scottish scene. This sparked the astonishing creativity of the Mossgiel years, as Burns's poetry vivified an informed, Enlightenment sensibility with the language of the community in which he lived.

In the same period Burns was pursuing sexual experience with similar enthusiasm. It worried his father in his final years, and it continued to worry his family at Mossgiel, but his pleasure in sex was unabashed. Eventually, inevitably, one of his girlfriends got pregnant: Elizabeth Paton, who had worked for the family at Lochlie. This brought Burns before the church authorities who were responsible for the enforcement of sexual discipline at the parish level. Burns had to pay a fine, and sit with Elizabeth in the 'stool of repentance' to be publicly admonished by the minister back in Tarbolton parish church. By the time the child was born in May 1785, the relationship had ended, and Burns had become engaged to Jean Armour, the daughter of a Mauchline stonemason. Jean was pregnant by March 1786. Hoping to avoid scandal, her parents hurried her out of the parish to relatives in Paisley, away from the prying eyes of the Kirk Session and, most importantly, away from Burns, with whom she was denied contact. In the eyes of Burns, Jean's apparent acquiescence in her parents' tactics looked like the breaking-off of their engagement. In the eyes of the respectable Armours, Robert Burns had no means of supporting their daughter and her child, with little money and no apparent prospects.

2. *The Kilmarnock edition*

Yet Burns did have prospects. His poems had been circulating in manuscript among his friends, and among his friends' friends. That he was widely known as a poet through this local network put him in a position to do something he could not otherwise have risked: publish a book. Rather than pay a printer to produce a volume in the hope that it would at least recoup its costs in the marketplace, Burns could invite 'subscriptions' which amounted to promises to buy the book in advance. And so he had a prospectus printed, dated 14 April 1786, and headed,

PROPOSALS,

FOR PUBLISHING BY SUBSCRIPTION,

SCOTCH POEMS,

BY ROBERT BURNS.

The Work to be elegantly Printed in One Volume, Octavo.
Price Stitched *Three Shillings.*

As the Author has not the most distant Mercenary view in Publishing,
as soon as so many Subscribers appear as will defray the necessary Expence,
the Work will be sent to the Press.

Three shillings, though still more than most people could afford, was relatively cheap for a new book in this format. The records of the printer, John Wilson of Kilmarnock, show that at least 400 copies were ordered in this way, justifying a print-run of 612 in total. Of those subscriptions, 145 were collected by Burns's friend in Ayr, the lawyer Robert Aiken; 72 by Kilmarnock wine merchant Robert Muir; 70 by Burns's brother Gilbert; 41 by Mauchline draper James Smith; and 40 by Mauchline lawyer Gavin Hamilton. *Poems, Chiefly in the Scottish Dialect* was published at Kilmarnock at the end of July, 1786.

Both the prospectus, and the title of the published volume, draw attention to the language in which Burns's poems are written. As the change from simply 'Scotch' to 'Chiefly' Scottish suggests, Burns's language is heterogeneous, shifting from Scots to English not only from one poem to the next but from one stanza or line to the next.

Sometimes, indeed, this shift is invisible on the page: what looks like the same word will require a Scottish vowel in one context, and an English vowel in another, to provide the rhyme. Allan Ramsay, more than anyone responsible for the revival of Scots as a literary language in the years after the Treaty of Union with England in 1707, identified this expanded range as the great advantage of the Scottish poet, in the 'Preface' to his *Poems* of 1721:

[G]ood Poetry may be in any Language. . . . [T]he Pronunciation [of Scots] is liquid and sonorous, and much fuller than the *English*, of which we are Masters, by being taught it in our Schools, and daily reading it; which being added to all our own native Words, of eminent Significancy, makes our Tongue by far the completest. (p. vii)

'Our Tongue', on Ramsay's account, is not one language to be contrasted with English: it is a language which has absorbed English into itself as an additional resource, and this provides a useful way of thinking about the language of Burns's verse. In Burns's case, even more than in Ramsay's, this linguistic range is paralleled by the variety of verse-forms, modes, and literary traditions on which the poetry draws. An effect of this is to put the reader into a succession of different relationships to the poetry's subject matter. For example, one of the verse-forms that Burns inherits from medieval Scotland is the 'Christ's Kirk on the Green' stanza, used for 'brawl' poems celebrating popular festivals and disorder (see headnote to 'The Holy Fair', p. 291). Such poems characteristically invite the reader into the community that is being described by demanding that they suspend their own moral attitudes to appreciate the energies and pleasures of a society in the moment of its recreation. Eighteenth-century examples like 'The Holy Fair' in the Kilmarnock *Poems* make an equivalent demand at the level of language, as the poem is consistently conducted in something like the language of the community it celebrates. The absence of moral distance means that no moral judgement can be drawn to round off the poem, so 'The Holy Fair' just ends with the end of the day that it chronicles. In contrast, 'The Cotter's Saturday night' quite explicitly distinguishes between its intended reader, one from the prosperous 'middling sort' such as its dedicatee Robert Aiken, and the cottar class which is its subject, with the speaker of the poem acting as explicator of the latter to the former. The subject matter is essentially the same as that of 'The Holy Fair': the lives of ordinary people in the Scottish countryside. But this matter is framed in the stanza form of Spenser's *The Faerie Queene*, promising the educated reader that it will be moralized in a way corresponding to the literary authority of this source. The language of the poem modulates according to the poet's task of social mediation: the English of the opening address to Aiken is followed by a specifically Scots vocabulary to describe everyday experience, which ebbs in turn as soon as the father pulls out the (English-language) Bible; the poet ends by turning this family into an example of Scotland's moral 'grandeur' (l. 163) and addressing a prayer to the nation and its God, all in English. To say that either 'The Holy Fair' or 'The Cotter's Saturday night' is more successful than the other is perhaps to miss the point: the joy of the Kilmarnock *Poems* lies in Burns's experimentation with the different voices, different genres, different personae and stances towards his material, opened up to him by his literary inheritance and the particular historical moment in which he was writing.

Burns frames this variety in several ways. For the title page of his book, Burns wrote an epigraph, advertising himself as a 'Simple Bard, unbroke by rules of Art', who, inspired by 'Nature' alone, 'pours the wild effusions of the heart'. The poetry that follows is full of delight in wild creatures and in the woods and rivers of his county. But clearly, Burns did not learn the vocabulary of 'the wild effusions of the heart', of 'Bards' and 'Nature', from nature. He acquired it from a mid-eighteenth-century British literary culture which had given up the previous era's deep investment in classical precedents in search of heightened emotional effects such as the sublime and the sentimental. The latter is a particularly important category for Burns. At just the point in the first 'Epistle to James Lapraik' where Burns claims he needs no learning to write poetry, merely 'ae spark o' Nature's fire', he is quoting from the high-priest of the sentimental, Laurence Sterne. Smith's *Theory of Moral Sentiments* (1759) had located the basis of ethics in our capacity to imagine the feelings and perceptions of others, and to imagine how we in turn must appear in their eyes. Some of the poems of the Kilmarnock volume invite us to share in the feelings of another in this way: 'The auld Farmer's . . . Salutation to his auld Mare', for example, or, most famously, 'To a Mouse'. And consistently in these poems and songs, the spontaneous human affections of 'the heart' are defined in opposition to material selfishness taken as the defining feature of a modern commercial society.

> Nae treasures, nor pleasures
>   Could make us happy lang;
> The *heart* ay's the part ay,
>   That makes us right or wrang. ('Epistle to Davie', ll. 67–70)

This opposition is particularly characteristic of the sentimental novel *The Man of Feeling* (1771) by Henry Mackenzie: 'a book I prize next to the Bible' wrote Burns to his old tutor in 1783.

Yet Burns does something very interesting with his sentimental model. *The Man of Feeling* imagines the attachments of 'the heart' as under siege, as eventually defeated, by 'the world' of economic reality, a world of greed and lies: emotional bonds between particular individuals cannot be generalized into an alternative to money as the organizing principle of society. The feelings cultivated by reading such fiction must be their own reward: the fiction itself warns that they cannot constitute a way of life. Burns's verse epistles in the Kilmarnock edition set out to prove otherwise. Ten lines before those quoted above from the 'Epistle to Davie', Burns imagines the flowers and birdsong of spring inspiring poetry:

> On braes when we please then,
> We'll sit and *sowth* a tune;
> Syne *rhyme* till't, we'll time till't,
> And sing't when we hae done.

The first-person *plural* is important here. In offering us this image of creativity as collaboration rather than individual inspiration, Burns also asserts the productivity, rather than the precariousness, of particular sentimental solidarities. This is more than a promise, for we have the poem in front of us as the first fruit of just this collaboration. It is part of the logic of the verse epistle as a genre that it makes the addressee a condition for the existence of the poem. This is obviously true of an epistle to a patron; but also of the Kilmarnock verse epistles, addressed to equals. Even Gavin Hamilton, whose help in getting the Kilmarnock volume published allows Burns to call him 'patron', is addressed *as* an equal ('A Dedication'). For the friendships of the verse epistles are not only literary constructions, offering, like Mackenzie's, an escape from the wider reality of modern society. Rather, they dramatize part of that reality, an already-existing social practice of mutual assistance in the clubs and lodges of Enlightenment Ayrshire; the social practice that, as we have seen, made it possible to publish *Poems, Chiefly in the Scottish Dialect*.

The sentimental sociability of the verse epistles is not the only mode that Burns appropriates from mid-century literary culture and adapts for his own purposes. The Kilmarnock *Poems* use the word 'Bard' (or the diminutive 'Bardie') no fewer than thirty times in the 235 pages between the title and the close of 'A Bard's Epitaph'. The word comes from the Celtic languages, where it just means 'poet'. In English, it had long been used to name the traditional singer of Scottish, Welsh, and, especially, Irish society, originally a man attached to a tribal chieftain whose virtues and victories he commemorated in song. In the middle of the eighteenth century, as part of the shift away from neo-classical literary values and the discovery or invention of indigenous origins for the 'British' nation, this figure had been revaluated and celebrated in Thomas Gray's Pindaric ode 'The Bard' (1757) and James Macpherson's prose-poems of 'Ossian', beginning with *Fragments of Ancient Poetry* (1760). Gray's Welsh bard is the last of his kind, and curses the invading army of Edward I which has murdered all his fellow-bards. Macpherson's Ossian too is the last of his kind, and laments the destruction of his tribe, his father and son included, in a third-century war. To be a bard in Gray's and Macpherson's sense is to mourn the destruction of the social context that gave your song its meaning. In appropriating the term, Burns puts this definition into reverse. For Burns, 'Bard' evokes the *possibility* that a delimited social context might provide the poet with his vocation, not the inevitability of that context's destruction. As with sentimentalism, Burns takes a contemporary literary category that assumes its own social impotence and uses it to claim a certain kind of social authority for himself.

How exactly Burns's social context might be delimited remained an open question at the publication of the Kilmarnock *Poems* in 1786. As we have seen, that volume's enabling condition was a specifically local network of friends and sponsors. When Burns's muse Coila visits him in 'The Vision', her 'mantle' shimmers with the landmarks of Kyle; but her 'robe' is tartan, and she identifies herself as the local agent of a nationwide system of muses overseeing Scottish life. As we have also seen, Burns's language and verse-forms often advertise their origins in a national (that is, Scottish) literary culture. When Ramsay revived the literary use of Scots in the 1720s he had in effect proposed that language, and the history of poetry written in that language, as the vehicle of a Scottish national identity, in the absence of political sovereignty after the Union, and as an alternative to the Presbyterian church, the most powerful national institution left after 1707. To write in the verse forms and modes bequeathed by Ramsay was already to accept a national role. Burns accordingly refers to himself as a 'Scotch Bard', as well as an Ayrshire one, in the Kilmarnock volume, and addresses Scottish MPs, for example, as spokesman for the Scottish people ('The Author's earnest cry and prayer'). What happened after the Kilmarnock edition confirmed Burns, not just as *a* 'Scotch Bard', but as *the* 'Scotch Bard', a position he occupies to this day.

3. The Edinburgh edition

The Kilmarnock edition of *Poems, Chiefly in the Scottish Dialect* probably made Burns the substantial sum of around £50. His genius in verse, and publication by subscription, had allowed him to turn the cultural capital of his education and the social capital of his friendships into actual money. In the summer of 1786 Burns still intended to leave this money for the support of his illegitimate children on his emigration to Jamaica. But the possibility of publishing a second, expanded edition also presented itself. Wilson, his Kilmarnock printer, wanted Burns to advance the cost of the paper for such a volume; Burns, unwilling to do this, planned a trip to Edinburgh, to see if he could make a better deal there. In the meantime, his local fame was beginning to be replicated at a national level. Not all his local contacts, after all, were only local people. Some were wealthy landowners who spent part or most of the year in their townhouses in the capital. Catrine, a few miles from Mauchline, was the summer home of Dugald Stewart, Professor of Moral Philosophy at Edinburgh University. He introduced Burns's work to the Edinburgh poet Thomas Blacklock, who got hold of the Kilmarnock book and immediately recommended that a second, larger edition should be arranged. James Cunningham, Earl of Glencairn, who had estates in Ayrshire, acquired a copy through his factor there and was impressed; another local landowner, James Dalrymple of Orangefield, who knew Burns through the Masons, was related to Glencairn by marriage. So when Burns set off for Edinburgh in late November 1786 he carried a letter of introduction from Dalrymple to this influential Scottish nobleman. A review of the Kilmarnock *Poems* had already appeared in the *Edinburgh Magazine* for the previous month (see Appendix 2 of the present volume).

On his arrival, Burns was lionized by literary Edinburgh. Some of the adulation was superficial and condescending. Scottish Enlightenment 'conjectural history' had proposed that poetry, rather than being the achievement of advanced civilizations like that of Rome or modern Europe, was rooted in the spontaneous expression of feeling, equated with a timeless 'human nature'. Not only, therefore, could it be found in the earliest, most 'primitive' or 'barbarous' states of human society, it was found there in a purer state, uncorrupted by the constraints imposed by later, more complex, social forms. Thus had Hugh Blair, Professor of Rhetoric and Belles Lettres at the University of Edinburgh, argued in his *Critical Dissertation on the Poems of Ossian* (1763). In claiming direct inspiration by Nature, and in adopting the

name of Bard, Burns had invited categorization in this way by his gen-
teel readers, with his difference in social class guaranteeing his close-
ness to nature as Ossian's distance in historical time had guaranteed
his. The re-socialization of these ideas by the poems themselves was
not what won their author access to Edinburgh 'society'.

Still, Burns enjoyed much of what Edinburgh had to offer. He made
many lasting friends in the city. He seized the opportunity for sexual
adventures, both consummated (with lower-class women) and uncon-
summated (with the middle-class Mrs McLehose, separated from her
husband, with whom Burns entered into a protracted epistolary flirta-
tion, writing to 'Clarinda' and signing himself 'Sylvander'). Most
importantly, there was the new edition of his poems, slightly expanded
to include some of the work that Burns had held back from the
Kilmarnock volume or written subsequently. Glencairn introduced
Burns to William Creech, probably the most important 'bookseller'
(that is, publisher) of the Scottish Enlightenment. The Edinburgh edi-
tion was published, like its predecessor, by subscription, but on a new,
national scale: Glencairn's influence helped secure commitments to
2,876 copies at five shillings a copy. Of those among the 1,521 names in
the volume's subscription list that have been identified, around 20 per
cent come from the (relatively easy to identify) land-owning classes,
and the rest from the 'middling sort' of professionals, merchants, and
manufacturers. Burns covered the costs of producing the book (to
rather higher standards than were possible at Kilmarnock) from the
money generated. Three thousand copies were printed and ready for
distribution by 17 April 1787. Five hundred of the subscriptions were
from Creech himself, who sold them from his shop for six shillings.
But Creech's real profit would come from the copyright, which he
bought from Burns for 100 guineas, and which secured him a share of
the takings from the London reprint of 1,500 copies later in 1787, and
from subsequent editions. Burns's profits came to him more slowly
than he would have liked, and it was not until February 1789 that his
accounts were finally settled with Creech for the Edinburgh edition,
but he eventually made about £450 in total.

The plan of slave-driving in Jamaica was finally abandoned after this
spectacular success, and Burns took advantage of his immediate free-
dom by enjoying a series of tours around Scotland, to the Highlands
and his father's ancestral north-east, and to the Borders: getting to
know the country of which he was now acclaimed the national poet.
But Burns does not seem to have considered the possibility of pursuing
writing as a career, for example under the permanent patronage of

Glencairn or another nobleman. Instead, he used the access to influential people that his fame had granted him to secure a government job as an exciseman, checking that manufacturers, importers, and retailers of taxable goods were cheating neither the government nor the public. On his Highland tour he met Robert Graham of Fintry, recently appointed a Commissioner to the Scottish Board of Excise: Burns wrote to him asking for his help. In eighteenth-century Britain, securing the influence or 'interest' of a friend in a high place was how you got a job in government service, and how you got promotion once you had the job. As Glencairn's patronage had made the Edinburgh edition possible, so Fintry's patronage got Burns his place in the Excise. Another contact among the gentry, Patrick Miller of Dalswinton, had earlier offered Burns the lease of a farm on his estate in Nithsdale, in Dumfriesshire. Burns inspected the farm, Ellisland, during his Border tour in the summer of 1787. Returning to Edinburgh via Mauchline, he slept with Jean: the Armours had been reconciled to their son-in-law by his new prosperity. Jean again became pregnant, and in February 1788 produced twins (she had one child surviving from the twins she bore in her previous pregnancy). Burns was commissioned into the Excise in July, and moved to Ellisland, to establish a dairy farm, work part-time in his customs job, and build a modern farmhouse to receive his wife and growing family.

4. The later career

With the publication of the Edinburgh edition, and his subsequent settling with Jean in Dumfriesshire, the second act of Burns's career comes to an end. It is this period that has given us the popular image of Burns: the ploughman-poet, the sociable man's man, the reckless lover. And yet his subsequent career is just as interesting. At this point, Burns seems to have lost all interest in making money from his poetry. He certainly continued to write and publish poems. He sent 18 new poems to Creech for inclusion in a third edition of his *Poems* in two volumes (1793), which also added the already-published 'Tam o' Shanter'. But as Creech held the copyright on this volume, the poet only received twenty complimentary copies in return. He also published poems in newspapers and magazines, and circulated his work among friends and patrons in manuscript form as he always had done, sometimes assembling collections of his work for this purpose. This type of production could be as substantial as the 'Glenriddell Manuscripts': two bound volumes into which Burns transcribed a wide selection of his poems and letters for the library of his friend and neighbour at Ellisland, Captain Robert Riddell. Poetry once again played a role in cultivating local relationships, as it had in Ayrshire, even while Burns remained a famous poet at a national level.

But this period also sees Burns devoting himself to a 'national' project quite different from his self-construction as 'Scotia's bard' in the *Poems*. Among the men he met in Edinburgh was a music publisher called James Johnson, who had begun a collection of Scottish songs in a series of volumes with 100 songs per volume. Burns jumped at the chance to contribute. The songs included in the *Poems* demonstrated his skill with song-lyric, and music was as central to the cultural life of Ayrshire as he found it was to Edinburgh's: both Jean and his mother were skilled and knowledgeable singers. There was time for Burns to add three songs to the first volume of *The Scots Musical Museum* in 1787. For the second volume he sent 41, and over half the total number of songs in Volumes III–V are by Burns. The six-volume collection, finished only in 1803, includes 223 songs from Burns's pen, and such was his influence with Johnson that he became in effect its editor as well. At the same time, Burns began working with another publisher, George Thomson, on his *Select Collection of Original Scotish Airs*. Johnson's *Museum* was produced as cheaply as possible: Stephen Clarke, an Edinburgh organist, added simple bass lines to the score for the voice; pages were printed from pewter plates onto cheap paper in a modest format. Thomson's *Collection* was an altogether more up-market production, providing a full and complex keyboard score as well as the vocal melody printed from copper plates in a large-format volume, and hiring composers as distinguished as Haydn and Beethoven to provide instrumental introductions. In both cases, Burns's work for these collections was collaborative in a more material sense than the *Poems* had been. It was also (more or less, during his lifetime) anonymous; and done without payment.

As to any remuneration, you may think my Songs either *above*, or *below* price; for they shall be the one or the other.—In the honest enthusiasm with which I embark in your undertaking, to talk of money, wages, fee, hire, &c. would be downright Sodomy of Soul! (Letter to Thomson, 16 Sept. 1792)

In the Kilmarnock and Edinburgh editions, Burns's desire to address a national audience, and his pursuit of economic security, had gone hand-in-hand. Now he kept these aspirations apart.

While Johnson gave Burns a free hand, the poet often disagreed with Thomson about the matching of tunes to lyrics and the propriety of using Scots in the latter. Their disagreements had the benefit of generating a copious correspondence from which we learn a great deal about Burns's attitude to song. We can therefore be quite clear about what Burns was *not* doing in his collaborations with the two men. He was not composing tunes, but writing new words, or amending existing words, for tunes that were, in the vast majority of cases, already published in other collections, of which Burns assembled a comprehensive library. By the same token, neither was he engaged in the antiquarian or anthropological pursuit of 'folklore'. Unlike, for example, Walter Scott in his *Minstrelsy of the Scottish Border* (1802–3), Burns did not understand himself to be recovering ancient artefacts preserved in a purely oral tradition, soon to be extinguished by the spread of literacy. Instead, he was collecting the productions of, and contributing to, a thriving contemporary musical culture in which the same songs might be circulating from singer to singer in a country district, and at the same time published in Edinburgh or London. (That Johnson calls his collection a 'Museum' should not mislead us: he is using this word in its original sense to mean a building dedicated to the Muses, not one in which the remnants of extinct societies are exhibited.) In the first 'Epistle to J. Lapraik', Burns describes hearing a song in an Ayrshire cottage at a 'rockin', a winter-evening's work-party at which stories are told and songs sung to accompany spinning and darning and other domestic tasks: a folkloric context, to be sure. But the song he hears has adapted for a tune, possibly of Irish origin, a poem in English from an Edinburgh magazine (see note to l. 13 of the 'Epistle', p. 319). Burns then took this song, re-wrote the lyric once again, this time into Scots, and published it in *The Scots Musical Museum* with a score for its accompaniment on a piano or a cello. Instances such as this demonstrate that for Burns and his collaborators, what made these songs 'Scottish' was not their preservation of a national 'tradition' dating from a pre-modern (and pre-Union) past; was not, indeed, a question of their origins at all. What gave them their national status was rather their ubiquity across the social hierarchy in the present day. They were sung at the keyboard in Edinburgh parlours and at the fireside in rural cottages alike; a ubiquity facilitated, rather than threatened, by popular literacy and the modern technology of print.

Of course, Burns was under no illusion that harmonies shared by rich and poor corresponded to harmony between them. A recurring feature of the poetry published in the Kilmarnock and Edinburgh volumes is their anger at the callous indifference of the wealthy towards the suffering of the labouring classes below them. In the context of the

1780s, this could be read as moral criticism of the individuals who occupied the upper ranks of the social hierarchy, rather than a political criticism of the hierarchy itself. In Ayrshire, after all, the politics which most directly affected Burns were church politics, and here Burns found himself in sympathy with the common-sense morality of the 'moderate' party, a party in tune with the priorities of educated gentlemen, and which defended the right of landowners to impose ministers on congregations on their estates; and in conflict with the orthodox theology and strict sexual discipline of the 'popular party', which drew its strongest support from Burns's own class of tenant farmers and self-employed artisans. But Burns's identification with the gentlemen's party in the church, and critique of gentlemanly attitudes to the poor, are both expressions of Burns's commitment to an Enlightenment ideology of 'improvement'. The loss of America had left the British elite divided and defensive, and made reform of a corrupt political system look both possible and necessary. But just as the American Revolution had been led by landed gentlemen in the name of rights and liberties supposedly embodied in the British constitution, so social conditions in Britain might be ameliorated if only landed gentlemen could be shamed into demonstrating the sort of moral leadership exhibited by Washington and Jefferson. The *Poems* can thus be read as advocating solidarity across the social ranks rather than their levelling; a solidarity Burns might imagine in terms of the apolitical 'brotherhood' of the Masonic Lodge and other institutions of enlightened sociability. In this respect, Burns was in tune with the movement, supported by many of his friends among the gentry, both in Ayrshire and Dumfriesshire, for political reform within the framework of the existing British constitution.

Such a reforming agenda seemed at first to receive a boost when constitutional reform got under way in France in the summer of 1789. In fact the effect of the French Revolution, driven forward as it was by the street-level actions of ordinary people, was to close down the reform movement in Britain for a generation. Its advocates found their moderate demands associated with the increasing violence of events in France, and themselves subject to surveillance and persecution from an increasingly paranoid British state. At just the period when Burns launched himself into the collaboration with Thomson, in the second half of 1792, the overthrow of the French monarchy by the people of Paris, and the unexpected triumph of the new republic over its enemies on the battlefield, were celebrated in the streets of many Scottish towns and cities with demands for 'liberty' in Britain as well (see headnote to 'The Tree of Liberty', p. 402). Burns, who had by this time given up the farm at Ellisland to work full-time for the Excise from a new home in Dumfries, had been openly enthusiastic about events in France. But he was a government employee, dependent on the income from his Excise duties to support his wife and children. The 'Year of Liberty' culminated for Burns in an accusation made to his superiors that he had been involved in a disturbance at the theatre in Dumfries at which 'God Save the King' had been booed, and the French Revolutionary anthem, 'Ça ira', called for in its place. The letters written by Burns in his (successful) attempt to avert dismissal are reproduced in Appendix 1 of this volume. And yet Burns continued to produce work whose rhetoric, while perfectly consistent with that of the *Poems* of the 1780s, was rendered unambiguously democratic by the transformed political context of the last decade of the eighteenth century. To demand respect for those who owned no property was now to take a political position, not merely a moral one; and a political position that could lose you your job, or worse. Some of these poems and songs were published anonymously in magazines and newspapers; some were not published until after his death. In the event, it was his increasingly precarious health, and not his political opinions, which came to threaten the Burns household with penury. An exciseman who could not perform his duties was not paid. Burns was laid low with a recurrence of depression in the winter of 1795–6, after the death of a daughter; a long-standing medical problem, combining rheumatic fever and a heart condition, wore him away in the new year, and he died on 12 July 1796.

5. *Burns in the public sphere*

There is a fourth act to the poetic career of Robert Burns. In the decades following his death, the poems that he had chosen not to publish were collected and printed for the first time. Most of this work had long circulated in manuscript among friends and patrons. The type of publication in which these poems first appeared, and the form they took there, is as much a part of the story of Burns's poetry as the history of the Kilmarnock and Edinburgh editions. It is too diverse a narrative to include in this introduction, and details can be found for each text in its headnote. At the same time, new collections of his work incorporated the poems of the Edinburgh edition, the previously anonymous songs, and the posthumously published material. In his 'People's Edition' of that year, Robert Chambers estimated that over 100 editions of the poems of Burns had been published by 1838, and this level of reproduction continued throughout the nineteenth century. The profound and sustained popularity across the English-speaking world that this indicates was partly a result of a widespread and often prosperous Scottish diaspora across the Empire and in the United States for whom the poems and songs of Burns represented a cherished memory of the old country. Part of Burns's continued popularity must also be connected to the increasing education and organization of working people, their demand for political representation where it was denied them, and their sense that in Burns they found the prophet of their democratic destiny. As his work was translated into other languages, this Burns became celebrated first across the continent of Europe, and then across the world.

> For a' that, and a' that,
> It's coming yet, for a' that;
> And man, and man, the world o'er,
> Shall brothers be, for a' that.

In this song from 1795, 'A man's a man for a' that', the local solidarity of Batchelor's Club and Masonic Lodge in the Ayrshire villages of Burns's young manhood swells into an aspiration to global fraternity. Just as the Kilmarnock edition claimed for its author a national role that he had not yet achieved, so this song dreams of an international solidarity whose promise, more than two centuries later, we have yet to fulfil. The continuing world-wide appeal of Burns's poetry, however it is read, and whatever values are attached to it, perhaps offers some hope that its fulfilment remains at least imaginable.

From the beginning, however, the story of Burns's poetry was often subsumed into the story of Burns the man. The first major edition of the complete works of Robert Burns was Dr James Currie's in 1800, and most of this text is taken up with a biography of the poet, in which the poems are introduced in the context of their composition. The effect is to subordinate the poetry to Currie's sometimes prurient interest in Burns's private life. Currie's incorporation of the poetry in the biography was replicated in many collections, including Robert Chambers's important editions in 1852 and 1856. The standard twentieth-century scholarly edition of Burns is James Kinsley's from 1968, to which the present volume's notes are deeply indebted. But mid-twentieth-century literary scholarship was interested in reconstructing the order and contexts in which the poems were *written*, and so Kinsley ordered the texts along the same biographical narrative as did Currie and Chambers. Kinsley was also committed (again, following the established scholarly practice of the time) to constructing an 'ideal' version of each text by collating its various versions in manuscript as well as print, to the end of producing a poem that corresponded as closely as possible to the poet's 'final intentions'. The paradoxical effect of these procedures is to completely efface the poet's intentions regarding the context in which his work was to be *read*; the context in which the poems were eventually read; and that different versions of the same poem may have been written for different contexts. That Burns wrote 'Man was made to mourn' almost immediately after 'The Fornicator' is quite interesting, but should not obscure the fact that the former appeared in the celebrated volume that made Burns famous, and the latter only in a book printed for private circulation among his friends after the author's death.

The present volume, following the nineteenth-century precedent of William Scott Douglas's 1871 and 1876 editions, is organized on the principle that the context in which a poem or a song first found its public is an important fact about that poem or song. This principle finds expression in two ways. First, each text is generally based on the first published version, whatever form that publication took (see 'Note on the Text'). Second, the texts are presented in order of publication rather than composition, beginning with the complete text of the Kilmarnock *Poems* of 1786. By following this principle, this volume aims to return Burns to history; not as an object of merely antiquarian interest, but because for Burns, as I hope this introduction has shown, poetry and song provided a means of living in history, not a picture of it, or an escape from it. The history in which Burns lived was in many ways the beginning of our own; we do him fullest justice when we seek in his work the resources to do the same.

CHRONOLOGY

1786 March: Jean's parents discover her pregnancy and send her to stay with relatives in Paisley. This confirms B's plan to emigrate to Jamaica.

July: threatened with a suit for damages from James Armour, B transfers his share of the Mossgiel lease to Gilbert. Publication at Kilmarnock of *Poems, Chiefly in the Scottish Dialect*.

September: Jean gives birth to twins; the girl will die the following year.

November: travels to Edinburgh to arrange publication of a second edition.

1787 April: publication of the Edinburgh edition of *Poems*.

May: touring the Borders. *The Scots Musical Museum*, Volume I.

August–October: touring the Highlands.

1788 February: *The Scots Musical Museum*, Volume II.

March: Jean gives birth to twin girls who both die within a month.

June: B settles at Ellisland farm on the river Nith in Dumfriesshire.

July: B commissioned into the Excise; takes up part-time duties.

December: Jean joins B at Ellisland with their son Robert.

1789 June: in Paris, declaration of a National Assembly.

July 14: storming of the Bastille prison.

August: B and Jean have a second son, Francis.

1790 February: *The Scots Musical Museum*, Volume III.

Edmund Burke, *Reflections on the Revolution in France*.

1791 April: a third son, William, born at Ellisland.

Autumn: B gives up Ellisland and moves the family into an apartment in Dumfries to work full-time as an exciseman.

Thomas Paine, *The Rights of Man*, a reply to Burke's attack on the revolution.

1792 May: British government moves against 'seditious writings' such as *Rights of Man*.

August: *The Scots Musical Museum*, Volume IV.

September: victories of the recently declared French Republic spark street celebrations and demonstrations.

November: birth of Elizabeth, who survives infancy, the first daughter with Jean to do so.

December: B reported to his superiors in the Excise for his radical sympathies.

Mary Wollstonecraft, *A Vindication of the Rights of Woman*.

1793 January: execution in Paris of Louis XVI.

February: a third edition of *Poems*, now in two volumes. France declares war on the United Kingdom.

May: first half-volume of Thomson's *Select Collection of Original Scotish Airs*.

August: sedition trials begin in Scotland, with sentencing of lawyer Thomas Muir to 14 years transportation to Australia.

1794 May: British government suspends Habeas Corpus, allowing for detention without charge.

August: B and Jean have a fourth son, James.

Another two-volume edition of B's *Poems* published.

December: B takes on duties of acting supervisor.

1795 January: B is a founder member of the Royal Dumfries Volunteers, a home-defence unit.

A bad harvest exacerbates political discontent. Government passes the Seditious Meetings Act and the Treasonable Practices Act: more repressive legislation.

September: Elizabeth, B and Jean's only daughter, dies.

December: B too ill to work, creating real financial hardship in the household.

1796 21 July: B dies in Dumfries; buried with full military honours by the Volunteers.

December: *The Scots Musical Museum*, Volume V.

NOTE ON THE TEXT

THE aim of this edition is to present the poems and songs of Burns in a form as close as is practicable to that in which readers first encountered them in the public realm during Burns's lifetime and in the century after his death. The copy-text is accordingly the first published version of each work, unless there is a particular reason for choosing a later one, in which case this is explained in the notes. Substantial emendations to the copy-text are made only on the basis of manuscript sources or authorial changes to later editions. Such emendations are also annotated. The body of each text on the following pages generally follows its copy-text in accidentals of spelling and punctuation, although the inconsistent use of quotation marks has been regularized by adopting single marks throughout. Capitalization follows the copy-texts from the Kilmarnock and Edinburgh editions, but has been regularized elsewhere, including the capitalization of the first word of each poem; the use of italics in naming tunes has also been regularized. The title at the head of each poem or song is that used in the copy-text, although on the contents page, and in the notes and index, a more familiar alternative may accompany this for the sake of clarity. Similarly, the name of the addressee of a verse epistle may, following the copy-text, be obscured with asterisks at the head of the poem, but the name is completed on the contents page and in references elsewhere. The only footnotes that appear on the same page as the text are those that appear in the copy-text, and are the work of the poet unless otherwise stated. The only additions to the page are line numbers for ease of reference, and the degree sign (°) to indicate a note at the end of the book.

Applying these principles is mostly straightforward in the case of work published during the poet's lifetime, or sent for publication in *The Scots Musical Museum* or the *Select Collection* before his death. Occasionally, a question arises regarding what counts as 'publication'. One of the lifetime copy-texts ('Here Lies Robert Fergusson Poet') is a tombstone. Another ('Written on a window in Stirling') is an anti-Burns tract, which obtained *its* copy-text from the transcription into a tourist's notebook of some graffiti written by Burns and subsequently destroyed by him (in this case, the window was clearly the first published version, alas no longer available for use as copy-text). In the case of posthumously published work, the criteria are put under much more serious strain. Was *The Merry Muses of Caledonia* in the public realm in 1799? It was printed, certainly, but for private circulation; it could be argued that this was not publication, but a sophistication of the private circulation in manuscript that many Burns texts underwent *before* publication. I have allowed the printed nature of the text to sway me in this instance, and the suspicion that printed books tend to get borrowed and mislaid, and fall into the wrong hands, and generally get around in a way that makes them public, even if they are not on open sale; and in a way that manuscripts, more carefully attended to, more intimately consumed, do not.

The posthumously published work is also much more prone to textual corruption. In the decades after the poet's death, some of the transcription from manuscript sources for hasty printing in chapbooks and magazines was careless. In this case it seems justified to correct the copy-text with reference to other sources, while pointing out, in the notes, that the poem on the page of this volume is not *quite* the poem first encountered in her tuppenny tract or monthly magazine by a contemporary reader. The limit case for this procedure proved to be 'A poet's welcome to his love-begotten daughter'. This exists in several good holograph manuscripts, all of them different from each other; its first published version, in a chapbook from 1799, differs in many ways from all the manuscripts, at one point simply contradicting them, apparently due to corruption of the text during transcription. But so many are these corruptions that to correct them all with reference to the manuscripts is not to produce a good reading version of the first published text, but to produce yet another version of the poem, too distant from the printed copy *and* from the manuscripts to count as a version of either of them. In this case, instead, the copy-text is the first complete publication of a reliable manuscript copy, which does not come about until the centenary of the poet's death.

The music provides other challenges. Attending to the textual circumstances in which songs were first published means distinguishing those that appeared with no more than the name of a tune below their title from those that were published with a score. In the first instance, Burns clearly expected the reader to fit the words to the tune themselves. This volume makes the same demand in such cases; but if Burns relied on his reader's musical knowledge, here the tune is offered in the notes, adapted from a contemporary compendium (almost always *The Scots Musical Museum*). Where the song was published with a score, in the *Museum* or in *A Select Collection of Original Scotish Airs*, this volume follows its copy-text in placing words and music alongside one another. Just as the verbal text follows its copy-text in accidentals of spelling, punctuation, and so on, so the scores here maintain accidentals of annotation: the deployment of slurs and beams, for example, will look odd to the modern musician's eye. On the other hand, Stephen Clarke's transcriptions for the *Museum* sometimes struggled with its small pages: syllables could not be arranged, or bass and treble notes aligned, in any consistent way, and this has been tidied up for the present volume. Without quite the same spatial restrictions, it has also been possible to extract each first verse from the score and include it also at the head of subsequent verses in the lyric, for easier appreciation of the song as a whole.

Music was not the only accompaniment to which Burns set his words. The self-conscious construction of a particular type of poetic identity in the *Poems* finds its visual equivalent in the engraving of the poet by John Beugo that appeared in the frontispiece of the Edinburgh editions from 1787 onwards. 'Tam o' Shanter' was written as the companion to a picture: an engraving of a ruin near the poet's birthplace, an old church his father had worked to restore. These images, like the tunes for the songs, shaped the way in which Burns's readers experienced his words, and are included here as another aspect of the material context in which his poetry was first encountered and enjoyed.

POEMS,

CHIEFLY IN THE

SCOTTISH DIALECT,

BY

ROBERT BURNS.

THE Simple Bard, unbroke by rules of Art,
He pours the wild effusions of the heart:
And if inspir'd, 'tis Nature's pow'rs inspire;
Her's all the melting thrill, and her's the kindling fire.

ANONYMOUS.°

KILMARNOCK:
PRINTED BY JOHN WILSON.
M,DCC,LXXXVI.

PREFACE

The following trifles are not the production of the Poet, who, with all the advantages of learned art, and perhaps amid the elegancies and idlenesses of upper life, looks down for a rural theme, with an eye to Theocrites or Virgil.° To the Author of this, these and other celebrated names their countrymen are, in their original languages, 'A fountain shut up, and a book sealed.'° Unacquainted with the necessary requisites for commencing Poet by rule, he sings the sentiments and manners, he felt and saw in himself and his rustic compeers around him, in his and their native language. Though a Rhymer from his earliest years, at least from the earliest impulses of the softer passions, it was not till very lately, that the applause, perhaps the partiality, of Friendship, wakened his vanity so far as to make him think any thing of his was worth showing; and none of the following works were ever composed with a view to the press. To amuse himself with the little creations of his own fancy, amid the toil and fatigues of a laborious life; to transcribe the various feelings, the loves, the griefs, the hopes, the fears, in his own breast; to find some kind of counterpoise to the struggles of a world, always an alien scene, a task uncouth to the poetical mind; these were his motives for courting the Muses, and in these he found Poetry to be it's own reward.

Now that he appears in the public character of an Author, he does it with fear and trembling. So dear is fame to the rhyming tribe, that even he, an obscure, nameless Bard, shrinks aghast, at the thought of being branded as 'An impertinent blockhead, obtruding his nonsense on the world; and because he can make a shift to jingle a few doggerel, Scotch rhymes together, looks upon himself as a Poet of no small consequence forsooth.'

It is an observation of that celebrated Poet,[1] whose divine Elegies do honor to our language, our nation, and our species, that 'Humility has depressed many a genius to a hermit, but never raised one to fame.' If any Critic catches at the word *genius*, the Author tells him, once for all, that he certainly looks upon himself as possest of some poetic abilities, otherwise his publishing in the manner he has done, would be a manœuvre below the worst character, which, he hopes, his worst enemy will ever give him: but to the genius of a Ramsay,° or the glorious

---

[1] Shenstone.°

dawnings of the poor, unfortunate Ferguson,° he, with equal unaffected sincerity, declares, that, even in his highest pulse of vanity, he has not the most distant pretensions. These two justly admired Scotch Poets he has often had in his eye in the following pieces; but rather with a view to kindle at their flame, than for servile imitation.

To his Subscribers,° the Author returns his most sincere thanks. Not the mercenary bow over a counter, but the heart-throbbing gratitude of the Bard, conscious how much he is indebted to Benevolence and Friendship, for gratifying him, if he deserves it, in that dearest wish of every poetic bosom—to be distinguished. He begs his readers, particularly the Learned and the Polite, who may honor him with a perusal, that they will make every allowance for Education and Circumstances of Life: but, if after a fair, candid, and impartial criticism, he shall stand convicted of Dulness and Nonsense, let him be done by, as he would in that case do by others—let him be condemned, without mercy, to contempt and oblivion.

THE TWA DOGS, A TALE

'TWAS in that place o' Scotland's isle,
That bears the name o' auld king COIL,°
Upon a bonie day in June,
When wearing thro' the afternoon,
Twa Dogs, that were na thrang at hame,
Forgather'd ance upon a time.

The first I'll name, they ca'd him *Cæsar*,
Was keepet for His Honor's pleasure;
His hair, his size, his mouth, his lugs,
Shew'd he was nane o' Scotland's dogs,   10
But whalpet some place far abroad,
Where sailors gang to fish for Cod.°

His locked, letter'd, braw brass-collar
Shew'd him the *gentleman* an' *scholar*;
But tho' he was o' high degree,
The fient a pride na pride had he,
But wad hae spent an hour caressan,
Ev'n wi' a Tinkler-gipsey's *messan*:
At Kirk or Market, Mill or Smiddie,
Nae tawted *tyke*, tho' e'er sae duddie,   20
But he wad stan't, as glad to see him,
An' stroan't on stanes an' hillocks wi' him.

The tither was a *ploughman's collie*,
A rhyming, ranting, raving billie,
Wha for his friend an' comrade had him,
And in his freaks had *Luath* ca'd him,
After some dog in *Highland sang*,[1]
Was made lang syne, lord knows how lang.

He was a gash an' faithfu' *tyke*,
As ever lap a sheugh or dyke.   30
His honest, sonsie, baws'nt face,
Ay gat him friends in ilka place;

---

[1] Cuchullin's dog in Ossian's Fingal.°

His breast was white, his towzie back,
Weel clad wi' coat o' glossy black;
His gawsie tail, wi' upward curl,
Hung owre his hurdies wi' a swirl.

Nae doubt but they were fain o' ither,
An' unco pack an' thick thegither;
Wi' social nose whyles snuff'd an' snowket;
Whyles mice and modewurks they howket;   40
Whyles scour'd awa in lang excursion,
An' worry'd ither in diversion;
Till tir'd at last wi' mony a farce,
They set them down upon their arse,°
An' there began a lang digression
About the *lords o' the creation.*

CÆSAR

I've aften wonder'd, honest *Luath,*
What sort o' life poor dogs like you have;
An' when the *gentry's* life I saw,
What way *poor bodies* liv'd ava.   50

Our *Laird* gets in his racked rents,°
His coals, his kane, an' a' his stents:
He rises when he likes himsel;
His flunkies answer at the bell;
He ca's his coach; he ca's his horse;
He draws a bonie, silken purse
As lang's my tail, whare thro' the steeks,
The yellow letter'd *Geordie* keeks.°

Frae morn to een it's nought but toiling,
At baking, roasting, frying, boiling;   60
An' tho' the gentry first are steghan,
Yet ev'n the *ha' folk* fill their peghan
Wi' sauce, ragouts, an' sic like trashtrie,°
That's little short o' downright wastrie.
Our *Whipper-in,* wee, blastet wonner,°
Poor, worthless elf, it eats a dinner,
Better than ony *Tenant-man*
His Honor has in a' the lan':

An' what poor *Cot-folk* pit their painch in,°
I own it's past my comprehension.°   70

LUATH

Trowth, Cæsar, whyles they're fash't enough;°
A *Cotter* howkan in a sheugh,
Wi' dirty stanes biggan a dyke,
Bairan a quarry, an' sic like,°
Himsel, a wife, he thus sustains,
A smytrie o' wee, duddie weans,
An' nought but his han'-daurk, to keep
Them right an' tight in thack an' raep.

An' when they meet wi' sair disasters,
Like loss o' health or want o' masters,   80
Ye maist wad think, a wee touch langer,
An' they maun starve o' cauld and hunger:
But how it comes, I never kent yet,
They're maistly wonderfu' contented;
An' buirdly chiels, and clever hizzies,
Are bred in sic a way as this is.

CÆSAR

But then, to see how ye're negleket,
How huff'd, an' cuff'd, an' disrespeket!
L—d man, our gentry care as little
For *delvers*, *ditchers*, an' sic cattle;   90
They gang as saucy by poor folk,
As I wad by a stinkan brock.

I've notic'd, on our Laird's *court-day*,°
An' mony a time my heart's been wae,
Poor *tenant bodies*, scant o' cash,
How they maun thole a *factor's* snash;
He'll stamp an' threaten, curse an' swear,
He'll *apprehend* them, *poind* their gear;°
While they maun stan', wi' aspect humble,
An' hear it a', an' fear an' tremble!   100

I see how folk live that hae riches;
But surely poor-folk maun be wretches!

LUATH

They're no sae wretched 's ane wad think;
Tho' constantly on poortith's brink,
They're sae accustom'd wi' the sight,
The view o't gies them little fright.

Then chance and fortune are sae guided,
They're ay in less or mair provided;
An' tho' fatigu'd wi' close employment,
A blink o' rest 's a sweet enjoyment.   110

The dearest comfort o' their lives,
Their grushie weans an' faithfu' wives;
The *prattling things* are just their pride,
That sweetens a' their fire-side.

An' whyles twalpennie-worth o' *nappy*
Can mak the bodies unco happy;
They lay aside their private cares,
To mind the Kirk and State affairs;
They'll talk o' *patronage* an' *priests*,°
Wi' kindling fury i' their breasts,   120
Or tell what new taxation's comin,
An' ferlie at the folk in LON'ON.

As bleak-fac'd Hallowmass returns,°
They get the jovial, rantan *Kirns*,
When *rural life*, of ev'ry station,
Unite in common recreation;
Love blinks, Wit slaps, an' social Mirth
Forgets there's *care* upo' the earth.

That *merry day* the year begins,
They bar the door on frosty win's;   130
The nappy reeks wi' mantling ream,
An' sheds a heart-inspiring steam;
The luntan pipe, an' sneeshin mill,
Are handed round wi' right guid will;
The cantie, auld folks, crackan crouse,
The young anes rantan thro' the house—

My heart has been sae fain to see them,
That I for joy hae barket wi' them.

Still it's owre true that ye hae said,
Sic game is now owre aften play'd;   140
There's monie a creditable *stock*
O' decent, honest, fawsont folk,
Are riven out baith root an' branch,
Some rascal's pridefu' greed to quench,°
Wha thinks to knit himsel the faster
In favor wi' some *gentle Master*,
Wha aiblins thrang a *parliamentin*,
For Britain's guid his saul indentin—°

CÆSAR

Haith lad ye little ken about it;
For Britain's guid! guid faith! I doubt it.   150
Say rather, gaun as PREMIERS lead him,°
An' saying *aye* or *no*'s they bid him:
At Operas an' Plays parading,
Mortgaging, gambling, masquerading:
Or maybe, in a frolic daft,
To HAGUE or CALAIS takes a waft,
To make a *tour* an' tak a whirl,
To learn *bon ton* an' see the worl'.°

There, at VIENNA or VERSAILLES,
He rives his father's auld entails;°   160
Or by MADRID he takes the rout,
To thrum *guittars* an' fecht wi' nowt;
Or down *Italian Vista* startles,
Wh—re-hunting amang groves o' myrtles:°
Then bowses drumlie *German-water*,°
To mak himsel look fair and fatter,
An' purge the bitter ga's an' cankers,
O' curst *Venetian* b—res an' ch—ncres.°

For Britain's guid! for her destruction!
Wi' dissipation, feud an' faction!   170

LUATH

Hech man! dear sirs! is that the gate,
They waste sae mony a braw estate!
Are we sae foughten and harass'd
For gear to gang that gate at last!

O would they stay aback frae courts,
An' please themsels wi' countra sports,
It wad for ev'ry ane be better,
The *Laird*, the *Tenant*, an' the *Cotter!*
For thae frank, rantan, ramblan billies,
Fient haet o' them 's ill hearted fellows;   180
Except for breakin o' their timmer,
Or speakin lightly o' their *Limmer*,
Or shootin of a hare or moorcock,°
The ne'er-a-bit they're ill to poor folk.

But will ye tell me, master *Cæsar*,
Sure *great folk's* life's a life o' pleasure?
Nae cauld nor hunger e'er can steer them,
The vera thought o't need na fear them.

CÆSAR

L——d man, were ye but whyles where I am,
The *gentles* ye wad neer envy them!   190

It's true, they need na starve or sweat,
Thro' Winter's cauld, or Summer's heat;
They've nae sair-wark to craze their banes,
An' fill *auld-age* wi' grips an' granes;
But *human-bodies* are sic fools,
For a' their colledges an' schools,
That when nae *real* ills perplex them,
They *mak* enow themsels to vex them;
An' ay the less they hae to sturt them,
In like proportion, less will hurt them.   200

A country fellow at the pleugh,
His *acre's* till'd, he's right eneugh;
A country girl at her wheel,

Her *dizzen's* done, she's unco weel;°
But Gentlemen, an' Ladies warst,
Wi' ev'n down *want o' wark* are curst.
They loiter, lounging, lank an' lazy;
Tho' deil-haet ails them, yet uneasy;
Their days, insipid, dull an' tasteless,
Their nights, unquiet, lang an' restless.   210

An' ev'n their sports, their balls an' races,
Their galloping thro' public places,
There's sic parade, sic pomp an' art,
The joy can scarcely reach the heart.

The *Men* cast out in *party-matches*,°
Then sowther a' in deep debauches.
Ae night, they're mad wi' drink an' wh——ring,
Niest day their life is past enduring.

The *Ladies* arm-in-arm in clusters,
As great an' gracious a' as sisters;   220
But hear their *absent thoughts* o' ither,
They're a' run deils an' jads thegither.
Whyles, owre the wee bit cup an' platie,
They sip the *scandal-potion* pretty;
Or lee-lang nights, wi' crabbet leuks,
Pore owre the devil's *pictur'd beuks*;°
Stake on a chance a farmer's stackyard,
An' cheat like ony *unhang'd blackguard*.

There's some exceptions, man an' woman;
But this is Gentry's life in common.   230

By this, the sun was out o' sight,
An' darker gloamin brought the night:
The *bum-clock* humm'd wi' lazy drone,
The kye stood rowtan i' the loan;
When up they gat an' shook their lugs,
Rejoic'd they were na *men* but *dogs*;
An' each took off his several way,
Resolv'd to meet some ither day.

SCOTCH DRINK

> *Gie him strong* Drink *until he wink,*
> *That's sinking in despair;*
> *An'* liquor *guid to fire his bluid,*
> *That's prest wi' grief an' care:*
> *There let him bowse an' deep carouse,*
> *Wi' bumpers flowing o'er,*
> *Till he forgets his* loves *or* debts,
> *An' minds his griefs no more.*

SOLOMON'S PROVERBS, xxxi. 6, 7.°

LET other Poets raise a fracas
'Bout vines, an' wines, an' druken *Bacchus,*°
An' crabbed names an' stories wrack us,
      An' grate our lug,
I sing the juice *Scotch bear* can mak us,
      In glass or jug.

O thou, my MUSE! guid, auld SCOTCH DRINK!
Whether thro' wimplin worms thou jink,°
Or, richly brown, ream owre the brink,
      In glorious faem,   10
Inspire me, till I *lisp* an' *wink*,
      To sing thy name!

Let husky Wheat the haughs adorn,
And Aits set up their awnie horn,
An' Pease an' Beans, at een or morn,
      Perfume the plain,
Leeze me on thee *John Barleycorn,*
      Thou king o' grain!

On thee aft Scotland chows her cood,
In souple scones, the wale o' food!°   20
Or tumbling in the boiling flood
      Wi' kail an' beef;
But when thou pours thy strong *heart's blood*,
      There thou shines chief.

Food fills the wame, an' keeps us livin;
Tho' life's a gift no worth receivin,
When heavy-dragg'd wi' pine an' grievin;
      But oil'd by thee,
The wheels o' life gae down-hill, scrievin,°
      Wi' rattlin glee.   30

Thou clears the head o' doited Lear;
Thou chears the heart o' drooping Care;
Thou strings the nerves o' Labor-sair,
      At's weary toil;
Thou ev'n brightens dark Despair,
      Wi' gloomy smile.

Aft, clad in massy, siller weed,
Wi' Gentles thou erects thy head;
Yet humbly kind, in time o' need,
      The *poor man's* wine;   40
His wee drap pirratch, or his bread,
      Thou kitchens fine.

Thou art the life o' public haunts;
But thee, what were our fairs and rants?
Ev'n godly meetings o' the saunts,°
      By thee inspir'd,
When gaping they besiege the *tents*,°
      Are doubly fir'd.

That *merry night* we get the corn in,
O sweetly, then, thou reams the horn in!   50
Or reekan on a *New-year-mornin*
      In cog or bicker,
An' just a wee drap *sp'ritual burn* in,°
      An' gusty sucker!

When Vulcan gies his bellys breath,°
An' Ploughmen gather wi' their graith,
O rare! to see thee fizz an' freath
      I' the lugget caup!
Then *Burnewin* comes on like Death
      At ev'ry chap.   60

Nae mercy, then, for airn or steel;
The brawnie, banie, ploughman-chiel
Brings hard owrehip, wi' sturdy wheel,
    The strong forehammer,
Till block an' studdie ring an' reel
    Wi' dinsome clamour.

When skirlin weanies see the light,
Thou maks the gossips clatter bright,°
How fumbling coofs their dearies slight,°
    Wae worth them for't!   70
While healths gae round to him wha, *tight*,
    Gies famous sport.°

When neebors anger at a plea,
An' just as wud as wud can be,
How easy can the *barley-brie*
    Cement the quarrel!
It's aye the cheapest Lawyer's fee
    To taste the barrel.

Alake! that e'er my *Muse* has reason,
To wyte her countrymen wi' treason!   80
But monie daily weet their weason
    Wi' liquors nice,
An' hardly, in a winter season,
    E'er spier her price.

Wae worth that *Brandy*, burnan trash!
Fell source o' monie a pain an' brash!
Twins monie a poor, doylt, druken hash
    O' half his days;
An' sends, beside, auld *Scotland's* cash
    To her warst faes.   90

Ye Scots wha wish auld Scotland well,
Ye chief, to you my tale I tell,
Poor, plackless devils like *mysel*,
    It sets you ill,
Wi' bitter, dearthfu' *wines* to mell,°
    Or foreign gill.

May *Gravels* round his blather wrench,
An' *Gouts* torment him, inch by inch,°
Wha twists his gruntle wi' a glunch
      O' sour disdain,   100
Out owre a glass o' *Whisky-punch*
      Wi' honest men!

O *Whisky!* soul o' plays an' pranks!
Accept a *Bardie's* gratefu' thanks!
When wanting thee, what tuneless cranks
      Are my poor Verses!
Thou comes—they rattle i' their ranks
      At ither's arses!

Thee *Ferintosh!* O sadly lost!°
Scotland lament frae coast to coast!   110
Now colic-grips, an' barkin hoast,
      May kill us a';
For loyal Forbes' *Charter'd boast*°
      Is ta'en awa!

Thae curst horse-leeches o' th' Excise,°
Wha mak the *Whisky stells* their prize!
Haud up thy han' *Deil!* ance, twice, *thrice!*
      There, sieze the blinkers!
An' bake them up in brunstane pies
      For poor d—n'd *Drinkers*.   120

Fortune, if thou'll but gie me still
Hale breeks, a scone, an' *whisky gill*,
An' rowth o' *rhyme* to rave at will,
      Tak a' the rest,
An' deal't about as thy blind skill
      Directs thee best.

THE AUTHOR'S EARNEST CRY AND PRAYER, TO THE RIGHT HONORABLE AND HONORABLE, THE SCOTCH REPRESENTATIVES IN THE HOUSE OF COMMONS

> *Dearest of Distillation! last and best!——*
> *——How art thou lost!——*
>
> PARODY ON MILTON°

YE *Irish lords*, ye *knights* an' *squires*,°
Wha *represent* our *Brughs* an' *Shires*,
An' dousely manage our affairs
        In *Parliament*,
To you a simple Bardie's pray'rs
        Are humbly sent.

Alas! my roupet *Muse* is haerse!
Your Honor's hearts wi' grief 'twad pierce,
To see her sittan on her arse
        Low i' the dust,   10
An' scriechan out prosaic verse,
        An' like to brust!

Tell them wha hae the chief direction,
Scotland an' *me's* in great affliction,
E'er sin' they laid that curst restriction
        On AQUAVITÆ;°
An' rouse them up to strong conviction,
        An' move their pity.

Stand forth and tell yon PREMIER YOUTH,°
The honest, open, naked truth: 20
Tell him o' mine an' Scotland's drouth,
        His servants humble:
The muckle devil blaw you south,
        If ye dissemble!

Does ony *great man* glunch an' gloom?°
Speak out an' never fash your thumb.
Let *posts* an' *pensions* sink or swoom

           Wi' them wha grant them:
If honestly they canna come,
           Far better want them.   30

  In gath'rin votes you were na slack,
Now stand as tightly by your tack:
Ne'er claw your lug, an' fidge your back,
           An' hum an' haw,
But raise your arm, an' tell your crack
           Before them a'.

  Paint Scotland greetan owre her thrissle;
Her *mutchkin stowp* as toom's a whissle;
An' d—mn'd Excise-men in a bussle,°
           Seizan a *Stell*,   40
Triumphant crushan't like a muscle
           Or laimpet shell.

  Then on the tither hand present her,
A blackguard *Smuggler*, right behint her,°
An' cheek-for-chow, a chuffie *Vintner*,
           Colleaguing join,
Picking her pouch as bare as Winter,
           Of a' kind coin.

  Is there, that bears the name o' SCOT,
But feels his heart's bluid rising hot,   50
To see his poor, auld Mither's *pot*,
           Thus dung in staves,°
An' plunder'd o' her hindmost groat,
           By gallows knaves?

  Alas! I'm but a nameless wight,
Trode i' the mire out o' sight!
But could I like MONTGOMERIES fight,°
           Or gab like BOSWELL,°
There's some *sark-necks* I wad *draw* tight,
           An' *tye* some *hose* well.   60

  God bless your Honors, can ye see't,
The kind, auld, cantie Carlin greet,

An' no get warmly to your feet,
          An' gar them hear it,
An' tell them, wi' a patriot-heat,
          Ye winna bear it?

Some o' you nicely ken the laws,
To round the period an' pause,
An' with rhetoric clause on clause
          To mak harangues;   70
Then echo thro' Saint Stephen's wa's°
          Auld Scotland's wrangs.

Dempster, a true-blue Scot I'se warran;°
Thee, aith-detesting, chaste *Kilkerran*;°
An' that glib-gabbet Highland Baron,
          The Laird o' *Graham*;°
And ane, a chap that's d—mn'd auldfarren,
          Dundas his name.°

Erskine, a spunkie norland billie;°
True Campbells, *Frederick* an' *Ilay*;°   80
An' Livistone, the bauld *Sir Willie*;°
          An' monie ithers,
Whom auld Demosthenes or Tully°
          Might own for brithers.

Arouse my boys! exert your mettle,
To get auld Scotland back her *kettle!*
Or faith! I'll wad my new pleugh-pettle,
          Ye'll see't or lang,
She'll teach you, wi' a reekan whittle,
          Anither sang.   90

This while she's been in crankous mood,
Her *lost Militia* fir'd her bluid;°
(Deil na they never mair do guid,
          Play'd her that pliskie!)
An' now she's like to rin red-wud
          About her *Whisky*.

An' L——d! if ance they pit her till't,
Her tartan petticoat she'll kilt,
An' durk an' pistol at her belt,°
    She'll tak the streets,° 100
An' rin her whittle to the hilt,
    I' th' first she meets!

For G——d-sake, Sirs! then speak her fair,
An' straik her cannie wi' the hair,
An' to the *muckle house* repair,°
    Wi' instant speed,
An' strive, wi' a' your Wit an' Lear,
    To get remead.

Yon ill-tongu'd tinkler, *Charlie Fox*,°
May taunt you wi' his jeers an' mocks; 110
But gie him't het, my hearty cocks!
    E'en cowe the cadie!°
An' send him to his dicing box,
    An' sportin lady.°

Tell yon guid bluid o' auld *Boconnock's*,°
I'll be his debt twa mashlum bonnocks,
An' drink his health in auld *Nanse Tinnock's*[1]
    Nine times a week,
If he some scheme, like tea an' winnocks,°
    Wad kindly seek. 120

Could he some *commutation* broach,
I'll pledge my aith in guid braid Scotch,
He need na fear their foul reproach
    Nor erudition,
Yon mixtie-maxtie, queer hotch-potch,
    The *Coalition*.°

Auld Scotland has a raucle tongue;
She's just a devil wi' a rung;
An' if she promise auld or young

---

[1] A worthy old Hostess of the Author's in *Mauchline*, where he sometimes studies Politics over a glass of guid, auld *Scotch Drink*.

To tak their part,   130
Tho' by the neck she should be strung,
She'll no desert.

And now, ye chosen FIVE AND FORTY,°
May still your Mither's heart support ye;
Then, tho' a *Minister* grow dorty,
          An' kick your place,°
Ye'll snap your fingers, poor an' hearty,
          Before his face.

God bless your Honors, a' your days,
Wi' sowps o' kail and brats o' claise,   140
In spite o' a' the thievish kaes
          That haunt St. *Jamie's!*°
Your humble Bardie sings an' prays
          While *Rab* his name is.

POSTSCRIPT

Let half-starv'd slaves in warmer skies,°
See future wines, rich-clust'ring, rise;
Their lot auld Scotland ne'er envies,
          But blythe an' frisky,
She eyes her freeborn, martial boys,
          Tak aff their Whisky.   150

What tho' their Phœbus kinder warms,
While Fragrance blooms an' Beauty charms!
When wretches range, in famish'd swarms,
          The scented groves,
Or hounded forth, *dishonor* arms
          In hungry droves.

Their *gun's* a burden on their shouther;
They downa bide the stink o' *powther*;
Their bauldest thought's a hank'ring swither,
          To stan' or rin,   160
Till skelp— a shot— they're aff, a' throw'ther,
          To save their skin.

But bring a SCOTCHMAN frae his hill,°
Clap in his cheek a *Highland gill*,
Say, such is royal GEORGE'S will,
   An' there's the foe,
He has nae thought but how to kill
   Twa at a blow.

Nae cauld, faint-hearted doubtings tease him;
Death comes, wi' fearless eye he sees him;   170
Wi' bluidy han' a welcome gies him;
   An' when he fa's,
His latest draught o' breathin lea'es him°
   In faint huzzas.

Sages their solemn een may steek,
An' raise a philosophic reek,
An' physically causes seek,
   In *clime* an' *season*,°
But tell me *Whisky's* name in Greek,
   I'll tell the reason.   180

SCOTLAND, my auld, respected Mither!
Tho' whyles ye moistify your leather,
Till whare ye sit, on craps o' heather,
   Ye tine your dam;°
FREEDOM and WHISKY gang thegither,
   Tak aff your *dram!*

THE HOLY FAIR

> *A robe of seeming truth and trust*
> *Hid crafty observation;*
> *And secret hung, with poison'd crust,*
> *The dirk of Defamation:*
> *A mask that like the gorget show'd,*
> *Dye-varying, on the pigeon;*
> *And for a mantle large and broad,*
> *He wrapt him in* Religion.
>
>   HYPOCRISY A-LA-MODE.°

I

UPON a simmer Sunday morn,
    When Nature's face is fair,
I walked forth to view the corn,
    An' snuff the callor air.
The rising sun, owre GALSTON Muirs,°
    Wi' glorious light was glintan;
The hares were hirplan down the furrs,
    The lav'rocks they were chantan
                Fu' sweet that day.

II

As lightsomely I glowr'd abroad,   10
    To see a scene sae gay,
Three *hizzies*, early at the road,
    Cam skelpan up the way.
Twa had manteeles o' dolefu' black,
    But ane wi' lyart lining;
The third, that gaed a wee a-back,
    Was in the fashion shining
                Fu' gay that day.

III

The *twa* appear'd like sisters twin,
    In feature, form an' claes;   20
Their visage wither'd, lang an' thin,
    An' sour as ony slaes:
The *third* cam up, hap-step-an'-loup,
    As light as ony lambie,
An' wi' a curchie low did stoop,
    As soon as e'er she saw me,
                Fu' kind that day.

IV

Wi' bonnet aff, quoth I, 'Sweet lass,
    'I think ye seem to ken me;
'I'm sure I've seen that bonie face,   30
    'But yet I canna name ye.'
Quo' she, an' laughan as she spak,
    An' taks me by the han's,

'Ye, for my sake, hae gien the feck
  'Of a' the *ten comman's*
            A screed some day.'

V

'My name is FUN—your cronie dear,°
  'The nearest friend ye hae;
'An' this is SUPERSTITION here,
  'An' that's HYPOCRISY.
'I'm gaun to ********* *holy fair*,°   40
  'To spend an hour in daffin:
'Gin ye'll go there, yon runkl'd pair,
  'We will get famous laughin
            At them this day.'

VI

Quoth I, 'With a' my heart, I'll do't;
  'I'll get my sunday's sark on,
'An' meet you on the holy spot;
  'Faith, we'se hae fine remarkin!'
Then I gaed hame at crowdie-time,   50
  An' soon I made me ready;
For roads were clad, frae side to side,
  Wi' monie a wearie body,
            In droves that day.

VII

Here, farmers gash, in ridin graith,
  Gaed hoddan by their cotters;
There, swankies young, in braw braid-claith,
  Are springan owre the gutters.
The lasses, skelpan barefit, thrang,
  In silks an' scarlets glitter;   60
Wi' *sweet-milk cheese*, in monie a whang,
  An' *farls*, bak'd wi' butter,
            Fu' crump that day.

VIII

When by the *plate* we set our nose,
  Weel heaped up wi' ha'pence,
A greedy glowr *black-bonnet* throws,°

An' we maun draw our tippence.
Then in we go to see the show,
    On ev'ry side they're gath'ran;
Some carryan dails, some chairs an' stools,   70
    An' some are busy bleth'ran
                    Right loud that day.

IX

Here stands a shed to fend the show'rs,
    An' screen our countra Gentry;
There, *racer Jess*, an' twathree wh——res,°
    Are blinkan at the entry.
Here sits a raw o' tittlan jads,
    Wi' heaving breasts an' bare neck;
An' there, a batch o' *Wabster lads*,
    Blackguarding frae K********ck°   80
                    For *fun* this day.

X

Here, some are thinkan on their sins,
    An' some upo' their claes;
Ane curses feet that fyl'd his shins,
    Anither sighs an' prays:
On this hand sits an *Elect* swatch,°
    Wi' screw'd-up, grace-proud faces;
On that, a set o' chaps, at watch,
    Thrang winkan on the lasses
                    To *chairs* that day.   90

XI

O happy is that man, an' blest!
    Nae wonder that it pride him!
Whase ain dear lass, that he likes best,
    Comes clinkan down beside him!
Wi' arm repos'd on the *chair-back*,
    He sweetly does compose him;
Which, by degrees, slips round her *neck*,
    An's loof upon her *bosom*
                    Unkend that day.

XII

Now a' the congregation o'er   100
   Is silent expectation;
For ****** speels the holy door,°
   Wi' tidings o' s—lv—t—n.°
Should *Hornie*, as in ancient days,°
   'Mang sons o' G— present him,
The vera sight o' ******'s face,
   To's ain *het hame* had sent him
         Wi' fright that day.

XIII

Hear how he clears the points o' Faith
   Wi' rattlin an' thumpin!   110
Now meekly calm, now wild in wrath,
   He's stampan, an' he's jumpan!
His lengthen'd chin, his turn'd up snout,
   His eldritch squeel an' gestures,
O how they fire the heart devout,
   Like *cantharidian* plaisters°
         On sic a day!

XIV

But hark! the *tent* has chang'd it's voice;°
   There's peace an' rest nae langer;
For a' the *real judges* rise,   120
   They canna sit for anger.
***** opens out his cauld harangues,°
   On *practice* and on *morals*;
An' aff the *godly* pour in thrangs,
   To gie the jars an' barrels
         A lift that day.

XV

What signifies his barren shine,
   Of *moral pow'rs* an' *reason*?
His English style, an' gesture fine,°
   Are a' clean out o' season.   130
Like SOCRATES or ANTONINE,°
   Or some auld pagan heathen,

The *moral man* he does define,
　　But ne'er a word o' *faith* in
　　　　　　That's right that day.

XVI

In guid time comes an antidote
　　Against sic poosion'd nostrum;
For *******, frae the water-fit,°
　　Ascends the *holy rostrum*:
See, up he's got the word o' G—,　　　　　　140
　　An' meek an' mim has view'd it,
While COMMON-SENSE has taen the road,°
　　An' aff, an' up the *Cowgate*°
　　　　　　Fast, fast that day.

XVII

Wee ****** neist, the Guard relieves,°
　　An' Orthodoxy raibles,
Tho' in his heart he weel believes,
　　An' thinks it auld wives' fables:
But faith! the birkie wants a *Manse*,
　　So, cannilie he hums them;　　　　　　150
Altho' his *carnal* Wit an' Sense
　　Like hafflins-wise o'ercomes him
　　　　　　At times that day.

XVIII

Now, butt an' ben, the Change-house fills,°
　　Wi' *yill-caup* Commentators:
Here's crying out for bakes an' gills,
　　An' there the pint-stowp clatters;
While thick an' thrang, an' loud an' lang,
　　Wi' *Logic*, an' wi' *Scripture*,
They raise a din, that, in the end,　　　　　　160
　　Is like to breed a rupture
　　　　　　O' wrath that day.

XIX

Leeze me on Drink! it gies us mair
　　Than either School or Colledge:
It kindles Wit, it waukens Lear,

It pangs us fou o' Knowledge.
Be't *whisky-gill* or *penny-wheep*,
    Or ony stronger potion,
It never fails, on drinkin deep,
    To kittle up our *notion*,   170
            By night or day.

XX

The lads an' lasses, blythely bent
    To mind baith *saul* an' *body*,
Sit round the table, weel content,
    An' steer about the *toddy*.
On this ane's dress, an' that ane's leuk,
    They're makin observations;
While some are cozie i' the neuk,
    An' forming *assignations*
            To meet some day.   180

XXI

But now the L—'s ain trumpet touts,°
    Till a' the hills are rairan,
An' echos back return the shouts;
    Black ****** is na spairan:°
His piercin words, like Highlan swords,
    Divide the joints an' marrow;°
His talk o' H—ll, whare devils dwell,
    Our vera 'Sauls does harrow'[1]
            Wi' fright that day!

XXII

A vast, unbottom'd, boundless *Pit*,   190
    Fill'd fou o' *lowan brunstane*,
Whase raging flame, an' scorching heat,
    Wad melt the hardest whun-stane!
The *half asleep* start up wi' fear,
    An' think they hear it roaran,
When presently it does appear,
    'Twas but some neebor *snoran*
            Asleep that day.

[1] Shakespeare's Hamlet.

XXIII

'Twad be owre lang a tale to tell,
    How monie stories past,
An' how they crouded to the yill,
    When they were a' dismist:
How drink gaed round, in cogs an' caups,
    Amang the furms an' benches;
An' *cheese* an' *bread*, frae women's laps,
    Was dealt about in lunches,
                An' dawds that day.

XXIV

In comes a gawsie, gash *Guidwife*,
    An' sits down by the fire,
Syne draws her *kebbuck* an' her knife;
    The lasses they are shyer.
The auld *Guidmen*, about the *grace*,
    Frae side to side they bother,
Till some ane by his bonnet lays,
    An' gies them't, like a *tether*,
                Fu' lang that day.

XXV

Waesucks! for him that gets nae lass,
    Or lasses that hae naething!
Sma' need has he to say a grace,
    Or melvie his braw claithing!
O *Wives* be mindfu', ance yoursel,
    How bonie lads ye wanted,
An' dinna, for a *kebbuck-heel*,
    Let lasses be affronted
                On sic a day!

XXVI

Now *Clinkumbell*, wi' rattlan tow,
    Begins to jow an' croon;
Some swagger hame, the best they dow,
    Some wait the afternoon.
At slaps the billies halt a blink,
    Till lasses strip their shoon:

Wi' *faith* an' *hope*, an' *love* an' *drink*,
 They're a' in famous tune
                    For crack that day.

XXVII

How monie hearts this day converts,
 O' sinners and o' Lasses!
Their hearts o' stane, gin night are gane,
 As saft as ony flesh is.
There's some are fou o' *love divine*;
 There's some are fou o' *brandy*;   240
An' monie jobs that day begin,
 May end in *Houghmagandie*
                    Some ither day.

ADDRESS TO THE DEIL

O Prince, O chief of many throned pow'rs,
That led th'embattl'd Seraphim to war—

                              MILTON°

O Thou, whatever title suit thee!
Auld Hornie, Satan, Nick, or Clootie,°
Wha in yon cavern grim an' sootie,
                    Clos'd under hatches,
Spairges about the brunstane cootie,
                    To scaud poor wretches!

 Hear me, *auld Hangie*, for a wee,
An' let poor, *damned bodies* bee;
I'm sure sma' pleasure it can gie,
                    Ev'n to a *deil*,   10
To skelp an' scaud poor dogs like me,
                    An' hear us squeel!

 Great is thy pow'r, an' great thy fame;
Far kend an' noted is thy name;
An' tho' yon *lowan heugh's* thy hame,
                    Thou travels far;

An' faith! thou's neither lag nor lame,
                    Nor blate nor scaur.

Whyles, ranging like a roaran lion,°
For prey, a' holes an' corners tryin;   20
Whyles, on the strong-wing'd Tempest flyin,
                    Tirlan the *kirks*;
Whyles, in the human bosom pryin,
                    Unseen thou lurks.

I've heard my rev'rend *Graunie* say,
In lanely glens ye like to stray;
Or where auld, ruin'd castles, gray,
                    Nod to the moon,
Ye fright the nightly wand'rer's way,
                    Wi' eldritch croon.   30

When twilight did my *Graunie* summon,
To say her pray'rs, douse, honest woman!
Aft 'yont the dyke she's heard you bumman,
                    Wi' eerie drone;
Or, rustling, thro' the boortries coman,
                    Wi' heavy groan.

Ae dreary, windy, winter night,
The stars shot down wi' sklentan light,
Wi' you, *mysel*, I gat a fright,
                    Ayont the lough;   40
Ye, like a *rash-buss*, stood in sight,
                    Wi' waving sugh.

The cudgel in my nieve did shake,
Each bristl'd hair stood like a stake,
When wi' an eldritch, stoor *quaick, quaick*,
                    Amang the springs,
Awa ye squatter'd like a *drake*,
                    On whistling wings.

Let *Warlocks* grim, an' wither'd *Hags*,°
Tell how wi' you on ragweed nags,   50
They skim the muirs an' dizzy crags,

Wi' wicked speed;
And in kirk-yards renew their leagues,
Owre howcket dead.

Thence, countra wives, wi' toil an' pain,
May plunge an' plunge the *kirn* in vain;
For Oh! the yellow treasure's taen
By witching skill;
An' dawtet, twal-pint *Hawkie's* gane
As yell's the Bill. 60

Thence, mystic knots mak great abuse,
On *Young-Guidmen*, fond, keen an' croose;
When the best *wark-lume* i' the house,
By cantraip wit,
Is instant made no worth a louse,
Just at the bit.

When thowes dissolve the snawy hoord,
An' float the jinglan icy boord,
Then, *Water-kelpies* haunt the foord,
By your direction, 70
An' nighted Trav'llers are allur'd
To their destruction.

An' aft your moss-traversing *Spunkies*
Decoy the wight that late an' drunk is:
The bleezan, curst, mischievous monkies
Delude his eyes,
Till in some miry slough he sunk is,
Ne'er mair to rise.

When MASONS' mystic *word* an' *grip*,°
In storms an' tempests raise you up, 80
Some cock or cat, your rage maun stop,
Or, strange to tell!
The *youngest Brother* ye wad whip
Aff straught to *H–ll*.

Lang syne in EDEN'S bonie yard,
When youthfu' lovers first were pair'd,

An' all the Soul of Love they shar'd,
                The raptur'd hour,
Sweet on the fragrant, flow'ry swaird,
                In shady bow'r.   90

Then you, ye auld, snick-drawing dog!
Ye cam to Paradise incog,
An' play'd on man a cursed brogue,
                (Black be your fa'!)
An' gied the infant warld a shog,
                'Maist ruin'd a'.

D'ye mind that day, when in a bizz,
Wi' reeket duds, an' reestet gizz,
Ye did present your smoutie phiz,
                'Mang better folk,   100
An' sklented on the *man of Uzz*,°
                Your spitefu' joke?

An' how ye gat him i' your thrall,
An' brak him out o' house an' hal',
While scabs an' botches did him gall,
                Wi' bitter claw,
An' lows'd his ill-tongu'd, wicked *Scawl*
                Was worst ava?

But a' your doings to rehearse,
Your wily snares an' fechtin fierce,   110
Sin' that day MICHAEL[1] did you pierce,°
                Down to this time,
Wad ding a *Lallan* tongue, or *Erse*,°
                In Prose or Rhyme.

An' now, auld *Cloots*, I ken ye're thinkan,
A certain *Bardie's* rantin, drinkin,
Some luckless hour will send him linkan,
                To your black pit;
But faith! he'll turn a corner jinkan,
                An' cheat you yet.   120

---

[1] Vide Milton, Book 6th.

> But fare-you-weel, auld *Nickie-ben*!
> O wad ye tak a thought an' men'!
> Ye aiblins might—I dinna ken—
>   Still hae a *stake*—
> I'm wae to think upo' yon den,
>   Ev'n for your sake!

THE DEATH AND DYING WORDS OF POOR MAILIE,
THE AUTHOR'S ONLY PET YOWE.
AN UNCO MOURNFU' TALE

> AS MAILIE, an' her lambs thegither,
> Was ae day nibbling on the tether,
> Upon her cloot she coost a hitch,
> An' owre she warsl'd in the ditch:
> There, groaning, dying, she did ly,
> When *Hughoc*[1] he cam doytan by.

> Wi' glowrin een, an' lifted han's,
> Poor *Hughoc* like a statue stan's;
> He saw her days were near hand ended,
> But, waes my heart! he could na mend it!   10
> He gaped wide, but naething spak,
> At length poor *Mailie* silence brak.

> 'O thou, whase lamentable face
> Appears to mourn my woefu' case!
> My *dying words* attentive hear,
> An' bear them to my *Master* dear.

> Tell him, if e'er again he keep
> As muckle gear as buy a *sheep*,
> O, bid him never tye them mair,
> Wi' wicked strings o' hemp or hair!°   20
> But ca them out to park or hill,
> An' let them wander at their will:
> So, may his flock increase an' grow
> To *scores* o' lambs, an' *packs* of woo'!°

[1] A neibor herd-callan.

Tell him, he was a Master kin',
An' ay was guid to me an' mine;
An' now my *dying* charge I gie him,°
My helpless *lambs*, I trust them wi' him.

O, bid him save their harmless lives,
Frae dogs an' tods, an' butchers' knives!   30
But gie them guid *cow-milk* their fill,
Till they be fit to fend themsel;
An' tent them duely, e'en an' morn,
Wi' taets o' *hay* an' ripps o' *corn*.

An' may they never learn the gaets,
Of ither vile, wanrestfu' *Pets*!
To slink thro' slaps, an' reave an' steal,
At stacks o' pease, or stocks o' kail.
So may they, like their great *forbears*,
For monie a year come thro' the sheers: 40
So *wives* will gie them bits o' bread,
An' *bairns* greet for them when they're dead.

My poor *toop-lamb*, my son an' heir,
O, bid him breed him up wi' care!
An' if he live to be a beast,
To pit some havins in his breast!
An' warn him ay at ridin time,°
To stay content wi' *yowes* at hame;
An' no to rin an' wear his cloots,
Like ither menseless, graceless brutes.   50

An' niest my *yowie*, silly thing,
Gude keep thee frae a *tether string*!
O, may thou ne'er forgather up,
Wi' onie blastet, moorlan *toop*;
But ay keep mind to moop an' mell,
Wi' sheep o' credit like thysel!

And now, *my bairns*, wi' my last breath,
I lea'e my blessin wi' you baith:
An' when ye think upo' your Mither,
Mind to be kind to ane anither.   60

Now, honest Hughoc, dinna fail,
To tell my Master a' my tale;
An' bid him burn this cursed *tether*,
An' for thy pains thou'se get my blather.'°

This said, poor *Mailie* turn'd her head,
An' clos'd her een amang the dead!

POOR MAILIE'S ELEGY

LAMENT in rhyme, lament in prose,
Wi' saut tears trickling down your nose;
Our *Bardie's* fate is at a close,
        Past a' remead!
The last, sad cape-stane of his woes;
        Poor Mailie's dead!

It's no the loss o' warl's gear,
That could sae bitter draw the tear,
Or make our *Bardie*, dowie, wear
        The mourning weed: 10
He's lost a friend and neebor dear,
        In *Mailie* dead.

Thro' a' the town she trotted by him;
A lang half-mile she could descry him;
Wi' kindly bleat, when she did spy him,
        She ran wi' speed:
A friend mair faithfu' ne'er came nigh him,
        Than *Mailie* dead.

I wat she was a *sheep* o' sense,
An' could behave hersel wi' mense: 20
I'll say't, she never brak a fence,
        Thro' thievish greed.
Our *Bardie*, lanely, keeps the spence
        Sin' *Mailie's* dead.

Or, if he wanders up the howe,
Her living image in *her yowe*,

Comes bleating till him, owre the knowe,
        For bits o' bread;
An' down the briny pearls rowe
        For *Mailie* dead.   30

She was nae get o' moorlan tips,
Wi' tauted ket, an' hairy hips;
For her forbears were brought in ships,
        Frae 'yont the TWEED:°
A bonier *fleesh* ne'er cross'd the clips
        Than *Mailie's* dead.

Wae worth that man wha first did shape,
That vile, wanchancie thing—*a raep!*
It maks guid fellows girn an' gape,
        Wi' chokin dread;   40
An' *Robin's* bonnet wave wi' crape
        For *Mailie* dead.

O, a' ye *Bards* on bonie DOON!°
An' wha on AIRE your chanters tune!°
Come, join the melancholious croon
        O' *Robin's* reed!
His heart will never get aboon!
        His *Mailie's* dead!

TO J. S****

Friendship, mysterious cement of the soul!
Sweet'ner of Life, and solder of Society!
I owe thee much—

                        BLAIR.°

DEAR S****, the sleest, pawkie thief,
That e'er attempted stealth or rief,
Ye surely hae some warlock-breef
        Owre human hearts;
For ne'er a bosom yet was prief
        Against your arts.

For me, I swear by sun an' moon,
And ev'ry star that blinks aboon,
Ye've cost me twenty pair o' shoon
      Just gaun to see you;   10
And ev'ry ither pair that's done,
      Mair taen I'm wi' you.

That auld, capricious carlin, *Nature*,
To mak amends for scrimpet stature,
She's turn'd you off, a human-creature
      On her *first* plan,
And in her freaks, on ev'ry feature,
      She's wrote, *the Man*.

Just now I've taen the fit o' rhyme,°
My barmie noddle's working prime,   20
My fancy yerket up sublime
      Wi' hasty summon:
Hae ye a leisure-moment's time
      To hear what's comin?

Some rhyme a neebor's name to lash;
Some rhyme, (vain thought!) for needfu' cash;
Some rhyme to court the countra clash,
      An' raise a din;
For me, an *aim* I never fash;
      I rhyme for *fun*.   30

The star that rules my luckless lot,
Has fated me the russet coat,°
An' damn'd my fortune to the groat;°
      But, in requit,
Has blest me with a *random-shot*
      O' countra wit.

This while my notion's taen a sklent,
To try my fate in guid, black *prent*;°
But still the mair I'm that way bent,
      Something cries, 'Hoolie!   40
'I red you, honest man, tak tent!
      'Ye'll shaw your folly.

'There's ither Poets, much your betters,
'Far seen in *Greek*, deep men o' *letters*,
'Hae thought they had ensur'd their debtors,
    'A' future ages;
'Now moths deform in shapeless tatters,
    'Their unknown pages.'

Then farewel hopes of Laurel-boughs,
To garland my poetic brows!   50
Henceforth, I'll rove where busy ploughs
    Are whistling thrang,
An' teach the lanely heights an' howes
    My rustic sang.

I'll wander on with tentless heed,
How never-halting moments speed,
Till fate shall snap the brittle thread;
    Then, all unknown,
I'll lay me with th' *inglorious dead*,°
    Forgot and gone!   60

But why, o' Death, begin a tale?
Just now we're living sound an' hale;
Then top and maintop croud the sail,
    Heave *Care* o'er-side!
And large, before Enjoyment's gale,
    Let's tak the tide.

This life, sae far's I understand,
Is a' enchanted fairy-land,
Where Pleasure is the Magic-wand,
    That, wielded right,   70
Maks Hours like Minutes, hand in hand,
    Dance by fu' light.

The *magic-wand* then let us wield;
For, ance that five an' forty's speel'd,
See, crazy, weary, joyless Eild,
    Wi' wrinkl'd face,
Comes hostan, hirplan owre the field,
    Wi' creeping pace.

When ance *life's day* draws near the gloamin,
Then fareweel vacant, careless roamin;   80
An' fareweel cheerfu' tankards foamin,
                    An' social noise;
An' fareweel dear, deluding woman,
                    The joy of joys!

O *Life!* how pleasant in thy morning,
Young Fancy's rays the hills adorning!
Cold-pausing Caution's lesson scorning,
                    We frisk away,
Like school-boys, at th' expected warning,
                    To joy and play.   90

We wander there, we wander here,
We eye the *rose* upon the brier,
Unmindful that the *thorn* is near,
                    Among the leaves;
And tho' the puny wound appear,
                    Short while it grieves.

Some, lucky, find a flow'ry spot,
For which they never toil'd nor swat;
They drink the *sweet* and eat the *fat*,
                    But care or pain;   100
And haply, eye the barren hut,
                    With high disdain.°

With steady aim, some Fortune chase;
Keen hope does ev'ry sinew brace;
Thro' fair, thro' foul, they urge the race,
                    And sieze the prey:
Then canie, in some cozie place,
                    They close the *day*.

And others, like your humble servan',
Poor wights! nae rules nor roads observin;   110
To right or left, eternal swervin,
                    They zig-zag on;
Till curst with Age, obscure an' starvin,
                    They aften groan.

Alas! what bitter toil an' straining—
But truce with peevish, poor complaining!
Is Fortune's fickle *Luna* waning?°
      E'en let her gang!
Beneath what light she has remaining,
      Let's sing our Sang.   120

My pen I here fling to the door,
And kneel, ye *Pow'rs*, and warm implore,°
'Tho' I should wander *Terra* o'er,
      'In all her climes,
'Grant me but this, I ask no more,
      'Ay rowth o' rhymes.

'Gie dreeping roasts to *countra Lairds*,
'Till icicles hing frae their beards;
'Gie fine braw claes to fine *Life-guards*,
      'And *Maids of Honor*;   130
'And yill an' whisky gie to *Cairds*,
      'Until they sconner.

'A *Title*, DEMPSTER merits it;°
'A *Garter* gie to WILLIE PIT;°
'Gie Wealth to some be-ledger'd Cit,°
      'In cent per cent;
'But give me real, sterling Wit,
      'And I'm content.

'While ye are pleas'd to keep me hale,
'I'll sit down o'er my scanty meal,   140
'Be't *water-brose*, or *muslin-kail*,
      'Wi' cheerfu' face,
'As lang's the Muses dinna fail
      'To say the grace.'

An anxious e'e I never throws
Behint my lug, or by my nose;
I jouk beneath Misfortune's blows
      As weel's I may;
Sworn foe to *sorrow*, *care*, and *prose*,
      I rhyme away.   150

O ye, douse folk, that live by rule,
Grave, tideless-blooded, calm and cool,
Compar'd wi' you—O fool! fool! fool!
        How much unlike!
Your hearts are just a standing pool,
        Your lives, a dyke!

Nae hare-brain'd, sentimental traces,°
In your unletter'd, nameless faces!
In *arioso* trills and graces°
        Ye never stray,   160
But *gravissimo*, solemn basses°
        Ye hum away.

Ye are sae *grave*, nae doubt ye're *wise*;
Nae ferly tho' ye do despise
The hairum-scairum, ram-stam boys,°
        The rambling squad:°
I see ye upward cast your eyes—
        —Ye ken the road—

Whilst I—but I shall haud me there—
Wi' you I'll scarce gang *ony where*—   170
Then *Jamie*, I shall say nae mair,
        But quat my sang,
Content *with* YOU to mak a *pair*,
        Whare'er I gang.

A DREAM

Thoughts, words and deeds, the Statute blames with reason;
But surely Dreams *were ne'er indicted Treason.*

ON READING, IN THE PUBLIC PAPERS, THE LAUREATE'S
ODE, WITH THE OTHER PARADE OF JUNE 4th, 1786, THE
AUTHOR WAS NO SOONER DROPT ASLEEP, THAN HE
IMAGINED HIMSELF TRANSPORTED TO THE BIRTH-DAY
LEVEE; AND, IN HIS DREAMING FANCY, MADE THE
FOLLOWING ADDRESS.

I

GUID-MORNIN to your MAJESTY!
    May heaven augment your blisses,
On ev'ry new *Birth-day* ye see,
    A humble Bardie wishes!°
My Bardship here, at your Levee,
    On sic a day as this is,
Is sure an uncouth sight to see,
    Amang thae Birth-day dresses
                Sae fine this day.

II

I see ye're complimented thrang,   10
    By many a *lord* an' *lady*;
'God save the King' 's a cukoo sang
    That's unco easy said ay:
The *Poets* too, a venal gang,
    Wi' rhymes weel-turn'd an' ready,
Wad gar you trow ye ne'er do wrang,
    But ay unerring steady,
                On sic a day.

III

For me! before a Monarch's face,
    Ev'n *there* I winna flatter;   20
For neither Pension, Post, nor Place,
    Am I your humble debtor:
So, nae reflection on YOUR GRACE,°
    Your Kingship to bespatter;
There's monie *waur* been o' the Race,
    And aiblins *ane* been better°
                Than You this day.

IV

'Tis very true, my sovereign King,
    My skill may weel be doubted;
But *Facts* are cheels that winna ding,   30
    An' downa be disputed:
Your *royal nest*, beneath *Your* wing,
    Is e'en right reft an' clouted,

And now the third part o' the string,
    An' less, will gang about it°
                Than did ae day.

V

Far be't frae me that I aspire
    To blame your Legislation,
Or say, ye wisdom want, or fire,
    To rule this mighty nation;   40
But faith! I muckle doubt, my SIRE,
    Ye've trusted 'Ministration,
To chaps, wha, in a *barn* or *byre*,
    Wad better fill'd their station
                Than *courts* yon day.

VI

And now Ye've gien auld *Britain* peace,
    Her broken shins to plaister;
Your sair taxation does her fleece,
    Till she has scarce a tester:
For me, thank God, my life's a *lease*,   50
    Nae *bargain* wearing faster,
Or faith! I fear, that, wi' the geese,
    I shortly boost to pasture
                I' the craft some day.°

VII

I'm no mistrusting *Willie Pit*,
    When taxes he enlarges,
(An' *Will's* a true guid fallow's get,°
    A Name not Envy spairges)
That he intends to pay your *debt*,°
    An' lessen a' your *charges*;   60
But, G—d-sake! let nae *saving-fit*
    Abridge your bonie *Barges*
                An' *Boats* this day.

VIII

Adieu, my LIEGE! may Freedom geck
    Beneath your high protection;
An' may Ye rax Corruption's neck,

And gie her for dissection!°
But since I'm here, I'll no neglect,
   In loyal, true affection,
To pay your QUEEN, with due respect,°   70
   My fealty an' subjection
          This great Birth-day.

IX

Hail, *Majesty most Excellent!*
   While Nobles strive to please Ye,
Will Ye accept a Compliment,
   A simple Bardie gies Ye?
Thae bonie Bairntime, Heav'n has lent,°
   Still higher may they heeze Ye
In bliss, till Fate some day is sent,
   For ever to release Ye   80
          Frae Care that day.

X

For you, young Potentate o' W—,°
   I tell your *Highness* fairly,
Down Pleasure's stream, wi' swelling sails,
   I'm tauld ye're driving rarely;
But some day ye may gnaw your nails,
   An' curse your folly sairly,
That e'er ye brak Diana's *pales*,°
   Or rattl'd dice wi' *Charlie*°
          By night or day.   90

XI

Yet aft a ragged *Cowte's* been known,
   To mak a noble *Aiver*;
So, ye may dousely fill a Throne,
   For a' their clish-ma-claver:
There, Him at *Agincourt* wha shone,
   Few better were or braver;
And yet, wi' funny, queer *Sir John*,[1]
   He was an unco shaver
          For monie a day.

---

[1] Sir John Falstaff, Vide Shakespeare.

XII

For you, right rev'rend O——,°   100
   Nane sets the *lawn-sleeve* sweeter,°
Altho' a ribban at your lug°
   Wad been a dress compleater:
As ye disown yon paughty dog,
   That *bears* the Keys of Peter,°
Then swith! an' get a *wife* to hug,
   Or trouth! ye'll stain the *Mitre*
              Some luckless day.

XIII

Young, royal TARRY-BREEKS,° I learn,
   Ye've lately come athwart her;   110
A glorious *Galley*,[1] stem and stern,
   Weel rigg'd for *Venus barter*;
But first hang out that she'll discern°
   Your *hymeneal Charter*,
Then heave aboard your *grapple airn*,
   An', large upon her *quarter*,
              Come full that day.

XIV

Ye lastly, bonie blossoms a',
   Ye *royal Lasses* dainty,°
Heav'n mak you guid as weel as braw,   120
   An' gie you *lads* a plenty:
But sneer na *British-boys* awa;
   For King's are unco scant ay,
An' German-Gentles are but *sma'*,°
   They're better just than *want ay*
              On onie day.

XV

God bless you a'! consider now,
   Ye're unco muckle dautet;
But ere the *course* o' life be through,
   It may be bitter sautet: 130

[1] Alluding to the Newspaper account of a certain royal Sailor's Amour.

An' I hae seen their *coggie* fou,
   That yet hae tarrow't at it,
But or the *day* was done, I trow,
   The laggen they hae clautet
      Fu' clean that day.

THE VISION

DUAN FIRST[1]

THE sun had clos'd the *winter-day*,
The Curlers quat their roaring play,°
And hunger'd Maukin taen her way
      To kail-yards green,°
While faithless snaws ilk step betray
      Whare she has been.

The Thresher's weary *flingin-tree*,
The lee-lang day had tir'd me;
And when the Day had clos'd his e'e,
      Far i' the West,   10
Ben i' the *Spence*, right pensivelie,
      I gaed to rest.

There, lanely, by the ingle-cheek,
I sat and ey'd the spewing reek,
That fill'd, wi' hoast-provoking smeek,
      The auld, clay biggin;°
And heard the restless rattons squeak
      About the riggin.

All in this mottie, misty clime,
I backward mus'd on wasted time,   20
How I had spent my *youthfu' prime*,
      An' done nae-thing,
But stringing blethers up in rhyme
      For fools to sing.

[1] Duan, a term of Ossian's for the different divisions of a digressive Poem. See his Cath-Loda, Vol. 2 of McPherson's Translation.

Had I to guid advice but harket,
I might, by this, hae led a market,
Or strutted in a Bank and clarket
           My *Cash-Account*;
While here, half-mad, half-fed, half-sarket,
           Is a' th' amount.   30

I started, mutt'ring blockhead! coof!
And heav'd on high my wauket loof,
To swear by a' yon starry roof,
           Or some rash aith,
That I, henceforth, would be *rhyme-proof*
           Till my last breath—

When click! the *string* the *snick* did draw;°
And jee! the door gaed to the wa';
And by my ingle-lowe I saw,
           Now bleezan bright,   40
A tight, outlandish *Hizzie*, braw,
           Come full in sight.

Ye need na doubt, I held my whisht;
The infant aith, half-form'd, was crusht;
I glowr'd as eerie's I'd been dusht,
           In some wild glen;
When sweet, like *modest Worth*, she blusht,
           And stepped ben.

Green, slender, leaf-clad *Holly-boughs*°
Were twisted, gracefu', round her brows,   50
I took her for some SCOTTISH MUSE,
           By that same token;
And come to stop those reckless vows,
           Would soon been broken.

A 'hare-brain'd, sentimental trace'°
Was strongly marked in her face;
A wildly-witty, rustic grace
           Shone full upon her;
Her *eye*, ev'n turn'd on empty space,
           Beam'd keen with *Honor*.   60

Down flow'd her robe, a *tartan* sheen,°
Till half a leg was scrimply seen;
And such a *leg!* my BESS, I ween,°
   Could only peer it;
Sae straught, sae taper, tight and clean,
    Nane else came near it.

Her *Mantle* large, of greenish hue,
My gazing wonder chiefly drew;
Deep *lights* and *shades*, bold-mingling, threw
   A lustre grand;   70
And seem'd, to my astonish'd view,
    A *well-known* Land.

Here, rivers in the sea were lost;
There, mountains to the skies were tost:
Here, tumbling billows mark'd the coast,
   With surging foam;
There, distant shone, *Art's* lofty boast,
    The lordly dome.

Here, DOON pour'd down his far-fetch'd floods;
There, well-fed IRWINE stately thuds:° 80
Auld, hermit AIRE staw thro' his woods,°
   On to the shore;
And many a lesser torrent scuds,
    With seeming roar.

Low, in a sandy valley spread,
An ancient BOROUGH rear'd her head;°
Still, as in *Scottish Story* read,
   She boasts a *Race*,
To ev'ry nobler virtue bred,
    And polish'd grace.°   90

DUAN SECOND

With musing-deep, astonish'd stare,
I view'd the heavenly-seeming *Fair*;
A whisp'ring *throb* did witness bear
   Of kindred sweet,
When with an elder Sister's air
    She did me greet.

'All hail! *my own* inspired Bard!
'In me thy native Muse regard!
'Nor longer mourn thy fate is hard,
        'Thus poorly low!   100
'I come to give thee such *reward*,
        'As *we* bestow.

  'Know, the great *Genius* of this Land,
'Has many a light, aerial band,°
'Who, all beneath his high command,
        'Harmoniously,
'As *Arts* or *Arms* they understand,
        'Their labors ply.

  'They SCOTIA'S Race among them share;
'Some fire the *Sodger* on to dare;   110
'Some rouse the *Patriot* up to bare°
        'Corruption's heart:
'Some teach the *Bard*, a darling care,
        'The tuneful Art.

  ''Mong swelling floods of reeking gore,
'They ardent, kindling spirits pour;
'Or, mid the venal Senate's roar,
        'They, sightless, stand,
'To mend the honest *Patriot-lore*,
        'And grace the hand.°   120

  'Hence, FULLARTON, the brave and young;°
'Hence, DEMPSTER'S truth-prevailing tongue;°
'Hence, sweet harmonious BEATTIE sung
        'His "Minstrel lays;"°
'Or tore, with noble ardour stung,
        'The *Sceptic's* bays.°

  'To lower Orders are assign'd,
'The humbler ranks of Human-kind,
'The rustic Bard, the lab'ring Hind,°
        'The Artisan;   130
'All chuse, as various they're inclin'd,
        'The various man.

'When yellow waves the heavy grain,
'The threat'ning *Storm*, some, strongly, rein;
'Some teach to meliorate the plain,
   'With *tillage-skill*;°
'And some instruct the Shepherd-train,
   'Blythe o'er the hill.

'Some hint the Lover's harmless wile;
'Some grace the Maiden's artless smile;   140
'Some soothe the Lab'rer's weary toil,
   'For humble gains,
'And make his *cottage-scenes* beguile
   'His cares and pains.

'Some, bounded to a district-space,
'Explore at large Man's *infant race*,
'To mark the embryotic trace,
   'Of *rustic Bard*;
'And careful note each op'ning grace,
   'A guide and guard.   150

'*Of these am I*—COILA my name;°
'And this district as mine I claim,
'Where once the *Campbell's*, chiefs of fame,°
   'Held ruling pow'r:
'I mark'd thy embryo-tuneful flame,
   'Thy natal hour.

'With future hope, I oft would gaze,
'Fond, on thy little, early ways,
'Thy rudely-caroll'd, chiming phrase,
   'In uncouth rhymes,   160
'Fir'd at the simple, artless lays
   'Of other times.

'I saw thee seek the sounding shore,
'Delighted with the dashing roar;
'Or when the *North* his fleecy store
   'Drove thro' the sky,
'I saw grim Nature's visage hoar,
   'Struck thy young eye.

'Or when the deep-green-mantl'd Earth,
'Warm-cherish'd ev'ry floweret's birth,   170
'And joy and music pouring forth,
   'In ev'ry grove,
'I saw thee eye the gen'ral mirth
    'With boundless love.

'When ripen'd fields, and azure skies,
'Call'd forth the *Reaper's* rustling noise,
'I saw thee leave their ev'ning joys,
   'And lonely stalk,
'To vent thy bosom's swelling rise,
    'In pensive walk.   180

'When *youthful Love*, warm-blushing, strong,
'Keen-shivering shot thy nerves along,
'Those accents, grateful to thy tongue,
   'Th' adored *Name*,
'I taught thee how to pour in song,
    'To soothe thy flame.

'I saw thy pulse's maddening play,
'Wild-send thee Pleasure's devious way,
'Misled by Fancy's *meteor-ray*,
   'By Passion driven;   190
'But yet the *light* that led astray,
    'Was *light* from Heaven.

'I taught thy manners-painting strains,
'The *loves*, the *ways* of simple swains,
'Till now, o'er all my wide domains,
   'Thy fame extends;
'And some, the pride of *Coila's* plains,
    'Become thy friends.

'Thou canst not learn, nor I can show,
'To paint with *Thomson's* landscape-glow;°   200
'Or wake the bosom-melting throe,
   'With *Shenstone's* art;°
'Or pour, with *Gray*, the moving flow,°
    'Warm on the heart.

'Yet all beneath th'unrivall'd Rose,
'The lowly Daisy sweetly blows;
'Tho' large the forest's Monarch throws
      'His army shade,
'Yet green the juicy Hawthorn grows,
      'Adown the glade.   210

'Then never murmur nor repine;
'Strive in thy *humble sphere* to shine;
'And trust me, not *Potosi's mine*,°
      'Nor *Kings regard*,
'Can give a bliss o'ermatching thine,
      'A *rustic Bard*.

'To give my counsels all in one,
'Thy *tuneful flame* still careful fan;
'Preserve *the dignity of Man*,
      'With Soul erect;   220
'And trust, the UNIVERSAL PLAN
      'Will all protect.

'*And wear thou this*'—She solemn said,
And bound the *Holly* round my head:
The polish'd leaves, and berries red,
      Did rustling play;
And, like a passing thought, she fled,
      In light away.

THE following POEM will, by many Readers, be well
enough understood; but, for the sake of those who are unac-
quainted with the manners and traditions of the country
where the scene is cast, Notes are added, to give some account
of the principal Charms and Spells of that Night, so big with
Prophecy to the Peasantry in the West of Scotland. The pas-
sion of prying into Futurity makes a striking part of the his-
tory of Human-nature, in it's rude state, in all ages and nations;
and it may be some entertainment to a philosophic mind, if
any such should honor the Author with a perusal, to see the
remains of it, among the more unenlightened in our own.

HALLOWEEN[1]

Yes! let the Rich deride, the Proud disdain,
The simple pleasures of the lowly train;
To me more dear, congenial to my heart,
One native charm, than all the gloss of art.

GOLDSMITH.°

I

UPON that *night*, when Fairies light,
  On *Cassilis Downans*[2] dance,°
Or owre the lays, in splendid blaze,
  On sprightly coursers prance;
Or for *Colean*,° the rout is taen,
  Beneath the moon's pale beams;
There, up the *Cove*,[3] to stray an' rove,
  Amang the rocks an' streams
          To sport that night.

II

Amang the bonie, winding banks,   10
  Where *Doon* rins, wimplin, clear,
Where BRUCE[4] ance rul'd the martial ranks,°
  An' shook his *Carrick* spear,
Some merry, friendly, countra folks,
  Together did convene,
To *burn* their nits, an' *pou* their stocks,
  An' haud their *Halloween*
          Fu' blythe that night.

[1] Is thought to be a night when Witches, Devils, and other mischief-making beings, are all abroad on their baneful, midnight errands: particularly, those aerial people, the Fairies, are said, on that night, to hold a grand Anniversary.

[2] Certain little, romantic, rocky, green hills, in the neighbourhood of the ancient seat of the Earls of Cassilis.

[3] A noted cavern near Colean-house, called the Cove of Colean; which, as well as Cassilis Downans, is famed, in country story, for being a favourite haunt of Fairies.

[4] The famous family of that name, the ancestors of ROBERT the great Deliverer of his country, were Earls of Carrick.

III

The lasses feat, an' cleanly neat,
    Mair braw than when they're fine;°   20
Their faces blythe, fu' sweetly kythe,
    Hearts leal, an' warm, an' kin':
The lads sae trig, wi' wooer-babs,
    Weel knotted on their garten,
Some unco blate, an' some wi' gabs,
    Gar lasses hearts gang startin
                Whyles fast at night.

IV

Then, first an' foremost, thro' the kail,
    Their *stocks*[1] maun a' be sought ance;
They steek their een, an' grape an' wale,   30
    For muckle anes, an' straught anes.
Poor hav'rel *Will* fell aff the drift,°
    An' wander'd thro' the *Bow-kail*,
An' pow't, for want o' better shift,
    A *runt* was like a sow-tail
                Sae bow't that night.

V

Then, straught or crooked, yird or nane,
    They roar an' cry a' throw'ther;
The vera *wee-things*, toddlan, rin,
    Wi' stocks out owre their shouther: 40
An' gif the *custock's* sweet or sour,
    Wi' joctelegs they taste them;
Syne coziely, aboon the door,
    Wi' cannie care, they've plac'd them
                To lye that night.

---

[1] The first ceremony of Halloween, is, pulling each a *Stock*, or plant of kail. They must go out, hand in hand, with eyes shut, and pull the first they meet with: its being big or little, straight or crooked, is prophetic of the size and shape of the grand object of all their Spells—the husband or wife. If any *yird*, or earth, stick to the root, that is *tocher*, or fortune; and the taste of the *custoc*, that is, the heart of the stem, is indicative of the natural temper and disposition. Lastly, the stems, or to give them their ordinary appellation, the *runts*, are placed somewhere above the head of the door; and the christian names of the people whom chance brings into the house, are, according to the priority of placing the *runts*, the names in question.

VI

The lasses staw frae 'mang them a',
  To pou their *stalks o' corn*;[1]
But *Rab* slips out, an' jinks about,
  Behint the muckle thorn:
He grippet *Nelly* hard an' fast;   50
  Loud skirl'd a' the lasses;
But her *tap-pickle* maist was lost,
  When kiutlan in the *Fause-house*[2]
      Wi' him that night.

VII

The auld Guidwife's weel-hoordet *nits*[3]
  Are round an' round divided,
An' monie lads an' lasses fates
  Are there that night decided:
Some kindle, couthie, side by side,
  An' *burn* thegither trimly;   60
Some start awa, wi' saucy pride,
  An' jump out owre the chimlie
      Fu' high that night.

VIII

Jean slips in twa, wi' tentie e'e;
  Wha 'twas, she wadna tell;
But this is *Jock*, an' this is *me*,
  She says in to hersel:
He bleez'd owre her, an' she owre him,
  As they wad never mair part,
Till fuff! he started up the lum,   70
  An' *Jean* had e'en a sair heart
      To see't that night.

[1] They go to the barn-yard, and pull each, at three several times, a stalk of Oats. If the third stalk wants the *top-pickle*, that is, the grain at the top of the stalk, the party in question will want the Maidenhead.

[2] When the corn is in a doubtful state, by being too green, or wet, the Stack-builder, by means of old timber, &c. makes a large apartment in his stack, with an opening in the side which is fairest exposed to the wind: this he calls a *Fause-house*.

[3] Burning the nuts is a favourite charm. They name the lad and lass to each particular nut, as they lay them in the fire; and according as they burn quietly together, or start from beside one another, the course and issue of the Courtship will be.

IX

Poor Willie, wi' his *bow-kail runt*,
    Was *brunt* wi' primsie *Mallie*;
An' *Mary*, nae doubt, took the drunt,
    To be compar'd to *Willie*:
Mall's nit lap out, wi' pridefu' fling,
    An' her ain fit, it brunt it;
While *Willie* lap, and swore by *jing*,
    'Twas just the way he wanted   80
                    To be that night.

X

Nell had the *Fause-house* in her min',
    She pits hersel an' *Rob* in;
In loving bleeze they sweetly join,
    Till white in ase they're sobbin:
Nell's heart was dancin at the view;
    She whisper'd *Rob* to leuk for't:
Rob, stownlins, prie'd her bonie mou,
    Fu' cozie in the neuk for't,
                    Unseen that night.   90

XI

But *Merran* sat behint their backs,
    Her thoughts on *Andrew Bell*;
She lea'es them gashan at their cracks,
    An' slips out by hersel:
She thro' the yard the nearest taks,
    An' for the *kiln* she goes then,°
An' darklins grapet for the *bauks*,
    And in the *blue-clue*[1] throws then,
                    Right fear't that night.

---

[1] Whoever would, with success, try this spell, must strictly observe these directions. Steal out, all alone, to the *kiln*, and, darkling, throw into the *pot*, a clew of blue yarn; wind it in a new clew off the old one; and towards the latter end, something will hold the thread: demand, *wha hauds?* i.e. who holds? and answer will be returned from the kiln-pot, by naming the christian and sirname of your future Spouse.

XII

An' ay she *win't*, an' ay she swat,   100
 I wat she made nae jaukin;
Till something *held* within the *pat*,
 Good L—d! but she was quaukin!
But whether 'twas the *Deil* himsel,
 Or whether 'twas a *bauk-en*',
Or whether it was *Andrew Bell*,
 She did na wait on talkin
    To spier that night.

XIII

Wee *Jenny* to her Graunie says,
 'Will ye go wi' me Graunie?   110
'I'll *eat the apple*[1] at the *glass*,
 'I gat frae uncle Johnie:'
She fuff't her pipe wi' sic a lunt,
 In wrath she was sae vap'rin,
She notic't na, an aizle brunt
 Her braw, new, worset apron
    Out thro' that night.

XIV

'Ye little Skelpie-limmer's-face!
 'I daur you try sic sportin,
'As seek the *foul Thief* onie place,   120
 'For him to spae your fortune:
'Nae doubt but ye may get a *sight!*
 'Great cause ye hae to fear it;
'For monie a ane has gotten a fright,
 'An' liv'd an' di'd deleeret,
    'On sic a night.

XV

'Ae Hairst afore the *Sherra-moor*,°
 'I mind't as weel's yestreen,

---

[1] Take a candle, and go, alone, to a looking glass; eat an apple before it, and some traditions say you should comb your hair all the time: the face of your conjugal companion, *to be*, will be seen in the glass, as if peeping over your shoulder.

'I was a gilpey then, I'm sure,
  'I was na past fyfteen: 130
'The Simmer had been cauld an' wat,
  'An' *Stuff* was unco green;
'An' ay a rantan *Kirn* we gat,
  'An' just on *Halloween*
         'It fell that night.

XVI

'Our *Stibble-rig* was *Rab McGraen*,
  'A clever, sturdy fallow;
'His Sin gat *Eppie Sim* wi' wean,
  'That liv'd in Achmacalla:°
'He gat *hemp-seed*,[1] I mind it weel,   140
  'An' he made unco light o't;
'But monie a day was *by himsel*,
  'He was sae sairly frighted
        'That vera night.'

XVII

Then up gat fechtan *Jamie Fleck*,
  An' he swoor by his conscience,
That he could *saw hemp-seed* a peck;
  For it was a' but nonsense:
The auld guidman raught down the pock,
  An' out a handfu' gied him;   150
Syne bad him slip frae 'mang the folk,
  Sometime when nae ane see'd him,
        An' try't that night.

XVIII

He marches thro' amang the stacks,
  Tho' he was something sturtan;
The *graip* he for a *harrow* taks,

---

[1] Steal out, unperceived, and sow a handful of hemp seed; harrowing it with any thing you can conveniently draw after you. Repeat, now and then, 'Hemp-seed I saw thee, Hemp-seed I saw thee; and him (or her) that is to be my true-love, come after me and pou thee.' Look over your left shoulder, and you will see the appearance of the person invoked, in the attitude of pulling hemp. Some traditions say, 'come after me and shaw thee,' that is, show thyself; in which case it simply appears. Others omit the harrowing, and say, 'come after me and harrow thee.'

An' haurls at his curpan:
And ev'ry now an' then, he says,
  'Hemp-seed I saw thee,
'An' her that is to be my lass,   160
  'Come after me an' draw thee
          'As fast this night.'

XIX

He whistl'd up *lord Lenox' march*,°
  To keep his courage cheary;
Altho' his hair began to arch,
  He was sae fley'd an' eerie:
Till presently he hears a squeak,
  An' then a grane an' gruntle;
He by his showther gae a keek,
  An' tumbl'd wi' a wintle   170
        Out owre that night.

XX

He roar'd a horrid murder-shout,
  In dreadfu' desperation!
An' young an' auld come rinnan out,
  An' hear the sad narration:
He swoor 'twas hilchan *Jean M*c*Craw*,
  Or crouchie *Merran Humphie*,
Till stop! she trotted thro' them a';
  An' wha was it but *Grumphie*
        Asteer that night?   180

XXI

Meg fain wad to the *Barn* gaen,
  To *winn three wechts o' naething*;[1]
But for to meet the Deil her lane,

[1] This charm must likewise be performed, unperceived and alone. You go to the *barn*, and open both doors; taking them off the hinges, if possible; for there is danger, that the Being, about to appear, may shut the doors, and do you some mischief. Then take that instrument used in winnowing the corn, which, in our country-dialect, we call a *wecht;* and go thro' all the attitudes of letting down corn against the wind. Repeat it three times; and the third time, an apparition will pass thro' the barn, in at the windy door, and out at the other, having both the figure in question and the appearance or retinue, marking the employment or station in life.

>   She pat but little faith in:
> She gies the Herd a pickle nits,
>   An' twa red cheeket apples,
> To watch, while for the *Barn* she sets,
>   In hopes to see *Tam Kipples*
>   That vera night.

XXII

> She turns the key, wi' cannie thraw,   190
>   An' owre the threshold ventures;
> But first on *Sawnie* gies a ca',
>   Syne bauldly in she enters:
> A *ratton* rattl'd up the wa',
>   An' she cry'd, L—d preserve her!
> An' ran thro' midden-hole an' a',
>   An' pray'd wi' zeal and fervour,
>   Fu' fast that night.

XXIII

> They hoy't out Will, wi' sair advice;
>   They hecht him some fine braw ane;   200
> It chanc'd the *Stack* he *faddom't thrice*,[10]
>   Was timmer-propt for thrawin:°
> He taks a swirlie, auld *moss-oak*,
>   For some black, grousome *Carlin;*
> An' loot a winze, an' drew a stroke,
>   Till skin in blypes cam haurlin
>   Aff's nieves that night.

XXIV

> A wanton widow *Leezie* was,
>   As cantie as a kittlen;
> But Och! that night, amang the shaws,   210
>   She gat a fearfu' settlin!
> She thro' the whins, an' by the cairn,
>   An' owre the hill gaed scrievin,

---

[1] Take an opportunity of going, unnoticed, to a *Bear-stack*, and fathom it three times round. The last fathom of the last time, you will catch in your arms, the appearance of your future conjugal yoke-fellow.

Whare *three Lairds' lan's met at a burn*,[1]
 To dip her *left sark-sleeve* in,
   Was bent that night.

XXV

Whyles owre a linn the burnie plays,
 As thro' the glen it wimpl't;
Whyles round a rocky scar it strays;
 Whyles in a wiel it dimpl't;   220
Whyles glitter'd to the nightly rays,
 Wi' bickerin, dancin dazzle;
Whyles cooket underneath the braes,
 Below the spreading hazle
   Unseen that night.

XXVI

Amang the brachens, on the brae,
 Between her an' the moon,
The Deil, or else an outler Quey,
 Gat up an' gae a croon:
Poor *Leezie's* heart maist lap the hool; 230
 Near lav'rock-height she jumpet,
But mist a fit, an' in the *pool*,
 Out owre the lugs she plumpet,
   Wi' a plunge that night.

XXVII

In order, on the clean hearth-stane,
 The *Luggies*[2] three are ranged;
And ev'ry time great care is taen,
 To see them duely changed:

---

[1] You go out, one or more, for this is a social spell, to a south-running spring or rivulet, where 'three Lairds' lands meet,' and dip your left shirt sleeve. Go to bed in sight of a fire, and hang your wet sleeve before it to dry. Ly awake; and sometime near midnight, an apparition, having the exact figure of the grand object in question, will come and turn the sleeve, as if to dry the other side of it.

[2] Take three dishes; put clean water in one, foul water in another, and leave the third empty: blindfold a person, and lead him to the hearth where the dishes are ranged; he (or she) dips the left hand: if by chance in the clean water, the future husband or wife will come to the bar of Matrimony, a Maid; if in the foul, a widow; if in the empty dish, it foretells, with equal certainty, no marriage at all. It is repeated three times; and every time the arrangement of the dishes is altered.

Auld, uncle *John*, wha *wedlock's joys*,
   Sin' *Mar's-year* did desire,°   240
Because he gat the toom dish thrice,
   He heav'd them on the fire,
                In wrath that night.

XXVIII

Wi' merry sangs, an' friendly cracks,
   I wat they did na weary;
And unco tales, an' funnie jokes,
   Their sports were cheap an' cheary:
Till *butter'd So'ns*,[1] wi' fragrant lunt,
   Set a' their gabs a steerin;
Syne, wi' a social glass o' strunt,   250
   They parted aff careerin
                Fu' blythe that night.

THE AULD FARMER'S NEW-YEAR-MORNING SALUTATION TO HIS AULD MARE, MAGGIE, ON GIVING HER THE ACCUSTOMED RIPP OF CORN TO HANSEL IN THE NEW-YEAR

A *Guid New-year* I wish you Maggie!
Hae, there's a ripp to thy auld baggie:
Tho' thou's howe-backet, now, an' knaggie,
      I've seen the day,
Thou could hae gaen like ony staggie
      Out owre the lay.

Tho' now thou's dowie, stiff an' crazy,
An' thy auld hide as white's a daisie,
I've seen thee dappl't, sleek an' glaizie,
      A bonie gray: 10
He should been tight that daur't to *raize* thee,
      Ance in a day.

Thou ance was i' the foremost rank,
A *filly* buirdly, steeve an' swank,

---

[1] Sowens, with butter instead of milk to them, is always the *Halloween Supper*.

An' set weel down a shapely shank,
        As e'er tread yird;
An' could hae flown out owre a stank,
        Like onie bird.

It's now some nine-an'-twenty-year,
Sin' thou was my *Guidfather's Meere*;   20
He gied me thee, o' tocher clear,
        An' fifty mark;°
Tho' it was sma', 'twas *weel-won* gear,
        An' thou was stark.

When first I gaed to woo my *Jenny*,
Ye then was trottan wi' your Minnie:
Tho' ye was trickie, slee an' funnie,
        Ye ne'er was donsie;
But hamely, tawie, quiet an' cannie,
        An' unco sonsie.   30

That *day*, ye pranc'd wi' muckle pride,
When ye bure hame my bonie *Bride*:
An' sweet an' gracefu' she did ride
        Wi' maiden air!
KYLE-STEWART I could bragged wide,°
        For sic a *pair*.

Tho' now ye dow but hoyte and hoble,
An' wintle like a saumont-coble,
That day, ye was a jinker noble,
        For heels an' win'!   40
An' ran them till they a' did wauble,
        Far, far behin'!

When thou an' I were young an' skiegh,
An' *Stable-meals* at Fairs were driegh,°
How thou wad prance, an' snore, an' scriegh,
        An' tak the road!
Towns-bodies ran, an' stood abiegh,
        An' ca't thee mad.

When thou was corn't, an' I was mellow,°
We took the road ay like a Swallow: 50
At *Brooses* thou had ne'er a fellow,
          For pith an' speed;
But ev'ry tail thou pay't them hollow,°
          Whare'er thou gaed.

The sma', droop-rumpl't, hunter cattle,°
Might aiblins waur't thee for a brattle;
But *sax Scotch mile*, thou try't their mettle,°
          An' gart them whaizle:
Nae whip nor spur, but just a wattle
          O' saugh or hazle.   60

Thou was a noble *Fittie-lan'*,
As e'er in tug or tow was drawn!
Aft thee an' I, in aught hours gaun,
          On guid March-weather,
Hae turn'd *sax rood* beside our han',°
          For days thegither.

Thou never braing't, an' fetch't, an' flisket,
But thy *auld tail* thou wad hae whisket,
An' spread abreed thy weel-fill'd *brisket*,
          Wi' pith an' pow'r,   70
Till sprittie knowes wad rair't an' risket,
          An' slypet owre.

When frosts lay lang, an' snaws were deep,
An' threaten'd *labor* back to keep,
I gied thy *cog* a wee-bit heap
          Aboon the timmer;°
I ken'd my *Maggie* wad na sleep,
          For that, or Simmer.

In *cart* or *car* thou never reestet;
The steyest brae thou wad hae fac't it;   80
Thou never lap, an' sten't, an' breastet,
          Then stood to blaw;
But just thy step a wee thing hastet,
          Thou snoov't awa.

My Pleugh is now thy *bairn-time* a';°
Four gallant brutes, as e'er did draw;
Forby sax mae, I've sell't awa,
   That thou hast nurst:
They drew me thretteen pund an' twa,
    The vera warst.   90

Monie a sair daurk we twa hae wrought,
An' wi' the weary warl' fought!
An' monie an *anxious day*, I thought
   We wad be beat!
Yet here to *crazy Age* we're brought,
   Wi' something yet.

An' think na', my auld, trusty *Servan'*,
That now perhaps thou's less deservin,
An' thy *auld days* may end in starvin',
   For my last fow,   100
A heapet *Stimpart*, I'll reserve ane
    Laid by for you.

We've worn to crazy years thegither;
We'll toyte about wi' ane anither;
Wi' tentie care I'll flit thy tether,
   To some hain'd rig,°
Whare ye may nobly rax your leather,
   Wi' sma' fatigue.

THE COTTER'S SATURDAY NIGHT

INSCRIBED TO R. A****, ESQ;

Let not Ambition mock their useful toil,
 Their homely joys, and destiny obscure;
Nor Grandeur hear, with a disdainful smile,
 The short and simple annals of the Poor.

      GRAY.°

I

MY lov'd, my honor'd, much respected friend,
No mercenary Bard his homage pays;

With honest pride, I scorn each selfish end,
    My dearest meed, a friend's esteem and praise:
To you I sing, in simple Scottish lays,
    The *lowly train* in life's sequester'd scene;
The native feelings strong, the guileless ways,
    What A**** in a *Cottage* would have been;
Ah! tho' his worth unknown, far happier there I ween!

II

November chill blaws loud wi' angry sugh;   10
    The short'ning winter-day is near a close;
The miry beasts retreating frae the pleugh;
    The black'ning trains o' craws to their repose:
The toil-worn COTTER frae his labor goes,
    This night his weekly moil is at an end,
Collects his *spades*, his *mattocks* and his *hoes*,
    Hoping the *morn* in ease and rest to spend,
And weary, o'er the moor, his course does hameward
        bend.°

III

At length his lonely *Cot* appears in view,
    Beneath the shelter of an aged tree;   20
The expectant *wee-things*, toddlan, stacher through
    To meet their *Dad*, wi' flichterin noise and glee.
His wee-bit ingle, blinkan bonilie,
    His clean hearth-stane, his thrifty *Wifie's* smile,
The *lisping infant*, prattling on his knee,
    Does a' his weary *kiaugh* and care beguile,°
And makes him quite forget his labor and his toil.

IV

Belyve, the *elder bairns* come drapping in,
    At *Service* out, amang the Farmers roun';°
Some ca' the pleugh, some herd, some tentie rin   30
    A cannie errand to a neebor town:
Their eldest hope, their *Jenny*, woman-grown,
    In youthfu' bloom, Love sparkling in her e'e,
Comes hame, perhaps, to shew a braw new gown,
    Or deposite her sair-won penny-fee,
To help her *Parents* dear, if they in hardship be.

V

With joy unfeign'd, *brothers* and *sisters* meet,
    And each for other's weelfare kindly spiers:
The social hours, swift-wing'd, unnotic'd fleet;
    Each tells the uncos that he sees or hears.   40
The Parents partial eye their hopeful years;
    Anticipation forward points the view;
The *Mother*, wi' her needle and her sheers,
    Gars auld claes look amaist as weel's the new;
The *Father* mixes a' wi' admonition due.

VI

Their Master's and their Mistress's command,
    The *youngkers* a' are warned to obey;
And mind their labors wi' an eydent hand,
    And ne'er, tho' out o' sight, to jauk or play:
'And O! be sure to fear the LORD alway!   50
    'And mind your *duty*, duely, morn and night!
'Lest in temptation's path ye gang astray,
    'Implore his *counsel* and assisting *might*:
'They never sought in vain that sought the LORD aright.'

VII

But hark! a rap comes gently to the door;
    Jenny, wha kens the meaning o' the same,
Tells how a neebor lad came o'er the moor,
    To do some errands, and convoy her hame.
The wily Mother sees the *conscious flame*
    Sparkle in *Jenny's* e'e, and flush her cheek,   60
With heart-struck, anxious care enquires his name,
    While *Jenny* hafflins is afraid to speak;
Weel-pleas'd the Mother hears, it's nae wild, worthless
        Rake.°

VIII

With kindly welcome, *Jenny* brings him ben;
    A *strappan youth*; he takes the Mother's eye;
Blythe *Jenny* sees the *visit's* no ill taen;
    The Father cracks of horses, pleughs and kye.
The *Youngster's* artless heart o'erflows wi' joy,

But blate and laithfu', scarce can weel behave;
The Mother, wi' a woman's wiles, can spy   70
    What makes the *youth* sae bashfu' and sae grave;
Weel-pleas'd to think her *bairn's* respected like the lave.

IX

O happy love! where love like this is found!
    O heart-felt raptures! bliss beyond compare!
I've paced much this weary, *mortal round*,
    And sage EXPERIENCE bids me this declare—
'If Heaven a draught of heavenly pleasure spare,
    'One *cordial* in this melancholy *Vale*,
''Tis when a youthful, loving, *modest* Pair,
    'In other's arms, breathe out the tender tale,   80
'Beneath the milk-white thorn that scents the ev'ning gale.'

X.

Is there, in human form, that bears a heart—
    A Wretch! a Villain! lost to love and truth!
That can, with studied, sly, ensnaring art,
    Betray sweet Jenny's unsuspecting youth?
Curse on his perjur'd arts! dissembling smooth!
    Are *Honor*, *Virtue*, *Conscience*, all exil'd?
Is there no Pity, no relenting Ruth,
    Points to the Parents fondling o'er their Child?
Then paints the *ruin'd Maid*, and *their* distraction wild!   90

XI

But now the Supper crowns their simple board,
    The healsome *Porritch*, chief of SCOTIA'S food:
The soupe their *only Hawkie* does afford,
    That 'yont the hallan snugly chows her cood:
The *Dame* brings forth, in complimental mood,
    To grace the lad, her weel-hain'd kebbuck, fell,
And aft he's prest, and aft he ca's it guid;
    The frugal *Wifie*, garrulous, will tell,
How 'twas a towmond auld, sin' Lint was i' the bell.

XII

The chearfu' Supper done, wi' serious face,   100
    They, round the ingle, form a circle wide;

The Sire turns o'er, with patriarchal grace,
　　The big *ha'-Bible*, ance his *Father's* pride:
His bonnet rev'rently is laid aside,
　　His *lyart haffets* wearing thin and bare;
Those strains that once did sweet in ZION glide,°
　　He wales a portion with judicious care;
'*And let us worship GOD!*' he says with solemn air.

XIII

They chant their artless notes in simple guise;
　　They tune their *hearts*, by far the noblest aim:　　110
Perhaps *Dundee's* wild-warbling measures rise,
　　Or plaintive *Martyrs*, worthy of the name;
Or noble *Elgin* beets the heaven-ward flame,°
　　The sweetest far of SCOTIA'S holy lays:
Compar'd with these, *Italian trills* are tame;°
　　The tickl'd ears no heart-felt raptures raise;
Nae unison hae they, with our CREATOR'S praise.

XIV

The priest-like Father reads the sacred page,
　　How *Abram* was the Friend of GOD on high;
Or, *Moses* bade eternal warfare wage,　　120
　　With *Amalek's* ungracious progeny;°
Or how the *royal Bard* did groaning lye,
　　Beneath the stroke of Heaven's avenging ire;°
Or *Job's* pathetic plaint, and wailing cry;°
　　Or rapt *Isaiah's* wild, seraphic fire;
Or other *Holy Seers* that tune the *sacred lyre*.°

XV

Perhaps the *Christian Volume* is the theme,°
　　How *guiltless blood* for *guilty man* was shed;
How HE, who bore in heaven the second name,
　　Had not on Earth whereon to lay His head:°　　130
How His first *followers* and *servants* sped;°
　　The *Precepts sage* they wrote to many a land:°
How *he*, who lone in *Patmos* banished,°
　　Saw in the sun a mighty angel stand;
And heard great *Bab'lon's* doom pronounc'd by
　　　　Heaven's command.

XVI

Then kneeling down to HEAVEN'S ETERNAL
    KING,
  The *Saint*, the *Father*, and the *Husband* prays:
Hope 'springs exulting on triumphant wing,'[1]
  That *thus* they all shall meet in future days:
There, ever bask in *uncreated rays*,°   140
  No more to sigh, or shed the bitter tear,
Together hymning their CREATOR'S praise,°
  In *such society*, yet still more dear;
While circling Time moves round in an eternal sphere.

XVII

Compar'd with *this*, how poor Religion's pride,
  In all the pomp of *method*, and of *art*,
When men display to congregations wide,
  Devotion's ev'ry grace, except the *heart!*
The POWER, incens'd, the Pageant will desert,
  The pompous strain, the sacredotal stole;   150
But haply, in some *Cottage* far apart,
  May hear, well pleas'd, the language of the *Soul*;
And in His *Book of Life* the Inmates poor enroll.°

XVIII

Then homeward all take off their sev'ral way;
  The youngling *Cottagers* retire to rest:
The Parent-pair their *secret homage* pay,
  And proffer up to Heaven the warm request,
That HE who stills the *raven's* clam'rous nest,
  And decks the *lily* fair in flow'ry pride,°
Would, in the way *His Wisdom* sees the best,   160
  For *them* and for their *little ones* provide;
But chiefly, in their hearts with *Grace divine* preside.

XIX

From scenes like these, old SCOTIA'S grandeur springs,°
  That makes her lov'd at home, rever'd abroad:
Princes and lords are but the breath of kings,°
  'An honest man's the noble work of GOD:'°

---

[1] Pope's Windsor Forest.

And *certes*, in fair Virtue's heavenly road,
　　The *Cottage* leaves the *Palace* far behind:
What is a lordling's pomp? a cumbrous load,
　　Disguising oft the *wretch* of human kind,　　　　170
Studied in arts of Hell, in wickedness refin'd!

XX

O SCOTIA! my dear, my native soil!
　　For whom my warmest wish to heaven is sent!
Long may thy hardy sons of *rustic toil*,
　　Be blest with health, and peace, and sweet content!
And O may Heaven their simple lives prevent
　　From *Luxury's* contagion, weak and vile!
Then howe'er *crowns* and *coronets* be rent,
　　A *virtuous Populace* may rise the while,°
And stand a wall of fire around their much-lov'd
　　ISLE.　　　　180

XXI

O THOU! who pour'd the *patriotic tide*,°
　　That stream'd thro' great, unhappy WALLACE'
　　　　heart;°
Who dar'd to, nobly, stem tyrannic pride,
　　Or *nobly die*, the second glorious part:
(The Patriot's GOD, peculiarly thou art,
　　His *friend, inspirer, guardian* and *reward!*)
O never, never SCOTIA'S realm desert,
　　But still the *Patriot*, and the *Patriot-Bard*,
In bright succesion raise, her *Ornament* and *Guard!*°

TO A MOUSE,
On turning her up in her Nest, with the Plough,
November, 1785

WEE, sleeket, cowran, tim'rous *beastie*,
O, what a panic's in thy breastie!
Thou need na start awa sae hasty,
　　　　Wi' bickering brattle!
I wad be laith to rin an' chase thee,
　　　　Wi' murd'ring *pattle!*

I'm truly sorry Man's dominion
Has broken Nature's social union,°
An' justifies that ill opinion,
        Which makes thee startle,   10
At me, thy poor, earth-born companion,
        An' *fellow-mortal!*

I doubt na, whyles, but thou may *thieve*;
What then? poor beastie, thou maun live!
A *daimen-icker* in a *thrave*
        'S a sma' request:
I'll get a blessin wi' the lave,
        An' never miss't!

Thy wee-bit *housie*, too, in ruin!
It's silly wa's the win's are strewin!   20
An' naething, now, to big a new ane,
        O' foggage green!
An' bleak *December's winds* ensuin,
        Baith snell an' keen!

Thou saw the fields laid bare an' wast,
An' weary *Winter* comin fast,
An' cozie here, beneath the blast,
        Thou thought to dwell,
Till crash! the cruel *coulter* past°
        Out thro' thy cell.   30

That wee-bit heap o' leaves an' stibble,
Has cost thee monie a weary nibble!
Now thou's turn'd out, for a' thy trouble,
        But house or hald,
To thole the Winter's *sleety dribble*,
        An' *cranreuch* cauld!

But Mousie, thou art no thy-lane,
In proving *foresight* may be vain:
The best laid schemes o' *Mice* an' *Men*,
        Gang aft agley,°
An' lea'e us nought but grief an' pain,   40
        For promis'd joy!

Still, thou art blest, compar'd wi' *me!*
The *present* only toucheth thee:
But Och! I *backward* cast my e'e,
              On prospects drear!
An' *forward*, tho' I canna *see*,
              I *guess* an' *fear!*°

EPISTLE TO DAVIE,

A BROTHER POET

January—

I

WHILE winds frae off BEN-LOMOND blaw,°
And bar the doors wi' driving snaw,
   And hing us owre the ingle,
I set me down, to pass the time,
And spin a verse or twa o' rhyme,
   In hamely, *westlin* jingle.
While frosty winds blaw in the drift,
   Ben to the chimla lug,
I grudge a wee the *Great-folk's* gift,
     That live sae bien an' snug: 10
       I tent less, and want less
         Their roomy fire-side;
       But hanker, and canker,
         To see their cursed pride.

II

It's hardly in a body's pow'r,
To keep, at times, frae being sour,
   To see how things are shar'd;
How *best o' chiels* are whyles in want,
While *Coofs* on countless thousands rant,°
   And ken na how to wair't;   20
But DAVIE lad, ne'er fash your head,
   Tho' we hae little gear,
We're fit to win our daily bread,
   As lang's we're hale and fier:

'Mair spier na, nor fear na,'[10]
    Auld age ne'er mind a feg;
The last o't, the warst o't,
    Is only but to beg.

III

To lye in kilns and barns at e'en,°
When banes are craz'd, and bluid is thin,   30
    Is, doubtless, great distress!
Yet then *content* could make us blest;
Ev'n then, sometimes we'd snatch a taste
    Of truest happiness.
The honest heart that's free frae a'
    Intended fraud or guile,
However Fortune kick the ba',
    Has ay some cause to smile:
        And mind still, you'll find still,
          A comfort this nae sma';   40
        Nae mair then, we'll care then,
          Nae *farther* we can *fa'*.

IV

What tho', like Commoners of air,
We wander out, we know not where,
    But either house or hal'?
Yet *Nature's* charms, the hills and woods,
The sweeping vales, and foaming floods,
    Are free alike to all.
In days when Daisies deck the ground,
    And Blackbirds whistle clear,   50
With honest joy, our hearts will bound,
    To see the *coming* year:
        On braes when we please then,
          We'll sit and *sowth* a tune;
        Syne *rhyme* till't, we'll time till't,°
          And sing't when we hae done.

V

It's no in titles nor in rank;
It's no in wealth like *Lon'on Bank*,

[1] Ramsay.

To purchase peace and rest;°
It's no in makin muckle, *mair*:   60
It's no in books; it's no in Lear,
     To make us truly blest:
If Happiness hae not her seat
     And center in the breast,
We may be *wise*, or *rich*, or *great*,
     But never can be *blest*:
          Nae treasures, nor pleasures
               Could make us happy lang;
          The *heart* ay's the part ay,
               That makes us right or wrang.   70

VI

Think ye, that sic as *you* and *I*,
Wha drudge and drive thro' wet and dry,
     Wi' never-ceasing toil;
Think ye, are we less blest than they,
Wha scarcely tent us in their way,
     As hardly worth their while?
Alas! how aft, in haughty mood,
     GOD'S creatures they oppress!
Or else, neglecting a' that's guid,
     They riot in excess!   80
          Baith careless, and fearless,
               Of either Heaven or Hell;
          Esteeming, and deeming,
               It a' an idle tale!

VII

Then let us chearfu' acquiesce;
Nor make our scanty Pleasures less,
     By pining at our state:
And, ev'n should Misfortunes come,
I, here wha sit, hae met wi' some,
     An's thankfu' for them yet.   90
They gie the wit of *Age* to *Youth*;
     They let us ken oursel;
They make us see the naked truth,
     The *real* guid and ill.
          Tho' losses, and crosses,

Be lessons right severe,
There's *wit* there, ye'll get there,
Ye'll find nae other where.

VIII

But tent me, DAVIE, *Ace o' Hearts!*
(To say aught less wad wrang the *cartes*,   100
    And flatt'ry I detest)
This life has joys for you and I;
And joys that riches ne'er could buy;
    And joys the very best.
There's a' the *Pleasures o' the Heart*,
    The *Lover* and the *Frien'*;
Ye hae your MEG, your dearest part,°
    And I my darling JEAN!
        It warms me, it charms me,
            To mention but her *name*:   110
        It heats me, it beets me,
            And sets me a' on flame!

IX

O, all ye *Pow'rs* who rule above!
O THOU, whose very self art *love*!
    THOU know'st my words sincere!
The *life blood* streaming thro' my heart,
Or my more dear *Immortal part*,
    Is not more fondly dear!
When heart-corroding care and grief
    Deprive my soul of rest,   120
Her dear idea brings relief,
    And solace to my breast.°
        Thou BEING, Allseeing,
            O hear my fervent pray'r!
        Still take her, and make her,
            THY most peculiar care!

X

All hail! ye tender feelings dear!
The smile of love, the friendly tear,
    The sympathetic glow!
Long since, this world's thorny ways   130

Had number'd out my weary days,°
   Had it not been for you!
Fate still has blest me with a friend,
   In ev'ry care and ill;
And oft a more *endearing* band,
   A *tye* more tender still.
     It lightens, it brightens,
       The tenebrific scene,°
     To meet with, and greet with,
       My DAVIE or my JEAN!   140

XI

O, how that *name* inspires my style!
The words come skelpan, rank and file,
   Amaist before I ken!
The ready measure rins as fine,
As *Phœbus* and the famous *Nine*°
   Were glowran owre my pen.
My spavet *Pegasus* will limp,°
   Till ance he's fairly het;
And then he'll hilch, and stilt, and jimp,
   And rin an unco fit: 150
     But least then, the beast then,
       Should rue this hasty ride,
     I'll light now, and dight now,
       His sweaty, wizen'd hide.

THE LAMENT

OCCASIONED BY THE UNFORTUNATE ISSUE
OF A FRIEND'S AMOUR

Alas! how oft does goodness wound itself!
And sweet Affection *prove the spring of Woe!*
               HOME.°

I

O Thou pale Orb, that silent shines,
   While care-untroubled mortals sleep!
Thou seest a *wretch*, who inly pines,
   And wanders here to wail and weep!

With Woe I nightly vigils keep,
    Beneath thy wan, unwarming beam;
And mourn, in lamentation deep,
    How *life* and *love* are all a dream!

II

I joyless view thy rays adorn,
    The faintly-marked, distant hill: 10
I joyless view thy trembling horn,
    Reflected in the gurgling rill.
My fondly-fluttering heart, be still!
    Thou busy pow'r, Remembrance, cease!
Ah! must the agonizing thrill,
    For ever bar returning Peace!

III

No idly-feign'd, poetic pains,
    My sad, lovelorn lamentings claim:
No shepherd's pipe—Arcadian strains;
    No fabled tortures, quaint and tame.   20
The *plighted faith*; the *mutual flame*;
    The *oft-attested Powers above*;
The *promis'd Father's tender name*;
    These were the pledges of my love!

IV

Encircled in her clasping arms,
    How have the raptur'd moments flown!
How have I wish'd for Fortune's charms,
    For her dear sake, and her's alone!
And, must I think it! is she gone,
    My secret-heart's exulting boast?   30
And does she heedless hear my groan?
    And is she ever, ever lost?

V

Oh! can she bear so base a heart,
    So lost to Honor, lost to Truth,
As from the *fondest lover* part,
    The *plighted husband* of her youth?
Alas! Life's path may be unsmooth!

Her way may lie thro' rough distress!
Then, who her pangs and pains will soothe,
  Her sorrows share and make them less?   40

VI

Ye winged Hours that o'er us past,
  Enraptur'd more, the more enjoy'd,
Your dear remembrance in my breast,
  My fondly-treasur'd thoughts employ'd.
That breast, how dreary now, and void,
  For her too scanty once of room!
Ev'n ev'ry *ray* of *Hope* destroy'd,
  And not a *Wish* to gild the gloom!

VII

The morn that warns th'approaching day,
  Awakes me up to toil and woe: 50
I see the hours, in long array,
  That I must suffer, lingering, slow.
Full many a pang, and many a throe,
  Keen Recollection's direful train,°
Must wring my soul, ere Phœbus, low,
  Shall kiss the distant, western main.

VIII

And when my nightly couch I try,
  Sore-harass'd out, with care and grief,
My toil-beat nerves, and tear-worn eye,
  Keep watchings with the nightly thief: 60
Or if I slumber, Fancy, chief,
  Reigns, hagard-wild, in sore afright:
Ev'n day, all-bitter, brings relief,
  From such a horror-breathing night.

IX

O! thou bright Queen, who, o'er th'expanse,
  Now highest reign'st, with boundless sway!
Oft has thy silent-marking glance
  Observ'd us, fondly-wand'ring, stray!
The time, unheeded, sped away,
  While Love's *luxurious pulse* beat high,   70

Beneath thy silver-gleaming ray,
    To mark the mutual-kindling eye.

X

Oh! scenes in strong remembrance set!
    Scenes, never, never to return!
Scenes, if in stupor I forget,
    Again I feel, again I burn!
From ev'ry joy and pleasure torn,
    Life's weary vale I'll wander thro';
And hopeless, comfortless, I'll mourn
    A faithless woman's broken vow.   80

DESPONDENCY, AN ODE

I

OPPRESS'D with grief, oppress'd with care,
A burden more than I can bear,
    I set me down and sigh:
O Life! Thou art a galling load,
Along a rough, a weary road,
    To wretches such as I!
Dim-backward as I cast my view,
    What sick'ning Scenes appear!
What Sorrows *yet* may pierce me thro',
    Too justly I may fear!   10
        Still caring, despairing,
            Must be my bitter doom;
        My woes here, shall close ne'er,
            But with the *closing tomb!*

II

Happy! ye sons of Busy-life,
Who, equal to the bustling strife,
    No other view regard!
Ev'n when the wished *end's* deny'd,
Yet while the busy *means* are ply'd,
    They bring their own reward: 20
Whilst I, a hope-abandon'd wight,

Unfitted with an *aim*,°
Meet ev'ry sad-returning night,
   And joyless morn the same.
      You, bustling and justling,
         Forget each grief and pain;
      I, listless, yet restless,
         Find ev'ry prospect vain.

III

How blest the Solitary's lot,
Who, all-forgetting, all-forgot,°   30
   Within his humble cell,
The cavern wild with tangling roots,
Sits o'er his newly-gather'd fruits,
   Beside his crystal well!°
Or haply, to his ev'ning thought,
   By unfrequented stream,
The *ways of men* are distant brought,
   A faint-collected dream:
      While praising, and raising
         His thoughts to Heaven on high,   40
      As wand'ring, meand'ring,
         He views the solemn sky.

IV

Than I, no *lonely Hermit* plac'd
Where never human footstep trac'd,
   Less fit to play the part,
The *lucky moment* to improve,
And *just* to stop, and *just* to move,
   With *self-respecting* art:
But ah! those pleasures, Loves and Joys,
   Which I too keenly taste,   50
The *Solitary* can despise,
   Can want, and yet be blest!
      He needs not, he heeds not,
         Or human love or hate;°
      Whilst I here, must cry here,
         At perfidy ingrate!

V

Oh, enviable, early days,
When dancing thoughtless Pleasure's maze,
    To Care, to Guilt unknown!
How ill exchang'd for riper times,   60
To feel the follies, or the crimes,
    Of others, or my own!
Ye tiny elves that guiltless sport,
    Like linnets in the bush,
Ye little know the ills ye court,
    When Manhood is your wish!
        The losses, the crosses,
            That *active man* engage;
        The fears all, the tears all,
            Of dim declining *Age!*   70

MAN WAS MADE TO MOURN, A DIRGE

I

WHEN chill November's surly blast
    Made fields and forests bare,
One ev'ning, as I wand'red forth,
    Along the banks of AIRE,
I spy'd a man, whose aged step
    Seem'd weary, worn with care;
His face was furrow'd o'er with years,°
    And hoary was his hair.

II

Young stranger, whither wand'rest thou?
    Began the rev'rend Sage;   10
Does thirst of wealth thy step constrain,°
    Or youthful Pleasure's rage?
Or haply, prest with cares and woes,
    Too soon thou hast began,
To wander forth, with me, to mourn
    The miseries of Man.

III

The Sun that overhangs yon moors,
　　Out-spreading far and wide,
Where hundreds labour to support
　　A haughty lordling's pride;
I've seen yon weary winter-sun
　　Twice forty times return;
And ev'ry time has added proofs,
　　That Man was made to mourn.

IV

O Man! while in thy early years,
　　How prodigal of time!
Mispending all thy precious hours,
　　Thy glorious, youthful prime!
Alternate Follies take the sway;
　　Licentious Passions burn;
Which tenfold force gives Nature's law,
　　That Man was made to mourn.

V

Look not alone on youthful Prime,
　　Or Manhood's active might;°
Man then is useful to his kind,
　　Supported is his right:
But see him on the edge of life,
　　With Cares and Sorrows worn,°
Then Age and Want, Oh! ill-match'd pair!°
　　Show Man was made to mourn.

VI

A few seem favourites of Fate,
　　In Pleasure's lap carest;
Yet, think not all the Rich and Great,
　　Are likewise truly blest.
But Oh! what crouds in ev'ry land,
　　All wretched and forlorn,
Thro' weary life this lesson learn,
　　That Man was made to mourn!

VII

Many and sharp the num'rous Ills
    Inwoven with our frame!°   50
More pointed still we make ourselves,
    Regret, Remorse and Shame!
And Man, whose heav'n-erected face,
    The smiles of love adorn,°
Man's inhumanity to Man°
    Makes countless thousands mourn!

VIII

See, yonder poor, o'erlabour'd wight,
    So abject, mean and vile,
Who begs a brother of the earth
    To give him leave to toil;   60
And see his lordly *fellow-worm*,
    The poor petition spurn,
Unmindful, tho' a weeping wife,
    And helpless offspring mourn.

IX

If I'm design'd yon lordling's slave,
    By Nature's law design'd,
Why was an independent wish
    E'er planted in my mind?°
If not, why am I subject to
    His cruelty, or scorn?   70
Or why has Man the will and pow'r
    To make his fellow mourn?

X

Yet, let not this too much, my Son,
    Disturb thy youthful breast:
This partial view of human-kind
    Is surely not the *last!*
The poor, oppressed, honest man
    Had never, sure, been born,
Had there not been some recompence
    To comfort those that mourn!   80

XI

O Death! the poor man's dearest friend,
   The kindest and the best!
Welcome the hour, my aged limbs
   Are laid with thee at rest!
The Great, the Wealthy fear thy blow,
   From pomp and pleasure torn;
But Oh! a blest relief for those°
   That weary-laden mourn!

WINTER, A DIRGE

I

THE Wintry West extends his blast,
   And hail and rain does blaw;
Or, the stormy North sends driving forth,
   The blinding sleet and snaw:
While, tumbling brown, the Burn comes down,
   And roars frae bank to brae;
And bird and beast, in covert, rest,
   And pass the heartless day.

II

'The sweeping blast, the sky o'ercast,'[1º]
   The joyless *winter-day*,   10
Let others fear, to me more dear,
   Than all the pride of May:
The Tempest's howl, it *soothes* my soul,
   My *griefs* it seems to join;
The leafless trees my fancy please,
   Their *fate* resembles mine!

III

Thou POW'R SUPREME, whose mighty Scheme,
   These *woes* of mine fulfil;
Here, firm, I rest, they *must* be best,
   Because they are *Thy* Will!   20

[1] Dr. Young.

Then all I want (Oh, do thou grant
   This one request of mine!)
Since to *enjoy* Thou dost deny,
   Assist me to *resign!*

A PRAYER,
IN THE PROSPECT OF DEATH

I

O THOU unknown, Almighty Cause°
   Of all my hope and fear!
In whose dread Presence, ere an hour,
   Perhaps I must appear!

II

If I have wander'd in those paths
   Of life I ought to shun;
As *Something*, loudly, in my breast,
   Remonstrates I have done;

III

Thou know'st that Thou hast formed me,
   With Passions wild and strong;   10
And list'ning to their witching voice
   Has often led me wrong.

IV

Where human *weakness* has come short,
   Or *frailty* stept aside,
Do Thou, ALL-GOOD, for such Thou art,
   In shades of darkness hide.

V

Where with *intention* I have err'd,
   No other plea I have,
But, *Thou art good*; and Goodness still°
   Delighteth to forgive.   20

TO A MOUNTAIN-DAISY,
*On turning one down, with the Plough, in April—*1786

WEE, modest, crimson-tipped flow'r,
Thou's met me in an evil hour;
For I maun crush amang the stoure
    Thy slender stem:
To spare thee now is past my pow'r,
    Thou bonie gem.

 Alas! it's no thy neebor sweet,
The bonie *Lark*, companion meet!
Bending thee 'mang the dewy weet!
    Wi's spreckl'd breast,   10
When upward-springing, blythe, to greet
    The purpling East.°

 Cauld blew the bitter-biting *North*
Upon thy early, humble birth;
Yet chearfully thou glinted forth
    Amid the storm,
Scarce rear'd above the *Parent-earth*
    Thy tender form.

 The flaunting *flow'rs* our Gardens yield,
High-shelt'ring woods and wa's maun shield, 20
But thou, beneath the random bield
    O' clod or stane,
Adorns the histie *stibble-field*,
    Unseen, alane.

 There, in thy scanty mantle clad,
Thy snawie bosom sun-ward spread,°
Thou lifts thy unassuming head
    In humble guise;
But now the *share* uptears thy bed,°
    And low thou lies!   30

 Such is the fate of artless Maid,
Sweet *flow'ret* of the rural shade!

By Love's simplicity betray'd,
        And guileless trust,
Till she, like thee, all soil'd, is laid
        Low i' the dust.

Such is the fate of simple Bard,
On Life's rough ocean luckless starr'd!
Unskilful he to note the card
        Of *prudent Lore*,   40
Till billows rage, and gales blow hard,
        And whelm him o'er!

Such fate to *suffering worth* is giv'n,
Who long with wants and woes has striv'n,
By human pride or cunning driv'n
        To Mis'ry's brink,
Till wrench'd of ev'ry stay but HEAV'N,°
        He, ruin'd, sink!

Ev'n thou who mourn'st the *Daisy's* fate,
That fate is thine—no distant date;   50
Stern Ruin's *plough-share* drives, elate,°
        Full on thy bloom,
Till crush'd beneath the *furrow's* weight,
        Shall be thy doom!

TO RUIN

I

ALL hail! inexorable lord!
At whose destruction-breathing word,
    The mightiest empires fall!
Thy cruel, woe-delighted train,
The ministers of Grief and Pain,
    A sullen welcome, all!
With stern-resolv'd, despairing eye,
    I see each aimed dart;
For one has cut my *dearest tye*,
    And quivers in my heart.   10

> Then low'ring, and pouring,
>   The *Storm* no more I dread;
> Tho' thick'ning, and black'ning,
>   Round my devoted head.

II

And thou grim Pow'r, by Life abhorr'd,
While Life a *pleasure* can afford,
  Oh! hear a wretch's pray'r!
Nor more I shrink appall'd, afraid;
I court, I beg thy friendly aid,
  To close this scene of care!   20
When shall my soul, in silent peace,
  Resign Life's *joyless* day?
My weary heart it's throbbings cease,
  Cold mould'ring in the clay?
    No fear more, no tear more,
      To stain my lifeless face,
    Enclasped, and grasped,
      Within thy cold embrace!

EPISTLE TO A YOUNG FRIEND

May—1786

I

I Lang hae thought, my youthfu' friend,
  A Something to have sent you,
Tho' it should serve nae other end
  Than just a kind memento;
But how the subject theme may gang,
  Let time and chance determine;
Perhaps it may turn out a Sang;
  Perhaps, turn out a Sermon.

II

Ye'll try the world soon my lad,
  And ANDREW dear believe me,   .10
Ye'll find mankind an unco squad,
  And muckle they may grieve ye:

For care and trouble set your thought,
    Ev'n when your end's attained;
And a' your views may come to nought,°
    Where ev'ry nerve is strained.

III

I'll no say, men are villains a';
    The real, harden'd wicked,
Wha hae nae check but *human law*,
    Are to a few restricked: 20
But Och, mankind are unco weak,
    An' little to be trusted;
If *Self* the wavering balance shake,
    It's rarely right adjusted!

IV

Yet they wha fa' in Fortune's strife,
    Their fate we should na censure,
For still th' *important end* of life,
    They equally may answer:
A man may hae an *honest heart*,
    Tho' Poortith hourly stare him;   30
A man may tak a neebor's part,
    Yet hae nae *cash* to spare him.

V

Ay free, aff han', your story tell,
    When wi' a bosom crony;
But still keep something to yoursel
    Ye scarcely tell to ony.
Conceal yoursel as weel's ye can
    Frae critical dissection;
But keek thro' ev'ry other man,
    Wi' sharpen'd, sly inspection.   40

VI

The *sacred lowe* o' weel plac'd love,
    Luxuriantly indulge it;
But never tempt th'*illicit rove*,°
    Tho' naething should divulge it:
I wave the quantum o' the sin;

The hazard of concealing;
But Och! it hardens *a' within*,
And petrifies the feeling!

VII

To catch Dame Fortune's golden smile,
　　Assiduous wait upon her;
And gather gear by ev'ry wile,
　　That's justify'd by Honor:
Not for to *hide* it in a *hedge*,
　　Nor for a *train-attendant*;
But for the glorious priviledge
　　Of being *independant*.

VIII

The *fear o' Hell's* a hangman's whip,
　　To haud the wretch in order;
But where ye feel your *Honor* grip,
　　Let that ay be your border:
It's slightest touches, instant pause—
　　Debar a' side-pretences;
And resolutely keep it's laws,
　　Uncaring consequences.

IX

The great CREATOR to revere,
　　Must sure become the *Creature*;
But still the preaching cant forbear,
　　And ev'n the rigid feature:
Yet ne'er with Wits prophane to range,
　　Be complaisance extended;
An *athiest-laugh's* a poor exchange
　　For *Deity offended!*

X

When ranting round in Pleasure's ring,
　　Religion may be blinded;
Or if she gie a *random-sting*,
　　It may be little minded;
But when on Life we're tempest-driven,
　　A Conscience but a canker—

50

60

70

A correspondence fix'd wi' Heav'n,
  Is sure a noble *anchor!*   80

XI

Adieu, dear, amiable Youth!
  Your *heart* can ne'er be wanting!
May Prudence, Fortitude and Truth
  Erect your brow undaunting!
In *ploughman phrase* 'GOD send you speed,'
  Still daily to grow wiser;
And may ye better reck the *rede*,
  Than ever did th' *Adviser!*°

ON A SCOTCH BARD
GONE TO THE WEST INDIES

A' Ye wha live by sowps o' drink,
A' ye wha live by crambo-clink,
A' ye wha live and never think,
        Come, mourn wi' me!
Our *billie's* gien us a' a jink,
        An' owre the Sea.

  Lament him a' ye rantan core,
Wha dearly like a random-splore;
Nae mair he'll join the *merry roar*,
        In social key;   10
For now he's taen anither shore,
        An' owre the Sea!

  The bonie lasses weel may wiss him,
And in their dear *petitions* place him:°
The widows, wives, an' a' may bless him,
        Wi' tearfu' e'e;
For weel I wat they'll sairly miss him
        That's owre the Sea!

  O Fortune, they hae room to grumble!
Hadst thou taen aff some drowsy bummle,°   20
Wha can do nought but fyke an' fumble,°

'Twad been nae plea;
But he was gleg as onie wumble,°
   That's owre the Sea!

Auld, cantie KYLE may weepers wear,°
An' stain them wi' the saut, saut tear:
'Twill mak her poor, auld heart, I fear,
   In flinders flee:°
He was her *Laureat* monie a year,
   That's owre the Sea!   30

He saw Misfortune's cauld *Nor-west*
Lang-mustering up a bitter blast;
A Jillet brak his heart at last,
   Ill may she be!
So, took a birth afore the mast,
   An' owre the Sea.

To tremble under Fortune's cummock,
On scarce a bellyfu' o' *drummock*,
Wi' his proud, independant stomach,
   Could ill agree;   40
So, row't his hurdies in a *hammock*,
   An' owre the Sea.

He ne'er was gien to great misguidin,
Yet coin his pouches wad na bide in;
Wi' him it ne'er was *under hidin*;
   He dealt it free:
The *Muse* was a' that he took pride in,
   That's owre the Sea.

Jamaica bodies, use him weel,
An' hap him in a cozie biel: 50
Ye'll find him ay a dainty chiel,
   An' fou o' glee:
He wad na wrang'd the vera *Diel*,
   That's owre the Sea.

Fareweel, my *rhyme-composing billie!*
Your native soil was right ill-willie;

But may ye flourish like a lily,
    Now bonilie!
I'll toast you in my hindmost *gillie*,
    Tho' owre the Sea!   60

A DEDICATION

TO G**** H******** Esq;

EXPECT na, Sir, in this narration,
A fleechan, fleth'ran *Dedication*,
To roose you up, an' ca' you guid,
An' sprung o' great an' noble bluid;
Because ye're sirnam'd like *His Grace*,°
Perhaps related to the race:
Then when I'm tir'd—and sae are *ye*,
Wi' monie a fulsome, sinfu' lie,
Set up a face, how I stop short,
For fear your modesty be hurt.   10

This may do—maun do, Sir, wi' them wha
Maun please the Great-folk for a wamefou;
For me! sae laigh I need na bow,
For, LORD be thanket, *I can plough*;
And when I downa yoke a naig,
Then, LORD be thanket, *I can beg*;°
Sae I shall say, an' that's nae flatt'rin,
It's just *sic Poet* an' *sic Patron*.

The Poet, some guid Angel help him,
Or else, I fear, some *ill ane* skelp him!   20
He may do weel for a' he's done yet,
But only—he's no just begun yet.

The Patron, (Sir, ye maun forgie me,
I winna lie, come what will o' me)
On ev'ry hand it will allow'd be,
He's just—nae better than he should be.

I readily and freely grant,
He downa see a poor man want;
What's no his ain, he winna tak it;
What ance he says, he winna break it;   30
Ought he can lend he'll no refus't,
Till aft his guidness is abus'd;
And rascals whyles that do him wrang,
Ev'n *that*, he does na mind it lang:
As Master, Landlord, Husband, Father,°
He does na fail his part in either.

But then, nae thanks to him for a' that;
Nae *godly symptom* ye can ca' that;
It's naething but a milder feature,
Of our poor, sinfu', corrupt Nature:°   40
Ye'll get the best o' moral works,
'Mang black *Gentoos*, and Pagan *Turks*,°
Or Hunters wild on *Ponotaxi*,°
Wha never heard of Orth–d–xy.°
That he's the poor man's friend in need,
The GENTLEMAN in word and deed,
It's no through terror of D–mn–t–n; ⎫
It's just a carnal inclination, ⎬
And Och! that's nae r–g–n–r–t–n!° ⎭

Morality, thou deadly bane,°   50
Thy tens o' thousands thou hast slain!
Vain is his hope, whase stay an' trust is,
In *moral* Mercy, Truth, and Justice!

No—stretch a point to catch a plack;°
Abuse a Brother to his back;
Steal through the *winnock* frae a wh–re,
But point the Rake that taks the *door*;°
Be to the Poor like onie whunstane,
And haud their noses to the grunstane;
Ply ev'ry art o' *legal* thieving;   60
No matter—stick to *sound believing*.

Learn three-mile pray'rs, an' half-mile graces,
Wi' weel-spread looves, an' lang, wry faces;

Grunt up a solemn, lengthen'd groan,
And damn a' Parties but your own;°
I'll warrant then, ye're nae Deceiver,
A steady, sturdy, staunch *Believer*.

O ye wha leave the springs o' C–lv–n,°
For *gumlie dubs* of your ain delvin!
Ye sons of Heresy and Error,   70
Ye'll *some day* squeel in quaking terror!
When Vengeance draws the sword in wrath,°
And in the fire throws the *sheath*;
When Ruin, with his sweeping *besom*,°
Just frets till Heav'n commission gies him;
While o'er the *Harp* pale Misery moans, ⎫
And strikes the ever-deep'ning tones,   ⎬
Still louder shrieks, and heavier groans!° ⎭

Your pardon, Sir, for this digression,
I maist forgat my *Dedication*;   80
But when Divinity comes cross me,
My readers then are sure to lose me.°

So Sir, you see 'twas nae daft vapour,
But I maturely thought it proper,
When a' my works I did review,
To *dedicate* them, Sir, to YOU:
Because (ye need na tak it ill)
I thought them something like *yoursel*.

Then patronize them wi' your favor,
And your Petitioner shall ever—   90
I had amaist said, *ever pray*,
But that's a word I need na say:
For prayin I hae little skill o't;
I'm baith dead-sweer, an' wretched ill o't;
But I'se repeat each poor man's *pray'r*,
That kens or hears about you, Sir—

'May ne'er Misfortune's gowling bark,
'Howl thro' the dwelling o' the CLERK!°
'May ne'er his gen'rous, honest heart,

'For that same gen'rous spirit smart!   100
'May K******'s far-honor'd name°
'Lang beet his hymeneal flame,
'Till H*******'s, at least a diz'n,
'Are frae their nuptial labors risen:
'Five bonie Lasses round their table,
'And sev'n braw fellows, stout an' able,
'To serve their King an' Country weel,
'By word, or pen, or pointed steel!
'May Health and Peace, with mutual rays,
'Shine on the ev'ning o' his days;   110
'Till his wee, curlie *John's* ier-oe,
'When ebbing life nae mair shall flow,
'The last, sad, mournful rites bestow!'

    I will not wind a lang conclusion,
With complimentary effusion:
But whilst your wishes and endeavours,
Are blest with Fortune's smiles and favours,
I am, Dear Sir, with zeal most fervent,
Your much indebted, humble servant.

    But if, which Pow'rs above prevent,   120
That iron-hearted Carl, *Want*,
Attended, in his grim advances,
By *sad mistakes*, and *black mischances*,
While hopes, and joys, and pleasures fly him,
Make you as poor a dog as I am,
Your *humble servant* then no more;
For who would humbly serve the Poor?
But by a poor man's hopes in Heav'n!
While recollection's pow'r is giv'n,
If, in the vale of humble life,   130
The victim sad of Fortune's strife,
I, through the tender-gushing tear,
Should recognise my *Master dear*,
If friendless, low, we meet together,
Then, Sir, your hand—my FRIEND and BROTHER.

TO A LOUSE,

On Seeing one on a Lady's Bonnet at Church

HA! whare ye gaun, ye crowlan ferlie!
Your impudence protects you sairly:
I canna say but ye strunt rarely,
          Owre *gawze* and *lace*;
Tho' faith, I fear ye dine but sparely,
          On sic a place.

Ye ugly, creepan, blastet wonner,
Detested, shunn'd, by saunt an' sinner,
How daur ye set your fit upon her,
          Sae fine a *Lady*!   10
Gae somewhere else and seek your dinner,
          On some poor body.

Swith, in some beggar's haffet squattle;
There ye may creep, and sprawl, and sprattle,°
Wi' ither kindred, jumping cattle,
          In shoals and nations;
Whare *horn* nor *bane* ne'er daur unsettle,°
          Your thick plantations.

Now haud you there, ye're out o' sight,
Below the fatt'rels, snug and tight,   20
Na faith ye yet! ye'll no be right,°
          Till ye've got on it,
The vera tapmost, towrin height
          O' *Miss's bonnet*.

My sooth! right bauld ye set your nose out,
As plump an' gray as onie grozet:
O for some rank, mercurial rozet,
          Or fell, red smeddum,°
I'd gie you sic a hearty dose o't,
          Wad dress your droddum!   30

I wad na been surpriz'd to spy
You on an auld wife's *flainen toy*;

Or aiblins some bit duddie boy,
    On's *wylecoat*;
But Miss's fine *Lunardi*, fye!°
    How daur ye do't?

O *Jenny* dinna toss your head,
An' set your beauties a' abread!
Ye little ken what cursed speed
    The blastie's makin! 40
Thae *winks* and *finger-ends*, I dread,
    Are notice takin!°

O wad some Pow'r the giftie gie us
To see oursels as others see us!°
It wad frae monie a blunder free us
    An' foolish notion:
What airs in dress an' gait wad lea'e us,
    And ev'n Devotion!

EPISTLE TO J. L*****K,

AN OLD SCOTCH BARD

April 1st, 1785

WHILE briers an' woodbines budding green,
An' Paitricks scraichan loud at e'en,
And morning Poossie whiddan seen,
    Inspire my Muse,
This freedom, in an *unknown* frien',
    I pray excuse.

On Fasteneen we had a rockin,°
To ca' the crack and weave our stockin;
And there was muckle fun and jokin,
    Ye need na doubt; 10
At length we had a hearty yokin,
    At *sang about*.

There was ae *sang*, amang the rest,°
Aboon them a' it pleas'd me best,
That some kind husband had addrest,

To some sweet wife:
It thirl'd the heart-strings thro' the breast,°
        A' to the life.

I've scarce heard ought describ'd sae weel,
What gen'rous, manly bosoms feel;
Thought I, 'Can this be *Pope*, or *Steele*,   20
        Or *Beattie's* wark;'°
They tald me 'twas an odd kind chiel
        About *Muirkirk*.

It pat me fidgean-fain to hear't,
An' sae about him there I spier't;
Then a' that kent him round declar'd,
        He had *ingine*,
That nane excell'd it, few cam near't,
        It was sae fine.   30

That set him to a pint of ale,
An' either douse or merry tale,
Or rhymes an' sangs he'd made himsel,
        Or witty catches,
'Tween Inverness and Tiviotdale,°
        He had few matches.

Then up I gat, an' swoor an aith,
Tho' I should pawn my pleugh an' graith,
Or die a cadger pownie's death,
        At some dyke-back,   40
A *pint* an' *gill* I'd gie them *baith*,
        To hear your crack.

But first an' foremost, I should tell,
Amaist as soon as I could spell,
I to the *crambo-jingle* fell,
        Tho' rude an' rough,
Yet crooning to a body's sel,
        Does weel eneugh.

I am nae *Poet*, in a sense,
But just a *Rhymer* like by chance,   50

An' hae to Learning nae pretence,
    Yet, what the matter?
Whene'er my Muse does on me glance,
    I jingle at her.

Your Critic-folk may cock their nose,
And say, 'How can you e'er propose,
'You wha ken hardly *verse* frae *prose*,
    'To mak a *sang?*
But by your leaves, my learned foes,
    Ye're maybe wrang.   60

What's a' your jargon o' your Schools,°
Your Latin names for horns an' stools;
If honest Nature made you *fools*,
    What sairs your Grammars?
Ye'd better taen up *spades* and *shools*,
    Or *knappin-hammers.*

A set o' dull, conceited Hashes,
Confuse their brains in *Colledge-classes!*
They *gang in* Stirks, and *come out* Asses,
    Plain truth to speak;   70
An' syne they think to climb Parnassus°
    By dint o' Greek!

Gie me ae spark o' Nature's fire,°
That's a' the learning I desire;
Then tho' I drudge thro' dub an' mire
    At pleugh or cart,
My Muse, tho' hamely in attire,
    May touch the heart.

O for a spunk o' ALLAN'S glee,°
Or FERGUSON'S, the bauld an' slee,°   80
Or bright L*****K'S, my friend to be,
    If I can hit it!
That would be *lear* eneugh for me,
    If I could get it.

Now, Sir, if ye hae friends enow,
Tho' *real friends* I b'lieve are few,

Yet, if your catalogue be fow,
        I'se no insist;
But gif ye want ae friend that's true,
        I'm on your list.   90

I winna blaw about *mysel*,
As ill I like my fauts to tell;
But friends an' folk that wish me well,
        They sometimes roose me;
Tho' I maun own, as monie still,
        As far abuse me.

There's ae *wee faut* they whiles lay to me,
I like the lasses—Gude forgie me!
For monie a Plack they wheedle frae me,
        At dance or fair: 100
Maybe some *ither thing* they gie me
        They weel can spare.

But MAUCHLINE Race or MAUCHLINE Fair,°
I should be proud to meet you there;
We'se gie ae night's discharge to *care*,
        If we forgather,
An' hae a swap o' *rhymin-ware*,°
        Wi' ane anither.

The *four-gill chap*, we'se gar him clatter,
An' kirs'n him wi' reekin water;   110
Syne we'll sit down an' tak our whitter,
        To chear our heart;
An' faith, we'se be *acquainted* better
        Before we part.

Awa ye selfish, warly race,
Wha think that havins, sense an' grace,
Ev'n love an' friendship should give place
        To *catch-the-plack!*°
I dinna like to see your face,
        Nor hear your crack.   120

But ye whom social pleasure charms,
Whose hearts the *tide of kindness* warms,

Who hold your *being* on the terms,
        'Each aid the others,'
Come to my bowl, come to my arms,
        My friends, my brothers!

But to conclude my lang epistle,
As my auld pen's worn to the grissle;
Twa lines frae you wad gar me fissle,
        Who am, most fervent,   130
While I can either sing, or whissle,
        Your friend and servant.

TO THE SAME

April 21st, 1785

WHILE new-ca'd kye rowte at the stake,°
An' pownies reek in pleugh or braik,
This hour on e'enin's edge I take,
        To own I'm debtor,
To honest-hearted, auld L*****K,
        For his kind *letter*.

Forjesket sair, with weary legs,
Rattlin the corn out-owre the rigs,
Or dealing thro' amang the naigs
        Their ten-hours bite,   10
My awkart Muse sair pleads and begs,°
        I would na write.

The tapetless, ramfeezl'd hizzie,
She's saft at best an' something lazy,
Quo' she, 'Ye ken we've been sae busy
        'This month an' mair,
'That trouth, my head is grown right dizzie,
        'An' something sair.'

Her dowf excuses pat me mad;
'Conscience,' says I, 'ye thowless jad!
'I'll write, an' that a hearty blaud,   20

'This vera night;
'So dinna ye affront your trade,
              'But rhyme it right.

'Shall bauld L*****K, the *king o' hearts*,
'Tho' mankind were a *pack o' cartes*,
'Roose you sae weel for your deserts,
              'In terms sae friendly,
'Yet ye'll neglect to shaw your parts
              'An' thank him kindly?'°   30

Sae I gat paper in a blink,
An' down gaed *stumpie* in the ink:°
Quoth I, 'Before I sleep a wink,
              'I vow I'll close it;
'An' if ye winna mak it clink,
              'By Jove I'll prose it!'

Sae I've begun to scrawl, but whether
In rhyme, or prose, or baith thegither,
Or some hotch-potch that's rightly neither,
              Let time mak proof;   40
But I shall scribble down some blether
              Just clean aff-loof.

My worthy friend, ne'er grudge an' carp,
Tho' Fortune use you hard an' sharp;
Come, kittle up your *moorlan harp*°
              Wi' gleesome touch!
Ne'er mind how Fortune *waft* an' *warp*;°
              She's but a b–tch.

She's gien me monie a jirt an' fleg,
Sin I could striddle owre a rig;   50
But by the L—d, tho' I should beg
              Wi' lyart pow,
I'll laugh, an' sing, an' shake my leg,
              As lang's I dow!

Now comes the *sax an' twentieth* simmer,
I've seen the bud upo' the timmer,

Still persecuted by the limmer
            Frae year to year;
But yet, despite the kittle kimmer,
            I, Rob, am here.   60

Do ye envy the *city-gent*,
Behint a kist to lie an' sklent,
Or purse-proud, big wi' cent per cent,
            An' muckle wame,
In some bit *Brugh* to represent°
            A *Bailie's* name?°

Or is't the paughty, feudal *Thane*,°
Wi' ruffl'd sark an' glancin cane,
Wha thinks himsel nae *sheep-shank bane*,
            But lordly stalks,   70
While caps an' bonnets aff are taen,
            As by he walks?

'O *Thou* wha gies us each guid gift!
'Gie me o' *wit* an' *sense* a lift,
'Then turn me, if *Thou* please, *adrift*,
            'Thro' Scotland wide;
'Wi' *cits* nor *lairds* I wadna shift,°
            'In a' their pride!'

Were this the *charter* of our state,
'On pain o' *hell* be rich an' great,'   80
Damnation then would be our fate,
            Beyond remead;
But, thanks to *Heav'n*, that's no the gate
            We learn our *creed*.

For thus the royal *Mandate* ran,
When first the human race began,
'The social, friendly, honest man,
            'Whate'er he be,
''Tis *he* fulfils *great Nature's plan*,
            'And none but *he*.'   90

O *Mandate,* glorious and divine!
The followers o' the ragged Nine,°
Poor, thoughtless devils! yet may shine
                    In glorious light,
While sordid sons o' Mammon's line
                    Are dark as night!

Tho' here they scrape, an' squeeze, an' growl,
Their worthless nievefu' of a *soul*
May in some *future carcase* howl,°
                    The forest's fright;   100
Or in some day-detesting *owl*
                    May shun the light.

Then may L*****K and B**** arise,
To reach their native, kindred skies,
And *sing* their pleasures, hopes an' joys,
                    In some mild sphere,
Still closer knit in friendship's ties
                    Each passing year!

TO W. S*****N, OCHILTREE

May——1785

I Gat your letter, winsome Willie;
Wi' gratefu' heart I thank you brawlie;
Tho' I maun say't, I wad be silly,
                    An' unco vain,
Should I believe, my coaxin billie,
                    Your flatterin strain.

But I'se believe ye kindly meant it,
I sud be laith to think ye hinted
Ironic satire, sidelins sklented,
                    On my poor Musie;   10
Tho' in sic phraisin terms ye've penn'd it,
                    I scarce excuse ye.

My senses wad be in a creel,°
Should I but dare a *hope* to speel,

Wi' *Allan*, or wi' *Gilbertfield*,°
        The braes o' fame;
Or *Ferguson*, the writer-chiel,°
        A deathless name.

(O *Ferguson!* thy glorious *parts*,
Ill-suited *law's* dry, musty arts!   20
My curse upon your whunstane hearts,
        Ye Enbrugh Gentry!
The tythe o' what ye waste at *cartes*
        Wad stow'd his pantry!)

Yet when a tale comes i' my head,
Or lasses gie my heart a screed,
As whiles they're like to be my dead,
        (O sad disease!)
I kittle up my *rustic reed*;
        It gies me ease.   30

Auld COILA, now, may fidge fu' fain,°
She's gotten *Bardies* o' her ain,
Chiels wha their chanters winna hain,°
        But tune their lays,
Till echoes a' resound again
        Her weel-sung praise.

Nae *Poet* thought her worth his while,
To set her name in measur'd style;
She lay like some unkend-of isle
        Beside *New Holland*,°   40
Or whare wild-meeting oceans *boil*
        Besouth *Magellan*.°

Ramsay an' famous *Ferguson*
Gied *Forth* an' *Tay* a lift aboon;
Yarrow an' *Tweed*, to monie a tune,°
        Owre Scotland rings;
While *Irwin, Lugar, Aire* an' *Doon*,
        Naebody sings.°

Th' *Illissus, Tiber, Thames* an' *Seine*,°
Glide sweet in monie a tunefu' line;   50
But *Willie* set your fit to mine,
          An' cock your crest,°
We'll gar our streams an' burnies shine
          Up wi' the best.

We'll sing auld COILA'S plains an' fells,
Her moors red-brown wi' heather bells,
Her banks an' braes, her dens an' dells,
          Where glorious WALLACE°
Aft bure the gree, as story tells,
          Frae Suthron billies.   60

At WALLACE' name, what Scottish blood,
But boils up in a spring-tide flood!
Oft have our fearless fathers strode
          By WALLACE' side,
Still pressing onward, red-wat-shod,
          Or glorious dy'd!

O sweet are COILA'S haughs an' woods,
When lintwhites chant amang the buds,
And jinkin hares, in amorous whids,
          Their loves enjoy,   70
While thro' the braes the cushat croods
          With wailfu' cry!

Ev'n winter bleak has charms to me,°
When winds rave thro' the naked tree;
Or frosts on hills of *Ochiltree*
          Are hoary gray;
Or blinding drifts wild-furious flee,
          Dark'ning the day!

O NATURE! a' thy shews an' forms
To feeling, pensive hearts hae charms!   80
Whether the Summer kindly warms,
          Wi' life an' light,
Or Winter howls, in gusty storms,
          The lang, dark night!

The *Muse*, nae *Poet* ever fand her,
Till by himsel he learn'd to wander,
Adown some trottin burn's meander,
    An' no think lang;
O sweet, to stray an' pensive ponder
    A heart-felt sang!   90

The warly race may drudge an' drive,
Hog-shouther, jundie, stretch an' strive,
Let me fair NATURE'S face descrive,
    And I, wi' pleasure,
Shall let the busy, grumbling hive
    Bum owre their treasure.

Fareweel, 'my rhyme-composing brither!'°
We've been owre lang unkenn'd to ither:
Now let us lay our heads thegither,
    In love fraternal: 100
May *Envy* wallop in a tether,
    Black fiend, infernal!

While Highlandmen hate tolls an' taxes;
While moorlan herds like guid, fat braxies;
While Terra firma, on her axis,
    Diurnal turns,
Count on a friend, in faith an' practice,
    In ROBERT BURNS.

POSTSCRIPT

My memory's no worth a preen;
I had amaist forgotten clean,
Ye bad me write you what they mean   110
    By this *new-light*,[1]°
'Bout which our *herds* sae aft hae been
    Maist like to fight.

In days when mankind were but callans,
At *Grammar*, *Logic*, an' sic talents,

[1] A cant-term for those religious opinions, which Dr. TAYLOR of Norwich has
defended so strenuously.

They took nae pains their speech to balance,
          Or rules to gie,
But spak their thoughts in plain, braid lallans,
          Like you or me.   120

In thae auld times, they thought the *Moon*,
Just like a sark, or pair o' shoon,
Woor by degrees, till her last roon
          Gaed past their viewin,
An' shortly after she was done
          They gat a new ane.

This past for certain, undisputed;
It ne'er cam i' their heads to doubt it,
Till chiels gat up an' wad confute it,
          An' ca'd it wrang;   130
An' muckle din there was about it,
          Baith loud an' lang.

Some *herds*, weel learn'd upo' the beuk,°
Wad threap auld folk the thing misteuk;
For 'twas the *auld moon* turn'd a newk
          An' out o' sight,
An' backlins-comin, to the leuk,
          She grew mair bright.

This was deny'd, it was affirm'd;
The *herds* an' *hissels* were alarm'd;   140
The rev'rend gray-beards rav'd an' storm'd,
          That beardless laddies
Should think they better were inform'd,
          Than their auld dadies.

Frae less to mair it gaed to sticks;°
Frae words an' aiths to clours an' nicks;
An' monie a fallow gat his licks,
          Wi' hearty crunt;
An' some, to learn them for their tricks,
          Were hang'd an' brunt.   150

This game was play'd in monie lands,
An' *auld-light* caddies bure sic hands,
That faith, the *youngsters* took the sands°
Wi' nimble shanks,
Till *Lairds* forbad, by strict commands,
Sic bluidy pranks.

But *new-light herds* gat sic a cowe,
Folk thought them ruin'd stick-an-stowe,
Till now amaist on ev'ry *knowe*
Ye'll find ane plac'd;   160
An' some, their *New-light* fair avow,
Just quite barefac'd.

Nae doubt the *auld-light flocks* are bleatan;
Their zealous *herds* are vex'd an' sweatan;
Mysel, I've ev'n seen them greetan
Wi' girnan spite,
To hear the *Moon* sae sadly lie'd on
By word an' write.°

But shortly they will cowe the louns!
Some *auld-light herds* in neebor towns   170
Are mind't, in things they ca' *balloons*,°
To tak a flight,
An' stay ae month amang the *Moons*
An' see them right.

Guid observation they will gie them;
An' when the *auld Moon's* gaun to lea'e them,
The hindmost *shaird*, they'll fetch it wi' them,
Just i' their pouch,
An' when the *new-light* billies see them,
I think they'll crouch!   180

Sae, ye observe that a' this clatter
Is naething but a 'moonshine matter;'°
But tho' dull *prose-folk* latin splatter
In logic tulzie,
I hope we, *Bardies*, ken some better
Than mind sic brulzie.

EPISTLE TO J. R******,
ENCLOSING SOME POEMS

O Rough, rude, ready-witted R******,
The wale o' cocks for fun an' drinkin!°
There's monie godly folks are thinkin,
        Your *dreams*[1] an' tricks°
Will send you, Korah-like, a sinkin,°
        Straught to auld Nick's.

Ye hae sae monie cracks an' cants,
And in your wicked, druken rants,
Ye mak a devil o' the *Saunts*,°
        An' fill them fou;
And then their failings, flaws an' wants,
        Are a' seen thro'.

Hypocrisy, in mercy spare it!
That *holy robe*, O dinna tear it!
Spare't for their sakes wha aften wear it,
        The lads in *black*;
But your curst wit, when it comes near it,
        Rives't aff their back.

Think, wicked Sinner, wha ye're skaithing:
It's just the *Blue-gown* badge an' claithing,
O' Saunts; tak that, ye lea'e them naething,
        To ken them by,
Frae ony unregenerate Heathen,°
        Like you or I.

I've sent you here, some rhymin ware,
A' that I bargain'd for, an' mair;
Sae when ye hae an hour to spare,
        I will expect,
Yon *Sang*[2] ye'll sen't, wi' cannie care,
        And no neglect.

10

20

30

---

[1] A certain humorous *dream* of his was then making a noise in the world.
[2] A *Song* he had promised the Author.

Tho' faith, sma' heart hae I to sing!
My Muse dow scarcely spread her wing:
I've play'd mysel a bonie *spring*,
        An' *danc'd* my fill!
I'd better gaen an' sair't the king,
        At Bunker's hill.°

'Twas ae night lately, in my fun,°
I gaed a rovin wi' the gun,
An' brought a *Paitrick* to the *grun'*,
        A bonie *hen*,   40
And, as the twilight was begun,
        Thought nane wad ken.

The poor, wee thing was *little hurt*;
I *straiket* it a wee for sport,
Ne'er thinkan they wad fash me for't;
        But, Deil-ma-care!
Somebody tells the *Poacher-Court*,°
        The hale affair.

Some auld, us'd hands had taen a note,
That *sic a hen* had got a *shot*;   50
I was suspected for the plot;
        I scorn'd to lie;
So gat the whissle o' my groat,
        An' pay't the *fee*.°

But by my *gun*, o' guns the wale,
An' by my *pouther* an' my *hail*,
An' by my *hen*, an' by her *tail*,
        I vow an' swear!
The *Game* shall pay, ower moor an' *dail*,
        For this, niest year.   60

As soon's the *clockin-time* is by,°
An' the *wee powts* begun to cry,
·L—d, I'se hae sportin by an' by,
        For my *gowd guinea*;
Tho' I should herd the *buckskin* kye°
        For't, in Virginia!

Trowth, they had muckle for to blame!
'Twas neither broken wing nor limb,
But twa-three *draps* about the *wame*
       Scarce thro' the *feathers*;   70
An' baith a *yellow George* to claim,°
       An' *thole* their *blethers!*

It pits me ay as mad's a hare;
So I can rhyme nor write nae mair;
But *pennyworths* again is fair,°
       When time's expedient:
Meanwhile I am, respected Sir,
       Your most obedient.

SONG

Tune—Corn Rigs are bonie

I

IT was upon a Lammas night,
  When corn rigs are bonie,
Beneath the moon's unclouded light,
  I held awa to Annie:°
The time flew by, wi' tentless heed,°
  Till 'tween the late and early;
Wi' sma' persuasion she agreed,
  To see me thro' the barley.

II

The sky was blue, the wind was still,
  The moon was shining clearly;   10
I set her down, wi' right good will,
  Amang the rigs o' barley:
I ken't her heart was a' my ain;
  I lov'd her most sincerely;
I kiss'd her owre and owre again,
  Amang the rigs o' barley.

III

I lock'd her in my fond embrace;
  Her heart was beating rarely:

My blessings on that happy place,   20
  Amang the rigs o' barley!
But by the moon and stars so bright,
  That shone that hour so clearly!°
She ay shall bless that happy night,
  Amang the rigs o' barley.

IV

I hae been blythe wi' Comrades dear;
  I hae been merry drinking;
I hae been joyfu' gath'rin gear;
  I hae been happy thinking: 30
But a' the pleasures e'er I saw,
  Tho' three times doubl'd fairly,
That happy night was worth them a',
  Amang the rigs o' barley.

CHORUS

  Corn rigs, an' barley rigs,
    An' corn rigs are bonie:
  I'll ne'er forget that happy night,
    Amang the rigs wi' Annie.

SONG,

COMPOSED IN AUGUST

Tune—*I had a horse, I had nae mair*

I

NOW westlin winds, and slaught'ring guns
  Bring Autumn's pleasant weather;°
And the moorcock springs, on whirring wings,°
  Amang the blooming heather:
Now waving grain, wide o'er the plain,
  Delights the weary Farmer;
And the moon shines bright, when I rove at night,
  To muse upon my Charmer.

II

The Partridge loves the fruitful fells;°
  The Plover loves the mountains;°   10

The Woodcock haunts the lonely dells;°
  The soaring Hern the fountains:
Thro' lofty groves, the Cushat roves,
  The path of man to shun it;°
The hazel bush o'erhangs the Thrush,
  The spreading thorn the Linnet.

III

Thus ev'ry kind their pleasure find,
  The savage and the tender;
Some social join, and leagues combine;
  Some solitary wander: 20
Avaunt, away! the cruel sway,
  Tyrannic man's dominion;
The Sportsman's joy, the murd'ring cry,°
  The flutt'ring, gory pinion!°

IV

But PEGGY dear, the ev'ning's clear,
  Thick flies the skimming Swallow;
The sky is blue, the fields in view,
  All fading-green and yellow:
Come let us stray our gladsome way,
  And view the charms of Nature;°   30
The rustling corn, the fruited thorn,
  And ev'ry happy creature.°

V

We'll gently walk, and sweetly talk,
  Till the silent moon shine clearly;°
I'll grasp thy waist, and fondly prest,°
  Swear how I love thee dearly:°
Not vernal show'rs to budding flow'rs,
  Not Autumn to the Farmer,
So dear can be, as thou to me,
  My fair, my lovely Charmer!   40

SONG

Tune—*Gilderoy*

I

FROM thee, ELIZA, I must go,
 And from my native shore:
The cruel fates between us throw
 A boundless ocean's roar;
But boundless oceans, roaring wide,
 Between my Love and me,
They never, never can divide
 My heart and soul from thee.

II

Farewell, farewell, ELIZA dear,
 The maid that I adore!
A boding voice is in mine ear,
 We part to meet no more!
But the latest throb that leaves my heart,°
 While Death stands victor by,
That throb, ELIZA, is thy part,
 And thine that latest sigh!

10

THE FAREWELL.

TO THE BRETHREN OF ST. JAMES'S LODGE, TARBOLTON

Tune—*Goodnight and joy be wi' you a'*

I

ADIEU! a heart-warm, fond adieu!
 Dear brothers of the *mystic tye!*
Ye favored, ye *enlighten'd* Few,°
 Companions of my social joy!
Tho' I to foreign lands must hie,
 Pursuing Fortune's slidd'ry ba',
With melting heart, and brimful eye,
 I'll mind you still, tho' far awa.

II

Oft have I met your social Band,
    And spent the chearful, festive night;   10
Oft, honor'd with supreme command,°
    Presided o'er the *Sons of light*:
And by that *Hieroglyphic* bright,°
    Which none but *Craftsmen* ever saw!
Strong Mem'ry on my heart shall write
    Those happy scenes when far awa!

III

May Freedom, Harmony and Love
    Unite you in the *grand Design*,
Beneath th' Omniscient Eye above,
    The glorious ARCHITECT Divine!°   20
That you may keep th' *unerring line*,
    Still rising by the *plummet's law*,
Till *Order* bright, completely shine,
    Shall be my Pray'r when far awa.

IV

And *YOU*, farewell! whose merits claim,°
    Justly that *highest badge* to wear!
Heav'n bless your honor'd, noble Name,
    To MASONRY and SCOTIA dear!
A last request, permit me here,
    When yearly ye assemble a',   30
One *round*, I ask it with a *tear*,
    To him, *the Bard, that's far awa.*

EPITAPHS AND EPIGRAMS°

EPITAPH ON A HENPECKED COUNTRY SQUIRE

As father Adam first was fool'd,
    A case that's still too common,
Here lyes a man a woman rul'd,
    The devil rul'd the woman.

EPIGRAM ON SAID OCCASION

O Death, hadst thou but spar'd his life,
  Whom we, this day, lament!
We freely wad exchang'd the *wife*,
  An' a' been weel content.

Ev'n as he is, cauld in his graff,
  The *swap* we yet will do't;
Tak thou the Carlin's carcase aff,
  Thou'se get the *saul* o' *boot*.

ANOTHER

One Queen Artemisa, as old stories tell,
When depriv'd of her husband she loved so well,
In respect for the love and affection he'd show'd her,
She reduc'd him to dust, and she drank up the Powder.

But Queen N**********, of a diff'rent complexion,
When call'd on to order the fun'ral direction,
Would have *eat* her dead lord, on a slender pretence,
Not to show her respect, but—*to save the expense*.

EPITAPHS

ON A CELEBRATED RULING ELDER

Here Sowter **** in Death does sleep;°
  To H—ll, if he's gane thither,
Satan, gie him thy gear to keep,
  He'll haud it weel thegither.

ON A NOISY POLEMIC

Below thir stanes lie Jamie's banes;
  O Death, it's my opinion,
Thou ne'er took such a bleth'ran b—tch,
  Into thy dark dominion!

ON WEE JOHNIE

Hic jacet wee *Johnie*

Whoe'er thou art, O reader, know,
　　That Death has murder'd Johnie;
An' here his *body* lies fu' low——
　　For *saul* he ne'er had ony.

FOR THE AUTHOR'S FATHER

O ye whose cheek the tear of pity stains,
　　Draw near with pious rev'rence and attend!
Here lie the loving Husband's dear remains,
　　The tender Father, and the gen'rous Friend.

The pitying Heart that felt for human Woe;
　　The dauntless heart that fear'd no human Pride;
The Friend of Man, to vice alone a foe;
　　'For ev'n his failings lean'd to Virtue's side.'[1]

FOR R.A. ESQ;

Know thou, O stranger to the fame
Of this much lov'd, much honor'd name!
(For none that knew him need be told)
A warmer heart Death ne'er made cold.

FOR G.H. ESQ;

The poor man weeps—here G—N sleeps,
　　Whom canting wretches blam'd:°
But with *such as he*, where'er he be,
　　May I be *sav'd* or *d—'d!*

---

[1] Goldsmith.

A BARD'S EPITAPH

IS there a whim-inspir'd fool,
Owre fast for thought, owre hot for rule,
Owre blate to seek, owre proud to snool,
        Let him draw near;
And o'er this grassy heap sing dool,
        And drap a tear.

Is there a Bard of rustic song,
Who, noteless, steals the crouds among,°
That weekly this area throng,
        O, pass not by!
But with a frater-feeling strong,°
        Here, heave a sigh.

Is there a man whose judgment clear,
Can others teach the course to steer,
Yet runs, himself, life's mad career,
        Wild as the wave,
Here pause—and thro' the starting tear,
        Survey this grave.

The poor Inhabitant below
Was quick to learn and wise to know,
And keenly felt the friendly glow,
        And *softer flame*;
But thoughtless follies laid him low,
        And stain'd his name!

Reader attend—whether thy soul
Soars fancy's flights beyond the pole,
Or darkling grubs this earthly hole,
        In low pursuit,
Know, prudent, cautious, *self-controul*
        Is Wisdom's root.

10

20

FINIS

A. Nasmyth pinxt.   I. Beugo sculpt.

ROBERT BURNS

POEMS,

CHIEFLY IN THE

SCOTTISH DIALECT.

BY

ROBERT BURNS.

EDINBURGH:

PRINTED FOR THE AUTHOR,

AND SOLD BY WILLIAM CREECH.

M,DCC,LXXXVII.

DEDICATION.

TO THE

NOBLEMEN AND GENTLEMEN

OF THE

CALEDONIAN HUNT.

MY LORDS, AND GENTLEMEN,

A Scottish Bard, proud of the name, and whose highest ambition is to sing in his Country's service, where shall he so properly look for patronage as to the illustrious Names of his native Land; those who bear the honours and inherit the virtues of their Ancestors?—The Poetic Genius of my Country found me as the prophetic bard Elijah did Elisha—at the plough; *and threw her inspiring* mantle over me.° *She bade me sing the loves, the joys, the rural scenes and rural pleasures of my natal Soil, in my native tongue: I tuned my wild, artless notes, as she inspired.—She whispered me to come*

to this ancient metropolis of Caledonia, and lay my Songs under your hon-
oured protection: I now obey her dictates.

Though much indebted to your goodness, I do not approach you, my
Lords and Gentlemen, in the usual stile of dedication, to thank you for past
favours; that path is so hackneyed by prostituted Learning, that honest
Rusticity is ashamed of it.—Nor do I present this Address with the venal
soul of a servile Author, looking for a continuation of those favours: I was
bred to the Plough, and am independent. I come to claim the common
Scottish name with you, my illustrious Countrymen; and to tell the world
that I glory in the title.—I come to congratulate my Country, that the
blood of her ancient heroes still runs uncontaminated; and that from your
courage, knowledge, and public spirit, she may expect protection, wealth,
and liberty.—In the last place, I come to proffer my warmest wishes to the
Great Fountain of Honour, the Monarch of the Universe, for your welfare
and happiness.

When you go forth to waken the Echoes, in the ancient and favourite
amusement of your Forefathers, may Pleasure ever be of your party; and
may Social-joy await your return! When harassed in courts or camps with
the justlings of bad men and bad measures, may the honest consciousness of
injured Worth attend your return to your native Seats; and may Domestic
Happiness, with a smiling welcome, meet you at your gates! May Corruption
shrink at your kindling indignant glance; and may tyranny in the Ruler
and licentiousness in the People equally find you an inexorable foe!

I have the honour to be,

  With the sincerest gratitude and highest respect,

   MY LORDS AND GENTLEMEN,

  Your most devoted humble servant,

    ROBERT BURNS.

EDINBURGH,
April 4. 1787.

THE BRIGS OF AYR

A POEM

Inscribed to J. B*********, *Esq;* AYR

THE simple Bard, rough at the rustic plough,
Learning his tuneful trade from ev'ry bough;
The chanting linnet, or the mellow thrush,
Hailing the setting sun, sweet, in the green thorn bush,
The soaring lark, the perching red-breast shrill,
Or deep-ton'd plovers, grey, wild-whistling o'er the hill;
Shall he, nurst in the Peasant's lowly shed,
To hardy Independence bravely bred,
By early Poverty to hardship steel'd,
And train'd to arms in stern Misfortune's field,   10
Shall he be guilty of their hireling crimes,
The servile, mercenary Swiss of rhymes?°
Or labour hard the panegyric close,°
With all the venal soul of dedicating Prose?
No! though his artless strains he rudely sings,
And throws his hand uncouthly o'er the strings,
He glows with all the spirit of the Bard,
Fame, honest fame, his great, his dear reward.°
Still, if some Patron's gen'rous care he trace,
Skill'd in the secret, to bestow with grace;   20
When B********* befriends his humble name,
And hands the rustic Stranger up to fame,
With heartfelt throes his grateful bosom swells,
The godlike bliss, to give, alone excels.

'Twas when the stacks get on their winter-hap,
And thack and rape secure the toil-won crap;
Potatoe-bings are snugged up frae skaith
Of coming Winter's biting, frosty breath;
The bees, rejoicing o'er their summer-toils,
Unnumber'd buds an' flow'rs' delicious spoils,   30
Seal'd up with frugal care in massive, waxen piles,
Are doom'd by Man, that tyrant o'er the weak,
The death o' devils, smoor'd wi' brimstone reek:°

The thund'ring guns are heard on ev'ry side,
The wounded coveys, reeling, scatter wide;
The feather'd field-mates, bound by Nature's tie,
Sires, mothers, children, in one carnage lie:
(What warm, poetic heart but inly bleeds,
And execrates man's savage, ruthless deeds!)
Nae mair the flow'r in field or meadow springs;   40
Nae mair the grove with airy concert rings,
Except perhaps the Robin's whistling glee,
Proud o' the height o' some bit half-lang tree:
The hoary morns precede the sunny days, ⎫
Mild, calm, serene, wide-spreads the noontide blaze, ⎬
While thick the gossamour waves wanton in the rays. ⎭

'Twas in that season; when a simple Bard,
Unknown and poor, simplicity's reward,
Ae night, within the ancient brugh of *Ayr*,
By whim inspir'd, or haply prest wi' care,   50
He left his bed and took his wayward rout,
And down by *Simpson's*[1] wheel'd the left about:
(Whether impell'd by all-directing Fate,
To witness what I after shall narrate;
Or whether, rapt in meditation high,
He wander'd out he knew not where nor why)
The drowsy *Dungeon-clock* had number'd two,°
And *Wallace-Tow'r*[2] had sworn the fact was true:°
The tide-swoln Firth, with sullen-sounding roar,
Through the still night dash'd hoarse along the shore: 60
All else was hush'd as Nature's closed e'e;
The silent moon shone high o'er tow'r and tree:°
The chilly Frost, beneath the silver beam,
Crept, gently-crusting, o'er the glittering stream.——

When, lo! on either hand the list'ning Bard,
The clanging sugh of whistling wings is heard;°
Two dusky forms dart thro' the midnight air,
Swift as the *Gos*[3] drives on the wheeling hare;
Ane on th' *Auld Brig* his airy shape uprears,

[1] A noted tavern at the *Auld Brig* end.   [2] The two steeples.
[3] The gos-hawk, or falcon.

The ither flutters o'er the *rising piers*: 70
Our warlock Rhymer instantly descry'd°
The Sprites that owre the *Brigs of Ayr* preside.
(That Bards are second-sighted is nae joke,
And ken the lingo of the sp'ritual folk;°
Fays, Spunkies, Kelpies, a', they can explain them,°
And ev'n the vera deils they brawly ken them).
Auld Brig appear'd of ancient Pictish race,
The vera wrinkles Gothic in his face:°
He seem'd as he wi' Time had warstl'd lang,
Yet, teughly doure, he bade an unco bang. 80
New Brig was buskit in a braw, new coat,
That he, at *Lon'on*, frae ane *Adams* got;°
In's hand five taper staves as smooth's a bead,°
Wi' virls an' whirlygigums at the head.°
The Goth was stalking round with anxious search,
Spying the time-worn flaws in ev'ry arch;
It chanc'd his new-come neebor took his e'e,
And e'en a vex'd and angry heart had he!
Wi' thieveless sneer to see his modish mien,
He, down the water, gies him this guid-een—— 90

AULD BRIG

I doubt na, frien', ye'll think ye're nae sheep-shank,
Ance ye were streekit owre frae bank to bank!
But gin ye be a Brig as auld as me,
Tho' faith, that date, I doubt, ye'll never see;
There'll be, if that date come, I'll wad a boddle,
Some fewer whigmeleeries in your noddle.

NEW BRIG

Auld Vandal, ye but show your little mense,°
Just much about it wi' your scanty sense;
Will your poor, narrow foot-path of a street,
Where twa wheel-barrows tremble when they meet, 100
Your ruin'd, formless bulk o' stane and lime,
Compare wi' bonie *Brigs* o' modern time?
There's men of taste wou'd tak the *Ducat-stream*,[1]
Tho' they should cast the vera sark and swim,

---

[1] A noted ford, just above the Auld Brig.

E'er they would grate their feelings wi' the view
Of sic an ugly, Gothic hulk as you.

AULD BRIG

Conceited gowk! puff'd up wi' windy pride!
This mony a year I've stood the flood an' tide;
And tho' wi' crazy eild I'm sair forfairn,
I'll be a *Brig* when ye're a shapeless cairn! 110
As yet ye little ken about the matter,
But twa-three winters will inform ye better.
When heavy, dark, continued, a'-day rains
Wi' deepening deluges o'erflow the plains;
When from the hills where springs the brawling *Coil*,
Or stately *Lugar's* mossy fountains boil,
Or where the *Greenock* winds his moorland course,
Or haunted *Garpal*[1] draws his feeble source,°
Arous'd by blustering winds an' spotting thowes,
In mony a torrent down the snaw-broo rowes; 120
While crashing ice, borne on the roaring speat,
Sweeps dams, an' mills, an' brigs, a' to the gate;
And from *Glenbuck*,[2] down to the *Ratton-key*,[3]
Auld *Ayr* is just one lengthen'd, tumbling sea;
Then down ye'll hurl, deil nor ye never rise!
And dash the gumlie jaups up to the pouring skies.
A lesson sadly teaching, to your cost,
That Architecture's noble art is lost!

NEW BRIG

Fine *architecture*, trowth, I needs must say't o't!
The L—d be thankit that we've tint the gate o't! 130
Gaunt, ghastly, ghaist-alluring edifices,
Hanging with threat'ning jut like precipices;
O'er-arching, mouldy, gloom-inspiring coves,
Supporting roofs, fantastic, stony groves:°
Windows and doors in nameless sculptures drest,
With order, symmetry, or taste unblest;
Forms like some bedlam Statuary's dream,

---

[1] The banks of the *Garpal Water* is one of the few places in the West of Scotland where those fancy-scaring beings, known by the name of *Ghaists*, still continue pertinaciously to inhabit.

[2] The source of the river of Ayr. [3] A small landing-place above the large key.

The craz'd creations of misguided whim;
Forms might be worshipp'd on the bended knee,
And still the *second dread command* be free,°
Their likeness is not found on earth, in air, or sea.   140
Mansions that would disgrace the building-taste
Of any mason reptile, bird, or beast;
Fit only for a doited Monkish race,
Or frosty maids forsworn the dear embrace,
Or Cuifs of later times, wha held the notion,
That sullen gloom was sterling, true devotion:
Fancies that our guid Brugh denies protection,
And soon may they expire, unblest with resurrection!°

AULD BRIG

O ye, my dear-remember'd, ancient yealings,°   150
Were ye but here to share my wounded feelings!
Ye worthy *Proveses*, an' mony a *Bailie*,°
Wha in the paths o' righteousness did toil ay;
Ye dainty *Deacons*, an' ye douce *Conveeners*,°
To whom our moderns are but causey-cleaners;
Ye godly *Councils* wha hae blest this town;
Ye godly *Brethren* o' the sacred gown,
Wha meekly gae your *hurdies* to the *smiters*;
And (what would now be strange) ye *godly Writers*:°
A' ye douce folk I've borne aboon the broo,   160
Were ye but here, what would ye say or do!
How would your spirits groan in deep vexation,
To see each melancholy alteration;
And, agonising, curse the time and place
When ye begat the base, degen'rate race!
Nae langer Rev'rend Men, their country's glory,
In plain, braid Scots hold forth a plain, braid story:
Nae langer thrifty Citizens, an' douce,
Meet owre a pint, or in the Council-house;
But staumrel, corky-headed, graceless Gentry,   170
The herryment and ruin of the country;
Men, three-parts made by Taylors and by Barbers,
Wha waste your weel-hain'd gear on d—d *new Brigs*
    and *Harbours!*°

NEW BRIG

Now haud you there! for faith ye've said enough,
And muckle mair than ye can mak to through.°
As for your Priesthood, I shall say but little,
Corbies and *Clergy* are a shot right kittle:°
But, under favor o' your langer beard,
Abuse o' Magistrates might weel be spar'd;
To liken them to your auld-warld squad,   180
I must needs say, comparisons are odd.
In *Ayr*, Wag-wits nae mair can have a handle
To mouth 'A Citizen,' a term o' scandal:°
Nae mair the Council waddles down the street,
In all the pomp of ignorant conceit;
Men wha grew wise priggin owre hops an' raisins,
Or gather'd lib'ral views in Bonds and Seisins.°
If haply Knowledge, on a random tramp,
Had shor'd them with a glimmer of his lamp,
And would to Common-sense for once betray'd them,   190
Plain, dull Stupidity stept kindly in to aid them.

———

What farther clishmaclaver might been said,
What bloody wars, if Spirites had blood to shed,
No man can tell; but, all before their sight,
A fairy train appear'd in order bright:
Adown the glittering stream they featly danc'd;°
Bright to the moon their various dresses glanc'd:
They footed o'er the wat'ry glass so neat,
The infant ice scarce bent beneath their feet:
While arts of Minstrelsy among them rung,   200
And soul-ennobling Bards heroic ditties sung.

———

O had *McLauchlan*,[1] thairm-inspiring Sage,°
Been there to hear this heavenly band engage,
When thro' his dear *Strathspeys* they bore with Highland rage;
Or when they struck old Scotia's melting airs,
The lover's raptur'd joys or bleeding cares;
How would his Highland lug been nobler fir'd,

[1] A well known performer of Scottish music on the violin.

And ev'n his matchless hand with finer touch inspir'd!
No guess could tell what instrument appear'd,
But all the soul of Music's self was heard;   210
Harmonious concert rung in every part,
While simple melody pour'd moving on the heart.

The Genius of the Stream in front appears,°
A venerable Chief advanc'd in years;
His hoary head with water-lilies crown'd,
His manly leg with garter tangle bound.°
Next came the loveliest pair in all the ring,
Sweet Female Beauty hand in hand with Spring;
Then, crown'd with flow'ry hay, came Rural Joy,
And Summer, with his fervid-beaming eye: 220
All-chearing Plenty, with her flowing horn,
Led yellow Autumn wreath'd with nodding corn;
Then Winter's time-bleach'd locks did hoary show,
By Hospitality with cloudless brow.°
Next follow'd Courage with his martial stride,
From where the *Feal* wild-woody coverts hide:°
Benevolence, with mild, benignant air,
A female form, came from the tow'rs of *Stair*:°
Learning and Worth in equal measures trode,
From simple *Catrine*, their long-lov'd abode:°   230
Last, white-rob'd Peace, crown'd with a hazle wreath,
To rustic Agriculture did bequeath
The broken, iron instruments of Death,°
At sight of whom our Sprites forgat their kindling wrath.

ADDRESS TO THE UNCO GUID,
OR THE
RIGIDLY RIGHTEOUS

My Son, these maxims make a rule,
    And lump them ay thegither;
The Rigid Righteous *is a fool,*
    The Rigid Wise *anither:*
The cleanest corn that e'er was dight

May hae some pyles o' caff in;
So ne'er a fellow-creature slight
For random fits o' daffin.

SOLOMON. — Eccles. ch. vii. vers. 16.°

I

O YE wha are sae guid yoursel,
    Sae pious and sae holy,
Ye've nought to do but mark and tell
    Your Neebours' fauts and folly!
Whase life is like a weel-gaun mill,
    Supply'd wi' store o' water,
The heaped happer's ebbing still,
    And still the clap plays clatter.°

II

Hear me, ye venerable Core,
    As counsel for poor mortals,
That frequent pass douce Wisdom's door
    For glaikit Folly's portals;
I, for their thoughtless, careless sakes
    Would here propone defences,
Their donsie tricks, their black mistakes,
    Their failings and mischances.

III

Ye see your state wi' theirs compar'd,
    And shudder at the niffer,
But cast a moment's fair regard
    What maks the mighty differ;
Discount what scant occasion gave,
    That purity ye pride in,
And (what's aft mair than a' the lave)
    Your better art o' hiding.

IV

Think, when your castigated pulse
    Gies now and then a wallop,
What ragings must his veins convulse,
    That still eternal gallop:
Wi' wind and tide fair i' your tail,

10

20

Right on ye scud your sea-way; 30
But, in the teeth o' baith to sail,
   It maks an unco leeway.

V

See Social-life and Glee sit down,
   All joyous and unthinking,
Till, quite transmugrify'd, they're grown
   Debauchery and Drinking:
O would they stay to calculate
   Th' eternal consequences;
Or your more dreaded h–ll to state,
   D–mnation of expences! 40

VI

Ye high, exalted, virtuous Dames,
   Ty'd up in godly laces,
Before ye gie poor *Frailty* names,
   Suppose a change o' cases;
A dear-lov'd lad, convenience snug,
   A treacherous inclination——
But, let me whisper i' your lug,
   Ye're aiblins nae temptation.

VII

Then gently scan your brother Man,°
   Still gentler sister Woman; 50
Tho' they may gang a kennin wrang,
   To step aside is human:
One point must still be greatly dark,
   The moving *Why* they do it;
And just as lamely can ye mark,
   How far perhaps they rue it.

VIII

Who made the heart, 'tis *He* alone
   Decidedly can try us,
He knows each chord its various tone,
   Each spring its various bias: 60
Then at the balance let's be mute,
   We never can adjust it;

What's *done* we partly may compute,
  But know not what's *resisted*.

TO A HAGGIS

FAIR fa' your honest, sonsie face,
Great Chieftan o' the Puddin-race!
Aboon them a' ye tak your place,
        Painch, tripe, or thairm:°
Weel are ye wordy of a *grace*
        As lang's my arm.

  The groaning trencher there ye fill,
Your hurdies like a distant hill,
Your *pin* wad help to mend a mill°
        In time o' need,   10
While thro' your pores the dews distil
        Like amber bead.°

  His knife see Rustic-labour dight,
An' cut you up wi' ready slight,
Trenching your gushing entrails bright
        Like onie ditch;
And then, O what a glorious sight,
        Warm-reekin, rich!

  Then, horn for horn they stretch an' strive,°
Deil tak the hindmost, on they drive,   20
Till a' their weel-swall'd kytes belyve
        Are bent like drums;
Then auld Guidman, maist like to rive,
        Bethankit hums.°

  Is there that owre his French *ragout*,
Or *olio* that wad staw a sow,
Or *fricassee* wad mak her spew°
        Wi' perfect sconner,
Looks down wi' sneering, scornfu' view
        On sic a dinner?   30

Poor devil! see him owre his trash,
As feckless as a wither'd rash,
His spindle shank a guid whip-lash,
        His nieve a nit;
Thro' bluidy flood or field to dash,
        O how unfit!

But mark the Rustic, *haggis-fed*,
The trembling earth resounds his tread,
Clap in his walie nieve a blade,
        He'll mak it whissle;   40
An' legs, an' arms, an' heads will sned,
        Like taps o' thrissle.°

Ye Pow'rs wha mak mankind your care,
And dish them out their bill o' fare,
Auld Scotland wants nae skinking ware
        That jaups in luggies;
But, if ye wish her gratefu' pray'r,
        Gie her a *Haggis!*°

JOHN BARLEYCORN[1]

A BALLAD

I

THERE was three kings into the east,
   Three kings both great and high,
And they hae sworn a solemn oath
   John Barleycorn should die.

II

They took a plough and plough'd him down,
   Put clods upon his head,
And they hae sworn a solemn oath
   John Barleycorn was dead.

---

[1] This is partly composed on the plan of an old song known by the same name.

III

But the chearful Spring came kindly on,
    And show'rs began to fall;
John Barleycorn got up again,
    And sore surpris'd them all.
10

IV

The sultry suns of Summer came,
    And he grew thick and strong,
His head weel arm'd wi' pointed spears,
    That no one should him wrong.

V

The sober Autumn enter'd mild,
    When he grew wan and pale;
His bending joints and drooping head
    Show'd he began to fail.
20

VI

His colour sicken'd more and more,
    He faded into age;
And then his enemies began
    To show their deadly rage.

VII

They've taen a weapon, long and sharp,
    And cut him by the knee;
Then ty'd him fast upon a cart,
    Like a rogue for forgerie.

VIII

They laid him down upon his back,
    And cudgell'd him full sore;°
They hung him up before the storm,
    And turn'd him o'er and o'er.°
30

IX

They filled up a darksome pit
    With water to the brim,°

They heaved in John Barleycorn,
   There let him sink or swim.

X

They laid him out upon the floor,
   To work him farther woe,
And still, as signs of life appear'd,
   They toss'd him to and fro.°   40

XI

They wasted, o'er a scorching flame,°
   The marrow of his bones;
But a Miller us'd him worst of all,
   For he crush'd him between two stones.°

XII

And they hae taen his very heart's blood,
   And drank it round and round;
And still the more and more they drank,
   Their joy did more abound.

XIII

John Barleycorn was a hero bold,
   Of noble enterprise,   50
For if you do but taste his blood,
   'Twill make your courage rise.

XIV

'Twill make a man forget his woe;
   'Twill heighten all his joy:
'Twill make the widow's heart to sing,
   Tho' the tear were in her eye.

XV

Then let us toast John Barleycorn,
   Each man a glass in hand;
And may his great posterity
   Ne'er fail in old Scotland!   60

A FRAGMENT

Tune—*Gilliecrankie*

I

WHEN *Guilford* good our Pilot stood,°
   An' did our hellim thraw, man,°
Ae night, at tea, began a plea,
   Within *America*, man:
Then up they gat the maskin-pat,
   And in the sea did jaw, man;°
An' did nae less, in full Congress,°
   Than quite refuse our law, man.

II

Then thro' the lakes *Montgomery* takes,°
   I wat he was na slaw, man;   10
Down *Lowrie's burn* he took a turn,
   And *C–rl–t–n* did ca', man:°
But yet, whatreck, he, at *Quebec*,
   Montgomery-like did fa', man,
Wi' sword in hand, before his band,
   Amang his en'mies a', man.°

III

Poor *Tammy G–ge* within a cage°
   Was kept at *Boston-ha'*, man;
Till *Willie H——e* took o'er the knowe°
   For *Philadelphia*, man: 20
Wi' sword an' gun he thought a sin
   Guid Christian bluid to draw, man;
But at *New-York*, wi' knife an' fork,
   Sir Loin he hacked sma', man.°

IV

B–rg——ne gaed up, like spur an' whip,°
   Till *Fraser* brave did fa', man;
Then lost his way, ae misty day,
   In *Saratoga* shaw, man.
C–rnw–ll–s fought as lang's he dought,°

An' did the Buckskins claw, man;°   30
But *Cl–nt–n's* glaive frae rust to save°
   He hung it to the wa', man.

V

Then *M–nt–gue*, an' *Guilford* too,°
   Began to fear a fa', man;
And *S–ckv–lle* doure, wha stood the stoure,°
   The German Chief to thraw, man:°
For Paddy *B–rke*, like ony Turk,°
   Nae mercy had at a', man;
An' *Charlie F–x* threw by the box,°
   An' lows'd his tinkler jaw, man.   40

VI

Then *R–ck–ngh–m* took up the game;°
   Till Death did on him ca', man;
When *Sh–lb–rne* meek held up his cheek,°
   Conform to Gospel law, man:
Saint Stephen's boys, wi' jarring noise,
   They did his measures thraw, man,
For *N–rth* an' *F–x* united stocks,°
   An' bore him to the wa', man.

VII

Then Clubs an' Hearts were *Charlie's* cartes,°
   He swept the stakes awa', man,   50
Till the Diamond's Ace, of *Indian* race,
   Led him a sair *faux pas*, man:°
The Saxon lads, wi' loud placads,°
   On *Chatham's Boy* did ca', man;°
An' Scotland drew her pipe an' blew,
   'Up, Willie, waur them a', man!'°

VIII

Behind the throne then *Gr–nv–lle's* gone,°
   A secret word or twa, man;
While slee *D–nd–s* arous'd the class°
   Be-north the Roman wa', man: 60
An' *Chatham's* wraith, in heav'nly graith,
   (Inspired Bardies saw, man)

Wi' kindling eyes cry'd, '*Willie*, rise!
'Would I hae fear'd them a', man!'

IX

But, word an' blow, *N–rth, F–x, and Co*.
  Gowff'd *Willie* like a ba', man,°
Till *Suthron* raise, an' coost their claise
  Behind him in a raw, man:°
An' *Caledon* threw by the drone,
  An' did her whittle draw, man;
An' swoor fu' rude, thro' dirt an' blood,
  To mak it guid in law, man.°

* * * * * * *

GREEN GROW'S THE RASHES

Songs from *The Scots Musical Museum*

GREEN GROWS THE RASHES

Andante

There's nought but care on ev'-ry han', In ev'-ry hour that pas-ses, O: What sig-ni-fies the life o' man, An' twere not for the las-ses, O?

Chorus

Green grow the rash-es, O; Green grow the rash-es, O; The sweet-est hours that e'er I spend, Are spent a-mang the las-ses, O.

There's nought but care on ev'ry han',
 In ev'ry hour that passes, O:
What signifies the life o' man,
 An' twere not for the lasses, O?

CHORUS: Green grow the rashes, O;
 Green grow the rashes, O;
 The sweetest hours that e'er I spend,
 Are spent amang the lasses, O.

The warly race may riches chase,
 An' riches still may fly them, O;   10
An' tho' at last they catch them fast,
 Their hearts can ne'er enjoy them, O.
 Green grow, &c.

But gie me a canny hour at e'en,
 My arms about my Dearie, O;
An' warly cares, an' warly men,
 May a' gae tapsalteerie, O!
 Green grow, &c.

For you sae douse! ye sneer at this,
 Ye'er nought but senseless asses, O:
The wisest Man the warl' saw,°
 He dearly lov'd the lasses, O.   20
 Green grow, &c.

Auld Nature swears, the lovely Dears
 Her noblest work she classes, O:
Her prentice han' she try'd on man,
 An' then she made the lasses, O.
 Green grow, &c.

THE BIRKS OF ABERFELDY

CHORUS: Bonny lassie, will ye go,
will ye go, will ye go,
bonny lassie, will ye go
to the Birks of Aberfeldy?

Now Simmer blinks on flowery braes,
And o'er the chrystal streamlets plays;
Come let us spend the lightsome days
In the birks of Aberfeldy.
Bonny lassie, &c.

The little birdies blythely sing,
While o'er their heads the hazels hing; 10
Or lightly flit on wanton wing
In the birks of Aberfeldy.
Bonny lassie, &c.

The braes ascend like lofty wa's,
The foamy stream deep-roaring fa's,
O'er-hung wi' fragrant-spreading shaws,
The birks of Aberfeldy.
Bonny lassie, &c.

The hoary cliffs are crown'd wi' flowers,
White o'er the linns the burnie pours,
And rising weets wi' misty showers
The birks of Aberfeldy. 20
Bonny lassie, &c.

Let Fortune's gifts at random flee,
They ne'er shall draw a wish frae me.
Supremely blest wi' love and thee
In the birks of Aberfeldy.
Bonny lassie, &c.

THE PLOUGHMAN

The Ploughman he's a bony lad,
His mind is ever true, jo,
His garters knit below his knee,
His bonnet it is blue, jo.°

CHORUS: Then up wi't a', my Ploughman lad,
And hey, my merry Ploughman;
Of a' the trades that I do ken,
Commend me to the Ploughman.

My Ploughman he comes hame at e'en,
    He's aften wat and weary: 10
Cast off the wat, put on the dry,
    And gae to bed, my Dearie.
        Up wi't a' &c.

I will wash my Ploughman's hose,
    And I will dress his o'erlay;
I will mak my Ploughman's bed,
    And chear him late and early.
        Up wi't a' &c.

I hae been east, I hae been west,
    I hae been at Saint Johnston,°
The boniest sight that e'er I saw
    Was th' Ploughman laddie dancin.   20
        Up wi't a' &c.

Snaw-white stockins on his legs,
    And siller buckles glancin;
A gude blue bannet on his head,
    And O but he was handsome!
        Up wi't a' &c.

Commend me to the Barn yard,
    And the Corn-mou, man;°
I never gat my Coggie fou
    Till I met wi' the Ploughman.
        Up wi't a' &c.

RATTLIN, ROARIN WILLIE

O Rattlin, roarin Willie,
  O he held to the fair,
An' for to sell his fiddle
  And buy some other ware;
But parting wi' his fiddle,
  The saut tear blin't his e'e;°
And Rattlin, roarin Willie
  Ye're welcome hame to me.

O Willie, come sell your fiddle,
  O sell your fiddle sae fine;   10
O Willie, come sell your fiddle,
  And buy a pint o' wine;
If I should sell my fiddle,
  The warl' would think I was mad,
For mony a rantin day
  My fiddle and I hae had.

As I cam by Crochallan°
  I cannily keekit ben,
Rattlin, roarin Willie
  Was sitting at yon boord-en',   20
Sitting at yon boord-en',
  And amang guid companie;
Rattlin, roarin Willie,
  Ye're welcome hame to me!

TIBBIE, I HAE SEEN THE DAY

Slowish

O Tib-bie, I hae seen the day, Ye would na been sae shy; For

laik o' gear ye light-ly me, But trowth, I care na by. Yes-

treen I met you on the moor, Ye spak na, but gaed by like stoure; Ye

geck at me be-cause I'm poor, But fient a hair care I.   O

Chorus

Tib-bie, I hae seen the day, Ye would na been sae shy; For

laik o' gear ye light-ly me, But trowth I care na by.

CHORUS: O Tibbie, I hae seen the day,
          Ye would na been sae shy;
          For laik o' gear ye lightly me,
          But trowth, I care na by.

Yestreen I met you on the moor,
Ye spak na, but gaed by like stoure;
Ye geck at me because I'm poor,
   But fient a hair care I.
     Tibbie, I hae &c.

I doubt na, lass, but ye may think,
Because ye hae the name o' clink,   10
That ye can please me at a wink,
   Whene'er ye like to try.
     Tibbie, I hae &c.

But sorrow tak him that's sae mean,
Altho' his pouch o' coin were clean,
Wha follows ony saucy quean
   That looks sae proud and high.
     Tibbie, I hae &c.

Altho' a lad were e'er sae smart,
If that he want the yellow dirt,
Ye'll cast your head anither airt,
   And answer him fu' dry.   20
     Tibbie, I hae &c.

But if he hae the name o' gear,
Ye'll fasten to him like a brier,
Tho' hardly he for sense or lear
   Be better than the kye.
     Tibbie, I hae &c.

But, Tibbie, lass, tak my advice,
Your daddie's gear maks you sae nice;
The deil a ane wad spier your price,
   Were ye as poor as I.
     Tibbie, I hae &c.

AY WAUKIN, O

Slow

Sim - mer's a plea - sant time, Flowers of ev' - ry co - lour; The
wa - ter rins o'er the heugh, And I long for my true lo - ver!
Ay wau - kin, O, Wau - kin still and wea - ry:
Sleep I can get nane, For think - ing on my Dear - ie.

Simmer's a pleasant time,
    Flowers of ev'ry colour;
The water rins o'er the heugh,
    And I long for my true lover!

CHORUS: Ay waukin, O,
        Waukin still and weary:
        Sleep I can get nane,
        For thinking on my Dearie.

When I sleep I dream,
    When I wauk I'm irie;   10
Sleep I can get nane
    For thinking on my Dearie.
        Ay waukin &c.

Lanely night comes on,
    A' the lave are sleepin:
I think on my bony lad
    And I bleer my een wi' greetin.
        Ay waukin &c.

MY LOVE SHE'S BUT A LASSIE YET

My love she's but a las-sie yet, My love she's but a las-sie yet, We'll let her stand a year or twa, She'll no be half sae sau-cy yet. I rue the day I sought her O, I rue the day I sought her O, Wha gets her needs na say he's woo'd, But he may say he's bought her O.

My love she's but a lassie yet,
My love she's but a lassie yet,
We'll let her stand a year or twa,
   She'll no be half sae saucy yet.

I rue the day I sought her O,
I rue the day I sought her O,
Wha gets her needs na say he's woo'd,
   But he may say he's bought her O.

Come draw a drap o' the best o't yet,
Come draw a drap o' the best o't yet: 10
Gae seek for pleasure whare ye will,
   But here I never misst it yet.

We're a' dry wi' drinking o't,
We're a' dry wi' drinking o't:
The minister kisst the fidler's wife,
   He could na preach for thinkin o't.

I LOVE MY JEAN

Of a' the airts the wind can blaw, I dear - ly like the west, For there the bo - ny Las - sie lives, The Las - sie I lo'e best: There's wild - woods grow, and ri - vers row, And mony a hill be - tween; But day and night my fan - cy's flight Is ever wi' my Jean. I see her in the de - wy flowers, I see her sweet and fair; I hear her in the tune - fu' birds, I hear her charm the air: There's

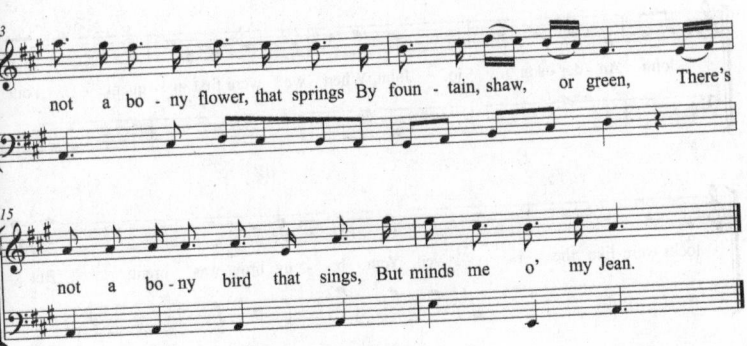

not a bo - ny flower, that springs By foun - tain, shaw, or green, There's

not a bo - ny bird that sings, But minds me o' my Jean.

Of a' the airts the wind can blaw,
    I dearly like the west,
For there the bony Lassie lives,
    The Lassie I lo'e best:
There's wild-woods grow, and rivers row,
    And mony a hill between;
But day and night my fancy's flight
    Is ever wi' my Jean.

I see her in the dewy flowers,
    I see her sweet and fair;   10
I hear her in the tunefu' birds,
    I hear her charm the air:
There's not a bony flower, that springs
    By fountain, shaw, or green,
There's not a bony bird that sings,
    But minds me o' my Jean.

JOHN ANDERSON MY JO

John Anderson my jo, John, When we were first ac-quent; Your
locks were like the ra-ven, Your bo-ny brow was brent; But
now your brow is beld, John, Your locks are like the snaw; But
bles-sings on your fro-sty pow, John An-der-son my Jo.

John Anderson my jo, John,
    When we were first acquent;
Your locks were like the raven,
    Your bony brow was brent;
But now your brow is beld, John,
    Your locks are like the snaw;
But blessings on your frosty pow,
    John Anderson my Jo.

John Anderson my jo, John,
    We clamb the hill the gither;   10
And mony a canty day John,
    We've had wi' ane anither:
Now we maun totter down, John,
    And hand in hand we'll go;
And sleep the gither at the foot,
    John Anderson my Jo.

CA' THE EWES TO THE KNOWES

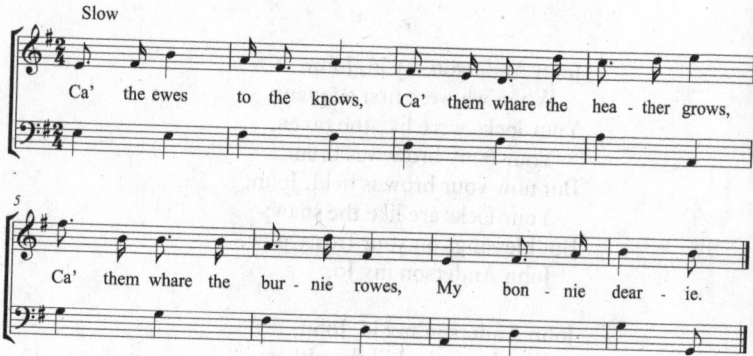

CHORUS: Ca' the ewes to the knows,
               Ca' them whare the heather grows,
               Ca' them whare the burnie rowes,
               My bonnie dearie.

As I gaed down the water-side,
   There I met my shepherd-lad,
He row'd me sweetly in his plaid,
   An he ca'd me his dearie.
      Ca' the ewes &c.

Will ye gang down the water-side
   And see the waves sae sweetly glide
Beneath the hazels spreading wide,
   The moon it shines fu' clearly.
      Ca' the ewes &c.

I was bred up at nae sic school,
   My shepherd-lad, to play the fool,
And a' the day to sit in dool,
   And nae body to see me.
      Ca' the ewes &c.

10

Ye sall get gowns and ribbons meet,
  Cauf-leather shoon upon your feet,
And in my arms ye'se lie and sleep,
  And ye sall be my dearie.   20
    Ca' the ewes &c.

If ye'll but stand to what ye've said,
  I'se gang wi' you, my shepherd-lad,
And ye may rowe me in your plaid,
  And I sall be your dearie.
    Ca' the ewes &c.

While waters wimple to the sea;
  While day blinks in the lift sae hie;
Till clay-cauld death sall blin' my e'e,
  Ye sall be my dearie.   30
    Ca' the ewes &c.

THE RANTIN DOG THE DADDIE O'T

Lively

O wha my ba - bie - clouts will buy, O Wha will tent me when I cry;

Wha will kiss me where I lie. The rant - in dog the dad - die o't.

O Wha will own he did the faut, O wha will buy the groan in maut, O

Wha will tell me how to ca't. The ran - tin dog the dad - die o't.

O wha my babie-clouts will buy,
O wha will tent me when I cry;
Wha will kiss me where I lie.
The rantin dog the daddie o't.

O wha will own he did the faut,
O wha will buy the groanin maut,°
O wha will tell me how to ca't.
The rantin dog the daddie o't.

When I mount the Creepie-chair,°
Wha will sit beside me there, 10
Gie me Rob, I'll seek nae mair,
The rantin dog the Daddie o't.

Wha will crack to me my lane;
Wha will mak me fidgin fain;
Wha will kiss me o'er again.
The rantin dog the Daddie o't.

TAM GLEN

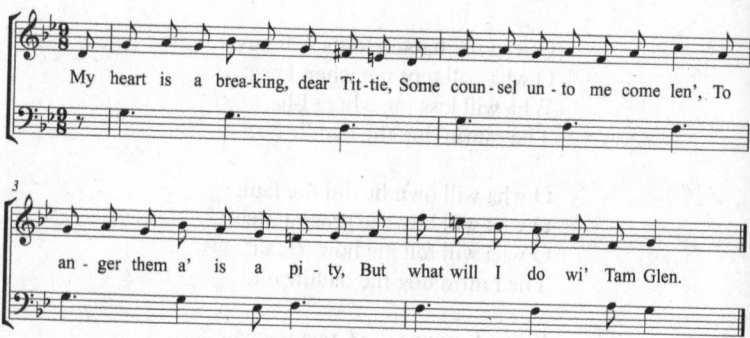

My heart is a brea-king, dear Tit-tie, Some coun-sel un-to me come len', To an-ger them a' is a pi-ty, But what will I do wi' Tam Glen.

My heart is a breaking, dear Tittie,
   Some counsel unto me come len',
To anger them a' is a pity,
   But what will I do wi' Tam Glen.

I'm thinking, wi' sic a braw fellow,
   In poortith I might mak a fen:
What care I in riches to wallow,
   If I mauna marry Tam Glen.

There's Lowrie the laird o' Dumeller,
   'Gude day to you brute' he comes ben: 10
He brags and he blaws o' his siller,
   But when will he dance like Tam Glen.

My Minnie does constantly deave me,
   And bids me beware o' young men;
They flatter, she says, to deceive me,
   But wha can think sae o' Tam Glen.

My Daddie says, gin I'll forsake him,
   He'll gie me gude hunder marks ten:°
But, if it's ordain'd I maun take him,
   O wha will I get but Tam Glen.   20

Yestreen at the Valentines' dealing,°
   My heart to my mou gied a sten;
For thrice I drew ane without failing,
   And thrice it was written, Tam Glen.

The last Halloween I was waukin
   My droukit sark-sleeve, as ye ken;°
His likeness cam up the house staukin,
   And the very grey breeks o' Tam Glen!

Come counsel, dear Tittie, don't tarry;
   I'll gie you my bonie black hen,   30
Gif ye will advise me to Marry
   The lad I lo'e dearly, Tam Glen.

MY TOCHERS THE JEWEL

O mei-kle thinks my Luve o' my beau-ty, And mei-kle thinks my Luve o' my kin; But lit-tle thinks my Luve, I ken braw-lie, My toch-er's the jew-el has charms for him. It's a' for the ap-ple he'll nour-ish the tree; It's a' for the hin-ey he'll che-rish the bee, My laddie's sae meik-le in love wi' the sil-ler, He can-na hae luve to spare for me.

O meikle thinks my Luve o' my beauty,
   And meikle thinks my Luve o' my kin;
But little thinks my Luve, I ken brawlie,
   My tocher's the jewel has charms for him.
It's a' for the apple he'll nourish the tree;
   It's a' for the hiney he'll cherish the bee,
My laddie's sae meikle in love wi' the siller,
   He canna hae luve to spare for me.

Your proffer o' luve's an airle-penny,°
   My tocher's the bargain ye wad buy;   10
But an ye be crafty, I am cunnin,
   Sae ye wi' anither your fortune maun try.
Ye're like to the timmer o' yon rotten wood,
   Ye're like to the bark o' yon rotten tree.
Ye'll slip frae me like a knotless thread,
   And ye'll crack your credit wi' mae nor me.

THERE'LL NEVER BE PEACE TILL JAMIE
COMES HAME

Slowish

By yon cas-tle wa' at the close of the day, I heard a man sing tho' his head it was grey; And as he was sing-ing the tears down came, There'll ne-ver be peace till Jam-ie comes hame. The Church is in ru-ins, the state is in jars, De-lu-sions, op-pres-sions, and mur-der-ous wars, We dare na weel say't, but we ken wha's to blame, There'll ne-ver be peace till Jam-ie comes hame.

By yon castle wa' at the close of the day,
I heard a man sing tho' his head it was grey;
And as he was singing the tears down came,
There'll never be peace till Jamie comes hame.
The Church is in ruins, the state is in jars,°
Delusions, oppressions, and murderous wars,
We dare na weel say't, but we ken wha's to blame,°
There'll never be peace till Jamie comes hame.

My seven braw sons for Jamie drew sword,°
And now I greet round their green beds in the yerd;   10
It brak the sweet heart of my faithfu' auld Dame,
There'll never be peace till Jamie comes hame.
Now life is a burden that bows me down,
Sin I tint my bairns, and he tint his crown;
But till my last moments my words are the same,
There'll never be peace till Jamie comes hame.

RORY DALL'S PORT

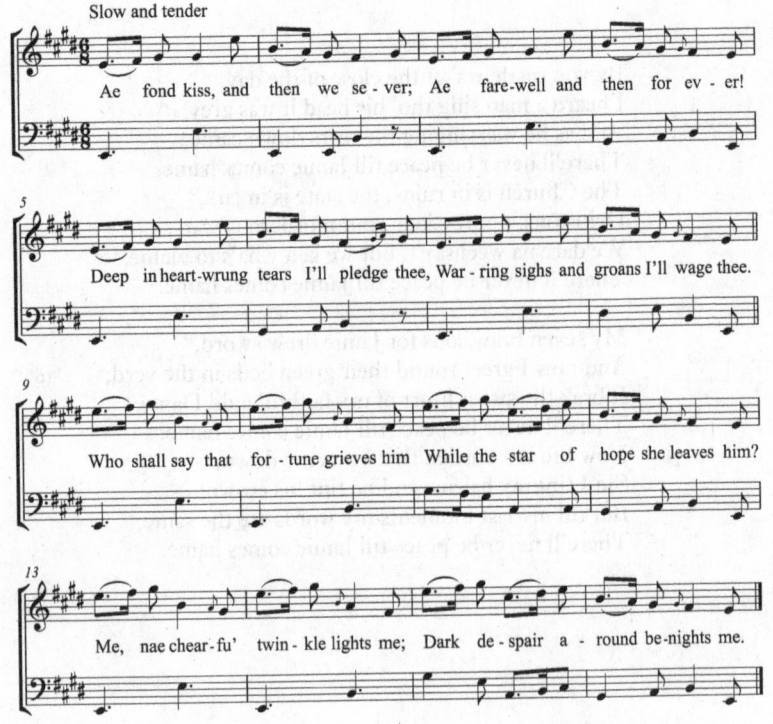

Slow and tender

Ae fond kiss, and then we se - ver; Ae fare-well and then for ev - er!

Deep in heart-wrung tears I'll pledge thee, War - ring sighs and groans I'll wage thee.

Who shall say that for - tune grieves him While the star of hope she leaves him?

Me, nae chear-fu' twin - kle lights me; Dark de - spair a - round be-nights me.

Ae fond kiss, and then we sever;
Ae farewell and then for ever!
Deep in heart-wrung tears I'll pledge thee,
Warring sighs and groans I'll wage thee.
Who shall say that fortune grieves him
While the star of hope he leaves him?
Me, nae chearfu' twinkle lights me;
Dark despair around benights me.

I'll ne'er blame my partial fancy,
Naething could resist my Nancy: 10
But to see her, was to love her;
Love but her, and love for ever.
Had we never lov'd sae kindly,
Had we never lov'd sae blindly,
Never met—or never parted,
We had ne'er been broken-hearted.

Fare thou weel, thou first and fairest!
Fare thee weel, thou best and dearest!
Thine be ilka joy and treasure,
Peace, Enjoyment, Love and Pleasure! 20
Ae fond kiss, and then we sever;
Ae fareweel, Alas! for ever!
Deep in heart-wrung tears I'll pledge thee,
Warring sighs and groans I'll wage thee.

BESS AND HER SPINNING WHEEL

Slow

O Leeze me on my spin-ning wheel, And leeze me on my rock and reel; Frae

tap to tae that cleeds me bien, And haps me fiel and warm at e'en! I'll

set me down and sing and spin, While laigh de - scends the sim - mer sun, Blest

wi' con - tent, and milk and meal, O leeze me on my spin-nin wheel.

O Leeze me on my spinning wheel,
And leeze me on my rock and reel;°
Frae tap to tae that cleeds me bien,
And haps me fiel and warm at e'en!
I'll set me down and sing and spin,
While laigh descends the simmer sun,
Blest wi' content, and milk and meal,
O leeze me on my spinnin wheel.

On ilka hand the burnies trot,°
And meet below my theekit cot;   10
The scented birk and hawthorn white
Across the pool their arms unite,
Alike to screen the birdie's nest,
And little fishes caller rest:
The sun blinks kindly in the biel',
Where, blythe I turn my spinnin wheel.

On lofty aiks the cushats wail,
And Echo cons the doolfu' tale;
The lintwhites in the hazel braes,
Delighted, rival ithers lays: 20
The craik amang the claver hay,°
The pairtrick whirrin o'er the ley,
The swallow jinkin round my shiel,
Amuse me at my spinnin wheel.

Wi' sma' to sell, and less to buy,
Aboon distress, below envy,
O wha wad leave this humble state,
For a' the pride of a' the great?
Amid their flairing, idle toys,
Amid their cumbrous, dinsome joys,   30
Can they the peace and pleasure feel
Of Bessy at her spinnin wheel!

YE JACOBITES BY NAME

Slowish

Ye Ja-co-bites by name give an ear, give an ear; Ye Ja-co-bites by name, give an ear; Ye Ja-co-bites by name Your fautes I will pro-claim Your doc-trines I maun blame, you shall hear.

Ye Jacobites by name give an ear, give an ear;
    Ye Jacobites by name, give an ear;
        Ye Jacobites by name
            Your fautes I will proclaim
            Your doctrines I maun blame,
                You shall hear.

What is Right, and what is Wrang, by the law, by the law?
    What is Right, and what is Wrang, by the law?
        What is Right, and what is Wrang?
            A short sword, and a lang,   10
                A weak arm, and a strang
                    For to draw.

What makes heroic strife, fam'd a far, fam'd a far?
    What makes heroic strife, fam'd a far?
        What makes heroic strife?
            To whet th' assassin's knife,
                Or hunt a Parent's life
                    Wi' bludie war.

Then let your schemes alone, in the state, in the state,
    Then let your schemes alone, in the state,   20
        Then let your schemes alone,
            Adore the rising sun,
                And leave a man undone
                    To his fate.

THE BANKS O' DOON

Slow and tender

Ye Banks and braes o' bo - nie Doon, How can ye bloom sae fresh and fair; How can ye chant, ye lit - tle birds, And I sae wea - ry fu' o' care! Thou'll break my heart thou warb - ling bird, That wan - tons thro' the flower-ing thorn: Thou minds me o' de - par - ted joys, De - par - ted ne - ver to re - turn.

Ye Banks and braes o' bonie Doon,
  How can ye bloom sae fresh and fair;
How can ye chant, ye little birds,
  And I sae weary fu' o' care!
Thou'll break my heart thou warbling bird,
  That wantons thro' the flowering thorn:
Thou minds me o' departed joys,
  Departed never to return.°

Oft hae I rov'd by bonie Doon,
  To see the rose and woodbine twine;   10
And ilka bird sang o' its luve,
  And fondly sae did I o' mine.
Wi' lightsome heart I pu'd a rose,
  Fu' sweet upon its thorny tree;
And my fause luver staw my rose,
  But, ah! he left the thorn wi' me.

SUCH A PARCEL OF ROGUES IN A NATION

Fare-weel to a' our Sco-tish fame, Fare-weel our an-cient glo-ry; Fare-weel ev-en to the Sco-tish name, Sae fam'd in mar-tial sto-ry. Now Sark rins o'er the Sol-way sands, And Tweed rins to the oc-ean To mark where Eng-land's pro-vince stands, Such a par-cel of rogues in a na-tion.

Fareweel to a' our Scotish fame,
  Fareweel our ancient glory;
Fareweel even to the Scotish name,
  Sae fam'd in martial story.
Now Sark runs o'er the Solway sands,
  And Tweed rins to the ocean°
To mark where England's province stands,
Such a parcel of rogues in a nation.

What force or guile could not subdue,
  Thro' many warlike ages,   10
Is wrought now by a coward few,
  For hireling traitors wages.
The English steel we could disdain,
  Secure in valour's station;
But English gold has been our bane,
Such a parcel of rogues in a nation!

O would, or I had seen the day
  That treason thus could fell us,
My auld grey head had lien in clay,
  Wi' Bruce and loyal Wallace!°   20
But pith and power, till my last hour,
  I'll mak this declaration;
We're bought and sold for English gold
Such a parcel of rogues in a nation.

AFTON WATER

Slow & tender

Flow gent-ly sweet A-fton a-mong thy green braes, Flow gent-ly, I'll sing thee a song in thy praise; My Ma-ry's a-sleep by thy mur-mur-ing stream, Flow gent-ly, sweet A-fton, dis-turb not her dream.

Flow gently sweet Afton among thy green braes,
Flow gently, I'll sing thee a song in thy praise;
My Mary's asleep by thy murmuring stream,
Flow gently, sweet Afton, disturb not her dream.

Thou stock dove whose echo resounds thro' the glen,
Ye wild whistling blackbirds in yon thorny den,°
Thou green crested lapwing thy screaming forbear,
I charge you disturb not my slumbering Fair.

How lofty, sweet Afton, thy neighbouring hills,
Far mark'd with the courses of clear, winding rills;   10
There daily I wander as noon rises high,
My flocks and my Mary's sweet Cot in my eye.

How pleasant thy banks and green vallies below,
Where wild in the woodlands the primroses blow;
There oft as mild ev'ning weeps over the lea,
The sweet scented birk shades my Mary and me.

Thy chrystal stream, Afton, how lovely it glides,
And winds by the cot where my Mary resides;
How wanton thy waters her snowy feet lave,
As gathering sweet flowerets she stems thy clear wave.   20

Flow gently, sweet Afton, among thy green braes,
Flow gently, sweet River, the theme of my lays;
My Mary's asleep by thy murmuring stream,
Flow gently, sweet Afton, disturb not her dream.

THE DEIL'S AWA WI' TH' EXCISEMAN

The deil cam fiddlin thro' the town,
 And danc'd awa wi' th' Exciseman;
And ilka wife cries, auld Mahoun,°
 I wish you luck o' the prize, man.

CHORUS: The deil's awa the deil's awa
    The deil's awa wi' the Exciseman,
    He's danc'd awa he's danc'd awa
    He's danc'd awa wi' the Exciseman.

We'll mak our maut and we'll brew our drink,
 We'll laugh, sing, and rejoice, man;   10
And mony braw thanks to the meikle black deil,
 That danc'd awa wi' th' Exciseman.
  The deil's awa, &c.

There's threesome reels, there's foursome reels,
 There's hornpipes and strathspeys, man,
But the ae best dance e'er cam to the Land°
 Was, the deil's awa wi' th' Exciseman.
  The deil's awa, &c.

A RED RED ROSE

O my Luve's like a red, red rose,
    That's newly sprung in June;
O my Luve's like the melodie
    That's sweetly play'd in tune.

As fair art thou, my bonie lass,
    So deep in luve am I;
And I will luve thee still, my Dear,
    Till a' the seas gang dry.

Till a' the seas gang dry, my Dear,
    And the rocks melt wi' the sun: 10
O I will love thee still my dear,
    While the sands o' life shall run.

And fare thee weel, my only Luve!
    And fare thee weel, a while!
And I will come again, my Luve,
    Tho' it were ten thousand mile!

AULD LANG SYNE

* Some Sing Kiss in place of Cup.

Should auld acquaintance be forgot
   And never brought to mind?
Should auld acquaintance be forgot,
   And auld lang syne!

CHORUS: For auld lang syne my jo,
      For auld lang syne,
      We'll tak a cup o' kindness yet
      For auld lang syne.

And surely ye'll be your pint stowp!
   And surely I'll be mine!   10
And we'll tak a cup o' kindness yet,
   For auld lang syne.
      For auld &c.

We twa hae run about the braes,
   And pou'd the gowans fine;
But we've wander'd mony a weary fitt,
   Sin auld lang syne.
      For auld &c.

We twa hae paidl'd in the burn,
   Frae morning sun till dine;
But seas between us braid hae roar'd,
   Sin auld lang syne.   20
      For auld &c.

And there's a hand, my trusty fiere!
   And gie's a hand o' thine!
And we'll tak a right gude-willie-waught,
   For auld lang syne.
      For auld &c.

COMIN THRO' THE RYE

Comin thro' the rye, poor body,
    Comin thro' the rye
She draigl't a' her petticoatie
    Comin thro' the rye.

CHORUS: Oh Jenny's a' weet poor body
      Jenny's seldom dry
      She draigl't a' her petticoatie
      Comin thro' the rye.

Gin a body meet a body
    Comin thro' the rye,
Gin a body kiss a body
    Need a body cry.
      Oh Jenny's a' weet &c.

    10

Gin a body meet a body
    Comin thro' the glen;
Gin a body kiss a body
    Need the warld ken!
      Oh Jenny's a' weet &c.

O LEAVE NOVELS &c

O leave novels, ye Mauchline belles,
    Ye're safer at your spinning wheel;
Such witching books, are baited hooks
    For rakish rooks like Rob Mossgiel.
Your fine Tom Jones and Grandisons°
    They make your youthful fancies reel
They heat your brains, and fire your veins
    And then you're prey for Rob Mossgiel.

Beware a tongue that's smoothly hung;
    A heart that warmly seems to feel;   10
That feelin heart but acks a part,
    'Tis rakish art in Rob Mossgiel.
The frank address, the soft caress,
    Are worse than poisoned darts of steel,
The frank address, and politesse,
    Are all finesse in Rob Mossgiel.

Songs from *A Select Collection of Original Scotish Airs, for the Voice*

DUNCAN GRAY CAME HERE TO WOO

Air—*Duncan Gray*

Dun-can Gray came here to woo, Ha ha the woo-ing o't On

Duncan Gray came here to woo,
    Ha, ha, the wooing o't;
On new-year's night, when we were fow,
    Ha, ha, the wooing o't.
Maggie coost her head fu' high,
    Look'd asklent and unco skeigh,
Gart poor Duncan stand abiegh;
    Ha, ha, the wooing o't.

Duncan fleech'd, and Duncan pray'd,
    Ha, ha, the wooing o't;   10
Meg was deaf as Ailsa Craig,[1]
    Ha, ha, the wooing o't.
Duncan sigh'd, baith out and in,
    Grat his een baith blear't and blin',
Spak o' louping o'er a linn;
    Ha, ha, the wooing o't.

Time and chance are but a tide,
    Ha, ha, the wooing o't;
Slighted love is sair to bide,
    Ha, ha, the wooing o't.   20
Shall I like a fool, quoth he,
    For a haughty hizzie die?
She may gae to—France for me!
    Ha, ha, the wooing o't.

How it comes, let Doctors tell,
    Ha, ha, the wooing o't;
Meg grew sick,—as he grew heal,
    Ha, ha, the wooing o't.
Something in her bosom wrings,
    For relief a sigh she brings;   30
And oh! her een they spak sic things!
    Ha, ha, the wooing o't.

[1] A great insulated rock to the south of the island of Arran. [note in Thomson]

Duncan was a lad o' grace,
   Ha, ha, the wooing o't;
Maggie's was a piteous case,
   Ha, ha, the wooing o't.
Duncan cou'd na be her death,
   Swelling pity smoor'd his wrath;
Now they're crouse and canty baith!
   Ha, ha, the wooing o't.   40

O WHISTLE, AND I'LL COME TO YOU, MY LAD

Air—*O whistle, and I'll come to you, my lad*

O WHISTLE, and I'll come to you, my lad,
O whistle, and I'll come to you, my lad;
Tho' father and mother and a' should gae mad,
O whistle and I'll come to you my lad.
But warily tent, when you come to court me,
And come na unless the back-yett be a-jee;
Syne up the back-style, and let naebody see,
And come, as ye were na coming to me,
And come, as ye were na coming to me.

O whistle, and I'll come to you, my lad,   10
O whistle, and I'll come to you, my lad;
Tho' father and mother and a' should gae mad,
O whistle and I'll come to you my lad.
At kirk, or at market, whene'er ye meet me,
Gang by me as tho' that ye car'd nae a flie;
But steal me a blink o' your bonie black e'e,
Yet look as ye were na looking at me,
Yet look as ye were na looking at me.

O whistle, and I'll come to you, my lad,
O whistle, and I'll come to you, my lad;   20
Tho' father and mother and a' should gae mad,
O whistle and I'll come to you my lad.
Ay vow and protest that ye carena for me,
And *whyles* ye may lightly my beauty a wee;
But court nae anither, tho' joking ye be,
For fear that she wyle your fancy frae me,
For fear that she wyle your fancy frae me.

Other poems and songs published in Burns's lifetime

WRITTEN ON A WINDOW IN STIRLING

HERE STEWARTS once in triumph reign'd,°
And laws for Scotia well ordain'd.°
But now unroof'd their palace stands;°
Their sceptre's fall'n to other's hands.°
The injur'd STEWART'S Line is gone,
A Race, outlandish, fills the throne:°
An ideot Race to honour lost,°
Who know them best despise them most.°

Here Lies
ROBERT FERGUSSON POET
Born September 5ᵗʰ 1751
Died October 16ᵗʰ 1774

No sculptur'd Marble here nor pompous lay°
No storied Urn nor animated Bust°
This simple Stone directs Pale Scotia's way
To pour her Sorrows o'er her Poets Dust.

ELEGY,
On the departed Year 1788

FOR lords or kings I dinna mourn,
E'en let them die—for that they're born:
But Oh! prodigious to reflect!
A TOWMONT, Sirs, is gane to wreck!
O EIGHTY-EIGHT, in thy sma' space,
What dire events hae taken place!
Of what enjoyments thou has reft us,
In what a pickle thou has left us!

The Spanish empire's tint a head;°
And my auld teethless Bautie's dead:°   10
The tulzie's teugh 'tween PITT and FOX,°
And our gudewife's wee birdy cocks;
The tane is game, a bludie devil,
But to the *hen birds* unco civil;°
The tither's dour, has nae sic breedin,
But better stuff ne'er claw'd a midden.

Ye *Ministers*, come mount the pupit,
And cry till ye be haerse and rupet;
For EIGHTY-EIGHT he wish'd you weel,
And gied you a' baith gear and meal;   20
E'en mony a plack and mony a peck,°
Ye ken yoursels, for little feck.

Ye *bonnie lasses*, dight your een
For some o' you hae tint a frien';
In EIGHTY-EIGHT, ye ken, was taen,
What ye'll ne'er hae to gie again.

Observe the vera nowt and sheep,
How dowf an' dowielie they creep;°
Nay even the yirth itsel does cry,
For *Embrugh* wells are grutten dry.°   30

O EIGHTY-NINE, thou'se but a bairn,
And no o'er auld, I hope, to learn!
Thou beardless boy, I pray tak care;
Thou now has got thy *Daddie's* chair;
Nae hand-cuff'd, mizzl'd, half-shackl'd *Regent*,°
But like himsel, a full free agent,
Be sure ye follow out the plan,
Nae waur than he did—honest man! }
As muckle better as you can.

JANUARY 1, 1789

ON CAPTAIN GROSE'S PRESENT
PEREGRINATIONS THROUGH SCOTLAND,
COLLECTING THE ANTIQUITIES OF THAT KINGDOM

HEAR, Land o' Cakes, and brither Scots,°
Frae Maiden-kirk to Johnie Groat's,°
If there's a hole in a' your coats,
    I rede you tent it;
A child's amang you taking notes,
     And faith, he'll prent it.

If in your bounds ye chance to light
Upon a fine, fat, fodgel wight,
O' stature short, but genius bright,
    That's he—mark weel!   10
And wow! he has an unco slight
     O' cawk and keel.°

At some auld houlet-haunted biggin,
Or kirk deserted by its riggin,
It's ten to ane ye'll find him snug in
    Some eldritch part,
Wi' deils, they say, Lord safe's, colleaguin
    At some black art.

Ilk ghaist that haunts auld ha' or chamer,
Ye gipsey-gang that deal in glamor,°   20
And you deep-read in Hell's black grammer,
    Warlocks and witches,
Ye'll quake at his conjuring hammer,
     Ye midnight bitches.

It's tauld he was a sodger bred,°
And ane would rather fa'n than fled;
But now he's quat the spurtle blade,°
    And dog-skin wallet,
And ta'en the—Antiquarian trade,
     I think they call it.   30

He hath a fouth o' auld nick-nackets;
Rousty airn-caps and gingling jackets,°
Would haud the Lothians three in tackets
      A towmont gude;
And parritch-pots and auld saut-backets,
      Afore the flood.

Of Eve's first fire he has a cinder;
Auld Tubalcain's fire-shool and fender;°
That which distinguished the gender
      O' Balaam's ass;°   40
A broomstick o' the Witch of Endor,°
      Weel shod wi' brass.

Besides, he'll cut you off fu' gleg
The shape of Adam's philibeg:°
The knife that cutet Abel's craig,°
      He'll prove you fully,
It was a faulding jockteleg,
      Or lang kail gully.

But would you see him in his glee,
(For meikle glee and fun has he),   50
Then set him down, and twa or three
      Gude fellows wi' him!
And port, O port! shine thou a wee,
      And then ye'll see him!

Now, by the powers o' verse and prose,
Thou art a dainty chield, O Gr——:
Whae'er o' thee shall ill suppose,
      They sair misca' thee:
I'd take the rascal by the nose,
      Would say, shame fa' thee.   60

August 11.

ALLOA CHURCH. AYRSHIRE.

TAM O' SHANTER. A TALE

WHEN chapmen billies leave the street,°
And drouthy neebors, neebors meet,
As market-days are wearing late,
And folk begin to tak the gate;
While we sit bowsing at the nappy,
And gettin fou, and unco happy,
We think na on the long Scots miles,°
The waters, mosses, slaps and styles,
That lie between us and our hame,
Where sits our sulky, sullen dame,   10
Gathering her brows, like gathering storm,
Nursing her wrath to keep it warm.

    This truth fand honest Tam o' Shanter,
As he frae Ayr ae night did canter;
(Auld Ayr, whom ne'er a town surpasses
For honest men and bonnie lasses.)

O Tam! hadst thou but been sae wise
As taen thy ain wife Kate's advice!
She tauld thee weel, thou was a skellum,
A bletherin, blusterin, drunken blellum;   20
That frae November till October,
Ae market-day thou was na sober;
That ilka melder, wi' the miller,°
Thou sat as long as thou had siller;
That every naig was ca'd a shoe on,
The smith and thee gat roarin fou on;
That at the L—d's house, even on Sunday,°
Thou drank wi' Kirkton Jean till Monday.—
She prophesied that, late or soon,
Thou wad be found deep-drown'd in Doon;   30
Or catch'd wi' warlocks in the mirk
By Aloway's old haunted kirk.

Ah, gentle dames! it gars me greet,
To think how mony counsels sweet,
How mony lengthen'd sage advices,
The husband frae the wife despises!

But to our tale:——Ae market-night,
Tam had got planted unco right,
Fast by an ingle bleezing finely,
Wi' reamin swats that drank divinely;°   40
And at his elbow, souter Johnie,
His ancient, trusty, drouthy cronie;
Tam lo'ed him like a vera brither,
They had been fou for weeks thegither.—
The night drave on wi' sangs and clatter,
And ay the ale was growing better:
The landlady and Tam grew gracious,
Wi' favors secret, sweet, and precious:
The souter tauld his queerest stories;
The landlord's laugh was ready chorus: 50
The storm without might rair and rustle,
Tam did na mind the storm a whistle.—
Care, mad to see a man sae happy,
E'en drown'd himself amang the nappy:
As bees flee hame, wi' lades o' treasure,

The minutes wing'd their way wi' pleasure:
Kings may be blest, but Tam was glorious;
O'er a' the ills o' life victorious!

But pleasures are like poppies spread,
You seize the flower, its bloom is shed;   60
Or like the snow falls in the river,
A moment white—then melts for ever;
Or like the borealis race,°
That flit ere you can point their place;
Or like the rainbow's lovely form,
Evanishing amid the storm.—°
Nae man can tether time or tide,
The hour approaches Tam maun ride;
That hour o' night's black arch the key-stane,
That dreary hour he mounts his beast in;   70
And sic a night he taks the road in
As ne'er poor sinner was abroad in.

The wind blew, as 'twad blawn its last;
The rattling showers rose on the blast;
The speedy gleams the darkness swallow'd
Loud, deep, and lang, the thunder bellow'd:
That night, a child might understand
The deil had business on his hand.

Weel mounted on his grey meare, Meg,
A better never lifted leg,   80
Tam skelpit on thro' dub and mire,
Despising wind, and rain, and fire:
Whyles holding fast his gude blue bonnet;°
Whyles crooning o'er an auld Scots sonnet;°
Whyles glowring round wi' prudent cares,
Lest bogles catch him unawares;
Kirk-Aloway was drawing nigh,
Where ghaists and houlets nightly cry.°

By this time he was cross the ford,
Where in the snaw the chapman smoor'd;   90
And past the birks and meikle stane,
Where drunken Charlie brak's neck-bane;

And thro' the whins, and by the cairn,
Where hunters fand the murder'd bairn;
And near the tree, aboon the well,
Where Mungo's mither hang'd hersel:°
Before him, Doon pours all his floods;
The doubling storm roars thro' the woods;°
The light'nings flash from pole to pole;
Near, and more near, the thunders roll:°   100
When, glimmering thro' groaning trees,
Kirk-Alloway seem'd in a bleeze;
Thro' ilka bore the beams were glancing,
And loud resounded mirth and dancing.

    Inspiring, bold John Barleycorn!
What dangers thou canst make us scorn:
Wi' tippeny, we fear nae evil;
Wi' usquabae, we'll face the devil!
The swats sae ream'd in Tammie's noddle,
Fair-play, he car'd na deils a boddle:°   110
But Maggy stood, right sair astonish'd,
Till by the heel and hand admonish'd,
She ventur'd forward on the light,
And, wow! Tam saw an unco sight!

    Warlocks and witches in a dance,
Nae cotillon brent new frae France,°
But hornpipes, jigs, strathspeys and reels,
Put life and mettle in their heels.—
A winnock-bunker in the East,°
There sat auld Nick in shape o' beast;   120
A towzie tyke, black, grim, and large,
To gie them music was his charge:
He screw'd the pipes and gart them skirl,°
Till roof and rafters a' did dirl.—
Coffins stood round, like open presses,
That shaw'd the dead in their last dresses;
And (by some devilish cantraip slight)
Each in its cauld hand held a light;
By which heroic Tam was able
To note upon the haly table,   130
A murderer's banes, in gibbet-airns;°

Twa span-lang, wee, unchristen'd bairns;°
A thief, new cutted frae a rape,
Wi' his last gasp his gab did gape;
Five tomahawks, wi' blood red-rusted;
Five scymitars, wi' murder crusted;
A garter which a babe had strangled;
A knife a father's throat had mangled,
Whom his ain son of life bereft,
The grey hairs yet stak to the heft: 140
Wi' mair of horrible and awefu',
That even to name wad be unlawfu':—°
Three lawyers' tongues, turn'd inside out,
Wi' lies seam'd like a beggar's clout;
Three priests' hearts, rotten, black as muck,
Lay stinking, vile, in every neuk.°

As Tammie glowr'd, amaz'd and curious,
The mirth and fun grew fast and furious:
The piper loud and louder blew;
The dancers quick and quicker flew;   150
They reel'd, they set, they cross'd, they cleekit,
Till ilka Carlin swat and reekit,
And coost her duddies on the wark,
And linkit at it in her sark.—

Now Tam! O Tam! had they been queans,
A' plump and strappin in their teens!
Their sarks, instead o' creeshie flainen,
Been snaw-white, seventeen-hunder linen;°
Thir breeks o' mine, my only pair,
That ance were plush o' gude blue hair,   160
I wad hae gien them off my hurdies
For ae blink o' the bonie burdies!
But withered beldams, auld and droll,
Rigwoodie hags wad spean a foal,°
Loupin and flingin on a crumock,
I wonder did na turn thy stomach.—

But Tam kend what was what fu' brawlie;
There was ae winsome wench and walie,°
That night enlisted in the core,

(Lang after kend on Carrick shore;   170
For mony a beast to dead she shot,
And perish'd mony a bonnie boat,
And shook baith meikle corn and bear
And kept the country-side in fear)—°
Her cutty-sark o' Paisley harn,°
That while a lassie she had worn,
In longitude tho' sorely scanty,
It was her best, and she was vauntie.—
Ah! little thought thy reverend graunie,
That sark she coft for her wee Nannie   180
Wi' twa pund Scots ('twas a' her riches)°
Should ever grac'd a dance o' witches!

But here my Muse her wing maun cour,
Sic flights are far beyond her power;
To sing how Nannie lap and flang,
(A souple jad she was and strang,)
And how Tam stood like ane bewitch'd,
And thought his vera een enrich'd;
Even Satan glowr'd, and fidg'd fu' fain,
And hotch'd, and blew wi' might and main;   190
Till first ae caper—syne anither—
Tam lost his reason a' thegither,
And roars out—'Weel done, cutty-sark!'
And in an instant all was dark;
And scarcely had he Maggie rallied,
When out the hellish legion sallied.—

As bees bizz out wi' angry fyke,
When plundering herds assail their byke;
As open pussie's mortal foes,°
When, pop, she starts before their nose;   200
As eager rins the market-croud,
When 'catch the thief!' resounds aloud;°
So Maggy rins, the witches follow,
Wi' mony an eldritch shout and hollo.—

Ah Tam! ah Tam! thou'll get thy fairin!
In hell they'll roast thee like a herrin!
In vain thy Kate awaits thy comin,

Kate soon will be a woefu' woman!!!
Now, do thy speedy utmost, Meg!
And win the key-stane o' the brig;°   210
There at them thou thy tail may toss,
A running stream they dare na cross!
But ere the key-stane she could make,
The fient a tail she had to shake;
For Nannie, far before the rest,
Hard upon noble Maggy prest,
And flew at Tam with furious ettle,
But little kend she Maggy's mettle!
Ae spring brought off her master hale,
But left behind her ain gray tail: 220
The carlin claught her by the rump,
And left poor Maggy scarce a stump.

Now wha this Tale o' truth shall read,
Ilk man and mother's son, take heed:
Whene'er to drink you are inclin'd,
Or cutty-sarks rin in your mind,
Think, ye may buy the joys o'er dear;
Remember TAM O' SHANTER'S MEARE!

EXTEMPORE

ON SOME LATE COMMEMORATIONS OF THE POET THOMSON

DOST thou not rise, indignant shade,
    And smile with spurning scorn,
When they wha would hae starv'd thy life,
    Thy senseless turf adorn?

They, wha about thee mak sic fyke,
    Now thou art but a name,
Wad seen thee d—n'd ere they had spar'd
    Ae plack to fill thy wame.

Helpless, alane, thou clamb the brae,
    Wi' meikle, meikle toil;   10

And claucht th' unfading garland there,
  Thy sair-won rightfu' spoil.°

And wear it there! and call aloud
  This axiom undoubted—
'Would'st thou hae Nobles' patronage?
  'First learn to live without it!!!'

'To wham hae routh, shall yet be given'—°
  Is every Patron's faith;
'But he, the friendless, needy wretch,
  'Shall lose the mite he hath.'   20

THE RIGHTS OF WOMAN

AN OCCASIONAL ADDRESS
SPOKEN, ON HER BENEFIT NIGHT, NOV. 26, AT DUMFRIES,
BY MISS FONTENELLE

WHILE Europe's eye is fix'd on mighty things,
The fate of empires, and the fall of kings;°
While quacks of state must each produce his plan,°
And even children lisp, The Rights of Man;°
Amid the mighty fuss, just let me mention,
The RIGHTS of WOMAN merit some attention—

First, in the sexes' intermix'd connection,
One sacred Right of Woman is, PROTECTION.
The tender flower that lifts its head, elate,
Helpless, must fall before the blasts of fate,   10
Sunk on the earth, deface'd its lovely form,
Unless your shelter ward th' impending storm.

Our second Right, but needless here is caution,
To keep that Right inviolate 's the fashion:
Each man of sense has it so full before him,
He'd die before he'd wrong it——'tis DECORUM.
There was indeed, in far less polish'd days,
A time when rough, rude man had naughty ways:
Would swagger, swear, get drunk, kick up a riot,°
Nay even thus invade a Lady's quiet.   20

Now, thank our stars! these Gothic times are fled;°
Now well-bred men—and you are all well-bred—
Most justly think (and we are much the gainers)
Such conduct neither spirit, wit, nor manners.°

For Right the third, our last, our best, our dearest,
That right to flutt'ring female hearts the nearest,
Which even the Rights of Kings in low prostration
Most humbly own——'tis dear, dear ADMIRATION!
In that blest sphere alone we live and move,
There taste that life of life, immortal Love!   30
Smiles, glances, tears, sighs, fits, flirtations, airs,
'Gainst such an host, what flinty savage dares—
When awful beauty joins with all her charms,
Who is so rash as rise in rebel arms?

Then truce with Kings, and truce with Constitutions,
With bloody armaments and revolutions;
Let MAJESTY your first attention summon,
Ah! cà ira! The Majesty of Woman!!!°

LAMENT
FOR
JAMES, EARL OF GLENCAIRN

THE wind blew hollow frae the hills,°
    By fits the sun's departing beam
Look'd on the fading yellow woods
    That wav'd o'er Lugar's winding stream:°
Beneath a craigy steep, a Bard,
    Laden with years and meikle pain,
In loud lament bewail'd his lord,
    Whom death had all untimely taen.

He lean'd him to an ancient aik,°
    Whose trunk was mould'ring down with years;   10
His locks were bleached white with time,
    His hoary cheek was wet wi' tears;
And as he touch'd his trembling harp,
    And as he tuned his doleful sang,

The winds, lamenting thro' their caves,
    To echo bore the notes alang.

'Ye scatter'd birds that faintly sing
    'The reliques of the vernal quire;
'Ye woods that shed on a' the winds
    'The honours of the aged year,°   20
'A few short months, and glad and gay,
    'Again ye'll charm the ear and e'e;
'But nocht in all-revolving time
    'Can gladness bring again to me.

'I am a bending aged tree,
    'That long has stood the wind and rain;
'But now has come a cruel blast,
    'And my last hald of earth is gane:
'Nae leaf o' mine shall greet the spring,
    'Nae simmer sun exalt my bloom;   30
'But I maun lie before the storm,
    'And ithers plant them in my room.

'I've seen sae mony changefu' years,
    'On earth I am a stranger grown;
'I wander in the ways of men,
    'Alike unknowing and unknown:°
'Unheard, unpitied, unreliev'd,
    'I bear alane my lade o' care,
'For silent, low, on beds of dust,
    'Lie a' that would my sorrows share.°   40

'And last, (the sum of a' my griefs!)
    'My noble master lies in clay;
'The flower amang our barons bold,
    'His country's pride, his country's stay:
'In weary being now I pine,
    'For all the life of life is dead,°
'And hope has left my aged ken,
    'On forward wing for ever fled.

'Awake thy last sad voice, my harp!
    'The voice of woe and wild despair!   50

'Awake, resound thy latest lay,
   'Then sleep in silence evermair!
'And thou, my last, best, only friend,
   'That fillest an untimely tomb,
'Accept this tribute from the Bard
   'Thou brought from fortune's mirkest gloom.

'In Poverty's low barren vale,
   'Thick mists, obscure, involv'd me round;
'Though oft I turned the wistful eye,
   'Nae ray of fame was to be found: 60
'Thou found'st me, like the morning sun
   'That melts the fogs in limpid air,°
'The friendless Bard and rustic song,
   'Became alike thy fostering care.

'O! why has Worth so short a date!
   'While villains ripen grey with time!
'Must thou, the noble, generous, great,
   'Fall in bold manhood's hardy prime!
'Why did I live to see that day?
   'A day to me so full of woe?   70
'O! had I met the mortal shaft
   'Which laid my benefactor low!

'The bridegroom may forget the bride,
   'Was made his wedded wife yestreen;
'The monarch may forget the crown
   'That on his head an hour has been;
'The mother may forget the child
   'That smiles sae sweetly on her knee;
'But I'll remember thee, Glencairn,°
   'And a' that thou hast done for me!'   80

BRUCE'S ADDRESS
TO HIS TROOPS, AT THE BATTLE OF BANNOCKBURN

SCOTS, wha hae wi' Wallace bled,
Scots, wham BRUCE has aften led,
Welcome to your gory bed,
    Or to glorious victorie!°

Now's the day, and now's the hour!
See the front o' battle lour!
See approach proud EDWARD's pow'r!
    EDWARD, chains and slaverie!°

Wha will be a traitor knave?
Wha can fill a coward's grave?   10
Wha sae base as be a slave?
    Traitor, coward, turn and flie!°

Wha for Scotland's King and Law,
FREEDOM's sword will strongly draw,°
Freeman stand or Freeman fa?
    CALEDONIAN! on wi' me!°

By Oppression's woes and pains!
By your sons in servile chains!
We will drain our dearest veins—
    But they shall—they SHALL *be free!*°   20

Lay the proud usurpers low;
Tyrants fall in every foe;
LIBERTY's in every blow!°
    Forward let us do or die!°

THE ELECTION: A NEW SONG
Tune—*Fy, let us a' to the Bridal*

FY, let us a' to K————,°
    For there will be bickerin there;
For *M——'s light horse* are to muster,°

And O, how the heroes will swear!
And there will be *M*—— commander,
 And *G*—— the battle to win;°
Like brothers they'll stand by each other,
 Sae knit in alliance and kin.°

And there will be black-nebbit *Johnie*,°
 The tongue o' the trump to them a'; 10
An he get na H–ll for his haddin,
 The Deil gets nae justice ava.
And there will be *K*————'s birkie,°
 A boy no sae black at the bane;
But as to his fine *Nabob* fortune,
 We'll e'en let the subject alane.

And there will be *W*——'s new *Sh*——*ff*,°
 Dame Justice fu' brawlie has sped;
She's gotten the heart of a *B*——,
 But, Lord! what's become o' the head? 20
And there will be *C*————, ESQUIRE,°
 Sae mighty in *C*————'s eyes:
A wight that will weather d–mn–tion,
 The Devil the prey will despise.

And there will be ————*ses* doughty,°
 New-christening towns far and near;°
Abjuring their democrat doings
 By kissin the a— of a *Peer*.°
And there will be *K*————, sae gen'rous,°
 Whase honour is proof to the storm; 30
To save them from stark reprobation,
 He lent them his name to the *Firm*.

But we winna mention *R*——*stle*,°
 The *body*, e'en let him escape:
He'd venture the gallows for siller,
 An 'twere na the cost o' the rape.
And where is our King's *L*—— *L*————*t*,°
 Sae fam'd for his *gratefu*' return?°
The billie is gettin his questions
 To say in *S–nt St–ph–n's* the morn.° 40

And there will be Lads o' the g–sp–l,
   M————, wha's as *gude* as he's *true*:°
And there will be *B————'s Apostle*,°
   Wha's mair o' the *black* than the *blue*:°
And there will be Folk frae *Saint MARY'S*,°
   A *house* o' great merit and note;
The deil ane but honours them highly,
   Tho' deil ane will gie them his vote.°

And there will be wealthy young *RICHARD*—°
   Dame Fortune should hing by the neck   50
For prodigal thriftless bestowing—
   His merit had won him respect.
And there will be rich brother *Nabobs*,°
   Tho' *Nabobs*, yet men of the first:
And there will be *C–ll–st–n's* whiskers,°
   And *Quintin*, o' lads not the warst.°

And there will be *Stamp-office Johnie*,°
   Tak tent how ye purchase a dram:
And there will be gay *C–ss–nc–ry*,°
   And there will be gleg *Colonel Tam*.°   60
And there will be trusty *KIROCHTREE*,°
   Whase honour was ever his law;
If the VIRTUES were packt in a parcel
   His WORTH might be sample for a'.

And can we forget the auld *MAJOR*,°
   Wha'll ne'er be forgot in the *Greys*;°
Our flatt'ry we'll keep for some other,
   HIM, only it's justice to praise.
And there will be maiden *K–lk–rr–n*,°
   And also *B–rsk–m–n's* gude Knight;°   70
And there will be roaring *B–rtwh–stle*,°
   Yet, luckily roars in the right.

And there, frae the *N–ddisd–le* border,°
   Will mingle the *M–xw–lls* in droves;
Teugh *Jockie*, staunch *Geordie*, and *Walie*,°
   That griens for the fishes and loaves.°
And there will be L–g–n M——d–w–l,°

    Sculdudry—and he will be there;°
And also the *Wild Scot o' Galloway*,
    Sogering, gunpowder *Bl—r*.°   80

Then hey the *chaste Int'rest* o' *B———*,°
    And hey for the blessins 'twill bring:
It may send *B———* to the *C————ns*,°
    In S–d–m 'twould make him a King.°
And hey for the sanctified *M———*,°
    Our land wha wi' Ch–p–ls has stor'd:°
He founder'd his horse amang harlots,
    But gied the auld naig to the L–rd!

THE DUMFRIES VOLUNTEERS—A BALLAD

Tune—*Push about the jorum*

DOES haughty Gaul invasion threat,
    Then let the louns bewaure, Sir,
There's WOODEN WALLS upon our seas,°
    And VOLUNTEERS on shore, Sir:
The Nith shall run to Corsincon,[1]°
    And Criffell[2] sink in Solway,
Ere we permit a foreign foe
    On British ground to rally.

O let us not, like snarling tykes,
    In wrangling be divided,   10
Till, slap! come in an *unco loun*,
    And wi' a rung decide it!
Be Britain still to Britain true,
    Amang oursels united;
For never but by British hands
    Must British wrongs be righted.

The *kettle* o' the Kirk and State,
    Perhaps a clout may fail in't,
But de'il a foreign tinkler loun
    Shall ever ca' a nail in't: 20

---

[1] A high hill at the source of the Nith.
[2] A high hill at the confluence of the Nith with Solway Firth.

Our FATHERS BLUDE the *kettle* bought,°
   And wha wad dare to spoil it,
By Heavens! the sacrilegious dog
   Shall fuel be to boil it!

The wretch that would a *tyrant* own,
   And th' wretch his true-sworn brother,
Who'd set the *mob* above the *throne*,°
   May they be damn'd together!
Who will not sing, GOD SAVE THE KING,
   Shall hang as high's the steeple;   30
But while we sing, GOD SAVE THE KING,
   We'll ne'er forget THE PEOPLE.°

SONG

Tune—For a' that, and a' that

WHAT tho' on hamely fare we dine,
   Wear hodden grey, and a' that:°
Gie fools their silk, and knaves their wine,
   A man's a man for a' that.
For a' that, and a' that,
Their tinsel shew, and a' that;
An honest man, tho' ne'er sae poor,
Is chief o' men for a' that.

Ye see yon birkie ca'd a lord,
   Wha struts and stares, and a' that,   10
Tho' hundreds worship at his word,
   He's but a cuif for a' that.
For a' that, and a' that,
His ribband, star, and a' that;°
A man of independent mind,
Can look, and laugh at a' that.

The king can make a belted knight,°
   A marquis, duke, and a' that,
But an honest man's aboon his might,
   Guid faith, he manna fa' that!   20
For a' that, and a' that,

His dignities, and a' that;°
The pith o' sense, and pride o' worth,
Are grander far than a' that.

Then let us pray, that come it may,
    As come it shall, for a' that;
When sense and worth, o'er a' the earth,
    Shall bear the gree, and a' that;
For a' that, and a' that,
It's coming yet, for a' that;   30
And man, and man, the world o'er,
Shall brothers be, for a' that.

Other poems and songs published posthumously

THE
JOLLY BEGGARS:
A CANTATA

RECITATIVO

WHEN lyart leaves bestrow the yird,
Or wavering like the Bauckie bird,[1]°
　Bedim cauld Boreas' blast;°
When hailstanes drive wi' bitter skyte,
And infant frosts begin to bite,
　In hoary cranreuch drest;
Ae night at e'en a merry core
　O' randie, gangrel bodies,
In Poosie-Nansie's held the splore,°
　To drink their orra duddies:　　　　　　　　10
　　　　Wi' quaffing and laughing,
　　　　　They ranted and they sang;
　　　　Wi' jumping and thumping,
　　　　　The vera girdle rang.

First, neist the fire, in auld red rags,°
Ane sat; weel brac'd wi' mealy bags,°
　And knapsack a' in order;
His doxy lay within his arm,
Wi' usquebae an' blankets warm,
　She blinket on her sodger:　　　　　　　　20
An' ay he gies the tozie drab
　The tither skelpin' kiss,
While she held up her greedy gab
　Just like an aumos dish.°
　　　　Ilk smack still, did crack still,
　　　　　Just like a cadger's whip,
　　　　Then staggering and swaggering°
　　　　　He roar'd this ditty up—

[1] The old Scotch name for the Bat.

AIR

Tune—*Soldier's Joy*°

I

I am a son of Mars who have been in many wars,
And show my cuts and scars wherever I come;   30
This here was for a wench, and that other in a trench,
When welcoming the French at the sound of the drum.
      Lal de daudle, &c.

II

My prenticeship I past where my leader breath'd his last,
When the bloody die was cast on the heights of Abram;°
I served out my trade when the gallant game was play'd,°
And the Moro low was laid at the sound of the drum.°
      Lal de daudle, &c.

III

I lastly was with Curtis, among the floating batt'ries,
And there I left for witness an arm and a limb;
Yet let my country need me, with Elliot to head me,°
I'd clatter on my stumps at the sound of a drum.   40
      Lal de daudle, &c.

IV

And now tho' I must beg with a wooden arm and leg,
And many a tatter'd rag hanging over my bum,
I'm as happy with my wallet, my bottle and my callet,°
As when I us'd in scarlet to follow a drum.
      Lal de daudle, &c.

V

What tho' with hoary locks, I must stand the winter shocks,
Beneath the woods and rocks oftentimes for a home,
When the tother bag I sell, and the tother bottle tell,°
I could meet a troop of hell, at the sound of a drum.
      Lal de daudle, &c.

RECITATIVO

He ended; and the kebars sheuk,
  Aboon the chorus roar;   50

While frighted rattons backward leuk,
　　And seek the benmost bore:
A fairy fiddler frae the neuk,°
　　He skirl'd out encore!
But up arose the martial chuck,
　　And laid the loud uproar.

AIR

Tune—*Soldier Laddie*°

I

I once was a maid, tho' I cannot tell when,
And still my delight is in proper young men;
Some one of a troop of dragoons was my daddie,
No wonder I'm fond of a sodger laddie.　　　　　　　60
　　　　　　　Sing, Lal de lal, &c.

II

The first of my loves was a swaggering blade,
To rattle the thundering drum was his trade;
His leg was so tight, and his cheek was so ruddy,
Transported I was with my sodger laddie.
　　　　　　　Sing, Lal de lal, &c.

III

But the godly old chaplain left him in the lurch,
The sword I forsook for the sake of the church;
He ventur'd the *soul*, and I risked the *body*,
'Twas then I prov'd false to my sodger laddie.
　　　　　　　Sing, Lal de lal, &c.

IV

Full soon I grew sick of my sanctified sot,
The regiment at large for a husband I got;　　　　　　70
From the gilded spontoon to the fife I was ready,°
I asked no more but a sodger laddie.
　　　　　　　Sing, Lal de lal, &c.

V

But the peace it reduc'd me to beg in despair,°
Till I met my old boy at a Cunningham fair;°

His *rags regimental* they flutter'd so gaudy,
My heart it rejoic'd at my sodger laddie.

> Sing, Lal de lal, &c.

VI

And now I have lived—I know not how long,
And still I can join in a cup or a song;
But whilst with both hands I can hold the glass steady,
Here's to thee, my hero, my sodger laddie.°   80

> Sing, Lal de lal, &c.

RECITATIVO

Then neist outspak a raucle carlin,
Wha kent fu' weel to cleek the sterling,
For mony a pursie she had hooked,
And had in mony a well been douked.°
Her love had been a Highland laddie,°
But weary fa' the waefu' woodie!
Wi' sighs and sobs she thus began
To wail her braw John Highlandman.

AIR

Tune—*O an ye were dead gudeman*°

I

A Highland lad my love was born,
The Lalland laws he held in scorn;
But he still was faithfu' to his clan,   90
My gallant, braw John Highlandman.

CHORUS

Sing, hey my braw John Highlandman!
Sing, ho my braw John Highlandman!
There's not a lad in a' the lan'
Was match for my John Highlandman.

II

With his philibeg an' tartan plaid,°
An' gude claymore down by his side,°
The ladies' hearts he did trepan,°

My gallant, braw John Highlandman.   100
            Sing, hey, &c.

III

We ranged a' from Tweed to Spey,°
An' liv'd like lords and ladies gay;
For a Lalland face he feared none,
My gallant, braw John Highlandman.
            Sing, hey, &c.

IV

They banish'd him beyond the sea,
But ere the bud was on the tree,
Adown my cheeks the pearls ran,
Embracing my John Highlandman.
            Sing, hey, &c.

V

But, oh! they catch'd him at the last,
And bound him in a dungeon fast;   110
My curse upon them every one,
They've hang'd my braw John Highlandman.
            Sing, hey, &c.

VI

And now a widow, I must mourn
The pleasures that will ne'er return;
No comfort but a hearty can,
When I think on John Highlandman.
            Sing, hey, &c.

RECITATIVO

A pigmy scraper wi' his fiddle,
Wha us'd to trysts and fairs to driddle,
Her strappan limb and gausy middle
      He reach'd nae higher,   120
Had hol'd his heartie like a riddle,
      An' blawn't on fire.

Wi' hand on haunch, an' upward e'e,
He croon'd his gamut, one, two, three,

Then in an Arioso key,°
   The wee Apollo°
Set off wi' *Allegretto* glee°
   His giga solo.°

AIR
Tune—*Whistle owre the lave o't*°

I

Let me ryke up to dight that tear,
An' go wi' me to be my dear,   130
An' then your every care and fear
  May whistle owre the lave o't.

CHORUS

I am a fiddler to my trade,
An' a' the tunes that e'er I play'd,
The sweetest still to wife or maid,
   Was whistle owre the lave o't.

II

At kirns an' weddings we'se be there,
An' O! sae nicely's we will fare;
We'll bouse about till Daddie Care
  Sing, whistle owre the lave o't.   140
      I am, &c.

III

Sae merrily's the banes we'll pyke,
An' sun oursells about the dyke,
An' at our leisure when ye like,
  We'll whistle owre the lave o't.
      I am, &c.

IV

But bless me wi' your heaven o' charms,
And while I kittle hair on thairms,°
Hunger, cauld, an' a' sic harms,
  May whistle owre the lave o't.
      I am, &c.

RECITATIVO

Her charms had struck a sturdy Caird,
   As weel as poor Gutscraper;   150
He taks the fiddler by the beard,
   And draws a roosty rapier.—
He swoor by a' was swearing worth,
   To speet him like a pliver,
Unless he wou'd from that time forth,
   Relinquish her for ever.

Wi' ghastly e'e, poor tweedle-dee
   Upon his hunkers bended,°
And pray'd for grace wi' ruefu' face,
   An' so the quarrel ended.   160
But tho' his little heart did grieve,
   When round the tinker prest her,
He feign'd to snirtle in his sleeve,
   When thus the Caird address'd her.

AIR

Tune—Clout the caudron°

I

My bonny lass I work in brass,
   A tinker is my station;
I've travell'd round all Christian ground
   In this my occupation.
I've ta'en the gold, I've been enroll'd°
   In many a noble squadron;   170
But vain they search'd, when off I march'd
   To go an' clout the caudron.

                              I've ta'en the gold, &c.

II

Despise that shrimp, that wither'd imp,
   Wi' a' his noise an' caprin',
An' tak' a share wi' those that bear
   The *budget* an' the *apron*.
An' *by* that stowp! my faith an' houpe,

An' *by* that dear Kilbaigie,[1]°
If e'er ye want, or meet wi' scant,
    May I ne'er weet my craigie.   180
                 An' by that stowp, &c.

RECITATIVO

The Caird prevail'd—th' unblushing fair°
    In his embraces sunk,
Partly wi' love o'ercome sae sair,
    An' partly she was drunk.
Sir Violino with an air,
    That show'd a man of spunk,
Wish'd *unison* between the pair,
    An' made the bottle clunk
          To their health that night.

But hurchin Cupid shot a shaft   190
    That play'd a dame a shavie,
The fiddler rak'd her fore and aft,
    Behint the chicken cavie.
Her lord, a wight o' Homer's[2] craft,
    Tho' limping wi' the spavie,
He hirpl'd up, an' lap like daft,
    An' shor'd them Dainty Davie
          O boot that night.°

He was a care-defying blade
    As ever Bacchus listed,°   200
Tho' Fortune sair upon him laid,
    His heart she ever miss'd it.
He had no wish but—to be glad,
    Nor want but—when he thristed;
He hated nought but—to be sad,
    And thus the muse suggested
          His sang that night.

---

[1] A peculiar sort of whisky so called: a great favourite with Poosie-Nansie's clubs.
[2] Homer is allowed to be the oldest ballad singer on record.

AIR

Tune—*For a' that, an' a' that*°

I

I am a bard of no regard,
   Wi' gentle folks, an' a' that;
But *Homer-like*, the glowran byke,   210
   Frae town to town I draw that.

CHORUS

For a' that, an' a' that,
   An' twice as muckle's a' that;
I've lost but ane, I've twa behin',
   I've *wife eneugh* for a' that.

II

I never drank the Muses' stank,
   Castalia's burn, an' a' that;°
But there it streams, and richly reams,°
   My *Helicon* I ca' that.

                    For a' that, &c.

III

Great love I bear to a' the fair,   220
   Their humble slave, an' a' that;
But lordly will, I hold it still°
   A mortal sin to thraw that.

                    For a' that, &c.

IV

In raptures sweet, this hour we meet,
   Wi' mutual love an' a' that;
But for how lang the *flie may stang*,
   Let *inclination* law that.

                    For a' that, &c.

V

Their tricks and craft have put me daft,
   They've ta'en me in, an' a' that;
But clear your decks, an' here's the *sex!*°   230
   I like the jads for a' that.

For a' that, an' a' that,
    An' twice as muckle's a' that;
My *dearest bluid*, to do them guid,
    They're welcome till't for a' that.

RECITATIVO

So sung the bard—and Nansie's wa's
Shook with a thunder of applause,
    Re-echo'd from each mouth;
They toom'd their pocks, an' pawn'd their duds,
They scarcely left to coor their fuds,   240
    To quench their lowan drouth.°
Then owre again, the jovial thrang,
    The poet did request
To lowse his pack an' wale a sang,
    A ballad o' the best:
        He, rising, rejoicing
            Between his twa *Deborahs*,°
        Looks round him, an' found them
            Impatient for the chorus.

AIR

Tune—*Jolly mortals fill your glasses*°

I

See! the smoking bowl before us,   250
    Mark our jovial ragged ring!
Round and round take up the chorus,
    And in raptures let us sing.

CHORUS

A fig for those by law protected!
Liberty's a glorious feast!
Courts for cowards were erected,
    Churches built to please the priest.

II

What is title? what is treasure?
    What is reputation's care?
If we lead a life of pleasure,   260

'Tis no matter *how* or *where!*
        A fig, &c.

III

With the ready trick and fable,
    Round we wander all the day;
And at night, in barn or stable,
    Hug our doxies on the hay.
                A fig, &c.

IV

Does the train-attended *carriage*
    Through the country lighter rove?
Does the sober bed of marriage
    Witness brighter scenes of love?
                A fig, &c.

V

Life is all a *variorum,*°
    We regard not how it goes;
Let them cant about *decorum*
    Who have character to lose.°
                A fig, &c.

270

VI

Here's to budgets, bags and wallets!
    Here's to all the wandering train!
Here's our ragged *brats* and *callets!*
    One and all cry out, Amen!

A fig for those by law protected!
    Liberty's a glorious feast!
Courts for cowards were erected,
    Churches built to please the priest.

280

HOLY WILLIE'S PRAYER:
A POEM

O THOU, wha in the heavens dost dwell,
Wha, as it pleases best thysel',

Sends ane to heaven and ten to hell,
          A' for thy glory,°
And no for ony guid or ill
          They've done afore thee!°

I bless and praise thy matchless might,
Whan thousands thou hast left in night,
That I am here afore thy sight,
          For gifts an' grace°   10
A burnin' an' a shinin' light,°
          To a' this place.

What was I, or my generation,°
That I should get such exaltation,
I wha deserve sic just damnation,
          For broken laws,
Five thousand years 'fore my creation,°
          Thro' Adam's cause.

When frae my mither's womb I fell,
Thou might hae plunged me in hell,   20
To gnash my gums, to weep and wail,
          In burnin' lake,°
Whar damned devils roar and yell,
          Chain'd to a stake.

Yet I am here a chosen sample,°
To show thy grace is great an' ample;
I'm here a pillar in thy temple,°
          Strong as a rock,
A guide, a buckler an' example°
          To a' thy flock.°   30

But yet, O L——d! confess I must,
At times I'm fash'd wi' fleshly lust;°
An' sometimes too, wi' warldly trust°
          Vile self gets in;
But thou remembers we are dust,°
          Defil'd in sin.

O L—d! yestreen, thou kens, wi' Meg,
Thy pardon I sincerely beg,
O! may it ne'er be a livin' plague
        To my dishonour,°   40
An' I'll ne'er lift a lawless l–g°
        Again upon her.

Besides, I farther maun allow,
Wi' Lizie's lass, three times I trow;
But, L—d, that Friday I was fow,
        When I came near her,
Or else, thou kens, thy *servant true*
        Wad ne'er hae steer'd her.°

Maybe thou lets this *fleshly thorn*°
Beset thy servant e'en and morn,   50
Lest he o'er high and proud shou'd turn,°
        'Cause he's sae *gifted*;
If sae, thy han' maun e'en be borne,°
        Until thou lift it.

L—d bless thy chosen in this place,
For *here* thou hast a *chosen race*;°
But G–d confound their stubborn face,
        And blast their name,°
Wha bring thy elders to disgrace
        An' public shame.   60

L—d mind G——n H———n's deserts,°
He drinks, an' swears, an' plays at cartes,°
Yet has sae mony takin' arts,°
        Wi' grit an' sma',
Frae G–d's ain priest the people's hearts°
        He steals awa'.

An' whan we chasten'd him therefore,
Thou kens how he bred sic a splore,
As set the warld in a roar
        O' laughin' at us;   70
Curse thou his basket and his store,°
        Kail an' potatoes.

L—d hear my earnest cry an' pray'r,
Against that presbyt'ry o' Ayr;
Thy strong right hand, L—d make it bare,°
      Upo' their heads,
L—d weigh it down, and dinna spare,
      For their misdeeds.

O L—d my G–d, that glib-tongu'd A——n,°
My very heart an' saul are quakin',   80
To think how we stood sweatin', shakin',°
      An' p—d wi' dread,
While he wi' hingin' lips and snakin'
      Held up his head.°

L—d in the day of vengeance try him,°
L—d visit them wha did employ him,°
An' pass not in thy mercy by 'em,°
      Nor hear their pray'r;
But for thy people's sake destroy 'em,
      And dinna spare.   90

But, L—d remember me and mine
Wi' mercies temp'ral and divine,
That I for gear and grace may shine,
      Excell'd by nane,
An' a' the glory shall be thine,
      Amen, Amen!

EXTEMPORE VERSES
ON
DINING WITH LORD DAER
Mossgiel, October 25th

THIS wot all ye whom it concerns,
I, rhymer Rab, alias BURNS,
      October twenty-third,
A ne'er to be forgotten day!
Sae far I sprachl'd up the brae,
      I dinner'd with a LORD.

I've been at drucken Writer's feasts;°
Nay, been bitch-fou 'mang godly Priests,
    (Wi' rev'rence be it spoken!)
I've even join'd the honour'd jorum,   10
When mighty Squireships o' the Quorum,°
    Their hydra drouth did sloken.

But wi' a LORD!—stand out my shin!°
A LORD—a PEER—an EARL'S SON—
    Up higher yet, my bonnet!
An' such a LORD—lang Scotch ell twa;°
Our PEERAGE he looks o'er them a',
    As I look o'er my sonnet.°

But, O! for Hogarth's magic pow'r,°
To shew Sir Bardie's willyart glowr,   20
    An' how he star'd an' stammer'd!
When goavan 's he'd been led wi' branks,
An' stumpan on his ploughman shanks,
    He in the parlour hammer'd.

'To meet good Stuart little pain is,°
'Or Scotia's sacred Demosthenes,'°
    Thinks I, 'They are but men!'
But 'Burns, my Lord'—Guid G–d! I doited;
My knees on ane anither knoited,
    As faultering I gaed ben!   30

I sidling shelter'd in a neuk,
An' at his Lordship staw a leuk,
    Like some portentous omen:
Except GOOD SENSE, an' SOCIAL GLEE,
An' (what surpris'd me) MODESTY,
    I marked nought uncommon.

I watch'd the symptoms o' the GREAT,°
The GENTLE PRIDE, the LORDLY STATE,
    The arrogant assuming;
The fient a pride, nae pride had he,   40
Nor sauce, nor state, that I could see,
    Mair than an honest Ploughman.

Then from his Lordship I shall learn,
Henceforth to meet with unconcern,
      One rank as well's another:
Nae honest, worthy man need care,
To meet wi' NOBLE, youthfu' DAER,
      For he but meets a BROTHER.

THE FORNICATER

Tune—*Clout the Cauldron*

YOU Jovial boys who love the joys,
   The blessfu' joys of lovers;
An' dare avow't wi daintless brow,°
   Whate'er the lass discovers;°
I pray draw near, and you shall hear,
   An' welcome in a *frater*,°
I've lately been on quarintine,
   A proven Fornicater.

Before the congregation wide,°
   I past the muster fairly;   10
My handsome Betsey by my side,
   We gat our ditty rarely.°
My downcast eye, by chance did spy,
   What made my mouth to water,
Those limbs sae clean, where I between°
   Commenced Fornicater.

Wi' ruefu' face and signs o' grace,
   I paid the buttock hire;°
The night was dark, and thro the park
   I cou'dna but convoy her;°   20
A parting kiss, what cou'd I less,
   My vows began to scatter;
Sweet Betsey fell, fal lal de ral!
   I am a Fornicater.

But, by the sun an' moon I swear,
   An' I'll fulfil ilk hair o't,

That while I own a single crown,
  She's welcome to a share o't;
My rogish boy, his mother's joy,
  An' darling of his *pater*,°   30
I for his sake the name will take,
  A harden'd Fornicater.°

NINE INCH WILL PLEASE A LADY

Tune—*The Quaker's wife*

COME rede me dame, come tell me, dame,
  My dame, come tell me truly,
What length o' graith, when weel ca'd hame,°
  Will sair a woman duly?
The carlin clew her wanton tail,
  Her wanton tail sae ready;
I learn't a sang in Annandale,°
  Nine inch will please a lady.

But for a coontrie c——t like mine,
  In sooth we're nae sae gentle;   10
We'll tak' twa thumb-bread to the nine,
  And that's a sonsie p——e.°
O leeze me on my Charlie-lad!
  I'll ne'er forget my Charlie!
Twa roarin handfu' and a daud,°
  He nidg't it in fu' rarely.°

But weary fa' the laithron doup,°
  And may it ne'er ken thrivin';
It's no the length that gars me loup,
  But its the double drivin'.   20
Come nidge me Tam, come nodge me Tam,
  Come nidge me o'er the nyvle;°
Come louse and lug your batterin' ram,
  And thrash him at my gyvel.°

POOR BODIES DO NAETHING BUT M–W

Tune—*The Campbells are commin'*

WHEN princes an' prelates,°
An' hot-headed zealates,
A' Europe had set in a low, a low,°
  The poor man lies down,
  Nor envies a crown,
But comforts himsel' wi' a m–w, a m–w.

  An' why shou'd na poor bodies m–w, m–w, m–w;
  An' why shou'd na poor bodies m–w;
  The rich they hae siller, an' houses, an' land,
  Poor bodies hae naething but m–w.   10

  When B—s—k's great prince°
  Gade a cruizin' to France,°
Republican billies to cow, cow, cow;
  Great B—s—k's strang prince
  Wadda shown better sense,
At hame wi his prin—ss to m–w, m–w, m–w.
          An' why, &c.

  The E–p——r swore,°
  By sea an' by shore,
At Paris to kick up a row, a row;
  But Paris ay ready,   20
  Just leugh at the laddie,
An' bade him gae hame an' gae m–w, m–w, m–w.
          An' why, &c.

  When the brave duke of Y—k°
  The Rhine first did pass,°
Republican armies to cow, cow, cow,
  They bade him gae hame,
  To his P—ss—n dame,°
An' gie her a kiss an' a m–w, a m–w.
          An' why, &c.

> Out over the Rhine,
>> Proud P—ss–a did shine,°   30
> To spend his last blood he did vow, vow, vow;
>> But F—d——k had better,°
>> Ne'er forded the water,
> But spent as he dought at a m–w, a m–w.
>>>> An' why, &c.

>> The black-headed eagle,°
>> As keen as a beagle,
> He hunted o'er height an' o'er howe, howe, howe,
>> In the braes of Gemap,°
>> He fell in trap,
> E'en let him come out as he dow, dow, dow.   40
>>>> An' why, &c.

>> When Kate laid her claws,
>> On poor St——l—s,°
> An' Poland was bent like a bow, a bow;°
>> May the diel in her a—e,
>> Ram a huge p—k o' brass,
> An' d—n her to h–ll wi' a m–w.
>>>> An' why, &c.°

POEM

ON PASTORAL POETRY

Hail Poesie! thou Nymph reserv'd!
In chase o' thee, what crouds hae swerv'd
Frae common sense, or sunk enerv'd
>>>> 'Mang heaps o' clavers;
And och! o'er aft thy joes hae starv'd,
>>>> Mid a' thy favors!

Say, Lassie, why thy train amang,
While loud, the trump's heroic clang,
And sock or buskin skelp alang°
>>>> To death or marriage;   10
Scarce ane has tried the shepherd-sang
>>>> But wi' miscarriage?

In Homer's craft Jock Milton thrives;°
Eschylus' pen Will Shakespeare drives;°
Wee Pope, the knurlin, 'till him rives
   Horatian fame;°
In thy sweet sang, Barbauld, survives
   Even Sappho's flame.°

But thee, Theocritus, wha matches?°
They're no herd's ballats, Maro's catches;°   20
Squire Pope but busks his skinklin patches
   O' heathen tatters:°
I pass by hunders, nameless wretches,
   That ape their betters.

In this braw age o' wit and lear,
Will nane the Shepherd's whistle mair
Blaw sweetly in its native air
   And rural grace;
And wi' the far-fam'd Grecian share
   A rival place?   30

Yes! there is ane; a Scottish callan!
There's ane; come forrit, honest Allan!°
Thou need na jouk behint the hallan,
   A chiel sae clever;
The teeth o' time may gnaw Tamtallan,°
   But thou's for ever.

Thou paints auld nature to the nines,
In thy sweet Caledonian lines;
Nae gowden stream thro' myrtles twines,
   Where Philomel,°   40
While nightly breezes sweep the vines,
   Her griefs will tell!

In gowany glens thy burnie strays,
Where bonnie lasses bleach their claes;
Or trots by hazelly shaws and braes,
   Wi' hawthorns gray,
Where blackbirds join the shepherd's lays
   At close o' day.

Thy rural loves are nature's sel;
Nae bombast spates o' nonsense swell;   50
Nae snap conceits, but that sweet spell
      O' witchin love,
That charm, that can the strongest quell,
      The sternest move.°

POETICAL INSCRIPTION,

FOR AN ALTAR TO INDEPENDENCE

*At Kerrouchtry, the seat of Mr. Heron, written in
Summer* 1795.

THOU of an independent mind
With soul resolved, with soul resigned;
Prepar'd power's proudest frown to brave,
Who wilt not be, nor have a slave;
Virtue alone who dost revere,
Thy own reproach alone dost fear,
Approach this shrine, and worship here.

ADDRESS TO A LADY

OH wert thou in the cauld blast,
   On yonder lea, on yonder lea;
My plaidie to the angry airt,
   I'd shelter thee, I'd shelter thee:
Or did misfortune's bitter storms
   Around thee blaw, around thee blaw,
Thy bield should be my bosom,
   To share it a', to share it a'.

Or were I in the wildest waste,
   Sae black and bare, sae black and bare,   10
The desart were a paradise,
   If thou wert there, if thou wert there.
Or were I monarch o' the globe,
   Wi' thee to reign, wi' thee to reign;
The brightest jewel in my crown,
   Wad be my queen, wad be my queen.

LINES
WRITTEN EXTEMPORE IN A LADY'S POCKET-BOOK

GRANT me, indulgent heaven, that I may live
To see the miscreants feel the pains they give;
Deal Freedom's sacred treasures free as air,
Till slave and despot be but things which were.

VERSES

*Written under the Portrait of Fergusson the Poet, in a copy of
that author's works presented to a young Lady, Edinburgh 19ᵗʰ
March, 1787, by the late celebrated Robert Burns.*

CURSE on ungrateful man that can be pleased,
And yet can starve the author of the pleasure!°
O thou my elder brother in misfortune,
By far my elder brother in the muse,°
With tears I pity thy unhappy fate!
Why is the bard unfitted for the world°
Yet has so keen a relish of its pleasures?

SONG

Tune—*The Weaver and his Shuttle, O*

MY father was a farmer upon the Carrick border, O°
And carefully he bred me in decency and order, O
He bade me act a manly part, though I had ne'er a farthing, O
For without an honest manly heart, no man was worth regarding, O.

Then out into the world my course I did determine, O
Tho' to be rich was not my wish, yet to be great was charming, O
My talents they were not the worst; nor yet my education: O
Resolv'd was I, at least to try, to mend my situation, O.

In many a way, and vain essay, I courted fortune's favor; O
Some cause unseen, still stept between, to frustrate each
    endeavour; O   10

Sometimes by foes I was o'erpower'd; sometimes by friends
   forsaken; O
And when my hope was at the top, I still was worst mistaken, O.

Then sore harrass'd, and tir'd at last, with fortune's vain delusion; O
I dropt my schemes, like idle dreams, and came to this
   conclusion; O
The past was bad, and the future hid; its good or ill untryed; O
But the present hour was in my pow'r, and so I would enjoy it, O.

No help, nor hope, nor view had I; nor person to befriend me; O
So I must toil, and sweat and moil, and labor to sustain me, O°
To plough and sow, to reap and mow, my father bred
   me early; O
For one, he said, to labor bred, was a match for fortune
   fairly, O.   20

Thus all obscure, unknown, and poor, thro' life I'm doom'd
   to wander, O
Till down my weary bones I lay in everlasting slumber: O
No view nor care, but shun whate'er might breed me pain
   or sorrow; O
I live to day, as well's I may, regardless of tomorrow, O.

But chearful still, I am as well, as a monarch in a palace, O
Tho' fortune's frown still hunts me down, with all her
   wonted malice; O
I make indeed, my daily bread, but ne'er can make it farther; O
But as daily bread is all I need, I do not much regard her, O.

When sometimes by my labor I earn a little money, O
Some unforeseen misfortune comes generally upon me; O   30
Mischance, mistake, or by neglect, or my good-natur'd folly; O
But come what will, I've sworn it still, I'll ne'er be
   melancholy, O.

All you who follow wealth and power with unremitting ardor, O
The more in this you look for bliss, you leave your view
   the farther; O
Had you the wealth Potosi boasts, or nations to adore you, O°
A chearful honest hearted clown I will prefer before you, O.

FRAGMENT

Tune—*Dainty Davie*

THERE was a lad was born in Kyle,[1]
But what na day o' what na style°
I doubt its hardly worth the while
    To be sae nice wi' *Robin.*°

Robin was a rovin' Boy,
    Rantin' rovin', rantin' rovin';
Robin was a rovin' Boy,
    Rantin' rovin' Robin.

Our monarch's hindmost year but ane°
Was five and twenty days begun,   10
'Twas then a blast o' Janwar Win'°
    Blew hansel in on *Robin.*°

The gossip keekit in his loof,°
Quo' scho wha lives will see the proof,
This waly boy will be nae coof,
    I think we'll ca' him *Robin.*

He'll hae misfortunes great and sma',
But ay a heart aboon them a';
He'll be a credit 'till us a',
    We'll a' be proud o' *Robin.*   20

But sure as three times three mak nine,
I see by ilka score and line,
This chap will dearly like our kin',
    So leeze me on thee *Robin.*

Guid faith quo' scho I doubt you Sir,
Ye'll gar the lasses lie aspar;°
But twenty fauts ye may hae waur
    So blessin's on thee, *Robin!*

[1] *Kyle*—a district of Ayrshire. [note in Cromek 1808]

> *Robin was a rovin' Boy,*
> *Rantin' rovin', rantin' rovin';*
> *Robin was a rovin' Boy,*
> *Rantin' rovin' Robin.*

30

ELEGY
On the Death Of Robert Ruisseaux[1]

Now Robin lies in his last lair,°
He'll gabble rhyme, nor sing nae mair,
Cauld poverty, wi' hungry stare,
                Nae mair shall fear him;
Nor anxious fear, nor cankert care
                E'er mair come near him.

To tell the truth, they seldom fash't him,
Except the moment that they crush't him;
For sune as chance or fate had husht 'em
                Tho' e'er sae short,
Then wi' a rhyme or song he lasht 'em,
                And thought it sport.—

Tho' he was bred to kintra wark,
And counted was baith wight and stark,
Yet that was never Robin's mark
                To mak a man;
But tell him, he was learn'd and clark,
                Ye roos'd him then![2]

10

SKETCH OF AN EPISTLE TO R. GRAHAM, Esq.
OF FINTRAY

FINTRAY, my stay in worldly strife,
Friend o' my muse, friend o' my life,
   Are ye as idle 's I am?
Come then, wi' uncouth, kintra fleg,

---

[1] *Ruisseaux*—a play on his own name. [note in Cromek 1808]
[2] *Ye roos'd*—ye prais'd. [note in Cromek 1808]

O'er Pegasus I'll fling my leg,
   And ye shall see me try him.

I'll sing the zeal Drumlanrig bears,°
Who left the all-important cares
   Of fiddles, whores and hunters;°
And bent on buying borough towns,°   10
Came shaking hands wi' wabster louns,°
   And kissing barefit bunters.°

Combustion through our boroughs rode,°
Whistling his roaring pack abroad,
   Of mad, unmuzzled lions;
As Queensberry buff and blue unfurled,°
And Westerha' and Hopeton hurled°
   To every Whig defiance.°

But Queensberry, cautious, left the war,
Th' unmanner'd dust might soil his star,°   20
   Besides, he hated bleeding;
But left behind him heroes bright,
Heroes in Cesarean fight,
   Or Ciceronian pleading.°

O, for a throat like huge Monsmeg,°
To muster o'er each ardent Whig°
   Beneath Drumlanrig's banner.
Heroes and heroines commix
All in the field of politics,
   To win immortal honour.   30

M^cM—rdo and his lovely spouse,°
(Th' enamour'd laurels kiss her brows),
   Led on the loves and graces;
She won each gaping Burgess' heart;°
While he, sub rosa, play'd his part°
   Among their wives and lasses.

Craigdarroch led a light-arm'd corps,°
Tropes, metaphors and figure pours,
   Like Hecla streaming thunder;°

Glenriddel, skill'd in rusty coins,°   40
Blew up each Tory's dark designs,°
   And bar'd the treason under.

In either wing two champions fought,
Redoubted Staig who set at nought°
   The wildest savage Tory;
And Walsh, who ne'er yet flinch'd his ground,°
High-wav'd his magnum-bonum round
   With Cyclopean fury.°

Miller brought up th' artillery ranks,°
The many-pounders of the Banks,   50
   Resistless desolation;
While Maxwelton, that baron bold,°
Mid Lawson's port entrench'd his hold,°
   And threaten'd worse damnation.

To these, what Tory hosts oppos'd;
With these, what Tory warriors clos'd,
   Surpasses my descriving.
Squadrons, extended long and large,
With furious speed rush'd to the charge,
   Like raging devils driving.   60

What verse can sing!—what prose narrate!
The butcher deeds of bloody fate
   Amid this mighty tulzie?
Grim horror girn'd; pale terror roar'd
As murther at his thrapple shor'd;
   And hell mixt in the brulzie!

As Highland craigs, by thunder cleft,
When light'nings fire the stormy lift,
   Hurl down wi' crashing rattle;
As flames amang a hundred woods;   70
As headlong foam a hundred floods;
   Such is the rage of battle.°

The stubborn Tories dare to die:
As soon the rooted oaks would fly,

Before th' approaching fellers,
The Whigs come on like ocean's roar,
When all his wintry billows pour
    Against the Buchan bullers.°

Lo, from the shades of death's deep night,
Departed Whigs enjoy the fight,   80
    And think on former daring!
The muffled murtherer of Charles
The Magna Charta flag unfurls,°
    All deadly gules its bearing.

Nor wanting ghosts of Tory fame;
Bold Scrimgeour follows gallant Graham:—°
    Auld Covenanters shiver—
(Forgive, forgive, much-wrong'd Montrose!°
While death and hell ingulph thy foes,
    Thou liv'st on high for ever!)   90

Still o'er the field the combat burns;
The Tories, Whigs, give way by turns;—
    But fate the word has spoken—
For woman's wit, or strength of man,
Alas! can do but what they can——
    The Tory ranks are broken!

O, that my e'en were flowing burns!
My voice a lioness that mourns
    Her darling cub's undoing!
That I might greet, that I might cry,   100
While Tories fall, while Tories fly,
    And furious Whigs pursuing!

What Whig but wails the good Sir James;
Dear to his country, by the names
    Friend, Patron, Benefactor!
Not Pulteney's wealth can Pulteney save!°
And Hopetoun falls, the generous, brave!
    And Stewart, bold as Hector!°

Thou, Pitt, shalt rue this overthrow;°
And Thurlow growl a curse of woe,°   110
    And Melville melt in wailing!°
Now Fox and Sheridan rejoice!°
And Burke shall sing, 'O Prince arise!°
    Thy power is all-prevailing!'

For your poor friend, the Bard, afar
He only hears and sees the war,°
    A cool spectator purely:°
So, when the storm the forest rends,
The robin in the hedge descends,
    And sober chirps securely.   120

Now for my friends and brethren's sakes,
And for my dear-lov'd land o' cakes,°
    I pray with holy fire:
Lord send a rough-shod troop o' hell,
O'er a' wad Scotland buy or sell,
    To grind them in the mire.

EPISTLE TO THE PRESIDENT OF THE
HIGHLAND SOCIETY,
RESPECTING FIVE HUNDRED HIGHLANDERS ATTEMPTING
TO EMIGRATE TO AMERICA

To the Right Honourable the Earl of B ****, President of
the Right Honourable and Honourable the Highland Society,
which met on the 23d of May last, at the Shakespeare,
Covent-Garden, to concert ways and means to frustrate the
designs of FIVE HUNDRED HIGHLANDERS who, as the
Society were informed by Mr. Mᶜ—— of A **** s, were so
audacious as to attempt an escape from their lawful lords
and masters, whose property they are, by emigrating from
the lands of Mr Macdonald of Glengary to the wilds of
Canada, in search of that fantastic thing—LIBERTY!

Long life, my Lord, an' health be yours,
Unskaith'd by hunger'd Highlan' boors!
Lord grant nae duddie, desperate beggar,

Wi' durk, claymore, or rusty trigger
May twin auld Scotland o' a life,
She likes—as *butchers* like a *knife!*

    Faith, you and A **** s were right°
To keep the Highlan' hounds in sight!
I doubt na! they wad bid nae better
Than let them ance out owre the water;   10
Then up amang thae lakes and seas
They'll mak what rules an' laws they please.
Some daring Hancocke, or a Franklin,°
May set their Highlan' bluid a–ranklin;
Some Washington again may head them,°
Or some Montgomery, fearless, lead them;°
Till God knows what may be effected,
When by such heads an' hearts directed:
Poor dunghill sons of dirt and mire,
May to Patrician rights aspire!   20
Nae sage North, now, nor sager Sackville,°
To watch an' premier owre the pack vile!
An' whare will ye get Howes and Clintons°
To bring them to a right repentance?
To cowe the rebel generation,
An' save the *honour* o' the nation!

    They! an' be d——d! what right hae they
To meat, or sleep, or light o' day?
Far less to riches, pow'r, or freedom,
But what your Lordships please to gie them?   30

But hear, my Lord! G **** hear!°
Your *hand's owre light on them,* I fear;
Your factors, grieves, trustees an' bailies,
I canna say but they do gailies;
They lay aside a' tender mercies,
An' tirl the hallions to the birsies;
Yet, while they're only poin'd and herriet,
They'll keep their stubborn Highland spirit:
But smash them! crash them a' to spails!
An' rot the dyvors i' the jails!   40
The young dogs, swinge them to the labour,

Let wark an' hunger mak them sober!
The hizzies, if they're oughtlins faussont,
Let them in Drury Lane be lesson'd!°
An' if the wives, an' dirty brats
Come thiggan at your doors an' yetts,
Flaffan wi' duds, an' grey wi' beese,°
Frightan awa your deucks and geese;
Get out a horse-whip, or a jowler,
The langest thong, the fiercest growler,   50
An' gar the tatter'd gipsies pack
Wi' a' their bastarts on their back!

Go on, my lord! I lang to meet you,
An' in my *house at hame* to greet you!
Wi' common lords ye shanna mingle,
The benmost newk beside the ingle
At my right hand assign'd your seat,
'Tween Herod's hip an' Polycrate,—°
Or, if ye on your station tarrow,
Between Almagro an' Pizarro;°   60
A seat, I'm sure ye're weel deservin't;
An' till ye come—your humble servant,
         BEELZEBUB.°

   June 1,
Anno Mundi 5790°

THE SELKIRK GRACE

SOME hae meat and canna eat,
   And some wad eat that want it.
But we hae meat and we can eat,
   And sae the Lord be thanket.

THE TREE OF LIBERTY

HEARD ye o' the tree o' France,
   I watna what's the name o't;
Around it a' the patriots dance,°
   Weel Europe kens the fame o't.

It stands where ance the Bastile stood,°
  A prison built by kings, man,
When Superstition's hellish brood°
  Kept France in leading strings, man.

Upo' this tree there grows sic fruit,
  Its virtues a' can tell, man;   10
It raises man aboon the brute,
  It maks him ken himsel, man.
Gif ance the peasant taste a bit,
  He's greater than a lord, man,
And wi' the beggar shares a mite
  O' a' he can afford, man.

This fruit is worth a' Afric's wealth,
  To comfort us 'twas sent, man:
To gie the sweetest blush o' health,
  And mak us a' content, man.   20
It clears the een, it cheers the heart,
  Maks high and low gude friends, man;
And he wha acts the traitor's part,
  It to perdition sends, man.

My blessings aye attend the chiel,
  Wha pitied Gallia's slaves, man,°
And staw'd a branch, spite o' the deil,
  Frae yont the western waves, man.°
Fair Virtue water'd it wi' care,
  And now she sees wi' pride, man,   30
How weel it buds and blossoms there,
  Its branches spreading wide, man.

But vicious folk aye hate to see
  The works o' Virtue thrive, man;
The courtly vermin's banned the tree,
  And grat to see it thrive, man;
King Loui' thought to cut it down,°
  When it was unco sma', man;
For this the watchman cracked his crown,
  Cut aff his head and a', man.°   40

A wicked crew syne, on a time,°
   Did tak a solemn aith, man,
It ne'er should flourish to its prime,
   I wat they pledged their faith, man,
Awa they gaed wi' mock parade,
   Like beagles hunting game, man,
But soon grew weary o' the trade,
   And wished they'd been at hame, man.

For Freedom, standing by the tree,
   Her sons did loudly ca', man;°   50
She sang a sang o' liberty,
   Which pleased them ane and a', man.
By her inspired, the new-born race
   Soon drew the avenging steel, man;
The hirelings ran—her foes gied chase,°
   And banged the despot weel, man.

Let Britain boast her hardy oak,
   Her poplar and her pine, man,
Auld Britain ance could crack her joke,
   And o'er her neighbours shine, man.   60
But seek the forest round and round,
   And soon 'twill be agreed, man,
That sic a tree can not be found,
   'Twixt London and the Tweed, man.°

Without this tree, alake this life
   Is but a vale o' woe, man;
A scene o' sorrow mixed wi' strife,
   Nae real joys we know, man.
We labour soon, we labour late,
   To feed the titled knave, man;   70
And a' the comfort we're to get,
   Is that ayont the grave, man.

Wi' plenty o' sic trees, I trow,
   The warld would live in peace, man;
The sword would help to mak a plough,
   The din o' war wad cease, man.
Like brethren in a common cause,

We'd on each other smile, man;
And equal rights and equal laws
    Wad gladden every isle, man.   80

Wae worth the loon wha wadna eat
    Sic halesome dainty cheer, man;
I'd gie the shoon frae aff my feet,
    To taste sic fruit, I swear, man.
Syne let us pray, auld England may
    Sure plant this far-famed tree, man;
And blythe we'll sing, and hail the day
    That gave us liberty, man.

'Ill-fated genius' [on Robert Fergusson]

ILL-FATED genius! Heaven-taught Fergusson!°
    What heart that feels and will not yield a tear,
To think life's sun did set ere well begun
    To shed its influence on thy bright career.
O why should truest worth and genius pine,
    Beneath the iron grasp of Want and Wo,
While titled knaves and idiot greatness shine
    In all the spendour Fortune can bestow!

A FRAGMENT—
ON GLENRIDDEL'S FOX BREAKING HIS CHAIN

THOU, Liberty, thou art my theme,
Not such as idle Poets dream,
Who trick thee up a Heathen goddess
That a fantastic cap and rod has:°
Such stale conceits are poor and silly;
I paint thee out, a Highland filly,
A sturdy, stubborn, handsome dapple,
As sleek's a mouse, as round's an apple,
That when thou pleasest can do wonders;
But when thy luckless rider blunders,   10
Or if thy fancy should demur there,
Wilt break thy neck ere thou go further.—

These things premis'd, I sing a fox,
Was caught among his native rocks,
And to a dirty kennel chain'd,
How he his liberty regain'd.——

Glenriddel, a Whig without a stain,°
A Whig in principle and grain,
Couldst thou enslave a free-born creature,
A native denizen of Nature?   20
How couldst thou with a heart so good,
(A better ne'er was sluic'd with blood)
Nail a poor devil to a tree,
That ne'er did harm to thine or thee?

The staunchest Whig Glenriddel was,
Quite frantic in his Country's cause;°
And oft was Reynard's prison passing,
And with his brother Whigs canvassing
The Rights of Men, the Powers of Women,°
With all the dignity of Freemen.——   30

Sir Reynard daily heard debates
Of Princes' kings' and Nations' fates;
With many rueful, bloody stories
Of tyrants, Jacobites and tories:°
From liberty how angels fell,
That now are galley slaves in hell;
How Nimrod first the trade began°
Of binding Slavery's chains on man;
How fell Semiramis, G—d d—mn her!°
Did first with sacreligious hammer,   40
(All ills till then were trivial matters)
For Man dethron'd forge hen-peck fetters;
How Xerxes, that abandon'd tory,°
Thought cutting throats was reaping glory,
Untill the stubborn Whigs of Sparta°
Taught him great Nature's Magna charta;°
How mighty Rome her fiat hurl'd,
Resistless o'er a bowing world,
And kinder than they did desire,
Polish'd mankind with sword and fire: 50

With much too tedious to relate,
Of Ancient and of Modern date,
But ending still how Billy Pit,
(Unlucky boy!) with wicked wit,
Has gagg'd old Britain, drain'd her coffer,°
As butchers bind and bleed a heifer.—

Thus wily Reynard by degrees,
In kennel listening at his ease,
Suck'd in a mighty stock of knowledge,
As much as some folks at a college.—   60
Knew Britain's rights and constitution,
Her aggrandizement, diminution,
How fortune wrought us good from evil;
Let no man then despise the devil,
As who should say, I ne'er can need him;
Since we to scoundrels owe our freedom.—

ODE [FOR GENERAL WASHINGTON'S BIRTHDAY]

No Spartan tube, no Attic shell,°
  No lyre Eolian I awake;°
'Tis Liberty's bold note I swell,
  Thy harp, Columbia, let me take.°
See gathering thousands, while I sing,
A broken chain, exulting, bring,
And dash it in a tyrant's face!°
And dare him to his very beard,
And tell him, he no more is feared,
  No more the Despot of Columbia's race.   10
A tyrant's proudest insults braved,
They shout, a People freed! They hail an Empire saved.

  Where is Man's godlike form?
Where is that brow erect and bold,
That eye that can, unmoved, behold
The wildest rage, the loudest storm,
That e'er created fury dared to raise!
Avaunt! thou caitiff, servile, base,
That tremblest at a Despot's nod,

Yet, crouching under th' iron rod,   20
Canst laud the arm that struck th' insulting blow!
Art thou of man's imperial line?
Dost boast that countenance divine?
Each sculking feature answers, No!
But come, ye sons of Liberty,
Columbia's offspring, brave as free,
In danger's hour still flaming in the van:
Ye know, and dare maintain, The Royalty of Man.

Alfred, on thy starry throne,°
Surrounded by the tuneful choir,   30
The Bards that erst have struck the patriot lyre,°
And roused the freeborn Briton's soul of fire,
    No more thy England own.—
Dare injured nations form the great design,
    To make detested tyrants bleed?°
Thy England execrates the glorious deed!
    Beneath her hostile banners waving,
    Every pang of honor braving,
England in thunder calls—'The Tyrant's cause is mine!'°
That hour accurst, how did the fiends rejoice,   40
And hell thro' all her confines raise th' exulting voice,
That hour which saw the generous English name°
Linkt with such damned deeds of everlasting shame!

Thee, Caledonia, thy wild heaths among,
Famed for the martial deed, the heaven-taught song,
    To thee, I turn with swimming eyes.—
Where is that soul of Freedom fled?
Immingled with the mighty Dead!
    Beneath that hallowed turf where WALLACE lies!°
Hear it not, Wallace, in thy bed of death!   50
    Ye babbling winds in silence sweep;
    Disturb not ye the hero's sleep,
Nor give the coward secret breath.—
Is this the ancient Caledonian form,
Firm as her rock, resistless as her storm?
Shew me that eye which shot immortal hate,
    Blasting the Despot's proudest bearing:
Shew me that arm which, nerved with thundering fate,

Braved Usurpation's boldest daring!°
Dark-quenched as yonder sinking star,   60
No more that glance lightens afar;
That palsied arm no more whirls on the waste of war.

A POET'S WELCOME TO HIS
LOVE-BEGOTTEN DAUGHTER
THE FIRST INSTANCE THAT ENTITLED HIM TO THE
VENERABLE APPELLATION OF FATHER

THOU's welcome, wean! Mishanter fa' me,
If thoughts o' thee or yet thy mammie
Shall ever daunton me or awe me,
                    My sweet, wee lady,
Or if I blush when thou shalt ca' me
                    Tyta or daddie!

What tho' they ca' me fornicator,°
An' tease my name in kintra clatter?
The mair they talk, I'm kend the better;
                    E'en let them clash!   10
An auld wife's tongue 's a feckless matter
                    To gie ane fash.

Welcome, my bonie, sweet, wee dochter!
Tho' ye come here a wee unsought for,
And tho' your comin I hae fought for
                    Baith kirk and queir;°
Yet, by my faith, ye're no unwrought for—
                    That I shall swear!

Sweet fruit o' monie a merry dint,
My funny toil is no a' tint: 20
Tho' thou cam to the warl' asklent,
                    Which fools may scoff at,
In my last plack thy part 's be in't
                    The better half o't.

Tho' I should be the waur bestead,
Thou 's be as braw and bienly clad,

And thy young years as nicely bred
   Wi' education,
As onie brat o' wedlock's bed
   In a' thy station.   30

Wee image o' my bonie Betty,°
As fatherly I kiss and daut thee,
As dear and near my heart I set thee,
   Wi' as guid will,
As a' the priests had seen me get thee
   That's out o' Hell.

Gude grant that thou may ay inherit
Thy mither's looks an' gracefu' merit,
An' thy poor, worthless daddie's spirit
   Without his failins!   40
'Twill please me mair to see thee heir it
   Than stocket mailins.°

And if thou be what I wad hae thee,
An' tak the counsel I shall gie thee,
I'll never rue my trouble wi' thee—
   The cost nor shame o't—
But be a loving father to thee,
   And brag the name o't.

APPENDIX 1

FROM THE LETTERS

[L125. To Dr John Moore, London]

Sir

For some months past I have been rambling over the country, partly on account of some little business I have to settle° in various places; but of late I have been confined with some lingering complaints originating as I take it in the stomach.—To divert my spirits a little in this miserable fog of Ennui, I have taken a whim to give you a history of MYSELF.—My name has made a small noise in the country; you have done me the honor to interest yourself very warmly in my behalf; and I think a faithful account of, what character of a man I am, and how I came by that character, may perhaps amuse you in an idle moment.—I will give you an honest narrative, though I know it will be at the expence of frequently being laughed at; for I assure you, Sir, I have, like Solomon whose character, excepting the trifling affair of WISDOM, I some-times think I resemble, I have, I say, like him 'Turned my eyes to behold Madness and Folly;'° and like him too, frequently shaken hands with their intoxicating friendship.—In the very polite letter Miss Williams° did me the honor to write me, she tells me you have got a complaint in your eyes.—I pray God that it may be removed; for considering that lady and you are my common friends, you will probably employ her to read this letter; and then goodnight to that esteem with which she was pleased to honor the Scotch Bard.—After you have perused these pages, should you think them trifling and impertinent, I only beg leave to tell you that the poor Author wrote them under some very twitching qualms of conscience, that, perhaps he was doing what he ought not to do: a predicament he has more than once been in before.—

I have not the most distant pretensions to what the pye-coated guardians of escutcheons° call, A Gentleman.—When at Edin^r last winter, I got acquainted in the Herald's Office, and looking through that granary of Honors I there found almost every name in the kingdom; but for me,

> '—My ancient but ignoble blood
> Has crept thro' Scoundrels ever since the flood'—°

Gules, Purpure, Argent,° &c. quite disowned me.—My Fathers rented land of the noble Kieths of Marshal,° and had the honor to share their fate.—I do not use the word, Honor, with any reference to Political principles; loyal and disloyal I take to be merely relative terms in that ancient and formidable court known in this Country by the name of CLUB-LAW.—Those who dare wel-come Ruin and shake hands with Infamy for what they sincerely believe to be the cause of their God or their King—'Brutus and Cassius are honorable men.'°—I mention this circumstance because it threw my father on the world at large; where after many years' wanderings and sojournings, he pickt up a pretty large quantity of Observation and Experience, to which I am indebted for most of my little pretensions to wisdom.—I have met with few who understood 'Men, their manners and their ways'° equal to him; but stubborn, ungainly Integrity, and headlong, ungovernable Irrascibillity are disqualifying circumstances: consequently I was born a very poor man's son.—For the first six or seven years of my life, my father was gardiner to a worthy gentleman of small estate in the neighbourhood of Ayr.—Had my father continued in that situation, I must have marched off to be one of the little underlings about a farm-house; but it was his dearest wish and prayer to have it in his power to keep his children under his own eye till they could discern between good and evil; so with the assistance of his generous Master my father ventured on a small farm in his estate.°—At these years I was by no means a favorite with any body.—I was a good deal noted for a retentive memory, a stubborn, sturdy something in my disposition, and an enthusiastic, idiot piety.—I say idiot piety, because I was then but a child.—Though I cost the schoolmaster some thrashings, I made an excellent English scholar; and against the years of ten or eleven, I was absolutely a Critic in substantives, verbs and particles.—In my infant and boyish days too, I owed much to an old Maid of my Mother's, remarkable for her ignorance, credulity and superstition.—She had, I suppose, the largest collection in the county of tales and songs concerning devils, ghosts, fairies, brownies, witches, warlocks, spunkies,° kelpies, elf-candles,° dead-lights,° wraiths, apparitions, cantraips, giants, inchanted towers, dragons and other trumpery.—This cultivated the latent seeds of Poesy; but had so strong an effect on my imagination, that to this hour, in my nocturnal rambles, I sometimes keep a sharp look-out in suspicious places; and though nobody can be more sceptical in these matters than I, yet it often takes an effort of Philosophy to shake off these idle terrors.—The earliest thing of Composition that I recollect taking pleasure in was, The vision of Mirza° and a hymn of Addison's beginning—'How are Thy servants blest, O Lord!' I particularly remember one half-stanza which was music to my boyish ear—

> 'For though in dreadful whirls we hung,
> 'High on the broken wave'—°

I met with these pieces in Mason's English Collection,° one of my schoolbooks.—The two first books I ever read in private, and which gave me more pleasure than any two books I ever read again, were, the life of Hannibal and the history of Sir William Wallace.°—Hannibal gave my young ideas such a turn that I used to strut in raptures up and down after the recruiting drum and bagpipe, and wish myself tall enough to be a soldier; while the story of Wallace poured a Scotish prejudice in my veins which will boil along there till the floodgates of life shut in eternal rest.—Polemical divinity about this time was putting the country half-mad; and I, ambitious of shining in conversation parties on sundays between sermons, funerals, &c. used in a few years more to puzzle

Calvinism with so much heat and indiscretion that I raised a hue and cry of heresy against me which has not ceased to this hour.—

My vicinity to Ayr was of great advantage to me.—My social disposition, when not checked by some modification of spited pride, like our catechism definition of Infinitude, was 'without bounds or limits.'°—I formed many connections with other Youngkers who possessed superiour advantages; the youngling Actors who were busy with the rehearsal of PARTS in which they were shortly to appear on that STAGE where, Alas! I was destined to druge behind the SCENES.—It is not commonly at these green years that the young Noblesse and Gentry have a just sense of the immense distance between them and their ragged Playfellows.—It takes a few dashes into the world to give the young Great man that proper, decent, unnoticing disregard for the poor, insignificant, stupid devils, the mechanics and peasantry around him; who perhaps were born in the same village.—My young Superiours never insulted the clouterly appearance of my ploughboy carcase, the two extremes of which were often exposed to all the inclemencies of all the seasons.—They would give me stray volumes of books; among them, even then, I could pick up some observations; and ONE, whose heart I am sure not even the MUNNY BEGUM'S scenes have tainted,° helped me to a little French.—Parting with these, my young friends and benefactors, as they dropped off for the east or west Indies, was often to me a sore affliction; but I was soon called to more serious evils.—My father's generous Master died; the farm proved a ruinous bargain; and, to clench the curse, we fell into the hands of a Factor who sat for the picture I have drawn of one in my Tale of two dogs.°—My father was advanced in life when he married; I was the eldest of seven children; and he, worn out by early hardship, was unfit for labour.—My father's spirit was soon irritated, but not easily broken.—There was a freedom in his lease in two years more, and to weather these two years we retrenched expences.—We lived very poorly; I was a dextrous Ploughman for my years; and the next eldest to me was a brother, who could drive the plough very well and help me to thrash.—A Novel-Writer might perhaps have viewed these scenes with some satisfaction, but so did not I: my indignation yet boils at the recollection of the scoundrel tyrant's insolent, threatening epistles, which used to set us all in tears.—

This kind of life, the chearless gloom of a hermit with the unceasing moil of a galley-slave, brought me to my sixteenth year; a little before which period I first committed the sin of RHYME. You know our country custom of coupling a man and woman together as Partners in the labors of Harvest.—In my fifteenth autumn, my Partner was a bewitching creature who just counted an autumn less.—My scarcity of English denies me the power of doing her justice in that language; but you know the Scotch idiom, She was a bonie, sweet, sonsie lass.—In short, she altogether unwittingly to herself, initiated me in a certain delicious Passion, which in spite of acid Disappointment, gin-horse Prudence° and bookworm Philosophy, I hold to be the first of human joys, our dearest pleasure here below.—How she caught the contagion I can't say; you medical folks talk much of infection by breathing the same air, the touch, &c.

but I never expressly told her that I loved her.—Indeed I did not well know myself, why I liked so much to loiter behind with her, when returning in the evening from our labors; why the tones of her voice made my heartstrings thrill like an Eolian harp;° and particularly, why my pulse beat such a furious ratann when I looked and fingered over her hand, to pick out the nettle-stings and thistles.—Among her other love-inspiring qualifications, she sung sweetly; and 'twas her favorite reel to which I attempted giving an embodied vehicle in rhyme.—I was not so presumtive as to imagine that I could make verses like printed ones, composed by men who had Greek and Latin; but my girl sung a song which was said to be composed by a small country laird's son, on one of his father's maids, with whom he was in love; and I saw no reason why I might not rhyme as well as he, for excepting smearing sheep and casting peats, his father living in the moors, he had no more Scholarcraft than I had.—

Thus with me began Love and Poesy; which at times have been my only, and till within this last twelvemonth have been my highest enjoyment.—My father struggled on till he reached the freedom in his lease, when he entered on a larger farm° about ten miles farther in the country.—The nature of the bargain was such as to throw a little ready money in his hand at the commencement, otherwise the affair would have been impractible.—For four years we lived comfortably here; but a lawsuit between him and his Landlord commencing, after three years tossing and whirling in the vortex of Litigation, my father was just saved from absorption in a jail by phthisical° consumption, which after two years promises, kindly stept in and snatch'd him away—'To where the wicked cease from troubling, and where the weary be at rest.'—°

It is during this climacterick° that my little story is most eventful.—I was, at the beginning of this period, perhaps the most ungainly, aukward being in the parish.—No Solitaire° was less acquainted with the ways of the world.—My knowledge of ancient story was gathered from Salmon's and Guthrie's geographical grammars;° my knowledge of modern manners, and of literature and criticism, I got from the Spectator.°—These, with Pope's works, some plays of Shakespear, Tull and Dickson on Agriculture,° The Pantheon,° Locke's Essay on the human understanding,° Stackhouse's history of the bible,° Justice's British Gardiner's directory,° Boyle's lectures,° Allan Ramsay's works,° Taylor's scripture doctrine of original sin,° a select Collection of English songs,° and Hervey's meditations° had been the extent of my reading.—The Collection of Songs was my vade mecum.°—I pored over them, driving my cart or walking to labor, song by song, verse by verse; carefully noting the true tender or sublime from affectation and fustian.—I am convinced I owe much to this for my critic-craft such as it is.—

In my seventeenth year, to give my manners a brush, I went to a country dancing school.—My father had an unaccountable antipathy against these meetings; and my going was, what to this hour I repent, in absolute defiance of his commands.—My father, as I said before, was the sport of strong passions: from that instance of rebellion he took a kind of dislike to me, which, I believe was one cause of that dissipation which marked my future years.—I only say,

Dissipation, comparative with the strictness and sobriety of Presbyterean country life; for though the will-o'-wisp meteors of thoughtless Whim were almost the sole lights of my path, yet early ingrained Piety and Virtue never failed to point me out the line of Innocence.—The great misfortune of my life was, never to have AN AIM.—I had felt early some stirrings of Ambition, but they were the blind gropings of Homer's Cyclops° round the walls of his cave: I saw my father's situation entailed on me perpetual labor.—The only two doors by which I could enter the fields of fortune were, the most niggardly economy, or the little chicaning art of bargain-making: the first is so contracted an aperture, I never could squeeze myself into it; the last, I always hated the contamination of the threshold.—Thus, abandoned of aim or view in life; with a strong appetite for sociability, as well from native hilarity as from a pride of observation and remark; a constitutional hypochondriac taint which made me fly solitude; add to all these incentives to social life, my reputation for bookish knowledge, a certain wild, logical talent, and a strength of thought something like the rudiments of good sense, made me generally a welcome guest; so 'tis no great wonder that always 'where two or three were met together, there was I in the midst of them.'° But far beyond all the other impulses of my heart was, un penchant á l'adorable moitiée du genre humain.°—My heart was compleatly tinder, and was eternally lighted up by some Goddess or other; and like every warfare in this world, I was sometimes crowned with success, and sometimes mortified with defeat.—At the plough, scythe or reap-hook I feared no competitor, and set Want at defiance: and as I never cared farther for my labors than while I was in actual exercise, I spent the evening in the way after my own heart.—A country lad rarely carries on an amour without an assisting confident.—I possessed a curiosity, zeal and intrepid dexterity in these matters which recommended me a proper Second in duels of that kind; and I dare say, I felt as much pleasure at being in the secret of half the amours in the parish, as ever did Premier at knowing the intrigues of half the courts of Europe.—

The very goosefeather in my hand seems instinctively to know the well-worn path of my imagination, the favorite theme of my song; and is with difficulty restrained from giving you a couple of paragraphs on the amours of my Compeers, the humble Inmates of the farm-house and cottage; but the grave sons of Science, Ambition or Avarice baptize these things by the name of Follies.—To the sons and daughters of labor and poverty they are matters of the most serious nature: to them, the ardent hope, the stolen interview, the tender farewell, are the greatest and most delicious part of their enjoyments.—

Another circumstance in my life which made very considerable alterations in my mind and manners was, I spent my seventeenth summer on a smuggling coast° a good distance from home at a noted school, to learn Mensuration, Surveying, Dialling,° &c. in which I made a pretty good progress.—But I made greater progress in the knowledge of mankind.—The contraband trade was at that time very successful; scenes of swaggering riot and roaring dissipation were as yet new to me; and I was no enemy to social life.—Here, though I learned to look unconcernedly on a large tavern-bill, and mix without fear in a drunken squabble, yet I went on with a high hand in my Geometry; till the sun entered Virgo,° a month which is always a carnival in my bosom, a charming Fillette who lived next door to the school overset my Trigonometry, and set me off in a tangent from the sphere of my studies.—I struggled on with my Sines and Co-sines for a few days more; but stepping out to the garden one charming noon, to take the sun's altitude, I met with my Angel,

> —'Like Proserpine gathering flowers,
> 'Herself a fairer flower'—°

It was vain to think of doing any more good at school.—The remaining week I staid, I did nothing but craze the faculties of my soul about her, or steal out to meet with her; and the two last nights of my stay in the country, had sleep been a mortal sin, I was innocent.—

I returned home very considerably improved.—My reading was enlarged with the very important addition of Thomson's and Shenstone's works; I had seen mankind in a new phasis;° and I engaged several of my schoolfellows to keep up a literary correspondence with me.—This last helped me much on in composition.—I had met with a collection of letters by the Wits of Queen Ann's reign,° and I pored over them most devoutly. I kept copies of any of my own letters that pleased me, and a comparison between them and the composition of most of my correspondents flattered my vanity.—I carried this whim so far that though I had not three farthings worth of business in the world, yet every post brought me as many letters as if I had been a broad, plodding son of Day-book & Ledger.—

My life flowed on much in the same tenor till my twenty third year.—Vive l'amour et vive la bagatelle,° were my sole principles of action.—The addition of two more Authors to my library gave me great pleasure; Sterne and Mᶜkenzie.— Tristram Shandy° and the Man of Feeling° were my bosom favorites.—Poesy was still a darling walk for my mind, but 'twas only the humour of the hour.—I had usually half a dozen or more pieces on hand; I took up one or other as it suited the momentary tone of the mind, and dismissed it as it bordered on fatigue.—My Passions when once they were lighted up, raged like so many devils, till they got vent in rhyme; and then conning over my verses, like a spell, soothed all into quiet.—None of the rhymes of those days are in print, except, Winter, a dirge,° the eldest of my printed pieces; The death of Poor Mailie,° John Barleycorn,° And songs first, second and third:° song second was the ebullition of that passion which ended the forementioned school-business.—

My twenty third year was to me an important era.—Partly thro' whim, and partly that I wished to set about doing something in life, I joined with a flax-dresser in a neighbouring town,° to learn his trade and carry on the business of manufacturing and retailing flax.—This turned out a sadly unlucky affair.—My Partner was a scoundrel of the first water who made money by the mystery of thieving; and to finish the whole, while we were given a welcoming carousal to the New year, our shop, by the drunken carelessness of my Partner's wife, took fire and was burnt to ashes;° and left me like a true Poet, not worth sixpence.—I was oblidged to give up business; the clouds of misfortune were gathering thick round my father's head, the darkest of which was, he was visibly far gone in a consumption; and to crown all, a belle-fille° whom I adored and who had pledged her soul to meet me in the field of matrimony, jilted me with peculiar circumstances of mortification.—The finishing evil that brought up the rear of this infernal file was my hypochondriac complaint being irritated to such a degree, that for three months I was in diseased state of body and mind, scarcely to be envied by the hopeless wretches who have just got their mittimus, 'Depart from me, ye Cursed.'—°

From this adventure I learned something of a town-life.—But the principal thing which gave my mind a turn was, I formed a bosom-friendship with a young fellow, the first created being I had ever seen, but a hapless son of misfortune.—He was the son of a plain mechanic; but a great Man in the neighbourhood taking him under his patronage gave him a genteel education with a view to bettering his situation in life.—The Patron dieing just as he was ready to launch forth into the world, the poor fellow in despair went to sea; where after a variety of good and bad fortune, a little before I was acquainted with him, he had been set ashore by an American Privateer on the wild coast of Connaught, stript of every thing.—I cannot quit this poor fellow's story without adding that he is at this moment Captain of a large westindiaman belonging to the Thames.—

This gentleman's mind was fraught with courage, independance, Magnanimity, and every noble, manly virtue.—I loved him, I admired him, to a degree of enthusiasm; and I strove to imitate him.—In some measure I succeeded: I had the pride before, but he taught it to flow in proper channels.—His knowledge of the world was vastly superiour to mine, and I was all attention to learn.— He was the only man I ever saw who was a greater fool than myself when WOMAN was the presiding star; but he spoke of a certain fashionable failing with levity, which hitherto I had regarded with horror.—Here his friendship did me a mischief; and the consequence was, that soon after I resumed the plough, I wrote the WELCOME inclosed.°—My reading was only encreased by two stray volumes of Pamela,° and one of Ferdinand Count Fathom,° which gave me some idea of Novels.—Rhyme, except some religious pieces which are in print, I had given up; but meeting with Fergusson's Scotch Poems,° I strung anew my wildly-sounding, rustic lyre with emulating vigour.—When my father died, his all went among the rapacious hell-hounds that growl in the kennel of justice; but we made a shift to scrape a little money in the family amongst us, with which, to keep us together, my brother and I took a neighbouring farm.°—My brother wanted my harebrained imagination as well as my social and amorous madness, but in good sense and every sober qualification he was far my superiour.—

I entered on this farm with a full resolution, 'Come, go to, I will be wise!'°— I read farming books; I calculated crops; I attended markets; and in short, in spite of 'The devil, the world and the flesh,' I believe I would have been a wise man; but the first year from unfortunately buying in bad seed, the second from a late harvest, we lost half of both our crops: this overset all my wisdom, and I returned 'Like the dog to his vomit, and the sow that was washed to her wallowing in the mire.'—°

I now began to be known in the neighbourhood as a maker of rhymes. The first of my poetic offspring that saw the light was a burlesque lamentation on a quarrel between two rev^d Calvinists,° both of them dramatis personae in my Holy Fair.—I had an idea myself that the piece had some merit; but to prevent the worst, I gave a copy of it to a friend who was very fond of these things, and told him I could not guess who was the Author of it, but that I thought it pretty clever.—With a certain side of both clergy and laity it met with a roar of applause.— Holy Willie's Prayer° next made its appearance, and alarmed the kirk-Session so much that they held three several meetings to look over their holy artillery, if any of it was pointed against profane Rhymers.—Unluckily for me, my idle wanderings led me, on another side, point blank within the reach of their heaviest metal.—This is the unfortunate story alluded to in my printed poem, The Lament.°—'Twas a shocking affair, which I cannot yet bear to recollect; and had very nearly given me one or two of the principal qualifications for a place among those who have lost the chart and mistake the reckoning of Rationality.—I gave up my part of the farm to my brother, as in truth it was only nominally mine; and made what little preparation was in my power for Jamaica.—Before leaving my native country for ever, I resolved to publish my Poems.—I weighed my productions as impartially as in my power; I thought they had merit; and 'twas a delicious idea that I would be called a clever fellow, even though it should never reach my ears a poor Negro-driver, or perhaps a victim to that inhospitable clime gone to the world of Spirits.— I can truly say that pauvre Inconnu° as I then was, I had pretty nearly as high an idea of myself and my works as I have at this moment.—It is ever my opinion that the great, unhappy mistakes and blunders, both in a rational and religious point of view, of which we see thousands daily guilty, are owing to their ignorance, or mistaken notions of themselves.—To know myself had been all along my constant study.—I weighed myself alone; I balanced myself with others; I watched every means of information how much ground I occupied both as a Man and as a Poet: I studied assiduously Nature's DESIGN where she seem'd to have intended the various LIGHTS and SHADES in my character.— I was pretty sure my Poems would meet with some applause; but at the worst, the roar of the Atlantic would deafen the voice of Censure, and the novelty of west-Indian scenes make me forget Neglect.—

I threw off six hundred copies, of which I had got subscriptions for about three hundred and fifty. My vanity was highly gratified by the reception I met with from the Publick; besides pocketing, all expences deducted, near twenty pounds.—This last came very seasonable, as I was about to indent myself° for want of money to pay my freight.—So soon as I was master of nine guineas, the price of wafting me to the torrid zone, I bespoke a passage in the very first ship that was to sail, for

'Hungry ruin had me in the wind'—°

I had for some time been sculking from covert to covert under all the terrors of a Jail; as some ill-advised, ungrateful people° had uncoupled the merciless legal Pack at my heels.—I had taken the last farewel of my few friends; my chest was on the road to Greenock;° I had composed my last song I should ever measure in Caledonia, 'The gloomy night is gathering fast,'° when a letter from D[r] Blacklock to a friend of mine° overthrew all my schemes by rousing my poetic ambition.—The Doctor belonged to a set of Critics for whose applause I had not even dared to hope. His idea that I would meet with every encouragement for a second edition fired me so much that away I posted to Edinburgh without a single acquaintance in town, or a single letter of introduction in my pocket.—The baneful Star that had so long shed its blasting influence in my Zenith, for once made a revolution to the Nadir;° and the providential care of a good God placed me under the patronage of one of his noblest creatures, the Earl of Glencairn:° 'Oublie moi, Grand Dieu, si jamais je l'oublie!'—°

I need relate no farther.—At Edin[r] I was in a new world: I mingled among many classes of men, but all of them new to me; and I was all attention 'to catch the manners living as they rise.'—°

You can now, Sir, form a pretty near guess what sort of a Wight° he is whom for some time you have honored with your correspondence.—That Fancy & Whim, keen Sensibility and riotous Passions may still make him zig-zag in his future path of life, is far from being improbable; but come what will, I shall answer for him the most determinate integrity and honor; and though his evil star should again blaze in his meridian with tenfold more direful influence, he may reluctantly tax Friendship with Pity but no more.—

My most respectful Compliments to Miss Williams.—Her very elegant and friendly letter I cannot answer at present, as my presence is requisite in Edinburgh, and I set off tomorrow.—

If you will oblidge me so highly and do me so much honor as now and then to drop me a letter, Please direct to me at Mauchline, Ayrshire.—

I have the honor to be, Sir,
your ever grateful humble serv[t]
R[OB][T] BURNS

Mauchline 2[d] August 1787

[L515]

Mr WILL[m] JOHNSTON, *Proprietor of the Edin[r] Gazetteer*°
Care of Mr Elliot, Bookseller Parliament-Square—Edin[r]

Sir,

I have just read your Prospectus of the Edin[r] Gazetteer.—If you go on in your Paper with the same spirit, it will, beyond all comparison, be the first Composition of the kind in Europe.—I beg leave to insert my name as a Subscriber; & if you have already published any papers, please send me them from the beginning.—Point out your own way of settling payments in this place, or I shall settle with you through the medium of my friend, Peter Hill, Bookseller in Edin[r].—

Go on, Sir! Lay bare, with undaunted heart & steady hand, that horrid mass of corruption called Politics & State-Craft! Dare to draw in their native colors these

'Calm, thinking VILLAINS whom no faith can fix'—°

whatever be the shiboleth of their pretended Party.—

The address, to me at Dumfries, will find,

Sir, your very humble Servt
ROB^T BURNS

Dumfries 13th Nov 1792

[L524. To Mrs Frances Dunlop]

Dumfries 6th Decr 1792°

I shall be in Ayrshire I think, next week; & if at all possible, I shall certainly, my much esteemed Friend, have the pleasure of visiting at Dunlop house.°— Alas, Madam! how seldom do we meet in this world that we have reason to congratulate ourselves on accessions of happiness!—I have not passed half the ordinary term of an old man's life, & yet I scarcely look over the obituary of a Newspaper that I do not see some names that I have known, & which I, & other acquaintances, little thought to meet with there so soon.—Every other instance of the mortality of our kind, makes us cast a horrid anxious look into the dreadful abyss of uncertainty, & shudder with apprehension for our own fate.—But of how different importance are the lives of different Individuals? Nay, of what importance is one period of the same life, more than another? A few years ago, I could have lain down in the dust, careless, as the book of Job elegantly says, 'Careless of the voice of the morning';° & now, not a few, & these most helpless, individuals, would, on losing me & my exertions, lose both their 'Staff & Shield.'°—By the way, these helpless ones have lately got an addition; M^{rs} B— having given me a fine girl° since I wrote you.—There is a charming passage in Thomson's Edward & Eleonora—

'The valiant, *in himself*, what can he suffer?
Or what does he regard his single woes?
But when, alas, he multiplies himself
To dearer selves, to the loved tender Fair,
To those whose bliss, whose beings hang upon him,
To helpless children! then, O then! he feels
The point of misery festering in his heart,
And weakly weeps his fortune like a coward'—°

As I am got in the way of quotations, I shall give you another from the same piece, peculiarly—Alas, too peculiarly apposite, my dear Madam, to your present frame of mind.—

'Who so unworthy but may proudly deck him
With his fair-weather virtue, that exults,

> Glad, o'er the summer main? the tempest comes,
> The rough winds rage aloud; when from the helm
> This virtue shrinks, & in a corner lies
> Lamenting—Heavens! if privileged from trial,
> How cheap a thing were virtue!'—°

I do not remember to have heard you mention Thomson's Dramas, as favorite walks of your reading.—Do you know, I pick up favorite quotations, & store them in my mind as ready armour, offensive, or defensive, amid the struggle of this turbulent existence.—Of these is one, a very favorite one, from Thomson's Alfred—

> 'Attach thee firmly to the virtuous deeds
> And offices of life: to life itself,
> With all its vain & transient joys, sit loose'—°

Probably I have quoted some of these to you formerly, as indeed when I write from the heart, I am apt to be guilty of these repetitions.—The compass of the heart, in the musical style of expression, is much more bounded, than the [illegible] reach of invention; so the notes of the former are extremely apt to run into similar passages; but in return for the paucity of its compass, its few notes are much more sweet.—I must still give you another quotation, which I am almost sure I have given you before, but I cannot resist the temptation.—The subject is Religion.—Speaking of its importance to mankind, the Author says,

> ''Tis this, my Friend, that streaks our morning bright;
> 'Tis this that gilds the horrors of our night.—
> When wealth forsakes us, & when friends are few;
> When friends are faithless, & when foes pursue;
> 'Tis this that wards the blow, or stills the smart,
> Disarms affliction, or repels its dart:
> Within the breast bids purest raptures rise,
> Bids smiling conscience spread her cloudless skies'—°

I see you are in for double Postage, so I shall e'en scribble out t'other sheet.—We, in this country, here have many alarms of the Reform, or rather the Republican spirit, of your part of the kingdom.—Indeed, we are a good deal in commotion ourselves, & in our Theatre here,° 'God save the king' has met with some groans & hisses, while Ça ira° has been repeatedly called for.—For me, I am a *Placeman*,° you know; a very humble one indeed, Heaven knows, but still so much so as to gag me from joining in the cry.—What my private sentiments are, you will find out without an Interpreter.—In the mean time, I have taken up the subject in another view, and the other day, for a pretty Actress's benefit-night, I wrote an Address, which I will give on the other page, called *The Rights of Woman*.°

I shall have the honour of receiving your criticisms in person at Dunlop.

[L528]

ROBERT GRAHAM Esquire *of Fintry Excise Office Edin'*

Dumfries Dec' 31ˢᵗ [1792]

Sir,

I have been surprised, confounded & distracted by Mʳ Mitchel, the Collector,° telling me just now, that he has received an order from your Honᵇˡᵉ Board to enquire into my political conduct, & blaming me as a person disaffected to Government.—Sir, you are a Husband—& a father—you know what you would feel, to see the much-loved wife of your bosom, & your helpless, prattling little ones, turned adrift into the world, degraded & disgraced from a situation in which they had been respectable & respected, & left almost without the necessary support of a miserable existence.—Alas, Sir! must I think that such, soon, will be my lot! And from the damned, dark insinuations of hellish, groundless Envy too!—I believe, Sir, I may aver it, & in the sight of Omnipotence, that I would not tell a deliberate Falsehood, no, not though even worse horrors, if worse can be, than those I have mentioned, hung over my head; & I say, that the allegation, whatever villain has made it, is a LIE! To the British Constitution, on Revolution principles,° next after my God, I am most devoutly attached!—

You, Sir, have been much & generously my Friend—Heaven knows how warmly I have felt the obligation, how gratefully I have thanked you.—Fortune, Sir, has made you powerful, & me impotent; has given you patronage, & me dependence.—I would not for my *single Self* call on your Humanity; were such my insular, unconnected situation, I would despise the tear that now swells in my eye—I could brave Misfortune, I could face Ruin: for at the worst, 'Death's thousand doors stand open;'° but, Good God! the tender concerns that I have mentioned, the claims & ties that I, at this moment, see & feel around me, how they ennerve Courage, & wither Resolution! To your patronage, as a man of some genius, you have allowed me a claim; & your esteem, as an honest Man, I know is my due: to these, Sir, permit me to appeal; & by these may I adjure you to save me from that misery which threatens to overwhelm me, & which, with my latest breath I will say it, I have not deserved.

Pardon this confused scrawl.—Indeed I know not well what I have written.—

I have the honor to be, Sir,
your deeply indebted
& ever grateful humble servᵗ
ROBᵀ BURNS

[L530. To Robert Graham of Fintry]

Dumfries 5ᵗʰ Janʳʸ 1793°

Sir,

I am this moment honored with your letter: with what feelings I received this other instance of your goodness, I shall not pretend to describe.—

Now, to the charges which Malice & Misrepresentation have brought against me.—

It has been said, it seems, that I not only belong to, but head a disaffected party in this place.—I know of no party in this place, either Republican or Reform, except an old party of Borough-Reform;° with which I never had any thing to do.—Individuals, both Republican & Reform, we have, though not many of either; but if they have associated, it is more than I have the least knowledge of: & if there exists such an association, it must consist of such obscure, nameless beings, as precludes any possibility of my being known to them, or they to me.—

I was in the playhouse one night, when Çà ira° was called for.—I was in the middle of the pit, & from the Pit the clamour arose.—One or two individuals with whom I occasionally associate were of the party, but I neither knew of the Plot, nor joined in the Plot; nor ever opened my lips to hiss, or huzza, that, or any other Political tune whatever.—I looked on myself as far too obscure a man to have any weight in quelling a Riot; at the same time, as a character of higher respectability, than to yell in the howlings of a rabble.—This was the conduct of all the first Characters in this place; & these Characters know, & will avow, that such was my conduct.—

I never uttered any invectives against the king.—His private worth, it is altogether impossible that such a man as I, can appreciate; and in his Public capacity, I always revered, & ever will, with the soundest loyalty, revere, the Monarch of Great-britain, as, to speak in Masonic, the sacred KEYSTONE OF OUR ROYAL ARCH CONSTITUTION.—

As to REFORM PRINCIPLES, I look upon the British Constitution, as settled at the Revolution, to be the most glorious Constitution on earth, or that perhaps the wit of man can frame; at the same time, I think, & you know what High and distinguished Characters have for some time thought so, that we have a good deal deviated from the original principles of that Constitution; particularly, that an alarming System of Corruption has pervaded the connection between the Executive Power and the House of Commons.—This is the Truth, the Whole truth, of my Reform opinions; opinions which, before I was aware of the complection of these innovating times, I too unguardedly (now I see it) sported with: but henceforth, I seal up my lips.—However, I never dictated to, corresponded with, or had the least connection with, any political association whatever—except, that when the Magistrates & principal inhabitants of this town, met to declare their attachment to the Constitution, & their abhorrence of Riot, which declaration you would see in the Papers, I, as I thought my duty as a Subject at large, & a Citizen in particular, called upon me, subscribed the same declaratory Creed.—

Of Johnston, the publisher of the Edinʳ Gazetteer,° I know nothing.— One evening in company with four or five friends, we met with his prospectus which we thought manly & independant; & I wrote to him, ordering his paper for us.—If you think that I act improperly in allowing his Paper to come addressed to me, I shall immediately countermand it.—I never, so judge me, God! wrote a line of prose for the Gazetteer in my life.—An occasional address, spoken by Miss Fontenelle on her benefit-night here, which I called, the Rights of Woman,° I sent to the Gazetteer; as also, some extempore stanzas on the Commemoration of Thomson:° both these I will subjoin for your perusal.—You will see they have nothing whatever to do with Politics.—At the time when I sent Johnston one of these poems, but which one, I do not remember, I inclosed, at the request of my warm & worthy friend, Robt Riddel Esq: of Glenriddel,° a prose Essay, signed Cato, written by him, & addressed to the delegates for the County Reform,° of which he was one for this County.—With the merits, or demerits, of that Essay I have nothing to do, farther than transmitting it in the same Frank,° which Frank he had procured me.—

As to France, I was her enthusiastic votary in the beginning of the business.—When she came to shew her old avidity for conquest, in annexing Savoy,° &c. to her dominions, & invading the rights of Holland,° I altered my sentiments.—A tippling Ballad which I made on the Prince of Brunswick's breaking up his camp,° & sung one convivial evening, I shall likewise send you, sealed up, as it is not every body's reading.—This last is not worth your perusal; but lest Mrs FAME should, as she has already done, use, & even abuse, her old priviledge of lying, you shall be the master of every thing, le pour et le contre, of my political writings & conduct.—

This, my honored Patron, is all.—To this statement I challenge disquisition.—Mistaken Prejudice, or unguarded Passion, may mislead, & often have misled me; but when called on to answer for my mistakes, though, I will say it, no man can feel keener compunction for his errors, yet, I trust, no man can be more superiour to evasion or disguise.—

I shall do myself the honor to thank Mrs Graham for her goodness, in a separate letter.—

If, Sir, I have been so fortunate as to do away these misapprehensions of my conduct & character, I shall with the confidence which you were wont to allow me, apply to your goodness on every opening in the way of business, where I think I with propriety may offer myself.—An instance that occurs just now; M^r M^{c}farlane, Supervisor of the Galloway District is & has been for some time, very ill.—I spoke to Mr Mitchel as to his wishes to forward my application for the job, but though he expressed & ever does express every kindness for me, he hesitates, in hopes that the disease may be of short continuance.—However, as it seems to be a paralytic affection, I fear that it may be some time ere he can take charge of so extended a District.—There is a great deal of fatigue, & very little business in the District; two things suitable enough to my hardy constitution, & inexperience in that line of life.—

I have the honor to be, Sir,

                    your ever grateful, as highly obliged humble serv^t
                                                    ROB^T BURNS

[L531]

Mʳˢ GRAHAM *of Fintry* [Dumfries, 5 January 1793]

To Mʳˢ Graham of Fintry, this little poem,° written in haste on the spur of the
occasion, & therefore inaccurate; but a sincere Compliment to that Sex, the
most amiable of the works of God—is most respectfully presented by—

THE AUTHOR

[L558]

JOHN FRANCIS ERSKINE of Mar

In the year 1792/93, when Royalist & Jacobin had set all Britain by the ears,
because I unguardedly, rather under the temptation of being witty than disaf-
fected, had declared my sentiments in favor of Parliamentary Reform, in the
manner of that time, I was accused to the Board of Excise of being a Republican;
& was very near being turned adrift in the wide world on that account.—
Mʳ Erskine of Mar, *a gentleman indeed*, wrote to my friend Glenriddell° to
know if I was really out of place on account of my Political principles; & if so,
he proposed a Subscription among the friends of Liberty for me, which he
offered to head, that I might be no pecuniary loser by my political
Integrity.—This was the more generous, as I had not the honor of being known
to Mʳ Erskine. I wrote him as follows.—

[Dumfries, 13 April 1793]

Sir,
    degenerate as Human Nature is said to be, & in many instances, worthless &
unprincipled it certainly is; still there are bright examples to the contrary;
examples, that even in the eye of Superiour Beings must shed a lustre on
the name of Man.—Such an example have I now before me, when you, Sir,
came forward to patronise & befriend a distant, obscure stranger; merely
because Poverty had made him helpless, & his British hardihood of mind had
provoked the arbitrary wantonness of Power.—My much esteemed friend,
Mʳ Riddell of Glenriddell, has just read me a paragraph of a letter he had from
you.—Accept, Sir, of the silent throb of gratitude; for words would but mock
the emotions of my soul.—
    You have been misinformed, as to my final dismission from the Excise: I still
am in the service.—Indeed, but for the exertions of a gentleman who must be
known to you, Mʳ Graham of Fintry, a gentleman who has ever been my warm
& generous friend, I had, without so much as a hearing, or the smallest previ-
ous intimation, been turned adrift, with my helpless family, to all the horrors
of Want.—Had I had any other resource, probably I might have saved them
the trouble of a dismissal; but the little money I gained by my Publication, is
almost every guinea embarked, to save from ruin an only brother;° who, though
one of the worthiest, is by no means one of the most fortunate of men.—

In my defence to their accusations, I said, that whatever might be my sentiments of Republics, ancient or modern, as to Britain, I abjured the idea.—That a Constitution which, in its original principles, experience had proved to be every way fitted for our happiness in society, it would he insanity to sacrifice to an untried, visionary theory.—That, in consideration of my being situated in a department, however humble, immediately in the hands of the people in power, I had forborne taking any active part, either personally, or as an author, in the present business of Reform.—But that, where I must declare my sentiments, I would say that there existed a system of corruption between the Executive Power & the Representative part° of the Legislature, which boded no good to our glorious Constitution; & which every patriotic Briton must wish to see amended.—Some such Sentiments as these I stated in a letter to my generous Patron, Mr Graham, which he laid before the Board at large, where it seems my last remark gave great offence; & one of our Supervisors general, a Mr Corbet, was instructed to enquire, on the spot, into my conduct, & to document me—'that *my* business was to *act*, not to think; & that whatever might be Men or Measures, it was my business to be silent & obedient'—Mr Corbet was likewise my steady friend; so, between Mr Graham & him, I have been partly forgiven: only, I understand that all hopes of my getting officially forward are blasted.—

Now, Sir, to the business in which I would more immediately interest you.—The partiality of my Countrymen has brought me forward as a man of genius, & has given me a Character to support.—In the Poet, I have avowed manly & independant sentiments, which I trust will be found in the Man.—Reasons of no less weight than the support of a wife & children have pointed out as the eligible, & indeed the only eligible line of life for me, my present occupation.—Still, my honest fame is my dearest concern; & a thousand times have I trembled at the idea of the degrading epithets that Malice, or Misrepresentation may affix to my name.—I have often, in blasting anticipation, listened to some future hackney Magazine Scribbler, with the heavy malice of savage stupidity, exulting in his hireling paragraphs that 'Burns, notwithstanding the fanfaronade of independance to be found in his works, & after having been held forth to Public View & Public Estimation as a man of some genius, yet, quite destitute of resources within himself to support this borrowed dignity, he dwindled into a paltry Exciseman; & slunk out the rest of his insignificant existence in the meanest of pursuits & among the vilest of mankind.'—

In your illustrious hands, Sir, permit me to lodge my strong disavowal & defiance of these slanderous falsehoods.—BURNS was a poor man, from birth; & an Exciseman, by necessity: but—I will say it!—the sterling of his honest worth, no poverty could debase; & his independant British mind, Oppression might bend, but could not subdue!—Have not I, to me, a more precious stake in my Country's welfare, than the richest Dukedom in it?—I have a large family of children, & the probability of more. I have three sons, whom, I see already, have brought with them into the world souls ill qualified to inhabit the bodies of Slaves.—Can I look tamely on, & see any machination to wrest from them, the birthright of my boys,° the little independant Britons in whose veins runs my own blood?—No! I will not!—should my heart stream around my attempt to defend it!—

Does any man tell me, that my feeble efforts can be of no service; & that it does not belong to my humble station to meddle with the concerns of a People?—I tell him, that it is on such individuals as I, that for the hand of support & the eye of intelligence, a Nation has to rest.—The uninformed mob may swell a Nation's bulk; & the titled, tinsel Courtly throng may be its feathered ornament, but the number of those who are elevated enough in life, to reason & reflect; & yet low enough to keep clear of the venal contagion of a Court; these are a Nation's strength.—

One small request more: when you have honored this letter with a perusal, please commit it to the flames.—BURNS, in whose behalf you have so generously interested yourself, I have here, in his native colours, drawn *as he is*; but should any of the people in whose hands is the very bread he eats, get the least knowledge of the picture, it would ruin the poor Bard for ever.—

My Poems having just come out in another edition, I beg leave to present you with a copy; as a small mark of that high esteem & ardent gratitude with which I have the honor to be—
Sir,

Your deeply indebted,
And ever devoted humble servant

APPENDIX 2

CONTEMPORARY REVIEWS OF THE KILMARNOCK *POEMS* (1786)

1. From *The Edinburgh Magazine, or Literary Miscellany, for October 1786*, pp. 284–5.

Poems, chiefly in the Scottish Dialect. By ROBERT BURNS, *Kilmarnock*

WHEN an author we know nothing of solicits our attention, we are but too apt to treat him with the same reluctant civility we show to a person who has come unbidden into company. Yet talents and address will gradually diminish the distance of our behaviour, and when the first unfavourable impression has worn off, the author may become a favourite, and the stranger a friend. The poems we have just announced may probably have to struggle with the pride of learning and the partiality of refinement; yet they are intitled to particular indulgence.

Who are you, Mr Burns? will some surly critic say. At what university have you been educated? what languages do you understand? what authors have you particularly studied? whether has Aristotle or Horace° directed your taste? who has praised your poems, and under whose patronage are they published? In short, what qualifications intitle you to instruct and entertain us? To the questions of such a catechism, perhaps honest Robert Burns would make no satisfactory answers. 'My good Sir, he might say, I am a poor country man; I was bred up at the school of Kilmarnock; I understand no languages but my own; I have studied Allan Ramsay and Ferguson.° My poems have been praised at many a fire-side; and I ask no patronage for them, if they deserve none. I have not looked on mankind *through the spectacle of books*. An ounce of mother-wit, you know, is worth a pound of clergy; and Homer and Ossian,° for any thing that I have heard, could neither write nor read.' The author is indeed a striking example of native genius bursting through the obscurity of poverty and the obstructions of laborious life. He is said to be a common ploughman; and when we consider him in this light, we cannot help regretting that wayward fate had not placed him in a more favoured situation. Those who view him with the severity of lettered criticism, and judge him by the fastidious rules of art, will discover that he has not the doric simplicity° of Ramsay, nor the brilliant imagination of Ferguson; but to those who admire the exertions of untutored fancy, and are blind to many faults for the sake of numberless beauties, his poems will afford singular gratification. His observations on human characters are acute and sagacious, and his descriptions are lively and just. Of rustic pleasantry he has a rich fund; and some of his softer scenes are touched with inimitable delicacy. He seems to be a boon companion, and often startles us with a dash of libertinism, which will keep some readers at a distance. Some of his subjects are serious, but those of the humorous kind are the best. It is not meant, however, to enter into a minute investigation of his merits, as the copious extracts we have subjoined will enable our readers to judge for themselves. The Character Horace gives to Osellus is particularly applicable to him.

Rusticus abnormis sapiens, crassaque Minerva.°

2. [Henry Mackenzie,] *The Lounger* No XCVII.
Saturday, Dec. 9. 1786.

To the feeling and the susceptible there is something wonderfully pleasing in the contemplation of genius, of that supereminent reach of mind by which some men are distinguished. In the view of highly superior talents, as in that of great and stupendous natural objects, there is a sublimity which fills the soul with wonder and delight, which expands it, as it were, beyond its usual bounds, and which, investing our nature with extraordinary powers, and extraordinary honours, interests our curiosity, and flatters our pride.

This divinity of genius, however, which admiration is fond to worship, is best arrayed in the darkness of distant and remote periods, and is not easily acknowledged in the present times, or in places with which we are perfectly acquainted. Exclusive of all the deductions which envy or jealousy may some-times be supposed to make, there is a familiarity in the near approach of persons around us, not very consistent with the lofty ideas which we wish to form of him who has led captive our imagination in the triumph of his fancy, over-powered our feelings with the tide of passion, or enlightened our reason with the investigation of hidden truths. It may be true, that 'in the olden time' genius had some advantages which tended to its vigour and its growth;° but it is not unlikely that, even in these degenerate days, it rises much oftener than it is observed; that in 'the ignorant present time' our posterity may find names which they will dignify, though we neglected, and pay to their memory those honours which their contemporaries had denied them.

There is, however, a natural, and indeed a fortunate vanity in trying to redress this wrong which genius is exposed to suffer. In the discovery of talents generally unknown, men are apt to indulge the same fond partiality as in all other discoveries which themselves have made; and hence we have had repeated instances of painters and of poets, who have been drawn from obscure situa-tions, and held forth to public notice and applause by the extravagant en-comiums of their introductors, yet in a short time have sunk again to their former obscurity; whose merit, though perhaps somewhat neglected, did not appear to have been much undervalued by the world, and could not support, by its own intrinsic excellence, that superior place which the enthusiasm of its patrons would have assigned it.

I know not if I shall be accused of such enthusiasm and partiality, when I introduce to the notice of my readers a poet of our own country, with whose writings I have lately become acquainted; but if I am not greatly deceived, I think I may safely pronounce him a genius of no ordinary rank. The person to whom I allude, is ROBERT BURNS, an *Ayrshire* Ploughman, whose poems were some time ago published in a country-town in the west of Scotland, with no other ambition, it would seem, than to circulate among the inhabitants of the county where he was born, to obtain a little fame from those who had heard of his talents. I hope I shall not be thought to assume too much, if I endeavour to place him in a higher point of view, to call for a verdict of his country on the merit of his works, and to claim for him those honours which their excellence appears to deserve.

In mentioning the circumstances of his humble station, I mean not to rest his pretensions solely on that title, or to urge the merits of his poetry when considered in relation to the lowness of his birth, and the little opportunity of improvement which his education could afford. These particulars, indeed, might excite our wonder at his productions; but his poetry, considered abstractedly, and without the apologies arising from his situation, seems to me fully intitled to command our feelings, and to obtain our applause. One bar, indeed, his birth and education have opposed to his fame, the language in which most of his poems are written. Even in Scotland, the provincial dialect which Ramsay and he have used is now read with a difficulty which greatly damps the pleasure of the reader: in England it cannot be read at all, without such a constant reference to a glossary, as nearly to destroy that pleasure.

Some of his productions, however, especially those of the grave style, are almost English. From one of those I shall first present my readers with an extract, in which I think they will discover a high tone of feeling, a power and energy of expression, particularly and strongly characteristic of the mind and the voice of the poet. 'Tis from his poem intitled the *Vision*, in which the genius of his native county, *Ayrshire*, is thus supposed to address him:

[quotes 'The Vision', ll. 205–40]

Of strains like the above, solemn and sublime, with that rapt and inspired melancholy in which the Poet lifts his eye 'above this visible diurnal sphere,' the Poems intitled, *Despondency*, the *Lament*, *Winter*, *a Dirge*, and the Invocation to *Ruin*, afford no less striking examples. Of the tender and the moral, specimens equally advantageous might be drawn from the elegiac verses, intitled *Man was made to mourn*, from *The Cottar's Saturday Night*, the Stanzas *To a Mouse*, or those *To a Mountain-Daisy*, on turning it down with the plough in April 1786. This last Poem I shall insert entire, not from its superior merit, but because its length suits the bounds of my Paper.

[quotes 'To a Mountain-Daisy' complete, glossing Scots words with English equivalents]

I have seldom met with an image more truly pastoral than that of the lark, in the second stanza. Such strokes as these mark the pencil of the poet, which delineates Nature with the precision of intimacy, yet with the delicate colouring of beauty and of taste.

The power of genius is not less admirable in tracing the manners, than in painting the passions, or in drawing the scenery of Nature. That intuitive glance with which a writer like *Shakespeare* discerns the characters of men, with which he catches the many-changing hues of life, forms a sort of problem in the science of mind, of which it is easier to see the truth than to assign the cause. Though I am very far from meaning to compare our rustic bard to Shakespeare, yet whoever will read his lighter and more humorous poems, his *Dialogue of the Dogs*, his *Dedication to G—— H——, Esq*; his *Epistles to a young Friend*, and to *W. S——n*, will perceive with what uncommon penetration and sagacity this Heaven-taught ploughman, from his humble and unlettered station, has looked upon men and manners.

Against some passages of those last-mentioned poems it has been objected, that they breathe a spirit of libertinism and irreligion. But if we consider the ignorance and fanaticism of the lower class of people in the country where these poems were written, a fanaticism of that pernicious sort which sets *faith* in opposition to *good works*,° the fallacy and danger of which, a mind so enlightened as our Poet's could not but perceive; we shall look upon his lighter Muse, not as the enemy of religion, (of which in several places he expresses the justest sentiments), but as the champion of morality, and the friend of virtue.

There are, however, it must be allowed, some exceptionable parts of the volume he has given to the public, which caution would have suppressed, or correction struck out; but Poets are seldom cautious, and our Poet had, alas! no friends or companions from whom correction could be obtained. When we reflect on his rank in life, the habits to which he must have been subject, and the society in which he must have mixed, we regret perhaps more than wonder, that delicacy should be so often offended in perusing a volume in which there is so much to interest and please us.

Burns possesses the spirit as well as the fancy of a Poet. That honest pride and independence of soul which are sometimes the Muse's only dower, break forth on every occasion in his works. It may be, then, I shall wrong his feelings, while I indulge my own, in calling the attention of the public to his situation and circumstances. That condition, humble as it was, in which he found content, and wooed the Muse, might not have been deemed uncomfortable; but grief and misfortunes have reached him there; and one or two of his poems hint, what I have learnt from some of his countrymen, that he has been obliged to form the resolution of leaving his native land, to seek under a West-Indian clime° that shelter and support which Scotland has denied him. But I trust means may be found to prevent this resolution from taking place; and that I do my country no more than justice, when I suppose her ready to stretch out her hand to cherish and retain this native Poet, whose 'wood-notes wild'° possess so much excellence. To repair the wrongs of suffering or neglected merit; to call forth genius from the obscurity in which it had pined indignant, and place it where it may profit or delight the world; these are exertions which give to wealth an enviable superiority, to greatness and to patronage a laudable pride.

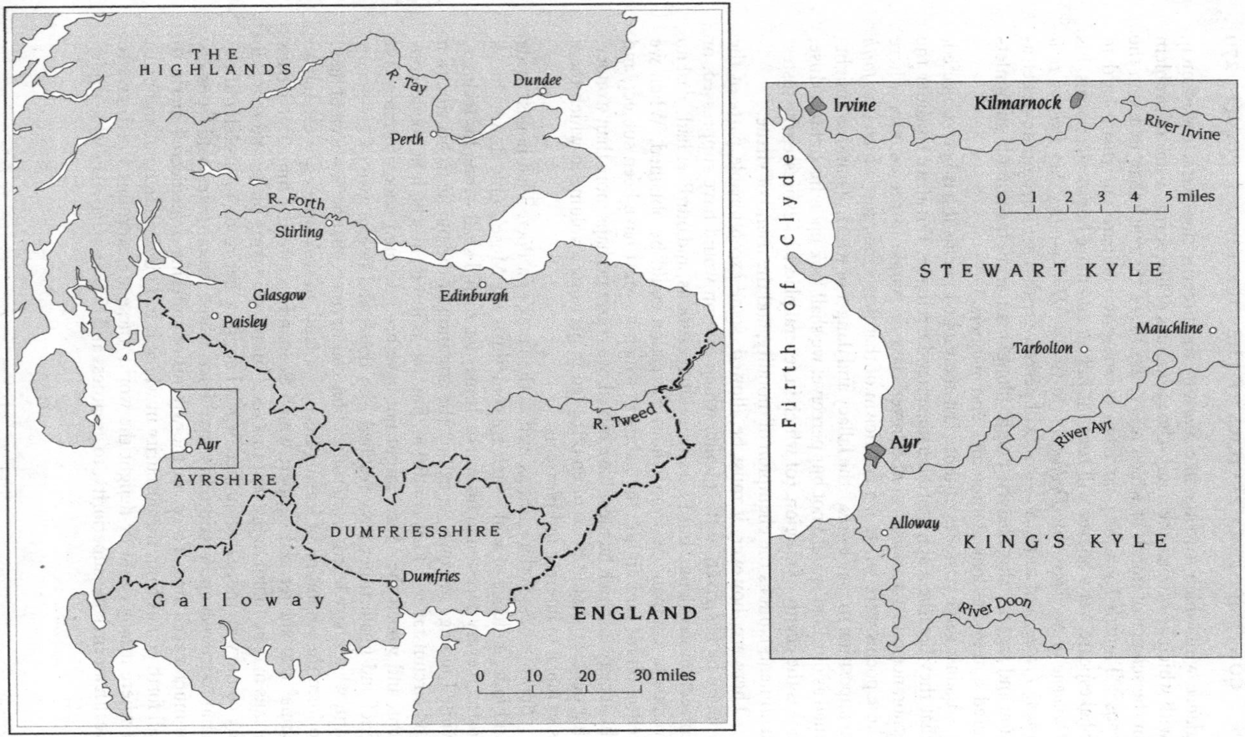

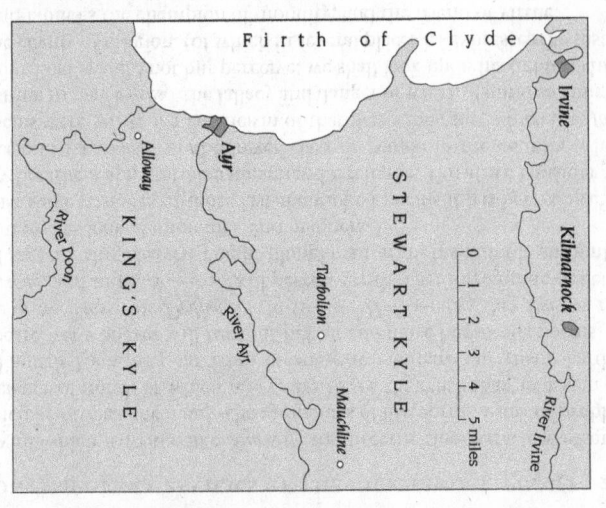

Southern Scotland, with (enlarged) Kyle District, Ayrshire

NOTES

THE notes are intended to indicate, as appropriate in each instance, the context in which each poem or song was produced and read, both material (the sorts of texts in which they appeared, and how they changed over time); literary (the forms they adopt from, and allusions they make to, previous literature); social (their role in the poet's correspondence, their relation to other social practices); and political (their stake in the conflicts of the time). They are not primarily intended to elucidate Scots vocabulary: in case of difficulty the reader should first consult the Glossary, and only if it fails to provide satisfaction should the notes be consulted instead.

Each note begins with a number preceded by the capital 'K'. This is the number of the text in James Kinsley's standard scholarly edition. As the present volume generally uses the titles under which these texts were first published, it was thought advisable to retain the reference to Kinsley's numbering in case of confusion; as Kinsley arranged his texts in likely order of composition, these numbers also give some sense of the relative priority of the texts. The debt of these notes to Kinsley in the matter of Burns's allusions to other eighteenth-century poets is enormous and I hope consistently acknowledged. Where a number is preceded by a capital 'L', this is a reference to a letter in G. Ross Roy's edition also listed below; again, by the number of the letter, not the page number of Roy's two-volume set.

EDITIONS OF BURNS REFERRED TO IN THE NOTES

Cunningham	*The Works of Robert Burns; with his life*, ed. Alan Cunningham. Eight volumes. London, 1834.
Douglas	*The Complete Poetical Works of Robert Burns*, ed. William Scott Douglas. Two volumes. Kilmarnock, 1876.
Henley and Henderson	*The Poetry of Robert Burns*, ed. William Ernest Henley and Thomas F. Henderson. Four volumes. London, 1896.
Kinsley	*The Poems and Songs of Robert Burns*, ed. James Kinsley. Oxford, 1968.
McGuirk	*Robert Burns: Selected Poems*, ed. Carol McGuirk. London, 1993.
Wallace	*The Life and Works of Robert Burns*, ed. Robert Chambers, revised William Wallace. Four volumes. Edinburgh and London, 1896.

OTHER ABBREVIATIONS

BE	*Burns Encyclopedia Online*: www.robertburns.org/encyclopedia
DNB	*Oxford Dictionary of National Biography*: www.oxforddnb.com

DSL	*Dictionary of the Scots Language*: www.dsl.ac.uk
Fergusson	Robert Fergusson, *The Poems of Robert Fergusson*, Vol. II, ed. Matthew P. McDiarmid (Edinburgh, 1956).
HPO	*History of Parliament Online*: www.historyofparliamentonline.org
Letters	*The Letters of Robert Burns*, ed. J. De Lancey Ferguson, 2nd edn. ed. G. Ross Roy (Oxford, 1985).
Lonsdale	Roger Lonsdale, ed., *The Poems of Thomas Gray, William Collins, Oliver Goldsmith* (London, 1969).
Macpherson	James Macpherson, *The Poems of Ossian and related works*, ed. Howard Gaskill (Edinburgh, 1996).
OED	*Oxford English Dictionary*: www.oed.co.uk
Pope	*The Poems of Alexander Pope*, ed. John Butt (London, 1989).
Ramsay	*The Works of Allan Ramsay*, Vols. I and II, ed. Burns Martin and John W. Oliver; Vols. III–V ed. Alexander M. Kinghorn and Alexander Law (Edinburgh, 1945–74).
SC	*A Select Collection of Original Scotish Airs, for the Voice*, ed. George Thomson, in six volumes (London, 1798–1841).
Shenstone	William Shenstone, *The Works in Verse and Prose, of William Shenstone Esq, in two volumes* (London 1764).
SMM	*The Scots Musical Museum*, ed. James Johnson, in six volumes (Edinburgh, 1787–1803).
Thomson	James Thomson, *The Seasons and The Castle of Indolence*, ed. James Sambrook (Oxford, 1987).
Young	Edward Young, *The Complaint: or, night thoughts on life, death, and immortality. A new edition, corrected by the author* (London, 1755).

Poems, Chiefly in the Scottish Dialect (Kilmarnock, 1786)

This volume, Burns's first, is usually referred to as the 'Kilmarnock edition': later, enlarged editions of the *Poems* were published in Edinburgh in 1787, 1793, and 1794. For the circumstances of its publication see the Introduction.

1 *Epigraph.* These are Burns's own words, but they are clearly informed by the following lines:

> *Nature!* informer of the poet's art,
> Whose force alone can raise or melt the heart,
> Thou art his guide; each passion, every line,
> Whate'er he draws to please, must all be thine.

These are ll. 27–30 of the 'Prologue' to James Thomson's tragedy *Sophonisba* (1730) by Alexander Pope; but as John Butt notes, they are probably by David Mallet, born Malloch (1701–65), another Scottish poet in Pope's circle (Pope 807).

3 *Preface*

Theocrites or Virgil. Theocritus, Greek pastoral poet who lived *c.*300–*c.*260 BC; Roman poet Publius Vergilius Maro (70–19 BC), author of the pastoral

Eclogues, and whose poems describing the routines of rural life, the *Georgics*, were an important model and source of authority for descriptive poetry in the eighteenth century.

'A fountain shut up, and a book sealed'. Burns conflates the Song of Songs 4: 12, 'A garden inclosed is my sister, my spouse; a spring shut up, a fountain sealed', with the more obviously relevant Isaiah 29: 11, 'And the vision of all is become unto you as the words of a book that is sealed, which men deliver to one that is learned, saying, Read this, I pray thee: and he saith, I cannot; for it is sealed'.

Shenstone. William Shenstone (1714–63), English nature-poet and essayist. The lines quoted are the closing advice to poets from Shenstone's essay 'On allowing Merit in Others': 'Banish the self-debasing principle, and scorn the disingenuity of readers. Humility has depressed many a genius into a hermit; but never yet raised one into a poet of eminence' (Shenstone Vol. II, 15).

Ramsay. Allan Ramsay (1684–1758), influential post-Union revivalist of poetry in Scots.

4 *Ferguson*. Robert Fergusson (1750–74), vivid chronicler of the Edinburgh scene who died in poverty. Burns arranged and paid for a stone to mark Fergusson's grave on his first visit to Edinburgh in 1786–7.

Subscribers. For publication by subscription see the Introduction to this volume.

5 *The Twa Dogs, a Tale*. K71. The first poem of the Kilmarnock edition is Burns's earliest composition in iambic tetrameter couplets, a form to which he will return, not often, but with great success, for example in 'Tam o' Shanter'. It had been used by Robert Fergusson for an earlier dialogue, 'Mutual Complaint of Plainstanes and Causey' in *Poems on Various Subjects* (1779; Fergusson 122–6).

l. 2. *auld king COIL*. 'Coilus, King of the Picts, from whom the district of Kyle is said to take its name', as Burns will explain in a footnote to 'The Vision' (see p. 302). For Kyle, see Map.

l. 12. *Where sailors gang to fish for Cod*. That is, Newfoundland, whose Grand Banks had been fished by Europeans for centuries.

l. 27 and footnote. *Cuchullin's dog in Ossian's Fingal*. *Fingal* is an epic prose-poem published by James Macpherson (1736–96) in 1761–2. Macpherson claimed that it was a translation of a poem composed and sung to the harp by Ossian, a third-century Gaelic bard, but was widely suspected of forgery: Burns alludes to the controversy in l. 28. Cuchullin is one of the heroic warriors of the tale.

6 l. 44. *arse*. The next two editions of *Poems*, published in Edinburgh in 1787 and 1793, gesture towards politeness with 'They sat them down upon their a—,'; then in the fourth edition of 1794 Burns replaces ll. 43–4 altogether with 'Until, wi' daffin weary grown, | Upon a knowe they sat them down'.

6 l. 51. *racked rents*. That is, excessive rents. Specifically, 'rack-rent' meant a rent approaching the total income that the rented land could generate for the tenant, leaving them little to live on. Rent inflation was a serious problem in Burns's Scotland.

l. 58. *Geordie*. The guinea, a gold coin displaying the monarch's head worth 21s.

l. 63. *ragouts*. French-style stews.

l. 65. *Whipper-in*. The Huntsman's assistant in managing a pack of foxhounds, responsible for keeping them together as a pack.

7 l. 69. *Cot-folk*. For cottars see headnote to 'The Cotter's Saturday night', p. 306.

l. 70. *I own it's past my comprehension*. The line, as Kinsley notes, is borrowed from Shenstone's 'The Price of an Equipage', where the bafflement is produced by a small farmer maintaining a coach and footmen. The next line explains: 'Yes, Sir, but DAMON has a pension—', that is, a government salary (Shenstone Vol. I, 219).

l. 71. *they're*. From the 1793 *Poems*, correcting Kilmarnock's 'their'.

l. 74. *Bairan*. In the context this clearly means 'digging', but neither Burns's glossaries nor *DSL* offer this as a possible sense.

l. 93. *court-day*. Usually refers to the day on which a court of justice meets, but here applied, perhaps ironically, to the quarter-days on which rents are due.

l. 98. *He'll apprehend them, poind their gear*. Ramsay had evoked the same fear in Act I scene ii of *The Gentle Shepherd*: 'With glooman Brow the Laird seeks in his Rent: | 'Tis no to gi'e . . . | *His Honour* mauna want, he poinds your Gear' (ll. 138–40; Ramsay Vol. II, 222).

8 l. 119. *patronage an' priests*. The Church of Scotland had been settled with a Presbyterian constitution, whereby the appointment of a parish minister requires the consent of the congregation, in 1690. But in 1711 the British parliament passed an act restoring 'lay patronage': that is, the inherited right of certain landowners, including the crown, to appoint ministers. This contradiction was a source of popular anger throughout the eighteenth century, especially in staunchly Presbyterian western counties such as Ayrshire, to the point where '[l]arge numbers of the rural lower orders left the Established Church in the 1760s and 1770s as a result of often violent patronage disputes which rent parishes asunder' (Brown, *Religion and Society*, 19).

l. 123. *Hallowmass*. The Feast of All Saints, 1 November.

9 l. 144. *Some rascal*. That is, a factor of the type mentioned at ll. 96f. In the biographical letter to John Moore of 2 August 1787 reproduced in Appendix 1, Burns says he had in mind the factor who harried his father at Mount Oliphant (p. 261).

l. 148. *For Britain's guid his saul indentin*. That politicians seeking election might 'indent' (contract, sell into servitude) their souls is an idea, Kinsley observes, that Burns gets from Fergusson's *The Election* ll. 120–1: 'their saul is lent, | For the town's gude indent' (Fergusson 190).

l. 151. *as PREMIERS lead him.* The ability of eighteenth-century administrations to secure the assent of parliament by offering MPs sinecures and other benefits was identified as 'corruption' in 'Patriot' or 'Country-Party' rhetoric, of which these lines are an example.

ll. 157–8. *To make a tour an' tak a whirl, | To learn bon ton an' see the worl'.* The 'Grand Tour' of France and Italy was typically the culmination of a young British gentleman's education, to encounter (among other things) elevated manners and the latest fashions, or 'bon-ton': as the phrase suggests, defined as French.

l. 160. *He rives his father's auld entails.* An 'entail' was a legal mechanism for maintaining the integrity of a landed estate in its passage from one generation to the next by preventing the current owner from selling or mortgaging it, in part or as a whole. But lawyers had long since found ways to get round these clauses in order to raise the ready cash of which pleasure-seeking young gentlemen were so often in short supply.

l. 164. *groves o' myrtles.* The myrtle is an evergreen shrub sacred to Venus in the pagan mythology.

l. 165. *German-water.* Mineral water from a German spa-town.

l. 168. *b—res an' ch—ncres.* Presumably bores, with bore in the sense of 'small hole' and meaning here the female sex (see headnote to 'Green Grow the Rashes', p. 340, for an instance of this metaphor); and chancres, the infectious lesions which are the first symptom of syphilis. In the 1787 Edinburgh edition and subsequently ll. 167–8 are replaced with 'An' clear the consequential sorrows, | Love-gifts of Carnival Signioras'.

10 ll. 181, 183. *breakin o' their timmer . . . Or shootin of a hare or moor-cock.* Eighteenth-century landowners were often aggressive in asserting their legal property rights in the face of the traditional claims of the poor to e.g. timber or game.

11 l. 204. *Her dizzen's done.* 'Dizzen' here means her 'hank or dozen cuts of yarn, the standard quantity allotted to a woman for a day's spinning' (*DSL*).

l. 215. *party-matches.* Perhaps gatherings of a local political faction or 'interest', or perhaps just social visits: not a phrase in *OED*.

l. 226. *the devil's pictur'd beuks.* Playing-cards, in the language in which gambling was denounced from the pulpit.

12 *Scotch Drink.* K77. In a letter of 20 March 1786 to Robert Muir of Kilmarnock Burns wrote, 'I am heartily sorry I had not the pleasure of seeing you as you returned thro Machline [Mauchline] . . . I here enclose you my SCOTCH DRINK, and "may the —— follow with a blessing for your edification."—I hope, sometime before we hear the Gowk, to have the pleasure of seeing you, at Kilm^k; when, I intend we shall have a gill between us, in a Mutchkin-stoup' (L23). The blank should be filled up with 'Deil'; the Gowk is the cuckoo, which first arrives in southern

Scotland in the second half of April. The verse form used here is the Standard Habbie stanza: see headnote to 'Poor Mailie's Elegy', p. 295, for its origins.

12 *Epigraph.* This is an extrapolation from King Lemuel's advice to his son in Proverbs 31: 6–7: 'Give strong drink unto him that is ready to perish, and wine unto those that be of heavy hearts. | Let him drink, and forget his poverty, and remember his misery no more.'

l. 2. *Bacchus.* The Roman god of wine.

l. 8. *wimplin worms.* McGuirk suggests this refers to 'the network of tubes at the top of a still' (McGuirk 232).

l. 20. *souple scones.* Thin barley scones were a treat compared to the staple oatcake.

13 ll. 28–9. *oil'd by thee,* | *The wheels o' life.* Kinsley notes the borrowing from Ramsay's 'Epistle to Robert Yarde': 'A cheerfu' Bottle' 'brawly oyls the Wheels of Life' (ll. 105, 108; Ramsay Vol. II, 60).

l. 45. *the saunts.* The orthodox in religion.

l. 47. *the tents.* A 'tent' in this sense is 'a moveable wooden pulpit, with steps and a canopy, erected in the open air, esp. at the half-yearly communion services when the congregation is too large for the church to contain', and metonymically the preacher himself (*DSL*). For the communion events alluded to here, see headnote to 'The Holy Fair', p. 291.

l. 53. *a wee drap sp'ritual burn.* Burn is 'the water used in brewing' (*DSL*).

l. 55. *Vulcan.* The Roman god of fire and smithying.

14 l. 68. *gossips.* The women of the neighbourhood, enjoying the traditional party with the howdie (midwife) at a birth.

l. 69. *fumbling.* Sexually impotent (*OED*).

ll. 70–2. In the 1787 Edinburgh edition and subsequently these lines are replaced with 'Wae worth the name! | Nae Howdie gets a social night, | Or plack frae them'.

l. 95. *dearthfu' wines.* This is a conjunction, Kinsley observes, borrowed from Ramsay's 'Last Speech of a Wretched Miser', l. 42 (Ramsay Vol. II, 63).

15 ll. 97–8. *Gravels . . . An' Gouts.* Gout is an arthritic condition of the joints, to which heavy drinking can contribute: the 'gravel' is a related condition in which crystals form in the urine, making its passage painful.

l. 109. *Ferintosh.* A famous whisky distilled on the Black Isle, north of Inverness.

l. 113. *loyal Forbes' Charter'd boast.* The Ferintosh distilleries belonged to Forbes of Culloden. At the Revolution in 1689, the then laird, Duncan Forbes, was an active and influential supporter of the new king, William; supporters of the deposed James VII ravaged the Ferintosh and Culloden estates in retaliation. In compensation the Scottish parliament granted

Forbes, in perpetuity, the privilege of distilling whisky at Ferintosh free of duty. This privilege disappeared under new (British) legislation in 1784 (see headnote to the following poem), leading to the closure of the Ferintosh distilleries shortly after.

l. 115. *Thae curst horse-leeches o' th' Excise*. That is, the customs officers responsible for enforcing payment of duty and destroying illicit stills. Burns would himself become an exciseman in 1788.

16 *The Author's earnest cry and prayer, to the right honorable and honorable, the Scotch representatives in the House of Commons*. K81. In the 1787 Edinburgh edition and subsequently Burns provides a footnote to the title: 'This was wrote before the Act anent the Scotch Distilleries, of session 1786; for which Scotland and the Author return their most grateful thanks'. An earlier act, in 1784, had tried to rationalize the excise laws, but ended up producing new restrictions that increased the rewards for illicit production and drove many legitimate distilleries out of business. This is the situation against which Burns's poem protests. The tax regime introduced in 1786 instead tended to reward more efficient production (though this in turn would end up causing a new set of problems).

Epigraph. Burns parodies Adam's response to Eve's account of her fall in Book VIII of John Milton's *Paradise Lost* (1667): 'O fairest of Creation, last and best | Of all Gods works . . . | How art thou lost, how on a sudden lost, | Defac't, defloured, and now to Death devote?' (ll. 896–7, 900–1).

l. 1. *Irish lords*. Under the terms of the Treaty of Union of 1707, Scottish peers elected from among themselves sixteen 'representative peers' to sit in the British House of Lords, the number limited in this way to reflect the much smaller population of Scotland; but the remaining Scottish peers, as peers, remained excluded from election to the House of Commons. Irish peers *could* be elected to the Commons for Scottish (as for English) constituencies.

l. 16. *AQUAVITÆ*. 'Water of life', Latin equivalent to the Gaelic *uisge beatha* from which the word 'whisky' is derived.

l. 19. *PREMIER YOUTH*. William Pitt the younger (b. 1759, the same year as Burns), backed by George III, had been confirmed as First Lord of the Treasury (and thus 'Premier' or 'Prime Minister') by the general election of 1784, and would remain in that office until 1801.

l. 25. *great man*. Since its use to describe prime minister Robert Walpole earlier in the century, this phrase had evoked ministerial power dominating the Commons through its distribution of offices and other rewards (the '*posts* an' *pensions*' of l. 27).

17 l. 39. *Excise-men*. See note to p. 15, l. 115.

l. 44. *A blackguard Smuggler*. The eighteenth-century British state's use of import duties to raise revenue created a thriving black economy along its coasts. Tea, brandy, rum, and tobacco were the main contraband involved. Burns mentions his personal encounter with this trade in the biographical letter to John Moore of 2 August 1787 reproduced in Appendix 1, p. 263.

17 l. 52. *dung in staves*. That is, staved in.

l. 57. *could I like MONGOMERIES fight*. A leading Ayrshire aristo-cratic family, distinguished on the royalist side in the seventeenth-century civil wars, and whose current head, Archibald, 11th Earl of Eglinton, had led a regiment in North America in the Seven Years War (1756–63).

l. 58. *BOSWELL*. James Boswell (1740–95), advocate; famous as friend of Samuel Johnson in London, but now back on the family's Ayrshire estate at Auchinleck and active in local politics.

18 l. 71. *Saint Stephen's wa's*. Until the old Palace of Westminster burnt down in 1834, its St Stephen's Chapel served as the debating chamber of the House of Commons.

l. 73. *Dempster*. George Dempster of Dunnichen (1732–1818), MP for the Perth district of burghs (Perth, Dundee, St Andrews, Forfar, and Cupar) 1761–90. 'From the start a frequent and passionate speaker' (*DNB*), and, in a period when Scottish MPs typically backed the govern-ment of the day, famous for speaking and voting independently (for example on the American War), earning him the nickname 'honest George'.

l. 74. *Kilkerran*. Sir Adam Fergusson of Kilkerran (1733–1813), MP for Ayrshire for ten years before his replacement by one of Pitt's people in 1784: he would regain the seat in the next election in 1790. 'An old woman who as a child had once seen Sir Adam in a temper described . . . how "Sir Adam cam out and he chappit on the ground wi' his stick, and says he, 'Dinna think that because I'm no swearin I'm no angry'"', hence 'aith-detesting' (Fergusson, *Lowland Lairds*, 94).

l. 76. *The Laird o' Graham*. James Graham (1755–1836). Barred as the eldest son of a Scottish peer from standing in Scotland, Graham was an MP for English seats until he succeeded his father as Duke of Montrose in 1790. He was active in promoting Scottish interests, and had a reputa-tion for independence until joining the government as a Lord of the Treasury in 1783. The Graham estates are around Loch Lomond in the southern Highlands, hence 'Highland Baron'.

l. 78. *Dundas*. Henry Dundas (1742–1811), MP for Midlothian 1774–90. As Lord Advocate 1775–84 Dundas gained powers of patronage across the Scottish political scene; on joining Pitt's new administration in 1784 he also became the government's all-powerful political manager in Scotland.

l. 79. *Erskine*. Thomas Erskine (1750–1823), brother of the Earl of Buchan (in north-east Scotland, hence a 'norland billie'): a London lawyer and talented courtroom speaker, but only very briefly an MP (for Portsmouth) in 1783–4.

l. 80. *True Campbells, Frederick and Ilay*. Frederick Campbell, brother of the Duke of Argyll, MP for the Glasgow district of burghs (Glasgow, Rutherglen, Dumbarton, and Renfrew) 1761–80, and then for Argyll

1781–99; Sir Ilay Campbell (1734–1823), no direct relation to Frederick, but a successor as MP for the Glasgow burghs in 1784: Dundas made him Lord Advocate in the same year and thus a principal agent of his power. Both Campbells were Pitt's men; neither seems to have been distinguished for eloquence.

l. 81. *Livistone, the bauld Sir Willie*. Sir William Augustus Cunynghame, proprietor of Milncraig in Ayrshire and Livingstone in Linlithgow, for which latter county he was MP 1774–90.

l. 83. *Demosthenes or Tully*. Famous classical orators: Demosthenes of Athens (384–322 BC); and the Roman Marcus Tullius Cicero (106–43 BC). Both died trying to defend their republics against, respectively, Alexander of Macedon and Mark Antony and his allies.

l. 92. *Her lost Militia fir'd her bluid*. When, two years into the Seven Years War in 1759, invasion by France had looked likely, the British government had revived the moribund local militias of England in response. A section of the Scottish elite, centred on literary and legal figures, campaigned for a militia to be established in Scotland as well, as a means of reviving the 'national spirit' and countering the alienating and feminizing effects of commercial society, as well as for defence. Acts were prepared for parliament in 1760 and 1762; the campaign was revived, during the American Revolutionary War, in 1776 and 1782. It came to nothing, due as much to hostility or indifference in Scotland as to the opposition of government: Scotland's militia was 'lost' only in the sense that it had not been won. James Graham had put forward the most recent bill, and most of the MPs Burns mentions in this poem had been active in the campaign at some point. See Robertson, *The Scottish Enlightenment and the Militia Issue*, chs. 4 and 5.

19 l. 99. *durk*. That is, dirk, the Highland dagger.

l. 100. *She'll tak the streets*. This poem's contrast between two modes of political agency—the parliamentary eloquence of land-owning gentlemen, and riot—reminds us that the MPs whom Burns addresses were elected by a tiny proportion of the population, and that street disorder was the only way in which ordinary people brought pressure to bear on their rulers. '[T]he tetchy sensibilities of a libertarian crowd defined, in the largest sense, the limits of what was politically possible,' writes E. P. Thompson of the period; 'the price which aristocracy and gentry paid for a limited monarchy and weak state was, perforce, the licence of the crowd'. Such licence did not threaten the existence of the social hierarchy itself: it 'bred riots but not rebellions: direct action but not democratic organizations' ('Patrician Society, Plebian Culture', 396, 403, 397).

l. 105. *the muckle house*. That is, parliament.

l. 109. *Charlie Fox*. Charles James Fox (1749–1806), populist leader of the opposition to Pitt's government; despite his current reforming agenda he had tasted power in 1783 as part of a coalition with Lord North, prime minister 1770–82 and a much more conservative figure than Pitt (see notes to p. 139, ll. 39ff.).

19   l. 112. *cadie*. Burns's glossary translates this as 'person' merely, but *DSL* notes that it can mean specifically a 'ragamuffin or rough fellow' (Fox had a reputation for scruffiness).

ll. 113–14. *his dicing box,* | *An' sportin lady*. *DNB* notes that Fox was 'the doyen of the gambling craze that disturbed so many family fortunes' in the period. 'Sporting lady', Kinsley notes, also means whore: Fox was notorious for a string of mistresses, but by this time had settled down with the experienced courtesan Elizabeth Armitstead.

l. 115. *yon guid blood o' auld Boconnock's*. Pitt again: his great-grandfather had been Governor of Madras, and used the fortune he made in India to buy the estate of Boconnoc in Cornwall. This gave him control of a seat in parliament and began the family's political rise.

l. 117 and footnote. *Nanse Tinnock's*. Nanse Tonnock kept a respectable tavern in Mauchline: on reading this poem, she denied that Burns had ever been a regular in her establishment.

l. 119. *tea and winnocks*. One of Pitt's priorities on coming to power was to pay off the United Kingdom's huge national debt, incurred in a long series of expensive wars with France. Reorganizing the tax system was part of his strategy. The 1784 Commutation Act slashed duty on tea to reduce the incentive for smuggling, and recouped the revenue with a tax on houses, calculated by the number of windows; hence '*commutation*' in l. 121.

l. 126. *The Coalition*. That is, the Fox–North coalition (see note to l. 109 above), the heavily defeated party of the 1784 election.

20   l. 133. *ye chosen FIVE AND FORTY*. By the terms of the Treaty of Union, the number of Scottish seats sending MPs to the Commons. Scotsmen could sit for English constituencies, as did James Graham (l. 76) and Thomas Erskine (l. 79).

ll. 135–6. *though a Minister grow dorty,* | *An' kick your place*. 'Place' here refers to any lucrative office or sinecure an MP might have been given by the executive in exchange for his vote, and 'kick' something like 'kick away from under you'; as well as suggesting a physical kick in a bodily place.

l. 142. *St. Jamie's*. That is, the Court: St James's Palace was the official London residence of the monarch.

l. 145. *half-starv'd slaves in warmer skies*. *Not* a reference to the chattel slaves of Britain's Caribbean colonies, or elsewhere in the Americas, but to southern Europeans: 'slaves', in the political idiom of eighteenth-century Britain, because subject to absolutist rulers (pre-eminently the kings of France and Spain) without the liberties supposedly guaranteed by the British constitution; and because Catholic, and thus subject to the Pope. The Postscript's association of liberty with a capacity for military service was a commonplace of early-modern political thought which had informed the mid-century militia debate (see note to l. 92 above).

21   l. 163. *bring a SCOTCHMAN frae his hill*. Scottish regiments, and in particular Highlanders (long suspected of disloyalty to the Hanoverian

regime because of their prominence in the Jacobite rebellions of 1715 and 1745–6), had proven valuable in two campaigns in North America: against France in the Seven Years War, and more recently against the United States in the Revolutionary War.

l. 173. *latest*. That is, last.

ll. 177–8. *physically causes seek,* | *In clime an' season*. The idea that cultural differences could be traced to differences of climate was much discussed by Enlightenment philosophers. As Kinsley notes, Burns could have come across it in Henry Mackenzie's essay in the *Mirror* no. 18 (27 March 1779) where he quotes its most famous formulation in Montesquieu's *De L'esprit des Lois* (1748); in its rejection by David Hume in his essay 'Of National Characters' (1741); or its discussion by Adam Ferguson in Part III, section i of *An Essay on the History of Civil Society* (1766).

l. 184. *dam*. A 'quantity of urine discharged at once' (*DSL*); to 'tine your dam' is to wet yourself.

ll. 183–6. In the fourth edition of 1794, Burns substituted a less shocking form of incontinence: 'Till when ye speak, ye aiblins blether; | Yet deil mak matter! | *Freedom* and *Whisky* gang thegither, | Tak aff your whitter'.

The Holy Fair. K70. In the 1787 Edinburgh edition and subsequently Burns provides a footnote to the title: '*Holy Fair* is a common phrase in the West of Scotland for a sacramental occasion'. The sacrament in question is Holy Communion, rarely celebrated more than two or three times a year in the Church of Scotland. In summer, a parish might hold a 'Communion Season' over several days, which other congregations were invited to attend and at which their ministers were invited to preach. Because a parish church could not hold so many people, this was an open-air occasion, and 'a highly popular event in seventeenth- and eighteenth-century Scotland, but it was more often an annual holiday than a holy event; thus, rarely more than 20 per cent of parishioners came forward to receive the sacrament' (Brown, *Religion and Society*, 73).

The verse form here is a version of the 'Christ's Kirk on the Green' stanza, named after a poem attributed to James I of Scotland, 'Chrystis Kirk of the Greene'. Burns would have come across this poem in Allan Ramsay's anthology *The Ever-Green: being a collection of Scots Poems, wrote by the ingenious before 1600* (1724), but also Ramsay's adaptation of it, with the addition of two further cantos, in his 1721 *Poems* (Ramsay Vol. I, 57–82). The form was also adopted by Robert Fergusson for 'Hallow-Fair', 'Leith Races', and 'The Election'. All of these poems celebrate communal holiday high-jinks of one kind or another. The ending of the final, short, line with 'that day' or 'that night' is conventional.

Epigraph. Kinsley ascribes these lines to Thomas Brown's 1704 comedy *The stage-Beaux toss'd in a blanket: or, hypocrisie alamode*, but they appear nowhere in Brown's play and are probably Burns's own. *A-LA-MODE*: in the current fashion.

22 l. 5. *owre GALSTON Muirs*. Galston is a village on the River Irvine, about seven miles north of Burns's farm at Mossgiel. The 1787 Edinburgh edition's 'owre', used here, corrects the Kilmarnock edition's 'our'.

23 l. 37. *My name is FUN*. The six introductory stanzas of this poem take their cue from the first five of 'Leith Races': the girl encountered by the speaker of Fergusson's poem similarly announces 'They ca' me MIRTH' (l. 32; Fergusson 161), and his agreement with her plan is equally enthusiastic.

l. 41. *I'm gaun to ********* holy fair*. The asterisks fit the name of Mauchline, the village just a mile from Mossgiel.

l. 66. *black-bonnet*. The officiating elder, responsible for gathering money in the collection-plate.

24 l. 75. *racer Jess*. According to Kinsley, the half-witted daughter of the 'Poosie Nansie' in whose Mauchline tavern the 'Jolly Beggars' gather in Burns's poem.

l. 80. *Blackguarding frae K*******ck*. To blackguard is 'to loaf, play the vagabond' (*OED*, though this line is its only example of the verb in this sense, so probably Burns's coinage). Kilmarnock, the nearest town, is about ten miles from Mauchline (see Map).

l. 86. *an Elect swatch*. In the 1787 Edinburgh edition and subsequently this becomes 'a Chosen swatch'. In either case, the reference is to those enjoying the inner conviction that they have been chosen or elected for salvation by God's grace (hence 'grace-proud' in l. 87) in accordance with the Kirk's Calvinist theology, as summarized in *The Westminster Confession of Faith* (1647): 'By the decree of God, for the manifestation of His glory, some men and angels are predestinated unto everlasting life; and others foreordained to everlasting death' (ch. III, para. iii).

25 l. 102. *For ****** speels the holy door*. The name elided here is that of (Alexander) Moodie, the orthodox minister of Riccarton parish in Kilmarnock (Kinsley), whom Burns had lampooned in an earlier satire, 'The Holy Tulzie' (K52).

l. 103. *tidings o' s—lv—t—n*. In the 1787 Edinburgh edition and subsequently Burns changes this (salvation) to d—mn—t—n (damnation). The change accords with the advice Burns was given by Revd Hugh Blair, Professor of Rhetoric and Belles Lettres at Edinburgh University; but Burns ignored almost all of Blair's other advice, and 'damnation' in any case better reflects the emphasis of orthodox preaching.

l. 104. *Hornie*. The Devil.

l. 116. *cantharidian plaisters*. The glossary to the 1787 Edinburgh edition helpfully explains 'cantharidian' as meaning 'made of cantharides': that is, Spanish Fly, the famous aphrodisiac. In the old medicine remedies were often applied by spreading them inside a bandage as a 'plaster'.

l. 118. *the tent*. See note to p. 13, l. 47.

l. 122. ******* opens out his cauld harangues*. The name elided here is that of (George) Smith, minister at Galston (Kinsley). A modernizing 'moderate', whose preaching attended to living a moral life, rather than the state of the listener's soul; orthodox Calvinism rejected mere 'good works' as a means to salvation (see note to p. 95, l. 50).

ll. 128–9. *Of moral pow'rs and reason?* | *His English style*. Smith's sermon draws on the terminology of the Enlightenment, and adopts the more genteel, less impassioned manner of the Anglican church. For the importance of '*reason*' in 'moderate' attitudes, see note to p. 109, l. 112.

l. 131. *SOCRATES or ANTONINE*. Respectively the Athenian philosopher (d. 399 BC) and hero of Plato's dialogues; and Marcus Aurelius Antoninus (AD 121–80), Roman Emperor and Stoic moralist.

26 l. 138. *For *******, frae the water-fit*. The name elided here is that of (William) Peebles, orthodox minister of the Newton parish in Ayr (Kinsley), on the right bank of the river where it enters the sea (hence 'water-fit').

l. 142. *COMMON-SENSE*. This stanza opens by adopting the rhetoric of the orthodox party, for whom Smith's worldly morals are 'poosion'd nostrum'; so 'common-sense' here could name Smith's moderate party in the church, as well as reasonableness in the abstract.

l. 143. *the Cowgate*. In the 1787 Edinburgh edition and subsequently Burns provides a footnote: 'A street so called, which faces the *tent* in ——', i.e. in Mauchline.

l. 145. *Wee ****** neist, the Guard relieves*. The name elided here is that of (Alexander) Miller, assistant minister at St Michael's parish church in Mauchline (Kinsley). More strictly orthodox ministers, including William Peebles (see note to l. 138 above) often claimed (it seems with some justification) that 'moderate' clergy publicly subscribed to the Westminster Confession only because subscription was a condition of a career in the established church, while regarding its doctrines with scepticism in private: Miller, Burns suggests, is one of these. See Kidd, 'Scotland's Invisible Enlightenment', 35, 41f.

l. 154. *Change-house*. 'A small inn or alehouse'; 'perhaps with reference to the changing of horses' for long-distance travellers (*DSL*).

27 l. 181. *the L——'s ain trumpet touts*. Among the many trumpets in the Bible, perhaps the most relevant is that of Revelation 1: 10–11: 'I was in the Spirit on the Lord's day, and heard behind me a great voice, as of a trumpet, Saying, I am Alpha and Omega, the first and the last'. Or, given the way in which this stanza proceeds, Ezekiel 33: 4: 'Then whosoever heareth the sound of the trumpet, and taketh not warning; if the sword come, and take him away, his blood shall be upon his own head'.

l. 184. *Black ****** is na spairan*. The name elided here is that of 'Black' John Russel (Kinsley). Russel was minister at the Old High Kirk in Kilmarnock, a terrifying disciplinarian, and the other target of Burns's 'Holy Tulzie'.

l. 185. *His piercin words, like Highlan swords,* | *Divide the joints an' marrow*. This alludes to Paul's Epistle to the Hebrews 4: 12: 'For the word of God is quick, and powerful, and sharper than any twoedged sword, piercing even to the dividing asunder of soul and spirit, and of the joints and marrow, and is a discerner of the thoughts and intents of the heart'.

27 l. 188 and footnote. *Our vera 'Sauls does harrow'*. In Shakespeare's tragedy, the ghost of Hamlet's father warns him: 'I could a tale unfold whose lightest word | Would harrow up thy soul, freeze thy young blood' (1. 5. 19–20).

29 *Address to the Deil.* K76.

Epigraph. Beelzebub's address to Satan in Book I, ll. 128–9 of *Paradise Lost* (1667).

ll. 1–2. *O Thou, whatever title suit thee! | Auld Hornie, Satan, Nick, or Clootie.* As Kinsley observes, this echoes the address to Jonathan Swift which Alexander Pope (1688–1744) added to *The Dunciad* in the 1729 Variorum edition, listing his friend's various personae: 'O thou! whatever Title please thine ear, | Dean, Drapier, Bickerstaff, or Gulliver!' (Book I, ll. 17–18; Pope 351).

30 l. 19. *like a roaran lion.* The image is from the First Epistle of Peter 5: 8: 'Be sober, be vigilant; because your adversary the Devil, as a roaring lion, walketh about, seeking whom he may devour'.

l. 49. *Let Warlocks grim, an' wither'd Hags.* Witchcraft had long since ceased to be recognized in official legal and religious practice: the Witchcraft Act had been repealed in 1736, and its last victim had been executed in 1727. But it had survived as the object of popular belief, or half-belief. The disruption of dairy production, and male impotence, as described in the following stanzas, were typical of the everyday frustrations ascribed to the malice of neighbours in league with the devil.

31 l. 79. *MASONS' mystic word an' grip.* Freemasonry had been established in Scotland at least since the formation of the Grand Lodge in 1736: Burns joined in 1781 (see also notes to 'The Farewell', below). Aside from its mystical mumbo-jumbo, it functioned as an organization for mutual assistance operating outside but parallel to the systems of family and political patronage that structured eighteenth-century British society, and therefore potentially useful for poorer brothers such as Burns. On first joining a Lodge as an Apprentice, brothers are given secret words and 'grips' (handshakes) in order to identify themselves as such to fellow masons. Although Freemasonry had a somewhat tangential relation to orthodox Christianity, and some rituals may have invoked a figure named 'Lucifer', in this stanza Burns is having fun with the accusation that Freemasons engaged in Devil-worship, not revealing any secrets of the Lodge.

32 l. 101. the *man of Uzz.* Job, 'perfect and upright', and very rich: the Book of Job begins when God puts everything of Job's in Satan's power to prove that His servant does not only obey Him because he is rewarded for it. Satan proceeds to visit every kind of devastation on Job's household, family, and body.

l. 111. *that day MICHAEL did you pierce.* Satan 'first knew pain' when the Archangel Michael cuts him with a sword during the War in Heaven in *Paradise Lost*, Book VI, ll. 325–8.

33 l. 113. *Wad ding a Lallan tongue, or Erse.* That is, would defeat both Scots and Gaelic to express.

The death and dying words of Poor Mailie, the Author's only Pet Yowe. An unco mournfu' Tale. K24. Based on a true incident, though readers will be relieved to know that Mailie in fact survived her fall into a ditch. The precedent for this sort of poem was 'The Last Dying Words of Bonny Heck, a Famous Grey-Hound in the Shire of Fife' by William Hamilton of Gilbertfield (d. 1751), published in the important collection *A Choice Collection of Comic and Serious Scots Poems both ancient and modern. By several hands* (Edinburgh, 1706). According to Kinsley, 'The death and dying words of Poor Mailie' was 'Burns's first significant essay in Scots'. 'Pet' here means quite specifically 'a lamb or sheep which has been hand-reared and kept separate from the flock' (*DSL*).

l. 20. *wicked strings o' hemp or hair.* Mailie is tethered, not because she is a 'pet', but to stop her wandering onto arable ground, an indication that this is an old-style, unenclosed, rural setting: see Leask, *Robert Burns and Pastoral*, 151.

l. 24. *packs of woo'.* A pack is 'a measure of wool, gen. 12 stones Scots weight' (*DSL*).

34 l. 27. *gie.* From the 1793 *Poems*, correcting Kilmarnock's 'gae'.

l. 47. *ridin time.* That is, 'the mating time of animals, esp. sheep' (*DSL*). In the 1787 Edinburgh edition and subsequently Burns substitutes for this line: 'An' warn him, what I winna name'.

35 l. 64. *thou'se get my blather.* Hughoc, useless in Mailie's crisis, is rewarded with almost the only part of a sheep not eaten in eighteenth-century Scotland. 'The bequest of the bladder, a thing of no worth, is a medieval death-bed joke . . . which probably survived in popular tradition' (Kinsley).

Poor Mailie's Elegy. K25. Here, Burns uses the 'Standard Habbie' stanza in its original, elegiac, form, with the last line always ending in 'dead': the stanzas of Robert Sempill's 'The Life and Death of the Piper of Kilbarchan, or the Epitaph of Habbie Simpson' (1690), from which it takes its name, end with the lines '*Hab Simpson's* dead', 'Sen *Habbi's* dead', 'But now he's dead', and so on. Ramsay and Fergusson had also used the stanza for elegies (comic and otherwise) in this form, but, like Burns, for other purposes too.

36 l. 34. *Frae 'yont the TWEED.* That is, Mailie belongs to one of the new breeds, such as the Cheviot, starting to be imported into Scotland from England (the river Tweed marks the border) to improve the wool-yield of the rougher native stock.

l. 43. *DOON.* The river Doon flows past Burns's birthplace, Alloway: see Map.

36 l. 44. *wha on AIRE your chanters tune*. The river Ayr flows past Mauchline, near Burns's farm at Mossgiel: see Map. A chanter is 'that pipe of a bagpipe, with finger-holes on which the melody is played' (*OED*).

To J. S****. K79. The addressee is James Smith (b. 1765), a draper in Mauchline, and one of Burns's best friends there: he collected 41 subscriptions for the Kilmarnock edition. This is Standard Habbie used for the other main purpose to which Ramsay and Fergusson had adapted it, the familiar verse epistle.

Epigraph. From Robert Blair's 1743 poem *The Grave*, ll. 88–90 (slightly altered).

37 l. 19. *fit o' rhyme*. McGuirk notes that Burns may have known Ben Jonson's 'A Fit of Rhyme against Rhyme', poem XXIX in *Underwoods* (1640).

l. 32. *the russet coat*. Russet is 'a coarse homespun woollen cloth of a reddish-brown, grey or neutral colour, formerly used for the dress of peasants and country-folk' (*OED*).

l. 33. *damn'd my fortune to the groat*. *DSL* notes that 'groat-man' was used, in 1795, to mean 'day-labourer, one who originally worked for a groat a day', though Burns was never in this situation.

l. 38. *guid, black prent*. Kinsley notes that the phrase is borrowed from Robert Fergusson, in 'Answer to Mr. J. S.'s Epistle': 'For whan in gude black print I saw thee | Wi' souple gab, | I skirl'd fou loud, "Oh wae befa' thee! | "But thou'rt a daub"' (ll. 3–6; Fergusson 71).

38 l. 59. *th' inglorious dead*. This recalls Thomas Gray's meditation on the graves of the poor in *Elegy Written in a Country Churchyard* (1751): 'Some mute inglorious Milton here may rest, | Some Cromwell guiltless of his Country's Blood' (ll. 59–60; Lonsdale 128).

39 l. 102. *high disdain*. McGuirk suggests this continues the echoes of Gray's *Elegy*, where the rich are requested not to hear 'The short and simple annals of the poor' with 'a disdainful smile' (ll. 32, 31; Lonsdale 123); lines that Burns uses in the epigraph to 'The Cotter's Saturday night'.

40 l. 117. *Luna*. The moon, representing change.

l. 122. *And kneel, ye Pow'rs*. The Kilmarnock edition, and all three subsequent editions published by Creech, open the quotation marks here:

> And kneel, 'Ye *Pow'rs*, and warm implore,

I follow Kinsley in adopting the present reading from Burns's manuscript.

l. 133. *DEMPSTER*. See note to p. 18, l. 73.

l. 134. *A Garter gie to WILLIE PIT*. That is, accession to the elite order of knighthood in the United Kingdom, the Order of the Garter. For 'Willie Pit', see note to p. 16, l. 19.

l. 135. *Cit.* In the eighteenth century, 'cit' (from 'citizen') was 'usually applied, more or less contemptuously, to a townsman as distinguished from a countryman, or to a tradesman or shopkeeper as distinguished from a gentleman' (*OED*).

41 l. 157. *sentimental traces.* 'Trace' is a word just coming into use to mean 'A mark or impression left on the face, the mind etc.': *OED*'s earliest example is from 1809 (6b). It had however been used by John Locke in something like this sense, to mean 'A change in the brain as the result of some mental experience' (*OED* 6d) in his *Essay Concerning Human Understanding* of 1690: 'The memory of Thoughts, is retained by the impressions that are made on the Brain, and the traces there left after such thinking' (Book II, ch. i, §15). Burns uses the phrase again in 'The Vision' l. 55, in describing Coila, his muse.

l. 159. *arioso.* Melodious (as a musical direction; Italian).

l. 161. *gravissimo.* Solemn (as a musical direction; Italian).

l. 165. *hairum-scairum.* 'Reckless, careless, heedless in action' (*OED*).

l. 166. *rambling.* This is changed to 'rattling' in the 1787 and 1793 editions, and then to 'rattlin' in 1794.

A Dream. K113. The monarch's birthday was a major event in the courtly calendar, and was marked by, among other things, a levee (a formal reception), and a birthday ode from the poet laureate (George III's current laureate was Thomas Warton). Burns's poem uses the 'Christ's Kirk on the Green' stanza typically used to describe more boisterous and plebeian occasions: see headnote to 'The Holy Fair', p. 291 above. A tighter rhyme-scheme is used here than in that poem, with only two rhymes (though often rough and ready) in all eight long lines.

42 l. 4. *Bardie.* In the 1793 and 1794 editions, the narrator becomes a slightly less humble-sounding 'Poet', both here and again in l. 76.

l. 23. *YOUR GRACE.* An older mode of address to a monarch, this had only been replaced by 'your Majesty' in Scottish usage at the Act of Union in 1707. Burns thus adopts a style never officially used to address a king of the House of Hanover, which acceded to the British throne in 1714.

ll. 25–6. *There's monie waur been o' the Race, | And aiblins ane been better.* Burns retained a sentimental loyalty to the long-lost cause of the House of Stuart (see notes to 'There'll never be peace till Jamie comes hame' and 'Written on a window in Stirling', pp. 344 and 349). Accordingly, this is usually taken as a reference to Charles Edward Stuart, the 'Bonnie Prince Charlie' who had attempted to win back the throne for his father James, from George's grandfather, in the Jacobite Rebellion of 1745–6. In this case, l. 26 has to mean 'perhaps one *would have* been better', since Charles was never king (at this point, he was living in exile in Rome: he died in early 1788).

43 ll. 34–5. *And now the third part o' the string, | An' less, will gang about it.* This is a reference to the British Empire's massive loss of territory, actual and potential, by the secession of the United States. The Treaty of

Paris which ended the Revolutionary War in 1783 had recognized the new republic's claim to all land east of the Mississippi and south of the Great Lakes.

43 l. 54. *I' the craft some day.* 'Craft', or croft, means the piece of cultivated land attached to the cottage, sometimes called the 'infield'.

l. 57. *Will's a true guid fallow's get.* Pitt was the offspring ('get') of William Pitt the elder, prime minister 1757–61 and again 1766–8. The elder Pitt was generally credited with Britain's successes in the Seven Years War, and respected for refusing ennoblement as reward for his services.

l. 59. *he intends to pay your debt.* See note to p. 19, l. 119.

44 l. 67. *dissection.* The bodies of the hanged were made available to surgeons for dissection in anatomy lessons.

l. 70. *your QUEEN.* George had married Charlotte of Mecklenburg-Strelitz (1744–1818), daughter of a German ducal family, the year after his accession to the throne in 1760.

l. 77. *Thae bonie Bairntime.* In her first 22 years of marriage Charlotte bore 15 children.

l. 82. *young Potentate o' W—.* George, Prince of Wales (1762–1830). As this stanza suggests, the heir to the throne was famously dedicated to dissipation.

l. 88. *brak Diana's pales.* Diana was the Roman goddess of chastity, so breaking into her sanctuary is a figure for sexual licence.

l. 89. *rattl'd dice wi' Charlie.* That is, with Charles James Fox MP, leader of the Opposition, for whom see notes to p. 19, ll. 109 and 113–14. His friendship with opposition politicians was another reason for the profound alienation between the Prince of Wales and his father.

l. 97 and footnote. *funny, queer Sir John.* As the footnote indicates, a reference to the loose-living Sir John Falstaff, companion to the young Prince Hal in Shakespeare's *Henry IV* plays. On acceding to the throne at the end of *Henry IV Part II*, Hal rejects his old companion, and goes on to become the hero-king who defeats the French at the battle of Agincourt in *Henry V*. Queer: here, 'amusing, funny, entertaining' (*DSL*).

45 l. 100. *right rev'rend O—.* The second son, Prince Frederick, Duke of York (1763–1827). The Hanoverian kings remained rulers of their native principality in Germany, retaining their historic rights and privileges there: George exercised one of these when he had Frederick, at six months old, 'elected' Prince-Bishop of Osnaburg (Osnabrück) to secure the substantial revenues attached to this position.

l. 101. *the lawn-sleeve.* Lawn was a type of fine linen used for the sleeves of a bishop's dress.

l. 102. *a ribban at your lug.* That is, the black cockade worn in the hats of officers in the Hanoverian army, in which Frederick was a Major-General.

ll. 104–5. *As ye disown yon paughty dog,* | *That bears the Keys of Peter.* That is, the Pope. The Bishopric of Osnaburg alternated between Protestant and Catholic incumbents, and Frederick of course was the former, and thus free to marry. His religious title did not inhibit him from adopting the same debauched lifestyle as his elder brother, and Burns's concern in the following lines is ironic. Frederick made the expected marriage with a German princess in 1791.

l. 109. *Young, royal TARRY-BREEKS.* Prince William Henry (1765–1837), the third son, who had been sent into the navy in 1779 (hence 'tarry-breeks': wooden ships were sealed with tar), 'chiefly to prevent him from falling under the influence of his eldest brother' (*DNB*). In the winter of 1785–6, William, at this point a lieutenant, was staying in Portsmouth with Sir Henry Martin, Commissioner to the Navy there, and fell in love with his host's daughter, Sarah: this is the 'Amour' referred to in Burns's footnote. William was keen to marry but the distance in rank made this impossible and they were quickly separated.

l. 113. *hang out.* 'To suspend (a sign, colours, or the like) . . . to display as a sign or signal' (*OED*): in this context, like a signal-flag from the mast of a ship.

l. 119. *Ye royal Lasses dainty.* There were six princesses in the royal brood.

ll. 123–4. *Kings are unco scant ay,* | *An' German-Gentles are but sma'.* In the event, Princess Charlotte married the King of Württemberg, and Princess Elizabeth married the Duke of Hesse-Homburg; Princess Mary married her cousin the Duke of Gloucester, and the other three never married.

46 *The Vision.* K62. This poem is divided into two 'duans': as Burns's footnote explains, a term taken from James Macpherson (see note to p. 5, l. 27). 'Cath-Loda', a poem in Macpherson's 1765 *Works of Ossian* Vol. II (Macpherson 305–20), is divided into three.

Duan First

l. 2. *roaring.* The sound of curling stones on ice.

ll. 3–4. *hunger'd Maukin taen her way* | *To kail-yards green.* As Kinsley notes, an image borrowed from James Thomson's 'Winter' (1726): 'The hare, | Though timorous of heart . . . the garden seeks, | Urged on by fearless want' (ll. 257–8, 260–1; Thomson 135–6).

l. 16. *The auld, clay biggin.* The houses of the poor were often at least partly built of clay plastered on a timber base. The cottage in which Burns was born was of this type; by 1786 Burns was living in the more substantial stone farmhouse at Mossgiel.

47 l. 37. *the string the snick did draw.* From outside, the latch was typically lifted by a string passing through a hole in the door.

l. 49. *Holly-boughs.* Coila will crown the speaker with holly as her parting gesture at l. 224. 'The Vision' borrows its title, though little else, from a

poem by Allan Ramsay, which masquerades as a sixteenth-century Scottish
poem among the genuine sixteenth-century Scottish poems he collected
in *The Ever Green* (1724). Coila's holly may be an allusion to the title of
Ramsay's collection.

47   l. 55. *A 'hare-brain'd, sentimental trace'.* Burns is quoting from his own
verse, namely 'To J. Smith', l. 157 (p. 41). 'Trace' is used again in some-
thing like the same sense in l. 147 of the present poem.

48   l. 61. *a tartan sheen.* The wearing of tartan in the Highlands had been
proscribed by law after the defeat of the Jacobites in 1746, because of its
association with the rebel clans; a proscription only recently repealed, in
1782. But tartan had been appropriated as a signifier of Scottishness gen-
erally in the aftermath of the Union of 1707, for example in Allan Ramsay's
poem 'Tartana, or the Plaid' (in the *Poems* of 1721; Ramsay Vol. I, 27–37).

l. 63. *BESS.* Usually identified with Elizabeth Paton, a servant at Burns's
father's farm at Lochlie, and the mother of Burns's first child, also
Elizabeth, born in May 1785 (see also note to p. 113, ll. 37–72). By then
Burns was already in love with Jean Armour, who would be his lover by the
end of the year, and would bear him twins little more than a month after
the publication of the Kilmarnock *Poems* in July 1786. In the Edinburgh
edition of 1787, and subsequently, 'my BESS, I ween' is replaced by 'my
bonny JEAN'.

ll. 79–80. *DOON . . . IRWINE.* The Doon and Irvine are rivers in
Ayrshire, and form the borders of Kyle, Burns's district: see Maps.

l. 81. *Auld, hermit AIRE staw thro' his woods.* In its reaches above and
below Mauchline the river Ayr flows through a winding, thickly-wooded
ravine.

l. 86. *An ancient BOROUGH.* Ayr, a Royal Burgh since 1205.

ll. 88–90. *a Race, | To ev'ry nobler virtue bred, | And polish'd grace.* These
lines seem to anticipate the seven stanzas that continue Duan First in the
Edinburgh edition of 1787 and subsequently, which offer examples of this
noble 'Race'; suggesting that Kinsley is right to say that these stanzas were
not a later composition, but a deleted section of the original draft.

> By stately tow'r, or palace fair,
> Or ruins pendent in the air,
> Bold stems of Heroes, here and there,
>   I could discern;
> Some seem'd to muse, some seem'd to dare,
>   With feature stern.
>
> My heart did glowing transport feel,
> To see a Race heroic wheel,
> And brandish round the deep-dy'd steel
>   In sturdy blows;
> While back-recoiling seem'd to reel
>   Their Suthron foes.

His COUNTRY'S SAVIOUR, mark him well!
Bold *Richardton's* heroic swell;
The chief on *Sark* who glorious fell,
        In high command;
And *He* whom ruthless Fates expel
        His native land.

There, where a sceptr'd *Pictish* shade
Stalk'd round his ashes lowly laid,
I mark'd a martial Race, pourtray'd
        In colours strong;
Bold, soldier-featur'd, undismay'd
        They strode along.

Thro' many a wild, romantic grove,
Near many a hermit-fancy'd cove,
(Fit haunts for Friendship or for Love,
        In musing mood)
An *aged Judge*, I saw him rove,
        Dispensing good.

With deep-struck, reverential awe,
The learned Sire and Son I saw,
To Nature's God and Nature's law
        They gave their lore,
This, all its source and end to draw,
        That, to adore.

Brydon's brave Ward I well could spy,
Beneath old *Scotia's* smiling eye;
Who call'd on Fame, low standing by,
        To hand him on,
Where many a Patriot-name on high
        And Hero shone.

In a series of footnotes, Burns identifies the 'Race heroic' with the Wallace family; 'His COUNTRY'S SAVIOUR' with William Wallace (d. 1305), a leader in Scotland's Wars of Independence from England (the 'Suthron'); Richardton with Adam Wallace of Richardton, 'cousin to the immortal preserver of Scottish independence'; and 'The chief on *Sark* who glorious fell' with 'Wallace, Laird of Craigie, who was second in command, under Douglas Earl of Ormond, at the famous battle on the banks of Sark, fought *anno* 1448. That glorious victory was principally owing to the judicious conduct and intrepid valour of the gallant Laird of Craigie, who died of his wounds after the action.' The earliest records of the Wallaces as a landed family relate to Ayrshire estates (Riccarton—'Richardton'—and Craigie are both near Kilmarnock), though the hero William held land further north, in Renfrewshire. The Sark is a stream on the border, and Craigie's battle was with an invading English army. On Burns's Wallace-worship see the letter of 2 August 1787 to

John Moore in Appendix 1, p. 260. A direct descendant of Craigie, Mrs Frances Dunlop (neé Wallace) was to become an important patron and correspondent of Burns. '*He* whom ruthless Fates expel | His native land' does not get a footnote: Kinsley suggests this refers to Mrs Dunlop's eldest son, in 'exile' in England after selling the Craigie estate to pay off his debts.

The 'sceptr'd Pictish shade', another footnote explains, is 'Coilus King of the Picts, from whom the district of Kyle is said to take its name' and who 'lies buried, as tradition says, near the family-seat of the Montgomeries of Coilsfield, where his burial-place is still shown' (for the Montgomeries see note to p. 17, l. 57). The 'wild, romantic grove' is the Ayr gorge at 'Barskimming, the seat of the Lord Justice Clerk': that is, Sir Thomas Miller, an improving landlord as well as a judge. The 'learned *Sire* and *Son*' are 'the late Doctor and present Professor Stewart': Dugald Stewart (1753–1828) attended to his father Matthew's duties as Professor of Mathematics at the University of Edinburgh in the years leading to the latter's death in 1785, when the son took up the chair of Moral Philosophy there. Their country house was at Catrine, a couple of miles outside Mauchline. Finally, '*Brydon's* brave Ward' is named as 'Colonel Fullarton': another improving local landlord, William Fullarton (1754–1808) had been conducted on the Grand Tour by Patrick Brydone (1741–1818), author of *A Tour through Sicily and Malta*. Fullarton had distinguished himself in the war with Mysore in India in 1782–3, leading a regiment raised on his Ayrshire estate.

Duan Second

49 l. 104. *many a light, aerial band*. As McGuirk suggests, this may be based on the 'machinery' of spirits deployed by Pope in 'The Rape of the Lock', including 'The light Militia of the lower Sky' (canto I, l. 42; Pope 219).

l. 111. *the Patriot*. In the rhetoric of eighteenth-century British politics, this means the representative who refuses the personal advantages offered by the executive in return for his support (cf. note to p. 16, l. 25) and holds ministers to account in the name of the nation.

l. 120. *And grace the hand*. In the Edinburgh edition of 1787, and subsequently, another extra stanza is added here:

> 'And when the Bard, or hoary Sage,
> 'Charm or instruct the future age,
> 'They bind the wild, Poetric rage
> 'In energy,
> 'Or point the inconclusive page
> 'Full on the eye.

l. 121. *FULLARTON*. Colonel William Fullarton (see note to ll. 88–90 above).

l. 122. *DEMPSTER*. See note to p. 18, l. 73.

ll. 123–4. *BEATTIE sung* | *His 'Minstrel lays'*. James Beattie (1735–1803), Professor of Moral Philosophy and Logic at Marischal College, Aberdeen. Beattie was highly influential on British Romantic culture, starting with Burns, as author of *The Minstrel: or, The Progress of Genius*, a poem in two books (1771, 1774) on the education of a poet.

l. 126. *The Sceptic's bays*. The sceptic is David Hume (1711–76). Beattie was also celebrated for his *Essay on the Nature and Immutability of Truth* (1770), a scathing (and unconvincing) rebuttal of the scepticism of Hume's *Treatise of Human Nature* (1739–40).

l. 129. *Hind*. 'A farm servant, an agricultural labourer' (*OED*).

50 ll. 135–6. *to meliorate the plain,* | *With tillage-skill*. The introduction of modern agricultural techniques, ongoing in Burns's Scotland, gets its own muse.

l. 151. *COILA*. In the stanzas added to Duan First in the Edinburgh edition of 1787, Burns will cite the legendary origins of the name of the district of Kyle in a Pictish king, Coilus (see note to ll. 88–90 above); the name of Burns's muse also recalls the Water of Coyle, a tributary of the Ayr.

l. 153. *the Campbell's, chiefs of fame*. Since the fourteenth century, a branch of the Campbell family had owned the extensive Loudon estate in Ayrshire, which included Mossgiel, the farm Burns was working with his brother in 1786. As 'chiefs of fame' Burns may be thinking of the Dukes of Argyll, chiefs of the Clan Campbell and decisive agents of government power in the West Highlands. Loudon was an Earldom in its own right, and the fourth Earl had fought both against the Jacobites and in North America in the Seven Years War; but the fifth Earl got himself into financial difficulties, and shot himself in April 1786, so that Burns's ultimate feudal superior at the time of the Kilmarnock edition was 6-year-old Flora Campbell, the fifth Earl's daughter.

51 l. 200. *Thomson's landscape-glow*. James Thomson (1700–48), Scottish-born, London-based author of the nature-descriptive *The Seasons* (1726–46).

l. 202. *Shenstone's art*. For Shenstone see note to Preface, p. 283.

l. 203. *Gray*. Thomas Gray (1716–71), author of elegies, odes, and bardic verse.

52 l. 213. *Potosi's mine*. The silver mine in what is now Bolivia, a source of massive wealth for the Spanish Empire.

53 *Halloween*. K73. Another adaptation of the 'Christ's Kirk on the Green' stanza used in 'The Holy Fair' and 'A Dream'. In the first stanza, and in the first four lines of stanzas III and VI, Burns does not rhyme the long lines in the usual way, but gives them each an internal rhyme of their own.

Epigraph. From Oliver Goldsmith (d. 1774), *The Deserted Village* (1770), ll. 251–4 (Lonsdale 686). Burns has capitalized the initials of 'rich' and 'proud', and changed Goldsmith's 'blessings' to more Burnsian 'pleasures'.

53 l. 2 and footnote. *Cassillis Downans*. Cassillis House, seat of the Kennedy family, stands at the sharp bend in the river Doon near Maybole. Nearby Dowan's Hill is topped by the remains of an ancient hill-fort, which attracted associations with supernatural activity.

l. 5 and footnote. *Colean*. In 1786 Culzean Castle (pronounced more or less as Burns spells it), another Kennedy property, on the coastal cliff-top west of Maybole, was in the process of being transformed to designs by Robert Adam on the orders of the tenth Earl of Cassillis. The caves below the castle referred to in the footnote had been extensively used by the ninth Earl for storing contraband, landed on the adjacent beaches.

l. 12. *Where BRUCE ance rul'd*. Robert de Brus became Earl of Carrick (that part of Ayrshire south of the river Doon) by marriage in 1271; his son Robert was crowned King of Scots in 1306, and went on to (eventually) defeat the English and re-establish Scotland's independence.

54 l. 20. *fine*. That is, in their finery.

l. 32. *fell aff the drift*. That is, fell off the herd, got left behind.

56 l. 96. *kiln*. A structure for drying grain, consisting of 'a lattice-work of beams supporting a bed of straw with the grain strewed upon it, and a lower chamber containing the fire' (*DSL*). Merran drops her ball of blue thread from the upper chamber into the fire chamber or 'kiln-pot' below (the '*pat*' of l. 102).

57 l. 127. *the Sherra-moor*. The battle of Sheriffmuir, near Stirling, between a government army under the Duke of Argyle and Jacobite rebels led by the Earl of Mar, in 1715. Inconclusive on the day, that was a bad enough result for the Jacobites to ensure the collapse of the rebellion a few months later.

58 l. 139. *Achmacalla*. As Kinsley comments, 'a place-name concocted to make the rhyme'.

59 l. 163. *lord Lenox' march*. A regimental march of the 25th Regiment of Foot, eventually to become the King's Own Scottish Borderers, and since 1762 under the command of Lord George Henry Lennox. The tune is in Sir Herbert Maxwell, ed., *The Lowland Scots Regiments* (Glasgow, 1918), 338.

60 l. 201. *the Stack he faddom't thrice*. For 'faddom't' Burns's 1787 glossary gives only 'fathomed', but *DSL* confirms that faddom means 'to encircle with the outstretched arms' as a means of measuring a quantity of e.g. peat, but also 'specif. of corn-stacks at *Halloween* to call up the apparition of one's future spouse'.

l. 202. *timmer-propt for thrawin*. Kinsley suggests 'propped with lengths of timber to prevent warping'.

62 l. 240. *Mar's-year*. 1715: see note to l. 127 above.

The auld Farmer's new-year-morning Salutation to his auld Mare, Maggie, on giving her the accustomed ripp of Corn to hansel in the new-year. K75. A hansel or handsel is 'a gift bestowed to commemorate an inaugural occasion, event, or season, e.g. the beginning of the year' (*DSL*); to hansel in the New Year is to give such a gift. Nigel Leask points out that Burns's title alludes to *The Farmer's New-Year Gift to his Countrymen, Heritors, and Farmers, for the Year 1757* by landowner Sir Archibald Grant of Monymusk, a work embodying a paternalistic relation between landowner and tenant which Burns transfers to that between master and horse (Leask, *Robert Burns and Pastoral*, 158).

63 l. 22. *fifty mark*. A mark was a unit of currency equivalent to 13*s*. 4*d*.; so 50 mark was £33 6*s*. 8*d*.

l. 35. *KYLE-STEWART*. Kyle district is historically divided by the river Ayr into Kyle Stewart to its north, and Kyle Regis or King's Kyle to its south: see Map.

l. 44. *Fairs*. That is, country fairs, market days.

64 l. 49. *mellow*. That is, tipsy.

l. 53. *pay't them hollow*. In the modern idiom, beat them hollow.

l. 55. *droop-rumpl't, hunter cattle*. This reading is from the 1787 Edinburgh edition, correcting the Kilmarnock text's 'droot-'. Hunters are horses bred for the recreational purposes of the gentry, not working horses like Maggie.

l. 57. *Scotch mile*. Its abolition as a standard measure by the Scottish parliament in 1685 meant that this had no statutory definition, but *OED* suggests 1976 yards, as opposed to the 1760 yards of the English mile.

l. 65. *sax rood*. A rood is a quarter-acre, so Maggie could plough an acre and a half in her eight-hour day.

ll. 75–6. *I gied thy cog a wee-bit heap | Aboon the timmer*. That is, heaped the grain in your (wooden) tub above the level of the rim.

65 l. 85. *My Pleugh*. That is, my plough *team*. These lines reflect the transitional stage reached by agricultural 'improvement' in Burns's Ayrshire. Horses, the faster, more specialized beast of burden, have replaced oxen; but the plough is still the old, heavy, wooden one, requiring four horses to pull it (l. 86), not the new lightweight iron one, which required only two.

l. 106. *To some hain'd rig*. The Kilmarnock edition glosses 'hain' as 'to save, to spare', but here it is used in a more specific sense: 'to enclose or protect a field or wood by a hedge or fence; to preserve grassland from cattle for hay or winter pasture' (*DSL*).

The Cotter's Saturday night. K72. For this poem Burns adopts the verse form invented by Edmund Spenser for his allegorical epic *The Faerie Queene* (1590, 1596). The Spenserian stanza had been revived in the eighteenth century, and used for widely varying purposes by many of the poets admired by Burns: by William Shenstone in 'The School-Mistress' (1737, enlarged 1742); by James Thomson in *The Castle of Indolence* (1748); and by James Beattie in *The Minstrel* (1770, 1774). The most important precedent for 'The Cotter's Saturday night', however, was Robert Fergusson's 'The Farmer's Ingle' (published posthumously in 1779), which used a simplified Spenserian stanza for a sympathetic description, in Scots, of evening in a rural cottage (Fergusson 136–40).

A 'cotter' or cottar rented a few acres of land on which to grow food for himself and his family; he paid rent in the form of labour for the land-owner. This class was rapidly vanishing from lowland Scotland in 1786, as such patches of land were incorporated into larger units farmed commer-cially by tenants employing waged labour where they could afford to do so. The domestic piety depicted in the poem certainly reflects the house-hold in which Burns grew up, but the family were always tenants, working substantial farms of between 70 and 120 acres.

The poem is inscribed to Robert Aiken (1739–1807), the prosperous Ayr solicitor who gathered almost a quarter (145) of the subscriptions that made the Kilmarnock edition possible. In a letter of early 1786 to John Kennedy, factor to the Earl of Dumfries at Cumnock (and brother-in-law of Burns's Mauchline friend Gavin Hamilton), Burns describes Aiken as now '[m]y chief Patron'; and enclosed with his next letter, at Kennedy's request, a copy of this poem (L21, 17 February; and L22, 3 March).

65 *Epigraph*. Thomas Gray, *Elegy Written in a Country Churchyard* (1751) ll. 29–32 (Lonsdale 122–3).

66 l. 18. *weary, o'er the moor, his course does hameward bend*. Echoes ll. 3–4 of Gray's *Elegy*: 'The plowman homeward plods his weary way, | And leaves the world to darkness and to me' (Lonsdale 117).

l. 26. *Does a' his weary kiaugh and care beguile*. In the later Edinburgh editions of 1793 and 1794 Burns changed this line to 'Does a' his weary carking cares beguile'. *DSL* suggests 'kiaugh' or 'kauch' is a specifically south-western word, from Dumfries and Galloway: its use here is the only example offered from an Ayrshire context.

l. 29. *At Service out, amang the Farmers roun'*. The older children are in full-time paid employment on neighbouring farms. Especially in areas like Ayrshire, farm-servants '[o]ften came of cottar families . . . [T]hrough life, the child of a cottar bound to give service for some days in the year, yet with that precious if insecure title to land, would move into full-time serv-ice for a period before marrying finally to the cottar pos-ition' (Gray, 'The Social Impact of Agrarian Change', 54). Burns avoided this kind of service as a child: see the biographical letter to John Moore of 2 August 1787 reproduced in Appendix 1, p. 260.

67 l. 63. *Rake*. That is, 'a fashionable or stylish man of dissolute or promis-cuous habits' (*OED*), which habits usually require ready cash, though the young Burns laughingly uses 'rakish' of himself in his song 'O leave novels, ye Mauchline belles' (included in this volume).

69 l. 106. *Those strains that once did sweet in ZION glide*. The Psalms of David.

ll. 111–13. *Dundee . . . Or plaintive Martyrs . . . Or noble Elgin*. The Church of Scotland published its authorized metrical translation of the Psalms in 1650, using a restricted number of verse-forms to facilitate setting them to music. 'Common Metre' verses have lines of eight syllables, then six, then eight, then six. 'Dundee', 'Martyrs', and 'Elgin' are three of the many tunes to which Common Metre psalms could be sung.

l. 115. *Italian trills*. The displacement of native styles of singing and music generally by fashionable Italian modes provoked great displeasure in eighteenth-century Scotland and England alike. See, for example, Robert Fergusson's 1773 'Elegy, on the Death of Scots Music': 'Now foreign sonnets bear the gree, | And crabbit queer variety | Of sound fresh sprung frae *Italy*, | A bastard breed!' (ll. 49–54; Fergusson 39).

l. 121. *Amalek's ungracious progeny*. Amalek, a Duke of Edom, is defeated by Joshua in Exodus 17; but his descendants keep coming back for more, on and off, throughout the first half of the Old Testament.

ll. 122–3. *the royal Bard . . . Beneath the stroke of Heaven's avenging ire*. When King David, putative author of the Psalms, gets another man's wife pregnant, and arranges for her husband to die in battle, God punishes him by having the child die (2 Samuel 11–12).

l. 124. *Job's pathetic plaint*. For Job see note to p. 32, l. 101.

l. 126. *other Holy Seers*. That is, one of the other sixteen books of the Prophets in the Protestant Bible.

l. 127. *the Christian Volume*. The New Testament.

l. 130. *whereon to lay His head*. Echoes Matthew 8: 20 and Luke 9: 58: 'And Jesus saith unto him, The foxes have holes, and the birds of the air have nests; but the Son of man hath not where to lay his head'. These first four lines evoke the 'theme' of the four gospels (Matthew, Mark, Luke, John).

l. 131. *How His first followers and servants sped*. As recorded in Acts.

l. 132. *The Precepts sage they wrote to many a land*. The Epistles of Paul, James, Peter, John, and Jude.

l. 133. *he, who lone in Patmos*. It was on the island of Patmos that St John the Divine had the visions recorded in the Book of Revelation, the last book of the New Testament. John sees 'an angel standing in the sun' (l. 134) at 19: 17; the fate of Babylon (l. 135) is the theme of the preceding chapter.

70 l. 138 and footnote. *Hope 'springs exulting on triumphant wing'*. As Burns notes, from Alexander Pope, *Windsor-Forest* (1713): 'See! from the Brake the whirring Pheasant springs, | And mounts exulting on triumphant Wings' (ll. 111–12). The pheasant is shot in the following couplet (Pope 199).

l. 140. *uncreated rays*. Kinsley notes an echo of Thomson's God in 'Summer' (1727): 'How shall I then attempt to sing of Him | Who, Light Himself, in uncreated light | Invested deep, dwells awfully retired | From mortal eye' (ll. 175–8; Thomson 42); and that Thomson is himself echoing the more convoluted formulation of the same idea at the start of *Paradise Lost*, Book III.

70 l. 142. *hymning their CREATOR'S praise*. Kinsley suggests that this echoes the celestial choir's celebration of the creation in *Paradise Lost* (1667): 'And touch't thir Golden Harps, & hymning prais'd | God and his works, Creatour him they sung' (Book VII, ll. 258–9).

l. 153. *His Book of Life*. See Paul's Epistle to the Philippians 4: 3: 'And I entreat thee also, true yokefellow, help those women which laboured with me in the gospel . . . and with other my fellowlabourers, whose names are in the book of life'.

ll. 158–9. *HE who stills the raven's clam'rous nest, | And decks the lily fair in flow'ry pride*. The conjunction suggests that Burns has in mind Luke's account of the Sermon on the Mount: 'Consider the ravens: for they neither sow nor reap; which neither have storehouse nor barn; and God feedeth them: how much more are ye better than the fowls?' (12: 24); 'Consider the lilies how they grow; they toil not, they spin not; and yet I say unto you, that Solomon in all his glory was not arrayed like one of these' (12: 27). Matthew's version (6: 26–9) doesn't mention ravens. Luke, and Burns, may also be remembering Job 38: 41: 'Who provideth for the raven his food? when his young ones cry unto God, they wander for lack of meat.'

l. 163. *From scenes like these, old SCOTIA'S grandeur springs*. Kinsley notes another echo of Thomson's 'Summer', this time of lines added in the 1744 edition of *The Seasons*: 'A simple scene! yet hence Britannia sees | Her solid grandeur rise' (ll. 423–4; Thomson 48). But the grandeur Thomson celebrates is political and economic, not moral, and the 'simple scene' is one of sheep-shearing, not prayer; his point being that wool exports were still, in 1744, the basis of Britain's material prosperity, as they had been since the Middle Ages.

l. 165. *Princes and lords are but the breath of kings*. Kinsley notes the echo of Goldsmith's *Deserted Village*: 'Princes and lords may flourish or may fade; | A breath can make them, as a breath has made; | But a bold peasantry, their country's pride, | When once destroy'd, can never be supply'd' (ll. 51–6; Lonsdale 678).

l. 166. *'An honest man's the noble work of GOD.'* Kinsley notes that Burns is quoting, and altering, Pope's *Essay on Man* Epistle IV here: 'A Wit's a feather, and a Chief a rod; | An honest Man's the noblest work of God' (ll. 246–7; Pope 543).

71 ll. 176–8. *Luxury's contagion . . . A virtuous Populace*. Burns here articulates an opposition at the core of the eighteenth-century critique of modern commercial society, inherited ultimately from Italian Renaissance political thinking. Commerce and empire enrich a nation, but their very material wealth ('luxury') morally weakens citizens by withdrawing them from the exercise of public duties ('virtue') into the enjoyment of merely personal pleasures. This ultimately allows political power to be gathered up by a single person (a 'tyrant'), so that citizens lose their liberties altogether. But the 'citizens' with which this theory is typically concerned are the land-owning and thus enfranchised elite who have public duties to neglect in the first place. Burns's lines here ascribe 'virtue' to the

unenfranchised poor instead, who, since *they* are not being enriched by commerce and empire, are not in danger of being corrupted either.

l. 181. *the patriotic tide*. 'Patriotic' names something more specific than 'loving one's country' here: in the rhetoric described in the previous note, the 'patriot' is one who stands up to the 'tyrant'. See l. 111 of 'The Vision' and note (p. 302), and the equation of Wallace and George Washington in the 'Ode on General Washington's Birthday': the American rebels understood themselves as 'patriots' in just this sense.

l. 182. *unhappy WALLACE' heart*. For William Wallace, see note to p. 48, ll. 88–90. 'Unhappy' in the old sense of 'unfortunate, unlucky, ill-fated; miserable in lot or circumstances' (*OED*): Wallace was betrayed, captured by the English king Edward I, then hanged, drawn, and quartered as a traitor. Kinsley points out that Thomson uses 'unhappy' of the 'Great patriot-hero' Wallace in a pair of lines (ll. 900–1) added to 'Autumn' in 1744 (Thomson 113).

l. 189. *her Ornament* and *Guard!*. Kinsley finds an echo of lines added to Thomson's 'Winter' in *The Seasons* of 1744: 'O thou, whose wisdom, solid yet refined, | Whose patriot virtues . . . Give thee with pleasing dignity to shine | At once the guardian, ornament, and joy | Of polished life' (ll. 656–7, 661–3; Thomson 146). The addressee is Lord Chesterfield; the speaker is 'the Rural Muse'.

To a Mouse. K69.

72 ll. 7–8. *Man's dominion | Has broken Nature's social union*. Kinsley finds the latter phrase in a related context in Pope's *Essay on Man*, Epistle III, where the speaker advises learning from the building skills of ants and bees: 'Here too all forms of social union find, | And hence let Reason, late, instruct Mankind: | Here subterranean works and cities see; | There towns aerial on the waving tree' (ll. 179–82; Pope 531). But perhaps more relevant is William Warburton's note to just this section of Pope's poem in his 1751 edition, which denounces the misinterpretation of the Bible which has allowed man to regard 'the whole animal creation . . . as being created for no use of their own, but for his only; and therefore treated them with the utmost barbarity. . . . It became one [i.e. Pope] who adhered to the Scripture account of Man's dominion to reprove this abuse of it' (59–60). See also notes to p. 116, ll. 19 and 22.

l. 29. *coulter*. The blade at the front of the plough, making the first, vertical, cut into the ground.

ll. 39–40. *The best laid schemes o' Mice an' Men, | Gang aft agley*. As Kinsley points out, the famous moral of this poem echoes a (rather more specific) sentiment in *The Grave* (1743), a widely read poem of the 'graveyard' school by Scottish minister Robert Blair (1699–1746): 'The best concerted Schemes Men lay for Fame | Die fast away' (ll. 185–6).

73 ll. 47–8. *forward, tho' I canna see, | I guess an' fear*. Kinsley notes that the contrast of the final stanza is borrowed from Samuel Johnson's philosophical tale *The History of Rasselas, Prince of Abyssinia* (1759), where the hero

asks, 'What . . . makes the difference between man and all the rest of the animal creation?' and finds the source of humanity's distinguishing unhappiness in the fact that 'I sometimes shrink at evils recollected, and sometimes start at evils anticipated' (ch. II). But as Carol McGuirk has observed, this conclusion is contradicted by what has been said of the mouse in the rest of the poem: it *has* been looking forward, it *has* been 'anticipating evil', in the shape of 'weary *Winter* comin fast' (l. 26); this is precisely why it was building a nest (*Robert Burns and the Sentimental Era*, 9).

73 *Epistle to Davie, a Brother Poet.* K51. David Siller (1760–1830) had been a teacher at Tarbolton, the nearest village to Burns's father's last farm at Lochlie; by 1786 he was a grocer in Irvine. A poet and a fiddler, he had been like Burns a member of the Tarbolton Batchelor's Club (see Introduction to this volume).

This poem uses the complex 'Cherrie and the Slae' stanza, so named after a poem in this form published in 1597 by Alexander Montgomerie (d. 1598), one of a circle of poets at the court of James VI. Burns would have found this poem in Volume II of Ramsay's anthology *The Ever-Green: being a collection of Scots Poems, wrote by the ingenious before 1600* (1724). He would also have come across Ramsay's own use of this form for half-serious verse epistle (e.g. 'To the Right Honourable, the Town-Council of Edinburgh'; 'To the Whin-Bush Club') in his 1721 *Poems* (Ramsay Vol. I, 208–9, 211–12).

l. 1. *BEN-LOMOND*. The southernmost high summit of the Scottish Highlands, due north of Ayrshire, across the Firth of Clyde.

l. 19. *countless thousands*. That is, on an income of many thousands of pounds per annum.

74 l. 25. *'Mair spier na, nor fear na'*. Burns quotes from the last four short lines (the 'wheel' of a 'Cherrie and the Slae' stanza) that close Ramsay's 'A Poet's Wish: An Ode' (in the 1721 *Poems*). The wish is for life and health to continue composing verse, expressed to the Oracle of Apollo, and the stanza quoted is the Oracle's reply: 'Mair speer na, and fear na, | But set thy Mind to rest, | Aspire ay still high'r ay, | And always hope the best' (ll. 53–6; Ramsay Vol. I, 244).

l. 29. *kilns*. Structures for drying grain: see note to p. 56, l. 96.

l. 55. *we'll time till't*. The Kilmarnock edition has no apostrophe in 'we'll': it is inserted in one of the two printings of the 1787 editions, disappears in 1793, and reappears in 1794. 'Well *timed* till't' (of the rhyme to the tune) would make good sense; but 'time' here is the verb in an old intransitive usage meaning 'to keep time to' (*OED* 3c), so I adopt 'we'll' here.

75 ll. 58–9. *It's no in wealth like Lon'on Bank, | To purchase peace and rest*. This perhaps recalls, to make a rather different point, Adam Smith's distinction between the rewards appropriate for industry, and for benevolence: 'What reward is most proper for promoting the practice of truth, justice, and humanity? The confidence, the esteem, and love of those we live with.

Humanity does not desire to be great, but to be beloved. It is not in being rich that truth and justice would rejoice, but in being trusted and believed, recompenses which those virtues must almost always acquire' (Smith, *Theory of Moral Sentiments*, 166–7).

76 l. 107. *Ye hae your MEG*. Siller's sweetheart was Margaret Orr, a servant at Stair House, twelve miles south-east of Irvine.

l. 121. *Her dear idea brings relief, | And solace to my breast*. Kinsley notes the echo of Shenstone's pastoral 'Elegy IX': 'But come, my friend, with taste, with science blest, | Restore thy dear idea to my breast' (ll. 45, 47). Shenstone's poem, like Burns's, praises love and friendship over the pursuit of wealth, though Shenstone's 'dear idea' is of the friend, not the lover (Shenstone Vol. I, 36).

77 l. 131. *Had number'd out my weary days*. Kinsley observes that the phrase recalls Laurence Sterne's *Sentimental Journey* (1768): 'Sweet pliability of man's spirit, that can at once surrender itself to illusions, which cheat expectation and sorrow of their weary moments!—long—long since had ye number'd out my days, had I not trod so great a part of them upon this enchanted ground' (87). The illusions Yorick celebrates are those of the imagination, not love.

l. 138. *tenebrific*. That is, 'dark, gloomy' (*OED*), but this seems to be Burns's coinage (from the older 'tenebrificous').

l. 145. *Phœbus and the famous Nine*. That is, Phoebus Apollo, Roman god of (among other things), music and poetry, and in this role leader of the nine Muses, goddesses who inspire the various arts.

l. 147. *My spavet Pegasus*. The winged horse of Greek mythology had become an image of poetry itself.

The Lament. Occasioned by the unfortunate issue of a friend's amour. K93. The subtitle's disclaimer notwithstanding, this poem has for its biographical context Burns's own enforced separation from a pregnant Jean Armour in early 1786; a situation unresolved when the Kilmarnock edition went to press (see Introduction to this volume, and the biographical letter to John Moore of 2 August 1787 reproduced in Appendix 1, p. 266).

The stanza form here is a version of the medieval 'ballade' stanza used by Chaucer and, in Scotland, Robert Henryson and William Dunbar. James VI, in his *Essayes of A Prentise in the Divine Art of Poesie* (1584), had described this stanza as suitable for 'any heich & graue subiectis, specially drawin out of learnit authoruis' and named it 'Ballat Royal'. Burns would have come across many poems using this rhyme scheme in Ramsay's *Ever-Green*, which made available to a modern readership a wide selection of fifteenth- and sixteenth-century Scottish poetry that had been preserved in the Bannatyne Manuscript (compiled in 1568), but most of these abandon the ten-syllable line of Chaucer and Henryson (cited by James) for an eight-syllable line (sometimes used by Dunbar). This is the model that Burns adopts: the *Ever-Green* poems often adopt it for a similar 'lover's complaint' theme.

77 *Epigraph.* Lady Randolph in John Home's 1757 play *Douglas: A Tragedy* Act I.

79 l. 54. *Keen Recollection's direful train.* Kinsley notes the echo of Goldsmith's *The Deserted Village*, when the speaker sees the 'ruined ground' where the cottage once stood: 'Remembrance wakes with all her busy train, | Swells at my breast and turns the past to pain' (ll. 80–1; Lonsdale 679).

80 *Despondency, an Ode.* K94. Another example of the 'Cherrie and the Slae' stanza: see headnote to 'Epistle to Davie', p. 310.

81 l. 22. *Unfitted with an aim.* Compare the biographical letter to John Moore of 2 August 1787 reproduced in Appendix 1, p. 263.

l. 30. *How blest the Solitary's lot, | Who, all-forgetting, all-forgot.* Kinsley points out the echo of Alexander Pope, 'Eloisa to Abelard' (1717): 'How happy is the blameless Vestal's lot! | The world forgetting, by the world forgot' (ll. 207–8; Pope 257).

ll. 31, 33–4. *Within his humble cell, || Sits o'er his newly-gathered fruits, | Beside his crystal well.* Kinsley spots that the phrasing here echoes ll. 3–4 of Thomas Parnell's poem 'The Hermit': 'the Cave his humble Cell, | His Food the Fruits, his Drink the chrystal Well': *Poems on Several Occasions* (Dublin, 1722), 123.

l. 54. *Or human love or hate.* The first 'or' means 'either'. See *OED*, 'or (conj.* 1)' 3: a poetic, but not specifically Scottish, usage.

82 *Man was made to Mourn, a Dirge.* K64. In the earliest manuscript copy of this poem Burns names a tune for which it was composed, 'Peggy Bawn'.

This score is adapted from the version of this Irish song in *The Scots Musical Museum* (509). A tune is not mentioned in any of the published editions of the present poem, but the stanza, with its alteration of tetrameter and trimeter lines, is typical of popular song, with the second quatrain of each stanza being sung to the second section of the tune.

l. 7. *furrow'd o'er with years.* Kinsley observes that Burns takes this phrase from Robert Blair's *The Grave*: 'Shatter'd with Age, and furrow'd o'er with Years' (l. 195: see note to p. 72, ll. 39–40). Blair is describing the pyramids.

l. 11. *Does thirst of wealth thy step constrain.* Kinsley notes the echo of a similar encounter between youth and experience in Shenstene's 'Elegy VII': 'Stranger, he said, amid this pealing rain, | Benighted, lonesome, whither wouldst thou stray? | Does wealth or pow'r thy weary step constrain? | Reveal thy wish, and let me point the way' (ll. 20–3). Shenstone's interlocutor knows whereof he speaks, being the ghost of Cardinal Wolsey, lord chancellor to Henry VIII, no less (Shenstone Vol. I, 28).

83 l. 34. *Manhood's active might.* Kinsley spots another phrase borrowed from Shenstone, this time 'Elegy XI', though Shenstone *contrasts* the imaginative joys of youth with the power of adulthood: 'Not all the force of manhood's active might, | Not all the craft to subtle age assign'd, | Not science shall extort that dear delight, | Which gay delusion gave the tender mind' (ll. 45–8; Shenstone Vol. I, 42).

ll. 37–8. *But see him on the edge of life, | With Cares and Sorrows worn.* As Kinsley points out, another echo of Blair's *The Grave*, describing the erosion of a memorial a few lines later: 'Worn on the Edge of Days, the Brass consumes, | The Busto moulders, and the deep-cut Marble, | . . . gives up its Charge' (ll. 203–5).

l. 39. *Then Age and Want, Oh! ill-match'd pair.* Kinsley suggests an echo of Edward Young's *Night Thoughts*, Night First: '*Want*, and incurable *Disease* (fell Pair!) | On hopeless Multitudes remorseless seize | At once; and make a Refuge of the Grave' (Young 8).

84 ll. 49–50: *the num'rous Ills | Inwoven with our frame.* This last phrase Kinsley finds in Young's *Night Thoughts*, Night Seventh, but there it is not ills but 'delicate Moralities of *Sense*', supplementing reason, which are 'By Skill Divine inwoven in our Frame' (Young 152).

ll. 53–4. *Man, whose heav'n-erected face, | The smiles of love adorn.* Kinsley observes the phrasing borrowed from Thomson's version of 'man', 'Who wears sweet smiles, and looks erect on Heaven'; Thomson contrasts this with man's inhumanity to *animals*, though, giving a different point to the word 'erect': 'Spring' (1728), l. 355 (Thomson 12).

ll. 55. *Man's inhumanity to Man.* Kinsley points to two parallels in *Night Thoughts*: 'And *Inhumanity* is caught from Man, | From smiling Man' (Young, Night Fifth, 82); 'Turn the World's History; what find we there, | But *Fortune*'s Sports, or *Nature*'s cruel Claims, | Or *Woman*'s Artifice, or *Man*'s Revenge, | And endless Inhumanities on Man?' (Young, Night Eighth, 186).

ll. 65–8. *If I'm designed yon lordling's slave . . . E'er planted in my mind?.* Kinsley identifies this with 'the stock complaint of the Restoration stage hero', giving as an example Arimant in John Dryden's heroic drama *Aureng-Zebe* (1675): 'Why am I thus to slavery design'd | And yet am cheated with a free-born mind?' (Act 3, ll. 43–4). But Arimant's 'slavery' is that of love for an imperious mistress, not a matter of low birth.

85   l. 87. *relief for those*. Changed to 'relief to those' in later copies of the 1787 edition and subsequently. These final lines again recall *Night Thoughts*: see note to l. 39 above.

Winter, a Dirge. K10. Like two other poems at this point in the Kilmarnock edition, 'A Prayer, in the Prospect of Death' and 'To Ruin', this is a very early composition, written in English, before Burns turned to Scots: in the biographical letter to John Moore of 2 August 1787 reproduced in Appendix 1, Burns refers to 'Winter' as 'the earliest of my printed pieces' (p. 264). Like its fellow 'dirge' 'Man was made to Mourn', manuscript versions, but no published version, set this poem to a tune, and it takes the same song-type stanza.

This is 'McPherson's Farewell', the tune of a ballad 'properly so called' (L586), published in *The Scots Musical Museum* as song 114, from which this score is adapted.

l. 9 and footnote. *'The sweeping blast, the sky o'ercast'*. Burns offers this as another borrowing from Edward Young, but it does not seem to correspond to anything in Young with the exactness suggested by the quotation marks. Kinsley suggests it is a general 'recollection' of the dimeter lines of *Ocean: An Ode* (1728): 'As from the North, | Now rushes forth | A Blast, that thunders in my lay' ('To the King', XIV); 'When rushes forth | The frowning *North* | On blackning billows, with what dread | My shudering soul | Beholds them rowl' (XIII), and so on. But the words might come from Young's 'The Force of Religion: or, Vanquished Love' (1714), a verse-narrative of the martyrdom of Lady Jane Grey. Jane's husband approaches with news of her father's execution 'like a gloomy Storm, at once to sweep, | And plunge her to the Bottom of the Deep'; a few lines later a new verse paragraph begins, 'Thus the fair Lily, when the Sky's o'ercast, | At first but shudders in the feeble Blast' (end of Book I).

86   *A Prayer, in the Prospect of Death*. K13. The stanza form here is also the Common Metre of the Scottish Metrical Psalms: see note to p. 69, ll. 111–13.

ll. 1, 19. *O THOU unknown, Almighty cause; But, Thou art good*. Kinsley notes that the poem begins and ends with echoes of the second stanza of Pope's 'The Universal Prayer' (1738), which is written in the same form: 'Thou Great First Cause, least Understood! | Who all my Sense confin'd | To know but this,—that Thou art Good, | And that my self am blind' (ll. 5–8; Pope 247).

87 *To a Mountain-Daisy*. K92. The Standard Habbie stanza is used here for sentimental apostrophe, as in 'To a Mouse'. This was another poem sent by Burns to John Kennedy, factor to the Earl of Dumfries (see headnote to 'The Cotter's Saturday night', p. 306): in the accompanying letter, he calls it 'the very latest of my productions.—I am a good deal pleas'd with some sentiments in it myself; as they are just the native, querulous feelings of a heart, which, as the elegantly melting Gray says, "Melancholy has marked for her own" ' (L28, 20 April 1786; the allusion is to Gray's 'Elegy' l. 120).

ll. 11–12. *to greet | The purpling East*. McGuirk suggests an echo of Milton's 'L'Allegro', where the lark sings 'From his watch-tower in the skies, | Till the dappled dawn doth rise' (ll. 43–4).

l. 26. *Thy snawie bosom sun-ward spread*. Kinsley detects an echo of Book II of James Beattie's *The Minstrel* (1774): 'One cultivated spot there was, that spread | Its flowery bosom to the noonday beam' (ll. 73–4).

l. 29. *share*. That is, the ploughshare, the blade that cuts the ground horizontally at the bottom of the furrow.

88 l. 47. *Till wrench'd of ev'ry stay but HEAV'N*. Kinsley spots the borrowing from Thomson's depiction in 'Autumn' of Lavinia who is 'deprived of all, | Of every stay save innocence and Heaven' (ll. 179–80; Thomson 94).

l. 51. *Stern Ruin's plough-share drives, elate*. Kinsley points out the borrowing from Young's vision of the Apocalypse in *Night Thoughts*: 'Stars rush; and final *Ruin* fiercely drives | Her Ploughshare o'er Creation!' (Young, Night Ninth, 230).

To Ruin. K12. The 'Cherrie and the Slae' stanza once again: see headnote to 'Epistle to Davie', p. 310.

89 *Epistle to a young Friend*. K105. The addressee is Andrew Aiken, son of Robert Aiken: see headnote to 'The Cotter's Saturday night', p. 306. The stanza form here, odd lines being tetrameters, rhyming in pairs, and even lines trimeters but with an additional syllable to give a feminine rhyme, is the stanza form of songs like 'Corn Rigs' and 'From thee Eliza I must go'.

90 l. 15. *views*. Here, 'view' is in the old sense of 'an aim or intention; a design or plan; an object or purpose' (*OED* II.12).

l. 43. *th' illicit rove*. Clearly, 'wandering' in a sexual sense.

92 ll. 87–8. *may ye better reck the rede, | Than ever did th' Adviser*. Kinsley points out the echo of Ophelia's objection to her brother's advice to guard her chastity 'Whiles like a puffed and reckless libertine | Himself the primrose path of dalliance treads | And recks not his own rede' in Shakespeare's *Hamlet* (1. 3. 49–51).

92 *On a Scotch Bard gone to the West Indies.* K100. For the whole of the year in which the Kilmarnock edition was published, 1786, Burns planned to take up a position as an overseer of slaves on a sugar plantation in Jamaica: see Introduction to this volume (his best friend in Mauchline, James Smith, *did* eventually go to Jamaica).

l. 14. *petitions.* Here in the sense of 'a solemn and humble prayer to God' (*OED*).

l. 20. *taen aff.* 'Take off' in the sense of 'lead away summarily' (*OED*).

l. 20. *bummle.* A bumble-bee, but also a traditional figure for the sexually incompetent: Kinsley quotes William Dunbar's 'The tua mariit Wemen and the Wedo', where one wife complains that her husband is 'ane bumbart, ane dron bee' (l. 91; *The Poems of William Dunbar*, ed. John Small, Vol. II, Edinburgh, 1893).

l. 21. *fumble.* Here with the specific connotation of sexual inadequacy: see note to p. 14, l. 69.

93 l. 23. *wumble.* That is, wimble. As a tool for piercing holes, this was a traditional metaphor for the penis: see headnote to 'Green Grow the Rashes', p. 340, for a related use.

l. 25. *KYLE.* Burns's district of Ayrshire, between the rivers Irvine and Doon: see Map.

l. 28. *In flinders flee.* 'An old alliterative phrase' found in ballads, notes Kinsley.

94 *A Dedication to G**** H*******, Esq;* K103. Gavin Hamilton (1751–1805) was Mauchline's solicitor, with James Smith one of Burns's best friends there, and frequently at odds with its Kirk Session (the governing body of a parish, consisting of minister and elders): see the headnote to 'Holy Willie's Prayer', p. 378, for an instance of this. Along with Smith and Robert Aiken, he was instrumental in getting the Kilmarnock *Poems* published, collecting 40 subscriptions. In placing a 'Dedication' to a 'patron' so late in the volume, instead of at its head, Burns may be alluding to Laurence Sterne's dedication in Volume I of *Tristram Shandy* (1759), which does not appear until chapter 8 (and does not name an individual, but offers itself for sale).

l. 5. *sirnam'd like His Grace.* That is, like the Duke of Hamilton, a powerful nobleman in the region.

ll. 11–16. *This may do—maun do, Sir . . . I can beg.* Burns quotes these lines in a letter to a local laird, John Arnot of Dalquhatswood, in an April 1786 letter inviting him to subscribe to the Kilmarnock *Poems*. Arnot declined, but was a subscriber to the Edinburgh edition of the following year.

95 l. 35. *Landlord.* Hamilton was in one sense Burns's landlord: he had subleased the farm at Mossgiel to Burns and his brother Gilbert since 1783.

ll. 39–40. *a milder feature, | Of our poor, sinfu', corrupt Nature.* Burns refuses the Calvinist insistence that *no* good can proceed from human nature, but only from the grace of God; and adopts instead the secular moral theory of the Enlightenment, which considers benevolence and compassion as natural to human beings (though perhaps placed in us by God). Compare the founding statement of the Church of Scotland's official doctrine, *The Westminster Confession of Faith* (1647) with the first sentence of Adam Smith's *The Theory of Moral Sentiments* (1759): 'From this original corruption [of Adam and Eve], whereby we are utterly indisposed, disabled, and made opposite to all good, and wholly inclined to all evil, do proceed all actual transgressions' (ch. VI, para. iv); 'How selfish soever man may be supposed, there are evidently some principles in his nature, which interest him in the fortune of others, and render their happiness necessary to him, though he derives nothing from it except the pleasure of seeing it' (Smith, *Theory of Moral Sentiments*, 9).

l. 42. *Gentoos.* 'Hindus, as opposed to Moslems. (Anglo-Indian, f. Portugese *gentio*, "gentile")' (Kinsley).

l. 43. *Ponotaxi.* A generic South American location.

l. 44. *Orth–d–xy.* That is, the orthodox Calvinism of the Kirk.

l. 49. *And Och! That's nae r–g–n–r–t–n.* Regeneration, that which distinguishes the elect whom God has chosen to save. *The Westminster Confession* continues: 'This corruption of nature, during this life, does remain in those that are regenerated; and although it be, through Christ, pardoned, and mortified; yet both itself, and all the motions thereof, are truly and properly sin' (ch. VI, para. v). This line was omitted in the 1787 Edinburgh and subsequent editions.

l. 50. *Morality, thou deadly bane.* This paragraph voices the Calvinist rejection of 'good works' (that is, moral living) as a means to salvation: 'Works done by unregenerate men, although for the matter of them they may be things which God commands; and of good use both to themselves and others: yet, because they proceed not from a heart purified by faith; nor are done in a right manner, according to the Word; not to a right end, the glory of God, they are therefore sinful and cannot please God, nor make a man meet to receive grace from God' (*Westminster Confession*, ch. XVI, para. vii). This and the next 28 lines constitute a 'digression' (l. 79) in which Burns ironically gives voice to the attitudes and practices which he thought Calvinist doctrine encouraged.

l. 54. *stretch a point to catch a plack.* Bend the truth to make a profit.

l. 57. *point.* That is, point out, or point at in accusation.

96 l. 65. *damn a' Parties but your own.* A glance at the divisions within the Kirk, between the 'moderate' party and the orthodox one.

l. 68. *C–lv–n.* Jean Calvin (1509–64), French Protestant reformer whose theology was the basis of Scottish Church doctrine.

l. 72. *When Vengeance draws the sword in wrath.* The 'day' of the previous line is clearly the Day of Judgement, but the imagery here comes from Ezekiel's prophesy of the destruction of Israel: 'That all flesh may know that I the LORD have drawn forth my sword out of its sheath: it shall not return any more' (21: 5).

96 l. 74. *Ruin, with his sweeping besom.* Another prophecy of apocalypse, visiting Babylon this time: 'I will also make it a possession for the bittern, and pools of water; and I will sweep it with the besom of destruction, saith the LORD of hosts' (Isaiah 14: 23).

ll. 76–8. *While o'er the Harp . . . and heavier groans.* Perhaps a dig at the quality of psalm-singing in the kirk (the Psalms often refer to accompaniment on this instrument, though singing in church was unaccompanied).

l. 82 *My readers then are sure to lose me.* 'Then' is changed to 'still' in the 1787 and subsequent editions. For the specific context of the anticlericalism shared by Burns and Hamilton, see headnote to 'Holy Willie's Prayer', p. 378.

l. 98. *the CLERK.* That is, the lawyer. 'Clerk' could mean simply 'a man (or woman) of book learning, one able to read and write'; similarly, 'an ordinary legal practitioner in country towns' like Hamilton was referred to as a 'writer' (*OED*).

97 l. 101. *K******'s far-honor'd name.* Hamilton's wife, Helen Kennedy.

98 *To a Louse.* K83.

l. 14. *sprawl.* 'To crawl from one place to another in a struggling or ungraceful manner' (*OED*).

l. 17. *horn nor bane.* Combs were made of horn or bone.

l. 21. *Na faith ye yet!.* 'Na faith!' is an expression of surprise; 'yet', here, is 'a cheer or rallying cry' (*DSL*).

l. 28. *red smeddum.* Powdered mercury, used as an insecticide.

99 l. 35. *Miss's fine Lunardi.* A fashionable type of bonnet, named after a recent Italian pioneer of balloon-flight: see note to p. 111, l. 171.

ll. 41–2. *Thae winks and finger-ends, I dread, | Are notice takin.* Others in the church have noticed the louse, not only the speaker.

ll. 43–4. *O wad some Pow'r the giftie gie us | To see oursels as others see us.* Burns's moral comes from Adam Smith: 'If we saw ourselves in the light in which others see us, or in which they would see us if they knew all, a reformation would generally be unavoidable. We could not otherwise endure the sight' (Smith, *Theory of Moral Sentiments*, 158–9).

Epistle to J. L*****k, an old Scotch Bard. K57. Usually referred to as the 'First Epistle to Lapraik'. John Lapraik (1727–1807) had lost his farm in 1772 as a result of the closure of the Ayr Bank (see Introduction to this volume), had been imprisoned for debt in 1785, and was now leasing a farm near the village of Muirkirk, about twelve miles up the valley of the Ayr from Mauchline. He went on to publish *Poems, on Several Occasions* in 1788.

l. 7. *On Fasteneen we had a rockin.* Fasteneen is Shrove Tuesday. Burns's glossary explains that a 'rockin' is 'a meeting on a winter evening': the name derives from 'rock' meaning distaff, the tool which held the unspun flax or wool during spinning. As the next line suggests, these could be work parties as well as social occasions.

l. 13. *ae sang*. The theme of married love identifies the song as Lapraik's 'When I upon thy bosom lean', published in his 1788 *Poems*. This is an adaptation to fit the tune 'Johnny's Grey Breeks' (see headnote to 'My Father was a Farmer', p. 391) of a poem published in *The Weekly Magazine, or Edinburgh Amusement* in October 1773, which begins 'When on thy bosom I recline': Kinsley suggests Lapraik may have been the author of this also. Burns in turn adapted Lapraik's lyric as song 205 in *The Scots Musical Museum*, set to a different tune.

100 l. 17. *It thirl'd the heart-strings thro' the breast*. As Kinsley notes, this echoes Peggy's praise of Patie, the titular *Gentle Shepherd* of Allan Ramsay's 1725 pastoral comedy: 'And then he speaks with sic a taking Art | His Words they thirle like Musick thro' my Heart' (i. 2. 96–7; Ramsay Vol. II, 221).

ll. 21–2. *Pope, or Steele, | Or Beattie's wark*. Alexander Pope (1688–1744), the greatest English poet of his time; Richard Steele (1672–1729), poet, playwright, and essayist. For Beattie see note to p. 49, l. 123. These comparisons reflect the fact that Lapraik's song is in English; Burns's adaptation will translate it into Scots.

l. 35. *'Tween Inverness and Tiviotdale*. Inverness is the Highland capital; the river Teviot is a tributary of the Tweed, in the Borders.

101 l. 61. *What's a' your jargon o' your Schools*. Kinsley observes that this borrows from John Pomfret, *Reason: A Poem* (1700): 'What's all the noisy Jargon of the Schools | But idle Nonsense of laborious Fools, | Who fetter *Reason* with perplexing Rules' (ll. 57–9). Pomfret is denouncing medieval scholastic philosophy.

l. 71. *Parnassus*. The mountain which, in Greek mythology, is the home of the Muses.

l. 73. *Gie me ae spark o' Nature's fire*. Kinsley notes the similarity with Tristram's prayer for authorial autonomy from regulation in Volume III (1761) of Laurence Sterne's *Tristram Shandy*: 'Great *Apollo!* If thou art in a giving humour,—give me,—I ask no more, but one stroke of native humour, with a single spark of thy own fire along with it,—and send *Mercury*, with the *rules* and *compasses*, if he can be spared, with my compliments to—no matter' (144). Burns's line also echoes Pope's 'Essay on Criticism' (1711) which argues exactly the opposite case. Having discussed Homer and Virgil, Pope's poem exclaims, 'Oh may some Spark of *your* Cœlestial Fire | The last, the meanest of your Sons inspire' (ll. 195–6; Pope 150). Homer and Virgil are indeed great because they follow '*Unerring Nature*, still divinely bright, | One *clear, unchang'd*, and *Universal* Light' (ll. 70–1); but Pope's Nature is not set in opposition to classical rules of composition, as in Burns and Sterne, but produces them: 'Those RULES of old *discover'd*, not *devis'd*, | Are *Nature* still, but *Nature Methodiz'd*' (ll. 88–9; Pope 146).

l. 79. *ALLAN'S glee*. That is, Allan Ramsay's: see note to Preface, p. 283.

101 l. 80. *FERGUSON'S*. That is, Robert Fergusson's: see note to Preface, p. 283.

102 l. 103. *MAUCHLINE*. The nearest village to Burns's farm at Mossgiel: see Maps.

l. 107. *rhymin-ware*. The phrase is borrowed from William Hamilton's third epistle to Ramsay, where he imagines himself as a pedlar of poetry: 'Sae little worth's my rhyming Ware, | My Pack I scarce dare apen mair' (ll. 49–50; Ramsay Vol. I, 129).

ll. 115–18. *Awa ye selfish, warly race . . . To catch-the-plack!.* The opposition of this and the following stanza recalls, as McGuirk points out, Shenstone's 'Elegy IX': 'Scorn'd be the wretch that quits his genial bowl, | His loves, his friendships, ev'n his self, resigns; | Perverts the sacred instinct of his soul, | And to a ducate's dirty sphere confines' (Shenstone Vol. I, 35).

103 *To the same.* K58. Usually known as the 'Second Epistle to Lapraik'.

l. 1. *at the stake.* The cows are 'tethered for milking' (Kinsley).

l. 11. *awkart.* Burns glosses this as simply 'awkward', but Kinsley goes further: 'cantankerous, perverse' (nothing like this in *DSL*).

104 ll. 27–30. *'Roose you sae weel for your deserts . . . An' thank him kindly?'*. Kinsley notes that this echoes a stanza in an earlier exchange of Standard Habbie 'Familiar Epistles', between Allan Ramsay and William Hamilton of Gilbertfield: 'Thy blyth and cheerfu' merry Muse, | Of Compliments is sae profuse; | For my good Haivins dis me roose | Sae very finely | It were ill Breeding to refuse | To thank her kindly' (Hamilton's Epistle III, ll. 25–30, in Ramsay's 1721 *Poems*; Ramsay Vol. II, 129).

l. 32. *stumpie.* 'The stump of a quill-pen, esp. one that has been much sharpened' (*DSL*).

l. 45. *your moorlan harp.* As its name suggests, Muirkirk is an upland district.

l. 47. *how Fortune waft an' warp.* On a loom, the warp threads are fixed vertically in the frame, and the waft thread woven through it horizontally. The point of the image perhaps lies in the sudden shifts involved in weaving on a hand-loom: the shooting of the shuttle to-and-fro, the movement of the frame back and forth.

105 l. 65. *Brugh.* That is, a burgh, a market-town.

l. 66. *A Baillie's name.* A baillie is a magistrate in a burgh.

l. 67. *feudal Thane.* 'Thane' is an ancient level of nobility which in fact vanished with the advent of feudalism properly so-called: Burns has found it in Shakespeare's *Macbeth*.

l. 77. *cits.* See note to p. 40, l. 135.

106 l. 92. *the ragged Nine.* Kinsley finds a precedent for describing the Muses as 'ragged' in William Congreve's comedy *Love for Love* (1710): 'as ragged as one of the Muses' (I. 1).

l. 99. *May in some future carcase howl.* The transfer of souls into new bodies after death (metempsychosis) is associated in the West with the beliefs ascribed to Pythagoras (d. *c.*495 BC); Plato (*c.*427–*c.*348 BC) describes a version of it at the end of the *Republic*.

To W. S******n, Ochiltree. K59. William Simson (1758–1815) was educated at Glasgow University and in 1786 was schoolmaster at Ochiltree, about five miles south of Mauchline on the Lugar water.

l. 13. *My senses wad be in a creel.* That is, 'in confusion, in a state of perplexity' (*DSL*).

107 l. 15. *Wi' Allan, or wi' Gilbertfield.* 'Allan' is Allan Ramsay (see note to Preface, p. 283), 'Gilbertfield' is Ramsay's close friend and collaborator, William Hamilton of Gilbertfield (d. 1759), most celebrated for his abridged and modernized version of Blind Harry's *Wallace*, making available to a modern audience this long fifteenth-century poem narrating the exploits of the hero of the Wars of Independence. These two are particularly relevant to this poem as the authors of 'Familiar Epistles between Lieutenant William Hamilton and Allan Ramsay', written in the same Standard Habbie stanza, published in Ramsay's 1721 *Poems* (Ramsay Vol. I, 115–34).

l. 17. *Ferguson, the writer-chiel.* Robert Fergusson (see note to Preface, p. 283): 'writer-chiel' refers to Fergusson's job in 1769–73 as a lawyer's clerk, 'copying legal documents at the rate of a penny a page' (*DNB*).

l. 31. *COILA.* Burns's muse, with responsibility for Kyle poets generally: see note to p. 50, l. 151.

l. 33. *chanters.* A chanter is 'that pipe of a bagpipe, with finger-holes on which the melody is played' (*OED*).

l. 40. *New Holland.* That is, Australia. The Dutch were the first Europeans to reach Australia: our current name for the continent was just coming into use in English in Burns's lifetime.

l. 42. *Magellan.* The Strait of Magellan is the passage between the southern tip of South America and the island of Tierra del Fuego. The Atlantic and Pacific oceans meet south of the latter, at the notoriously stormy Cape Horn.

ll. 44–5. *Forth an' Tay . . . Yarrow an' Tweed.* Eastward-flowing Scottish rivers: see Map (the Yarrow is a tributary of the Tweed). Ramsay praises '*Tay* and *Tweed's* smooth Streams' in 'A Poet's Wish' in the 1721 *Poems* (l. 10; Ramsay Vol. I, 243). Fergusson hymns Forth, Tweed, and Tay in 'The Rivers of Scotland. An Ode', and both the Tweed and the Yarrow in ll. 25–30 of 'Elegy on the Death of Scots Music', both in his 1773 *Poems* (Fergusson 40–6, 38).

ll. 47–8. *While Irwin, Lugar, Aire an' Doon,* | *Naebody sings.* These are all Ayrshire rivers. The Lugar flows into the Ayr just south of Mauchline; for the others, see Map. Kinsley points out that Burns's complaint about their poetic neglect relative to the bigger east-flowing rivers named in ll. 44–5 takes its turn after Fergusson's about the poetic neglect of the latter in comparison to the classical rivers of Italy, in 'Hame content. A satire' of 1779: 'The ARNO and the TIBUR lang | Hae run fell clear in Roman sang; | But, save the reverence of Schools! | They're baith but lifeless dowy pools. | Dought they compare wi' bonny Tweed, | As clear as ony lammer-bead? | Or are their shores more sweet and gay | Than Fortha's haughs or banks o' Tay?' (ll. 75–82; Fergusson 159).

108 l. 49. *Th' Illissus, Tiber, Thames, an' Seine.* The river Ilissos skirted the walls of classical Athens; the Tiber runs through Rome. For parallels with Burns's comparisons here, see the lines from Fergusson above, and also a poem in Ramsay's 1728 *Poems*, 'Epistle from Mr. William Starrat': 'Give me the Muse that calls past Ages back, | And shaws proud Southren Sangsters their Mistake, | That frae their *Thames* can fetch the Laurel North, | And big *Parnassus* on the Frith of *Forth*' (ll. 19–22; Ramsay Vol. II, 70).

l. 52. *cock your crest.* Cf. the phrase '*to set up one's crest*, to assume an air of importance or self-confidence' (*DSL*): Kinsley suggests the image is of two pipers setting up their pipes and playing together.

l. 58. *WALLACE.* See note to p. 48, ll. 88–90.

l. 73. *Ev'n winter bleak has charms to me.* Kinsley hears an echo of Thomson's 'Autumn', describing the man of rural retirement, 'from all the stormy passions free': 'Even winter wild to him is full of bliss' (l. 1327; Thomson 125).

109 l. 97. *Fareweel, 'my rhyme-composing brither!'.* The Kilmarnock edition closes the quotation marks after 'composing'; the present text follows the 1793 and 1794 editions where this is sorted out.

ll. 109–86. *POSTSCRIPT.* In this section of Burns's epistle he gets round to replying to Simson's own, which had asked about the context of 'The Holy Tulzie' (K52), a poem satirizing the conflict between two clergymen in Kilmarnock, both of the orthodox party in the church, Alexander Moodie and John Russel (see notes to p. 25, l. 102, p. 27, l. 184). The 'Postscript' here is a straightforward allegory of orthodoxy's conflict with theological revisionism, and nothing to do with the intra-party conflict in Kilmarnock ridiculed in the earlier poem.

l. 112 and footnote. *new-light; Dr. TAYLOR of Norwich.* John Taylor (1694–1761), minister of a Presbyterian congregation in Norwich in the east of England, 'a profound influence on Scottish theology' and a 'totem to the liberal wing of the Kirk' (Kidd, 'Scotland's Invisible Enlightenment', 48) through his work *The Scripture-Doctrine of Original Sin proposed to free and candid Examination*, published in 1740 (Burns mentions reading this book in the biographical letter to John Moore of 2 August 1787 reproduced in Appendix 1, p. 262). English Presbyterians, like their Scottish co-religionists, held to the Calvinist theology summarized in the Westminster Confession of Faith (see note to p. 95, ll. 39–40 and *passim*), which placed great emphasis on the inherent sinfulness of human nature unless redeemed by the grace of God. Taylor's book rejected this by confirming common-sense notions of innocence and guilt: 'And therefore if we understand, that it is *unjust*, that the Innocent should be under Displeasure, or a Curse . . . then God understands it to be so too. And pray, consider seriously what a God he must be, who can be displeased with, and curse his innocent Creatures, even before they have a Being' (p. 151). This move of course involves assessing God's intentions by the standards of human justice and rationality, and for orthodox Calvinism such faculties were as fallen, and thus as inadequate, as every other aspect of human nature. Taylor argues, on the contrary, that while the Genesis account of the Fall speaks of God punishing Adam and Eve with mortality, there is 'Not one Word of a Curse upon their Souls, upon the Powers of their Minds, their Understanding and Reason. Not one Word of darkening or weakening their rational Powers; not one Word of clogging those with any additional Difficulties' (19). Burns adopts one use of 'New Light' current in the period, to name the illumination that human reason can shed on God's purposes in the eyes of the Kirk's modernizing, 'moderate' faction; 'New Light' or 'New Licht' can mean other things in other contexts.

110 l. 133. *Some herds.* Burns picks up the traditional figure of clergymen as shepherds, their congregations as flocks, also deployed in 'The Holy Tulzie'. The particular 'herds' referred to in this line are the moderate ministers.

l. 145. *it gaed to sticks.* It went to cudgels; that is, it got violent.

111 l. 153. *took the sands.* To 'take the sands' is 'to make for the sea, to flee the country, to "clear out"' (*DSL*).

l. 168. *By word an' write.* By word of mouth, and in writing: as Kinsley notes, 'an old conjunction'.

l. 171. *things they ca' balloons.* A very recent invention. James Tytler had made the first balloon flight in Britain in Edinburgh in 1784, and the Italian pioneer Vincenzo Lunardi made several flights in Scotland in 1785.

l. 182. *moonshine.* Here, 'vain, empty, foolish; worthless' (*OED*).

112 *Epistle to J. R******, enclosing some Poems.* K47. John Rankine (d. 1810) was tenant of Adamhill farm, Tarbolton. His friendship with Burns dates from the period of the family's tenure of nearby Lochlie (Rankine was, like Burns, a member of the Tarbolton Masonic Lodge: see notes to 'The Farewell', below), though this poem, Burns's first verse epistle, dates from after Burns and his family moved to Mossgiel. It is not known which poems originally accompanied the present text to Rankine. It was however the third poem sent by Burns to John Kennedy, factor to the Earl of Dumfries (after 'The Cotter's Saturday night' and 'To a Mountain-Daisy) in May 1786: the accompanying letter announces that 'In about three or four weeks I shall probably set the Press agoing' with his first printed work (L30 [3], 16 May).

l. 2. *cocks.* 'Cock' here in the sense of 'one who fights with pluck and spirit. Hence a familiar term of appreciation among the vulgar' (*OED*).

112 l. 4 footnote. *A certain humorous dream of his was then making a noise in the world.* The 1787 Edinburgh and subsequent editions change 'world' for the more modest 'country-side'. In explanation of the dream, Cunningham passes on the story of Rankine and his landlord, named only as 'Lord K—', who 'was in the practice of calling all his familiar acquaintances "brutes," and sometimes "damned brutes."—... Once, in company, his lordship having indulged in this rudeness more than his wont, turned to Rankine and exclaimed, "Brute, are ye dumb? have ye no queer, sly story to tell us?"—"I have nae story," said Rankine, "but last night I had an odd dream."—"Out with it, by all means," said the other. "Aweel, ye see," said Rankine, "I dreamed I was dead, and that for keeping other than good company on earth I was damned. When I knocked at hell-door, wha should open it but the deil; he was in a rough humour, and said, 'Wha may ye be, and what's your name?'—'My name,' quoth I, 'is John Rankine, and my dwelling-place was Adam-Hill.'—'Gae wa' wi',' quoth Satan, 'ye canna be here; ye're ane of Lord K—'s damned brutes—hell's fou o' them already!'" This sharp rebuke, it is said, polished for the future his lordship's speech' (Cunningham Vol. II, 283–4).

l. 5. *Korah-like.* In Numbers, Korah leads the rebellious sons of Levi against the authority of Moses. Moses announces that the Lord will make an example of them: 'And the earth opened her mouth, and swallowed them up, and their houses, and all the men that appertained unto Korah, and all their goods. They, and all that appertained to them, went down alive into the pit, and the earth closed upon them; and they perished from among the congregation' (16: 32–3).

l. 9. *mak a devil o' the Saunts.* The 'saunts' are the orthodox in religion. Kinsley connects this to another story of Rankine's humour, apparently passed on by his youngest daughter, and related by Robert Chambers: 'Rankine amused the fancy of Burns by a trick which he played upon a "sanctimonious professor" [i.e. one professing a religious life] whom he invited to a jorum of toddy in his farm-house. "The hot-water kettle had, by pre-arrangement, been primed with proof-whisky, so that the more water Rankine's guest added to his purpose of diluting it, the more potent the liquor became"' (Wallace Vol. I, 120).

l. 23. *unregenerate.* Applies to those not redeemed by the grace of God: see note to p. 95, l. 50.

113 l. 36. *Bunker's hill.* That is, at the Battle of Bunker Hill near Boston in 1775, early in the American Revolutionary War. A victory on the field for the British army, but at such cost that it served as a victory for the rebels in terms of propaganda and morale.

ll. 37–72. *'Twas ae night lately, in my fun . . . An' thole their blethers.* What follows is an allegory of Burns's affair with Elizabeth Paton, a servant-girl, in 1784; her pregnancy; its discovery by the church authorities; and Burns's punishment by them for 'fornication': sex out of wedlock.

l. 47. *the Poacher-Court*. That is, the Kirk Session: the minister and the elders of a parish, responsible for supervising the morals of the congregation.

l. 54. *An' pay't the fee*. As a punishment for fornication, both parties had to take their place in the 'stool of repentance', seats raised or in a gallery in front of the pulpit, there to be publicly admonished by the minister on three successive Sundays; the man also had to pay a fine. See Burns's account of this experience in 'The Fornicater' (included in this volume).

l. 61. *As soon's the clockin-time is by*. That is, as soon as Elizabeth has had the child. Burns will celebrate this event in 'A Poet's welcome to his love-begotten Daughter' (included in this volume).

l. 65. *the buckskin kye*. 'Buckskin' is a term used of Americans. Kinsley suggests that the 'kye' (cattle) 'are probably plantation slaves'.

114 l. 71. *a yellow George*. A guinea, a gold coin displaying the monarch's head, worth 21*s*.

l. 75. *pennyworths*. That is, 'money's worth, value for money, return for one's payment or trouble' (*OED*).

Song [It was upon a Lammas night]. K8. The three songs included at this point in the Kilmarnock edition are among Burns's earliest compositions: see the biographical letter to John Moore of 2 August 1787 reproduced in Appendix 1, p. 264.

Tune: Corn Rigs are bonie.

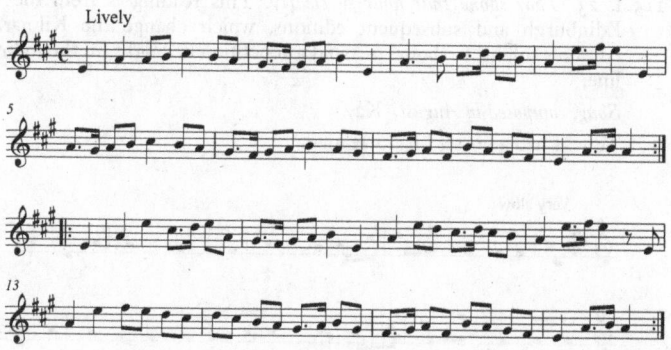

On the account of James Dick, the origins of this tune seem to lie in London, where it appears in a 1680 play by Thomas D'Urfey with a song called 'Sawney was tall and of noble race'; as 'A Northern Song' in a 1681 collection; as 'Sawney will never be my love again' in 1685; and the tune alone is titled 'Sawney' in 1687 (*Songs of Robert Burns*, ed. Dick, 353). 'There was, in London in the 1680s, a flourishing genre called

"Scotch songs"; these were somewhat debased popular songs of allegedly Scottish origin, some with fake tunes, all with fake words, and Londoners liked them because they were refreshingly different from the classical productions of Purcell and Lully.' The male character in these songs is usually called 'Sawney', the name for a stage-Scotsman (Johnson, *Music and Society*, 130–1). The tune became popular in Scotland under the present title as the setting for the closing song of Allan Ramsay's 1725 pastoral comedy *The Gentle Shepherd*, 'My Patie is a lover gay', included in the first volume of *The Scots Musical Museum* as song 93 (from which the score above is adapted). Burns could have found the score in several of the collections, including James Oswald's *Caledonian Pocket Companion*, Vol. II (1745), 22.

114   l. 4. *I held awa to Annie.* *DSL*'s meanings for 'haud awa' are 'to keep away, keep out or off' and 'to continue on one's way, go away' (though these are listed as east-coast usages).

l. 5. *tentless heed.* Reading 'heed' as the English word, it has been suggested (e.g. in Wallace Vol. I, 97) that this is an oxymoron, 'tentless' meaning, precisely, 'heedless'. The Kilmarnock edition of 1786, and the first Edinburgh edition of 1787, give the final word as 'head', and Wallace suggests that the intended word is the Scots 'heid', meaning 'head', but pronounced like 'heed'. Against this is the use in both editions of 'tentless heed' in 'To J. Smith', l. 55. Following this precedent; because 'head' invites a mistaken pronunciation from the modern reader; and in the absence of any textual authority for 'heid', I take the present reading from the 1793 and 1794 editions.

115   l. 23. *That shone that hour so clearly.* This reading is from the 1787 Edinburgh and subsequent editions, which change the Kilmarnock edition's 'night' to 'hour' to avoid a repetition of 'night' in the following line.

Song, composed in August. K2.

Tune: I had a horse, I had nae mair.

The tune was published, with its traditional words, as song 185 in *The Scots Musical Museum*, and the score above is adapted from this version. The present song was republished as song 351 in *The Scots Musical Museum* set to a different tune, 'When the King comes o'er the water', and re-titled with its first line. For the *SMM* version Burns altered some of the vocabulary in the ways listed below, mostly by substituting Scots words for English ones. George Thomson substituted 'sportsmen's' for 'slaught'ring' and added three lines to the end of each stanza to make it fit a third tune, 'Ally Croaker', to produce song 93 in the *Select Collection* (1799).

ll. 1–2. *slaught'ring guns | Bring Autumn's pleasant weather*. The open season for red grouse ('muir-fowl') began, then as now, on 12 August; for partridge, on 1 September. Kinsley observes that Burns is remembering two lines from Alexander Pope's description of Autumn in *Windsor-Forest* (1713): 'When milder Autumn Summer's Heat succeeds' (l. 97; Pope 198) and 'With slaught'ring Guns th'unweary'd Fowler roves' (l. 125; Pope 199).

l. 3. *And*. Deleted in the 1787 and subsequent editions of *Poems*.

l. 9. *The Partridge loves the fruitful fells*. 'The Paitrick lo'es the fruitfu' fells' in *SMM*.

l. 10. *The Plover loves*. 'The Plover lo'es' in *SMM*.

116 l. 11. *The Woodcock haunts the lonely dells*. These are 'lanely dells' in *SMM*. Another echo of *Windsor-Forest*, as Kinsley notes: 'And lonely Woodcocks haunt the watry Glade' (l. 128; Pope 199).

l. 14. *The path of man*. 'The path o' man' in *SMM*.

ll. 19–23. *Some social join . . . Tyrannic man's dominion; | The Sportsman's joy*. For the contrast of 'social' nature and 'man's dominion' see note to p. 72, ll. 7–8. Kinsley notes that this opposition also occurs in Thomson, where 'the rude clamour of the sportsman's joy' is rejected as a subject for poetry: his muse is instead 'most delighted when she social sees | The whole mixed animal creation round | Alive and happy', unlike 'the steady tyrant, man' ('Autumn', ll. 360, 381–3, 390; Thomson 98–9).

l. 24. *The flutt'ring, gory pinion*. Another image adapted from Pope's 'Windsor-Forest', as Kinsley observes: the shot pheasant 'Flutters in Blood, and panting beats the Ground' (l. 114; Pope 199).

l. 30. *the charms of Nature*. The 'charms o' Nature' in *SMM*.

l. 32. *ev'ry happy creature*. Becomes 'ilka happy creature' in *SMM*.

l. 34. *Till the silent moon*. 'While the silent moon' in *SMM*.

l. 35. *I'll grasp thy waist*. 'I'll clasp thy waist' in *SMM*.

l. 36. *how I love thee*. Becomes 'how I lo'e thee' in *SMM*.

Song [From thee, Eliza, I must go]. K9.

Tune: Gilderoy.

The tune takes its name from a seventeenth-century English ballad about a Highland outlaw: this tune seems to become attached to it in Scotland a bit later (*Songs of Robert Burns*, ed. Dick, 359–60). Burns could have found the score in several of the collections, including James Oswald's *Caledonian Pocket Companion*, Vol. V (1753), 20; the score given here is adapted from song 66 of *The Scots Musical Museum*. Burns's lyric was set to another tune and republished in George Thomson's *Select Collection of Original Scotish Airs* for 1793 (song 15).

117 l. 13. *latest.* That is, last.

The Farewell. To the Brethren of St. James's Lodge, Tarbolton. K115.

Tune: Good night and joy be wi' you a'.

The tune is that of the Scottish traditional song of parting (until it was replaced, largely thanks to Burns, by 'Auld Lang Syne'). Burns would have found the score in James Oswald's *Caledonian Pocket Companion*, Vol. IV (1752), 32: the score given here is adapted from

The Scots Musical Museum. At Burns's request, Johnson ended the *Museum* with this as song no. 600, giving the traditional words as part of the score, followed by Burns's verses. The traditional words are as follows:

> The night is my departing night,
>   The morn's the day I maun awa:
> There's no a friend or fae o' mine
>   But wishes that I were awa.—
> What I hae done, for lake o' wit,
>   I never, never can reca':
> I trust ye're a' my friends as yet,
>   Gude night and joy be wi' you a'!

But instead of following this rhyme scheme, with every second line rhyming, Burns uses the B rhyme of the first quatrain as the A rhyme of the second quatrain to produce the ballade stanza already used in 'The Lament'.

On Freemasonry, see note to p. 31, l. 79. Burns joined the Tarbolton Lodge in 1781, and was elected Depute Master in 1784. The occasion of the poem is Burns's prospective departure for Jamaica, also anticipated in 'On a Scotch Bard gone to the West Indies'.

l. 3. *Ye favored, ye enlighten'd Few.* The second 'ye' appears in neither the 1786 Kilmarnock nor 1787 Edinburgh editions. I take this reading from the 1793 version: necessary for the metre, unless 'favored' is given three syllables.

118 l. 11. *honour'd with supreme command.* As Depute Master Burns would have chaired meetings in the absence of the Grand Master.

l. 13. *that Hieroglyphic bright.* Freemasonry is very fond of symbols and diagrams, interpreted allegorically.

l. 20. *ARCHITECT Divine.* Freemasonry imagines God in terms consistent with the craft from which it claims descent and borrows its symbols (such as, in the following two lines, the plumb-line used by builders to establish a true vertical).

l. 25. *YOU.* The person wearing the '*highest badge*' of Grand Master of the Tarbolton Lodge was Captain James Montgomerie of Coilsfield, local landowner and one of the Montgomerie family mentioned in l. 57 of 'The Author's earnest cry and prayer' (see note to this line on p. 288). One of the major attractions of Freemasonry was that it could bring a member of an influential noble family like Montgomerie, and a struggling tenant farmer like Burns, into mutually respectful social contact.

EPITAPHS AND EPIGRAMS. This title does not appear at this point in the Kilmarnock or Edinburgh editions; it is inserted to correspond with the heading in the Contents.

Epitaph on a henpecked Country Squire; Epigram on said occasion; Another. K96, K97, K98. These are the only verses in the Kilmarnock edition of 1786 to be omitted in the Edinburgh edition of 1787 and subsequently. The 'henpecked' squire was, according to a note Burns made in a copy of these poems, William Campbell of Netherplace (the 'N**********' of the third of these verses), near Mauchline (Kinsley).

The first stanza of the third poem repeats a story told of Artemisia II of Caria in western Anatolia (d. 350 BC).

119 On a *celebrated ruling Elder*. K32.

l. 1. *Sowter* ****. A sowter or souter is a cobbler. The missing name is presumably 'John'.

On a noisy Polemic. K33. 'Polemic' here is in the now very unusual sense of polemicist: 'a person who argues or writes in opposition to another, or who takes up a controversial position; a controversialist' (*OED*). 'Jamie' is James Humphrey (d. 1844), a stonemason in the Mauchline-Tarbolton area, and a theological sparring-partner of the poet's.

On Wee Johnie. K34. Probably, suggests Kinsley, John Wilson, schoolmaster and clerk to the Kirk Session in Tarbolton.

120 *For the Author's Father*. K35. On the death of William Burnes, see Introduction to this volume.

l. 8 and footnote. *'For ev'n his failings lean'd to Virtue's side'*. 'Thus to relieve the wretched was his pride, | And even his failings leaned to virtue's side': the village parson from Oliver Goldsmith's *The Deserted Village*, ll. 163–4 (Lonsdale 683).

For R.A. Esq. K36. For Robert Aiken, see headnote to 'The Cotter's Saturday night', p. 306.

For G.H. Esq. K37. For Gavin Hamilton, see headnote to 'A Dedication to Gavin Hamilton', p. 316.

l. 2. *canting wretches*. Specifically, Mauchline Kirk Session, with whom Hamilton had 'a long-running feud' (Crawford, *The Bard*, 170). See headnote to 'Holy Willie's Prayer', p. 378.

A Bard's Epitaph. K104. Thomas Gray ends 'An Elegy Written in a Country Churchyard' (1751) with an 'Epitaph' which seems to be for the poet (Lonsdale 138–40); Alexander Pope ends 'Elegy to the Memory of an Unfortunate Lady' (1717) by imagining his own eventual death (Pope 264).

121 l. 8. *Who, noteless, steals the crouds among*. The image of the poet is borrowed from Shenstone, who contrasts him with the self-advertising 'fool': 'But ill-star'd sense, nor gay nor loud, | Steals soft, on tip-toe, through the crowd'. 'The Progress of Taste; or, the Fate of Delicacy. A Poem on the Temper and Studies of the Author; and how great a Misfortune it is for a Man of small Estate to have much Taste', ll. 41–2 (Shenstone Vol. I, 264).

l. 11. *frater*. Brother (Latin), comrade (*OED*).

From *Poems, Chiefly in the Scottish Dialect* (Edinburgh, 1787)

For the circumstances of this volume's publication, see Introduction. It included all the poems of the Kilmarnock edition except the epitaph and epigrams on a hen-pecked country squire, plus 19 additional poems, of which five are included here. It also included a new dedication, a list of 1,527 subscribers, a greatly expanded glossary (on which the present volume's is based), and a frontispiece with an engraving of the poet, reproduced here. There were two printings: during the printing of the second batch of sheets, after the type for the first batch had been broken up, it was decided to extend the print-run; the type for the first batch was re-set, and discrepancies inevitably crept in. The two printings are known by one of these discrepancies, at l. 45 of 'To a Haggis', where 'skinking' became 'stinking'. The present texts follow the 'skinking' copy.

122 *Frontispiece*. The publisher of the Edinburgh edition, William Creech, commissioned a half-length portrait of Burns in oils by Alexander Nasmyth (1758–1840), which is now the best-known image of the poet. This engraving was based on Nasmyth's painting, but Burns also sat for the engraver, John Beugo, and it may be the better likeness. For the vast majority of Burns's early readers, the engraving, not the painting, provided their only idea of the poet's appearance.

123 *Dedication. To the Noblemen and Gentlemen of the Caledonian Hunt*. The Caledonian Hunt was a sporting and social association for the Scottish aristocracy and gentry, organizing (for example) balls and race meetings. At the instigation of the Earl of Glencairn (see headnote to 'Lament for James, Earl of Glencairn', p. 359) the Hunt subscribed collectively to a second edition of Burns's poems: it is allocated 100 copies at the top of the list of subscribers.

as the prophetic bard Elijah did Elisha . . . and threw her inspiring mantle over me. The Lord tells the aged prophet Elijah to anoint Elisha as his successor, and he finds him 'plowing with twelve yoke of oxen before him, and he with the twelfth: and Elijah passed by him, and cast his mantle upon him' (1 Kings 19: 19).

125 *The Brigs of Ayr*. K120. Work began in May 1786 on a new bridge across the river at Ayr to carry the ever-increasing traffic of this expanding commercial centre. This poem is dedicated to merchant and banker John Ballantine (1743–1812), the town's Dean of Guild, the burgh magistrate responsible for the regulation of trade, and an initiator of civic improvements such as this. Ballantine had offered to help Burns when it looked possible that a second edition of the *Poems* might be published at Kilmarnock.

The most obvious model for a dialogue between parts of the public highway is Robert Fergusson's 'Mutual Complaint of Plainstanes and Causey'. Here Burns's couplets pair iambic pentameter lines rather than the tetrameters used in that poem (and familiar in Burns's work from 'The Twa Dogs'); following instead the model of other dialogues from Fergusson's *Poems on Various Subjects* (1779), 'The Ghaists' and 'A Drink Eclogue'. But Burns also uses a twelve-syllable line (an alexandrine) in this poem, often to end his paragraphs.

l. 12. *mercenary Swiss*. Switzerland, like some other poor, mountainous countries, had a history of exporting soldiers for hire, and had long been a by-word in this way.

125   l. 13. *close*. 'The closing passage of a speech, argument etc.' (*OED* 1b).

l. 18. *honest Fame*. Kinsley notes precedents in the last line of Pope's 'Temple of Fame' (1715): 'Oh grant an honest Fame, or grant me none!' (l. 524; Pope 188); and towards the end of Goldsmith's 'Deserted Village' (1770), where poetry is 'Unfit, in these degenerate times of shame, | To catch the heart, or strike for honest fame' (ll. 409–10; Lonsdale 694).

l. 33. *The death o' devils, smoor'd wi' brimstone reek*. Burns's language, suggests Kinsley, recalls the end of William Dunbar's 'Dance of the Sevin Deidly Synnis' (*c*.1507), where the Gaelic damned so deafen the Devil 'That in the deipest Pot of Hell | He smorit them all with Smuke' (Ramsay's version in *The Ever Green* [1724], Vol. II, 246).

126   l. 57. *Dungeon-clock*. The 'New' or 'High' Tolbooth in the Sandgate combined, as was usual, meeting-space for the council above, the town jail below, and a belfry; a steeple had been added in 1726. No longer standing.

l. 58 and footnote. *Wallace-Tow'r*. Also known as the 'Auld Tower', an old fortified house on the High Street to which a belfry had been added in 1731. There seems to be no historical basis for its association with William Wallace. Not the building of this name on the same site today. Burns's footnote refers to 'Dungeon-clock' as well as 'Wallace Tow'r'.

l. 62. *The silent moon shone high o'er tow'r and tree*. Echoes the opening verse of 'Mary's Dream' by John (a.k.a. Alexander) Lowe (1750–98), later collected as song 37 of *The Scots Musical Museum*: 'The moon had climb'd the highest hill | which rises o'er the source of Dee, | And from the eastern summit shed | her silver light on tow'r and tree'.

l. 66. *The clanging sugh of whistling wings*. As Kinsley observes, Pope's translation of Homer's *Odyssey* has Jove's eagles 'clang their wings, and hovering beat the sky' (II, l. 176).

127   l. 71. *warlock*. Apparently in *OED*'s weaker Scottish sense of 'magician, conjurer': see following note.

l. 74. *the sp'ritual folk*. In a letter of 18 November 1786 Burns mentions 'those visionary Bards . . . who hold commerce with aerial beings' (L56).

l. 75. *Fays, Spunkies*. Fairies and will-o'-the-wisps.

ll. 77–8. *of ancient Pictish race, | The vera wrinkles Gothic*. 'Gothic' here might mean, as later at l. 107, 'medieval, pre-modern' in a general sense. The Auld Brig was built in 1470, but its style is not specifically Gothic in the architectural meaning of the term. Some early eighteenth-century accounts describe the Picts (the 'Caledonians' encountered by the Romans) as 'Gothic' in an ethnic sense, speaking a Germanic language and originating from Northern Europe: for example, Robert Sibbald in *The History, Ancient and Modern, of the Sheriffdoms of Fife and Kinross* (1710) argues that 'the *Picts* . . . were of a *Gothish* Extract' (p. 18). Burns picks up on this at l. 97. The more obvious assumption, that they were of the same Celtic stock as the other inhabitants of ancient Britain, was also current.

l. 82. *ane Adams.* Robert Adam (1728–92), the great Scottish architect, based in London since 1758, although his plan for the bridge had not been taken up, and it was being constructed instead to a design by its builder, Alexander Steven.

l. 83. *five taper staves.* This is obscure. The New Bridge had five arches, and this line may imagine them, or the scaffolding holding them up during construction, in terms of the staves of a barrel.

l. 84. *virls an' whirlygigums.* Presumably the neo-classical decoration gracing the upper part of the bridge.

l. 97. *Vandal.* That is, barbarian: the Vandals were the Germanic tribe who sacked Rome in 455.

128 ll. 115–18. *Coil . . . Lugar . . . Greenock . . . Garpal.* Tributaries of the Ayr.

l. 134. *Supporting roofs, fantastic, stony groves.* A manuscript copy has a dash in place of the first comma, making it clear that fantastic, stony groves are supporting roofs, rather than stony groves supporting roofs fantastic.

129 l. 140. *the second dread command.* 'Thou shalt not make unto thee any graven image, or any likeness of any thing that is in heaven above, or that is in the earth beneath, or that is in the water under the earth' (Exodus 20: 4).

ll. 146–9. *Cuifs of later times . . . unblest with resurrection!.* Even while mocking medieval monasticism, the enlightened New Brig gets in a dig at the manners fostered by the orthodox Calvinist clergy, and praises Ayr for choosing moderate ministers instead.

l. 150. *yealings.* Contemporaries by age (*OED*).

l. 152. *Provoses . . . Bailie.* That is, Priors (of monastic houses); and a magistrate in a Scottish town.

l. 154. *Deacons . . . Conveeners.* Deacon was one of many ecclesiastical ranks that disappeared under Presbyterian church government; a Convener is chairman of council meetings.

l. 159. *Writers.* That is, lawyers, perhaps specialists in canon law, before the Reformation; to be contrasted with the scepticism towards the modern church shown by Burns's lawyer friends like Robert Aiken and Gavin Hamilton.

l. 173. *Harbours.* Improving the quays at the mouth of the Ayr, especially to facilitate the export of coal to Ireland, was an ongoing concern.

130 l. 175. *mak to through.* 'make good, prove' (*OED*). The present instance is *OED*'s only example of this usage, which does not appear in *DSL*.

l. 177. *a shot right kittle.* A tricky target.

l. 183. *'A Citizen'.* See note to p. 40, l. 135.

l. 187. *Seisins.* In Scots Law, a seisin is 'the instrument by which the possession of feudal property is proved' (*OED*).

l. 196. *featly.* 'Nimbly' (*OED*), an archaism used, Kinsley notes, by Dryden and Pope in similar contexts, e.g. 'So featly tripp'd the light-foot Ladies round' (Pope, 'January and May' l. 620; Pope 93).

130 l. 202. *McLauchlan.* James McLauchlan, Highland fiddler and composer much in demand among the Ayrshire gentry.

131 l. 213. *The Genius of the Stream.* Recalls the appearance of the river-gods in Milton's *Lycidas* of 1638 ('Camus', for the river Cam in Cambridge, at l. 103), and Pope's 'Windsor Forest' of 1713 ('Old Father *Thames*' at ll. 329–33; Pope 206–7).

l. 216. *tangle.* i.e. seaweed.

ll. 217–24. *Next came the loveliest pair . . . Hospitality with cloudless brow.* Kinsley suggests that this conventional procession of the seasons especially recalls the unfinished Book VII of Spenser's *The Faerie Queene*, canto vii, verses 28–31.

ll. 225–6. *Courage . . . the Feal.* The Water of Fail is a stream running past Tarbolton into the river Ayr, through the Coilsfield estate of Hugh Montgomerie, one of the military family noted at l. 57 of 'The Author's earnest cry and prayer' above. Hugh had served in the American Revolutionary War and was currently MP for Ayrshire.

ll. 227–8. *Benevolence . . . tow'rs of Stair.* Stair House, close to the Ayr a few miles downstream from Coilsfield, was owned by Major-General Alexander Stewart and his wife Catherine; it is the latter, the recipient of two of Burns's manuscript collections, who is figured here.

ll. 229–30. *Learning and Worth . . . Catrine.* Catrine, on the Ayr upstream from Mauchline, was the home of Professor Dugald Stewart; see note to p. 48, l. 90, and headnote to 'Extempore Verses on Dining with Lord Daer', p. 382.

ll. 232–3. *To rustic Agriculture did bequeath | The broken, iron instruments of Death.* 'And he shall judge among the nations, and shall rebuke many people: and they shall beat their swords into plowshares, and their spears into pruninghooks: nation shall not lift up sword against nation, neither shall they learn war any more' (Isaiah 2: 4).

Address to the Unco Guid, or the Rigidly Righteous. K39. The verse form here is the song stanza used in the Kilmarnock volume for another poem of moral advice, 'Epistle to a Young Friend'.

132 *Epigraph.* 'All things have I seen in the days of my vanity: there is a just man that perisheth in his righteousness, and there is a wicked man that prolongeth his life in his wickedness. Be not righteous over much; neither make thyself over wise: why shouldest thou destroy thyself?' (The son of David in Ecclesiastes 7: 15–16). Burns's verse paraphrase of verse 16 makes a rather different point. As McGuirk suggests, the New Testament offers a better gloss on Burns's poem, when the Pharisees bring to Jesus a woman condemned to be stoned to death for adultery, and he says, 'He that is without sin among you, let him first cast a stone at her' (John 8: 7).

l. 8. *still the clap plays clatter.* The clapper of a mill shakes or knocks the hopper to feed grain down to the mill-stones.

133 l. 49. *scan.* In *OED*'s sense 2: 'to judge by a certain rule or standard'; or sense 3, 'examine'. This word is used in a similar context in Goldsmith's

Deserted Village, describing the parson who offers hospitality to vagrants: 'Pleased with his guests, the good man learned to glow, | And quite forgot their vices in their woe; | Careless their merits or their faults to scan, | His pity gave ere charity began' (ll. 159–62; Lonsdale 683). *OED* observes that sense 2 sometimes alludes to its first sense of 'scan', 'To analyse (verse) by determining the nature and number of the component feet or the number and prosodic value of the syllables'.

134 *To a Haggis.* K136. This poem is unique among those added to the *Poems* for the edition of 1787 in having been previously published, in the *Caledonian Mercury* newspaper for 19 December 1786, and the *Scots Magazine* for the following January. A haggis is chopped offal mixed with oatmeal, suet, and onion, seasoned and stuffed in a sheep's stomach, and boiled. A dish native to all of northern Britain in Burns's time, but already thought of as distinctively Scottish.

l. 4. *Painch, tripe, or thairm.* All refer to the stomach or intestines of an animal.

l. 9. *Your pin.* Such a thing as a 'pudding-pin' existed, perhaps used in sealing and serving the haggis. 'Mrs Haliburton . . . sat bolt upright, her lips skewered up and twisted, as if by a pudding-pin' (Christian Isobel Johnstone, *Elizabeth de Bruce* [1827], 226). The term was also used to signify something trivial, perhaps informing the pin's mock-heroic transformation in these lines.

ll. 11–12. *distil | Like amber bead.* Oil of amber was distilled from the raw material for medical uses.

l. 19. *horn for horn.* That is, spoon for spoon (spoons were carved from horn).

l. 24. *Bethankit.* A blessing: here, the grace after the meal.

ll. 25–7. *ragout . . . olio . . . fricassee.* All of these are highly seasoned stews of meat and vegetables: olio is of Spanish or Portuguese origin, the other two are French.

135 ll. 39–42. *Clap in his walie nieve a blade . . . Like taps o' thrissle.* Kinsley notes that Fergusson makes a similar case for Scottish fare, in this case kail and bannocks, in 'The Farmer's Ingle': 'On sickan food has mony a doughty deed | By Caledonia's ancestors been done' in defending the country from the Romans and the Danes (ll. 37–8; Fergusson 138). It is also the case made by Burns for whisky in the 'Postscript' to 'The Author's earnest cry and prayer', ll. 163–74.

ll. 43–8. The *Caledonian Mercury* and *Scots Magazine* versions have an alternative last stanza:

> Ye Powers wha gie us a' that's gude,
> Still bless auld Caledonia's brood
> Wi' great John Barkeycorn's heart's blude
>   In stowps or luggies;
> And on our board that king o' food
>   A glorious Haggice.

135 *John Barleycorn. A Ballad.* K23. The tradition on which Burns draws in this poem is very old. The personification of barley as Allan-a-Maut, and the allegory of his being fostered, murdered, and his blood invigorating his murderers, appears in a poem in the sixteenth-century Bannatyne manuscript; the fertility myth underlying it is immeasurably older (see Kinsley). Burns expands on his source material by paying more attention to the actual processing of the grain. The malting process described is the first stage of making both whisky and beer, before distillation (for whisky) or the addition of hops (for beer).

136 l. 30. *cudgell'd.* Threshing, to beat the grain from the stalks.

l. 32. *turn'd him o'er and o'er.* Winnowing, to remove the chaff from the grain.

ll. 33–4. *a darksome pit | With water.* Soaking in a tub.

137 ll. 39–40. *as signs of life appeared, | They toss'd him to and fro.* The wet grain is allowed to germinate on the malting floor, and raked to ensure this happens evenly.

l. 41. *wasted o'er a scorching flame.* The germinating grain is then dried in a kiln, completing the malting process.

l. 44. *crush'd him between two stones.* The malt is then ground into 'grist' (to which water and yeast will be added to begin fermentation).

138 *A Fragment.* K38. Also known as 'Ballad on the American War' and by its first line.

Tune: Gillicrankie (better known as Killiekrankie).

Burns transcribed a version of this old Jacobite song (see headnote to 'There'll never be peace', p. 344) for *The Scots Musical Museum* as song 292. As well as the tune, Burns adopts for this poem the internal rhyme used in the first and third lines of its chorus and third verse ('Or I had fed an Athole Gled | On th' braes o' Killiecrankie, O') and makes it a consistent structuring principle in his stanzas.

l. 1. *Guilford.* Frederick North, second Earl of Guilford (1732–92), usually referred to as Lord North, prime minister 1770–82.

l. 2. *hellim*. Simply 'a common Sc. pronunciation of Eng. *helm*, tiller' (*DSL*): this line is the only instance that *DSL* cites.

ll. 3–6. *Ae night, at tea . . . And in the sea did jaw*. To assist the East India Company North allowed it to export its tea direct to the American colonies to be sold by authorized merchants there, without passing through a British port or paying the duty this would incur; instead, a tax would be levied on the tea in America to pay for colonial administration. This programme was imposed without consultation with the colonies themselves; threatened to make colonial government financially independent of the governed; and undercut other traders in tea, both legitimate and illegitimate. On 16 December 1773 protesters in Boston seized the cheap tea from three Company ships and dumped it overboard: the 'Boston Tea Party'.

l. 7. *full Congress*. In September 1774 twelve of the thirteen colonies sent delegates to a Continental Congress in Philadelphia to demand the repeal of punitive legislation passed by North's government in response to events in Boston, and agreed to work for the repeal of all British colonial legislation passed since the end of the war with France in 1763. The Second Continental Congress assembled in May the following year, by which time fighting had already broken out between colonial militias and the British army. It was this Congress which declared the independence of the United States from Britain on 4 July 1776.

l. 9. *Montgomery*. Richard Montgomery was the Irish-born leader of the first campaign by the Continental Army in the Revolutionary War, an invasion of Quebec from Lake Champlain in late 1775.

l. 12. *C–rl–t–n*. General Guy Carlton (1724–1808), the Governor of Quebec, narrowly escaped capture after evacuating Montreal, and Montgomery's forces continued down the St Lawrence ('*Lowrie's burn*').

ll. 13–16. *he, at Quebec . . . Amang his en'mies a', man*. Montgomery was killed in a failed attempt to storm Quebec city on 31 December: 'Montgomery-like . . . Wi' sword in hand' connects him to the militarily-inclined Montgomeries (no relation) of Burns's own county (see note to p. 17, l. 57).

l. 17. *Tammy G–ge*. General Thomas Gage (1721–87), commander-in-chief of the British army in America and Governor of Massachusetts, sent his soldiers out of Boston in April 1775 to capture rebel arms. The skirmishes this provoked at Lexington and Concord began the war, and drove the British force back into Boston, where Gage then found himself penned in by the New England militias.

l. 19. *Willie H—e*. General Sir William Howe (1729–1814), who succeeded Gage as commander-in-chief in October 1775. With 'a deep affection for American colonists' (*DNB*) he pulled his punches in the months after the Declaration of Independence and pursued the possibility of a negotiated settlement from his base at New York. Even when this failed he avoided any strategy likely to crush the rebellion outright, instead mounting an expedition to Philadelphia in the summer of 1777 (Burns's verse obscures this chronology).

138 l. 24. *Sir Loin.* That sirloin of beef is so called because this cut was knighted by an epicure monarch is a 'fictitious etymology' dating back at least to the seventeenth century, says *OED*.

l. 25. *B–rg—ne.* General John Burgoyne (1723–92), commander of the British army in Canada. In the autumn of 1777 he led his forces south via Lake Champlain, planning to link up with Howe's army advancing from New York. But Howe had ignored this plan in favour of his Philadelphia expedition, and Burgoyne instead found American forces under General Gates blocking his way. An attempt to break through was defeated at the battle of Bemis Heights: Burns mentions Simon Fraser, a career soldier from Inverness and one of Burgoyne's brigade commanders, killed in this action. At Saratoga, surrounded and short of supplies, Burgoyne was forced to surrender his entire army to the Americans.

l. 29. *C–rnw–ll–s.* General Charles Cornwallis (1738–1805) led successful operations in the southern colonies in the summer of 1780, but in the autumn of 1781 became trapped in his base at Yorktown on the Virginia coast by a Franco-American army on land and a large French naval force at sea.

139 l. 30. *Buckskins.* The rebel troops (and Americans in general, as at l. 65 of 'Epistle to J. Rankine').

l. 31. *Cl–nt–n's glaive.* General Sir Henry Clinton (1730–95) succeeded Howe as commander-in-chief on the latter's resignation in 1778. He was slow to send forces from New York to relieve Cornwallis at Yorktown: Cornwallis surrendered on 19 October 1781, effectively ending the war. Clinton's ships then turned back without engaging the superior French fleet. 'Glaive' means sword: a poetic archaism.

l. 33. *M–nt–gue.* John Montagu (1718–92), fourth Earl of Sandwich. First Lord of the Admiralty under North; he took the blame for the naval situation which led to the disaster at Yorktown.

l. 35. *S–ckv–lle.* George Sackville Germain (1716–85), Secretary of State for the American Colonies in North's government and 'the driving force in the execution of global strategy' during the war (*DNB*).

ll. 35–6. *wha stood the stoure, | The German Chief to thraw.* Sackville's strategy was often frustrated by his generals in America: Wallace glosses 'stoure' as 'brunt of the struggle' and suggests that the 'German Chief' refers to the 'commander of the Hessian auxiliaries' deployed there (Wallace Vol. II, 64). Kinsley instead reads these lines as a reference back to the event that almost finished Sackville's career two decades earlier, his alleged disobedience of a (very imprecise) order from his commanding officer, Prince Ferdinand of Brunswick, at the battle of Minden in 1759; an incident used against him for the rest of his life.

l. 37. *Paddy B–rke.* Edmund Burke (1729–97), MP for Malton: only 'Paddy' because he was Irish.

l. 39. *Charlie F–x.* Charles James Fox: see note to p. 19, l. 109 and *passim*. As country gentlemen lost faith in the North government over its handling of the American war, the opposition scented blood: in the House of Commons, the angry eloquence of Burke and Fox linked this crisis to the ability of the King's ministers to corrupt the independence of parliament through Treasury money and powers of patronage.

l. 41. *R–ck–ngh–m*. Charles Watson-Wentworth (1730–82), second Marquess of Rockingham, who had been prime minister in 1765–6 and then led the anti-North faction that included Fox and Burke in the Commons. When North resigned in March 1782, Rockingham took his place, but died in July of that year.

l. 43. *Sh–lb–rne meek held up his cheek*. William Petty (1737–1805), second Earl of Shelburne, was the leader of the other faction in opposition to North. He entered government in alliance with Rockingham in 1782, and replaced the latter as prime minister on his death, inheriting the thankless task of concluding a peace treaty with the United States and France. His policy in the negotiations was to concede everything demanded by the Americans, to ensure that France, the real enemy, gained next to nothing from their very expensive war. Burns jokingly explains this policy as an example of Christian charity ('resist not evil: but whosoever shall smite thee on thy right cheek, turn to him the other also', Matthew 5: 39). Later events proved its wisdom, but it caused outrage among MPs ('Saint Stephen's Boys': see note to p. 18, l. 71). In the words of one historian, 'The country would accept peace because it needed it, but then condemn the man who had made it' (Watson, *Reign of George III*, 257).

l. 47. *N–rth an' F–x united stocks*. Shelburne resigned in February 1783; Fox then formed a coalition government with the man who had been until recently their common enemy, Lord North, under the nominal premiership of the Duke of Portland.

l. 49. *Clubs an' Hearts were Charlie's cartes*. Perhaps representing Fox's combination of ruthless political manoeuvring and personal charm. For Fox's gambling, see note to p. 19, ll. 113–14.

ll. 51–2. *Till the Diamond's Ace, of Indian race, | Led him a sair faux pas*. Burke and Fox prepared a bill reforming the relationship of the East India Company to the Crown, to prevent governments from using its influence over appointments to Company jobs as a means of controlling MPs. But Fox and Burke were by now widely seen as 'factious': that is, serving only the interest of their own political friends and allies, rather than that of the nation as a whole. In this light, Fox's India Bill looked like an attempt to put Indian patronage permanently in the hands of Foxites, replacing a tyranny of the Crown with a tyranny of party, and the Commons began to turn against them.

l. 53. *placads*. 'Placad' is the Scots equivalent of 'placard', but here with the specific meaning of 'summons, call. Rare. Appar. orig. in some 18th c. Jacobite song adapted by Burns and Scott' (*DSL*).

l. 54. *Chatham's Boy*. William Pitt the younger (see note to p. 16, l. 19) was the second son of William Pitt the elder (see note to p. 43, l. 57), who was made Earl of Chatham in 1766. Pitt had been first brought into government by Shelburne, and resigned with him; now those opposed to the India Bill, including the King, began to line up Pitt as an alternative prime minister.

139 l. 56. *'Up, Willie, waur them a', man!'*. 'Up an' waur them a', Willie' was a Jacobite song on the Battle of Sheriffmuir (see note to p. 57, l. 127), a version of which Burns adapted as song 188 for *The Scots Musical Museum*.

l. 57. *Behind the throne then Gr–nv–lle's gone*. George Grenville, third Earl Temple (1753–1813) communicated to the House of Lords the King's view 'that he should consider all who voted for it [Fox's India Bill] as his enemies'. The Lords duly rejected it on 17 December 1783, allowing the King to dismiss Fox and North and appoint Pitt as First Lord of the Treasury.

l. 59. *slee D–nd–s*. For Henry Dundas see note to p. 18, l. 78. A key ally of Pitt's, working to secure him support among Scottish MPs; the 'Roman wa'' is Hadrian's, running across England to the south of the border with Scotland.

140 ll. 65–6. *N–rth, F–x, and Co.* | *Gowff'd Willie like a ba'*. Although Pitt was now prime minister, Fox retained control of the Commons, and Pitt's measures were repeatedly voted down there in the following months.

ll. 67–8. *and coost their claise* | *Behind him in a raw*. The image seems to be of men stripping for a fight. Pitt came to convince as a 'Patriot' politician, governing independently of factional interests, and Fox's majorities in the Commons were steadily whittled away even before the general election in the spring of 1784.

l. 72. *To mak it guid in law*. Established by the constitutionally dubious tactics described in the note to l. 57, Pitt's government was made 'guid in law' by the 1784 election to the extent that it gave him a majority in the Commons of around 120; Dundas's efforts made the Pittite victory particularly convincing in Scotland ('*Caledon*').

Songs from *The Scots Musical Museum*

For a description of this publication, and Burns's role in it, see the Introduction to this volume.

142 *Green grow the Rashes*. K45; song 77 in *SMM* Vol. I (1787), with the attribution 'The words by Mʳ R. Burns'.

The tune is traditional, recorded as early as 1627, as are the first two lines of the chorus. In Burns's time this seems mostly to have been used for bawdy lyrics: there are two such sets in *The Merry Muses of Caledonia* (see headnote to 'The Fornicater', p. 383), one collected by Burns, and another probably by him, where the chorus continues 'The lasses they hae wimble bores, | The widows they hae gashes, O' (K124). In the present version, sexual pleasure provides a perspective from which the priorities of commercial society can be criticized. These words were also published in the second, Edinburgh, edition of *Poems Chiefly in the Scottish Dialect* in the same year under the title 'Green grow the Rashes. A Fragment' (hence, presumably, the exception to Burns's usual rule of anonymity in *SMM*). The title above the song in *SMM* is the name of the tune (as that above 'Ae Fond Kiss' is 'Rory Dall's Port'), as derived from the chorus of the traditional lyric, which, following a Scottish usage, has 'grows', not 'grow'; the index in *SMM*, like the Edinburgh *Poems*, changes this to 'grow' after Burns's chorus.

143 l. 19. *The wisest Man the warl' saw.* Solomon, the Old Testament king proverbial for wisdom, granted by God 'a wise and an understanding heart' in 1 Kings 3: 12; and who 'loved many strange women' and had 'seven hundred wives, princesses, and three hundred concubines' (1 Kings 11: 1, 3).

144 *The Birks of Aberfeldy.* K170; song 113 in *SMM* Vol. I (1787), with no attribution, but signed 'B'.

The tune is that of an older song, 'The Birks of Abergeldie', recorded in the late seventeenth century and common in the eighteenth-century collections: Johnson also prints its chorus and three, much simpler, stanzas, in which the seducer's promises are more material ('Ye shall get a gown of silk, | And coat of calinmancoe') and the bonny lassie answers back ('Na, kind Sir, I dare nae gang, | My Minnie she'll be angry'). Abergeldie is on Deeside in the north-east; Aberfeldy is on the upper Tay, where Burns wrote this song on his Highland tour earlier in 1787.

146 *The Ploughman.* K205; song 165 in *SMM* Vol. II (1788), with no attribution.

The tune is in several of the eighteenth-century collections. Burns borrows stanzas 2 and 3 from the lyric in David Herd, *Ancient and Modern Scots Songs* (1769), 317–18; like Herd before him he also has an eye on the bawdy version later published in *The Merry Muses of Caledonia* (1799), where ploughing is an extended metaphor for sex.

l. 4. *His bonnet it is blue.* The flat round cap of blue wool was the traditional headgear of Scottish farmers and farm labourers.

147 l. 18. *Saint Johnston.* An old name for Perth.

l. 26. *Corn-mou.* 'A pile of unthreshed grain stored in a barn' (*DSL*).

148 *Rattlin, roarin Willie.* K216; song 194 in *SMM* Vol. II (1788), with no attribution.

Another tune dating from at least the late seventeenth century. The first two stanzas are traditional: Burns adds a third to turn it into a celebration of his own convivial circle.

149 l. 6. *The saut tear blin't his e'e.* A mock-heroic moment. As Kinsley notes, this is a phrase typical of tragic ballads, e.g. *Mary Hamilton*: 'But when she cam to the gallows-foot, | The saut tear blinded her ee' (Child, *English and Scottish Popular Ballads* no. 173, version M, ll. 23–4).

149 l. 17. *Crochallan*. The Crochallan Fencibles was a drinking club founded in Edinburgh by William Smellie, a printer, which met in a tavern in Anchor Close owned by Daunie Douglas. Douglas was famous for singing the Gaelic song 'Crodh Chailein' (Colin's Cattle), which gave the club the first part of its name. The second is the designation for the militias raised for home defence since the American Revolutionary War, members of the club adopting mock-military rank. Mention of the Crochallan here turns 'Willie' into a specific figure, its president 'Colonel' William Dunbar, a lawyer.

150 *Tibbie, I hae seen the day*. K6; song 196 in *SMM* Vol. II (1788), with no attribution, but signed 'X'.

The tune, named in *SMM*, is 'Invercauld's Reel', found in several eighteenth-century collections of Strathspeys. As Kinsley's number indicates, this is one of Burns's earliest pieces, composed when he was 17 or 18.

152 *Ay waukin, O*. K287; song 213 in *SMM* Vol. III (1790), with no attribution.

An old tune, and words that also draw on traditional materials. The second and third verses, with only five syllables in the first line, are scored with an alternative first bar in the text:

154 *My love she's but a Lassie yet*. K293; song 225 in *SMM* Vol. III (1790), with no attribution.

The first stanza is traditional, and had been attached to this tune, 'Miss Farquarson's Reel', before Burns; he turns it into a drinking song, with the last stanza borrowed from another version of 'Green grows the Rashes'.

156 *I Love my Jean*. K227; song 235 in *SMM* Vol. III (1790), with no attribution, but signed 'R'.

The first line is sometimes used as the title. The index in *SMM* comments 'Music by Marshall', but William Marshall's 'Miss Admiral Gordon's Strathspey' is in turn based on an older tune. Written for Burns's wife, Jean (née Armour); George Thomson emphasized this autobiographical context in renaming the tune 'The Poet's ain Jean' for publication in the *Select Collection* in 1805.

158 *John Anderson my Jo*. K302; song 260 in *SMM* Vol. III (1790), with no attribution, but signed 'B'.

A very old tune, long attached to this title; but the version circulating in eighteenth-century Scotland was a wife's brisk complaint about her ageing husband's impotence, as reflected in the lyric included in *The Merry Muses of Caledonia*: 'John Anderson, my jo, John, | When first that ye began, | Ye had as good a tail-tree, | As ony other man', and so on.

Burns slows down the tune, and, as with 'Green grows the Rashes', turns a bawdy song into something very different. Republished in Thomson's *Select Collection* in 1799.

160 *Ca' the ewes to the knowes.* K185; song 264 in *SMM* Vol. III (1790), with no attribution. 'Ewes' must be pronounced as it is usually spelt in Scots, 'yowes'.

Kinsley designates this version the 'A' text. This is a rare instance of Burns 'collecting' a traditional song from an oral source, rather than writing new lyrics, or adapting old ones, for already-published tunes. His source was Revd John Clunie, at the time of his meeting Burns in 1787 a schoolmaster in Fife; writing to Thomson in 1794, Burns says that Clunie 'sung it charmingly; & at my request, Mr Clarke took it down from his singing.—When I gave it to Johnson, I added some Stanzas to the song and mended others, but still it will not do for you' (L636). Right enough, a 'B' text (K456), revised further for Thomson, never appeared in the *Select Collection*. The verse needs to fit in five syllables before the second bar, where the chorus has only three, so the score offers separate notation for this:

162 *The rantin dog the Daddie o't.* K80; song 277 in *SMM* Vol. III (1790), with no attribution, but signed 'Z', which the Index tells us designates 'old verses, with corrections or additions' rather than a particular author: Burns is trying to distance himself from what are clearly his words.

The tune is named in *SMM* as 'East nook o' Fife'. The words follow the pattern of a lyric by Allan Ramsay, 'The Cordial' (Ramsay Vol. III, 40–1), whose tune is known by the first line of Ramsay's song, 'Where will bonny Annie lie', and sometimes proposed as an alternative setting for the present song. I have made consistent the random capitalization of 'wha' in the score. Included, as it stands, in *The Merry Muses of Caledonia*.

163 l. 6. *groanin maut.* 'Ale brewed to celebrate a birth' (*DSL*).

l. 9. *Creepie-chair.* The stool of repentance, in church, where those guilty of 'fornication' stood to be publicly rebuked: see note to p. 133, l. 54. Compare also the same experience narrated from the male point of view in 'The Fornicater' from *The Merry Muses of Caledonia* (in this volume).

164 *Tam Glen.* K236; song 296 in *SMM* Vol. III (1790), with no attribution.

The tune is 'The Merry Beggars', an English tune from the opera *The Jovial Crew* (1731) which had found its way into Oswald's *Caledonian Pocket Companion*. The lyric was republished in the *Select Collection* in 1799 set to 'The Muckin' o' Geordie's Byre': one of Thomson's favourite tunes, but a setting never suggested by Burns.

165 l. 18. *hunder marks ten.* The mark or merk was an old unit of Scottish currency, equivalent to 13s. 4d.

165 l. 21. *the Valentines' dealing*. 'A custom observed on St.Valentine's eve whereby the names of the members of a company of both sexes are written on slips of paper and then chosen by lot by the opposite sex, the person whose name was drawn supposedly becoming the drawer's sweetheart for the year' (*DSL*).

l. 26. *My droukit sark-sleeve*. Another way of discovering your destined partner: 'You go out . . . to a south-running spring or rivulet . . . and dip your left shirt sleeve. Go to bed in sight of a fire, and hang your wet sleeve before it to dry. Ly awake; and sometime near midnight, an apparition, having the exact figure of the grand object in question, will come and turn the sleeve, as if to dry the other side of it' (Burns's note to 'Halloween' in the Kilmarnock *Poems*, p. 61).

166 *My Tochers the Jewel*. K345; song 312 in *SMM* Vol. IV (1792), with no attribution, but signed 'B'.

The tune is 'The Muckin' o' Geordie's Byre', which dates from the early eighteenth century, and is found in many of the song collections of the period. The last four lines of the lyric, and possibly others, are borrowed from traditional materials. Thomson republished this song in the *Select Collection*, 1799.

167 l. 9. *airle-penny*. 'Payment as a token of engagement of services, or as the preliminary to the striking of a bargain' (*DSL*).

168 *There'll never be peace till Jamie comes hame*. K326; song 315 in *SMM* Vol. IV (1792), with no attribution.

The tune is in Oswald's *Caledonian Pocket Companion* Vol. I, 20. Sending this song to his friend Alexander Cunningham, an Edinburgh lawyer, in March 1791, Burns introduces it thus: 'You must know a beautiful Jacobite Air, There'll never be peace till Jamie comes hame.—When Political combustion ceases to be the object of Princes and Patriots, it then, you know, becomes the lawful prey of Historians & Poets.—' He continues, 'If you like the air, & if the stanzas hit your fancy, you cannot imagine, my dear Friend, how much you would oblige me if by the charms of your delightful voice you would give my honest effusion to "The memory of joys that are past," to the few friends whom you indulge in that pleasure.—' (L442).

'Jacobites' were loyalists of the exiled King James, VII of Scotland and II of England (deposed by William and Mary in 1688); and after his death in 1701 of his son, also James (d. 1766). Jacobite sentiment remained widespread in Scottish song even as political commitment to a Stuart restoration shrivelled.

169 l. 5. *The Church is in ruins*. James was driven out in 1688 for being a Catholic, and for having a son and heir whom he could raise a Catholic. But many Jacobites were adherents of the 'national' church as they understood it: high-church Anglicans in England, opposed to tolerance for dissenting Protestant denominations; and Episcopalians in Scotland, opposed to the Presbyterian constitution confirmed for the Church of Scotland in 1690.

l. 7. *we ken wha's to blame.* Either William, or the House of Hanover, the German Protestant princely family on whom the British crown was settled on the death of James VII's childless, but Protestant, daughters Mary and Anne. George of Hanover acceded to the throne on Anne's death in 1714 as George I.

l. 9. *for Jamie drew sword.* John Graham of Claverhouse raised forces for the elder James that defeated government forces at Killiecrankie in 1689; and there were two significant uprisings in Scotland in support of the younger James, in 1715 and in 1745–6.

170 *Rory Dall's Port [Ae fond kiss].* K337; song 347 in *SMM* Vol. IV (1792), with no attribution, but signed 'X'.

SMM gives as the title the name of the tune, which is in Oswald's *Caledonian Pocket Companion*, Vol. VIII, 24: 'port' is Gaelic for 'tune', and Rory Dall is the traditional name of the harper of the MacLeods at Dunvegan on Skye. This tune is very different to the one to which Burns's words are usually sung today.

The song is associated with Burns's relationship with Mrs Agnes McLehose, whom he met in Edinburgh in 1787 when she had been separated from her lawyer husband for many years. Herself a poet, they entered into an intense sentimental relationship conducted mostly through the exchange of letters and verse. Burns adapted two of McLehose's poems for publication as lyrics in *SMM* Vol. II (186, 'Talk not of love' and 190, 'To a Blackbird', both 'By a Lady'), a volume which also included his own song (198) 'Clarinda' sung by 'Sylvander': pseudonyms the pair used in their letters. McLehose broke with Burns on learning of his marriage to Jean Armour later in 1788; but contact was renewed in late 1791, just before McLehose made the dangerous crossing to Jamaica in a failed attempt at reconciliation with her husband. Anticipation of this journey clearly prompted the three poems of farewell to 'Nancy' of which this is one. Yet the letter in which Burns sent them to McLehose frames them in a quite different way: 'I have yours, my ever dearest Nancy, this moment.—I have just ten minutes before the Post goes, & these I shall employ in sending you some Songs I have just been composing to different tunes for the Collection of Songs, of which you have three volumes—& of which you *shall* have the fourth.—' (L486).

172 *Bess and her Spinning Wheel.* K365; song 360 in *SMM* Vol. IV (1792), with no attribution.

The tune is called 'Sweet's the lass that loves me' in the *Caledonian Pocket Companion*, Vol. V, 10 but dates from around 1700.

l. 2. *rock and reel.* The distaff, the tool which held the unspun flax or wool during spinning, and the reel onto which it was spun.

173 l. 9. *the burnies trot.* In the sense of 'to flow rapidly and noisily, to purl, ripple' (*DSL*).

l. 21. *craik.* Corncrake.

174 *Ye Jacobites by Name.* K371; song 371 in *SMM* Vol. IV (1792), with no attribution.

The tune had been published in an English collection of 1719–20: in the list of songs for inclusion in *SMM* drawn up by Burns and Johnson, its title is given as 'Up, Black-nebs by Name, alias Ye Jacobites by Name'. 'Black-neb' is a (usually derogatory) name for a democrat, sympathetic to the aims of the French Revolution (for 'Jacobites' see headnote to 'There'll never be peace till Jamie comes hame', p. 344). Both titles promise a song inciting political action from those content with the mere name of a party: the song delivers something much more ambivalent.

176 *The Banks o' Doon*. K328; song 374 in *SMM* Vol. IV (1792), with no attribution, but signed 'B'.

This, Kinsley's 'B' text, is the song now known under this title, and was published again in Thomson's *Select Collection* in 1798; the earlier 'A' text was written for a different tune. The present tune is 'The Caledonian Hunt's Delight', first published in Niel Gow's second volume of *Strathspey Reels* (1788). For the river Doon, see Map.

177 ll. 7–8. *departed joys, | Departed never to return*. Kinsley suggests an echo of Robert Blair's *The Grave* (1743): 'Of Joys departed | Not to return, how painful the Remembrance!' (ll. 109–10).

178 *Such a parcel of rogues in a nation*. K375; song 378 in *SMM* Vol. IV (1792), with no attribution.

The specific 'rogues' accused here are the 31 Scottish Commissioners who negotiated a Treaty of Union between the English and Scottish parliaments in 1706. Headed by the Duke of Queensberry, they included two directors of the Bank of Scotland and the Provost of Edinburgh as well as noblemen. Most stood to gain financially from the terms of the Treaty, which included compensation for the losses incurred by investors in Scotland's calamitous colonial venture in Central America the previous decade. Securing the assent of the Scottish parliament to its own abolition in 1707 also required considerable bribery, so this song's targets can be understood to include a large part of Scotland's politically enfranchised class, as well as the Commissioners. The Union was deeply unpopular with ordinary Scots, and Burns has adapted a song, both words and music, from around that time: the tune is in the *Caledonian Pocket Companion*, Vol. IV, 26.

179 ll. 5–6. *Now Sark runs o'er the Solway sands, | And Tweed rins to the ocean*. The river Sark marks the western end of the border between England and Scotland, and runs into the Solway Firth; the river Tweed, as it approaches the North Sea, forms its eastern end.

l. 20. *Bruce and loyal Wallace*. Robert Bruce, King of Scots 1306–29, and William Wallace (d. 1305), leaders of Scotland's Wars of Independence from England.

180 *Afton Water*. K257; song 386 in *SMM* Vol. IV (1792), with no attribution, but signed 'B'.

Burns sent this lyric to his friend and patron Mrs Dunlop in February 1789, with these words: 'There is a small river, Afton, that falls into Nith, near New-Cumnock, which has some charming, wild, romantic scenery on its banks.—I have a particular pleasure in those little pieces of poetry such as our Scots songs, &c. where the names and landskip-features of rivers, lakes, or woodlands, that one knows, are introduced.—I attempted a compliment of that kind, to Afton, as follows: I mean it for Johnson's Musical Museum.—' (L310).

181 ll. 5–6: *Thou stock dove . . . Ye wild whistling blackbirds in yon thorny den.* Kinsley suggests that the birds are borrowed from James Thomson's 'Spring': 'The blackbird whistles from the thorny brake' at l. 604, and 'the stock-dove breathes | A melancholy murmur through the whole' at l. 613; the stock-dove first appears in the second edition of 1730 (Thomson 19).

182 *The Deil's awa wi' th' Exciseman.* K386; song 399 in *SMM* Vol. IV (1792), with no attribution.

In early 1792 Burns sent this song to John Leven, a General Supervisor in the Excise Office at Edinburgh, and thus one of Burns's superiors. The letter is mostly Excise business, but ends, 'Mr Mitchell mentioned to you a ballad which I composed & sung at one of his Excise-court dinners: here it is.—' (L500). The tune is in the *Caledonian Pocket Companion*, Vol. VIII, 21, though it also appears in an earlier, English collection: in his letter Burns gives its name as 'Madam Cassey'.

183 l. 3. *Mahoun.* The devil.

l. 15. *the ae best dance.* 'Before a superlative, ae adds emphasis' explains *DSL.*

184 *A red red Rose.* K453; song 402 in *SMM* Vol. V (1796), with no attribution, but the 'Old Set' (see below) is signed 'R'.

The tune is 'Major Graham', from Niel Gow's first volume of *Strathspey Reels* (1784). This three-part tune requested by Burns creates a problem for setting the words: in performance, one of those parts has to be repeated to accommodate all four stanzas. The full lyric, as reproduced here, appears in song 403, an 'Old Set' of these words to a different (but, as Kinsley notes, no more traditional) tune. The lyric borrows from traditional materials but reorganized by Burns. In a letter to Alexander Cunningham with the song in late 1793, Burns describes giving it to Pietro Urbani, the Milanese-born composer and teacher who was himself publishing a collection of Scottish songs in Edinburgh: '—I likewise gave him a simple old Scots song which I had pickt up in this country [i.e. Dumfriesshire], which he promised to set in a suitable manner.—I would not even have given him this, had there been any of Mr Thomson's airs, *suitable to it,* unoccupied' (L593A). Thomson republished the song to the same tune in the *Select Collection* in 1799.

186 *Auld lang syne.* K240; song 413 in *SMM* Vol. V (1796), with no attribution, but signed 'Z' (signifying 'old verses, with corrections or additions').

The tune is in the *Caledonian Pocket Companion*, Vol. III, 21, and dates from at least 1700. How much of that lyric is Burns's invention has been debated: the title, and a version of the chorus, had certainly long been in circulation. In his own comments Burns consistently attributes the song to an earlier source. In a letter to Mrs Dunlop in 1788, Burns describes it as 'an old song & tune which has often thrilled thro' my soul'; and at the end of the transcription he adds, 'Light be the turf on the breast of the heaven-inspired Poet who composed this glorious Fragment! There is more of the fire of native genius in it, than in half a dozen of modern English Bacchanalians' (L290). Writing to Thomson five years later he comments, 'The air is but mediocre; but the following song, the old Song of the olden times, & which has never been in print, nor even in manuscript, untill I took it down from an old man's singing; is enough to recommend any air—' (L586). However, McGuirk suggests this may be a deliberate policy of self-effacement on Burns's part, rather than an accurate reflection of how this lyric came into being (McGuirk, p. 251). Thomson published it in the *Select Collection* in 1799 with the tune 'O can ye labour lea' to which it is now usually sung.

188 *Comin thro' the rye.* K560; song 417 in *SMM* Vol. V (1796), with no attribution, but signed 'B'.

Johnson calls this the '1ˢᵗ Sett.' of this song; song 418 gives a second song under this title with variant words and different music. Burns's song is a variation on a widely circulating sexually suggestive *topos*: there is an explicitly bawdy version in *The Merry Muses of Caledonia*. In a manuscript list Burns names the tune as 'Miller's Wedding—a Strathspey'.

190 *O leave novels &c.* K43; song 573 in *SMM* Vol. VI (1803), with the attribution 'By Burns'.

A song from early in Burns's career, as suggested by his reference to himself as 'Rob Mossgiel': Mossgiel was the farm Burns shared with his brother Gilbert in 1783–6, and Scottish farmers were routinely known by the names of their farms in this way. The tune has not been traced.

191 l. 5. *Tom Jones and Grandisons. The History of Tom Jones, a Foundling* (1749) by Henry Fielding; *The History of Sir Charles Grandison* (1753–4) by Samuel Richardson. Tom is a spontaneous and warm-hearted hero whose sexual adventures land him in trouble; Sir Charles is a model of masculine chastity. But the particularities of these texts are less relevant here than Burns's play with the idea, often expressed throughout the century, that reading novels warped young women's expectations of their lives in ways that left them vulnerable to seduction by more knowing men; a possibility often acted out in the plots of novels themselves. In Burns's favourite, Henry Mackenzie's *The Man of Feeling*, for example, prostitute Emily Atkins recounts her original seduction and betrayal by a young gentleman whose figure, address, and conversation 'were not unlike those warm ideas of an accomplished man which my favourite novels had taught me to form' (p. 43).

Songs from *A Select Collection of Original Scotish Airs, for the Voice*

For a description of this publication, and Burns's relationship to it, see the Introduction to this volume.

192 *Duncan Gray came here to woo.* K394; song 48 in *SC* Vol. I (1798). Attribution under the title, 'Written for this work by Mr Robert Burns'.

The tune is traditional, and traditionally used for sexual comedy. There is an explicitly bawdy version in *The Merry Muses of Caledonia*, possibly 'mended' by Burns; Burns also wrote a cleverly suggestive lyric for *The Scots Musical Museum*, Vol. II (1788) song 160, keeping the repeated line of the bawdy version, 'Ha, ha the girdin o't'. This song differs from both earlier versions in replacing premarital sex with 'wooing'; but like Burns's earlier version for *SMM*, and unlike the bawdy version, the story ends with a happy marriage.

196 *O whistle, and I'll come to you, my lad.* K420; song 94 in *SC* Vol. II (1799). Attribution under the title, 'Written for this work by Mr Robert Burns'.

The first four lines of each stanza, and the tune, are traditional. Burns had already published a very basic version of this song in *The Scots Musical Museum*, Vol. II (1788) as song 106, adding to the first four lines only another repeating four ('Come down the back stairs when ye come to court me; | | And come as ye were na' coming to me').

Other poems and songs published in Burns's lifetime

199 *Written on a window in Stirling.* K166A. These lines were first 'published' by Burns on the window of his room in an inn at Stirling, etched with a diamond-tipped stylus, in August 1787, on his way north to tour the Highlands. But they were copied by other hands and circulated in manuscript, and first printed the following year, as evidence for the prosecution in a 24-page pamphlet, *Animadversions on some Poets and Poetasters of the present age, especially R—T B—S, and J—N L—K. By James Maxwell, Poet in Paisley*. Maxwell (1720–1800) was best known for a metrical version of the Psalms (1773), and attacks Burns for impiety in, for example, 'The Cotter's Saturday night' and 'The Holy Fair'. The present text is then offered on page 8 as 'Another Specimen of the same Author, said to be written on a Window in Stirling'. It is followed by three verse 'answers' to Burns's denunciation of the reigning dynasty. The first, by Revd George Hamilton, begins, 'Thus wretches rail, whom sordid gain | Has dragg'd in faction's gilded chain'; and ends, 'These few rash lines shall damn thy name, | And blast thy hopes of future fame' (ll. 13–14). The other two, 'By another hand', both end by bidding Burns back to his master in hell, and the second contains an outright threat: 'For this thy life in danger stands, | If thou art found within his lands', that is, the King's (ll. 13–14). Burns's poem was already being held against him by potential sponsors in his quest for a job in the Excise (see Introduction). He wrote to Mrs McLehose: 'I have almost given up on the excise idea. . . . I have been question'd like a child about my matters, and blamed and schooled for my Inscription on Stirling window' (L189, 27 January 1788). William Scott Douglas tells the story that, on a return visit two months after the first, Burns went back to the inn 'and dashed out the pane with the butt-end of his riding-switch' (Douglas Vol. II, 309). In the Glenriddell manuscript (see Introduction) Burns's title for 'these imprudent lines' is 'Written by Somebody in the window of an inn at Stirling on seeing the Royal Palace in ruins'.

199 l. 1. *STEWARTS*. The royal family of Scotland from Robert II (r. 1371–90), and of England from the accession of James VI as James I of England in 1603, to Anne (d. 1714). Stirling Castle was the principal base for the Stewart court until the departure of James for London.

l. 2. *for Scotia well*. The version in the Glenriddell manuscript has 'for Scotland's weal': Maxwell may have worked from a corrupted copy, or Burns may have amended the line in the later version (see note to l. 4).

l. 3. *unroof'd*. Burns is referring to the collapse ten years earlier, from natural causes, of the ceiling in the King's Inner Hall, the royal presence chamber (the castle was garrisoned, and not otherwise a ruin).

l. 4. *other's hands*. The manuscript version has 'other hands' and then inserts two additional lines: 'Fallen indeed, and to the earth, | Whence grovelling reptiles take their birth.—' Kinsley suggests that these 'appear to be Burns's addition for the Glenriddell MS'.

l. 6. *A Race, outlandish*. The House of Hanover. With no children surviving the ageing Anne, a 1701 act of the English parliament settled the succession on this German princely family as the nearest Protestants in line, to preclude the restoration of Anne's father, the Catholic James II and VII, deposed in 1688, or his Catholic son. George of Hanover accordingly became George I of Great Britain and Ireland on Anne's death in 1714; his great-grandson, George III, was the reigning monarch in Burns's lifetime.

l. 7. *ideot*. This spelling was still current.

ll. 7–8. *An ideot Race to honour lost, | Who know them best despise them most*. Two major editions, published in 1834 while the throne was still filled by this outlandish race, confessedly omit these lines, condemning their 'severe and improper remarks' (*The Works of Robert Burns*, ed. James Hogg and William Motherwell, Vol. II, 71); 'What was improper in the days of Burns is not proper now' (Cunningham Vol. III, 294). Allan Cunningham does however add Burns's 'Reply' to the Revd Hamilton's 'Answer', and his mocking 'Reproof' to his own poem (K166C), appealing to the legal authority of the great (Scottish-born) English judge, William Murray (1704–93), Earl of Mansfield:

> RASH mortal, and slanderous Poet, thy name
> Shall no longer appear in the records of fame;
> Dost not know that old Mansfield, who writes like the Bible,
> Says the more 'tis a truth, Sir, the more 'tis a libel?

Here Lies Robert Fergusson Poet. K142. Fergusson, Burns's most important inspiration for poetry in Scots, had died penniless in the Edinburgh insane asylum (probably on 17, not 16, October 1774) and been buried in an unmarked grave at Canongate Church. On his first visit to Edinburgh Burns wrote to the Bailies of the Canongate 'for your permission to lay a simple stone over his revered ashes, to remain an unalienable property to his deathless fame' (L81, 6 February 1787). The stone was eventually erected, at Burns's expense, in August 1789, and the present text is taken from the inscription. On the back of the letter to the Bailies Burns wrote a version with two additional stanzas:

> She mourns, sweet, tuneful youth, thy hapless fate,
>   Tho' all the pow'rs of song thy fancy fired;
> Yet Luxury and Wealth lay by in state,
>   And thankless starv'd what they so much admir'd.
>
> This humble tribute with a tear he gives,
>   A brother Bard, he can no more bestow;
> But dear to fame thy Song immortal lives,
>   A nobler monument than Art can show.

These were eventually published in Alexander Smith, *The Poetical Works of Robert Burns* (1865), Vol. I, 348. See also the posthumously published 'Verses, Written under the Portrait of Fergusson the Poet' and 'Ill-fated genius!'

l. 1. *No sculptur'd Marble here.* Still the case, but a bronze Fergusson now strolls out of the gates of the kirkyard: David Annand's statue was unveiled in 2004.

l. 2. *No storied Urn nor animated Bust.* In the manuscript version this is in quotation marks, adapted as it is from Gray's 'Elegy Written in a Country Churchyard': 'Can storied urn or animated bust | Back to its mansion call the fleeting breath?' (ll. 41–2; Lonsdale 125).

Elegy, On the departed Year 1788. K250. Published in the *Edinburgh Evening Courant* for Saturday, 10 January 1789. The *Courant* was a newspaper published three times a week, selling for 3*d*., in the usual format of a single sheet folded once with text carried in four columns on each page: the outside pages carried mostly advertisements and commercial news, the inside spread mostly foreign and domestic politics and social notices. This poem appeared on page 3 in column 3 and was signed 'Thomas A Linn' (a 'linn' is a waterfall, hence an appropriate pen-name for 'Burns').

200 l. 9. *The Spanish empire's tint a head.* Charles III, King of Spain (b. 1716), had died on 14 December after a 29-year reign.

l. 10. *Bautie.* 'A name given to a dog' (*DSL*).

l. 11. *The tulzie's teugh 'tween PITT and FOX.* William Pitt the younger, the prime minister; and Charles James Fox, the leader of the opposition (see notes to p. 16, l. 19, p. 19, l. 109 and *passim*); on the cause of the 'tulzie' see note to l. 35 below.

l. 14. *to the hen birds unco civil.* Referring to Fox's mistresses.

l. 21. *mony a plack and mony a peck.* Church of Scotland clergy were paid in a combination of money and agricultural produce, mostly oats.

l. 28. *dowielie.* When this poem was republished in Thomas Stewart's *Poems Ascribed to Robert Burns* (1801) this was replaced by 'dowie now'; in R. H. Cromek's *Reliques of Robert Burns* (1808), with 'daviely'. Right enough, 'dowielie' does not appear in the *Dictionary of the Scots Language*, while the two alternatives do; and 'dowf and dowie' is a common pairing. But Burns might be coining a new word, taking the adjective 'dowie' and adding 'lie' to make it an adverb.

200 l. 30. *Embrugh wells are grutten dry.* A hard winter had frozen much of Edinburgh's water supply.

l. 35. *Nae hand-cuff'd, mizzl'd, half-shackl'd Regent.* George III had become mentally incapacitated the previous November. The issue of the *Courant* in which this poem appeared carried, on the facing page, a report of the ongoing 'tulzie' in the House of Commons over the terms on which George's eldest son might be appointed Prince Regent. Fox wanted the younger George granted full monarchical powers; Pitt wanted him 'half-shackl'd' to prevent the prince dismissing Pitt and asking his friend Fox to form a new government (which, the prince assumed, would then pay off his considerable debts). The King recovered before any legislation was passed: Burns wrote an 'Ode to the departed Regency Bill' in March.

201 *On Captain Grose's present Peregrinations through Scotland.* K275. Published in the *Edinburgh Evening Courant* for Thursday, 27 August 1789; once again on page 3 in column 3, and again signed 'Thomas A Linn'.

Francis Grose (1731–91) had published *The Antiquities of England and Wales* in 1772–87, a set of engravings of mostly medieval buildings with accompanying explanatory text. Burns met him on his second trip to Scotland to make sketches and collect information for *The Antiquities of Scotland*, of which the first volume appeared in 1789. They became firm friends and collaborators (see headnote to 'Tam o' Shanter', below). When this poem was included in the two-volume edition of the *Poems* in 1793, the title was amended to 'On the Late Captain Grose's Peregrinations . . .' (Vol. II, 219).

201 l. 1. *Land o' Cakes.* That is, of oatcakes or bannocks.

l. 2. *Frae Maiden-kirk to Johnie Groat's.* Maidenkirk in Wigtownshire is the most southerly of Scottish parishes; John o'Groats in Caithness is traditionally taken as its most northerly community.

ll. 11–12. *an unco slight | O' cawk and keel.* Unusual skill with chalk and pencil, i.e. drawing.

l. 20. *glamor.* Magic. 'When Devil, Wizards, or Juglers deceive the Sight, they are said to cast *Glamour* o'er the Eyes of the Spectator' (glossary to Ramsay's 1721 *Poems*; Ramsay Vol. I, 254).

l. 25. *a sodger bred.* Grose served in the British Army 1747–51, and remained a Captain in the Surrey Militia.

l. 27. *the spurtle blade.* A 'spurtle' can be a flat implement for turning oatcakes, a spatula; but by extension 'a (broad) sword, used jocularly or in disparagement' (*DSL*).

202 l. 32. *gingling jackets.* Mail coats, medieval armour.

l. 38. *Tubalcain*. Zillah's son, 'an instructor of every artificer in brass and iron' (Genesis 4: 22).

l. 40. *Balaam's ass*. Shying away from an armed angel that Balaam can't see, the Lord lets his ass talk back to Balaam when he beats it for this disobedience (Numbers 22: 21–30).

l. 41. *the Witch of Endor*. When Saul gets no supernatural guidance from the Lord, he sends instead for 'a woman that hath a familiar spirit' from Endor (1 Samuel 28).

l. 44. *philibeg*. The *fèileadh beag* (Gaelic) is the kilt, an early eighteenth-century invention.

l. 45. *Abel*. The younger son of Adam and Eve, murdered by his brother Cain in Genesis 4: 8.

203 *Tam o' Shanter*. K321. This poem first appeared in three publications in the Spring of 1791. It was commissioned by Francis Grose (see headnote to 'On Captain Grose's present Peregrinations', p. 352) for the second volume of *The Antiquities of Scotland*, to accompany the etching (included here) and description (see below) for Alloway Church in the Ayrshire section (pp. 199–201); but it was also published in *The Edinburgh Magazine, or, Literary Miscellany*, for March; and in the *Edinburgh Herald* newspaper for 18 March, where it takes up more than two whole columns out of four on the front page. In both periodicals the title is 'Aloway Kirk; or, Tam o'Shanter. A Tale'. The present text is based on Grose's book, this being the context for which the poem was originally written.

Grose's account of Alloway Church is as follows:

> This church stands by the river, a small distance from the bridge of Doon, on the road leading from Maybole to Ayr. About a century ago it was united to the parish of Ayr; since which time it has fallen to ruins. It is one of the eldest parishes in Scotland, and still retains these privileges: the minister of Ayr is obliged to marry and baptise in it, and also here to hold his parochial catechisings. The magistrates attempted, some time ago, to take away the bell; but were repulsed by the Alloites, *vi & armis*.

There is a footnote to the chapter heading which introduces the poem thus:

> This church is also famous for being the place wherein the witches and warlocks used to hold their infernal meetings, or sabbaths, and prepare their magical unctions; here too they used to amuse themselves with dancing to the pipes of the muckle-horned Deel. Diverse stories of these horrid rites are still current; one of which my worthy friend Mr. Burns has here favoured me with in verse.

The poem is contained in this footnote, in two columns; but it is a footnote that takes over almost all of the three pages devoted to Alloway Kirk, with Grose's text only occupying two or three lines along the top of each.

When this poem was included in the two-volume edition of the *Poems* in 1793, Burns added an epigraph: '*Of Brownyis and of Bogillis full is this buke.*' This is l. 18 from the Prologue to Book VI of Gavin Douglas's *Eneados*, his translation of Virgil's *Aeneid* into Scots (completed 1513; a modern edition had appeared in 1710). For Burns's attitude to 'brownies and bogles' see his letter to Dr Moore in Appendix 1, p. 260.

203 l. 1. *chapmen billies.* Pedlars, as in Fergusson's 'Hallow Fair', ll. 28–9: 'Here chapmen billies tak their stand, | An' shaw their *bonny wallies*' (Fergusson 90).

l. 7. *long Scots miles.* See note to p. 64, l. 57.

204 l. 23. *melder.* 'The grinding of one customer's load of corn at a mill' (*DSL*).

l. 28. *the L—d's house.* The name of a pub. This seems to refer to the village inn at Kirkoswald in Carrick (south of the Doon, Tam's part of Ayrshire) run by Jean Kennedy (hence 'Kirkton Jean') and her sister, and known as 'the Leddies' House' after them. But Burns needs a monosyllable here, so we are left to imagine a pub called 'The Lord's House'.

l. 40. *reamin swats.* A conjunction spotted by Kinsley in Ramsay's 'Elegy on Lucky Wood', l. 34 (Ramsay Vol. I, 19).

205 l. 63. *the borealis race.* The aurora borealis, or northern lights.

l. 66. *Evanishing.* A self-consciously 'literary' word, as Kinsley observes, which Burns could have found in the mouth of Sir William in Ramsay's *Gentle Shepherd*, 3. 4. 117: 'Cares evanish like a Morning Dream' (Ramsay Vol. II, 251).

l. 83. *his gude blue bonnet.* The flat round cap of blue wool was the traditional headgear of Scottish tenant farmers and farm labourers.

l. 84. *sonnet.* Here clearly just meaning 'song'. *DSL* suspects that this becomes a Scottish usage only because of its appearance in this line. On the other hand, the English word derives from the Italian *sonetto*, which means 'little song'.

l. 88. *nightly.* As Kinsley notes, in its now-obsolete sense of 'at or by night; during the night' (*OED* 2) rather than 'every night'.

206 ll. 90–6. *Where in the snaw . . . Mungo's mither hang'd hersel.* 'These calamities are to be attributed to witchcraft', observes Kinsley (III, 1358), referring to the (not quite so terrible) misfortunes blamed on Mause in Ramsay's *The Gentle Shepherd*, 2. 3. 31–50, e.g. 'When *Watie* wander'd ae Night thro' the Shaw, | And tint himsell amaist amang the Snaw; | When *Mungo*'s Mear stood still, and swat with Fright, | When he brought East the *Howdy* under Night' (Ramsay Vol. II, 231).

l. 98. *The doubling storm.* In the now-defunct sense of 'resounding, echoing'. Kinsley, and *OED*, offer the precedent of Pope's 'Temple of Fame' (1715), l. 333: 'Thro' the big Dome the doubling Thunder bounds' (Pope 183).

ll. 99–100. *The light'nings flash from pole to pole;* | *Near, and more near, the thunders roll.* This is a neo-classical formula borrowed, Kinsley notes, from Dryden and Pope, for example in the latter's translation of the *Odyssey*: 'Then Jove in anger bids his thunder roll, | And forky lightnings flash from pole to pole' (XII, ll. 485–6).

l. 110. *Fair-play.* 'In justice to him' (Kinsley).

l. 116. *cotillon.* Cotillion could name several types of fashionable dance.

l. 119. *A winnock-bunker.* (In) a window-seat (*DSL*).

l. 123. *He screw'd the pipes.* The drones of a bagpipe are tuned by turning them.

l. 131. *gibbet-airns.* The bodies of hanged criminals were hung up in chains on gibbets as a warning to others.

207 l. 132. *Twa span-lang . . . bairns.* Kinsley suggests that this phrase, followed as it is a few lines later by a reference to a 'strangled' child (l. 137), suggests an echo of *The Grave* (1743) by Robert Blair, where the inmates of the churchyard include 'the *Child* | Of a Span long, that never saw the Sun, | Nor press'd the Nipple, strangled in Life's Porch' (ll. 517–19).

ll. 141–2. *awefu' . . . unlawfu'.* Kinsley points out that this rhyme is borrowed from Ramsay, 'A Tale of Three Bonnets', canto I, ll. 173–4: 'Sae tho the Aith we took was awfu', | To keep it now appears unlawfu'' (Ramsay Vol. III, 13).

ll. 143–6. *Three lawyers' tongues . . . in every neuk.* When this poem was included in the two-volume edition of the *Poems* in 1793 these lines were cut, on the advice of Alexander Fraser Tytler, an Edinburgh lawyer and historian, who argued that the shift into social satire distracted from the effect of pure horror.

l. 158. *seventeen-hunder.* 'Hunder' just means hundred, but in weaving more specifically 'a unit for denoting the fineness of a web . . . and hence the fineness of the cloth itself' (*DSL*). The other examples cited by *DSL* are between six and twelve, so seventeen must be very fine indeed.

l. 164. *spean.* Wean, but 'in transferred use, of creating an aversion to food through disgust, fear or the like' (*DSL*).

l. 168. *There was a winsome wench and walie.* Almost quoting, as Kinsley notes, Ramsay's 'A Tale of Three Bonnets', canto I, l. 83: 'She was a winsome Wench and waly' (Ramsay Vol. III, 10).

208 ll. 171–4. *For mony a beast to dead she shot . . . And kept the country-side in fear.* Another of the calamities laid at Mause's door in Ramsay's *The Gentle Shepherd*, 2. 3, is '*Bawsy* shot to dead upon the Green' (Ramsay Vol. II, 231), 'bawsy' being a name for 'a horse or a cow having a white stripe or patch on the face' (*DSL*).

l. 175. *Paisley harn.* Harn is 'coarse linen cloth made from the refuse of flax or hemp' which 'labouring people use for shirts' (*DSL*, quoting a 1795 account). Paisley was a major centre of Scottish textile production: as we learn from ll. 178–9, Nannie's sark has been bought, not home-made.

208 l. 81. *twa pund Scots.* There had been no separate Scottish currency since the union of 1707, at which point the Scottish pound was worth 1s. 8d. in English currency. But the term 'pund Scots' survived to mean this amount: so Nannie's sark has cost 3s. 4d.

ll. 197–202. *As bees bizz out . . . When 'catch the thief!' resounds aloud.* The similes here follow the 'As . . . When . . .' form of the Homeric or epic simile, and, as Kinsley points out, Burns may be borrowing the first two from Pope's translation of the *Iliad* (1715–20): 'As Wasps, provok'd by Children in their Play, | Pour from their Mansions', describing the Greeks pouring from their tents (XVI. 314–15); and 'As when two skilful Hounds the Lev'ret winde', describing the Greek pursuit of a Trojan spy (X. 427).

l. 199. *open.* 'Of a hound: to bay or cry loudly when on a scent or in sight of the quarry' (*OED*).

209 l. 210. *the key-stane o' the brig.* 'It is a well known fact that witches, or any evil spirits, have no power to follow a poor wight any farther than the middle of the next running stream.—It may be proper likewise to mention to the benighted traveller, that when he falls in with *bogles,* whatever danger may be in his going forward, there is much more hazard in turning back' (Burns's footnote in the 1793 edition: Vol. II, 61).

Extempore on some late commemorations of the poet Thomson. K332. First published in *The Edinburgh Gazetteer* newspaper for Friday, 23 November 1792, in the first column on the back page, signed 'Thomas à Rhymer'. This issue of the *Gazetteer* was only its second: bi-weekly publication was planned but at this stage it appeared every Friday, price 3½d. It had been launched by Captain William Johnston (d. 1817), who had helped found the Scottish Friends of the People the previous July, an association, mostly of lawyers and landowners, dedicated to 'restoring our constitution to its original purity' through reforms aimed at preventing the 'corruption' of parliamentarians by governments (Brims, 'From Reformers to "Jacobins" ', 35). Since then, a French Republic had been declared, and its army had unexpectedly triumphed over the Prussian and Austrian forces intent on destroying it (the present poem is followed by another, not by Burns, 'On the retreat of the Duke of Brunswick': see note to p. 237, l. 11). This had inspired an explosion of political activity among ordinary people too (see also headnote to 'The Tree of Liberty', p. 403). The many political pamphlets circulating in this period included, in the west of Scotland, some purporting to reproduce thirteenth-century prophecies by Thomas the Rhymer of a time when 'after terrible convulsions in church and state, military, civil and religious despots would be forced to flee in shame' (Brims, 'From Reformers to "Jacobins" ', 37): this may inform Burns's choice of pseudonym. Johnson's paper quickly became a crucial 'vehicle for the circulation of radical addresses and motions . . . as well as the dissemination of information about radical activities throughout the British Isles' (*DNB*), and unusually balanced coverage of events of France. Burns was enthusiastic from the start: see his letter to Johnston of 13 November in Appendix 1, p. 267f. The number for 23 November covered, under the headline 'TRIAL OF THE KING', the ongoing debate in the National Convention in Paris regarding the fate of the imprisoned Louis XVI; the establishment of a 'Society of Friends to Liberty and Equality' in Flanders, after the French had driven out its Austrian overlords; and, sharing the back page with this poem, a list of the toasts made at the Revolution Society in Sheffield on the anniversary of the 1688 Revolution in Britain. Although Johnston's paper consistently advocated the reform, not the overthrow, of the British constitution, by February he had been sentenced to three months in prison for reporting a sedition trial. By the end of the year his successor as editor had been charged with seditious libel, and the last issue appeared in January 1794. Burns's connection to the paper threatened to cause him problems, too: see the letter to Fintry dated 5 January 1793 in Appendix 1, p. 271f.

The commemorations to which the poem refers were for James Thomson (1700–48), author of *The Seasons*, at Ednam, his birthplace, in Roxburghshire, in September 1791. They were the idea of David Erskine, Earl of Buchan (1742–1829), who had erected a monument to the poet: Burns wrote a poem for the occasion, as requested, but did not attend.

210 ll. 11–12. *th' unfading garland there,* | *Thy sair-won rightful spoil.* Buchan's event was to culminate in crowning a bust of Thomson with a laurel-wreath. Burns's 'Address, to the Shade of Thomson, on crowning his Bust . . . with Bays' ends with a reference to 'that wreath thou well hast won' (K 331, l. 18).

l. 17. *'To wham hae routh, shall yet be given'.* Matthew, Mark, and Luke all report Jesus's explanation for talking in parables that only some can understand: 'For whosoever hath, to him shall be given, and he shall have more abundance: but whosoever hath not, from him shall be taken away even that he hath' (Matthew 13: 12).

The Rights of Woman. K390. First published in the third issue of *The Edinburgh Gazetteer* (see headnote to 'Extempore on some late commemorations of the poet Thomson', p. 356), Friday, 30 November 1792. The news pages of this number are dominated by coverage of the continuing French campaign in Flanders, speeches in the National Convention in Paris, and the Russian invasion of Poland; the editorial on page 3 begins publication of the 'Scotch Pension list', revealing the incomes paid by the government to various prominent Scots. Burns's poem appears in the first column on the back page, unsigned. This column continues with a letter from his friend and former neighbour Robert Riddell of Glenriddell, signed 'Cato', urging the Scottish landed class to press for constitutional reform, and sent with Burns's poem as explained in the letter to Fintry of 5 January 1793 in Appendix 1, p. 272. Burns also sent a copy of this poem to his friend and patron Mrs Dunlop in a letter of 6 December (see Appendix 1, p. 269); early editors reproduced it in that context, starting with Currie in 1800 (Vol. II, 418–19).

Title. The Rights of Woman by Mary Wollstonecraft (1759–97) had appeared at the start of the year. Wollstonecraft argues against the education for subordination typically given to girls, one that prevents the full development of their talents and virtues.

210 *Subtitle.* Louisa Fontenelle (1773–99) was a well-known actress, at this point working with George Sutherland's company at the theatre which had opened in Dumfries the previous September. A 'benefit night' was a performance from which a share of the box-office takings went to a specified performer; benefit nights were built into the schedules of eighteenth-century theatres. Burns wrote several occasional pieces for the theatre at Dumfries.

l. 2. *the fall of kings.* Louis XVI had been deposed by a popular uprising in Paris on 10 August; a French Republic was declared on 22 September.

l. 3. *While quacks of state must each produce his plan.* Since September, France had been governed by a National Convention elected to debate and decide on a new constitution for the country. The *Edinburgh Gazetteer* pressed for constitutional reform in Britain, but the editorial of the previous issue had warned that, 'Whilst we cease not to remind the people of this country, of the utility, and even absolute necessity, of a Reform in the representation of the Commons, they will not forget that it is only a rational measure we are engaged in indicating. Schemes, splendid and captivating in theory, but impracticable or destructive in execution, may indeed please the imagination whilst reviewing the gay vision, but can have no tendency to serve the real interests of the community' (pp. 2–3).

l. 4. *The Rights of Man.* The title of a book published in two parts (1791, 1792) by Thomas Paine (1737–1809), defending the rational critique of inherited power against Edmund Burke's reactionary polemic, *Reflections on the Revolution in France* (1790). Paine argued for a transformation of the British state far beyond the reforms campaigned for by Johnston, Riddell, and their friends. His book had achieved an unprecedentedly wide readership, with cheap editions selling for 6*d*., and abridgements for 1½*d*., since the government had issued a proclamation against seditious writings in May with the intention of suppressing it. As this issue of the *Gazetteer* reported, Paine was now in Paris, having been elected to the National Convention.

l. 19. *kick up a riot.* Currie's note to l. 24 identifies this with the aristocratic 'roar of Folly and Dissipation' (Burns's words in L645, 29 October 1794) which accompanied the Caledonian Hunt's balls and races: the Hunt had met in Dumfries in the autumn of 1792. But at the same time, elsewhere in Scotland, street disorder had been coming from the other end of the social scale, prompted by the triumph of the French Republic's army in Flanders: see headnote to 'The Tree of Liberty', p. 403. The constitutional reformers of the *Gazetteer*, while also enthused by events on the Continent, were anxious to distance themselves from popular law-breaking. This issue of the paper reports the meeting of 'The Convention of Delegates from the Societies of the Friends of the People in and around Edinburgh' on 28 November which elected as vice-president Thomas Muir of Hunters Hill, one of the founders of the Scottish organization (for which see headnote to 'Extempore on some late commemorations of the poet Thomson', p. 356). This meeting also resolved to publish its decision 'That the name or names of any person or persons belonging to the Associated Friends of the People, who may be found guilty of rioting, of creating or aiding sedition or tumult, shall be expunged from the books of the Society' (p. 3, col. 4).

211 l. 21. *Gothic.* Here, 'barbarous, rude, uncouth, unpolished, in bad taste' (*OED*).

l. 24. *Such conduct neither spirit, wit, nor manners.* In Currie's edition there is a footnote to this line: 'Ironical allusion to the saturnalia of the *Caledonian Hunt*' (see note to Dedication to the Edinburgh *Poems*, p. 331).

l. 38. *Ah! cà ira!.* The title of the French revolutionary anthem is 'Ça ira' ('So it will be'): the *Gazetteer* presumably lacked cedillas in its type. In the letter to Mrs Dunlop with this poem, Burns notes that there had been calls for this song in place of 'God Save the King' in the Dumfries theatre (see Appendix 1, p. 269).

Lament for James, Earl of Glencairn. K334. First published in the third edition of *Poems, Chiefly in the Scottish Dialect*, an expanded version of the Edinburgh edition published in two volumes by Creech in 1793; this poem appears in Vol. II, pp. 188–93.

James Cunningham, fourteenth Earl of Glencairn (1749–91), was Burns's most important early patron. When he first travelled to Edinburgh in November 1786 Burns was given a letter of introduction to Glencairn by an Ayrshire landowner and fellow mason who was married to Glencairn's sister. The nobleman had already read and been impressed by the Kilmarnock *Poems*. He in turn introduced Burns to many useful connections, including William Creech, the bookseller who would produce the Edinburgh editions of the *Poems*, and arranged for the Caledonian Hunt to subscribe *en masse* to the new volume (see note to Dedication to the Edinburgh *Poems*, p. 331). On leaving the city Burns wrote to him: 'I came to this town without friend or acquaintance, but I met with your Lordship; and to YOU, Your good family I owe in a great measure all that at present I am and have' (L103, 4 May 1787). Glencairn had been one of the Representative Scottish Peers (see note to p. 16, l. 1) in the House of Lords in 1780–4, where he aligned himself with Charles James Fox. He died on 30 January 1791; Burns first sent this poem to a friend on 10 March.

l. 1. *THE wind blew hollow.* Kinsley observes that 'hollow winds' blow through scenes of loss in Pope: 'The hollow Winds thro' naked Temples roar' ('Windsor Forest', l. 68; Pope 197); 'The darksom pines . . . Wave high, and murmur to the hollow wind' ('Eloisa to Abelard' ll. 155–6; Pope 256).

l. 4. *Lugar's winding stream.* A tributary of the river Ayr.

l. 9. *He lean'd him to an ancient aik.* The association of an aged, friendless bard, mourning the loss of his friends, with an aged oak, comes from Ossian in Macpherson's poems: 'I, like an ancient oak on Morven,

I moulder alone in my place. The blast hath lopped my branches away; and I tremble at the wings of the north' (*Fragments of Ancient Poetry* [1760], VII; Macpherson 16).

212 ll. 19–20. *Ye woods that shed ... The honours of the aged year.* Kinsley notes the borrowing from Thomson's 'Winter': 'Low waves the rooted forest, vexed, and sheds | What of its tarnished honours yet remain—' (ll. 181–2; Thomson 134).

l. 36. *Alike unknowing and unknown.* The structure mirrors another line from Pope's 'Eloisa to Abelard': 'The world forgetting, by the world forgot' (l. 208; Pope 257).

ll. 39–40. *silent, low, on beds of dust | Lie a' that would my sorrows share.* As Kinsley spots, an echo of Cuchullin's words in 'Fingal' (1761–2), Book III: 'Pale, silent, low on bloody beds, are they who were my friends!' (Macpherson 76).

l. 46. *all the life of life is dead.* Kinsley notes that this borrows from James Thomson's song, 'For ever Fortune wilt thou prove', l. 8: 'And all the life of life is gone?' (*Poems on Several Occasions* [1750], 16).

213 ll. 61–2. *the morning sun | That melts the fogs in limpid air.* As Kinsley observes, this condenses Thomson's lines in 'Summer': 'the potent sun | Melts into limpid air the high-raised clouds | And morning fogs' (ll. 199–201; Thomson 42).

ll. 77–9: *The mother may forget the child ... But I'll remember thee, Glencairn.* 'Can a woman forget her sucking child, that she should not have compassion on the son of her womb? yea, they may forget, yet will I not forget thee' (Isaiah 49: 15).

Bruce's Address to his Troops. K425. First published in the London daily *Morning Chronicle* for 8 May 1794, on page 3. Under the owner-editorship of James Perry (born Pirie, in Aberdeen) this was the widely read national journal of the opposition, now reduced in parliament to a core of loyalists around Charles James Fox after it split over Fox's sympathy for the French Revolution: Burns's poem appears alongside reports of the second reading in parliament of a bill to lend £2.5 million to the King of Prussia, since February 1793 Britain's ally in the war with France, and of initial French success in their offensive against the allies in the Low Countries. Charges of seditious libel eventually earned Perry a prison sentence. In March Burns had turned down an offer of regular work for Perry's paper, mindful that his political alignment had once before (see letters of December 1792 and January 1793 in Appendix 1, p. 270f) threatened his government job: 'My prospect in the Excise is something; at least, it is, encumbered as I am with the welfare, the very existence, of near half-a-score of helpless individuals, what I dare not sport with.' Accordingly, while the paper could publish the song, 'let them insert it as a thing they have met with by accident, & unknown to me' (L620B). It appeared anonymously, with the following introduction: 'If the following warm and animating Ode was not written near the time to which it applies, it is one of the most faithful imitations of the simple and beautiful style of the Scottish Bards we ever read, and we know but of one *living* Poet to whom to ascribe it.'

Burns sent the first version of this song to George Thomson at the end of August 1793, to be set to the tune 'Hey tutti taiti'. This was best known as a drinking song, included as song 170 in *SMM* from which the score below is adapted:

'There is a tradition, which I have met with in many parts of Scotland', Burns told Thomson, that this tune 'was Robert Bruce's March at the battle of Bannock-burn', the 1314 victory that secured Bruce the Scottish throne independent of Edward II of England (L582). Burns explains in the same letter that he had been inspired by 'the accidental recollection of that glorious struggle for Freedom, associated with the glowing ideas of some other struggles of the same nature, *not quite so ancient*' (the French Republic had just introduced mass conscription, the *levée en masse*, in response to the new coalition ranged against it). However, Thomson preferred an old Jacobite tune, 'Lewis Gordon', already published in *SMM* as song 86 in Vol. I, from which the score below is adapted.

This tune, however, required an extra two syllables in the final line of the stanza. Burns obliged (I have noted the additional words in the notes below), and when Thomson suggested further alterations, Burns replied, 'My Ode pleases me so much that I cannot alter it. . . . I am exceedingly obliged to you for putting me on reconsidering it: as I think I have much improved it' (L587).

This version of the text, with the longer final line in each stanza, was the song that Burns sent to Mrs Dunlop in December (L605), and that Burns agreed could be published in the *Morning Chronicle* in the spring of the following year (the London paper clearly did not know what to make of the name that appeared below the title on the manuscript they had been sent, so that a subheading reads '*Scene*—LEWIS GARDEN'). This is also the version of the song which appears, with 'Lewis Gordon' identified as the tune, in chapbooks (see headnote to 'The Jolly Beggars', p. 371) later in the decade. But collections of Burns's work, starting with James Currie's in 1800, have invariably taken their text from the first letter to Thomson, with the shorter final line, set to 'Hey tutti taiti'.

214 l. 4. *glorious.* Should be omitted to make this line fit the original tune, 'Hey tutti taiti'.

l. 8. *EDWARD.* Should be omitted to make this line fit the original tune.

l. 12. *Traitor, coward, turn and flie.* The line for 'Hey tutti taiti' is 'Let him turn and flee'.

l. 14. *FREEDOM's sword.* On the page facing this poem appears a letter to the editor from 'A Friend of Mankind' which concludes, 'Whatever be the ultimate fate of the French revolutionists, the friends of freedom must ever consider them as the authors of the greatest attempt that has hitherto been made in the cause of man' (2).

l. 16. *CALEDONIAN! on wi' me.* The line for 'Hey tutti taiti' is 'Let him follow me'.

l. 20. *But they shall—they* SHALL *be free!.* Omit a 'they shall' to make this line fit the original tune.

ll. 21–3. *Lay the proud usurpers low ... LIBERTY's in every blow!.* In a manuscript note Burns observes that these lines borrow 'a Couplet worthy of Homer' from William Hamilton's 1722 modernization of Blind Harry's fifteenth-century epic poem *Wallace*: 'A false Usurper sinks in every Foe, | And Liberty returns with ev'ry blow' at the battle of Biggar in Book VI, ch. II (*A New Edition of the Life and Heroick Actions of the renoun'd Sir William Wallace*, 122).

l. 24. *Forward.* Should be omitted to make this line fit the original tune.

The Election: a new song. K492. This is one of three songs that Burns wrote to support Patrick Heron of Kerroughtrie (d. 1803) in his successful campaign for the parliamentary seat of the Stewartry of Kirkcudbright in Spring 1795. Burns wrote a fourth 'Heron ballad' (as they are known) for the General Election the following year, when Heron was re-elected. They were published, anonymously, as 'broadsides': single sheets of cheap paper, in this case printed on one side only. This text follows the copy in the Abbotsford Library. The Heron ballads were first republished in two 1834 *Works of Robert Burns*, the one edited by James Hogg and William Motherwell (in Vol. I), the other by Cunningham (in Vol. III).

Tune: Fy, let us a' to the Bridal.

This score has been adapted from song 58 in *The Scots Musical Museum*, 'The Blithsome Bridal'. Burns's lyric follows the form of this traditional song: 'And there will be Saundy the sutor, | And Will wi' the meikle mou, | And there will be Tam the blutter, | With Andrew the tinkler, I trow' (stanza 2), and so on.

The member of parliament for a county was elected by its 'freeholders' of land over a certain extent (nothing prevented a landowner voting in more than one county on this basis). At the previous election in 1790 there were 154 qualified freeholders in Kirkcudbrightshire. They were obliged to attend a meeting in the county town between 12 and 2 on the designated day in order to cast their votes, and it is this assembly that Burns is anticipating in the present ballad. The election followed the death of the previous MP, Major-General Alexander Stewart of Cairn (see note to p. 131, ll. 227–8), grandson of an Earl of Galloway. It was not a contest between national political parties, but between rival local 'interests' (networks of patronage, influence, and family alliance). Heron headed one such interest; John Stewart, seventh Earl of Galloway (d. 1806), headed another, and through his brother-in-law James Murray of Broughton was backing Thomas Gordon of Balmaghie, Murray's nephew, for the seat. Heron too was a wealthy landowner, with family estates in England and other business interests (he was co-founder in 1769 of the Ayr Bank which collapsed four years later); but he also enjoyed the support of Secretary of State Henry Dundas, who managed the election of Scottish MPs for the government. The *History of Parliament* records Heron being returned unopposed, which suggests that Balmaghie must have withdrawn from the contest when his defeat looked inevitable.

l. 1. *K————*. Kirkcudbright (pronounced 'kirk*oo*brie'). The county town of one of the two shires making up the historic region of Galloway (the other being Wigtownshire, to the west).

214 l. 3. *M*———. Murray. James Murray of Cally and Broughton (d. 1799), a grandson of the fifth Earl of Galloway, was one of the wealthiest landowners in south-west Scotland.

l. 6. *G*———. Gordon. Thomas Gordon of Balmaghie (d. 1806), nephew of Murray, and Heron's opponent.

l. 8. *Sae knit in alliance and kin.* Ten years before Murray had deserted his wife Catherine, sister of the Earl of Galloway, for his mistress, Grace Johnston, who was his nephew Gordon's sister's daughter, and thus his own great-niece. Remarkably, this did not destroy his political alliance with Galloway, nor dent the two men's confidence in being able to impose their candidate on the county. When sending Heron two of his election ballads (probably including this one) in March, Burns comments:

> To pillory on Parnassus the rank reprobation of character, the utter dereliction of all principle, in a profligate junto which has not only outraged virtue, but violated common decency; which, spurning even hypocrisy as paltry iniquity below their daring;—to unmask their flagitiousness to the broadest day—to deliver such over to their merited fate, is surely not merely innocent, but laudable; is not only propriety, but virtue.—You have already, as your auxiliary, the sober detestation of mankind on all your opponents; and I swear by the lyre of Thalia to muster on your side all the votaries of honest laughter, and fair, candid ridicule! (L660)

215 l. 9. *black-nebbit Johnie.* John Bushby (d. 1802), banker and sheriff clerk of Dumfries, factor on the Galloway and Broughton estates, and manager of their political interest. 'Black-nebbit' is ironic: a black-neb was a democrat.

l. 13. *K*————'s *birkie*. Kempleton. William Bushby of Kempleton (d. 1813), John's brother, had been ruined by the fall of Heron's bank, gone to India, and returned with a fortune. A 'nabob' (l. 15) was just such a wealthy returnee: the wealth was usually assumed to be the product of oppression and corruption in India, which its deployment in parliamentary politics threatened to reproduce in Britain.

l. 17. *W*———'s *new Sh*———*ff*. Wigtown's new sheriff was another Bushby, John's son John Bushby Maitland of Eccles (b. 1767).

l. 21. *C*———. Cardonness. David Maxwell of Cardoness (d. 1825) was a very wealthy Kirkcudbrightshire landowner.

l. 25. ———*ses doughty*. Douglases. 'Doughty' traditionally attached to this surname, from the old ballad 'The Battle of Otterburn': 'The doughty earl of Douglas rode | Into England, to catch a prey'. But Sir William Douglas and James Douglas of Orchardton, referred to here, were not descended from medieval warlords, but, from humble beginnings, had made a fortune in trade and manufacturing.

l. 26. *New-christening towns far and near.* Having extended the town of Carlinwark around his cotton mills Sir William had it renamed 'Castle Douglas'; he also built mills in Newton Stewart in Wigtownshire which then became 'Newton Douglas'.

l. 28. *kissin the a— of a Peer.* Arse. The peer is Galloway, to whom the Douglases paid court; what their previous 'democrat doings' might have been is not clear.

l. 29. *K————, sae gen'rous.* Kenmure. John Gordon of Kenmure (1750–1840) had been MP for the constituency: Burns and a friend had stayed with the family on a tour.

l. 33. *R——stle.* Redcastle. Walter Sloan Lawrie of Redcastle, near Castle Douglas.

l. 37. *L— L————t.* Lord Lieutenant, the King's representative in the county; in this case George Stewart, styled Lord Garlies, the eldest son of the Earl of Galloway.

l. 38. *Sae fam'd for his gratefu' return.* This might refer to the controversy over the writ (see following note).

ll. 39–40. *getting his questions | To say in S—nt St–ph–n's the morn.* St Stephen's Chapel was the old debating chamber of the House of Commons. Galloway managed to delay the Sheriff's execution of the writ calling the election to gain time for his campaign; Garlies was called to account for this by parliament. To 'get one's questions' is 'to memorise the Catechism' (*DSL*): that is, Garlies is preparing his *answers.*

l. 42. *M————.* Muirhead. Revd James Muirhead, minister of Urr, but also freeholder of the Logan estate.

l. 43. *B————'s Apostle.* Buittle. Revd George Maxwell, minister of Buittle.

l. 44. *mair o' the black than the blue.* 'Not true blue' suggests Wallace (Vol. IV, 199).

l. 45. *Folk frae Saint MARY's.* Saint Mary's Isle is a peninsula just south of Kirkcudbright town, and seat of the Earl of Selkirk, a man of reformist instincts whose eldest son Burns greatly admired (see headnote to 'Extempore Verses on Dining with Lord Daer', p. 382). Scottish peers and their eldest sons could not vote in Scottish elections; but Selkirk's younger sons John, Dunbar, and Thomas were freeholders of the county and could.

216 l. 48. *Tho' deil ane will gie them his vote.* A survey of Scottish county politics in 1788 reported that Selkirk 'has never interested himself in politicks, or affected to be at the head of any interest in the County' (Elphinstone, ed., *View of the Political State of Scotland*, 194).

l. 49. *young RICHARD.* Richard Alexander Oswald of Auchencruive (b. 1771), nephew to Lord Methven and heir to a fortune built by his father in the Atlantic slave-trade. The names from this point on are those of Heron's supporters.

l. 53. *rich brother Nabobs.* David Anderson of St Germains in East Lothian and his brother James of Lincluden, who returned to Scotland in 1785–6 after successful careers in the East India Company.

l. 55. *C–ll–st–n's whiskers.* Collieston. William Copeland of Collieston and Mollins: 'remarkable for large whiskers', says a contemporary commentary.

216 l. 56. *Quintin*. Quintin McAdam of Waterside (b. 1763), nephew of John McAdam of Craigengillan near Mauchline, an early friend to Burns.

l. 57. *Stamp-office Johnie*. John Syme (1755–1831), a close friend of Burns's. Another victim of the collapse of Heron's bank, he held the sinecure position of 'distributor of stamps' in Dumfries: these were the stamps confirming that duty had been paid on taxable stuffs, hence the warning in the following line.

l. 59. *C–ss–nc–ry*. Cassencary. Colonel Alexander Muir Mackenzie of Cassencarry.

l. 60. *gleg Colonel Tam*. Lieutenant-Colonel Thomas Goldie of Goldielea.

l. 61. *trusty KIROCHTREE*. Patrick Heron of Kerroughtrie, the candidate: see headnote.

l. 65. *the auld MAJOR*. The candidate's brother, Major Basil Heron of Drumnaught.

l. 66. *the Greys*. The Greys were the Royal North British Dragoons, Major Heron's cavalry regiment.

l. 69. *maiden K–lk–rr–n*. Kilkerran. Sir Adam Fergusson of Kilkerran, MP for Ayrshire. 'Maiden' because he never married, but see also note to p. 18, l. 74.

l. 70. *B–rsk–m–n's gude Knight*. Barskimming. Sir William Miller of Glenlee (in Kirkcudbrightshire), Barskimming (in Ayrshire), and the legal dynasty.

l. 71. *roaring B–rtwh–stle*. Alexander Birtwhistle, merchant, part-owner of cotton mills in Gatehouse of Fleet, and Provost of Kirkcudbright town.

l. 73. *N–ddisd–le border*. Niddisdale or Nithsdale is the western division of Dumfriesshire: the lowest part of the river Nith, at Dumfries town, forms the border with Kirkcudbrightshire, and the estates mentioned below are on the Stewartry side.

ll. 74–5. *M–xw–lls . . . Teuch Jockie, staunch Geordie, and Walie*. John Maxwell of Terraughty, 'the Maxwels' veteran Chief' of an earlier Burns poem ('To Terraughty', K325); George Maxwell of Carruchan; and Wellwood Maxwell of Barncleugh, son-in-law to John (these men were not otherwise related).

l. 76. *griens*. This is 'greens' in the broadside text (corrected by hand in the Abbotsford copy).

l. 77. *L–g–n M–d–w–l*. Lieutenant-Colonel Andrew McDouall (or McDowall) of Logan (b. 1758), MP for Wigtownshire.

l. 78. *Sculdudry*. 'fornication' (*DSL*). McDouall was notorious for the consequences of a ten-year affair with Margaret Kennedy, a niece of Burns's friend Gavin Hamilton (and for whom Burns wrote the song 'Young Peggy', K65). Margaret was just 16 when McDouall seduced her, but when she bore him a surviving child he denied promising her marriage in that event. Her relatives had taken him to court in 1794; the case was concluded in 1801, with £3,000 damages awarded to the daughter (Margaret having died in the meantime).

l. 80. *Sogering, gunpowder Bl—r.* Presumably Lieutenant John Blair, younger of Borgue.

217   l. 81. *the chaste Int'rest o' B——.* Broughton.

l. 83. *send B—— to the C————ns.* Balmaghie; Commons.

l. 84. *S–d–m.* Sodom.

l. 85. *the sanctified M——.* Murray.

l. 86. *Ch–p–ls.* Chapels. Perhaps a reference to the facilities of Murray's planned village at Gatehouse of Fleet, in ironic contrast to his bad moral example.

The Dumfries Volunteers. K484. First published in the *Edinburgh Evening Courant* (see headnote to 'Elegy, On the departed Year 1788', p. 351) for 4 May 1795, 'By Mr. Burns', on page 3, column 4, which it shares with descriptions of army deserters. Elsewhere in this issue we find a debate in the House of Lords on the Prince of Wales's debts, and an editorial on the war:

> Peace continues still to be generally talked of. It is indeed so desirable an event, and the very sound carries with it such a charm, that it operates on men's minds as a reality, when we fear in the present instance, it will prove only a shadow. If we reflect for a moment on the kind of language always held out by his MAJESTY's Ministers in regard to the necessity of prosecuting the war, so long as the Revolutionary Government in France continues to exist, and on the measures now pursued to carry it on with redoubled vigour, we shall find no cause to believe that a peace is at all in agitation. (3)

Tune: Push about the jorum.

Burns's lyric was republished posthumously as song 546 in *The Scots Musical Museum*, from which this score is adapted. In *SMM*, the last two lines of each stanza are repeated as a chorus ('We'll ne'er permit . . .' etc.) to accompany the last four bars of the present score. The poem was published in many other newspapers, including the *Dumfries Journal* (5 May) and the *Caledonian Mercury* (7 May).

The withdrawal of Prussia from the coalition in April 1795 had allowed the French unchallenged occupation of the whole of the Low Countries, their fleets and harbours, exposing the long coastline of Britain to assault as never before; but there was no immediate threat of invasion by France at this time. The government had called for counties to organize their own forces in May of the previous year, more to suppress internal disorder and rebellion than to repel any external threat, thus freeing the regular army for service elsewhere. The offer to constitute the Royal Dumfries Volunteers, signed by 90 men, including Burns, on 3 February 1795 and sent to the King's representative in Dumfriesshire, the Lord Lieutenant, makes no mention of an anti-invasion role:

> We the subscribers, all inhabitants of the burgh and neighbourhood of Dumfries, within the County of Dumfries, do hereby declare our sincere attachment to the person and government of His Majesty King George the Third; our respect for the happy Constitution of Great Britain; and our firm resolution on every occasion to protect the lives and properties of ourselves and our fellow-subjects from every attempt of the ambitious and turbulent who threaten to overturn the laws of our country, and who, by anarchy, sedition, and bloodshed may endeavour to destroy the sacred bonds of society; and, as we are of opinion that the only way we can obtain a speedy and honourable peace is by the Government vigorously carrying on the present war, humbly submit the following proposals to His Majesty for the purpose of forming ourselves into a Volunteer Corps, in order to support the internal peace and good order of the town, as well as to give energy to the measures of Government . . . (reproduced in Will, *Robert Burns as a Volunteer*, 43–4)

As an employee of the Crown Burns could not avoid joining; given his detestation of the government of William Pitt, he cannot have relished the idea of becoming its policeman. In practice, on the other hand, the Volunteers were a self-organizing body of men such as Burns had always enjoyed participating in: they determined the conditions of their service (e.g. 'the Corps shall not be obliged to march more than five miles from the town of Dumfries', Will 45); they elected their own officers; and discipline and other matters were administered by a committee, of which Burns was elected a member in August. This very independence caused misgivings in government, and Volunteer units were eventually replaced by a drafted Militia firmly under the authority of country gentlemen. The Royal Dumfries Volunteers gave Burns a military funeral in July 1796, it seems against his dying wishes.

217   l. 3. *WOODEN WALLS*. A conventional metonym for the Royal Navy. This issue of the *Courant* includes a report to the French National Convention,

putting a brave face on the narrow British naval victory at Genoa in March.

l. 5. *Nith.* The river Nith runs through Dumfries.

l. 21. *Our FATHERS BLUDE the kettle bought.* See the mention of 'our ancestors' in the Perth loyal address extracted below.

218 ll. 25, 27. *that would a tyrant own,* | | *Who'd set the mob above the throne.* For another example of the equivalence of these dangers, see Burns's closing wish for the nobility and gentry of Scotland in the Dedication to the Edinburgh *Poems*: 'may tyranny in the Ruler and licentiousness in the People equally find you an inexorable foe!' (p. 124).

ll. 31–2. *while we sing, GOD SAVE THE KING,* | *We'll ne'er forget THE PEOPLE.* It has been suggested that Burns here echoes the words of 'a most elegant and forcible speech' by Thomas Muir, co-founder in Scotland of the Association of the Friends of the People (see headnote to 'Extempore on some late commemorations of the poet Thomson', p. 356), as Scottish delegate to a meeting of the Friends of the Liberty of the Press in London the previous year, when he said

> That with respect to Loyalty, he was not exceeded by any one, if by Loyalty, Affection to the Constitution was intended; but if the word meant, (as he feared it did at present) an inclination to perpetuate abuse, or to rivet still more tightly the yoke of oppression about the necks of his countrymen, he feared he had but little of it; he honoured, he loved his Sovereign, but he could not on that account forget the People. (*Morning Post,* 16 January 1793, 3)

The same qualification was frequently, if less eloquently, expressed in the declarations of loyalty published by the more reform-minded public bodies in the same period. For example, on 18 December 1792 a town meeting in Perth had resolved to 'express and make public our loyalty and attachment to his Majesty' and to

> a Constitution which we love and revere as a monument of political wisdom, equally glorious to our ancestors, by whom it was framed, and happy for us who enjoy the enviable advantages of it; but, in our opinion, its stability would be rendered more permanent, and liberty better secured, if the House of Commons were a more general as well as a truer Representation of the People. (*Morning Chronicle,* 28 December 1792, 2)

Song [A man's a man for a' that]. K482. First published, anonymously, in the *Glasgow Magazine* for August 1795, p. 115. This was only the third issue of the radical monthly. As well as Burns's song it included a second instalment of a biography of Thomas Muir (see note above), now serving a 14-year sentence in Botany Bay for sedition; the act passed by the legislature of Virginia in 1785 guaranteeing freedom of religion; and a third instalment of a retrospect of recent history, covering Britain's 'scandalous' (p. 117) support for Continental absolutism against the French Republic. This ends with the consequences of Britain's campaign against the French West Indies: complaints had been made in parliament about the disruption to Britain's own Caribbean trade. This issue of the *Glasgow Magazine* concludes:

> The arms of Great Britain, when carried into distant countries, have seldom been celebrated for justice or humanity. The desolated regions of the East [i.e. British-controlled India] confirm this deplorable truth; and it appears, that the same system of rapacity and cruelty had been adopted in the West. . . . Legislators, as such, should have no private interest, but should feel an equal concern for every portion of the people subject to their authority, however distant, and in whatever capacity: And of what consequence are the present disappointments of the West India merchants, compared with the miseries of millions of Africans, whom their infamous trafic has reduced to slavery, or of those millions in the East, who have perished without their assistance or sympathy? (119)

Manuscript versions, including the one which Burns sent to George Thomson for the *Select Collection* in January 1795, begin with an additional stanza:

> Is there, for honest poverty
>   That hangs his head, and a' that;
> The coward-slave, we pass him by,
>   We dare be poor for a' that!
> For a' that, and a' that.
> Our toils obscure, and a' that,
> The rank is but the guinea's stamp,
> The man's the gowd for a' that.

This is the version printed in all the nineteenth-century collections which reproduce the letters to Thomson, starting with Currie's in 1800 (Vol. IV, 216–17); and also in the 1799 Stewart and Meikle chapbook that includes *Holy Willie's Prayer*. The present version was republished in *The Oracle* newspaper for 2 June 1796 and *The Scots Magazine* for August 1797, in both cases attributed to Burns.

Tune: For a' that and a' that.

Burns had already set a lyric to this tune for his 'cantata' 'Love and Liberty', later published as 'The Jolly Beggars'; part of which had already appeared as song 290 of *The Scots Musical Museum*, from which this score is adapted.

218 l. 2. *hodden grey*. 'Coarse homespun, undyed woollen cloth, of a greyish colour, due to a mixture of white and black wool . . . Freq. used . . . to describe one dressed in simple rustic fashion, or a homely unaffected individual' (*DSL*).

l. 14. *His ribband, star, and a' that*. The sash and chest insignia of an order of nobility. Compare this stanza to Thomas Paine, *The Rights of Man*, Vol. I (1791):

> Titles are but nick-names, and every nick-name is a title. The thing is perfectly harmless in itself; but it marks a sort of foppery in the human character, which degrades it. It reduces man into the diminutive of man in things which are great, and the counterfeit of woman in things which are little. It talks about its fine *blue ribbon* like a girl, and shows its new *garter* like a child. A certain writer, of some antiquity, says, 'When I was a child, I thought as a child; but when I became a man, I put away childish things'. (*Rights of Man, Common Sense, and Other Political Writings*, 131)

The blue riband and the garter are insignia of the Order of the Garter, the highest order of chivalry in Britain. The 'writer of some antiquity' is Paul: 1 Corinthians 13: 11.

l. 17. *The king*. The five-stanza version substitutes 'A prince'.

219 l. 22. *His*. The five-stanza version substitutes 'Their'.

Other poems and songs published posthumously

220 *The Jolly Beggars*. K84. This, and the following two texts, were first published in 1799 by Stewart and Meikle of Glasgow in 'chapbooks': small-format pamphlets of, in this case, 16 pages, often containing works by more than one author, and sold for 2*d*. each. In each of them the title-page attributes these works to 'Robert Burns, The Ayrshire Poet' (a version of 'A Poet's welcome to his love-begotten daughter' also appeared in these pamphlets: see headnote to that poem, p. 407). In the printing used here, 'The Jolly Beggars; or, Tatterdemallions. A Cantata' takes up 14 pages, the other two containing poems by other writers. This title is the publishers' invention: it seems that the only title in the manuscript from which they worked was 'A Cantata', but the other extant manuscript is entitled 'Love and Liberty: A Cantata', and this is generally adopted in modern editions. Burns's title borrows from Pope's celebration of extra-marital love in 'Eloisa to Abelard' (1717): 'Oh happy state! when souls each other draw, | When love is liberty, and nature, law' (ll. 91–2; Pope 254). The publishers' title evokes the many traditional songs about beggars, and the multi-character songs *The Happy Beggars* and *The Merry Beggars* in the later editions of Allan Ramsay's *Tea-Table Miscellany*, Vol. IV (10th edition of 1740, pp. 348–9 and 374–5); in constructing a more extended sequence on this theme, Burns clearly also had in mind the ballad-opera form of John Gay's *The Beggar's Opera* (1728), the songs of which enter Ramsay's collection in the same edition. From the start the *Tea-Table Miscellany*

included a short 'Scots Cantata' consisting of two recitatives and two airs (Ramsay Vol. III, 36–7).

'Love and Liberty' was written in 1785–6. It seems that an early draft or drafts included several more songs, and characters to sing them, than in the version published in 1799. One of these, sung by a 'merry-andrew' or clown and introduced by its own recitative, later came into the hands of the publisher Thomas Stewart, and he inserted it into the existing text at l. 80, after the camp follower's song, in his 1802 *Stewart's Edition of Burns's Poems*.

220 RECITATIVO. *Recitative* is the type of delivery, between speaking and singing, used to fill in the dialogue and narration between songs in eighteenth-century opera. This one takes the 'Cherrie and the Slae' stanza already used by Burns for e.g. the 'Epistle to Davie' in the Kilmarnock *Poems* (see headnote to that poem, p. 310).

l. 2. *wavering*. 'Waver' can mean 'flutter' (*OED* sense 3).

l. 3. *Boreas*. The North Wind.

l. 9. *Poosie-Nansie's*. 'The Hostess of a noted Caravansary in M——, well known to and much frequented by the lowest orders of Travellers and Pilgrims' (Burns's note in the manuscripts): i.e. an inn in Mauchline.

l. 15. *red rags*. The remains of a British army uniform.

l. 16. *brac'd*. 'Surrounded, encompassed' (*OED*); possibly also 'burdened': the old soldier has been carrying bags of meal as well as his knapsack. Kinsley points out that 'oatmeal was the common alms', so the implication may be that the soldier has been very successful in attracting charity.

l. 24. *aumos dish*. 'Alms-dish' explains Burns in a manuscript note. Robert Chambers notes in his editions that 'The Scottish beggars used to carry a large wooden dish for the reception of any alms which took the shape of food' (1838, p. 30).

l. 27. *Then staggering and swaggering*. Kinsley spots that this line is borrowed from this section, the 'wheel', of another 'Cherrie and the Slae' stanza, in Ramsay's 'The Vision', stanza xix: 'Quhen staggirand and swaggirand | They stoyter Hame to sleip' (ll. 263–4; Ramsay Vol. III, 90).

221 ll. 29–48. *Tune—Soldier's Joy*.

This score is adapted from Alexander McGlashan's *A Collection of Scots Measures* (1781), 32; it appears in a couple of other eighteenth-century collections. I follow *Low* (pp. 128–9) in putting the high strain first, for the verse; the last eight bars are for 'lal de daudle' etc.

l. 34. *the heights of Abram.* General James Wolfe's 1759 victory over the French on the Plains of Abraham, a plateau above the St Lawrence outside Quebec, established British control of Canada, but Wolfe himself was killed.

l. 35. *I served out my trade.* Completed my apprenticeship (*OED* 'serve' 2a).

l. 36. *the Moro low was laid.* At the other end of the American theatre of the Seven Years War, the storming of El Morro, the Spanish fortress on Cuba, secured Havana for British troops in 1762.

ll. 37, 39. *with Curtis, among the floating batt'ries . . . with Elliot to head me.* During the war with France and Spain that accompanied the American Revolutionary War, General George Eliot's British garrison held Gibraltar against a three-year Spanish siege, aided by naval forces under Roger Curtis, who led a marine brigade during the destruction of the naval batteries bombarding the peninsula in 1782.

l. 43. *my wallet, my bottle and my callet.* A wallet is 'a bag for holding provisions . . . a pedlar's pack, or the like'; a callet is 'a lewd woman, trull, strumpet, drab' (both *OED*).

l. 47. *tell.* In something like *OED*'s sense 21a, 'To count out (pieces of money) in payment; hence, to pay (money)'; except this has to mean 'pay *for*'. The soldier sells a spare bag of meal he has been given as alms to pay for an extra bottle of whisky.

222 l. 53. *fairy.* Here just meaning 'delicate, finely formed' (*OED*).

ll. 57–80. *Tune—Soldier Laddie.*

This is a seventeenth-century tune which Burns could have found in a number of the collections, including *Orpheus Caledonius*, Vol. II (1733), 27.

The present score is adapted from song 323 in *The Scots Musical Museum*, where the singer does *not* follow the camp: 'And when he comes hame, he'll make me a Lady, | My blessings gang wi' my soger laddie'. Burns's version was included in *The Merry Muses of Caledonia* (1799). The last eight bars are for 'lal de lal' etc.

222 l. 71. *spontoon to the fife*. A spontoon was 'a species of half-pike or halberd carried by infantry officers' (*OED*); the fife would have been played by a boy.

l. 73. *the peace*. The Peace of Paris, in 1783, that ended the American Revolutionary War and the war with France and Spain that accompanied it.

l. 74. *Cunningham*. The district of Ayrshire north of the River Irvine: see Map.

223 l. 80. At this point Stewart's 1802 edition inserted the following, from a manuscript fragment (a 'merry-andrew' is a clown):

> Recitative
>
> Poor Merry-Andrew, in a neuk,
>   Sat guzzling wi' a Tinkler-hizzie;
> They mind't na wha the chorus teuk
>   Between themsels they were sae busy:
> At length wi' drink an' courting dizzy,
>   He stoiter'd up an' made a face;
> Then turn'd, an' laid a smack on Grizzie,
>   Syne tun'd his pipes wi' grave grimace.
>
> Air. Tune, Auld Sir Symon.
>
> Sir Wisdom's a fool when he's fou;
>   Sir Knave is a fool in a Session;
> He's there but a 'prentice, I trow,
>   But I am a fool by profession.
>
> My Grannie she bought me a beuk,
>   And I held awa' to the school;
> I fear I my talent misteuk,
>   But what will ye hae of a fool.
>
> For drink I would venture my neck;
>   A hizzie's the half o' my Craft:
> But what could ye other expect
>   Of ane that's avowedly daft.
>
> I, ance, was ty'd up like a stirk,
>   For civilly swearing and quaffing;
> I, ance, was abus'd i' the kirk
>   For towsing a lass i' my daffin.
>
> Poor Andrew that tumbles for sport,
>   Let nae body name wi' a jeer;
> There's even, I'm tauld, i' the Court
>   A Tumbler ca'd the Premier.

> Observ'd ye yon reverend lad
>   Mak faces to tickle the Mob;
> He rails at our mountebank squad,
>   It's rivalship just i' the job.
>
> And now my conclusion I'll tell,
>   For faith I'm confoundedly dry:
> The chiel that's a fool for himsel,
>   Gude L—d, he's far dafter than I.

l. 84. *douked*. From the manuscript; 'ducked' in the 1799 text, but clearly pronounced as the Scots word.

l. 85. *love*. This is 'dove' in the 1799 text, but this is a misreading (easily made) of the poet's handwriting in the manuscript.

ll. 89–116. *Tune—O an ye were dead gudeman.*

Burns could have found the tune in James Oswald's *Caledonian Pocket Companion*, Vol. IV (1752), 24. This score is adapted from song 409 of *The Scots Musical Museum*, where, the gudeman being dead, 'I wad bestow my widowhood | upon a ranton Highlandman'; Burns's lyric has more in common with songs celebrating the Highland Jacobite rebels of 1715 and 1745.

l. 97. *his philibeg an' tartan plaid*. The *fèileadh beag* (Gaelic) is the kilt, developed earlier in the century to dress the legs, leaving the plaid, originally used to cover the whole body, to be carried instead as cloak and bedding.

l. 98. *claymore*. *Claidheamh mòr* (Gaelic): broadsword.

l. 99. *trepan*. 'to catch in a trap; to entrap, ensnare, beguile' (*OED*).

224 l. 101. *Tweed to Spey*. The river Tweed flows through south-east Scotland, one stage forming the border with England; the river Spey runs north-east through the central Highlands.

225 l. 125. *Arioso*. Melodious; 'Used of instrumental music, it describes a sustained, vocal style' (*OED*).

l. 126. *Apollo*. Here in his capacity as god of music.

l. 127. *Allegretto*. Italian musical term meaning 'somewhat brisk' (*OED*).

l. 128. *giga*. Italian musical term for 'piece of music, of a lively character, in two strains or sections, each of which is repeated' (*OED*); but the fiddler is probably just playing a jig. Kinsley notes the echo of Ramsay's 'The Life and Acts of, or, An Elegy on Patie Burnie, The Famous Fidler of Kinghorn' in his 1721 *Poems*, where a standard Habbie stanza describes the first fiddle, 'On which *Apollo*, | With meikle Pleasure play'd himself | Baith Jig and Solo' (ll. 52 –4; Ramsay Vol. I, 188).

ll. 129–48. *Tune—Whistle owre the lave o't.*

The tune is in several of the eighteenth-century collections, and, Burns told Thomson, 'said to be by a John Bruce, a celebrated violin-player, in Dumfries about the beginning of this century' (L644, 19 October 1794). In Burns's version for *The Scots Musical Museum* song 249 (on which the score above is based), the title phrase comes in place of what cannot be said ('Now we're married, spier nae mair, | But Whistle o'er . . .') and to express an acceptance of fate ('Wiser men than me's beguil'd | So Whistle o'er . . .'). The present song was included in *The Merry Muses of Caledonia* (1799).

l. 146. *thairms*. Burns explains in a manuscript note, 'small guts = fiddle strings'.

226 l. 158. *hunkers*. Burns explains in a manuscript note, 'the position of one going to sit down on the floor'; a squat.

ll. 165–80. *Tune—Clout the caudron.*

Burns could have found this tune in *Orpheus Caledonius*, Vol. II (1733), 25; as the title suggests, it was used for songs about the services offered by tinkers, usually with a layer of sexual innuendo. The score above is adapted from song 23 in *The Scots Musical Museum*.

l. 169. *I've ta'en the gold.* That is, accepted the bounty for joining the army.

227 l. 178. *Kilbaigie.* 'Keilbaigie' in the 1799 text: another simple misreading of the poet's handwriting. The distillery in question was at Kilbagie in Clackmannanshire.

ll. 182–207. *RECITATIVO.* This recitative takes the 'Christ's Kirk' stanza used by Burns in 'The Holy Fair', 'A Dream', and 'Halloween' in the Kilmarnock *Poems*.

ll. 197–8. *An' shor'd them Dainty Davie | O boot.* 'Shore' means 'offer, present with as a mark of favour' (*DSL*). 'Dainty Davie' seems to be functioning here as a euphemism for sex; the poet is in effect wishing the couple all the best in their encounter (although the 'lord' of the 'dame' involved, he has two others in reserve, as we learn in l. 214).

l. 200. *listed.* That is, enlisted.

228 ll. 208–35. *Tune—For a' that an' a' that.* For a score, see notes to 'A man's a man for a' that', p. 370. Burns used the last three verses of the present lyric in another version published as song 290 of *The Scots Musical Museum*, from which this score is adapted. The 'Jolly Beggars' version was included in *The Merry Muses of Caledonia* (1799) under the title 'I am a Bard'.

ll. 216–17. *I never drank the Muses' stank, | Castalia's burn.* Castalia is a spring in Greek mythology that could inspire the gift of poetry in those who heard its sound or drank its waters: it is placed on either Mount Parnassus or on Mount Helicon (l. 220). The wording here suggests a renaissance convention to Kinsley, with examples from Sir David Lindsay's *Ane dialoge* of 1554 ('I did never sleep on Pernasso . . . Nor drank I never | Off Hylicon', ll. 226, 230–1), and Sir Philip Sidney's sonnet 74 in *Astrophil and Stella* of 1591 ('I never drank of Aganippe well', l. 1).

l. 218. *But there it streams, and richly reams.* More immediately, Fergusson also substitutes drink as the fount of poetic inspiration: 'O *Muse*, be kind, and dinna fash us | To flee awa' beyont Parnassus, | Nor seek for *Helicon* to wash us, | That heath'nish spring; | Wi' Highland whisky scour our hawses, | And gar us sing' ('The King's Birth-Day in Edinburgh', ll. 13–18; Fergusson 52).

l. 222. *will.* In *OED*'s sense 2, 'carnal desire or appetite'.

l. 230. *clear your decks.* In preparation for a toast.

229 l. 241. *To quench their lowan drouth.* The 1799 text has a space after this line, corresponding to a page-break in the manuscript, turning the first six lines into a stanza in their own right. In fact the final recitative has returned to the 'Cherrie and the Slae' stanza of the opening one.

229 l. 247. *his twa Deborahs*. Deborah is a prophetess in the Book of Judges. Kinsley points to Judges 5: 12, 'Awake, awake, Deborah: awake, awake, utter a song'; but also relevant to the bard's companions might be Deborah's answer to Barak: 'I will surely go with thee: notwithstanding the journey that thou takest shall not be for thine honour' (Judges 4: 9).

ll. 250–81. *Tune—Jolly Mortals fill your glasses.*

Burns would have known a song of this title in Joseph Ritson's *Select Collection of English Songs* (1783), Vol. II, song xvii: the score above is adapted from this source.

230 l. 270. *variorum*. A Scottish usage, says *OED*, meaning 'a varying or changing scene'.

l. 273. *character*. From the manuscript: 'characters' in the 1799 text. 'The estimate formed of a person's qualities; reputation . . . favourable estimate, good repute' (*OED*).

Holy Willie's Prayer. K53. Stewart and Meikle's chapbook follows this poem with more works by Burns, namely 'Letter to John Goudie' (usually known as 'Epistle to John Goldie') and six song-lyrics (all but the second and last included in the present volume): 'Duncan Gray', 'The lass that made the bed to me', 'A man's a man for a' that', 'Of a' the airts', 'Now westlin' winds', and 'I gaed a waefu' gate yestreen'. This text follows the version 'Printed by Chapman and Lang' (on the title page).

The manuscript versions add an epigraph from Pope ('And send the Godly in a pet to pray—', *The Rape of the Lock*, canto IV, l. 64; Pope 234); some also add a prologue explaining the background to the poem, for example the 'Argument' in the Glenriddell copy:

> Holy Willie was a rather oldish batchelor Elder in the parish of Mauchline, & much & justly famed for that polemical chattering which ends in tippling Orthodoxy, & for that Spiritualized Bawdry which refines to Liquorish Devotion.—In a Sessional process with a gentleman in Mauchline, a M^r. Gavin Hamilton, Holy Willie, and his priest, father Auld, after full hearing of the Presbytry of Ayr, came off but second best; owing partly to the oratorical powers of M^r. Robt. Aiken, M^r. Hamilton's Counsel; but chiefly to M^r. Hamilton's being one of the most irreproachable & truly respectable characters in the country.— On losing his Process, the Muse overheard him at his devotions as follows—

For Hamilton see the headnote to 'A Dedication to Gavin Hamilton', p. 316; for Aiken, the headnote to 'The Cotter's Saturday night', p. 306). The charges brought against Hamilton by the Session of his church in August 1784 included missing attendance at church, travelling on a Sunday, and neglecting family worship. The Presbytery of Ayr, the next level up in the government of the church, was in the control of its 'moderate' faction, perhaps predisposed to find in favour of the 'respectable' 'gentleman' Hamilton, and in January 1785 it duly did so. On the Mauchline Session's reaction to this poem, see the letter to John Moore of 2 August 1787 in Appendix 1, p. 266.

231 l. 4. *A' for thy glory.* This is the orthodox Calvinism of the Church of Scotland, as set out in *The Westminster Confession of Faith* (1647): 'By the decree of God, for the manifestation of His glory, some men and angels are predestinated unto everlasting life; and others foreordained to everlasting death' (ch. III, para. iii).

ll. 5–6. *And no for ony guid or ill | They've done afore thee!.* 'Those of mankind that are predestinated unto life, God . . . hath chosen in Christ unto everlasting glory, out of His mere free grace and love, without any foresight of faith or good works, or perseverance in either of them' (*Westminster Confession*, ch. III, para. v).

l. 10. *For gifts an' grace.* For Paul, 'Having then gifts differing according to the grace that is given to us' explains why different individuals have different roles in the church (Romans 12: 6).

l. 11. *A burnin' an' a shinin' light.* The words of Jesus, describing John the Baptist; 'He was a burning and a shining light' (John 5: 35).

l. 13. *generation.* Here, 'ancestry, lineage, descent' (*OED*).

l. 17. *Five thousand years.* The manuscript versions have 'Sax thousand': the date of the creation of the world, including Adam and Eve, had been dated to 4004 BC, so 6,000 is a closer approximation to the age of humanity in 1784.

l. 22. *burnin' lake.* John sees the devil 'cast into the lake of fire and brimstone' in Revelation 20: 10; the chains and stake of l. 24 are the sort of additional details beloved of orthodox preachers.

l. 25. *Yet I am here a chosen sample.* '. . . men, attending the will of God revealed in His Word, and yielding obedience thereunto, may, from the certainty of their effectual vocation, be assured of their eternal election' (*Westminster Confession*, ch. III, para. viii). Willie may be taken as an example of this assurance.

l. 27. *a pillar in thy temple.* Another echo of Revelation: 'Him that overcometh will I make a pillar in the temple of my God, and he shall go no more out: and I will write upon him the name of my God, and the name of the city of my God, which is new Jerusalem' (3: 12).

231 l. 29. *buckler.* In the Old Testament, the Lord, or his truth, is a buckler (shield) to the faithful (e.g. 2 Samuel 22: 31; Psalms 18 and 91; Proverbs 2: 7).

l. 30. *To a' thy flock.* When this poem was reprinted in *Stewart's Edition of Burns's Poems* (1802), an additional stanza appeared after this line:

> O L——d thou kens what zeal I bear,
> When drinkers drink, and swearers swear,
> And singin' there, and dancin' here,
> > Wi' great an' sma';
> For I am keepet by thy fear,
> > Free frae them a'.——

As with the 'merry andrew' section added to 'The Jolly Beggars' in the same volume, Stewart seems to have got hold of a discarded manuscript fragment, though in this case the fragment has not survived.

l. 32. *fleshly lust.* 'The Lord knoweth how to deliver the godly out of temptations, and to reserve the unjust unto the day of judgment to be punished: But chiefly them that walk after the flesh in the lust of uncleanness, and despise government' (2 Peter 2: 9–10).

l. 33. *trust.* 'a duty or office . . . entrusted to one' (*OED*).

l. 35. *thou remembers we are dust.* In Genesis 2: 7, God 'formed man of the dust of the ground'; and in Psalm 103, 'Like as a father pitieth his children, so the Lord pitieth them that fear him. For he knoweth our frame; he remembereth that we are dust'.

232 ll. 37–48. *O L——d! yestreen . . . Wad ne'er hae steer'd her.* In Robert Chambers's editions of 1838, 1851, and 1856 these two stanzas are omitted and replaced by a row of asterisks, without explanation.

ll. 39–40. *a livin' plague, | To my dishonour.* That is, a child.

l. 41. *l–g.* Leg.

l. 49. *this fleshly thorn.* Willie in this stanza takes Paul as his type, who explains in the second Epistle to the Corinthians that 'lest I should be exalted above measure through the abundance of the revelations, there was given to me a thorn in the flesh, the messenger of Satan to buffet me, lest I should be exalted above measure' (12: 7). Manuscript versions have Paul's 'buffet' in place of 'beset' in l. 50.

l. 51. *o'er.* From the manuscripts; the 1799 text used here has 'our' (another printing has 'owre').

l. 53. *borne.* From the manuscripts; the 1799 text has 'born'.

l. 56. *a chosen race.* The doctrine of predestination made Israel's status as a 'chosen people' in the Old Testament a paradigm for Calvinists.

l. 58. *blast.* Here, 'to bring infamy upon', or 'to strike or visit with the wrath and curse of heaven' (*OED*).

l. 61. *G——n H————n.* Gavin Hamilton (see headnote above); but the line scans better if the first name is abbreviated to the familiar 'Gaun', as in the manuscripts.

l. 62. *cartes.* From the manuscripts; the 1799 text has 'carts'.

l. 63. *takin' arts.* For this usage, cf. Peggy's praise of Patie, in Allan Ramsay's 1725 pastoral comedy *The Gentle Shepherd*: 'And then he speaks with sic a taking Art | His Words they thirle like Musick thro' my Heart' (1. 2. 96–7; Ramsay Vol. II, 221).

l. 65. *ain.* From the manuscripts; the 1799 text has 'an'.

l. 71. *Curse thou his basket and his store.* In Deuteronomy 28, 'thy basket and thy store', along with many other things, shall be either 'blessed' (28: 5), or 'cursed' (28: 17), depending on whether thou wilt or wilt not 'hearken unto the voice of the Lord thy God' (28: 15).

233 l. 75. *Thy strong right hand.* 'Thy right hand, O Lord, is become glorious in power: thy right hand, O Lord, hath dashed in pieces the enemy' (Exodus 15: 6).

l. 79. *A——n.* Aiken (see headnote above), Hamilton's lawyer.

l. 81. *we.* That is, Willie and his minister, Revd Auld.

l. 83–4: *While he wi' hingin' lips and snakin' | Held up his head.* At this point the manuscripts describe Auld, Willie's ally, rather than Aiken, his enemy: 'While Auld wi' hingin lip gaed sneaking | And hid his head!' In 1876 William Scott Douglas, with access to the Glenriddell manuscript and taking the present text as the earlier version, comments

> It seems to me that the Bard had latterly been induced to alter—and in our humble opinion, to spoil—this stanza, by the importunity of Dumfriesshire friends who could not form an intelligible idea of the word 'snakin' as used in the original Ayrshire copies . . . where [it] has the very opposite meaning [from the English 'sneaking'], namely *exulting.* The picture in the early version is truly grand. The orator observes the effect of his eloquence on his client's persecutors, and rears his head like a leopard after hitting a damaging blow with his forepaw; the under jaw firmly lowers itself, while the nostrils distend, and from the palate of the speaker escapes a sound of defiance and contempt for his opponent. This is what Burns calls 'snakin'.' It may not be found in any Scotch Dictionary; but every Ayrshire man, and hundreds in other lowland and even highland counties of Scotland, understand the word so, when read in the connection referred to. (Douglas Vol. II, 437–8)

DSL has no record of 'snaking' in this sense other than Scott Douglas's claim; in the entry for 'snaik' ('to prowl, snuff about looking for food') it suggests Burns perhaps meant to use *this* word in a figurative sense to mean 'snuffling, sniffing contemptuously'.

l. 85. *day of vengeance.* The Old Testament prophets mention this, for example Jeremiah: 'For this is the day of the Lord God of hosts, a day of vengeance, that he may avenge him of his adversaries: and the sword shall devour, and it shall be satiate and made drunk with their blood' (46: 10).

233   l. 86. *visit them*. That is, punish them. A biblical usage, as in Jeremiah again: 'the Lord doth not accept them; he will now remember their iniquity, and visit their sins' (14: 10).

l. 87. *pass not in thy mercy by 'em*. A usage from the minor prophet Amos, where the Lord warns, 'The end is come upon my people of Israel; I will not again pass by them any more' (8: 2).

Extempore verses on dining with Lord Daer. K127. Accompanied in the 1799 Stewart and Meikle chapbook by 'The Dominie Depos'd; or, some reflections on his Intrigue with a young lass. By William Forbes, A.M. Late School-master at Petercoulter'. The Burns text comes from a letter to Dr John Mackenzie, the surgeon in Mauchline and a close friend, and the chapbook follows the poem with the letter:

DEAR SIR

I NEVER spent an afternoon among great folks, with half that pleasure, as when in company with you I had the honour of paying my devoirs to that plain, honest, worthy man, the Professor. I would be delighted to see him perform acts of kindness and friendship, though I were not the object, he does it with such a grace.—I think his character, divided into ten parts, stands thus—four parts Socrates—four parts Nathaniel—and two parts Shakespeare's Brutus.

The foregoing verses were really extempore, but a little corrected since. They may entertain you a little, with the help of that partiality with which you are so good as favour [*sic*] the performances of,

DEAR SIR,
Your very humble servant
ROBERT BURNS.

'The Professor' was Dugald Stewart (1753–1828), Professor of Moral Philosophy at the University of Edinburgh. Impressed by the Kilmarnock edition, Stewart invited Burns to dinner at Catrine House, his country home near Mauchline, on 23 October 1786, where his former student Basil William Douglas, styled Lord Daer (1763–94), was also a guest. Daer, eldest surviving son of the Earl of Selkirk, was an improving landlord and proponent of political reform; he went on to be active in the radical circles of the early 1790s.

The poem is written in a 'tail-rhyme' stanza: Burns could have found forms in Chaucer and Dunbar, but just this type, where a trimeter 'tail' follows a rhyming couplet of tetrameter lines in a six-line stanza, had been used by William Collins for some of his *Odes on Several Descriptive and Allegoric Subjects* (1746) and by Thomas Gray for 'Ode on the Death of a Favourite Cat' (1753).

234   l. 7. *Writers*. That is, lawyers.

l. 11. *Quorum*. Justices of the Peace as a body, in contexts where a certain number have to be present for their decision to be binding.

l. 13. *stand out my shin!*. *DSL* offers 'to *set* or *turn out the brunt side o one's shin*: to be proud of oneself, to hold one's head high, be quite uplifted'; 'to set out the shin' means 'to walk proudly' in *OED*.

l. 16. *lang Scotch ell*. The Scotch ell, a measure of length, at 37 inches, was actually shorter than the English one, at 45.

l. 18. *sonnet*. Song: see note to p. 205, l. 84.

l. 19. *Hogarth*. William Hogarth (1697–1764), painter and engraver of 'modern moral subjects' such as *The Rake's Progress* and *Marriage à-la-mode*.

l. 25. *good Stuart*. Dugald Stewart: see headnote above. The editions of Currie and Cunningham omit this stanza.

l. 26. *Scotia's sacred Demosthenes*. Demosthenes (d. 322 BC), the great Athenian orator; Henley and Henderson suggest (Vol. II, 342) that this refers to Hugh Blair, who seems to have attended this dinner as well. Blair was Professor of Rhetoric and Belles Lettres at Edinburgh University.

l. 37. *I watch'd*. That is, watched *for* (something expected): *OED* 4d.

235 *The Fornicater*. K61. This and the following two songs appear in a volume entitled *The Merry Muses of Caledonia; a collection of favourite Scots songs, Ancient and Modern; selected for use of the Crochallan Fencibles*. Printed for private distribution, the title-page names no publisher; one of the extant copies gives the date as 1799, but was probably produced the following year. The title page has an epigraph:

> Say, Puritan, can it be wrong,
> To dress plain truth in witty song?
> What honest Nature says, we should do;
> What every lady does,—or would do.

Burns was a member of the Crochallan Fencibles (see note to p. 149, l. 17), collected bawdy songs and shared them with like-minded friends, and is certainly the author, in whole or in part, of many of the 85 songs in *Merry Muses*. It is impossible to say if his involvement in the production of this volume went any further, but his name remained associated with it even as other material was added in the following century-and-a-half of its unofficial circulation, until a more liberal age permitted its open publication (in the United States in 1964, and in Great Britain in 1965).

This song, the first in the volume (pp. 3–4), is certainly by Burns: a manuscript in his hand exists (in which 'fornicator' is spelt correctly), and the lyric describes the experience of public penance for 'fornication' allegorized in 'Epistle to J. Rankine' in the Kilmarnock edition. An avowedly bowdlerized version was published in 1876 by Scott Douglas.

Tune: Clout the Cauldron. For a score, see notes to p. 226, ll. 165–80.

235 l. 3. *daintless*. The manuscript has 'dauntless'. The present version perhaps reflects a vernacular pronunciation, although it does not appear in *DSL*.

l. 4. *Whate'er the lass discovers*. The verb in the sense of 'divulge, reveal, disclose to knowledge (anything secret or unknown)' or 'reveal the identity of (a person)' (*OED* 4, 6): for example, to the Church Session. The manuscript has 'When the bonny lass discovers', which Kinsley glosses as 'reveals her pregnancy', although this is not a usage listed in *OED* or *DSL*.

l. 6. *frater*. Brother (Latin).

l. 9. *Before the congregation wide*. For punishment in the 'stool of repentance', see note to p. 113, ll. 37–72; and see the experience narrated in the woman's voice in 'The rantin dog the daddie o't' from *SMM*.

l. 12. *ditty*. 'The matter of charge, or ground of indictment, against a person accused of a crime' (*DSL*).

l. 15. *limbs*. This reading is from the manuscript. The *Merry Muses* text has 'lambs': probably a mistake.

l. 18. *buttock hire*. 'A fine exacted by the church in cases of fornication' (*DSL*).

l. 20. *convoy*. The manuscript has 'convey'.

ll. 25–32. *But, by the sun an' moon I swear...A harden'd Fornicater*. Compare the sentiments expressed towards the real 'Betsey', Elizabeth Paton, and her daughter in 'A poet's welcome to his love-begotten daughter' in this volume.

236 l. 30. *pater*. Father (Latin).

l. 32. *A harden'd Fornicater*. The manuscript has two more stanzas, not included in *Merry Muses*. 'Tipt you off blue-boram' means 'given you syphilis'; 'esse Mater' means 'to become a mother'.

> Ye wenching blades whose hireling jades
> Have tipt you off blue-boram,
> I tell ye plain, I do disdain
> To rank you in the Quorum;
> But a bony lass upon the grass
> To teach her esse Mater,
> And no reward but for regard,
> O that's a Fornicator.
>
> Your warlike Kings and Heros bold,
> Great Captains and Commanders;
> Your mighty Cèsars fam'd of old,
> And Conquering Alexanders;
> In fields they fought and laurels bought

> And bulwarks strong did batter,
> But still they grac'd our noble list
> And ranked Fornicator!!!

Nine inch will please a lady. K252. Probably by Burns (ll. 5–7 survive in his handwriting), starting from a traditional scenario; *Merry Muses*, 32–4.

Tune: The Quaker's wife.

In L567 (June 1793) Burns recommends this tune to Thomson for his song 'Blythe hae I been on yon hill'; but the version Thomson uses has an altered second part. The present score reflects the traditional tune, and is adapted from 'Merrily dance the Quaker' in *A Collection of Scots Reels or Country Dances* published by Robert Bremner (1759).

l. 3. *graith.* Here, tackle.

l. 7. *Annandale.* The eastern district of Dumfriesshire.

l. 12. *p——e.* Pintle, i.e. cock.

l. 15. *and a daud.* 'Daud' can mean 'a lump of any solid matter' (*DSL*); or this phrase might just mean 'and then some'.

l. 16. *He nidg't it in.* *DSL* has 'press, squeeze' among its meanings for 'knidge'.

l. 17. *laithron.* 'Lazy, loitering' (*DSL*). This reading is from the manuscript: *Merry Muses* has 'laithern'.

l. 22. *nyvle.* Navel.

l. 24. *gyvel.* Gable-end, used figuratively here, suggests *DSL*, for the pudendum.

237 *Poor bodies do naething but m—w.* K395. Also known as 'Why shouldna poor folk mowe?' and by its first line. For 'mow' or 'mowe' *DSL* offers 'copulate'; the British-English 'shag' might be a closer equivalent, except a 'mow' can also be enjoyed by livestock. *Merry Muses*, 80–3.

Tune: The Campbells are coming.

Burns made a version of the old Jacobite song for *The Scots Musical Museum*, song 299, from which this score is adapted. The chorus is traditionally sung to the lower part of the tune; *Low* sets it to the higher in this instance.

Most of this is certainly by Burns. Several manuscript versions exist in his hand: one sent to his Edinburgh friend Robert Cleghorn in a letter of 12 December 1792 ('a song, just finished this moment'), L527; another in L632 of July 1794 to George Thomson, editor of the *Select Collection*, who marked in the margin, 'What a pity this is not publishable'. But stanzas 4 and 6 of the present text appear in none of them, and have been added by others; the stanzas by Burns also reveal many changes which cannot be attributed to him, only a few of which I have noted below.

237 l. 1. *WHEN*. 'While' in the manuscripts: see note to l. 46 below.

l. 3. *had*. This is 'hae' in the manuscripts: see note to l. 46 below.

l. 11. *B—s—k's great prince*. Brunswick (Braunschweig, in Germany). Charles William Ferdinand, Duke of Brunswick and brother-in-law to George III, invaded France with a mostly Prussian and Austrian army in August 1792, intending to reverse the revolution and restore Louis XVI to his full powers. The invasion was halted by the French at Valmy on 20 September.

l. 12. *Gade*. 'Cam' in the manuscripts: see note to l. 46 below.

l. 17. *The E—p——r swore*. 'Emperor' may refer to Francis II, Holy Roman (that is, German) Emperor, another leader of the anti-revolutionary coalition; or his father Leopold II, who in August 1791 had, with the King of Prussia, made a joint declaration of their readiness to punish France for any harm visited on Louis XVI and his family (though Leopold died before the war began).

l. 23. *the brave duke of Y—k*. York. Britain joined the coalition in February 1793. Frederick, Duke of York and Albany, second son of George III, commanded the British contingent in the coalition armies in the spring and summer of that year.

l. 24. *The Rhine first did pass.* In the copy of *Merry Muses* in the National Library of Scotland, Victorian editor William Scott Douglas has annotated this terrible line with an alternative: 'At the Rhine fell to work'. Douglas included a few heavily bowdlerized stanzas from this song in his 1876 *Complete Poetical Works.*

l. 27. *his P—ss—n dame.* Prussian. In 1791 Frederick had married Princess Frederica Charlotte, daughter of the King of Prussia.

238 l. 30. *Proud P—ss—a.* Prussia.

l. 32. *F—d——k.* King Frederick-William II, one of the leaders of the Coalition.

l. 35. *The black-headed eagle.* A black double-headed eagle was the emblem of the Empire.

l. 38. *the braes of Gemap.* French forces, invading the Austrian Netherlands, defeated the Imperial army at Jemappes on 6 November 1792.

ll. 41–2. *Kate laid her claws, | On poor St——l—s.* Stanislaus. Stanisław August Poniatowski, last King of the Polish-Lithuanian Commonwealth, had sided with his reformist parliament to produce a modernizing Constitution for Poland, partly inspired by events in France, in 1791. The Polish nobility rebelled, and the following year Catherine the Great, Empress of Russia ('Kate'), sent in her troops to reassert Russian hegemony and aristocratic privilege; Stanisław then went over to the reactionary side. Decades earlier, Catherine and Stanisław had been lovers.

l. 43. *was.* This is 'has' in the manuscript: see following note.

l. 46. *An' why, &c.* The manuscript versions end with an additional stanza (I have added line-breaks to replicate the form of the stanza in *Merry Muses*):

> But truce with commotions
> And new-fangled notions,
> A bumper I trust you'll allow:
> Here's George our gude king
> And Charlotte his queen,
> And lang may they tak a gude mowe!

Burns wrote this song during the attempts to destroy the new regimes in France and Poland that it describes. If the preceding stanzas implicitly explain the belligerence of Charles, Francis, and Frederick-William as a substitute for sex, this last stanza reassures the British reader that the United Kingdom will remain at peace, given the famous attention of 'Farmer George' to his connubial duties (in her first 22 years of marriage Charlotte had borne 15 children). Although Burns retains this stanza in the song he sends to Thomson in 1794, this meaning had been lost, because Britain had by then entered the war. The *Merry Muses* text updates the song for wartime, omitting this closing reassurance, adding the reference to the Duke of York's campaign in stanza 4, and making the changes noted in ll. 1, 3, 12, and 43 to more consistently place these events in the past (Poland, for example, had not merely 'bent like a bow' by 1799, but had vanished from the map entirely, in the Third Partition of 1795).

Poem on Pastoral Poetry. K82. This, and the following two texts, were first published in *The Works of Robert Burns; with an account of his life, and a criticism on his writings. In four volumes* (London and Edinburgh, 1800), Vol. IV. Researched and edited by Dr James Currie, this was the first major collection not only of Burns's poetry and songs but also of his correspondence. This poem appears at pp. 359–61. This title is Currie's invention: a manuscript version gives the title only as 'Sketch'. Burns had used the Standard Habbie stanza to talk *about* poetry before, for example in the Epistles to John Lapraik.

238 l. 9. *sock or buskin*. Originally, the low shoe (*soccus*) worn by comic actors, in contrast to the high thick-soled boot (*buskin* in renaissance English) worn by the actors in ancient Athenian tragedy; metonyms for comic and tragic theatre respectively.

239 l. 13. *Homer's craft*. Epic poetry, its greatest modern instance being Milton's *Paradise Lost* (1667).

l. 14. *Eschylus*. Athenian playwright (d. *c*.456 BC), author of tragedies including the series known as the *Oresteia*.

ll. 15–16. *Wee Pope . . . Horatian fame*. Disease left Alexander Pope (1688–1744) with restricted growth and a hunchback. He appears here as the pre-eminent satirist of the modern age, in the tradition of the Roman poet Quintus Horatius Flaccus (65–8 BC), known in English as Horace.

ll. 17–18. *Barbauld . . . E'en Sappho's flame*. Anna Lætitia Barbauld, née Aiken (1743–1825), at this point probably the best-known female poet writing in English; Sappho, d. *c*.570 BC, Greek poet hugely admired in antiquity, though only fragments of her work now survive.

l. 19. *Theocritus*. Currie's 1800 text has 'Theopocritus', a mistake corrected in the second edition of the following year. A third-century BC Greek poet, his *Bucolics* are credited with initiating the pastoral tradition in European poetry. Living in Sicily, Theocritus wrote in the Doric version of Greek rather than the language of Athens. In his Preface to his 1721 *Poems*, Allan Ramsay appeals to this as a precedent for writing in Scots: 'The *Scotticisms*, which perhaps may offend some over-nice Ear, give new Life and Grace to the Poetry, and become their Place as well as the *Doric* Dialect of *Theocritus*, so much admired by the best Judges' (Ramsay Vol. I, xix).

l. 20. *herd's ballats, Maro's catches*. This makes perfect sense as it stands: the sort of ballads composed or sung by a shepherd or cattleherd, contrasted with the work of the Roman poet Publius Vergilius Maro (70–19 BC), known as Virgil in English, whose pastoral *Eclogues* are modelled on Theocritus. But the manuscript has 'Herd's', which has suggested to some that Burns means the songs collected in *Ancient and Modern Scottish Songs* (1769) by David Herd (d. 1810).

ll. 21–2. *skinklin patches | O' heathen tatters.* Pope's *Pastorals* are teenage works, modelled on and frequently borrowing from Virgil's *Eclogues*.

l. 32. *Allan.* Allan Ramsay (1686–1758), author of the verse drama *The Gentle Shepherd* (1725; later turned into a ballad-opera) which naturalizes pastoral conventions in Scots.

l. 35. *Tamtallan.* The impressive ruins of Tantallon castle stand on an East-Lothian clifftop.

l. 40. *Philomel.* A pastoral-conventional name for the nightingale: in Greek myth, Philomela is raped and her tongue cut out to prevent her accusing her rapist: she is eventually turned into a nightingale by the gods. The nightingale is not a species native to Scotland.

240 ll. 43–54. *In gowany glens thy burnie strays... The sternest move.* The manuscript version has these two stanzas in reverse order.

Poetical Inscription for an Altar to Independence. K505. First published in Currie's *Works of Robert Burns* (1800), Vol. IV, p. 369. For Patrick Heron of Heron and Kerroughtrie, see headnote to 'The Election', p. 363; this poem was written around the same time.

Address to a Lady. K524. First published in Currie's *Works of Robert Burns* (1800), Vol. IV, p. 381. The title is again Currie's invention: universally known by its first line. It took another seventy years before these words were matched to the air for which they were written, at least in print. Currie does not mention a tune; Cunningham (Vol. V) assigns them to 'Lass o' Livingstone'. Eventually, in the 1850s, Robert Chambers tracked down Jessy Lewars, who as a girl had helped out in the Burns household during the poet's final illness. She told him that Burns had offered to write words for any tune she cared to play for him on the piano, and these lines were the result. But in Volume IV of his 1856 edition, Chambers identified this tune as 'The Wren's Nest' in *The Scots Musical Museum*, Vol. V, song 406. It was in fact another tune included in that volume, 'Lennox love to Blantyre', paired there with a lyric called 'The Wren' as song 483. This is the source of the score below.

Slowish

Chambers's mistake was rectified by William Scott Douglas in his *Complete Poetical Works of Robert Burns* (1871), Vol. II.

241 *Lines written extempore in a lady's pocket-book.* K412. Written in June 1793; first published by Thomas Stewart in *Poems Ascribed to Robert Burns, the Ayrshire Bard* (Glasgow, 1801), 74. This volume collected most of the poems Stewart and Meikle had published in their chapbook series and added many others. See also headnote to 'The Tree of Liberty', p. 402. The form is that strongly associated with Pope: iambic pentameter ('heroic') couplets.

Verses, Written under the Portrait of Fergusson the Poet. K143. First published in *The Scots Magazine*, LXV (November 1803). An up-market but unchallenging monthly, this issue includes a biographical essay on the seventeenth-century physician Sir Andrew Balfour, and a series of extracts from recent books about the East Indies, including an account of the fall of Seringapatam to British forces in 1799. The present poem appears on p. 798 without any more comment than appears in the subtitle; it is followed by another piece inscribed by Burns in the same source, the very early 'Tragic Fragment' (K5). The *Scots Magazine* text has been mangled in transcription. A facsimile of the holograph inscription can be found in Henley and Henderson Vol. II, between pages 408 and 409. The poem is a rare excursion for Burns into blank verse.

l. 2. *pleasure!*. The exclamation mark is from the holograph: the text published in 1803 has only a comma.

l. 4. *muse*. From the holograph: the 1803 text has 'Muses'.

l. 6. *unfitted for*. This is taken from the holograph. The 1803 text has 'unpitied for', which makes no sense; nineteenth-century editions change this to 'unpitied by', until the correct reading appears in 1896.

Song [My father was a farmer]. K21. This, and following two texts, were first published in *Reliques of Robert Burns; consisting chiefly of original letters, poems and critical observations on Scottish songs, collected and published by R. H. Cromek* (London, 1808). All three texts come from the notebooks, now known as the First and Second Commonplace Books, in which Burns jotted ideas and drafts beginning in April 1783. Cromek combined material from these two manuscript volumes, and claimed to reproduce the resulting text in its entirety, explaining that 'It has been the chief object in making this collection, not to omit any thing which might illustrate the character and feelings of the bard at different periods of his life' (p. 315). 'My father was a farmer' appears on pp. 330–1. It is a very early production, and in the First Commonplace Book Burns introduces it with a comment dated April 1784: 'The Following Song is a wild Rhapsody, miserably deficient in Versification, but as the sentiments are the genuine feelings of my heart, for that reason I have a particular pleasure in conning it over' (p. 329). The long lines of this poem can be thought of as pairs of shorter iambic tetrameter lines conjoined, the first often structured with an internal rhyme, the second ending on a feminine rhyme with 'O' completing the measure.

Tune: The Weaver and his shuttle O, also known as Jockey's (or Johnny's) grey breeks.

This score is adapted from *The Scots Musical Museum* song 27, 'The Gentle Swain'. It allows for the repetition of the last two lines of verse in the last eight bars: we have no indication that this is what Burns expected in setting these words to this tune.

l. 1. *My father was a farmer upon the Carrick border.* Cromek has 'Father' and 'Farmer': the present text follows his manuscript source which uses lower case for both initials. Carrick is the southernmost district of Ayrshire, across the river Doon from Burns's native Kyle: see Map.

242 l. 18. *moil.* 'To make oneself wet and muddy' (*OED*). This reading is from the manuscript: Cromek has 'broil'.

l. 35. *Potosi.* The silver mine in present-day Bolivia, the source of great wealth to the Spanish Empire.

243 *Fragment [There was a lad was born in Kyle].* K140. Also known as 'Rantin rovin Robin'. This song and the following 'Elegy' come from a section of Cromek's version of the Commonplace Book headed 'EGOTISMS from my own Sensations'. It begins, 'I don't well know what is the reason of it, but some how or other though I am, when I have a mind, pretty generally beloved; yet, I never could get the art of commanding respect.—I imagine it is owing to my being deficient in what Sterne calls "that understrapping virtue of discretion."—I am so apt to a *lapsus linguæ*, that I sometimes think the character of a certain great man, I have read of somewhere, is

very much *apropos* to myself—that he was a compound of great talents and great folly. N.B. To try if I can discover the causes of this wretched infirmity, and, if possible, to mend it' (Cromek, pp. 339–40; Burns quotes *Tristram Shandy*, Vol. VI, p. 351). The song appears on pp. 341–2, and comes from the Second Commonplace Book, begun in Edinburgh in 1787 at the height of Burns's celebrity there.

The tune, 'Dainty Davie', dates from the seventeenth century. It is used for song 34 of *The Scots Musical Museum*, from whence the score below is adapted:

In 1871 William Scott Douglas (in *Complete Poetical Works*, Vol. II) observed that it was 'almost universally' sung to a different tune, 'O an ye were dead gudeman' (see note to p. 223, ll. 89–116).

243   l. 2. *what na day o' what na style.* 'what na' means 'which, of two or more' (*DSL*). Britain had switched from the Julian to the Gregorian calendars in 1752; dates calculated in the old and new 'styles' differ by 11 days in consequence.

l. 4. *nice.* In the now obsolete sense of 'particular, strict, or careful with regard to a specific point or thing' (*OED*).

l. 9. *Our monarch's hindmost year but ane.* George III ascended the throne in 1760.

l. 11. *Janwar Win'.* A note in Cromek's source text, the Second Commonplace Book, but not included by him, explains: 'January 25, 1759, the date of my bardship's vital existence.—R.B'.

l. 12. *hansel.* 'A gift bestowed to commemorate an inaugural occasion, event or season, e.g. the beginning of the year . . . with the idea of bringing good-luck to the recipient' (*DSL*).

l. 13. *keekit.* Cromek has 'keckit': clearly a compositor's mistake.

l. 26. *Ye'll gar the lasses lie aspar.* That is, 'aspread, with legs apart' (*DSL*). This is from the Second Commonplace Book: Cromek has 'Ye gar the lasses ****'.

244 *Elegy on the Death of Robert Ruisseaux.* K141. First published in Cromek, p. 343, from the Second Commonplace Book. 'Ruisseaux' is French for 'streams' and hence an equivalent for 'burns'. The Standard Habbie stanza again used for its original purpose, humorous elegy.

l. 1. *lair.* 'The resting place of a corpse; a grave, tomb' (*OED*).

Sketch of an Epistle to R. Graham, Esq. of Fintray. K318. Written in 1790, and sent in a letter to its addressee on 10 June; first published in *The Edinburgh Magazine, and Literary Miscellany* for April 1811. This journal had merged with the very similar *Scots Magazine* in 1804 (it was also known by this older name) and was published by the prestigious Archibald Constable and Co., responsible for the mighty *Edinburgh Review*, the *Encyclopaedia Britannica*, and Walter Scott. The April issue includes extracts from travellers' accounts of China and Nepal; 'Memoirs of the Progress of Manufactures, Chemistry, Science, and the Fine Arts'; an 'Account of the Establishment of the present System of Public Education in Scotland', extracted from a new history of the Reformation; a letter describing 'Recent Improvements in Glasgow'; and a review of 'A Sketch of the State of British India, with a view of pointing out the best means of civilizing its Inhabitants, and diffusing the knowledge of Christianity throughout the Eastern World'. Burns's poem appears on pp. 294–5. Beneath the title we are told that 'The following poem, from the pen of the celebrated Robert Burns, has never before been published.' The poem is written in the same type of tail-rhyme stanza as the 'Extempore verses on dining with Lord Daer': see headnote to that poem, p. 382.

In two of the manuscripts the title is 'Epistle to Robt. Graham of Fintry on the close of the disputed Election between Sir J. Johnston and Captn. Miller, for the Dumfries district of Boroughs' of 1790; this poem is sometimes (for example in Hogg and Motherwell's 1834 edition) grouped with the 1795 Heron poems as an 'Election ballad'. Those towns that had political rights as 'Royal Burghs' were grouped in fours or fives to elect MPs: in this case Dumfries, Kirkcudbright, Annan, Lochmaben, and Sanquhar ('The Five Carlins' of Burns's ballad on this election, K269). In contested elections, each town council first voted on which candidate to support; then a delegate from each town would cast their vote at the election itself. County elections (see headnote to 'The Election', p. 363) were vulnerable to the ability of great landowners to create votes by parcelling out their lands to their allies; but burgh elections, like the administration of the burghs themselves, were simply and openly corrupt, with bribery routine and violence unremarkable, and the Dumfries Burghs contest of 1790 was notorious even by these low standards. Miller's patron, the Duke of Queensberry, doled out £8,000; Johnstone's people spent £12,000, secured the vote of Lochmaben by kidnapping a hostile member of its finely hung council, and still lost the election 2–3 (for details see *HPO*).

Title. Robert Graham (1749–1815) was factor on some large estates in Perthshire and Forfarshire. He had sold the family's Fintry estate in Forfarshire in 1780 to pay off personal debts, but retained the designation.

He became a Commissioner of the Scottish Board of Excise in 1787, and in this capacity was in a position to help Burns in his career when he became an exciseman the following year: in his letters Burns often refers to Fintry as his 'patron'. It was to Fintry that Burns turned when his political alignments threatened his job: see Appendix 1, p. 270f. Burns wrote several poems addressed to him: the present text is sometimes known as the 'Second Epistle to Fintry'.

245 l. 7. *Drumlanrig*. The Dumfriesshire seat of William Douglas, fourth Duke of Queensberry (1724–1810), at the head of the most powerful 'interest' in the county, though rarely there in person.

l. 9. *Of fiddles, whores and hunters*. Queensberry was a generous patron of both musicians and prostitutes; he also owned a famous racing stud ('hunters' are a type of horse). The *Edinburgh Magazine* was using a manuscript that Burns had sent to his friends the McMurdos, where this line reads 'Of Princes and their darlings'. The four other surviving manuscripts have the present reading: John McMurdo was Chamberlain to Queensberry at Drumlanrig, so Burns clearly chose to pull his punches in that particular version.

l. 10. *buying*. This becomes 'winning' in the *Edinburgh Magazine* text, for the same reason.

l. 11. *wabster louns*. Weavers, an important demographic in town life, self-employed artisans working at home.

l. 12. *bunters*. This becomes 'carlins' in the *Edinburgh Magazine* text, to rhyme with 'darlings'; 'bunter' in Samuel Johnson's sense, being roughly synonymous with 'carlin': 'used, by way of contempt, for any low vulgar woman' (*OED*). The present version of this stanza was first published in Cunningham Vol. III, 161, in a note after the poem.

ll. 7–12. *I'll sing the zeal Drumlanrig bears . . . And kissing barefit bunters*. Burns drafted an alternative beginning for this poem, incorporating the present second stanza, which continues after the first stanza thus:

> But where shall I gae rin a ride,
> That I may splatter nane beside?
>   I wad na be uncivil:
> In manhood's various paths and ways
> There's aye some doytan body strays,
>   And I ride like the devil.—
>
> Say, I break off wi' a' my birr,
> And down yon dark, deep alley spur,
>   Where Theologics dander:
> Alas! curst wi' eternal fogs,
> And damn'd in everlasting bogs,
>   As sure's the creed I'll blunder!

I'll stain a Band, or jaup a gown,
Or rin my reckless, guilty crown
 Against the haly door:
Sair do I rue my luckless fate,
When, as the Muse an' Deil would hae't,
 I rade that road before.—

Suppose I take a spurt, and mix
Amang the wilds o' Politicks
 Electors and Elected,
Where dogs at Court (sad sons of bitches!)
Septennially a madness touches
 Till all the Land's infected.—

I'll sing the zeal Drumlanrig bears,
Who left the all-important cares
 Of fiddles, whores and hunters;
And bent on buying borough towns,
Came shaking hands wi' wabster louns,
 And kissing barefit bunters.

All-hail! Drumlanrig's haughty Grace,
Discarded remnant of a Race,
 Once godlike great in story:
Thy fathers' virtues all contrasted;
The very name of D—— blasted;
 Thine that inverted glory.—

Hate, Envy, oft the Douglas bore,
But thou hast superadded more,
 And sunk them in Contempt:
Follies and Crimes have stained the name,
But Queensberry thine the virgin claim,
 From aught of Good exempt.—

Great was the drinking, dancing, singing,
Bonfireing, racketing and ringing,

The manuscript ends with those two lines. This fragment was first published in Douglas Vol. II, pp. 418–19, separately from the rest of the poem.

l. 13. *Combustion.* A word used in Burns's letter to Mrs Dunlop: see note to l. 117 below.

l. 16. *buff and blue.* The colours of the opposition to William Pitt's government. Charles James Fox and his supporters began wearing blue coats with buff waistcoats in imitation of Washington's army, to signal their sympathy with the rebels, during the American war. Queensberry had been a 'mentor' to the young Fox, at least at the card-table and the race-track. But Queensbury had been extending his influence in the burghs with the backing of Henry Dundas, Pitt's right-hand man and manager of Scottish elections; and once in parliament, Queensberry's candidate, Patrick Miller (d. 1845), seems to have voted against the government only twice. On the other hand, Miller was well enough connected in opposition circles to communicate to Burns the prospect of a job with the *Morning Chronicle* in 1794: see headnote to 'Bruce's Address to his Troops', p. 360.

245   l. 17. *Westerha' and Hopeton.* Sir James Johnstone of Westerhall (1726–94), the sitting member for the constituency, head of a rival interest to Queensberry's. Johnstone's political career had been founded on the fortune he had made in India. As an MP he seems to have been a model of 'independence', the political virtue most highly regarded by Burns; only in his opposition to reform of the burghs themselves was he resolutely with the government (see *HPO*). John Hope, fourth Earl of Hopetoun (d. 1823), backed Johnstone.

l. 18. *Whig.* See note to ll. 82–3 below for the inheritance evoked by this name.

l. 20. *his star.* The insignia of his rank as a duke.

ll. 23–4. *Cesarean fight, | Or Ciceronian pleading.* Contrasting the Roman general and conqueror of Gaul, Gaius Julius Caesar (d. 44 BC), and the great orator and defender of the Republic, Marcus Tullius Cicero (d. 43 BC).

l. 25. *Monsmeg.* Mons Meg, the 20-inch-calibre fifteenth-century cannon, built in Mons, Flanders, but long resident at Edinburgh Castle where it was fired to mark ceremonial occasions; in 1790 it was languishing in London.

l. 26. *muster.* The grammar here suggests this verb must be in the sense of 'talk volubly and incessantly' (*DSL*), but there is clearly also a play on 'come together . . . in preparation for battle' (of an army: *OED*).

l. 31. *M^cM—rdo and his lovely spouse.* Burns's friends John and Jean McMurdo: see note to l. 9 above. They were on the winning, Queensberry, side, as the victor's 'laurels' of the next line reminds us.

l. 34. *Burgess.* A freeman of the town.

l. 35. *sub rosa.* That is, ' "under the rose", in secret, secretly' (*OED*). This reading is from most of the manuscripts: the *Edinburgh Magazine* text has 'all-conquering' here, removing the innuendo in deference to the McMurdos for whom its version was written (see notes to ll. 9 and 10 above).

l. 37. *Craigendarroch.* Alexander Fergusson of Craigendarroch (d. 1796), Dumfriesshire landowner and lawyer; allied to the Queensberry interest.

l. 39. *Hecla.* The Icelandic volcano. A major eruption had continued from April 1766 till May 1768.

246 l. 40. *Glenriddel, skill'd in rusty coins.* Burns's friend and neighbour the antiquarian Captain Robert Riddell of Glenriddell (see headnote to 'On Glenriddel's Fox breaking his chain', p. 404).

l. 41. *each Tory's dark designs.* Here, and at l. 45, the term 'Tory' is introduced in the context of the agency of Miller's supporters, Glenriddell and Staig. For the political lineage evoked by this term, see note to l. 86 below; but no serious politician called themselves a Tory in this period, when the name was 'a term of political abuse' (Kidd, 'Burns and Politics', 64). Glenriddell and Staig see themselves as opposing 'Tories' because that is what self-defined Whigs call their enemies, and the poem ironically adopts this usage (for another example of Burns's ironic take on 'Whigs', see 'On Glenriddel's Fox breaking his chain').

l. 44. *Redoubted Staig.* David Staig (1740–1824), Provost of Dumfries for twenty years, on and off. 'A popular and energetic public figure' (*BE*).

l. 46. *Walsh.* John Walsh, Sheriff Substitute for the County.

ll. 47–8. *his magnum-bonum round | With Cyclopean fury.* A magnum-bonum is 'a bottle containing two quarts of wine or spirits' says *DSL* (Latin, 'a great good'). The reference is to the enraged Polyphemos after Odysseus and his men have blinded him in his single eye to secure their escape in Homer's *Odyssey* Book IX.

l. 49. *Miller.* A footnote in one of the manuscripts, and the reference to banks in the next line, identify this as Patrick Miller, senior of Dalswinton, father of the Queensberry candidate, a banker, and Burns's landlord at Ellisland.

l. 52. *Maxwelton, that baron bold.* Sir Robert Laurie, fifth baronet of Maxwelton, MP for the county of Dumfries 1774–1804. In the Queensberry interest, and so on Miller's side, but also a supporter of the government.

l. 53. *Lawson.* 'A famous wine merchant' (Burns's manuscript footnote).

ll. 70–2: *As flames amang a hundred woods . . . Such is the rage of battle.* Kinsley spots the echo of Macpherson's 'Fingal', ii: 'As a hundred winds in Lochlin's groves, as fire in the firs of a hundred hills; so loud, so ruinous and vast the ranks of men are hewn down' (Macpherson 67–8).

247 l. 78. *the Buchan bullers.* A collapsed cave in the sea-cliffs near Peterhead in the north-east, where a heavy swell can produce violent breakers.

ll. 82–3. *The muffled murtherer of Charles | The Magna Charta flag unfurls.* Eighteenth-century 'Whigs' could define themselves as the descendants of the parliamentary resistance to the Stuart monarchs of the seventeenth century, which often justified itself with reference to the rights extracted from King John in the Magna Carta (the Great Charter) of 1215. The expulsion of James II and VII in the 'Revolution' of 1688–9, and the transfer of the throne to the House of Hanover in 1714, were seen as the culmination of this struggle; this triumphalist history usually skated over parliament's execution of Charles I in 1649 during the civil war. The executioner was masked.

247 l. 86. *Bold Scrimgeour follows gallant Graham.* John Scrymgeour, first Earl of Dundee (d. 1668), joined Charles's army in 1648; James Graham, first Marquis of Montrose (d. 1650), raised an army for Charles in Scotland in 1644. But the figure who might make 'Auld Covenanters shiver' (l. 87) was a different Graham, John, first Viscount Dundee (d. 1689), notorious in south-west Scotland as the ruthless enemy of those who defended their presbyterian church against the Stuart regime in the 1670s and 1680s. Burns's footnotes to one of the manuscripts confirm that he has conflated the two Dundees. These were 'Tories' in the original sense, for whom loyalty to the monarch was the paramount political virtue.

l. 88. *much-wrong'd Montrose.* Captured by Scottish parliamentary forces, Montrose was hanged in Edinburgh in 1650, his head displayed there and his limbs sent to other Scottish towns.

l. 106. *Not Pulteney's wealth can Pulteney save.* Sir James's brother William had become one of the richest commoners in Britain in 1767: an improbable series of deaths in her family had made his wife Frances heir to the fortune of her uncle, William Pulteney, Earl of Bath, if the couple changed their name to his.

l. 108. *Stewart.* 'William Stewart of Hillside' says Burns in a manuscript note.

248 l. 109. *Pitt.* William Pitt the younger (1759–1806), prime minister.

l. 110. *Thurlow.* Edward, first Baron Thurlow (1731–1806), lord chancellor: 'the ferocity of his demeanour could inspire respect, and sometimes fear' (*DNB*).

l. 111. *Melville.* Henry Dundas of Melville castle (1742–1811), treasurer of the navy, commissioner of the board of control, Pitt's right-hand man and his manager of Scotland.

l. 112. *Fox and Sheridan.* Charles James Fox (1749–1806), leader of the opposition; Richard Brinsley Sheridan (1751–1816), an MP as well as a playwright and a close friend and ally of Fox.

l. 113. *Burke shall sing, 'O Prince arise!'.* Edmund Burke MP (1729–97) had been a close ally of Fox and Sheridan since the American war, including their attempts the previous year to have the Prince of Wales made Regent when his father George III became mentally ill: see note to p. 200, l. 35. But Burke had since split with his friends over the French Revolution.

l. 116. *He only hears and sees the war.* The *Edinburgh Magazine* has 'He hears, and only hears the war' which has no manuscript authority; then prints a row of '&c's and stops. From this point the present text follows Cunningham's version (see note to l. 12 above), which completes this stanza, and supplies the final stanza in the endnote to the poem.

l. 117. *A cool spectator purely.* Burns wrote to Mrs Dunlop from Ellisland:

> I have just got a summons to attend with my men-servants armed as well as we can, on Monday at one o'clock in the *morning* to escort

Capt[n] Miller from Dalswinton in to Dumfries to be a Candidate for our Boroughs which chuse their Member that day.—The Duke of Queensberry & the Nithsdale Gentlemen who are almost all friends to the Duke's Candidate, the said Capt[n], are to raise all Nithsdale on the same errand.—The Duke of Buccleugh's, Earl of Hopeton's people, in short, the Johnstons, Jardines, and all the Clans of Annandale, are to attend Sir James Johnston who is the other Candidate, on the same account.—This is no exaggeration.— . . . What will be the event, I know not.—I shall go to please my Landlord, & to see the Combustion; but instead of trusting to the strength of Man, I shall trust to the heels of my horse, which are among the best in Nithsdale. (L403, 9 July 1790)

John Bushby (see note to p. 215, l. 9), managing the final election as sheriff-clerk, kept the three delegates for Miller in the courthouse overnight before the vote, to protect them from a mob of (he claimed) four thousand, 'one half at least armed with bludgeons', and called in the army to maintain order (*HPO*).

l. 122. *land o' cakes.* That is, oatcakes: meaning Scotland.

Epistle to the President of the Highland Society. K108. Written in 1786; first published in *The Edinburgh Magazine, and Literary Miscellany* for February 1818 under the present title, but usually known as the 'Address of Beelzebub'. This issue also includes an essay 'On whether Pope was a poet'; letters on popular superstitions and proposing a philharmonic society for Edinburgh; a continuation of a review of Walter Scott's novel *Rob Roy*; and some natural history. Burns's poem appears on pp. 130–1, between a continuation of an essay on the life and writings of James Hogg and a discussion of the original ballad of 'Rob Roy'. It is introduced with a long letter to the editor:

I was happy to observe in your last Number, a complete copy of a song by Burns ['Here's a Health to them that's awa',' K391] which the public had hitherto only seen in an imperfect state [in Cromek's *Reliques*, 1808]. It is well to preserve in some secure and accessible repository all such reliques and memorials of remarkable men, as are either interesting on account of their intrinsic merit, or that serve in any degree to illustrate the state of our national literature and manners,—though perhaps unworthy of a place in more classical collections. With this view, I enclose for your Magazine another production of our great Scottish poet, which has not yet appeared in print. You will find several indifferent enough lines in it, and one or two rather rough expressions, but nothing, I think, that can offend any true old-fashioned unsophisticated Scotchman, or even the more fastidious *Southron*, who has not lost all remembrance of Fielding, or who has learned to estimate the irresistible naïveté of the author of Waverley. In one word, while I deprecate as much as any one can the injudicious zeal of such editors as

Cromek . . . yet I consider it a duty to preserve from oblivion every production which the public has a claim to inherit as the legacy of departed genius, unless its publication be offensive to right feeling, or derogatory to the talents and character of the author. These remarks may perhaps appear disproportioned to the importance of the following careless effusion, but you will at least recognize in it something of the unpruned vigour of Burns' genius,—the rustic but keen severity of his sarcasm,—and the manly detestation of oppression (real or supposed) which so strongly characterized him. The internal evidences of its authenticity are sufficiently obvious; but for your more complete satisfaction, I enclose the original in his own handwriting. It was given to me by a friend who got it many years ago from the well known 'ready-witted Rankin,' the poet's early and intimate acquaintance. I am, &c.   R.W.

Ayr, Jan. 30, 1818.

The Highland Society, an organization of Highland landowners, met in London on 23 May 1786 to discuss

the encouragement of the fisheries in the Highlands, &c. Three thousand pounds were immediately subscribed by eleven gentlemen present for this particular purpose. The Earl of Breadalbane informed the meeting that five hundred persons had agreed to emigrate from the estates of Mr MᶜDonald of Glengarry; that they had subscribed money, purchased ships, &c., to carry their design into effect. The noblemen and gentlemen agreed to co-operate with government to frustrate their design; and to recommend to the principal noblemen and gentlemen in the Highlands to endeavour to prevent emigration, by improving the fisheries, agriculture, and manufactures, and particularly to enter into a subscription for that purpose.

This is the account of the meeting that Burns read in the *Edinburgh Advertiser* of 30 May. John Campbell, Earl of Breadalbane (1762–1834), was currently one of the Scottish representative peers in the House of Lords; Thomas Mackenzie of Highfield had been laird of Applecross since 1774; and Duncan Macdonell of Glengarry (d. 1788) was 'chief' of clan Macdonell. Within ten years one of the 'improvements' proposed was requiring the mass eviction of tenants to make way for sheep runs, a process that was reaching a climax by the time this poem was published in the *Edinburgh Magazine*; and emigration, far from being prevented, was sometimes forced on the evicted.

249 l. 7. *A* **** *s*. Applecross.

l. 13. *Hancocke, or a Franklin.* John Hancock (1737–93), President of the Continental Congress at the signing of the Declaration of Independence in 1776; Benjamin Franklin (1706–90), scientist, inventor, and writer who helped draft the Declaration.

l. 15. *Washington*. George Washington (1732–99), commander in the war with Britain and first President of the new state.

l. 16. *Montgomery*. Richard Montgomery (1738–75), a retired British soldier who led a rebel unit to capture Montreal but was killed attacking Quebec in the opening of the war.

l. 21. *North*. Frederick, Lord North (1713–92), prime minister 1770–82 and thus responsible for the failure in America; *Sackville*: George, first Viscount Sackville (1716–85), Secretary of State for American Affairs during the war.

l. 23. *Howes and Clintons*. William, fifth Viscount Howe (1729–1814), the general in charge of British forces; Sir Henry Clinton (1738–95), general whose inability to relieve the siege of General Cornwallis's army at Yorktown led to its surrender and the final British collapse in 1781. These references are of course ironic: Howe and Clinton had failed to bring the American rebels 'to a right repentance'.

l. 31. *G *****. Glengarry.

250 l. 44. *Drury Lane*. At one end of Covent Garden (where the Highland Society had met); both names were synonymous with prostitution.

l. 47. *Flaffan wi' duds*. Kinsley notes the echo of Fergusson's 'The Ghaists', where the ghost of George Heriot, wealthy merchant and philanthropist in the reign of James VI, mourns the effect of the union with England on the finances of his hospital: 'Hale interest for my fund can scantly now | Cleed a' my callants backs, and stap their mou'. | How maun their weyms wi' sairest hunger slack, | Their duds in targets flaff upo' their back' (ll. 73–6; Fergusson 143).

l. 58. *'Tween Herod's hip an' Polycrate*. Herod was king of Judea under Rome at the time of Christ's birth; Polycrates was king of Samos in the Aegean in the mid sixth century BC.

l. 60. *Almagro an' Pizarro*. Diego D'Almargo (1475–1538) and Francisco Pizarro (1478–1541), leaders of the brutal Spanish conquest of Peru.

Beelzebub. 'The prince of the devils' (Matthew 12: 24) in the New Testament, and Satan's lieutenant in *Paradise Lost*.

Anno Mundi 5790. That is, 1786, plus the 4004 years traditionally calculated to have elapsed between the creation of the world and the birth of Christ: Beelzebub of course does not count years from the latter.

The Selkirk Grace. K531. First published in *The Works of Robert Burns; with his life. In eight volumes*, ed. Alan Cunningham (1834), Vol. III, p. 311. Cunningham's note claims: 'On a visit to St. Mary's Isle, the Earl of Selkirk requested Burns to say grace at dinner. These were the words he uttered—they were applauded then, and have since been known in Galloway by the name of "The Selkirk Grace." ' An almost identical version appeared the same year in *The Works of Robert Burns*, ed. The Ettrick Shepherd [James Hogg] and William Motherwell, Vol. II p. 78, entitled 'A Grace, spoken at the table of the Earl of Selkirk', and in Chambers's edition of 1838. The earliest written version of the grace to have survived is in the papers of James Grierson of Dalgoner (1753–1843), who knew the poet at Ellisland, though he only began collecting Burns material in 1805. Grierson's version is in English, apart from the last line; his is the text used by Kinsley. See the article by J. A. Mackay in *Burns Chronicle*, 98 (1989), 24–8.

250 *The Tree of Liberty*. K625. First published in *The Poetical Works of Robert Burns*, ed. Robert Chambers (1838), 86–7: 'Here printed for the first time, from a MS. in the possession of Mr James Duncan, Mosesfield, near Glasgow'. Only 148 pages long with the text in two columns on each page, Chambers's first edition aimed to be 'the cheapest, so that it may be expected to find its way where hitherto none but the most inferior editions, or none at all, have been introduced' ('Preface', 3): he would later refer to it as the 'People's Edition'.

Many have doubted that this poem is by Burns: the manuscript on which Chambers based it, in Burns's handwriting, has been lost. But some of the doubts seem grounded in political distaste, and there is no obvious reason to doubt Chambers's account of his source. He included it in both his subsequent editions. In his 1856–7 *Life and Works of Robert Burns* he introduces it with a discussion of Burns's anger at the war with France: 'Being . . . little apt to think his words of great consequence, it is to be feared that he was much less cautious in the expression of his opinions than was necessary for his escaping censure. We have already had some of these escapes of political sentiment before us. Some others have survived till these times on the breath of tradition and otherwise' (p. 77). Chambers then offers the poem included in the present volume as 'Lines written extempore in a lady's pocket-book' as one of two examples, and continues,

> It is far from likely that the whole of the democratic effusions of Burns have come down to us. For many years, that kind of authorship was attended with so much reproach, that men of humanity studied to conceal rather than to expose the evidence by which it could be proved against him. And even after the poor bard's death, the interests of his young family demanded of all the admirers of his name, that nothing should be brought forward which was calculated to excite a political jealousy regarding him. Hence, for many years there was a mystery observed on this subject. During that time, of course, many manuscripts might perish. As things now stand—the whole matter being looked on as only a curious piece of literary history—there can be no great objection to the publication of any piece of the kind which may have chanced to be preserved. There is one which, but for the manner in which it introduces the name of the unfortunate Louis XVI., might have now been read without any pain, as containing only the feelings of a man who looked too sanguinely upon the popular cause in France:— (p. 78)

The following poem is 'The Tree of Liberty'. Although Chambers's text does not name a tune, the stanza form, with the repetition of 'man' in every second line, is that of Burns's 'Fragment' on the American war from the Edinburgh *Poems*, which is written to fit the tune 'Killiecrankie'.

Title. Thomas Paine had published a poem called 'Liberty Tree' in the *Pennsylvania Magazine* in 1775. There, the tree is planted by the first colonists, and 'The fame of its fruit drew the nations around, | To seek out this peacable shore'; but now 'all the tyrranical pow'rs, | King, commons, and lords, are uniting amain, | To cut down this guardian of ours' (ll. 11–12, 26–8; *Works of Thomas Paine*, ed. Carey, 385–6). The practice of planting a young tree as part of a ritual declaring a community's liberation was formalized during the revolution in France: it seems to have developed from the use of maypoles in rural areas as gestures of collective defiance of landlords (see Ozouf 1988). In the autumn of 1792, the new republic's army defeated a Prussian invasion at Valmy (20 September) and then turned north to overwhelm the Austrians at Jemappes (6 November) and seize what had been the Austrian Netherlands (present-day Belgium). The news of General Dumouriez's arrival in Brussels triggered popular celebration and protest in many Scottish towns, often accompanied by street disorder. This sometimes involved, for example, burning an effigy of Henry Dundas, the government's hated manager of Scottish politics. In Fife and the north-east (Dundee, Stonehaven, Aberdeen, Fochabers) it included the erection of liberty trees. The one in Dundee carried a sign saying 'Liberty and Equality, no sinecures' (Harris, 'Political Protests', 66).

l. 3. *patriots*. That is, partisans of the 'country' or the 'nation' as opposed to the king.

251 l. 5. *It stands where ance the Bastile stood*. Symbolically, at least. The Bastille prison in Paris was stormed on 14 July 1789: King Louis XVI having lost control of his capital city to its people, the revolution at this point became irreversible. The Bastille was quickly demolished: I can find no record of a liberty tree being planted on the site.

l. 7. *Superstition's hellish brood*. The French Catholic church, closely integrated in the pre-revolutionary absolutist state.

l. 26. *Gallia*. France, 'Gaul' in Roman times.

l. 28. *Frae yont the western waves*. The poem understands the American Revolution as an inspiration for the French one.

l. 37. *King Loui' thought to cut it down*. Louis XVI went along with the reforms imposed on him by the new government, even as his Austrian in-laws prepared to reverse the revolution by force of arms. But on 21–2 June 1791, he fled with his queen in the direction of Austrian territory; was recognized, stopped at Varennes, and brought back to Paris, deeply suspected as an enemy of the state of which he remained, for another year, head.

l. 40. *Cut aff his head*. Louis was sent to the guillotine on 21 January 1793; his queen followed in October. At a time of European war, 'What is there in the delivering over a perjured Blockhead & an unprincipled Prostitute into the hands of the hangman, that it should arrest for a moment, attention [?]' Burns asked Mrs Dunlop on 12 January 1795 (L649); at which point she stopped answering his letters.

252 l. 41. *A wicked crew*. The Coalition of European monarchies ranged against the French republic, with Austria and Prussia at its core, but after the execution of Louis including Britain as well.

ll. 49–50. *Freedom . . . Her sons did loudly ca'*. Perhaps referring to the mass mobilization with which the French republic countered the expanded coalition against it in 1793.

l. 55. *The hirelings ran*. The Prussian and Austrian armies included many mercenaries. In fact important victories were thin on the ground in the year following Louis's execution; but the republic survived.

l. 64. *Tweed*. The river that marks the border between England and Scotland.

253 *'Ill-fated genius' [on Robert Fergusson]*. K144. First published in *The Life and Works of Robert Burns*, ed. Robert Chambers, in four volumes, Vol. III (1852), on p. 221, where Chambers tells us it was 'inscribed . . . in a copy of *The World*', a literary journal which ran 1753–6 and was frequently reprinted in book form.

l. 1. *Heaven-taught Fergusson*. The epithet is borrowed from Henry Mackenzie's description of Burns in *The Lounger*: see Appendix 2, p. 279. Fergusson in fact spent four years at the University of St Andrews.

A Fragment—On Glenriddel's Fox breaking his chain. K527. Only known from the Glenriddell manuscripts (see Introduction to this volume). First published in an account of those manuscripts by Henry A. Bright in 1874, and in an edition of Burns's poetry by William Scott Douglas in his *Complete Poetical Works of Robert Burns* (1876), Vol. II, pp. 441–3. The absence of any other surviving source for this poem, probably written in 1790, suggests that Burns thought of it as to some extent private between himself and Glenriddell. The present text is taken from the Glenriddell manuscript itself: the Scott Douglas text follows it very accurately, only tidying up some punctuation, capitalization and so on.

Title. Burns's farm at Ellisland in Dumfriesshire, to which he moved in 1788, was less than a mile down the river Nith from Friar's Carse, the home of Captain Robert Riddell of Glenriddell (1755–94). Despite the disparity in rank and income they had a lot in common: Riddell too was interested in song, collecting traditional tunes and composing his own, as well as enjoying wider antiquarian interests, and they collaborated in establishing a local library. Of more relevance to the present poem is their shared opposition politics: Glenriddell was an exponent of reform of the House of Commons franchise for both counties and burghs.

l. 4. *cap and rod*. The Phrygian cap, a cone of soft felt with the top pushed to one side: associated with liberty as the (reputed) marker of a freed slave in the Roman empire; slaves were freed by an official laying a rod on the individual's head while reciting a formula declaring him or her free. A goddess of liberty with a Phrygian cap was already appearing in the iconography of the French Revolution.

254 l. 17. *a Whig without a stain.* For this term, see note to p. 247, ll. 82 –3. In reference to reformers like Glenriddell, the term signifies a veneration for an idealized version of the principles of government established by the 'Revolution' of 1688–9 which imposed limits on the powers of the monarch, and a desire to rid the present political system of the corruption that has allowed ministerial power, exercised on behalf of the King, to slide the constitutional balance back towards 'tyranny'.

l. 26. *his Country's cause.* Not just Scotland or Britain, but 'the Country' (represented by landed gentlemen like Glenriddell) as opposed to 'the Court' (the king's ministers).

l. 29. *The Rights of Men.* Thomas Paine's book *The Rights of Man* had probably not yet been published when this poem was written, but the rhetoric of 'natural rights' goes back at least to John Locke's *Two Treatises on Government* (1690), an important theorization of Whig political values.

l. 34. *tyrants, Jacobites, and tories.* 'Tyranny' was a bugbear of Whig rhetoric; for Jacobites, see headnote to 'There'll never be peace till Jamie comes hame' from *The Scots Musical Museum* on p. 168; for Tories, see note to p. 246, l. 41.

l. 37. *Nimrod.* 'And Cush begat Nimrod: he began to be a mighty one in the earth. And the beginning of his kingdom was Babel, and Erech, and Accad, and Calneh, in the land of Shinar' (Genesis 10: 8, 10): the first mention of kingship in the Bible.

l. 39. *Semiramis.* An Assyrian queen who appears in Greek and Roman stories as a type of feminine political power.

l. 43. *Xerxes.* The Persian king (d. 465 BC) who invaded Greece in 480 BC.

l. 45. *the stubborn Whigs of Sparta.* The absolute commitment of the Spartans to civic life, making the rise of tyrants impossible, was a touchstone for Whig ideology. Spartan forces played the leading role in the defeat of Xerxes's forces at Plataea and Mycale (479 BC).

l. 46. *Magna charta.* See note to p. 247, ll. 82–3.

255 ll. 53–5. *Billy Pit . . . Has gagg'd old Britain, drain'd her coffer.* William Pitt the younger (1759–1806), prime minister. Pitt's priority at this point was getting the public finances in order, which meant new taxes: see note to p. 19, l. 119.

Ode. K451. A draft fragment of this poem (corresponding to the last verse paragraph) was published in Currie's 1800 *Works of Robert Burns*, as part of a letter to Mrs Dunlop of 25 June 1794, where Burns refers to his projected 'irregular Ode for Gen¹ Washington's birth-day' (L628); this fragment was republished in many nineteenth-century editions. Yet, although two manuscripts existed, the complete poem was only published in 1874 (in *Notes and Queries*, 5 March, pp. 242–3); and first included in an edition of Burns's work by William Scott Douglas in his *Complete Poetical Works of Robert Burns* (1876), Vol. II, pp. 426–8, under the title given in the letter to Mrs Dunlop. This text follows the transcription of one of the manuscripts in *Autograph Poems and Letters of Robert Burns in the collection of R. B. Adam* (Buffalo, NY, 1922), 38–40. George Washington, leader of the Continental Army in the Revolutionary War and first President of the United States, was born on 22 February 1732.

255 l. 1. *tube . . . shell*. Figures for wind-instruments and thus for song. Sparta and Athens were rival city-states in classical Greece, often imagined as the originators of political liberty. This line recalls the opening of 'Ode to Liberty' by William Collins (1746): 'Who shall awake the Spartan fife . . .?'; the singer continues, 'Let not my shell's misguided power | E'er draw thy sad, thy mindful tears' (ll. 1, 15; Lonsdale 442, 444). Collins's ode is an example of the *translatio imperii* or *translatio studii*, a poem that traces the progress of liberty (or power or learning) from Greece through Rome to its modern home in Britain. Burns's poem is a variation on this theme, imagining Liberty abandoning Britain in turn, and finding a home yet further west.

l. 2. *lyre Eolian*. Aeolus was the Greek god of the winds, and an Aeolian harp was 'a stringed instrument producing musical sounds on exposure to a-current of air' (*OED*); it is possible Burns was thinking of the Aeolian islands, another part of Greece.

l. 4. *Columbia*. That is, America: the continent discovered by Christopher Columbus.

l. 7. *And dash it in a tyrant's face!*. The 'tyrant' is of course George III.

256 l. 29. *Alfred*. King of the West Saxons (*c.*848–99) who united the English kingdoms in their struggle against Danish invaders. He had been re-imagined as the prototype patriot-prince in Thomson and Mallet's opposition masque *Alfred* (1740): 'If not to raise our drooping *English* name, | To . . . make this land | Renown'd for peaceful arts to bless mankind, | And generous war to humble proud oppressors: | If not to build on an eternal base, | On liberty and laws, the public weal: | If not for these great ends I am ordain'd, | May I ne'er idly fill the throne of *England!*' (1. 5, p. 19).

l. 31. *The Bards that erst have struck the patriot lyre*. Perhaps including the Bard who appears at the end of *Alfred* to sing 'Rule Britannia': 'The nations, not so blest as thee, | Must in their turns, to tyrants fall' etc. (2. 5, p. 42). 'Patriot' has a quite specific meaning in eighteenth-century political rhetoric, as when the Hermit foresees a time 'when guardian laws | Are by the patriot, in the glowing senate, | Won from corruption' (1. 5, p. 19).

l. 35. *To make detested tyrants bleed*. The French Republic had executed the erstwhile Louis XVI in January 1793.

l. 39. *'The Tyrant's cause is mine!'*. When Britain went to war with France in February, it was entering a military and political alliance with absolutist monarchies such as Prussia, Austria, and Spain. The US government was of course sympathetic to the Republic.

l. 42. *the generous English name*. Perhaps recalls the 'English name' and 'generous war' of Alfred's speech, quoted above.

l. 49. *WALLACE*. William Wallace (d. 1305), one of the Guardians of Scotland who led armies against the occupying forces of Edward I of England in the Wars of Independence.

257 ll. 58–9. *that arm which . . . Braved Usurpation's boldest daring!*. In *Alfred*, the Hermit prophesies to the king a time 'when th' impatient arm | Of liberty, invincible, shall scourge | The tyrants of mankind' (1. 5, p. 17).

A poet's welcome to his love-begotten daughter. K60. A version of this poem was first published in one of Stewart and Meikle's chapbooks in 1799, then reprinted in some of the earlier nineteenth-century editions, beginning with Stewart's own in 1801 and again in *The Works of Robert Burns*, ed. The Ettrick Shepherd [James Hogg] and William Motherwell, Vol. II (1834); more morally fastidious editors (Currie, Cromek, Cunningham, Chambers) ignored it. But this version of the poem was either mangled in transcription, or came from an already-corrupted manuscript, since lost; it also omitted two of the eight stanzas in the present text (the fifth and sixth). There are three surviving manuscripts, and each arranges the poem's stanzas in a different order. The version in the Glenriddell manuscript was the first to be used in a printed edition, William Scott Douglas's *Complete Poetical Works of Robert Burns* (1876); but *that* version omits the present stanza 7. So the present text follows *The Poetry of Robert Burns*, ed. William Ernest Henley and Thomas F. Henderson (1896), Vol. 2, 37–9, who seem to have been the first to examine all the surviving manuscripts to select the most complete. Henley and Henderson number their stanzas: I have omitted this.

For Burns's affair with Elizabeth Paton in 1784, see notes to p. 48, l. 63 and p. 113, ll. 37–72. A daughter, also Elizabeth, was born on 22 May 1785. She was brought up by Burns's mother until the poet's death, when she moved back in with her own mother, by then married with other children. Burns sent a copy of this poem to a friend in a letter of 2 July 1787 (L118); another was enclosed in the letter to John Moore included in Appendix 1 (see p. 265).

l. 7. *fornicator*. The Kirk's name for a sexual miscreant: see 'The Fornicater' in this volume for Burns's mocking appropriation of the term.

l. 16. *Baith kirk and queir*. That is, against the whole body of the church (the 'queir' or choir being the eastern part of an old cruciform churchbuilding).

258 l. 31. *bonie Betty*. Elizabeth Paton.

l. 42. *stocket mailins*. That is, rented land ready-stocked with cattle.

Appendix 1. From the Letters

The texts of these letters are taken from *The Letters of Robert Burns*, ed. J. De Lancey Ferguson and G. Ross Roy (Oxford, 1985). They are slightly simplified from that source by the omission of deleted words and of square brackets around interpolated sections.

259 *L125. To Dr John Moore, 2 August 1787.* Addressee: John Moore (1729–1802), born in Stirling, had studied medicine at the University of Glasgow. A varied career included posts as surgeon in the army and to the British ambassador in Paris. He settled in London in 1778, where he wrote travel and medical books. He had recently published a well-received novel, *Zeluco* (1786). Frances Dunlop (see headnote to L524 below) had sent him a copy of the Kilmarnock *Poems* and Moore had got in touch with the poet.

some little business I have to settle. Burns refers to his northern tour of that summer: he had taken the opportunity to chase up subscription money due for the Edinburgh edition.

'Turned my eyes to behold Madness and Folly'. Ecclesiastes 2: 12. This book of the Old Testament is supposedly written by Solomon, proverbial for his wisdom; Burns resembles him because Solomon 'loved many strange women' (1 Kings 11: 1).

Miss Williams. Helen Maria Williams (1762–1827), a poet from the radical culture of English Presbyterianism. At this point Williams seems to have been acting as Moore's amanuensis. She would later move to Paris to experience the Revolution at first hand, as recorded in *Letters from France* (1790–6).

escutcheons. An escutcheon is the shield in a coat-of-arms: the badge of (supposedly) long-held gentility.

'My ancient but ignoble blood . . . since the flood'. Pope's 'Essay on Man', Epistle IV: 'Go! If your ancient, but ignoble blood | Has crept thro' scoundrels ever since the flood' (ll. 211–12; Pope 542).

Gules, Purpure, Argent. More heraldic jargon, for the colours used in a coat-of-arms: red, purple, silver.

Kieths of Marshal. George Keith, styled tenth Earl Marshall (1692/3–1778), forfeited the family estates, in the north-east of Scotland, for his deep involvement in the Jacobite rising of 1715.

'Brutus and Cassius are honorable men'. Mark Antony uses this phrase ironically of Caesar's assassins in Act 3, scene 2 of Shakespeare's *Julius Caesar*, ll. 75f.

260 *'Men, their manners and their ways'.* Pope again, in 'January and May': 'Sir, I have liv'd a Courtier all my Days, | And study'd Men, their Manners, and their Ways' (ll. 156–7; Pope 80).

a small farm. Mount Oliphant, to which the Burns family moved in 1766, was 70 acres (Leask 16).

brownies . . . spunkies. A brownie is, in this case, a goblin or evil spirit; a spunkie is a will-o'-the-wisp.

elf-candles. 'A spark or flash of light thought to be of supernatural origin' (*DSL*).

dead-lights. 'The name given by the peasantry to the luminous appearance which is sometimes observed over putrescent animal bodies' (*DSL*).

The vision of Mirza. An essay first published by Joseph Addison in *The Spectator*, 159 (1711), which takes the form of an ancient oriental account of a philosophical vision.

'For though in dreadful whirls . . . | High on the broken wave'. The lines quoted are from Joseph Addison's 'Hymn. On the Conclusion of his Travels'; *The Poetical Works of the Right Honourable Joseph Addison Esq.* (Glasgow, 1750), 203–4.

Mason's English Collection. Arthur Masson, *A Collection of Prose and Verse, from the Best English Authors. For the Use of Schools* (Edinburgh, 1764).

the life of Hannibal and the history of Sir William Wallace. The Life of Hannibal, translated from the French of M. Dacier (London, 1737); and *A New Edition of the Life and Heroick Actions of the renoun'd Sir William Wallace* (Glasgow, 1722), William Hamilton's modernization of Blind Harry's fifteenth-century epic poem *Wallace.*

261 *'without bounds or limits'.* Burns is remembering Thomas Watson's handbook to the theology of the Shorter Catechism, *A Body of Practical Divinity,* at the question 'What Kind of Spirit is God?': 'God's Omnipresency; the Greek Word for Infinite, signifies without Bounds or Limits' (the fourth edition, corrected and amended; Glasgow 1741, 34).

not even the MUNNY BEGUM'S *scenes have tainted.* A reference to the notorious political and economic corruption of British-controlled Bengal. Governor-General Warren Hastings appointed, as guardian of the heir of a Bengal noble family, Munny Begum, the boy's father's chief concubine. An Indian minister accused Hastings of taking a bribe in the case; Hastings had him charged with forging the evidence, found guilty, and hanged. This was one of several scandals that led to Hastings's trial in parliament, which began in 1788.

a Factor who sat for the picture I have drawn of one in my Tale of two dogs. See 'The Twa Dogs', ll. 93–100 (p. 7).

gin-horse Prudence. A gin-horse is one used to drive a mill. 'There is a species of the Human genus that I call, the Gin-horse Class: what enviable dogs they are!—Round, & round, & round they go . . . without an idea or wish beyond their circle; fat, sleek, stupid, patient, quiet & contented' (L600A to Maria Riddell, 1793).

262 *Eolian harp.* 'A stringed instrument producing musical sounds on exposure to a current of air' (*OED*).

a larger farm. Lochlie, near Tarbolton: 130 acres (Leask 16).

phthisical. Tubercular.

'To where the wicked cease from troubling, and where the weary be at rest'. Job 3: 17.

climacterick. 'A critical period or moment in . . . a person's life or career' (*OED*).

Solitaire. Recluse.

262 *Salmon's and Guthrie's geographical grammars.* William Guthrie, *A New Geographical, Historical, and Commercial Grammar; and Present State of the Several Kingdoms of the World* (London, 1770); Thomas Salmon, *A New Geographical and Historical Grammar* (London, 1749).

The Spectator. The essay-journal published daily in London by Joseph Addison and Richard Steele in 1711–13; much collected and anthologized.

Tull and Dickson on Agriculture. Jethro Tull, *The New Horse-Houghing Husbandry: or, An Essay on the Principles of Tillage and Vegetation* (London, 1731), a pioneering description of agricultural improvement; Alan Dickson, *A Treatise of Agriculture* (Edinburgh, 1762 and 1769).

The Pantheon. François Pomey, *The Pantheon: Representing the Fabulous Histories of the Pagan Gods and Most Illustrious Heroes, in a Short, Plain and Familiar Method by way of Dialogue*, trans. Andrew Tooke (London 1698, with many reprints through the following century).

Locke's Essay on the human understanding. John Locke, *An Essay Concerning Human Understanding* (London, 1690).

Stackhouse's history of the bible. Thomas Stackhouse, *A New History of the Holy Bible, from the Beginning of the World, to the Establishment of Christianity* (London, 1733).

Justice's British Gardiner's directory. Sir James Justice, *The British Gardener's New Director; Chiefly adapted to the Climate of the Northern Countries.* A fourth edition appeared in Dublin in 1765.

Boyle's lectures. Probably a collection of the work of Robert Boyle (1627–91) in either science or religion, although I can find no such collection with this title.

Allan Ramsay's works. Perhaps the two-volume set published in London in 1751 and 1761.

Taylor's scripture doctrine of original sin. John Taylor, *The Scripture-Doctrine of Original Sin proposed to free and candid Examination* (London, 1740). See note to p. 109, l. 112.

a select Collection of English songs. Joseph Ritson, *A Select Collection of English Songs* (London, 1783).

Hervey's meditations. James Hervey, *Meditations and Contemplations. In Two Volumes* (London, 1748 and reprinted many times).

vade mecum. 'A book or manual suitable for carrying about with one for ready reference' from the Latin 'go with me' (*OED*).

263 *the blind gropings of Homer's Cyclops.* Referring to the giant Polyphemos after Odysseus and his men blinded him in his single eye to secure their escape from his cave in Homer's *Odyssey* Book IX.

'where two or three were met together, there was I in the midst of them'. Jesus at Matthew 18: 20: 'For where two or three are gathered together in my name, there am I in the midst of them'.

un penchant á l'adorable moitiée du genre humain. A liking for the adorable half of the human kind.

a smuggling coast. The coast of Carrick, the southern district of Ayrshire, has plenty of hidden coves and caves suited to the landing of contraband. Burns studied at Kirkoswald in Carrick, about 15 miles from his home at Mount Oliphant.

Mensuration . . . Dialling. Mensuration is 'the branch of geometry that deals with the measurement of lengths, areas, and volumes'; to dial is 'to survey or lay out with the aid of a dial or miner's or surveyor's compass' (*OED*).

264 *the sun entered Virgo.* The sun enters this constellation in the last week of August.

'Like Proserpine gathering flowers | Herself a fairer flower'. Milton, *Paradise Lost*, Book IV, ll. 269–70 (with 'Like' for 'where'). In Greek myth Proserpina is kidnapped by the God of the Underworld, her absence throwing the world into winter.

phasis. 'Phase', in the sense associated with the changing appearance of the moon.

letters by the Wits of Queen Ann's reign. John Newbery, *Letters On the most common, as well as important, Occasions in Life, by Cicero, Pliny, Voltaire, Balzac, St. Evremont, Locke, Ld Lansdowne, Temple, Dryden, Garth, Pope, Gay, Swift, Rowe, and Other Writers of distinguish'd Merit; [with] A Dissertation on the Epistolary Style; With proper Directions for addressing Persons of Rank and Eminence. For the Use of young Gentlemen and Ladies* (London 1756).

Vive l'amour et vive la bagatelle. Long live love, and long live fun.

Tristram Shandy. Laurence Sterne, *The Life and Opinions of Tristram Shandy, Gentleman* (1760–7).

the Man of Feeling. Henry Mackenzie, *The Man of Feeling* (1771).

Winter, a dirge. See p. 85.

The death of Poor Mailie. See p. 33.

John Barleycorn. See p. 135.

songs first, second and third. Referring to the songs of the Kilmarnock *Poems*: 'It was upon a Lammas night', 'Now westlin winds, and slaught'ring guns', and 'From thee, Eliza, I must go' (pp. 114–117).

flax-dresser in a neighbouring town. The town was Irvine: see Map. Processing locally-grown flax into thread for linen was an important industry in Ayrshire. 'Dressing' flax meant combing out impurities to ready it for spinning.

burnt to ashes. Flax was notoriously flammable, and great care needed to be taken to avoid accidents like this.

265 *a belle-fille.* Burns clearly just means 'a pretty girl'.

265 *their mittimus, 'Depart from me, ye Cursed'*. 'Mittimus' originally referred to a type of legal document but came to mean 'a dismissal from an office or situation; a notice to quit' (*OED*). Burns quotes Matthew 25: 14.

the WELCOME inclosed. The poem included in this volume as 'A poet's welcome to his love-begotten daughter', p. 257; Burns refers to his affair with Elizabeth Paton, servant at Lochlie.

Pamela. Samuel Richardson, *Pamela; or, Virtue Rewarded* (1740).

Ferdinand count Fathom. Tobias Smollett, *Ferdinand Count Fathom* (1753).

Fergusson's Scotch Poems. Robert Fergusson, *Poems on Various Subjects*, published posthumously by Thomas Ruddiman, Edinburgh in 1779. Burns owned the third, 1785 edition of this two-volume set.

a neighbouring farm. Mossgiel, near Mauchline (118 acres).

'Come, go to, I will be wise!'. The editors of the *Letters* suggest that Burns is remembering Ecclesiastes 7: 23: 'I said, I will be wise; but it was far from me'.

'Like the dog to his vomit, and the sow that was washed to her wallowing in the mire'. The second Epistle of Peter 2: 22, describing backsliders: 'it is happened unto them according to the true proverb, The dog is turned to his own vomit again; and the sow that was washed to her wallowing in the mire'.

266 *rev^d Calvinists.* The orthodox Kilmarnock ministers Alexander Moodie and 'Black' John Russel (see notes to p. 25, l. 102 and p. 27, l. 184), whose feud is the target of Burns's 'burlesque lamentation' 'The Holy Tulzie' (K52: not included in the present volume).

Holy Willie's Prayer. See p. 230.

The Lament. See p. 77. The 'shocking affair' was his separation from Jean Armour by her parents.

pauvre Inconnu. Poor unknown.

I was about to indent myself. That is, commit himself in advance to work for a certain period on arrival in Jamaica until the cost of his passage was paid off.

'Hungry ruin had me in the wind'. Burns adapts a line from Thomas Otway's play, *The History and Fall of Caius Marius* (1680), where Marius describes Rome before he rescued it, 'When it lay trembling like a hunted Prey, | And hungry Ruine had it in the Wind' (Act 1, scene 1).

some ill-advised, ungrateful people. The Armours, again. In July 1786, as the *Poems* went to press, and Jean approached her time, 'James Armour realised that the Burns who had always seemed such a waster might have some money after all. . . . He set about getting a warrant requiring Burns to hand over a large sum of money or face jail with his assets confiscated' (Crawford, *The Bard*, 222).

267 *Greenock.* A major Atlantic port on the Firth of Clyde.

'The gloomy night is gathering fast'. Burns cites his song of this title, not included in the present volume, which he had published in the Edinburgh edition (K122).

a letter from Dr Blacklock to a friend of mine. Thomas Blacklock (1721–91), a celebrated Edinburgh poet and scholar. Blacklock's letter was to Ayrshire minister George Lawrie, who passed it on to Gavin Hamilton, who showed it to his friend Burns (Crawford, *The Bard*, 228).

Zenith . . . Nadir. The points in the heavens directly above the observer (from where astrology credits a star or planet with its greatest influence) and directly below (from where it has least).

Earl of Glencairn. For this important patron see headnote to 'Lament for James, Earl of Glencairn', p. 359.

'Oublie moi, Grand Dieu, si jamais je l'oublie!'. 'Forget me, Great God, if ever I forget it!'; that is, forget God's providential care in this instance.

'to catch the manners living as they rise'. In the first Epistle of the *Essay on Man*, Pope invites his friend Bolingbroke to 'Expatiate free o'er all this scene of Man . . . Eye Nature's walks, shoot Folly as it flies, | And catch the Manners living as they rise' (ll. 5, 13–14; Pope 504).

Wight. Fellow (a poetic archaism).

L515. To William Johnston, 13 November 1792. Addressee: For Captain William Johnston see headnote to 'Extempore on some late commemorations of the poet Thomson', p. 356.

268 *'Calm, thinking VILLAINS whom no faith can fix'*. From Alexander Pope, 'The Temple of Fame': 'Calm, thinking Villains, whom no Faith cou'd fix, | Of crooked Counsels and dark Politicks' (ll. 410–11; Pope 185).

L524. To Mrs Frances Dunlop, 6 December 1792. Addressee: Frances Anna Wallace (1730–1815), widow of John Dunlop of Dunlop (d. 1785). Mrs Dunlop had found consolation in the Kilmarnock *Poems* after the death of her husband, and after her spendthrift eldest son had sold off the Craigie estate which she had brought into the marriage and which had descended to her family from a cousin of William Wallace. Her friendship with the poet 'produced more letters than he addressed to any other single individual' (*Letters* 451).

Dunlop house. Dunlop is towards the northern end of Ayrshire: a long way from Burns in Dumfries.

'Careless of the voice of the morning'. This is not, as Burns claims, from the Book of Job, but from 'Carthon: A Poem' in Macpherson's 1765 *Works of Ossian* (Macpherson 134).

'Staff and Shield'. Perhaps recalling 1 Samuel 17: 7: 'And the staff of his spear was like a weaver's beam . . . and one bearing a shield went before him.'

a fine girl. Elizabeth Riddell Burns, born on 21 November. Her death three years later caused Burns desperate anguish.

268 *'The valiant in himself . . . like a coward'*. Prince Edward's lines in James Thomson's tragedy *Edward and Eleonora* (published 1739, though banned from the stage), Act 4, scene 7, ll. 44–51.

269 *'Who so unworthy . . . How cheap a thing were virtue'*. Gloster in the same play and the following scene, ll. 30–6.

'Attach thee firmly . . . sit loose'. The Hermit's advice to the king in Thomson's masque *Alfred* (1740), Act 1, scene 5.

' 'Tis this, my Friend . . . cloudless skies'. From a commendatory verse to the frequently reprinted James Hervey, *Meditations and Contemplations. In Two Volumes* (London, 1748), I, p. xvii.

our Theatre here. A theatre had opened in Dumfries in September 1792.

Ça ira. The anthem of the French revolutionaries ('So it will be').

a Placeman. That is, a government employee, dependent on the approval of his superiors.

The Rights of Woman. See p. 210.

270 *L528. To Robert Graham of Fintry, 31 December 1792*. Addressee: see note to title of 'Sketch of an Epistle to R. Graham, Esq. of Fintray', p. 393.

Collector. This was the excise post responsible for oversight of a county.

Revolution principles. That is, the principles of the division of powers between King, Lords, and Commons established in the Revolution of 1688–9.

Death's thousand doors stand open. From *The Grave* (1743), l. 394, a widely-read poem of the 'graveyard' school by Scottish minister Robert Blair, describing the prospects for 'the Wretch | That's weary of the World, and tir'd of Life' (ll. 389–90).

L530. To Robert Graham of Fintry, 5 January 1793.

271 *Borough-Reform*. This refers to the campaign to rid the town councils of their self-perpetuating, oligarchic power-structures. Burns acknowledges the local survival of a reform movement only where it was opposed to the most flagrant variety of corruption in the system.

Çà ira. The anthem of the French revolutionaries ('So it will be').

Edin' Gazetteer. See headnotes to 'Extempore on some late commemorations of the poet Thomson', p. 356, and L515 to William Johnston, above.

272 *The Rights of Woman*. See p. 210.

The Commemoration of Thomson. See p. 209.

Robt Riddel Esq: of Glenriddel. See note to the title of 'A Fragment—On Glenriddel's Fox breaking his chain', p. 404.

County Reform. The campaign to rid parliamentary elections for the counties of such abuses as the creation of votes by the great proprietors through the fictional distribution of their land among their allies.

Frank. The mark of postage paid, before the invention of adhesive stamps.

Savoy. Savoy was occupied and formally annexed to France in November 1792; it had previously belonged to the King of Sardinia.

invading the rights of Holland. The status of the Dutch Republic had been settled by treaty in 1788, with Britain and Prussia the guarantors: in November 1792 the government in Paris broke this treaty, set on a course that would lead to war with Britain.

A tippling ballad . . . on the Prince of Brunswick's breaking up his camp. This is a version of the song 'Poor bodies do naething but m–w' (see p. 237) which Burns had already sent to Robert Cleghorn, and which would eventually be published, with additions and subtractions, in *The Merry Muses of Caledonia* (1799).

273 *L531. To Mrs Graham of Fintry, 5 January 1793.* Addressee: Margaret Elizabeth Mylne of Mylnefield (1754–1816) had married Fintry in 1773: they had 14 children.

this little poem. Burns enclosed a copy of 'The Rights of Woman' (see p. 210).

L558. To John Francis Erskine, 13 April 1793. Addressee: John Francis Erskine (1741–1825) was the eldest son of an aristocratic family and later 27th Earl of Mar and 12th Lord Erskine. This exchange of letters was the only contact between Erskine and Burns.

This text is taken from the Glenriddell manuscript (see Introduction), into which Burns made a copy of this letter a year or two later, prefacing it with the explanation given here.

my friend Glenriddell. Robert Riddell of Glenriddell: see note to the title of 'A Fragment—On Glenriddel's Fox breaking his chain', p. 404.

to save from ruin an only brother. That is, Gilbert, still farming Mossgiel (their younger brothers John and William had died in 1785 and 1790).

274 *Executive Power & the Representative part.* That is, between the king's ministers and the House of Commons.

275 *my boys.* Burns is thinking of his three sons with Jean Armour; a fourth had been born to an Edinburgh servant girl, Jenny Clow, in 1788.

Appendix 2. Contemporary Reviews of the Kilmarnock Poems (1786)

276 *From The Edinburgh Magazine, or Literary Miscellany, for October 1786, pp. 284–5.* This was the first notice taken in print of Burns's work. The author is probably the magazine's publisher, James Sibbald (Crawford, *The Bard*, 234–5). Further poems by Burns appeared in the next two editions as well, and in January Burns wrote to Sibbald to thank him for his support: 'The warmth with which you have befriended an obscure man and young Author, in your last three Magazines—I can only say, Sir, I feel the weight of the obligation, and wish I could express my sense of it' (L71).

276 *Aristotle or Horace*. Here in their capacity as literary critics: Aristotle (384–322 BC) as author of the *Poetics*; Quintus Horatius Flaccus (65–8 BC) as author of the *Ars Poetica*.

Allan Ramsay and Ferguson. Allan Ramsay (1684–1758), influential post-Union revivalist of poetry in Scots; Robert Fergusson (1750–74), vivid chronicler of the Edinburgh scene: both important precedents for Burns's work in Scots.

Homer and Ossian. James Macpherson claimed Ossian, a bard in Gaelic myth, as the third-century author of the pieces 'translated' as *Fragments of Ancient Poetry* (1760) which had been preserved by oral tradition in the Highlands. These were in fact mostly prose-paraphrases of sixteenth-century heroic verse; Macpherson went on to attribute his two epic poems 'Fingal' and 'Temora' to the same source, completing 'Ossian' 's claim to be the 'Northern Homer'.

doric simplicity. Theocritus wrote in the Doric version of Greek rather than the language of Athens. In his Preface to his 1721 *Poems*, Allan Ramsay appeals to this as a precedent for writing in Scots: 'The *Scotticisms*, which perhaps may offend some over-nice Ear, give new Life and Grace to the Poetry, and become their Place as well as the *Doric* Dialect of *Theocritus*, so much admired by the best Judges' (Ramsay Vol. I, p. xix).

277 *Rusticus abnormis sapiens, crassaque Minerva*. Horace again, in *Satire* 2.2: 'a peasant, an independent sage of homespun wisdom' (translation from Frank Stack, *Pope and Horace* (1985), 60). On pp. 285–8 the *Edinburgh Magazine* then reproduces 'Address to the Deil' complete; 'Epistle to J. Lapriak, an old Scotch Bard', ll. 43–78; 'The Holy Fair', stanzas IX–XI, XXI–XXII, and XXVI–XXVII; and 'Halloween', stanzas VII–VIII, XIII–XIV, and XVII–XXVII.

The Lounger No XCVII. Saturday, Dec. 9. 1786. *The Lounger* was a single-sheet essay-journal in the style of Addison and Steele's *Spectator*; most of its numbers are by Henry Mackenzie (1745–1831), including this one. A lawyer by training, the success of his sentimental novel *The Man of Feeling* (1771) and his other activities made him an important arbiter of taste in literary Edinburgh. Burns wrote to him in May 1787: 'I leave Edin^r tomorrow morning, and send you this to assure you that no little petulant self-conceit, no distance or absence shall ever make me forget how much I owe You' (L101).

'in the olden time' genius had some advantages which tended to its vigour and its growth. This recalls the theory of Hugh Blair, Professor of Rhetoric and Belles Lettres at Edinburgh University, which drew on the 'conjectural history' of his contemporaries to explain the origins of poetry: 'In the infancy of society, men live scattered and dispersed, in the midst of solitary rural scenes, where the beauties of nature are their chief entertainment. . . . Their passions have nothing to restrain them: their imagination has nothing to check it. They display themselves to one another without disguise: and converse and act in the uncovered simplicity of nature. As their feelings are strong, so their language, of itself, assumes a poetical

turn' ('A Critical Dissertation upon the Poems of Ossian'; Macpherson 345). As society develops, 'the understanding is more exercised; the imagine, less' and so poetry declines (346).

279 *faith in opposition to good works.* A point of Calvinist orthodoxy: see note to p. 95, l. 50.

a West-Indian clime. In 1786 Burns was planning to emigrate to Jamaica.

'wood-notes wild'. In Milton's 'L'Allegro' (*c.*1631), the happy man goes to the theatre to hear 'sweetest Shakespeare fancy's child, | Warble his native wood-notes wild' (ll. 133–4). In 1794 Burns wrote to his Edinburgh friend Alexander Cunningham (L620, 3 March):

> There is one commission that I must trouble you with.—I lately lost a valuable Seal, a present from a departed friend, which vexes me very much.—I have gotten one of your Highland pebbles, which I fancy would make a very decent one; & I want to cut my armorial bearings on it: will you be so obliging as enquire what will be the expence of such a business? . . . On a field, azure, a holly-bush, seeded, proper, in base; a Shepherd's pipe & crook, Saltier-wise, also proper, in chief.—On a wreath of the colors, a woodlark perching on a sprig of bay-tree, proper, for Crest.—Two Mottoes: Round the top of the Crest—'Wood-notes wild'—At the bottom of the Shield, in the usual place—
> 'Better a wee bush than nae bield.'—

FURTHER READING

IMPORTANT OR USEFUL EDITIONS OF BURNS'S WORK,
IN ORDER OF PUBLICATION

The Works of Robert Burns; with an account of his life, and a criticism on his writings, ed. James Currie, in four volumes (London: Cadell and Davies, 1800).

Poems Ascribed to Robert Burns, the Ayrshire Bard, not contained in any previous edition of his works hitherto published, ed. Thomas Stewart (Glasgow: Thomas Stewart, 1801).

Stewart's Edition of Burns's Poems, including a number of original pieces never before published, ed. Thomas Stewart (Glasgow: Thomas Stewart, 1802).

Reliques of Robert Burns; consisting chiefly of original letters, poems, and critical observations on Scottish songs, ed. R. H. Cromek (London: Cadell and Davies, 1808).

The Works of Robert Burns, with his life, ed. Allan Cunningham. In eight volumes (London: Cochrane, 1834).

The Works of Robert Burns, ed. The Ettrick Shepherd [James Hogg] and William Motherwell, in six volumes (Glasgow: Fullarton, 1834–6).

The Poetical Works of Robert Burns, ed. Robert Chambers (Edinburgh: Chambers, 1838).

The Life and Works of Robert Burns, ed. Robert Chambers, in four volumes (Edinburgh: Chambers, 1851; revised and expanded 1856–7).

The Poetical Works of Robert Burns, ed. Alexander Smith, in two volumes (London: Macmillan, 1865).

The Complete Poetical Works of Robert Burns, arranged in the order of their first publication, ed. William Scott Douglas, in two volumes (Kilmarnock: McKie, 1871; revised and expanded 1876).

The Life and Works of Robert Burns, ed. Robert Chambers, revised William Wallace, in four volumes (Edinburgh and London, 1896).

The Poetry of Robert Burns, ed. William Ernest Henley and Thomas F. Henderson, in four volumes (London: Jack, 1896).

The Songs of Robert Burns, now first printed with the melodies for which they were written, ed. James C. Dick (London: H. Froude, 1903).

The Merry Muses of Caledonia, ed. James Barke, Sydney Goodsir Smith, and J. De Lancey Ferguson (1959; reprinted with a new introduction by Valentina Bold, Edinburgh: Luath, 2009).

The Poems and Songs of Robert Burns, ed. James Kinsley (Oxford: Clarendon Press, 1968).

The Letters of Robert Burns, ed. J. De Lancey Ferguson, second edition ed. G. Ross Roy, in two volumes (Oxford: Clarendon Press, 1985).

The Kilmarnock Poems, ed. Donald A. Low (London: Dent, 1985).

The Songs of Robert Burns, ed. Donald A. Low (London: Routledge, 1993).

Robert Burns: Selected Poems, ed. Carol McGuirk (London: Penguin, 1993).

BIOGRAPHY

Crawford, Robert, *The Bard: Robert Burns, a Biography* (London: Jonathan Cape, 2009).

Mackay, James, *Burns: A Biography of Robert Burns* (Edinburgh: Mainstream, 1992).

Will, William, *Robert Burns as a Volunteer. Some fresh facts which further help to confound the poet's critics* (Glasgow, 1919).

BACKGROUND

Adam, Charles Elphinstone, ed., *A View of the Political State of Scotland in the Last Century. A confidential report on the political opinions, family connections, or personal circumstances of the 2662 county voters in 1788* (Edinburgh: David Douglas, 1887).

Brims, J., 'From Reformers to "Jacobins": The Scottish Association of the Friends of the People', in Tom Devine, ed., *Conflict and Stability in Scottish Society 1700–1830* (Edinburgh: John Donald, 1990), 31–50.

Brown, Callum G., *Religion and Society in Scotland since 1707* (Edinburgh: Edinburgh University Press, 1997).

Clark, Ian D. L., 'From Protest to Reaction: The Moderate Regime in the Church of Scotland, 1752–1805', in N. T. Phillipson and Rosalind Mitchison, eds., *Scotland in the Age of Improvement* (Edinburgh: Edinburgh University Press, 1970), 200–24.

Clive, John, 'The Social Background of the Scottish Renaissance', in N. T. Phillipson and Rosalind Mitchison, eds., *Scotland in the Age of Improvement* (Edinburgh: Edinburgh University Press, 1970), 225–44.

Crawford, Robert, *Devolving English Literature* (Oxford: Oxford University Press, 1992).

Daiches, David, *The Paradox of Scottish Culture: The Eighteenth-Century Experience* (Oxford: Oxford University Press, 1964).

Davis, Leith, 'At "sang about": Scottish Song and the Challenge to British Culture', in Leith Davis, Ian Duncan, and Janet Sorensen, eds., *Scotland and the Borders of Romanticism* (Cambridge: Cambridge University Press, 2004), 188–203.

Dwyer, John, *Virtuous Discourse: Sensibility and Community in Late Eighteenth-Century Scotland* (Edinburgh: John Donald, 1987).

—— 'Introduction—A "Peculiar Blessing": Social Converse in Scotland from Hutchison to Burns', in John Dwyer and Richard B. Sher, eds., *Sensibility and Society in Eighteenth-Century Scotland* (Edinburgh: Mercat Press, 1993), 1–22.

Fergusson, James, *Lowland Lairds* (London: Faber and Faber, 1949).

Gray, Malcolm, 'The Social Impact of Agrarian Change in the Rural Lowlands', in Tom Devine and Rosalind Mitchison, eds., *People and Society in Scotland, Volume I: 1760–1830* (Edinburgh: John Donald, 1988), 53–69.

Harris, Bob, 'Political Protests in the Year of Liberty, 1792', in Bob Harris, ed., *Scotland in the Age of the French Revolution* (Edinburgh: John Donald, 2005), 49–78.

Johnson, David, *Music and Society in Lowland Scotland in the Eighteenth Century* (1972; Edinburgh: Mercat Press, 2003).

Kidd, Colin, 'Scotland's Invisible Enlightenment: Subscription and Heterodoxy in the Eighteenth-Century Kirk', *Records of the Scottish Church History Society* 30 (2000), 28–59.

—— 'Burns and Politics', in Gerard Carruthers, ed., *The Edinburgh Companion to Robert Burns* (Edinburgh: Edinburgh University Press, 2009), 61–73.

Kinghorn, Alexander M., and Low, Alexander, eds., *Poems by Allan Ramsay and Robert Fergusson* (Edinburgh: Scottish Academic Press, 1985).

Mackenzie, Henry, *The Man of Feeling*, ed. Brian Vickers (1771; Oxford: Oxford University Press, 1987).

McLachlan, Christopher, ed., *Before Burns: Eighteenth-Century Scottish Poetry* (Edinburgh: Canongate, 2002).

Newman, Steve, 'The Scots Songs of Allan Ramsay: "Lyrick" Transformation, Popular Culture, and the Boundaries of the Scottish Enlightenment', *Modern Language Quarterly* 63.3 (Sept. 2002), 277–314.

Ozouf, Mona, *Festivals and the French Revolution*, trans. Alan Sheridan (Cambridge, MA: Harvard University Press, 1988).

Paine, Thomas, *The Works of Thomas Paine, Secretary for Foreign Affairs, to the Congress of the United States, in the late war*, ed. James Carey, in two volumes (Philadelphia: Carey, 1797).

—— *Rights of Man, Common Sense, and Other Political Writings*, ed. Mark Philp (Oxford: Oxford University Press, 1995).

Robertson, John, *The Scottish Enlightenment and the Militia Issue* (Edinburgh: John Donald, 1985).

Sher, Richard, *Church and University in the Scottish Enlightenment: The Moderate Literati of Edinburgh* (Edinburgh: Edinburgh University Press, 1985).

—— *The Enlightenment and the Book: Scottish Authors and their Publishers in Eighteenth-Century Britain, Ireland, and America* (Chicago: University of Chicago Press, 2006).

Smith, Adam, *The Theory of Moral Sentiments* (1759; Oxford: Oxford University Press, 1976).

Sterne, Laurence, *The Life and Opinions of Tristram Shandy, Gentleman*, ed. Ian Campbell Ross (1759–67; Oxford: Oxford University Press, 1983).

—— *A Sentimental Journey*, ed. Ian Jack (1768; Oxford: Oxford University Press, 1968).

Thompson, E. P., 'Patrician Society, Plebeian Culture', *Journal of Social History* 7.4 (Summer 1974), 382–405.

Watson, Steven, *The Reign of George III* (Oxford: Oxford University Press, 1960).

CRITICISM

Ashmead, John, and Davidson, John, 'Words, Music and Emotion in the Love Songs of Robert Burns', in John Dwyer and Richard B. Sher, eds., *Sensibility* and Society in Eighteenth-Century Scotland (Edinburgh: Mercat Press, 1993), 225–42.

Bentman, Raymond, 'Robert Burns's Use of Scottish Diction', in Frederick W. Hilles and Harold Bloom, eds., From Sensibility to Romanticism: Essays Presented to Frederick A. Pottle (Oxford: Oxford University Press, 1965), 239–58. Reprinted in Carol McGuirk, ed., Critical Essays on Robert Burns (New York: G. K. Hall, 1998), 79–94.

Burke, Tim, 'Robert Burns', in John Goodridge, ed., Eighteenth-Century Labouring-Class Poets (London: Pickering and Chatto, 2002), 103–15.

Butler, Marilyn, 'Burns and Politics', in Robert Crawford, ed., Robert Burns and Cultural Authority (Edinburgh: Edinburgh University Press, 1997), 86–112.

Butt, John, 'The Revival of Scottish Vernacular Poetry', in Frederick W. Hilles and Harold Bloom, eds., From Sensibility to Romanticism: Essays Presented to Frederick A. Pottle (Oxford: Oxford University Press, 1965), 219–37.

Carruthers, Gerard, Robert Burns (Tavistock: Northcote House, 2006).

—— ed., The Edinburgh Companion to Robert Burns (Edinburgh: Edinburgh University Press, 2009).

Crawford, Robert, ed., Robert Burns and Cultural Authority (Edinburgh: Edinburgh University Press, 1997).

Crawford, Thomas, Burns: A Study of the Poems and Songs (Edinburgh: Oliver and Boyd, 1960).

—— Society and the Lyric: A Study of the Song Culture of Eighteenth-Century Scotland (Edinburgh: Scottish Academic Press, 1979).

Daiches, David, Robert Burns (London: G. Bell and Sons, 1952).

Damrosch, Leo, 'Burns, Blake, and the Recovery of Lyric', Studies in Romanticism 21 (Winter 1982), 637–60.

Davie, Cedric Thorpe, 'Robert Burns, Writer of Songs', in Donald Low, ed., Critical Essays on Robert Burns (London: Routledge and Kegan Paul, 1975), 157–84.

Davis, Leith, 'The Poetry of Nature and the Nature of Poetry: Robert Burns and William Wordsworth', in Acts of Union: Scotland and the Literary Negotiation of the British Nation, 1707–1830 (Stanford CA: Stanford University Press, 1998), 107–43.

—— 'Re-presenting Scotia: Robert Burns and the Imagined Community of Scotland', in Carol McGuirk, ed., Critical Essays on Robert Burns (New York: G. K. Hall, 1998), 63–76.

Fielding, Penny, 'Burns's Topographies', in Leith Davis, Ian Duncan, and Janet Sorensen, eds., Scotland and the Borders of Romanticism (Cambridge: Cambridge University Press, 2004), 170–87.

Jack, R. D. S., and Noble, Andrew, eds., The Art of Robert Burns (London: Vision, 1982).

Leask, Nigel, 'Burns, Wordsworth, and the Politics of Vernacular Poetry', in Peter de Bolla, Nigel Leask, and David Simpson, eds., Land, Nation and Culture, 1740–1840: Thinking the Republic of Taste (Basingstoke: Palgrave Macmillan, 2005), 202–22.

—— 'Robert Burns and Scottish Common Sense Philosophy', in Gavin Budge, ed., *Romantic Empiricism: Poetics and the Philosophy of Common Sense, 1780–1830* (Lewisburg, PA: Bucknell University Press, 2007), 64–87.

—— *Robert Burns and Pastoral: Poetry and Improvement in Late Eighteenth-Century Scotland* (Oxford: Oxford University Press, 2010).

Low, Donald A., ed., *Robert Burns: The Critical Heritage* (London: Routledge and Kegan Paul, 1974).

—— ed., *Critical Essays on Robert Burns* (London: Routledge and Kegan Paul, 1975).

—— *Robert Burns* (Edinburgh: Scottish Academic Press, 1986).

McGinty, Walter, *Robert Burns and Religion* (Aldershot: Ashgate, 2003).

McGuirk, Carol, *Robert Burns and the Sentimental Era* (Athens, GA: University of Georgia Press, 1985).

—— 'Scottish Hero, Scottish Victim: Myths of Robert Burns', in Andrew Hook, ed., *The History of Scottish Literature, Volume 2: 1660–1800* (Aberdeen: Aberdeen University Press, 1987), 219–38.

—— 'Poor Bodies: Robert Burns and the Melancholy of Anatomy', in Carol McGuirk, ed., *Critical Essays on Robert Burns* (New York: G. K. Hall, 1998), 32–48.

—— '"The Rhyming Trade": Fergusson, Burns, and the Marketplace', in Robert Crawford, ed., *'Heaven-Taught Fergusson': Robert Burns's Favourite Scottish Poet* (Phantassie: Tuckwell, 2003), 135–59.

McIlvanney, Liam, *Burns the Radical: Poetry and Politics in Late Eighteenth-Century Scotland* (Phantassie: Tuckwell, 2002).

Mathison, Hamish, 'Robert Burns and National Song', in David Duff and Catherine Jones, eds., *Scotland, Ireland, and the Romantic Aesthetic* (Lewisburg, PA: Bucknell University Press, 2007), 77–92.

Murphy, Peter, 'Robert Burns', in *Poetry as an Occupation and an Art in Britain, 1760–1830* (Cambridge: Cambridge University Press, 1993), 49–93.

Radcliffe, David Hill, 'Imitation, Popular Literacy and "The Cotter's Saturday Night"', in Carol McGuirk, ed., *Critical Essays on Robert Burns* (New York: G. K. Hall, 1998), 251–79.

Simpson, Kenneth, ed., *Love and Liberty. Robert Burns: A Bicentenary Celebration* (Phantassie: Tuckwell, 1997).

Skoblow, Jeffrey, *'Dooble tongue': Scots, Burns, Contradiction* (Newark: University of Delaware Press, 2001).

Weston, John C., 'Burns's Use of the Scots Verse-Epistle Form', *Philological Quarterly* 49.2 (April 1970), 188–210.

—— 'Robert Burns's Satire', in Andrew Noble and R. D. S. Jack, eds., *The Art of Robert Burns* (London: Vision, 1982; reprinted in Carol McGuirk, ed., *Critical Essays on Robert Burns*. New York: G. K. Hall, 1998), 117–33.

GLOSSARY

This glossary is based on the one included in the Edinburgh editions of *Poems, Chiefly in the Scottish Dialect*. Most definitions below are taken from this glossary: these are marked with (E) only where they are juxtaposed with definitions marked (K) from the much smaller glossary appended to the 1786 Kilmarnock edition; with definitions from *Dictionary of the Scots Language* (*DSL*) or from Kinsley's 1968 edition (Kinsley); or with expansions, definitions, or examples of my own, marked (ed.). Definitions in the Kilmarnock glossary were almost always taken over into the Edinburgh glossary, though sometimes in amended form. The meanings given of these words in Scots is generally in addition to, not instead of, any meanings they may have in English.

The Kilmarnock glossary is prefaced with the following explanation: 'Words that are universally known, and those that differ from the English only by the elision of letters by apostrophes, or by varying the termination of the verb, are not inserted. The terminations may be thus known; the participle present, instead of *ing*, ends, in the Scotch Dialect, in *an* or *in*; in *an*, particularly, when the verb is composed of the participle present, and any of the tenses of the auxiliary, *to be*. The past time and participle past are usually made by shortening the *ed* into '*t*.'

The Edinburgh glossary replaces this with advice on pronunciation: 'The *ch* and *gh* have always the guttural sound. The sound of the English diphthong *oo*, is commonly spelled *ou*. The French *u*, a sound which often occurs in the Scotch language, is marked *oo*, or *ui*. The *a* in genuine Scotch words, except when forming a diphthong, or followed by an *e* mute after a single consonant, sounds generally like the broad English *a* in *wall*. The Scotch diphthongs, *ae*, always, and *ea* very often, sound like the French *é* masculine. The Scotch diphthong *ey*, sounds like the Latin *ei*.'

a' all
aback behind, away (K); away, aloof (E)
abiegh at a distance (K); at a shy distance (E)
aboon above, up
abread, abreed abroad, in sight
ack to act (ed.)
ae one (K)
aff off
aff-loof unpremeditated
aft, aften oft
afore before
agley wide of the aim (K); off the right line, wrong (E)
aiblins perhaps
aik oak (ed.)

ain own
airn iron
airt point of the compass, quarter, direction (*DSL*)
aith an oath
aits oats
aiver an old horse (K)
aizle a red ember (K); a hot cinder (E)
a-jee to one side, aside, off the straight (*DSL*)
alake alas
alane alone
amaist almost
amang among
an' and, if (E)
ance once
ane one, an (K)

anither another

as as if, e.g. as they would never part: as if they would never part (ed.)

ase ashes (K)

asklent asquint, on the slant, on one side (*DSL*)

aspar apart, aspread, with legs apart (*DSL*)

aught eight

auld old

auldfarren sagacious, cunning, prudent

ava at all, of all (K)

awa away

awkart aukward

awn the beard of oats, etc. (K)

awnie bearded (E)

ay, aye yes; always (ed.)

ayont beyond

ba' ball

backlins-comin coming back, returning

bad did bid (E); bade (ed.)

baggie the belly

bairan baring (K)

bairn a child

bairn-time a family of children, a brood

baith both

bake a biscuit (*DSL*)

bane bone

banie, bainie bony (K); having large bones, stout (E)

bang attack, onslaught (*DSL*); bide a bang: endure an onslaught (ed.)

barefit bare-footed

barkin barking

barmie of or like barm (E); i.e. yeast (ed.)

batch a crew, a gang

bauk a crossbeam

bauk-en' the end of a beam

bauld bold

bauldly boldly

baws'nt having a white stripe down the face (K)

be't be it

bear barley (ed.)

bee to let be, to leave in quiet (K); to give over, to cease (E)

beese beasts; specifically body and head vermin (*DSL*)

beet to add fuel to fire

behint, behin' behind

beld bald (*DSL*)

bellys bellows (K)

belyve by and by

ben into the spence or parlour

benmaist furthest in, in the second inner room (*DSL*)

besom broom (ed.)

bestead, bestad situated, circumstanced (*DSL*)

beuk a book

bicker (1) a kind of wooden dish, a short race

bicker (2) to move quickly, to run, to rush (*DSL*)

bid desire (*DSL*); bid nae better than: want nothing more than to (ed.)

bide (1) stay; bade: did stay

bide (2) tolerate, stand (usually in the negative: canna, downa); bade: endured (*DSL*)

biel, bield shelter (K)

bien wealthy, plentiful

big (v) to build

biggin (n) a building (K); a building, a house (E)

biggit builded

bill bull

billie a brother, a young fellow

birk birch-tree (ed.)

birkie a clever fellow

birr force, energy, enthusiasm (*DSL*)

birsie bristle, hair (*DSL*)

birth berth (ed.)

bit crisis, nick of time (E); at the bit: at the critical point (*DSL*)

bizz a bustle, to buzz

blastet worthless (K)

blastie a shrivell'd dwarf; a term of contempt

blather the bladder (K)

blaud a flat piece of anything; to flap

blate bashful, sheepish

blaw to blow, to boast (E); boasting, e.g. muckle blaw (ed.)

blellum 'an idle talking fellow' (*DSL*)

blether to talk idly; nonsense (E); in latter sense esp. as blethers (ed.)

bleth'ran, bleth'rin talking idly

bleezan, bleezin blazing

bleeze blaze

blin' blind (ed.)

blink a glance, an amorous leer, a short space of time (K); a little while, a smiling look; to look kindly, to shine by fits (E)

blinker a term of contempt

blinkin smirking

blue-gown one of those beggars who get annually, on the King's birthday, a blue cloke or gown with a badge

bluid blood

bluidy bloody

blype a shred of cloth, etc. (K); a shred, a large piece (E)

bodies people, folk; a body: one, e.g. a body's sel: oneself (ed.)

bodle a small old coin

bogle a ghost, spectre, or phantom, causing fright (*DSL*)

bonie, bony handsome, beautiful

bonilie handsomely, beautifully

bonnock a kind of thin cake of bread

boord a board (E); i.e. table (ed.)

boortrie the shrub elder, planted much of old in the hedges of barn-yards, etc.

boost behoved (K); behoved, must needs (E), e.g. I shortly boost to pasture: I shortly must to pasture, i.e. I shortly must go to pasture (ed.)

boot o' boot: into the bargain (Kinsley)

botch an angry tumour

bow-kail cabbage

bow't bended, crooked

bowse to drink deeply, booze (ed.)

brachens fern (E); i.e. bracken

brae a declivity, a precipice, the slope of a hill

braid broad

braik a kind of harrow

braindge to run swiftly forward

braindge't reeled forward

braing to rush forward recklessly, to plunge (*DSL*)

brainge to draw unsteadily (K)

brak broke, made insolvent

branks a kind of halter, or bridle, for horses or cows (*DSL*)

brash a sudden illness (K)

brat a worn shred of cloth (K)

brats coarse clothes, rags

brattle a short race, hurry, fury

braw fine, handsome

brawlie, brawly very well, finely, heartily

braxie a morkin sheep (K); that is, a sheep that has died by disease or accident (*DSL*)

bread, breid breadth (ed.)

breastet sprung forward (K); did spring up or forward (E)

breef an invulnerable charm (K); an invulnerable or irresistible spell (E)

breeks breeches

brent (1) smooth, unwrinkled (*DSL*)

brent (2) bold, shameless (*DSL*)

brie juice, liquid (E); barley-brie: whisky (ed.)

brisket the breast, the bosom

brither a brother

brock a badger (*DSL*)

brogue an affront (K); a hum, a trick (E)

broo liquid or moisture of any kind (*DSL*)

broose a race at country weddings who shall first reach the bridegroom's house on returning from church

brugh a burgh

brulzie, bruilzie a broil, a combustion

brunstane brimstone

brunt did burn

brust to burst

buckskin an inhabitant of Virginia

buirdly stout-made, broad-built

bum-clock a humming beetle that flies in the summer evening

bumman, bummin humming as bees

bure did bear (E); bure the gree: held or won first supremacy; bure sic hands: fought so vigorously (Kinsley)

burn water, a rivulet

Burnewin *q.d.* burn the wind, a Blacksmith (K)

busk to adorn, to deck, to dress up (*DSL*)

busle, bussle a bustle; to bustle

but without (E); in this sense often in combination with or, e.g. but house or hald (ed.)

but and ben the country kitchen and parlour (K)

by himsel lunatic, distracted (E); i.e. beside himself (ed.)

byke a swarm or crowd of people (*DSL*)

byre cow-stable

ca' to call, to drive (K); i.e. to drive horses, livestock, etc.; ca' hame: drive home (ed.)

cadie, caddie a person, a young fellow

cadger a carrier

cairds tinkers (K)

cairn a loose heap of stones (K)

callan a boy

caller fresh, sound (E); esp of air, food etc. (ed.)

cannie gentle, mild, dextrous; cannily: dextrously, gently

cant a merry old story (*DSL*)

cantie, canty chearful, merry

cantraip a charm, a spell

cape stane cope stone (K)

careerin chearfully

carl a fellow; a man of the common folk, not a gentleman (*DSL*)

carlin a stout old woman

cartes cards

caudron cauldron, pot (ed.)

cauf calf

cauld cold

caup a small, wooden dish with two lugs, or handles (K); a wooden drinking vessel (E)

cavie hen-coop (*DSL*)

chamer parlour, best room or spare room in a house, often an upper room (*DSL*)

chanter a part of a bagpipe (E); i.e. that part which can be played separately of the bag and drones (ed.)

chap (1) a person, a fellow

chap (2) a blow (E), e.g. with a tool, or on a door etc. (ed.)

chap (3) a measure of drink (ed.)

chapman pedlar (ed.)

chiel, cheel a young fellow

chimla, chimlie a fire grate

chimla lug the fireside

chow to chew; cheek-for-chow: side by side

chuffie fat-faced (K)

claes, claise cloaths

claith cloth

claithing cloathing

clarket, clarkit wrote (E); to record in writing, to enter up in a book (*DSL*)

clash an idle tale, the story of the day

clatter to tell idle stories; an idle story

claught to grasp, seize forcibly, clutch (*DSL*)

claut to clean, to scrape

clavers clover (*DSL*)

claw to scratch

cleed clothe (*DSL*)

cleek (1) seize, snatch, steal, pilfer (*DSL*)

cleek (2) in dancing, to link arms and whirl round (*DSL*) clew (1) scratched (ed.)

clew, clue (2) ball (of thread or yarn) (ed.)

clink money, cash (*DSL*)

clinkan, clinkin jerking, clinking

clinkumbell who rings the church bell

clips shears

clish-ma-claver idle conversation

clock to hatch; a beetle

clockin hatching

cloot the hoof of a cow, sheep, etc.

clootie, cloots an old name for the Devil (E). From the Devil's cloven hoof: 'clootie' means 'cloven' (*DSL*)

clour a bump or swelling after a blow

clout a patch; to mend or patch, especially pots and shoes (*DSL*); cloths (ed.)

coble a fishing boat

coft bought (*DSL*)

cog, coggie a small wooden dish without handles (K)

colic-grips the pains or gripes of colic, a bowel condition (ed.)

collie a general and sometimes a particular name for country curs (K)

cood the cud

coof, cuif a blockhead, a ninny

cooket, cookit appeared and disappeared by fits

coor (1) cover or protect (*DSL*)

coor (2) crouch, cringe, cower (*DSL*)

coost did cast

cootie a pretty large wooden dish (K)

core corps, party, clan

corky-headed, -heidit feather-brained, empty-headed (*DSL*)

corn't fed with oats

cotter the inhabitant of a cot house or cottage

countra country

couthie kind, loving

cove cavern

cowe to terrify, to keep under; to lop; a fright, a branch of furze, broom, etc.

cowran, cowrin cowering

cowte colt

crabbet, crabbit crabbed, fretful

crack conversation, to converse (K); a story, an entertaining tale (*DSL*)

craft, croft a field near a house, in old husbandry

craig neck; throat, gullet (*DSL*)

crambo-clink, crambo-jingle rhymes, doggerel verses

crank a harsh, grating sound (K); the noise of an ungreased wheel (E)

crankous fretting, peevish (K); fretful, captious (E)

cranreuch the hoar frost

crap a crop, the top (E); craps o' heather: heather tips, heather shoots (ed.)

craw a crow

crazy frail or infirm; hence craz'd (ed.)

creel a basket; to have one's wits in a creel: to be crazed, to be fascinated

creeshie greasy, dirty (*DSL*)

crood, croud to coo as a dove

croon a hollow, continued moan (K); to make a noise like the continued roar of a bull, to hum a tune (E)

crooning humming (E)

croose, crouse chearful, courageous; crously: chearfully, courageously

crouch to bow low (*DSL*)

crouchie crook-backed (K)

crowdie-time breakfast time

crowl to creep (K)

crump hard and brittle, spoken of bread

crunt a blow on the head with a cudgel

cummock a short staff (K); a short staff with a crooked head (E)

curchie a courtesy (E); i.e. a curtsy (ed.)

curling a well-known game on ice; curler: a player at ice

curpan, curpin the crupper (K)

Cushat the dove or wood pigeon

custock the stem of kail or cabbage (*DSL*)

cutty short, diminutive

cutty sark a short chemise or undergarment (*DSL*)

daffin merriment, foolishness

daft merry, giddy, foolish

dails deals, i.e. planks to be used for tables or benches (ed.)

daimen now and then, seldom (K)

dainty pleasant, good humoured, agreeable

darg, daurk a day's labour (K); han'-daurk: manual labour (ed.)

darklins darkling (E); i.e. in the dark (ed.)

daud, dawd the noise of one falling flat, a large piece of bread, &c. (K)

daur dare

daur't dared

daut, dawt to caress, to fondle (K)

dead death (Kinsley)

dead-sweer very loath, averse (K)

dearthfu' dear (E), i.e. 'costly, expensive': *OED* suggests this is Burns's coinage (ed.)

deave to bother, to annoy; esp. to annoy or weary by constantly talking or asking questions (*DSL*)

Deil the Devil (ed.)

Deil-ma-care! no matter! for all that! (E); deil ane: not one (ed.)

deleeret delirious (K)

descrive to describe

dight to wipe, to clean corn from chaff; cleaned from chaff

ding to worst, to push (E); be shifted, be worn out (Kinsley), e.g. facts are cheels that winna ding (ed.)

dinna do not

dirl shake, cause to vibrate (*DSL*)

disrespeket disrespected

diz'n, dizzen a dozen

doit (v) to be enfeebled or confused in mind, absent-minded (*DSL*)

doited stupified, hebetated

donsie unlucky, dangerous (K)

dool sorrow; to sing dool, to lament, to mourn

dorty saucy, nice

douce, douse sober, wise, prudent

doup buttocks (*DSL*)

dow am *or* are able to, can; downa: am *or* are not able to, cannot

dowf, dowff pithless, wanting force

dowie crazy and dull (K); worn with grief, fatigue, etc. (E)

doylt, doylte stupified, hebetated (K)

doyte to go drunkenly or stupidly (K)

draigle soil, bespatter (*DSL*)

drap a drop; to drop

draw to pull out; draw a stroke: raise a hand for a blow (*DSL*)

dreep to ooze, to drop

dreigh tardy, long-delayed (*DSL*)

dribble drizzling, slaver

driddle to toddle, dawdle, saunter (*DSL*)

drift a drove

droddum the breech (E), i.e. the posterior, esp. as object of chastisement (ed.)

droll half-witted, slightly crazed (*DSL*)

droop-rumpl't that droops at the crupper (E), i.e. of a horse, at its rump (ed.)

droukit drenched, soaked (*DSL*)

drouth thirst, drought

druken drunken

drumlie muddy

drummock meal and water mixed raw (K)

drunt pet, pettish humor (K); pet, sour humour (E)

dub a small pond

duds rags of clothes (K)

duddie ragged

dung worsted, pushed, driven (E), i.e. past tense of ding (ed.)

durk dirk, dagger (ed.)

dush to push as a bull, ram, &c. (K)

dyke low dry-stone wall (ed.)
dyvor debtor, bankrupt (*DSL*)

e'e the eye; een: the eyes
e'en, e'enin evening
eerie frighted, particularly the dread of spirits (K); frightened, dreading spirits (E)
eild old age (K)
eldritch fearful, horrid, ghastly (K)
en' end (ed.)
eneugh enough
enow enough (ed.)
ettle aim, purpose, design, object (*DSL*)
eydent constant, busy (K); diligent (E)

fa' (1) fall, lot (K); to fall (E); befall, e.g. in phrases of imprecation (shame fa' thee) or good wishes (*DSL*)
fa' (2) to have something fall to one's share; hence, gen. with canna, mauna, etc., to venture to obtain, win, come by (*DSL*)
faddom't fathomed
fae a foe
faem foam (K)
fain fond (of); eager (to); amorous; gladly (*DSL*), e.g. wad fain: would dearly (ed.)
fairin fairing, a present (E); specifically one bought at a fair (*DSL*)
fallow fellow
fand did find (E), found (ed.)
fareweel farewell
farl a cake of bread
fash trouble, care; to trouble, to care for (E); bother, bother about (ed.)
fatt'rels ribband ends, &c. (K)
fauld fold; sheep-pen (*DSL*)
fause false (ed.)
fause-hoose a conical structure of wooden props built inside a corn-stack to facilitate drying (*DSL*)

faussont, fawsont decent, orderly (K); decent, seemly (E)
faut fault (E); harm, injury (*DSL*)
fear to frighten, to scare (*DSL*)
fear't frightened
fearfu' frightful
feat neat, spruce
fecht to fight (K)
feck (1) value, worth, return, result (*DSL*)
feck (2) (large) number or portion (*DSL*)
feckless ineffective, weak, paltry (*DSL*)
feg fig (E); as in expressions such as ne'er mind a feg (ed.)
fell keen, biting (E)
fen, fend an effort, attempt, shift, esp. to maintain oneself. Freq. in phr. to mak a fen (*DSL*)
fetch to stop suddenly in the draught, and then come on too hastily [of a draught-horse] (K); to pull by fits (E)
ferlie, ferly a wonder, to wonder; also a term of contempt (K)
fidge to fidget; fidgin: fidgeting (E); fidgean-fain: restlessly eager (ed.)
fiel comfortable, cosy; soft, smooth and pleasant to the touch (*DSL*)
fier sound, healthy (K); esp. in expression hale and fier (*DSL*); a brother, a friend (E)
fient, fiend, a petty oath (E); a strong negative (*DSL*); e.g. the fient a pride: not a bit of pride; fient haet: not one (ed.)
fissle to make a russling noise, to fidget; a bustle
fit, fitt a foot (ed.)
fittie-lan' the near horse of the hindmost pair in the plough (K); from 'fit-o-land', the horse 'treading the unploughed land while its neighbour walks in the furrow' (Kinsley)
fizz to make a hissing noise like fermentation

flaff flap, flutter (*DSL*)

flainen flannel

flair flatter; brag, boast (*DSL*)

flee fly (ed.)

fleech to supplicate in a flattering manner

fleesh fleece (K)

fleg a kick, a random blow

flether to decoy by fair words

fleth'ran flattering

fley to frighten (K)

flichter to flutter (K); to flutter as young nestlings when their dam approaches (E)

flinders shreds, broken pieces

flingin-tree a flail

flisk to fret at the yoke (K)

fliskit fretted (E)

flit transport from one place to another (*DSL*)

flunkies livery servants (K)

fodgel plump, buxom, well-built (*DSL*)

foggage grass which grows among crops, and is fed on by horses and cattle after the crop is removed (*DSL*)

forbad forbade (ed.)

forbears ancestors (K), forefathers (E)

forby, forbye besides (K)

forfairn distressed, worn out, jaded

forgat forgot (ed.)

forgather to meet, to encounter with

forgie forgive (ed.)

forjesket jaded (K)

foord ford

foughten troubled, harassed

fouth abundance, plenty (*DSL*)

fow, fou, fu' (1) full, drunk &c. (K)

fow (2) a bushel (K)

frae from (ed.)

freath froath (K); i.e. froth (ed.)

fud the human posteriors, the buttocks (*DSL*)

fuff to blow intermittedly (K)

funnie full of merriment

fur, furr a furrow

furm a form, a bench

fyke trifling cares; to piddle, to be in a fuss about trifles (E); (n) fuss (ed.)

fyle to dirty, to soil (K)

ga' gall, pustule, sore (Kinsley)

gab the mouth; to speak boldly (K); to speak boldly or pertly (E)

gae to go; gaed: went; gaen or gane: gone; gaun: going

gaet, gate way, manner, practice (K); way, manner, road (E)

gailies fairly well, pretty well (*DSL*)

gang to go, to walk

gangrel a tramp, vagrant, vagabond (*DSL*)

gar to make, to force to (E); e.g. gar you trow: make you believe (ed.)

garten a garter

gash wise, sagacious, talkative; to converse (K)

gat got (ed.)

gate, or gaet way, manner, road

gawsie, gaucy jolly, large (K)

gear riches, goods of any kind

geck to toss the head in pride or wantonness (K)

gentles great folks

geordie a guinea

get a child, a young one

gie to give; gied: gave; gi'en: given

gif if, whether (*DSL*)

gilpey a young girl (K)

gin (conj.) if, against

gin (prep.) by, before (*DSL*), e.g. gin night: by the time night comes (ed.)

girdle iron griddle for making scones, oatcakes, etc. (*DSL*)

girn to grin; to twist the features in rage, agony, etc.

gizz a wig (K); a periwig (E)

glaikit stupid, foolish; thoughtless, irresponsible, flighty, frivolous (gen. applied to women) (*DSL*)

glaizie smooth, glittering (K); glittering, smooth like glass (E)

gleg sharp, ready

glib-gabbet that speaks smoothly and readily

glint to peep (K)

gloamin the twilight

glowr to stare, to look; a stare, a look

glunch a frown; to frown (K)

goave, gove to stare stupidly or vacantly (*DSL*)

gowd gold

gowf (v) to hit or strike with the open hand (*DSL*)

gowk a fool or simpleton; the cuckoo (*DSL*)

graff grave (*DSL*)

graip a pronged instrument for cleaning stables

haet fient haet: a petty oath of

graith accoutrements, furniture, dress

grane, grain a groan; to groan

grape to grope

grapet groped

grat cried, wept (ed.)

graunie a grandmother

great intimate, familiar

gree to agree; to bear the gree: to be decidedly the victor

greet to shed tears, to weep

grippet catched, seized

grips gripes, colic pains (ed.)

grissle gristle

groat to get the whissle of one's groat: to play a losing game

grousome loathsomely grim (K)

grozet a gooseberry

grumphie a sow

grun' ground

grunstane a grindstone

gruntle the visage; a grunting noise (K)

grushie of thick, stout growth (K); thick, of thriving growth (E)

guid, gude good

guid-een good evening

Guidfather, Guidmither father-in-law and mother-in-law

Guidman, Guidwife the master and mistress of the house; Young Guidman, a man newly married

guid-mornin good morrow

guidwillie, guid-willie kindly, hearty, cordial, generous, open-handed (*DSL*)

gully large knife (*DSL*)

gumlie muddy

gusty tasteful (E); i.e. tasty (ed.)

ha' hall (E); ha'-Bible: the great bible that lies in the hall (E); ha' folk: servants (*DSL*)

haddin, haudin possessions, means of support, property, inheritance (*DSL*)

haerse horse (ed.)

haet fient haet: a petty oath of negation, nothing (E); e.g. fient haet o' them: not one of them; deil-haet ails them: damn-all ails them (ed.)

haffet the temple, the side of the head

hafflins nearly half, partly

haggis a kind of pudding boiled in the stomach of a cow or sheep

hail small shot (*DSL*)

hain to save, to spare (K)

hairst harvest

haith a petty oath

hal, or hald hold, hiding place (K); an abiding place (E)

hale whole, tight, healthy

hallan a particular partition wall in a cottage (E); specifically sheltering the living-space from the door, or between the human accommodation and that for animals (*DSL*)

hallions a person of slovenly dress or appearance, a good-for-nothing idler, a rascal (*DSL*)

hame home; hameward: homeward; hamely: homely

han', haun hand

hap to wrap, to cover

hap-step-an'-lowp hop, skip and leap

hash a term of contempt (K); a sot (E)

haud to hold

haughs low-lying rich lands, valleys

haurl to drag, to peel (K)

haverel a quarter-wit (K); a half-witted person; half-witted (E)

havins good manners, decorum, good sense

Hawkie a cow, properly one with a white face

healsome healthful, wholesome

hech! Oh! strange!

hecht to forebode (K); to foretell something that is to be got or given; foretold; the thing foretold (E)

heeze to elevate, to raise

hersel herself

herrin a herring

het hot

heugh a crag, a coal-pit (K)

hie high

hing to hang

hilch to hobble, to halt

himsel himself

hirpl to walk crazily, to creep

hirplan, hirplin creeping

hissel so many cattle as one person can attend

histie dry, chapt, barren (K)

hitch a loop, a knot

hizzie hussy, a young girl

hoast, host to cough

hoddan the motion of a sage country farmer on an old cart horse (K)

hogshouther to justle with the shoulder (K); a kind of horse play by justling with the shoulder (E)

hool outer skin or case

hoolie slowly, leisurely; Hoolie! take leisure! stop!

hoord a hoard; to hoard

Hornie one of the many names of the Devil

hotch to fidget, to hitch about with impatience or discomfort (DSL)

Houghmagandie a species of gender composed of the masculine and feminine united (K); fornication (E)

houlet owl (ed.)

howe hollow (K); a hollow or dell (E)

howe-backet sunk in the back, spoken of a horse etc.

howk to dig (K)

howket, howcket (adj) digged (E)

hoy to urge incessantly (K); to urge (E)

hoyte a motion between a trot and a gallop (K); to amble crazily (E)

huff to hector, bully; to scold, chide, storm at (OED)

hurchin an uncouth person; occasionally applied to a mischievous child (DSL)

hurdies the loins, the crupper

I' in

icker an ear of corn (K)

ier-oe a great grand child (K)

ilk, ilka each

ill-willie malicious, unkind (K); malicious, niggardly (E)

ingine genius (K); genius, ingenuity (E)

ingle fire, fire-place (E)

ingle-cheek the fireside, chimney-corner (DSL)

irie melancholy (DSL)

I'se I shall or will

ither other, one another

jad, jade also a familiar term among country folk for a giddy young girl

jauk to dally at work (K); to dally, to trifle (E)

jaup (n) a quantity of liquid suddenly spilt or thrown in the air (DSL)

jaup (v) (1) to splash or ripple in a container, spill over (DSL)

jaup (v) (2) to splash, bespatter, e.g. with mud or water (DSL)

jaw to pour out abruptly, splash, spill, throw (DSL)

jillet a jilt, a giddy girl

jimp to jump, slender in the waist, handsome

jingle to rhyme (OED)

jink to dodge, to turn a corner; a sudden turning a corner

jinker that turns quickly, a gay sprightly girl, a wag

jirt a jerk

jundie to justle (K)

jo sweetheart, lover (*DSL*)

jocteleg a kind of knife (K)

jouk to stoop (K); to stoop, to bow the head (E)

jow a verb, which includes both the swinging motion and pealing sound of a large bell

jowler a heavy-jawed dog of the hound type (*DSL*)

kae a daw (K); i.e. a jackdaw (ed.)

kail coleworts; a kind of broth

kain, kane fowls, etc. paid as rent by a farmer

kebar, caber beam, rafter (*DSL*)

kebbuck a cheese

keek a peep; to peep

kelpies a sort of mischievous spirits, said to haunt fords and ferries at night, especially in storms

ken to know; kend, kent, ken't: knew

kenning, kenning a very little of anything, a trifle (*DSL*)

ket a hairy, ragged fleece of wool (K)

kiaugh carking anxiety (K); 'carking' means harassing or vexing (ed.)

kilt to truss up the cloaths

kimmer a young girl, a gossip

kin' kind

kintra country (ed.)

kirk church (ed.)

kirn the harvest supper; a churn; to churn

kirsen to christen (K)

kist chest, shop-counter

kitchen any thing that eats with bread; to serve for soup, gravy, &c. (E); to give a relish or flavour to, to season (*DSL*)

kittle to tickle; ticklish, likely

kittlen a young cat

kiutle to cuddle, to caress, to fondle (K)

knaggie like knags or points of rock

knappin-hammer a hammer for breaking stones

knoit knock, beat, strike sharply (*DSL*)

knowe a small round hillock

kye cows

kyte stomach, belly (*DSL*)

kythe to discover, to show one's self

laggen the angle at the bottom of a wooden dish (K)

Lalland lowland (ed.)

lampet, laimpit a kind of shell-fish (E); i.e. a limpet (ed.)

laigh low

laik, lake lack, want, deficiency (*DSL*)

laith loath

laithfu' bashful (K)

laithron, laidron a term of abuse for a lazy, loutish person (*DSL*)

laird a landowner (ed.)

lallan lowland; Lallans, Scotch dialect

lan' land, estate

lane lone; my lane, thy lane, &c.: myself alone, thyself alone, &c.

lanely lonely

lang long; to think lang: to long, to weary (E); lang syne: long ago (ed.)

lap did leap

lave the rest, the remainder, the others

laverock, lav'rock the lark

lay, lea untilled ground left fallow, pasture (Kinsley)

lea'e leave

leal loyal, true (K)

lear, pronounced lare learning

lee-lang live-long

leeze me on a term of congratulatory endearment (K); from lief is me: dear is to me (*DSL*)

leuk a look; to look

lien lain, did lie (ed.)

lift (1) the sky

lift (2) a load, a consignment of goods (*DSL*)

lightly sneeringly; to sneer at

limmer a woman of easy virtue (K); a kept-mistress, a strumpet (E)

link to trip along (K)

linn a waterfall

lint flax; lint in the bell: flax in flower

lintwhite a linnet

loan the place of milking

lo'e love (ed.)

loof the palm of the hand, pl. looves

loot did let (K); let out, uttered (Kinsley)

lough loch, lake (ed.)

loun a fellow; a ragamuffin; a woman of easy virtue

loup jump (ed.)

lowe flame; to flame (K)

lowse to loose

lug the ear; a handle

luggie, lugget caup a small wooden dish with one handle (K)

lum the chimney

lunch a large piece of cheese, flesh, etc.

lunt smoke; to smoke (K); a column of smoke; to smoke (E)

lyart grey (K); of a mixed colour, grey (E); usually of hair (ed.)

mae more

mair more

maist, 'maist most; almost

mak to make

Mallie Molly

mang, 'mang among

manteele a mantle (K)

mashlum meslin, mixed corn

maskin-pat tea-pot (*DSL*)

maukin a hare

maun must

maut malt, specifically as the basis of ale or whisky (*DSL*)

meere a mare

meikle, mickle much (ed.)

mell to meddle with (K)

melvie to soil with meal (K); to coat with a film of meal or flour, as a miller's clothes (*DSL*)

men' mend

mense good breeding (K); good breeding, decorum (E)

menseless ill-bred, rude, impudent

messan, messin a small dog

midden a dunghill

midden-hole a gutter at the bottom of the dunghill

mim prim, affectedly meek

min', mind mind; remembrance (E); remember (ed.)

mind't mind it; resolved, intending

minnie mother, dam

mishanter mishap, unfortunate accident, disaster (*DSL*)

misteuk mistook

mither a mother

mixtie-maxtie confusedly mixed

mizzle muzzle (*DSL*)

modewurk a mole (K)

monie, mony many

moop to nibble as a sheep (K)

moorcock grouse (ed.)

moorlan of or belonging to moors

morn the next day, tomorrow

mottie full of motes

mou the mouth

muckle, meikle great, big; much

muslin-kail broth made up simply of water, barley, and greens (K)

mutchkin an English pint

mysel myself

na no, not, nor

nae no, not any

naething nothing

naig a horse

nane none

nappy strong ale (*DSL*)

near hand nearly, almost (*DSL*)

neebor a neighbour

negleket neglected

neuk, newk nook

niest next

nieve the fist (K)

niffer an exchange or barter (*DSL*)

nit a nut

noddle brain (ed.)

norland of or belonging to the North

noteless unnoticed, unknown

nowt, nowte black cattle (K)

o' of

o'erlay a neck-cloth worn by men, which hung down before, and was tied behind (*DSL*)

o't of it

onie, ony any

or is often used for ere, before (E), e.g. or lang: before long (ed.)

orra spare, extra, odd, superfluous (*DSL*)

oughtlins in any way, at all, in the least degree (*DSL*)

oursel, oursels ourselves

outler lying in the fields, not housed at night (K)

owre over (K); over, too (E)

owrehip a way of fetching a blow with a hammer over the arm

pack (1) intimate, familiar (K); twelve stones of wool (E)

pack (2) gar them pack: send them packing (ed.)

painch the paunch (K)

paitrick, pairtrick a partridge

pang to cram (K)

parratch, porritch pottage (K); oatmeal pudding, a well-known Scotch dish (E)

pat did put; a pot

pattle, pettle the plough-staff (K); an implement with a spatulate blade, usually carried on a plough for clearing the mould-board of soil (*DSL*)

paughty proud, saucy (K); proud, haughty (E)

paukie, pawkie cunning, fly

pay't paid; beat

peghan the crop of fowls, the stomach (K)

penny-wheep small beer (K)

phiz face (*OED*)

phraise fair speeches, flattery; to flatter

phraisin flattery

pickle a small quantity

pine pain, care (K); pain, uneasiness (E)

pintle penis (*DSL*)

pit to put (E); also make as in e.g. it pits me mad (ed.)

plack an old Scotch coin; plackless: pennyless

pleugh a plough; pleugh-pettle: a plough-staff

pliskie trick (K)

pliver plover (*DSL*)

pock bag (*DSL*)

poind to seize and sell the goods of a debtor in lieu of debt

poortith poverty

poosion to poison; to spoil, to render unpalatable or nauseating (*DSL*)

Poossie, pussie a hare or cat

pout, powt a chicken

pouther, powther powder

pow the head, the skull

pownies a little horse

pou, pow, pu to pull

pouch pocket (*DSL*)

preen a pin

prent print

prie to taste

prief proof (K)

prig to haggle over the price, to bargain (*DSL*)

primsie affectedly nice (K); demure, precise (E)

pund pound, pounds

pyke pick (out or off) (*DSL*)

quat quit, did quit (K)

quakin, quaikin quaking (K)

queer amusing, funny, entertaining (*DSL*)

quey a cow from one year to two years old

raep, rape rope (K)

ragweed the plant ragwort

raible to repeat by rote (K); to rattle nonsense (E)

rair to roar; rair't: roared (E); rairan: roaring (ed.)

raize to madden, to enflame

ramfeezl'd overspent (K); fatigued, overspent (E)

ram-stam thoughtless (K); forward, thoughtless (E)

randie rough and belligerent in manner, riotous, ruffianly, aggressive, esp. of a beggar who uses intimidation to extort alms (*DSL*)

rant a romp or boistrous frolic; to romp, roister, make merry (*DSL*)

rarely excellent, very well

rash a rush; rash-buss: a bush of rashes

ratton a rat

raucle stout, clever (K); rash, stout, fearless (E)

raught did reach (K)

raw a row (E); i.e. a line in order (ed.)

rax to stretch

ream (n) cream (E)

ream (v) to form a froth or foam, to mantle (*DSL*)

reave to rob

reck to take heed (K)

red-wud stark mad

rede counsel, to counsel (K)

reek smoke; to smoke

reeket smoked, smoky

reest to be restive (K); to stand restive (E)

reestet (1) stood restive

reestet (2) shrivelled (K); stunted, withered (E)

reft split, cleft (*OED*)

remead remedy

requit requital

restricked restricted

rief reaving (K)

rig a ridge (E); specifically, the unit of ploughed land, twenty or more feet across, and raised about three feet high in the middle, sloping down on either side to aid drainage (Kinsley)

riggin the roof (*DSL*)

rin to run, to melt

ringwoodie, rigwiddie ill-favoured (a word used of a witch) (*DSL*)

ripp a handful of unthreshed corn, &c. (K)

risk to make a noise like the breaking of small roots with the plough

rive (1) to wrench from its place, uproot, dig up, force out (*DSL*)

rive (2) to tear, rend, rip, lacerate (*DSL*)

rockin a meeting on a winter evening (K)

roon a shred, a remnant

roose to praise, to commend

roun' round, in the circle of neighbourhood

roupet, rupet hoarse, as with a cold

row, rowe to roll, to wrap

row't rolled, wrapped

rowt, rowte to bellow (K); to low, to bellow (E)

rowth, routh plenty

rozet rosin

rung a cudgel

runkle a wrinkle (K)

runt the stem of the colewort or cabbage

ryke, reak reach, stretch (*DSL*)

's is

sae so

saft soft

sair (adj) sore (K); hence sairly (ed.)

sair (v) serve

sall shall (ed.)

sang a song

sark a shirt

sarkit provided in shirts

saugh the willow

saul soul

saumont salmon

saunt a saint (K)

saut salt; saut-bucket: a small wooden box for holding salt, kept near the kitchen fireplace (*DSL*)

saw to sow (E); i.e. seed (ed.)

sax six

scaud to scald

scaur apt to be scared

scawl a scold (K)

scho she (*DSL*)

scone a kind of bread

sconner to loathe (K); a loathing; to loathe (E); to feel surfeited or nauseated (*DSL*)

scraich to scream as a hen, partridge, etc.

screed to tear (K); to tear; a rent (E)

screigh, scriegh to cry shrilly (K)

scriech a scream; to scream

scrieve to run smoothly and swiftly (K); to glide swiftly along (E)

scrievin gleesomely, swiftly (E)

scrimp scant; to stint (K)

'se shall, e.g. I'se: I shall (ed.)

see'd did see

sel self; a body's sel: one's self alone

sen' send

servan' servant

set set off, start out (*DSL*); ill-set: badly-disposed (*DSL*); it sets you ill: it puts you in a false position (ed.)

settlin to get a settlin: to be frighted into quietness

shaird a shred, a shard (E)

shaver a humorous mischievous wag (K)

shavie a trick, practical joke, imposition, swindle (*DSL*)

shaw a little wood; to show (K); to show; a small wood in a hollow place (E)

sheen bright (K); bright, shining (E)

sheep-shank to think one's self nae sheep-shank: to be conceited

sheugh a ditch, a trench

shiel temporary or roughly-made house or shed (*DSL*)

shift (1) the crop grown in any particular season in a system of crop rotation (*DSL*)

shift (2) to change places with (*DSL*)

shog shock

shool a shovel

shoon shoes

shore to offer, present as a mark of favour; threaten, bode unpleasant consequences (for) (*DSL*)

shouther, showther the shoulder

sic such

sidelins sidelong, slanting

siller silver; money

silly deserving pity or compassion; hapless, helpless; (of things) flimsy, unsubstantial (*DSL*)

simmer summer

sin son

sin', sin since (E)

skaith to damage, to injure; an injury (E)

skeigh, skiegh (of horses) mettlesome, fiery, proud (K); proud, nice, high-mettled (E)

skelp to strike, to slap; to walk with a smart tripping step; a smart stroke (E)

skelpie deserving to be smacked; skelpie-limmer: a mischievous girl, a little hussy (*DSL*)

skinking easily poured, thinly diluted; skinking ware: thin clear soups, potages, consommés, or the like (*DSL*)

skinkle to glitter, gleam, sparkle, scintillate, to have a bright showy appearance (*DSL*)

skirl a shrill cry (K); to shriek, to cry shrilly (E)

skyte a sudden, sharp, glancing blow, so as to make what strikes rebound in a slanting direction from that which is struck (*DSL*)

sklent (v) to slant, to fib (K); slant; to run aslant, to deviate from truth; sklented: ran or hit in an oblique direction; sklentin: slanting (E)

slae sloe

slap a gate, a breach in a fence

slee sly; sleest: slyest

sleeket sleek

sliddery, slidd'ry slippery

slype to fall over like a wet furrow (K); to fall over like a wet furrow from the plough (E)

sma' small (K); a small quantity or amount, little, not much (*DSL*)

smeddum powder of any kind (K); dust, powder (E)

smeek smoke (*DSL*)

smiddie smithy

smoor, smuir to be choked, stifled, suffocated; esp. to perish by being buried in a snowdrift (*DSL*)

smoutie smutty, obscene, ugly

smytrie a numerous collection of small individuals (K)

snash abusive language (K); abuse, Billingsgate (E)

snaw snow; to snow

sned to chop, to lop off; to cut off the tops and roots of turnips etc. (*DSL*)

sneeshin snuff; sneeshin-mill: snuff-box

snell bitter, biting

snick the latchet of a door

snick-drawing trick-contriving (K); literally 'latch-lifting' (ed.); to draw a sneck (fig.): to insinuate oneself into an affair surreptitiously; to act in a crafty stealthy manner (*DSL*)

snirtle snigger, make a noise through the nose when attempting to stifle laughter (*DSL*)

snool one whose spirit is broken with oppressive slavery; to submit tamely, to sneak

snoove to go smoothly and constantly; to sneak

snoov't went smoothly

snowk to scent or snuff as a dog, horse, &c.

sodger soldier (ed.)

sonsie having sweet, engaging looks; lucky, jolly

sooth truth; a petty oath

soupe, sowp a spoonful, a small quantity of any thing liquid (E); a drink, something to drink (ed.)

souple flexible, swift

souter shoemaker, cobbler (*DSL*)

sowens type of porridge made from fermented oat-husks and meal (ed.)

sowth to try over a tune with a low whistle

sowther to cement, to solder (K)

spae to prophesy, to divine

spail chip or sliver of wood, splinter (*DSL*)

spairge to spurt about like water or mire; to soil (K); to dash; to soil as with mire (E)

spak did speak

spavet having the spavin (E); i.e. in horses: an arthritic condition causing lameness (ed.); spavie: this condition, also jocularly applied to human beings (*DSL*)

speel to climb

speet spit (meat, fish, etc.) (ed.)

spence the country parlour

spier to ask, to enquire

splatter a splutter; to splutter

splore a ramble (K); a frolic, and riot, a noise (E)

sprachle, sprauchle to move or make one's way laboriously or in a hasty, clumsy manner, esp. in an upward direction (*DSL*)

sprattle to scramble

spreckl'd spotted, speckled

spring a quick reel in music, a Scotch reel

sprit a tough-rooted plant something like rushes

sprittie rushy (K); full of sprits (E)

spunk fire, mettle, wit (E); a spark of light; tinder-stick (ed.)

spunkie fiery; will o' wisp (K); mettlesome, fiery; will o' wisp or *ignis fatuus* (E)

squad a crew, a party

squatter to flutter in water (K); to flutter in water as a wild duck &c. (E)

squattle to sprawl

stacher to stagger

stack a rick of corn, hay, etc.

staggie diminutive of stag (K)

stan' to stand

stane a stone

stank a pool of standing water (K)

stark stout

startle to run as cattle stung by the gadfly

stauk stalk, stride (*DSL*)

staumrel awkward, blundering, stupid (*DSL*)

staw (1) did steal (E); i.e. moved stealthily (ed.)

staw (2) to surfeit, satiate, sicken, or disgust with excess of food (*DSL*)

steek to shut; a stitch

steer to molest, to stir

steeve firm (K); firm, compacted (E)

stegh to cram the belly (K)

stell a still

sten to rear as a horse (K)

stents tribute, dues of any kind

stey steep

stibble stubble

stibble-rig the reaper who takes the lead (K)

stick-an-stowe totally, altogether

stilt to halt, to limp

stimpart the eighth part of a Winchester bushel (E); i.e. a measure of grain (ed.)

stirk a cow or bullock a year old

stock a plant of colewort, cabbage, etc.

stoor sounding hollow, strong, and hoarse

stoup, stowp a kind of jug or dish with a handle

stoure dust, more particularly dust in motion

stownlins by stealth

straik to stroke

strappan tall and handsome

straught straight

streek to stretch (*DSL*)

striddle to straddle

stroan to pour out like a spout (K); to spout, to piss; stroan't: spouted, pissed (E)

strunt spiritous liquor of any kind; to walk sturdily

studdie an anvil

stuff corn or pulse of any kind

sturt trouble; to molest

sturtan frightened

sucker sugar

sud should

sugh the continued rushing noise of wind or water

suthron southern; an old name for the English nation

swaird sward (E); that is, grass-covered ground, turf (*OED* 'greensward')

swall swell (*DSL*)

swank stately, jolly

swankie a tight strapping young fellow or girl

swat did sweat

swatch a sample

swats newly-brewed weak beer (*DSL*)

sweer lazy, averse; dead-sweer: extremely averse

swinge to beat, whip, flog, belabour, drive with blows (*DSL*)

swirlie knaggy, full of knots (E); 'knaggy' means 'knotty, rough, rugged' (*OED*)

swith! get away (K); i.e. as an exclamation (ed.)

swoom swim (*DSL*)

swoor swore, did swear

syne since, ago, then (K); lang syne: long ago (ed.)

tack a lease or tenancy, esp. the leasehold tenure of a farm; an agreement or compact in general (*DSL*)

tae toe (ed.)

taen taken (ed.)

taet a small quantity (K)

tak to take (E); tak aff: to drink to the bottom, or at one draught (*OED*)

tald, tauld told

tane e.g. the tane and the tither: the one and the other (ed.)

tap the top (E)

tapetless unthinking (K); heedless, foolish (E)

tapsalteerie upside down, topsy-turvey, in(to) utter confusion or disorder (*DSL*)

tarrow to murmur at one's allowance (K)

tarry-breeks a sailor

tauted, tawted matted together (K); matted together, spoken of hair or wool (E)

tawie that handles quietly (K); that allows itself to peaceably be handled, spoken of a horse, cow, etc. (E)

ten hours bite a slight feed to the horses while in the yoke in the forenoon

tent (1) a field pulpit

tent (2) heed, caution; to take heed (E); in the latter sense a transitive verb: attend to, take care of; tak tent: take care (ed.)

tentie heedful, cautious

tentless heedless

teugh tough (ed.)

thack thatch; thack an' raep: all kinds of necessaries, particularly clothes (K)

thae these

thairm gut, intestine; as used for e.g. sausage-skin, or fiddle-strings (ed.)

theekit thatched (ed.)

thegither together

themsel, themsels themselves

thysel thyself

thick intimate, familiar

thig to beg, ask for charity (*DSL*)

thir these

thirl to thrill

thirl'd thrilled, vibrated

thole to suffer, to endure

thowe thaw (K)

thowless slack, pithless (K); slack, lazy (E)

thrang throng, a crowd

thrapple windpipe, gullet (*DSL*)

thrave a measure of cut grain, consisting of twenty-four sheaves (*DSL*)

thraw to sprain; to twist; to contradict (E); for thrawin: to prevent warping (Kinsley)

threap to maintain by dint of assertion

thrissle thistle

throw'ther pell-mell, confusedly

thud to make a loud, intermittent noise

tight competent, capable, alert, vigorous (*DSL*)

till to (ed.); till't: to it (E)

timmer timber

tinkler tinker

tip, toop a ram

tippeny weak ale sold at twopence the Scots pint (*DSL*)

tither other (ed.)

tine to lose

tint lost

tirl to knock gently, to uncover (K); to make a slight noise, to uncover (E)

tittle to whisper

tocher a marriage portion (E); i.e. a dowry (ed.)

tod a fox

toddle to totter like the walk of a child

toom empty

toun, town a hamlet; a farmhouse

tout the blast of a horn or trumpet; to blow a horn, &c.

tow a rope

towmond, towmont a twelvemonth

towze, touse to pull or knock about, treat or handle roughly (*DSL*)

towzie rough, shaggy

toy a very old fashion of female
  head-dress

toyte to walk like old age (K); to totter
  like old age (E)

tozie, tosie (1) cosy, snug, agreeably
  warm; (2) merry and elevated in
  drink (*DSL*)

trashtrie trash (K)

trig spruce, neat

trimly excellently

trode trodden (ed.)

trow to believe

trowth truth; a petty oath

tug raw hide, of which, in old
  times, plough traces were frequently
  made

tulzie a quarrel; to quarrel, to fight

twa two

'twad it would

twal twelve; twalpennie-worth: a
  small quantity, a penny-worth

twathree a few

twin to part

tyke a dog

unco strange; uncouth; very; very
  great; predigious

uncos news

under hidin in hiding (*DSL*)

unkenn'd unknown

upo' upon

usquabae whisky, from the Gaelic
  uisge beatha: water of life (ed.)

vap'rin vapouring (E); i.e. acting in
  a fantastic or ostentatious manner
  (*OED*)

vauntie proud, boastful, vain (*DSL*)

vera very

wa' wall; wa's: walls

wabster a weaver

wad (1) would; wadna: would not (E);
  can mean would *have*, e.g: wad been:
  would have been; wad stan't: would
  have stood (ed.)

wad (2) to bet; a bet, a pledge (E)

wae woe; sorrowful (E); wae worth:
  may ill betide (*DSL*)

waesucks! waes me! alas! O the pity!

waft the woof (E); i.e. those threads at
  right angles to the warp threads in a
  textile (ed.)

wair to lay out, to spend (K)

wale choice; to choose (E);
  in former usage also in sense of 'the
  best' (ed.)

walie big and strong; plump, buxom,
  thriving (*DSL*)

wallop to make violent struggling
  movements (*DSL*)

wame the belly

wamefou' a bellyfull

wanchancie unlucky

wanrestfu' restless

wark (1) work, labour (*DSL*)

wark (2) a building, esp. of a public or
  imposing kind (*DSL*)

warl', warld world (E); warl's gear:
  earthly possessions (ed.)

warly worldly, eager on amassing
  wealth

warran a warrant; to warrant

warsl'd wrestled

warst worst

wast waste (ed.)

wastrie prodigality

wat wet; I wat: I wot, I know (E);
  red-wat-shod: up to the ankles in
  blood (*DSL*)

water-brose brose made simply of
  meal and water (K) [i.e.] without the
  addition of milk, butter, &c. (E)

water-kelpies a sort of mischievous
  spirits that are said to haunt
  fords, &c. (K)

wattle a twig, a wand

wauble to swing (K); to swing, to
  reel (E)

waught a long pull, swig, or gulp of
  any drink; gude-willie-waught: such
  a draught taken with good-will, a
  hearty or cordial swig (*DSL*)

wauken to awake

wauket thickened as fullers do cloth (K)

waur worse; to worst (E); in latter sense e.g. waur't thee: give you the worst of it (ed.)

we'se we shall

wean, weanie child

wearie monie a wearie body: many a different person (E) (not a sense listed in *DSL*: ed.)

weary fa' the devil take—, confound— (to express exasperation) (*DSL*)

weason weasand (E); i.e. gullet (ed.)

wecht a wooden hoop with skin stretched over it, used in winnowing grain (*DSL*)

wee little; wee-things: little ones; wee-bit: a small matter (E); a wee: a short time (ed.)

weel well; weelfare: welfare

ween to surmise, guess, imagine (*DSL*): already an archaic/literary usage in eighteenth-century English, but seems to have retained more general currency in Scots (ed.)

weeper a broad white cuff worn by widows (*OED*)

weet rain; wetness (E); to wet, to moisten (ed.)

westlin westerly (*DSL*)

wha who

whaizle to wheeze (K)

whalpet whelped

whang a piece of cheese, bread, etc.

whare where

whare'er wherever

whase whose

wheep to fly nimbly; to jerk; penny wheep: small beer

whid the motion of a hare running but not frightened; a lie (E)

whiddan running as a hare or coney (E)

whigmeleerie a piece of ornamentation, used with depreciatory force, gew-gaw, bauble (*DSL*)

whisht! silence!; to hold one's whisht: to be silent

whisk to sweep (K); to sweep; to lash (E)

whissle a whistle; to whistle (E); to get the whissle of one's groat: to play a losing game (E); to be paid in one's own coin, to get one's just deserts (*DSL*)

whitter a hearty draught of liquor

whittle a knife (*DSL*)

whunstane a whin-stone

whyles whiles, sometimes

wi' with

wiel a small whirlpool (K)

wifie a diminutive or endearing term for wife

wight (1) person; (2) sturdy, vigorous, brisk, energetic (*DSL*)

willyart awkward, shy, bashful (*DSL*)

wimple to meander

win to wind, to winnow

win't winded, as a bottom of yarn (E); i.e. wound (ed.)

win' wind; win's: winds

winn to winnow

winna will not

winnock a window

wintle a wavering, swinging motion (K); a staggering motion; to stagger; to reel (E)

winze an oath (K)

wiss wish

wonner wonder, a term of contempt (K)

woo' wool

woodie, widdie a twig or wand of willow or other tough but flexible wood, or several of these twisted or interlaced to make a cord or rope and used for various purposes (*DSL*)

wooer-bab the garter knotted below the knee with a couple of loops and ends (K); i.e. on the *male* leg: a sign of the wearer's intention to propose marriage (*DSL*)

woor wore (ed.)

wordy worthy (ed.)

worset worsted

wrack to vex, to trouble (K); to tease, to vex (E)

wrang wrong; to wrong

wud mad, distracted

wumble a wimble (E);
i.e. a gimlet, a tool for drilling small holes (ed.)

wylecoat a flannel vest

wyte blame; to blame

ye is frequently used for the singular (K); this pronoun is frequently used for Thou (E)

yell dry, spoken of a cow (K); barren, that gives no milk (E)

yerk to lash, to jerk

yestreen yesternight

yett gate (*DSL*)

yill ale

yird, yerd, yirth earth

yokin yoking; a bout

yon that, those (of distant objects) (ed.)

'yont beyond

young-guidman a new married man (K)

yoursel yourself

yowe a ewe

INDEX OF TITLES

Entries in italics link titles used by James Kinsley in his edition (see Further Reading) to their titles in this edition.

INDEX OF FIRST LINES

The Oxford World's Classics Website

www.worldsclassics.co.uk

- Browse the full range of Oxford World's Classics online

- Sign up for our monthly e-alert to receive information on new titles

- Read extracts from the Introductions

- Listen to our editors and translators talk about the world's greatest literature with our Oxford World's Classics audio guides

- Join the conversation, follow us on Twitter at OWC_Oxford

- Teachers and lecturers can order inspection copies quickly and simply via our website

www.worldsclassics.co.uk

American Literature

British and Irish Literature

Children's Literature

Classics and Ancient Literature

Colonial Literature

Eastern Literature

European Literature

Gothic Literature

History

Medieval Literature

Oxford English Drama

Philosophy

Poetry

Politics

Religion

The Oxford Shakespeare

A complete list of Oxford World's Classics, including Authors in Context, Oxford English Drama, and the Oxford Shakespeare, is available in the UK from the Marketing Services Department, Oxford University Press, Great Clarendon Street, Oxford OX2 6DP, or visit the website at www.oup.com/uk/worldsclassics.

In the USA, visit www.oup.com/us/owc for a complete title list.

Oxford World's Classics are available from all good bookshops. In case of difficulty, customers in the UK should contact Oxford University Press Bookshop, 116 High Street, Oxford OX1 4BR.

CHARLES DICKENS	A Tale of Two Cities
GEORGE DU MAURIER	Trilby
MARIA EDGEWORTH	Castle Rackrent
GEORGE ELIOT	Daniel Deronda
	The Lifted Veil and Brother Jacob
	Middlemarch
	The Mill on the Floss
	Silas Marner
SUSAN FERRIER	Marriage
ELIZABETH GASKELL	Cranford
	The Life of Charlotte Brontë
	Mary Barton
	North and South
	Wives and Daughters
GEORGE GISSING	New Grub Street
	The Odd Women
EDMUND GOSSE	Father and Son
THOMAS HARDY	Far from the Madding Crowd
	Jude the Obscure
	The Mayor of Casterbridge
	The Return of the Native
	Tess of the d'Urbervilles
	The Woodlanders
WILLIAM HAZLITT	Selected Writings
JAMES HOGG	The Private Memoirs and Confessions of a Justified Sinner
JOHN KEATS	The Major Works
	Selected Letters
CHARLES MATURIN	Melmoth the Wanderer
JOHN RUSKIN	Selected Writings
WALTER SCOTT	The Antiquary
	Ivanhoe

though constrained to shield and aid the bad. Ask me no more questions, sir; but believe that I am rather to be pitied than condemned. I must leave my house to-morrow, for while I stay there, it is haunted. My future dwelling, if I am to live in peace, must be a secret. If my poor boy should ever stray this way, do not tempt him to disclose it or have him watched when he returns; for if we are hunted, we must fly again. And now this load is off my mind, I beseech you—and you, dear Miss Haredale, too—to trust me if you can, and think of me kindly as you have been used to do. If I die and cannot tell my secret even then (for that may come to pass), it will sit the lighter on my breast in that hour for this day's work; and on that day, and every day until it comes, I will pray for and thank you both, and trouble you no more."

With that, she would have left them, but they detained her, and with many soothing words and kind entreaties besought her to consider what she did, and above all to repose more freely upon them, and say what weighed so sorely on her mind. Finding her deaf to their persuasions, Mr. Haredale suggested, as a last resource, that she should confide in Emma, of whom, as a young person and one of her own sex, she might stand in less dread than of himself. From this proposal, however, she recoiled with the same indescribable repugnance she had manifested when they met. The utmost that could be wrung from her was, a promise that she would receive Mr. Haredale at her own house next evening, and in the mean time re-consider her determination and their dissuasions—though any change on her part, as she told them, was quite hopeless. This condition made at last, they reluctantly suffered her to depart, since she would neither eat nor drink within the house; and she, and Barnaby, and Grip, accordingly went out as they had come, by the private stair and garden gate; seeing and being seen of no one by the way.

It was remarkable in the raven that during the whole interview he had kept his eye on his book with exactly the air of a very sly human rascal, who, under the mask of pretending to read hard, was listening to everything. He still appeared to have the conversation very strongly in his mind, for although, when they were alone again, he issued orders for the instant preparation of innumerable kettles for purposes of tea, he was thoughtful, and rather seemed to do so from an abstract sense of duty, than with any regard to making himself agreeable, or being what is commonly called good company.

herself to the remainder of her task, she spoke from this time \
firmer voice and heightened courage.

"Heaven is my witness, as my own heart is—and yours, &
young lady, will speak for me, I know—that I have lived, since th
time we all have bitter reason to remember, in unchanging devotior
and gratitude to this family. Heaven is my witness that go where I
may, I shall preserve those feelings unimpaired. And it is my witness,
too, that they alone impel me to the course I must take, and from
which nothing now shall turn me, as I hope for mercy."

"These are strange riddles," said Mr. Haredale.

"In this world, sir," she replied, "they may, perhaps, never be
explained. In another, the Truth will be discovered in its own good
time. And may that time," she added in a low voice, "be far distant!"

"Let me be sure," said Mr. Haredale, "that I understand you, for I
am doubtful of my own senses. Do you mean that you are resolved
voluntarily to deprive yourself of those means of support you have
received from us so long—that you are determined to resign the
annuity we settled on you twenty years ago—to leave house, and
home, and goods, and begin life anew—and this, for some secret
reason or monstrous fancy which is incapable of explanation, which
only now exists, and has been dormant all this time? In the name of
God, under what delusion are you labouring?"

"As I am deeply thankful," she made answer, "for the kindness of
those, alive and dead, who have owned this house; and as I would not
have its roof fall down and crush me, or its very walls drip blood, my
name being spoken in their hearing; I never will again subsist upon
their bounty, or let it help me to subsistence. You do not know," she
added, suddenly, "to what uses it may be applied; into what hands it
may pass. I do, and I renounce it."

"Surely," said Mr. Haredale, "its uses rest with you."

"They did. They rest with me no longer. It may be—it *is*—
devoted to purposes that mock the dead in their graves. It never can
prosper with me. It will bring some other heavy judgment on th
head of my dear son, whose innocence will suffer for his mother
guilt."

"What words are these!" cried Mr. Haredale, regarding her w
wonder. "Among what associates have you fallen? Into what
have you ever been betrayed?"

"I am guilty, and yet innocent; wrong, yet right; good in inte

They were to return by the coach. As there was an interval of full two hours before it started, and they needed rest and some refreshment, Barnaby begged hard for a visit to the Maypole. But his mother, who had no wish to be recognized by any of those who had known her long ago, and who feared besides that Mr. Haredale might, on second thoughts, despatch some messenger to that place of entertainment in quest of her, proposed to wait in the churchyard instead. As it was easy for Barnaby to buy and carry thither such humble viands as they required, he cheerfully assented, and in the churchyard they sat down to take their frugal dinner.

Here again, the raven was in a highly reflective state; walking up and down when he had dined, with an air of elderly complacency which was strongly suggestive of his having his hands under his coat-tails; and appearing to read the tombstones with a very critical taste. Sometimes, after a long inspection of an epitaph, he would strop his beak upon the grave to which it referred, and cry in his hoarse tones, "I'm a devil, I'm a devil, I'm a devil!" but whether he addressed his observations to any supposed person below, or merely threw them off as a general remark, is matter of uncertainty.

It was a quiet pretty spot, but a sad one for Barnaby's mother; for Mr. Reuben Haredale lay there, and near the vault in which his ashes rested, was a stone to the memory of her own husband, with a brief inscription recording how and when he had lost his life. She sat here, thoughtful and apart, until their time was out, and the distant horn told that the coach was coming.

Barnaby, who had been sleeping on the grass, sprung up quickly at the sound; and Grip, who appeared to understand it equally well, walked into his basket straightway, entreating society in general (as though he intended a kind of satire upon them in connexion with churchyards) never to say die on any terms. They were soon on the coach-top and rolling along the road.

It went round by the Maypole, and stopped at the door. Joe was from home, and Hugh came sluggishly out to hand up the parcel that it called for. There was no fear of old John coming out. They could see him from the coach-roof fast asleep in his cosey bar. It was a part of John's character. He made a point of going to sleep at the coach's time. He despised gadding about; he looked upon coaches as things that ought to be indicted; as disturbers of the peace of mankind; as restless, bustling, busy, horn-blowing contrivances, quite beneath the

dignity of men, and only suited to giddy girls that did nothing but chatter and go a-shopping. "We know nothing about coaches here, sir," John would say, if any unlucky stranger made inquiry touching the offensive vehicles; "we don't book for 'em; we'd rather not; they're more trouble than they're worth, with their noise and rattle. If you like to wait for 'em you can; but we don't know anything about 'em; they may call and they may not—there's a carrier—he was looked upon as quite good enough for us, when *I* was a boy."

She dropped her veil as Hugh climbed up, and while he hung behind, and talked to Barnaby in whispers. But neither he nor any other person spoke to her, or noticed her, or had any curiosity about her; and so, an alien, she visited and left the village where she had been born, and had lived a merry child, a comely girl, a happy wife— where she had known all her enjoyment of life, and had entered on its hardest sorrows.

CHAPTER THE TWENTY-SIXTH.

"AND you're not surprised to hear this, Varden?" said Mr. Hare-dale. "Well! You and she have always been the best friends, and you should understand her if anybody does."

"I ask your pardon, sir," rejoined the locksmith. "I didn't say I understood her. I wouldn't have the presumption to say that of any woman. It's not so easily done. But I am not so much surprised, sir, as you expected me to be, certainly."

"May I ask why not, my good friend?"

"I have seen, sir," returned the locksmith with evident reluctance, "I have seen in connexion with her, something that has filled me with distrust and uneasiness. She has made bad friends; how, or when, I don't know; but that her house is a refuge for one robber and cut-throat at least, I am certain. There, sir! Now it's out."

"Varden!"

"My own eyes, sir, are my witnesses, and for her sake I would be willingly half-blind, if I could but have the pleasure of mistrusting 'em. I have kept the secret till now, and it will go no further than yourself, I know; but I tell you that with my own eyes—broad awake—I saw, in the passage of her house one evening after dark, the highwayman who robbed and wounded Mr. Edward Chester, and on the same night threatened me."

"And you made no effort to detain him?" said Mr. Haredale quickly.

"Sir," returned the locksmith, "she herself prevented me—held me, with all her strength, and hung about me until he had got clear off." And having gone so far, he related circumstantially all that had passed upon the night in question.

This dialogue was held in a low tone in the locksmith's little parlour, into which honest Gabriel had shown his visitor on his arrival. Mr. Haredale had called upon him to entreat his company to the widow's, that he might have the assistance of his persuasion and influence; and out of this circumstance the conversation had arisen.

"I forbore," said Gabriel, "from repeating one word of this to anybody, as it could do her no good and might do her great harm. I thought and hoped, to say the truth, that she would come to me, and talk to me about it, and tell me how it was; but though I have purposely put myself in her way more than once or twice, she has never touched upon the subject—except by a look. And indeed," said the good-natured locksmith, "there was a good deal in the look, more than could have been put into a great many words. It said among other matters 'Don't ask me anything' so imploringly, that I didn't ask her anything. You'll think me an old fool I know, sir. If it's any relief to call me one, pray do."

"I am greatly disturbed by what you tell me," said Mr. Haredale, after a silence. "What meaning do you attach to it?"

The locksmith shook his head, and looked doubtfully out of window at the failing light.

"She cannot have married again," said Mr. Haredale.

"Not without our knowledge surely, sir."

"She may have done so, in the fear that it would lead, if known, to some objection or estrangement. Suppose she married incautiously—it is not improbable, for her existence has been a lonely and monotonous one for many years—and the man turned out a ruffian, she would be anxious to screen him, and yet would revolt from his crimes. This might be. It bears strongly on the whole drift of her discourse yesterday, and would quite explain her conduct. Do you suppose Barnaby is privy to these circumstances?"

"Quite impossible to say, sir," returned the locksmith, shaking his head again: "and next to impossible to find out from him. If what you suppose is really the case, I tremble for the lad—a notable person, sir, to put to bad uses—"

"It is not possible, Varden," said Mr. Haredale, in a still lower tone of voice than he had spoken yet, "that we have been blinded and deceived by this woman from the beginning? It is not possible that this connexion was formed in her husband's lifetime, and led to his and my brother's—"

"Good God, sir," cried Gabriel, interrupting him, "don't entertain such dark thoughts for a moment. Five-and-twenty years ago, where was there a girl like her? A gay, handsome, laughing, bright-eyed damsel! Think what she was, sir. It makes my heart ache now, even now, though I'm an old man with a woman for a daughter, to think what she was, and what she is. We all change, but that's with Time; Time does his work honestly, and I don't mind him. A fig for Time, sir. Use him well, and he's a hearty fellow, and scorns to have you at a disadvantage. But care and suffering (and those have changed her) are devils, sir—secret, stealthy, undermining devils—who tread down the brightest flowers in Eden, and do more havoc in a month than Time does in a year. Picture to yourself for one minute what Mary was before they went to work with her fresh heart and face—do her that justice—and say whether such a thing is possible."

"You're a good fellow, Varden," said Mr. Haredale, "and are quite right. I have brooded on that subject so long, that every breath of suspicion carries me back to it. You are quite right."

"It isn't, sir," cried the locksmith with brightened eyes, and sturdy, honest voice; "it isn't because I courted her before Rudge, and failed, that I say she was too good for him. She would have been as much too good for me. But she *was* too good for him; he wasn't free and frank enough for her. I don't reproach his memory with it, poor fellow; I only want to put her before you as she really was. For myself, I'll keep her old picture in my mind; and thinking of that, and what has altered her, I'll stand her friend, and try to win her back to peace. And damme, sir," cried Gabriel, "with your pardon for the word, I'd do the same if she had married fifty highwaymen in a twelvemonth; and think it in the Protestant Manual too, though Martha said it wasn't, tooth and nail, till doomsday!"

If the dark little parlour had been filled with a dense fog, which, clearing away in an instant, left it all radiance and brightness, it could not have been more suddenly cheered than by this outbreak on the part of the hearty locksmith. In a voice nearly as full and round as his own, Mr. Haredale cried "Well said!" and bade him come away without more parley. The locksmith complied right willingly; and both getting into a hackney-coach* which was waiting at the door, drove off straightway.

They alighted at the street corner, and dismissing their conveyance, walked to the house. To their first knock at the door there was no response. A second met with the like result. But in answer to the third, which was of a more vigorous kind, the parlour window-sash was gently raised, and a musical voice cried:

"Haredale, my dear fellow, I am extremely glad to see you. How very much you have improved in your appearance since our last meeting! I never saw you looking better. *How* do you do?"

Mr. Haredale turned his eyes towards the casement whence the voice proceeded, though there was no need to do so, to recognize the speaker, and Mr. Chester waved his hand, and smiled a courteous welcome.

"The door will be opened immediately," he said. "There is nobody but a very dilapidated female to perform such offices. You will excuse her infirmities? If she were in a more elevated station of society, she would be gouty. Being but a hewer of wood and drawer of water, she is rheumatic. My dear Haredale, these are natural class distinctions, depend upon it."

Mr. Haredale, whose face resumed its lowering and distrustful look the moment he heard the voice, inclined his head stiffly, and turned his back upon the speaker.

"Not opened yet!" said Mr. Chester. "Dear me! I hope the aged soul has not caught her foot in some unlucky cobweb by the way. She is there at last! Come in, I beg!"

Mr. Haredale entered, followed by the locksmith. Turning with a look of great astonishment to the old woman who had opened the door, he inquired for Mrs. Rudge—for Barnaby. They were both gone, she replied, wagging her ancient head, for good. There was a gentleman in the parlour, who perhaps could tell them more. That was all *she* knew.

"Pray, sir," said Mr. Haredale, presenting himself before this new tenant, "where is the person whom I came here to see?"

"My dear friend," he returned, "I have not the least idea."

"Your trifling is ill-timed," retorted the other in a suppressed tone and voice, "and its subject ill-chosen. Reserve it for those who are your friends, and do not expend it on me. I lay no claim to the distinction, and have the self-denial to reject it."

"My dear, good sir," said Mr. Chester, "you are heated with walking. Sit down, I beg. Our friend is—"

"Is but a plain honest man," returned Mr. Haredale, "and quite unworthy of your notice."

"Gabriel Varden by name, sir," said the locksmith bluntly.

"A worthy English yeoman!" said Mr. Chester. "A most worthy yeoman, of whom I have frequently heard my son Ned—darling fellow—speak, and have often wished to see. Varden, my good friend, I am glad to know you. You wonder now," he said, turning languidly to Mr. Haredale, "to see me here. Now, I am sure you do."

Mr. Haredale glanced at him—not fondly or admiringly—smiled, and held his peace.

"The mystery is solved in a moment," said Mr. Chester; "in a moment. Will you step aside with me one instant. You remember our little compact in reference to Ned, and your dear niece, Haredale? You remember the list of assistants in their innocent intrigue? You remember these two people being among them? My dear fellow, congratulate yourself, and me. I have bought them off."

"You have done what?" said Mr. Haredale.

"Bought them off," returned his smiling friend. "I have found it necessary to take some active steps towards setting this boy and girl attachment quite at rest, and have begun by removing these two agents. You are surprised? Who *can* withstand the influence of a little money! They wanted it, and have been bought off. We have nothing more to fear from them. They are gone."

"Gone!" echoed Mr. Haredale. "Where?"

"My dear fellow—and you must permit me to say again, that you never looked so young; so positively boyish as you do to-night—the Lord knows where; I believe Columbus himself wouldn't find them. Between you and me they have their hidden reasons, but upon that point I have pledged myself to secrecy. She appointed to see you here to-night I know, but found it inconvenient, and couldn't wait. Here is the key of the door. I am afraid you'll find it inconveniently large; but as the tenement is yours, your good-nature will excuse that, Haredale, I am certain!"

CHAPTER THE TWENTY-SEVENTH.

Mr. HAREDALE stood in the widow's parlour with the door-key in his hand, gazing by turns at Mr. Chester and at Gabriel Varden, and occasionally glancing downward at the key as in the hope that of its own accord it would unlock the mystery; until Mr. Chester, putting on his hat and gloves, and sweetly inquiring whether they were walking in the same direction, recalled him to himself.

"No," he said. "Our roads diverge—widely, as you know. For the present, I shall remain here."

"You will be hipped,* Haredale; you will be miserable, melancholy, utterly wretched," returned the other. "It is a place of the very last description for a man of your temper. I know it will make you very miserable."

"Let it," said Mr. Haredale, sitting down; "and thrive upon the thought. Good night!"

Feigning to be wholly unconscious of the abrupt wave of the hand which rendered this farewell tantamount to a dismissal, Mr. Chester retorted with a bland and heartfelt benediction, and inquired of Gabriel in what direction *he* was going.

"Yours, sir, would be too much honour for the like of me," replied the locksmith, hesitating.

"I wish you to remain here a little while, Varden," said Mr. Haredale without looking towards them. "I have a word or two to say to you."

"I will not intrude upon your conference another moment," said Mr. Chester with inconceivable politeness. "May it be satisfactory to you both! God bless you!" So saying, and bestowing upon the locksmith a most refulgent smile, he left them.

"A deplorably constituted creature, that rugged person," he said, as he walked along the street; "he is an atrocity that carries its own punishment along with it—a bear that gnaws himself. And here is one of the inestimable advantages of having a perfect command over one's inclinations. I have been tempted in these two short interviews, to draw upon that fellow, fifty times. Five men in six would have yielded to the impulse. By suppressing mine, I wound him deeper and more keenly than if I were the best swordsman in all Europe, and he the worst. You are the wise man's very last resource," he said, tapping the hilt of his weapon; "we can but appeal to you when all else is said and done. To come to you before, and thereby spare our adversaries so much, is a barbarian mode of warfare, quite unworthy any man with the remotest pretensions to delicacy of feeling, or refinement."

He smiled so very pleasantly as he communed with himself after this manner, that a beggar was emboldened to follow him for alms, and to dog his footsteps for some distance. He was gratified by the circumstance, feeling it complimentary to his power of feature, and as a reward suffered the man to follow him until he called a chair, when he graciously dismissed him with a fervent blessing.

"Which is as easy as cursing," he wisely added, as he took his seat, "and more becoming to the face.—To Clerkenwell, my good creatures, if you please!" The chairmen were rendered quite vivacious by having such a courteous burden, and to Clerkenwell they went at a fair round trot.

Alighting at a certain point he had indicated to them upon the road, and paying them something less than they had expected from a fare of such gentle speech, he turned into the street in which the locksmith dwelt, and presently stood beneath the shadow of the Golden Key. Mr. Tappertit, who was hard at work by lamp-light, in a corner of the workshop, remained unconscious of his presence until a hand upon his shoulder made him start and turn his head.

"Industry," said Mr. Chester, "is the soul of business, and the keystone of prosperity. Mr. Tappertit, I shall expect you to invite me to dinner when you are Lord Mayor of London."

"Sir," returned the 'prentice, laying down his hammer, and rubbing his nose on the back of a very sooty hand, "I scorn the Lord Mayor and everything that belongs to him. We must have another state of society, sir, before you catch me being Lord Mayor. How de do sir?"

"The better, Mr. Tappertit, for looking into your ingenuous face once more. I hope you are well."

"I am as well, sir," said Sim, standing up to get nearer to his ear, and whispering hoarsely, "as any man can be under the aggravations to which I am exposed. My life's a burden to me. If it wasn't for wengeance, I'd play at pitch and toss with it on the losing hazard."

"Is Mrs. Varden at home?" said Mr. Chester.

"Sir," returned Sim, eyeing him over with a look of concentrated expression,—"she is. Did you wish to see her?"

Mr. Chester nodded.

"Then come this way, sir," said Sim, wiping his face upon his apron. "Follow me, sir.—Would you permit me to whisper in your ear, one half a second?"

"By all means."

Mr. Tappertit raised himself on tiptoe, applied his lips to Mr. Chester's ear, drew back his head without saying anything, looked hard at him, applied them to his ear again, again drew back, and finally whispered—"The name is Joseph Willet. Hush! I say no more."

Having said that much, he beckoned the visitor with a mysterious aspect to follow him to the parlour door, where he announced him in the voice of a gentleman-usher. "Mr. Chester."

"And not Mr. Ed'dard, mind," said Sim, looking into the door again and adding this by way of postscript in his own person; "it's his father."

"But do not let his father," said Mr. Chester, advancing hat in hand, as he observed the effect of this last explanatory announcement, "do not let his father be any check or restraint on your domestic occupations, Miss Varden."

"Oh! Now! There! An't I always a saying it!" exclaimed Miggs, clapping her hands. "If he an't been and took Missis for her own daughter. Well, she *do* look like it, that she do. Ony think of that, mim!"

"Is it possible" said Mr. Chester in his softest tones, "that this is Mrs. Varden! I am amazed. That is not your daughter, Mrs. Varden? No, no. Your sister."

"My daughter, indeed sir," returned Mrs. V., blushing with great juvenility.

"Ah, Mrs. Varden!" cried the visitor. "Ah, ma'am—humanity is indeed a happy lot, when we can repeat ourselves in others, and still be young as they. You must allow me to salute you—the custom of the country, my dear madam—your daughter too."

Dolly showed some reluctance to perform this ceremony, but was sharply reproved by Mrs. Varden, who insisted on her undergoing it that minute. For pride, she said with great severity, was one of the seven deadly sins, and humility and lowliness of heart were virtues. Wherefore she desired that Dolly would be kissed immediately, on pain of her just displeasure; at the same time giving her to understand that whatever she saw her mother do, she might safely do herself, without being at the trouble of any reasoning or reflection on the subject—which, indeed, was offensive and undutiful, and in direct contravention of the church catechism.

Thus admonished, Dolly complied, though by no means willingly; for there was a broad, bold look of admiration in Mr. Chester's face, refined and polished though it sought to be, which distressed her very much. As she stood with downcast eyes, not liking to look up and meet his, he gazed upon her with an approving air, and then turned to her mother.

"My friend Gabriel (whose acquaintance I only made this very evening) should be a happy man, Mrs. Varden."

"Ah!" sighed Mrs. V., shaking her head.

"Ah!" echoed Miggs.

"Is that the case?" said Mr. Chester, compassionately. "Dear me!"

"Master has no intentions sir," murmured Miggs as she sidled up to him, "but to be as grateful as his natur will let him, for everythink he owns which it is in his powers to appreciate. But we never sir"—said Miggs, looking sideways at Mrs. Varden, and interlarding her discourse with a sigh—"we never know the full value of *some* wines and fig-trees till we lose 'em.* So much the worse sir, for them as has the slighting of 'em on their consciences when they're gone to be in full blow elsewhere." And Miss Miggs cast up her eyes to signify where that might be.

As Mrs. Varden distinctly heard, and was intended to hear, all that Miggs said, and as these words appeared to convey in metaphorical terms a presage or foreboding that she would at some early period droop beneath her trials and take an easy flight towards the stars, she immediately began to languish, and taking a volume of the Manual from a neighbouring table, leant her arm upon it as though she were Hope and that her Anchor.* Mr. Chester perceiving this, and seeing how the volume was lettered on the back, took it gently from her hand, and turned the fluttering leaves.

"My favourite book, dear madam. How often, how very often in his early life—before he can remember"—(this clause was strictly true) "have I deduced little easy moral lessons from its pages, for my dear son Ned! You know Ned?"

Mrs. Varden had that honour, and a fine affable young gentleman he was.

"You're a mother, Mrs. Varden" said Mr. Chester, taking a pinch of snuff, "and you know what I, as a father, feel, when he is praised. He gives me some uneasiness—much uneasiness—he's of a roving nature, ma'am—from flower to flower—from sweet to sweet—but his is the butterfly time of life, and we must not be hard upon such trifling."

He glanced at Dolly. She was attending evidently to what he said. Just what he desired!

"The only thing I object to in this little trait of Ned's, is," said Mr. Chester, "—and the mention of his name reminds me, by the way, that I am about to beg the favour of a minute's talk with you alone—the only thing I object to in it, is, that it *does* partake of insincerity. Now, however I may attempt to disguise the fact from myself in my affection for Ned, still I always revert to this—that if we are not sincere, we are nothing. Nothing upon earth. Let us be sincere, my dear madam—"

"—and Protestant," murmured Mrs. Varden.

"—and Protestant above all things. Let us be sincere and Protestant, strictly moral, strictly just (though always with a leaning towards mercy), strictly honest, and strictly true, and we gain—it is a slight point, certainly, but still it is something tangible; we throw up a groundwork and foundation, so to speak, of goodness, on which we may afterwards erect some worthy superstructure."

Now, to be sure, Mrs. Varden thought, here is a perfect character. Here is a meek, righteous, thorough-going Christian, who, having mastered all these qualities, so difficult of attainment; who, having dropped a pinch of salt on the tails of all the cardinal virtues, and caught them every one; makes light of their possession, and pants for more morality. For the good woman never doubted (as many good men and women never do), that this slighting kind of profession, this setting so little store by great matters, this seeming to say, "I am not proud, I am what you hear, but I consider myself no better than other people; let us change the subject, pray"—was perfectly genuine and true. He so contrived it, and said it in that way that it appeared to have been forced from him, and its effect was marvellous.

Aware of the impression he had made—few men were quicker than he at such discoveries—Mr. Chester followed up the blow by propounding certain virtuous maxims, somewhat vague and general in their nature, doubtless, and occasionally partaking of the character of truisms, worn a little out at elbow, but delivered in so charming a voice and with such uncommon serenity and peace of mind, that they answered as well as the best. Nor is this to be wondered at; for as hollow vessels produce a far more musical sound in falling than those which are substantial, so it will oftentimes be found that sentiments which have nothing in them make the loudest ringing in the world, and are the most relished.

Mr. Chester, with the volume gently extended in one hand, and with the other planted lightly on his breast, talked to them in the most delicious manner possible; and quite enchanted all his hearers, notwithstanding their conflicting interests and thoughts. Even Dolly, who, between his keen regards and her eyeing over by Mr. Tappertit, was put quite out of countenance, could not help owning within herself that he was the sweetest-spoken gentleman she had ever seen. Even Miss Miggs, who was divided between admiration of Mr.

Chester and a mortal jealousy of her young mistress, had sufficient leisure to be propitiated. Even Mr. Tappertit, though occupied as we have seen in gazing at his heart's delight, could not wholly divert his thoughts from the voice of the other charmer. Mrs. Varden, to her own private thinking, had never been so improved in all her life; and when Mr. Chester, rising and craving permission to speak with her apart, took her by the hand and led her at arm's length up stairs to the best sitting-room, she almost deemed him something more than human.

"Dear madam," he said, pressing her hand delicately to his lips; "be seated."

Mrs. Varden called up quite a courtly air, and became seated.

"You guess my object?" said Mr. Chester, drawing a chair towards her. "You divine my purpose? I am an affectionate parent, my dear Mrs. Varden."

"That I am sure you are sir," said Mrs. V.

"Thank you," returned Mr. Chester, tapping his snuff-box lid. "Heavy moral responsibilities rest with parents, Mrs. Varden."

Mrs. Varden slightly raised her hands, shook her head, and looked at the ground as though she saw straight through the globe, out at the other end, and into the immensity of space beyond.

"I may confide in you," said Mr. Chester, "without reserve. I love my son, ma'am, dearly; and loving him as I do, I would save him from working certain misery. You know of his attachment to Miss Haredale. You have abetted him in it, and very kind of you it was to do so. I am deeply obliged to you—most deeply obliged to you—for your interest in his behalf; but my dear ma'am, it is a mistaken one, I do assure you."

Mrs. Varden stammered that she was sorry—

"Sorry, my dear ma'am," he interposed. "Never be sorry for what is so very amiable, so very good in intention, so perfectly like yourself. But there are grave and weighty reasons, pressing family considerations, and apart even from these, points of religious difference, which interpose themselves, and render their union impossible; utterly im-possible. I should have mentioned these circumstances to your husband; but he has—you will excuse my saying this so freely—he has *not* your quickness of apprehension or depth of moral sense. What an extremely airy house this is, and how beautifully kept! For one like myself—a widower so long—these tokens of female care and superintendence have inexpressible charms."

Mrs. Varden began to think (she scarcely knew why) that the young Mr. Chester must be in the wrong, and the old Mr. Chester must be in the right.

"My son Ned," resumed her tempter with his most winning air, "has had, I am told, your lovely daughter's aid, and your open-hearted husband's."

"—Much more than mine sir," said Mrs. Varden; "a great deal more. I have often had my doubts. It's a—"

"A bad example," suggested Mr. Chester. "It is. No doubt it is. Your daughter is at that age when to set before her an encouragement for young persons to rebel against their parents on this most important point, is particularly injudicious. You are quite right. I ought to have thought of that myself, but it escaped me, I confess—so far superior are your sex to ours, dear madam, in point of penetration and sagacity."

Mrs. Varden looked as wise as if she had really said something to deserve this compliment—firmly believed she had, in short—and her faith in her own shrewdness increased considerably.

"My dear ma'am," said Mr. Chester, "you embolden me to be plain with you. My son and I are at variance on this point. The young lady and her natural guardian differ upon it, also. And the closing point is, that my son is bound by his duty to me, by his honour, by every solemn tie and obligation, to marry some one else."

"Engaged to marry another lady!" quoth Mrs. Varden, holding up her hands.

"My dear madam, brought up, educated, and trained, expressly for that purpose. Expressly for that purpose.—Miss Haredale, I am told, is a very charming creature."

"I am her foster-mother, and should know—the best young lady in the world," said Mrs. Varden.

"I have not the smallest doubt of it. I am sure she is. And you, who have stood in that tender relation towards her, are bound to consult her happiness. Now, can I—as I have said to Haredale, who quite agrees—can I possibly stand by, and suffer her to throw herself away (although she *is* of a catholic family), upon a young fellow who, as yet, has no heart at all? It is no imputation upon him to say he has not, because young men who have plunged deeply into the frivolities and conventionalities of society, very seldom have. Their hearts never grow, my dear ma'am, till after thirty. I don't believe, no, I do *not* believe, that I had any heart myself when I was Ned's age."

"Oh sir," said Mrs. Varden, "I think you must have had. It's impossible that you, who have so much now, can ever have been without any."

"I hope," he answered, shrugging his shoulders meekly, "I have a little; I hope, a very little—Heaven knows! But to return to Ned; I have no doubt you thought, and therefore interfered benevolently in his behalf, that I objected to Miss Haredale. How very natural! My dear madam, I object to him—to him—emphatically to Ned himself."

Mrs. Varden was perfectly aghast at the disclosure.

"He has, if he honourably fulfils this solemn obligation of which I have told you—and he must be honourable, dear Mrs. Varden, or he is no son of mine—a fortune within his reach. He is of most expensive, ruinously expensive habits; and if, in a moment of caprice and wilfulness, he were to marry this young lady, and so deprive himself of the means of gratifying the tastes to which he has been so long accustomed, he would—my dear madam, he would break the gentle creature's heart. Mrs. Varden, my good lady, my dear soul, I put it to you—is such a sacrifice to be endured? Is the female heart a thing to be trifled with in this way? Ask your own, my dear madam. Ask your own, I beseech you."

"Truly," thought Mrs. Varden, "this gentleman is a saint. But," she added aloud, and not unnaturally, "if you take Miss Emma's lover away, sir, what becomes of the poor thing's heart then?"

"The very point," said Mr. Chester, not at all abashed, "to which I wished to lead you. A marriage with my son, whom I should be compelled to disown, would be followed by years of misery; they would be separated, my dear madam, in a twelvemonth. To break off this attachment, which is more fancied than real, as you and I know very well, will cost the dear girl but a few tears, and she is happy again. Take the case of your own daughter, the young lady down stairs, who is your breathing image"—Mrs. Varden coughed and simpered—"there is a young man, (I am sorry to say, a dissolute fellow, of very indifferent character,) of whom I have heard Ned speak—Bullet was it—Pullet—Mullet—"

"There is a young man of the name of Joseph Willet, sir," said Mrs. Varden, folding her hands loftily.

"That's he," cried Mr. Chester. Suppose this Joseph Willet now, were to aspire to the affections of your charming daughter, and were to engage them."

"It would be like his impudence," interposed Mrs. Varden, bridling, "to dare to think of such a thing!"

"My dear madam, that's the whole case. I know it would be like his impudence. It is like Ned's impudence to do as he has done; but you would not on that account, or because of a few tears from your beautiful daughter, refrain from checking their inclinations in their birth. I meant to have reasoned thus with your husband when I saw him at Mrs. Rudge's this evening—"

"My husband," said Mrs. Varden, interposing with emotion, "would be a great deal better at home than going to Mrs. Rudge's so often. I don't know what he does there. I don't see what occasion he has to busy himself in her affairs at all, sir."

"If I don't appear to express my concurrence in those last sentiments of yours," returned Mr. Chester, "quite so strongly as you might desire, it is because his being there, my dear madam, and not proving conversational, led me hither, and procured me the happiness of this interview with one, in whom the whole management, conduct, and prosperity of her family are centred, I perceive."

With that he took Mrs. Varden's hand again, and having pressed it to his lips with the high-flown gallantry of the day—a little burlesqued to render it the more striking in the good lady's unaccustomed eyes—proceeded in the same strain of mingled sophistry, cajolery, and flattery, to entreat that her utmost influence might be exerted to restrain her husband and daughter from any further promotion of Edward's suit to Miss Haredale, and from aiding or abetting either party in any way. Mrs. Varden was but a woman, and had her share of vanity, obstinacy, and love of power. She entered into a secret treaty of alliance, offensive and defensive, with her insinuating visitor; and really did believe, as many others would have done who saw and heard him, that in so doing she furthered the ends of truth, justice, and morality, in a very uncommon degree.

Overjoyed by the success of his negotiation, and mightily amused within himself, Mr. Chester conducted her down stairs in the same state as before; and having repeated the previous ceremony of salutation, which also as before comprehended Dolly, took his leave; first completing the conquest of Miss Miggs's heart, by inquiring if "this young lady" would light him to the door.

"Oh, mim," said Miggs, returning with the candle. "Oh gracious me, mim, there's a gentleman! Was there ever such a angel to talk as he is—and such a sweet-looking man! So upright and noble, that he seems to despise the very ground he walks on; and yet so mild and condescending, that he seems to say 'but I will take notice on it too.' And to think of his taking you for Miss Dolly, and Miss Dolly for your sister—Oh, my goodness me, if I was master wouldn't I be jealous of him!"

Mrs. Varden reproved her handmaid for this vain-speaking; but very gently and mildly—quite smilingly indeed—remarking that she was a foolish, giddy, light-headed girl, whose spirits carried her beyond all bounds, and who didn't mean half she said, or she would be quite angry with her.

"For my part," said Dolly, in a thoughtful manner, "I half believe

Mr. Chester is something like Miggs in that respect. For all his politeness and pleasant speaking, I am pretty sure he was making game of us, more than once."

"If you venture to say such a thing again, and to speak ill of people behind their backs in my presence, Miss," said Mrs. Varden, "I shall insist upon your taking a candle and going to bed directly. How dare you, Dolly? I'm astonished at you. The rudeness of your whole behaviour this evening has been disgraceful. Did anybody ever hear," cried the enraged matron, bursting into tears, "of a daughter telling her own mother she has been made game of!"

What a very uncertain temper Mrs. Varden's was!

CHAPTER THE TWENTY-EIGHTH.

REPAIRING to a noted coffee-house in Covent Garden when he left the locksmith's, Mr. Chester sat long over a late dinner, entertaining himself exceedingly with the whimsical recollection of his recent proceedings, and congratulating himself very much on his great cleverness. Influenced by these thoughts, his face wore an expression so benign and tranquil, that the waiter in immediate attendance upon him felt he could almost have died in his defence, and settled in his own mind (until the receipt of the bill, and a very small fee for very great trouble disabused it of the idea) that such an apostolic customer was worth half-a-dozen of the ordinary run of visitors, at least.

A visit to the gaming-table—not as a heated, anxious venturer, but one whom it was quite a treat to see staking his two or three pieces in deference to the follies of society, and smiling with equal benevolence on winners and losers—made it late before he reached home. It was his custom to bid his servant go to bed at his own time unless he had orders to the contrary, and to leave a candle on the common stair. There was a lamp on the landing by which he could always light it when he came home late, and having a key of the door about him he could enter and go to bed at his pleasure.

He opened the glass of the dull lamp, whose wick, burnt up and swollen like a drunkard's nose, came flying off in little carbuncles at the candle's touch, and scattering hot sparks about rendered it matter of some difficulty to kindle the lazy taper; when a noise, as of a man snoring deeply some steps higher up, caused him to pause and listen. It was the heavy breathing of a sleeper, close at hand. Some fellow had lain down on the open staircase, and was slumbering soundly. Having lighted the candle at length and opened his own door, he softly ascended, holding the taper high above his head, and peering cautiously about; curious to see what kind of man had chosen so comfortless a shelter for his lodging.

With his head upon the landing and his great limbs flung over half-a-dozen stairs, as carelessly as though he were a dead man whom drunken bearers had thrown down by chance, there lay Hugh, face uppermost, his long hair drooping like some wild weed upon his wooden pillow, and his huge chest heaving with the sounds which so unwontedly disturbed the place and hour.

He who came upon him so unexpectedly was about to break his rest by thrusting him with his foot, when, glancing at his upturned face, he arrested himself in the very action, and stooping down and shading the candle with his hand, examined his features closely. Close as his first inspection was, it did not suffice, for he passed the light, still carefully shaded as before, across and across his face, and yet observed him with a searching eye.

While he was thus engaged, the sleeper, without any starting or turning round, awoke. There was a kind of fascination in meeting his steady gaze so suddenly, which took from the other the presence of mind to withdraw his eyes, and forced him, as it were, to meet his look. So they remained staring at each other, until Mr. Chester at last broke silence, and asked him in a low voice, why he lay sleeping there.

"I thought," said Hugh, struggling into a sitting posture and gazing at him intently, still, "that you were a part of my dream. It was a curious one. I hope it may never come true, master."

"What makes you shiver?"

"The—the cold, I suppose," he growled, as he shook himself, and rose. "I hardly know where I am yet."

"Do you know me?" said Mr. Chester.

"Ay. I know you," he answered. "I was dreaming of you—we're not where I thought we were. That's a comfort."

He looked round him as he spoke, and in particular looked above his head, as though he half expected to be standing under some object which had had existence in his dream. Then he rubbed his eyes and shook himself again, and followed his conductor into his own rooms.

Mr. Chester lighted the candles which stood upon his dressing-table, and wheeling an easy chair towards the fire, which was yet burning, stirred up a cheerful blaze, sat down before it, and bade his uncouth visitor "Come here," and draw his boots off.

"You have been drinking again, my fine fellow," he said, as Hugh went down on one knee, and did as he was told.

"As I'm alive, master, I've walked the twelve long miles, and waited here I don't know how long, and had no drink between my lips since dinner-time at noon."

"And can you do nothing better, my pleasant friend, than fall asleep, and shake the very building with your snores?" said Mr. Chester. "Can't you dream in your straw at home, dull dog as you are, that you need come here to do it?—Reach me those slippers, and tread softly."

Hugh obeyed in silence.

"And harkee, my dear young gentleman," said Mr. Chester, as he put them on, "the next time you dream, don't let it be of me, but of some dog or horse with whom you are better acquainted. Fill the glass once—you'll find it and the bottle in the same place—and empty it to keep yourself awake."

Hugh obeyed again—even more zealously—and having done so, presented himself before his patron.

"Now," said Mr. Chester, "what do you want with me?"

"There was news to-day," returned Hugh. "Your son was at our house—came down on horseback. He tried to see the young woman, but couldn't get sight of her. He left some letter or some message which our Joe had charge of, but he and the old one quarrelled about it when your son had gone, and the old one wouldn't let it be delivered. He says (that's the old one does) that none of his people shall interfere and get him into trouble. He's a landlord, he says, and lives on everybody's custom."

"He is a jewel," smiled Mr. Chester, "and the better for being a dull one.—Well?"

"Varden's daughter—that's the girl I kissed—"

"—and stole the bracelet from upon the king's highway," said Mr. Chester, composedly. "Yes; what of her?"

"She wrote a note at our house to the young woman, saying she lost the letter I brought to you, and you burnt. Our Joe was to carry it, but the old one kept him at home all next day, on purpose that he shouldn't. Next morning he gave it to me to take; and here it is."

"You didn't deliver it then, my good friend?" said Mr. Chester, twirling Dolly's note between his finger and thumb, and feigning to be surprised.

"I supposed you'd want to have it," retorted Hugh. "Burn one, burn all, I thought."

"My devil-may-care acquaintance," said Mr. Chester—"really if you do not draw some nicer distinctions, your career will be cut short with most surprising suddenness. Don't you know that the letter you brought to me, was directed to my son who resides in this very place? And can you descry no difference between his letters and those addressed to other people?"

"If you don't want it," said Hugh, disconcerted by this reproof, for he had expected high praise, "give it me back, and I'll deliver it. I don't know how to please you, master."

"I shall deliver it," returned his patron, putting it away after a moment's consideration, "myself. Does the young lady walk out, on fine mornings?"

"Mostly—about noon is her usual time."

"Alone?"

"Yes, alone."

"Where?"

"In the grounds before the house.—Them that the footpath crosses."

"If the weather should be fine, I may throw myself in her way to-morrow, perhaps," said Mr. Chester, as coolly as if she were one of his ordinary acquaintance. "Mr. Hugh, if I should ride up to the Maypole door, you will do me the favour only to have seen me once. You must suppress your gratitude, and endeavour to forget my for-bearance in the matter of the bracelet. It is natural it should break out, and it does you honour; but when other folks are by, you must, for your own sake and safety, be as like your usual self as though you owed me no obligation whatever, and had never stood within these walls. You comprehend me?"

Hugh understood him perfectly. After a pause he muttered that he hoped his patron would involve him in no trouble about this last letter; for he had kept it back solely with the view of pleasing him. He was continuing in this strain, when Mr. Chester with a most beneficent and patronising air cut him short by saying:

"My good fellow, you have my promise, my word, my sealed bond (for a verbal pledge with me is quite as good), that I will always protect you so long as you deserve it. Now, do set your mind at rest. Keep it at ease, I beg of you. When a man puts himself in my power so thoroughly as you have done, I really feel as though he had a kind of claim upon me. I am more disposed to mercy and forbearance under such circumstances than I can tell you, Hugh. Do look upon me as your protector, and rest assured, I entreat you, that on the subject of that indiscretion, you may preserve, as long as you and I are friends, the lightest heart that ever beat within a human breast. Fill that glass once more to cheer you on your road homewards—I am really quite ashamed to think how far you have to go—and then God bless you for the night."

"They think," said Hugh, when he had tossed the liquor down, "that I am sleeping soundly in the stable. Ha ha ha! The stable door is shut, but the steed's gone, master."

"You are a most convivial fellow," returned his friend, "and I love your humour of all things. Good night! Take the greatest possible care of yourself, for my sake!"

It was remarkable that during the whole interview, each had endeavoured to catch stolen glances of the other's face, and had never looked full at it. They interchanged one brief and hasty glance as Hugh went out, averted their eyes directly, and so separated. Hugh closed the double doors behind him, carefully and without noise; and Mr. Chester remained in his easy chair, with his gaze intently fixed upon the fire.

"Well!" he said, after meditating for a long time—and said with a deep sigh and an uneasy shifting of his attitude, as though he dismissed some other subject from his thoughts, and returned to that which had held possession of them all the day—"the plot thickens; I have thrown the shell; it will explode, I think, in eight-and-forty hours, and should scatter these good folks amazingly. We shall see!"

He went to bed and fell asleep, but had not slept long when he started up and thought that Hugh was at the outer door, calling in a strange voice, very different from his own, to be admitted. The delusion was so strong upon him, and was so full of that vague terror of the night in which such visions have their being, that he rose, and taking his sheathed sword in his hand, opened the door, and looked out upon the staircase, and towards the spot where Hugh had lain asleep; and even spoke to him by name. But all was dark and quiet, and creeping back to bed again, he fell, after an hour's uneasy watching, into a second sleep, and woke no more till morning.

CHAPTER THE TWENTY-NINTH.

THE thoughts of worldly men are for ever regulated by a moral law of gravitation, which, like the physical one, holds them down to earth. The bright glory of day, and the silent wonders of a starlit night, appeal to their minds in vain. There are no signs in the sun, or in the moon, or in the stars, for their reading. They are like some wise men, who, learning to know each planet by its Latin name, have quite forgotten such small heavenly constellations as Charity, Forbearance, Universal Love, and Mercy, although they shine by night and day so brightly that the blind may see them; and who, looking upward at the spangled sky, see nothing there but the reflection of their own great wisdom and book-learning.

It is curious to imagine these people of the world, busy in thought, turning their eyes toward the countless spheres that shine above us, and making them reflect the only images their minds contain. The man who lives but in the breath of princes, has nothing in his sight but stars for courtiers' breasts. The envious man beholds his neighbours' honours even in the sky; to the money-hoarder, and the mass of worldly folk, the whole great universe above glitters with sterling coin—fresh from the mint—stamped with the sovereign's head—coming always between them and heaven, turn where they may. So do the shadows of our own desires stand between us and our better angels, and thus their brightness is eclipsed.

Everything was fresh and gay, as though the world were but that morning made, when Mr. Chester rode at a tranquil pace along the Forest road. Though early in the season, it was warm and genial weather; the trees were budding into leaf, the hedges and the grass were green, the air was musical with songs of birds, and high above them all the lark poured out her richest melody. In shady spots, the morning dew sparkled on each young leaf and blade of grass; and where the sun was shining, some diamond drops yet glistened brightly, as in unwillingness to leave so fair a world, and have such brief existence. Even the light wind, whose rustling was as gentle to the ear as softly-falling water, had its hope and promise; and, leaving a pleasant fragrance in its track as it went fluttering by, whispered of its intercourse with Summer, and of his happy coming.

The solitary rider went glancing on among the trees, from sunlight into shade and back again, at the same even pace—looking about him, certainly, from time to time, but with no greater thought of the day or the scene through which he moved, than that he was fortunate (being choicely dressed) to have such favourable weather. He smiled very complacently at such times, but rather as if he were satisfied with himself than with anything else; and so went riding on, upon his chesnut cob, as pleasant to look upon as his own horse, and probably far less sensitive to the many cheerful influences by which he was surrounded.

In course of time, the Maypole's massive chimneys rose upon his view: but he quickened not his pace one jot, and with the same cool gravity rode up to the tavern porch. John Willet, who was toasting his red face before a great fire in the bar, and who, with surpassing foresight and quickness of apprehension, had been thinking, as he looked at the blue sky, that if that state of things lasted much longer, it might ultimately become necessary to leave off fires and throw the windows open, issued forth to hold his stirrup; calling lustily for Hugh.

"Oh, you're here, are you, sir?" said John, rather surprised by the quickness with which he appeared. "Take this here valuable animal into the stable, and have more than particular care of him if you want to keep your place. A mortal lazy fellow, sir; he needs a deal of looking after."

"But you have a son," returned Mr. Chester, giving his bridle to Hugh as he dismounted, and acknowledging his salute by a careless motion of his hand towards his hat. "Why don't you make *him* useful?"

"Why, the truth is, sir," replied John with great importance, "that my son—what, you're a listening are you, villain?"

"Who's listening?" returned Hugh angrily. "A treat, indeed, to hear *you* speak! Would you have me take him in till he's cool?"

"Walk him up and down further off then, sir," cried old John, "and when you see me and a noble gentleman entertaining ourselves with talk, keep your distance. If you don't know your distance, sir," added Mr. Willet, after an enormously long pause, during which he fixed his great dull eyes on Hugh, and waited with exemplary patience for any little property in the way of ideas that might be coming to him, "we'll find a way to teach you, pretty soon."

Hugh shrugged his shoulders scornfully, and in his reckless swaggering way, crossed to the other side of the little green, and there, with the bridle slung loosely over his shoulder, led the horse to and fro, glancing at his master every now and then from under his bushy eyebrows, with as sinister an aspect as one would desire to see.

Mr. Chester, who, without appearing to do so, had eyed him attentively during this brief dispute, stepped into the porch, and turning abruptly to Mr. Willet, said,

"You keep strange servants, John."

"Strange enough to look at sir, certainly," answered the host; "but out of doors; for horses, dogs, and the like of that; there an't a better man in England than is that Maypole Hugh yonder. He an't fit for indoors," added Mr. Willet, with the confidential air of a man who felt his own superior nature, "*I* do that; but if that chap had only a little imagination, sir—"

"He's an active fellow now, I dare swear," said Mr. Chester, in a musing tone, which seemed to suggest that he would have said the same had there been nobody to hear him.

"Active, sir!" retorted John, with quite an expression in his face; "that chap! Hallo, there! You, sir! Bring that horse here, and go and hang my wig on the weathercock, to show this gentleman whether you're one of the lively sort or not."

Hugh made no answer, but throwing the bridle to his master, and snatching his wig from his head, in a manner so unceremonious and hasty that the action discomposed Mr. Willet not a little, though performed at his own special desire, climbed nimbly to the very summit of the maypole before the house, and hanging the wig upon the weathercock, sent it twirling round like a roasting jack. Having achieved this performance, he cast it on the ground, and sliding down the pole with inconceivable rapidity, alighted on his feet almost as soon as it had touched the earth.

"There, sir," said John, relapsing into his usual stolid state, "you won't see that at many houses, besides the Maypole, where there's good accommodation for man and beast—nor that neither, though that with him is nothing."

This last remark bore reference to his vaulting on horseback, as upon Mr. Chester's first visit, and quickly disappearing by the stable gate.

"That with him is nothing," repeated Mr. Willet, brushing his wig with his wrist, and inwardly resolving to distribute a small charge for dust and damage to that article of dress, through the various items of his guest's bill; "he'll get out of a'most any winder in the house. There never was such a chap for flinging himself about and never hurting his bones. It's my opinion, sir, that it's pretty nearly all owing to his not having any imagination; and that if imagination could be (which it can't) knocked into him, he'd never be able to do it any more. But we was a talking, sir, about my son."

"True, Willet, true," said his visitor, turning again towards the landlord with his accustomed serenity of face. "My good friend, what about him?"

It has been reported that Mr. Willet, previously to making answer, winked. But as he never was known to be guilty of such lightness of conduct either before or afterwards, this may be looked upon as a malicious invention of his enemies—founded, perhaps, upon the undisputed circumstance of his taking his guest by the third breast button of his coat, counting downwards from the chin, and pouring his reply into his ear:

"Sir," whispered John, with dignity, "I know my duty. We want no love-making here, sir, unbeknown to parents. I respect a certain young gentleman, taking him in the light of a young gentleman; I respect a certain young lady, taking her in the light of a young lady; but of the two as a couple, I have no knowledge, sir, none whatever. My son, sir, is upon his patrole."

"I thought I saw him looking through the corner window but this moment," said Mr. Chester, who naturally thought that being on patrole, implied walking about somewhere.

"No doubt you did, sir," returned John. "He is upon his patrole of honour, sir, not to leave the premises. Me and some friends of mine that use the Maypole of an evening, sir, considered what was best to be done with him, to prevent his doing anything unpleasant in opposing your desires; and we've put him on his patrole. And what's more, sir, he won't be off his patrole for a pretty long time to come, I can tell you that."

When he had communicated this bright idea, which had had its origin in the perusal by the village cronies of a newspaper, containing, among other matters, an account of how some officer pending the sentence of some court-martial had been enlarged on parole, Mr. Willet drew back from his guest's ear, and without any visible alteration of feature, chuckled thrice audibly. This nearest approach to a laugh in which he ever indulged (and that but seldom and only on extreme occasions), never even curled his lip or effected the smallest change in—no, not so much as a slight wagging of—his great, fat, double chin, which at these times, as at all others, remained a perfect desert in the broad map of his face; one changeless, dull, tremendous blank.

Lest it should be matter of surprise to any, that Mr. Willet adopted this bold course in opposition to one whom he had often entertained, and who had always paid his way at the Maypole gallantly, it may be remarked that it was his very penetration and sagacity in this respect, which occasioned him to indulge in those unusual demonstrations of jocularity, just now recorded. For Mr. Willet, after carefully balancing father and son in his mental scales, had arrived at the distinct conclusion that the old gentleman was a better sort of a customer than the young one. Throwing his landlord into the same scale, which was already turned by this consideration, and heaping upon him, again, his strong desires to run counter to the unfortunate Joe, and his opposition as a general principle to all matters of love and matrimony, it went down to the very ground straightway, and sent the light cause of the younger gentleman flying upwards to the ceiling. Mr. Chester was not the kind of man to be by any means dim-sighted to Mr. Willet's motives, but he thanked him as graciously as if he had been one of the most disinterested martyrs that ever shone on earth; and leaving him, with many complimentary reliances on his great taste and judgment, to prepare whatever dinner he might deem most fitting the occasion, bent his steps towards the Warren.

Dressed with more than his usual elegance; assuming a gracefulness of manner, which, though it was the result of long study, sat easily upon him and became him well; composing his features into their most serene and prepossessing expression; and setting in short that guard upon himself, at every point, which denoted that he attached no slight importance to the impression he was about to make; he entered the bounds of Miss Haredale's usual walk. He had not gone far, or looked about him long, when he descried coming towards him, a female figure. A glimpse of the form and dress as she crossed a little wooden bridge which lay between them, satisfied him that he had found her whom he desired to see. He threw himself in her way, and a very few paces brought them close together.

He raised his hat from his head, and yielding the path, suffered her to pass him. Then, as if the idea had but that moment occurred to him, he turned hastily back and said in an agitated voice:

"I beg pardon—do I address Miss Haredale?"

She stopped in some confusion at being so unexpectedly accosted by a stranger; and answered "Yes."

"Something told me," he said, *looking* a compliment to her beauty, "that it could be no other. Miss Haredale, I bear a name which is not unknown to you—which it is a pride, and yet a pain to me to know, sounds pleasantly in your ears. I am a man advanced in life, as you see. I am the father of him whom you honour and distinguish above all other men. May I for weighty reasons which fill me with distress, beg but a minute's conversation with you here?"

Who that was inexperienced in deceit, and had a frank and youthful heart, could doubt the speaker's truth—could doubt it too, when the voice that spoke, was like the faint echo of one she knew so well, and so much loved to hear? She inclined her head, and stopping, cast her eyes upon the ground.

"A little more apart—among these trees. It is an old man's hand, Miss Haredale; an honest one, believe me."

She put hers in it as he said these words, and suffered him to lead her to a neighbouring seat.

"You alarm me, sir," she said in a low voice. "You are not the bearer of any ill news, I hope?"

"Of none that you anticipate," he answered, sitting down beside her. "Edward is well—quite well. It is of him I wish to speak, certainly; but I have no misfortune to communicate."

She bowed her head again, and made as though she would have begged him to proceed; but said nothing.

"I am sensible that I speak to you at a disadvantage, dear Miss Haredale. Believe me that I am not so forgetful of the feelings of my younger days as not to know that you are little disposed to view me with favour. You have heard me described as cold-hearted, calculating, selfish—"

"I have never, sir"—she interposed with an altered manner and a firmer voice; "I have never heard you spoken of in harsh or disrespectful terms. You do a great wrong to Edward's nature if you believe him capable of any mean or base proceeding."

"Pardon me, my sweet young lady, but your uncle—"

"Nor is it my uncle's nature either," she replied, with a heightened colour in her cheek. "It is not his nature to stab in the dark, nor is it mine to love such deeds."

She rose as she spoke, and would have left him; but he detained her with a gentle hand, and besought her in such persuasive accents to hear him but another minute, that she was easily prevailed upon to comply, and so sat down again.

"And it is," said Mr. Chester, looking upward, and apostrophising the air;* "it is this frank, ingenuous, noble nature, Ned, that you can wound so lightly. Shame—shame upon you, boy!"

She turned towards him quickly, and with a scornful look and flashing eyes. There were tears in Mr. Chester's, but he dashed them hurriedly away, as though unwilling that his weakness should be known, and regarded her with mingled admiration and compassion.

"I never until now," he said, "believed, that the frivolous actions of a young man could move me like these of my own son. I never knew till now, the worth of a woman's heart, which boys so lightly win, and lightly fling away. Trust me, dear young lady, that I never until now did know your worth; and though an abhorrence of deceit and falsehood has impelled me to seek you out, and would have done so had you been the poorest and least gifted of your sex, I should have lacked the fortitude to sustain this interview could I have pictured you to my imagination as you really are."

Oh! If Mrs. Varden could have seen the virtuous gentleman as he said these words, with indignation sparkling from his eyes—if she could have heard his broken, quavering voice—if she could have beheld him as he stood bare-headed in the sunlight, and with unwonted energy poured forth his eloquence!

With a haughty face, but pale and trembling too, Emma regarded him in silence. She neither spoke nor moved, but gazed upon him as though she would look into his heart.

"I throw off," said Mr. Chester, "the restraint which natural affection would impose on some men, and reject all bonds but those of truth and duty. Miss Haredale, you are deceived; you are deceived by your unworthy lover, and my unworthy son."

Still she looked at him steadily, and still said not one word.

"I have ever opposed his professions of love for you; you will do me the justice, dear Miss Haredale, to remember that. Your uncle and myself were enemies in early life, and if I had sought retaliation, I might have found it here. But as we grow older, we grow wiser—better, I would fain hope—and from the first, I have opposed him in this attempt. I foresaw the end, and would have spared you, if I could."

"Speak plainly, sir," she faultered. "You deceive me, or are deceived yourself. I do not believe you—I cannot—I should not."

"First," said Mr. Chester, soothingly, "for there may be in your mind some latent angry feeling to which I would not appeal, pray take this letter. It reached my hands by chance, and by mistake, and should have accounted to you (as I am told) for my son's not answering some other note of yours. God forbid, Miss Haredale," said the good gentleman, with great emotion, "that there should be in your gentle breast one causeless ground of quarrel with him. You should know, and you will see, that he was in no fault here."

There appeared something so very candid, so scrupulously honourable, so very truthful and just in this course—something which rendered the upright person who resorted to it, so worthy of belief—that Emma's heart, for the first time, sunk within her. She turned away, and burst into tears.

"I would," said Mr. Chester, leaning over her, and speaking in mild and quite venerable accents; "I would, dear girl, it were my task to banish, not increase, those tokens of your grief. My son, my erring son,—I will not call him deliberately criminal in this, for men so young, who have been inconstant twice or thrice before, act without reflection, almost without a knowledge of the wrong they do,—will break his plighted faith to you; has broken it even now. Shall I stop here, and having given you this warning, leave it to be fulfilled; or shall I go on?"

"You will go on, sir," she answered, "and speak more plainly yet, in justice both to him and me."

"My dear girl," said Mr. Chester, bending over her more affectionately still; "whom I would call my daughter, but the fates forbid, Edward seeks to break with you upon a false and most unwarrantable pretence. I have it on his own showing; in his own hand. Forgive me, if I have had a watch upon his conduct; I am his father; I had a regard for your peace and his honour, and no better resource was left me. There lies on his desk at this moment, ready for transmission to you, a letter, in which he tells you that our poverty—our poverty; his and mine, Miss Haredale—forbids him to pursue his claim upon your hand; in which he offers, voluntarily proposes, to free you from your pledge; and talks magnanimously (men do so, very commonly, in such cases) of being in time more worthy your regard—and so forth. A letter, to be plain, in which he not only jilts you—pardon the word; I would summon to your aid your pride and dignity—not only jilts you, I fear, in favour of the object whose slighting treatment first inspired his brief passion for yourself and gave it birth in wounded vanity, but affects to make a merit and a virtue of the act."

She glanced proudly at him once more, as by an involuntary impulse, and with a swelling breast rejoined, "If what you say be true, he takes much needless trouble, sir, to compass his design. He is very tender of my peace of mind. I quite thank him."

"The truth of what I tell you, dear young lady," he replied, "you will test by the receipt or non-receipt of the letter of which I speak.—Haredale, my dear fellow, I am delighted to see you, although we meet under singular circumstances, and upon a melancholy occasion. I hope you are very well."

At these words the young lady raised her eyes, which were filled with tears; and seeing that her uncle indeed stood before them, and being quite unequal to the trial of hearing or of speaking one word more, hurriedly withdrew, and left them. They stood looking at each other, and at her retreating figure, and for a long time neither of them spoke.

"What does this mean? Explain it," said Mr. Haredale at length. "Why are you here, and why with her?"

"My dear friend," rejoined the other, resuming his accustomed manner with infinite readiness, and throwing himself upon the bench with a weary air, "you told me not very long ago, at that delightful old tavern of which you are the esteemed proprietor (and a most charming establishment it is for persons of rural pursuits and in robust health, who are not liable to take cold), that I had the head and heart of an evil spirit in all matters of deception. I thought at the time; I really did think; you flattered me. But now I begin to wonder at your discernment, and vanity apart, do honestly believe you spoke the truth. Did you ever counterfeit extreme ingenuousness and honest indignation? My dear fellow, you have no conception if you never did, how faint the effort makes one."

Mr. Haredale surveyed him with a look of cold contempt. "You may evade an explanation, I know," he said, folding his arms. "But I must have it. I can wait."

"Not at all. Not at all, my good fellow. You shall not wait a moment," returned his friend, as he lazily crossed his legs. "The simplest thing in the world. It lies in a nutshell. Ned has written her a letter—a boyish, honest, sentimental composition, which remains as yet in his desk, because he hasn't had the heart to send it. I have taken a liberty, for which my parental affection and anxiety are a sufficient excuse, and possessed myself of the contents. I have described them to your niece (a most enchanting person, Haredale; quite an angelic creature), with a little colouring and description adapted to our purpose. It's done. You may be quite easy. It's all over. Deprived of their adherents and mediators; her pride and jealousy roused to the utmost; with nobody to undeceive her, and you to confirm me; you will find that their intercourse will close with her answer. If she receives Ned's letter by to-morrow noon, you may date their parting from to-morrow night. No thanks I beg; you owe me none. I have acted for myself; and if I have forwarded our compact with all the ardour even you could have desired, I have done so selfishly, indeed."

"I curse the compact, as you call it, with my whole heart and soul," returned the other. "It was made in an evil hour. I have bound myself to a lie; I have leagued myself with you; and though I did so with a righteous motive, and though it cost me such an effort as haply few men know, I hate and despise myself for the deed."

"You are very warm," said Mr. Chester with a languid smile.

"I *am* warm. I am maddened by your coldness. 'Death, Chester, if your blood ran warmer in your veins, and there were no restraints upon me, such as those that hold and drag me back—well; it is done; you tell me so, and on such a point I may believe you. When I am most remorseful for this treachery, I will think of you and your marriage, and try to justify myself in such remembrances, for having torn asunder Emma and your son, at any cost. Our bond is cancelled now, and we may part."

Mr. Chester kissed his hand gracefully; and with the same tranquil face he had preserved throughout—even when he had seen his companion so tortured and transported by his passion that his whole frame was shaken—lay in his lounging posture on the seat and watched him as he walked away.

"My scape-goat and my drudge at school," he said, raising his head to look after him; "my friend of later days, who could not keep his mistress when he had won her, and threw me in her way to carry off the prize; I triumph in the present and the past. Bark on, ill-favoured ill-conditioned cur; fortune has ever been with me—I like to hear you."

The spot where they had met, was in an avenue of trees. Mr. Haredale not passing out on either hand, had walked straight on. He chanced to turn his head when at some considerable distance, and seeing that his late companion had by that time risen and was looking after him, stood still as though he half expected him to follow, and waited for his coming up.

"It *may* come to that one day, but not yet," said Mr. Chester, waving his hand, as though they were the best of friends, and turning away. "Not yet, Haredale. Life is pleasant enough to me; dull and full of heaviness to you. No. To cross swords with such a man—to indulge his humour unless upon extremity—would be weak indeed."

For all that, he drew his sword as he walked along, and in an absent humour ran his eye from hilt to point full twenty times. But thoughtfulness begets wrinkles; remembering this, he soon put it up, smoothed his contracted brow, hummed a gay tune with greater gaiety of manner, and was his unruffled self again.

CHAPTER THE THIRTIETH.

A HOMELY proverb recognises the existence of a troublesome class of persons who, having an inch conceded them, will take an ell.* Not to quote the illustrious examples of those heroic scourges of mankind, whose amiable path in life has been from birth to death through blood, and fire, and ruin, and who would seem to have existed for no better purpose than to teach mankind that as the absence of pain is pleasure, so the earth, purged of their presence, may be deemed a blessed place—not to quote such mighty instances, it will be sufficient to refer to old John Willet.

Old John having long encroached a good standard inch, full measure, on the liberty of Joe, and having snipped off a Flemish ell* in the matter of the parole, grew so despotic and so great, that his thirst for conquest knew no bounds. The more young Joe submitted, the more absolute old John became. The ell soon faded into nothing. Yards, furlongs, miles,* arose; and on went old John in the pleasantest manner possible, trimming off an exuberance in this place, shearing away some liberty of speech or action in that, and conducting himself in his small way with as much high mightiness and majesty, as the most glorious tyrant that ever had his statue reared in the public ways, of ancient or of modern times.

As great men are urged on to the abuse of power (when they need urging, which is not often), by their flatterers and dependents, so old John was impelled to these exercises of authority by the applause and admiration of his Maypole cronies, who, in the intervals of their nightly pipes and pots, would shake their heads and say that Mr. Willet was a father of the good old English sort; that there were no new-fangled notions or modern ways in him; that he put them in mind of what their fathers were when they were boys; that there was no mistake about him; that it would be well for the country if there were more like him, and more was the pity that there were not; with many other original remarks of that nature. Then they would condescendingly give Joe to understand that it was all for his good, and he would be thankful for it one day; and in particular, Mr. Cobb would acquaint him, that when he was his age, his father thought no more of giving him a parental kick, or a box on the ears, or a cuff on the head, or some little admonition of that sort, than he did of any other ordinary duty of life; and he would further remark, with looks of great significance, that but for this judicious bringing up, he might have never been the man he was at that present speaking: which was probable enough, as he was, beyond all question, the dullest dog of the party. In short, between old John and old John's friends, there never was an unfortunate young fellow so bullied, badgered, worried, fretted, and brow-beaten; so constantly beset, or made so tired of his life, as poor Joe Willet.

This had come to be the recognised and established state of things; but as John was very anxious to flourish his supremacy before the eyes of Mr. Chester, he did that day exceed himself, and did so goad and chafe his son and heir, that but for Joe's having made a solemn vow to keep his hands in his pockets when they were not otherwise engaged, it is impossible to say what he might have done with them. But the longest day has an end, and at length Mr. Chester came down stairs to mount his horse, which was ready at the door.

As old John was not in the way at the moment, Joe, who was sitting in the bar ruminating on his dismal fate and the manifold perfections of Dolly Varden, ran out to hold the guest's stirrup and assist him to mount. Mr. Chester was scarcely in the saddle, and Joe was in the very act of making him a graceful bow, when old John came diving out of the porch, and collared him.

"None of that, sir," said John, "none of that, sir. No breaking of patroles. How dare you come out of the door, sir, without leave? You're trying to get away, sir, are you, and to make a traitor of yourself again? What do you mean, sir?"

"Let me go, father," said Joe, imploringly, as he marked the smile upon their visitor's face, and observed the pleasure his disgrace afforded him. "This is too bad. Who wants to get away?"

"Who wants to get away!" cried John, shaking him. "Why you do, sir, you do. You're the boy, sir," added John, collaring with one hand, and aiding the effect of a farewell bow to the visitor with the other, "that wants to sneak into houses, and stir up differences between noble gentlemen and their sons, are you, eh? Hold your tongue, sir."

Joe made no effort to reply. It was the crowning circumstance of his degradation. He extricated himself from his father's grasp, darted an angry look at the departing guest, and returned into the house.

"But for her," thought Joe, as he threw his arms upon a table in the common room, and laid his head upon them, "but for Dolly, who I couldn't bear should think me the rascal they would make me out to be if I ran away, this house and I should part to-night."

It being evening by this time, Solomon Daisy, Tom Cobb, and Long Parkes, were all in the common room too, and had from the window been witnesses of what had just occurred. Mr. Willet joining them soon afterwards, received the compliments of the company with great composure, and lighting his pipe, sat down among them.

"We'll see, gentlemen," said John, after a long pause, "who's the master of this house, and who isn't. We'll see whether boys are to govern men, or men are to govern boys."

"And quite right too," assented Solomon Daisy with some approving nods; "quite right, Johnny. Very good, Johnny. Well said, Mr. Willet. Brayvo, sir."

John slowly brought his eyes to bear upon him, looked at him for a long time, and finally made answer, to the unspeakable consternation of his hearers, "When I want encouragement from you, sir, I'll ask you for it. You let me alone, sir. I can get on without you, I hope. Don't you tackle me, sir, if you please."

"Don't take it ill, Johnny; I didn't mean any harm," pleaded the little man.

"Very good, sir," said John, more than usually obstinate after his late success. "Never mind, sir. I can stand pretty firm of myself, sir, I believe, without being shored up by you." And having given utterance to this retort, Mr. Willet fixed his eyes upon the boiler, and fell into a kind of tobacco-trance.

The spirits of the company being somewhat damped by this embarrassing line of conduct on the part of their host, nothing more was said for a long time; but at length Mr. Cobb took upon himself to remark, as he rose to knock the ashes out of his pipe, that he hoped Joe would thenceforth learn to obey his father in all things; that he had found, that day, he was not one of the sort of men who were to be trifled with; and that he would recommend him, poetically speaking, to mind his eye for the future.

"I'd recommend you, in return," said Joe, looking up with a flushed face, "not to talk to me."

"Hold your tongue, sir," cried Mr. Willet, suddenly rousing himself, and turning round.

"I won't, father," cried Joe, smiting the table with his fist, so that the jugs and glasses rung again; "these things are hard enough to bear from you; from anybody else I never will endure them any more. Therefore I say, Mr. Cobb, don't talk to me."

"Why, who are you," said Mr. Cobb, sneeringly, "that you're not to be talked to, eh, Joe?"

To which Joe returned no answer, but with a very ominous shake of the head, resumed his old position, which he would have peacefully preserved until the house shut up at night, but that Mr. Cobb, stimulated by the wonder of the company at the young man's presumption, retorted with sundry taunts, which proved too much for flesh and blood to bear. Crowding into one moment the vexation and the wrath of years, Joe started up, overturned the table, fell upon his long enemy, pummelled him with all his might and main, and finished by driving him with surprising swiftness against a heap of spittoons in one corner; plunging into which, head foremost, with a tremendous crash, he lay at full length among the ruins, stunned and motionless. Then, without waiting to receive the compliments of the bystanders on the victory he had won, he retreated to his own bedchamber, and considering himself in a state of siege, piled all the portable furniture against the door by way of barricade.

"I have done it now," said Joe, as he sat down upon his bedstead and wiped his heated face. "I knew it would come at last. The Maypole and I must part company. I'm a roving vagabond—she hates me for evermore—it's all over!"

CHAPTER THE THIRTY-FIRST.

ONDERING on his unhappy lot, Joe sat and listened for a long time, expecting every moment to hear their creaking footsteps on the stairs, or to be greeted by his worthy father with a summons to capitulate unconditionally, and deliver himself up straightway. But neither voice nor footstep came; and though some distant echoes, as of closing doors and people hurrying in and out of rooms, resounding from time to time through the great passages, and penetrating to his remote seclusion, gave note of unusual commotion down stairs, no nearer sound disturbed his place of retreat, which seemed the quieter for these far-off noises, and was as dull and full of gloom as any hermit's cell.

It came on darker and darker. The old-fashioned furniture of the chamber, which was a kind of hospital for all the invalided moveables in the house, grew indistinct and shadowy in its many shapes; chairs and tables, which by day were as honest cripples as need be, assumed a doubtful and mysterious character; and one old leprous screen of faded India leather and gold binding, which had kept out many a cold breath of air in days of yore and shut in many a jolly face, frowned on him with a spectral aspect, and stood at full height in its allotted corner, like some gaunt ghost who waited to be questioned. A portrait opposite the window—a queer, old grey-eyed general, in an oval frame—seemed to wink and dose as the light decayed, and at length, when the last faint glimmering speck of day went out, to shut its eyes in good earnest, and fall sound asleep. There was such a hush and mystery about everything, that Joe could not help following its example; and so went off into a slumber likewise, and dreamed of Dolly, till the clock of Chigwell church struck two.

Still nobody came. The distant noises in the house had ceased, and out of doors all was quiet too; save for the occasional barking of some deep-mouthed dog, and the shaking of the branches by the night wind. He gazed mournfully out of window at each well-known object as it lay sleeping in the dim light of the moon; and creeping back to his former seat, thought about the late uproar, until, with long thinking of, it seemed to have occurred a month ago. Thus, between dosing, and thinking, and walking to the window and look- ing out, the night wore away; the grim old screen, and the kindred chairs and tables, began slowly to reveal themselves in their accus- tomed forms; the grey-eyed general seemed to wink and yawn and rouse himself; and at last he was broad awake again, and very uncomfortable and cold and haggard he looked, in the dull grey light of morning.

The sun had begun to peep above the forest trees, and already flung across the curling mist bright bars of gold, when Joe dropped from his window on the ground below, a little bundle and his trusty stick, and prepared to descend himself.

It was not a very difficult task; for there were so many projections and gable ends in the way, that they formed a series of clumsy steps, with no greater obstacle than a jump of some few feet at last. Joe, with his stick and bundle on his shoulder, quickly stood on the firm earth, and looked up at the old Maypole, it might be for the last time.

He didn't apostrophise it, for he was no great scholar. He didn't curse it, for he had little ill-will to give to anything on earth. He felt more affectionate and kind to it than ever he had done in all his life before, so said with all his heart, "God bless you!" as a parting wish, and turned away.

He walked along at a brisk pace, big with great thoughts of going for a soldier and dying in some foreign country where it was very hot and sandy, and leaving God knows what unheard-of wealth in prize-money to Dolly, who would be very much affected when she came to know of it; and full of such youthful visions, which were sometimes sanguine and sometimes melancholy, but always had her for their main point and centre, pushed on vigorously until the noise of London sounded in his ears, and the Black Lion hove in sight.

It was only eight o'clock then, and very much astonished the Black Lion was, to see him come walking in with dust upon his feet at that early hour, with no grey mare to bear him company. But as he ordered breakfast to be got ready with all speed, and on its being set before him gave indisputable tokens of a hearty appetite, the Lion received him, as usual, with a hospitable welcome; and treated him with those marks of distinction, which, as a regular customer, and one within the freemasonry of the trade, he had a right to claim.

This Lion or landlord,—for he was called both man and beast, by reason of his having instructed the artist who painted his sign, to convey into the features of the lordly brute whose effigy it bore, as near a counterpart of his own face as his skill could compass and devise,—was a gentleman almost as quick of apprehension, and of almost as subtle a wit, as the mighty John himself. But the difference between them lay in this; that whereas Mr. Willet's extreme sagacity and acuteness were the efforts of unassisted nature, the Lion stood indebted, in no small amount, to beer; of which he swigged such copious draughts, that most of his faculties were utterly drowned and washed away, except the one great faculty of sleep, which he retained in surprising perfection. The creaking Lion over the house-door was, therefore, to say the truth, rather a drowsy, tame, and feeble lion; and as these social representatives of a savage class are usually of a conventional character (being depicted, for the most part, in impossible attitudes and of unearthly colours), he was fre-quently supposed by the more ignorant and uninformed among the neighbours, to be the veritable portrait of the host as he appeared on the occasion of some great funeral ceremony or public mourning.

"What noisy fellow is that in the next room?" said Joe, when he had disposed of his breakfast, and had washed and brushed himself.

"A recruiting serjeant," replied the Lion.

Joe started involuntarily. Here was the very thing he had been dreaming of, all the way along.

"And I wish," said the Lion, "he was anywhere else but here. The party make noise enough, but they don't call for much. There's great cry there, Mr. Willet, but very little wool.* Your father wouldn't like 'em, *I* know."

Perhaps not much under any circumstances. Perhaps if he could have known what was passing at that moment in Joe's mind, he would have liked them still less.

"Is he recruiting for a—for a fine regiment?" said Joe, glancing at a little round mirror that hung in the bar.

"I believe he is," replied the host. "It's much the same thing, whatever regiment he's recruiting for. I'm told there an't a deal of difference between a fine man and another one, when they're shot through and through."

"They're not all shot," said Joe.

"No," the Lion answered, "not all. Those that are—supposing it's done easy—are the best off in my opinion."

"Ah!" retorted Joe, "but you don't care for glory."

"For what?" said the Lion.

"Glory."

"No," returned the Lion, with supreme indifference. "I don't. You're right in that, Mr. Willet. When Glory comes here, and calls for anything to drink and changes a guinea to pay for it, I'll give it him for nothing. It's my belief, sir, that the Glory's arms wouldn't do a very strong business."

These remarks were not at all comforting. Joe walked out, stopped at the door of the next room, and listened. The serjeant was describing a military life. It was all drinking, he said, except that there were frequent intervals of eating and love-making. A battle was the finest thing in the world—when your side won it—and Englishmen always did that. "Supposing you should be killed, sir?" said a timid voice in one corner. "Well, sir, supposing you should be," said the serjeant, "what then? Your country loves you, sir; his Majesty King George the Third loves you; your memory is honoured, revered, respected; everybody's fond of you, and grateful to you; your name's wrote down at full length in a book in the War-office. Damme, gentlemen, we must all die some time, or another, eh?"

The voice coughed, and said no more.

Joe walked into the room. A group of half-a-dozen fellows had gathered together in the tap-room, and were listening with greedy ears. One of them, a carter in a smockfrock, seemed wavering and disposed to enlist. The rest, who were by no means disposed, strongly urged him to do so (according to the custom of mankind), backed the serjeant's arguments, and grinned among themselves. "I say nothing, boys," said the serjeant, who sat a little apart, drinking his liquor. "For lads of spirit"—here he cast an eye on Joe—"this is the time. I don't want to inveigle you. The king's not come to that, I hope. Brisk young blood is what we want; not milk and water. We won't take five men out of six. We want top-sawyers, we do. I'm not a-going to tell tales out of school, but, damme, if every gentleman's son that carries arms in our corps, through being under a cloud and having little differences with his relations, was counted up"—here his eye fell on Joe again, and so good-naturedly, that Joe beckoned him out. He came directly.

"You're a gentleman, by G—!" was his first remark, as he slapped him on the back. "You're a gentleman in disguise. So am I. Let's swear a friendship."

Joe didn't exactly do that, but he shook hands with him, and thanked him for his good opinion.

"You want to serve," said his new friend. "You shall. You were made for it. You're one of us by nature. What'll you take to drink?"

"Nothing just now," replied Joe, smiling faintly. "I haven't quite made up my mind."

"A mettlesome fellow like you, and not made up his mind!" cried the serjeant. "Here—let me give the bell a pull, and you'll make up your mind in half a minute, I know."

"You're right so far"—answered Joe, "for if you pull the bell here, where I'm known, there'll be an end of my soldiering inclinations in no time. Look in my face. You see me, do you?"

"I do," replied the serjeant with an oath, "and a finer young fellow or one better qualified to serve his king and country, I never set my—" he used an adjective in this place—"eyes on."

"Thank you" said Joe, "I didn't ask you for want of a compliment, but thank you all the same. Do I look like a sneaking fellow or a liar?"

The serjeant rejoined with many choice asseverations that he didn't; and that if his (the serjeant's) own father were to say he did, he would run the old gentleman through the body cheerfully, and consider it a meritorious action.

Joe expressed his obligations, and continued, "You can trust me then, and credit what I say. I believe I shall enlist into your regiment to-night. The reason I don't do so now is, because I don't want until to-night, to do what I can't recal. Where shall I find you, this evening?"

His friend replied with some unwillingness, and after much ineffectual entreaty having for its object the immediate settlement of the business, that his quarters would be at the Crooked Billet in Tower-street; where he would be found waking until midnight, and sleeping until breakfast-time to-morrow.

"And if I do come—which it's a million to one, I shall—when will you take me out of London?" demanded Joe.

"To-morrow morning, at half after eight o' clock" replied the serjeant. "You'll go abroad—a country where it's all sunshine and plunder—the finest climate in the world."

"To go abroad," said Joe, shaking hands with him, "is the very thing I want. You may expect me."

"You're the kind of lad for us," cried the serjeant, holding Joe's hand in his, in the excess of his admiration. "You're the boy to push your fortune. I don't say it because I bear you any envy, or would take away from the credit of the rise you'll make, but if I had been bred and taught like you, I'd have been a colonel by this time."

"Tush man!" said Joe, "I'm not so young as that. Needs must when the devil drives; and the devil that drives me is an empty pocket and an unhappy home. For the present, good-bye."

"For king and country!" cried the serjeant, flourishing his cap.

"For bread and meat!" cried Joe, snapping his fingers. And so they parted.

He had very little money in his pocket; so little indeed, that after paying for his breakfast (which he was too honest and perhaps too proud to score up to his father's charge) he had but a penny left. He had courage, notwithstanding, to resist all the affectionate importunities of the serjeant, who waylaid him at the door with many protestations of eternal friendship, and did in particular request that he would do him the favour to accept of only one shilling as a temporary accommodation. Rejecting his offers both of cash and credit, Joe walked away with stick and bundle as before, bent upon getting through the day as he best could, and going down to the locksmith's in the dusk of the evening; for it should go hard, he had resolved, but he would have a parting word with charming Dolly Varden.

He went out by Islington and so on to Highgate, and sat on many stones and gates, but there were no voices in the bells to bid him turn. Since the time of noble Whittington,* fair flower of merchants, bells have come to have less sympathy with humankind. They only ring for money and on state occasions. Wanderers have increased in number; ships leave the Thames for distant regions, carrying from stem to stern no other cargo; the bells are silent; they ring out no entreaties or regrets; they are used to it and have grown worldly.

Joe bought a roll, and reduced his purse to the condition (with a difference) of that celebrated purse of Fortunatus,* which, whatever were its favoured owner's necessities, had one unvarying amount in it. In these real times, when all the Fairies are dead and buried, there are still a great many purses which possess that quality. The sum-total they contain is expressed in arithmetic by a circle, and whether it be added to or multiplied by its own amount, the result of the problem is more easily stated than any known in figures.

Evening drew on at last. With the desolate and solitary feeling of one who had no home or shelter, and was alone utterly in the world for the first time, he bent his steps towards the locksmith's house. He had delayed till now, knowing that Mrs. Varden sometimes went out alone, or with Miggs for her sole attendant, to lectures in the evening; and devoutly hoping that this might be one of her nights of moral culture.

He had walked up and down before the house, on the opposite side of the way, two or three times, when as he returned to it again, he caught a glimpse of a fluttering skirt at the door. It was Dolly's—to whom else could it belong? no dress but hers had such a flow as that. He plucked up his spirits, and followed it into the workshop of the Golden Key.

His darkening the door caused her to look round. Oh that face! "If it hadn't been for that," thought Joe, "I should never have walked into poor Tom Cobb. She's twenty times handsomer than ever. She might marry a Lord!"

He didn't say this. He only thought it—perhaps looked it also. Dolly was glad to see him, and was *so* sorry her father and mother were away from home. Joe begged she wouldn't mention it on any account.

Dolly hesitated to lead the way into the parlour, for there it was nearly dark; at the same time she hesitated to stand talking in the workshop, which was yet light and open to the street. They had got by some means, too, before the little forge; and Joe having her hand in his (which he had no right to have, for Dolly only gave it him to shake), it was so like standing before some homely altar being married, that it was the most embarrassing state of things in the world.

"I have come," said Joe, "to say good-bye—to say good-bye for I don't know how many years; perhaps for ever. I am going abroad."

Now this was exactly what he should not have said. Here he was, talking like a gentleman at large who was free to come and go and roam about the world at his pleasure, when that gallant coachmaker had vowed but the night before that Miss Varden held him bound in adamantine chains; and had positively stated in so many words that she was killing him by inches, and that in a fortnight more or thereabouts he expected to make a decent end and leave the business to his mother.

Dolly released her hand and said "Indeed!" She remarked in the same breath that it was a fine night, and in short, betrayed no more emotion than the forge itself.

"I couldn't go" said Joe, "without coming to see you. I hadn't the heart to."

Dolly was more sorry than she could tell, that he should have taken so much trouble. It was such a long way, and he must have such a deal to do. And how *was* Mr. Willet—that dear old gentleman—

"Is this all you say!" cried Joe.

All! Good gracious, what did the man expect! She was obliged to take her apron in her hand and run her eyes along the hem from corner to corner, to keep herself from laughing in his face;—not because his gaze confused her—not at all.

Joe had small experience in love affairs, and had no notion how different young ladies are at different times; he had expected to take Dolly up again at the very point where he had left her after that delicious evening ride, and was no more prepared for such an alteration than to see the sun and moon change places. He had buoyed himself up all day with an indistinct idea that she would certainly say

"Don't go," or "Don't leave us," or "Why do you go?" or "Why do you leave us?" or would give him some little encouragement of that sort; he had even entertained the possibility of her bursting into tears, of her throwing herself into his arms, of her falling down in a fainting-fit without previous word or sign; but any approach to such a line of conduct as this, had been so far from his thoughts that he could only look at her in silent wonder.

Dolly in the mean while, turned to the corners of her apron, and measured the sides, and smoothed out the wrinkles, and was as silent as he. At last after a long pause, Joe said good-bye. "Good-bye"—said Dolly—with as pleasant a smile as if he were going into the next street, and were coming back to supper; "good-bye."

"Come," said Joe, putting out both his hands, "Dolly, dear Dolly, don't let us part like this. I love you dearly, with all my heart and soul; with as much truth and earnestness as ever man loved woman in this world, I do believe. I am a poor fellow, as you know—poorer now than ever, for I have fled from home, not being able to bear it any longer, and must fight my own way without help. You are beautiful, admired, are loved by everybody, are well off and happy; and may you ever be so! Heaven forbid I should ever make you otherwise; but give me a word of comfort. Say something kind to me. I have no right to expect it of you, I know, but I ask it because I love you, and shall treasure the slightest word from you all through my life. Dolly, dearest, have you nothing to say to me?"

No. Nothing. Dolly was a coquette by nature, and a spoilt child. She had no notion of being carried by storm in this way. The coach-maker would have been dissolved in tears, and would have knelt down, and called himself names, and clasped his hands, and beat his breast, and tugged wildly at his cravat, and done all kinds of poetry. Joe had no business to be going abroad. He had no right to be able to do it. If he was in adamantine chains, he couldn't.

"I have said good-bye," said Dolly, "twice. Take your arm away directly, Mr. Joseph, or I'll call Miggs."

"I'll not reproach you," answered Joe, "it's my fault, no doubt. I have thought sometimes that you didn't quite despise me, but I was a fool to think so. Every one must, who has seen the life I have led—you most of all. God bless you!"

He was gone, actually gone. Dolly waited a little while, thinking he would return, peeped out at the door, looked up the street and down as well as the increasing darkness would allow, came in again, waited a little longer, went up stairs humming a tune, bolted herself in, laid her head down on her bed, and cried as if her heart would break. And yet such natures are made up of so many contradictions, that if Joe Willet had come back that night, next day, next week, next month, the odds are a hundred to one she would have treated him in the very same manner, and have wept for it afterwards with the very same distress.

She had no sooner left the workshop than there cautiously peered out from behind the chimney of the forge, a face which had already emerged from the same concealment twice or thrice, unseen, and which, after satisfying itself that it was now alone, was followed by a leg, a shoulder, and so on by degrees, until the form of Mr. Tappertit stood confessed, with a brown-paper cap stuck negligently on one side of its head, and its arms very much a-kimbo.

"Have my ears deceived me," said the 'Prentice, "or do I dream! am I to thank thee, Fortun', or to cus thee—which?"

He gravely descended from his elevation, took down his piece of looking-glass, planted it against the wall upon the usual bench, twisted his head round, and looked closely at his legs.

"If they're a dream," said Sim, "let sculptures have such wisions, and chisel 'em out when they wake. This is reality. Sleep has no such limbs as them. Tremble, Willet, and despair. She's mine! She's mine!"

With these triumphant expressions, he seized a hammer and dealt a heavy blow at a vice, which in his mind's eye represented the sconce or head of Joseph Willet. That done, he burst into a peal of laughter which startled Miss Miggs even in her distant kitchen, and dipping his head into a bowl of water, had recourse to a jack-towel inside the closet door, which served the double purpose of smothering his feelings and drying his face.

Joe, disconsolate and down-hearted, but full of courage too, on leaving the locksmith's house made the best of his way to the Crooked Billet, and there inquired for his friend the serjeant, who, expecting no man less, received him with open arms. In the course of five minutes after his arrival at that house of entertainment, he was enrolled among the gallant defenders of his native land; and within half an hour, was regaled with a steaming supper of boiled tripe and onions, prepared, as his friend assured him more than once, at the express command of his most Sacred Majesty the King. To this meal, which tasted very savoury after his long fasting, he did ample justice; and when he had followed it up, or down, with a variety of loyal and patriotic toasts, he was conducted to a straw mattress in a loft over the stable, and locked in there for the night.

The next morning, he found that the obliging care of his martial friend had decorated his hat with sundry parti-coloured streamers, which made a very lively appearance; and in company with that officer, and three other military gentlemen newly enrolled, who were under a cloud so dense that it only left three shoes, a boot, and a coat and a half visible among them, repaired to the river-side. Here they were joined by a corporal and four more heroes, of whom two were drunk and daring, and two sober and penitent, but each of whom, like Joe, had his dusty stick and bundle. The party embarked in a passage-boat bound for Gravesend, whence they were to proceed on foot to Chatham; the wind was in their favour, and they soon left London behind them, a mere dark mist—a giant phantom in the air.

CHAPTER THE THIRTY-SECOND.

MISFORTUNES, saith the adage, never come singly. There is little doubt that troubles are exceedingly gregarious in their nature, and flying in flocks, are apt to perch capriciously; crowding on the heads of some poor wights until there is not an inch of room left on their unlucky crowns, and taking no more notice of others who offer as good resting-places for the soles of their feet, than if they had no existence. It may have happened that a flight of troubles brooding over London, and looking out for Joseph Willet, whom they couldn't find, darted down hap-hazard on the first young man that caught their fancy, and settled on him instead. However this may be, certain it is that on the very day of Joe's departure they swarmed about the ears of Edward Chester, and did so buzz and flap their wings, and persecute him, that he was most profoundly wretched.

It was evening, and just eight o'clock, when he and his father, having wine and dessert set before them, were left to themselves for the first time that day. They had dined together, but a third person had been present during the meal, and until they met at table they had not seen each other since the previous night.

Edward was reserved, and silent. Mr. Chester was more than usually gay; but not caring, as it seemed, to open a conversation with one whose humour was so different, he vented the lightness of his spirit in smiles and sparkling looks, and made no effort to awaken his attention. So they remained for some time: the father lying on a sofa with his accustomed air of graceful negligence; the son seated opposite to him with downcast eyes, busied, it was plain, with painful and uneasy thoughts.

"My dear Edward," said Mr. Chester at length, with a most engaging laugh, "do not extend your drowsy influence to the decanter. Suffer *that* to circulate, let your spirits be never so stagnant."

Edward begged his pardon, passed it, and relapsed into his former state.

"You do wrong not to fill your glass," said Mr. Chester, holding up his own before the light. "Wine in moderation—not in excess, for that makes men ugly—has a thousand pleasant influences. It brightens the eyes, improves the voice, imparts a new vivacity to one's thoughts and conversation: you should try it, Ned."

"Ah father!" cried his son, "if—"

"My good fellow," interposed the parent hastily, as he set down his glass, and raised his eyebrows with a startled and horrified expression, "for heaven's sake don't call me by that obsolete and ancient name. Have some regard for delicacy. Am I grey, or wrinkled, do I go on crutches, have I lost my teeth, that you adopt such a mode of address? Good God, how very coarse!"

"I was about to speak to you from my heart, sir," returned Edward, "in the confidence which should subsist between us; and you check me in the outset."

"Now *do*, Ned, *do* not," said Mr. Chester, raising his delicate hand imploringly, "talk in that monstrous manner. About to speak from your heart! Don't you know that the heart is an ingenious part of our formation—the centre of the blood-vessels and all that sort of thing—which has no more to do with what you say or think, than your knees have? How can you be so very vulgar and absurd? These anatomical allusions should be left to gentlemen of the medical profession. They are really not agreeable in society. You quite surprise me, Ned."

"Well! there are no such things to wound, or heal, or have regard for. I know your creed, sir, and will say no more," returned his son.

"There again," said Mr. Chester, sipping his wine, "you are wrong. I distinctly say there are such things. We know there are. The hearts of animals—of bullocks, sheep, and so forth—are cooked and devoured, as I am told, by the lower classes, with a vast deal of relish. Men are sometimes stabbed to the heart, shot to the heart; but as to speaking from the heart, or to the heart, or being warm-hearted, or cold-hearted, or broken-hearted, or being all heart, or having no heart—pah! these things are nonsense, Ned."

"No doubt, sir," returned his son, seeing that he paused for him to speak. "No doubt."

"There's Haredale's niece, your late flame," said Mr. Chester, as a careless illustration of his meaning. "No doubt in your mind she was all heart once. Now she has none at all. Yet she is the same person, Ned, exactly."

"She is a changed person, sir," cried Edward, reddening; "and changed by vile means, I believe."

"You have had a cool dismissal, have you?" said his father. "Poor Ned! I told you last night what would happen.—May I ask you for the nut-crackers?"

"She has been tampered with, and most treacherously deceived," cried Edward, rising from his seat. "I never will believe that the knowledge of my real position, given her by myself, has worked this change. I know she is beset and tortured. But though our contract is at an end, and broken past all redemption; though I charge upon her want of firmness and want of truth, both to herself and me; I do not now, and never will believe, that any sordid motive, or her own unbiassed will, has led her to this course—never!"

"You make me blush," returned his father gaily, "for the folly of your nature, in which—but we never know ourselves—I devoutly hope there is no reflection of my own. With regard to the young lady herself, she has done what is very natural and proper, my dear fellow; what you yourself proposed, as I learn from Haredale; and what I predicted—with no great exercise of sagacity—she would do. She supposed you to be rich, or at least quite rich enough; and found you poor. Marriage is a civil contract; people marry to better their worldly condition and improve appearances; it is an affair of house and furniture, of liveries, servants, equipage, and so forth. The lady being poor and you poor also, there is an end of the matter. You cannot enter upon these considerations, and have no manner of business with the ceremony. I drink her health in this glass, and respect and honour her for her extreme good sense. It is a lesson to you. Fill yours, Ned."

"It is a lesson," returned his son, "by which I hope I may never profit, and if years and their experience impress it on—"

"Don't say on the heart," interposed his father.

"On men whom the world and its hypocrisy have spoiled," said Edward warmly, "Heaven keep me from its knowledge."

"Come, sir," returned his father, raising himself a little on the sofa, and looking straight towards him; "we have had enough of this. Remember, if you please, your interest, your duty, your moral obligations, your filial affections, and all that sort of thing, which it is so very delightful and charming to reflect upon; or you will repent it."

"I shall never repent the preservation of my self-respect, sir," said Edward. "Forgive me if I say that I will not sacrifice it at your bidding, and that I will not pursue the track which you would have me take, and to which the secret share you have had in this late separation, tends."

His father rose a little higher still, and looking at him as though curious to know if he were quite resolved and earnest, dropped gently down again, and said in the calmest voice—eating his nuts meanwhile,

"Edward, my father had a son, who being a fool like you, and, like you, entertaining low and disobedient sentiments, he disinherited and cursed one morning after breakfast. The circumstance occurs to me with a singular clearness of recollection this evening. I remember eating muffins at the time, with marmalade. He led a miserable life (the son, I mean) and died early; it was a happy release on all accounts; he degraded the family very much. It is a sad circumstance, Edward, when a father finds it necessary to resort to such strong measures."

"It is," replied Edward, "and it is sad when a son, proffering him his love and duty in their best and truest sense, finds himself repelled at every turn, and forced to disobey. Dear father," he added, more earnestly though in a gentler tone, "I have reflected many times on what occurred between us when we first discussed this subject. Let there be a confidence between us; not in terms, but truth. Hear what I have to say."

"As I anticipate what it is, and cannot fail to do so, Edward," returned his father coldly, "I decline. I couldn't possibly. I am sure it would put me out of temper, which is a state of mind I can't endure. If you intend to mar my plans for your establishment in life, and the preservation of that gentility and becoming pride, which our family have so long sustained—if, in short, you are resolved to take your own course, you must take it, and my curse with it. I am very sorry, but there's really no alternative."

"The curse may pass your lips," said Edward, "but it will be but empty breath. I do not believe that any man on earth has greater power to call one down upon his fellow—least of all, upon his own child—than he has to make one drop of rain or flake of snow fall from the clouds above us at his impious bidding. Beware, sir, what you do."

"You are so very irreligious, so exceedingly undutiful, so horribly profane," rejoined his father, turning his face lazily towards him, and cracking another nut, "that I positively must interrupt you here. It is quite impossible we can continue to go on, upon such terms as these. If you will do me the favour to ring the bell, the servant will show you to the door. Return to this roof no more, I beg you. Go, sir, since you have no moral sense remaining; and go to the Devil, at my express desire. Good day."

Edward left the room without another word or look, and turned his back upon the house for ever.

The father's face was slightly flushed and heated, but his manner was quite unchanged, as he rang the bell again, and addressed his servant on his entrance.

"Peak—if that gentleman who has just gone out—"

"I beg your pardon, sir, Mr. Edward?"

"Were there more than one, dolt, that you ask the question?—If that gentleman should send here for his wardrobe, let him have it, do you hear? If he should call himself at any time, I'm not at home. You'll tell him so, and shut the door."

So, it soon got whispered about, that Mr. Chester was very unfortunate in his son, who had occasioned him great grief and sorrow. And the good people who heard this and told it again, marvelled the more at his equanimity and even temper, and said what an amiable nature that man must have, who, having undergone so much, could be so placid and so calm. And when Edward's name was spoken, Society shook its head and laid its finger on its lip, and sighed, and looked very grave; and those who had sons about his age, waxed wrathful and indignant, and hoped, for Virtue's sake, that he was dead. And the world went on turning round, as usual, for five years, concerning which this Narrative is silent.

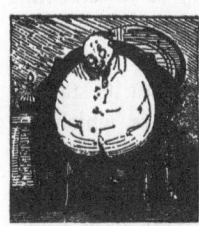

CHAPTER THE THIRTY-THIRD.

NE wintry evening, early in the year of our Lord one thousand seven hundred and eighty, a keen north wind arose as it grew dark, and night came on with black and dismal looks. A bitter storm of sleet, sharp, dense, and icy-cold, swept the wet streets, and rattled on the trembling windows. Signboards, shaken past endurance in their creaking frames, fell crashing on the pavement; old tottering chimneys reeled and staggered in the blast; and many a steeple rocked again that night, as though the earth were troubled.

It was not a time for those who could by any means get light and warmth, to brave the fury of the weather. In coffee-houses of the better sort, guests crowded round the fire, forgot to be political, and told each other with a secret gladness that the blast grew fiercer every minute. Each humble tavern by the water-side, had its group of uncouth figures round the hearth; who talked of vessels foundering at sea, and all hands lost, related many a dismal tale of shipwreck and drowned men, and hoped that some they knew were safe, and shook their heads in doubt. In private dwellings, children clustered near the blaze; listening with timid pleasure to tales of ghosts and goblins, and tall figures clad in white standing by bedsides, and people who had gone to sleep in old churches and being overlooked had found themselves alone there at the dead hour of the night: until they shuddered at the thought of the dark rooms up-stairs, yet loved to hear the wind moan too, and hoped it would continue bravely. From time to time these happy in-door people stopped to listen, or one held up his finger and cried "Hark!" and then, above the rumbling in the chimney, and the fast pattering on the glass, was heard a wailing, rushing sound, which shook the walls as though a giant's hand were on them; then a hoarse roar as if the sea had risen; then such a whirl and tumult that the air seemed mad; and then, with a lengthened howl, the waves of wind swept on, and left a moment's interval of rest.

Cheerily, though there were none abroad to see it, shone the Maypole light that evening. Blessings on the red—deep, ruby, glowing red—old curtain of the window; blending into one rich stream of brightness, fire and candle, meat, drink, and company, and gleaming like a jovial eye upon the bleak waste out of doors! Within, what carpet like its crunching sand, what music merry as its crackling logs, what perfume like its kitchen's dainty breath, what weather genial as its hearty warmth! Blessings on the old house, how sturdily it stood! How did the vexed wind chafe and roar about its stalwart roof; how did it pant and strive with its wide chimneys, which still poured forth from their hospitable throats, great clouds of smoke, and puffed defiance in its face; how above all, did it drive and rattle at the casement, emulous to extinguish that cheerful glow, which would not be put down and seemed the brighter for the conflict.

The profusion too, the rich and lavish bounty, of that goodly tavern! It was not enough that one fire roared and sparkled on its spacious hearth; in the tiles which paved and compassed it, five hundred flickering fires burnt brightly also. It was not enough that one red curtain shut the wild night out, and shed its cheerful influence on the room. In every saucepan lid, and candlestick, and vessel of copper, brass, or tin that hung upon the walls, were countless ruddy hangings, flashing and gleaming with every motion of the blaze, and offering, let the eye wander where it might, interminable vistas of the same rich colour. The old oak wainscoting, the beams, the chairs, the seats, reflected it in a deep, dull glimmer. There were fires and red curtains in the very eyes of the drinkers, in their buttons, in their liquor, in the pipes they smoked.

Mr. Willet sat in what had been his accustomed place five years before, with his eyes on the eternal boiler; and had sat there since the clock struck eight, giving no other signs of life than breathing with a loud and constant snore (though he was wide awake), and from time to time putting his glass to his lips, or knocking the ashes out of his pipe, and filling it anew. It was now half-past ten. Mr. Cobb and long Phil Parkes were his companions, as of old, and for two mortal hours and a half, none of the company had pronounced one word.

Whether people, by dint of sitting together in the same place and the same relative positions, and doing exactly the same things for a great many years, acquire a sixth sense, or some unknown power of influencing each other which serves them in its stead, is a question for philosophy to settle. But certain it is that old John Willet, Mr. Parkes, and Mr. Cobb, were one and all firmly of opinion that they were very jolly companions—rather choice spirits than otherwise; that they looked at each other every now and then as if there were a perpetual interchange of ideas going on among them; that no man considered himself or his neighbour by any means silent; and that each of them nodded occasionally when he caught the eye of another, as if he would say "You have expressed yourself extremely well, sir, in relation to that sentiment, and I quite agree with you."

The room was so very warm, the tobacco so very good, and the fire so very soothing, that Mr. Willet by degrees began to doze; but as he had perfectly acquired, by dint of long habit, the art of smoking in his sleep, and as his breathing was pretty much the same, awake or asleep, saving that in the latter case he sometimes experienced a slight difficulty in respiration (such as a carpenter meets with when he is planing and comes to a knot), neither of his companions was aware of the circumstance, until he met with one of these impediments and was obliged to try again.

"Johnny's dropped off" said Mr. Parkes in a whisper.

"Fast as a top" said Mr. Cobb.

Neither of them said any more until Mr. Willet came to another knot—one of surpassing obduracy—which bade fair to throw him into convulsions, but which he got over at last without waking, by an effort quite superhuman.

"He sleeps uncommon hard" said Mr. Cobb.

Mr. Parkes, who was possibly a hard-sleeper himself, replied with some disdain "Not a bit on it;" and directed his eyes towards a handbill pasted over the chimney-piece, which was decorated at the top with a woodcut representing a youth of tender years running away very fast, with a bundle over his shoulder at the end of a stick, and—to carry out the idea—a finger-post and a mile-stone beside him. Mr. Cobb likewise turned his eyes in the same direction, and surveyed the placard as if that were the first time he had ever beheld it. Now, this was a document which Mr. Willet had himself indited* on the disappearance of his son Joseph, acquainting the nobility and gentry and the public in general with the circumstances of his having left his home; describing his dress and appearance; and offering a reward of five pounds to any person or persons who would pack him up and return him safely to the Maypole at Chigwell, or lodge him in any of his Majesty's jails until such time as his father should come and claim him. In this advertisement Mr. Willet had obstinately persisted, despite the advice and entreaties of his friends, in describing his son as a "young boy;" and furthermore as being from eighteen inches to a couple of feet shorter than he really was: two circumstances which perhaps accounted in some degree, for its never having been productive of any other effect than the transmission to Chigwell at various times and at a vast expense, of some five-and-forty runaways varying from six years old to twelve.

Mr. Cobb and Mr. Parkes looked mysteriously at this composition, at each other, and at old John. From the time he had pasted it up with his own hands, Mr. Willet had never by word or sign alluded to the subject, or encouraged any one else to do so. Nobody had the least notion what his thoughts or opinions were, connected with it; whether he remembered it or forgot it; whether he had any idea that such an event had ever taken place. Therefore, even while he slept, no one ventured to refer to it in his presence; and for such sufficient reasons, these his chosen friends were silent now.

Mr. Willet had got by this time into such a complication of knots, that it was perfectly clear he must wake or die. He chose the former alternative, and opened his eyes.

"If he don't come in five minutes," said John, "I shall have supper without him."

The antecedent of this pronoun had been mentioned for the last time at eight o'clock. Messrs. Parkes and Cobb being used to this style of conversation, replied without difficulty that to be sure Solomon was very late, and they wondered what had happened to detain him.

"He an't blown away, I suppose," said Parkes. "It's enough to carry a man of his figure off his legs, and easy too. Do you hear it? It blows great guns, indeed. There'll be many a crash in the Forest to-night, I reckon, and many a broken branch upon the ground to-morrow."

"It won't break anything in the Maypole, I take it, sir," returned old John. "Let it try. I give it leave—what's that?"

"The wind," cried Parkes. "It's howling like a Christian, and has been all night long."

"Did you ever, sir," asked John, after a minute's contemplation, "hear the wind say 'Maypole?'"

"Why, what man ever did?" said Parkes.

"Nor 'ahoy' perhaps?" added John.

"No. Nor that neither."

"Very good, sir," said Mr. Willet, perfectly unmoved; "then if that was the wind just now, and you'll wait a little time without speaking, you'll hear it say both words very plain."

Mr. Willet was right. After listening for a few moments, they could clearly hear, above the roar and tumult out of doors, this shout repeated; and that with a shrillness and energy, which denoted that it came from some person in great distress or terror. They looked at each other, turned pale, and held their breath. No man stirred.

It was in this emergency, that Mr. Willet displayed something of that strength of mind and plenitude of mental resource, which rendered him the admiration of all his friends and neighbours. After looking at Messrs. Parkes and Cobb for some time in silence, he clapped his two hands to his cheeks, and sent forth a roar which made the glasses dance and rafters ring—a long-sustained, discordant bellow, that rolled onward with the wind, and startling every echo, made the night a hundred times more boisterous—a deep, loud, dismal bray, that sounded like a human gong. Then, with every vein in his head and face swoln with the great exertion, and his countenance suffused with a lively purple, he drew a little nearer to the fire, and turning his back upon it, said with dignity:

"If that's any comfort to anybody, they're welcome to it. If it an't, I'm sorry for 'em. If either of you two gentlemen likes to go out and see what's the matter, you can. I'm not curious, myself."

While he spoke the cry drew nearer and nearer, footsteps passed the window, the latch of the door was raised, it opened, was violently shut again, and Solomon Daisy, with a lighted lantern in his hand, and the rain streaming from his disordered dress, dashed into the room.

A more complete picture of terror than the little man presented, it would be difficult to imagine. The perspiration stood in beads upon his face, his knees knocked together, his every limb trembled, the power of articulation was quite gone; and there he stood, panting for breath, gazing on them with such livid ashy looks, that they were infected with his fear, though ignorant of its occasion, and, reflecting his dismayed and horror-stricken visage, stared back again without venturing to question him; until old John Willet, in a fit of temporary insanity, made a dive at his cravat, and, seizing him by that portion of his dress, shook him to and fro until his very teeth appeared to rattle in his head.

"Tell us what's the matter, sir," said John, "or I'll kill you. Tell us what's the matter, sir, or in another second, I'll have your head under the biler. How dare you look like that? Is anybody a following of you? What do you mean? Say something, or I'll be the death of you, I will."

Mr. Willet, in his frenzy, was so near keeping his word to the very letter (Solomon Daisy's eyes already beginning to roll in an alarming manner, and certain guttural sounds, as of a choking man, to issue from his throat), that the two bystanders, recovering in some degree, plucked him off his victim by main force, and placed the little clerk of Chigwell in a chair. Directing a fearful gaze all round the room, he implored them in a faint voice to give him some drink; and above all to lock the house-door and close and bar the shutters of the room, without a moment's loss of time. The latter request did not tend to re-assure his hearers, or to fill them with the most comfortable sensations; they complied with it, however, with the greatest expedition; and having handed him a bumper of brandy-and-water, nearly boiling hot, waited to hear what he might have to tell them.

"Oh, Johnny," said Solomon, shaking him by the hand. "Oh, Parkes. Oh, Tommy Cobb. Why did I leave this house to-night! On the nineteenth of March—of all nights in the year, on the nineteenth of March!"

They all drew closer to the fire. Parkes, who was nearest to the door, started and looked over his shoulder. Mr. Willet, with great indignation, inquired what the devil he meant by that—and then said, "God forgive me," and glanced over his own shoulder, and came a little nearer.

"When I left here to-night," said Solomon Daisy, "I little thought what day of the month it was. I have never gone alone into the church after dark on this day, for seven-and-twenty years. I have heard it said that as we keep our birthdays when we are alive, so the ghosts of dead people, who are not easy in their graves, keep the day they died upon.—How the wind roars!"

Nobody spoke. All eyes were fastened on Solomon.

"I might have known," he said, "what night it was, by the foul weather. There's no such night in the whole year round as this is, always. I never sleep quietly in my bed on the nineteenth of March."

"Go on," said Tom Cobb, in a low voice. "Nor I neither."

Solomon Daisy raised his glass to his lips; put it down upon the floor with such a trembling hand that the spoon tinkled in it like a little bell; and continued thus:

"Have I ever said that we are always brought back to this subject in some strange way, when the nineteenth of this month comes round? Do you suppose it was by accident, I forgot to wind up the church-clock? I never forget it at any other time, though it's such a clumsy thing that it has to be wound up every day. Why should it escape my memory on this day of all others?

"I made as much haste down there as I could when I went from here, but I had to go home first for the keys; and the wind and rain being dead against me all the way, it was pretty well as much as I could do at times to keep my legs. I got there at last, opened the church-door, and went in. I had not met a soul all the way, and you may judge whether it was dull or not. Neither of you would bear me company. If you could have known what was to come, you'd have been in the right.

"The wind was so strong, that it was as much as I could do to shut the church-door by putting my whole weight against it; and even as it was, it burst wide open twice, with such strength that any of you would have sworn, if you had been leaning against it, as I was, that somebody was pushing on the other side. However, I got the key turned, went into the belfry, and wound up the clock—which was very near run down, and would have stood stock-still in half an hour.

"As I took up my lantern again to leave the church, it came upon me all at once that this was the nineteenth of March. It came upon me with a kind of shock, as if a hand had struck the thought upon my forehead; at the very same moment, I heard a voice outside the tower—rising from among the graves."

Here old John precipitately interrupted the speaker, and begged that if Mr. Parkes (who was seated opposite to him and was staring directly over his head) saw anything, he would have the goodness to mention it. Mr. Parkes apologised, and remarked that he was only listening; to which Mr. Willet angrily retorted, that his listening with that kind of expression in his face was not agreeable, and that if he couldn't look like other people, he had better put his pocket-handkerchief over his head. Mr. Parkes with great submission pledged himself to do so, if again required, and John Willet turning to Solomon desired him to proceed. After waiting until a violent gust of wind and rain, which seemed to shake even that sturdy house to its foundation, had passed away, the little man complied:

"Never tell me that it was my fancy, or that it was any other sound which I mistook for that I tell you of. I heard the wind whistle through the arches of the church. I heard the steeple strain and creak. I heard the rain as it came driving against the walls. I felt the bells shake. I saw the ropes sway to and fro. And I heard that voice."

"What did it say?" asked Tom Cobb.

"I don't know what; I don't know that it spoke. It gave a kind of cry, as any one of us might do, if something dreadful followed us in a dream, and came upon us unawares; and then it died off: seeming to pass quite round the church."

"I don't see much in that," said John, drawing a long breath, and looking round him like a man who felt relieved.

"Perhaps not," returned his friend, "but that's not all."

"What more do you mean to say, sir, is to come?" asked John, pausing in the act of wiping his face upon his apron. "What are you a going to tell us of next?"

"What I saw."

"Saw!" echoed all three, bending forward.

"When I opened the church-door to come out," said the little man, with an expression of face which bore ample testimony to the sincerity of his conviction, "when I opened the church-door to come out, which I did suddenly, for I wanted to get it shut again before another gust of wind came up, there crossed me—so close, that by stretching out my finger I could have touched it—something in the likeness of a man. It was bare-headed to the storm. It turned its face without stopping, and fixed its eyes on mine. It was a ghost—a spirit."

"Whose?" they all three cried together.

In the excess of his emotion (for he fell back trembling in his chair, and waved his hand as if entreating them to question him no further,) his answer was lost on all but old John Willet, who happened to be seated close beside him.

"Who!" cried Parkes and Tom Cobb, looking eagerly by turns at Solomon Daisy and at Mr. Willet. "Who was it?"

"Gentlemen," said Mr. Willet after a long pause, "you needn't ask. The likeness of a murdered man. This is the nineteenth of March."

A profound silence ensued.

"If you'll take my advice," said John, "we had better, one and all, keep this a secret. Such tales would not be liked at the Warren. Let us keep it to ourselves for the present time at all events, or we may get into trouble, and Solomon may lose his place. Whether it was really as he says, or whether it wasn't, is no matter. Right or wrong, nobody would believe him. As to the probabilities, I don't myself think," said Mr. Willet, eyeing the corners of the room in a manner which showed that, like some other philosophers, he was not quite easy in his theory, "that a ghost as had been a man of sense in his lifetime, would be out a-walking in such weather—I only know that *I* wouldn't, if I was one."

But this heretical doctrine was strongly opposed by the other three, who quoted a great many precedents to show that bad weather was the very time for such appearances; and Mr. Parkes (who had had a ghost in his family, by the mother's side) argued the matter with so much ingenuity and force of illustration, that John was only saved from having to retract his opinion by the opportune appearance of supper, to which they applied themselves with a dreadful relish. Even Solomon Daisy himself, by dint of the elevating influences of fire, lights, brandy, and good company, so far recovered as to handle his knife and fork in a highly creditable manner, and to display a capacity both of eating and drinking, such as banished all fear of his having sustained any lasting injury from his fright.

Supper done, they crowded round the fire again, and, as is common on such occasions, propounded all manner of leading questions calculated to surround the story with new horrors and surprises. But Solomon Daisy, notwithstanding these temptations, adhered so steadily to his original account, and repeated it so often, with such slight variations, and with such solemn asseverations of its truth and reality, that his hearers were (with good reason) more astonished than at first. As he took John Willet's view of the matter in regard to the propriety of not bruiting the tale abroad, unless the spirit should appear to him again, in which case it would be necessary to take immediate counsel with the clergyman, it was solemnly resolved that it should be hushed up and kept quiet. And as most men like to have a secret to tell which may exalt their own importance, they arrived at this conclusion with perfect unanimity.

As it was by this time growing late, and was long past their usual hour of separating, the cronies parted for the night. Solomon Daisy, with a fresh candle in his lantern, repaired homewards under the escort of long Phil Parkes and Mr. Cobb, who were rather more nervous than himself. Mr. Willet, after seeing them to the door, returned to collect his thoughts with the assistance of the boiler, and to listen to the storm of wind and rain, which had not yet abated one jot of its fury.

CHAPTER THE THIRTY-FOURTH.

BEFORE old John had looked at the boiler quite twenty minutes, he got his ideas into a focus, and brought them to bear upon Solomon Daisy's story. The more he thought of it, the more impressed he became with a sense of his own wisdom, and a desire that Mr. Haredale should be impressed with it likewise. At length, to the end that he might sustain a principal and important character in the affair; and might have the start of Solomon and his two friends, through whose means he knew the adventure, with a variety of exaggerations, would be known to at least a score of people, and most likely to Mr. Haredale himself, by breakfast-time to-morrow; he determined to repair to the Warren before going to bed.

"He's my landlord," thought John, as he took a candle in his hand, and setting it down in a corner out of the wind's way, opened a casement in the rear of the house, looking towards the stables. "We haven't met of late years so often as we used to do—changes are taking place in the family—it's desirable that I should stand as well with them, in point of dignity, as possible—the whispering about of this here tale will anger him—it's good to have confidences with a gentleman of his natur', and set one's-self right besides. Halloa there! Hugh—Hugh. Hal-loa!"

When he had repeated this shout a dozen times, and startled every pigeon from its slumbers, a door in one of the ruinous old buildings opened, and a rough voice demanded what was amiss now, that a man couldn't even have his sleep in quiet.

"What! Haven't you sleep enough, growler, that you're not to be knocked up for once?" said John.

"No," replied the voice, as the speaker yawned and shook himself. "Not half enough."

"I don't know how you *can* sleep, with the wind a bellowsing and roaring about you, making the tiles fly like a pack of cards," said John; "but no matter for that. Wrap yourself up in something or another, and come here, for you must go as far as the Warren with me. And look sharp about it."

Hugh, with much low growling and muttering, went back into his lair; and presently re-appeared, carrying a lantern and a cudgel, and enveloped from head to foot in an old, frowsy, slouching horse-cloth. Mr. Willet received this figure at the back door, and ushered him into the bar, while he wrapped himself in sundry greatcoats and capes, and so tied and knotted his face in shawls and handkerchiefs, that how he breathed was a mystery.

"You don't take a man out of doors at near midnight in such weather, without putting some heart into him, do you, master?" said Hugh.

"Yes I do, sir," returned Mr. Willet. "I put the heart (as you call it) into him when he has brought me safe home again, and his standing steady on his legs an't of so much consequence. So hold that light up, if you please, and go on a step or two before, to show the way."

Hugh obeyed with a very indifferent grace, and a longing glance at the bottles. Old John, laying strict injunctions on his cook to keep the doors locked in his absence, and to open to nobody but himself on pain of dismissal, followed him into the blustering darkness out of doors.

The way was wet and dismal, and the night so black, that if Mr. Willet had been his own pilot, he would have walked into a deep horsepond within a few hundred yards of his own house, and would certainly have terminated his career in that ignoble sphere of action. But Hugh, who had a sight as keen as any hawk's, and, apart from that endowment, could have found his way blindfold to any place within a dozen miles, dragged old John along, quite deaf to his remonstrances, and took his own course without the slightest reference to, or notice of, his master. So they made head against the wind as they best could; Hugh crushing the wet grass beneath his heavy tread, and stalking on after his ordinary savage fashion; John Willet following at arm's length, picking his steps, and looking about him, now for bogs and ditches, and now for such stray ghosts as might be wandering abroad, with looks of as much dismay and uneasiness as his immoveable face was capable of expressing.

At length they stood upon the broad gravel-walk before the Warren-house. The building was profoundly dark, and none were moving near it save themselves. From one solitary turret-chamber, however, there shone a ray of light; and towards this speck of comfort in the cold, cheerless, silent scene, Mr. Willet bade his pilot lead him.

"The old room," said John, looking timidly upward; "Mr. Reuben's own apartment, God be with us! I wonder his brother likes to sit there, so late at night—on this night too."

"Why, where else should he sit?" asked Hugh, folding the lantern to his breast, to keep the candle from the wind, while he trimmed it with his fingers. "It's snug enough, an't it?"

"Snug!" said John indignantly. "You have a comfortable idea of snugness, you have, sir. Do you know what was done in that room, you ruffian?"

"Why, what is it the worse for that!" cried Hugh, looking into John's fat face. "Does it keep out the rain, and snow, and wind, the less for that? Is it less warm or dry, because a man was killed there? Ha, ha, ha! Never believe it, master. One man's no such matter as that comes to."

Mr. Willet fixed his dull eyes on his follower, and began—by a species of inspiration—to think it just barely possible that he was something of a dangerous character, and that it might be advisable to get rid of him one of these days. He was too prudent to say anything, with the journey home before him; and therefore turned to the iron gate before which this brief dialogue had passed, and pulled the handle of the bell that hung beside it. The turret in which the light appeared being at one corner of the building, and only divided from the path by one of the garden-walks, upon which this gate opened, Mr. Haredale threw up the window directly, and demanded who was there.

"Begging pardon, sir," said John, "I knew you sat up late, and made bold to come round, having a word to say to you."

"Willet—is it not?"

"Of the Maypole—at your service, sir."

Mr. Haredale closed the window, and withdrew. He presently appeared at a door in the bottom of the turret, and coming across the garden-walk, unlocked the gate and let them in.

"You are a late visitor, Willet. What is the matter?"

"Nothing to speak of, sir," said John; "an idle tale, I thought you ought to know of; nothing more."

"Let your man go forward with the lantern, and give me your hand. The stairs are crooked and narrow.—Gently with your light, friend. You swing it like a censer."*

Hugh, who had already reached the turret, held it more steadily, and ascended first, turning round from time to time to shed his light downward on the steps. Mr. Haredale following next, eyed his lowering face with no great favour; and Hugh, looking down on him, returned his glances with interest, as they climbed the winding stair.

It terminated in a little anti-room adjoining that from which they had seen the light. Mr. Haredale entered first, and led the way through it into the latter chamber, where he seated himself at a writing-table from which he had risen when they rang the bell.

"Come in," he said, beckoning to old John, who remained bowing at the door. "Not you, friend," he added hastily to Hugh, who entered also. "Willet, why do you bring that fellow here?"

"Why, sir," returned John, elevating his eyebrows, and lowering his voice to the tone in which the question had been asked him, "he's a good guard, you see."

"Don't be too sure of that," said Mr. Haredale, looking towards him as he spoke. "I doubt it. He has an evil eye."

"There's no imagination in his eye," returned Mr. Willet, glancing over his shoulder at the organ in question, "certainly."

"There is no good there, be assured," said Mr. Haredale. "Wait in that little room, friend, and close the door between us."

Hugh shrugged his shoulders, and with a disdainful look, which showed, either that he had overheard, or that he guessed the purport of their whispering, did as he was told. When he was shut out, Mr. Haredale turned to John, and bade him go on with what he had to say, but not to speak too loud, for there were quick ears yonder.

Thus cautioned, Mr. Willet, in an oily whisper, recited all that he had heard and said that night; laying particular stress upon his own sagacity, upon his great regard for the family, and upon his solicitude for their peace of mind and happiness. The story moved his auditor much more than he had expected. Mr. Haredale often changed his attitude, rose and paced the room, returned again, desired him to repeat, as nearly as he could, the very words that Solomon had used, and gave so many other signs of being disturbed and ill at ease, that even Mr. Willet was surprised.

"You did quite right," he said, at the end of a long conversation, "to bid them keep this story secret. It is a foolish fancy on the part of this weak-brained man, bred in his fears and superstition. But Miss Haredale, though she would know it to be so, would be disturbed by it if it reached her ears; it is too nearly connected with a subject very painful to us all, to be heard with indifference. You were most prudent, and have laid me under a great obligation. I thank you very much."

This was equal to John's most sanguine expectations; but he would have preferred Mr. Haredale's looking at him when he spoke, as if he really did thank him, to his walking up and down, speaking by fits and starts, often stopping with his eyes fixed on the ground, moving hurriedly on again, like one distracted, and seeming almost unconscious of what he said or did.

This, however, was his manner; and it was so embarrassing to John that he sat quite passive for a long time, not knowing what to do. At length he rose. Mr. Haredale stared at him for a moment as though he had quite forgotten his being present, then shook hands with him, and opened the door. Hugh, who was, or feigned to be, fast asleep on the anti-chamber floor, sprang up on their entrance, and throwing his cloak about him, grasped his stick and lantern, and prepared to descend the stairs.

"Stay," said Mr. Haredale. "Will this man drink?"

"Drink! He'd drink the Thames up, if it was strong enough, sir," replied John Willet. "He'll have something when he gets home. He's better without it, now, sir."

"Nay. Half the distance is done," said Hugh. "What a hard master you are! I shall go home the better for one glassful, half-way. Come!"

As John made no reply, Mr. Haredale brought out a glass of liquor, and gave it to Hugh, who, as he took it in his hand, threw part of it upon the floor.

"What do you mean by splashing your drink about a gentleman's house, sir?" said John.

"I'm drinking a toast," Hugh rejoined, holding the glass above his head, and fixing his eyes on Mr. Haredale's face; "a toast to this house and its master." With that he muttered something to himself, and drank the rest, and setting down the glass, preceded them without another word.

John was a good deal scandalised by this observance, but seeing that Mr. Haredale took little heed of what Hugh said or did, and that his thoughts were otherwise employed, he offered no apology, and went in silence down the stairs, across the walk, and through the garden-gate. They stopped upon the outer side for Hugh to hold the light while Mr. Haredale locked it on the inner; and then John saw with wonder (as he often afterwards related), that he was very pale, and that his face had changed so much and grown so haggard since their entrance, that he almost seemed another man.

They were in the open road again, and John Willet was walking on behind his escort, as he had come, thinking very steadily of what he had just now seen, when Hugh drew him suddenly aside, and almost at the same instant three horsemen swept past—the nearest brushed his shoulder even then—who, checking their steeds as suddenly as they could, stood still, and waited for their coming up.

CHAPTER THE THIRTY-FIFTH.

WHEN John Willet saw that the horsemen wheeled smartly round, and drew up three abreast in the narrow road, waiting for him and his man to join them, it occurred to him with unusual precipitation that they must be highwaymen; and had Hugh been armed with a blunderbuss, in place of his stout cudgel, he would certainly have ordered him to fire it off at a venture, and would, while the word of command was obeyed, have consulted his own personal safety in immediate flight. Under the circumstances of disadvantage, however, in which he and his guard were placed, he deemed it prudent to adopt a different style of generalship, and therefore whispered his attendant to address them in the most peaceable and courteous terms. By way of acting up to the spirit and letter of this instruction, Hugh stepped forward, and flourishing his staff before the very eyes of the rider nearest to him, demanded roughly what he and his fellows meant by so nearly galloping over them, and why they scoured the king's highway at that late hour of night.

The man whom he addressed was beginning an angry reply in the same strain, when he was checked by the horseman in the centre, who, interposing with an air of authority, inquired in a somewhat loud but not harsh or unpleasant voice:

"Pray, is this the London road?"

"If you follow it right, it is," replied Hugh roughly.

"Nay, brother," said the same person, "you're but a churlish English-man, if Englishman you be—which I should much doubt but for your tongue. Your companion, I am sure, will answer me more civilly. How say you, friend?"

"I say it *is* the London road, sir," answered John. "And I wish," he added in a subdued voice, as he turned to Hugh, "that you was in any other road, you vagabond. Are you tired of your life, sir, that you go a-trying to provoke three great neck-or-nothing chaps, that could keep on running over us, back'ards and for'ards, till we was dead, and then take our bodies up behind 'em, and drown us ten miles off?"

"How far is it to London?" inquired the same speaker.

"Why, from here sir," answered John, persuasively, "it's thirteen very easy mile."

The adjective was thrown in, as an inducement to the travellers to ride away with all speed; but instead of having the desired effect, it elicited from the same person, the remark, "Thirteen miles! That's a long distance!" which was followed by a short pause of indecision.

"Pray," said the gentleman, "are there any inns hereabouts?"

At the word "inns," John plucked up his spirit in a surprising manner; his fears rolled off like smoke; all the landlord stirred within him.

"There are no inns," rejoined Mr. Willet, with a strong emphasis on the plural number; "but there's a Inn—one Inn—the Maypole Inn. That's a Inn indeed. You won't see the like of that Inn often."

"You keep it perhaps?" said the horseman, smiling.

"I do, sir," replied John, greatly wondering how he had found this out.

"And how far is the Maypole from here?"

"About a mile"—John was going to add that it was the easiest mile in all the world, when the third rider, who had hitherto kept a little in the rear, suddenly interposed:

"And have you one excellent bed, landlord? Hem! A bed that you can recommend—a bed that you are sure is well aired—a bed that has been slept in by some perfectly respectable and unexceptionable person?"

"We don't take in no tagrag and bobtail* at our house, sir," answered John. "And as to the bed itself—"

"Say, as to three beds," interposed the gentleman who had spoken before; "for we shall want three if we stay, though my friend only speaks of one."

"No, no, my lord; you are too good, you are too kind; but your life is of far too much importance to the nation in these portentous times, to be placed upon a level with one so useless and so poor as mine. A great cause, my lord, a mighty cause, depends on you. You are its leader and its champion, its advanced guard and its van. It is the cause of our altars and our homes, our country and our faith. Let *me* sleep on a chair—the carpet—anywhere. No one will repine if *I* take cold or fever. Let John Grueby* pass the night beneath the open sky—no one will repine for *him*. But forty thousand men of this our island in the wave (exclusive of women and children) rivet their eyes and thoughts on Lord George Gordon;* and every day, from the rising up of the sun to the going down of the same, pray for his health and vigour. My lord," said the speaker, rising in his stirrups, "it is a glorious cause, and must not be forgotten. My lord, it is a mighty cause, and must not be endangered. My lord, it is a holy cause, and must not be deserted."

"It *is* a holy cause," exclaimed his lordship, lifting up his hat with great solemnity. "Amen!"

"John Grueby," said the long-winded gentleman, in a tone of mild reproof, "his lordship said Amen."

"I heard my lord, sir," said the man, sitting like a statue on his horse.

"And do not *you* say Amen, likewise?"

To which John Grueby made no reply at all, but sat looking straight before him.

"You surprise me, Grueby," said the gentleman. "At a crisis like the present, when Queen Elizabeth, that maiden monarch, weeps within her tomb, and Bloody Mary,* with a brow of gloom and shadow, stalks triumphant—"

"Oh, sir," cried the man, gruffly, "where's the use of talking of Bloody Mary, under such circumstances as the present, when my lord's wet through and tired with hard riding? Let's either go on to London, sir, or put up at once; or that unfort'nate Bloody Mary will have more to answer for—and she's done a deal more harm in her grave than she ever did in her lifetime, I believe."

By this time Mr. Willet, who had never heard so many words

spoken together at one time, or delivered with such volubility and emphasis as by the long-winded gentleman; and whose brain, being wholly unable to sustain or compass them, had quite given itself up for lost; recovered so far as to observe that there was ample accommodation at the Maypole for all the party: good beds; neat wines; excellent entertainment for man and beast; private rooms for large or small parties; dinners dressed upon the shortest notice; choice stabling, and a lock-up coach-house: and, in short, to run over such recommendatory scraps of language as were painted up on various portions of the building, and which, in the course of some forty years, he had learnt to repeat with tolerable correctness. He was considering whether it was at all possible to invent any novel sentences to the same purpose, when the gentleman who had spoken first, turning to him of the long wind, exclaimed, "What say you, Gashford?* Shall we tarry at this house he speaks of, or press forward? You shall decide."

"I would submit, my lord, then," returned the person he appealed to, in a silky tone, "that your health and spirits—so important, under Providence, to our great cause, our pure and truthful cause"—here his lordship pulled off his hat again, though it was raining hard—"require refreshment and repose."

"Go on before, landlord, and show the way," said Lord George Gordon; "we will follow at a footpace."

"If you'll give me leave, my lord," said John Grueby, in a low voice, "I'll change my proper place, and ride before you. The looks of the landlord's friend are not over honest, and it may be as well to be cautious with him."

"John Grueby is quite right," interposed Mr. Gashford, falling back hastily. "My lord, a life so precious as yours must not be put in peril. Go forward, John, by all means. If you have any reason to suspect the fellow, blow his brains out."

John made no answer, but looking straight before him, as his custom seemed to be when the secretary spoke, bade Hugh push on, and followed close behind him. Then came his lordship, with Mr. Willet at his bridle rein; and, last of all, his lordship's secretary—for that, it seemed, was Gashford's office.

Hugh strode briskly on, often looking back at the servant, whose horse was close upon his heels, and glancing with a leer at his holster case of pistols, by which he seemed to set great store. He was a square-built, strong-made, bull-necked fellow, of the true English breed; and as Hugh measured him with his eye, he measured Hugh, regarding him meanwhile with a look of bluff disdain. He was much older than the Maypole man, being to all appearance five-and-forty; but was one of those self-possessed, hard-headed, imperturbable fellows, who, if they ever are beat at fisty-cuffs, or other kind of warfare, never know it, and go on coolly till they win.

"If I led you wrong now," said Hugh, tauntingly, "you'd—ha ha ha!—you'd shoot me through the head, I suppose."

John Grueby took no more notice of this remark than if he had been deaf and Hugh dumb; but kept riding on, quite comfortably, with his eyes fixed on the horizon.

"Did you ever try a fall with a man when you were young, master?" said Hugh. "Can you make any play at single-stick?"*

John Grueby looked at him sideways with the same contented air, but deigned not a word in answer.

"—Like this?" said Hugh, giving his cudgel one of those skilful flourishes, in which the rustic of that time delighted. "Whoop!"

"—Or that," returned John Grueby, beating down his guard with his whip, and striking him on the head with its butt end. "Yes, I played a little once. You wear your hair too long; I should have cracked your crown if it had been a little shorter."

It was a pretty smart, loud-sounding rap, as it was, and evidently astonished Hugh; who, for the moment, seemed disposed to drag his new acquaintance from his saddle. But his face betokening neither malice, triumph, rage, nor any lingering idea that he had given him offence; his eyes gazing steadily in the old direction, and his manner being as careless and composed as if he had merely brushed away a fly; Hugh was so puzzled, and so disposed to look upon him as a customer of almost supernatural toughness, that he merely laughed, and cried "Well done!" then, sheering off a little, led the way in silence.

Before the lapse of many minutes the party halted at the Maypole door. Lord George and his secretary quickly dismounting, gave their horses to their servant, who, under the guidance of Hugh, repaired to the stables. Right glad to escape from the inclemency of the night, they followed Mr. Willet into the common room, and stood warming themselves and drying their clothes before the cheerful fire, while he busied himself with such orders and preparations as his guest's high quality required.

As he bustled in and out of the room, intent on these arrange-
ments, he had an opportunity of observing the two travellers, of
whom, as yet, he knew nothing but the voice. The Lord, the great
personage, who did the Maypole so much honour, was about the
middle height, of a slender make, and sallow complexion, with an
aquiline nose, and long hair of a reddish brown, combed perfectly
straight and smooth about his ears, and slightly powdered, but with-
out the faintest vestige of a curl. He was attired, under his greatcoat,
in a full suit of black, quite free from any ornament, and of the most
precise and sober cut. The gravity of his dress, together with a
certain lankness of cheek and stiffness of deportment, added nearly
ten years to his age, but his figure was that of one not yet past thirty.
As he stood musing in the red glow of the fire, it was striking to
observe his very bright large eye, which betrayed a restlessness of
thought and purpose, singularly at variance with the studied com-
posure and sobriety of his mien, and with his quaint and sad apparel.
It had nothing harsh or cruel in its expression; neither had his face,
which was thin and mild, and wore an air of melancholy; but it was
suggestive of an indefinable uneasiness, which infected those who
looked upon him, and filled them with a kind of pity for the man:
though why it did so, they would have had some trouble to explain.

Gashford, the secretary, was taller, angularly made, high-
shouldered, bony, and ungraceful. His dress, in imitation of his
superior, was demure and staid in the extreme; his manner, formal
and constrained. This gentleman had an overhanging brow, great
hands and feet and ears, and a pair of eyes that seemed to have made
an unnatural retreat into his head, and to have dug themselves a cave
to hide in. His manner was smooth and humble, but very sly and
slinking. He wore the aspect of a man who was always lying in wait
for something that *wouldn't* come to pass; but he looked patient—
very patient—and fawned like a spaniel dog. Even now, while he
warmed and rubbed his hands before the blaze, he had the air of one
who only presumed to enjoy it in his degree as a commoner; and
though he knew his lord was not regarding him, he looked into his
face from time to time, and, with a meek and deferential manner,
smiled as if for practice.

Such were the guests whom old John Willet, with a fixed and
leaden eye, surveyed a hundred times, and to whom he now
advanced with a state candlestick in each hand, beseeching them to

follow him into a worthier chamber. "For my lord," said John—it is odd enough, but certain people seem to have as great a pleasure in pronouncing titles as their owners have in wearing them—"this room, my lord, isn't at all the sort of place for your lordship, and I have to beg your lordship's pardon for keeping you here, my lord, one minute."

With this address, John ushered them up stairs into the state apartment, which, like many other things of state, was cold and comfortless. Their own footsteps, reverberating through the spacious room, struck upon their hearing with a hollow sound; and its damp and chilly atmosphere was rendered doubly cheerless by contrast with the homely warmth they had deserted.

It was of no use, however, to propose a return to the place they had quitted, for the preparations went on so briskly that there was no time to stop them. John, with the tall candlesticks in his hands, bowed them up to the fire-place; Hugh, striding in with a lighted brand and pile of fire-wood, cast it down upon the hearth, and set it in a blaze; John Grueby (who had a great blue cockade* in his hat, which he appeared to despise mightily) brought in the portmanteau he had carried on his horse, and placed it on the floor; and presently all three were busily engaged in drawing out the screen, laying the cloth, inspecting the beds, lighting fires in the bedrooms, expediting the supper, and making everything as cosy and as snug as might be, on so short a notice. In less than an hour's time, supper had been served, and ate, and cleared away; and Lord George and his secretary, with slippered feet, and legs stretched out before the fire, sat over some hot mulled wine together.

"So ends, my lord," said Gashford, filling his glass with great complacency, "the blessed work of a most blessed day."

"And of a blessed yesterday," said his lordship, raising his head.

"Ah!"—and here the secretary clasped his hands—"a blessed yesterday indeed! The Protestants of Suffolk are godly men and true. Though others of our countrymen have lost their way in darkness, even as we, my lord, did lose our road to-night, theirs is the light and glory."

"Did I move them, Gashford?" said Lord George.

"Move them, my lord! Move them! They cried to be led on against the Papists, they vowed a dreadful vengeance on their heads, they roared like men possessed—"

"But not by devils," said his lord.

"By devils! my lord! By angels."

"Yes—oh surely—by angels, no doubt," said Lord George, thrusting his hands into his pockets, taking them out again to bite his nails, and looking uncomfortably at the fire. "Of course by angels—eh Gashford?"

"You do not doubt it, my lord?" said the secretary.

"No—No" returned his lord. "No. Why should I? I suppose it would be decidedly irreligious to doubt it—wouldn't it Gashford? Though there certainly were," he added, without waiting for an answer, "some plaguy ill-looking characters among them."

"When you warmed," said the secretary, looking sharply at the other's downcast eyes, which brightened slowly as he spoke; "when you warmed into that noble outbreak: when you told them that you were never of the luke-warm or the timid tribe, and bade them take heed that they were prepared to follow one who would lead them on, though to the very death; when you spoke of a hundred and twenty thousand men across the Scottish border* who would take their own redress at any time, if it were not conceded; when you cried 'Perish the Pope and all his base adherents; the penal laws against them shall never be repealed* while Englishmen have hearts and hands'—and waved your own and touched your sword; and when they cried 'No Popery!' and you cried 'No; not even if we wade in blood,' and they threw up their hats and cried 'Hurrah! not even if we wade in blood; No Popery! Lord George! Down with the Papists—Vengeance on their heads:' when this was said and done, and a word from you, my lord, could raise or still the tumult—ah! then I felt what greatness was indeed, and thought, When was there ever power like this of Lord George Gordon's!"

"It's a great power. You're right. It is a great power!" he cried with sparkling eyes. "But—dear Gashford—did I really say all that?"

"And how much more!" cried the secretary, looking upwards. "Ah! how much more!"

"And I told them what you say, about the one hundred and forty thousand men in Scotland, did I!" he asked with evident delight. "That was bold."

"Our cause is boldness. Truth is always bold."

"Certainly. So is religion. She's bold, Gashford?"

"The true religion is, my lord."

"And that's ours," he rejoined, moving uneasily in his seat, and biting his nails as though he would pare them to the quick. "There can be no doubt of ours being the true one. You feel as certain of that as I do, Gashford, don't you?"

"Does my lord ask *me*," whined Gashford, drawing his chair nearer with an injured air, and laying his broad flat hand upon the table; "*me*," he repeated, bending the dark hollows of his eyes upon him with an unwholesome smile, "who, stricken by the magic of his eloquence in Scotland but a year ago, abjured the errors of the Romish church, and clung to him as one whose timely hand had plucked me from a pit?"

"True. No—No. I—I didn't mean it," replied the other, shaking him by the hand, rising from his seat, and pacing restlessly about the room. "It's a proud thing to lead the people, Gashford," he added as he made a sudden halt.

"By force of reason too," returned the pliant secretary.

"Ay, to be sure. They may cough, and jeer, and groan in

Parliament, and call me fool and madman, but which of them can raise this human sea and make it swell and roar at pleasure? Not one."

"Not one," repeated Gashford.

"Which of them can say for his honesty, what I can say for mine; which of them has refused a minister's bribe* of one thousand pounds a year, to resign his seat in favour of another? Not one."

"Not one," repeated Gashford again—taking the lion's share of the mulled wine between whiles.

"And as we are honest, true, and in a sacred cause, Gashford," said Lord George with a heightened colour and in a louder voice, as he laid his fevered hand upon his shoulder, "and are the only men who regard the mass of people out of doors, or are regarded by them, we will uphold them to the last; and will raise a cry against these un-English Papists which shall re-echo through the country, and roll with a noise like thunder. I will be worthy of the motto on my coat of arms, 'Called and chosen and faithful.'"*

"Called" said the secretary, "by Heaven."

"I am."

"Chosen by the people."

"Yes."

"Faithful to both."

"To the block!"

It would be difficult to convey an adequate idea of the excited manner in which he gave these answers to the secretary's promptings; of the rapidity of his utterance, or the violence of his tone and gesture; in which, struggling through his Puritan's demeanour,* was something wild and ungovernable which broke through all restraint. For some minutes he walked rapidly up and down the room, then stopping suddenly, exclaimed,

"Gashford—*You* moved them yesterday too. Oh yes! You did."

"I shone with a reflected light my lord," replied the humble secretary, laying his hand upon his heart. "I did my best."

"You did well," said his master, "and are a great and worthy instrument. If you will ring for John Grueby to carry the portmanteau into my room, and will wait here while I undress, we will dispose of business as usual, if you're not too tired."

"Too tired my lord!—But this is his consideration! Christian from head to foot." With which soliloquy, the secretary tilted the jug, and looked very hard into the mulled wine, to see how much remained.

John Willet and John Grueby appeared together. The one bearing the great candlesticks, and the other the portmanteau, showed the deluded lord into his chamber; and left the secretary alone, to yawn and shake himself, and finally to fall asleep before the fire.

"Now Mr. Gashford sir," said John Grueby in his ear, after what appeared to him a moment of unconsciousness; "my lord's abed."

"Oh. Very good John," was his mild reply. "Thank you John. Nobody need sit up. I know my room."

"I hope you're not a going to trouble your head to-night, or my lord's head neither, with anything more about Bloody Mary," said John. "I wish the blessed old creetur had never been born."

"I said you might go to bed, John," returned the secretary. "You didn't hear me, I think."

"Between Bloody Marys, and blue cockades, and glorious Queen Besses, and no Poperys, and Protestant associations,* and making of speeches," pursued John Grueby, looking, as usual, a long way off, and taking no notice of this hint, "my lord's half off his head. When we go out o' doors, such a set of ragamuffins comes a shouting after us 'Gordon for ever!' that I'm ashamed of myself and don't know where to look. When we're in-doors, they come a roaring and screaming about the house like so many devils; and my lord instead of ordering them to be drove away, goes out into the balcony and demeans himself by making speeches to 'em, and calls 'em 'Men of England,' and 'Fellow-countrymen,' as if he was fond of 'em and thanked 'em for coming. I can't make it out, but they're all mixed up somehow or another with that unfort'nate Bloody Mary, and call her name out till they're hoarse. They're all Protestants too—every man and boy among 'em: and Protestants is very fond of spoons I find, and silver plate in general, whenever area-gates is left open accidentally. I wish that was the worst of it, and that no more harm might be to come; but if you don't stop these ugly customers in time, Mr. Gashford, (and I know you; you're the man that blows the fire) you'll find 'em grow a little bit too strong for you. One of these evenings, when the weather gets warmer and Protestants are thirsty, they'll be pulling London down,—and I never heerd that Bloody Mary went as far as *that*."

Gashford had vanished long ago, and these remarks had been

bestowed on empty air. Not at all discomposed by the discovery, John Grueby fixed his hat on, wrong side foremost that he might be unconscious of the shadow of the obnoxious cockade, and withdrew to bed; shaking his head in a very gloomy and prophetic manner until he reached his chamber.

CHAPTER THE THIRTY-SIXTH.

GASHFORD, with a smiling face, but still with looks of profound deference and humility, betook himself towards his master's room, smoothing his hair down as he went, and humming a psalm tune. As he approached Lord George's door, he cleared his throat and hummed more vigorously.

There was a remarkable contrast between this man's occupation at the moment, and the expression of his countenance, which was singularly repulsive and malicious. His beetling brow almost obscured his eyes; his lip was curled contemptuously; his very shoulders seemed to sneer in stealthy whisperings with his great flapped ears.

"Hush!" he muttered softly, as he peeped in at the chamber-door. "He seems to be asleep. Pray Heaven he is! Too much watching, too much care, too much thought—ah! Lord preserve him for a martyr! He is a saint, if ever saint drew breath on this bad earth."

Placing his light upon a table, he walked on tiptoe to the fire, and sitting in a chair before it with his back towards the bed, went on communing with himself like one who thought aloud:

"The saviour of his country and his country's religion, the friend of his poor countrymen, the enemy of the proud and harsh; beloved of the rejected and oppressed, adored by forty thousand bold and loyal English hearts—what happy slumbers his should be!" And here he sighed, and warmed his hands, and shook his head as men do when their hearts are full, and heaved another sigh, and warmed his hands again.

"Why, Gashford?" said Lord George, who was lying broad awake, upon his side, and had been staring at him from his entrance.

"My—my lord," said Gashford, starting and looking round as though in great surprise. "I have disturbed you!"

"I have not been sleeping."

"Not sleeping!" he repeated, with assumed confusion. "What can

I say for having in your presence given utterance to thoughts—but they were sincere—they were sincere!" exclaimed the secretary, drawing his sleeve in a hasty way across his eyes; "and why should I regret your having heard them?"

"Gashford," said the poor lord, stretching out his hand with manifest emotion. "Do not regret it. You love me well, I know—too well. I don't deserve such homage."

Gashford made no reply, but grasped the hand and pressed it to his lips. Then rising, and taking from the trunk a little desk, he placed it on a table near the fire, unlocked it with a key he carried in his pocket, sat down before it, took out a pen, and, before dipping it in the inkstand, sucked it—to compose the fashion of his mouth perhaps, on which a smile was hovering yet.

"How do our numbers stand since last enrolling-night?" inquired Lord George. "Are we really forty thousand strong, or do we still speak in round numbers when we take the Association at that amount?"

"Our total now exceeds that number by a score and three," Gashford replied, casting his eyes upon his papers.

"The funds?"

"Not *very* improving; but there is some manna in the wilderness,* my lord. Hem! On Friday night the widows' mites dropped in. 'Forty scavengers, three and fourpence. An aged pew-opener of St. Martin's parish, sixpence. A bell-ringer of the established church, sixpence. A Protestant infant, newly born, one halfpenny. The United Link Boys, three shillings—one bad. The anti-popish prisoners in Newgate, five and fourpence. A friend in Bedlam,* half-a-crown. Dennis the hangman,* one shilling.'"

"That Dennis," said his lordship, "is an earnest man. I marked him in the crowd in Welbeck Street, last Friday."

"A good man," rejoined the secretary; "a staunch, sincere, and truly zealous man."

"He should be encouraged," said Lord George. "Make a note of Dennis. I'll talk with him."

Gashford obeyed, and went on reading from his list:

"'The Friends of Reason, half-a-guinea. The Friends of Liberty, half-a-guinea. The Friends of Peace, half-a-guinea. The Friends of Charity, half-a-guinea. The Friends of Mercy, half-a-guinea. The Associated Rememberers of Bloody Mary, half-a-guinea. The United Bull-Dogs, half-a-guinea.'"

"The United Bull-Dogs," said Lord George, biting his nails most horribly, "are a new society, are they not?"

"Formerly the 'Prentice Knights, my lord. The indentures of the old members expiring by degrees, they changed their name, it seems, though they still have 'prentices among them, as well as workmen."

"What is their president's name?" inquired Lord George.

"President," said Gashford, reading, "Mr. Simon Tappertit."

"I remember him. The little man, who sometimes brings an elderly sister to our meetings, and sometimes another female too, who is conscientious, I have no doubt, but not well-favoured?"

"The very same, my lord."

"Tappertit is an earnest man," said Lord George thoughtfully. "Eh, Gashford?"

"One of the foremost among them all, my lord. He snuffs the battle from afar, like the war-horse. He throws his hat up in the street as if he were inspired, and makes most stirring speeches from the shoulders of his friends."

"Make a note of Tappertit," said Lord George Gordon. "We may advance him to a place of trust."

"That," rejoined the secretary, doing as he was told, "is all—except Mrs. Varden's box (fourteenth time of opening), seven shillings and sixpence in silver and copper, and half-a-guinea in gold; and Miggs (being the saving of a quarter's wages), one-and-threepence."

"Miggs," said Lord George. "Is that a man?"

"The name is entered on the list as a woman," replied the secretary. "I think she is the tall spare female of whom you spoke just now, my lord, as not being well-favoured, who sometimes comes to hear the speeches—along with Tappertit and Mrs. Varden."

"Mrs. Varden is the elderly lady then, is she!"

The secretary nodded, and rubbed the bridge of his nose with the feather of his pen.

"She is a zealous sister," said Lord George. "Her collection goes on prosperously, and is pursued with fervour. Has her husband joined?"

"A malignant,"* returned the secretary, folding up his papers. "Unworthy such a wife. He remains in outer darkness, and steadily refuses."

"The consequences be upon his own head!—Gashford!"

"My lord!"

"You don't think," he turned restlessly in his bed as he spoke, "these people will desert me, when the hour arrives? I have spoken boldly for them, ventured much, suppressed nothing. They'll not fall off, will they?"

"No fear of that, my lord," said Gashford, with a meaning look, which was rather the involuntary expression of his own thoughts than intended as any confirmation of his words, for the other's face was turned away. "Be sure there is no fear of that."

"Nor," he said with a more restless motion than before, "of their—but they *can* sustain no harm from leaguing for this purpose. Right is on our side, though Might may be against us. You feel as sure of that as I—honestly, you do?"

The secretary was beginning with "You do not doubt," when the other interrupted him, and impatiently rejoined:

"Doubt. No. Who says I doubt? If I doubted, should I cast away relatives, friends, everything, for this unhappy country's sake; this unhappy country," he cried, springing up in bed, after repeating the phrase "unhappy country's sake" to himself, at least a dozen times, "forsaken of God and man, delivered over to a dangerous confederacy of Popish powers;* the prey of corruption, idolatry, and despotism! Who says I doubt? Am I called, and chosen, and faithful? Tell me. Am I, or am I not?"

"To God, the country, and yourself," cried Gashford.

"I am. I will be. I say again, I will be: to the block. Who says as much! Do you? Does any man alive?"

The secretary drooped his head with an expression of perfect acquiescence in anything that had been said or might be; and Lord George gradually sinking down upon his pillow, fell asleep.

Although there was something very ludicrous in his vehement manner, taken in conjunction with his meagre aspect and ungraceful presence, it would scarcely have provoked a smile in any man of kindly feeling; or even if it had, he would have felt sorry and almost angry with himself next moment, for yielding to the impulse. This lord was sincere in his violence and in his wavering. A nature prone to false enthusiasm, and the vanity of being a leader, were the worst qualities apparent in his composition. All the rest was weakness— sheer weakness; and it is the unhappy lot of thoroughly weak men, that their very sympathies, affections, confidences—all the qualities which in better constituted minds are virtues—dwindle into foibles, or turn into downright vices.

Gashford, with many a sly look towards the bed, sat chuckling at his master's folly, until his deep and heavy breathing warned him that he might retire. Locking his desk, and replacing it within the trunk (but not before he had taken from a secret lining two printed handbills) he cautiously withdrew; looking back, as he went, at the pale face of the slumbering man, above whose head the dusty plumes that crowned the Maypole couch, waved drearily and sadly as though it were a bier.

Stopping on the staircase to listen that all was quiet, and to take off his shoes lest his footsteps should alarm any light sleeper who might be near at hand, he descended to the ground floor, and thrust one of his bills beneath the great door of the house. That done, he crept softly back to his own chamber, and from the window let another fall—carefully wrapped round a stone to save it from the wind—into the yard below.

They were addressed on the back "To every Protestant into whose hands this shall come," and bore within, what follows:

"Men and Brethren. Whoever shall find this letter, will take it as a warning to join, without delay, the friends of Lord George Gordon. There are great events at hand; and the times are dangerous and troubled. Read this carefully, keep it clean, and drop it somewhere else. For King and Country. Union."

"More seed, more seed," said Gashford as he closed the window. "When will the harvest come!"

CHAPTER THE THIRTY-SEVENTH.

To surround anything, however monstrous or ridiculous, with an air of mystery, is to invest it with a secret charm, and power of attraction which to the crowd is irresistible. False priests, false prophets, false doctors, false patriots, false prodigies of every kind, veiling their proceedings in mystery, have always addressed themselves at an immense advantage to the popular credulity, and have been, perhaps, more indebted to that resource in gaining and keeping for a time the upper hand of Truth and Common Sense, than to any half-dozen items in the whole catalogue of imposture. Curiosity is, and has been from the creation of the world, a master-passion. To awaken it, to gratify it by slight degrees, and yet leave something always in suspense, is to establish the surest hold that can be had, in wrong, on the unthinking portion of mankind.

If a man had stood on London Bridge, calling till he was hoarse, upon the passers-by, to join with Lord George Gordon, although for an object which no man understood, and which in that very incident had a charm of its own,—the probability is, that he might have influenced a score of people in a month. If all zealous Protestants had been publicly urged to join an association for the avowed purpose of singing a hymn or two occasionally, and hearing some indifferent speeches made, and ultimately of petitioning Parliament not to pass an act for abolishing the penal laws against Roman Catholic priests, the penalty of perpetual imprisonment denounced against those who educated children in that persuasion, and the disqualification of all members of the Romish church to inherit real property in the United Kingdom by right of purchase or descent,—matters so far removed from the business and bosoms of the mass, might perhaps have called together a hundred people. But when vague rumours got abroad, that in this Protestant association a secret power was mustering against the government for undefined and mighty purposes; when the air was filled with whispers of a confederacy among the Popish powers to degrade and enslave England, establish an inquisition in London, and turn the pens of Smithfield market* into stakes and cauldrons; when terrors and alarms which no man understood were perpetually broached, both in and out of Parliament, by one enthusiast who did not understand himself, and by-gone bugbears which had lain quietly in their graves for centuries, were raised again to haunt the ignorant and credulous; when all this was done, as it were, in the dark, and secret invitations to join the Great Protestant Association in defence of religion, life, and liberty, were dropped in the public ways, thrust under the house-doors, tossed in at windows, and pressed into the hands of those who trod the streets by night; when they glared from every wall, and shone on every post and pillar, so that stocks and stones appeared infected with the common fear, urging all men to join together blindfold in resistance of they knew not what, they knew not why;—then the mania spread indeed, and the body, still increasing every day, grew forty thousand strong.

So said, at least, in this month of March 1780, Lord George

Gordon, the association's president. Whether it was the fact or otherwise, few men knew, or cared to ascertain. It had never made any public demonstration; had scarcely ever been heard of, save through him; had never been seen; and was supposed by many to be the mere creature of his disordered brain. He was accustomed to talk largely about numbers of men—stimulated, as it was inferred, by certain successful disturbances, arising out of the same subject, which had occurred in Scotland* in the previous year; was looked upon as a cracked-brained member of the lower house, who attacked all parties and sided with none, and was very little regarded. It was known that there was discontent abroad—there always is; he had been accustomed to address the people by placard, speech, and pamphlet, upon other questions; nothing had come, in England, of his past exertions, and nothing was apprehended from his present. Just as he has come upon the reader, he had come, from time to time, upon the public, and been forgotten in a day; as suddenly as he appears in these pages, after a blank of five long years, did he and his proceedings begin to force themselves, about this period, upon the notice of thousands of people, who had mingled in active life during the whole interval, and who, without being deaf or blind to passing events, had scarcely ever thought of him before.

"My lord," said Gashford in his ear, as he drew the curtains of his bed betimes; "my lord!"

"Yes—who's that? What is it?"

"The clock has struck nine," returned the secretary, with meekly-folded hands. "You have slept well? I hope you have slept well? If my prayers are heard, you are refreshed indeed."

"To say the truth, I have slept so soundly," said Lord George, rubbing his eyes and looking round the room, "that I don't remember quite—what place is this?"

"My lord!" cried Gashford, with a smile.

"Oh!" returned his superior. "Yes. You're not a Jew then?"

"A Jew!" exclaimed the pious secretary, recoiling.

"I dreamed that we were Jews, Gashford. You and I—both of us—Jews with long beards."

"Heaven forbid, my lord! We might as well be Papists."

"I suppose we might," returned the other, very quickly. "Eh? You really think so, Gashford?"

"Surely I do," the secretary cried, with looks of great surprise.

"Humph!" he muttered. "Yes, that seems reasonable."

"I hope, my lord—" the secretary began.

"Hope!" he echoed, interrupting him. "Why do you say, you hope? There's no harm in thinking of such things."

"Not in dreams," returned the secretary.

"In dreams! No, nor waking either."

—"'Called, and chosen, and faithful,'" said Gashford, taking up Lord George's watch which lay upon a chair, and seeming to read the inscription on the seal, abstractedly.

It was the slightest action possible, not obtruded on his notice, and apparently the result of a moment's absence of mind, not worth remark. But as the words were uttered, Lord George, who had been going on impetuously, stopped short, reddened, and was silent. Apparently quite unconscious of this change in his demeanour, the wily secretary stepped a little apart, under pretence of pulling up the window-blind, and returning, when the other had had time to recover, said:

"The holy cause goes bravely on, my lord. I was not idle, even last night. I dropped two of the hand-bills before I went to bed, and both are gone this morning. Nobody in the house has mentioned the circumstance of finding them, though I have been down stairs full half-an-hour. One or two recruits will be their first fruit, I predict; and who shall say how many more, with Heaven's blessing on your inspired exertions!"

"It was a famous device in the beginning," replied Lord George; "an excellent device, and did good service in Scotland. It was quite worthy of you. You remind me not to be a sluggard, Gashford, when the vineyard is menaced with destruction, and may be trodden down by papist feet. Let the horses be saddled in half-an-hour. We must be up and doing!"

He said this with a heightened colour, and in a tone of such enthusiasm, that the secretary deemed all further prompting needless, and withdrew.

—"Dreamed he was a Jew," he said thoughtfully, as he closed the bedroom door. "He may come to that before he dies. It's like enough. Well! After a time, and provided I lost nothing by it, I don't see why that religion shouldn't suit me as well as any other. There are rich men among the Jews; shaving is very troublesome;—yes, it would suit me well enough. For the present, though, we must be Christian to the core. Our prophetic motto will suit all creeds in their turn, that's a comfort." Reflecting on this source of consolation, he reached the sitting-room, and rang the bell for breakfast.

Lord George was quickly dressed (for his plain toilet was easily made), and as he was no less frugal in his repasts than in his Puritan attire, his share of the meal was soon despatched. The secretary, however, more devoted to the good things of this world, or more intent on sustaining his strength and spirits for the sake of the Protestant cause, ate and drank to the last minute, and required indeed some three or four reminders from John Grueby, before he could resolve to tear himself away from Mr. Willet's plentiful providing.

At length he came down stairs, wiping his greasy mouth, and having paid John Willet's bill, climbed into his saddle. Lord George, who had been walking up and down before the house talking to himself with earnest gestures, mounted his horse; and returning old John Willet's stately bow, as well as the parting salutation of a dozen idlers whom the rumour of a live lord being about to leave the Maypole had gathered round the porch, they rode away, with stout John Grueby in the rear.

If Lord George Gordon had appeared in the eyes of Mr. Willet over-night, a nobleman of somewhat quaint and odd exterior, the impression was confirmed this morning, and increased a hundred fold. Sitting bolt upright upon his bony steed, with his long, straight hair, dangling about his face and fluttering in the wind; his limbs all angular and rigid, his elbows stuck out on either side ungracefully, and his whole frame jogged and shaken at every motion of his horse's feet; a more grotesque or more ungainly figure can hardly be conceived. In lieu of whip, he carried in his hand a great gold-headed cane, as large as any footman carries in these days; and his various modes of holding this unwieldy weapon—now upright before his face like the sabre of a horse-soldier, now over his shoulder like a musket, now between his finger and thumb, but always in some uncouth and awkward fashion—contributed in no small degree to the absurdity of his appearance. Stiff, lank, and solemn, dressed in an unusual manner, and ostentatiously exhibiting—whether by design or accident—all his peculiarities of carriage, gesture, and conduct; all the qualities, natural and artificial, in which he differed from other men; he might have moved the sternest looker-on to laughter, and fully provoked the smiles and whispered jests which greeted his departure from the Maypole inn.

Quite unconscious, however, of the effect he produced, he trotted on beside his secretary, talking to himself nearly all the way, until they came within a mile or two of London, when now and then some passenger went by who knew him by sight, and pointed him out to some one else, and perhaps stood looking after him, or cried in jest or earnest as it might be, "Hurrah Geordie! No Popery!" At which he would gravely pull off his hat, and bow. When they reached the town and rode along the streets, these notices became more frequent; some laughed, some hissed, some turned their heads and smiled, some wondered who he was, some ran along the pavement by his side and cheered. When this happened in a crush of carts and chairs and coaches, he would make a dead stop, and pulling off his hat cry "Gentlemen, No Popery!" to which the gentlemen would respond with lusty voices, and with three times three; and then, on he would go again with a score or so of the raggedest, following at his horse's heels, and shouting till their throats were parched.

The old ladies too—there were a great many old ladies in the streets, and these all knew him. Some of them—not those of the highest rank, but such as sold fruit from baskets and carried burdens—clapped their shrivelled hands, and raised a weazen, piping, shrill "Hurrah my Lord." Others waved their hands, or handkerchiefs, or shook their fans or parasols, or threw up windows and called in haste to those within, to come and see. All these marks of popular esteem, he received with profound gravity and respect; bowing very low, and so frequently that his hat was more off his head than on; and looking up at the houses as he passed along, with the air of one who was making a public entry, and yet was not puffed-up or proud.

So they rode (to the deep and unspeakable disgust of John Grueby) the whole length of Whitechapel, Leadenhall-street, and Cheapside, and into Saint Paul's Churchyard. Arriving close to the cathedral, he halted; spoke to Gashford; and looking upward at its lofty dome, shook his head, as though he said "The Church in Danger!" Then to be sure, the bystanders stretched their throats indeed; and he went on again with mighty acclamations from the mob, and lower bows than ever.

So along the Strand, up Swallow-street, into the Oxford-road, and thence to his house in Welbeck-street, near Cavendish-square,* whither he was attended by a few dozen idlers; of whom he took leave on the steps with this brief parting "Gentlemen, No Popery. Good day. God bless you." This being rather a shorter address than they expected, was received with some displeasure, and cries of "A speech! a speech!" which might have been complied with, but that John Grueby, making a mad charge upon them with all three horses, on his way to the stables, caused them to disperse into the adjoining fields, where they presently fell to pitch and toss, chuck-farthing, odd or even, dog-fighting, and other Protestant recreations.*

In the afternoon Lord George came forth again, dressed in a black velvet coat, and trousers and waistcoat of the Gordon plaid, all of the same Quaker cut; and in this costume, which made him look a dozen times more strange and singular than before, went down on foot to Westminster. Gashford, meanwhile, bestirred himself in business matters; with which he was still engaged when, shortly after dusk, John Grueby entered and announced a visitor.

"Let him come in" said Gashford.

"Here! come in!" growled John to somebody without; "You're a Protestant, an't you?"

"*I* should think so," replied a deep, gruff voice.

"You've the looks of it," said John Grueby. "I'd have known you for one, anywhere." With which remark he gave the visitor admission, retired, and shut the door.

The man who now confronted Gashford, was a squat, thickset personage, with a low retreating forehead, a coarse shock head of hair, and eyes so small and near together, that his broken nose alone seemed to prevent their meeting and fusing into one of the usual size. A dingy handkerchief twisted like a cord about his neck, left its great veins exposed to view, and they were swoln and starting, as though with gulping down strong passions, malice, and ill-will. His dress was of threadbare velveteen—a faded, rusty, whitened black, like the ashes of a pipe or a coal fire after a day's extinction; discoloured with the soils of many a stale debauch, and reeking yet with pot-house odours. In lieu of buckles at his knees, he wore unequal loops of packthread; and in his grimy hands he held a knotted stick, the knob of which was carved into a rough likeness of his own vile face. Such was the visitor who doffed his three-cornered hat in Gashford's presence, and waited, leering, for his notice.

"Ah! Dennis!" cried the secretary. "Sit down."

"I see my lord down yonder—" cried the man, with a jerk of his thumb towards the quarter that he spoke of, "and he says to me, says my lord, 'If you've nothing to do, Dennis, go up to my house and talk with Muster Gashford.' Of course I'd nothing to do, you know. These an't my working hours. Ha ha! I was a taking the air when I see my lord, that's what I was doing. I takes the air by night, as the howls does, Muster Gashford."

"And sometimes in the day-time, eh?" said the secretary—"when you go out in state, you know."

"Ha ha!" roared the fellow, smiting his leg; "for a gentleman as 'ull say a pleasant thing in a pleasant way, give me Muster Gashford agin' all London and Westminster! My lord an't a bad 'un at that, but he's a fool to you. Ah to be sure,—when I go out in state."

"And have your carriage," said the secretary; "and your chaplain, eh? and all the rest of it?"

"You'll be the death of me," cried Dennis with another roar, "you will. But what's in the wind now, Muster Gashford," he asked hoarsely, "Eh? Are we to be under orders to pull down one of them Popish chapels—or what?"

"Hush!" said the secretary, suffering the faintest smile to play upon his face. "Hush! God bless me, Dennis! We associate, you know, for strictly peaceable and lawful purposes."

"*I* know, bless you," returned the man, thrusting his tongue into his cheek; "I entered a' purpose, didn't I!"

"No doubt," said Gashford, smiling as before. And when he said so, Dennis roared again, and smote his leg still harder, and falling into fits of laughter, wiped his eyes with the corner of his neckerchief, and cried "Muster Gashford again all England—hollow!"

"Lord George and I were talking of you last night," said Gashford, after a pause. "He says you are a very earnest fellow."

"So I am," returned the hangman.

"And that you truly hate the Papists."

"So I do," and he confirmed it with a good round oath. "Lookye here, Muster Gashford," said the fellow, laying his hat and stick upon the floor, and slowly beating the palm of one hand with the fingers of the other; "Ob-serve. I'm a constitutional officer that works for my living, and does my work creditable. Do I, or do I not?"

"Unquestionably."

"Very good. Stop a minute. My work, is sound, Protestant, constitutional, English work. Is it, or is it not?"

"No man alive can doubt it."

"Nor dead neither. Parliament says this here—says Parliament 'If any man, woman, or child, does anything which goes again a certain number of our acts'—how many hanging laws may there be at this present time, Muster Gashford? Fifty?"

"I don't exactly know how many," replied Gashford, leaning back in his chair and yawning; "a great number though."

"Well; say fifty. Parliament says 'If any man, woman, or child, does anything again any one of them fifty acts, that man, woman, or child, shall be worked off by Dennis.' George the Third steps in when they number very strong at the end of a sessions, and says, 'These are too many for Dennis. I'll have half for *my*self* and Dennis shall have half for *him*self;' and sometimes he throws me in one over that I don't expect, as he did three year ago, when I got Mary Jones,* a young woman of nineteen who come up to Tyburn with a infant at her breast, and was worked off for taking a piece of cloth off the counter of a shop in Ludgate-hill, and putting it down again when the shopman see her; and who had never done any harm before, and only tried to do that, in consequence of her husband having been pressed three weeks previous, and she being left to beg, with two young children—as was proved upon the trial. Ha ha!—Well! That being the law and the practice of England, is the glory of England, an't it Muster Gashford?"

"Certainly," said the secretary.

"And in times to come," pursued the hangman, "if our grandsons should think of their grandfathers' times, and find these things altered, they'll say 'Those were days indeed, and we've been going down hill ever since.'*—Won't they Muster Gashford?"

"I have no doubt they will," said the secretary.

"Well then, look here," said the hangman. "If these papists gets into power, and begins to boil and roast instead of hang, what becomes of my work! If they touch my work that's a part of so many laws, what becomes of the laws in general, what becomes of the religion, what becomes of the country!—Did you ever go to church, Muster Gashford?"

"Ever!" repeated the secretary with some indignation; "of course."

"Well," said the ruffian, "I've been once—twice, counting the time I was christened—and when I heard the Parliament prayed for, and thought how many new hanging laws they made every sessions, I considered that *I* was prayed for. Now mind, Muster Gashford," said the fellow, taking up his stick and shaking it with a ferocious air, "I mustn't have my Protestant work touched, nor this here Protestant state of things altered in no degree, if I can help it; I mustn't have no Papists interfering with me, unless they come to me to be worked off in course of law; I mustn't have no biling, no roasting, no frying—nothing but hanging. My lord may well call me an earnest fellow. In support of the great Protestant principle of having plenty of that, I'll," and here he beat his club upon the ground, "burn, fight, kill—do anything you bid me, so that it's bold and devilish— though the end of it was, that I got hung myself.—There, Muster Gashford!"

He appropriately followed up this frequent prostitution of a noble word to the vilest purposes, by pouring out in a kind of ecstacy, at least a score of most tremendous oaths; then wiped his heated face upon his neckerchief, and cried, "No Popery! I'm a religious man, by G—!"

Gashford had leant back in his chair, regarding him with eyes so sunken, and so shadowed by his heavy brows, that for aught the hangman saw of them, he might have been stone blind. He remained smiling in silence for a short time longer, and then said, slowly and distinctly:

"You are indeed an earnest fellow, Dennis—a most valuable fellow—the staunchest man I know of in our ranks. But you must calm yourself; you must be peaceful, lawful, mild as any lamb. I am sure you will be though."

"Ay, ay, we shall see, Muster Gashford, we shall see. You won't have to complain of me," returned the other, shaking his head.

"I am sure I shall not," said the secretary in the same mild tone, and with the same emphasis. "We shall have, we think, about next month, or May, when this Papist relief bill comes before the house, to convene our whole body for the first time. My lord has thoughts of our walking in procession through the streets—just as an innocent display of strength—and accompanying our petition down to the door of the House of Commons."

"The sooner, the better," said Dennis, with another oath.

"We shall have to draw up in divisions, our numbers being so large; and, I believe I may venture to say," resumed Gashford, affecting not to hear the interruption, "though I have no direct instructions to that effect—that Lord George has thought of you as an excellent leader for one of these parties. I have no doubt you would be an admirable one."

"Try me," said the fellow, with an ugly wink.

"You would be cool, I know," pursued the secretary, still smiling, and still managing his eyes so that he could watch him closely, and really not be seen in turn, "obedient to orders, and perfectly temperate. You would lead your party into no danger, I am certain."

"I'd lead them, Muster Gashford"—the hangman was beginning in a reckless way, when Gashford started forward, laid his finger on his lips, and feigned to write, just as the door was opened by John Grueby.

"Oh!" said John, looking in; "here's another Protestant."

"Some other room, John," cried Gashford in his blandest voice. "I am engaged just now."

But John had brought this new visitor to the door, and he walked in unbidden, as the words were uttered; giving to view the form and features, rough attire, and reckless air, of Hugh.

CHAPTER THE THIRTY-EIGHTH.

THE secretary put his hand before his eyes to shade them from the glare of the lamp, and for some moments looked at Hugh with a frowning brow, as if he remembered to have seen him lately, but could not call to mind where, or on what occasion. His uncertainty was very brief, for before Hugh had spoken a word, he said, as his countenance cleared up:

"Ay, ay, I recollect. It's quite right, John, you needn't wait. Don't go, Dennis."

"Your servant, master," said Hugh, as Grueby disappeared.

"Yours friend," returned the secretary in his smoothest manner. "What brings *you* here? We left nothing behind us, I hope?"

Hugh gave a short laugh, and thrusting his hand into his breast, produced one of the handbills, soiled and dirty from lying out of doors all night, which he laid upon the secretary's desk after flattening it upon his knee, and smoothing out the wrinkles with his heavy palm.

"Nothing but that, master. It fell into good hands, you see."

"What is this!" said Gashford, turning it over with an air of perfectly natural surprise. " Where did you get it from, my good fellow; what does it mean? I don't understand this at all."

A little disconcerted by this reception, Hugh looked from the secretary to Dennis, who had risen and was standing at the table too, observing the stranger by stealth, and seeming to derive the utmost satisfaction from his manners and appearance. Considering himself silently appealed to by this action, Mr. Dennis shook his head thrice, as if to say of Gashford, "No. He don't know anything at all about it. I know he don't. I'll take my oath he don't;" and hiding his profile from Hugh with one long end of his frowzy neckerchief, nodded and chuckled behind this screen in extreme approval of the secretary's proceedings.

"It tells the man that finds it, to come here, don't it?" asked Hugh. "I'm no scholar, myself, but I showed it to a friend, and he said it did."

"It certainly does," said Gashford, opening his eyes to their utmost width; "really this is the most remarkable circumstance I have ever known. How did you come by this piece of paper, my good friend?"

"Muster Gashford," wheezed the hangman under his breath, "agin all Newgate!"

Whether Hugh heard him, or saw by his manner that he was being played upon, or perceived the secretary's drift of himself, he came in his blunt way to the point at once.

"Here!" he said, stretching out his hand and taking it back; "never mind the bill, or what it says, or what it don't say. You don't know anything about it, master,—no more do I,—no more does he," glancing at Dennis. "None of us know what it means, or where it comes from: there's an end of that. Now, I want to make one against the Catholics, I'm a No-Popery man, and ready to be sworn in. That's what I've come here for."

"Put him down on the roll, Muster Gashford," said Dennis approvingly. "That's the way to go to work—right to the end at once, and no palaver."

"What's the use of shooting wide of the mark, eh, old boy!" cried Hugh.

"My sentiments all over!" rejoined the hangman. "This is the sort of chap for my division, Muster Gashford. Down with him, sir. Put him on the roll. I'd stand godfather to him, if he was to be christened in a bonfire, made of the ruins of the Bank of England."

With these and other expressions of confidence of the like flattering kind, Mr. Dennis gave him a hearty slap on the back, which Hugh was not slow to return.

"No Popery, brother!" cried the hangman.

"No Property, brother!" responded Hugh.

"Popery, Popery," said the secretary with his usual mildness.

"It's all the same!" cried Dennis. "It's all right. Down with him, Muster Gashford. Down with everybody, down with everything! Hurrah for the Protestant religion! That's the time of day, Muster Gashford!"

The secretary regarded them both with a very favourable expression of countenance, while they gave loose to these and other demonstrations of their patriotic purpose; and was about to make some remark aloud, when Dennis, stepping up to him, and shading his mouth with his hand, said, in a hoarse whisper, as he nudged him with his elbow:

"Don't split upon a constitutional officer's profession, Muster Gashford. There are popular prejudices, you know, and he mightn't like it. Wait till he comes to be more intimate with me. He's a fine-built chap, an't he?"

"A powerful fellow indeed!"

"Did you ever, Muster Gashford," whispered Dennis, with a horrible kind of admiration, such as that with which a cannibal might regard his intimate friend, when hungry,—"did you ever"—and here he drew still closer to his ear, and fenced his mouth with both his open hands—"see such a throat as his? Do but cast your eye upon it. There's a neck for stretching, Muster Gashford!"

The secretary assented to this proposition with the best grace he could assume—it is difficult to feign a true professional relish: which is eccentric sometimes—and after asking the candidate a few unimportant questions, proceeded to enrol him a member of the Great Protestant Association of England. If anything could have exceeded Mr. Dennis's joy on the happy conclusion of this ceremony, it would have been the rapture with which he received the announcement that the new member could neither read nor write: those two arts being (as Mr. Dennis swore) the greatest possible curse a civilised community could know, and militating more against the professional emoluments and usefulness of the great constitutional office he had the honour to hold, than any adverse circumstances that could present themselves to his imagination.

The enrolment being completed, and Hugh having been informed by Gashford, in his peculiar manner, of the peaceful and strictly lawful objects contemplated by the body to which he now belonged—during which recital Mr. Dennis nudged him very much with his elbow, and made divers remarkable faces—the secretary gave them both to understand that he desired to be alone. Therefore they took their leaves without delay, and came out of the house together.

"Are you walking, brother?" said Dennis.

"Ay!" returned Hugh. "Where you will."

"That's social," said his new friend. "Which way shall we take? Shall we go and have a look at doors that we shall make a pretty good clattering at, before long—eh, brother?"

Hugh answering in the affirmative, they went slowly down to Westminster, where both houses of Parliament were then sitting. Mingling in the crowd of carriages, horses, servants, chairmen, link-boys, porters, and idlers of all kinds, they lounged about; while Hugh's new friend pointed out to him significantly the weak parts of the building, how easy it was to get into the lobby, and so to the very door of the House of Commons; and how plainly, when they marched down there in grand array, their roars and shouts would be heard by the members inside; with a great deal more to the same purpose, all of which Hugh received with manifest delight.

He told him, too, who some of the Lords and Commons were, by name, as they came in and out; whether they were friendly to the Papists or otherwise; and bade him take notice of their liveries and equipages, that he might be sure of them, in case of need. Sometimes he drew him close to the windows of a passing carriage, that he might see its master's face by the light of the lamps; and, both in respect of people and localities, he showed so much acquaintance with everything around, that it was plain he had often studied there before; as indeed, when they grew a little more confidential, he confessed he had.

Perhaps the most striking part of all this was, the number of people—never in groups of more than two or three together—who seemed to be skulking about the crowd for the same purpose. To the greater part of these, a slight nod or a look from Hugh's companion was sufficient greeting; but, now and then, some man would come and stand beside him in the throng, and, without turning his head or appearing to communicate with him, would say a word or two in a low voice, which he would answer in the same cautious manner. Then they would part, like strangers. Some of these men often reappeared again unexpectedly in the crowd close to Hugh, and, as they passed by, pressed his hand, or looked him sternly in the face; but they never spoke to him, nor he to them; no, not a word.

It was remarkable, too, that whenever they happened to stand where there was any press of people, and Hugh chanced to be look-ing downward, he was sure to see an arm stretched out—under his own perhaps, or perhaps across him—which thrust some paper into the hand or pocket of a bystander, and was so suddenly withdrawn that it was impossible to tell from whom it came; nor could he see in any face, on glancing quickly round, the least confusion or surprise.

They often trod upon a paper like the one he carried in his breast, but his companion whispered him not to touch it or to take it up,—not even to look towards it,—so there they let them lie, and passed on.

When they had paraded the street and all the avenues of the building in this manner for near two hours, they turned away, and his friend asked him what he thought of what he had seen, and whether he was prepared for a good hot piece of work if it should come to that. "The hotter the better," said Hugh, "I'm prepared for any-thing."—"So am I," said his friend, "and so are many of us;" and they shook hands upon it with a great oath, and with many terrible imprecations on the Papists.

As they were thirsty by this time, Dennis proposed that they should repair together to the Boot,* where there was good company and strong liquor. Hugh yielding a ready assent, they bent their steps that way with no loss of time.

This Boot was a lone house of public entertainment, situated in the fields at the back of the Foundling Hospital;* a very solitary spot at that period, and quite deserted after dark. The tavern stood at some distance from any high road, and was approachable only by a

dark and narrow lane; so that Hugh was much surprised to find several people drinking there, and great merriment going on. He was still more surprised to find among them almost every face that had caught his attention in the crowd; but his companion having whispered him outside the door, that it was not considered good manners at the Boot to appear at all curious about the company, he kept his own counsel, and made no show of recognition.

Before putting his lips to the liquor which was brought for them, Dennis drank in a loud voice the health of Lord George Gordon, President of the Great Protestant Association; which toast Hugh pledged likewise, with corresponding enthusiasm. A fiddler who was present, and who appeared to act as the appointed minstrel of the company, forthwith struck up a Scotch reel; and that in tones so invigorating, that Hugh and his friend (who had both been drinking before) rose from their seats as by previous concert, and, to the great admiration of the assembled guests, performed an extemporaneous No-Popery Dance.

CHAPTER THE THIRTY-NINTH.

HE applause which the performance of Hugh and his new friend elicited from the company at The Boot, had not yet subsided, and the two dancers were still panting from their exertions, which had been of a rather extreme and violent character, when the party was reinforced by the arrival of some more guests, who, being a detachment of United Bulldogs, were received with very flattering marks of distinction and respect.

The leader of this small party—for, including himself, they were but three in number—was our old acquaintance, Mr. Tappertit, who seemed, physically speaking, to have grown smaller with years (particularly as to his legs, which were stupendously little), but who, in a moral point of view, in personal dignity and self-esteem, had swelled into a giant. Nor was it by any means difficult for the most unobservant person to detect this state of feeling in the quondam 'Prentice, for it not only proclaimed itself impressively and beyond mistake in his majestic walk and kindling eye, but found a striking means of revelation in his turned-up nose, which scouted all things of earth with deep disdain, and sought communion with its kindred skies.

Mr. Tappertit, as chief or captain of the Bulldogs, was attended by his two lieutenants; one, the tall comrade of his younger life; the other, a 'Prentice Knight in days of yore—Mark Gilbert, bound in the olden time to Thomas Curzon of the Golden Fleece. These gentlemen, like himself, were now emancipated from their 'Prentice thraldom, and served as journeymen; but they were, in humble emulation of his great example, bold and daring spirits, and aspired to a distinguished state in great political events. Hence their connexion with the Protestant Association of England, sanctioned by the name of Lord George Gordon; and hence their present visit to The Boot.

"Gentlemen!" said Mr. Tappertit, taking off his hat as a great General might in addressing his troops. "Well met. My Lord does me and you the honour to send his compliments per self."

"You've seen my Lord too, have you?" said Dennis. *I* see him this afternoon."

"My duty called me to the Lobby* when our shop shut up; and I saw him there, sir," Mr. Tappertit replied, as he and his Lieutenants took their seats. "How do *you* do?"

"Lively, master, lively," said the fellow. "Here's a new brother, regularly put down in black and white by Muster Gashford; a credit to the cause; one of the stick-at-nothing sort; one arter my own heart. D'ye see him? Has he got the looks of a man that'll do, do you think?" he cried, as he slapped Hugh on the back.

"Looks or no looks," said Hugh, with a drunken flourish of his arm, "I'm the man you want. I hate the Papists, every one of 'em. They hate me and I hate them. They do me all the harm they can, and I'll do them all the harm *I* can. Hurrah!"

"Was there ever," said Dennis, looking round the room, when the echo of his boisterous voice had died away; "was there ever such a game boy! Why, I mean to say, brothers, that if Muster Gashford had gone a hundred mile and got together fifty men of the common run, they wouldn't have been worth this one."

The greater part of the company implicitly subscribed to this opinion, and testified their faith in Hugh, by nods and looks of great significance. Mr. Tappertit sat and contemplated him for a long time in silence, as if he suspended his judgment; then drew a little nearer to him, and eyed him over more carefully; then went close up to him, and took him apart into a dark corner.

"I say," he began, with a thoughtful brow, "haven't I seen you before?"

"It's like you may," said Hugh, in his careless way. "I don't know; shouldn't wonder."

"No, but it's very easily settled," returned Sim. "Look at me. Did you ever see *me* before? You wouldn't be likely to forget it, you know, if you ever did. Look at me. Don't be afraid; I won't do you any harm. Take a good look—steady now."

The encouraging way in which Mr. Tappertit made this request, and coupled it with an assurance that he needn't be frightened, amused Hugh mightily—so much indeed, that he saw nothing at all of the small man before him, through closing his eyes in a fit of hearty laughter, which shook his great broad sides until they ached again.

"Come!" said Mr. Tappertit, growing a little impatient under this disrespectful treatment. "Do you know me, feller?"

"Not I," cried Hugh. "Ha ha ha! Not I! But I should like to."

"And yet I'd have wagered a seven-shilling piece,"* said Mr. Tappertit, folding his arms, and confronting him with his legs wide apart and firmly planted on the ground, "that you once were hostler at the Maypole."

Hugh opened his eyes on hearing this, and looked at him in great surprise.

"—And so you were, too," said Mr. Tappertit, pushing him away, with a condescending playfulness. "When did *my* eyes ever deceive—unless it was a young woman! Don't you know me now?"

"Why it an't—" Hugh faltered.

"An't it," said Mr. Tappertit. "Are you sure of that? You remember G. Varden, don't you?"

Certainly Hugh did, and he remembered D. Varden too; but that he didn't tell him.

"You remember coming down there, before I was out of my time, to ask after a vagabond that had bolted off, and left his disconsolate father a prey to the bitterest emotions, and all the rest of it—don't you?" said Mr. Tappertit.

"Of course I do!" cried Hugh. "And I saw you there."

"Saw me there!" said Mr. Tappertit. "Yes, I should think you did see me there. The place would be troubled to go on without me. Don't you remember my thinking you liked the vagabond, and on that account going to quarrel with you; and then finding you detested him worse than poison, going to drink with you? Don't you remember that?"

"To be sure!" cried Hugh.

"Well! and are you in the same mind now?" said Mr. Tappertit.

"Yes!" roared Hugh.

"You speak like a man," said Mr. Tappertit, "and I'll shake hands with you." With these conciliatory expressions he suited the action to the word; and Hugh meeting his advances readily, they performed the ceremony with a show of great heartiness.

"I find," said Mr. Tappertit, looking round on the assembled guests, "that brother What's-his-name and I are old acquaintance.— You never heard anything more of that rascal, I suppose, eh?"

"Not a syllable," replied Hugh. "I never want to. I don't believe I ever shall. He's dead long ago, I hope."

"It's to be hoped, for the sake of mankind in general and the happiness of society, that he is," said Mr. Tappertit, rubbing his palm upon his legs, and looking at it between whiles. "Is your other hand at all cleaner? Much the same. Well, I'll owe you another shake. We'll suppose it done, if you've no objection."

Hugh laughed again, and with such thorough abandonment to his mad humour, that his limbs seemed dislocated, and his whole frame in danger of tumbling to pieces; but Mr. Tappertit, so far from receiving this extreme merriment with any irritation, was pleased to regard it with the utmost favour, and even to join in it, so far as one of his gravity and station could, with any regard to that decency and decorum which men in high places are expected to maintain.

Mr. Tappertit did not stop here, as many public characters might have done, but calling up his brace of lieutenants, introduced Hugh to them with high commendation; declaring him to be a man who, at such times as those in which they lived, could not be too much cherished. Further, he did him the honour to remark, that he would be an acquisition of which even the United Bulldogs might be proud; and finding, upon sounding him, that he was quite ready and willing to enter the society (for he was not at all particular, and would have leagued himself that night with anything, or anybody, for any purpose whatsoever), caused the necessary preliminaries to be gone into upon the spot. This tribute to his great merit delighted no man more than Mr. Dennis, as he himself proclaimed with several rare and surprising oaths; and indeed it gave unmingled satisfaction to the whole assembly.

"Make anything you like of me!" cried Hugh, flourishing the can he had emptied more than once. "Put me on any duty you please. I'm your man. I'll do it. Here's my captain—here's my leader. Ha ha ha! Let him give me the word of command, and I'll fight the whole Parliament House single-handed, or set a lighted torch to the King's Throne itself!" With that, he smote Mr. Tappertit on the back, with such violence that his little body seemed to shrink into a mere nothing; and roared again until the very foundlings near at hand were startled in their beds.

In fact, a sense of something whimsical in their companionship seemed to have taken entire possession of his rude brain. The bare fact of being patronised by a great man whom he could have crushed with one hand, appeared in his eyes so eccentric and humorous, that a kind of ferocious merriment gained the mastery over him, and quite subdued his brutal nature. He roared and roared again; toasted Mr. Tappertit a hundred times; declared himself a Bulldog to the core; and vowed to be faithful to him to the last drop of blood in his veins.

All these compliments Mr. Tappertit received as matters of course—flattering enough in their way, but entirely attributable to his vast superiority. His dignified self-possession only delighted Hugh the more; and in a word, this giant and dwarf struck up a friendship which bade fair to be of long continuance, as the one held it to be his right to command, and the other considered it an exquisite pleasantry to obey. Nor was Hugh by any means a passive follower, who scrupled to act without precise and definite orders; for when Mr. Tappertit mounted on an empty cask which stood by way of rostrum in the room, and volunteered a speech upon the alarming crisis then at hand, he placed himself beside the orator, and though he grinned from ear to ear at every word he said, threw out such expressive hints to scoffers in the management of his cudgel, that those who were at first the most disposed to interrupt, became remarkably attentive, and were the loudest in their approbation.

It was not all noise and jest, however, at The Boot, nor were the whole party listeners to the speech. There were some men at the other end of the room (which was a long, low-roofed chamber) in earnest conversation all the time; and when any of this group went out, fresh people were sure to come in soon afterwards and sit down in their places, as though the others had relieved them on some watch or duty; which it was pretty clear they did, for these changes took place by the clock, at intervals of half an hour. These persons whispered very much among themselves, and kept aloof, and often looked round, as jealous of their speech being overheard; some two or three among them entered in books what seemed to be reports from the others; when they were not thus employed, one of them would turn to the newspapers which were strewn upon the table, and from the Saint James's Chronicle, the Herald, Chronicle,* or Public Advertiser, would read to the rest in a low voice some passage having reference to the topic in which they were all so deeply interested. But the great attraction was a pamphlet called The Thunderer,* which espoused their own opinions, and was supposed at that time to emanate directly from the Association. This was always in request; and whether read aloud, to an eager knot of listeners, or by some

solitary man, was certain to be followed by stormy talking and excited looks.

In the midst of all his merriment, and admiration of his captain, Hugh was made sensible by these and other tokens, of the presence of an air of mystery, akin to that which had so much impressed him out of doors. It was impossible to discard a sense that something serious was going on, and that under the noisy revel of the public-house, there lurked unseen and dangerous matter. Little affected by this, however, he was perfectly satisfied with his quarters and would have remained there till morning, but that his conductor rose soon after midnight, to go home; Mr. Tappertit following his example, left him no excuse to stay. So they all three left the house together: roaring a No-Popery song until the fields resounded with the dismal noise.

"Cheer up, captain!" cried Hugh, when they had roared themselves out of breath. "Another stave!"

Mr. Tappertit, nothing loath, began again; and so the three went staggering on, arm-in-arm, shouting like madmen, and defying the watch with great valour. Indeed this did not require any unusual bravery or boldness, as the watchmen of that time, being selected for the office on account of excessive age and extraordinary infirmity, had a custom of shutting themselves up tight in their boxes on the first symptoms of disturbance, and remaining there until they disappeared. In these proceedings, Mr. Dennis, who had a gruff voice and lungs of considerable power, distinguished himself very much, and acquired great credit with his two companions.

"What a queer fellow you are!" said Mr. Tappertit. "You're so precious sly and close. Why don't you ever tell what trade you're of?"

"Answer the captain instantly," cried Hugh, beating his hat down on his head; "why don't you ever tell what trade you're of?"

"I'm of as gen-teel a calling, brother, as any man in England—as light a business as any gentleman could desire."

"Was you 'prenticed to it?" asked Mr. Tappertit.

"No. Natural genius," said Mr. Dennis. "No 'prenticing. It come by natur'. Muster Gashford knows my calling. Look at that hand of mine—many and many a job that hand has done, with a neatness and dex-terity, never known afore. When I look at that hand," said Mr. Dennis, shaking it in the air, "and remember the helegant bits of work it has turned off, I feel quite molloncholy to think it should ever grow old and feeble. But sich is life!"

He heaved a deep sigh as he indulged in these reflections, and putting his fingers with an absent air on Hugh's throat, and particularly under his left ear, as if he were studying the anatomical development of that part of his frame, shook his head in a despondent manner and actually shed tears.

"You're a kind of artist, I suppose—eh!" said Mr. Tappertit.

"Yes," rejoined Dennis; "yes—I may call myself a artist—a fancy workman—art improves natur'—that's my motto."

"And what do you call this?" said Mr. Tappertit taking his stick out of his hand.

"That's my portrait atop," Dennis replied; "d'ye think it's like?"

"Why—it's a little too handsome," said Mr. Tappertit. "Who did it? You?"

"I!" repeated Dennis, gazing fondly on his image. "I wish I had the talent. That was carved by a friend of mine, as is now no more. The very day afore he died, he cut that with his pocket-knife from memory! 'I'll die game,' says my friend, 'and my last moments shall be dewoted to making Dennis's picter'.' That's it."

"That was a queer fancy, wasn't it?" said Mr. Tappertit.

"It *was* a queer fancy," rejoined the other, breathing on his fictitious nose, and polishing it with the cuff of his coat, "but he was a queer subject altogether—a kind of gipsy—one of the finest, stand-up men, you ever see. Ah! He told me some things that would startle you a bit, did that friend of mine, on the morning when he died."

"You were with him at the time, were you?" said Mr. Tappertit.

"Yes," he answered with a curious look, "I was there. Oh! yes certainly, I was there. He wouldn't have gone off half as comfortable without me. I had been with three or four of his family under the same circumstances. They were all fine fellows."

"They must have been fond of you," remarked Mr. Tappertit, looking at him sideways.

"I don't know that they was exactly fond of me," said Dennis, with a little hesitation, "but they all had me near 'em when they departed. I come in for their wardrobes too. This very hankecher that you see round my neck, belonged to him that I've been speaking of—him as did that likeness."

Mr. Tappertit glanced at the article referred to, and appeared to think that the deceased's ideas of dress were of a peculiar and by no means an expensive kind. He made no remark upon the point, however, and suffered his mysterious companion to proceed without interruption.

"These smalls," said Dennis, rubbing his legs; "these very smalls—they belonged to a friend of mine that's left off sich incumbrances for ever: this coat too—I've often walked behind this coat, in the streets, and wondered whether it would ever come to me: this pair of shoes have danced a hornpipe for another man, afore my eyes, full half-a-dozen times at least: and as to my hat," he said, taking it off, and twirling it round upon his fist—"Lord! I've seen this hat go up Holborn on the box of a hackney-coach—ah, many and many a day!"

"You don't mean to say their old wearers are *all* dead, I hope?" said Mr. Tappertit, falling a little distance from him, as he spoke.

"Every one of 'em," replied Dennis. "Every man Jack!"

There was something so very ghastly in this circumstance, and it appeared to account, in such a very strange and dismal manner, for his faded dress—which, in this new aspect, seemed discoloured by the earth from graves—that Mr. Tappertit abruptly found he was going another way, and, stopping short, bade him good night with the utmost heartiness. As they happened to be near the Old Bailey,* and Mr. Dennis knew there were turnkeys in the lodge with whom he could pass the night, and discuss professional subjects of common interest among them before a rousing fire, and over a social glass, he separated from his companions without any great regret, and warmly shaking hands with Hugh, and making an early appointment for their meeting at The Boot, left them to pursue their road.

"That's a strange sort of man," said Mr. Tappertit, watching the hackney-coachman's hat as it went bobbing down the street. "I don't know what to make of him. Why can't he have his smalls made to order, or wear live clothes at any rate?"

"He's a lucky man, captain," cried Hugh. "I should like to have such friends as his."

"I hope he don't get 'em to make their wills, and then knock 'em on the head," said Mr. Tappertit, musing. "But come. The United B.'s expect me. On!—What's the matter?"

"I quite forgot," said Hugh, who had started at the striking of a neighbouring clock. "I have somebody to see to-night—I must turn back directly. The drinking and singing put it out of my head. It's well I remembered it!"

Mr. Tappertit looked at him as though he were about to give utterance to some very majestic sentiments in reference to this act of desertion, but as it was clear, from Hugh's hasty manner, that the engagement was one of a pressing nature, he graciously forbore, and gave him his permission to depart immediately, which Hugh acknowledged with a roar of laughter.

"Good night, captain!" he cried. "I am yours to the death, remember!"

"Farewell!" said Mr. Tappertit, waving his hand. "Be bold and vigilant!"

"No Popery, captain!" roared Hugh.

"England in blood first!" cried his desperate leader. Whereat Hugh cheered and laughed, and ran off like a greyhound.

"That man will prove a credit to my corps," said Simon, turning thoughtfully upon his heel. "And let me see. In an altered state of society—which must ensue if we break out and are victorious—when the locksmith's child is mine, Miggs must be got rid of somehow, or she'll poison the tea-kettle one evening when I'm out. He might marry Miggs, if he was drunk enough. It shall be done. I'll make a note of it."

CHAPTER THE FORTIETH.

LITTLE thinking of the plan for his happy settlement in life which had suggested itself to the teeming brain of his provident commander, Hugh made no pause until Saint Dunstan's giants* struck the hour above him, when he worked the handle of a pump which stood hard by, with great vigour, and thrusting his head under the spout, let the water gush upon him until a little stream ran down from every uncombed hair, and he was wet to the waist. Considerably refreshed by this ablution, both in mind and body, and almost sobered for the time, he dried himself as he best could; then crossed the road, and plied the knocker of the Middle Temple gate.

The night-porter looked through a small grating in the portal with a surly eye, and cried "Halloa!" which greeting Hugh returned in kind, and bade him open quickly.

"We don't sell beer here," cried the man; "what else do you want?"

"To come in," Hugh replied, with a kick at the door.

"Where to go to?"

"Paper-Buildings."

"Whose chambers?"

"Sir John Chester's." Each of which answers, he emphasised with another kick.

After a little growling on the other side, the gate was opened, and he passed in: undergoing a close inspection from the porter as he did so.

"*You* wanting Sir John, at this time of night!" said the man.

"Ay!" said Hugh. "I! What of that?"

"Why, I must go with you and see that you do, for I don't believe it."

"Come along then."

Eyeing him with suspicious looks, the man, with key and lantern, walked on at his side, and attended him to Sir John Chester's door, at which Hugh gave one knock, that echoed through the dark staircase like a ghostly summons, and made the dull light tremble in the drowsy lamp.

"Do you think he wants me now?" said Hugh.

Before the man had time to answer, a footstep was heard within, a light appeared, and Sir John, in his dressing-gown and slippers, opened the door.

"I ask your pardon, Sir John," said the porter, pulling off his hat. "Here's a young man says he wants to speak to you. It's late for strangers. I thought it best to see that all was right."

"Aha?" cried Sir John, raising his eyebrows. "It's you, messenger, is it? Go in. Quite right, friend. I commend your prudence highly. Thank you. God bless you. Good night."

To be commended, thanked, God-blessed, and bade good night by one who carried "Sir" before his name, and wrote himself M.P. to boot, was something for a porter. He withdrew with much humility and reverence. Sir John followed his late visitor into the dressing-room, and sitting in his easy chair before the fire, and moving it so that he could see him as he stood, hat in hand, beside the door, looked at him from head to foot.

The old face, calm and pleasant as ever; the complexion, quite juvenile in its bloom and clearness; the same smile; the wonted precision and elegance of dress; the white, well-ordered teeth; the delicate hands; the composed and quiet manner; everything as it used to be: no marks of age or passion, envy, hate, or discontent: all unruffled and serene, and quite delightful to behold.

He wrote himself M.P.—but how? Why, thus. It was a proud family—more proud, indeed, than wealthy. He had stood in danger of arrest; of bailiffs, and a jail—a vulgar jail, to which the common people with small incomes went. Gentlemen of ancient houses have no privilege of exemption from such cruel laws—unless they are of one great house, and then they have. A proud man of his stock and kindred had the means of sending him there. He offered—not indeed to pay his debts, but to let him sit for a close borough* until his own son came of age, which, if he lived, would come to pass in twenty years. It was quite as good as an Insolvent Act,* and infinitely more genteel. So Sir John Chester was a member of Parliament.

But how Sir John? Nothing so simple, or so easy. One touch with a sword of state, and the transformation is effected. John Chester Esquire, M.P. attended court—went up with an address—headed a deputation. Such elegance of manner, so many graces of deportment, such powers of conversation, could never pass unnoticed. Mr. was too common for such merit. A man so gentlemanly should have been—but Fortune is capricious—born a Duke: just as some dukes should have been born labourers. He caught the fancy of the king, knelt down a grub, and rose a butterfly. John Chester Esquire was knighted and became Sir John.

"I thought when you left me this evening, my esteemed acquaintance," said Sir John after a pretty long silence, "that you intended to return with all despatch?"

"So I did, Master."

"And so you have?" he retorted, glancing at his watch. "Is that what you would say?"

Instead of replying, Hugh changed the leg on which he leant, shuffled his cap from one hand to the other, looked at the ground, the wall, the ceiling, and finally at Sir John himself; before whose pleasant face he lowered his eyes again, and fixed them on the floor.

"And how have you been employing yourself in the mean while?" quoth Sir John, lazily crossing his legs. "Where have you been? what harm have you been doing?"

"No harm at all, Master," growled Hugh, with humility. "I have only done as you ordered."

"As I *what?*" returned Sir John.

"Well then," said Hugh uneasily, "as you advised, or said I ought, or said I might, or said that you would do, if you was me. Don't be so hard upon me, master."

Something like an expression of triumph in the perfect control he had established over this rough instrument, appeared in the knight's face for an instant; but it vanished directly, as he said—paring his nails while speaking:

"When you say I ordered you, my good fellow, you imply that I directed you to do something for me—something I wanted done—something for my own ends and purposes—you see? Now I am sure I needn't enlarge upon the extreme absurdity of such an idea, however unintentional; so, please—" and here he turned his eyes upon him—"to be more guarded. Will you?"

"I meant to give you no offence," said Hugh. "I don't know what to say. You catch me up so very short."

"You will be caught up much shorter, my good friend—infinitely shorter—one of these days, depend upon it," replied his patron, calmly. "By-the-bye, instead of wondering why you have been so long, my wonder should be why you came at all. Why did you?"

"You know, master," said Hugh, "that I couldn't read the bill I found, and that supposing it to be something particular from the way it was wrapped up, I brought it here."

"And could you ask no one else to read it, Bruin?"* said Sir John.

"No one that I could trust with secrets, master. Since Barnaby Rudge was lost sight of for good and all—and that's five year ago—I haven't talked with any one but you."

"You have done me honour, I am sure."

"I have come to and fro, master, all through that time, when there was anything to tell, because I knew that you'd be angry with me if I stayed away," said Hugh, blurting the words out, after an embarrassed silence; "and because I wished to please you, if I could, and not to have you go against me. There. That's the true reason why I came to-night. You know that, master, I am sure."

"You are a specious fellow," returned Sir John, fixing his eyes upon him, "and carry two faces under your hood, as well as the best. Didn't you give me in this room, this evening, any other reason; no dislike of anybody who has slighted you, lately, on all occasions, abused you, treated you with rudeness; acted towards you, more as if you were a mongrel dog than a man like himself?"

"To be sure I did!" cried Hugh, his passion rising, as the other meant it should; "and I say it all over now, again. I'd do anything to have some revenge on him—anything. And when you told me that he and all the Catholics would suffer from those who joined together under that handbill, I said I'd make one of 'em, if their master was the devil himself. I *am* one of 'em. See whether I am as good as my word and turn out to be among the foremost, or no. I mayn't have much head, master, but I've head enough to remember those that use me ill. You shall see, and so shall he, and so shall hundreds more, how my spirit backs me when the time comes. My bark is nothing to my bite. Some that I know, had better have a wild lion among 'em than me, when I am fairly loose—they had!"

The knight looked at him with a smile of far deeper meaning than ordinary; and pointing to the old cupboard, followed him with his eyes while he filled and drank a glass of liquor; and smiled when his back was turned, with deeper meaning yet.

"You are in a blustering mood, my friend," he said, when Hugh confronted him again.

"Not I, master!" cried Hugh. "I don't say half I mean. I can't. I haven't got the gift. There are talkers enough among us; I'll be one of the doers."

"Oh! you have joined those fellows then?" said Sir John, with an air of most profound indifference.

"Yes. I went up to the house you told me of, and got put down upon the muster. There was another man there, named Dennis—"

"Dennis, eh!" cried Sir John, laughing. "Ay, ay! a pleasant fellow, I believe?"

"A roaring dog, master—one after my own heart—hot upon the matter too—red hot."

"So I have heard," replied Sir John carelessly. "You don't happen to know his trade, do you?"

"He wouldn't say," cried Hugh. "He keeps it secret."

"Ha ha!" laughed Sir John. "A strange fancy—a weakness with some persons—you'll know it one day, I dare swear."

"We're intimate already," said Hugh.

"Quite natural! And have been drinking together, eh?" pursued

Sir John. "Did you say what place you went to in company, when you left Lord George's?"

Hugh had not said or thought of saying, but he told him; and this inquiry being followed by a long train of questions, he related all that had passed both in and out of doors, the kind of people he had seen, their numbers, state of feeling, mode of conversation, apparent expectations and intentions. His questioning was so artfully contrived, that he seemed even in his own eyes to volunteer all this information rather than to have it wrested from him; and he was brought to this state of feeling so naturally, that when Sir John yawned at length and declared himself quite wearied out, he made a rough kind of excuse for having talked so much.

"There—get you gone," said Sir John, holding the door open in his hand. "You have made a pretty evening's work. I told you not to do this. You may get into trouble. You'll have an opportunity of revenging yourself on your proud friend Haredale, though, and for that, you'd hazard anything I suppose?"

"I would," retorted Hugh, stopping in his passage out, and looking back; "but what do *I* risk! What do I stand a chance of losing, master? Friends, home? A fig for 'em all; I have none; they are nothing to me. Give me a good scuffle; let me pay off old scores in a bold riot where there are men to stand by me; and then use me as you like—it don't matter much to me what the end is!"

"What have you done with that paper?" said Sir John.

"I have it here, master."

"Drop it again as you go along; it's as well not to keep such things about you."

Hugh nodded, and touching his cap with an air of as much respect as he could summon up, departed.

Sir John, fastening the doors behind him, went back to his dressing-room, and sat down once again before the fire, at which he gazed for a long time, in earnest meditation.

"This happens fortunately," he said, breaking into a smile, "and promises well. Let me see. My relative and I, who are the most Protestant fellows in the world, give our worst wishes to the Roman Catholic cause; and to Saville, who introduces their bill,* I have a personal objection besides; but as each of us has himself for the first article in his creed, we cannot commit ourselves by joining with a very extravagant madman, such as this Gordon most undoubtedly is.

Now really, to foment his disturbances in secret, through the medium of such a very apt instrument as my savage friend here, may further our real ends; and to express at all becoming seasons, in moderate and polite terms, a disapprobation of his proceedings, though we agree with him in principle, will certainly be to gain a character for honesty and uprightness of purpose, which cannot fail to do us infinite service, and to raise us into some importance. Good! So much for public grounds. As to private considerations, I confess that if these vagabonds *would* make some riotous demonstration (which does not appear impossible), and *would* inflict some little chastisement on Haredale as a not inactive man among his sect, it would be extremely agreeable to my feelings, and would amuse me beyond measure. Good again! Perhaps better!"

When he came to this point, he took a pinch of snuff; then beginning slowly to undress, he resumed his meditations, by saying with a smile:

"I fear, I *do* fear exceedingly, that my friend is following fast in the footsteps of his mother. His intimacy with Mr. Dennis is very ominous. But I have no doubt he must have come to that end any way. If I lend him a helping hand, the only difference is, that he may, upon the whole, possibly drink a few gallons, or puncheons, or hogsheads, less in this life than he otherwise would. It's no business of mine. It's a matter of very small importance!"

So he took another pinch of snuff, and went to bed.

CHAPTER THE FORTY-FIRST.

FROM the workshop of the Golden Key, there issued forth a tinkling sound, so merry and good-humoured, that it suggested the idea of some one working blithely, and made quite pleasant music. No man who hammered on at a dull monotonous duty, could have brought such cheerful notes from steel and iron; none but a chirping, healthy, honest-hearted fellow, who made the best of everything, and felt kindly towards everybody, could have done it for an instant. He might have been a coppersmith, and still been musical. If he had sat in a jolting waggon, full of rods of iron, it seemed as if he would have brought some harmony out of it.

Tink, tink, tink—clear as a silver bell, and audible at every pause of the streets' harsher noises, as though it said, "I don't care; nothing puts me out; I am resolved to be happy." Women scolded, children squalled, heavy carts went rumbling by, horrible cries proceeded from the lungs of hawkers; still it struck in again, no higher, no lower, no louder, no softer; not thrusting itself on people's notice a bit the more for having been outdone by louder sounds—tink, tink, tink, tink, tink.

It was a perfect embodiment of the still small voice, free from all cold, hoarseness, huskiness, or unhealthiness of any kind; foot-passengers slackened their pace, and were disposed to linger near it; neighbours who had got up splenetic that morning, felt good-humour stealing on them as they heard it, and by degrees became quite sprightly; mothers danced their babies to its ringing; still the same magical tink, tink, tink, came gaily from the workshop of the Golden Key.

Who but the locksmith could have made such music! A gleam of sun shining through the unsashed window, and chequering the dark workshop with a broad patch of light, fell full upon him, as though attracted by his sunny heart. There he stood working at his anvil, his face all radiant with exercise and gladness, his sleeves turned up, his wig pushed off his shining forehead—the easiest, freest, happiest man in all the world. Beside him sat a sleek cat, purring and winking in the light, and falling every now and then into an idle doze, as from excess of comfort. Toby looked on from a tall bench hard by; one beaming smile, from his broad nut-brown face down to the slack-baked buckles in his shoes. The very locks that hung around had something jovial in their rust, and seemed like gouty gentlemen of hearty natures, disposed to joke on their infirmities. There was nothing surly or severe in the whole scene. It seemed impossible that any one of the innumerable keys could fit a churlish strong-box or a prison-door. Cellars of beer and wine, rooms where there were fires, books, gossip, and cheering laughter—these were their proper sphere of action. Places of distrust, and cruelty, and restraint, they would have left quadruple-locked for ever.

Tink, tink, tink. The locksmith paused at last, and wiped his brow. The silence roused the cat, who, jumping softly down, crept to the door, and watched with tiger eyes a bird-cage in an opposite window. Gabriel lifted Toby to his mouth, and took a hearty draught.

Then, as he stood upright, with his head flung back, and his portly chest thrown out, you would have seen that Gabriel's lower man was clothed in military gear. Glancing at the wall beyond, there might have been espied, hanging on their several pegs, a cap and feather, broad-sword, sash, and coat of scarlet; which any man learned in such matters would have known from their make and pattern to be the uniform of a serjeant in the Royal East-London Volunteers.*

As the locksmith put his mug down, empty, on the bench whence it had smiled on him before, he glanced at these articles with a laughing eye, and looking at them with his head a little on one side, as though he would get them all into a focus, said, leaning on his hammer:

"Time was, now, I remember, when I was like to run mad with the desire to wear a coat of that colour. If any one (except my father) had called me a fool for my pains, how I should have fired and fumed! But what a fool I must have been, sure-ly!"

"Ah!" sighed Mrs. Varden, who had entered unobserved. "A fool indeed. A man at your time of life, Varden, should know better now."

"Why, what a ridiculous woman you are, Martha," said the locksmith, turning round with a smile.

"Certainly," replied Mrs. V. with great demureness. "Of course I am. I know that, Varden. Thank you."

"I mean—" began the locksmith.

"Yes," said his wife, "I know what you mean. You speak quite plain enough to be understood, Varden. It's very kind of you to adapt yourself to my capacity, I am sure."

"Tut, tut, Martha," rejoined the locksmith; "don't take offence at nothing. I mean, how strange it is of you to run down volunteering, when it's done to defend you and all the other women, and our own fireside and everybody else's, in case of need."

"It's unchristian," cried Mrs. Varden, shaking her head.

"Unchristian!" said the locksmith. "Why, what the devil—"

Mrs. Varden looked at the ceiling, as in expectation that the consequence of this profanity would be the immediate descent of the four-post bedstead on the second floor, together with the best sitting-room on the first; but no visible judgment occurring, she heaved a deep sigh, and begged her husband, in a tone of resignation, to go on, and by all means to blaspheme as much as possible, because he knew she liked it.

The locksmith did for a moment seem disposed to gratify her, but he gave a great gulp, and mildly rejoined:

"I was going to say, what on earth do you call it unchristian for? Which would be most unchristian, Martha—to sit quietly down and let our houses be sacked by a foreign army, or to turn out like men and drive 'em off? Shouldn't I be a nice sort of a Christian, if I crept into a corner of my own chimney and looked on while a parcel of whiskered savages bore off Dolly—or you—?"

When he said "or you," Mrs. Varden, despite herself, relaxed into a smile. There was something complimentary in the idea. "In such a state of things as that, indeed—" she simpered.

"As that!" repeated the locksmith. "Well, that would be the state of things directly. Even Miggs would go. Some black tambourine-player, with a great turban on, would be bearing *her* off, and, unless the tambourine-player was proof against kicking and scratching, it's my belief he'd have the worst of it. Ha ha ha! I'd forgive the tambourine-player. I wouldn't have him interfered with on any account, poor fellow." And here the locksmith laughed again so heartily, that tears came into his eyes—much to Mrs. Varden's indignation, who thought the capture of so sound a Protestant and estimable a private character as Miggs by a pagan negro, a circumstance too shocking and awful for contemplation.

The picture Gabriel had drawn, indeed, threatened serious consequences, and would indubitably have led to them, but luckily at that moment a light footstep crossed the threshold, and Dolly, running in, threw her arms round her old father's neck and hugged him tight.

"Here she is at last!" cried Gabriel. "And how well you look, Doll, and how late you are, my darling!"

How well she looked? Well? Why, if he had exhausted every laudatory adjective in the dictionary, it wouldn't have been praise enough. When and where was there ever, such a plump, roguish, comely, bright-eyed, enticing, bewitching, captivating, maddening little puss in all this world, as Dolly! What was the Dolly of five years ago, to the Dolly of that day! How many coachmakers, saddlers, cabinet-makers, and professors of other useful arts, had deserted their fathers, mothers, sisters, brothers, and, worst of all, their cousins, for the love of her! How many unknown gentlemen—supposed to be of mighty fortunes, if not titles—had waited round the corner after dark, and tempted Miggs the incorruptible, with golden guineas, to deliver offers of marriage folded up in love-letters! How many disconsolate fathers and substantial tradesmen had waited on the locksmith for the same purpose, with dismal tales of how their sons had lost their appetites, and taken to shut themselves up in dark bedrooms, and wandering in desolate suburbs with pale faces, and all because of Dolly Varden's loveliness and cruelty! How many young men, in all previous times of unprecedented steadiness, had turned suddenly wild and wicked for the same reason, and, in an ecstasy of unrequited love, taken to wrench off door-knockers, and invert the boxes of rheumatic watchmen! How had she recruited the king's service, both by sea and land, through rendering desperate his loving subjects between the ages of eighteen and twenty-five! How many young ladies had publicly professed, with tears in their eyes, that for their tastes she was much too short, too tall, too bold, too cold, too stout, too thin, too fair, too dark—too everything but handsome! How many old ladies, taking counsel together, had thanked Heaven their daughters were not like her, and had hoped she might come to no harm, and had thought she would come to no good, and had wondered what people saw in her, and had arrived at the conclusion that she was "going off" in her looks, or had never come on in them, and that she was a thorough imposition and a popular mistake!

And yet here was this same Dolly Varden, so whimsical and hard to please that she was Dolly Varden still, all smiles and dimples and pleasant looks, and caring no more for the fifty or sixty young fellows who at that very moment were breaking their hearts to marry her, than if so many oysters had been crossed in love and opened afterwards.

Dolly hugged her father as has been already stated, and having hugged her mother also, accompanied both into the little parlour where the cloth was already laid for dinner, and where Miss Miggs—a trifle more rigid and bony than of yore—received her with a sort of hysterical gasp, intended for a smile. Into the hands of that young virgin, she delivered her bonnet and walking dress (all of a dreadful, artful, and designing kind), and then said with a laugh, which rivalled the locksmith's music, "How glad I always am to be at home again!"

"And how glad we always are, Doll," said her father, putting back the dark hair from her sparkling eyes, "to have you at home. Give me a kiss."

If there had been anybody of the male kind there to see her do it— but there was not—it was a mercy.

"I don't like your being at the Warren," said the locksmith, "I can't bear to have you out of my sight. And what is the news over yonder, Doll?"

"What news there is, I think you know already," replied his daughter. "I am sure you do though."

"Ay?" cried the locksmith. "What's that?"

"Come, come," said Dolly, "you know very well. I want you to tell me why Mr. Haredale—oh, how gruff he is again, to be sure!—has been away from home for some days past, and why he is travelling about (we know he *is* travelling, because of his letters) without telling his own niece why or wherefore."

"Miss Emma doesn't want to know, I'll swear," returned the locksmith.

"I don't know that," said Dolly; "but *I* do, at any rate. Do tell me. Why is he so secret, and what is this ghost story, which nobody is to tell Miss Emma, and which seems to be mixed up with his going away? Now I see you know, by your colouring so."

"What the story means, or is, or has to do with it, I know no more than you, my dear," returned the locksmith, "except that it's some foolish fear of little Solomon's—which has, indeed, no meaning in it, I suppose. As to Mr. Haredale's journey, he goes, as I believe—"

"Yes," said Dolly.

"As I believe," resumed the locksmith, pinching her cheek, "on business, Doll. What it may be, is quite another matter. Read Blue Beard,* and don't be too curious, pet; it's no business of yours or mine, depend upon that; and here's dinner, which is much more to the purpose."

Dolly might have remonstrated against this summary dismissal of the subject, notwithstanding the appearance of dinner, but at the mention of Blue Beard Mrs. Varden interposed, protesting she could not find it in her conscience to sit tamely by, and hear her child recommended to peruse the adventures of a Turk and Mussulman— far less of a fabulous Turk, which she considered that Potentate to be. She held that, in such stirring and tremendous times as those in which they lived, it would be much more to the purpose if Dolly became a regular subscriber to the Thunderer, where she would have an opportunity of reading Lord George Gordon's speeches word for word, which would be a greater comfort and solace to her, than a hundred and fifty Blue Beards ever could impart. She appealed in support of this proposition to Miss Miggs, then in waiting, who said that indeed the peace of mind she had derived from the perusal of that paper generally, but especially of one article of the very last week as ever was, entitled "Great Britain drenched in gore," exceeded all belief; the same composition, she added, had also wrought such a comforting effect on the mind of a married sister of hers, then resident at Golden Lion Court, number twenty-sivin, second bell-handle on the right-hand doorpost, that, being in a delicate state of health, and in fact expecting an addition to her family, she had been seized with fits directly after its perusal, and had raved of the Inquisition ever since; to the great improvement of her husband and friends. Miss Miggs went on to say that she would recommend all those whose hearts were hardened to hear Lord George themselves, whom she commended first, in respect of his steady Protestantism, then of his oratory, then of his eyes, then of his nose, then of his legs, and lastly of his figure generally, which she looked upon as fit for any statue, prince, or angel, to which sentiment Mrs. Varden fully subscribed.

Mrs. Varden having cut in, looked at a box upon the mantel-shelf, painted in imitation of a very red-brick dwelling-house, with a yellow roof; having at top a real chimney, down which voluntary subscribers dropped their silver, gold, or pence, into the parlour; and on the door the counterfeit presentment* of a brass plate, whereon was legibly inscribed "Protestant Association:"—and looking at it, said, that it was to her a source of poignant misery to think that Varden never had, of all his substance, dropped anything into that temple, save once in secret—as she afterwards discovered—two fragments of tobacco-pipe, which she hoped would not be put down to his last account. That Dolly, she was grieved to say, was no less backward in her contributions, better loving, as it seemed, to purchase ribbons and such gauds, than to encourage the great cause, then in such heavy tribulation; and that she did entreat her (her father she much feared could not be moved) not to despise, but imitate, the bright example of Miss Miggs, who flung her wages, as it were, into the very countenance of the Pope, and bruised his features with her quarter's money.

"Oh, mim," said Miggs, "don't relude to that. I had no intentions, mim, that nobody should know. Such sacrifices as I can make, are quite a widder's mite. It's all I have," cried Miggs with a great burst of tears—for with her they never came on by degrees—"but it's made up to me in other ways; it's well made up."

This was quite true, though not perhaps in the sense that Miggs intended. As she never failed to keep her self-denial full in Mrs. Varden's view, it drew forth so many gifts of caps and gowns and other articles of dress, that upon the whole the red-brick house was perhaps the best investment for her small capital she could possibly have hit upon; returning her interest, at the rate of seven or eight per cent. in money, and fifty at least in personal repute and credit.

"You needn't cry, Miggs," said Mrs. Varden, herself in tears; "you needn't be ashamed of it, though your poor mistress *is* on the same side."

Miggs howled at this remark, in a peculiarly dismal way, and said she knowed that master hated her. That it was a dreadful thing to live in families and have dislikes, and not give satisfactions. That to make divisions was a thing she could not abear to think of, neither could her feelings let her do it. That if it was master's wishes as she and him should part, it was best they should part, and she hoped he might be the happier for it, and always wishes him well, and that he might find somebody as would meet his dispositions. It would be a hard trial, she said, to part from such a missis, but she could meet any suffering when her conscience told her she was in the rights, and therefore she was willing even to go that lengths. She did not think, she added, that she could long survive the separations, but, as she was hated and looked upon unpleasant, perhaps her dying as soon as possible would be the best endings for all parties. With this affecting conclusion, Miss Miggs shed more tears, and sobbed abundantly.

"Can you bear this, Varden?" said his wife in a solemn voice, laying down her knife and fork.

"Why, not very well, my dear," rejoined the locksmith, "but I try to keep my temper."

"Don't let there be words on my account, mim," sobbed Miggs. "It's much the best that we should part. I wouldn't stay—oh, gracious me!—and make dissensions, not for a annual gold mine, and found in tea and sugar."

Lest the reader should be at any loss to discover the cause of Miss Miggs's deep emotion, it may be whispered apart that, happening to be listening, as her custom sometimes was, when Gabriel and his wife conversed together, she had heard the locksmith's joke relative to the foreign black who played the tambourine, and bursting with the spiteful feelings which the taunt awoke in her fair breast, exploded in the manner we have witnessed. Matters having now arrived at a crisis, the locksmith as usual, and for the sake of peace and quietness, gave in.

"What are you crying for, girl?" he said. "What's the matter with you? What are you talking about hatred for? *I* don't hate you; I don't hate anybody. Dry your eyes and make yourself agreeable, in Heaven's name, and let us all be happy while we can."

The allied powers deeming it good generalship to consider this a sufficient apology on the part of the enemy, and confession of having been in the wrong, did dry their eyes and take it in good part. Miss Miggs observed that she bore no malice, no not to her greatest foe, whom she rather loved the more indeed, the greater persecution she sustained. Mrs. Varden approved of this meek and forgiving spirit in high terms, and incidentally declared as a closing article of agreement, that Dolly should accompany her to the Clerkenwell branch of the association, that very night. This was an extraordinary instance of her great prudence and policy; having had this end in view from the first, and entertaining a secret misgiving that the locksmith (who was bold when Dolly was in question) would object, she had backed Miss Miggs up to this point, in order that she might have him at a disadvantage. The manœuvre succeeded so well that Gabriel only made a wry face, and with the warning he had just had, fresh in his mind, did not dare to say one word.

The difference ended, therefore, in Miggs being presented with a gown by Mrs. Varden and half-a-crown by Dolly, as if she had eminently distinguished herself in the paths of morality and goodness. Mrs. V., according to custom, expressed her hope that Varden would take a lesson from what had passed and learn more generous conduct for the time to come; and the dinner being now cold and nobody's appetite very much improved by what had passed, they went on with it, as Mrs. Varden said, "like Christians."

As there was to be a grand parade of the Royal East London Volunteers that afternoon, the locksmith did no more work; but sat down comfortably with his pipe in his mouth, and his arm round his pretty daughter's waist, looking lovingly on Mrs. V. from time to time, and exhibiting from the crown of his head to the sole of his foot, one smiling surface of good humour. And to be sure, when it was time to dress him in his regimentals, and Dolly, hanging about him in all kinds of graceful winning ways, helped to button and buckle and brush him up and get him into one of the tightest coats that ever was made by mortal tailor, he was the proudest father in all England.

"What a handy jade it is!" said the locksmith to Mrs. Varden, who stood by with folded hands—rather proud of her husband too—while Miggs held his cap and sword at arm's length, as if mistrusting that the latter might run some one through the body of its own accord; "but never marry a soldier Doll, my dear."

Dolly didn't ask why not, or say a word indeed, but stooped her head down very low to tie his sash.

"I never wear this dress," said honest Gabriel, "but I think of poor

Joe Willet. I loved Joe; he was always a favourite of mine. Poor Joe!—Dear heart, my girl, don't tie me in so tight."

Dolly laughed—not like herself at all—the strangest little laugh that could be—and held her head down lower still.

"Poor Joe!" resumed the locksmith, muttering to himself; "I always wish he had come to me. I might have made it up between them, if he had. Ah! old John made a great mistake in his way of acting by that lad—a great mistake.—Have you nearly tied that sash, my dear?"

What an ill-made sash it was! There it was, loose again and trailing on the ground. Dolly was obliged to kneel down, and recommence at the beginning.

"Never mind young Willet, Varden," said his wife frowning; "you might find some one more deserving to talk about, I think."

Miss Miggs gave a great sniff to the same effect.

"Nay, Martha," cried the locksmith, "don't let us bear too hard upon him. If the lad is dead indeed, we'll deal kindly by his memory."

"A runaway and a vagabond!" said Mrs. Varden.

Miss Miggs expressed her concurrence as before.

"A runaway, my dear, but not a vagabond," returned the locksmith in a gentle tone. "He behaved himself well, did Joe—always—and was a handsome manly fellow. Don't call him a vagabond, Martha."

Mrs. Varden coughed—and so did Miggs.

"He tried hard to gain your good opinion, Martha, I can tell you," said the locksmith smiling, and stroking his chin. "Ah! that he did. It seems but yesterday that he followed me out to the Maypole door one night, and begged me not to say how like a boy they used him—say here, at home, he meant, though at the time, I recollect, I didn't understand. 'And how's Miss Dolly, sir?' says Joe," pursued the locksmith, musing sorrowfully, "Ah! Poor Joe!"

"Well, I declare," cried Miggs. "Oh! Goodness gracious me!"

"What's the matter now?" said Gabriel, turning sharply to her.

"Why, if here an't Miss Dolly," said the handmaid, stooping down to look into her face, "a giving way to floods of tears. Oh mim! oh sir. Raly it's give me such a turn," cried the susceptible damsel, pressing her hand upon her side to quell the palpitation of her heart, "that you might knock me down with a feather."

The locksmith, after glancing at Miss Miggs as if he could have wished to have a feather brought straightway, looked on with a broad stare while Dolly hurried away, followed by that sympathising young woman: then turning to his wife, stammered out, "Is Dolly ill? Have *I* done anything? Is it my fault?"

"Your fault!" cried Mrs V. reproachfully. "There—You had better make haste out."

"What have I done?" said poor Gabriel. "It was agreed that Mr. Edward's name was never to be mentioned, and I have not spoken of him, have I!"

Mrs. Varden merely replied that she had no patience with him, and bounced off after the other two. The unfortunate locksmith wound his sash about him, girded on his sword, put on his cap, and walked out.

"I am not much of a dab at my exercise," he said under his breath, "but I shall get into fewer scrapes at that work than at this. Every man came into the world for something; my department seems to be to make every woman cry without meaning it. It's rather hard!"

But he forgot it before he reached the end of the street, and went on with a shining face, nodding to the neighbours, and showering about his friendly greetings like mild spring rain.

CHAPTER THE FORTY-SECOND.

THE Royal East London Volunteers made a brilliant sight that day: formed into lines, squares, circles, triangles, and what not, to the beating of drums and the streaming of flags; and performed a vast number of complex evolutions, in all of which Serjeant Varden bore a conspicuous share. Having displayed their military prowess to the utmost in these warlike shows, they marched in glittering order to the Chelsea Bun-house,* and regaled in the adjacent taverns until dark. Then at sound of drum they fell in again, and returned amidst the shouting of His Majesty's lieges to the place from whence they came.

The homeward march being somewhat tardy,—owing to the unsoldierlike behaviour of certain corporals, who, being gentlemen of sedentary pursuits in private life and excitable out of doors, broke several windows with their bayonets, and rendered it imperative on the commanding officer to deliver them over to a strong guard, with whom they fought at intervals as they came along,—it was nine o'clock when the locksmith reached home. A hackney-coach was waiting near his door; and as he passed it, Mr. Haredale looked from the window and called him by his name.

"The sight of you is good for sore eyes, sir," said the locksmith, stepping up to him. "I wish you had walked in though, rather than waited here."

"There is nobody at home, I find," Mr. Haredale answered; "besides, I desired to be as private as I could."

"Humph!" muttered the locksmith, looking round at his house. "Gone with Simon Tappertit to that precious Branch, no doubt."

Mr. Haredale invited him to come into the coach, and, if he were not tired or anxious to go home, to ride with him a little way that they might have some talk together. Gabriel cheerfully complied, and the coachman mounting his box drove off.

"Varden," said Mr. Haredale after a minute's pause, "you will be amazed to hear what errand I am on; it will seem a very strange one."

"I have no doubt it's a reasonable one, sir, and has a meaning in it," replied the locksmith; "or it would not be yours at all. Have you just come back to town, sir?"

"But half an hour ago."

"Bringing no news of Barnaby, or his mother?" said the locksmith dubiously. "Ah! you needn't shake your head, sir. It was a wild-goose chase. I feared that, from the first. You exhausted all reasonable means of discovery when they went away. To begin again after so long a time has passed is hopeless, sir—quite hopeless."

"Why, where are they?" he returned impatiently. "Where can they be? Above ground?"

"God knows," rejoined the locksmith, "many that I knew above it five years ago, have their beds under the grass now. And the world is a wide place. It's a hopeless attempt, sir, believe me. We must leave the discovery of this mystery, like all others, to time, and accident, and Heaven's pleasure."

"Varden, my good fellow," said Mr. Haredale, "I have a deeper meaning in my present anxiety to find them out, than you can fathom. It is not a mere whim; it is not the casual revival of my old wishes and desires; but an earnest, solemn purpose. My thoughts and dreams all tend to it, and fix it in my mind. I have no rest by day or night; I have no peace or quiet; I am haunted."

His voice was so altered from its usual tones, and his manner bespoke so much emotion, that Gabriel, in his wonder, could only sit and look towards him in the darkness, and fancy the expression of his face.

"Do not ask me," continued Mr. Haredale, "to explain myself. If I were to do so, you would think me the victim of some hideous fancy. It is enough that this is so, and that I cannot—no, I can not—lie quietly in my bed, without doing what will seem to you incomprehensible."

"Since when, sir," said the locksmith after a pause, "has this uneasy feeling been upon you?"

Mr. Haredale hesitated for some moments, and then replied: "Since the night of the storm. In short, since the last nineteenth of March."

As though he feared that Varden might express surprise, or reason with him, he hastily went on:

"You will think, I know, I labour under some delusion. Perhaps I do. But it is not a morbid one; it is a wholesome action of the mind, reasoning on actual occurrences. You know the furniture remains in Mrs. Rudge's house, and that it has been shut up, by my orders, since she went away, save once a-week or so, when an old neighbour visits it to scare away the rats. I am on my way there now."

"For what purpose?" asked the locksmith.

"To pass the night there," he replied; "and not to-night alone, but many nights. This is a secret which I trust to you in case of any unexpected emergency. You will not come, unless in case of strong necessity, to me; from dusk to broad day I shall be there. Emma, your daughter, and the rest, suppose me out of London, as I have been until within this hour. Do not undeceive them. This is the errand I am bound upon. I know I may confide it to you, and I rely upon your questioning me no further at this time."

With that, as if to change the theme, he led the astounded locksmith back to the night of the Maypole highwayman, to the robbery of Edward Chester, to the reappearance of the man at Mrs. Rudge's house, and to all the strange circumstances which afterwards occurred. He even asked him carelessly about the man's height, his face, his figure, whether he was like any one he had ever seen—like

Hugh, for instance, or any man he had known at any time—and put many questions of that sort, which the locksmith, considering them as mere devices to engage his attention and prevent his expressing the astonishment he felt, answered pretty much at random.

At length they arrived at the corner of the street in which the house stood, where Mr. Haredale, alighting, dismissed the coach. "If you desire to see me safely lodged," he said, turning to the locksmith with a gloomy smile, "you can."

Gabriel, to whom all former marvels had been nothing in comparison with this, followed him along the narrow pavement in silence. When they reached the door, Mr. Haredale softly opened it with a key he had about him, and closing it when Varden entered, they were left in thorough darkness.

They groped their way into the ground-floor room. Here Mr. Haredale struck a light, and kindled a pocket taper he had brought with him for the purpose. It was then, when the flame was full upon him, that the locksmith saw for the first time how haggard, pale, and changed he looked; how worn and thin he was; how perfectly his whole appearance coincided with all that he had said so strangely as they rode along. It was not an unnatural impulse in Gabriel, after what he had heard, to note curiously the expression of his eyes. It was perfectly collected and rational;—so much so, indeed, that he felt ashamed of his momentary suspicion, and drooped his own when Mr. Haredale looked towards him, as if he feared they would betray his thoughts.

"Will you walk through the house?" said Mr. Haredale, with a glance towards the window, the crazy shutters of which were closed and fastened. "Speak low."

There was a kind of awe about the place, which would have rendered it difficult to speak in any other manner. Gabriel whispered "Yes," and followed him up stairs.

Everything was just as they had seen it last. There was a sense of closeness from the exclusion of fresh air, and a gloom and heaviness around, as though long imprisonment had made the very silence sad. The homely hangings of the beds and windows had begun to droop; the dust lay thick upon their dwindling folds; and damps had made their way through ceiling, wall, and floor. The boards creaked beneath their tread as if resenting the unaccustomed intrusion; nimble spiders, paralysed by the taper's glare, checked the motion of their hundred legs upon the wall, or dropped like lifeless things upon the ground; the death-watch ticked aloud; and the scampering feet of rats and mice rattled behind the wainscot.

As they looked about them on the decaying furniture, it was strange to find how vividly it presented those to whom it had belonged, and with whom it was once familiar. Grip seemed to perch again upon his high-backed chair; Barnaby to crouch in his old favourite corner by the fire; the mother to resume her usual seat, and watch him as of old. Even when they could separate these objects from the phantoms of the mind which they invoked, the latter only glided out of sight, but lingered near them still; for then they seemed to lurk in closets and behind the doors, ready to start out and suddenly accost them in their well-remembered tones.

They went down stairs, and again into the room they had just now left. Mr. Haredale unbuckled his sword and laid it on the table, with a pair of pocket pistols; then told the locksmith he would light him to the door.

"But this is a dull place, sir," said Gabriel, lingering; "may no one share your watch?"

He shook his head, and so plainly evinced his wish to be alone, that Gabriel could say no more. In another moment the locksmith was standing in the street, whence he could see that the light once more travelled up-stairs, and soon returning to the room below, shone brightly through the chinks in the shutters.

If ever man were sorely puzzled and perplexed, the locksmith was, that night. Even when snugly seated by his own fireside, with Mrs. Varden opposite in a night-cap and night-jacket, and Dolly beside him (in a most distracting dishabille) curling her hair, and smiling as if she had never cried in all her life and never could—even then, with Toby at his elbow and his pipe in his mouth, and Miggs (but that perhaps was not much) falling asleep in the back-ground, he could not quite discard his wonder and uneasiness. So, in his dreams—still there was Mr. Haredale, haggard and careworn, listening in the solitary house to every sound that stirred, with the taper shining through the chinks until the day should turn it pale and end his lonely watching.

CHAPTER THE FORTY-THIRD.

NEXT morning brought no satisfaction to the locksmith's thoughts, nor next day, nor the next, nor many others. Often after nightfall he entered the street, and turned his eyes towards the well-known house; and as surely as he did so, there was the solitary light, still gleaming through the crevices of the window-shutter, while all within was motionless, noiseless, cheerless, as a grave. Unwilling to hazard Mr. Haredale's favour by disobeying his strict injunction, he never ventured to knock at the door or to make his presence known in any way. But whenever strong interest and curiosity combined, attracted him to the spot—which was not seldom—the light was always there.

If he could have known what passed within, the knowledge would have yielded him no clue to this mysterious vigil. At twilight, Mr. Haredale shut himself up, and at daybreak he came forth. He never missed a night, always came and went alone, and never varied his proceedings in the least degree.

The manner of his watch was this. At dusk, he entered the house in the same way as when the locksmith bore him company, kindled a light, went through the rooms, and narrowly examined them. That done, he returned to the chamber on the ground-floor, and laying his sword and pistols on the table, sat by it until morning.

He usually had a book with him, and often tried to read, but never fixed his eyes or thoughts upon it for five minutes together. The slightest noise without doors, caught his ear; a step upon the pavement seemed to make his heart leap.

He was not without some refreshment during the long lonely hours; generally carrying in his pocket a sandwich of bread and meat, and a small flask of wine. The latter, diluted with large quantities of water, he drank in a heated, feverish way, as though his throat were dried up; but he scarcely ever broke his fast, by so much as a crumb of bread.

If this voluntary sacrifice of sleep and comfort had its origin, as the locksmith on consideration was disposed to think, in any superstitious expectation of the fulfilment of a dream or vision connected with the event on which he had brooded for so many years, and if he waited for some ghostly visitor who walked abroad when men lay sleeping in their beds, he showed no trace of fear or wavering. His stern features expressed the most inflexible resolution; his brows were puckered, and his lips compressed, with deep and settled purpose; and when he started at a noise and listened, it was not with the start of fear but hope, and catching up his sword as though the hour had come at last, he would clutch it in his tight-clenched hand, and listen, with sparkling eyes and eager looks, until it died away.

These disappointments were numerous, for they ensued on almost every sound, but his constancy was not shaken. Still, every night he was at his post, the same stern, sleepless, sentinel; and still night passed and morning dawned, and he must watch again.

This went on for weeks; he had taken a lodging at Vauxhall* in which to pass the day and rest himself; and from this place, when the tide served, he usually came to London Bridge from Westminster by water, in order that he might avoid the busy streets.

One evening, shortly before twilight, he came his accustomed road upon the river's bank, intending to pass through Westminster Hall into Palace Yard,* and there take boat to London Bridge as usual. There was a pretty large concourse of people assembled round the

Houses of Parliament, looking at the members as they entered and departed, and giving vent to rather noisy demonstrations of approval or dislike, according to their known opinions. As he made his way among the throng, he heard once or twice the No-Popery cry, which was then becoming pretty familiar to the ears of most men; but holding it in very slight regard, and observing that the idlers were of the lowest grade, he neither thought nor cared about it, but made his way along, with perfect indifference.

There were many little knots and groups of persons in Westminster Hall: some few looking upward at its noble ceiling, and at the rays of evening light, tinted by the setting sun, which streamed in aslant through its small windows, and growing dimmer by degrees, were quenched in the gathering gloom below; some, noisy passengers, mechanics going home from work, and otherwise, who hurried quickly through, waking the echoes with their voices, and soon darkening the small door in the distance, as they passed into the street beyond; some, in busy conference together on political or private matters, pacing slowly up and down with eyes that sought the ground, and seeming, by their attitudes, to listen earnestly from head to foot. Here, a dozen squabbling urchins made a very Babel in the air; there, a solitary man, half clerk, half mendicant, paced up and down with hungry dejection in his look and gait; at his elbow passed an errand-lad, swinging his basket round and round, and with his shrill whistle riving the very timbers of the roof; while a more observant schoolboy, half-way through, pocketed his ball, and eyed the distant beadle as he came looming on. It was that time of evening when, if you shut your eyes and open them again, the darkness of an hour appears to have gathered in a second. The smooth-worn pavement, dusty with footsteps, still called upon the lofty walls to reiterate the shuffle and the tread of feet unceasingly, save when the closing of some heavy door resounded through the building like a clap of thunder, and drowned all other noises in its rolling sound.

Mr. Haredale, glancing only at such of these groups as he passed nearest to, and then in a manner betokening that his thoughts were elsewhere, had nearly traversed the Hall, when two persons before him caught his attention. One of these, a gentleman in elegant attire, carried in his hand a cane, which he twirled in a jaunty manner as he loitered on; the other, an obsequious, crouching, fawning figure, listened to what he said—at times throwing in an humble word himself—and, with his shoulders shrugged up to his ears, rubbed his hands submissively, or answered at intervals by an inclination of the head, half-way between a nod of acquiescence, and a bow of most profound respect.

In the abstract there was nothing very remarkable in this pair, for servility waiting on a handsome suit of clothes and a cane—not to speak of gold and silver sticks, or wands of office—is common enough. But there was that about the well-dressed man, yes, and about the other likewise, which struck Mr. Haredale with no pleasant feeling. He hesitated, stopped, and would have stepped aside and turned out of his path, but at the moment, the other two faced about quickly, and stumbled upon him before he could avoid them.

The gentleman with the cane lifted his hat and had begun to tender an apology, which Mr. Haredale had begun as hastily to acknowledge and walk away, when he stopped short and cried, "Haredale! Gad bless me, this is strange indeed!"

"It is," he returned impatiently; "yes—a—"

"My dear friend," cried the other, detaining him, "why such great speed? One minute, Haredale, for the sake of old acquaintance."

"I am in haste," he said. "Neither of us has sought this meeting. Let it be a brief one. Good night!"

"Fie, fie!" replied Sir John (for it was he), "how very churlish! We were speaking of you. Your name was on my lips—perhaps you heard me mention it? No? I am sorry for that. I am really sorry.— You know our friend here, Haredale? This is really a most remarkable meeting!"

The friend, plainly very ill at ease, had made bold to press Sir John's arm, and to give him other significant hints that he was desirous of avoiding this introduction. As it did not suit Sir John's purpose, however, that it should be evaded, he appeared quite unconscious of these silent remonstrances, and inclined his hand towards him as he spoke, to call attention to him more particularly.

The friend, therefore, had nothing for it, but to muster up the pleasantest smile he could, and to make a conciliatory bow, as Mr. Haredale turned his eyes upon him. Seeing that he was recognised, he put out his hand in an awkward and embarrassed manner, which was not mended by its contemptuous rejection.

"Mr. Gashford!" said Haredale, coldly. "It is as I have heard then. You have left the darkness for the light, sir, and hate those whose opinions you formerly held, with all the bitterness of a renegade. You are an honour, sir, to any cause. I wish the one you espouse at present, much joy of the acquisition it has made."

The secretary rubbed his hands and bowed, as though he would disarm his adversary by humbling himself before him. Sir John Chester again exclaimed, with an air of great gaiety, "Now, really, this is a most remarkable meeting!" and took a pinch of snuff with his usual self-possession.

"Mr. Haredale," said Gashford, stealthily raising his eyes, and letting them drop again when they met the other's steady gaze, "is too conscientious, too honourable, too manly, I am sure, to attach unworthy motives to an honest change of opinions, even though it implies a doubt of those he holds himself. Mr. Haredale is too just, too generous, too clear-sighted in his moral vision, to—"

"Yes, sir?" he rejoined with a sarcastic smile, finding that the secretary stopped. "You were saying"—

Gashford meekly shrugged his shoulders, and looking on the ground again, was silent.

"No, but let us really," interposed Sir John at this juncture, "let us really, for a moment, contemplate the very remarkable character of this meeting. Haredale, my dear friend, pardon me if I think you are not sufficiently impressed with its singularity. Here we stand, by no previous appointment or arrangement, three old schoolfellows, in Westminster Hall: three old boarders in a remarkably dull and shady seminary at Saint Omer's,* where you, being Catholics and of necessity educated out of England, were brought up; and where I, being a promising young Protestant at that time, was sent to learn the French Tongue from a native of Paris!"

"Add to the singularity, Sir John," said Mr. Haredale, "that some of you Protestants of promise are at this moment leagued in yonder building, to prevent our having the surpassing and unheard-of privilege of teaching our children to read and write—here—in this land, where thousands of us enter your service every year, and to preserve the freedom of which, we die in bloody battles abroad, in heaps: and that others of you, to the number of some thousands as I learn, are led on to look on all men of my creed as wolves and beasts of prey, by this man Gashford. Add to it, besides, the bare fact that this man lives in society, walks the streets in broad day—I was about to say, holds up his head, but that he does not—and it will be strange, and very strange, I grant you."

"Oh! you are hard upon our friend," replied Sir John, with an engaging smile. "You are really very hard upon our friend!"

"Let him go on, Sir John," said Gashford, fumbling with his gloves. "Let him go on. I can make allowances, Sir John. I am honoured with your good opinion, and I can dispense with Mr. Haredale's. Mr. Haredale is a sufferer from the penal laws, and I can't expect his favour."

"You have so much of my favour, sir," retorted Mr. Haredale, with a bitter glance at the third party in their conversation, "that I am glad to see you in such good company. You are the essence of your great Association, in yourselves."

"Now, there you mistake," said Sir John, in his most benignant way. "There—which is a most remarkable circumstance for a man of your punctuality and exactness, my dear Haredale—you fall into an error. I don't belong to the body; I have an immense respect for its members, but I don't belong to it; although I am, it is certainly true, the conscientious opponent of your being relieved. I feel it my duty to be so; it is a most unfortunate necessity; and cost me a bitter struggle.—Will you try this box? If you don't object to a trifling infusion of a very chaste scent, you'll find its flavour exquisite."

"I ask your pardon, Sir John," said Mr. Haredale, declining the proffer with a motion of his hand, "for having ranked you among the humble instruments who are obvious and in all men's sight. I should have done more justice to your genius. Men of your capacity plot in secrecy and safety, and leave exposed posts to the duller wits."

"Don't apologise, for the world," replied Sir John sweetly; "old friends like you and I may be allowed some freedoms, or the deuce is in it."

Gashford, who had been very restless all this time, but had not once looked up, now turned to Sir John, and ventured to mutter something to the effect that he must go, or my Lord would perhaps be waiting. "Don't distress yourself, good sir," said Mr. Haredale, "I'll take my leave, and put you at your ease—" which he was about to do without further ceremony, when he was stayed by a buzz and murmur at the upper end of the hall, and, looking in that direction, saw Lord George Gordon coming on, with a crowd of people round him.

There was a lurking look of triumph, though very differently expressed, in the faces of his two companions, which made it a natural impulse on Mr. Haredale's part not to give way before this leader, but to stand there while he passed. He drew himself up to his full height, and, clasping his hands behind him, looked on with a proud and scornful aspect, while Lord George slowly advanced (for the press was great about him) towards the spot where they were standing.

He had left the House of Commons but that moment, and had come straight down into the Hall, bringing with him, as his custom was, intelligence of what had been said that night in reference to the Papists, and what petitions had been presented in their favour, and who had supported them, and when the bill was to be brought in, and when it would be advisable to present their own Great Protestant petition. All this he told the persons about him in a loud voice, and with great abundance of ungainly gesture. Those who were nearest him made comments to each other, and vented threats and murmurings; those who were outside the crowd cried "Silence," and "Stand back," or closed in upon the rest, endeavouring to make a forcible exchange of places: and so they came driving on in a very disorderly and irregular way, as it is the manner of a crowd to do.

When they were very near to where the Secretary, Sir John, and Mr. Haredale stood, Lord George turned round and, making a few remarks of a sufficiently violent and incoherent kind, concluded with the usual sentiment, and called for three cheers to back it. While these were in the act of being given with great energy, he extricated himself from the press, and stepped up to Gashford's side. Both he and Sir John being well known to the populace, they fell back a little, and left the four standing together.

"Mr. Haredale, Lord George," said Sir John Chester, seeing that the nobleman regarded him with an inquisitive look. "A Catholic gentleman unfortunately—most unhappily a Catholic—but an esteemed acquaintance of mine, and once of Mr. Gashford's. My dear Haredale, this is Lord George Gordon."

"I should have known that, had I been ignorant of his lord-ship's person," said Mr. Haredale. "I hope there is but one gentleman in England who, addressing an ignorant and excited throng, would speak of a large body of his fellow-subjects in such injurious language as I heard this moment. For shame, my lord, for shame!"

"I cannot talk to you, sir," replied Lord George in a loud voice, and waving his hand in a disturbed and agitated manner; "we have nothing in common."

"We have much in common—many things—all that the Almighty gave us," said Mr. Haredale; "and common charity, my lord, not to say common sense and common decency, should teach you to refrain from these proceedings. If every one of those men had arms in their hands at this moment, as they have them in their heads, I would not leave this place without telling you that you disgrace your station."

"I don't hear you, sir," he replied in the same manner as before; "I can't hear you. It is indifferent to me what you say. Don't retort, Gashford," for the secretary had made a show of wishing to do so; "I can hold no communion with the worshippers of idols."

As he said this, he glanced at Sir John, who lifted his hands and eyebrows, as if deploring the intemperate conduct of Mr. Haredale, and smiled in admiration of the crowd, and of their leader.

"*He* retort!" cried Haredale. "Look you here, my Lord. Do you know this man?"

Lord George replied by laying his hand upon the shoulder of his cringing secretary, and viewing him with a smile of confidence.

"This man," said Mr. Haredale, eyeing him from top to toe, "who in his boyhood was a thief, and has been from that time to this, a servile, false, and truckling knave: this man, who has crawled and crept through life, wounding the hands he licked, and biting those he fawned upon: this sycophant, who never knew what honour, truth, or courage meant; who robbed his benefactor's daughter of her virtue, and married her to break her heart, and did it, with stripes and cruelty: this creature, who has whined at kitchen windows for the broken food, and begged for halfpence at our chapel doors: this apostle of the faith, whose tender conscience cannot bear the altars where his vicious life was publicly denounced—Do you know this man, my Lord?"

"Oh, really—you are very, very hard upon our friend!" exclaimed Sir John.

"Let Mr. Haredale go on," said Gashford, upon whose unwholesome face the perspiration had broken out during this speech, in blotches of wet; "I don't mind him, Sir John; it's quite as indifferent to me what he says, as it is to my Lord; if he reviles my Lord, as you have heard, Sir John, how can *I* hope to escape?"

"Is it not enough, my Lord," Mr. Haredale continued, "that I, as good a gentleman as you, must hold my property, such as it is, by a trick at which the state connives* because of these hard laws; and that we may not teach our youth in schools the common principles of right and wrong; but must we be denounced and ridden by such men as this! Here is a man to head your No-Popery cry, my Lord. For shame. For shame!"

The infatuated nobleman had glanced more than once at Sir John Chester, as if to inquire whether there was any truth in these statements concerning Gashford, and Sir John had as often plainly answered by a shrug or look, "Oh dear me! no." He now said, in the same loud key, and in the same strange manner as before:

"I have nothing to say, sir, in reply, and no desire to hear anything more. I beg you won't obtrude your conversation, or these personal attacks, upon me any further. I shall not be deterred from doing my duty to my country and my countrymen, by any such attempts, whether they proceed from emissaries of the Pope or not, I assure you. Come, Gashford!"

They had walked on a few paces while speaking, and were now at the Hall-door, through which they passed together. Mr. Haredale, without any leave-taking, turned away to the river-stairs, which were close at hand, and hailed the only boatman who remained there.

But the throng of people—the foremost of whom had heard every word that Lord George Gordon said, and among all of whom the rumour had been rapidly dispersed that the stranger was a Papist who was bearding him for his advocacy of the popular cause—came pouring out pell-mell, and, forcing the nobleman, his secretary, and Sir John Chester on before them, so that they appeared to be at their head, crowded to the top of the stairs where Mr. Haredale waited until the boat was ready, and there stood still, leaving him on a little clear space by himself.

They were not silent, however, though inactive. At first some indistinct mutterings arose among them, which were followed by a hiss or two, and these swelled by degrees into a perfect storm. Then one voice said, "Down with the Papists!" and there was a pretty general cheer, but nothing more. After a lull of a few moments, one man cried out, "Stone him;" another, "Duck him;" another, in a stentorian voice, "No Popery!" This favourite cry the rest re-echoed, and the mob, which might have been two hundred strong, joined in a general shout.

Mr. Haredale had stood calmly on the brink of the steps, until they made this demonstration, when he looked round contemptuously, and walked at a slow pace down the stairs. He was pretty near the boat, when Gashford, as if without intention, turned about, and directly afterwards a great stone was thrown by some hand in the crowd, which struck him on the head, and made him stagger like a drunken man.

The blood sprung freely from the wound, and trickled down his coat. He turned directly, and rushing up the steps with a boldness and passion which made them all fall back, demanded:

"Who did that? Show me the man who hit me."

Not a soul moved; except some in the rear who slunk off, and, creeping to the other side of the way, looked on like indifferent spectators.

"Who did that?" he repeated. "Show me the man who did it. Dog, was it you? It was your deed, if not your hand—I know you."

He threw himself on Gashford as he said the words, and hurled him to the ground. There was a sudden motion in the crowd, and some laid hands upon him, but his sword was out, and they fell off again.

"My Lord—Sir John"—he cried, "draw, one of you—you are responsible for this outrage, and I look to you. Draw, if you are gentlemen." With that he struck Sir John upon the breast with the flat of his weapon, and with a burning face and flashing eyes stood upon his guard; alone, before them all.

For an instant, for the briefest space of time the mind can readily conceive, there was a change in Sir John's smooth face, such as no

man ever saw there. The next moment, he stepped forward, and laid one hand on Mr. Haredale's arm, while with the other he endeavoured to appease the crowd.

"My dear friend, my good Haredale, you are blinded with passion—it's very natural, extremely natural—but you don't know friends from foes."

"I know them all, sir, I can distinguish well—"he retorted, almost mad with rage. "Sir John, my Lord—do you hear me? Are you cowards?"

"Never mind, sir," said a man, forcing his way between and pushing him towards the stairs with friendly violence, "never mind asking that. For God's sake, get away. What *can* you do against this number? And there are as many more in the next street, who'll be round directly"—indeed they began to pour in as he said the words—"you'd be giddy from that cut, in the first heat of a scuffle. Now do retire, sir, or take my word for it you'll be worse used than you would be if every man in the crowd was a woman, and that woman Bloody Mary. Come, sir, make haste—as quick as you can."

Mr. Haredale, who began to turn faint and sick, felt how sensible this advice was, and descended the steps with his unknown friend's assistance. John Grueby (for John it was) helped him into the boat, and giving her a shove off which sent her thirty feet into the tide, bade the waterman pull away like a Briton; and walked up again as composedly as if he had just landed.

There was at first a slight disposition on the part of the mob to resent this interference; but John looking particularly strong and cool, and wearing besides Lord George's livery, they thought better of it, and contented themselves with sending a shower of small missiles after the boat, which plashed harmlessly in the water, for she had by this time cleared the bridge, and was darting swiftly down the centre of the stream.

From this amusement, they proceeded to giving Protestant knocks at the doors of private houses, breaking a few lamps, and assaulting some stray constables. But it being whispered that a detachment of Life Guards* had been sent for, they took to their heels with great expedition, and left the street quite clear.

CHAPTER THE FORTY-FOURTH.

WHEN the concourse separated, and, dividing into chance clusters, drew off in various directions, there still remained upon the scene of the late disturbance, one man. This man was Gashford, who, bruised by his late fall, and hurt in a much greater degree by the indignity he had undergone, and the exposure of which he had been the victim, limped up and down, breathing curses and threats of vengeance.

It was not the secretary's nature to waste his wrath in words. While he vented the froth of his malevolence in these effusions, he kept a steady eye on two men, who, having disappeared with the rest when the alarm was spread, had since returned, and were now visible in the moonlight, at no great distance, as they walked to and fro, and talked together.

He made no move towards them, but waited patiently on the dark side of the street, until they were tired of strolling backwards and forwards and walked away in company. Then he followed, but at some distance: keeping them in view, without appearing to have that object, or being seen by them.

They went up Parliament Street, past Saint Martin's church, and away by Saint Giles's to Tottenham Court Road, at the back of which, upon the western side, was then a place called the Green Lanes.* This was a retired spot, not of the choicest kind, leading into the fields. Great heaps of ashes; stagnant pools, overgrown with rank grass and duckweed; broken turnstiles; and the upright posts of palings long since carried off for firewood, which menaced all heedless walkers with their jagged and rusty nails; were the leading features of the landscape: while here and there a donkey, or a ragged horse, tethered to a stake, and cropping off a wretched meal from the coarse stunted turf, were quite in keeping with the scene, and would have suggested (if the houses had not done so sufficiently, of themselves) how very poor the people were who lived in the crazy huts adjacent, and how fool-hardy it might prove for one who carried money, or wore decent clothes, to walk that way alone, unless by daylight.

Poverty has its whims and shows of taste, as wealth has. Some of these cabins were turreted, some had false windows painted on their rotten walls; one had a mimic clock, upon a crazy tower of four feet high, which screened the chimney; each in its little patch of ground had a rude seat or arbour. The population dealt in bones, in rags, in broken glass, in old wheels, in birds, and dogs. These, in their several ways of stowage, filled the gardens; and shedding a perfume, not of the most delicious nature, in the air, filled it besides with yelps, and screams, and howling.

Into this retreat, the secretary followed the two men whom he had held in sight; and here he saw them safely lodged, in one of the meanest houses, which was but a room, and that of small dimensions. He waited without, until the sound of their voices, joined in a discordant song, assured him they were making merry; and then approaching the door, by means of a tottering plank which crossed the ditch in front, knocked at it with his hand.

"Muster Gashford!" said the man who opened it, taking his pipe from his mouth, in evident surprise. "Why, who'd have thought of this here honor! Walk in, Muster Gashford—walk in, sir."

Gashford required no second invitation, and entered with a gracious air. There was a fire in the rusty grate (for though the spring was pretty far advanced, the nights were cold), and on a stool beside it Hugh sat smoking. Dennis placed a chair, his only one, for the secretary, in front of the hearth; and took his seat again upon the stool he had left, when he rose to give the visitor admission.

"What's in the wind now, Muster Gashford?" he said, as he resumed his pipe, and looked at him askew. "Any orders from head-quarters? Are we going to begin? What is it, Muster Gashford?"

"Oh, nothing, nothing," rejoined the secretary, with a friendly nod to Hugh. "We have broken the ice, though. We had a little spurt to-day—eh, Dennis?"

"A very little one," growled the hangman. "Not half enough for me."

"Nor me either!" cried Hugh. "Give us something to do with life in it—with life in it, Master. Ha, ha!"

"Why, you wouldn't," said the secretary, with his worst expression of face, and in his mildest tones, "have anything to do, with—with death in it?"

"I don't know that," replied Hugh. "I'm open to orders. I don't care; not I."

"Nor I!" vociferated Dennis.

"Brave fellows!" said the secretary, in as pastor-like a voice as if he were commending them for some uncommon act of valour and generosity. "By the bye"—and here he stopped and warmed his hands: then suddenly looked up—"who threw that stone to-day?"

Mr. Dennis coughed and shook his head, as who should say, "A mystery indeed!" Hugh sat and smoked in silence.

"It was well done!" said the secretary, warming his hands again. "I should like to know that man."

"Would you?" said Dennis, after looking at his face to assure himself that he was serious. "Would you like to know that man, Muster Gashford?"

"I should indeed," replied the secretary.

"Why then, Lord love you," said the hangman, in his hoarsest chuckle, as he pointed with his pipe to Hugh, "there he sets. That's the man. My stars and halters, Muster Gashford," he added in a whisper, as he drew his stool close to him and jogged him with his elbow, "what a interesting blade he is! He wants as much holding in as a thorough-bred bulldog. If it hadn't been for me to-day, he'd have had that 'ere Roman down, and made a riot of it, in another minute."

"And why not?" cried Hugh in a surly voice, as he overheard this last remark. "Where's the good of putting things off? Strike while the iron's hot; that's what I say."

"Ah!" retorted Dennis, shaking his head, with a kind of pity for his friend's ingenuous youth: "but suppose the iron an't hot, brother? You must get people's blood up afore you strike, and have 'em in the humour. There wasn't quite enough to provoke 'em to-day, I tell you. If you'd had your way, you'd have spoilt the fun to come, and ruined us."

"Dennis is quite right," said Gashford, smoothly. "He is perfectly correct. Dennis has great knowledge of the world."

"I ought to have, Muster Gashford, seeing what a many people I've helped out of it, eh?" grinned the hangman, whispering the words behind his hand.

The secretary laughed at this jest as much as Dennis could desire, and when he had done, said, turning to Hugh:

"Dennis's policy was mine, as you may have observed. You saw, for instance, how I fell when I was set upon. I made no resistance. I did nothing to provoke an outbreak. Oh dear no!"

"No, by the Lord Harry!"* cried Dennis with a noisy laugh, "you went down very quiet, Muster Gashford—and very flat besides. I thinks to myself at the time 'it's all up with Muster Gashford!' I never see a man lay flatter nor more still—with the life in him—than you did to-day. He's a rough 'un to play with, is that 'ere Papist, and that's the fact."

The secretary's face, as Dennis roared with laughter, and turned his wrinkled eyes on Hugh who did the like, might have furnished a study for the devil's picture. He sat quite silent until they were serious again, and then said, looking round:

"We are very pleasant here; so very pleasant, Dennis, that but for my Lord's particular desire that I should sup with him, and the time being very near at hand, I should be inclined to stop, until it would be hardly safe to go homeward. I come upon a little business—yes, I do—as you supposed. It's very flattering to you; being this. If we ever should be obliged—and we can't tell, you know—this is a very uncertain world"—

"I believe you, Muster Gashford," interposed the hangman with a grave nod. "The uncertainties as I've seen in reference to this here state of existence, the unexpected contingencies as have come about!—Oh my eye!" And feeling the subject much too vast for expression, he puffed at his pipe again, and looked the rest.

"I say," resumed the secretary, in a slow, impressive way; "we can't tell what may come to pass; and if we should be obliged, against our wills, to have recourse to violence, my Lord (who has suffered terribly to-day, as far as words can go) consigns to you two—bearing in mind my recommendation of you both, as good staunch men, beyond all doubt and suspicion—the pleasant task of punishing this Haredale. You may do as you please with him, or his; provided that you show no mercy, and no quarter, and leave no two beams of his house standing where the builder placed them. You may sack it, burn it, do with it as you like, but it must come down; it must be razed to the ground; and he, and all belonging to him, left as shelterless as new-born infants whom their mothers have exposed. Do you understand me?" said Gashford, pausing, and pressing his hands together gently.

"Understand you, master!" cried Hugh. "You speak plain now. Why, this *is* hearty!"

"I knew you would like it," said Gashford, shaking him by the hand; "I thought you would. Good night! Don't rise, Dennis: I would rather find my way alone. I may have to make other visits here, and it's pleasant to come and go without disturbing you. I can find my way perfectly well. Good night!"

He was gone, and had shut the door behind him. They looked at each other, and nodded approvingly: Dennis stirred up the fire.

"This looks a little more like business!" he said.

"Ay, indeed!" cried Hugh; "this suits me!"

"I've heerd it said of Muster Gashford," said the hangman, thoughtfully, "that he'd a surprising memory and wonderful firmness—that he never forgot, and never forgave.—Let's drink his health!"

Hugh readily complied; pouring no liquor on the floor when he drank this toast; and they pledged the secretary as a man after their own hearts, in a bumper.

CHAPTER THE FORTY-FIFTH.

WHILE the worst passions of the worst men were thus working in the dark, and the mantle of religion, assumed to cover the ugliest deformities, threatened to become the shroud of all that was good and peaceful in society, a circumstance occurred which once more altered the position of two persons from whom this history has long been separated, and to whom it must now return.

In a small English country town, the inhabitants of which supported themselves by the labour of their hands in plaiting and preparing straw for those who made bonnets and other articles of dress and ornament from that material,—concealed under an assumed name, and living in a quiet poverty which knew no change, no pleasures, and few cares but that of struggling on from day to day in the one great toil for bread,—dwelt Barnaby and his mother. Their poor cottage had known no stranger's foot since they sought the shelter of its roof five years before; nor had they in all that time held any commerce or communication with the old world from which they had fled. To labour in peace, and devote her labour and her life to her poor son, was all the widow sought. If happiness can be said at any time to be the lot of one on whom a secret sorrow preys, she was happy now. Tranquillity, resignation, and her strong love of him who needed it so much, formed the small circle of her quiet joys; and while that remained unbroken, she was contented.

For Barnaby himself, the time which had flown by, had passed him like the wind. The daily suns of years had shed no brighter gleam of reason on his mind; no dawn had broken on his long, dark night. He would sit sometimes—often for days together—on a low seat by the fire or by the cottage door, busy at work (for he had learnt the art his mother plied), and listening, God help him, to the tales she would repeat, as a lure to keep him in her sight. He had no recollection of these little narratives; the tale of yesterday was new upon the morrow; but he liked them at the moment; and when the humour held him, would remain patiently within doors, hearing her stories like a little child, and working cheerfully from sunrise until it was too dark to see.

At other times,—and then their scanty earnings were barely sufficient to furnish them with food, though of the coarsest sort,—he would wander abroad from dawn of day until the twilight deepened into night. Few in that place, even of the children, could be idle, and he had no companions of his own kind. Indeed there were not many who could have kept up with him in his rambles, had there been a legion. But there were a score of vagabond dogs belonging to the neighbours, who served his purpose quite as well. With two or three of these, or sometimes with a full half-dozen barking at his heels, he would sally forth on some long expedition that consumed the day; and though, on their return at nightfall, the dogs would come home limping and sore-footed, and almost spent with their fatigue, Barnaby was up and off again at sunrise with some new attendants of the same class, with whom he would return in like manner. On all these travels, Grip, in his little basket at his master's back, was a constant member of the party, and when they set off in fine weather and in high spirits, no dog barked louder than the raven.

Their pleasures on these excursions were simple enough. A crust of bread and scrap of meat, with water from the brook or spring, sufficed for their repast. Barnaby's enjoyments were, to walk, and run, and leap, till he was tired; then to lie down in the long grass, or by the growing corn, or in the shade of some tall tree, looking upward at the light clouds as they floated over the blue surface of the sky, and listening to the lark as she poured out her brilliant song. There were wild-flowers to pluck—the bright red poppy, the gentle harebell, the cowslip, and the rose. There were birds to watch; fish; ants; worms; hares or rabbits, as they darted across the distant pathway in the wood and so were gone: millions of living things to have an interest in, and lie in wait for, and clap hands and shout in memory of, when they had disappeared. In default of these, or when they wearied, there was the merry sunlight to hunt out, as it crept in aslant through leaves and boughs of trees, and hid far down—deep, deep, in hollow places—like a silver pool, where nodding branches seemed to bathe and sport; sweet scents of summer air breathing over fields of beans or clover; the perfume of wet leaves or moss; the life of waving trees, and shadows always changing. When these or any of them tired, or in excess of pleasing tempted him to shut his eyes, there was slumber in the midst of all these soft delights, with the gentle wind murmuring like music in his ears, and everything around melting into one delicious dream.

Their hut—for it was little more—stood on the outskirts of the town, at a short distance from the high road, but in a secluded place, where few chance passengers strayed at any season of the year. It had a plot of garden-ground attached, which Barnaby, in fits and starts of working, trimmed, and kept in order. Within doors and without, his mother laboured for their common good; and hail, rain, snow, or sunshine, found no difference in her.

Though so far removed from the scenes of her past life, and with so little thought or hope of ever visiting them again, she seemed to have a strange desire to know what happened in the busy world. Any old newspaper, or scrap of intelligence from London, she caught at with avidity. The excitement it produced was not of a pleasurable kind, for her manner at such times expressed the keenest anxiety and dread; but it never faded in the least degree. Then, and in stormy winter nights, when the wind blew loud and strong, the old expression came into her face, and she would be seized with a fit of trembling, like one who had an ague. But Barnaby noted little of this; and putting a great constraint upon herself, she usually recovered her accustomed manner before the change had caught his observation.

Grip was by no means an idle or unprofitable member of the humble household. Partly by dint of Barnaby's tuition, and partly by pursuing a species of self-instruction common to his tribe, and exerting his powers of observation to the utmost, he had acquired a degree of sagacity which rendered him famous for miles round. His conversational powers and surprising performances were the

universal theme: and as many persons came to see the wonderful
raven, and none left his exertions unrewarded—when he con-
descended to exhibit, which was not always, for genius is capri-
cious—his earnings formed an important item in the common stock.
Indeed, the bird himself appeared to know his value well; for though
he was perfectly free and unrestrained in the presence of Barnaby
and his mother, he maintained in public an amazing gravity, and
never stooped to any other gratuitous performances than biting the
ankles of vagabond boys (an exercise in which he much delighted),
killing a fowl or two occasionally, and swallowing the dinners of
various neighbouring dogs, of whom the boldest held him in great
awe and dread.

Time had glided on in this way, and nothing had happened to
disturb or change their mode of life, when, one summer's night in
June, they were in their little garden, resting from the labours of the
day. The widow's work was yet upon her knee, and strewn upon the
ground about her; and Barnaby stood leaning on his spade, gazing at
the brightness in the west, and singing softly to himself.

"A brave evening, mother! If we had, chinking in our pockets, but a few specks of that gold which is piled up yonder in the sky, we should be rich for life."

"We are better as we are," returned the widow with a quiet smile. "Let us be contented, and we do not want and need not care to have it, though it lay shining at our feet."

"Ay!" said Barnaby, resting with crossed arms on his spade, and looking wistfully at the sunset, "that's well enough, mother; but gold's a good thing to have. I wish that I knew where to find it. Grip and I could do much with gold, be sure of that."

"What would you do?" she asked.

"What! A world of things. We'd dress finely—you and I, I mean; not Grip—keep horses, dogs, wear bright colours and feathers, do no more work, live delicately and at our ease. Oh, we'd find uses for it, mother, and uses that would do us good. I would I knew where gold was buried. How hard I'd work to dig it up!"

"You do not know," said his mother, rising from her seat and laying her hand upon his shoulder, "what men have done to win it, and how they have found, too late, that it glitters brightest at a distance, and turns quite dim and dull when handled."

"Ay, ay; so you say; so you think," he answered, still looking eagerly in the same direction. "For all that, mother, I should like to try."

"Do you not see," she said, "how red it is? Nothing bears so many stains of blood, as gold. Avoid it. None have such cause to hate its name as we have. Do not so much as think of it, dear love. It has brought such misery and suffering on your head and mine as few have known, and God grant few may have to undergo. I would rather we were dead and laid down in our graves, than you should ever come to love it."

For a moment Barnaby withdrew his eyes and looked at her with wonder. Then, glancing from the redness in the sky to the mark upon his wrist as if he would compare the two, he seemed about to question her with earnestness, when a new object caught his wandering attention, and made him quite forgetful of his purpose.

This was a man with dusty feet and garments, who stood, bareheaded, behind the hedge that divided their patch of garden from the pathway, and leant meekly forward as if he sought to mingle with their conversation, and waited for his time to speak. His face was turned towards the brightness, too, but the light that fell upon it showed that he was blind, and saw it not.

"A blessing on those voices!" said the wayfarer. "I feel the beauty of the night more keenly, when I hear them. They are like eyes to me. Will they speak again, and cheer the heart of a poor traveller?"

"Have you no guide?" asked the widow, after a moment's pause.

"None but that," he answered, pointing with his staff towards the sun: "and sometimes a milder one at night, but she is idle now."

"Have you travelled far?"

"A weary way and long," rejoined the traveller as he shook his head. "A weary, weary, way. I struck my stick just now upon the bucket of your well—be pleased to let me have a draught of water, lady."

"Why do you call me lady?" she returned. "I am as poor as you."

"Your speech is soft and gentle, and I judge by that," replied the man. "The coarsest stuffs and finest silks, are—apart from the sense of touch—alike to me. I cannot judge you by your dress."

"Come round this way," said Barnaby, who had passed out at the garden gate and now stood close beside him. "Put your hand in mine. You're blind and always in the dark, eh? Are you frightened in the dark? Do you see great crowds of faces, now? Do they grin and chatter?"

"Alas!" returned the other, "I see nothing. Waking or sleeping, nothing."

Barnaby looked curiously at his eyes, and touching them with his fingers, as an inquisitive child might do, led him towards the house.

"You have come a long distance," said the widow, meeting him at the door. "How have you found your way so far?"

"Use and necessity are good teachers, as I have heard—the best of any," said the blind man, sitting down upon the chair to which Barnaby had led him, and putting his hat and stick upon the red-tiled floor. "May neither you nor your son ever learn under them. They are rough masters."

"You have wandered from the road, too," said the widow, in a tone of pity.

"Maybe, maybe," returned the blind man with a sigh, and yet with something of a smile upon his face, "that's likely. Handposts and milestones are dumb, indeed, to me. Thank you the more for this rest, and this refreshing drink!"

As he spoke, he raised the mug of water to his mouth. It was clear, and cold, and sparkling, but not to his taste nevertheless, or his thirst was not very great, for he only wetted his lips and put it down again.

He wore, hanging with a long strap round his neck, a kind of scrip or wallet, in which to carry food. The widow set some bread and cheese before him, but he thanked her, and said that through the kindness of the charitable he had broken his fast once since morning, and was not hungry. When he had made her this reply, he opened his wallet, and took out a few pence, which was all it appeared to contain.

"Might I make bold to ask," he said, turning towards where Barnaby stood looking on, "that one who has the gift of sight, would lay this out for me in bread to keep me on my way? Heaven's blessing on the young feet that will bestir themselves in aid of one so helpless as a sightless man!"

Barnaby looked at his mother, who nodded assent; in another moment he was gone upon his charitable errand. The blind man sat listening with an attentive face, until long after the sound of his retreating footsteps was inaudible to the widow, and then said, suddenly, and in a very altered tone:

"There are various degrees and kinds of blindness, widow. There is the connubial blindness, ma'am, which perhaps you may have observed in the course of your own experience, and which is a kind of wilful and self-bandaging blindness. There is the blindness of party, ma'am, and public men, which is the blindness of a mad bull in the midst of a regiment of soldiers clothed in red. There is the blind confidence of youth, which is the blindness of young kittens, whose eyes have not yet opened on the world; and there is that physical blindness, ma'am, of which I am, contrairy to my own desire, a most illustrious example. Added to these, ma'am, is that blindness of the intellect, of which we have a specimen in your interesting son, and which, having sometimes glimmerings and dawnings of the light, is scarcely to be trusted as a total darkness. Therefore, ma'am, I have taken the liberty to get him out of the way for a short time, while you and I confer together, and this precaution arising out of the delicacy of my sentiments towards yourself, you will excuse me, ma'am, I know."

Having delivered himself of this speech with many flourishes of manner, he drew from beneath his coat a flat stone bottle, and holding the cork between his teeth, qualified his mug of water with a plentiful infusion of the liquor it contained. He politely drained the bumper to her health, and the ladies, and setting it down empty, smacked his lips with infinite relish.

"I am a citizen of the world, ma'am," said the blind man, corking his bottle, "and if I seem to conduct myself with freedom, it is the way of the world. You wonder who I am, ma'am, and what has brought me here. Such experience of human nature as I have, leads me to that conclusion, without the aid of eyes by which to read the movements of your soul as depicted in your feminine features. I will satisfy your curiosity immediately, ma'am; im-mediately." With that he slapped his bottle on its broad back, and having put it under his garment as before, crossed his legs and folded his hands, and settled himself in his chair, previous to proceeding any further.

The change in his manner was so unexpected, the craft and wickedness of his deportment were so much aggravated by his condition—for we are accustomed to see in those who have lost a human sense, something in its place almost divine—and this alteration bred so many fears in her whom he addressed, that she could not pronounce one word. After waiting, as it seemed, for some remark or answer, and waiting in vain, the visitor resumed:

"Madam, my name is Stagg. A friend of mine who has desired the honour of meeting with you any time these five years past, has commissioned me to call upon you. I should be glad to whisper that gentleman's name in your ear.—Zounds, ma'am, are you deaf? Do you hear me say that I should be glad to whisper my friend's name in your ear?"

"You need not repeat it," said the widow, with a stifled groan; "I see too well from whom you come."

"But as a man of honour, ma'am," said the blind man, striking himself on the breast, "whose credentials must not be disputed, I take leave to say that I *will* mention that gentleman's name. Ay, ay," he added, seeming to catch with his quick ear the very motion of her hand, "but not aloud. With your leave ma'am, I desire the favour of a whisper."

She moved towards him, and stooped down. He muttered a word in her ear; and, wringing her hands, she paced up and down the room like one distracted. The blind man, with perfect composure, produced his bottle again, mixed another glass-full; put it up as before; and, drinking from time to time, followed her with his face in silence.

"You are slow in conversation, widow," he said after a time, pausing in his draught. "We shall have to talk before your son."

"What would you have me do?" she answered. "What do you want?"

"We are poor, widow, we are poor," he retorted, stretching out his right hand, and rubbing his thumb upon its palm.

"Poor!" she cried. "And what am I?"

"Comparisons are odious," said the blind man. "I don't know, I don't care. I say that we are poor. My friend's circumstances are indifferent, and so are mine. We must have our rights, widow, or we must be bought off. But you know that, as well as I, so where's the use of talking?"

She still walked wildly to and fro. At length, stopping abruptly before him, she said:

"Is he near here?"

"He is. Close at hand."

"Then I am lost!"

"Not lost, widow," said the blind man, calmly; "only found. Shall I call him?"

"Not for the world," she answered, with a shudder.

"Very good," he replied, crossing his legs again, for he had made as though he would rise and walk to the door. "As you please, widow. His presence is not necessary that I know of. But both he and I must live; to live, we must eat and drink; to eat and drink, we must have money:—I say no more."

"Do you know how pinched and destitute I am?" she retorted. "I do not think you do, or can. If you had eyes, and could look around you on this poor cabin, you would have pity on me. Oh! let your heart be softened by your own affliction, friend, and have some sympathy with mine."

The blind man snapped his fingers as he answered:

"—Beside the question, ma'am, beside the question. I have the softest heart in the world, but I can't live upon it. Many a gentleman lives well upon a soft head, who would find a heart of the same quality a very great drawback. Listen to me. This is a matter of business, with which sympathies and sentiments have nothing to do. As a mutual friend, I wish to arrange it in a satisfactory manner, if

possible; and thus the case stands.—If you are very poor now, it's your own choice. You have friends who, in case of need, are always ready to help you. My friend is in a more destitute and desolate situation than most men, and, you and he being linked together in a common cause, he naturally looks to you to assist him. He has boarded and lodged with me a long time (for as I said just now, I am very soft-hearted), and I quite approve of his entertaining this opinion. You have always had a roof over your head; he has always been an outcast. You have your son to comfort and assist you; he has nobody at all. The advantages must not be all one side. You are in the same boat, and we must divide the ballast a little more equally."

She was about to speak, but he checked her, and went on.

"The only way of doing this, is by making up a little purse now and then for my friend; and that's what I advise. He bears you no malice that I know of, ma'am: so little, that although you have treated him harshly more than once, and driven him, I may say, out of doors, he has that regard for you that I believe, even if you disappointed him now, he would consent to take charge of your son, and to make a man of him."

He laid a great stress on these latter words, and paused as if to find out what effect they had produced. She only answered by her tears.

"He is a likely lad," said the blind man, thoughtfully, "for many purposes, and not ill-disposed to try his fortune in a little change and bustle, if I may judge from what I heard of his talk with you to-night.—Come. In a word, my friend has pressing necessity for twenty pounds. You, who can give up an annuity, can get that sum for him. It's a pity you should be troubled. You seem very comfortable here, and it's worth that much to remain so. Twenty pounds, widow, is a moderate demand. You know where to apply for it; a post will bring it you.—Twenty pounds!"

She was about to answer him again, but again he stopped her.

"Don't say anything hastily; you might be sorry for it. Think of it a little while. Twenty pounds—of other people's money—how easy! Turn it over in your mind, I'm in no hurry. Night's coming on, and if I don't sleep here, I shall not go far. Twenty pounds! Consider of it, ma'am, for twenty minutes; give each pound a minute; that's a fair allowance. I'll enjoy the air the while, which is very mild and pleasant in these parts."

With these words, he groped his way to the door, carrying his chair with him. Then seating himself, under a spreading honeysuckle, and stretching his legs across the threshold so that no person could pass in or out without his knowledge, he took from his pocket a pipe, flint, steel and tinder-box, and began to smoke. It was a lovely evening, of that gentle kind, and at that time of year, when the twilight is most beautiful. Pausing now and then to let his smoke curl slowly off, and to sniff the grateful fragrance of the flowers, he sat there at his ease—as though the cottage were his proper dwelling, and he had held undisputed possession of it all his life—waiting for the widow's answer and for Barnaby's return.

CHAPTER THE FORTY-SIXTH.

WHEN Barnaby returned with the bread, the sight of the pious old pilgrim smoking his pipe and making himself so thoroughly at home, appeared to surprise even him; the more so as that worthy person, instead of putting up the loaf in his wallet as a scarce and precious article, tossed it carelessly on the table, and producing his bottle, bade him sit down and drink.

"For I carry some comfort you see," he said. "Taste that. Is it good?"

The water stood in Barnaby's eyes as he coughed from the strength of the draught, and answered in the affirmative.

"Drink some more," said the blind man; "don't be afraid of it. You don't taste anything like that, often, eh?"

"Often!" cried Barnaby. "Never!"

"Too poor?" returned the blind man with a sigh. "Ay. That's bad. Your mother, poor soul, would be happier if she was richer, Barnaby."

"Why, so I tell her—the very thing I told her just before you came to-night, when all that gold was in the sky," said Barnaby, drawing his chair nearer to him, and looking eagerly in his face. "Tell me. Is there any way of being rich, that I could find out?"

"Any way! A hundred ways."

"Ay, ay?" he returned. "Do you say so? What are they?—Nay, mother, it's for your sake I ask; not mine;—for yours, indeed. What are they?"

The blind man turned his face, on which there was a smile of triumph, to where the widow stood in great distress; and answered,

"Why, they are not to be found out by stay-at-homes, my good friend."

"By stay-at-homes!" cried Barnaby, plucking at his sleeve. "But I am not one. Now, there you mistake. I am often out before the sun, and travel home when he has gone to rest. I am away in the woods before the day has reached the shady places, and am often there when the bright moon is peeping through the boughs, and looking down upon the other moon that lives in the water. As I walk along, I try to find, among the grass and moss, some of that small money for which she works so hard and used to shed so many tears. As I lie asleep in the shade, I dream of it—dream of digging it up in heaps; and spying it out, hidden under bushes; and seeing it sparkle, as the dew-drops do, among the leaves. But I never find it. Tell me where it is. I'd go there, if the journey were a whole year long, because I know she would be happier when I came home and brought some with me. Speak again. I'll listen to you if you talk all night."

The blind man passed his hand lightly over the poor fellow's face, and finding that his elbows were planted on the table, that his chin rested on his two hands, that he leaned eagerly forward, and that his whole manner expressed the utmost interest and anxiety, paused for a minute as though he desired the widow to observe this fully, and then made answer:

"It's in the world, bold Barnaby, the merry world; not in solitary places like those you pass your time in, but in crowds, and where there's noise and rattle."

"Good! good!" cried Barnaby, rubbing his hands. "Yes! I love that. Grip loves it too. It suits us both. That's brave!"

"—The kind of places," said the blind man, "that a young fellow likes, and in which a good son may do more for his mother, and himself to boot, in a month, than he could here in all his life—that is, if he had a friend, you know, and some one to advise with."

"You hear this, mother?" cried Barnaby, turning to her with delight. "Never tell me we shouldn't heed it, if it lay shining at our feet. Why do we heed it so much now? Why do you toil from morning until night?"

"Surely," said the blind man, "surely. Have you no answer, widow? Is your mind," he slowly added, "not made up yet?"

"Let me speak with you," she answered, "apart."

"Lay your hand upon my sleeve," said Stagg, rising from the table; "and lead me where you will. Courage, bold Barnaby. We'll talk more of this: I've a fancy for you. Wait there till I come back. Now, widow."

She led him out at the door, and into the little garden, where they stopped.

"You are a fit agent," she said, in a half breathless manner, "and well represent the man who sent you here."

"I'll tell him that you said so," Stagg retorted. "He has a regard for you, and will respect me the more (if possible) for your praise. We must have our rights, widow."

"Rights! Do you know," she said, "that a word from me—"

"Why do you stop?" returned the blind man calmly, after a long pause. "Do I know that a word from you would place my friend in the last position of the dance of life? Yes, I do. What of that? It will never be spoken, widow."

"You are sure of that?"

"Quite—so sure, that I don't come here to discuss the question. I say we must have our rights, or we must be bought off. Keep to that point, or let me return to my young friend, for I have an interest in the lad, and desire to put him in the way of making his fortune. Bah! you needn't speak," he added hastily; "I know what you would say: you have hinted at it once already. Have I no feeling for you, because I am blind? No, I have not. Why do you expect me, being in darkness, to be better than men who have their sight—why should you? Is the hand of God more manifest in my having no eyes, than in your having two? It's the cant of you folks to be horrified if a blind man robs, or lies, or steals; oh yes, it's far worse in him, who can barely live on the few halfpence that are thrown to him in your crowded streets, than in you, who can see, and work, and are not dependent on the mercies of the world. A curse on you! You who have seven senses may be wicked at your pleasure; we who have six, and want the most important, are to live and be moral on our affliction. The true charity and justice of rich to poor, all the world over!"

He paused a moment when he had said these words, and caught the sound of money, jingling in her hand.

"Well?" he cried, quickly resuming his former manner. "That should lead to something. The point, widow?"

"First answer me one question," she replied. "You say he is close at hand. Has he left London?"

"Being close at hand, widow, it would seem he has," returned the blind man.

"I mean, for good? You know that."

"Yes, for good. The truth is, widow, that his making a longer stay there might have had disagreeable consequences. He has come away for that reason."

"Listen," said the widow, telling some money out, upon a bench beside them. "Count."

"Six," said the blind man, listening attentively. "Any more?"

"They are the savings" she answered "of five years. Six guineas."

He put out his hand for one of the coins; felt it carefully, put it between his teeth, rung it on the bench; and nodded to her to proceed.

"These have been scraped together and laid by, lest sickness or death should separate my son and me. They have been purchased at the price of much hunger, hard labour, and want of rest. If you *can* take them—do—on condition that you leave this place upon the instant, and enter no more into that room, where he sits now, expecting your return."

"Six guineas" said the blind man, shaking his head, "though of the fullest weight that were ever coined, fall very far short of twenty pounds, widow."

"For such a sum, as you know, I must write to a distant part of the country. To do that, and receive an answer, I must have time."

"Two days?" said Stagg.

"More."

"Four days?"

"A week. Return on this day week, at the same hour, but not to the house. Wait at the corner of the lane."

"Of course," said the blind man, with a crafty look, "I shall find you there?"

"Where else can I take refuge? Is it not enough that you have made a beggar of me, and that I have sacrificed my whole store, so hardly earned, to preserve this home?"

"Humph!" said the blind man, after some consideration. "Set me with my face towards the point you speak of, and in the middle of the road. Is this the spot?"

"It is."

"On this day week at sunset. And think of him within doors.—For the present, good night."

She made him no answer, nor did he stop for any. He went slowly away, turning his head from time to time, and stopping to listen, as if he were curious to know whether he was watched by any one. The shadows of night were closing fast around, and he was soon lost in the gloom. It was not, however, until she had traversed the lane from end to end, and made sure that he was gone, that she re-entered the cottage, and hurriedly barred the door and window.

"Mother!" said Barnaby. "What is the matter? Where is the blind man?"

"He is gone."

"Gone!" he cried, starting up. "I must have more talk with him. Which way did he take?"

"I don't know," she answered, folding her arms about him. "You must not go out to-night. There are ghosts and dreams abroad."

"Ay?" said Barnaby, in a frightened whisper.

"It is not safe to stir. We must leave this place to-morrow."

"This place! This cottage—and the little garden mother!"

"Yes! To-morrow morning at sunrise. We must travel to London; lose ourselves in that wide place—there would be some trace of us in any other town—then travel on again, and find some new abode."

Little persuasion was required to reconcile Barnaby to anything that promised change. In another minute, he was wild with delight; in another, full of grief at the prospect of parting with his friends the dogs; in another, wild again; then he was fearful of what she had said to prevent his wandering abroad that night, and full of terrors and strange questions. His light-heartedness in the end surmounted all his other feelings, and lying down in his clothes to the end that he might be ready on the morrow, he soon fell fast asleep before the poor turf fire.

His mother did not close her eyes, but sat beside him, watching. Every breath of wind sounded in her ears like that dreaded footstep at the door, or like that hand upon the latch, and made the calm summer night, a night of horror. At length the welcome day appeared. When she had made the little preparations which were needful for their journey, and had prayed upon her knees with many tears, she roused Barnaby, who jumped up gaily at her summons.

His clothes were few enough, and to carry Grip was a labour of love. As the sun shed his earliest beams upon the earth, they closed the door of their deserted home, and turned away. The sky was blue and bright. The air was fresh and filled with a thousand perfumes. Barnaby looked upward, and laughed with all his heart.

But it was a day he usually devoted to a long ramble, and one of the dogs—the ugliest of them all—came bounding up, and jumping round him in the fulness of his joy. He had to bid him go back in a surly tone, and his heart smote him while he did so. The dog retreated; turned with a half-incredulous, half-imploring look; came a little back; and stopped.

It was the last appeal of an old companion and a faithful friend— cast off. Barnaby could bear no more, and as he shook his head and waved his playmate home, he burst into tears.

"Oh mother, mother, how mournful he will be when he scratches at the door, and finds it always shut!"

There was such a sense of home in the thought, that though her own eyes overflowed she would not have obliterated the recollection of it, either from her own mind or from his, for the wealth of the whole wide world.

CHAPTER THE FORTY-SEVENTH.

IN the exhaustless catalogue of Heaven's mercies to mankind, the power we have of finding some germs of comfort in the hardest trials must ever occupy the foremost place; not only because it supports and upholds us when we most require to be sustained, but because in this source of consolation there is something, we have reason to believe, of the divine spirit; something of that goodness which detects amidst our own evil doings, a redeeming quality; something which, even in our fallen nature, we possess in common with the angels; which had its being in the old time when they trod the earth, and lingers on it yet, in pity.

How often, on their journey, did the widow remember with a grateful heart, that out of his deprivation Barnaby's cheerfulness and affection sprung! How often did she call to mind that but for that, he might have been sullen, morose, unkind, far removed from her—vicious, perhaps, and cruel! How often had she cause for comfort, in his strength, and hope, and in his simple nature! Those feeble powers of mind which rendered him so soon forgetful of the past, save in brief gleams and flashes,—even they were a comfort now. The world to him was full of happiness; in every tree, and plant, and flower, in every bird, and beast, and tiny insect whom a breath of summer wind laid low upon the ground, he had delight. His delight was hers; and where many a wise son would have made her sorrowful, this poor light-hearted idiot filled her breast with thankfulness and love.

Their stock of money was low, but from the hoard she had told into the blind man's hand, the widow had withheld one guinea. This, with the few pence she possessed besides, was to two persons of their frugal habits, a goodly sum in bank. Moreover they had Grip in company; and when they must otherwise have changed the guinea, it was but to make him exhibit outside an alehouse door, or in a village street, or in the grounds or gardens of a mansion of the better sort, and scores, who would have given nothing in charity, were ready to bargain for more amusement from the talking bird.

One day—for they moved slowly, and although they had many rides in carts and waggons, were on the road a week—Barnaby, with Grip upon his shoulder and his mother following, begged permission at a trim lodge to go up to the great house, at the other end of the avenue, and show his raven. The man within was inclined to give them admittance, and was indeed about to do so, when a stout gentleman with a long whip in his hand, and a flushed face which seemed to indicate that he had had his morning's draught, rode up to the gate, and called in a loud voice and with more oaths than the occasion seemed to warrant to have it opened directly.

"Who hast thou got here?" said the gentleman angrily, as the man threw the gate wide open, and pulled off his hat, "who are these? Eh? ar't a beggar, woman?"

The widow answered with a curtsey, that they were poor travellers.

"Vagrants," said the gentleman, "vagrants and vagabonds. Thee wish to be made acquainted with the cage, dost thee—the cage, the stocks, and the whipping-post?* Where dost come from?"

She told him in a timid manner,—for he was very loud, hoarse, and red-faced,—and besought him not to be angry, for they meant no harm and would go upon their way that moment.

"Don't be too sure of that," replied the gentleman, "we don't allow vagrants to roam about this place. I know what thou want'st—stray linen drying on hedges, and stray poultry, eh? What hast got in that basket, lazy hound?"

"Grip, Grip, Grip—Grip the clever, Grip the wicked, Grip the knowing—Grip, Grip, Grip," cried the raven, whom Barnaby had shut up on the approach of this stern personage. "I'm a devil I'm a devil I'm a devil, Never say die Hurrah Bow wow wow, Polly put the kettle on we'll all have tea."

"Take the virmin out, scoundrel," said the gentleman; "and let me see him."

Barnaby, thus condescendingly addressed, produced his bird, but not without much fear and trembling, and set him down upon the ground; which he had no sooner done than Grip drew fifty corks at least, and then began to dance; at the same time eyeing the gentleman with surprising insolence of manner, and screwing his head so much on one side that he appeared desirous of screwing it off upon the spot.

The cork-drawing seemed to make a greater impression on the gentleman's mind, than the raven's power of speech, and was indeed particularly adapted to his habits and capacity. He desired to have that done again, but despite his being very peremptory, and notwithstanding that Barnaby coaxed to the utmost, Grip turned a deaf ear to the request, and preserved a dead silence.

"Bring him along," said the gentleman, pointing to the house. But Grip, who had watched the action, anticipated his master, by hopping on before them;—constantly flapping his wings, and screaming "cook!" meanwhile, as a hint perhaps that there was company coming, and a small collation would be acceptable.

Barnaby and his mother walked on, on either side of the gentleman on horseback, who surveyed each of them from time to time in a proud and coarse manner, and occasionally thundered out some question, the tone of which alarmed Barnaby so much that he could find no answer, and, as a matter of course, could make him no reply. On one of these occasions, when the gentleman appeared disposed to exercise his horsewhip, the widow ventured to inform him in a low voice and with tears in her eyes, that her son was of weak mind.

"An idiot, eh?" said the gentleman looking at Barnaby as he spoke. "And how long hast been an idiot?"

"She knows," was Barnaby's timid answer, pointing to his mother—"I—always, I believe."

"From his birth," said the widow.

"I don't believe it," cried the gentleman, "not a bit of it. It's an excuse not to work. There's nothing like flogging to cure that disorder. I'd make a difference in him in ten minutes, I'll be bound."

"Heaven has made none in more than twice ten years, sir," said the widow mildly.

"Then why han't you shut him up? we pay enough for county institutions,* damn 'em. But thou'd rather drag him about to excite charity—of course. Ay, I know thee."

Now, this gentleman had various endearing appellations among his intimate friends. By some he was called "a country gentleman of the true school," by some "a fine old country gentleman," by some "a sporting gentleman," by some "a thorough-bred Englishman," by some "a genuine John Bull;" but they all agreed in one respect, and that was, that it was a pity there were not more like him, and that because there were not, the country was going to rack and ruin every day. He was in the commission of the peace, and could write his name almost legibly; but his greatest qualifications were, that he was more severe with poachers, was a better shot, a harder rider, had better horses, kept better dogs, could eat more solid food, drink more strong wine, go to bed every night more drunk and get up every morning more sober, than any man in the county. In knowledge of horseflesh he was almost equal to a farrier, in stable learning he surpassed his own head groom, and in gluttony not a pig on his estate was a match for him. He had no seat in Parliament himself, but he was extremely patriotic, and usually drove his voters up to the poll with his own hands. He was warmly attached to the church, and never appointed to the living in his gift any but a three-bottle man and a first-rate fox-hunter. He mistrusted the honesty of all poor people who could read and write, and had a secret jealousy of his own wife (a young lady whom he had married for what his friends called "the good old English reason," that her father's property adjoined his own) for possessing those accomplishments in a greater degree than himself. In short, Barnaby being an idiot, and Grip a creature of mere brute instinct, it would be very hard to say what this gentleman was.

He rode up to the door of a handsome house approached by a great flight of steps, where a man was waiting to take his horse, and led the way into a large hall, which, spacious as it was, was tainted with the fumes of last night's stale debauch. Great-coats, riding-whips, bridles, topboots, spurs, and such gear, were strewn about on all sides, and formed, with some huge stags' antlers, and a few portraits of dogs and horses, its principal embellishments.

Throwing himself into a great chair (in which, by the bye, he often snored away the night, when he had been, according to his admirers, a finer country gentleman than usual) he bade the man tell his mistress to come down: and presently there appeared, a little flurried, as it seemed, by the unwonted summons, a lady much younger than himself, who had the appearance of being in delicate health, and not too happy.

"Here! Thou'st no delight in following the hounds as an English-woman should have," said the gentleman. "See to this here. That'll please thee perhaps."

The lady smiled, sat down at a little distance from him, and glanced at Barnaby with a look of pity.

"He's an idiot, the woman says," observed the gentleman, shaking his head; "I don't believe it."

"Are you his mother?" asked the lady.

She answered yes.

"What's the use of asking *her?*" said the gentleman, thrusting his hands into his breeches pockets. "She'll tell thee so, of course. Most likely he's hired, at so much a day. There. Get on. Make him do something."

Grip having by this time recovered his urbanity, condescended, at Barnaby's solicitation, to repeat his various phrases of speech, and to go through the whole of his performances with the utmost success. The corks, and the never say die, afforded the gentleman so much delight that he demanded the repetition of this part of the entertainment, until Grip got into his basket, and positively refused to say another word, good or bad. The lady too, was much amused with him; and the closing point of his obstinacy so delighted her husband that he burst into a roar of laughter, and demanded his price.

Barnaby looked as though he didn't understand his meaning. Probably he did not.

"His price," said the gentleman, rattling the money in his pockets, "what dost want for him? How much?"

"He's not to be sold," replied Barnaby, shutting up the basket in a great hurry, and throwing the strap over his shoulder. "Mother, come away."

"Thou seest how much of an idiot he is, book-learner," said the gentleman, looking scornfully at his wife. "He can make a bargain. What dost want for him, old woman?"

"He is my son's constant companion," said the widow. "He is not to be sold, sir, indeed."

"Not to be sold!" cried the gentleman, growing ten times redder, hoarser, and louder than before. "Not to be sold!"

"Indeed no," she answered. "We have never thought of parting with him, sir, I do assure you."

He was evidently about to make a very passionate retort, when a few murmured words from his wife happening to catch his ear, he turned sharply round, and said, "Eh? What?"

"We can hardly expect them to sell the bird, against their own desire," she faltered. "If they prefer to keep him—"

"Prefer to keep him!" he echoed. "These people, who go tramping about the country, a pilfering and vagabondizing on all hands, prefer to keep a bird, when a landed proprietor and a justice asks his price! That old woman's been to school. I know she has. Don't tell me no," he roared to the widow, "I say, yes."

Barnaby's mother pleaded guilty to the accusation, and hoped there was no harm in it.

"No harm!" said the gentleman. "No. No harm. No harm, ye old rebel, not a bit of harm. If my clerk was here, I'd set ye in the stocks, I would, or lay ye in jail for prowling up and down, on the look-out for petty larcenies, ye limb of a gipsy. Here, Simon, put these pilferers out, shove 'em into the road, out with 'em! Ye don't want to sell the bird, ye that come here to beg, don't ye? If they an't out in double-quick, set the dogs upon 'em!"

They waited for no further dismissal, but fled precipitately, leaving the gentleman to storm away by himself (for the poor lady had already retreated), and making a great many vain attempts to silence Grip, who, excited by the noise, drew corks enough for a city feast as they hurried down the avenue, and appeared to congratulate himself beyond measure on having been the cause of the disturbance. When they had nearly reached the lodge, another servant, emerging from the shrubbery, feigned to be very active in ordering them off, but this man put a crown into the widow's hand, and whispering that his lady sent it, thrust them gently from the gate.

This incident only suggested to the widow's mind, when they halted at an alehouse some miles further on, and heard the justice's character as given by his friends, that perhaps something more than capacity of stomach and tastes for the kennel and the stable, were required to form either a perfect country gentleman, a thorough-bred Englishman, or a genuine John Bull; and that possibly the terms were sometimes misappropriated, not to say disgraced. She little thought then, that a circumstance so slight would ever influence their future fortunes; but time and experience enlightened her in this respect.

"Mother," said Barnaby, as they were sitting next day in a wagon which was to take them to within ten miles of the capital, "we're going to London first, you said. Shall we see that blind man there?"

She was about to answer "Heaven forbid!" but checked herself, and told him No, she thought not; why did he ask?

"He's a wise man," said Barnaby, with a thoughtful countenance. "I wish that we may meet with him again. What was it that he said of crowds? That gold was to be found where people crowded, and not among the trees and in such quiet places? He spoke as if he loved it; London is a crowded place; I think we shall meet him there."

"But why do you desire to see him, love?" she asked.

"Because," said Barnaby, looking wistfully at her, "he talked to me about gold, which is a rare thing, and say what you will, a thing you would like to have, I know. And because he came and went away so strangely—just as white-headed old men come sometimes to my bed's foot in the night, and say what I can't remember when the bright day returns. He told me he'd come back. I wonder why he broke his word!"

"But you never thought of being rich or gay, before, dear Barnaby. You have always been contented."

He laughed and bade her say that again, then cried, "Ay ay—oh yes," and laughed once more. Then something passed that caught his fancy, and the topic wandered from his mind, and was succeeded by another just as fleeting.

But it was plain from what he had said, and from his returning to the point more than once that day, and on the next, that the blind man's visit, and indeed his words, had taken strong possession of his mind. Whether the idea of wealth had occurred to him for the first time on looking at the golden clouds that evening—and images were often presented to his thoughts by outward objects quite as remote and distant; or whether their poor and humble way of life had suggested it, by contrast, long ago; or whether the accident (as he would deem it) of the blind man's pursuing the current of his own remarks, had done so at the moment; or he had been impressed by the mere circumstance of the man being blind, and, therefore, unlike any one with whom he had talked before; it was impossible to tell. She tried every means to discover, but in vain; and the probability is that Barnaby himself was equally in the dark.

It filled her with uneasiness to find him harping on this string, but all that she could do, was to lead him quickly to some other subject, and to dismiss it from his brain. To caution him against their visitor, to show any fear or suspicion in reference to him, would only be, she feared, to increase that interest with which Barnaby regarded him, and to strengthen his desire to meet him once again. She hoped, by plunging into the crowd, to rid herself of her terrible pursuer, and then, by journeying to a distance and observing increased caution, if that were possible, to live again unknown, in secrecy and peace.

They reached, in course of time, their halting-place within ten miles of London, and lay there for the night, after bargaining to be carried on for a trifle next day, in a light van which was returning empty, and was to start at five o'clock in the morning. The driver was punctual, the road good—save for the dust, the weather being very hot and dry—and at seven in the forenoon of Friday the second of June,* one thousand seven hundred and eighty, they alighted at the foot of Westminster Bridge, bade their conductor farewell, and stood alone, together, on the scorching pavement. For the freshness which night sheds upon such busy thoroughfares had already departed, and the sun was shining with uncommon lustre.

CHAPTER THE FORTY-EIGHTH.

UNCERTAIN where to go next, and bewildered by the crowd of people who were already astir, they sat down in one of the recesses on the bridge, to rest. They soon became aware that the stream of life was all pouring one way, and that a vast throng of persons were crossing the river from the Middlesex to the Surrey shore, in un-usual haste and evident excitement. They were, for the most part, in knots of two or three, or sometimes half-a-dozen; they spoke little together—many of them were quite silent; and hurried on as if they had one absorbing object in view, which was common to them all.

They were surprised to see that nearly every man in this great concourse, which still came pouring past, without slackening in the least, wore in his hat a blue cockade; and that the chance passengers who were not so decorated, appeared timidly anxious to escape observation or attack, and gave them the wall* as if they would con-ciliate them. This, however, was natural enough, considering their inferiority in point of numbers; for the proportion of those who wore blue cockades, to those who were dressed as usual, was at least forty or fifty to one. There was no quarrelling, however: the blue cockades went swarming on, passing each other when they could, and making all the speed that was possible in such a multitude; and exchanged nothing more than looks, and very often not even those, with such of the passers-by as were not of their number.

At first, the current of people had been confined to the two path-ways, and but a few more eager stragglers kept the road. But after half an hour or so, the passage was completely blocked up by the great press, which, being now closely wedged together, and impeded by the carts and coaches it encountered, moved but slowly, and was sometimes at a stand for five or ten minutes together.

After the lapse of nearly two hours, the numbers began to dimin-ish visibly, and gradually dwindling away, by little and little, left the bridge quite clear, save that, now and then, some hot and dusty man with the cockade in his hat, and his coat thrown over his shoulder, went panting by, fearful of being too late, or stopped to ask which way his friends had taken, and being directed, hastened on again like one refreshed. In this comparative solitude, which seemed quite strange and novel after the late crowd, the widow had for the first time an opportunity of inquiring of an old man who came and sat beside them, what was the meaning of that great assemblage.

"Why, where have you come from," he returned, "that you haven't heard of Lord George Gordon's great association? This is the day that he presents the petition against the Catholics, God bless him!"

"What have all these men to do with that?" she asked.

"What have they to do with it!" the old man replied. "Why, how you talk! Don't you know his Lordship has declared he won't present it to the house at all, unless it is attended to the door by forty thousand good and true men* at least? There's a crowd for you!"

"A crowd indeed!" said Barnaby. "Do you hear that, mother!"

"And they're mustering yonder, as I am told," resumed the old man, "nigh upon a hundred thousand strong. Ah! Let Lord George alone. He knows his power. There'll be a good many faces inside them three windows over there," and he pointed to where the House of Commons overlooked the river, "that'll turn pale when good Lord George gets up this afternoon, and with reason too. Ay, ay. Let his Lordship alone. Let him alone. *He* knows!" And so, with much mumbling and chuckling and shaking of his forefinger, he rose, with the assistance of his stick, and tottered off.

"Mother!" said Barnaby, "that's a brave crowd he talks of. Come!"

"Not to join it!" cried his mother.

"Yes, yes," he answered, plucking at her sleeve. "Why not? Come!"

"You don't know," she urged, "what mischief they may do, where they may lead you, what their meaning is. Dear Barnaby, for my sake—"

"For your sake!" he cried, patting her hand. "Well! It *is* for your sake, mother. You remember what the blind man said, about the gold. Here's a brave crowd! Come! Or wait till I come back—yes, yes, wait here."

She tried with all the earnestness her fears engendered, to turn him from his purpose, but in vain. He was stooping down to buckle on his shoe, when a hackney-coach passed them rather quickly, and a voice inside called to the driver to stop.

"Young man," said a voice within.

"Who's that?" cried Barnaby, looking up.

"Do you wear this ornament?" returned the stranger, holding out a blue cockade.

"In Heaven's name, no. Pray do not give it him!" exclaimed the widow.

"Speak for yourself, woman," said the man within the coach, coldly. "Leave the young man to his choice; he's old enough to make it, and to snap your apron-strings. He knows, without your telling, whether he wears the sign of a loyal Englishman or not."

Barnaby, trembling with impatience, cried "Yes! yes, yes, I do," as he had cried a dozen times already. The man threw him a cockade, and crying "Make haste to Saint George's Fields,"* ordered the coachman to drive on fast; and left them.

With hands that trembled with his eagerness to fix the bauble in his hat, Barnaby was adjusting it as he best could, and hurriedly replying to the tears and entreaties of his mother, when two gentlemen passed on the opposite side of the way. Observing them, and seeing how Barnaby was occupied, they stopped, whispered together for an instant, turned back, and came over to them.

"Why are you sitting here?" said one of them, who was dressed in a plain suit of black, wore long lank hair, and carried a great cane. "Why have you not gone with the rest?"

"I am going, sir," replied Barnaby, finishing his task, and putting his hat on with an air of pride. "I shall be there directly."

"Say my Lord, young man, when his Lordship does you the honour of speaking to you," said the second gentleman mildly. "If you don't know Lord George Gordon when you see him, it's high time you should."

"Nay, Gashford," said Lord George, as Barnaby pulled off his hat again and made him a low bow, "it's no great matter on a day like this, which every Englishman will remember with delight and pride. Put on your hat, friend, and follow us, for you lag behind and are late. It's past ten now. Didn't you know that the hour of assembling was ten o'clock?"

Barnaby shook his head and looked vacantly from one to the other.

"You might have known it, friend" said Gashford, "it was perfectly understood. How came you to be so ill informed?"

"He cannot tell you, sir," the widow interposed. "It's of no use to ask him. We are but this morning come from a long distance in the country, and know nothing of these matters."

"The cause has taken a deep root, and has spread its branches far and wide," said Lord George to his secretary. "This is a pleasant hearing. I thank Heaven for it!"

"Amen!" cried Gashford with a solemn face.

"You do not understand me, my Lord," said the widow. "Pardon me, but you cruelly mistake my meaning. We know nothing of these matters. We have no desire or right to join in what you are about to do. This is my son, my poor afflicted son, dearer to me than my own life. In mercy's name, my Lord, go your way alone, and do not tempt him into danger!"

"My good woman," said Gashford, "how can you!—Dear me!— What do you mean by tempting, and by danger? Do you think his Lordship is a roaring lion, going about and seeking whom he may devour? God bless me!"

"No, no, my Lord, forgive me," implored the widow, laying both her hands upon his breast, and scarcely knowing what she did, or said, in the earnestness of her supplication, "but there are reasons why you should hear my earnest, mother's prayer, and leave my son with me. Oh do! He is not in his right senses, he is not, indeed!"

"It is a bad sign of the wickedness of these times," said Lord George, evading her touch, and colouring deeply, "that those who cling to the truth and support the right cause, are set down as mad. Have you the heart to say this of your own son, unnatural mother!"

"I am astonished at you!" said Gashford, with a kind of meek severity. "This is a very sad picture of female depravity."

"He has surely no appearance," said Lord George, glancing at Barnaby, and whispering in his secretary's ear, "of being deranged? And even if he had, we must not construe any trifling peculiarity into madness. Which of us"—and here he turned red again—"would be safe, if that were made the law!"

"Not one," replied the secretary; "in that case, the greater the zeal, the truth, and talent; the more direct the call from above; the clearer would be the madness. With regard to this young man, my Lord," he added, with a lip that slightly curled as he looked at Barnaby, who stood twirling his hat, and stealthily beckoning them to come away, "he is as sensible and self-possessed as any one I ever saw."

"And you desire to make one of this great body?" said Lord George, addressing him; "and intended to make one, did you?"

"Yes—yes," said Barnaby, with sparkling eyes. "To be sure I did! I told her so myself."

"I see," replied Lord George, with a reproachful glance at the unhappy mother. "I thought so. Follow me and this gentleman, and you shall have your wish."

Barnaby kissed his mother tenderly on the cheek, and bidding her be of good cheer, for their fortunes were both made now, did as he was desired. She, poor woman, followed too—with how much fear and grief it would be hard to tell.

They passed quickly through the Bridge-road, where the shops were all shut up (for the passage of the great crowd and the expectation of their return had alarmed the tradesmen for their goods and windows), and where, in the upper stories, all the inhabitants were congregated, looking down into the street below, with faces variously expressive of alarm, of interest, expectancy, and indignation. Some of these applauded, and some hissed; but regardless of these interruptions—for the noise of a vast congregation of people at a little distance, sounded in his ears like the roaring of a sea—Lord George

Gordon quickened his pace, and presently arrived before St. George's Fields.

They were really fields at that time, and of considerable extent. Here an immense multitude was collected, bearing flags of various kinds and sizes, but all of the same colour—blue, like the cockades— some sections marching to and fro in military array, and others drawn up in circles, squares, and lines. A large portion, both of the bodies which paraded the ground, and of those which remained stationary, were occupied in singing hymns or psalms. With whomsoever this originated, it was well done; for the sound of so many thousand voices in the air must have stirred the heart of any man within him, and could not fail to have a wonderful effect upon enthusiasts, however mistaken.

Scouts had been posted in advance of the great body, to give notice of their leader's coming. These falling back, the word was quickly passed through the whole host, and for a short interval there ensued a profound and death-like silence, during which the mass was so still and quiet, that the fluttering of a banner caught the eye, and became a circumstance of note. Then they burst into a tremendous shout, into another, and another; and the air seemed rent and shaken, as if by the discharge of cannon.

"Gashford!" cried Lord George, pressing his secretary's arm tight within his own, and speaking with as much emotion in his voice, as in his altered face, "I am called indeed, now. I feel and know it. I am the leader of a host. If they summoned me at this moment with one voice to lead them on to death, I'd do it—Yes, and fall first myself!"

"It is a proud sight," said the secretary. "It is a noble day for England, and for the great cause throughout the world. Such homage, my Lord, as I, an humble but devoted man, can render—"

"What are you doing!" cried his master, catching him by both hands; for he had made a show of kneeling at his feet; "Do not unfit me, dear Gashford, for the solemn duty of this glorious day—" the tears stood in the eyes of the poor gentleman as he said the words.— "Let us go among them; we have to find a place in some division for this new recruit—give me your hand."

Gashford slid his cold insidious palm into his master's grasp, and so, hand in hand, and followed still by Barnaby and by his mother too, they mingled with the concourse.

They had by this time taken to their singing again, and as their leader passed between their ranks, they raised their voices to their utmost. Many of those who were banded together to support the religion of their country, even unto death, had never heard a hymn or psalm in all their lives. But these fellows having for the most part strong lungs, and being naturally fond of singing, chanted any ribaldry or nonsense that occurred to them, feeling pretty certain that it would not be detected in the general chorus, and not caring very much if it were. Many of these voluntaries were sung under the very nose of Lord George Gordon, who, quite unconscious of their burden, passed on with his usual stiff and solemn deportment, very much edified and delighted by the pious conduct of his followers.

So they went on and on, up this line, down that, round the exterior of this circle, and on every side of that hollow square; and still there were lines, and squares, and circles out of number to review. The day being now intensely hot, and the sun striking down his fiercest rays upon the field, those who carried heavy banners began to grow faint and weary; most of the number assembled were fain to pull off their neckcloths, and throw their coats and waistcoats open; and some, towards the centre, quite overpowered by the excessive heat, which was of course rendered more unendurable by the multitude around them, lay down upon the grass, and offered all they had about them for a drink of water. Still, no man left the ground, not even of these who were so distressed; still Lord George, streaming from every pore, went on with Gashford; and still Barnaby and his mother followed close behind them.

They had arrived at the top of a long line of some eight hundred men in single file, and Lord George had turned his head to look back, when a loud cry of recognition—in that peculiar and half-stifled tone which a voice has, when it is raised in the open air and in the midst of a great concourse of persons—was heard, and a man stepped with a shout of laughter from the rank, and smote Barnaby on the shoulders with his heavy hand.

"How now!" he cried. "Barnaby Rudge! Why, where have you been hiding for these hundred years!"

Barnaby had been thinking within himself that the smell of the trodden grass brought back his old days at cricket, when he was a young boy and played on Chigwell Green. Confused by this sudden and boisterous address, he stared in a bewildered manner at the man, and could scarcely say "What! Hugh!"

"Hugh!" echoed the other; "ay, Hugh—Maypole Hugh! You remember my dog? He's alive now, and will know you, I warrant. What, you wear the colour, do you? Well done! Ha ha ha!"

"You know this young man, I see," said Lord George.

"Know him, my Lord! as well as I know my own right hand. My captain knows him. We all know him."

"Will you take him into your division?"

"It hasn't in it a better, nor a nimbler, nor a more active man, than Barnaby Rudge," said Hugh. "Show me the man who says it has. Fall in, Barnaby. He shall march, my Lord, between me and Dennis; and he shall carry," he added, taking a flag from the hand of a tired man who tendered it, "the gayest silken streamer in this valiant army."

"In the name of God, no!" shrieked the widow, darting forward. "Barnaby—my Lord—see—he'll come back—Barnaby—Barnaby!"

"Women in the field!" cried Hugh, stepping between them, and holding her off. "Holloa! My captain there!"

"What's the matter here?" cried Simon Tappertit, bustling up in a great heat. "Do you call this order?"

"Nothing like it, captain," answered Hugh, still holding her back with his outstretched hand. "It's against all orders. Ladies are carrying off our gallant soldiers from their duty. The word of command, captain! They're filing off the ground. Quick!"

"Close!" cried Simon, with the whole power of his lungs. "Form! March!"

She was thrown to the ground; the whole field was in motion; Barnaby was whirled away into the heart of a dense mass of men, and she saw him no more.

CHAPTER THE FORTY-NINTH.

HE mob had been divided from its first assemblage into four divisions; the London, the Westminster, the Southwark, and the Scotch.* Each of these divisions being subdivided into various bodies, and these bodies being drawn up in various forms and figures, the general arrangement was, except to the few chiefs and leaders, as unintelligible as the plan of a great battle to the meanest soldier in the field. It was not without its method, however; for, in a very short space of time after being put in motion, the crowd had resolved itself into three great parties, and were prepared, as had been arranged, to cross the river by different bridges, and make for the House of Commons in separate detachments.

At the head of that division which had Westminster Bridge* for its approach to the scene of action, Lord George Gordon took his post; with Gashford at his right hand, and sundry ruffians, of most unpromising appearance, forming a kind of staff about him. The conduct of a second party, whose route lay by Blackfriars,* was entrusted to a committee of management, including perhaps a dozen men: while the third, which was to go by London Bridge,* and through the main streets, in order that their numbers and their serious intentions might be the better known and appreciated by the citizens, were led by Simon Tappertit (assisted by a few subalterns, selected from the Brotherhood of United Bull-dogs), Dennis the hangman, Hugh, and some others.

The word of command being given, each of these great bodies took the road assigned to it, and departed on its way, in perfect order and profound silence. That which went through the City greatly exceeded the others in number, and was of such prodigious extent that when the rear began to move, the front was nearly four miles in advance, notwithstanding that the men marched three abreast and followed very close upon each other.

At the head of this party, in the place where Hugh, in the madness of his humour, had stationed him, and walking between that dangerous companion and the hangman, went Barnaby; as many a man among the thousands who looked on that day afterwards remembered well. Forgetful of all other things in the ecstacy of the moment, his face flushed and his eyes sparkling with delight, heedless of the weight of the great banner he carried, and mindful only of its flashing in the sun and rustling in the summer breeze, on he went, proud, happy, elated past all telling:—the only light-hearted, undesigning creature, in the whole assembly.

"What do you think of this?" asked Hugh, as they passed through the crowded streets, and looked up at the windows which were thronged with spectators. "They have all turned out to see our flags and streamers? Eh, Barnaby? Why, Barnaby's the greatest man of all the pack! His flag's the largest of the lot, the brightest too. There's nothing in the show, like Barnaby. All eyes are turned on him. Ha ha ha!"

"Don't make that din, brother," growled the hangman, glancing with no very approving eyes at Barnaby as he spoke: "I hope he don't think there's nothing to be done, but carrying that there piece of blue rag, like a boy at a breaking-up. You're ready for action I hope, eh? You, I mean," he added, nudging Barnaby roughly with his elbow. "What are you staring at? Why don't you speak?"

Barnaby had been gazing at his flag, and looked vacantly from his questioner to Hugh.

"He don't understand your way," said the latter. "Here, I'll explain it to him. Barnaby old boy, attend to me."

"I'll attend," said Barnaby, looking anxiously round; "but I wish I could see her somewhere."

"See who?" demanded Dennis in a gruff tone. "You an't in love I hope, brother? That an't the sort of thing for us, you know. We mustn't have no love here."

"She would be proud indeed to see me now, eh Hugh?" said Barnaby. "Wouldn't it make her glad to see me at the head of this brave show? She'd cry with joy, I know she would. Where *can* she be? She never sees me at my best, and what do I care to be gay and fine if *she's* not by?"

"Why, what palaver's this?" asked Mr. Dennis with supreme disdain. "We an't got no sentimental members among us, I hope."

"Don't be uneasy, brother," cried Hugh, "he's only talking of his mother."

"Of his what?" said Mr. Dennis with a strong oath.

"His mother."

"And have I combined myself with this here section, and turned out on this here memorable day, to hear men talk about their mothers!" growled Mr. Dennis with extreme disgust. "The notion of a man's sweetheart's bad enough, but a man's mother!—" and here his disgust was so extreme that he spat upon the ground, and could say no more.

"Barnaby's right," cried Hugh with a grin, "and I say it. Lookee, bold lad. If she's not here to see, it's because I've provided for her, and sent half a dozen gentlemen, every one of 'em with a blue flag (but not half as fine as yours), to take her, in state, to a grand house all hung round with gold and silver banners, and everything else you please, where she'll wait till you come, and want for nothing."

"Ay!" said Barnaby, his face beaming with delight: "have you indeed? That's a good hearing. That's fine! Kind Hugh!"

"But nothing to what will come, bless you," retorted Hugh, with a wink at Dennis, who regarded his new companion in arms with great astonishment.

"No, indeed?" cried Barnaby.

"Nothing at all," said Hugh. "Money, cocked hats and feathers, red coats and gold lace; all the fine things there are, ever were, or will be; will belong to us if we are true to that noble gentleman—the best man in the world, carry our flags for a few days, and keep 'em safe. That's all we've got to do."

"Is that all?" cried Barnaby with glistening eyes, as he clutched his pole the tighter; "I warrant you I keep this one safe, then. You have put it in good hands. You know me, Hugh. Nobody shall wrest this flag away."

"Well said!" cried Hugh. "Ha ha! Nobly said! That's the old stout Barnaby, that I have climbed and leaped with many and many a day—I knew I was not mistaken in Barnaby.—Don't you see man," he added in a whisper, as he slipped to the other side of Dennis, "that the lad's a natural, and can be got to do anything, if you take him the right way. Letting alone the fun he is, he's worth a dozen men, in earnest, as you'd find if you tried a fall with him. Leave him to me. You shall soon see whether he's of use or not."

Mr. Dennis received these explanatory remarks with many nods and winks, and softened his behaviour towards Barnaby from that moment. Hugh, laying his finger on his nose, stepped back into his former place, and they proceeded in silence.

It was between two and three o'clock in the afternoon when the three great parties met at Westminster, and, uniting into one huge mass, raised a tremendous shout. This was not only done in token of their presence, but as a signal to those on whom the task devolved, that it was time to take possession of the lobbies of both Houses, and of the various avenues of approach, and of the gallery stairs. To the last-named place, Hugh and Dennis, still with their pupil between them, rushed straightway; Barnaby having given his flag into the hands of one of their own party, who kept them at the outer door. Their followers pressing on behind, they were borne as on a great wave to the very doors of the gallery, whence it was impossible to retreat, even if they had been so inclined, by reason of the throng which choked up the passages. It is a familiar expression in describing a great crowd, that a person might have walked upon the people's heads. In this case it was actually done; for a boy who had by some means got among the concourse, and was in imminent danger of suffocation, climbed to the shoulders of a man beside him and walked upon the people's hats and heads into the open street; traversing in his passage the whole length of two staircases and a long gallery. Nor was the swarm without less dense; for a basket which had been tossed into the crowd, was jerked from head to head, and shoulder to shoulder, and went spinning and whirling on above them, until it was lost to view, without ever once falling in among them or coming near the ground.

Through this vast throng, sprinkled doubtless here and there with honest zealots, but composed for the most part of the very scum and refuse of London, whose growth was fostered by bad criminal laws, bad prison regulations, and the worst conceivable police,*—such of the members of both Houses of Parliament as had not taken the precaution to be already at their posts, were compelled to fight and force their way. Their carriages were stopped and broken; the wheels wrenched off; the glasses shivered to atoms; the panels beaten in; drivers, footmen, and masters, pulled from their seats and rolled in the mud. Lords, commoners, and reverend Bishops, with little distinction of person or party, were kicked and pinched and hustled; passed from hand to hand through various stages of ill-usage; and sent to their fellow senators at last with their clothes hanging in ribands about them, their bagwigs torn off, themselves speechless and breathless, and their persons covered with the powder which had been cuffed and beaten out of their hair. One Lord was so long in the hands of the populace, that the Peers as a body resolved to sally forth and rescue him, and were in the act of doing so, when he happily appeared among them covered with dirt and bruises, and hardly to be recognized by those who knew him best. The noise and uproar were on the increase every moment. The air was filled with execrations, hoots, and howlings. The mob raged and roared, like a mad monster as it was, unceasingly, and each new outrage served to swell its fury.

Within doors, matters were even yet more threatening. Lord George—preceded by a man who carried the immense petition on a porter's knot* through the lobby to the door of the House of

Commons, where it was received by two officers of the house who rolled it up to the table ready for presentation—had taken his seat at an early hour, before the Speaker went to prayers.* His followers pouring in at the same time, the lobby and all the avenues were immediately filled, as we have seen: thus the members were not only attacked in their passage through the streets, but were set upon within the very walls of Parliament; while the tumult, both within and without, was so great, that those who attempted to speak could scarcely hear their own voices; far less consult upon the course it would be wise to take in such extremity, or animate each other to dignified and firm resistance. So sure as any member, just arrived, with dress disordered and dishevelled hair, came struggling through the crowd in the lobby, it yelled and screamed in triumph; and when the door of the house, partially and cautiously opened by those within for his admission, gave them a momentary glimpse of the interior, they grew more wild and savage, like beasts at the sight of prey, and made a rush against the portal which strained its locks and bolts in their staples, and shook the very beams.

The stranger's gallery,* which was immediately above the door of the house, had been ordered to be closed on the first rumour of disturbance, and was empty; save that now and then Lord George took his seat there, for the convenience of coming to the head of the stairs which led to it, and repeating to the people what had passed within. It was on these stairs that Barnaby, Hugh, and Dennis were posted. There were two flights, short, steep, and narrow, running parallel to each other, and leading to two little doors communicating with a low passage which opened on the gallery. Between them was a kind of well, or unglazed skylight, for the admission of light and air into the lobby, which might be some eighteen or twenty feet below.

Upon one of these little staircases—not that at the head of which Lord George appeared from time to time, but the other—Gashford stood with his elbow on the bannister, and his cheek resting on his hand, with his usual crafty aspect. Whenever he varied this attitude in the slightest degree—so much as by the gentlest motion of his arm—the uproar was certain to increase, not merely there, but in the lobby below; from which place no doubt, some man who acted as fugleman* to the rest, was constantly looking up and watching him.

"Order!" cried Hugh, in a voice which made itself heard even above the roar and tumult, as Lord George appeared at the top of the staircase. "News! News from my Lord!"

The noise continued, notwithstanding his appearance, until Gashford looked round. There was silence immediately—even among the people in the passages without, and on the other staircases, who could neither see nor hear, but to whom, notwithstanding, the signal was conveyed with marvellous rapidity.

"Gentlemen" said Lord George, who was very pale and agitated, "We must be firm. They talk of delays, but we must have no delays. They talk of taking your petition into consideration next Tuesday, but we must have it considered now. Present appearances look bad for our success, but we must succeed and will!"

"We must succeed and will!" echoed the crowd. And so among their shouts and cheers and other cries, he bowed to them and retired, and presently came back again. There was another gesture from Gashford, and a dead silence directly.

"I am afraid," he said, this time, "that we have little reason, gentlemen, to hope for any redress from the proceedings of Parliament. But we must redress our own grievances, we must meet again, we must put our trust in Providence, and it will bless our endeavours."

This speech being a little more temperate than the last, was not so favourably received. When the noise and exasperation were at their height, he came back once more, and told them that the alarm had gone forth for many miles round; that when the King heard of their assembling together in that great body, he had no doubt His Majesty would send down private orders to have their wishes complied with; and—with the manner of his speech as childish, irresolute, and uncertain as his matter—was proceeding further, when two gentlemen suddenly appeared at the door where he stood, and pressing past him and coming a step or two lower down upon the stairs, confronted the people.

The boldness of this action quite took them by surprise. They were not the less disconcerted, when one of the gentlemen, turning to Lord George, spoke thus—in a loud voice that they might hear him well, but quite coolly and collectedly.

"You may tell these people, if you please, my Lord, that I am General Conway* of whom they have heard; and that I oppose this petition, and all their proceedings, and yours. I am a soldier, you may tell them; and I will protect the freedom of this place with my sword. You see, my Lord, that the members of this house are all in arms to-day; you know that the entrance to it is a narrow one; you cannot be ignorant that there are men within these walls who are determined to defend that pass to the last, and before whom many lives must fall if your adherents persevere. Have a care what you do."

"And my Lord George," said the other gentleman, addressing him in like manner, "I desire them to hear this, from me—Colonel Gordon*—your near relation. If a man among this crowd, whose uproar strikes us deaf, crosses the threshold of the House of Commons, I swear to run my sword that moment—not into his, but into your body!"

With that, they stepped back again, keeping their faces towards the crowd; took each an arm of the misguided nobleman; drew him into the passage, and shut the door; which they directly locked and fastened on the inside.

This was so quickly done, and the demeanour of both gentlemen—who were not young men either—was so gallant and resolute, that the crowd faltered and stared at each other with irresolute and timid looks. Many tried to turn towards the door; some of the faintest-hearted cried that they had best go back, and called to those behind to give way; and the panic and confusion were increasing rapidly, when Gashford whispered Hugh.

"What now!" Hugh roared aloud, turning towards them. "Why go back? Where can you do better than here, boys! One good rush against these doors and one below at the same time, will do the business. Rush on, then! As to the door below, let those stand back who are afraid. Let those who are not afraid, try who shall be the first to pass it. Here goes! Look out down there!"

Without the delay of an instant, he threw himself headlong over the bannisters into the lobby below. He had hardly touched the ground when Barnaby was at his side. The chaplain's assistant, and some members who were imploring the people to retire, immediately withdrew; and then, with a great shout, both crowds threw themselves against the doors pell-mell, and besieged the House in earnest.

At that moment, when a second onset must have brought them into collision with those who stood on the defensive within, in which case great loss of life and bloodshed would inevitably have ensued,— the hindmost portion of the crowd gave way, and the rumour spread from mouth to mouth that a messenger had been despatched by water for the military, who were forming in the street. Fearful of sustaining a charge in the narrow passages in which they were so closely wedged together, the throng poured out as impetuously as they had flocked in. As the whole stream turned at once, Barnaby and Hugh went with it: and so, fighting and struggling and trampling on fallen men and being trampled on in turn themselves, they and the whole mass floated by degrees into the open street, where a large detachment of the Guards, both horse and foot, came hurrying up; clearing the ground before them so rapidly that the people seemed to melt away as they advanced.

The word of command to halt being given, the soldiers formed across the street; the rioters, breathless and exhausted with their late exertions, formed likewise, though in a very irregular and disorderly manner. The commanding officer rode hastily into the open space between the two bodies, accompanied by a magistrate and an officer of the House of Commons, for whose accommodation a couple of troopers had hastily dismounted. The Riot Act was read,* but not a man stirred.

In the first rank of the insurgents, Barnaby and Hugh stood side by side. Somebody had thrust into Barnaby's hands when he came out into the street, his precious flag; which, being now rolled up and tied round the pole, looked like a giant quarter-staff as he grasped it firmly and stood upon his guard. If ever man believed with his whole heart and soul that he was engaged in a just cause, and that he was bound to stand by his leader to the last, poor Barnaby believed it of himself and Lord George Gordon.

After an ineffectual attempt to make himself heard, the magistrate gave the word and the Horse Guards came riding in among the crowd. But even then he galloped here and there, exhorting the people to disperse; and, although heavy stones were thrown at the men, and some were desperately cut and bruised, they had no orders but to make prisoners of such of the rioters as were the most active, and to drive the people back with the flat of their sabres. As the horses came in among them, the throng gave way at many points, and the Guards, following up their advantage, were rapidly clearing the ground, when two or three of the foremost, who were in a manner cut off from the rest by the people closing round them, made straight towards Barnaby and Hugh, who had no doubt been pointed out as the two men who dropped into the lobby; laying about them now with some effect, and inflicting on the more turbulent of their opponents, a few slight flesh wounds, under the influence of which a man dropped, here and there, into the arms of his fellows, amid much groaning and confusion.

At the sight of gashed and bloody faces, seen for a moment in the crowd, then hidden by the press around them, Barnaby turned pale and sick. But he stood his ground, and grasping his pole more firmly yet, kept his eye fixed upon the nearest soldier—nodding his head meanwhile, as Hugh, with a scowling visage, whispered in his ear.

The soldier came spurring on, making his horse rear as the people pressed about him, cutting at the hands of those who would have grasped his rein and forced his charger back, and waving to his comrades to follow—and still Barnaby, without retreating an inch, waited for his coming. Some called to him to fly, and some were in the very act of closing round him, to prevent his being taken, when the pole swept the air above the people's heads, and the man's saddle was empty in an instant.

Then he and Hugh turned and fled; the crowd opening to let them pass, and closing up again so quickly that there was no clue to the course they had taken. Panting for breath, hot, dusty, and exhausted with fatigue, they reached the river-side in safety, and getting into a boat with all despatch were soon out of any immediate danger.

As they glided down the river, they plainly heard the people cheering; and supposing they might have forced the soldiers to retreat, lay upon their oars for a few minutes, uncertain whether to return or not. But the crowd passing along Westminster Bridge, soon assured them that the populace were dispersing; and Hugh rightly guessed from this, that they had cheered the magistrate for offering to dismiss the military on condition of their immediate departure to their several homes; and that he and Barnaby were better where they were. He advised, therefore, that they should proceed to Blackfriars, and, going ashore at the bridge, make the best of their way to the Boot; where there was not only good entertainment and safe lodging, but where they would certainly be joined by many of their late companions. Barnaby assenting, they decided on this course of action, and pulled for Blackfriars accordingly.

They landed at a critical time, and fortunately for themselves at the right moment. For, coming into Fleet Street, they found it in an unusual stir; and inquiring the cause, were told that a body of Horse Guards had just galloped past, and that they were escorting some rioters whom they had made prisoners, to Newgate for safety. Not at all ill-pleased to have so narrowly escaped the cavalcade, they lost no more time in asking questions, but hurried to the Boot with as much speed as Hugh considered it prudent to make, without appearing singular or attracting an inconvenient share of public notice.

CHAPTER THE FIFTIETH.

THEY were among the first to reach the tavern, but they had not been there many minutes, when several groups of men who had formed part of the crowd, came straggling in. Among them were Simon Tappertit and Mr. Dennis; both of whom, but especially the latter, greeted Barnaby with the utmost warmth, and paid him many compliments on the prowess he had shown.

"Which," said Dennis, with an oath, as he rested his bludgeon in a corner with his hat upon it, and took his seat at the same table with them, "it does me good to think of. There was a opportunity! But it led to nothing. For my part, I don't know what would. There's no spirit among the people in these here times. Bring something to eat and drink here. I'm disgusted with humanity."

"On what account?" asked Mr. Tappertit, who had been quenching his fiery face in a half-gallon can. "Don't you consider this a good beginning, mister?"

"Give me security that it an't an ending," rejoined the hangman. "When that soldier went down, we might have made London ours; but no;—we stand, and gape, and look on—the justice (I wish he had had a bullet in each eye, as he would have had, if we'd gone to work my way) says, 'My lads, if you'll give me your word to disperse, I'll order off the military,'—our people set up a hurrah, throw up the game with the winning cards in their hands, and skulk away like a pack of tame curs as they are. Ah!" said the hangman, in a tone of deep disgust, "it makes me blush for my feller creeturs. I wish I had been born a ox, I do!"

"You'd have been quite as agreeable a character if you had been, I think," returned Simon Tappertit, going out in a lofty manner.

"Don't be too sure of that," rejoined the hangman, calling after him; "if I was a horned animal at the present moment, with the smallest grain of sense, I'd toss every man in this company, excepting them two," meaning Hugh and Barnaby, "for his manner of conducting himself this day."

With which mournful review of their proceedings, Mr. Dennis sought consolation in cold boiled beef and beer; but without at all relaxing the grim and dissatisfied expression of his face, the gloom of which was rather deepened than dissipated by their grateful influence.

The company who were thus libelled might have retaliated by strong words, if not by blows, but they were dispirited and worn out. The greater part of them had fasted since morning; all had suffered extremely from the excessive heat; and, between the day's shouting, exertion, and excitement, many had quite lost their voices, and so much of their strength that they could hardly stand. Then they were uncertain what to do next, fearful of the consequences of what they had done already, and sensible that after all they had carried no point, but had indeed left matters worse than they had found them. Of those who had come to the Boot, many dropped off within an hour; such of them as were really honest and sincere, never, after the morning's experience, to return, or to hold any communication with their late companions. Others remained but to refresh themselves, and then went home desponding; others who had theretofore been regular in their attendance, avoided the place altogether. The half-dozen prisoners whom the Guards had taken, were magnified by report into half a hundred at least; and their friends, being faint and sober, so slackened in their energy, and so drooped beneath these dispiriting influences, that by eight o'clock in the evening, Dennis, Hugh, and Barnaby, were left alone. Even they were fast asleep upon the benches, when Gashford's entrance roused them.

"Oh! You *are* here then?" said the secretary. "Dear me!"

"Why, where should we be, Muster Gashford!" Dennis rejoined as he rose into a sitting posture.

"Oh nowhere, nowhere," he returned with excessive mildness. "The streets are filled with blue cockades. I rather thought you might have been among them. I am glad you are not."

"You have orders for us, master, then?" said Hugh.

"Oh dear, no. Not I. No orders, my good fellow. What orders should I have? You are not in my service."

"Muster Gashford," remonstrated Dennis, "we belong to the cause, don't we?"

"The cause!" repeated the secretary, looking at him in a sort of abstraction. "There is no cause. The cause is lost."

"Lost!"

"Oh yes. You have heard, I suppose? The petition is rejected by a hundred and ninety-two, to six.* It's quite final. We might have spared ourselves some trouble: that, and my Lord's vexation, are the only circumstances I regret. I am quite satisfied in all other respects."

As he said this, he took a penknife from his pocket, and putting his hat upon his knee, began to busy himself in ripping off the blue cockade which he had worn all day; at the same time humming a psalm tune which had been very popular in the morning, and dwelling on it with a gentle regret.

His two adherents looked at each other, and at him, as if they were at a loss how to pursue the subject. At length Hugh, after some elbowing and winking between himself and Mr. Dennis, ventured to stay his hand, and to ask him why he meddled with that riband in his hat.

"Because," said the secretary, looking up with something between a snarl and a smile, "because to sit still and wear it, or fall asleep and wear it, or run away and wear it, is a mockery. That's all, friend."

"What would you have us do, master!" cried Hugh.

"Nothing," returned Gashford, shrugging his shoulders; "nothing. When my Lord was reproached and threatened for standing by you, I, as a prudent man, would have had you do nothing. When the soldiers were trampling you under their horses' feet, I would have had you do nothing. When one of them was struck down by a daring hand, and I saw confusion and dismay in all their faces, I would have had you do nothing—just what you did, in short. This is the young man who had so little prudence and so much boldness. Ah! I am sorry for him."

"Sorry, master!" cried Hugh.

"Sorry, Muster Gashford!" echoed Dennis.

"In case there should be a proclamation out to-morrow, offering five hundred pounds, or some such trifle, for his apprehension; and in case it should include another man who dropped into the lobby from the stairs above," said Gashford, coldly; "still, do nothing."

"Fire and fury, master!" cried Hugh, starting up. "What have we done, that you should talk to us like this!"

"Nothing," returned Gashford with a sneer. "If you are cast into prison; if the young man—" here he looked hard at Barnaby's attentive face—"is dragged from us and from his friends; perhaps from people whom he loves, and whom his death would kill; is thrown into jail, brought out and hanged before their eyes; still, do nothing. You'll find it your best policy, I have no doubt."

"Come on!" cried Hugh, striding towards the door. "Dennis—Barnaby—come on!"

"Where? To do what?" said Gashford, slipping past him, and standing with his back against it.

"Anywhere! Anything!" cried Hugh. "Stand aside, master, or the window will serve our turn as well. Let us out!"

"Ha ha ha! You are of such—of such an impetuous nature," said Gashford, changing his manner for one of the utmost good fellowship and the pleasantest raillery; "you are such an excitable creature—but you'll drink with me before you go?"

"Oh, yes—certainly," growled Dennis, drawing his sleeve across his thirsty lips. "No malice, brother. Drink with Muster Gashford!"

Hugh wiped his heated brow, and relaxed into a smile. The artful secretary laughed outright.

"Some liquor here! Be quick, or he'll not stop, even for that. He is a man of such desperate ardour!" said the smooth secretary, whom Mr. Dennis corroborated with sundry nods and muttered oaths—"Once roused, he is a fellow of such fierce determination!"

Hugh poised his sturdy arm aloft, and clapping Barnaby on the back, bade him fear nothing. They shook hands together—poor Barnaby evidently possessed with the idea that he was among the most virtuous and disinterested heroes in the world—and Gashford laughed again.

"I hear," he said smoothly, as he stood among them with a great measure of liquor in his hand, and filled their glasses as quickly and as often as they chose, "I hear—but I cannot say whether it be true or false—that the men who are loitering in the streets to-night, are half disposed to pull down a Romish chapel or two, and that they only want leaders. I even heard mention of those in Duke Street Lincoln's-Inn Fields, and in Warwick Street Golden Square;* but common report, you know—You are not going?"

—"To do nothing, master, eh?" cried Hugh. "No jails and halter for Barnaby and me. They must be frightened out of that. Leaders are wanted, are they? Now boys!"

"A most impetuous fellow!" cried the secretary. "Ha ha! A courageous, boisterous, most vehement fellow! A man who—"

There was no need to finish the sentence, for they had rushed out of the house, and were far beyond hearing. He stopped in the middle of a laugh, listened, drew on his gloves, and, clasping his hands behind him, paced the deserted room for a long time, then bent his steps towards the busy town, and walked into the streets.

They were filled with people, for the rumour of that day's proceedings had made a great noise. Those persons who did not care to leave home, were at their doors or windows, and one topic of discourse prevailed on every side. Some reported that the riots were effectually put down; others that they had broken out again: some said that Lord George Gordon had been sent under a strong guard to the Tower; others that an attempt had been made upon the King's life, that the soldiers had been again called out, and that the noise of musketry in a distant part of the town had been plainly heard within an hour. As it grew darker, these stories became more direful and mysterious; and often, when some frightened passenger ran past with tidings that the rioters were not far off, and were coming up, the doors were shut and barred, lower windows made secure, and as much consternation engendered, as if the city were invaded by a foreign army.

Gashford walked stealthily about, listening to all he heard, and diffusing or confirming, whenever he had an opportunity, such false intelligence as suited his own purpose; and, busily occupied in this way, turned into Holborn* for the twentieth time, when a great many women and children came flying along the street—often panting and looking back—and the confused murmur of numerous voices struck upon his ear. Assured by these tokens, and by the red light which began to flash upon the houses on either side, that some of his friends were indeed approaching, he begged a moment's shelter at a door which opened as he passed, and running with some other persons to an upper window, looked out upon the crowd.

They had torches among them, and the chief faces were distinctly visible. That they had been engaged in the destruction of some building was sufficiently apparent, and that it was a Catholic place of worship was evident from the spoils they bore as trophies, which were easily recognisable for the vestments of priests, and rich fragments of altar furniture. Covered with soot, and dirt, and dust, and lime; their garments torn to rags; their hair hanging wildly about them; their hands and faces jagged and bleeding with the wounds of rusty nails; Barnaby, Hugh, and Dennis hurried on before them all, like hideous madmen. After them, the dense throng came fighting on: some singing; some shouting in triumph; some quarreling among themselves; some menacing the spectators as they passed; some with great wooden fragments, on which they spent their rage as if they had been alive, rending them limb from limb, and hurling the scattered morsels high into the air; some in a drunken state, unconscious of the hurts they had received from falling bricks, and stones, and beams; one borne upon a shutter, in the very midst, covered with a dingy cloth, a senseless, ghastly heap. Thus—a vision of coarse faces, with here and there a blot of flaring, smoky light; a dream of demon heads and savage eyes, and sticks and iron bars uplifted in the air, and whirled about; a bewildering horror, in which so much was seen, and yet so little, which seemed so long and yet so short, in which there were so many phantoms, not to be forgotten all through life, and yet so many things that could not be observed in that distracting glimpse—it flitted onward, and was gone.

As it passed away upon its work of wrath and ruin, a piercing scream was heard. A knot of persons ran towards the spot; Gashford, who just then emerged into the street, among them. He was on the outskirts of the little concourse, and could not see or hear what passed within; but one who had a better place, informed him that a widow woman had descried her son among the rioters.

"Is that all?" said the secretary, turning his face homewards. "Well! I think this looks a little more like business!"

CHAPTER THE FIFTY-FIRST.

PROMISING as these outrages were to Gashford's view, and much like business as they looked, they extended that night no farther. The soldiers were again called out, again they took half-a-dozen prisoners, and again the crowd dispersed after a short and bloodless scuffle. Hot and drunken though they were, they had not yet broken all bounds and set all law and government at defiance. Something of their habitual deference to the authority erected by society for its own preservation yet remained among them, and had its majesty been vindicated in time, the secretary would have had to digest a bitter disappointment.

By midnight, the streets were clear and quiet, and, save that there stood in two parts of the town, a heap of nodding walls and pile of rubbish, where there had been at sunset a rich and handsome building, everything wore its usual aspect. Even the Catholic gentry and tradesmen, of whom there were many, resident in different parts of the City and its suburbs, had no fear for their lives or property, and but little indignation for the wrong they had already sustained in the plunder and destruction of their temples of worship. An honest confidence in the government under whose protection they had lived for many years, and a well-founded reliance on the good feeling and right thinking of the great mass of the community, with whom, notwithstanding their religious differences, they were every day in habits of confidential, affectionate, and friendly intercourse, re-assured them, even under the excesses that had been committed; and convinced them that they who were Protestants in anything but the name, were no more to be considered as abettors of these disgraceful occurrences, than they themselves were chargeable with the uses of the block, the rack, the gibbet, and the stake, in cruel Mary's reign.*

The clock was on the stroke of one, when Gabriel Varden, with his lady and Miss Miggs, sat waiting in the little parlour. This fact; the toppling wicks of the dull, wasted candles; the silence that prevailed; and above all the nightcaps of both maid and matron, were sufficient evidence that they had been prepared for bed some time ago, and had some strong reason for sitting up so far beyond their usual hour.

If any other corroborative testimony had been required, it would have been abundantly furnished in the actions of Miss Miggs, who, having arrived at that restless state and sensitive condition of the nervous system which are the result of long watching, did, by a constant rubbing and tweaking of her nose, a perpetual change of position (arising from the sudden growth of imaginary knots and knobs in her chair), a frequent friction of her eyebrows, the incessant recurrence of a small cough, a small groan, a gasp, a sigh, a sniff, a spasmodic start, and by other demonstrations of that nature, so file down and rasp, as it were, the patience of the locksmith, that after looking at her in silence for some time, he at last broke out into this apostrophe:

"Miggs my good girl, go to bed—do go to bed. You're really worse than the dripping of a hundred water-butts outside the window, or the scratching of as many mice behind the wainscot. I can't bear it. Do go to bed, Miggs. To oblige me—do."

"You haven't got nothing to untie sir," returned Miss Miggs, "and therefore your requests does not surprise me. But Missis has—and while you set up, mim"—she added, turning to the locksmith's wife, "I couldn't, no not if twenty times the quantity of cold water was aperiently running down my back at this moment, go to my bed with a quiet spirit."

Having spoken these words, Miss Miggs made divers efforts to rub her shoulders in an impossible place, and shivered from head to foot; thereby giving the beholders to understand that the imaginary cascade was still in full flow, but that a sense of duty upheld her under that, and all other sufferings, and nerved her to endurance.

Mrs. Varden being too sleepy to speak, and Miss Miggs having, as the phrase is, said her say, the locksmith had nothing for it but to sigh and be as quiet as he could.

But to be quiet with such a basilisk* before him, was impossible. If he looked another way, it was worse to feel that she was rubbing her cheek, or twitching her ear, or winking her eye, or making all kinds of extraordinary shapes with her nose, than to see her do it. If she was for a moment free from any of these complaints, it was only because of her foot being asleep, or of her arm having got the fidgets, or of her leg being doubled up with the cramp, or of some other horrible disorder which racked her whole frame. If she did enjoy a moment's ease, then with her eyes shut and her mouth wide open she would be seen to sit very stiff and upright in her chair; then to nod a little way forward, and stop with a jerk; then to nod a little further forward, and stop with another jerk; then to recover herself; then to come forward again—lower—lower—lower—by very slow degrees, until, just as it seemed impossible that she could preserve her balance for another instant, and the locksmith was about to call out in an agony, to save her from dashing down upon her forehead and fracturing her skull, then, all of a sudden and without the smallest notice, she would come upright and rigid again with her eyes open, and in her countenance an expression of defiance, sleepy but yet most obstinate, which plainly said "I've never once closed 'em since I looked at you last, and I'll take my oath of it!"

At length, after the clock had struck two, there was a sound at the street door as if somebody had fallen against the knocker by accident. Miss Miggs immediately jumping up and clapping her hands, cried with a drowsy mingling of the sacred and profane, "Ally Looyer Mim! there's Simmuns's knock!"

"Who's there?" said Gabriel.

"Me!" cried the well-known voice of Mr. Tappertit. Gabriel opened the door, and gave him admission.

He did not cut a very insinuating figure; for a man of his stature suffers in a crowd; and having been active in yesterday morning's work, his dress was literally crushed from head to foot: his hat being beaten out of all shape, and his shoes trodden down at heel like slippers. His coat fluttered in strips about him, the buckles were torn away both from his knees and feet, half his neckerchief was gone, and the bosom of his shirt was rent to tatters. Yet notwithstanding all these personal disadvantages; despite his being very weak from heat and fatigue; and so begrimed with mud and dust that he might have been in a case, for anything of the real texture (either of his skin or apparel) that the eye could discern; he stalked haughtily into the parlour, and throwing himself into a chair, and endeavouring to thrust his hands into the pockets of his small-clothes, which were turned inside out and displayed upon his legs, like tassels, surveyed the household with a gloomy dignity.

"Simon," said the locksmith gravely, "How comes it that you return home at this time of night, and in this condition? Give me an assurance that you have not been among the rioters, and I am satisfied."

"Sir," replied Mr. Tappertit, with a contemptuous look, "I wonder at *your* assurance in making such demands."

"You have been drinking," said the locksmith.

"As a general principle, and in the most offensive sense of the words, sir," returned his journeyman with great self-possession, "I consider you a liar. In that last observation you have unintentionally—unintentionally, sir—struck upon the truth."

"Martha," said the locksmith, turning to his wife, and shaking his head sorrowfully, while a smile at the absurd figure before him still played upon his open face, "I trust it may turn out that this poor lad is not the victim of the knaves and fools we have so often had words about, and who have done so much harm this day. If he has been at Warwick Street or Duke Street to-night—"

"He has been at neither, sir," cried Mr. Tappertit in a loud voice, which he suddenly dropped into a whisper as he repeated, with eyes fixed upon the locksmith, "he has been at neither."

"I am glad of it, with all my heart," said the locksmith in a serious tone; "for if he had been, and it could be proved against him, Martha, your great association would have been to him the cart that draws men to the gallows and leaves them hanging in the air. It would, as sure as we're alive!"

Mrs. Varden was too much scared by Simon's altered manner and appearance, and by the accounts of the rioters which had reached her ears that night, to offer any retort, or to have recourse to her usual matrimonial policy. Miss Miggs, wrung her hands, and wept.

"He was not at Duke Street or at Warwick Street, G. Varden," said Simon, sternly; "but he *was* at Westminster. Perhaps, sir, he kicked a county member, perhaps sir he tapped a lord—you may stare, sir, I repeat it—blood flowed from noses, and perhaps he tapped a lord. Who knows? This," he added, putting his hand into his waistcoat-pocket, and taking out a large tooth, at sight of which both Miggs and Mrs. Varden screamed, "this was a bishop's. Beware, G. Varden!"

"Now, I would rather," said the locksmith hastily, "have paid five hundred pounds, than had this come to pass. You idiot, do you know what peril you stand in?"

"I know it, sir," replied his journeyman, "and it is my glory. I was there, everybody saw me there. I was conspicuous, and prominent. I will abide the consequences."

The locksmith, really disturbed and agitated, paced to and fro in silence—glancing at his former 'prentice every now and then—and at length stopping before him, said:

"Get to bed, and sleep for a couple of hours that you may wake penitent, and with some of your senses about you. Be sorry for what you have done, and we will try to save you. If I call him by five o'clock," said Varden, turning hurriedly to his wife, "and he washes himself clean and changes his dress, he may get to the Tower Stairs, and away by the Gravesend tide-boat,* before any search is made for him. From there he can easily get on to Canterbury, where your cousin will give him work till this storm has blown over. I am not sure that I do right in screening him from the punishment he deserves, but he has lived in this house, man and boy, for a dozen years, and I should be sorry if for this one day's work he made a miserable end. Lock the front door Miggs, and show no light towards the street when you go up stairs. Quick, Simon! Get to bed!"

"And do you suppose, sir," retorted Mr. Tappertit, with a thickness and slowness of speech which contrasted forcibly with the rapidity and earnestness of his kind-hearted master—"and do you suppose, sir, that I am base and mean enough to accept your servile proposition?—Miscreant!"

"Whatever you please, Sim, but get to bed. Every minute is of consequence. The light here, Miggs!"

"Yes yes, oh do! Go to bed directly," cried the two women together.

Mr. Tappertit stood upon his feet, and pushing his chair away to show that he needed no assistance, answered, swaying himself to and fro, and managing his head as if it had no connexion whatever with his body:

"You spoke of Miggs, sir—Miggs may be smothered!"

"Oh Simmun!" ejaculated that young lady in a faint voice. "Oh mim! Oh sir! Oh goodness gracious, what a turn he has give me!"

"This family may *all* be smothered, sir," returned Mr. Tappertit, after glancing at her with a smile of ineffable disdain, "excepting Mrs. V. I have come here, sir, for her sake this night. Mrs. Varden, take this piece of paper. It's a protection, ma'am. You may need it."

With these words he held out at arm's length, a dirty, crumpled scrap of writing. The locksmith took it from him, opened it, and read as follows:*

'All good friends to our cause, I hope will be particular, and do no injury to the property of any true Protestant. I am well assured that the proprietor of this house is a staunch and worthy friend to the cause.

   'GEORGE GORDON.'

"What's this!" said the locksmith, with an altered face.

"Something that'll do you good service, young feller," replied his journeyman, "as you'll find. Keep that safe, and where you can lay your hand upon it in an instant. And chalk 'No Popery' on your door to-morrow night, and for a week to come—that's all."

"This is a genuine document," said the locksmith, "I know, for I have seen the hand before. What threat does it imply? What devil is abroad?"

"A fiery devil," retorted Sim; "a flaming, furious devil. Don't you put yourself in its way, or you're done for, my buck. Be warned in time, G. Varden. Farewell!"

But here the two women threw themselves in his way—especially Miss Miggs, who fell upon him with such fervour that she pinned him against the wall—and conjured him in moving words not to go forth till he was sober; to listen to reason; to think of it; to take some rest, and then determine.

"I tell you," said Mr. Tappertit, "that my mind is made up. My bleeding country calls me, and I go! Miggs, if you don't get out of the way, I'll pinch you."

Miss Miggs, still clinging to the rebel, screamed once vociferously—but whether in the distraction of her mind, or because of his having executed his threat, is uncertain.

"Release me," said Simon, struggling to free himself from her chaste, but spider-like embrace. "Let me go! I have made arrangements for you in an altered state of society, and mean to provide for you comfortably in life—there! Will that satisfy you?"

"Oh Simmun!" cried Miss Miggs. "Oh my blessed Simmun! Oh mim, what are my feelings at this conflicting moment!"

Of a rather turbulent description, it would seem; for her nightcap had been knocked off in the scuffle, and she was on her knees upon the floor, making a strange revelation of blue and yellow curl-papers, straggling locks of hair, tags of staylaces, and strings of it's impossible to say what; panting for breath, clasping her hands, turning her eyes upwards, shedding abundance of tears, and exhibiting various other symptoms of the acutest mental suffering.

"I leave," said Simon, turning to his master, with an utter disregard of Miggs's maidenly affliction, "a box of things up stairs. Do what you like with 'em. *I* don't want 'em. I'm never coming back here, any more. Provide yourself, sir, with a journeyman; I'm my country's journeyman; henceforward that's *my* line of business."

"Be what you like in two hours' time, but now go up to bed," returned the locksmith, planting himself in the doorway. "Do you hear me? Go to bed!"

"I hear you, and defy you, Varden," rejoined Simon Tappertit.

"This night, sir, I have been in the country, planning an expedition which shall fill your bell-hanging soul with wonder and dismay. The plot demands my utmost energy. Let me pass!"

"I'll knock you down if you come near the door," replied the locksmith. "You had better go to bed!"

Simon made no answer, but gathering himself up as straight as he could, plunged head foremost at his old master, and the two went driving out into the workshop together, plying their hands and feet so briskly that they looked like half-a-dozen, while Miggs and Mrs. Varden screamed for twelve.

It would have been easy for Varden to knock his old 'prentice down, and bind him hand and foot; but as he was loath to hurt him in his then defenceless state, he contented himself with parrying his blows when he could, taking them in perfect good part when he could not, and keeping between him and the door, until a favourable opportunity should present itself for forcing him to retreat up stairs, and shutting him up in his own room. But in the goodness of his heart, he calculated too much upon his adversary's weakness, and forgot that drunken men who have lost the power of walking steadily, can often run. Watching his time, Simon Tappertit made a cunning show of falling back, staggered unexpectedly forward, brushed past him, opened the door (he knew the trick of that lock well), and darted down the street like a mad dog. The locksmith paused for a moment in the excess of his astonishment, and then gave chace.

It was an excellent season for a run, for at that silent hour the streets were deserted, the air was cool, and the flying figure before him distinctly visible at a great distance, as it sped away, with a long gaunt shadow following at its heels. But the short-winded locksmith had no chance against a man of Sim's youth and spare figure, though the day had been when he could have run him down in no time. The space between them rapidly increased, and as the rays of the rising sun streamed upon Simon in the act of turning a distant corner, Gabriel Varden was fain to give up, and sit down on a door-step to fetch his breath. Simon meanwhile, without once stopping, fled at the same degree of swiftness to the Boot, where, as he well knew, some of his company were lying, and at which respectable hostelry— for he had already acquired the distinction of being in great peril of the law—a friendly watch had been expecting him all night, and was even now on the look-out for his coming.

"Go thy ways, Sim, go thy ways," said the locksmith, as soon as he could speak. "I have done my best for thee, poor lad, and would have saved thee, but the rope is round thy neck, I fear."

So saying, and shaking his head in a very sorrowful and disconsolate manner, he turned back, and soon re-entered his own house, where Mrs. Varden and the faithful Miggs had been anxiously expecting his return.

Now Mrs. Varden (and by consequence Miss Miggs likewise) was impressed with a secret misgiving that she had done wrong; that she had, to the utmost of her small means, aided and abetted the growth of disturbances, the end of which it was impossible to foresee; that she had led remotely to the scene which had just passed; and that the locksmith's time for triumph and reproach had now arrived indeed. And so strongly did Mrs. Varden feel this, and so crest-fallen was she in consequence, that while her husband was pursuing their lost journeyman, she secreted under her chair the little red-brick dwelling-house with the yellow roof, lest it should furnish new occasion for reference to the painful theme; and now hid the same still farther, with the skirts of her dress.

But it happened that the locksmith had been thinking of this very article on his way home, and that, coming into the room and not seeing it, he at once demanded where it was.

Mrs. Varden had no resource but to produce it, which she did with many tears, and broken protestations that if she could have known—

"Yes, yes," said Varden, "of course—I know that. I don't mean to reproach you, my dear. But recollect from this time that all good things perverted to evil purposes, are worse than those which are naturally bad. A thoroughly wicked woman, is wicked indeed. When religion goes wrong, she is very wrong, for the same reason. Let us say no more about it, my dear."

So he dropped the red-brick dwelling-house on the floor, and setting his heel upon it, crushed it into pieces. The halfpence, and sixpences, and other voluntary contributions, rolled about in all directions, but nobody offered to touch them, or to take them up.

"That," said the locksmith, "is easily disposed of, and I would to Heaven that everything growing out of the same society could be settled as easily."

"It happens very fortunately, Varden," said his wife, with her handkerchief to her eyes, "that in case any more disturbances should happen—which I hope not; I sincerely hope not—"

"I hope so too, my dear."

"—That in case any should occur, we have the piece of paper which that poor misguided young man brought."

"Ay, to be sure," said the locksmith, turning quickly round. "Where is that piece of paper?"

Mrs. Varden stood aghast as he took it from her outstretched hand, tore it into fragments, and threw them under the grate.

"Not use it!" she said.

"Use it!" cried the locksmith. "No! Let them come and pull the roof about our ears; let them burn us out of house and home; I'd neither have the protection of their leader, nor chalk their howl upon my door, though, for not doing it, they shot me on my own threshold. Use it! Let them come and do their worst. The first man who crosses my door-step on such an errand as theirs, had better be a hundred miles away. Let him look to it. The others may have their will. I wouldn't beg or buy them off, if, instead of every pound of iron in the place, there was a hundred weight of gold. Get you to bed, Martha. I shall take down the shutters and go to work."

"So early!" said his wife.

"Ay," replied the locksmith cheerily, "so early. Come when they may, they shall not find us skulking and hiding, as if we feared to take our portion of the light of day, and left it all to them. So pleasant dreams to you, my dear, and cheerful sleep!"

With that he gave his wife a hearty kiss, and bade her delay no longer, or it would be time to rise before she lay down to rest. Mrs. Varden quite amiably and meekly walked up stairs, followed by Miggs, who, although a good deal subdued, could not refrain from sundry stimulative coughs and sniffs by the way, or from holding up her hands in astonishment at the daring conduct of master.

CHAPTER THE FIFTY-SECOND.

A MOB is usually a creature of very mysterious existence, particularly in a large city. Where it comes from or whither it goes, few men can tell. Assembling and dispersing with equal suddenness, it is as difficult to follow to its various sources as the sea itself; nor does the parallel stop here, for the ocean is not more fickle and uncertain, more terrible when roused, more unreasonable, or more cruel.

The people who were boisterous at Westminster upon the Friday morning, and were eagerly bent upon the work of devastation in Duke Street and Warwick Street at night, were, in the mass, the same. Allowing for the chance accessions of which any crowd is morally sure in a town where there must always be a large number of idle and profligate persons, one and the same mob was at both places. Yet they spread themselves in various directions when they dispersed in the afternoon, made no appointment for re-assembling, had no definite purpose or design, and indeed, for anything they knew, were scattered beyond the hope of future union.

At the Boot, which, as has been shown, was in a manner the head quarters of the rioters, there were not, upon this Friday night, a dozen people. Some slept in the stable and outhouses, some in the common room, some two or three in beds. The rest were in their usual homes or haunts. Perhaps not a score in all lay in the adjacent fields and lanes, and under haystacks, or near the warmth of brick-kilns, who had not their accustomed place of rest beneath the open sky. As to the public ways within the town, they had their ordinary

nightly occupants, and no others; the usual amount of vice and wretchedness, but no more.

The experience of one evening, however, had taught the reckless leaders of disturbance, that they had but to show themselves in the streets, to be immediately surrounded by materials which they could only have kept together when their aid was not required, at great risk, expense, and trouble. Once possessed of this secret, they were as confident as if twenty thousand men, devoted to their will, had been encamped about them, and assumed a confidence which could not have been surpassed, though that had really been the case. All day, Saturday, they remained quiet. On Sunday, they rather studied how to keep their men within call, and in full hope, than to follow out, by any very fierce measure, their first day's proceedings.

"I hope," said Dennis, as, with a loud yawn, he raised his body from a heap of straw on which he had been sleeping, and supporting his head upon his hand, appealed to Hugh on Sunday morning, "that Muster Gashford allows some rest? Perhaps he'd have us at work again already, eh?"

"It's not his way to let matters drop, you may be sure of that," growled Hugh in answer. "I'm in no humour to stir yet, though. I'm as stiff as a dead body, and as full of ugly scratches as if I had been fighting all day yesterday with wild cats."

"You've so much enthusiasm, that's it," said Dennis, looking with great admiration at the uncombed head, matted beard, and torn hands and face of the wild figure before him; "you're such a devil of a fellow. You hurt yourself a hundred times more than you need, because you will be foremost in everything, and will do more than the rest."

"For the matter of that," returned Hugh, shaking back his ragged hair and glancing towards the door of the stable in which they lay; "there's one yonder as good as me. What did I tell you about him? Did I say he was worth a dozen, when you doubted him?"

Mr. Dennis rolled lazily over upon his breast, and resting his chin upon his hand in imitation of the attitude in which Hugh lay, said, as he too looked towards the door:

"Ay ay, you knew him brother, you knew him. But who'd suppose to look at that chap now, that he could be the man he is! Isn't it a thousand cruel pities, brother, that instead of taking his nat'ral rest and qualifying himself for further exertions in this here *h*onorable cause, he should be playing at soldiers like a boy? And his cleanliness too!" said Mr. Dennis, who certainly had no reason to entertain a fellow feeling with anybody who was particular on that score: "what weaknesses he's guilty of, with respect to his cleanliness! At five o'clock this morning, there he was at the pump, though any one would think he had gone through enough the day before yesterday, to be pretty fast asleep at that time. But no—when I woke for a minute or two, there he was at the pump, and if you'd have seen him sticking them peacock's feathers into his hat when he'd done washing—ah! I'm sorry he's such a imperfect character, but the best on us is incomplete in some pint of view or another."

The subject of this dialogue and of these concluding remarks which were uttered in a tone of philosophical meditation, was, as the reader will have divined, no other than Barnaby, who, with his flag in his hand, stood sentry in the little patch of sunlight at the distant door, or walked to and fro outside, singing softly to himself, and keeping time to the music of some clear church bells. Whether he stood still, leaning with both hands on the flag-staff, or, bearing it upon his shoulder, paced slowly up and down, the careful arrangement of his poor dress, and his erect and lofty bearing, showed how high a sense he had of the great importance of his trust, and how happy and how proud it made him. To Hugh and his companion, who lay in a dark corner of the gloomy shed, he, and the sunlight, and the peaceful Sabbath sound to which he made response, seemed like a bright picture framed by the door, and set off by the stable's blackness. The whole formed such a contrast to themselves, as they lay wallowing, like some obscene animals, in their squalor and wickedness on the two heaps of straw, that for a few moments they looked on without speaking, and felt almost ashamed.

"Ah!" said Hugh at length, carrying it off with a laugh: "He's a rare fellow is Barnaby, and can do more, with less rest, or meat, or drink, than any of us. As to his soldiering, *I* put him on duty there."

"Then there was a object in it, and a proper good one too, I'll be sworn," retorted Dennis with a broad grin, and an oath of the same quality. "What was it, brother?"

"Why, you see," said Hugh, crawling a little nearer to him, "that our noble captain yonder, came in yesterday morning rather the worse for liquor, and was—like you and me—ditto last night."

Dennis looked to where Simon Tappertit lay coiled upon a truss of hay, snoring profoundly, and nodded.

"And our noble captain," continued Hugh with another laugh, "our noble captain and I, have planned for to-morrow a roaring expedition, with good profit in it."

"Against the papists?" asked Dennis, rubbing his hands.

"Ay, against the papists—against one of 'em at least, that some of us, and I for one, owe a good heavy grudge to."

"Not Muster Gashford's friend that he spoke to us about in my house, eh?" said Dennis, brimfull of pleasant expectation.

"The same man," said Hugh.

"That's your sort," cried Mr. Dennis, gaily shaking hands with him, "that's the kind of game. Let's have rewenges and injuries, and all that, and we shall get on twice as fast. Now you talk, indeed!"

"Ha ha ha! The captain," added Hugh, "has thoughts of carrying off a woman in the bustle, and—ha ha ha!—and so have I!"

Mr. Dennis received this part of the scheme with a wry face, observing that as a general principle he objected to women altogether, as being unsafe and slippery persons on whom there was no calculating with any certainty, and who were never in the same mind for four-and-twenty hours at a stretch. He might have expatiated on this suggestive theme at much greater length, but that it occurred to him to ask what connexion existed between the proposed expedition and Barnaby's being posted at the stable door as sentry; to which Hugh cautiously replied in these words:

"Why, the people we mean to visit, were friends of his once upon a time, and I know that much of him to feel pretty sure that if he thought we were going to do them any harm, he'd be no friend to our side, but would lend a ready hand to the other. So I've persuaded him (for I know him of old) that Lord George has picked him out to guard this place to-morrow while we're away, and that it's a great honour—and so he's on duty now, and as proud of it as if he was a general. Ha ha! What do you say to me for a careful man as well as a devil of a one?"

Mr. Dennis exhausted himself in compliments, and then added, "But about the expedition itself—"

"About that," said Hugh, "you shall hear all particulars from me and the great captain conjointly and both together—for see, he's waking up. Rouse yourself lion-heart. Ha ha! Put a good face upon it, and drink again. Another hair of the dog that bit you, captain! Call for drink! There's enough of gold and silver cups and candlesticks buried underneath my bed," he added, rolling back the straw, and pointing to where the ground was newly turned, "to pay for it, if it was a score of casks full. Drink captain!"

Mr. Tappertit received these jovial promptings with a very bad grace, being much the worse, both in mind and body, for his two nights of debauch, and but indifferently able to stand upon his legs. With Hugh's assistance, however, he contrived to stagger to the pump; and having refreshed himself with an abundant draught of cold water, and a copious shower of the same refreshing liquid on his head and face, he ordered some rum and milk to be served; and upon that innocent beverage and some biscuits and cheese made a pretty hearty meal. That done, he disposed himself in an easy attitude on the ground beside his two companions (who were carousing after their own tastes), and proceeded to enlighten Mr. Dennis in reference to to-morrow's project.

That their conversation was an interesting one, was rendered manifest by its length, and by the close attention of all three. That it was not of an oppressively grave character, but was enlivened by various pleasantries arising out of the subject, was clear from their loud and frequent roars of laughter, which startled Barnaby on his post, and made him wonder at their levity. But he was not summoned to join them, until they had eaten, and drunk, and slept, and talked together for some hours; not, indeed, until the twilight; when they informed him that they were about to make a slight demonstration in the streets—just to keep the people's hands in, as it was Sunday night, and the public might otherwise be disappointed—and that he was free to accompany them, if he would.

Without the slightest preparation, saving that they carried clubs and wore the blue cockade, they sallied out into the streets; and, with no more settled design than that of doing as much mischief as they could, paraded them at random. Their numbers rapidly increasing, they soon divided into parties; and agreeing to meet by-and-by, in the fields near Welbeck Street, scoured the town in various directions. The largest body, and that which augmented with the greatest rapidity, was the one to which Hugh and Barnaby belonged. This took its way towards Moorfields,* where there was a rich chapel,* and in which neighbourhood several Catholic families were known to reside.

Beginning with the private houses so occupied, they broke open the doors and windows; and while they destroyed the furniture and left but the bare walls, made a sharp search for tools and engines of destruction, such as hammers, pokers, axes, saws, and such like instruments. Many of the rioters made belts of cord, of handkerchiefs, or any material they found at hand, and wore these weapons as openly as pioneers upon a field-day. There was not the least disguise or concealment—indeed, on this night, very little excitement or hurry. From the chapels, they tore down and took away the very altars, benches, pulpits, pews, and flooring; from the dwelling-houses, the very wainscoting and stairs. This Sunday evening's recreation they pursued like mere workmen who had a certain task to do, and did it. Fifty resolute men might have turned them at any moment; a single company of soldiers could have scattered them like dust; but no man interposed, no authority restrained them, and, except by the terrified persons who fled from their approach, they were as little heeded as if they were pursuing their lawful occupations with the utmost sobriety and good conduct.

In the same manner, they marched to the place of rendezvous agreed upon, made great fires in the fields, and reserving the most valuable of their spoils, burnt the rest. Priestly garments, images of saints, rich stuffs and ornaments, altar-furniture and household

goods, were cast into the flames, and shed a glare on the whole country round; but they danced, and howled, and roared about these fires till they were tired, and were never for an instant checked.

As the main body filed off from this scene of action, and passed down Welbeck Street, they came upon Gashford, who had been a witness of their proceedings, and was walking stealthily along the pavement. Keeping up with him, and yet not seeming to speak, Hugh muttered in his ear:

"Is this better, master?"

"No," said Gashford. "It is not."

"What would you have?" said Hugh. "Fevers are never at their height at once. They must get on by degrees."

"I would have you," said Gashford, pinching his arm with such malevolence that his nails seemed to meet in the skin; "I would have you put some meaning into your work. Fools! Can you make no better bonfires than of rags and scraps? Can you burn nothing whole?"

"A little patience, master," said Hugh. "Wait but a few hours, and you shall see. Look for a redness in the sky, to-morrow night."

With that, he fell back into his place beside Barnaby; and when the secretary looked after him, both were lost in the crowd.

CHAPTER THE FIFTY-THIRD.

THE next day was ushered in by merry peals of bells, and by the firing of the Tower guns; flags were hoisted on many of the church-steeples; the usual demonstrations were made, in honour of the anniversary of the King's birth-day; and every man went about his pleasure or business, as if the city were in perfect order, and there were no half-smouldering embers in its secret places which on the approach of night would kindle up again, and scatter ruin and dismay abroad. The leaders of the riot, rendered still more daring by the success of last night and by the booty they had acquired, kept steadily together, and only thought of implicating the mass of their followers so deeply that no hope of pardon or reward might tempt them to betray their more notorious confederates into the hands of justice.

Indeed, the sense of having gone too far to be forgiven, held the

timid together no less than the bold. Many, who would readily have
pointed out the foremost rioters and given evidence against them,
felt that escape by that means was hopeless, when their every act had
been observed by scores of people who had taken no part in the
disturbances; who had suffered in their persons, peace, or property,
by the outrages of the mob; who would be most willing witnesses;
and whom the government would, no doubt, prefer to any King's
evidence* that might be offered. Many of this class had deserted their
usual occupations on the Saturday morning; some had been seen by
their employers, active in the tumult; others knew they must be
suspected, and that they would be discharged if they returned;
others had been desperate from the beginning, and comforted them-
selves with the homely proverb, that, being hung at all, they might as
well be hung for a sheep as a lamb. They all hoped and believed, in a
greater or less degree, that the government they seemed to have
paralyzed, would, in its terror, come to terms with them in the end,
and suffer them to make their own conditions. The least sanguine
among them reasoned with himself that, at the worst, they were too
many to be all punished, and that he had as good a chance of escape
as any other man. The great mass never reasoned or thought at all,
but were stimulated by their own headlong passions, by poverty, by
ignorance, by the love of mischief, and the hope of plunder.

One other circumstance is worthy of remark; and that is, that from
the moment of their first outbreak at Westminster, every symptom of
order or preconcerted arrangement among them, vanished. When
they divided into parties and ran to different quarters of the town, it
was on the spontaneous suggestion of the moment. Each party
swelled as it went along, like rivers as they roll towards the sea; new
leaders sprang up as they were wanted, disappeared when the neces-
sity was over, and reappeared at the next crisis. Each tumult took
shape and form, from the circumstances of the moment; sober
workmen going home from their day's labour, were seen to cast down
their baskets of tools and become rioters in an instant; mere boys on
errands did the like. In a word, a moral plague ran through the city.
The noise, and hurry, and excitement, had for hundreds and hun-
dreds an attraction they had no firmness to resist. The contagion
spread, like a dread fever: an infectious madness, as yet not near
its height, seized on new victims every hour, and society began to
tremble at their ravings.

It was between two and three o'clock in the afternoon when Gashford looked into the lair described in the last chapter, and seeing only Barnaby and Dennis there, inquired for Hugh.

He was out, Barnaby told him; had gone out more than an hour ago; and had not yet returned.

"Dennis!" said the smiling secretary, in his smoothest voice, as he sat down cross-legged on a barrel, "Dennis!"

The hangman struggled into a sitting posture directly, and with his eyes wide open, looked towards him.

"How do you do, Dennis?" said Gashford, nodding. "I hope you have suffered no inconvenience from your late exertions, Dennis?"

"I always will say of you, Muster Gashford," returned the hangman, staring at him, "that that 'ere quiet way of yours might almost wake a dead man. It is," he added with a muttered oath—still staring at him in a thoughtful manner—"so awful sly!"

"So distinct, eh Dennis?"

"Distinct!" he answered, scratching his head, and keeping his eyes upon the secretary's face; "I seem to hear it, Muster Gashford, in my wery bones."

"I am very glad your sense of hearing is so sharp, and that I succeed in making myself so intelligible," said Gashford, in his unvarying, even tone. "Where is your friend?"

Mr. Dennis looked round as in expectation of beholding him asleep upon his bed of straw; then remembering that he had seen him go out, replied:

"I can't say where he is, Muster Gashford, I expected him back afore now. I hope it isn't time that we was busy, Muster Gashford?"

"Nay," said the secretary, "who should know that as well as you? How can *I* tell you, Dennis? You are perfect master of your own actions, you know, and accountable to nobody—except sometimes to the law, eh?"

Dennis, who was very much baffled by the cool matter-of-course manner of this reply, recovered his self-possession on his professional pursuits being referred to, and pointing towards Barnaby, shook his head and frowned.

"Hush!" cried Barnaby.

"Ah! Do hush about that, Muster Gashford," said the hangman in a low voice, "pop'lar prejudices—you always forget—well, Barnaby, my lad, what's the matter?"

"I hear him coming," he answered: "Hark! Do you mark that? That's his foot! Bless you, I know his step, and his dog's too. Tramp, tramp, pit-pat, on they come together, and, ha ha ha!—and here they are!" he cried joyfully, welcoming Hugh with both hands, and then patting him fondly on the back, as if instead of being the rough companion he was, he had been one of the most prepossessing of men. "Here he is, and safe too! I am glad to see him back again, old Hugh!"

"I'm a Turk if he don't give me a warmer welcome always than any man of sense," said Hugh, shaking hands with him with a kind of ferocious friendship, strange enough to see. "How are you, boy?"

"Hearty!" cried Barnaby, waving his hat. "Ha ha ha! And merry too Hugh! And ready to do anything for the good cause, and the right, and to help the kind, mild, pale-faced gentleman—the Lord they use so ill—eh, Hugh?"

"Ay!" returned his friend, dropping his hand, and looking at Gashford for an instant with a changed expression before he spoke to him. "Good day, master!"

"And good day to you," replied the secretary, nursing his leg. "And many good days—whole years of them, I hope. You are heated."

"So would you have been, master," said Hugh, wiping his face, "if you'd been running here as fast as I have."

"You know the news then? Yes, I supposed you would have heard it."

"News! what news!"

"You don't?" cried Gashford, raising his eyebrows with an exclamation of surprise. "Dear me! Come; then I *am* the first to make you acquainted with your distinguished position, after all. Do you see the King's Arms a-top?" he smilingly asked, as he took a large paper from his pocket, unfolded it, and held it out for Hugh's inspection.

"Well!" said Hugh. "What's that to me?"

"Much. A great deal," replied the secretary. "Read it."

"I told you, the first time I saw you, that I couldn't read," said Hugh, impatiently. "What in the Devil's name's inside of it?"

"It is a proclamation from The King in Council," said Gashford, "dated to-day, and offering a reward of five hundred pounds—five hundred pounds is a great deal of money, and a large temptation to some people—to any one who will discover the person or persons most active in demolishing those chapels on Friday night."

"Is that all?" cried Hugh, with an indifferent air. "I knew of that."

"Truly I might have known you did," said Gashford, smiling, and folding up the document again. "Your friend, I might have guessed—indeed I did guess—was sure to tell you."

"My friend!" stammered Hugh, with an unsuccessful effort to appear surprised. "What friend?"

"Tut tut—do you suppose I don't know where you have been?" retorted Gashford, rubbing his hands, and beating the back of one on the palm of the other, and looking at him with a cunning eye. "How dull you think me! Shall I say his name?"

"No," said Hugh, with a hasty glance towards Dennis.

"You have also heard from him, no doubt," resumed the secretary, after a moment's pause, "that the rioters who have been taken (poor fellows) are committed for trial, and that some very active witnesses have had the temerity to appear against them. Among others—" and here he clenched his teeth, as if he would suppress, by force, some violent words that rose upon his tongue; and spoke very slowly. "Among others, a gentleman who saw the work going on in Warwick Street; a Catholic gentleman; one Haredale."

Hugh would have prevented his uttering the word, but it was out already. Hearing the name, Barnaby turned swiftly round.

"Duty, duty, bold Barnaby!" cried Hugh, assuming his wildest and most rapid manner, and thrusting into his hand his staff and flag which leant against the wall. "Mount guard without loss of time, for we are off upon our expedition. Up, Dennis, and get ready. Take care that no one turns the straw upon my bed, brave Barnaby; we know what's underneath it—eh? Now, master, quick! What you have to say, say speedily, for the little captain and a cluster of 'em are in the fields, and only waiting for us. Sharp's the word, and strike's the action. Quick!"

Barnaby was not proof against this bustle and despatch. The look of mingled astonishment and anger which had appeared in his face when he turned towards them, faded from it, as the words passed from his memory, like breath from a polished mirror; and grasping the weapon which Hugh forced upon him, he proudly took his station at the door, beyond their hearing.

"You might have spoiled our plans, master," said Hugh. "*You*, too, of all men!"

"Who would have supposed that *he* would be so quick?" urged Gashford.

"He's as quick sometimes—I don't mean with his hands, for that you know, but with his head—as you, or any man," said Hugh. "Dennis, it's time we were going; they're waiting for us; I came to tell you. Reach me my stick and belt. Here! Lend a hand, master. Fling this over my shoulder, and buckle it behind, will you?"

"Brisk as ever!" said the secretary, adjusting it for him as he desired.

"A man need be brisk to-day; there's brisk work a-foot."

"There is, is there?" said Gashford. He said it with such a provoking assumption of ignorance, that Hugh, looking over his shoulder and angrily down upon him, replied:

"Is there! You know there is! Who knows better than you, master, that the first great step to be taken is to make examples of these witnesses, and frighten all men from appearing against us or any of our body, any more?"

"There's one we know of," returned Gashford, with an expressive smile, "who is at least as well informed upon that subject as you or I."

"If we mean the same gentleman, as I suppose we do," Hugh rejoined, softly, "I tell you this—he's as good and quick information about everything as—" here he paused and looked round, as if to make quite sure that the person in question was not within hearing—"as Old Nick himself. Have you done that, master? How slow you are!"

"It's quite fast now," said Gashford, rising. "I say—you didn't find that your friend disapproved of to-day's little expedition? Ha ha ha! It is fortunate it jumps so well with the witness' policy; for, once planned, it must have been carried out. And now you are going, eh?"

"Now we are going, master!" Hugh replied. "Any parting words?"

"Oh dear, no," said Gashford sweetly. "None!"

"You're sure?" cried Hugh, nudging the grinning Dennis.

"Quite sure, eh, Muster Gashford?" chuckled the hangman.

Gashford paused a moment, struggling with his caution and his malice; then putting himself between the two men, and laying a hand upon the arm of each, said, in a cramped whisper:

"Do not, my good friends—I am sure you will not—forget our talk one night—in your house, Dennis—about this person. No mercy, no quarter, no two beams of his house to be left standing where the builder placed them! Fire, the saying goes, is a good servant, but a bad master. Make it *his* master; he deserves no better. But I am sure you will be firm, I am sure you will be very resolute, I am sure you will remember that he thirsts for your lives, and those of all your brave companions. If you ever acted like stanch fellows, you will do so to-day. Won't you, Dennis—won't you, Hugh?"

The two looked at him, and at each other; then bursting into a roar of laughter, brandished their staves above their heads, shook hands, and hurried out.

When they had been gone a little time, Gashford followed. They were yet in sight, and hastening to that part of the adjacent fields in which their fellows had already mustered; Hugh was looking back, and flourishing his hat to Barnaby, who, delighted with his trust, replied in the same manner, and then resumed his pacing up and down before the stable-door, where his feet had worn a path already. And when Gashford himself was far distant, and looked back for the last time, he was still walking to and fro, with the same measured tread; the most devoted and the blithest champion that ever maintained a post, and felt his heart lifted up with a brave sense of duty, and determination to defend it to the last.

Smiling at the simplicity of the poor idiot, Gashford betook himself to Welbeck Street by a different path from that which he knew the rioters would take, and sitting down behind a curtain in one of the upper windows of Lord George Gordon's house, waited impatiently for their coming. They were so long, that although he knew it had been settled they should come that way, he had a misgiving they must have changed their plans and taken some other route. But at length the roar of voices was heard in the neighbouring fields, and soon afterwards they came thronging past, in a great body.

However, they were not all, nor nearly all, in one body, but were, as he soon found, divided into four parties, each of which stopped before the house to give three cheers, and then went on; the leaders crying out in what direction they were going, and calling on the spectators to join them. The first detachment, carrying, by way of banners, some relics of the havoc they had made in Moorfields, proclaimed that they were on their way to Chelsea, whence they would return in the same order, to make of the spoil they bore, a great bonfire, near at hand. The second gave out that they were bound for Wapping, to destroy a chapel; the third, that their place of destination was East Smithfield, and their object the same. All this was done in broad, bright, summer day. Gay carriages and chairs stopped to let them pass, or turned back to avoid them; people on foot stood aside in doorways, or perhaps knocked and begged permission to stand at a window, or in the hall, until the rioters had passed: but nobody interfered with them; and directly they had gone by, everything went on as usual.

There still remained the fourth body, and for that the secretary looked with a most intense eagerness. At last it came up. It was numerous, and composed of picked men; for as he gazed down among them, he recognised many upturned faces which he knew well—those of Simon Tappertit, Hugh, and Dennis in the front, of course. They halted and cheered, as the others had done; but when they moved again, they did not, like them, proclaim what design they had. Hugh merely raised his hat upon the bludgeon he carried, and glancing at a spectator on the opposite side of the way, was gone.

Gashford followed the direction of his glance instinctively, and saw, standing on the pavement, and wearing the blue cockade, Sir John Chester. He held his hat an inch or two above his head, to propitiate the mob; and, resting gracefully on his cane, smiling pleasantly, and displaying his dress and person to the very best advantage, looked on in the most tranquil state imaginable. For all that, and quick and dexterous as he was, Gashford had seen him recognise Hugh with the air of a patron. He had no longer any eyes for the crowd, but fixed his keen regards upon Sir John.

He stood in the same place and posture, until the last man in the concourse had turned the corner of the street; then very deliberately took the blue cockade out of his hat; put it carefully in his pocket, ready for the next emergency; refreshed himself with a pinch of snuff; put up his box; and was walking slowly off, when a passing carriage stopped, and a lady's hand let down the glass. Sir John's hat was off again immediately. After a minute's conversation at the carriage-window, in which it was apparent that he was vastly entertaining on the subject of the mob, he stepped lightly in, and was driven away.

The secretary smiled, but he had other thoughts to dwell upon, and soon dismissed the topic. Dinner was brought him, but he sent it down untasted; and, in restless pacings up and down the room, and constant glances at the clock, and many futile efforts to sit down and read, or go to sleep, or look out of the window, consumed four weary hours. When the dial told him thus much time had crept away, he stole up stairs to the top of the house, and coming out upon the roof sat down, with his face towards the east.

Heedless of the fresh air that blew upon his heated brow, of the pleasant meadows from which he turned, of the piles of roofs and chimneys upon which he looked, of the smoke and rising mist he vainly sought to pierce, of the shrill cries of children at their evening sports, the distant hum and turmoil of the town, the cheerful country breath that rustled past to meet it, and to droop, and die; he watched, and watched, till it was dark—save for the specks of light that twinkled in the streets below and far away—and, as the darkness deepened, strained his gaze and grew more eager yet.

"Nothing but gloom in that direction, still!" he muttered restlessly. "Dog! where is the redness in the sky, you promised me!"

CHAPTER THE FIFTY-FOURTH.

RUMOURS of the prevailing disturbances had by this time begun to be pretty generally circulated through the towns and villages round London, and the tidings were everywhere received with that appetite for the marvellous and love of the terrible which have probably been among the natural characteristics of mankind since the creation of the world. These accounts, however, appeared, to many persons at that day, as they would to us at the present, but that we know them to be matter of history, so monstrous and improbable, that a great number of those who were resident at a distance, and who were credulous enough on other points, were really unable to bring their minds to believe that such things could be; and rejected the intelligence they received on all hands, as wholly fabulous and absurd.

Mr. Willet—not so much, perhaps, on account of his having argued and settled the matter with himself, as by reason of his constitutional obstinacy—was one of those who positively refused to entertain the current topic for a moment. On this very evening, and perhaps at the very time when Gashford kept his solitary watch, old John was so red in the face with perpetually shaking his head in contradiction of his three ancient cronies and pot companions, that he was quite a phenomenon to behold; and lighted up the Maypole Porch wherein they sat together, like a monstrous carbuncle in a fairy tale.

"Do you think, sir," said Mr. Willet, looking hard at Solomon Daisy, for it was his custom in cases of personal altercation to fasten upon the smallest man in the party—"do you think sir, that I'm a born fool?"

"No, no, Johnny," returned Solomon, looking round upon the little circle of which he formed a part: "We all know better than that. You're no fool Johnny. No, no!"

Mr. Cobb and Mr. Parkes shook their heads in unison, muttering "No, no, Johnny, not you!" But as such compliments had usually the effect of making Mr. Willet rather more dogged than before, he surveyed them with a look of deep disdain, and returned for answer:

"Then what do you mean by coming here, and telling me that this evening you're a going to walk up to London together—you three—you—and have the evidence of your own senses? An't," said Mr. Willet, putting his pipe in his mouth with an air of solemn disgust, "an't the evidence of *my* senses enough for you?"

"But we haven't got it Johnny," pleaded Parkes, humbly.

"You haven't got it sir?" repeated Mr. Willet, eyeing him from top to toe. "You haven't got it, sir? You *have* got it, sir. Don't I tell you that His blessed Majesty King George the Third would no more stand a rioting and rollicking in his streets, than he'd stand being crowed over by his own Parliament?"

"Yes Johnny, but that's your sense—not your senses," said the adventurous Mr. Parkes.

"How do *you* know?" retorted John with great dignity. "You're a contradicting pretty free, you are sir. How do *you* know which it is? I'm not aware I ever told you, sir."

Mr. Parkes, finding himself in the position of having got into metaphysics without exactly seeing his way out of them, stammered forth an apology and retreated from the argument. There then ensued a silence of some ten minutes or quarter of an hour, at the expiration of which period Mr. Willet was observed to rumble and shake with laughter, and presently remarked, in reference to his late adversary, "that he hoped he had tackled him enough." Thereupon Messrs. Cobb and Daisy laughed, and nodded, and Parkes was looked upon as thoroughly and effectually put down.

"Do you suppose if all this was true, that Mr. Haredale would be constantly away from home, as he is?" said John, after another silence. "Do you think he wouldn't be afraid to leave his house with them two young women in it, and only a couple of men, or so?"

"Ay, but then you know," returned Solomon Daisy, "his house is a goodish way out of London, and they do say that the rioters won't go more than two mile, or three at farthest, off the stones. Besides, you know, some of the Catholic gentlefolks have actually sent trinkets and such-like down here for safety—at least, so the story goes."

"The story goes!" said Mr. Willet testily. "Yes, sir. The story goes that you saw a ghost last March. But nobody believes it."

"Well!" said Solomon, rising, to divert the attention of his two friends, who tittered at this retort: "believed or disbelieved, it's true; and true or not, if we mean to go to London, we must be going at once. So shake hands, Johnny, and good night."

"I shall shake hands," returned the landlord, putting his into his pockets, "with no man as goes to London on such nonsensical errands."

The three cronies were therefore reduced to the necessity of shaking his elbows; having performed that ceremony, and brought from the house their hats, and sticks, and great-coats, they bade him good night and departed; promising to bring him on the morrow full and true accounts of the real state of the city, and if it were quiet, to give him the full merit of his victory.

John Willet looked after them, as they plodded along the road in the rich glow of a summer evening; and knocking the ashes out of his pipe, laughed inwardly at their folly, until his sides were sore. When he had quite exhausted himself—which took some time, for he laughed as slowly as he thought and spoke—he sat himself comfortably with his back to the house, put his legs upon the bench, then his apron over his face, and fell sound asleep.

How long he slept, matters not; but it was for no brief space, for when he awoke, the rich light had faded, the sombre hues of night were falling fast upon the landscape, and a few bright stars were already twinkling over-head. The birds were all at roost, the daisies on the green had closed their fairy hoods, the honeysuckle twining round the porch exhaled its perfume in a twofold degree, as though it lost its coyness at that silent time and loved to shed its fragrance on the night; the ivy scarcely stirred its deep green leaves. How tranquil, and how beautiful it was!

Was there no sound in the air, besides the gentle rustling of the trees and the grasshopper's merry chirp? Hark! Something very faint and distant, not unlike the murmuring in a sea-shell. Now it grew louder, fainter now, and now it altogether died away. Presently—it came again, subsided, came once more; grew louder, fainter, swelled into a roar. It was on the road, and varied with its windings. All at once it burst into a distinct sound—the voices, and the tramping feet of many men.

It is questionable whether old John Willet, even then, would have thought of the rioters, but for the cries of his cook and housemaid, who ran screaming up stairs and locked themselves into one of the old garrets,—shrieking dismally when they had done so, by way of rendering their place of refuge perfectly secret and secure. These two females did afterwards depone that Mr. Willet in his consternation uttered but one word, and called that up the stairs in a stentorian voice, six distinct times. But as this word was a monosyllable, which, however inoffensive when applied to the quadruped it denotes, is highly reprehensible when used in connexion with females of unimpeachable character, many persons were inclined to believe that the young women laboured under some hallucination caused by excessive fear; and that their ears deceived them.

Be this as it may, John Willet, in whom the very uttermost extent of dull-headed perplexity supplied the place of courage, stationed himself in the porch, and waited for their coming up. Once, it dimly occurred to him that there was a kind of door to the house, which had a lock and bolts; and at the same time some shadowy ideas of shutters to the lower windows, flitted through his brain. But he stood stock still, looking down the road in the direction in which the noise was rapidly advancing, and did not so much as take his hands out of his pockets.

He had not to wait long. A dark mass, looming through a cloud of dust, soon became visible; the mob quickened their pace; shouting and whooping like savages, they came rushing on pell-mell; and in a few seconds he was bandied from hand to hand, in the heart of a crowd of men.

"Halloa!" cried a voice he knew, as the man who spoke came cleaving through the throng. "Where is he? Give him to me. Don't hurt him. How now, old Jack! Ha ha ha!"

Mr. Willet looked at him, and saw it was Hugh; but he said nothing, and thought nothing.

"These lads are thirsty and must drink!" cried Hugh, thrusting him back towards the house. "Bustle, Jack, bustle. Show us the best—the very best—the over-proof that you keep for your own drinking, Jack!"

John faintly articulated the words, "Who's to pay?"

"He says 'Who's to pay!'" cried Hugh, with a roar of laughter which was loudly echoed by the crowd. Then turning to John, he added, "Pay! Why, nobody."

John stared round at the mass of faces—some grinning, some fierce, some lighted up by torches, some indistinct, some dusky and shadowy: some looking at him, some at his house, some at each other—and while he was, as he thought, in the very act of doing so, found himself, without any consciousness of having moved, in the bar; sitting down in an arm-chair, and watching the destruction of his property, as if it were some queer play or entertainment, of an astonishing and stupefying nature, but having no reference to himself—that he could make out—at all.

Yes. Here was the bar—the bar that the boldest never entered without special invitation—the sanctuary, the mystery, the hallowed ground: here it was, crammed with men, clubs, sticks, torches, pistols; filled with a deafening noise, oaths, shouts, screams, hootings; changed all at once into a bear-garden, a madhouse, an infernal temple: men darting in and out, by door and window, smashing the glass, turning the taps, drinking liquor out of China punchbowls, sitting astride of casks smoking private and personal pipes, cutting down the sacred grove of lemons, hacking and hewing at the celebrated cheese, breaking open inviolable drawers, putting things in their pockets which didn't belong to them, dividing his own money before his own eyes, wantonly wasting, breaking, pulling down and tearing up: nothing quiet, nothing private: men everywhere—above, below, overhead, in the bedrooms, in the kitchen, in the yard, in the stables—clambering in at windows when there were doors wide open; dropping out of windows when the stairs were handy; leaping over the banisters into chasms of passages: new faces and figures presenting themselves every instant—some yelling, some singing, some fighting, some breaking glass and crockery, some laying the dust with the liquor they couldn't drink, some ringing the bells till they pulled them down, others beating them with pokers till they beat them into fragments: more men still—more, more, more—swarming on like insects: noise, smoke, light, darkness, frolic, anger, laughter, groans, plunder, fear, and ruin!

Nearly all the time while John looked on at this bewildering scene, Hugh kept near him; and though he was the loudest, wildest, most destructive villain there, he saved his old master's bones a score of times. Nay, even when Mr. Tappertit, excited by liquor, came up,

and in assertion of his prerogative politely kicked John Willet on the shins, Hugh bade him return the compliment; and if old John had had sufficient presence of mind to understand this whispered direction, and to profit by it, he might no doubt, under Hugh's protection, have done so with impunity.

At length the band began to reassemble outside the house, and to call to those within, to join them, for they were losing time. These murmurs increasing, and attaining a very high pitch, Hugh, and some of those who yet lingered in the bar, and who plainly were the leaders of the troop, took counsel together apart as to what was to be done with John, to keep him quiet until their Chigwell work was over. Some proposed to set the house on fire and leave him in it; others that he should be reduced to a state of temporary insensibility, by knocking on the head; others that he should be sworn to sit where he was until to-morrow at the same hour; others again that he should be gagged and taken off with them, under a sufficient guard. All these propositions being overruled, it was concluded, at last, to bind him in his chair, and the word was passed for Dennis.

"Look'ee here, Jack!" said Hugh, striding up to him: "We're going to tie you, hand and foot, but otherwise you won't be hurt. D'ye hear?"

John Willet looked at another man, as if he didn't know which was the speaker, and muttered something about an ordinary every Sunday at two o'clock.

"You won't be hurt I tell you, Jack—do you hear me?" roared Hugh, impressing the assurance upon him by means of a heavy blow on the back. "He's so dead scared, he's wool-gathering, I think. Ha ha! Give him a drop of something to drink here. Hand over, one of you."

A glass of liquor being passed forward, Hugh poured the contents down old John's throat. Mr. Willet feebly smacked his lips, thrust his hand into his pocket, and inquired what was to pay; adding, as he looked vacantly round, that he believed there was a trifle of broken glass—

"He's out of his senses for the time, it's my belief," said Hugh, after shaking him, without any visible effect upon his system, until his keys rattled in his pocket. "Where's that Dennis?"

The word was again passed, and presently Mr. Dennis, with a long cord bound about his middle, something after the manner of a friar, came hurrying in, attended by a body-guard of half-a-dozen of his men.

"Come! Be alive here!" cried Hugh, stamping his foot upon the ground. "Make haste!"

Dennis, with a wink and a nod, unwound the cord from about his person, and raising his eyes to the ceiling, looked all over it, and round the walls and cornice, with a curious eye; then shook his head.

"Move man, can't you!" cried Hugh, with another impatient stamp of his foot. "Are we to wait here till the cry has gone for ten miles round, and our work's interrupted?"

"It's all very fine talking, brother," answered Dennis, stepping towards him; "but unless—" and here he whispered in his ear— "unless we do it over the door, it can't be done at all in this here room."

"What can't?" Hugh demanded.

"What can't!" retorted Dennis. "Why, the old man can't."

"Why, you weren't going to hang him?" cried Hugh.

"No, brother!" returned the hangman, with a stare. "What else?"

Hugh made no answer, but snatching the rope from his companion's hand, proceeded to bind old John himself; but his very first move was so bungling and unskilful, that Mr. Dennis entreated, almost with tears in his eyes, that he might be permitted to perform the duty. Hugh consenting, he achieved it in a twinkling.

"There!" he said, looking mournfully at John Willet, who displayed no more emotion in his bonds than he had shown out of them. "That's what I call pretty, and workmanlike. He's quite a picter now. But, brother, just a word with you—now that he's ready trussed, as one may say, wouldn't it be better for all parties if we was to work him off? It would read uncommon well in the newspapers, it would indeed. The public would think a great deal more on us!"

Hugh, inferring what his companion meant, rather from his gestures than his technical mode of expressing himself (to which, as he was ignorant of his calling, he wanted the clue), rejected this proposition for the second time, and gave the word "Forward!" which was echoed by a hundred voices from without.

"To the Warren!" shouted Dennis as he ran out, followed by the rest. "A witness's house, my lads!"

A loud yell followed, and the whole throng hurried off, mad for pillage and destruction. Hugh lingered behind for a few moments to stimulate himself with more drink, and to set all the taps running, a few of which had accidentally been spared; then glancing round the despoiled and plundered room, through whose shattered window the rioters had thrust the Maypole itself,—for even that had been sawn down,—lighted a torch; clapped the mute and motionless John Willet on the back; and waving it above his head, and uttering a fierce shout, hastened after his companions.

CHAPTER THE FIFTY-FIFTH.

JOHN WILLET, left alone in his dismantled bar, continued to sit staring about him; awake as to his eyes, certainly, but with all his powers of reason and reflection in a sound and dreamless sleep. He looked round upon the room which had been for years, and was within an hour ago, the pride of his heart; and not a muscle of his face was moved. The night, without, looked black and cold through the dreary gaps in the casement; the precious liquids, now nearly leaked away, dripped with a hollow sound upon the floor; the May-pole peered ruefully in through the broken window, like the bowsprit of a wrecked ship; the ground might have been the bottom of the sea, it was so strewn with precious fragments. Currents of air rushed in, as the old doors jarred and creaked upon their hinges; the candles flickered and guttered down, and made long winding-sheets;* the cheery deep-red curtains flapped and fluttered idly in the road; even the stout Dutch kegs, overthrown and lying empty in dark corners, seemed the mere husks of good fellows whose jollity had departed, and who could kindle with a friendly glow no more. John saw this desolation, and yet saw it not. He was perfectly contented to sit there staring at it, and felt no more indignation or discomfort in his bonds than if they had been robes of honour. So far as he was personally concerned, old Time lay snoring, and the world stood still.

Save for the dripping from the barrels, the rustling of such light fragments of destruction as the wind affected, and the dull creaking of the open doors, all was profoundly quiet: indeed these sounds, like the ticking of the death-watch in the night, only made the silence they invaded deeper and more apparent. But quiet or noisy, it was all one to John. If a train of heavy artillery could have come up and commenced ball practice outside the window, it would have been all the same to him. He was a long way beyond surprise. A ghost couldn't have overtaken him.

By and by he heard a footstep—a hurried, and yet cautious foot-step—coming on towards the house. It stopped, advanced again, then seemed to go quite round it. Having done that, it came beneath the window, and a head looked in.

It was strongly relieved against the darkness outside by the glare of the guttering candles. A pale, worn, withered face; the eyes—but that was owing to its gaunt condition—unnaturally large and bright; the hair a grizzled black. It gave a searching glance all round the room, and a deep voice said:

"Are you alone in this house?"

John made no sign, though the question was repeated twice, and he heard it distinctly. After a moment's pause, the man got in at the window. John was not at all surprised at this, either. There had been so much getting in and out of window in the course of the last hour or so, that he had quite forgotten the door, and seemed to have lived among such exercises from infancy.

The man wore a large, dark, faded cloak, and a slouched hat; he walked up close to John, and looked at him. John returned the compliment with interest.

"How long have you been sitting thus?" said the man.

John considered, but nothing came of it.

"Which way have the party gone?"

Some wandering speculations relative to the fashion of the stranger's boots, got into Mr. Willet's mind by some accident or other, but they got out again in a hurry, and left him in his former state.

"You would do well to speak," said the man: "you may keep a whole skin, though you have nothing else left that can be hurt. Which way have the party gone?"

"That!" said John, finding his voice all at once, and nodding with perfect good faith—he couldn't point; he was so tightly bound—in exactly the opposite direction to the right one.

"You lie!" said the man angrily, and with a threatening gesture. "I came that way. You would betray me."

It was so evident that John's imperturbability was not assumed, but was the result of the late proceedings under his roof, that the man stayed his hand in the very act of striking him, and turned away.

John looked after him without so much as a twitch in a single nerve of his face. He seized a glass, and holding it under one of the little casks until a few drops were collected, drank them greedily off; then dashing it down upon the floor impatiently, he took the vessel in his hands and drained it into his throat. Some scraps of bread and meat were scattered about, and on these he fell next; eating them with great voracity, and pausing every now and then to listen for some fancied noise outside. When he had refreshed himself in this manner with violent haste, and raised another barrel to his lips, he pulled his hat upon his brow as though he were about to leave the house, and turned to John.

"Where are your servants?"

Mr. Willet indistinctly remembered to have heard the rioters calling to them to throw the key of the room in which they were, out of window, for their keeping. He therefore replied, "Locked up."

"Well for them if they remain quiet, and well for you if you do the like," said the man. "Now show me the way the party went."

This time Mr. Willet indicated it correctly. The man was hurrying to the door, when suddenly there came towards them on the wind, the loud and rapid tolling of an alarm bell, and then a bright and vivid glare streamed up, which illumined, not only the whole chamber, but all the country.

It was not the sudden change from darkness to this dreadful light, it was not the sound of distant shrieks and shouts of triumph, it was not this dread invasion of the serenity and peace of night, that drove the man back as though a thunderbolt had struck him. It was the Bell. If the ghastliest shape the human mind has ever pictured in its wildest dreams had risen up before him, he could not have staggered backward from its touch, as he did from the first sound of that loud iron voice. With eyes that started from his head, his limbs convulsed, his face most horrible to see, he raised one arm high up into the air, and holding something visionary, back and down, with his other hand, drove at it as though he held a knife and stabbed it to the heart. He clutched his hair, and stopped his ears, and travelled madly round and round; then gave a frightful cry, and with it rushed away: still, still, the Bell tolled on and seemed to follow him—louder and louder, hotter and hotter yet. The glare grew brighter, the roar of voices deeper; the crash of heavy bodies falling, shook the air; bright streams of sparks rose up into the sky; but louder than them all— rising faster far, to Heaven—a million times more fierce and furious—pouring forth dreadful secrets after its long silence—speaking the language of the dead—the Bell—the Bell!

What hunt of spectres could surpass that dread pursuit and flight! Had there been a legion of them on his track, he could have better borne it. They would have had a beginning and an end, but here all space was full. The one pursuing voice was everywhere: it sounded in the earth, the air; shook the long grass, and howled among the trembling trees. The echoes caught it up, the owls hooted as it flew upon the breeze, the nightingale was silent and hid herself among the thickest boughs: it seemed to goad and urge the angry fire, and lash it into madness; everything was steeped in one prevailing red; the glow was everywhere; nature was drenched in blood: still the remorseless crying of that awful voice—the Bell, the Bell!

It ceased; but not in his ears. The knell was at his heart. No work of man had ever voice like that which sounded there, and warned him that it cried unceasingly to Heaven. Who could hear that bell, and not know what it said! There was murder in its every note— cruel, relentless, savage murder—the murder of a confiding man, by one who held his every trust. Its ringing summoned phantoms from their graves. What face was that, in which a friendly smile changed to a look of half incredulous horror, which stiffened for a moment into one of pain, then changed again into an imploring glance at Heaven, and so fell idly down with upturned eyes, like the dead stags he had often peeped at when a little child: shrinking and shuddering—there was a dreadful thing to think of now!— and clinging to an apron as he looked! He sank upon the ground, and grovelling down as if he would dig himself a place to hide in, covered his face and ears: but no, no, no—a hundred walls and roofs of brass would not shut out that bell, for in it spoke the wrathful voice of God, and from that, the whole wide universe could not afford a refuge!

While he rushed up and down, not knowing where to turn, and while he lay crouching there, the work went briskly on indeed. When they left the Maypole, the rioters formed into a solid body, and advanced at a quick pace to the Warren. Rumour of their approach having gone before, they found the garden doors fast closed, the windows made secure, and the house profoundly dark: not a light being visible in any portion of the building. After some fruitless ringing at the bells, and beating at the iron gates, they drew off a few paces to reconnoitre, and confer upon the course it would be best to take.

Very little conference was needed, when all were bent upon one desperate purpose, infuriated with liquor, and flushed with successful riot. The word being given to surround the house, some climbed the gates, or dropped into the shallow trench and scaled the garden wall, while others pulled down the solid iron fence, and while they made a breach to enter by, made deadly weapons of the bars. The house being completely encircled, a small number of men were despatched to break open a tool-shed in the garden; and during their absence on this errand, the remainder contented themselves with knocking violently at the doors, and calling to those within, to come down and open them on peril of their lives.

No answer being returned to this repeated summons, and the detachment who had been sent away, coming back with an accession of pickaxes, spades, and hoes, they,—together with those who had such arms already, or carried (as many did) axes, poles, and crowbars,—struggled into the foremost rank, ready to beset the doors and windows. They had not at this time more than a dozen lighted torches among them; but when these preparations were completed, flaming links were distributed and passed from hand to hand with such rapidity, that, in a minute's time, at least two-thirds of the whole roaring mass, bore, each man in his hand, a blazing brand. Whirling these about their heads they raised a loud shout, and fell to work upon the doors and windows.

Amidst the clattering of heavy blows, the rattling of broken glass, the cries and execrations of the mob, and all the din and turmoil of the scene, Hugh and his friends kept together at the turret door where Mr. Haredale had last admitted him and old John Willet; and spent their united force on that. It was a strong old oaken door, guarded by good bolts and a heavy bar, but it soon went crashing in upon the narrow stairs behind, and made, as it were, a platform to facilitate their tearing up into the rooms above. Almost at the same moment, a dozen other points were forced, and at every one the crowd poured in like water.

A few armed servant-men were posted in the hall, and when the rioters forced an entrance there, they fired some half-a-dozen shots. But these taking no effect, and the concourse coming on like an army of devils, they only thought of consulting their own safety, and retreated, echoing their assailants' cries, and hoping in the confusion to be taken for rioters themselves; in which stratagem they succeeded, with the exception of one old man who was never heard of again, and was said to have had his brains beaten out with an iron bar (one of his fellows reported that he had seen the old man fall), and to have been afterwards burnt in the flames.

The besiegers being now in complete possession of the house, spread themselves over it from garret to cellar, and plied their demon labours fiercely. While some small parties kindled bonfires underneath the windows, others broke up the furniture and cast the fragments down to feed the flames below; where the apertures in the wall (windows no longer) were large enough, they hurled out tables, chests of drawers, beds, mirrors, pictures, and flung them whole into the fire; while every fresh addition to the blazing masses was received with shouts, and howls, and yells, which added new and dismal terrors to the conflagration. Those who had axes and had spent their fury on the moveables, chopped and tore down the doors and window frames, broke up the flooring, hewed away the rafters, and buried men who lingered in the upper rooms, in heaps of ruins. Some searched the drawers, the chests, the boxes, writing-desks, and closets, for jewels, plate, and money; while others less mindful of gain and more mad for destruction, cast their whole contents into the court-yard without examination, and called to those below, to heap them on the blaze. Men who had been into the cellars, and had staved the casks, rushed to and fro stark mad, setting fire to all they saw—often to the dresses of their own friends—and kindling the building in so many parts that some had no time for escape, and were seen, with drooping hands and blackened faces, hanging senseless on the window-sills to which they had crawled, until they were sucked and drawn into the burning gulf. The more the fire crackled and raged, the wilder and more cruel the men grew; as though moving in that element they became fiends, and changed their earthly nature for the qualities that give delight in hell.

The burning pile, revealing rooms and passages red hot, through gaps made in the crumbling walls; the tributary fires that licked the outer bricks and stones, with their long forked tongues, and ran up to meet the glowing mass within; the shining of the flames upon the villains who looked on and fed them; the roaring of the angry blaze, so bright and high that it seemed in its rapacity to have swallowed up the very smoke; the living flakes the wind bore rapidly away and hurried on with, like a storm of fiery snow; the noiseless breaking of great beams of wood, which fell like feathers on the heap of ashes, and crumbled in the very act to sparks and powder; the lurid tinge that overspread the sky, and the darkness, very deep by contrast, which prevailed around; the exposure to the coarse, common gaze, of every little nook which usages of home had made a sacred place, and the destruction by rude hands of every little household favourite which old associations made a dear and precious thing: all this taking place—not among pitying looks and friendly murmurs of compassion, but brutal shouts and exultations, which seemed to make the very rats who stood by the old house too long, creatures with some claim upon the pity and regard of those its roof had sheltered:— combined to form a scene never to be forgotten by those who saw it and were not actors in the work, so long as life endured.

And who were they? The alarm-bell rang—and it was pulled by no faint or hesitating hands—for a long time; but not a soul was seen. Some of the insurgents said that when it ceased, they heard the shrieks of women, and saw some garments fluttering in the air, as a party of men bore away no unresisting burdens. No one could say that this was true or false, in such an uproar; but where was Hugh? Who among them had seen him, since the forcing of the doors? The cry spread through the body. Where was Hugh?

"Here!" he hoarsely cried, appearing from the darkness; out of breath, and blackened with the smoke. "We have done all we can; the fire is burning itself out; and even the corners where it hasn't spread, are nothing but heaps of ruins. Disperse my lads, while the coast's clear; get back by different ways; and meet as usual!" With that he disappeared again,—contrary to his wont, for he was always first to advance, and last to go away,—leaving them to follow homewards as they would.

It was not an easy task to draw off such a throng. If Bedlam gates had been flung open wide, there would not have issued forth such maniacs as the frenzy of that night had made. There were men there, who danced and trampled on the beds of flowers as though they trod down human enemies; and wrenched them from the stalks, like savages who twisted human necks. There were men who cast their lighted torches in the air, and suffered them to fall upon their heads and faces, blistering the skin with deep unseemly burns. There were men who rushed up to the fire, and paddled in it with their hands as if in water; and others who were restrained by force from plunging in, to gratify their deadly longing. On the skull of one drunken lad— not twenty, by his looks—who lay upon the ground with a bottle to his mouth, the lead from the roof came streaming down in a shower of liquid fire, white hot; melting his head like wax. When the scattered parties were collected, men—living yet, but singed as with hot irons—were plucked out of the cellars, and carried off upon the shoulders of others, who strove to wake them as they went along, with ribald jokes, and left them, dead, in the passages of hospitals. But of all the howling throng not one learnt mercy from, or sickened at, these sights; nor was the fierce, besotted, senseless rage of one man glutted.

Slowly, and in small clusters, with hoarse hurrahs and repetitions of their usual cry, the assembly dropped away. The last few red-eyed stragglers reeled after those who had gone before; the distant noise of men calling to each other, and whistling for others whom they missed, grew fainter and fainter; at length even these sounds died away, and silence reigned alone.

Silence indeed! The glare of the flames had sunk into a fitful, flashing light; and the gentle stars, invisible till now, looked down upon the blackening heap. A dull smoke hung upon the ruin, as though to hide it from those eyes of Heaven; and the wind forbore to move it. Bare walls, roof open to the sky—chambers, where the beloved dead had many and many a fair day risen to new life and energy; where so many dear ones had been sad and merry; which were connected with so many thoughts and hopes, regrets and changes—all gone. Nothing left but a dull and dreary blank—a smouldering heap of dust and ashes—the silence and solitude of utter desolation.

CHAPTER THE FIFTY-SIXTH.

THE Maypole cronies, little dreaming of the change so soon to come upon their favourite haunt, struck through the Forest path upon their way to London; and avoiding the main road, which was hot and dusty, kept to the bye paths and the fields. As they drew nearer to their destination, they began to make inquiries of the people whom they passed, concerning the riots, and the truth or falsehood of the stories they had heard. The answers went far beyond any intelligence that had spread to quiet Chigwell. One man told them that that afternoon the Guards, conveying to Newgate some rioters who had been re-examined, had been set upon by the mob and compelled to retreat; another, that the houses of two witnesses near Clare Market* were about to be pulled down when he came away; another, that Sir George Saville's house in Leicester Fields was to be burned that night, and that it would go hard with Sir George if he fell into the people's hands, as it was he who had brought in the Catholic bill. All accounts agreed that the mob were out, in stronger numbers and more numerous parties than had yet appeared; that the streets were unsafe; that no man's house or life was worth an hour's purchase; that the public consternation was increasing every moment; and that many families had already fled the city. One fellow who wore the popular colour, damned them for not having cockades in their hats, and bade them set a good watch to-morrow-night upon the prison doors, for the locks would have a straining; another asked if they were fire-proof, that they walked abroad without the distinguishing mark of all good and true men; and a third who rode on horseback, and was quite alone, ordered them to throw, each man a shilling, in his hat, towards the support of the rioters. Although they were afraid to refuse compliance with this demand, and were much alarmed by these reports, they agreed, having come so far, to go forward, and see the real state of things with their own eyes. So they pushed on quicker, as men do who are excited by portentous news; and ruminating on what they had heard, spoke little to each other.

It was now night, and as they came nearer to the city they had dismal confirmation of this intelligence in three great fires, all close together, which burnt fiercely and were gloomily reflected in the sky. Arriving in the immediate suburbs, they found that almost every house had chalked upon its door in large characters "No Popery," that the shops were shut, and that alarm and anxiety were depicted in every face they passed.

Noting these things with a degree of apprehension which neither of the three cared to impart, in its full extent, to his companions, they came to a turnpike gate, which was shut. They were passing through the turnstile on the path, when a horseman rode up from London at a hard gallop, and called to the toll-keeper in a voice of great agitation, to open quickly in the name of God.

The adjuration was so earnest and vehement, that the man, with a lantern in his hand, came running out—toll-keeper though he was— and was about to throw the gate open, when happening to look behind him, he exclaimed, "Good Heaven, what's that! Another Fire!"

At this, the three turned their heads, and saw in the distance— straight in the direction whence they had come—a broad sheet of flame, casting a threatening light upon the clouds, which glimmered as though the conflagration were behind them, and showed like a wrathful sunset.

"My mind misgives me," said the horseman, "or I know from what far building those flames come. Don't stand aghast, my good fellow. Open the gate!"

"Sir," cried the man, laying his hand upon his horse's bridle as he let him through: "I know you now, sir; be advised by me; do not go on. I saw them pass, and know what kind of men they are. You will be murdered."

"So be it!" said the horseman, looking intently towards the fire, and not at him who spoke. "Leave go!"

"But Sir—Sir," cried the man, grasping at his rein more tightly yet, "if you do go on, wear the blue riband. Here, sir," he added, taking one from his own hat, and speaking so earnestly that the tears stood in his eyes: "it's necessity, not choice, that makes me wear it: it's love of life and home, sir. Wear it for this one night, sir; only for this one night."

"Do!" cried the three friends, pressing round his horse. "Mr. Haredale—worthy sir—good gentleman—pray be persuaded."

"Who's that?" cried Mr. Haredale, stooping down to look. "Did I hear Daisy's voice?"

"You did, sir," cried the little man. "Do be persuaded, sir. This gentleman says very true. Your life may hang upon it."

"Are you," said Mr. Haredale abruptly, "afraid to come with me?"

"I, sir?—N-n-no."

"Put that riband in your hat. If we meet the rioters, swear that I took you prisoner for wearing it. I will tell them so with my own lips; for as I hope for mercy when I die, I will take no quarter from them, nor shall they have quarter from me, if we come hand to hand tonight. Up here—behind me—quick! Clasp me tight round the body, and fear nothing."

In an instant they were riding away, at full gallop, in a dense cloud of dust, and speeding on like hunters in a dream.

It was well the good horse knew the road he traversed, for never once—no, never once in all the journey—did Mr. Haredale cast his eyes upon the ground, or turn them, for an instant, from the light towards which they sped so madly. Once he said in a low voice "It *is* my house," but that was the only time he spoke. When they came to dark and doubtful places, he never forgot to put his hand upon the little man to hold him more securely on his seat, but he kept his head erect and his eyes fixed on the fire, then, and always.

The road was dangerous enough, for they went the nearest way— headlong—far from the highway—by lonely lanes and paths, where waggon-wheels had worn deep ruts; where hedge and ditch hemmed in the narrow strip of ground; and tall trees, arching overhead, made it profoundly dark. But on, on, on, with neither stop nor stumble, till they reached the Maypole door, and could plainly see that the Fire began to fade, as if for want of fuel.

"Down—for one moment—for but one moment," said Mr. Haredale, helping Daisy to the ground, and following himself. "Willet—Willet—where are my niece and servants—Willet!"

Crying out to him distractedly, he rushed into the bar.—The landlord bound and fastened to his chair; the place dismantled, stripped, and pulled about his ears;—nobody could have taken shelter here.

He was a strong man, accustomed to restrain himself, and suppress his strong emotions; but this preparation for what was to follow—though he had seen that fire burning, and knew that his house must be razed to the ground—was more than he could bear. He covered his face with his hands for a moment, and turned away his head.

"Johnny, Johnny," said Solomon—and the simple-hearted fellow cried outright, and wrung his hands—"Oh dear old Johnny, here's a change. That the Maypole bar should come to this, and we should live to see it! The old Warren too, Johnny—Mr. Haredale—oh, Johnny, what a piteous sight this is!"

Pointing to Mr. Haredale as he said these words, little Solomon Daisy put his elbows on the back of Mr. Willet's chair, and fairly blubbered on his shoulder.

While Solomon was speaking, old John sat, mute as a stock-fish, staring at him with an unearthly glare, and displaying, by every possible symptom, entire and most complete unconsciousness. But when Solomon was silent again, John followed, with his great round eyes, the direction of his looks, and did appear to have some dawning distant notion that somebody had come to see him.

"You know us, don't you, Johnny?" said the little clerk, rapping himself on the breast. "Daisy, you know—Chigwell Church—bell-ringer—little desk on Sundays—eh, Johnny?"

Mr. Willet reflected for a few moments, and then muttered, as it were mechanically: "Let us sing to the praise and glory of—"

"Yes, to be sure," cried the little man, hastily; "that's it—that's me, Johnny. You're all right now, an't you? Say you're all right, Johnny."

"All right?" pondered Mr. Willet, as if that were a matter entirely between himself and his conscience. "All right? Ah!"

"They haven't been misusing you with sticks, or pokers, or any other blunt instruments,—have they, Johnny?" asked Solomon, with a very anxious glance at Mr. Willet's head. "They didn't beat you, did they?"

John knitted his brow; looked downwards, as if he were mentally engaged in some arithmetical calculation; then upwards, as if the total would not come at his call; then at Solomon Daisy, from his eyebrow to his shoe-buckle; then very slowly round the bar. And then a great, round, leaden-looking, and not at all transparent tear, came rolling out of each eye, and he said, as he shook his head:

"If they'd only had the goodness to murder me, I'd have thanked 'em kindly."

"No, no, no, don't say that, Johnny," whimpered his little friend. "It's very—very bad, but not quite so bad as that. No, no!"

"Look'ee here, sir!" cried John, turning his rueful eyes on Mr. Haredale, who had dropped on one knee, and was hastily beginning to untie his bonds. "Look'ee here, sir! The very Maypole—the old dumb Maypole—stares in at the winder, as if it said, 'John Willet, John Willet, let's go and pitch ourselves in the nighest pool of water as is deep enough to hold us; for our day is over!'"

"Don't, Johnny, don't," cried his friend: no less affected by this mournful effort of Mr. Willet's imagination, than by the sepulchral tone in which he had spoken for the Maypole. "Please don't, Johnny!"

"Your loss is great, and your misfortune a heavy one," said Mr. Haredale, looking restlessly towards the door: "and this is not a time to comfort you. If it were, I am in no condition to do so. Before I leave you, tell me one thing, and try to tell me truly and plainly, I implore you. Have you seen, or heard of Emma?"

"No!" said Mr. Willet.

"Nor any one, but these blood-hounds?"

"No!"

"They rode away, I trust in Heaven, before these dreadful scenes began," said Mr. Haredale, who, between his agitation, his eagerness to mount his horse again, and the dexterity with which the cords were tied, had scarcely yet undone one knot. "A knife, Daisy."

"You didn't," said John, looking about, as though he had lost his pocket-handkerchief or some such slight article—"either of you gentlemen—see a—a coffin anywheres, did you?"

"Willet!" cried Mr. Haredale. Solomon dropped the knife, and instantly becoming limp from head to foot, exclaimed "Good gracious!"

"—Because," said John, not at all regarding them, "a dead man called a little time ago, on his way yonder. I could have told you what name was on the plate, if he had brought his coffin with him, and left it behind. If he didn't, it don't signify."

His landlord, who had listened to these words with breathless attention, started that moment to his feet; and, without a word, drew Solomon Daisy to the door, mounted his horse, took him up behind again, and flew rather than galloped towards the pile of ruins, which that day's sun had shone upon, a stately house. Mr. Willet stared after them, listened, looked down upon himself to make quite sure that he was still unbound, and, without any manifestation of impatience, disappointment, or surprise, gently relapsed into the condition from which he had so imperfectly recovered.

Mr. Haredale tied his horse to the trunk of a tree, and grasping his companion's arm, stole softly along the footpath, and into what had been the garden of his house. He stopped for an instant to look upon its smoking walls, and at the stars that shone through roof and floor upon the heap of crumbling ashes. Solomon glanced timidly in his face, but his lips were tightly pressed together, a resolute and stern expression sat upon his brow, and not a tear, a look, or gesture indicating grief, escaped him.

He drew his sword; felt for a moment in his breast, as though he carried other arms about him; then grasping Solomon by the wrist again, went with a cautious step all round the house. He looked into every doorway and gap in the wall; retraced his steps at every rust- ling of the air among the leaves; and searched in every shadowed nook with outstretched hands. Thus they made the circuit of the building: but they returned to the spot from which they had set out, without encountering any human being, or finding the least trace of any concealed straggler.

After a short pause, Mr. Haredale shouted twice or thrice. Then cried aloud, "Is there any one in hiding here, who knows my voice! There is nothing to fear now. If any of my people are near, I entreat them to answer!" He called them all by name; his voice was echoed in many mournful tones; then all was silent as before.

They were standing near the foot of the turret, where the alarm- bell hung. The fire had raged there, and the floors had been sawn, and hewn, and beaten down, besides. It was open to the night; but a part of the staircase still remained, winding upwards from a great mound of dust and cinders. Fragments of the jagged and broken steps offered an insecure and giddy footing here and there, and then were lost again, behind protruding angles of the wall, or in the deep shadows cast upon it by other portions of the ruin; for by this time the moon had risen, and shone brightly.

As they stood here, listening to the echoes as they died away, and hoping in vain to hear a voice they knew, some of the ashes in this turret slipped and rolled down. Startled by the least noise in that melancholy place, Solomon looked up at his companion's face, and saw that he had turned towards the spot, and that he watched and listened keenly.

He covered the little man's mouth with his hand, and looked again. Instantly, with kindling eyes, he bade him on his life keep still, and neither speak nor move. Then holding his breath, and stooping down, he stole into the turret, with his drawn sword in his hand, and disappeared.

Terrified to be left there by himself, under such desolate circumstances, and after all he had seen and heard that night, Solomon would have followed, but there had been something in Mr. Haredale's manner and his look, the recollection of which held him spell-bound. He stood rooted to the spot; and scarcely venturing to breathe, looked up with mingled fear and wonder.

Again the ashes slipped and rolled—very, very softly—again—and then again, as though they crumbled underneath the tread of a stealthy foot. And now a figure was dimly visible; climbing very softly; and often stopping to look down: now it pursued its difficult way; and now it was hidden from the view again.

It emerged once more, into the shadowy and uncertain light—higher now, but not much, for the way was steep and toilsome, and its progress very slow. What phantom of the brain did he pursue; and why did he look down so constantly? He knew he was alone. Surely his mind was not affected by that night's loss and agony. He was not about to throw himself headlong from the summit of the tottering wall. Solomon turned sick, and clasped his hands. His limbs trembled beneath him, and a cold sweat broke out upon his pallid face.

If he complied with Mr. Haredale's last injunction now, it was because he had not the power to speak or move. He strained his gaze, and fixed it on a patch of moonlight, into which, if he continued to ascend, he must soon emerge. When he appeared there, he would try to call to him.

Again the ashes slipped and crumbled; some stones rolled down, and fell with a dull heavy sound upon the ground below. He kept his eyes upon the piece of moonlight. The figure was coming on, for its shadow was already thrown upon the wall. Now it appeared—and now looked round at him—and now—

The horror-stricken clerk uttered a scream that pierced the air, and cried "The ghost again! The ghost!"

Long before the echo of that cry had died away, another form rushed out into the light, flung itself upon the foremost one, knelt down upon its breast, and clutched its throat with both hands.

"Villain!" cried Mr. Haredale, in a terrible voice—for it was he. "Dead and buried, as all men supposed through your infernal arts, but reserved by Heaven for this—at last—at last—I have you. You, whose hands are red with my brother's blood, and that of his faithful servant, shed to conceal your own atrocious guilt—You, Rudge, double murderer and monster, I arrest you in the name of God, who has delivered you into my hands. Nay. Though you had the strength of twenty men," he added, as he writhed and struggled, "you could not escape me, or loosen my grasp to-night!"

CHAPTER THE FIFTY-SEVENTH.

ARNABY, armed as we have seen, continued to pace up and down before the stable-door; glad to be alone again, and heartily rejoicing in the unaccustomed silence and tranquillity. After the whirl of noise and riot in which the last two days had been passed, the pleasures of solitude and peace were enhanced a thousandfold. He felt quite happy; and as he leaned upon his staff and mused, a bright smile overspread his face, and none but cheerful visions floated into his brain.

Had he no thoughts of her, whose sole delight he was, and whom he had unconsciously plunged in such bitter sorrow and such deep affliction? Oh, yes. She was at the heart of all his cheerful hopes and proud reflections. It was she whom all this honour and distinction were to gladden; the joy and profit were for her. What delight it gave her to hear of the bravery of her poor boy! Ah! He would have known that without Hugh's telling him. And what a precious thing it was to know she lived so happily, and heard with so much pride (he pictured to himself her look when they told her) that he was in such high esteem: bold among the boldest, and trusted before them all. And when these frays were over, and the good Lord had conquered his enemies, and they were all at peace again, and he and she were rich, what happiness they would have in talking of these troubled times when he was a great soldier: and when they sat alone together in the tranquil twilight, and she had no longer reason to be anxious for the morrow, what pleasure would he have in the reflection that this was his doing—his—poor foolish Barnaby's; and in patting her on the cheek, and saying with a merry laugh, "Am I silly now, mother—am I silly now?"

With a lighter heart and step, and eyes the brighter for the happy tear that dimmed them for a moment, Barnaby resumed his walk; and singing gaily to himself, kept guard upon his quiet post.

His comrade Grip, the partner of his watch, though fond of basking in the sunshine, preferred to-day to walk about the stable; having a great deal to do in the way of scattering the straw, hiding under it such small articles as had been casually left about, and haunting Hugh's bed, to which he seemed to have taken a particular attachment. Sometimes Barnaby looked in and called him, and then he came hopping out; but he merely did this as a concession to his master's weakness, and soon returned again to his own grave pursuits: peering into the straw with his bill, and rapidly covering up the place, as if he were whispering secrets to the earth and burying them; constantly busying himself upon the sly; and affecting, whenever Barnaby came past, to look up in the clouds and have nothing whatever on his mind: in short, conducting himself, in many respects, in a more than usually thoughtful, deep, and mysterious manner.

As the day crept on, Barnaby, who had no directions forbidding him to eat and drink upon his post, but had been, on the contrary, supplied with a bottle of beer and a basket of provisions, determined to break his fast, which he had not done since morning. To this end, he sat down on the ground before the door, and putting his staff across his knees in case of alarm or surprise, summoned Grip to dinner.

This call, the bird obeyed with great alacrity; crying, as he sidled up to his master, "I'm a devil, I'm a devil, I'm a Polly, I'm a kettle, I'm a Protestant, No Popery!" Having learnt this latter sentiment from the gentry among whom he had lived of late, he delivered it with uncommon emphasis.

"Well said, Grip!" cried his master, as he fed him with the daintiest bits. "Well said, old boy!"

"Never say die, bow wow wow, keep up your spirits, Grip Grip Grip. Holloa! We'll all have tea, I'm a Protestant kettle, No Popery!" cried the raven.

"Gordon for ever, Grip!" cried Barnaby.

The raven, placing his head upon the ground, looked at his master sideways, as though he would have said, "Say that again!" Perfectly understanding his desire, Barnaby repeated the phrase a great many times. The bird listened with profound attention; sometimes repeating the popular cry in a low voice, as if to compare the two, and try if it would at all help him to this new accomplishment; sometimes flapping his wings, or barking; and sometimes in a kind of desperation drawing a multitude of corks, with extraordinary viciousness.

Barnaby was so intent upon his favourite, that he was not at first aware of the approach of two persons on horseback, who were riding at a foot-pace, and coming straight towards his post. When he perceived them, however, which he did when they were within some fifty yards of him, he jumped hastily up, and ordering Grip within doors, stood with both hands on his staff, waiting until he should know whether they were friends or foes.

He had hardly done so, when he observed that those who advanced were a gentleman and his servant; almost at the same moment, he recognised Lord George Gordon, before whom he stood uncovered, with his eyes turned towards the ground.

"Good day!" said Lord George, not reining in his horse until he was close beside him. "Well!"

"All quiet, sir, all safe!" cried Barnaby. "The rest are away—they went by that path—that one. A grand party!"

"Ay?" said Lord George, looking thoughtfully at him. "And you?"—

"Oh! They left me here to watch—to mount guard—to keep everything secure till they come back. I'll do it, sir, for your sake. You're a good gentleman; a kind gentleman—ay, you are. There are many against you, but we'll be a match for them, never fear!"

"What's that?" said Lord George—pointing to the raven who was peeping out of the stable-door—but still looking thoughtfully, and in some perplexity, it seemed, at Barnaby.

"Why, don't you know!" retorted Barnaby, with a wondering laugh. "Not know what *he* is! A bird, to be sure. My bird—my friend—Grip."

"A devil, a kettle, a Grip, a Polly, a Protestant—no Popery!" cried the raven.

"Though, indeed," added Barnaby, laying his hand upon the neck of Lord George's horse, and speaking softly: "you had good reason to ask me what he is, for sometimes it puzzles me—and I am used to him—to think he's only a bird. Ha ha ha! He's my brother, Grip is—always with me—always talking—always merry—eh, Grip?"

The raven answered by an affectionate croak, and hopping on his master's arm, which he held downward for that purpose, submitted with an air of perfect indifference to be fondled, and turned his restless, curious eye, now upon Lord George, and now upon his man.

Lord George, biting his nails in a discomfited manner, regarded Barnaby for some time in silence; then beckoning to his servant, said:

"Come hither, John."

John Grueby touched his hat, and came.

"Have you ever seen this young man before?" his master asked, in a low voice.

"Twice, my Lord," said John. "I saw him in the crowd last night and Saturday."

"Did—did it seem to you that his manner was at all wild, or strange?" Lord George demanded, faltering.

"Mad," said John, with emphatic brevity.

"And why do you think him mad, sir?" said his master, speaking in a peevish tone. "Don't use that word too freely. Why do you think him mad?"

"My Lord," John Grueby answered, "look at his dress, look at his eyes, look at his restless way, hear him cry 'No Popery!' Mad, my Lord."

"So because one man dresses unlike another," returned his angry master, glancing at himself, "and happens to differ from other men in his carriage and manner, and to advocate a great cause which the corrupt and irreligious desert, he is to be accounted mad, is he?"

"Stark, staring, raving mad, my Lord," returned the unmoved John.

"Do you say this to my face?" cried his master, turning sharply upon him.

"To any man, my Lord, who asks me," answered John.

"Mr. Gashford, I find, was right," said Lord George; "I thought him prejudiced, though I ought to have known a man like him better, than to have supposed it possible!"

"I shall never have Mr. Gashford's good word, my Lord," replied John, touching his hat respectfully, "and I don't covet it."

"You are an ill-conditioned, most ungrateful fellow," said Lord George: "a spy, for anything I know. Mr. Gashford is perfectly correct, as I might have felt convinced he was. I have done wrong to retain you in my service. It is a tacit insult to him as my choice and confidential friend to do so, remembering the cause you sided with, on the day he was maligned at Westminster. You will leave me to-night—nay, as soon as we reach home. The sooner, the better."

"If it comes to that, I say so too, my Lord. Let Mr. Gashford have his will. As to my being a spy, my Lord, you know me better than to believe it, I am sure. I don't know much about causes. My cause is the cause of one man against two hundred; and I hope it always will be."

"You have said quite enough," returned Lord George, motioning him to go back. "I desire to hear no more."

"If you'll let me add another word, my Lord," returned John Grueby, "I'd give this silly fellow a caution not to stay here by himself. The proclamation is in a good many hands already, and it's well known that he was concerned in the business it relates to. He had better get to a place of safety if he can, poor creature."

"You hear what this man says?" cried Lord George, addressing Barnaby, who had looked on and wondered while this dialogue passed. "He thinks you may be afraid to remain upon your post, and are kept here perhaps against your will. What do you say?"

"I think, young man," said John, in explanation, "that the soldiers may turn out and take you; and that if they do, you will certainly be hung by the neck till you're dead—dead—dead. And I think you'd better go from here, as fast as you can. That's what *I* think."

"He's a coward, Grip, a coward!" cried Barnaby, putting the raven on the ground, and shouldering his staff. "Let them come! Gordon for ever! Let them come!"

"Ay!" said Lord George, "let them! Let us see who will venture to attack a power like ours; the solemn league* of a whole people. *This* a madman! You have said well, very well. I am proud to be the leader of such men as you.

Barnaby's heart swelled within his bosom as he heard these words. He took Lord George's hand and carried it to his lips; patted his horse's crest, as if the affection and admiration he had conceived for the man extended to the animal he rode; then unfurled his flag, and proudly waving it, resumed his pacing up and down.

Lord George, with a kindling eye and glowing cheek, took off his hat, and flourishing it above his head, bade him exultingly Farewell!—then cantered off at a brisk pace; after glancing angrily round to see that his servant followed. Honest John set spurs to his horse and rode after his master, but not before he had again warned Barnaby to retreat, with many significant gestures, which indeed he continued to make, and Barnaby to resist, until the windings of the road concealed them from each other's view.

Left to himself again with a still higher sense of the importance of his post, and stimulated to enthusiasm by the special notice and encouragement of his leader, Barnaby walked to and fro in a delicious trance rather than as a waking man. The sunshine which prevailed around was in his mind. He had but one desire ungratified. If she could only see him now!

The day wore on; its heat was gently giving place to the cool of evening; a light wind sprung up, fanning his long hair, and making the banner rustle pleasantly above his head. There was a freedom and freshness in the sound and in the time, which chimed exactly with his mood. He was happier than ever.

He was leaning on his staff looking towards the declining sun, and reflecting with a smile that he stood sentinel at that moment over buried gold, when two or three figures appeared in the distance, making towards the house at a rapid pace, and motioning with their hands as though they urged its inmates to retreat from some approaching danger. As they drew nearer, they became more earnest in their gestures; and they were no sooner within hearing, than the foremost among them cried that the soldiers were coming up.

At these words, Barnaby furled his flag, and tied it round the pole.

His heart beat high while he did so, but he had no more fear or thought of retreating than the pole itself. The friendly stragglers hurried past him, after giving him notice of his danger, and quickly passed into the house, where the utmost confusion immediately prevailed. As those within hastily closed the windows and the doors, they urged him by looks and signs to fly without loss of time, and called to him many times to do so; but he only shook his head indignantly in answer, and stood the firmer on his post. Finding that he was not to be persuaded, they took care of themselves; and leaving the place with only one old woman in it, speedily withdrew.

As yet there had been no symptom of the news having any better foundation than in the fears of those who brought it, but the Boot had not been deserted five minutes, when there appeared, coming across the fields, a body of men who, it was easy to see, by the glitter of their arms and ornaments in the sun, and by their orderly and regular mode of advancing—for they came on as one man—were soldiers. In a very little time, Barnaby knew that they were a strong detachment of the Foot Guards, having along with them two gentlemen in private clothes, and a small party of Horse; the latter brought up the rear, and were not in number more than six or eight.

They advanced steadily; neither quickening their pace as they came nearer, nor raising any cry, nor showing the least emotion or anxiety. Though this was a matter of course in the case of regular troops, even to Barnaby, there was something particularly impressive and disconcerting in it to one accustomed to the noise and tumult of an undisciplined mob. For all that, he stood his ground not a whit the less resolutely, and looked on undismayed.

Presently, they marched into the yard, and halted. The commanding officer despatched a messenger to the horsemen, one of whom came riding back. Some words passed between them, and they glanced at Barnaby; who well remembered the man he had unhorsed at Westminster, and saw him now before his eyes. The man being speedily dismissed, saluted, and rode back to his comrades, who were drawn up apart at a short distance.

The officer then gave the word to prime and load. The heavy ringing of the musket-stocks upon the ground, and the sharp and rapid rattling of the ramrods in their barrels, were a kind of relief to Barnaby, deadly though he knew the purport of such sounds to be. When this was done, other commands were given, and the soldiers instantaneously formed in single file all round the house and stables; completely encircling them in every part, at a distance, perhaps, of some half-dozen yards; at least that seemed in Barnaby's eyes to be about the space left between himself and those who confronted him. The horsemen remained drawn up by themselves as before.

The two gentlemen in private clothes who had kept aloof, now rode forward, one on either side the officer. The proclamation having been produced and read by one of them, the officer called on Barnaby to surrender.

He made no answer, but stepping within the door, before which he had kept guard, held his pole crosswise to protect it. In the midst of a profound silence, he was again called upon to yield.

Still he offered no reply. Indeed he had enough to do, to run his eye backward and forward along the half-dozen men who immediately fronted him, and settle hurriedly within himself at which of them he would strike first, when they pressed on him. He caught the eye of one in the centre, and resolved to hew that fellow down, though he died for it.

Again there was a dead silence, and again the same voice called upon him to deliver himself up.

Next moment he was back in the stable, dealing blows about him like a madman. Two of the men lay stretched at his feet: the one he had marked, dropped first—he had a thought for that, even in the hot blood and hurry of the struggle. Another blow—another! Down, mastered, wounded in the breast by a heavy blow from the butt-end of a gun (he saw the weapon in the act of falling)—breathless—and a prisoner.

An exclamation of surprise from the officer recalled him, in some degree, to himself. He looked round. Grip, after working in secret all the afternoon, and with redoubled vigour while everybody's attention was distracted, had plucked away the straw from Hugh's bed, and turned up the loose ground with his iron bill. The hole had been recklessly filled to the brim, and was merely sprinkled with earth. Golden cups, spoons, candlesticks, coined guineas—all the riches were revealed.

They brought spades and a sack; dug up everything that was hidden there; and carried away more than two men could lift. They handcuffed him and bound his arms, searched him, and took away all he had. Nobody questioned or reproached him, or seemed to have much curiosity about him. The two men he had stunned, were carried off by their companions in the same business-like way in which everything else was done. Finally, he was left under a guard of four soldiers with fixed bayonets, while the officer directed in person the search of the house and the other buildings connected with it.

This was soon completed. The soldiers formed again in the yard; he was marched out, with his guard about him; and ordered to fall in, where a space was left. The others closed up all round, and so they moved away, with the prisoner in the centre.

When they came into the streets, he felt he was a sight; and looking up as they passed quickly along, could see people running to the windows a little too late, and throwing up the sashes to look after him. Sometimes he met a staring face beyond the heads about him, or under the arms of his conductors, or peering down upon him from a waggon-top or coach-box; but this was all he saw, being surrounded by so many men. The very noises of the streets seemed muffled and subdued; and the air came stale and hot upon him, like the sickly breath of an oven.

Tramp, tramp. Tramp, tramp. Heads erect, shoulders square, every man stepping in exact time—all so orderly and regular—nobody looking at him—nobody seeming conscious of his presence,—he could hardly believe he was a Prisoner. But at the word, though only thought, not spoken, he felt the handcuffs galling his wrists, the cord pressing his arms to his sides: the loaded guns levelled at his head; and those cold, bright, sharp, shining points turned towards him, the mere looking down at which, now that he was bound and helpless, made the warm current of his life run cold.

CHAPTER THE FIFTY-EIGHTH.

THEY were not long in reaching the barracks, for the officer who commanded the party was desirous to avoid rousing the people by the display of military force in the streets, and was humanely anxious to give as little opportunity as possible for any attempt at rescue; knowing that it must lead to bloodshed and loss of life, and that if the civil authorities by whom he was accompanied, empowered him to order his men to fire, many innocent persons would probably fall, whom curiosity or idleness had attracted to the spot. He therefore led the party briskly on, avoiding with a merciful prudence the more public and crowded thoroughfares, and pursuing those which he deemed least likely to be infested by disorderly persons. This wise proceeding not only enabled them to gain their quarters without any interruption, but completely baffled a body of rioters who had assembled in one of the main streets, through which it was considered certain they would pass, and who remained gathered together for the purpose of releasing the prisoner from their hands, long after they had deposited him in a place of security, closed the barrack gates, and set a double guard at every entrance for its better protection.

Arrived at this place, poor Barnaby was marched into a stone-floored room, where there was a very powerful smell of tobacco, a strong thorough draft of air, and a great wooden bedstead, large enough for a score of men. Several soldiers in undress were lounging about, or eating from tin-cans; military accoutrements dangled on rows of pegs along the whitewashed wall; and some half-dozen men lay fast asleep upon their backs, snoring in concert. After remaining here just long enough to note these things, he was marched out again, and conveyed across the parade-ground to another portion of the building.

Perhaps a man never sees so much at a glance as when he is in a situation of extremity. The chances are a hundred to one, that if Barnaby had lounged in at the gate to look about him, he would have lounged out again with a very imperfect idea of the place, and would have remembered very little about it. But as he was taken handcuffed across the gravelled area, nothing escaped his notice. The dry, arid look of the dusty square, and of the bare brick building; the clothes hanging at some of the windows; and the men in their shirt-sleeves and braces, lolling with half their bodies out of the others; the green sun-blinds at the officers' quarters, and the little scanty trees in front; the drummer-boys practising in a distant court-yard; the men on drill on the parade; the two soldiers carrying a basket between them, who winked to each other as he went by, and slily pointed to their throats; the spruce Sergeant who hurried past with a cane in his hand, and under his arm a clasped book with a vellum cover; the fellows in the ground-floor rooms, furbishing and brushing up their different articles of dress, who stopped to look at him, and whose voices as they spoke together echoed loudly through the empty galleries and passages;—everything, down to the stand of muskets before the guard-house, and the drum with a pipe-clayed belt attached, in one corner, impressed itself upon his observation, as though he had noticed them in the same place a hundred times, or had been a whole day among them, in place of one brief hurried minute.

He was taken into a small paved back yard, and there they opened a great door, plated with iron, and pierced some five feet above the ground with a few holes to let in air and light. Into this dungeon he was walked straightway; and having locked him up there, and placed a sentry over him, they left him to his meditations.

The cell, or black hole, for it had those words painted on the door, was very dark, and having recently accommodated a drunken deserter, by no means clean. Barnaby felt his way to some straw at the further end, and looking towards the door, tried to accustom himself to the gloom, which, coming from the bright sunshine out of doors, was not an easy task.

There was a kind of portico or colonnade outside, and this obstructed even the little light that at the best could have found its way through the small apertures in the door. The footsteps of the sentinel echoed monotonously as he paced its stone pavement to and fro (reminding Barnaby of the watch he had so lately kept himself); and as he passed and repassed the door, he made the cell for an instant so black by the interposition of his body, that his going away again seemed like the appearance of a new ray of light, and was quite a circumstance to look for.

When the prisoner had sat sometime upon the ground, gazing at the chinks, and listening to the advancing and receding footsteps of his guard, the man stood still upon his post. Barnaby, quite unable to think, or to speculate on what would be done with him, had been lulled into a kind of doze by his regular pace; but his stopping roused him; and then he became aware that two men were in conversation under the colonnade, and very near the door of his cell.

How long they had been talking there, he could not tell, for he had fallen into an unconsciousness of his real position, and when the footsteps ceased, was answering aloud some question which seemed to have been put to him by Hugh in the stable, though of the fancied purport, either of question or reply, notwithstanding that he awoke with the latter on his lips, he had no recollection whatever. The first words that reached his ears, were these:

"Why is he brought here then, if he has to be taken away again, so soon?"

"Why where would you have him go! Damme, he's not as safe anywhere as among the king's troops, is he? What *would* you do with him? Would you hand him over to a pack of cowardly civilians, that shake in their shoes till they wear the soles out, with trembling at the threats of the ragamuffins he belongs to?"

"That's true enough."

"True enough!—I'll tell you what. I wish, Tom Green, that I was a commissioned instead of a non-commissioned officer, and that I had the command of two companies—only two companies—of my own regiment. Call me out to stop these riots—give me the needful authority, and half-a-dozen rounds of ball cartridge—"

"Ay!" said the other voice. "That's all very well, but they won't give the needful authority. If the magistrate won't give the word, what's the officer to do?"*

Not very well knowing, as it seemed, how to overcome this difficulty, the other man contented himself with damning the magistrates.

"With all my heart," said his friend.

"Where's the use of a magistrate?" returned the other voice. "What's a magistrate in this case, but an impertinent, unnecessary, unconstitutional sort of interference? Here's a proclamation. Here's a man referred to in that proclamation. Here's proof against him, and a witness on the spot. Damme! Take him out and shoot him, sir. Who wants a magistrate?"

"When does he go before Sir John Fielding?"* asked the man who had spoken first.

"To-night at eight o'clock," returned the other. "Mark what follows. The magistrate commits him to Newgate. Our people take him to Newgate. The rioters pelt our people. Our people retire before the rioters. Stones are thrown, insults are offered, not a shot's fired. Why? Because of the magistrates. Damn the magistrates!"

When he had in some degree relieved his mind by cursing the magistrates in various other forms of speech, the man was silent, save for a low growling, still having reference to those authorities, which from time to time escaped him.

Barnaby, who had wit enough to know that this conversation concerned, and very nearly concerned, himself, remained perfectly quiet until they ceased to speak, when he groped his way to the door, and peeping through the air-holes, tried to make out what kind of men they were, to whom he had been listening.

The one who condemned the civil power in such strong terms, was a serjeant—engaged just then, as the streaming ribands in his cap announced, on the recruiting service. He stood leaning sideways against a pillar nearly opposite the door, and as he growled to himself, drew figures on the pavement with his cane. The other man had his back towards the dungeon, and Barnaby could only see his form. To judge from that, he was a gallant, manly, handsome fellow, but he had lost his left arm. It had been taken off between the elbow and the shoulder, and his empty coat-sleeve hung across his breast.

It was probably this circumstance which gave him an interest beyond any that his companion could boast of, and attracted Barnaby's attention. There was something soldierly in his bearing, and he wore a jaunty cap and jacket. Perhaps he had been in the service at one time or other. If he had, it could not have been very long ago, for he was but a young fellow now.

"Well, well," he said thoughtfully; "let the fault be where it may, it makes a man sorrowful to come back to old England, and see her in this condition."

"I suppose the pigs will join 'em next," said the serjeant, with an imprecation on the rioters, "now that the birds have set 'em the example."

"The birds!" repeated Tom Green.

"Ah—birds," said the serjeant testily; "that's English, an't it?"

"I don't know what you mean."

"Go to the guard-house, and see. You'll find a bird there, that's got their cry as pat as any of 'em, and bawls 'No Popery,' like a man—or like a devil, as he says he is. I shouldn't wonder. The devil's loose in London somewhere. Damme if I wouldn't twist his neck round, on the chance, if I had *my* way."

The young man had taken two or three hasty steps away, as if to go and see this creature, when he was arrested by the voice of Barnaby.

"It's mine," he called out, half laughing and half weeping—"my pet, my friend Grip. Ha ha ha! Don't hurt him, he has done no harm. I taught him; it's my fault. Let me have him, if you please. He's the only friend I have left now. He'll not dance, or talk, or whistle for you, I know; but he will for me, because he knows me, and loves me—though you wouldn't think it—very well. You wouldn't hurt a bird, I'm sure. You're a brave soldier, sir, and wouldn't harm a woman or a child—no, no, nor a poor bird, I am certain."

This latter adjuration was addressed to the serjeant, whom Barnaby judged from his red coat to be high in office, and able to seal Grip's destiny by a word. But that gentleman, in reply, surlily damned him for a thief and rebel as he was, and with many disinterested imprecations on his own eyes, liver, blood, and body, assured him that if it rested with him to decide, he would put a final stopper on the bird, and his master too.

"You talk boldly to a caged man," said Barnaby, in anger. "If I was on the other side of the door and there were none to part us, you'd change your note—ay, you may toss your head—you would! Kill the bird—do. Kill anything you can, and so revenge yourself on those who with their bare hands untied could do as much to you!"

Having vented this defiance, he flung himself into the furthest corner of his prison, and muttering, "Good bye, Grip—good bye, dear old Grip!" shed tears for the first time since he had been taken captive; and hid his face in the straw.

He had had some fancy at first, that the one armed man would help him, or would give him a kind word in answer. He hardly knew why, but he hoped and thought so. The young fellow had stopped when he called out, and checking himself in the very act of turning round, stood listening to every word he said. Perhaps he built his feeble trust on this; perhaps on his being young, and having a frank and honest manner. However that might be, he built on sand. The other went away directly he had finished speaking, and neither answered him, nor returned. No matter. They were all against him here; he might have known as much. Good bye, old Grip, good bye!

After some time, they came and unlocked the door, and called to him to come out. He rose directly, and complied, for he would not have *them* think he was subdued or frightened. He walked out like a man, and looked haughtily from face to face.

None of them returned his gaze or seemed to notice it. They marched him back to the parade by the way they had brought him, and there they halted, among a body of soldiers, at least twice as numerous as that which had taken him prisoner in the afternoon.

The officer he had seen before, bade him in a few brief words take notice that if he attempted to escape, no matter how favourable a chance he might suppose he had, certain of the men had orders to fire upon him, that moment. They then closed round him as before, and marched him off again.

In the same unbroken order they arrived at Bow-street, followed and beset on all sides by a crowd which was continually increasing. Here he was placed before a blind gentleman, and asked if he wished to say anything. Not he. What had he got to tell them? After a very little talking, which he was careless of and quite indifferent to, they told him he was to go to Newgate, and took him away.

He went out into the street, so surrounded and hemmed in on every side by soldiers, that he could see nothing; but he knew there was a great crowd of people, by the murmur; and that they were not friendly to the soldiers, was soon rendered evident by their yells and hisses. How often and how eagerly he listened for the voice of Hugh! No. There was not a voice he knew among them all. Was Hugh a prisoner too? Was there no hope!

As they came nearer and nearer to the prison, the hootings of the people grew more violent; stones were thrown; and every now and then, a rush was made against the soldiers, which they staggered under. One of them, close before him, smarting under a blow upon the temple, levelled his musket, but the officer struck it upwards with his sword, and ordered him on peril of his life to desist. This was the last thing he saw with any distinctness, for directly afterwards he was tossed about, and beaten to and fro, as though in a tempestuous sea. But go where he would, there were the same guards about him. Twice or thrice he was thrown down, and so were they; but even then, he could not elude their vigilance for a moment. They were up again, and had closed about him, before he, with his wrists so tightly bound, could scramble to his feet. Fenced in, thus, he felt himself hoisted to the top of a low flight of steps, and then for a moment he caught a glimpse of the fighting in the crowd, and of a few red coats sprinkled together, here and there, struggling to rejoin their fellows. Next moment, everything was dark and gloomy, and he was standing in the prison lobby; the centre of a group of men.

A smith was speedily in attendance, who rivetted upon him a set of heavy irons. Stumbling on as well as he could, beneath the unusual burden of these fetters, he was conducted to a strong stone cell, where, fastening the door with locks, and bolts, and chains, they left him, well secured; having first, unseen by him, thrust in Grip, who, with his head drooping and his deep black plumage rough and rumpled, appeared to comprehend and to partake, his master's fallen fortunes.

CHAPTER THE FIFTY-NINTH.

IT is necessary at this juncture to return to Hugh, who, having, as we have seen, called to the rioters to disperse from about the Warren, and meet again as usual, glided back into the darkness from which he had emerged, and reappeared no more that night.

He paused in the copse which sheltered him from the observation of his mad companions, and waited to ascertain whether they drew off at his bidding, or still lingered and called to him to join them. Some few, he saw, were indisposed to go away without him, and made towards the spot where he stood concealed as though they were about to follow in his footsteps, and urge him to come back; but these men, being in their turn called to by their friends, and in truth not greatly caring to venture into the dark parts of the grounds where they might be easily surprised and taken, if any of the neighbours or retainers of the family were watching them from among the trees, soon abandoned the idea, and hastily assembling such men as they found of their mind at the moment, straggled off.

When he was satisfied that the great mass of the insurgents were imitating this example, and that the ground was rapidly clearing, he plunged into the thickest portion of the little wood; and crashing the branches as he went, made straight towards a distant light: guided by that, and by the sullen glow of the fire behind him.

As he drew nearer and nearer to the twinkling beacon towards which he bent his course, the red glare of a few torches began to reveal itself, and the voices of men speaking together in a subdued tone, broke the silence, which, save for a distant shouting now and then, already prevailed. At length he cleared the wood and, springing across a ditch, stood in a dark lane, where a small body of ill-looking vagabonds, whom he had left there some twenty minutes before, waited his coming with impatience.

They were gathered round an old post-chaise or chariot, driven by one of themselves, who sat postilion-wise upon the near horse. The blinds were drawn up, and Mr. Tappertit and Dennis kept guard at the two windows. The former assumed the command of the party, for he challenged Hugh as he advanced towards them; and when he did so, those who were resting on the ground about the carriage rose to their feet and clustered round him.

"Well!" said Simon, in a low voice; "is all right?"

"Right enough," replied Hugh, in the same tone. "They're dispersing now—had begun before I came away."

"And is the coast clear?"

"Clear enough before our men, I take it," said Hugh. " There are not many who, knowing of their work over yonder, will want to meddle with 'em to-night.—Who's got some drink here?"

Everybody had some plunder from the cellar; half-a-dozen flasks and bottles were offered directly. He selected the largest, and putting it to his mouth, sent the wine gurgling down his throat. Having emptied it, he threw it down, and stretched out his hand for another, which he emptied likewise, at a draught. Another was given him, and this he half emptied too. Reserving what remained, to finish with, he asked:

"Have you got anything to eat, any of you? I'm as ravenous as a hungry wolf. Which of you was in the larder—come!"

"I was, brother," said Dennis, pulling off his hat, and fumbling in the crown. "There's a matter of cold venison pasty somewhere or another here, if that'll do."

"Do!" cried Hugh, seating himself on the pathway. "Bring it out! Quick! Show a light here, and gather round! Let me sup in state, my lads. Ha ha ha!"

Entering into his boisterous humour, for they all had drunk deeply and were as wild as he, they crowded about him, while two of their number who had torches, held them up, one on either side of him, that his banquet might not be despatched in the dark. Mr. Dennis, having by this time succeeded in extricating from his hat a great mass of pasty, which had been wedged in so tightly that it was not easily got out, put it before him; and Hugh, having borrowed a notched and jagged knife from one of the company, fell to work upon it vigorously.

"I should recommend you to swallow a little fire every day, about an hour afore dinner, brother," said Dennis, after a pause. "It seems to agree with you, and to stimulate your appetite."

Hugh looked at him, and at the blackened faces by which he was surrounded, and, stopping for a moment to flourish his knife above his head, answered with a roar of laughter.

"Keep order there, will you?" said Simon Tappertit.

"Why, isn't a man allowed to regale himself, noble captain," retorted his lieutenant, parting the men who stood between them, with his knife, that he might see him, "to regale himself a little bit, after such work as mine? What a hard captain! What a strict captain! What a tyrannical captain! Ha ha ha!"

"I wish one of you fellers would hold a bottle to his mouth to keep him quiet," said Simon, "unless you want the military to be down upon us."

"And what if they are down upon us!" retorted Hugh. "Who cares? Who's afraid? Let 'em come, I say, let 'em come. The more, the merrier. Give me bold Barnaby at my side, and we two will settle the military, without troubling any of you. Barnaby's the man for the military. Barnaby's health!"

But as the majority of those present, were by no means anxious for a second engagement that night, being already weary and exhausted, they sided with Mr. Tappertit, and pressed him to make haste with his supper, for they had already delayed too long. Knowing, even in the height of his frenzy, that they incurred great danger by lingering so near the scene of the late outrages, Hugh made an end of his meal without more remonstrance, and rising, stepped up to Mr. Tappertit and smote him on the back.

"Now then," he cried, "I'm ready. There are brave birds inside this cage, eh? Delicate birds,—tender, loving, little doves. I caged 'em—I caged 'em—one more peep!"

He thrust the little man aside as he spoke, and mounting on the steps which were half let down, pulled down the blind by force, and stared into the chaise like an ogre into his larder.

"Ha ha ha! and did you scratch, and pinch, and struggle, pretty mistress?" he cried, as he grasped a little hand that sought in vain to free itself from his grip: "you, so bright-eyed, and cherry-lipped, and daintily made? But I love you better for it, mistress. Ay, I do. You should stab me and welcome, so that it pleased you, and you had to cure me afterwards. I love to see you proud and scornful. It makes you handsomer than ever; and who so handsome as you at any time, my pretty one!"

"Come!" said Mr. Tappertit, who had waited during this speech with considerable impatience. "There's enough of that. Come down."

The little hand seconded this admonition by thrusting Hugh's great head away with all its force, and drawing up the blind, amidst his noisy laughter, and vows that he must have another look, for the last glimpse of that sweet face had provoked him past all bearing. However, as the suppressed impatience of the party now broke out into open murmurs, he abandoned this design, and taking his seat upon the bar, contented himself with tapping at the front windows of the carriage, and trying to steal a glance inside; Mr. Tappertit, mounting the steps and hanging on by the door, issued his directions to the driver with a commanding voice and attitude; the rest got up behind, or ran by the side of the carriage, as they could; some, in imitation of Hugh, endeavoured to see the face he had praised so highly, and were reminded of their impertinence by hints from the cudgel of Mr. Tappertit. Thus they pursued their journey by circuitous and winding roads; preserving, except when they halted to take breath, or to quarrel about the best way of reaching London, pretty good order and tolerable silence.

In the mean time, Dolly—beautiful, bewitching, captivating little Dolly—her hair dishevelled, her dress torn, her dark eyelashes wet with tears, her bosom heaving—her face, now pale with fear, now crimsoned with indignation—her whole self a hundred times more beautiful in this heightened aspect than ever she had been before— vainly strove to comfort Emma Haredale, and to impart to her the consolation of which she stood in so much need herself. The soldiers were sure to come; they must be rescued; it would be impossible to convey them through the streets of London, when they set the threats of their guards at defiance, and shrieked to the passengers for help. If they did this, when they came into the more frequented ways, she was certain—she was quite certain—they must be released. So poor Dolly said, and so poor Dolly tried to think; but the invariable conclusion of all such arguments was, that Dolly burst into tears; cried, as she wrung her hands, what would they do or think, or who would comfort them, at home, at the Golden Key; and sobbed most piteously.

Miss Haredale, whose feelings were usually of a quieter kind than Dolly's, and not so much upon the surface, was dreadfully alarmed, and indeed had only just recovered from a swoon. She was very pale, and the hand which Dolly held was quite cold; but she bade her, nevertheless, remember that, under Providence, much must depend upon their own discretion; that if they remained quiet and lulled the vigilance of the ruffians into whose hands they had fallen, the chances of their being able to procure assistance when they reached the town, were very much increased; that unless society were quite unhinged, a hot pursuit must be immediately commenced; and that her uncle, she might be sure, would never rest until he had found them out and rescued them. But as she said these latter words, the idea that he had fallen in a general massacre of the Catholics that night—no very wild or improbable supposition, after what they had seen and undergone—struck her dumb; and, lost in the horrors they had witnessed, and those they might be yet reserved for, she sat incapable of thought, or speech, or outward show of grief: as rigid, and almost as white and cold, as marble.

Oh, how many, many times, in that long ride, did Dolly think of her old lover—poor, fond, slighted Joe! How many, many times, did she recall that night when she ran into his arms from the very man now projecting his hateful gaze into the darkness where she sat, and leering through the glass, in monstrous admiration! And when she thought of Joe, and what a brave fellow he was, and how he would have rode boldly up, and dashed in among these villains now, yes, though they were double the number—and here she clenched her little hand, and pressed her foot upon the ground—the pride she felt for a moment in having won his heart, faded in a burst of tears, and she sobbed more bitterly than ever.

As the night wore on, and they proceeded by ways which were quite unknown to them—for they could recognise none of the objects of which they sometimes caught a hurried glimpse—their fears increased; nor were they without good foundation; it was not difficult for two beautiful young women to find, in their being borne they knew not whither, by a band of daring villains who eyed them as some among these fellows did, reasons for the worst alarm. When they at last entered London by a suburb with which they were wholly unacquainted, it was past midnight, and the streets were dark and empty. Nor was this the worst, for the carriage stopping in a lonely spot, Hugh suddenly opened the door, jumped in, and took his seat between them.

It was in vain they cried for help. He put his arm about the neck of each, and swore to stifle them with kisses if they were not as silent as the grave.

"I come here to keep you quiet," he said, "and that's the means I shall take. So don't be quiet, pretty mistresses—make a noise—do—and I shall like it all the better."

They were proceeding at a rapid pace, and apparently with fewer attendants than before, though it was so dark (the torches being extinguished) that this was mere conjecture. They shrunk from his touch, each into the farthest corner of the carriage; but shrink as Dolly would, his arm encircled her waist, and held her fast. She neither cried nor spoke, for terror and disgust deprived her of the power; but she plucked at his hand as though she would die in the effort to disengage herself; and crouching on the ground, with her head averted and held down, repelled him with a strength she wondered at as much as he. The carriage stopped again.

"Lift this one out," said Hugh to the man who opened the door, as he took Miss Haredale's hand, and felt how heavily it fell. "She's fainted."

"So much the better," growled Dennis—it was that amiable gentleman. "She's quiet. I always like 'em to faint, unless they're very tender and composed."

"Can you take her by yourself?" asked Hugh.

"I don't know till I try. I ought to be able to; I've lifted up a good many in my time," said the hangman. "Up then! She's no small weight, brother; none of these here fine gals are. Up again! Now we have it."

Having by this time hoisted the young lady into his arms, he staggered off with his burden.

"Look ye, pretty bird," said Hugh, drawing Dolly towards him. "Remember what I told you—a kiss for every cry. Scream, if you love me, darling. Scream once, mistress. Pretty mistress, only once, if you love me."

Thrusting his face away with all her force, and holding down her head, Dolly submitted to be carried out of the chaise, and borne after Miss Haredale into a miserable cottage, where Hugh, after hugging her to his breast, set her gently down upon the floor.

Poor Dolly! Do what she would, she only looked the better for it, and tempted them the more. When her eyes flashed angrily, and her ripe lips slightly parted, to give her rapid breathing vent, who could resist it? When she wept and sobbed as though her heart would break, and bemoaned her miseries in the sweetest voice that ever fell upon a listener's ear, who could be insensible to the little winning pettishness which now and then displayed itself even in the sincerity and earnestness of her grief? When, forgetful for a moment of herself, as she was now, she fell on her knees beside her friend, and bent over her, and laid her cheek to hers, and put her arms about her, what mortal eyes could have avoided wandering to the delicate bodice, the streaming hair, the neglected dress, the perfect abandonment and unconsciousness of the blooming little beauty? Who could look on and see her lavish caresses and endearments, and not desire to be in Emma Haredale's place; to be either her or Dolly; either the hugging or the hugged? Not Hugh. Not Dennis.

"I tell you what it is, young women," said Mr. Dennis, "I an't much of a lady's man myself, nor am I a party in the present business further than lending a willing hand to my friends: but if I see much more of this here sort of thing, I shall become a principal instead of a accessory. I tell you candidly."

"Why have you brought us here?" said Emma. "Are we to be murdered?"

"Murdered!" cried Dennis, sitting down upon a stool, and regarding her with great favour. "Why, my dear, who'd murder sich chickabiddies as you? If you was to ask me, now, whether you was brought here to be married, there might be something in it."

And here he exchanged a grin with Hugh, who removed his eyes from Dolly for the purpose.

"No, no," said Dennis, "there'll be no murdering, my pets. Nothing of that sort. Quite the contrary."

"You are an older man than your companion, sir," said Emma, trembling. "Have you no pity for us? Do you not consider that we are women?"

"I do indeed, my dear," retorted Dennis. "It would be very hard not to, with two such specimens afore my eyes. Ha ha! Oh yes, I consider that. We all consider that, Miss."

He shook his head waggishly, leered at Hugh again, and laughed very much, as if he had said a polite thing, and rather thought he was coming out.

"There'll be no murdering, my dear. Not a bit on it. I tell you what though, brother," said Dennis, cocking his hat for the convenience of scratching his head, and looking gravely at Hugh, "it's worthy of notice, as a proof of the amazing equalness and dignity of our law, that it don't make no distinction between men and women. I've heerd the judge say, sometimes, to a highwayman or housebreaker as had tied the ladies neck and heels—you'll excuse me making mention of it, my darlings—and put 'em in a cellar, that he showed no consideration to women. Now, I say that there judge didn't know his business, brother; and that if I had been that there highwayman or housebreaker, I should have made answer: 'What are you a talking of, my lord? I showed the women as much consideration as the law does, and what more would you have me do?' If you was to count up in the newspapers the number of females as have been worked off in this here city alone, in the last ten year," said Mr. Dennis thoughtfully, "you'd be surprised at the total—quite amazed, you would. There's a dignified and equal thing; a beautiful thing! But we've no security for its lasting. Now that they've begun to favour these here Papists, I shouldn't wonder if they went and altered even *that*, one of these days. Upon my soul, I shouldn't."

This subject, perhaps from being of too exclusive and professional a nature, failed to interest Hugh as much as his friend had anticipated. But he had no time to pursue it, for at this crisis Mr. Tappertit entered precipitately; at sight of whom Dolly uttered a scream of joy, and fairly threw herself into his arms.

"I knew it, I was sure of it!" cried Dolly. "My dear father's at the door. Thank God, thank God! Bless you, Sim. Heaven bless you for this!"

Simon Tappertit, who had at first implicitly believed that the locksmith's daughter, unable any longer to suppress her secret passion for himself, was about to give it full vent in its intensity, and to declare that she was his for ever, looked extremely foolish when she said these words;—the more so, as they were received by Hugh and Dennis with a loud laugh, which made her draw back, and regard him with a fixed and earnest look.

"Miss Haredale," said Sim, after a very awkward silence, "I hope you're as comfortable as circumstances will permit of. Dolly Varden, my darling—my own, my lovely one—I hope *you're* pretty comfortable likewise."

Poor little Dolly! She saw how it was; hid her face in her hands; and sobbed more bitterly than ever.

"You meet in me, Miss V.," said Simon, laying his hand upon his breast, "not a 'prentice, not a workman, not a slave, not the victim of your father's tyrannical behaviour, but the leader of a great people, the captain of a noble band, in which these gentlemen are, as I may say, corporals and serjeants. You behold in me, not a private individual, but a public character; not a mender of locks, but a healer of the wounds of his unhappy country. Dolly V., sweet Dolly V., for how many years have I looked forward to this meeting! For how many years has it been my intention to exalt and ennoble you! I redeem it. Behold in me, your husband. Yes, beautiful Dolly—charmer—enslaver—S. Tappertit is all your own!"

As he said these words he advanced towards her. Dolly retreated till she could go no farther, and then sank down upon the floor. Thinking it very possible that this might be maiden modesty, Simon essayed to raise her; on which Dolly, goaded to desperation, wound her hands in his hair, and crying out amidst her tears that he was a dreadful little wretch, and always had been, shook, and pulled, and beat him, until he was fain to call for help, most lustily. Hugh had never admired her half so much as at that moment.

"She's in an excited state to-night," said Simon, as he smoothed his rumpled feathers, "and don't know when she's well off. Let her be by herself till to-morrow, and that'll bring her down a little. Carry her into the next house!"

Hugh had her in his arms directly. It might be that Mr. Tappertit's heart was really softened by her distress, or it might be that he felt it in some degree indecorous that his intended bride should be struggling in the grasp of another man. He commanded him, on second thoughts, to put her down again; and looked moodily on as

she flew to Miss Haredale's side, and clinging to her dress, hid her flushed face in its folds.

"They shall remain here together till to-morrow," said Simon, who had now quite recovered his dignity—"till to-morrow. Come away!"

"Ay!" cried Hugh. "Come away, captain. Ha ha ha!"

"What are you laughing at?" demanded Simon sternly.

"Nothing, captain, nothing," Hugh rejoined; and as he spoke, and clapped his hand upon the shoulder of the little man, he laughed again, for some unknown reason, with tenfold violence.

Mr. Tappertit surveyed him from head to foot with lofty scorn (this only made him laugh the more), and turning to the prisoners, said:

"You'll take notice, ladies, that this place is well watched on every side, and that the least noise is certain to be attended with unpleasant consequences. You'll hear—both of you—more of our intentions to-morrow. In the mean time, don't show yourselves at the window, or appeal to any of the people you may see pass it; for if you do, it'll be known directly that you come from a Catholic house, and all the exertions our men can make, may not be able to save your lives."

With this last caution, which was true enough, he turned to the door, followed by Hugh and Dennis. They paused for a moment, going out, to look at them clasped in each other's arms, and then left the cottage; fastening the door, and setting a good watch upon it, and indeed all round the house.

"I say," growled Dennis, as they walked away in company, "that's a dainty pair. Muster Gashford's one is as handsome as the other, eh?"

"Hush!" said Hugh, hastily. "Don't you mention names. It's a bad habit."

"I wouldn't like to be *him*, then (as you don't like names), when he breaks it out to her; that's all," said Dennis. "She's one of them fine, black-eyed, proud gals, as I wouldn't trust at such times with a knife too near 'em. I've seen some of that sort, afore now. I recollect one that was worked off, many year ago—and there was a gentleman in that case too—that says to me, with her lip a trembling, but her hand as steady as ever I see one; 'Dennis, I'm near my end, but if I had a dagger in these fingers, and he was within my reach, I'd strike him dead afore me;'—ah, she did—and she'd have done it too!"

"Strike who dead?" demanded Hugh.

"How should I know, brother?" answered Dennis. "*She* never said; not she."

Hugh looked for a moment, as though he would have made some further inquiry into this incoherent recollection; but Simon Tappertit, who had been meditating deeply, gave his thoughts a new direction.

"Hugh!" said Sim. "You have done well to-day. You shall be rewarded. So have you, Dennis.—There's no young woman *you* want to carry off, is there?"

"N—no," returned that gentleman, stroking his grizzled beard, which was some two inches long. "None in partickler, I think."

"Very good," said Sim; "then we'll find some other way of making it up to you. As to you, old boy"—he turned to Hugh—"you shall have Miggs (her that I promised you, you know) within three days. Mind. I pass my word for it."

Hugh thanked him heartily; and as he did so, his laughing fit returned with such violence that he was obliged to hold his side with one hand, and to lean with the other on the shoulder of his small captain, without whose support he would certainly have rolled upon the ground.

CHAPTER THE SIXTIETH.

THE three worthies turned their faces towards the Boot, with the intention of passing the night in that place of rendezvous, and of seeking the repose they so much needed in the shelter of their old den; for now that the mischief and destruction they had purposed were achieved, and their prisoners were safely bestowed for the night, they began to be conscious of exhaustion, and to feel the wasting effects of the madness which had led to such deplorable results.

Notwithstanding the lassitude and fatigue which oppressed him now, in common with his two companions, and indeed with all who had taken an active share in that night's work, Hugh's boisterous merriment broke out afresh whenever he looked at Simon Tappertit, and vented itself—much to that gentleman's indignation—in such shouts of laughter as bade fair to bring the watch upon them, and involve them in a skirmish, to which in their present worn-out condition they might prove by no means equal. Even Mr. Dennis, who was not at all particular on the score of gravity or dignity, and who had a great relish for his young friend's eccentric humours, took occasion to remonstrate with him on this imprudent behaviour, which he held to be a species of suicide, tantamount to a man's working himself off without being overtaken by the law, than which he could imagine nothing more ridiculous or impertinent.

Not abating one jot of his noisy mirth for these remonstrances, Hugh reeled along between them, having an arm of each, until they hove in sight of the Boot, and were within a field or two of that convenient tavern. He happened by great good luck to have roared and shouted himself into silence by this time. They were proceeding onward without noise, when a scout who had been creeping about the ditches all night, to warn any stragglers from encroaching further on what was now such dangerous ground, peeped cautiously from his hiding-place, and called to them to stop.

"Stop! and why?" said Hugh.

Because (the scout replied) the house was filled with constables and soldiers; having been surprised, that afternoon. The inmates had fled or been taken into custody, he could not say which. He had prevented a great many people from approaching nearer, and he believed they had gone to the markets and such places to pass the night. He had seen the distant fires, but they were all out now. He had heard the people who passed and repassed, speaking of them too, and could report that the prevailing opinion was one of apprehension and dismay. He had not heard a word of Barnaby—didn't even know his name—but it had been said in his hearing that some man had been taken and carried off to Newgate. Whether this was true or false, he could not affirm.

The three took counsel together, on hearing this, and debated what it might be best to do. Hugh, deeming it possible that Barnaby was in the hands of the soldiers, and at that moment under detention at the Boot, was for advancing stealthily, and firing the house; but his companions, who objected to such rash measures unless they had a crowd at their backs, represented that if Barnaby were taken he had assuredly been removed to a stronger prison: they would never have dreamed of keeping him all night in a place so weak and open to attack. Yielding to this reasoning, and to their persuasions, Hugh consented to turn back, and to repair to Fleet Market; for which place, it seemed, a few of their boldest associates had shaped their course, on receiving the same intelligence.

Feeling their strength recruited and their spirits roused now that there was a new necessity for action, they hurried away, quite forgetful of the fatigue under which they had been sinking but a few minutes before; and soon arrived at their place of destination.

Fleet Market, at that time, was a long irregular row of wooden sheds and pent-houses, occupying the centre of what is now called Farringdon Street. They were jumbled together in a most unsightly fashion, in the middle of the road; to the great obstruction of the thoroughfare and the annoyance of passengers, who were fain to make their way, as they best could, among carts, baskets, barrows, trucks, casks, bulks, and benches, and to jostle with porters, hucksters, waggoners, and a motley crowd of buyers, sellers, pickpockets, vagrants, and idlers. The air was perfumed with the stench of rotten leaves and faded fruit; the refuse of the butchers' stalls, and offal and garbage of a hundred kinds: it was indispensable to most public conveniences in those days, that they should be public nuisances likewise; and Fleet Market maintained the principle to admiration.

To this place, perhaps because its sheds and baskets were a tolerable substitute for beds, or perhaps because it afforded the means of a hasty barricade in case of need, many of the rioters had straggled, not only that night, but for two or three nights before. It was now broad day, but the morning being cold, a group of them were gathered round a fire in a public-house, drinking hot purl,* and smoking pipes, and planning new schemes for to-morrow.

Hugh and his two friends being known to most of these men, were received with signal marks of approbation, and inducted into the most honourable seats. The room-door was closed and fastened to keep intruders at a distance, and then they proceeded to exchange news.

"The soldiers have taken possession of the Boot, I hear," said Hugh. "Who knows anything about it?"

Several cried that they did; but the majority of the company having been engaged in the assault upon the Warren, and all present having been concerned in one or other of the night's expeditions, it proved that they knew no more than Hugh himself; having been merely warned by each other, or by the scout, and knowing nothing of their own knowledge.

"We left a man on guard there to-day," said Hugh, looking round him, "who is not here. You know who it is—Barnaby, who brought the soldier down, at Westminster. Has any man seen or heard of him?"

They shook their heads, and murmured an answer in the negative, as each man looked round and appealed to his fellow; when a noise was heard without, and a man was heard to say that he wanted Hugh—that he must see Hugh.

"He is but one man," cried Hugh to those who kept the door; "let him come in."

"Ay, ay!" muttered the others. "Let him come in. Let him come in."

The door was accordingly unlocked and opened. A one-armed man, with his head and face tied up with a bloody cloth as though he had been severely beaten, his clothes torn, and his remaining hand grasping a thick stick, rushed in among them, and panting for breath, demanded which was Hugh.

"Here he is," replied the person he inquired for. "I am Hugh. What do you want with me?"

"I have a message for you," said the man. "You know one Barnaby."

"What of him? Did he send the message?"

"Yes. He's taken. He's in one of the strong cells in Newgate. He defended himself as well as he could, but was overpowered by numbers. That's his message."

"When did you see him?" asked Hugh, hastily.

"On his way to prison, where he was taken by a party of soldiers. They took a by-road, and not the one we expected. I was one of the few who tried to rescue him, and he called to me, and told me to tell Hugh where he was. We made a good struggle, though it failed. Look here!"

He pointed to his dress, and to his bandaged head, and still panting for breath, glanced round the room; then faced towards Hugh again.

"I know you by sight," he said, "for I was in the crowd on Friday, and on Saturday, and yesterday, but I didn't know your name. You're a bold fellow, I know. So is he. He fought like a lion to-night, but it was of no use. *I* did my best, considering that I want this limb."

Again he glanced inquisitively round the room—or seemed to do so, for his face was nearly hidden by the bandage—and again facing sharply towards Hugh, grasped his stick as if he half expected to be set upon, and stood on the defensive.

If he had any such apprehension, however, he was speedily re-assured by the demeanour of all present. None thought of the bearer of the tidings. He was lost in the news he brought. Oaths, threats, and execrations, were vented on all sides. Some cried that if they bore this tamely, another day would see them all in jail; some, that they should have rescued the other prisoners, and this would not have happened. One man cried in a loud voice, "Who'll follow me to Newgate!" and there was a loud shout, and general rush towards the door.

But Hugh and Dennis stood with their backs against it, and kept them back, until the clamour had so far subsided that their voices could be heard, when they called to them together that to go now, in broad day, would be madness; and that if they waited until night and arranged a plan of attack, they might release, not only their own companions, but all the prisoners, and burn down the jail.

"Not that jail alone," cried Hugh, "but every jail in London. They shall have no place to put their prisoners in. We'll burn them all down; make bonfires of them every one! Here!" he cried, catching at the hangman's hand. "Let all who're men here, join with us. Shake hands upon it. Barnaby out of jail, and not a jail left standing! Who joins?"

Every man there. And they swore a great oath to release their friends from Newgate next night; to force the doors and burn the jail; or perish in the fire themselves.

CHAPTER THE SIXTY-FIRST.

ON that same night—events so crowd upon each other in convulsed and distracted times, that more than the stirring incidents of a whole life often become compressed into the compass of four-and-twenty hours—on that same night, Mr. Haredale, having strongly bound his prisoner, with the assistance of the sexton, and forced him to mount his horse, conducted him to Chigwell; bent upon procuring a conveyance to London from that place, and carrying him at once before a Justice. The disturbed state of the town would be, he knew, a sufficient reason for demanding the murderer's committal to prison before daybreak, as no man could answer for the security of any of the watch-houses or ordinary places of detention; and to convey a prisoner through the streets when the mob were again abroad, would not only be a task of great danger and hazard, but would be to challenge an attempt at rescue. Directing the sexton to lead the horse, he walked close by the murderer's side, and in this order they reached the village about the middle of the night.

The people were all awake and up, for they were fearful of being burnt in their beds, and sought to comfort and assure each other by watching in company. A few of the stoutest-hearted were armed and gathered in a body on the green. To these, who knew him well, Mr. Haredale addressed himself, briefly narrating what had happened, and beseeching them to aid in conveying the criminal to London before the dawn of day.

But not a man among them dared to help him by so much as the motion of a finger. The rioters, in their passage through the village, had menaced with their fiercest vengeance any person who should aid in extinguishing the fire, or render the least assistance to him, or any catholic whomsoever. Their threats extended to their lives and all that they possessed. They were assembled for their own protection, and could not endanger themselves by lending any aid to him. This they told him, not without hesitation and regret, as they kept aloof in the moonlight and glanced fearfully at the ghostly rider, who, with his head drooping on his breast and his hat slouched down upon his brow, neither moved nor spoke.

Finding it impossible to persuade them, and indeed hardly knowing how to do so after what they had seen of the fury of the crowd, Mr. Haredale besought them that at least they would leave him free to act for himself, and would suffer him to take the only chaise and pair of horses that the place afforded. This was not acceded to without some difficulty, but in the end they told him to do what he would, and to go away from them in heaven's name.

Leaving the sexton at the horse's bridle, he drew out the chaise with his own hands, and would have harnessed the horses, but that the postboy of the village—a soft-hearted, good-for-nothing, vagabond kind of fellow—was moved by his earnestness and passion, and, throwing down a pitchfork with which he was armed, swore that the rioters might cut him into mince-meat if they liked, but he would not stand by and see an honest gentleman who had done no wrong, reduced to such extremity, without doing what he could to help him. Mr. Haredale shook him warmly by the hand, and thanked him from his heart. In five minutes' time the chaise was ready, and this good scapegrace* in his saddle. The murderer was put inside, the blinds were drawn up, the sexton took his seat upon the bar, Mr. Haredale mounted his horse and rode close beside the door; and so they started in the dead of night, and in profound silence, for London.

The consternation was so extreme that even the horses which had escaped the flames at the Warren, could find no friends to shelter them. They passed them on the road, browzing on the stunted grass; and the driver told them, that the poor beasts had wandered to the village first, but had been driven away, lest they should bring the vengeance of the crowd on any of the inhabitants.

Nor was this feeling confined to such small places, where the people were timid, ignorant, and unprotected. When they came near London they met, in the grey light of morning, more than one poor catholic family who, terrified by the threats and warnings of their neighbours, were quitting the city on foot, and who told them they could hire no cart or horse for the removal of their goods, and had been compelled to leave them behind, at the mercy of the crowd. Near Mile-end* they passed a house, the master of which, a catholic gentleman of small means, having hired a waggon to remove his furniture by midnight, had had it all brought down into the street, to wait the vehicle's arrival, and save time in the packing. But the man with whom he made the bargain, alarmed by the fires that night, and by the sight of the rioters passing his door, had refused to keep it: and the poor gentleman, with his wife and servant and their little children, were sitting trembling among their goods in the open street, dreading the arrival of day and not knowing where to turn or what to do.

It was the same, they heard, with the public conveyances. The panic was so great that the mails and stage-coaches were afraid to carry passengers who professed the obnoxious religion. If the drivers knew them, or they admitted that they held that creed, they would not take them, no, though they offered large sums; and yesterday, people had been afraid to recognise catholic acquaintance in the streets, lest they should be marked by spies, and burnt out, as it was called, in consequence. One mild old man—a priest, whose chapel was destroyed; a very feeble, patient, inoffensive creature—who was trudging away, alone, designing to walk some distance from town, and then try his fortune with the coaches, told Mr. Haredale that he feared he might not find a magistrate who would have the hardihood to commit a prisoner to jail, on his complaint. But notwithstanding these discouraging accounts they went on, and reached the Mansion House* soon after sunrise.

Mr. Haredale threw himself from his horse, but he had no need to knock at the door, for it was already open, and there stood upon the step a portly old man, with a very red, or rather purple face, who, with an anxious expression of countenance, was remonstrating with some unseen person up-stairs, while the porter essayed to close the door by degrees and get rid of him. With the intense impatience and excitement natural to one in his condition, Mr. Haredale thrust himself forward and was about to speak, when the fat old gentleman interposed:

"My good sir," said he, "pray let me get an answer. This is the sixth time I have been here. I was here five times yesterday. My house is threatened with destruction. It is to be burned down to-night, and was to have been last night, but they had other business on their hands. Pray let me get an answer."

"My good sir," returned Mr. Haredale, shaking his head, "my house is burned to the ground. But God forbid that yours should be. Get your answer. Be brief, in mercy to me."

"Now, you hear this, my Lord?"—said the old gentleman, calling up the stairs, to where the skirt of a dressing-gown fluttered on the landing-place. "Here is a gentleman here, whose house was actually burnt down last night."

"Dear me, dear me," replied a testy voice, "I am very sorry for it, but what am I to do? I can't build it up again. The chief magistrate of the city can't go and be a rebuilding of people's houses, my good sir. Stuff and nonsense!"

"But the chief magistrate of the city can prevent people's houses from having any need to be rebuilt, if the chief magistrate's a man, and not a dummy—can't he, my Lord?" cried the old gentleman in a choleric manner.

"You are disrespectable, sir," said the Lord Mayor*—"leastways, disrespectful I mean."

"Disrespectful, my Lord!" returned the old gentleman. "I was respectful five times yesterday. I can't be respectful for ever. Men can't stand on being respectful when their houses are going to be burnt over their heads, with them in 'em. What am I to do, my Lord? *Am* I to have any protection!"

"I told you yesterday, sir," said the Lord Mayor, "that you might have an alderman in your house, if you could get one to come."

"What the devil's the good of an alderman?" returned the choleric old gentleman.

"—To awe the crowd, sir," said the Lord Mayor.

"Oh Lord ha' mercy!" whimpered the old gentleman, as he wiped his forehead in a state of ludicrous distress, "to think of sending an alderman to awe a crowd! Why, my Lord, if they were even so many babies, fed on mother's milk, what do you think they'd care for an alderman! Will *you* come?"

"I!" said the Lord Mayor, most emphatically: "Certainly not."

"Then what," returned the old gentleman, "what am I to do? Am

I a citizen of England? Am I to have the benefit of the laws? Am I to have any return for the King's Taxes?"

"I don't know, I am sure," said the Lord Mayor; "what a pity it is you're a catholic! Why couldn't you be a protestant, and then you wouldn't have got yourself into such a mess? I'm sure I don't know what's to be done.—There are great people at the bottom of these riots.*—Oh dear me, what a thing it is to be a public character!—You must look in again in the course of the day.—Would a javelin-man* do?—Or there's Philips the constable,—*he's* disengaged,—he's not very old for a man at his time of life, except in his legs, and if you put him up at a window he'd look quite young by candle-light, and might frighten 'em very much.—Oh dear!—well,—we'll see about it."

"Stop!" cried Mr. Haredale, pressing the door open as the porter strove to shut it, and speaking rapidly, "My Lord Mayor, I beg you not to go away. I have a man here, who committed a murder eight-and-twenty years ago. Half-a-dozen words from me, on oath, will justify you in committing him to prison for re-examination. I only seek, just now, to have him consigned to a place of safety. The least delay may involve his being rescued by the rioters."

"Oh dear me!" cried the Lord Mayor. "God bless my soul—and body—oh Lor!—well I!—there are great people at the bottom of these riots, you know.—You really mustn't."

"My Lord," said Mr. Haredale, "the murdered gentleman was my brother; I succeeded to his inheritance; there were not wanting slanderous tongues at that time, to whisper that the guilt of this most foul and cruel deed was mine—mine, who loved him, as he knows, in Heaven, dearly. The time has come, after all these years of gloom and misery, for avenging him, and bringing to light a crime so artful and so devilish that it has no parallel. Every second's delay on your part loosens this man's bloody hands again, and leads to his escape. My Lord, I charge you hear me, and despatch this matter on the instant."

"Oh dear me!" cried the chief magistrate; "these an't business hours, you know—I wonder at you—how ungentlemanly it is of you—you mustn't—you really mustn't.—And I suppose *you* are a catholic too?"

"I am," said Mr. Haredale.

"God bless my soul, I believe people turn catholics a' purpose to vex and worrit me," cried the Lord Mayor. "I wish you wouldn't come here; they'll be setting the Mansion House afire next, and we shall have you to thank for it. You must lock your prisoner up, sir—give him to a watchman—and—and call again at a proper time. Then we'll see about it!"

Before Mr. Haredale could answer, the sharp closing of a door and drawing of its bolts, gave notice that the Lord Mayor had retreated to his bedroom, and that further remonstrance would be unavailing. The two clients retreated likewise, and the porter shut them out into the street.

"That's the way he puts me off," said the old gentleman, "I can get no redress and no help. What are you going to do, sir?"

"To try elsewhere," answered Mr. Haredale, who was by this time on horseback.

"I feel for you, I assure you—and well I may, for we are in a common cause," said the old gentleman. "I may not have a house to offer you to-night, let me tender it while I can. On second thoughts though," he added, putting up a pocket-book he had produced while speaking, "I'll not give you a card, for if it was found upon you, it might get you into trouble. Langdale*—that's my name—vintner and distiller—Holborn Hill—you're heartily welcome, if you'll come."

Mr. Haredale bowed his head, and rode off, close beside the chaise as before; determining to repair to the house of Sir John Fielding, who had the reputation of being a bold and active magistrate, and fully resolved, in case the rioters should come upon them, to do execution on the murderer with his own hands, rather than suffer him to be released.

They arrived at the magistrate's dwelling, however, without molestation (for the mob, as we have seen, were then intent on deeper schemes), and knocked at the door. As it had been pretty generally rumoured that Sir John was proscribed by the rioters, a body of thief-takers* had been keeping watch in the house all night. To one of them, Mr. Haredale stated his business, which appearing to the man of sufficient moment to warrant his arousing the justice, procured him an immediate audience.

No time was lost in committing the murderer to Newgate; then a new building,* recently completed at a vast expense, and considered to be of enormous strength. The warrant being made out, three of the thief-takers bound him afresh (he had been struggling, it seemed, in the chaise, and had loosened his manacles); gagged him, lest they should meet with any of the mob, and he should call to them for help; and seated themselves, along with him, in the carriage. These men being all well armed, made a formidable escort; but they drew up the blinds again, as though the carriage were empty, and directed Mr. Haredale to ride forward, that he might not attract attention by seeming to belong to it.

The wisdom of this proceeding was sufficiently obvious, for as they hurried through the city they passed among several groups of men, who, if they had not supposed the chaise to be quite empty, would certainly have stopped it. But those within keeping quite close, and the driver tarrying to be asked no questions, they reached the prison without interruption, and, once there, had him out, and safe within its gloomy walls, in a twinkling.

With eager eyes and strained attention, Mr. Haredale saw him chained, and locked and barred up in his cell. Nay, when he had left the jail, and stood in the free street, without, he felt the iron plates upon the doors, with his hands, and drew them over the stone wall, to assure himself that it was real; and to exult in its being so strong, and rough, and cold. It was not until he turned his back upon the jail, and glanced along the empty streets, so lifeless and quiet in the bright morning, that he felt the weight upon his heart; that he knew he was tortured by anxiety for those he had left at home; and that home itself was but another bead in the long rosary of his regrets.*

CHAPTER THE SIXTY-SECOND.

THE prisoner, left to himself, sat down upon his bedstead: and resting his elbows on his knees, and his chin upon his hands, remained in that attitude for hours. It would be hard to say, of what nature his reflections were. They had no distinctness, and, saving for some flashes now and then, no reference to his condition or the train of circumstances by which it had been brought about. The cracks in the pavement of his cell, the chinks in the wall where stone was joined to stone, the bars in the window, the iron ring upon the floor,—such things as these, subsiding strangely into one another, and awakening an indescribable kind of interest and amusement, engrossed his whole mind; and although at the bottom of his every thought there was an uneasy sense of guilt, and dread of death, he

felt no more than that vague consciousness of it, which a sleeper has
of pain. It pursues him through his dreams, gnaws at the heart of all
his fancied pleasures, robs the banquet of its taste, music of its
sweetness, makes happiness itself unhappy, and yet is no bodily sen-
sation, but a phantom without shape, or form, or visible presence;
pervading everything, but having no existence; recognizable every-
where, but nowhere seen, or touched, or met with face to face, until
the sleep is past, and waking agony returns.

After a long time, the door of his cell opened. He looked up; saw
the blind man enter; and relapsed into his former position.

Guided by his breathing, the visitor advanced to where he sat; and
stopping beside him, and stretching out his hand to assure himself
that he was right, remained, for a good space, silent.

"This is bad, Rudge. This is bad," he said at length.

The prisoner shuffled with his feet upon the ground in turning
his body from him, but made no other answer.

"How were you taken?" he asked. "And where? You never told me
more than half your secret. No matter; I know it now. How was it,
and where, eh?" he asked again, coming still nearer to him.

"At Chigwell," said the other.

"At Chigwell! How came you there?"

"Because I went there, to avoid the man I stumbled on," he answered. "Because I was chased and driven there, by him and Fate. Because I was urged to go there, by something stronger than my own will. When I found him watching in the house she used to live in, night after night, I knew I never could escape him—never! and when I heard the Bell—"

He shivered; muttered that it was very cold; paced quickly up and down the narrow cell; and sitting down again, fell into his old posture.

"You were saying," said the blind man, after another pause, "that when you heard the Bell—"

"Let it be, will you?" he retorted in a hurried voice. "It hangs there yet."

The blind man turned a wistful and inquisitive face towards him, but he continued to speak, without noticing him.

"I went to Chigwell, in search of the mob. I have been so hunted and beset by this man, that I knew my only hope of safety lay in joining them. They had gone on before; I followed them, when it left off."

"When what left off?"

"The Bell. They had quitted the place. I hoped that some of them might be still lingering among the ruins, and was searching for them when I heard—" he drew a long breath, and wiped his forehead with his sleeve—"his voice."

"Saying what?"

"No matter what. I don't know. I was then at the foot of the turret, where I did the—"

"Ay," said the blind man, nodding his head with perfect composure, "I understand."

"I climbed the stair, or so much of it as was left; meaning to hide till he had gone. But he heard me; and followed almost as soon as I set foot upon the ashes."

"You might have hidden in the wall, and thrown him down, or stabbed him," said the blind man.

"Might I? Between that man and me, was one who led him on—I saw it, though he did not—and raised above his head a bloody hand. It was in the room above that *he* and I stood glaring at each other on the night of the murder, and before he fell he raised his hand like that, and fixed his eyes on me. I knew the chase would end there."

"You have a strong fancy," said the blind man, with a smile.

"Strengthen yours with blood, and see what it will come to."

He groaned, and rocked himself, and looking up for the first time, said, in a low, hollow voice:

"Eight-and-twenty years! Eight-and-twenty years! He has never changed in all that time, never grown older, nor altered in the least degree. He has been before me in the dark night, and the broad sunny day; in the twilight, the moonlight, the sunlight, the light of fire, and lamp, and candle; and in the deepest gloom. Always the same! In company, in solitude, on land, on shipboard; sometimes leaving me alone for months, and sometimes always with me. I have seen him, at sea, come gliding in the dead of night along the bright reflection of the moon in the calm water; and I have seen him, on quays and market-places, with his hand uplifted, towering, the centre of a busy crowd, unconscious of the terrible form that had its silent stand among them. Fancy! Are you real? Am I? Are these iron fetters, rivetted on me by the smith's hammer, or are they fancies I can shatter at a blow?"

The blind man listened in silence.

"Fancy! Do I fancy that I killed him? Do I fancy that as I left the chamber where he lay, I saw the face of a man peeping from a dark door, who plainly showed me by his fearful looks that he suspected what I had done? Do I remember that I spoke fairly to him—that I drew nearer—nearer yet—with the hot knife in my sleeve? Do I fancy how *he* died? Did he stagger back into the angle of the wall into which I had hemmed him, and, bleeding inwardly, stand, not fall, a corpse before me? Did I see him, as I see you now, erect and on his feet—but dead!"

The blind man, who knew that he had risen, motioned him to sit down again upon his bedstead; but he took no notice of the gesture.

"It was then I thought, for the first time, of fastening the murder upon him. It was then I dressed him in my clothes, and dragged him down the back stairs to the piece of water. Do I remember listening to the bubbles that came rising up when I had rolled him in? Do I remember wiping the water from my face, and because the body splashed it there, in its descent, feeling as if it *must* be blood?

"Did I go home when I had done? And oh, my God! how long it

took to do! Did I stand before my wife, and tell her? Did I see her fall upon the ground; and, when I stooped to raise her, did she thrust me back with a force that cast me off as if I had been a child, staining the hand with which she clasped my wrist? Is *that* fancy?

"Did she go down upon her knees, and call on Heaven to witness that she and her unborn child renounced me from that hour; and did she, in words so solemn that they turned me cold—me, fresh from the horrors my own hands had made—warn me to fly while there was time; for though she would be silent, being my wretched wife, she would not shelter me? Did I go forth that night, abjured of God and man, and anchored deep in hell; to wander at my cable's length about the earth, and surely be drawn down at last?"

"Why did you return?" said the blind man.

"Why is blood red? I could no more help it, than I could live without breath. I struggled against the impulse, but I was drawn back, through every difficult and adverse circumstance, as by a mighty engine. Nothing could stop me. The day and hour were none of my choice. Sleeping and waking, I had been among the old haunts for years—had visited my own grave. Why did I come back? Because this jail was gaping for me, and he stood beckoning at the door."

"You were not known?" said the blind man.

"I was a man who had been twenty-two years dead. No. I was not known."

"You should have kept your secret better."

"*My* secret? *Mine?* It was a secret, any breath of air could whisper at its will. The stars had it in their twinkling, the water in its flowing, the leaves in their rustling, the seasons in their return. It lurked in strangers' faces, and their voices. Everything had lips on which it always trembled—*My* secret!"

"It was revealed by your own act at any rate," said the blind man.

"The act was not mine. I did it, but it was not mine. I was obliged at times to wander round, and round, and round that spot. If you had chained me up when the fit was on me, I should have broken away, and gone there. As truly as the loadstone draws iron towards it, so he, lying at the bottom of his deep grave, could draw me near him when he would. Was that fancy? Did I like to go there, or did I strive and wrestle with the power that forced me?"

The blind man shrugged his shoulders, and smiled incredulously.

The prisoner again resumed his old attitude, and for a long time both were mute.

"I suppose then," said his visitor, at length breaking silence, "that you are penitent and resigned; that you desire to make peace with everybody (in particular, with your wife who has brought you to this); and that you ask no greater favour than to be carried to Tyburn as soon as possible? That being the case, I had better take my leave. I am not good enough to be company for you."

"Have I not told you," said the other fiercely, "that I have striven and wrestled with the power that brought me here? Has my whole life, for eight-and-twenty years, been one perpetual struggle and resistance, and do you think I want to lie down and die? Do all men shrink from death—I most of all!"

"That's better said. That's better spoken, Rudge—but I'll not call you that again—than anything you have said yet," returned the blind man, speaking more familiarly, and laying his hand upon his arm. "Lookye,—I never killed a man myself, for I have never been placed in a position that made it worth my while. Farther, I am not an advocate for killing men, and I don't think I should recommend it or like it—for it's very hazardous—under any circumstances. But as you had the misfortune to get into this trouble before I made your acquaintance, and as you have been my companion, and have been of use to me for a long time now, I overlook that part of the matter, and am only anxious that you shouldn't die unnecessarily. Now I do not consider that at present it is at all necessary."

"What else is left me?" returned the prisoner. "To eat my way through these walls with my teeth?"

"Something easier than that," returned his friend. "Promise me that you will talk no more of these fancies of yours—idle, foolish things, quite beneath a man—and I'll tell you what I mean."

"Tell me," said the other.

"Your worthy lady with the tender conscience; your scrupulous, virtuous, punctilious, but not blindly affectionate wife—"

"What of her?"

"Is now in London."

"A curse upon her, be she where she may!"

"That's natural enough. If she had taken her annuity as usual, you would not have been here, and we should have been better off. But that's apart from the business. She's in London. Scared, as I suppose, and have no doubt, by my representation when I waited upon her, that you were close at hand (which I, of course, urged only as an inducement to compliance, knowing that she was not pining to see you), she left that place, and travelled up to London."

"How do you know?"

"From my friend the noble captain—the illustrious general—the bladder, Mr. Tappertit. I learnt from him the last time I saw him, which was yesterday, that your son who is called Barnaby—not after his father I suppose—"

"Death! does that matter now!"

"—You are impatient," said the blind man calmly; "it's a good sign, and looks like life—that your son Barnaby had been lured away from her by one of his companions who knew him of old, at Chigwell; and that he is now among the rioters."

"And what is that to me? If father and son be hanged together, what comfort shall I find in that?"

"Stay—stay, my friend," returned the blind man, with a cunning look, "you travel fast to journeys' ends. Suppose I track my lady out, and say thus much: 'You want your son, ma'am—good. I, knowing those who tempt him to remain among them, can restore him to you, ma'am—good. You must pay a price, ma'am, for his restoration— good again. The price is small, and easy to be paid—dear ma'am, that's best of all.'"

"What mockery is this?"

"Very likely, she may reply in those words. 'No mockery at all,' I answer: 'Madam, a person said to be your husband (identity is difficult of proof after the lapse of many years) is in prison, his life in peril—the charge against him, murder. Now, ma'am, your husband has been dead a long, long time. The gentleman never can be confounded with him, if you will have the goodness to say a few words, on oath, as to when he died, and how; and that this person (who I am told resembles him in some degree) is no more he than I am. Such testimony will set the question quite at rest. Pledge yourself to me to give it, ma'am, and I will undertake to keep your son (a fine lad) out of harm's way until you have done this trifling service, when he shall be delivered up to you, safe and sound. On the other hand, if you decline to do so, I fear he will be betrayed, and handed over to the law, which will assuredly sentence him to suffer death. It is, in fact, a choice between his life and death. If you refuse, he swings. If you comply, the timber is not grown, nor the hemp sown, that shall do him any harm.'"

"There is a gleam of hope in this!" cried the prisoner, starting up.

"A gleam!" returned his friend, "a noon-blaze; a full and glorious daylight. Hush! I hear the tread of distant feet. Rely on me."

"When shall I hear more?"

"As soon as I do. I should hope, to-morrow. They are coming to say that our time for talk is over. I hear the jingling of the keys. Not another word of this just now, or they may overhear us."

As he said these words, the lock was turned, and one of the prison turnkeys appearing at the door, announced that it was time for visitors to leave the jail.

"So soon!" said Stagg, meekly. "But it can't be helped. Cheer up, friend. This mistake will soon be set at rest, and then you are a man again! If this charitable gentleman will lead a blind man (who has nothing in return but prayers) to the prison-porch, and set him with his face towards the west, he will do a worthy deed. Thank you, good sir. I thank you very kindly."

So saying, and pausing for an instant at the door to turn his grinning face towards his friend, he departed.

When the officer had seen him to the porch, he returned, and again unlocking and unbarring the door of the cell, set it wide open, informing its inmate that he was at liberty to walk in the adjacent yard, if he thought proper, for an hour.

The prisoner answered with a sullen nod; and being left alone again, sat brooding over what he had heard, and pondering upon the hopes the recent conversation had awakened; gazing abstractedly, the while he did so, on the light without, and watching the shadows thrown by one wall on another, and on the stone-paved ground.

It was a dull, square yard, made cold and gloomy by high walls, and seeming to chill the very sunlight. The stone, so bare, and rough, and obdurate, filled even him with longing thoughts of meadow-land and trees; and with a burning wish to be at liberty. As he looked, he rose, and leaning against the doorpost, gazed up at the bright blue sky, smiling even on that dreary home of crime. He seemed, for a moment, to remember lying on his back in some sweet-scented place, and gazing at it through moving branches, long ago.

His attention was suddenly attracted by a clanking sound—he knew what it was, for he had startled himself by making the same noise in walking to the door. Presently a voice began to sing, and he saw the shadow of a figure on the pavement. It stopped—was silent all at once, as though the person for a moment had forgotten where he was, but soon remembered—and so, with the same clanking noise, the shadow disappeared.

He walked out into the court and paced it to and fro; startling the echoes, as he went, with the harsh jangling of his fetters. There was a door near his, which, like his, stood ajar.

He had not taken half-a-dozen turns up and down the yard, when, standing still to observe this door, he heard the clanking sound again. A face looked out of the grated window—he saw it very dimly, for the cell was dark and the bars were heavy—and directly afterwards, a man appeared, and came towards him.

For the sense of loneliness he had, he might have been in the jail a year. Made eager by the hope of companionship, he quickened his pace, and hastened to meet the man half way—

What was this! His son!

They stood face to face, staring at each other. He shrinking and cowed, despite himself; Barnaby struggling with his imperfect memory, and wondering where he had seen that face, before. He was not uncertain long, for suddenly he laid hands upon him, and striving to bear him to the ground, cried:

"Ah! I know! You are the robber!"

He said nothing in reply at first, but held down his head, and struggled with him silently. Finding the younger man too strong for him, he raised his face, looked close into his eyes, and said,

"I am your father."

God knows what magic the name had for his ears; but Barnaby released his hold, fell back, and looked at him aghast. Suddenly he sprung towards him, put his arms about his neck, and pressed his head against his cheek.

Yes, yes, he was; he was sure he was. But where had he been so long, and why had he left his mother by herself, or worse than by herself, with her poor foolish boy? And had she really been as happy as they said. And where was she? Was she near there? She was not happy now, and he in jail? Ah, no.

Not a word was said in answer; but Grip croaked loudly, and hopped about them, round and round, as if enclosing them in a magic circle, and invoking all the powers of mischief.

CHAPTER THE SIXTY-THIRD.

DURING the whole of this day, every regiment in or near the metropolis was on duty in one or other part of the town; and the regulars and militia, in obedience to the orders which were sent to every barrack and station within twenty-four hours' journey, began to pour in by all the roads. But the disturbances had attained to such a formidable height, and the rioters had grown, with impunity, to be so audacious and so daring, that the sight of this great force, continually augmented by new arrivals, instead of operating as a check, stimulated them to outrages of greater hardihood than any they had yet committed; and helped to kindle a flame in London, the like of which had never been beheld, even in its ancient and rebellious times.

All yesterday, and on this day likewise, the commander-in-chief* endeavoured to arouse the magistrates to a sense of their duty, and in particular the Lord Mayor, who was the faintest-hearted and most timid of them all. With this object, large bodies of the soldiery were several times despatched to the Mansion House to await his orders: but as he could, by no threats or persuasions, be induced to give any; and as the men remained in the open street, fruitlessly for any good purpose, and thrivingly for a very bad one; these laudable attempts did harm rather than good. For the crowd, becoming speedily acquainted with the Lord Mayor's temper, did not fail to take advantage of it, by boasting that even the civil authorities were opposed to the Papists, and could not find it in their hearts to molest those who were guilty of no other offence. These vaunts they took care to make within the hearing of the soldiers; and they, being naturally loath to quarrel with the people, received their advances kindly enough: answering, when they were asked if they desired to fire upon their countrymen, "No, they would be damned if they did;" and showing much honest simplicity, and good-nature. The feeling that the military were No Popery men, and were ripe for disobeying orders and joining the mob, soon became very prevalent in consequence. Rumours of their disaffection, and of their leaning towards the popular cause, spread from mouth to mouth with astonishing rapidity; and whenever they were drawn up idly in the streets or squares, there was sure to be a crowd about them, cheering, and shaking hands, and treating them with a great show of confidence and affection.

By this time, the crowd was everywhere; all concealment and disguise were laid aside, and they pervaded the whole town. If any man among them wanted money, he had but to knock at the door of a dwelling-house, or walk into a shop, and demand it in the rioters' name; and his demand was instantly complied with. The peaceable citizens being afraid to lay hands upon them, singly and alone, it may be easily supposed that when gathered together in bodies, they were perfectly secure from interruption. They assembled in the streets, traversed them at their will and pleasure, and publicly concerted their plans. Business was quite suspended; the greater part of the shops were closed; most of the houses displayed a blue flag in token of their adherence to the popular side; and even the Jews in Houndsditch, Whitechapel, and those quarters,* wrote upon their doors or window-shutters "This House is a True Protestant." The crowd was the law, and never was the law held in greater dread, or more implicitly obeyed.

It was about six o'clock in the evening, when a vast mob poured into Lincoln's Inn Fields by every avenue, and divided—evidently in pursuance of a previous design—into several parties. It must not be understood that this arrangement was known to the whole crowd, but that it was the work of a few leaders; who, mingling with the men as they came upon the ground, and calling to them to fall into this or that party, effected it as rapidly as if it had been determined on by a council of the whole number, and every man had known his place.

It was perfectly notorious to the assemblage that the largest body, which comprehended about two-thirds of the whole, was designed for the attack on Newgate. It comprehended all the rioters who had been conspicuous in any of their former proceedings; all those whom they recommended as daring hands and fit for the work; all those whose companions had been taken in the riots; and a great number of people who were relatives or friends of felons in the jail. This last class included, not only the most desperate and utterly abandoned villains in London, but some who were comparatively innocent. There was more than one woman there, disguised in man's attire, and bent upon the rescue of a child or brother. There were the two sons of a man who lay under sentence of death, and who was to be executed along with three others, on the next day but one. There was a great party of boys whose fellow pickpockets were in the prison; and at the skirts of all, a score of miserable women, outcasts from the world, seeking to release some other fallen creature as miserable as themselves, or moved by a general sympathy perhaps—God knows—with all who were without hope, and wretched.

Old swords, and pistols without ball or powder; sledge-hammers, knives, axes, saws, and weapons pillaged from the butchers' shops; a forest of iron bars and wooden clubs; long ladders for scaling the walls, each carried on the shoulders of a dozen men; lighted torches; tow smeared with pitch, and tar, and brimstone;* staves roughly plucked from fence and paling; and even crutches torn from crippled beggars in the streets; composed their arms. When all was ready, Hugh and Dennis, with Simon Tappertit between them, led the way. Roaring and chafing like an angry sea, the crowd pressed after them.

Instead of going straight down Holborn to the jail, as all expected, their leaders took the way to Clerkenwell, and rushing down a quiet street, halted before a locksmith's house—the Golden Key.

"Beat at the door," cried Hugh to the men about him. "We want one of his craft to-night. Beat it in, if no one answers."

The shop was shut. Both door and shutters were of a strong and sturdy kind, and they knocked without effect. But the impatient crowd raising a cry of "Set fire to the house!" and torches being passed to the front, an upper window was thrown open, and the stout old locksmith stood before them.

"What now, ye villains!" he demanded. "Where is my daughter?"

"Ask no questions of us, old man," retorted Hugh, waving his comrades to be silent, "but come down, and bring the tools of your trade. We want you."

"Want me!" cried the locksmith, glancing at the regimental dress he wore: "Ay, and if some that I could name possessed the hearts of mice, ye should have had me long ago. Mark me, my lad—and you about him do the same. There are a score among ye whom I see now and know, who are dead men from this hour. Begone! and rob an undertaker's while you can! You'll want some coffins before long."

"Will you come down?" cried Hugh.

"Will you give me my daughter, ruffian?" cried the locksmith.

"I know nothing of her," Hugh rejoined. "Burn the door!"

"Stop!" cried the locksmith, in a voice that made them falter—presenting, as he spoke, a gun. "Let an old man do that. You can spare him better."

The young fellow who held the light, and who was stooping down before the door, rose hastily at these words, and fell back. The locksmith ran his eye along the upturned faces, and kept the weapon levelled at the threshold of his house. It had no other rest than his shoulder, but was as steady as the house itself.

"Let the man who does it, take heed to his prayers," he said firmly; "I warn him."

Snatching a torch from one who stood near him, Hugh was stepping forward with an oath, when he was arrested by a shrill and piercing shriek, and, looking upward, saw a fluttering garment on the house-top.

There was another shriek, and another, and then a shrill voice cried, "Is Simmun below!" At the same moment a lean neck was stretched over the parapet, and Miss Miggs, indistinctly seen in the gathering gloom of evening, screeched in a frenzied manner, "Oh! dear gentlemen, let me hear Simmuns's answer from his own lips. Speak to me, Simmun. Speak to me!"

Mr. Tappertit, who was not at all flattered by this compliment, looked up, and bidding her hold her peace, ordered her to come down and open the door, for they wanted her master, and would take no denial.

"Oh good gentlemen!" cried Miss Miggs. "Oh my own precious, precious Simmun—"

"Hold your nonsense, will you!" retorted Mr. Tappertit; "and come down and open the door.—G. Varden, drop that gun, or it will be worse for you."

"Don't mind his gun," screamed Miggs. "Simmun and gentlemen, I poured a mug of table-beer right down the barrel."

The crowd gave a loud shout, which was followed by a roar of laughter.

"It wouldn't go off, not if you was to load it up to the muzzle," screamed Miggs. "Simmun and gentlemen, I'm locked up in the front attic, through the little door on the right hand when you think you've got to the very top of the stairs—and up the flight of corner steps, being careful not to knock your heads against the rafters, and not to tread on one side in case you should fall into the two-pair bedroom through the lath and plasture,* which do not bear, but the contrairy. Simmun and gentlemen, I've been locked up here for safety, but my endeavours has always been, and always will be, to be on the right side—the blessed side—and to prenounce the Pope of Babylon,* and all her inward and her outward workings, which is Pagin. My sentiments is of little consequences, I know," cried Miggs, with additional shrillness, "for my positions is but a servant, and as sich, of humilities; still I gives expressions to my feelings, and places my reliances on them which entertains my own opinions!"

Without taking much notice of these outpourings of Miss Miggs after she had made her first announcement in relation to the gun, the crowd raised a ladder against the window where the locksmith stood, and notwithstanding that he closed, and fastened, and defended it manfully, soon forced an entrance by shivering the glass and breaking in the frames. After dealing a few stout blows about him, he found himself defenceless, in the midst of a furious crowd, which overflowed the room and softened off in a confused heap of faces at the door and window.

They were very wrathful with him (for he had wounded two men), and even called out to those in front, to bring him forth and hang him on a lamp-post. But Gabriel was quite undaunted, and looked from Hugh and Dennis, who held him by either arm, to Simon Tappertit, who confronted him.

"You have robbed me of my daughter," said the locksmith, "who is far, far dearer to me than my life; and you may take my life, if you will. I bless God that I have been enabled to keep my wife free of this scene; and that He has made me a man who will not ask mercy at such hands as yours."

"And a wery game old gentleman you are," said Mr. Dennis, approvingly; "and you express yourself like a man. What's the odds, brother, whether it's a lamp-post to-night, or a feather-bed ten year to come, eh?"

The locksmith glanced at him disdainfully, but returned no other answer.

"For my part," said the hangman, who particularly favoured the lamp-post suggestion, "I honour your principles. They're mine exactly. In such sentiments as them," and here he emphasized his discourse with an oath, "I'm ready to meet you or any man half-way.—Have you got a bit of cord anywheres handy? Don't put yourself out of the way, if you haven't. A handkecher will do."

"Don't be a fool, master," whispered Hugh, seizing Varden roughly by the shoulder; "but do as you're bid. You'll soon hear what you're wanted for. Do it!"

"I'll do nothing at your request, or that of any scoundrel here," returned the locksmith. "If you want any service from me, you may spare yourselves the pains of telling me what it is. I tell you, before-hand, I'll do nothing for you."

Mr. Dennis was so affected by this constancy on the part of the staunch old man, that he protested—almost with tears in his eyes— that to balk his inclinations would be an act of cruelty and hard dealing to which he, for one, never could reconcile his conscience. The gentleman, he said, had avowed in so many words that he was ready for working off; such being the case, he considered it their duty, as a civilised and enlightened crowd, to work him off. It was not often, he observed, that they had it in their power to accommodate themselves to the wishes of those from whom they had the mis-fortune to differ. Having now found an individual who expressed a desire which they could reasonably indulge, (and for himself he was free to confess that in his opinion that desire did honour to his feelings), he hoped they would decide to accede to his proposition before going any further. It was an experiment which, skilfully and dexterously performed, would be over in five minutes, with great comfort and satisfaction to all parties; and though it did not become him (Mr. Dennis) to speak well of himself, he trusted he might be allowed to say that he had practical knowledge of the subject, and, being naturally of an obliging and friendly disposition, would work the gentleman off with a deal of pleasure.

These remarks, which were addressed in the midst of a frightful din and turmoil to those immediately about him, were received with great favour; not so much, perhaps, because of the hangman's elo-quence, as on account of the locksmith's obstinacy. Gabriel was in imminent peril, and he knew it; but he preserved a steady silence; and would have done so, if they had been debating whether they should roast him at a slow fire.

As the hangman spoke, there was some stir and confusion on the ladder; and directly he was silent—so immediately upon his holding his peace, that the crowd below had no time to learn what he had been saying, or to shout in response—some one at the window cried:

"He has a grey head. He is an old man: Don't hurt him!"

The locksmith turned, with a start, towards the place from which the words had come, and looked hurriedly at the people who were hanging on the ladder and clinging to each other.

"Pay no respect to my grey hair, young man," he said, answering the voice and not any one he saw. "I don't ask it. My heart is green enough to scorn and despise every man among you,—band of robbers that you are!"

This incautious speech by no means tended to appease the ferocity of the crowd. They cried again to have him brought out; and it would have gone hard with the honest locksmith, but that Hugh reminded them, in answer, that they wanted his services, and must have them.

"So, tell him what we want," he said to Simon Tappertit, "and quickly. And open your ears, master, if you would ever use them after to-night."

Gabriel folded his arms, which were now at liberty, and eyed his old 'prentice in silence.

"Lookye, Varden," said Sim, "we're bound for Newgate."

"I know you are," returned the locksmith. "You never said a truer word than that."

"To burn it down, I mean," said Simon, "and force the gates, and set the prisoners at liberty. You helped to make the lock of the great door."

"I did," said the locksmith. "You owe me no thanks for that—as you'll find before long."

"Maybe," returned his journeyman, "but you must show us how to force it."

"Must I!"

"Yes; for you know, and I don't. You must come along with us, and pick it with your own hands."

"When I do," said the locksmith quietly, "my hands shall drop off at the wrists, and you shall wear them, Simon Tappertit, on your shoulders for epaulettes."

"We'll see that," cried Hugh, interposing, as the indignation of the crowd again burst forth. "You fill a basket with the tools he'll want, while I bring him down stairs. Open the doors below, some of you. And light the great captain, others! Is there no business afoot, my lads, that you can do nothing but stand and grumble?"

They looked at one another, and quickly dispersing, swarmed over the house, plundering and breaking, according to their custom, and carrying off such articles of value as happened to please their fancy. They had no great length of time for these proceedings, for the basket of tools was soon prepared and slung over a man's shoulders. The preparations being now completed, and everything ready for the attack, those who were pillaging and destroying in the other rooms were called down to the workshop. They were about to issue forth, when the man who had been last up stairs, stepped forward, and asked if the young woman in the garret (who was making a terrible noise, he said, and kept on screaming without the least cessation) was to be released?

For his own part, Simon Tappertit would certainly have replied in the negative, but the mass of his companions, mindful of the good service she had done in the matter of the gun, being of a different opinion, he had nothing for it but to answer, Yes. The man, accordingly, went back again to the rescue, and presently returned with Miss Miggs, limp and doubled up, and very damp from much weeping.

As the young lady had given no tokens of consciousness on their way down stairs, the bearer reported her either dead or dying; and being at some loss what to do with her, was looking round for a convenient bench or heap of ashes on which to place her senseless form, when she suddenly came upon her feet by some mysterious means, thrust back her hair, stared wildly at Mr. Tappertit, cried "My Simmuns's life is not a wictim!" and dropped into his arms with such promptitude that he staggered and reeled some paces back, beneath his lovely burden.

"Oh bother!" said Mr. Tappertit. "Here. Catch hold of her, somebody. Lock her up again; she never ought to have been let out."

"My Simmun!" cried Miss Miggs, in tears, and faintly. "My for ever, ever blessed Simmun!"

"Hold up, will you," said Mr. Tappertit, in a very unresponsive tone, "I'll let you fall if you don't. What are you sliding your feet off the ground for?"

"My angel Simmuns!" murmured Miggs—"he promised—"

"Promised! Well, and I'll keep my promise," answered Simon, testily. "I mean to provide for you, don't I? Stand up!"

"Where am I to go? What is to become of me after my actions of this night!" cried Miggs. "What resting-places now remains but in the silent tombs!"

"I wish you was in the silent tombs, I do," cried Mr. Tappertit, "and boxed up tight, in a good strong one. Here," he cried to one of the by-standers, in whose ear he whispered for a moment: "Take her off, will you. You understand where?"

The fellow nodded; and taking her in his arms, notwithstanding her broken protestations, and her struggles (which latter species of opposition, involving scratches, was much more difficult of resistance), carried her away. They who were in the house poured out into the street; the locksmith was taken to the head of the crowd, and required to walk between his two conductors; the whole body was put in rapid motion; and without any shouting or noise they bore down straight on Newgate, and halted in a dense mass before the prison gate.

CHAPTER THE SIXTY-FOURTH.

BREAKING the silence they had hitherto preserved, they raised a great cry as soon as they were ranged before the jail, and demanded to speak with the governor. Their visit was not wholly unexpected, for his house, which fronted the street, was strongly barricaded, the wicket-gate of the prison was closed up, and at no loophole or grating was any person to be seen. Before they had repeated their summons many times, a man appeared upon the roof of the governor's house, and asked what it was they wanted.

Some said one thing, some another, and some only groaned and hissed. It being now nearly dark, and the house high, many persons in the throng were not aware that any one had come to answer them, and continued their clamour until the intelligence was gradually diffused through the whole concourse. Ten minutes or more elapsed before any one voice could be heard with tolerable distinctness; during which interval the figure remained perched alone, against the summer-evening sky, looking down into the troubled street.

"Are you," said Hugh at length, "Mr. Akerman,* the head jailer here?"

"Of course he is, brother," whispered Dennis. But Hugh, without minding him, took his answer from the man himself.

"Yes," he said. "I am."

"You have got some friends of ours in your custody, master."

"I have a good many people in my custody." He glanced downward, as he spoke, into the jail: and the feeling that he could see into the different yards, and that he overlooked everything which was hidden from their view by the rugged walls, so lashed and goaded the mob, that they howled like wolves.

"Deliver up our friends," said Hugh, "and you may keep the rest."

"It's my duty to keep them all. I shall do my duty."

"If you don't throw the doors open, we shall break 'em down," said Hugh; "for we will have the rioters out."

"All I can do, good people," Akerman replied, "is to exhort you to disperse; and to remind you that the consequences of any disturbance in this place, will be very severe, and bitterly repented by most of you, when it is too late."

He made as though he would retire when he had said these words, but he was checked by the voice of the locksmith.

"Mr. Akerman," cried Gabriel, "Mr. Akerman."

"I will hear no more from any of you," replied the governor, turning towards the speaker, and waving his hand.

"But I am not one of them," said Gabriel. "I am an honest man, Mr. Akerman; a respectable tradesman—Gabriel Varden, the locksmith. You know me?"

"You among the crowd!" cried the governor in an altered voice.

"Brought here by force—brought here to pick the lock of the great door for them," rejoined the locksmith. "Bear witness for me, Mr. Akerman, that I refuse to do it; and that I will not do it, come what may of my refusal. If any violence is done to me, please to remember this."

"Is there no way of helping you?" said the governor.

"None, Mr. Akerman. You'll do your duty, and I'll do mine. Once again, you robbers and cut-throats," said the locksmith, turning round upon them, "I refuse. Howl till you're hoarse. I refuse."

"Stay—stay!" said the jailer, hastily. "Mr. Varden, I know you for a worthy man, and one who would do no unlawful act except upon compulsion—"

"Upon compulsion, sir," interposed the locksmith, who felt that the tone in which this was said, conveyed the speaker's impression that he had ample excuse for yielding to the furious multitude who beset and hemmed him in, on every side, and among whom he stood, an old man, quite alone; "upon compulsion, sir, I'll do nothing."

"Where is that man," said the keeper, anxiously, "who spoke to me just now?"

"Here!" Hugh replied.

"Do you know what the guilt of murder is, and that by keeping that honest tradesman at your side you endanger his life!"

"We know it very well," he answered, "for what else did we bring him here? Let's have our friends, master, and you shall have your friend. Is that fair, lads?"

The mob replied to him with a loud Hurrah!

"You see how it is, sir?" cried Varden. "Keep 'em out, in King George's name. Remember what I have said. Good night!"

There was no more parley. A shower of stones and other missiles compelled the keeper of the jail to retire; and the mob, pressing on, and swarming round the walls, forced Gabriel Varden close up to the door.

In vain the basket of tools was laid upon the ground before him, and he was urged in turn by promises, by blows, by offers of reward, and threats of instant death, to do the office for which they had brought him there. "No," cried the sturdy locksmith, "I will not!"

He had never loved his life so well as then, but nothing could move him. The savage faces that glared upon him, look where he would; the cries of those who thirsted, like wild animals, for his blood; the sight of men pressing forward, and trampling down their fellows, as they strove to reach him, and struck at him above the heads of other men, with axes and with iron bars; all failed to daunt him. He looked from man to man, and face to face, and still, with quickened breath and lessening colour, cried firmly, "I will not!"

Dennis dealt him a blow upon the face which felled him to the ground. He sprung up again like a man in the prime of life, and with the crimson pouring from his forehead, caught him by the throat.

"You cowardly dog!" he said: "Give me my daughter. Give me my daughter."

They struggled together. Some cried "Kill him," and some (but they were not near enough) strove to trample him to death. Tug as he would at the old man's wrists, the hangman could not force him to unclench his hands.

"Is this all the return you make me, you ungrateful monster?" he articulated with great difficulty, and with many oaths.

"Give me my daughter!" cried the locksmith, who was now as fierce as those who gathered round him: "Give me my daughter!"

He was down again, and up, and down once more, and buffeting with a score of them, who bandied him from hand to hand, when one tall fellow, fresh from a slaughter-house, whose dress and great thigh-boots smoked hot with grease and blood, raised a pole-axe, and swearing a horrible oath, aimed it at the old man's uncovered head. At that instant, and in the very act, he fell himself, as if struck by lightning, and over his body a one-armed man came darting to the locksmith's side. Another man was with him, and both caught the locksmith roughly in their grasp.

"Leave him to us!" they cried to Hugh—struggling, as they spoke, to force a passage backward through the crowd. "Leave him to us. Why do you waste your whole strength on such as he, when a couple

of men can finish him in as many minutes! You lose time. Remember the prisoners! remember Barnaby!"

The cry ran through the mob. Hammers began to rattle on the walls; and every man strove to reach the prison, and be among the foremost rank. Fighting their way through the press and struggle, as desperately as if they were in the midst of enemies rather than their own friends, the two men retreated with the locksmith between them, and dragged him through the very heart of the concourse.

And now the strokes began to fall like hail upon the gate, and on the strong building; for those who could not reach the door, spent their fierce rage on anything—even on the great blocks of stone, which shivered their weapons into fragments, and made their hands and arms to tingle as if the walls were active in their stout resistance, and dealt them back their blows. The clash of iron ringing upon iron, mingled with the deafening tumult and sounded high above it, as the great sledge-hammers rattled on the nailed and plated door: the sparks flew off in showers; men worked in gangs, and at short intervals relieved each other, that all their strength might be devoted to the work; but there stood the portal still, as grim and dark and strong as ever, and, saving for the dints upon its battered surface, quite unchanged.

While some brought all their energies to bear upon this toilsome task; and some, rearing ladders against the prison, tried to clamber to the summit of the walls they were too short to scale; and some again engaged a body of police a hundred strong, and beat them back and trod them under foot by force of numbers; others besieged the house on which the jailer had appeared, and, driving in the door, brought out his furniture, and piled it up against the prison gate, to make a bonfire which should burn it down. As soon as this device was understood, all those who had laboured hitherto, cast down their tools and helped to swell the heap; which reached half-way across the street, and was so high, that those who threw more fuel on the top, got up by ladders. When all the keeper's goods were flung upon this costly pile, to the last fragment, they smeared it with the pitch, and tar, and rosin they had brought, and sprinkled it with turpentine. To all the woodwork round the prison doors they did the like, leaving not a joist or beam untouched. This infernal christening performed, they fired the pile with lighted matches and with blazing tow, and then stood by, awaiting the result.

The furniture being very dry, and rendered more combustible by wax and oil, besides the arts they had used, took fire at once. The flames roared high and fiercely, blackening the prison wall, and twining up its lofty front like burning serpents. At first, they crowded round the blaze, and vented their exultation only in their looks: but when it grew hotter and fiercer—when it crackled, leaped, and roared, like a great furnace—when it shone upon the opposite houses, and lighted up not only the pale and wondering faces at the windows, but the inmost corners of each habitation—when, through the deep red heat and glow, the fire was seen sporting and toying with the door, now clinging to its obdurate surface, now gliding off with fierce inconstancy and soaring high into the sky, anon returning to fold it in its burning grasp and lure it to its ruin—when it shone and gleamed so brightly that the church clock of St. Sepulchre's,* so often pointing to the hour of death, was legible as in broad day, and the vane upon its steeple-top glittered in the unwonted light like something richly jewelled—when blackened stone and sombre brick grew ruddy in the deep reflection, and windows shone like burnished gold, dotting the longest distance in the fiery vista with their specks of brightness—when wall and tower, and roof and chimney-stack, seemed drunk, and in the flickering glare appeared to reel and stagger—when scores of objects, never seen before, burst out upon the view, and things the most familiar put on some new aspect—then the mob began to join the whirl, and with loud yells, and shouts, and clamour, such as happily is seldom heard, bestirred themselves to feed the fire, and keep it at its height.

Although the heat was so intense that the paint on the houses over against the prison, parched and crackled up, and swelling into boils, as it were from excess of torture, broke and crumbled away; although the glass fell from the window-sashes, and the lead and iron on the roofs blistered the incautious hand that touched them, and the sparrows in the eaves took wing, and, rendered giddy by the smoke, fell fluttering down upon the blazing pile; still the fire was tended unceasingly by busy hands, and round it, men were going always. They never slackened in their zeal, or kept aloof, but pressed upon the flames so hard, that those in front had much ado to save themselves from being thrust in; if one man swooned or dropped, a dozen struggled for his place, and that, although they knew the pain, and thirst, and pressure, to be unendurable. Those who fell down in fainting-fits, and were not crushed or burnt, were carried to an inn-yard close at hand, and dashed with water from a pump; of which buckets full were passed from man to man among the crowd; but such was the strong desire of all to drink, and such the fighting to be first, that, for the most part, the whole contents were spilled upon the ground, without the lips of one man being moistened.

Meanwhile, and in the midst of all the roar and outcry, those who were nearest to the pile, heaped up again the burning fragments that came toppling down, and raked the fire about the door, which, although a sheet of flame, was still a door fast locked and barred, and kept them out. Great pieces of blazing wood were passed, besides, above the people's heads to such as stood about the ladders, and some of these, climbing up to the topmost stave, and holding on with one hand by the prison wall, exerted all their skill and force to cast these firebrands on the roof, or down into the yards within. In many instances their efforts were successful; which occasioned a new and appalling addition to the horrors of the scene: for the prisoners within, seeing from between their bars that the fire caught in many places and thrived fiercely, and being all locked up in strong cells for the night, began to know that they were in danger of being burnt alive. This terrible fear, spreading from cell to cell and from yard to yard, vented itself in such dismal cries and wailings, and in such dreadful shrieks for help, that the whole jail resounded with the noise; which was loudly heard even above the shouting of the mob and roaring of the flames, and was so full of agony and despair, that it made the boldest tremble.

It was remarkable that these cries began in that quarter of the jail which fronted Newgate Street, where, it was well known, the men who were to suffer death on Thursday were confined. And not only were these four who had so short a time to live, the first to whom the dread of being burnt occurred, but they were, throughout, the most importunate of all: for they could be plainly heard, notwithstanding the great thickness of the walls, crying that the wind set that way, and that the flames would shortly reach them; and calling to the officers of the jail to come and quench the fire from a cistern which was in their yard, and full of water. Judging from what the crowd without the walls could hear from time to time, these four doomed wretches never ceased to call for help; and that with as much distraction, and in as great a frenzy of attachment to existence, as though each had an honoured, happy life before him, instead of eight-and-forty hours of miserable imprisonment, and then a violent and shameful death.

But the anguish and suffering of the two sons of one of these men, when they heard, or fancied that they heard, their father's voice, is past description. After wringing their hands and rushing to and fro as if they were stark mad, one mounted on the shoulders of his brother and tried to clamber up the face of the high wall, guarded at the top with spikes and points of iron. And when he fell among the crowd, he was not deterred by his bruises, but mounted up again, and fell again, and, when he found the feat impossible, began to beat the stones and tear them with his hands, as if he could that way make a breach in the strong building, and force a passage in. At last, they clove their way among the mob about the door, though many men, a dozen times their match, had tried in vain to do so, and were seen, in—yes, in—the fire, striving to prize it down, with crowbars.

Nor were they alone affected by the outcry from within the prison. The women who were looking on, shrieked loudly, beat their hands together, stopped their ears; and many fainted: the men who were not near the walls and active in the siege, rather than do nothing, tore up the pavement of the street, and did so with a haste and fury they could not have surpassed if that had been the jail, and they were near their object. Not one living creature in the throng was for an instant still. The whole great mass were mad.

A shout! Another! Another yet, though few knew why, or what it meant. But those around the gate had seen it slowly yield, and drop from its topmost hinge. It hung on that side by but one, but it was upright still, because of the bar, and its having sunk, of its own weight, into the heap of ashes at its foot. There was now a gap at the top of the doorway, through which could be descried a gloomy passage, cavernous and dark. Pile up the fire!

It burnt fiercely. The door was red-hot, and the gap wider. They vainly tried to shield their faces with their hands, and standing as if in readiness for a spring, watched the place. Dark figures, some crawling on their hands and knees, some carried in the arms of others, were seen to pass along the roof. It was plain the jail could hold out no longer. The keeper, and his officers, and their wives and children, were escaping. Pile up the fire!

The door sank down again: it settled deeper in the cinders— tottered—yielded—was down!

As they shouted again, they fell back, for a moment, and left a clear space about the fire that lay between them and the jail entry. Hugh leapt upon the blazing heap, and scattering a train of sparks into the air, and making the dark lobby glitter with those that hung upon his dress, dashed into the jail.

The hangman followed. And then so many rushed upon their track, that the fire got trodden down and thinly strewn about the street; but there was no need of it now, for, inside and out, the prison was in flames.

CHAPTER THE SIXTY-FIFTH.

URING the whole course of the terrible scene which was now at its height, one man in the jail suffered a degree of fear and mental torment which had no parallel in the endurance, even of those who lay under sentence of death.

When the rioters first assembled before the building, the murderer was roused from sleep—if such slumbers as his, may have that blessed name—by the roar of voices, and the struggling of a great crowd. He started up as these sounds met his ear, and, sitting on his bedstead, listened.

After a short interval of silence the noise burst out again. Still listening attentively, he made out, in course of time, that the jail was besieged by a furious multitude. His guilty conscience instantly arrayed these men against himself, and brought the fear upon him that he would be singled out, and torn to pieces.

Once impressed with the terror of this conceit, everything tended to confirm and strengthen it. His double crime, the circumstances under which it had been committed, the length of time that had elapsed, and its discovery in spite of all, made him as it were, the visible object of the Almighty's wrath. In all the crime and vice and moral gloom of the great pest-house of the capital, he stood alone, marked and singled out by his great guilt, a Lucifer among the devils. The other prisoners were a host, hiding and sheltering each other—a crowd like that without the walls. He was one man against the whole united concourse; a single, solitary, lonely man, from whom the very captives in the jail fell off and shrunk appalled.

It might be that the intelligence of his capture having been bruited abroad, they had come there purposely to drag him out and kill him in the street; or it might be that they were the rioters, and, in pursuance of an old design, had come to sack the prison. But in either case he had no belief or hope that they would spare him. Every shout they raised, and every sound they made, was a blow upon his heart. As the attack went on, he grew more wild and frantic in his terror: tried to pull away the bars that guarded the chimney and prevented him from climbing up: called loudly on the turnkeys to cluster round the cell and save him from the fury of the rabble; or put him in some dungeon underground, no matter of what depth, how dark it was, or loathsome, or beset with rats and creeping things, so that it hid him and was hard to find.

But no one came, or answered him. Fearful, even while he cried to them, of attracting attention, he was silent. By and bye, he saw, as he looked from his grated window, a strange glimmering on the stone walls and pavement of the yard. It was feeble at first, and came and went, as though some officers with torches were passing to and fro upon the roof of the prison. Soon it reddened, and lighted brands came whirling down, spattering the ground with fire, and burning sullenly in corners. One rolled beneath a wooden bench, and set it in a blaze; another caught a water-spout, and so went climbing up the wall, leaving a long straight track of fire behind it. After a time, a slow thick shower of burning fragments, from some upper portion of the prison which was blazing nigh, began to fall before his door. Remembering that it opened outwards, he knew that every spark which fell upon the heap, and in the act lost its bright life, and died an ugly speck of dust and rubbish, helped to entomb him in a living grave. Still, though the jail resounded with shrieks and cries for help,—though the fire bounded up as if each separate flame had had a tiger's life, and roared as though, in every one, there were a hungry voice—though the heat began to grow intense, and the air suffocating, and the clamour without increased, and the danger of his situation even from one merciless element was every moment more extreme,—still he was afraid to raise his voice again, lest the crowd should break in, and should, of their own ears or from the information given them by the other prisoners, get the clue to his place of confinement. Thus fearful alike, of those within the prison and of those without; of noise and silence; light and darkness; of being released, and being left there to die; he was so tortured and tormented, that nothing man has ever done to man in the horrible caprice of power and cruelty, exceeds his self-inflicted punishment.

Now, now, the door was down. Now they came rushing through the jail, calling to each other in the vaulted passages; clashing the iron gates dividing yard from yard; beating at the doors of cells and wards; wrenching off bolts and locks and bars; tearing down the doorposts to get men out; endeavouring to drag them by main force through gaps and windows where a child could scarcely pass; whooping and yelling without a moment's rest; and running through the heat and flames as if they were cased in metal. By their legs, their arms, the hair upon their heads, they dragged the prisoners out. Some threw themselves upon the captives as they got towards the door, and tried to file away their irons; some danced about them with a frenzied joy, and rent their clothes, and were ready, as it seemed, to tear them limb from limb. Now a party of a dozen men came darting through the yard into which the murderer cast fearful glances from his darkened window; dragging a prisoner along the ground whose dress they had nearly torn from his body in their mad eagerness to set him free, and who was bleeding and senseless in their hands. Now a score of prisoners ran to and fro, who had lost themselves in the intricacies of the prison, and were so bewildered with the noise and glare that they knew not where to turn or what to do, and still cried out for help, as loudly as before. Anon some famished wretch whose theft had been a loaf of bread, or scrap of butcher's meat, came skulking past, barefooted,—going slowly away because that jail, his house, was burning; not because he had any other, or had friends to meet, or old haunts to revisit, or any liberty to gain, but liberty to starve and die. And then a knot of highwaymen went trooping by, conducted by the friends they had among the crowd, who muffled their fetters as they went along, with handkerchiefs and bands of hay, and wrapped them up in coats and cloaks, and gave them drink from bottles, and held it to their lips, because of their handcuffs which there was no time to remove. All this, and Heaven knows how much more, was done amidst a noise, a hurry, and distraction, like nothing that we know of, even in our dreams; which seemed for ever on the rise, and never to decrease for the space of a single instant.

He was still looking down from his window upon these things, when a band of men with torches, ladders, axes, and many kinds of weapons, poured into the yard, and hammering at his door, enquired if there were any prisoner within. He left the window when he saw them coming, and drew back into the remotest corner of the cell; but although he returned them no answer, they had a fancy that some one was within, for they presently set ladders against it, and began to tear away the bars at the casement; not only that, indeed, but with pickaxes to hew down the very stones in the wall.

As soon as they had made a breach at the window, large enough for the admission of a man's head, one of them thrust in a torch and looked all round the room. He followed this man's gaze until it rested on himself, and heard him demand why he had not answered, but made him no reply.

In the general surprise and wonder, they were used to this; for without saying anything more, they enlarged the breach until it was large enough to admit the body of a man, and then came dropping down upon the floor, one after another, until the cell was full. They caught him up among them, handed him to the window, and those who stood upon the ladders cast him down upon the pavement of the yard. Then the rest came out, one after another, and, bidding him fly, and lose no time, or the way would be choked up, hurried away to rescue others.

It seemed not a minute's work from first to last. He staggered to his feet, incredulous of what had happened, when the yard was filled again, and a crowd rushed on, hurrying Barnaby among them. In another minute—not so much: another minute! the same instant, with no lapse or interval between! he and his son were being passed from hand to hand, through the dense crowd in the street, and were glancing backward at a burning pile which some one said was Newgate.

From the moment of their first entrance into the prison, the crowd dispersed themselves about it, and swarmed into every chink and crevice, as if they had a perfect acquaintance with its innermost parts, and bore in their minds an exact plan of the whole. For this immediate knowledge of the place, they were, no doubt, in a great degree indebted to the hangman, who stood in the lobby, directing some to go this way, some that, and some the other; and who materially assisted in bringing about the wonderful rapidity with which the release of the prisoners was effected.

But this functionary of the law reserved one important piece of intelligence, and kept it snugly to himself. When he had issued his instructions relative to every other part of the building, and the mob were dispersed from end to end, and busy at their work, he took a bundle of keys from a kind of cupboard in the wall, and going by a private passage near the chapel (it joined the governor's house, and was then on fire), betook himself to the condemned cells, which were a series of small, strong, dismal rooms, opening on a low gallery, guarded, at the end at which he entered, by a strong iron wicket, and at its opposite extremity by two doors and a thick grate. Having double locked the wicket, and assured himself that the other entrances were well secured, he sat down on a bench in the gallery, and sucked the head of his stick, with an air of the utmost complacency, tranquillity, and contentment.

It would have been strange enough, a man's enjoying himself in this quiet manner, while the prison was burning, and such a tumult was cleaving the air, though he had been outside the walls. But here, in the very heart of the building, and moreover with the prayers and cries of the four men under sentence sounding in his ears, and their hands, stretched out through the gratings in their cell doors, clasped in frantic entreaty before his very eyes, it was particularly remarkable. Indeed, Mr. Dennis appeared to think it an uncommon circumstance, and to banter himself upon it; for he thrust his hat on one side as some men do when they are in a waggish humour, sucked the head of his stick with a higher relish, and smiled as though he would say, "Dennis, you're a rum dog; you're a queer fellow; you're capital company, Dennis, and quite a character!"

He sat in this way for some minutes, while the four men in the cells, who were certain that somebody had entered the gallery, but could not see who, gave vent to such piteous entreaties as wretches in their miserable condition may be supposed to have been inspired with: urging, whoever it was, to set them at liberty, for the love of Heaven; and protesting, with great fervour, and truly enough, perhaps, for the time, that if they escaped, they would amend their ways, and would never, never, never again do wrong before God or man, but would lead penitent and sober lives, and sorrowfully repent the crimes they had committed. The terrible energy with which they spoke, would have moved any person, no matter how good or just (if any good or just person could have strayed into that sad place that night), to have set them at liberty; and, while he would have left any other punishment to its free course, to have saved them from this last dreadful and repulsive penalty; which never turned a man inclined to evil, and has hardened thousands who were half inclined to good.

Mr. Dennis, who had been bred and nurtured in the good old school, and had administered the good old laws on the good old plan, always once and sometimes twice every six weeks, for a long time, bore these appeals with a deal of philosophy. Being at last, however, rather disturbed in his pleasant reflection by their repetition, he rapped at one of the doors with his stick, and cried:

"Hold your noise there, will you?"

At this they all cried together that they were to be hanged on the next day but one; and again implored his aid.

"Aid! For what!" said Mr. Dennis, playfully rapping the knuckles of the hand nearest him.

"To save us!" they cried.

"Oh, certainly," said Mr. Dennis, winking at the wall in the absence of any friend with whom he could humour the joke. "And so you're to be worked off, are you brothers?"

"Unless we are released to-night," one of them cried, "we are dead men!"

"I tell you what it is," said the hangman, gravely; "I'm afraid my friend that you're not in that 'ere state of mind that's suitable to your condition, then; you're not a going to be released: don't think it— Will you leave off that 'ere indecent row? I wonder you an't ashamed of yourselves, I do."

He followed up this reproof by rapping every set of knuckles one after the other, and having done so, resumed his seat again with a cheerful countenance.

"You've had law," he said, crossing his legs and elevating his eyebrows: "laws have been made a' purpose for you; a wery handsome prison's been made a' purpose for you; a parson's kept a' purpose for you; a constitootional officer's appointed a' purpose for you; carts is maintained a' purpose for you—and yet you're not contented!—*Will* you hold that noise, you sir in the furthest?"

A groan was the only answer.

"So well as I can make out," said Mr. Dennis, in a tone of mingled badinage and remonstrance, "there's not a man among you. I begin to think I'm on the opposite side, and among the ladies; though for the matter of that, I've seen a many ladies face it out, in a manner that did honour to the sex.—You in number two, don't grind them teeth of yours. Worse manners," said the hangman, rapping at the door with his stick, "I never see in this place afore. I'm ashamed on you. You're a disgrace to the Bailey!"

After pausing for a moment to hear if anything could be pleaded in justification, Mr. Dennis resumed, in a sort of coaxing tone:

"Now look'ee here, you four. I'm come here to take care of you, and see that you an't burnt instead of the other thing. It's no use your making any noise, for you won't be found out by them as has broken in, and you'll only be hoarse when you come to the speeches,—which is a pity. What I say in respect to the speeches always is, 'Give it mouth.' That's my maxim. Give it mouth. I've heerd," said the hangman, pulling off his hat to take his handkerchief from the crown and wipe his face, and then putting it on again a little more on one side than before, "I've heerd a eloquence on them boards—you know what boards I mean—and have heerd a degree of mouth given to them speeches, that they was as clear as a bell, and as good as a play. There's a pattern! And always, when a thing of this nature's to come off, what I stand up for, is, a proper frame of mind. Let's have a proper frame of mind, and we can go through with it, creditable—pleasant—sociable. Whatever you do, and I address myself, in particular, to you in the furthest, never snivel. I'd sooner by half, though I lose by it, see a man tear his clothes a' purpose to spile 'em before they come to me, than find him snivelling. It's ten to one a better frame of mind, every way!"

While the hangman addressed them to this effect, in the tone and

with the air of a pastor in familiar conversation with his flock, the
noise had been in some degree subdued; for the rioters were busy in
conveying the prisoners to the Sessions House,* which was beyond
the main walls of the prison, though connected with it, and the
crowd were busy, too, in passing them from thence along the street.
But when he had got thus far in his discourse, the sound of voices in
the yard showed plainly that the mob had returned and were coming
that way; and directly afterwards a violent crashing at the grate
below, gave note of their attack upon the cells (as they were called) at
last.

It was in vain the hangman ran from door to door, and covered the
grates, one after another, with his hat, in futile efforts to stifle the
cries of the four men within; it was in vain he dogged their out-
stretched hands, and beat them with his stick, or menaced them with
new and lingering pains in the execution of his office; the place
resounded with their cries. These, together with the feeling that they
were now the last men in the jail, so worked upon and stimulated the
besiegers, that in an incredibly short space of time they forced the
strong grate down below, which was formed of iron rods two inches
square, drove in the two other doors, as if they had been but deal
partitions, and stood at the end of the gallery with only a bar or two
between them and the cells.

"Halloa!" cried Hugh, who was the first to look into the dusky
passage: "Dennis before us! Well done, old boy. Be quick, and open
here, or we shall be suffocated in the smoke, going out."

"Go out at once, then," said Dennis. "What do you want here?"

"Want!" echoed Hugh. "The four men."

"Four devils!" cried the hangman. "Don't you know they're left
for death on Thursday? Don't you respect the law—the constitoo-
tion—nothing? Let the four men be."

"Is this a time for joking?" cried Hugh. "Do you hear 'em? Pull
away these bars that have got fixed between the door and the ground;
and let us in."

"Brother," said the hangman in a low voice, as he stooped under
pretence of doing what Hugh desired, but only looked up in his face,
"can't you leave these here four men to me, if I've the whim? You do
what you like, and have what you like of everything for your share,
give me my share. I want these four men left alone, I tell you!"

"Pull the bars down, or stand out of the way," was Hugh's reply.

"You can turn the crowd if you like, you know that well enough, brother," said the hangman, slowly. "What! You *will* come in, will you?"

"Yes."

"You won't let these men alone, and leave 'em to me? You've no respect for nothing—haven't you?" said the hangman, retreating to the door by which he had entered, and regarding his companion with an ugly scowl. "You *will* come in, will you, brother?"

"I tell you, yes. What the devil ails you? Where are you going?"

"No matter where I'm going," rejoined the hangman, looking in again at the iron wicket, which he had nearly shut upon himself, and held ajar. "Remember where you're coming. That's all!"

With that, he shook his likeness at Hugh, and giving him a grin, compared with which his usual smile was amiable, disappeared, and shut the door.

Hugh paused no longer, but goaded alike by the cries of the convicts, and by the impatience of the crowd, warned the man immediately behind him—the way was only wide enough for one abreast—to stand back, and wielded a sledge hammer with such strength, that after a few blows the iron bent and broke, and gave them free admittance.

If the two sons of one of these men, of whom mention has been made, were furious in their zeal before, they had now the wrath and vigour of lions. Calling to the man within each cell, to keep as far back as he could, lest the axes crashing through the door should wound him, a party went to work upon each one, to beat it in by sheer strength, and force the bolts and staples from their hold. But although these two lads had the weakest party, and the worst armed, and did not begin until after the others, having stopped to whisper to him through the grate, that door was the first open, and that man the first out. As they dragged him into the gallery to knock off his irons, he fell down among them, a mere heap of chains, and was carried out in that state on men's shoulders with no sign of life.

The release of these four wretched creatures, and conveying them, astounded and bewildered, into the street so full of life—a spectacle they had never thought to see again, until they emerged from solitude and silence upon that last journey, when the air should be heavy with the pent-up breath of thousands, and the streets and houses should be built and roofed with human faces, not with bricks and tiles and stones—was the crowning horror of the scene. Their pale and haggard looks, and hollow eyes; their staggering feet, and hands stretched out as if to save themselves from falling; their wandering and uncertain air; the way they heaved and gasped for breath, as though in water, when they were first plunged into the crowd; all marked them for the men. No need to say "this one was doomed to die;" there were the words broadly stamped and branded on his face. The crowd fell off, as if they had been laid out for burial, and had risen in their shrouds; and many were seen to shudder, as though they had been actually dead men, when they chanced to touch or brush against their garments.

At the bidding of the mob, the houses were all illuminated that night—lighted up from top to bottom as at a time of public gaiety and joy. Many years afterwards, old people who lived in their youth near this part of the city, remembered being in a great glare of light, within doors and without, and as they looked, timid and frightened children, from the windows, seeing *a face* go by. Though the whole great crowd and all its other terrors had faded from their recollection, this one object remained; alone, distinct, and well-remembered. Even in the unpractised minds of infants, one of these doomed men darting by, and but an instant seen, was an image of force enough to dim the whole concourse; to find itself an all-absorbing place, and hold it ever after.

When this last task had been achieved, the shouts and cries grew fainter; the clank of fetters, which had resounded on all sides as the prisoners escaped, was heard no more; all the noises of the crowd subsided into a hoarse and sullen murmur as it passed into the distance; and when the human tide had rolled away, a melancholy heap of smoking ruins marked the spot where it had lately chafed and roared.

CHAPTER THE SIXTY-SIXTH.

ALTHOUGH he had had no rest upon the previous night, and had watched with little intermission for some weeks past, sleeping only in the day by starts and snatches, Mr. Haredale, from the dawn of morning until sunset, sought his niece in every place where he deemed it possible she could have taken refuge. All day long, nothing, save a draught of water, passed his lips; though he prosecuted his inquiries far and wide, and never so much as sat down, once.

In every quarter he could think of; at Chigwell and in London; at the houses of the trades'-people with whom he dealt, and of the friends he knew; he pursued his search. A prey to the most harrowing anxieties and apprehensions, he went from magistrate to magistrate, and finally to the Secretary of State.* The only comfort he received was from this minister, who assured him that the Government, being now driven to the exercise of the extreme prerogatives of the Crown, were determined to exert them; that a proclamation would probably be out upon the morrow, giving to the military, discretionary and unlimited power in the suppression of the riots; that the sympathies of the King, the Administration, and both Houses of Parliament, and indeed of all good men of every religious persuasion, were strongly with the Catholics; and that justice should be done them at any cost or hazard. He told him, further, that other persons whose houses had been burnt, had for a time lost sight of their children or their relatives, but had in every case, within his knowledge, succeeded in discovering them; that his complaint should be remembered, and fully stated in the instructions given to the officers in command, and to all the inferior myrmidons of justice;* and that everything that could be done to help him, should be done, with a good-will and in good faith.

Grateful for this consolation, feeble as it was in its reference to the past, and little hope as it afforded him in connexion with the subject of distress which lay nearest to his heart; and really thankful for the interest the minister expressed, and seemed to feel, in his condition; Mr. Haredale withdrew. He found himself, with the night coming on, alone in the streets; and destitute of any place in which to lay his head.

He entered an hotel near Charing Cross, and ordered some refreshment and a bed. He saw that his faint and worn appearance attracted the attention of the landlord and his waiters; and thinking that they might suppose him to be penniless, took out his purse, and laid it on the table. It was not that, the landlord said, in a faltering voice. If he were one of those who had suffered by the rioters, he durst not give him entertainment. He had a family of children, and had been twice warned to be careful in receiving guests. He heartily prayed his forgiveness, but what could he do?

Nothing. No man felt that, more sincerely than Mr. Haredale. He told the man as much, and left the house.

Feeling that he might have anticipated this occurrence, after what he had seen at Chigwell in the morning, where no man dared to touch a spade, though he offered a large reward to all who would come and dig among the ruins of his house, he walked along the Strand; too proud to expose himself to another refusal, and of too generous a spirit to involve in distress or ruin any honest tradesman who might be weak enough to give him shelter. He wandered into one of the streets by the side of the river, and was pacing in a thoughtful manner up and down, thinking, strangely, of things that had happened long ago, when he heard a servant-man at an upper window call to another on the opposite side of the street, that the mob were setting fire to Newgate.

To Newgate! where that man was! His failing strength returned, his energies came back with tenfold vigour, on the instant. If it were possible—if they should set the murderer free—was he, after all he had undergone, to die with the suspicion of having slain his own brother, dimly gathering about him—

He had no consciousness of going to the jail; but there he stood, before it. There was the crowd, wedged and pressed together in a dense, dark, moving mass; and there were the flames soaring up into the air. His head turned round and round, lights flashed before his eyes, and he struggled hard with two men.

"Nay, nay," said one. "Be more yourself, my good sir. We attract attention here. Come away. What can you do among so many men?"

"The gentleman's always for doing something," said the other, forcing him along as he spoke. "I like him for that. I do like him for that."

They had by this time got him into a court, hard by the prison. He looked from one to the other, and as he tried to release himself, felt that he tottered on his feet. He who had spoken first, was the old gentleman whom he had seen at the Lord Mayor's. The other was John Grueby, who had stood by him so manfully at Westminster.

"What does this mean?" he asked them, faintly. "How came we together?"

"On the skirts of the crowd," returned the distiller; "but come with us. Pray come with us. You seem to know my friend here?"

"Surely," said Mr. Haredale, looking in a kind of stupor at John.

"He'll tell you then," returned the old gentleman, "that I am a man to be trusted. He's my servant. He was lately (as you know, I have no doubt) in Lord George Gordon's service; but he left it, and brought, in pure good-will to me and others, who are marked by the rioters, such intelligence as he had picked up, of their designs."

—"On one condition, please, sir," said John, touching his hat. "No evidence against my Lord—a misled man—a kind-hearted man, sir. My Lord never intended this."

"The condition will be observed, of course," rejoined the old distiller. "It's a point of honour. But come with us, sir; pray come with us."

John Grueby added no entreaties, but he adopted a different kind of persuasion, by putting his arm through one of Mr. Haredale's, while his master took the other, and leading him away with all speed.

Sensible, from a strange lightness in his head, and a difficulty in fixing his thoughts on anything, even to the extent of bearing his companions in his mind for a minute together without looking at them, that his intellect was affected by the agitation and suffering through which he had passed, and to which he was still a prey, Mr. Haredale let them lead him where they would. As they went along, he was conscious of having no command over what he said or thought, and that he had a fear of going mad.

The distiller lived, as he had told him when they first met, on Holborn Hill, where he had great storehouses and drove a large trade. They approached his house by a back entrance, lest they should attract the notice of the crowd, and went into an upper room which faced towards the street; the windows, however, in common with those of every other room in the house, were boarded up inside, that out of doors all might appear quite dark.

By the time they had laid him on a sofa in this chamber, Mr. Haredale was perfectly insensible; but John immediately fetching a surgeon, who took from him a large quantity of blood, he gradually came to himself. As he was for the time too weak to walk, they had no difficulty in persuading him to remain there all night, and got him to bed without loss of time. That done, they gave him a cordial and some toast, and presently a pretty strong composing-draught, under the influence of which he soon fell into a lethargy, and, for a time, forgot his troubles.

The vintner, who was a very hearty old fellow and a worthy man, had no thoughts of going to bed himself, for he had received several threatening warnings from the rioters, and had indeed gone out that evening to try and gather from the conversation of the mob whether his house was to be the next attacked. He sat all night in an easy-chair in the same room—dozing a little now and then—and received from time to time the reports of John Grueby and two or three other trust-worthy persons in his employ, who went out into the streets as scouts; and for whose entertainment an ample allowance of good cheer (which the old vintner, despite his anxiety, now and then attacked himself) was set forth in an adjoining chamber.

These accounts were of a sufficiently-alarming nature from the first; but as the night wore on, they grew so much worse, and involved such a fearful amount of riot and destruction, that in comparison with these new tidings all the previous disturbances sunk to nothing.

The first intelligence that came, was of the taking of Newgate, and the escape of all the prisoners, whose track, as they made up Holborn and into the adjacent streets, was proclaimed to those citizens who were shut up in their houses, by the rattling of their chains, which formed a dismal concert, and was heard in every direction: as though so many forges were at work. The flames too shone so brightly through the vintner's skylights, that the rooms and staircases below were nearly as light as in broad day; while the distant shouting of the mob seemed to shake the very walls and ceilings.

At length they were heard approaching the house, and some minutes of terrible anxiety ensued. They came close up, and stopped before it; but after giving three loud yells, went on. And although they returned several times that night, creating new alarms each time, they did nothing there; having their hands full. Shortly after they had gone away for the first time, one of the scouts came running in with the news that they had stopped before Lord Mansfield's house in Bloomsbury square.*

Soon afterwards there came another, and another, and then the first returned again: and so, by little and little, their tale was this:— That the mob gathering round Lord Mansfield's house, had called on those within to open the door, and receiving no reply (for Lord and Lady Mansfield were at that moment escaping by the backway), forced an entrance according to their usual custom. That they then began to demolish it with great fury, and setting fire to it in several parts, involved in a common ruin the whole of the costly furniture, the plate and jewels, a beautiful gallery of pictures, the rarest collection of manuscripts ever possessed by any one private person in the world, and worse than all, because nothing could replace this loss, the great Law Library, on almost every page of which were notes in the Judge's own hand, of inestimable value,—being the results of the study and experience of his whole life. That while they were howling and exulting round the fire, a troop of soldiers, with a magistrate among them, came up, and being too late (for the mischief was by that time done), began to disperse the crowd. That the riot act being read, and the crowd still resisting, the soldiers received orders to fire, and levelling their muskets shot dead at the first discharge six men and a woman, and wounded many persons; and loading again directly, fired another volley, but over the people's heads it was supposed, as none were seen to fall. That thereupon, and daunted by the shrieks and tumult, the crowd began to disperse, and the soldiers went away: leaving the killed and wounded on the ground: which they had no sooner done than the rioters came back again, and taking up the dead bodies, and the wounded people, formed into a rude procession, having the bodies in the front. That in this order, they paraded off with a horrible merriment; fixing weapons in the dead men's hands to make them look as if alive; and preceded by a fellow ringing Lord Mansfield's dinner-bell with all his might.

The scouts reported further, that this party meeting with some others who had been at similar work elsewhere, they all united into one, and drafting off a few men with the killed and wounded, marched away to Lord Mansfield's country seat at Caen Wood,* between Hampstead and Highgate; bent upon destroying that house likewise, and lighting up a great fire there, which from that height should be seen all over London. But in this, they were disappointed, for a party of horse having arrived before them, they retreated faster than they went, and came straight back to town.

There being now a great many parties in the streets, each went to work according to its humour, and a dozen houses were quickly blazing, including those of Sir John Fielding and two other justices,* and four in Holborn—one of the greatest thoroughfares in

London—which were all burning at the same time, and burned until they went out of themselves, for the people cut the engine hose, and would not suffer the firemen to play upon the flames. At one house near Moorfields, they found in one of the rooms some canary birds in cages, and these they cast into the fire alive. The poor little creatures screamed, it was said, like infants, when they were flung upon the blaze; and one man was so touched that he tried in vain to save them, which roused the indignation of the crowd, and nearly cost him his life.

At this same house, one of the fellows who went through the rooms, breaking the furniture and helping to destroy the building, found a child's doll—a poor toy—which he exhibited at the window to the mob below, as the image of some unholy saint which the late occupants had worshipped. While he was doing this, another man

with an equally tender conscience (they had both been foremost in throwing down the canary birds for roasting alive), took his seat on the parapet of the house, and harangued the crowd from a pamphlet circulated by the association, relative to the true principles of Christianity. Meanwhile the Lord Mayor, with his hands in his pockets, looked on as an idle man might look at any other show, and seem mightily satisfied to have got a good place.

Such were the accounts brought to the old vintner by his servants as he sat at the side of Mr. Haredale's bed; having been unable even to doze, after the first part of the night; being too much disturbed by his own fears; by the cries of the mob, the light of the fires, and the firing of the soldiers. Such, with the addition of the release of all the prisoners in the New Jail at Clerkenwell,* and as many robberies of passengers in the streets, as the crowd had leisure to indulge in, were the scenes of which Mr. Haredale was happily unconscious, and which were all enacted before midnight.*

CHAPTER THE SIXTY-SEVENTH.

WHEN darkness broke away and morning began to dawn, the town wore a strange aspect indeed.

Sleep had scarcely been thought of all night. The general alarm was so apparent in the faces of the inhabitants, and its expression was so aggravated by want of rest (few persons, with any property to lose, having dared to go to bed since Monday), that a stranger coming into the streets would have supposed some mortal pest or plague was raging. In place of the usual cheerfulness and animation of morning, everything was dead and silent. The shops remained unopened, offices and warehouses were shut, the coach and chair stands were deserted, no carts or waggons rumbled through the slowly waking streets, the early cries were all hushed; a universal gloom prevailed. Great numbers of people were out, even at day-break, but they flitted to and fro as though they shrank from the sound of their own footsteps; the public ways were haunted rather than frequented; and round the smoking ruins people stood apart from one another and in silence; not venturing to condemn the rioters, or to be supposed to do so, even in whispers.

At the Lord President's in Piccadilly, at Lambeth Palace, at the

Lord Chancellor's in Great Ormond Street,* in the Royal Exchange, the Bank, the Guildhall*, the Inns of Court, the Courts of Law, and every chamber fronting the streets near Westminster Hall and the Houses of Parliament, parties of soldiers were posted before daylight. A body of Horse-Guards paraded Palace-yard; an encampment was formed in the Park, where fifteen hundred men and five battalions of Militia* were under arms; the Tower was fortified, the draw-bridges were raised, the cannon loaded and pointed, and two regiments of artillery busied in strengthening the fortress and preparing it for defence. A numerous detachment of soldiers were stationed to keep guard at the New-River Head,* which the people had threatened to attack, and where, it was said, they meant to cut off the main-pipes, so that there might be no water for the extinction of the flames. In the Poultry, and on Cornhill,* and at several other leading points, iron chains were drawn across the street; parties of soldiers were distributed in some of the old city churches while it was yet dark; and in several private houses (among them, Lord Rockingham's in Grosvenor Square*); which were blockaded as though to sustain a siege, and had guns pointed from the windows. When the sun rose, it shone into handsome apartments filled with armed men; the furniture hastily heaped away in corners, and made of little or no account, in the terror of the time—on arms glittering in city chambers, among desks and stools, and dusty books—into little smoky church-yards in odd lanes and byeways, with soldiers lying down among the tombs, or lounging under the shade of the one old tree, and their pile of muskets sparkling in the light—on solitary sentries pacing up and down in court-yards, silent now, but yesterday resounding with the din and hum of business—everywhere on guard-rooms, garrisons, and threatening preparations.

As the day crept on, still stranger things were witnessed in the streets. The gates of the King's Bench and Fleet Prisons* being opened at the usual hour, were found to have notices affixed to them, announcing that the rioters would come that night to burn them down. The Wardens, too well knowing the likelihood there was of this promise being fulfilled, were fain to set their prisoners at liberty, and give them leave to move their goods; so, all day, such of them as had any furniture were occupied in conveying it, some to this place, some to that, and not a few to the brokers' shops, where they gladly sold it, for any wretched price those gentry chose to give. There were some broken men among these debtors who had been in jail so long, and were so miserable and destitute of friends, so dead to the world, and utterly forgotten and uncared for, that they implored their jailors not to set them free, and to send them, if need were, to some other place of custody. But they, refusing to comply, lest they should incur the anger of the mob, turned them into the streets, where they wandered up and down hardly remembering the ways untrodden by their feet so long, and crying—such abject things those rotten-hearted jails had made them—as they slunk off in their rags, and dragged their slip-shod feet along the pavement.

Even of the three hundred prisoners who had escaped from New-gate, there were some—a few, but there were some—who sought their jailors out and delivered themselves up: preferring imprisonment and punishment to the horrors of such another night as the last. Many of the convicts, drawn back to their old place of captivity by some indescribable attraction, or by a desire to exult over it in its downfall and glut their revenge by seeing it in ashes, actually went back in broad noon, and loitered about the cells. Fifty were retaken at one time on this next day, within the prison walls; but their fate did not deter others, for there they went in spite of everything, and there they were taken in twos and threes, twice or thrice a day, all through the week. Of the fifty just mentioned, some were occupied in endeavouring to rekindle the fire; but in general they seemed to have no object in view but to prowl and lounge about the old place: being often found asleep in the ruins, or sitting talking there, or even eating and drinking, as in a choice retreat.

Besides the notices on the gates of the Fleet and the King's Bench, many similar announcements were left, before one o'clock at noon, at the houses of private individuals; and further, the mob proclaimed their intention of seizing on the Bank, the Mint, the Arsenal at Woolwich,* and the Royal Palaces. The notices were seldom delivered by more than one man, who, if it were at a shop, went in, and laid it, with a bloody threat perhaps, upon the counter; or if it were at a private house, knocked at the door, and thrust it in the servant's hand. Notwithstanding the presence of the military in every quarter of the town, and the great force in the Park, these messengers did their errands with impunity all through the day. So did two boys who went down Holborn alone, armed with bars taken from the railings of Lord Mansfield's house, and demanded money for the rioters. So did a tall man on horseback who made a collection for the same purpose in Fleet Street, and refused to take anything but gold.

A rumour had now got into circulation, too, which diffused a greater dread all through London, even than these publicly-announced intentions of the rioters, though all men knew that if they were successfully effected, there must ensue a national bankruptcy and general ruin. It was said that they meant to throw the gates of Bedlam open, and let all the madmen loose. This suggested such dreadful images to the people's minds, and was indeed an act so fraught with new and unimaginable horrors in the contemplation, that it beset them more than any loss or cruelty of which they could foresee the worst, and drove many sane men nearly mad themselves.

So the day passed on: the prisoners moving their goods; people running to and fro in the streets, carrying away their property; groups standing in silence round the ruins; all business suspended; and the soldiers disposed as has been already mentioned, remaining quite inactive. So the day passed on, and dreaded night drew near again.

At last, at seven o'clock in the evening, the privy council* issued a solemn proclamation that it was now necessary to employ the military, and that the officers had most direct and effectual orders, by an immediate exertion of their utmost force, to repress the disturbances; and warning all good subjects of the king to keep themselves, their servants, and apprentices, within doors that night. There was then delivered out to every soldier on duty, thirty-six rounds of powder and ball; the drums beat; and the whole force was under arms at sunset.

The city authorities, stimulated by these vigorous measures, held a common council;* passed a vote thanking the military associations who had tendered their aid to the civil authorities; accepted it; and placed them under the direction of the two sheriffs. At the queen's palace,* a double guard, the yeomen on duty, the groom-porters, and all other attendants, were stationed in the passages and on the staircases at seven o'clock, with strict instructions to be watchful on their posts all night; and all the doors were locked. The gentlemen of the Temple, and the other Inns, mounted guard within their gates, and strengthened them with the great stones of the pavement, which they took up for the purpose. In Lincoln's Inn, they gave up the hall and commons to the Northumberland militia,* under the command of Lord Algernon Percy;* in some few of the city wards, the burgesses turned out, and without making a very fierce show, looked brave enough. Some hundreds of stout gentlemen threw themselves, armed to the teeth, into the halls of the different companies,* double-locked and bolted all the gates, and dared the rioters (among themselves) to come on at their peril. These arrangements being all made simultaneously, or nearly so, were completed by the time it got dark; and then the streets were comparatively clear, and were guarded at all the great corners and chief avenues by the troops: while parties of the officers rode up and down in all directions, ordering chance stragglers home, and admonishing the residents to keep within their houses, and, if any firing ensued, not to approach the windows. More chains were drawn across such of the thoroughfares as were of a nature to favour the approach of a great crowd, and at each of these points a considerable force was stationed. All these precautions having been taken and it being now quite dark, those in command awaited the result in some anxiety: and not without a hope that such vigilant demonstrations might of themselves dishearten the populace, and prevent any further outrages.

But in this reckoning they were cruelly mistaken, for in half an hour, or less, as though the setting in of night had been their pre-concerted signal, the rioters having previously, in small parties, prevented the lighting of the street lamps, rose like a great sea; and that in so many places at once, and with such inconceivable fury, that those who had the direction of the troops knew not, at first, where to turn or what to do. One after another, new fires blazed up in every quarter of the town, as though it were the intention of the insurgents to wrap the city in a circle of flames, which, contracting by degrees, should burn the whole to ashes; the crowd swarmed and roared in every street; and none but rioters and soldiers being out of doors, it seemed to the latter as if all London were arrayed against them, and they stood alone against the town.

In two hours, six-and-thirty fires were raging—six-and-thirty great conflagrations: among them the Borough Clink in Tooley-street,* the King's Bench, the Fleet, and the New Bridewell.* In almost every street, there was a battle; and in every quarter the muskets of the troops were heard above the shouts and tumult of the mob. The firing began in the Poultry, where the chain was drawn across the road, where nearly a score of people were killed on the first discharge. Their bodies having been hastily carried into St. Mildred's church* by the soldiers, they fired again, and following fast upon the crowd, who began to give way when they saw the execution that was done, formed across Cheapside, and charged them at the point of the bayonet.

The streets were now a dreadful spectacle indeed: while the shouts of the rabble, the shrieks of women, the cries of the wounded, and the constant firing, formed a deafening and an awful accompaniment to the sights which every corner presented. Wherever the road was obstructed by the chains, there the fighting and the loss of life were greatest; but there was hot work and bloodshed in almost every leading thoroughfare, and in every one the same appalling scenes occurred.

At Holborn Bridge,* and on Holborn Hill, the confusion was greater than in any other part; for the crowd that poured out of the city in two great streams, one by Ludgate Hill, and one by Newgate-street, united at that spot, and formed a mass so dense, that at every volley the people seemed to fall in heaps. At this place a large detachment of soldiery were posted, who fired, now up Fleet Market, now up Holborn, now up Snow Hill—constantly raking the streets in each direction. At this place too, several large fires were burning, so that all the terrors of that terrible night seemed to be concentrated in this one spot.

Full twenty times, the rioters, headed by one man who wielded an axe in his right hand, and bestrode a brewer's horse of great size and strength, caparisoned with fetters taken out of Newgate, which clanked and jingled as he went, made an attempt to force a passage at this point, and fire the vintner's house. Full twenty times they were repulsed with loss of life, and still came back again: and though the fellow at their head was marked and singled out by all, and was a conspicuous object as the only rioter on horseback, not a man could hit him. So surely as the smoke cleared away, so surely there was he; calling hoarsely to his companions, brandishing his axe above his head, and dashing on as though he bore a charmed life,* and was proof against ball and powder.

This man was Hugh; and in every part of the riot, he was seen. He headed two attacks upon the Bank, helped to break open the Toll-houses on Blackfriars Bridge,* and cast the money into the street:

fired two of the prisons with his own hand: was here, and there, and everywhere—always foremost—always active—striking at the soldiers, cheering on the crowd, making his horse's iron music heard through all the yell and uproar: but never hurt or stopped. Turn him at one place, and he made a new struggle in another; force him to retreat at this point, and he advanced on that, directly. Driven from Holborn for the twentieth time, he rode at the head of a great crowd straight upon Saint Paul's, attacked a guard of soldiers who kept watch over a body of prisoners within the iron railings, forced them to retreat, rescued the men they had in custody, and with this accession to his party, came back again, mad with liquor and excitement, and hallooing them on like a demon.

It would have been no easy task for the most careful rider to sit a horse in the midst of such a throng and tumult; but though this madman rolled upon his back (he had no saddle) like a boat upon the sea, he never for an instant lost his seat, or failed to guide him where he would. Through the very thickest of the press, over dead bodies and burning fragments, now on the pavement, now in the road, now riding up a flight of steps to make himself the more conspicuous to his party, and now forcing a passage through a mass of human beings, so closely wedged together that it seemed as if the edge of a knife would scarcely part them,—on he went, as though he could surmount all obstacles by the mere exercise of his will. And perhaps his not being shot was in some degree attributable to this very circumstance; for his extreme audacity, and the conviction that he must be one of those to whom the proclamation referred, inspired the soldiers with a desire to take him alive, and diverted many an aim which otherwise might have been more near the mark.

The vintner and Mr. Haredale, unable to sit quietly listening to the terrible noise without seeing what went on, had climbed to the roof of the house; and hiding behind a stack of chimneys, were looking cautiously down into the street, almost hoping that after so many repulses the rioters would be foiled, when a great shout proclaimed that a party were coming round the other way; and the dismal jingling of those accursed fetters warned them next moment that they too were led by Hugh. The soldiers had advanced into Fleet Market and were dispersing the people there; so that they came on with hardly any check, and were soon before the house.

"All's over now," said the vintner. "Fifty thousand pounds will be scattered in a minute. We must save ourselves. We can do no more, and shall have reason to be thankful if we do as much."

Their first impulse was, to clamber along the roofs of the houses, and, knocking at some garret window for admission, pass down that way into the street, and so escape. But another fierce cry from below, and a general upturning of the faces of the crowd, apprised them that they were discovered, and even that Mr. Haredale was recognised; for Hugh, seeing him plainly in the bright glare of the flames, which in that part made it as light as day, called to him by his name, and swore to have his life.

"Leave me here," said Mr. Haredale, "and in Heaven's name, my good friend, save yourself! Come on!" he muttered, as he turned towards Hugh and faced him without any further effort at concealment: "This roof is high, and if we grapple, we will die together!"

"Madness," said the honest vintner, pulling him back, "sheer madness. Hear reason sir. My good sir, hear reason. I could never make myself heard by knocking at a window now; and even if I could, no one would be bold enough to connive at my escape. Through the cellars, there's a kind of passage into the back street by which we roll casks in and out. We shall have time to get down there, before they can force an entry. Do not delay an instant, but come with me—for both our sakes—for mine—my dear good sir!"

As he spoke, and drew Mr. Haredale back, they had both a glimpse of the street. It was but a glimpse, but it showed them the crowd, gathering and clustering round the house: some of the armed men pressing to the front to break down the doors and windows, some bringing brands from the nearest fire, some with lifted faces following their course upon the roof and pointing them out to their companions, all raging and roaring like the flames they lighted up. They saw some men howling and thirsting for the treasures of strong liquor which they knew were stored within; they saw others, who had been wounded, sinking down into the opposite doorways and dying, solitary wretches, in the midst of all the vast assemblage; here a frightened woman trying to escape; and there a lost child; and there a drunken ruffian, unconscious of the death-wound on his head, raving and fighting to the last. All these things, and even such trivial incidents as a man with his hat off, or turning round, or stooping down, or shaking hands with another, they marked distinctly; yet in a glance so brief, that, in the act of stepping back, they lost the whole, and saw but the pale faces of each other, and the red sky above them.

Mr. Haredale yielded to the entreaties of his companion—more because he was resolved to defend him to the last, than for any thought he had of his own life, or any care he entertained for his own safety—and quickly re-entering the house, they descended the stairs together. Loud blows were thundering on the shutters, crowbars were already thrust beneath the door, the glass fell from the sashes, a deep light shone through every crevice, and they heard the voices of the foremost in the crowd so close to every chink and keyhole, that they seemed to be hoarsely whispering their threats into their very ears. They had but a moment reached the bottom of the cellar-steps and shut the door behind them, when the mob broke in.

The vaults were profoundly dark, and having no torch or candle— for they had been afraid to carry one, lest it should betray their place of refuge—they were obliged to grope with their hands. But they were not long without light, for they had not gone far when they heard the crowd forcing the door; and, looking back among the low-arched passages, could see them in the distance, hurrying to and fro with flashing links, broaching the casks, staving the great vats, turning off upon the right hand and the left, into the different cellars, and lying down to drink at the channels of strong spirits which were already flowing fast upon the ground.

They hurried on, not the less quickly for this; and had reached the only vault which lay between them and the passage out, when suddenly, from the direction in which they were going, a strong light gleamed upon their faces; and before they could slip aside, or turn back, or hide themselves, two men (one bearing a torch) came upon them, and cried in an astonished whisper, "Here they are!"

At the same instant they pulled off what they wore upon their heads. Mr. Haredale saw before him Edward Chester, and then saw, when the vintner gasped his name, Joe Willet.

Ay, the same Joe, though with an arm the less, who used to make the quarterly journey on the grey mare to pay the bill to the purple-faced vintner; and that very same purple-faced vintner, formerly of Thames Street, now looked him in the face, and challenged him by name.

"Give me your hand," said Joe softly, taking it whether the astonished vintner would or no. "Don't fear to shake it, man; it's a

friendly one and a hearty one, though it has no fellow. Why, how well you look and how bluff you are! And you—God bless you, sir. Take heart, take heart. We'll find them. Be of good cheer; we have not been idle."

There was something so honest and frank in Joe's speech, that Mr. Haredale put his hand in his involuntarily, though their meeting was suspicious enough. But his glance at Edward Chester, and that gentleman's keeping aloof, were not lost upon Joe, who said bluntly, glancing at Edward while he spoke:

"Times are changed, Mr. Haredale, and times have come when we ought to know friends from enemies, and make no confusion of names. Let me tell you that but for this gentleman, you would most likely have been dead by this time, or badly wounded at the best."

"What do you say?" asked Mr. Haredale.

"I say," said Joe, "first, that it was a bold thing to be in the crowd at all disguised as one of them; though I won't say much about that, on second thoughts, for that's my case too. Secondly, that it was a brave and glorious action—that's what I call it—to strike that fellow off his horse before their eyes!"

"What fellow! Whose eyes!"

"What fellow, sir!" cried Joe: "a fellow who has no good-will to you, and who has the daring and devilry in him of twenty fellows. I know him of old. Once in the house, *he* would have found you, here or anywhere. The rest owe you no particular grudge, and, unless they see you, will only think of drinking themselves dead. But we lose time. Are you ready?"

"Quite," said Edward. "Put out the torch, Joe, and go on. And be silent, there's a good fellow."

"Silent or not silent," murmured Joe, as he dropped the flaring link upon the ground, crushed it with his foot, and gave his hand to Mr. Haredale, "it was a brave and glorious action;—no man can alter that."

Both Mr. Haredale and the worthy vintner were too amazed and too much hurried to ask any further questions, so followed their conductors in silence. It seemed, from a short whispering which presently ensued between them and the vintner relative to the best way of escape, that they had entered by the back-door, with the connivance of John Grueby, who watched outside with the key in his pocket, and whom they had taken into their confidence. A part of the crowd coming up that way, just as they entered, John had double-locked the door again, and made off for the soldiers, so that means of retreat was cut from under them.

However, as the front door had been forced, and this minor crowd, being anxious to get at the liquor, had no fancy for losing time in breaking down another, but had gone round and got in from Holborn with the rest, the narrow lane in the rear was quite free of people. So when they had crawled through the passage indicated by the vintner (which was a mere shelving-trap for the admission of casks), and had managed with some difficulty to unchain and raise the door at the upper end, they emerged into the street without being observed or interrupted. Joe still holding Mr. Haredale tight, and Edward taking the same care of the vintner, they hurried through the streets at a rapid pace; occasionally standing aside to let some fugitives go by, or to keep out of the way of the soldiers who followed them, and whose questions, when they halted to put any, were speedily stopped by one whispered word from Joe.

CHAPTER THE SIXTY-EIGHTH.

WHILE Newgate was burning on the previous night, Barnaby and his father, having been passed among the crowd from hand to hand, stood in Smithfield, on the outskirts of the mob, gazing at the flames like men who had been suddenly roused from sleep. Some moments elapsed before they could distinctly remember where they were, or how they got there; or recollected that while they were standing idle and listless spectators of the fire, they had tools in their hands which had been hurriedly given them that they might free themselves from their fetters.

Barnaby, heavily ironed as he was, if he had obeyed his first impulse, or if he had been alone, would have made his way back to the side of Hugh, who to his clouded intellect now shone forth with the new lustre of being his preserver and truest friend. But his father's terror of remaining in the streets, communicated itself to him when he comprehended the full extent of his fears, and impressed him with the same eagerness to fly to a place of safety.

In a corner of the market among the pens for cattle, Barnaby knelt down, and pausing every now and then to pass his hand over his father's face, or look up to him with a smile, knocked off his irons. When he had seen him spring, a free man, to his feet, and had given vent to the transport of delight which the sight awakened, he went to work upon his own, which soon fell rattling down upon the ground, and left his limbs unfettered.

Gliding away together when this task was accomplished, and passing several groups of men, each gathered round a stooping figure to hide him from those who passed, but unable to repress the clanking sound of hammers, which told that they too were busy at the same work,—the two fugitives made towards Clerkenwell, and passing thence to Islington, as the nearest point of egress, were quickly in the fields. After wandering about for a long time, they found in a pasture near Finchley a poor shed, with walls of mud, and roof of grass and brambles, built for some cow-herd, but now deserted. Here they lay down for the rest of the night.

They wandered up and down when it was day, and once Barnaby went off alone to a cluster of little cottages two or three miles away,

to purchase bread and milk. But finding no better shelter, they
returned to the same place, and lay down again to wait for night.

Heaven alone can tell, with what vague thoughts of duty, and
affection; with what strange promptings of nature, intelligible to him
as to a man of radiant mind and most enlarged capacity; with what
dim memories of children he had played with when a child himself,
who had prattled of their fathers, and of loving them, and being
loved; with how many half-remembered, dreamy associations of his
mother's grief and tears and widowhood; he watched and tended this
man. But that a vague and shadowy crowd of such ideas came slowly
on him; that they taught him to be sorry when he looked upon his
haggard face, that they overflowed his eyes when he stooped to kiss
him on the cheek, that they kept him waking in a tearful gladness,
shading him from the sun, fanning him with leaves, soothing him
when he started in his sleep—ah! what a troubled sleep it was—and
wondering when *she* would come to join them and be happy, is the
Truth. He sat beside him all that day; listening for her footstep in
every breath of air, looking for her shadow on the gently-waving
grass, twining the hedge flowers for her pleasure when she came, and
his when he awoke; and stooping down from time to time to listen to
his mutterings, and wonder why he was so restless in that quiet
place. The sun went down, and night came on, and he was still quite
tranquil; busied with these thoughts, as if there were no other people
in the world, and the dull cloud of smoke hanging on the immense
city in the distance, hid no vices, no crimes, no life or death, or
causes of disquiet—nothing but clear air.

But the hour had now come when he must go alone to find out the
blind man (a task that filled him with delight,) and bring him to that
place; taking especial care that he was not watched or followed on his
way back. He listened to the directions he must observe, repeated
them again and again; and after twice or thrice returning to surprise
his father with a light-hearted laugh, went forth, at last, upon his
errand: leaving Grip, whom he had carried from the jail in his arms,
to his care.

Fleet of foot, and anxious to return, he sped swiftly on towards
the city, but could not reach it before the fires began and made the
night angry with their dismal lustre. When he entered the town—it
might be that he was changed by going there without his late com-
panions, and on no violent errand; or by the beautiful solitude in

which he had passed the day, or by the thoughts that had come upon him,—but it seemed peopled by a legion of devils. This flight and pursuit, this cruel burning and destroying, these dreadful cries and stunning noises, were they the good Lord's noble cause!

Though almost stupefied by the bewildering scene, still he found the blind man's house. It was shut up and tenantless. He waited for a long while, but no one came. At last he withdrew; and as he knew by this time that the soldiers were firing, and many people must have been killed, he went down into Holborn, where he heard the great crowd was, to try if he could find Hugh, and persuade him to avoid the danger, and return with him.

If he had been stunned and shocked before, his horror was increased a thousand-fold when he got into this vortex of the riot, and not being an actor in the terrible spectacle, had it all before his eyes. But there, in the midst, towering above them all, close before the house they were attacking now, was Hugh on horseback, calling to the rest!

Sickened by the sights surrounding him on every side, and by the heat and roar, and crash, he forced his way among the crowd (where many recognised him, and with shouts pressed back to let him pass), and in time was nearly up with Hugh, who was savagely threatening some one, but whom, or what he said he could not, in the great confusion, understand. At that moment the crowd forced their way into the house, and Hugh—it was impossible to see by what means, in such a concourse—fell headlong down.

Barnaby was beside him when he staggered to his feet. It was well he made him hear his voice, or Hugh, with his uplifted axe, would have cleft his skull in twain.

"Barnaby—you! Whose hand was that, that struck me down?"

"Not mine."

"Whose!—I say, whose!" he cried, reeling back, and looking wildly round. "What are we doing? Where is he? Show me!"

"You are hurt," said Barnaby—as indeed he was, in the head, both by the blow he had received, and by his horse's hoof. "Come away with me."

As he spoke, he took the horse's bridle in his hand, turned him, and dragged Hugh several paces. This brought them out of the crowd, which was pouring from the street into the vintner's cellars.

"Where's—where's Dennis?" said Hugh, coming to a stop, and

checking Barnaby with his strong arm. "Where has he been all day? What did he mean by leaving me as he did, in the jail, last night? Tell me, you—d'ye hear!"

With a flourish of his dangerous weapon, he fell down upon the ground like a log. After a minute, though already frantic with drinking and with the wound in his head, he crawled to a stream of burning spirit which was pouring down the kennel, and began to drink at it as if it were a brook of water.

Barnaby drew him away, and forced him to rise. Though he could neither stand nor walk, he involuntarily staggered to his horse, climbed upon his back, and clung there. After vainly attempting to divest the animal of his clanking trappings, Barnaby sprang up behind him, snatched the bridle, turned into Leather Lane, which was close at hand, and urged the frightened horse into a heavy gallop.

He looked back once before he left the street; and looked upon a sight not easily to be erased, even from his remembrance, so long as he had life.

The vintner's house, with a half a dozen others near at hand, was one great, glowing blaze. All night, no one had essayed to quench the flames or stop their progress; but now a body of soldiers were actively engaged in pulling down two old wooden houses, which were every moment in danger of taking fire, and which could scarcely fail, if they were left to burn, to extend the conflagration immensely. The tumbling down of nodding walls and heavy blocks of wood, the hooting and the execrations of the crowd, the distant firing of other military detachments, the distracted looks and cries of those whose habitations were in danger, the hurrying to and fro of frightened people with their goods; the reflections in every quarter of the sky, of deep, red, soaring flames, as though the last day had come and the whole universe were burning; the dust, and smoke, and drift of fiery particles, scorching and kindling all it fell upon; the hot unwholesome vapour, the blight on everything; the stars, and moon, and very sky, obliterated;—made up such a sum of dreariness and ruin, that it seemed as if the face of Heaven were blotted out, and night, in its rest and quiet, and softened light, never could look upon the earth again.

But there was a worse spectacle than this—worse by far than fire and smoke, or even the rabble's unappeasable and maniac rage. The gutters of the street and every crack and fissure in the stones, ran with scorching spirit; which, being dammed up by busy hands, overflowed the road and pavement, and formed a great pool, in which the people dropped down dead by dozens. They lay in heaps all round this fearful pond, husbands and wives, fathers and sons, mothers and daughters, women with children in their arms and babies at their breasts, and drank until they died. While some stooped with their lips to the brink and never raised their heads again, others sprang up from their fiery draught, and danced, half in a mad triumph, and half in the agony of suffocation, until they fell, and steeped their corpses in the liquor that had killed them. Nor was even this the worst or most appalling kind of death that happened on this fatal night. From the burning cellars, where they drank out of hats, pails, buckets, tubs, and shoes, some men were drawn, alive, but all alight from head to foot; who, in their unendurable anguish and suffering, making for anything that had the look of water, rolled, hissing, in this hideous lake, and splashed up liquid fire which lapped in all it met with as it ran along the surface, and neither spared the living nor the dead. On this last night of the great riots—

for the last night it was—the wretched victims of a senseless outcry, became themselves the dust and ashes of the flames they had kindled, and strewed the public streets of London.

With all he saw in this last glance fixed indelibly upon his mind, Barnaby hurried from the city which inclosed such horrors; and, holding down his head that he might not even see the glare of the fires upon the quiet landscape, was soon in the still country roads.

He stopped at about half-a-mile from the shed where his father lay, and with some difficulty making Hugh sensible that he must dismount, sunk the horse's furniture in a pool of stagnant water, and turned the animal loose. That done, he supported his companion as well as he could, and led him slowly forward.

CHAPTER THE SIXTY-NINTH.

IT was the dead of night, and very dark, when Barnaby, with his stumbling companion, approached the place where he had left his father; but he could see him stealing away into the gloom, distrustful even of him, and rapidly retreating. After calling to him twice or thrice that there was nothing to fear, but without effect, he suffered Hugh to sink upon the ground, and followed, to bring him back.

He continued to creep away, until Barnaby was close upon him; then turned, and said in a terrible, though suppressed voice:

"Let me go. Do not lay hands upon me. Stand back. You have told her; and you and she together, have betrayed me!"

Barnaby looked at him, in silence.

"You have seen your mother!"

"No," cried Barnaby, eagerly. "Not for a long time—longer than I can tell. A whole year, I think. Is she here?"

His father looked upon him stedfastly for a few moments, then said—drawing nearer to him as he spoke, for, seeing his face, and hearing his words, it was impossible to doubt his truth:

"What man is that?"

"Hugh—Hugh. Only Hugh. You know him. *He* will not harm you. Why, you're afraid of Hugh! Ha ha ha! Afraid of gruff, old, noisy Hugh!"

"What man is he, I ask you," he rejoined so fiercely, that Barnaby stopped in his laugh, and shrinking back, surveyed him with a look of terrified amazement.

"Why, how stern you are! You make me fear you, though you are my father—I never feared her. Why do you speak to me so?"

—"I want," he answered, putting away the hand which his son, with a timid desire to propitiate him, laid upon his sleeve,—"I want an answer, and you give me only jeers and questions. Who have you brought with you to this hiding-place, poor fool; and where is the blind man?"

"I don't know where. His house was close shut. I waited, but no person came; that was no fault of mine. This is Hugh—brave Hugh, who broke into that ugly jail, and set us free. Aha! You like him now, do you? You like him now!"

"Why does he lie upon the ground?"

"He has had a fall, and has been drinking. The fields and trees go round, and round, and round, with him, and the ground heaves under his feet. You know him? You remember? See!"

They had by this time returned to where he lay, and both stooped over him to look into his face.

"I recollect the man," his father murmured. "Why did you bring him here?"

"Because he would have been killed if I had left him over yonder. They were firing guns, and shedding blood. Does the sight of blood turn you sick, father? I see it does, by your face. That's like me— What are you looking at?"

"At nothing!" said the murderer softly, as he started back a pace or two, and gazed with sunken jaw and staring eyes above his son's head. "At nothing!"

He remained in the same attitude and with the same expression on his face for a minute or more; then glanced slowly round as if he had lost something; and went shivering back, towards the shed.

"Shall I bring him in, father?" asked Barnaby, who had looked on, wondering.

He only answered with a suppressed groan, and lying down upon the ground, wrapped his cloak about his head, and shrunk into the darkest corner.

Finding that nothing would rouse Hugh now, or make him sensible for a moment, Barnaby dragged him along the grass, and laid him on a little heap of refuse hay and straw which had been his own bed; first having brought some water from a running stream hard by, and washed his wound, and laved his hands and face. Then he lay down himself, between the two, to pass the night; and looking at the stars, fell fast asleep.

Awakened early in the morning, by the sunshine, and the songs of birds, and hum of insects, he left them sleeping in the hut, and walked into the sweet and pleasant air. But he felt that on his jaded senses, oppressed and burdened with the dreadful scenes of last night, and many nights before, all the beauties of opening day, which he had so often tasted, and in which he had had such deep delight, fell heavily. He thought of the blithe mornings when he and the dogs went bounding on together through the woods and fields; and the recollection filled his eyes with tears. He had no consciousness, God help him, of having done wrong, nor had he any new perception of the merits of the cause in which he had been engaged, or those of the men who advocated it; but he was full of cares now, and regrets, and dismal recollections, and wishes (quite unknown to him before) that this or that event had never happened, and that the sorrow and suffering of so many people had been spared. And now he began to think how happy they would be—his father, mother, he, and Hugh—if they rambled away together, and lived in some lonely place, where there were none of these troubles; and that perhaps the blind man, who had talked so wisely about gold, and told him of the great secrets he knew, could teach them how to live without being pinched and griped by want. As this occurred to him, he was the more sorry that he had not seen him last night; and he was still brooding over this regret, when his father came, and touched him on the shoulder.

"Ah!" cried Barnaby, starting from his fit of thoughtfulness. "Is it only you?"

"Who should it be?"

"I almost thought," he answered, "it was the blind man. I must have some talk with him, father."

"And so must I, for without seeing him, I don't know where to fly or what to do; and lingering here, is death. You must go to him again, and bring him here."

"Must I!" cried Barnaby, delighted; "that's brave, father. That's what I want to do."

"But you must bring only him, and none other. And though you wait at his door a whole day and night, still you must wait, and not come back without him."

"Don't you fear that," he cried gaily. "He shall come, he shall come."

"Trim off these gewgaws," said his father, plucking the scraps of ribbon and the feathers from his hat, "and over your own dress, wear my cloak. Take heed how you go, and they will be too busy in the streets to notice you. Of your coming back you need take no account, for he'll manage that, safely."

"To be sure!" said Barnaby. "To be sure he will! A wise man, father, and one who can teach us to be rich! Oh! I know him, I know him."

He was speedily dressed; and, as well disguised as he could be, with a lighter heart he then set off upon his second journey; leaving Hugh, who was still in a drunken stupor, stretched upon the ground within the shed, and his father walking to and fro before it.

The murderer, full of anxious thoughts, looked after him, and paced up and down, disquieted by every breath of air that whispered among the boughs, and by every light shadow thrown by the passing clouds upon the daisied ground. He was anxious for his safe return, and yet, though his own life and safety hung upon it, felt a relief while he was gone. In the intense selfishness which the constant presence before him of his great crimes, and their consequences here and hereafter, engendered, every thought of Barnaby, as his son, was swallowed up and lost. Still, his presence was a torture and reproach; in his wild eyes, there were terrible images of that guilty night; with his unearthly aspect, and his half-formed mind, he seemed to the murderer a creature who had sprung into existence from his victim's blood. He could not bear his look, his voice, his touch; and yet was forced, by his own desperate condition and his only hope of cheating the gibbet, to have him by his side, and to know that he was inseparable from his single chance of escape.

He walked to and fro, with little rest, all day, revolving these things in his mind; and still Hugh lay, unconscious, in the shed. At length, when the sun was setting, Barnaby returned, leading the blind man, and talking earnestly to him as they came along together.

The murderer advanced to meet them, and bidding his son go on and speak to Hugh, who had just then staggered to his feet, took his place at the blind man's elbow, and slowly followed, towards the shed.

"Why did you send *him?*" said Stagg. "Don't you know it was the way to have him lost, as soon as found?"

"Would you have had me come myself?" returned the other.

"Humph! Perhaps not. I was before the jail on Tuesday night, but missed you in the crowd. I was out last night, too. There was good work last night—gay work—profitable work"—he added, rattling the money in his pockets.

"Have you—"

—"Seen your good lady? Yes."

"Do you mean to tell me more, or not?"

"I'll tell you all," returned the blind man, with a laugh. "Excuse me—but I love to see you so impatient. There's energy in it."

"Does she consent to say the word that may save me?"

"No," returned the blind man emphatically, as he turned his face towards him. "No. Thus it is. She has been at death's door since she lost her darling—has been insensible, and I know not what. I tracked her to a hospital, and presented myself (with your leave) at her bedside. Our talk was not a long one, for she was weak, and there being people near, I was not quite easy. But I told her all that you and I agreed upon; and pointed out the young gentleman's position, in strong terms. She tried to soften me, but that, of course (as I told her), was lost time. She cried and moaned, you may be sure; all women do. Then, of a sudden, she found her voice and strength, and said that Heaven would help her and her innocent son; and that to Heaven she appealed against us—which she did; in really very pretty language, I assure you. I advised her, as a friend, not to count too much upon assistance from any such distant quarter—recommended her to think of it—told her where I lived—said I knew she would send to me before noon, next day—and left her, either in a faint or shamming."

When he had concluded this narration, during which he had made several pauses, for the convenience of cracking and eating nuts, of which he seemed to have a pocketful, the blind man pulled a flask from his pocket, took a draught himself, and offered it to his companion.

"You won't, won't you?" he said, feeling that he pushed it from him. "Well! Then the gallant gentleman who's lodging with you, will. Hallo, bully!"

"Death!" said the other, holding him back. "Will you tell me what I am to do!"

"Do! Nothing easier. Make a moonlight flitting in two hours' time with the young gentleman (he's quite ready to go; I have been giving him good advice as we came along), and get as far from London as you can. Let me know where you are, and leave the rest to me. She *must* come round; she can't hold out long; and as to the chances of your being retaken in the meanwhile, why it wasn't one man who got out of Newgate, but three hundred. Think of that, for your comfort."

"We must support life.—How?"

"How!" repeated the blind man. "By eating and drinking. And how get meat and drink, but by paying for it! Money!" he cried, slapping his pocket. "Is money the word? Why, the streets have been running money. Devil send that the sport's not over yet, for these are jolly times; golden, rare, roaring, scrambling times. Hallo, bully! Hallo! Hallo! Drink, bully, drink. Where are ye there! Hallo!"

With such vociferations, and with a boisterous manner which bespoke his perfect abandonment to the general licence and disorder, he groped his way towards the shed, where Hugh and Barnaby were sitting on the ground, and entered.

"Put it about!" he cried, handing his flask to Hugh. "The kennels run with wine and gold. Guineas and strong water flow from the very pumps. About with it, don't spare it!"

Exhausted, unwashed, unshorn; begrimed with smoke and dust; his hair clotted with blood; his voice quite gone, so that he spoke in whispers; his skin parched up by fever; his whole body bruised, and cut, and beaten about; Hugh still took the flask, and raised it to his lips. He was in the act of drinking, when the front of the shed was suddenly darkened, and Dennis stood before them.

"No offence, no offence," said that personage in a conciliatory tone, as Hugh stopped in his draught, and eyed him, with no pleasant look, from head to foot. "No offence, brother. Barnaby here too, eh? How are you, Barnaby? And two other gentlemen! Your humble servant, gentlemen. No offence to *you* either, I hope. Eh, brothers?"

Notwithstanding that he spoke in this very friendly and confident manner, he seemed to have considerable hesitation about entering, and remained outside the roof. He was rather better dressed than usual: wearing the same suit of thread-bare black, it is true, but having round his neck an unwholesome-looking cravat of a yellowish white; and on his hands great leather gloves, such as a gardener might wear in following his trade. His shoes were newly greased, and ornamented with a pair of rusty iron buckles; the packthread at his knees had been renewed; and where he wanted buttons, he wore pins. Altogether, he had something the look of a tipstaff, or a bailiff's follower,* desperately faded, but who had a notion of keeping up the appearance of a professional character, and making the best of the worst means.

"You're very snug here," said Mr. Dennis, pulling out a mouldy pocket-handkerchief, which looked like a decomposed halter; and wiping his forehead in a nervous manner.

"Not snug enough to prevent your finding us, it seems," Hugh answered, sulkily.

"Why, I'll tell you what, brother," said Dennis, with a friendly smile, "when you don't want me to know which way you're riding, you must wear another sort of bells on your horse. Ah! I know the sound o' them you wore last night, and have got quick ears for 'em, that's the truth. Well, but how are you, brother?"

He had by this time approached, and now ventured to sit down by him.

"How am I?" answered Hugh. "Where were you yesterday? Where did you go when you left me in the jail? Why did you leave me? And what did you mean by rolling your eyes and shaking your fist at me, eh?"

"I shake my fist!—at you, brother!" said Dennis, gently checking Hugh's uplifted hand, which looked threatening.

"Your stick, then; it's all one."

"Lord love you, brother, I meant nothing. You don't understand me by half. I shouldn't wonder now," he added, in the tone of a desponding and an injured man, "but you thought, because I wanted them chaps left in the prison, that I was a going to desert the banners?"

Hugh told him, with an oath, that he did.

"Well!" said Mr. Dennis mournfully, "if you an't enough to make a man mistrust his feller-creeturs, I don't know what is. Desert the banners, eh! Me! Ned Dennis, as was so christened by his own father!—Is this axe your'n, brother?"

"Yes, that's mine," said Hugh, in the same sullen manner as before; "it might have hurt you, if you had come in its way once or twice last night. Put it down."

"Might have hurt me!" said Mr. Dennis, still keeping it in his hand, and feeling the edge with an air of abstraction. "Might have hurt me! and me exerting myself all the time to the wery best advantage. Here's a world! And you're not a going to ask me to take a sup out of that 'ere bottle, eh?"

Hugh tossed it towards him. As he raised it to his lips, Barnaby jumped up, and motioning them to be silent, looked eagerly out.

"What's the matter, Barnaby?" said Dennis, glancing at Hugh and dropping the flask, but still holding the axe in his hand.

"Hush!" he answered softly. "What do I see glittering behind the hedge?"

"What!" cried the hangman, raising his voice to its highest pitch, and laying hold of him and Hugh. "Not—not SOLDIERS, surely!"

That moment, the shed was filled with armed men; and a body of horse, galloping into the field, drew up before it.

"There!" said Dennis, who remained untouched among them when they had seized their prisoners; "it's them two young ones, gentlemen, that the proclamation puts a price on. This other's an escaped felon.—I'm sorry for it, brother," he added, in a tone of resignation, addressing himself to Hugh; "but you've brought it on yourself; you forced me to do it; you wouldn't respect the soundest constitootional principles, you know; you went and wiolated the wery frame-work of society. I had sooner have given away a trifle in charity than done this, I would upon my soul.—If you'll keep fast hold on 'em, gentlemen, I think I can make a shift to tie 'em better than you can."

But this operation was postponed for a few moments by a new occurrence. The blind man, whose ears were quicker than most people's sight, had been alarmed, before Barnaby, by a rustling in the bushes, under cover of which the soldiers had advanced. He retreated instantly—had hidden somewhere for a minute—and probably in his confusion mistaking the point at which he had emerged, was now seen running across the open meadow.

An officer cried directly that he had helped to plunder a house last night. He was loudly called on, to surrender. He ran the harder, and in a few seconds would have been out of gun-shot. The word was given, and the men fired.

There was a breathless pause and a profound silence, during which all eyes were fixed upon him. He had been seen to start at the discharge, as if the report had frightened him. But he neither stopped nor slackened his pace in the least, and ran on full forty yards further. Then, without one reel or stagger, or sign of faintness, or quivering of any limb, he dropped.

Some of them hurried up to where he lay;—the hangman with them. Everything had passed so quickly, that the smoke was not yet scattered, but curled slowly off in a little cloud, which seemed like the dead man's spirit moving solemnly away. There were a few drops of blood upon the grass—more, when they turned him over—that was all.

"Look here! Look here!" said the hangman, stooping one knee beside the body, and gazing up with a disconsolate face at the officer and men. "Here's a pretty sight!"

"Stand out of the way," replied the officer. "Serjeant! see what he had about him."

The man turned his pockets out upon the grass, and counted, besides some foreign coins and two rings, five-and-forty guineas in gold. These were bundled up in a handkerchief and carried away; the body remained there for the present, but six men and the serjeant were left to take it to the nearest public-house.

"Now then, if you're going," said the serjeant, clapping Dennis on the back, and pointing after the officer who was walking towards the shed.

To which Mr. Dennis only replied, "Don't talk to me!" and then repeated what he had said before, namely "Here's a pretty sight!"

"It's not one that you care for much, I should think," observed the serjeant coolly.

"Why, who," said Mr. Dennis, rising, "should care for it, if I don't?"

"Oh! I didn't know you was so tender-hearted," said the serjeant. "That's all!"

"Tender-hearted!" echoed Dennis. "Tender-hearted! Look at this man. Do you call *this* constitootional? Do you see him shot through and through instead of being worked off like a Briton? Damme, if I know which party to side with. You're as bad as the other. What's to become of the country if the military power's to go a superseding the ciwilians in this way? Where's this poor fellow-creetur's rights as a citizen, that he didn't have *me* in his last moments! I was here. I was willing. I was ready. These are nice times, brother, to have the dead crying out against us in this way, and sleep comfortably in our beds arterwards; wery nice!"

Whether he derived any material consolation from binding the prisoners, is uncertain; most probably he did. At all events his being summoned to that work, diverted him, for the time, from these painful reflections, and gave his thoughts a more congenial occupation.

They were not all three carried off together, but in two parties; Barnaby and his father, going by one road in the centre of a body of foot; and Hugh, fast bound upon a horse, and strongly guarded by a troop of cavalry, being taken by another.

They had no opportunity for the least communication, in the short interval which preceded their departure; being kept strictly apart. Hugh only observed that Barnaby walked with a drooping head among his guard, and, without raising his eyes, that he tried to wave his fettered hand when he passed. For himself, he buoyed up his courage as he rode along, with the assurance that the mob would force his jail wherever it might be, and set him at liberty. But when they got into London, and more especially into Fleet Market, lately the stronghold of the rioters, where the military were rooting out the last remnant of the crowd, he saw that this hope was gone, and felt that he was riding to his death.

CHAPTER THE SEVENTIETH.

MR. DENNIS having despatched this piece of business without any personal hurt or inconvenience, and having now retired into the tranquil respectability of private life, resolved to solace himself with half an hour or so of female society. With this amiable purpose in his mind, he bent his steps towards the house where Dolly and Miss Haredale were still confined, and whither Miss Miggs had also been removed by order of Mr. Simon Tappertit.

As he walked along the streets with his leather gloves clasped behind him, and his face indicative of cheerful thought and pleasant calculation, Mr. Dennis might have been likened unto a farmer ruminating among his crops, and enjoying by anticipation the bountiful gifts of Providence. Look where he would, some heap of ruins afforded him rich promise of a working off; the whole town appeared to have been ploughed, and sown, and nurtured by most genial weather; and a goodly harvest was at hand.

Having taken up arms and resorted to deeds of violence, with the great main object of preserving the Old Bailey in all its purity, and the gallows in all its pristine usefulness and moral grandeur, it would perhaps be going too far to assert that Mr. Dennis had ever distinctly contemplated and foreseen this happy state of things. He rather looked upon it as one of those beautiful dispensations which are inscrutably brought about for the behoof and advantage of good men. He felt, as it were, personally referred to, in this prosperous ripening for the gibbet; and had never considered himself so much the pet and favourite child of Destiny, or loved that lady so well or with such a calm and virtuous reliance, in all his life.

As to being taken up, himself, for a rioter, and punished with the rest, Mr. Dennis dismissed that possibility from his thoughts as an idle chimera; arguing that the line of conduct he had adopted at

Newgate, and the service he had rendered that day, would be more than a set-off against any evidence which might identify him as a member of the crowd: that any charge of companionship which might be made against him by those who were themselves in danger, would certainly go for nought: and that if any trivial indiscretion on his part should unluckily come out, the uncommon usefulness of his office, at present, and the great demand for the exercise of its functions, would certainly cause it to be winked at, and passed over. In a word, he had played his cards throughout, with great care; had changed sides at the very nick of time; had delivered up two of the most notorious rioters, and a distinguished felon to boot; and was quite at his ease.

Saving—for there is a reservation; and even Mr. Dennis was not perfectly happy—saving for one circumstance; to wit, the forcible detention of Dolly and Miss Haredale, in a house almost adjoining his own. This was a stumbling-block, for if they were discovered and released, they could, by the testimony they had it in their power to give, place him in a situation of great jeopardy; and to set them at liberty, first extorting from them an oath of secrecy and silence, was a thing not to be thought of. It was more, perhaps, with an eye to the danger which lurked in this quarter, than from his abstract love of conversation with the sex, that the hangman, quickening his steps, now hastened into their society; cursing the amorous natures of Hugh and Mr. Tappertit with great heartiness, at every step he took.

When he entered the miserable room in which they were confined, Dolly and Miss Haredale withdrew in silence to the furthest corner. But Miss Miggs, who was particularly tender of her reputation, immediately fell upon her knees and began to scream very loud, crying "What will become of me!"—"Where is my Simmuns!" "Have mercy, good gentleman, on my sex's weakness!"—with other doleful lamentations of that nature, which she delivered with great propriety and decorum.

"Miss, Miss," whispered Dennis, beckoning to her with his forefinger, "come here—I won't hurt you. Come here, my lamb, will you?"

On hearing this tender epithet, Miss Miggs, who had left off screaming directly he opened his lips, and had listened to him attentively, began again: crying "Oh I'm his lamb! He says I'm his lamb! Oh gracious, why wasn't I born old and ugly? Why was I ever made to be the youngest of six, and all of 'em dead and in their blessed graves, excepting one married sister, which is settled in Golden Lion Court, number twenty-sivin, second bell-handle on the—!"

"Don't I say I an't a going to hurt you?" said Dennis, pointing to a chair. "Why Miss, what's the matter?"

"I don't know what mayn't be the matter!" cried Miggs, clasping her hands distractedly. "Anything may be the matter!"

"But nothing is, I tell you," said the hangman. "First stop that noise and come and sit down here, will you, chuckey?"

The coaxing tone in which he said these latter words might have failed in its object, if he had not accompanied them with sundry sharp jerks of his thumb over one shoulder, and with divers winks and thrustings of his tongue into his cheek, from which signals the damsel gathered that he sought to speak to her apart, concerning Miss Haredale and Dolly. Her curiosity being very powerful, and her jealousy by no means inactive, she arose, and with a great deal of shivering and starting back, and much muscular action among all the small bones in her throat, gradually approached him.

"Sit down," said the hangman.

Suiting the action to the word, he thrust her rather suddenly and prematurely into a chair; and designing to reassure her by a little harmless jocularity, such as is adapted to please and fascinate the sex, converted his right forefinger into an ideal bradawl or gimlet,* and made as though he would screw the same into her side—whereat Miss Miggs shrieked again, and discovered symptoms of faintness.

"Lovey, my dear," whispered Dennis, drawing his chair close to hers. "When was your young man here last, eh?"

"*My* young man, good gentleman!" answered Miggs in a tone of exquisite distress.

"Ah! Simmuns, you know—him?" said Dennis.

"Mine indeed!" cried Miggs, with a burst of bitterness—and as she said it, she glanced towards Dolly. "*Mine*, good gentleman!"

This was just what Mr. Dennis wanted, and expected.

"Ah!" he said, looking so soothingly, not to say amorously on Miggs, that she sat, as she afterwards remarked, on pins and needles of the sharpest Whitechapel kind; not knowing what intentions might be suggesting that expression to his features: "I was afraid of that. *I* saw as much, myself. It's her fault. She *will* entice 'em."

"I wouldn't," cried Miggs, folding her hands and looking upwards with a kind of devout blankness, "I wouldn't lay myself out as she does; I wouldn't be as bold as her; I wouldn't seem to say to all male creeturs 'come and kiss me'"—and here a shudder quite convulsed her frame—"for any earthly crowns as might be offered. Worlds," Miggs added solemnly, "should not reduce me. No. Not if I was Wenis."

"Well but you are Wenus you know," said Mr. Dennis, confidentially.

"No, I am not, good gentleman," answered Miggs, shaking her head with an air of self-denial which seemed to imply that she might be if she chose, but she hoped she knew better. "No I am not, good gentleman. Don't charge me with it."

Up to this time, she had turned round every now and then to where Dolly and Miss Haredale had retired, and uttered a scream, or groan, or laid her hand upon her heart and trembled excessively, with a view of keeping up appearances, and giving them to understand that she conversed with the visitor, under protest and on compulsion, and at a great personal sacrifice, for their common good. But at this point, Mr. Dennis looked so very full of meaning, and gave such a singularly expressive twitch to his face as a request to her to come still nearer to him, that she abandoned these little arts and gave him her whole and undivided attention.

"When was Simmuns here, I say?" quoth Dennis, in her ear.

"Not since yesterday morning; and then only for a few minutes. Not all day, the day before."

"You know he meant all along to carry off that one?" said Dennis, indicating Dolly by the slightest possible jerk of his head:—"And to hand you over to somebody else."

Miss Miggs, who had fallen into a terrible state of grief when the first part of this sentence was spoken, recovered a little at the second, and seemed by the sudden check she put upon her tears, to intimate that possibly this arrangement might meet her views; and that it might, perhaps, remain an open question.

"—But unfort'nately," pursued Dennis, who observed this: "somebody else was fond of her too, you see; and even if he wasn't, somebody else is took for a rioter, and it's all over with him."

Miss Miggs relapsed.

"Now, I want," said Dennis, "to clear this house, and to see you righted. What if I was to get her off, out of the way, eh?"

Miss Miggs, brightening again, rejoined, with many breaks and pauses from excess of feeling, that temptations had been Simmuns's bane. That it was not his faults, but hers (meaning Dolly's). That men did not see through these dreadful arts as women did, and therefore was caged and trapped, as Simmun had been. That she had no personal motives to serve—far from it—on the contrary, her intentions was good towards all parties. But forasmuch as she knowed that Simmun, if united to any designing and artful minxes (she would name no names, for that was not her dispositions)—to *any* designing and artful minxes—must be made miserable and unhappy for life, she *did* incline towards prewentions. Such, she added, was her free confessions. But as this was private feelings, and might perhaps be looked upon as wengeance, she begged the gentleman would say no more. Whatever he said, wishing to do her duty by all mankind, even by them as had ever been her bitterest enemies, she would not listen to him. With that she stopped her ears, and shook her head from side to side, to intimate to Mr. Dennis that though he talked until he had no breath left, she was as deaf as any adder.

"Lookee here, my sugar-stick," said Mr. Dennis; "if your view's the same as mine, and you'll only be quiet and slip away at the right time, I can have the house clear to-morrow, and be out of this trouble.—Stop though! there's the other."

"Which other, sir?" asked Miggs—still with her fingers in her ears and her head shaking obstinately.

"Why, the tallest one, yonder," said Dennis, as he stroked his chin, and added, in an under tone to himself, something about not crossing Muster Gashford.

Miss Miggs replied (still being profoundly deaf) that if Miss Haredale stood in the way at all, he might make himself quite easy on that score; as she had gathered, from what passed between Hugh and Mr. Tappertit when they were last there, that she was to be removed alone (not by them, by somebody else), to-morrow night.

Mr. Dennis opened his eyes very wide at this piece of information, whistled once, considered once, and finally slapped his head once and nodded once, as if he had got the clue to this mysterious removal, and so dismissed it. Then he imparted his design concerning Dolly to Miss Miggs, who was taken more deaf than before, when he began; and so remained, all through.

The notable scheme was this. Mr. Dennis was immediately to seek out from among the rioters, some daring young fellow (and he had one in his eye, he said), who, terrified by the threats he could hold out to him, and alarmed by the capture of so many who were no better and no worse than he, would gladly avail himself of any help to get abroad, and out of harm's way, with his plunder, even though his journey were incumbered by an unwilling companion; indeed, the unwilling companion being a beautiful girl, would probably be an additional inducement and temptation. Such a person found, he proposed to bring him there on the ensuing night, when the tall one was taken off, and Miss Miggs had purposely retired; and then that Dolly should be gagged, muffled in a cloak, and carried in any handy conveyance down to the river's side; where there were abundant means of getting her smuggled snugly off in any small craft of doubtful character, and no questions asked. With regard to the expense of this removal, he would say, at a rough calculation, that two or three silver tea or coffee pots, with something additional for drink (such as a muffineer, or toast-rack), would more than cover it. Articles of plate of every kind having been buried by the rioters in several lonely parts of London, and particularly, as he knew, in St. James's Square,* which, though easy of access, was little frequented after dark, and had a convenient piece of water in the midst, the needful funds were close at hand, and could be had upon the shortest notice. With regard to Dolly, the gentleman would exercise his own discretion. He would be bound to do nothing but take her away, and keep her away; all other arrangements and dispositions would rest entirely with himself.

If Miss Miggs had had her hearing, no doubt she would have been greatly shocked by the indelicacy of a young female's going away with a stranger, by night (for her moral feelings, as we have said, were of the tenderest kind); but directly Mr. Dennis ceased to speak, she reminded him that he had only wasted breath. She then went on to say (still with her fingers in her ears) that nothing less than a severe practical lesson would save the locksmith's daughter from utter ruin; and that she felt it, as it were, a moral obligation and a sacred duty to the family, to wish that some one would devise one for her reformation. Miss Miggs remarked, and very justly, as an abstract sentiment which happened to occur to her at the moment, that she dared to say the locksmith and his wife would murmur, and repine, if they were ever, by forcible abduction, or otherwise, to lose their child: but that we seldom knew, in this world, what was best for us; such being our sinful and imperfect natures, that very few arrived at that clear understanding.

Having brought their conversation to this satisfactory end, they parted: Dennis, to further his design, and take another walk about his farm; Miss Miggs, to launch, when he left her, into such a burst of mental anguish (which she gave them to understand was occasioned by certain tender things he had had the presumption and audacity to say), that little Dolly's heart was quite melted. Indeed, she said and did so much to soothe the outraged feelings of Miss Miggs, and looked so beautiful while doing so, that if that young maid had not had ample vent for her surpassing spite, in a knowledge of the mischief that was brewing, she must have scratched her features, on the spot.

CHAPTER THE SEVENTY-FIRST.

ALL next day, Emma Haredale, Dolly, and Miggs, remained cooped up together in what had now been their prison for so many days, without seeing any person, or hearing any sound but the murmured conversation, in an outer room, of the men who kept watch over them. There appeared to be more of these fellows than there had been hitherto; and they could no longer hear the voices of women, which they had before plainly distinguished. Some new excitement, too, seemed to prevail among them; for there was much stealthy going in and out, and a constant questioning of those who were newly arrived. They had previously been quite reckless in their behaviour; often making a great uproar; quarrelling among themselves, fighting, dancing, and singing. They were now very subdued and silent; conversing almost in whispers, and stealing in and out with a soft and stealthy tread, very different from the boisterous trampling in which their arrivals and departures had hitherto been announced to the trembling captives.

Whether this change was occasioned by the presence among them of some person of authority in their ranks, or by any other cause, they were unable to decide. Sometimes they thought it was in part attributable to there being a sick man in the chamber, for last night there had been a shuffling of feet, as though a burden were brought in, and afterwards a moaning noise. But they had no means of ascertaining the truth: for any question or entreaty on their parts only provoked a storm of brutal execrations, or something worse; and they were too happy to be left alone, unassailed by threats or admiration, to risk even that comfort, by any voluntary communication with those who held them in durance.

It was sufficiently evident, both to Emma and to the locksmith's poor little daughter herself, that she, Dolly, was the great object of attraction; and that so soon as they should have leisure to indulge in the softer passion, Hugh and Mr. Tappertit would certainly fall to blows for her sake: in which latter case, it was not very difficult to foresee whose prize she would become. With all her old horror of that man revived, and deepened into a degree of aversion and abhorrence which no language can describe; with a thousand old recollections and regrets, and causes of distress, anxiety, and fear, besetting her on all sides; poor Dolly Varden—sweet, blooming, buxom Dolly—began to hang her head, and fade, and droop, like a beautiful flower. The colour fled from her cheeks, her courage forsook her, her gentle heart failed. Unmindful of all her provoking caprices, forgetful of all her conquests and inconstancy, with all her winning little vanities quite gone, she nestled all the livelong day in Emma Haredale's bosom; and, sometimes calling on her dear old grey-haired father, sometimes on her mother, and sometimes even on her old home, pined slowly away, like a poor bird in its cage.

Light hearts, light hearts, that float so gaily on a smooth stream, that are so sparkling and buoyant in the sunshine—down upon fruit, bloom upon flowers, blush in summer air, life of the winged insect, whose whole existence is a day—how soon ye sink in troubled water! Poor Dolly's heart—a little, gentle, idle, fickle thing; giddy, restless, fluttering; constant to nothing but bright looks, and smiles, and laughter—Dolly's heart was breaking.

Emma had known grief, and could bear it better. She had little comfort to impart, but she could soothe and tend her, and she did so; and Dolly clung to her like a child to its nurse. In endeavouring to inspire her with some fortitude, she increased her own; and though the nights were long, and the days dismal, and she felt the wasting influence of watching and fatigue, and had perhaps a more defined and clear perception of their destitute condition and its worst dangers, she uttered no complaint. Before the ruffians, in whose power they were, she bore herself so calmly, and with such an appearance, in the midst of all her terror, of a secret conviction that they dared not harm her, that there was not a man among them but held her in some degree of dread; and more than one believed she had a weapon hidden in her dress, and was prepared to use it.

Such was their condition when they were joined by Miss Miggs; who gave them to understand that she too had been taken prisoner, because of her charms; and detailed such feats of resistance she had performed (her virtue having given her supernatural strength), that they felt it quite a happiness to have her for a champion. Nor was this the only comfort they derived at first from Miggs's presence and society: for that young lady displayed such resignation and long-suffering, and so much meek endurance, under her trials; and breathed in all her chaste discourse a spirit of such holy confidence and resignation, and devout belief that all would happen for the best;

that Emma felt her courage strengthened by the bright example, never doubting but that everything she said was true, and that she, like them, was torn from all she loved, and agonized by doubt and apprehension. As to poor Dolly, she was roused, at first, by seeing one who came from home; but when she heard under what circumstances she had left it, and in whose hands her father had fallen, she wept more bitterly than ever, and refused all comfort.

Miss Miggs was at some trouble to reprove her for this state of mind, and to entreat her to take example by herself, who, she said, was now receiving back, with interest, tenfold the amount of her subscriptions to the red-brick dwelling-house, in the articles of peace of mind and a quiet conscience. And, while on serious topics, Miss Miggs considered it her duty to try her hand at the conversion of Miss Haredale; for whose improvement she launched into a polemical address of some length, in the course whereof, she likened herself unto a chosen missionary, and that young lady to a cannibal in darkness. Indeed she returned so often to these subjects, and so frequently called upon them to take a lesson from her,—at the same time vaunting and, as it were, rioting in, her huge unworthiness, and abundant excess of sin,—that, in the course of a short time, she became, in that small chamber, rather a nuisance than a comfort, and rendered them, if possible, even more unhappy than they had been before.

The night had now come; and for the first time (for their jailers had been regular in bringing food and candles), they were left in darkness. Any change in their condition in such a place inspired new fears; and when some hours had passed, and the gloom was still unbroken, Emma could no longer repress her alarm.

They listened attentively. There was the same murmuring in the outer room, and now and then a moan which seemed to be wrung from a person in great pain, who made an effort to subdue it, but could not. Even these men seemed to be in darkness too; for no light shone through the chinks in the door, nor were they moving, as their custom was, but quite still: the silence being unbroken by so much as the creaking of a board.

At first, Miss Miggs wondered greatly in her own mind who this sick person might be; but arriving, on second thoughts, at the conclusion that he was a part of the schemes on foot, and an artful device soon to be employed with great success, she opined, for Miss

Haredale's comfort, that it must be some misguided Papist who had been wounded: and this happy supposition encouraged her to say, under her breath, "Ally Looyer!" several times.

"Is it possible," said Emma, with some indignation, "that you who have seen these men committing the outrages you have told us of, and who have fallen into their hands, like us, can exult in their cruelties!"

"Personal considerations, Miss," rejoined Miggs, "sinks into nothing, afore a noble cause. Ally Looyer! Ally Looyer! Ally Looyer, good gentlemen!"

It seemed, from the shrill pertinacity with which Miss Miggs repeated this form of acclamation, that she was calling the same through the keyhole of the door; but in the profound darkness she could not be seen.

"If the time has come—Heaven knows it may come at any moment—when they are bent on prosecuting the designs, whatever they may be, with which they have brought us here, can you still encourage, and side with them?" demanded Emma.

"I thank my goodness-gracious-blessed-stars I can, Miss," returned Miggs, with increased energy. "Ally Looyer, good gentlemen!"

Even Dolly, cast down and disappointed as she was, revived at this, and bade Miggs hold her tongue directly.

"*Which*, was you pleased to observe, Miss Varsen?" said Miggs, with a strong emphasis on the irrelative pronoun.

Dolly repeated her request.

"Ho, gracious me!" cried Miggs, with hysterical derision. "Ho, gracious me! Yes, to be sure I will. Ho yes! I am a abject slave, and a toiling, moiling, constant-working, always-being-found-fault-with, never-giving-satisfactions, nor-having-no-time-to-clean-oneself, potter's wessel*—an't I, Miss! Ho yes! My situations is lowly, and my capacities is limited, and my duties is to humble myself afore the base degenerating daughters of their blessed mothers as is fit to keep companies with holy saints but is born to persecutions from wicked relations—and to demean myself before them as is no better than Infidels—an't it, Miss! Ho yes! My only becoming occupations is to help young flaunting pagins to brush and comb and titivate their-selves into whitening and suppulchres,* and leave the young men to think that there an't a bit of padding in it nor no pinching ins nor fillings out nor pomatums* nor deceits nor earthly wanities—an't it, Miss! Yes, to be sure it is—ho yes!"

Having delivered these ironical passages with a most wonderful volubility, and with a shrillness perfectly deafening (especially when she jerked out the interjections), Miss Miggs, from mere habit, and not because weeping was at all appropriate to the occasion, which was one of triumph, concluded by bursting into a flood of tears, and calling in an impassioned manner on the name of Simmuns.

What Emma Haredale and Dolly would have done, or how long Miss Miggs, now that she had hoisted her true colours, would have gone on waving them before their astonished senses, it is impossible to tell. Nor is it necessary to speculate on these matters, for a startling interruption occurred at that moment, which took their whole attention by storm.

This was a violent knocking at the door of the house, and then its sudden bursting open; which was immediately succeeded by a scuffle in the room without, and the clash of weapons. Transported with the hope that rescue had at length arrived, Emma and Dolly shrieked aloud for help; nor were their shrieks unanswered; for after a hurried interval, a man, bearing in one hand a drawn sword, and in the other a taper, rushed into the chamber where they were confined.

It was some check upon their transport to find in this person an entire stranger, but they appealed to him, nevertheless, and besought him, in impassioned language, to restore them to their friends.

"For what other purpose am I here?" he answered, closing the door, and standing with his back against it. "With what object have I made my way to this place, through difficulty and danger, but to preserve you?"

With a joy for which it was impossible to find adequate expression, they embraced each other, and thanked Heaven for this most timely aid. Their deliverer stepped forward for a moment to put the light upon the table, and immediately returning to his former position against the door, bared his head, and looked on smilingly.

"You have news of my uncle, Sir?" said Emma, turning hastily towards him.

"And of my father and mother?" added Dolly.

"Yes," he said. "Good news."

"They are alive and unhurt?" they both cried at once.

"Yes, and unhurt," he rejoined.

"And close at hand?"

"I did not say close at hand," he answered smoothly; "they are at no great distance. *Your* friends, sweet one," he added, addressing Dolly, "are within a few hours' journey. You will be restored to them, I hope, to-night."

"My uncle, Sir—" faltered Emma.

"Your uncle, dear Miss Haredale, happily—I say happily, because he has succeeded where many of our creed have failed, and is safe— has crossed the sea, and is out of Britain."

"I thank God for it," said Emma, faintly.

"You say well. You have reason to be thankful: greater reason than it is possible for you, who have seen but one night of these cruel outrages, to imagine."

"Does he desire," said Emma, "that I should follow him?"

"Do you ask if he desires it?" cried the stranger in surprise. "If he desires it! But you do not know the danger of remaining in England, the difficulty of escape, or the price hundreds would pay to secure the means, when you make that inquiry. Pardon me. I had forgotten that you could not, being prisoner here."

"I gather, Sir," said Emma, after a moment's pause, "from what you hint at, but fear to tell me, that I have witnessed but the beginning, and the least, of the violence to which we are exposed; and that it has not yet slackened in its fury?"

He shrugged his shoulders, shook his head, lifted up his hands; and with the same smooth smile, which was not a pleasant one to see, cast his eyes upon the ground, and remained silent.

"You may venture, Sir, to speak plain," said Emma, "and to tell me the worst. We have undergone some preparation for it already."

But here Dolly interposed, and entreated her not to hear the worst, but the best; and besought the gentleman to tell them the best, and to keep the remainder of his news until they were safe among their friends again.

"It is told in three words," he said, glancing at the locksmith's daughter with a look of some displeasure. "The people have risen, to a man, against us; the streets are filled with soldiers, who support them and do their bidding. We have no protection but from above, and no safety but in flight; and that is a poor resource; for we are watched on every hand, and detained here, both by force and fraud. Miss Haredale, I cannot bear—believe me, that I cannot bear—by speaking of myself, or what I have done, or am prepared to do, to seem to vaunt my services before you. But, having powerful Protestant connexions, and having my whole wealth embarked with theirs in shipping and commerce, I happily possessed the means of saving your uncle. I have the means of saving you; and in redemption of my sacred promise, made to him, I am here; pledged not to leave you until I have placed you in his arms. The treachery or penitence of one of the men about you, led to the discovery of your place of confinement; and that I have forced my way here, sword in hand, you see."

"You bring," said Emma, faltering, "some note or token from my uncle?"

"No, he doesn't," cried Dolly, pointing at him earnestly: "now I am sure he doesn't. Don't go with him for the world!"

"Hush, pretty fool—be silent," he replied, frowning angrily upon her. "No, Miss Haredale, I have no letter, nor any token of any kind; for while I sympathise with you, and such as you, on whom misfortune so heavy and so undeserved has fallen, I value my life. I carry, therefore, no writing which, found upon me, would lead to its certain loss. I never thought of bringing any other token, nor did Mr. Haredale think of entrusting me with one: possibly because he had good experience of my faith and honesty, and owed his life to me."

There was a reproof conveyed in these words, which, to a nature like Emma Haredale's, was well addressed. But Dolly, who was differently constituted, was by no means touched by it; and still conjured her, in all the terms of affection and attachment she could think of, not to be lured away.

"Time presses," said their visitor, who, although he sought to express the deepest interest, had something cold and even in his speech, that grated on the ear; "and danger surrounds us. If I have exposed myself to it, in vain, let it be so; but if you and he should ever meet again, do me justice. If you decide to remain (as I think you do), remember, Miss Haredale, that I left you, with a solemn caution, and acquitting myself of all the consequences to which you expose yourself."

"Stay, sir!" cried Emma—"one moment, I beg you. Cannot we"— and she drew Dolly closer to her—"cannot we go together?"

"The task of conveying one female in safety through such scenes as we must encounter, to say nothing of attracting the attention of those who crowd the streets," he answered, "is enough. I have said that she will be restored to her friends to-night. If you accept the service I tender, Miss Haredale, she shall be instantly placed in safe conduct, and that promise redeemed. Do you decide to remain? People of all ranks and creeds are flying from the town, which is sacked from end to end. Let me be of use in some quarter. Do you stay, or go?"

"Dolly," said Emma, in a hurried manner, "my dear girl, this is our last hope. If we part now, it is only that we may meet again in happiness and honour. I will trust to this gentleman."

"No—no—no!" cried Dolly, clinging to her. "Pray, pray, do not!"

"You hear," said Emma, "that to-night—only to-night—within a few hours—oh, think of that!—you will be among those who would die of grief to lose you, and are now plunged in the deepest misery for your sake. Pray for me, dear girl, as I will for you; and never forget the many quiet hours we have passed together. Say one 'God bless you!' Say that at parting, sister!"

But Dolly could say nothing; no, not when Emma kissed her cheek a hundred times, and covered it with tears, could she do more than hang upon her neck, and sob, and clasp, and hold her tight.

"We have time for no more of this," cried the man, unclenching her hands, and throwing her roughly off, as he drew Emma Haredale towards the door: "Now! Quick, outside there! are you ready?"

"Ay!" cried a loud voice, which made him start. "Quite ready! Stand back here, for your lives!"

And in an instant he was felled like an ox in the butcher's shambles—struck down as though a block of marble had fallen from the roof and crushed him—and cheerful light, and beaming faces came pouring in—and Emma was clasped in her uncle's embrace; and Dolly, with a shriek that pierced the air, fell into the arms of her father and mother.

What fainting there was, what laughing, what crying, what sobbing, what smiling; how much questioning, no answering, all talking together, all beside themselves with joy; what kissing, congratulating, embracing, shaking of hands; and falling into all these raptures, over and over and over again; no language can describe.

At length, and after a long time, the old locksmith went up and fairly hugged two strangers, who had stood apart and left them to

themselves; and then they saw—whom? Yes, Edward Chester and Joseph Willet.

"See here!" cried the locksmith. "See here! where would any of us have been without these two? Oh, Mr. Edward, Mr. Edward—oh, Joe, Joe, how light, and yet how full, you have made my old heart to-night!"

"It was Mr. Edward that knocked him down, sir," said Joe: "I longed to do it, but I gave it up to him. Come, you brave and honest gentleman! Get your senses together, for you haven't long to lie here."

He had his foot upon the breast of their sham deliverer, in the absence of a spare arm; and gave him a gentle roll as he spoke. Gashford, for it was no other, crouching yet malignant, raised his scowling face, like sin subdued, and pleaded to be gently used.

"I have access to all my lord's papers, Mr. Haredale," he said, in a submissive voice: Mr. Haredale keeping his back towards him, and not once looking round: "there are very important documents among them. There are a great many in secret drawers, and distributed in various places, known only to my lord and me. I can give some very valuable information, and render important assistance to any inquiry. You will have to answer it, if I receive ill usage."

"Pah!" cried Joe, in deep disgust. "Get up, man; you're waited for, outside. Get up, do you hear?"

Gashford slowly rose; and picking up his hat, and looking with a baffled malevolence, yet with an air of despicable humility, all round the room, crawled out.

"And now, gentlemen," said Joe, who seemed to be the spokesman of the party, for all the rest were silent; "the sooner we get back to the Black Lion, the better, perhaps."

Mr. Haredale nodded assent; and drawing his niece's arm through his, and taking one of her hands between his own, passed out straightway; followed by the locksmith, Mrs. Varden, and Dolly—who would scarcely have presented a sufficient surface for all the hugs and caresses they bestowed upon her though she had been a dozen Dollys. Edward Chester and Joe followed.

And did Dolly never once look behind—not once? Was there not one little fleeting glimpse of the dark eyelash, almost resting on her flushed cheek, and of the downcast sparkling eye it shaded? Joe thought there was—and he is not likely to have been mistaken; for there were not many eyes like Dolly's, that's the truth.

The outer room, through which they had to pass, was full of men; among them, Mr. Dennis in safe keeping; and there had been since yesterday, lying in hiding behind a wooden screen which was now thrown down, Simon Tappertit, the recreant Prentice; burnt and bruised, and with a gun-shot wound in his body; and his legs—his perfect legs, the pride and glory of his life, the comfort of his whole existence—crushed into shapeless ugliness. Wondering no longer at the moans they had heard, Dolly kept closer to her father, and shuddered at the sight: but neither bruises, burns, nor gun-shot wound, nor all the torture of his shattered limbs, sent half so keen a pang to Simon's breast, as Dolly passing out, with Joe for her preserver.

A coach was ready at the door, and Dolly found herself safe and whole inside, between her father and mother; with Emma Haredale and her uncle, quite real, sitting opposite. But there was no Joe, no Edward; and they had said nothing. They had only bowed once, and kept at a distance. Dear heart! what a long way it was, to the Black Lion.

CHAPTER THE SEVENTY-SECOND.

THE Black Lion was so far off, and occupied such a length of time in the getting at, that notwithstanding the strong presumptive evidence she had about her of the late events being real and of actual occurrence, Dolly could not divest herself of the belief that she must be in a dream which was lasting all night. Nor was she quite certain that she saw and heard with her own proper senses, even when the coach, in the fullness of time, stopped at the Black Lion, and the host of that tavern approached in a gush of cheerful light to help them to dismount, and give them hearty welcome.

There too, at the coach door, one on one side, one upon the other, were already Edward Chester and Joe Willet, who must have followed in another coach: and this was such a strange and unaccountable proceeding, that Dolly was the more inclined to favour the idea of her being fast asleep. But when Mr. Willet appeared—old John himself—so heavy-headed and obstinate, and with such a double chin as the liveliest imagination could never in its boldest flights have conjured up in all its vast proportions—then she stood corrected, and unwillingly admitted to herself that she was broad awake.

And Joe had lost an arm—he—that well-made, handsome, gallant fellow! As Dolly glanced towards him, and thought of the pain he must have suffered, and the far-off places in which he had been wandering; and wondered who had been his nurse, and hoped that whoever it was, she had been as kind and gentle and considerate as she would have been; the tears came rising to her bright eyes, one by one, little by little, until she could keep them back no longer, and so, before them all, wept bitterly.

"We are all safe now, Dolly," said her father, kindly. "We shall not be separated any more. Cheer up, my love, cheer up!"

The locksmith's wife knew better perhaps, than he, what ailed her daughter. But Mrs. Varden being quite an altered woman—for the riots had done that good—added her word to his, and comforted her with similar representations.

"Mayhap," said Mr. Willet senior, looking round upon the

company, "she's hungry. That's what it is, depend upon it—I am, myself."

The Black Lion, who, like old John, had been waiting supper past all reasonable and conscionable hours, hailed this as a philosophical discovery of the profoundest and most penetrating kind; and the table being already spread, they sat down to supper straightway.

The conversation was not of the liveliest nature, nor were the appetites of some among them very keen. But in both these respects, old John more than atoned for any deficiency on the part of the rest, and very much distinguished himself.

It was not in point of actual talkativeness that Mr. Willet shone so brilliantly, for he had none of his old cronies to "tackle," and was rather timorous of venturing on Joe; having certain vague misgivings within him, that he was ready on the shortest notice, and on receipt of the slightest offence, to fell the Black Lion to the floor of his own parlour, and immediately withdraw to China or some other remote and unknown region, there to dwell for evermore; or at least until he had got rid of his remaining arm and both legs, and perhaps an eye or so, into the bargain. It was with a peculiar kind of pantomime that Mr. Willet filled up every pause; and in this he was considered by the Black Lion, who had been his familiar for some years, quite to surpass and go beyond himself, and outrun the expectations of his most admiring friends.

The subject that worked in Mr. Willet's mind, and occasioned these demonstrations, was no other than his son's bodily disfigurement, which he had never yet got himself thoroughly to believe, or comprehend. Shortly after their first meeting, he had been observed to wander, in a state of great perplexity, to the kitchen, and to direct his gaze towards the fire, as if in search of his usual adviser in all matters of doubt and difficulty. But there being no boiler at the Black Lion, and the rioters having so beaten and battered his own that it was quite unfit for further service, he wandered out again, in a perfect bog of uncertainty and mental confusion; and in that state took the strangest means of resolving his doubts: such as feeling the sleeve of his son's great-coat as deeming it possible that his arm might be there; looking at his own arms and those of everybody else, as if to assure himself that two and not one was the usual allowance; sitting by the hour together in a brown study, as if he were endeavouring to recal Joe's image in his younger days, and to remember whether he really had in those times one arm or a pair; and employing himself in many other speculations of the same kind.

Finding himself, at this supper, surrounded by faces with which he had been so well acquainted in old times, Mr. Willet recurred to the subject with uncommon vigour; apparently resolved to understand it now or never. Sometimes, after every two or three mouthfuls, he laid down his knife and fork, and stared at his son with all his might—particularly at his maimed side; then he looked slowly round the table until he caught some person's eye, when he shook his head with great solemnity, patted his shoulder, winked, or as one may say—for winking was a very slow process with him—went to sleep with one eye for a minute or two; and so, with another solemn shaking of his head, took up his knife and fork again, and went on eating. Sometimes he put his food into his mouth abstractedly, and, with all his faculties concentrated on Joe, gazed at him in a fit of stupefaction as he cut his meat with one hand, until he was recalled to himself by symptoms of choking on his own part, and was by that means restored to consciousness. At other times he resorted to such small devices as asking him for the salt, the pepper, the vinegar, the mustard—anything that was on his maimed side—and watching him as he handed it. By dint of these experiments, he did at last so satisfy and convince himself, that, after a longer silence than he had yet maintained, he laid down his knife and fork on either side his plate, drank a long draught from a tankard beside him, still keeping his eyes on Joe, and, leaning backward in his chair and fetching a long breath, said, as he looked all round the board:

"It's been took off!"

"By George!" said the Black Lion, striking the table with his hand, "he's got it!"

"Yes sir," said Mr. Willet, with the look of a man who felt that he had earned a compliment, and deserved it. "That's where it is. It's been took off."

"Tell him where it was done," said the Black Lion to Joe.

"At the defence of the Savannah,* father."

"At the defence of the Salwanner," repeated Mr. Willet, softly; again looking round the table.

"In America, where the war is," said Joe.

"In America where the war is," repeated Mr. Willet. "It was took off in the defence of the Salwanners in America where the war is."

Continuing to repeat these words to himself in a low tone of voice (the same information had been conveyed to him in the same terms, at least fifty times before), Mr. Willet arose from table; walked round to Joe; felt his empty sleeve all the way up, from the cuff, to where the stump of his arm remained; shook his hand; lighted his pipe at the fire, took a long whiff, walked to the door; turned round once when he had reached it, wiped his left eye with the back of his forefinger, and said, in a faltering voice; "My son's arm—was took off—at the defence of the—Salwanners—in America—where the war is"—with which words he withdrew, and returned no more that night.

Indeed, on various pretences, they all withdrew one after another, save Dolly, who was left sitting there alone. It was a great relief to be alone, and she was crying to her heart's content, when she heard Joe's voice at the end of the passage, bidding somebody good night.

Good night! Then he was going elsewhere—to some distance, perhaps. To what kind of home *could* he be going, now that it was so late!

She heard him walk along the passage, and pass the door. But there was a hesitation in his footsteps. He turned back—Dolly's heart beat high—he looked in.

"Good night!"—he didn't say Dolly, but there was comfort in his not saying Miss Varden.

"Good night!" sobbed Dolly.

"I am sorry you take on so much, for what is past and gone," said Joe kindly. "Don't. I can't bear to see you do it. Think of it no longer. You are safe and happy now."

Dolly cried the more.

"You must have suffered very much within these few days—and yet you're not changed, unless it's for the better. They said you were, but I don't see it. You were—you were always very beautiful" said Joe, "but you are more beautiful than ever, now. You are indeed. There can be no harm in my saying so, for you must know it. You are told so very often, I am sure."

As a general principle, Dolly *did* know it, and *was* told so, very often. But the coach-maker had turned out, years ago, to be a special donkey; and whether she had been afraid of making similar discoveries in others, or had grown by dint of long custom to be careless of compliments generally, certain it is that although she cried so much, she was better pleased to be told so now, than ever she had been in all her life.

"I shall bless your name," sobbed the locksmith's little daughter, "as long as I live. I shall never hear it spoken without feeling as if my heart would burst. I shall remember it in my prayers every night and morning till I die!"

"Will you?" said Joe, eagerly. "Will you indeed? It makes me—well, it makes me very glad and proud to hear you say so."

Dolly still sobbed, and held her handkerchief to her eyes. Joe still stood, looking at her.

"Your voice," said Joe, "brings up old times so pleasantly, that for the moment, I feel as if that night—there can be no harm in talking of that night now—had come back, and nothing had happened in the mean time. I feel as if I hadn't suffered any hardships, but had knocked down poor Tom Cobb only yesterday, and had come to see you with my bundle on my shoulder before running away.—You remember?"

Remember! But she said nothing. She raised her eyes for an instant. It was but a glance; a little, tearful, timid glance. It kept Joe silent though, for a long time.

"Well!" he said stoutly, "it was to be otherwise, and was. I have been abroad, fighting all the summer and frozen up all the winter, ever since. I have come back as poor in purse as I went, and crippled for life besides. But, Dolly, I would rather have lost this other arm—ay, I would rather have lost my head—than have come back to find you dead, or anything but what I always pictured you to myself, and what I always hoped and wished to find you. Thank God for all!"

Oh how much, and how keenly, the little coquette of five years ago, felt now! She had found her heart at last. Never having known its worth till now, she had never known the worth of his. How priceless it appeared!

"I did hope once," said Joe, in his homely way, "that I might come back a rich man, and marry you. But I was a boy then, and have long known better than that. I am a poor, maimed, discharged soldier, and must be content to rub through life as I can. I can't say, even now, that I shall be glad to see you married, Dolly; but I *am* glad—yes, I am, and glad to think I can say so—to know that you are admired and courted, and can pick and choose for a happy life. It's a comfort to me to know that you'll talk to your husband about me; and I hope the time will come when I may be able to like him, and to shake hands with him, and to come and see you as a poor friend who knew you when you were a girl. God bless you!"

His hand *did* tremble; but for all that, he took it away again, and left her.

CHAPTER THE SEVENTY-THIRD.

By this Friday night—for it was on Friday in the riot week, that Emma and Dolly were rescued, by the timely aid of Joe and Edward Chester—the disturbances were entirely quelled, and peace and order were restored to the affrighted city. True, after what had happened, it was impossible for any man to say how long this better state of things might last, or how suddenly new outrages, exceeding even those so lately witnessed, might burst forth and fill its streets with ruin and bloodshed; for this reason, those who had fled from the recent tumults still kept at a distance, and many families, hitherto unable to procure the means of flight, now availed themselves of the calm, and withdrew into the country. The shops, too, from Tyburn to Whitechapel, were still shut; and very little business was transacted in any of the places of great commercial resort. But, notwithstanding, and in spite of the melancholy forebodings of that numerous class of society who see with the greatest clearness into the darkest perspectives; the town remained profoundly quiet. The strong military force disposed in every advantageous quarter, and stationed at every commanding point, held the scattered fragments of the mob in check; the search after rioters was prosecuted with unrelenting vigour; and if there were any among them so desperate and reckless as to be inclined, after the terrible scenes they had beheld, to venture forth again, they were so daunted by these resolute measures, that they quickly shrunk into their hiding-places, and had no thought but for their personal safety.

In a word, the crowd was utterly routed. Upwards of two hundred had been shot dead* in the streets. Two hundred and fifty more were lying, badly wounded, in the hospitals; of whom seventy or eighty died within a short time afterwards. A hundred were already in custody, and more were taken every hour. How many perished in the conflagrations, or by their own excesses, is unknown; but that numbers found a terrible grave in the hot ashes of the flames they had kindled, or crept into vaults and cellars to drink in secret or to nurse their sores, and never saw the light again, is certain. When the embers of the fires had been black and cold for many weeks, the labourers' spades proved this beyond a doubt.

Seventy-two private houses and four strong jails* were destroyed in the four great days of these riots. The total loss of property, as estimated by the sufferers, was one hundred and fifty-five thousand pounds; at the lowest and least partial estimate of disinterested persons, it exceeded one hundred and twenty-five thousand pounds.* For this immense loss, compensation was soon afterwards made out of the public purse, in pursuance of a vote of the House of Commons; the sum being levied on the various wards in the city, on the county, and the borough of Southwark. Both Lord Mansfield and Lord Saville, however, who had been great sufferers, refused to accept of any compensation whatever.

The House of Commons, sitting on Tuesday with locked and guarded doors, had passed a resolution to the effect that, as soon as the tumults subsided, it would immediately proceed to consider the petitions presented from many of his majesty's Protestant subjects, and would take the same into its serious consideration. While this question was under debate, Mr. Herbert,* one of the members present, indignantly rose and called upon the House to observe that Lord George Gordon was then sitting under the gallery with the blue cockade, the signal of rebellion, in his hat. He was not only obliged, by those who sat near, to take it out; but, offering to go into the street to pacify the mob with the somewhat indefinite assurance that the House was prepared to give them "the satisfaction they sought," was actually held down in his seat by the combined force of several members. In short, the disorder and violence which reigned triumphant out of doors, penetrated into the senate, and there, as elsewhere, terror and alarm prevailed, and ordinary forms were for the time forgotten.

On the Thursday, both Houses had adjourned until the following Monday se'ennight,* declaring it impossible to pursue their deliberations with the necessary gravity and freedom, while they were surrounded by armed troops. And now that the rioters were dispersed, the citizens were beset with a new fear; for, finding the public thoroughfares and all their usual places of resort filled with soldiers entrusted with the free use of fire and sword, they began to lend a greedy ear to the rumours which were afloat of martial law being declared, and to dismal stories of prisoners having been seen hanging on lamp-posts in Cheapside and Fleet-street. These terrors being promptly dispelled by a Proclamation declaring that all the rioters in custody would be tried by a special commission in due course of law, a fresh alarm was engendered by its being whispered abroad that French money had been found on some of the rioters, and that the disturbances had been fomented by foreign powers who sought to compass the overthrow and ruin of England. This report, which was strengthened by the diffusion of anonymous hand-bills, but which, if it had any foundation at all, probably owed its origin to the circumstance of some few coins which were not English money having been swept into the pockets of the insurgents with other miscellaneous booty, and afterwards discovered on the prisoners or the dead bodies,—caused a great sensation; and men's minds being in that excited state when they are most apt to catch at any shadow of apprehension, was bruited about with much industry.

All remaining quiet, however, during the whole of this Friday, and on this Friday night, and no new discoveries being made, confidence began to be restored, and the most timid and desponding breathed again. In Southwark, no fewer than three thousand of the inhabitants formed themselves into a watch, and patrolled the streets every hour. Nor were the citizens slow to follow so good an example: and it being the manner of peaceful men to be very bold when the danger is over, they were abundantly fierce and daring; not scrupling to question the stoutest passenger with great severity, and carrying it with a very high hand over all errand-boys, servant-girls, and 'prentices.

As day deepened into evening, and darkness crept into the nooks and corners of the town as if it were mustering in secret and gathering strength to venture into the open ways, Barnaby sat in his dungeon, wondering at the silence, and listening in vain for the noise and outcry which had ushered in the night of late. Beside him, with his hand in hers, sat one in whose companionship he felt at peace and tranquil. She was worn, and altered; full of grief; and heavy-hearted; but the same to him.

"Mother," he said, after a long silence: "how long,—how many days and nights,—shall I be kept here?"

"Not many, dear. I hope not many."

"You hope! Ay, but your hoping will not undo these chains. *I* hope, but they don't mind that. Grip hopes, but who cares for Grip?"

The raven gave a short, dull, melancholy croak. It said "Nobody," as plainly as a croak could speak.

"Who cares for Grip, excepting you and me?" said Barnaby, smoothing the bird's rumpled feathers with his hand. "He never speaks in this place; he never says a word in jail; he sits and mopes all day in this dark corner, dozing sometimes, and sometimes looking at the light that creeps in through the bars, and shines in his bright eye as if a spark from those great fires had fallen into the room and was burning yet. But who cares for Grip?"

The raven croaked again—Nobody.

"And by the way," said Barnaby, withdrawing his hand from the bird, and laying it upon his mother's arm, as he looked eagerly in her face; "if they kill me—they may, I heard it said they would—what will become of Grip when I am dead?"

The sound of the word, or the current of his own thoughts, suggested to Grip his old phrase "Never say die!" But he stopped short in the middle of it, drew a dismal cork, and subsided into a faint croak, as if he lacked the heart to get through the shortest sentence.

"Will they take *his* life as well as mine?" said Barnaby. "I wish they would. If you and I and he could die together, there would be none to feel sorry, or to grieve for us. But do what they will, I don't fear them mother."

"They will not harm you," she said, her tears choking her utterance. "They never will harm you when they know all. I am sure they never will."

"Oh! Don't you be too sure of that," cried Barnaby, with a strange pleasure in the belief that she was self-deceived, and in his own sagacity. "They have marked me, mother, from the first. I heard them say so to each other when they brought me to this place last night; and I believe them. Don't you cry for me. They said that I was bold, and so I am, and so I will be. You may think that I am silly, but I can die as well as another.—I have done no harm, have I?" he added quickly.

"None before Heaven," she answered.

"Why then," said Barnaby, "let them do their worst. You told me once—you—when I asked you what death meant, that it was nothing to be feared, if we did no harm—Aha! mother, you thought I had forgotten that!"

His merry laugh and playful manner smote her to the heart. She drew him closer to her, and besought him to talk to her in whispers and to be very quiet, for it was getting dark, and their time was short, and she would soon have to leave him for the night.

"You will come to-morrow?" said Barnaby.

Yes. And every day. And they would never part again.

He joyfully replied that this was well, and what he wished, and what he had felt quite certain she would tell him: and then he asked her where she had been so long; and why she had not come to see him when he was a great soldier; and ran through the wild schemes he had had for their being rich and living prosperously; and, with some faint notion in his mind that she was sad and he had made her so, tried to console and comfort her, and talked of their former life and his old sports and freedom: little dreaming that every word he uttered only increased her sorrow, and that her tears fell faster at the freshened recollection of their lost tranquillity.

"Mother," said Barnaby, as they heard the man approaching to close the cells for the night, "when I spoke to you just now about my father you cried 'Hush!' and turned away your head. Why did you do so? Tell me why, in a word. You thought *he* was dead. You are not sorry that he is alive and has come back to us. Where is he? Here?"

"Do not ask any one where he is, or speak about him," she made answer.

"Why not?" said Barnaby. "Because he is a stern man and talks roughly? Well! I don't like him, or want to be with him by myself; but why not speak about him?"

"Because I am sorry that he is alive; sorry that he has come back; and sorry that he and you have ever met. Because, dear Barnaby, the endeavour of my life has been to keep you two asunder."

"Father and son asunder! Why?"

"He has," she whispered in his ear, "he has shed blood. The time has come when you must know it. He has shed the blood of one who loved him well, and trusted him, and never did him wrong in word or deed."

Barnaby recoiled in horror, and glancing at his stained wrist for an instant, wrapped it, shuddering, in his dress.

"But," she added hastily as the key turned in the lock, "and although we shun him, he is your father, dearest, and I am his wretched wife. They seek his life, and he will lose it. It must not be by our means; nay, if we could win him back to penitence, we should be bound to love him yet. Do not seem to know him, except as one who fled with you from the jail; and if they question you about him, do not answer them. God be with you through the night, dear boy! God be with you!"

She tore herself away, and in a few seconds Barnaby was alone. He stood for a long time rooted to the spot, with his face hidden in his hands; then flung himself, sobbing, upon his miserable bed.

But the moon came slowly up in all her gentle glory, and the stars looked out; and through the small compass of the grated window, as through the narrow crevice of one good deed in a murky life of guilt, the face of Heaven shone bright and merciful. He raised his head; gazed upward at the quiet sky, which seemed to smile upon the earth in sadness, as if the night, more thoughtful than the day, looked down in sorrow on the sufferings and evil deeds of men; and felt its peace sink deep into his heart. He, a poor idiot, caged in his narrow cell, was as much lifted up to God, while gazing on that mild light, as the freest and most favoured man in all the spacious city; and in his ill-remembered prayer, and in the fragment of the childish hymn, with which he sung and crooned himself asleep, there breathed as true a spirit as ever studied homily expressed, or old cathedral arches echoed.

As his mother crossed a yard on her way out, she saw, through a grated door which separated it from another court, her husband, walking round and round, with his hands folded on his breast, and his head hung down. She asked the man who conducted her, if she might speak a word with this prisoner. Yes, but she must be quick, for he was locking up for the night, and there was but a minute or so to spare. Saying this, he unlocked the door, and bade her go in.

It grated harshly as it turned upon its hinges, but he was deaf to the noise, and still walked round and round the little court, without raising his head or changing his attitude in the least. She spoke to him, but her voice was weak, and failed her. At length she put herself in his track, and when he came near, stretched out her hand and touched him.

He started backward, trembling from head to foot; but seeing who it was, demanded why she came there. Before she could reply, he spoke again.

"Am I to live or die? Do you murder too, or spare?"

"My son—our son," she answered, "is in this prison."

"What is that to me?" he cried, stamping impatiently on the stone pavement. "I know it. He can no more aid me than I can aid him. If you are come to talk of him, begone!"

As he spoke he resumed his walk, and hurried round the court as before. When he came again to where she stood, he stopped, and said,

"Am I to live or die? Do you repent?"

"Oh!—do *you?*" she answered. "Will you, while time remains? Do not believe that I could save you, if I dared."

"Say if you would," he answered with an oath, as he tried to disengage himself and pass on. "Say if you would."

"Listen to me for one moment," she returned; "for but a moment. I am but newly risen from a sick-bed, from which I never hoped to rise again. The best among us think at such a time of good intentions half-performed and duties left undone. If I have ever, since that fatal night, omitted to pray for your repentance before death—if I omitted, even then, anything which might tend to urge it on you when the horror of your crime was fresh—if, in our later meeting, I yielded to the dread that was upon me, and forgot to fall upon my knees and solemnly adjure you, in the name of him you sent to his account with Heaven, to prepare for the retribution which must come, and which is stealing on you now—I humbly before you, and in the agony of supplication in which you see me, beseech that you will let me make atonement."

"What is the meaning of your canting words?" he answered roughly. "Speak so that I may understand you."

"I will," she answered, "I desire to. Bear with me for a moment more. The hand of Him who set his curse on murder, is heavy on us now. You cannot doubt it. Our son, our innocent boy, on whom His anger fell before his birth, is in this place in peril of his life—brought here by your guilt; yes, by that alone, as Heaven sees and knows, for he has been led astray in the darkness of his intellect, and that is the terrible consequence of your crime."

"If you come, woman-like, to load me with reproaches—" he muttered, again endeavouring to break away.

"—I do not. I have a different purpose. You must hear it. If not to-night, to-morrow; if not to-morrow, at another time. You *must* hear it. Husband, escape is hopeless—impossible."

"You tell me so, do you?" he said, raising his manacled hand, and shaking it. "You!"

"Yes," she said, with indescribable earnestness. "But why?"

"To make me easy in this jail. To make the time 'twixt this and death, pass pleasantly. Ha ha! For my good—yes, for my good, of course," he said, grinding his teeth, and smiling at her with a livid face.

"Not to load you with reproaches," she replied; "not to aggravate the tortures and miseries of your condition; not to give you one hard word; but to restore you to peace and hope. Husband, dear husband, if you will but confess this dreadful crime; if you will but implore forgiveness of Heaven and of those whom you have wronged on earth; if you will dismiss these vain uneasy thoughts, which never can be realised, and will rely on Penitence and on the Truth; I promise you, in the great name of the Creator, whose image you have defaced, that He will comfort and console you. And for myself," she cried, clasping her hands, and looking upward, "I swear before Him, as He knows my heart and reads it now, that from that hour I will love and cherish you as I did of old, and watch you night and day in the short interval that will remain to us, and soothe you with my truest love and duty, and pray, with you, that one threatening judgment may be averted, and that our boy may be spared to bless God, in his poor way, in the free air and sunlight!"

He fell back and gazed at her while she poured out these words, as though he were for a moment awed by her manner, and knew not what to do. But rage and fear soon got the mastery of him, and he spurned her from him.

"Begone!" he cried. "Leave me! You plot, do you! You plot to get speech with me, and let them know I am the man they say I am. A curse on you and on your boy."

"On him the curse has already fallen," she replied, wringing her hands.

"Let it fall heavier. Let it fall on one and all. I hate ye both. The worst has come to me. The only comfort that I seek or I can have, will be the knowledge that it comes to you. Begone!"

She would have urged him gently, even then, but he menaced her with his chain.

"I say begone—I say it for the last time; and do not tempt me. The gallows has me in its grasp, and it is a black phantom that may urge me on to something more, before it coils its arm about my throat. Begone! I curse the hour that I was born, the man I slew, and all the living world!"

In a paroxysm of wrath, and terror, and the fear of death, he broke from her, and rushed into the darkness of his cell, where he cast himself jangling down upon the stone floor, and smote it with his ironed hands. The man returned to lock the dungeon door, and having done so, carried her away.

On that warm, balmy night in June, there were glad faces and light hearts in all quarters of the town; and sleep, banished by the late horrors, was doubly welcomed. On that night, families made merry in their houses, and greeted each other on the common danger they had escaped; and those who had been denounced, ventured into the streets; and they who had been plundered, got good shelter. Even the timorous Lord Mayor, who was summoned that night before the Privy Council to answer for his conduct, came back contented; observing to all his friends that he had got off very well with a reprimand, and repeating with huge satisfaction his memorable defence before the Council, "that such was his temerity, he thought death would have been his potion."

On that night, too, more of the scattered remnants of the mob were traced to their lurking-places, and taken; and in the hospitals, and deep among the ruins they had made, and in the ditches, and the fields, many unshrouded wretches lay dead: envied by those who had been active in the disturbances, and pillowed their doomed heads in the temporary jails.

And in the Tower, in a dreary room, whose thick stone walls shut out the hum of life, and made a stillness which the records left by former prisoners with those silent witnesses seemed to deepen and intensify; remorseful for every act that had been done by every man among the cruel crowd; feeling for the time their guilt his own, and their lives put in peril by himself; and finding, amidst such reflections, little comfort in fanaticism, or in his fancied call; sat the unhappy author of all—Lord George Gordon.

He had been made prisoner that evening. "If you are sure it's me

you want," he said to the officer, who waited outside with the warrant for his arrest on a charge of High Treason,* "I am ready to accompany you—" which he did without resistance. He was conducted first before the Privy Council, and afterwards to the Horse Guards, and then was taken by way of Westminster Bridge, and back over London Bridge (for the purpose of avoiding the main streets), to the Tower, under the strongest guard ever known to enter its gates with a single prisoner.

Of all his forty thousand men, not one remained to bear him company. Friends, dependents, followers,—none were there. His fawning secretary had played the traitor; and he whose weakness had been goaded and urged on by so many for their own purposes, was desolate and alone.

CHAPTER THE SEVENTY-FOURTH.

MR. DENNIS, having been made prisoner late in the evening, was removed to a neighbouring round-house* for that night, and carried before a justice for examination on the next day, Saturday. The charges against him being numerous and weighty, and it being in particular proved, by the testimony of Gabriel Varden, that he had shown a special desire to take his life, he was committed for trial. Moreover he was honoured with the distinction of being considered a chief among the insurgents, and received from the magistrate's lips the complimentary assurance that he was in a position of imminent danger, and would do well to prepare himself for the worst.

To say that Mr. Dennis's modesty was not somewhat startled by these honours, or that he was altogether prepared for so flattering a reception, would be to claim for him a greater amount of stoical philosophy than even he possessed. Indeed this gentleman's stoicism was of that not uncommon kind, which enables a man to bear with exemplary fortitude the afflictions of his friends, but renders him, by way of counterpoise, rather selfish and sensitive in respect of any that happen to befall himself. It is therefore no disparagement to the great officer in question to state, without disguise or concealment, that he was at first very much alarmed, and that he betrayed divers emotions of fear, until his reasoning powers came to his relief, and set before him a more hopeful prospect.

In proportion as Mr. Dennis exercised these intellectual qualities with which he was gifted, reviewing his best chances of coming off handsomely and with small personal inconvenience, his spirits rose, and his confidence increased. When he remembered the great estimation in which his office was held, and the constant demand for his services; when he bethought himself, how the Statute Book regarded him as a kind of Universal Medicine applicable to men, women, and children, of every age and variety of criminal constitution; and how high he stood, in his official capacity, in the favour of the Crown, and both Houses of Parliament, the Mint, the Bank of England, and the Judges of the land; when he recollected that whatever ministry was in or out, he remained their peculiar pet and panacea, and that for his sake England stood single and conspicuous among the civilised nations of the earth: when he called these things to mind and dwelt upon them, he felt certain that the national gratitude *must* relieve him from the consequences of his late proceedings, and would certainly restore him to his old place in the happy social system.

With these crumbs, or as one may say, with these whole loaves of comfort to regale upon, Mr. Dennis took his place among the escort that awaited him, and repaired to jail with a manly indifference. Arriving at Newgate, where some of the ruined cells had been hastily fitted up for the safe keeping of rioters, he was warmly received by the turnkeys, as an unusual and interesting case, which agreeably relieved their monotonous duties. In this spirit, he was fettered with great care, and conveyed into the interior of the prison.

"Brother," cried the hangman, as, following an officer, he traversed under these novel circumstances the remains of passages with which he was well acquainted, "am I going to be along with anybody?"

"If you'd have left more walls standing, you'd have been alone," was the reply. "As it is, we're cramped for room, and you'll have company."

"Well," returned Dennis, "I don't object to company, brother. I rather like company. I was formed for society, I was."

"That's rather a pity, an't it?" said the man.

"No," answered Dennis, "I'm not aware that it is. Why should it be a pity, brother?"

"Oh! I don't know," said the man carelessly. "I thought that was what you meant. Being formed for society, and being cut off in your flower, you know—"

"I say," interposed the other quickly, "what are you talking of? Don't! Who's a going to be cut off in their flowers?"

"Oh, nobody particular. I thought you was, perhaps," said the man.

Mr. Dennis wiped his face, which had suddenly grown very hot, and remarking in a tremulous voice to his conductor that he had always been fond of his joke, followed him in silence until he stopped at a door.

"This is my quarters, is it?" he asked, facetiously.

"This is the shop, sir," replied his friend.

He was walking in, but not with the best possible grace, when he suddenly stopped, and started back.

"Halloa!" said the officer. "You're nervous."

"Nervous!" whispered Dennis in great alarm. "Well I may be. Shut the door."

"I will, when you're in," returned the man.

"But I can't go in there," whispered Dennis. "I can't be shut up with that man. Do you want me to be throttled, brother?"

The officer seemed to entertain no particular desire on the subject one way or other, but briefly remarking that he had his orders, and intended to obey them, pushed him in, turned the key, and retired.

Dennis stood trembling with his back against the door, and involuntarily raising his arm to defend himself, stared at a man, the only other tenant of the cell, who lay, stretched at his full length, upon a stone bench, and who paused in his deep breathing as if he were about to wake. But he rolled over on one side, let his arm fall negligently down, drew a long sigh, and murmuring indistinctly, fell fast asleep again.

Relieved in some degree by this, the hangman took his eyes for an instant from the slumbering figure, and glanced round the cell in search of some 'vantage-ground or weapon of defence. There was nothing moveable within it, but a clumsy table which could not be displaced without noise, and a heavy chair. Stealing on tiptoe towards this latter piece of furniture, he retired with it into the remotest corner, and intrenching himself behind it, watched the enemy with the utmost vigilance and caution.

The sleeping man was Hugh; and perhaps it was not unnatural for Dennis to feel in a state of very uncomfortable suspense, and to wish with his whole soul that he might never wake again. Tired of standing, he crouched down in his corner after some time, and rested on the cold pavement; but although Hugh's breathing still proclaimed that he was sleeping soundly, he could not trust him out of his sight for an instant. He was so afraid of him, and of some sudden onslaught, that he was not content to see his closed eyes through the chair-back, but every now and then, rose stealthily to his feet, and peered at him with outstretched neck, to assure himself that he really was still asleep, and was not about to spring upon him when he was off his guard.

He slept so long and so soundly, that Mr. Dennis began to think he might sleep on until the turnkey visited them. He was congratulating himself upon these promising appearances, and blessing his stars with much fervour, when one or two unpleasant symptoms manifested themselves: such as another motion of the arm, another sigh, a restless tossing of the head. Then, just as it seemed that he was about to fall heavily to the ground from his narrow bed, Hugh's eyes opened.

It happened that his face was turned directly towards his unexpected visitor. He looked lazily at him for some half-dozen seconds without any aspect of surprise or recognition; then suddenly jumped up, and with a great oath pronounced his name.

"Keep off, brother, keep off!" cried Dennis, dodging behind the chair. "Don't do me a mischief. I'm a prisoner like you. I haven't the free use of my limbs. I'm quite an old man. Don't hurt me!"

He whined out the last three words in such piteous accents, that Hugh, who had dragged away the chair, and aimed a blow at him with it, checked himself, and bade him get up.

"I'll get up certainly, brother," cried Dennis, anxious to propitiate him by any means in his power. "I'll comply with any request of yours, I'm sure. There—I'm up now. What can I do for you? Only say the word, and I'll do it."

"What can you do for me!" cried Hugh, clutching him by the collar with both hands, and shaking him as though he were bent on stopping his breath by that means. "What have you done for me?"

"The best. The best that could be done," returned the hangman.

Hugh made him no answer, but shaking him in his strong gripe until his teeth chattered in his head, cast him down upon the floor, and flung himself on the bench again.

"If it wasn't for the comfort it is to me, to see you here," he muttered, "I'd have crushed your head against it; I would."

It was some time before Dennis had breath enough to speak, but as soon as he could resume his propitiatory strain, he did so.

"I did the best that could be done, brother," he whined; "I did indeed. I was forced with two bayonets and I don't know how many bullets on each side of me, to point you out. If you hadn't been taken, you'd have been shot; and what a sight that would have been—a fine young man like you!"

"Will it be a better sight now?" asked Hugh, raising his head, with such a fierce expression, that the other durst not answer him just then.

"A deal better," said Dennis meekly, after a pause. "First, there's all the chances of the law,* and they're five hundred strong. We may get off scot-free. Unlikelier things than that, have come to pass. Even if we shouldn't, and the chances fail, we can but be worked off once: and when it's well done, it's so neat, so skilful, so captivating, if that don't seem too strong a word, that you'd hardly believe it could be brought to sich perfection. Kill one's fellow-creeturs off, with muskets!—Pah!" and his nature so revolted at the bare idea, that he spat upon the dungeon pavement.

His warming on this topic, which to one unacquainted with his pursuits and tastes appeared like courage; together with his artful suppression of his own secret hopes, and mention of himself as being in the same condition with Hugh; did more to soothe that ruffian than the most elaborate arguments could have done, or the most abject submission. He rested his arms upon his knees, and stooping forward, looked from beneath his shaggy hair at Dennis, with something of a smile upon his face.

"The fact is, brother," said the hangman, in a tone of greater confidence, "that you got into bad company. The man that was with you was looked after more than you, and it was him I wanted. As to me, what have I got by it? Here we are, in one and the same plight."

"Lookee, rascal," said Hugh, contracting his brows, "I'm not altogether such a shallow blade but I know you expected to get something by it, or you would not have done it. But it's done, and you're here, and it will soon be all over with you and me; and I'd as soon die as live, or live as die. Why should I trouble myself to have revenge on you? To eat, and drink, and go to sleep, as long as I stay here, is all I care for. If there was but a little more sun to bask in, than can find its way into this cursed place, I'd lie in it all day, and not trouble myself to sit or stand up once. That's all the care I have for myself. Why should I care for *you?*"

Finishing this speech with a growl like the yawn of a wild beast, he stretched himself upon the bench again, and closed his eyes once more.

After looking at him in silence for some moments, Dennis, who was greatly relieved to find him in this mood, drew the chair towards his rough couch and sat down near him—taking the precaution, however, to keep out of the range of his brawny arm.

"Well said, brother; nothing could be better said," he ventured to observe. "We'll eat and drink of the best, and sleep our best, and make the best of it every way. Anything can be got for money. Let's spend it merrily."

"Ay," said Hugh, coiling himself into a new position.—"Where is it?"

"Why, they took mine from me at the lodge," said Mr. Dennis; "but mine's a peculiar case."

"Is it? They took mine too."

"Why then, I tell you what, brother," Dennis began. "You must look up your friends—"

"My friends!" cried Hugh, starting up and resting on his hands. "Where are my friends?"

"Your relations then," said Dennis.

"Ha ha ha!" laughed Hugh, waving one arm above his head. "He talks of friends to me—talks of relations to a man whose mother died the death in store for her son, and left him, a hungry brat, without a face he knew in all the world! He talks of this to me!"

"Brother," cried the hangman, whose features underwent a sudden change, "you don't mean to say—"

"I mean to say" Hugh interposed, "that they hung her up at Tyburn. What was good enough for her, is good enough for me. Let them do the like by me as soon as they please—the sooner the better. Say no more to me. I'm going to sleep."

"But I want to speak to you; I want to hear more about that," said Dennis, changing colour.

"If you're a wise man," growled Hugh, raising his head to look at him with a savage frown, "you'll hold your tongue. I tell you I'm going to sleep."

Dennis venturing to say something more in spite of this caution, the desperate fellow struck at him with all his force; and missing him, lay down again with many muttered oaths and imprecations, and turned his face towards the wall. After two or three ineffectual twitches at his dress, which he was hardy enough to venture upon, notwithstanding his dangerous humour, Mr. Dennis, who burnt, for reasons of his own, to pursue the conversation, had no alternative but to sit as patiently as he could: waiting his further pleasure.

CHAPTER THE SEVENTY-FIFTH.

 MONTH has elapsed,—and we stand in the bed-chamber of Sir John Chester. Through the half-opened window, the Temple Garden looks green and pleasant; the placid river, gay with boat and barge, and dimpled with the plash of many an oar, sparkles in the distance; the sky is blue and clear; and the summer air steals gently in, filling the room with perfume. The very town, the smoky town, is radiant. High roofs and steeple tops, wont to look black and sullen, smile a cheerful grey; every old gilded vane, and ball, and cross, glitters anew in the bright morning sun; and high among them all Saint Paul's towers up, showing its lofty crest in burnished gold.

Sir John was breakfasting in bed. His chocolate and toast stood upon a little table at his elbow; books and newspapers lay ready to his hand, upon the coverlet; and, sometimes pausing to glance with an air of tranquil satisfaction round the well-ordered room, and sometimes to gaze indolently at the summer sky, he ate, and drank, and read the news, luxuriously.

The cheerful influence of the morning seemed to have some effect, even upon his equable temper. His manner was unusually gay; his smile more placid and agreeable than usual; his voice more clear and pleasant. He laid down the newspaper he had been reading; leaned back upon his pillow with the air of one who resigned himself to a train of charming recollections; and after a pause, soliloquized as follows:

"And my friend the centaur, goes the way of his mama! I am not surprised. And his mysterious friend Mr. Dennis, likewise! I am not surprised. And my old postman, the exceedingly free-and-easy young madman of Chigwell! I am quite rejoiced. It's the very best thing that could possibly happen to him."

After delivering himself of these remarks, he fell again into his smiling train of reflection; from which he roused himself at length to finish his chocolate, which was getting cold, and ring the bell for more.

The new supply arriving, he took the cup from his servant's hand; and saying, with a charming affability, "I am obliged to you, Peak," dismissed him.

"It is a remarkable circumstance," he said, dallying lazily with the teaspoon, "that my friend the madman should have been within an ace of escaping, on his trial; and it was a good stroke of chance (or, as the world would say, a providential occurrence) that the brother of my Lord Mayor should have been in court, with other country justices, into whose very dense heads curiosity had penetrated. For though the brother of my Lord Mayor was decidedly wrong; and established his near relationship to that amusing person beyond all doubt, in stating that my friend was sane, and had, to his knowledge, wandered about the country with a vagabond parent, avowing revolutionary and rebellious sentiments; I am not the less obliged to him for volunteering that evidence. These insane creatures make such very odd and embarrassing remarks, that they really ought to be hanged, for the comfort of society."

The country justice had indeed turned the wavering scale against poor Barnaby, and solved the doubt that trembled in his favour. Grip little thought how much he had to answer for.

"They will be a singular party," said Sir John, leaning his head upon his hand, and sipping his chocolate; "a very curious party. The hangman himself; the centaur; and the madman. The centaur would make a very handsome preparation in Surgeons' Hall,* and would benefit science extremely. I hope they have taken care to bespeak him.—Peak, I am not at home, of course, to anybody but the hair-dresser."

This reminder to his servant was called forth by a knock at the door, which the man hastened to open. After a prolonged murmur of question and answer, he returned; and as he cautiously closed the room-door behind him, a man was heard to cough in the passage.

"Now, it is of no use, Peak," said Sir John, raising his hand in deprecation of his delivering any message; "I am not at home. I cannot possibly hear you. I told you I was not at home, and my word is sacred. Will you never do as you are desired?"

Having nothing to oppose to this reproof, the man was about to withdraw, when the visitor who had given occasion to it, probably rendered impatient by delay, knocked with his knuckles at the chamber-door, and called out that he had urgent business with Sir John Chester, which admitted of no delay.

"Let him in," said Sir John. "My good fellow," he added, when the door was opened, "how come you to intrude yourself in this extraordinary manner upon the privacy of a gentleman? How can you be so wholly destitute of self-respect as to be guilty of such remarkable ill-breeding?"

"My business, Sir John, is not of a common kind, I do assure you," returned the person he addressed. "If I have taken any uncommon course to get admission to you, I hope I shall be pardoned on that account."

"Well! we shall see; we shall see;" returned Sir John, whose face cleared up when he saw who it was, and whose prepossessing smile was now restored. "I am sure we have met before," he added, in his most winning tone, "but really I forget your name."

"My name is Gabriel Varden, sir."

"Varden, of course, Varden," returned Sir John, tapping his forehead. "Dear me, how very defective my memory becomes! Varden to be sure—Mr. Varden the locksmith. You have a charming wife, Mr. Varden, and a most beautiful daughter. They are well?"

Gabriel thanked him, and said they were.

"I rejoice to hear it," said Sir John. "Commend me to them when you return, and say that I wished I were fortunate enough to convey, myself, the salute which I entrust you to deliver. And what," he asked very sweetly, after a moment's pause, "can I do for you? You may command me, freely."

"I thank you Sir John," said Gabriel, with some pride in his manner, "but I have come to ask no favour of you, though I come on business.—Private," he added, with a glance at the man who stood looking on, "and very pressing business."

"I cannot say you are the more welcome for being independent, and having nothing to ask of me," returned Sir John, graciously, "for I should have been happy to render you a service; still, you are welcome on any terms. Oblige me with some more chocolate, Peak—and don't wait."

The man retired, and left them alone.

"Sir John," said Gabriel, "I am a working-man, and have been, all my life. If I don't prepare you enough for what I have to tell; if I come to the point too abruptly; and give you a shock, which a gentleman could have spared you, or at all events lessened very much, I hope you will give me credit for meaning well. I wish to be careful and considerate, and I trust that in a straight-forward person like me, you'll take the will for the deed."

"Mr. Varden," returned the other, perfectly composed under this exordium; "I beg you'll take a chair. Chocolate, perhaps, you don't relish? Well! it *is* an acquired taste, no doubt."

"Sir John," said Gabriel, who had acknowledged with a bow the invitation to be seated, but had not availed himself of it; "Sir John"—he dropped his voice and drew nearer to the bed—"I am just now come from Newgate—"

"Good Gad!" cried Sir John, hastily sitting up in bed; "from Newgate, Mr. Varden! How could you be so very imprudent as to come from Newgate! Newgate, where there are jail-fevers, and ragged people, and barefooted men and women, and a thousand horrors! Peak, bring the camphor, quick! Heaven and earth, Mr. Varden, my dear, good soul, how *could* you come from Newgate?"

Gabriel returned no answer, but looked on in silence while Peak (who had entered opportunely with the hot chocolate) ran to a drawer, and returning with a bottle, sprinkled his master's dressing-gown and the bedding; and besides moistening the locksmith himself, plentifully, described a circle round about him on the carpet. When he had done this, he again retired; and Sir John, reclining in an easy attitude upon his pillow, once more turned a smiling face towards his visitor.

"You will forgive me, Mr. Varden, I am sure, for being at first a little sensitive both on your account and my own. I confess I was startled, notwithstanding your delicate preparation. Might I ask you to do me the favour not to approach any nearer?—You have really come from Newgate!"

The locksmith inclined his head.

"In-deed! And now, Mr. Varden, all exaggeration and embellishment apart," said Sir John Chester, confidentially, as he sipped his chocolate, "what kind of place *is* Newgate?"

"A strange place, Sir John," returned the locksmith, "of a sad and doleful kind. A strange place, where many strange things are heard and seen; but few more strange than that I come to tell you of. The case is urgent. I am sent here."

"Not—no, no—not from the jail?"

"Yes, Sir John; from the jail."

"And my good, credulous, open-hearted friend," said Sir John, setting down his cup, and laughing,—"by whom?"

"By a man called Dennis—for many years the hangman, and to-morrow morning the hanged," returned the locksmith.

Sir John had expected—had been quite certain from the first— that he would say he had come from Hugh, and was prepared to meet him on that point. But this answer occasioned him a degree of astonishment, which for the moment he could not, with all his command of feature, prevent his face from expressing. He quickly subdued it, however, and said in the same light tone:

"And what does the gentleman require of me? My memory may be at fault again, but I don't recollect that I ever had the pleasure of an introduction to him, or that I ever numbered him among my personal friends, I do assure you, Mr. Varden."

"Sir John," returned the locksmith, gravely, "I will tell you, as nearly as I can, in the words he used to me, what he desires that you should know, and what you ought to know without a moment's loss of time."

Sir John Chester settled himself in a position of greater repose, and looked at his visitor with an expression of face which seemed to say, "This is an amusing fellow! I'll hear him out."

"You may have seen in the newspapers, Sir," said Gabriel,

pointing to the one which lay by his side, "that I was a witness against this man upon his trial some days since; and that it was not his fault I was alive, and able to speak to what I knew."

"*May* have seen!" cried Sir John. "My dear Mr. Varden, you are quite a public character, and live in all men's thoughts most deservedly. Nothing can exceed the interest with which I read your testimony, and remembered that I had the pleasure of a slight acquaintance with you.—I hope we shall have your portrait published?"

"This morning, Sir," said the locksmith, taking no notice of these compliments, "early this morning, a message was brought to me from Newgate, at this man's request, desiring that I would go and see him, for he had something particular to communicate. I needn't tell you that he is no friend of mine, and that I had never seen him, until the rioters beset my house."

Sir John fanned himself gently with the newspaper, and nodded.

"I knew, however, from the general report," resumed Gabriel, "that the order for his execution to-morrow, went down to the prison last night; and looking upon him as a dying man, I complied with his request."

"You are quite a Christian, Mr. Varden," said Sir John; "and in that amiable capacity, you increase my desire that you should take a chair."

"He said," continued Gabriel, looking steadily at the knight, "that he had sent to me, because he had no friend or companion in the whole world, (being the common hangman), and because he believed, from the way in which I had given my evidence, that I was an honest man, and would act truly by him. He said that, being shunned by every one who knew his calling, even by people of the lowest and most wretched grade; and finding, when he joined the rioters, that the men he acted with had no suspicion of it (which I believe is true enough, for a poor fool of an old 'prentice of mine was one of them); he had kept his own counsel, up to the time of his being taken and put in jail."

"Very discreet of Mr. Dennis," observed Sir John with a slight yawn, though still with the utmost affability, "but—except for your admirable and lucid manner of telling it, which is perfect—not very interesting to me."

"When," pursued the locksmith, quite unabashed and wholly

regardless of these interruptions, "when he was taken to the jail, he found that his fellow-prisoner, in the same room, was a young man, Hugh by name, a leader in the riots, who had been betrayed and given up by himself. From something which fell from this unhappy creature in the course of the angry words they had at meeting, he discovered that his mother had suffered the death to which they both are now condemned.—The time is very short, Sir John."

The knight laid down his paper fan, replaced his cup upon the table at his side, and, saving for the smile that lurked about his mouth, looked at the locksmith with as much steadiness as the locksmith looked at him.

"They have been in prison now, a month. One conversation led to many more; and the hangman soon found, from a comparison of time, and place, and dates, that he had executed the sentence of the law upon this woman, himself. She had been tempted by want—as so many people are—into the easy crime of passing forged notes. She was young and handsome; and the traders who employ men, women, and children in this traffic, looked upon her as one who was well adapted for their business, and who would probably go on without suspicion for a long time. But they were mistaken; for she was stopped in the commission of her very first offence, and died for it. She was of gipsy blood, Sir John—"

It might have been the effect of a passing cloud which obscured the sun, and cast a shadow on his face; but the knight turned deadly pale. Still he met the locksmith's eye, as before.

"She was of gipsy blood, Sir John," repeated Gabriel, "and had a high, free spirit. This, and her good looks, and her lofty manner, interested some gentlemen who were easily moved by dark eyes; and efforts were made to save her. They might have been successful, if she would have given them any clue to her history. But she never would, or did. There was reason to suspect that she would make an attempt upon her life. A watch was set upon her night and day; and from that time she never spoke again—"

Sir John stretched out his hand towards his cup. The locksmith going on, arrested it half way.

—"Until she had but a minute to live. Then she broke silence, and said, in a low firm voice which no one heard but this executioner, for all other living creatures had retired and left her to her fate, 'If I had a dagger within these fingers and he was within my reach, I would strike him dead before me, even now!' The man asked 'Who?'—she said, The father of her boy."

Sir John drew back his outstretched hand, and seeing that the locksmith paused, signed to him with easy politeness and without any new appearance of emotion, to proceed.

"It was the first word she had ever spoken, from which it could be understood that she had any relative on earth. 'Was the child alive?' he asked. 'Yes.' He asked her where it was, its name, and whether she had any wish respecting it. She had but one, she said. It was that the boy might live and grow, in utter ignorance of his father, so that no arts might teach him to be gentle and forgiving. When he became a man, she trusted to the God of their tribe to bring the father and the son together, and revenge her through her child. He asked her other questions, but she spoke no more. Indeed, he says she scarcely said this much to him, but stood with her face turned upwards to the sky, and never looked towards him once."

Sir John took a pinch of snuff; glanced approvingly at an elegant little sketch, entitled "Nature," on the wall; and raising his eyes to the locksmith's face again, said, with an air of courtesy and patronage, "You were observing, Mr. Varden—"

"That she never," returned the locksmith, who was not to be diverted by any artifice from his firm manner, and his steady gaze, "that she never looked towards him once, Sir John; and so she died, and he forgot her. But, some years afterwards, a man was sentenced to die the same death, who was a gipsy too; a sunburnt, swarthy fellow, almost a wild man; and while he lay in prison, under sentence, he, who had seen the hangman more than once while he was free, cut an image of him on his stick, by way of braving death, and showing those who attended on him, how little he cared or thought about it. He gave this stick into his hands at Tyburn, and told him then, that the woman I have spoken of had left her own people to join a fine gentleman, and that, being deserted by him, and cast off by her old friends, she had sworn within her own proud breast, that whatever her misery might be, she would ask no help of any human being. He told him that she had kept her word to the last; and that, meeting even him in the streets—he had been fond of her once, it seems—she had slipped from him by a trick, and he never saw her again, until, being in one of the frequent crowds at Tyburn, with some of his rough companions, he had been driven almost mad by seeing, in the criminal under another name, whose death he had come to witness, herself. Standing in the same place in which she had stood, he told the hangman this, and told him, too, her real name, which only her own people and the gentleman for whose sake she had left them, knew.—That name he will tell again, Sir John, to none but you."

"To none but me!" exclaimed the knight, pausing in the act of raising his cup to his lips with a perfectly steady hand, and curling up his little finger for the better display of a brilliant ring with which it was ornamented: "but me!—My dear Mr. Varden, how very preposterous, to select me for his confidence! With you at his elbow, too, who are so perfectly trustworthy."

"Sir John, Sir John," returned the locksmith, "at twelve to-morrow, these men die. Hear the few words I have to add, and do not hope to deceive me; for though I am a plain man of humble station, and you are a gentleman of rank and learning, the truth raises me to your level, and by its power I KNOW that you anticipate the disclosure with which I am about to end, and that you believe this doomed man, Hugh, to be your son."

"Nay," said Sir John, bantering him with a gay air; "the wild gentleman, who died so suddenly, scarcely went as far as that, I think?"

"He did not," returned the locksmith, "for she had bound him by some pledge, known only to these people, and which the worst among them respect, not to tell your name: but, in a fantastic pattern on the stick, he had carved some letters, and when the hangman asked it, he bade him, especially if he should ever meet with her son in after life, remember that place well."

"What place?"

"Chester."

The knight finished his cup of chocolate with an appearance of infinite relish, and carefully wiped his lips upon his handkerchief.

"Sir John," said the locksmith, "this is all that has been told to me; but since these two men have been left for death, they have conferred together, closely. See them, and hear what they can add. See this Dennis, and learn from him what he has not trusted to me. If you, who hold the clue to all, want corroboration (which you do not), the means are easy."

"And to what," said Sir John Chester, rising on his elbow, after smoothing the pillow for its reception; "my dear, good-natured, estimable Mr. Varden—with whom I cannot be angry if I would—to what does all this tend?"

"I take you for a man, Sir John, and I suppose to some pleading of natural affection in your breast," returned the locksmith indignantly. "I suppose to the straining of every nerve, and the exertion of all the influence you have, or can make, in behalf of your miserable son, and the man who has disclosed his existence to you. At the worst, I suppose to your seeing your son, and awakening him to a sense of his crime and danger. He has no such sense now. Think what his life must have been, when he said in my hearing, that if I moved you to anything, it would be to hastening his death, and ensuring his silence, if you had it in your power!"

"And have you, my good Mr. Varden," said Sir John in a tone of mild reproof, "have you really lived to your present age, and remained so very simple and credulous, as to approach a gentleman of established character with such credentials as these, from desperate men in their last extremity, catching at any straw? Oh dear! Oh fie, fie!"

The locksmith was going to interpose, but he stopped him:

"On any other subject, Mr. Varden, I shall be delighted—I shall be charmed—to converse with you, but I owe it to my own character not to pursue this topic for another moment."

"Think better of it, Sir, when I am gone," returned the locksmith; "think better of it, Sir. Although you have, thrice within as many weeks, turned your lawful son, Mr. Edward, from your door; you may have time, you may have years, to make your peace with *him*, Sir John: but that twelve o'clock will soon be here, and soon be past for ever."

"I thank you very much," returned the knight, kissing his delicate hand to the locksmith, "for your guileless advice; and I only wish, my good soul, although your simplicity is quite captivating, that you had a little more worldly wisdom. I never so much regretted the arrival of my hair-dresser as I do at this moment. God bless you! Good morning! You'll not forget my message to the ladies, Mr. Varden? Peak, show Mr. Varden to the door."

Gabriel said no more, but gave the knight a parting look, and left him. As he quitted the room, Sir John's face changed; and the smile gave place to a haggard and anxious expression, like that of a weary actor jaded by the performance of a difficult part. He rose from his bed with a heavy sigh, and wrapped himself in his morning-gown.

"So, she kept her word," he said, "and was constant to her threat! I would I had never seen that dark face of hers,—I might have read these consequences in it, from the first. This affair would make a noise abroad, if it rested on better evidence; but as it is, and by not joining the scattered links of the chain, I can afford to slight it.— Extremely distressing to be the parent of such an uncouth creature! Still, I gave him very good advice: I told him he would certainly be hanged: I could have done no more if I had known of our relationship; and there are a great many fathers who have never done as much for *their* natural children.—The hair-dresser may come in, Peak!"

The hair-dresser came in; and saw in Sir John Chester (whose accommodating conscience was soon quieted by the numerous precedents that occurred to him in support of his last observation), the same imperturbable, fascinating, elegant gentleman he had seen yesterday, and many yesterdays before.

CHAPTER THE SEVENTY-SIXTH.

As the locksmith walked slowly away from Sir John Chester's chambers, he lingered under the trees which shaded the path, almost hoping that he might be summoned to return. He had turned back thrice, and still loitered at the corner, when the clocks struck twelve.

It was a solemn sound, and not merely for its reference to tomorrow; for he knew that in that chime the murderer's knell was rung. He had seen him pass along the crowded street, amidst the execrations of the throng: had marked his quivering lip, and trembling limbs; the ashy hue upon his face, his clammy brow, the wild distraction of his eye—the fear of death that swallowed up all other thoughts, and gnawed without cessation at his heart and brain. He had marked the wandering look, seeking for hope, and finding, turn where it would, despair. He had seen the remorseful, pitiful, desolate creature, riding, with his coffin by his side, to the gibbet. He knew that to the last he had been an unyielding, obdurate man; that in the savage terror of his condition he had hardened, rather than relented, to his wife and child; and that the last words which had passed his white lips were curses on them as his foes.

Mr. Haredale had determined to be there, and see it done. Nothing but the evidence of his own senses could satisfy that gloomy thirst for retribution which had been gathering upon him for so many years. The locksmith knew this, and when the chimes had ceased to vibrate, hurried away to meet him.

"For these two men," he said, as he went, "I can do no more. Heaven have mercy on them!—Alas! I say I can do no more for them, but whom *can* I help? Mary Rudge will have a home, and a firm friend when she most wants one; but Barnaby—poor Barnaby— willing Barnaby—what aid can I render him? There are many, many men of sense, God forgive me," cried the honest locksmith, stopping in a narrow court to pass his hand across his eyes, "I could better afford to lose than Barnaby. We have always been good friends, but I never knew, till now, how much I loved the lad."

There were not many in the great city who thought of Barnaby that day, otherwise than as an actor in a show which was to take place to-morrow. But if the whole population had had him in their minds, and had wished his life to be spared, not one among them could have done so with a purer zeal or greater singleness of heart than the good locksmith.

Barnaby was to die. There was no hope. It is not the least evil attendant upon the frequent exhibition of this last dread punishment, of Death, that it hardens the minds of those who deal it out, and makes them, though they be amiable men in other respects, indifferent to, or unconscious of, their great responsibility. The word had gone forth that Barnaby was to die. It went forth every month, for lighter crimes. It was a thing so common, that very few were startled by the awful sentence, or cared to question its propriety. Just then, too, when the law had been so flagrantly outraged, its dignity must be asserted. The symbol of its dignity,—stamped upon every page of the criminal statute-book,—was the gallows; and Barnaby was to die.

They had tried to save him. The locksmith had carried petitions and memorials to the fountain-head, with his own hands. But the well was not one of mercy, and Barnaby was to die.

From the first She had never left him, save at night, and with her beside him, he was as usual contented. On this last day, he was more

elated and more proud than he had been yet; and when she dropped
the book she had been reading to him aloud, and fell upon his neck,
he stopped in his busy task of folding a piece of crape about his hat,
and wondered at her anguish. Grip uttered a feeble croak, half in
encouragement, it seemed, and half in remonstrance, but he wanted
heart to sustain it, and lapsed abruptly into silence.

With them, who stood upon the brink of the great gulf which
none can see beyond, Time, so soon to lose itself in vast Eternity,
rolled on like a mighty river, swoln and rapid as it nears the sea. It
was morning but now; they had sat and talked together in a dream;
and here was evening. The dreadful hour of separation, which even
yesterday had seemed so distant, was at hand.

They walked out into the court-yard, clinging to each other, but
not speaking. Barnaby knew that the jail was a dull, sad, miserable
place, and looked forward to to-morrow, as to a passage from it to
something bright and beautiful. He had a vague impression too, that
he was expected to be brave—that he was a man of great con-
sequence, and that the prison people would be glad to make him

weep: he trod the ground more firmly as he thought of this, and bade her take heart and cry no more, and feel how steady his hand was. "They call me silly, mother. They shall see—to-morrow!"

Dennis and Hugh were in the court-yard. Hugh came forth from his cell as they did, stretching himself as though he had been sleeping. Dennis sat upon a bench in a corner, with his knees and chin huddled together, and rocked himself to and fro like a person in severe pain.

The mother and son remained on one side of the court, and these two men upon the other. Hugh strode up and down, glancing fiercely every now and then at the bright summer sky, and looking round, when he had done so, at the walls.

"No reprieve, no reprieve! Nobody comes near us. There's only the night left now!" moaned Dennis faintly, as he wrung his hands. "Do you think they'll reprieve me in the night, brother? I've known reprieves come in the night, afore now. I've known 'em come as late as five, six, and seven o'clock in the morning. Don't you think there's a good chance yet,—don't you? Say you do. Say *you* do, young man," whined the miserable creature, with an imploring gesture towards Barnaby, "or I shall go mad!"

"Better be mad than sane, here," said Hugh. "*Go* mad."

"But tell me what you think. Somebody tell me what he thinks!" cried the wretched object,—so mean, and wretched, and despicable, that even Pity's self might have turned away at sight of such a being in the likeness of a man—"isn't there a chance for me,—isn't there a good chance for me? Isn't it likely they may be doing this to frighten me? Don't you think it is? Oh!" he almost shrieked, as he wrung his hands, "won't anybody give me comfort?"

"You ought to be the best, instead of the worst," said Hugh, stopping before him. "Ha, ha, ha! See the hangman, when it comes home to him!"

"You don't know what it is," cried Dennis, actually writhing as he spoke: "I do. That I should come to be worked off! I! I! That *I* should come!"

"And why not?" said Hugh, as he thrust back his matted hair to get a better view of his late associate. "How often, before I knew your trade, did I hear you talking of this as if it was a treat?"

"I an't unconsistent," screamed the miserable creature; "I'd talk so again, if I was hangman. Some other man has got my old opinions at this minute. That makes it worse. Somebody's longing to work me off. I know by myself that somebody must be!"

"He'll soon have his longing," said Hugh, resuming his walk. "Think of that, and be quiet."

Although one of these men displayed, in his speech and bearing, the most reckless hardihood; and the other, in his every word and action, testified such an extreme of abject cowardice that it was humiliating to see him; it would be difficult to say which of them would most have repelled and shocked an observer. Hugh's was the dogged desperation of a savage at the stake; the hangman was reduced to a condition little better, if any, than that of a hound with the halter round his neck. Yet, as Mr. Dennis knew and could have told them, these were the two commonest states of mind in persons brought to their pass. Such was the wholesome growth of the seed sown by the law, that this kind of harvest was usually looked for, as a matter of course.

In one respect they all agreed. The wandering and uncontrollable train of thought, suggesting sudden recollections of things distant and long forgotten and remote from each other—the vague restless craving for something undefined, which nothing could satisfy—the swift flight of the minutes, fusing themselves into hours, as if by enchantment—the rapid coming of the solemn night—the shadow of death always upon them, and yet so dim and faint, that objects the meanest and most trivial started from the gloom beyond, and forced themselves upon the view—the impossibility of holding the mind, even if they had been so disposed, to penitence and preparation, or of keeping it to any point while that hideous fascination tempted it away—these things were common to them all, and varied only in their outward tokens.

"Fetch me the book I left within—upon your bed," she said to Barnaby, as the clock struck. "Kiss me first!"

He looked in her face, and saw there, that the time was come. After a long embrace, he tore himself away, and ran to bring it to her; bidding her not stir till he came back. He soon returned, for a shriek recalled him,—but she was gone.

He ran to the yard gate, and looked through. They were carrying her away. She had said her heart would break. It was better so.

"Don't you think," whimpered Dennis, creeping up to him, as he stood with his feet rooted to the ground, gazing at the blank walls—

"don't you think there's still a chance? It's a dreadful end; it's a terrible end for a man like me. Don't you think there's a chance? I don't mean for you, I mean for me. Don't let *him* hear us" (meaning Hugh); "he's so desperate."

"Now then," said the officer, who had been lounging in and out with his hands in his pockets, and yawning as if he were in the last extremity for some subject of interest: "it's time to turn in, boys."

"Not yet," cried Dennis, "not yet. Not for an hour yet."

"I say,—your watch goes different from what it used to," returned the man. "Once upon a time it was always too fast. It's got the other fault now."

"My friend," cried the wretched creature, falling on his knees, "my dear friend—you always were my dear friend—there's some mistake. Some letter has been mislaid, or some messenger has been stopped upon the way. He may have fallen dead. I saw a man once, fall down dead in the street, myself, and he had papers in his pocket. Send to enquire. Let somebody go to enquire. They never will hang me. They never can.—Yes, they will," he cried, starting to his feet with a terrible scream. "They'll hang me by a trick, and keep the pardon back. It's a plot against me. I shall lose my life!" And uttering another yell, he fell in a fit upon the ground.

"See the hangman when it comes home to him!" cried Hugh again, as they bore him away—"Ha ha ha! Courage, bold Barnaby, what care we? Your hand! They do well to put us out of the world, for if we got loose a second time, we wouldn't let them off so easy, eh? Another shake! A man can die but once. If you wake in the night, sing that out lustily, and fall asleep again. Ha ha ha!"

Barnaby glanced once more through the grate into the empty yard; and then watched Hugh as he strode to the steps leading to his sleeping-cell. He heard him shout, and burst into a roar of laughter, and saw him flourish his hat. Then he turned away himself, like one who walked in his sleep; and, without any sense of fear or sorrow, lay down on his pallet, listening for the clock to strike again.

CHAPTER THE SEVENTY-SEVENTH.

THE time wore on: the noises in the streets became less frequent by degrees, until silence was scarcely broken save by the bells in church towers, marking the progress—softer and more stealthy while the city slumbered—of that Great Watcher with the hoary head, who never sleeps or rests. In the brief interval of darkness and repose which feverish towns enjoy, all busy sounds were hushed; and those who awoke from dreams lay listening in their beds, and longed for dawn, and wished the dead of the night were past.

Into the street outside the jail's main wall, workmen came straggling at this solemn hour, in groups of two or three, and meeting in the centre cast their tools upon the ground and spoke in whispers. Others soon issued from the jail itself, bearing on their shoulders, planks, and beams: these materials being all brought forth, the rest bestirred themselves, and the dull sound of hammers began to echo through the stillness.

Here and there among this knot of labourers, one, with a lantern or a smoky link, stood by to light his fellows at their work, and by its doubtful aid, some might be dimly seen taking up the pavement of the road, while others held great upright posts, or fixed them in the holes thus made for their reception. Some dragged slowly on towards the rest, an empty cart, which they brought rumbling from the prison yard; while others erected strong barriers across the street. All were busily engaged. Their dusky figures moving to and fro, at that unusual hour, so active and so silent, might have been taken for those of shadowy creatures toiling at midnight on some ghostly unsubstantial work, which, like themselves, would vanish with the first gleam of day, and leave but morning mist and vapour.

While it was yet dark, a few lookers-on collected, who had plainly come there for the purpose and intended to remain: even those who had to pass the spot on their way to some other place, lingered, and lingered yet, as though the attraction of that were irresistible. Meanwhile the noise of saw and mallet went on briskly, mingled with the clattering of boards on the stone pavement of the road, and sometimes with the workmen's voices as they called to one another. Whenever the chimes of the neighbouring church were heard—and that was every quarter of an hour—a strange sensation, instantaneous and indescribable, but perfectly obvious, seemed to pervade them all.

Gradually, a faint brightness appeared in the east, and the air, which had been very warm all through the night, felt cool and chilly. Though there was no daylight yet, the darkness was diminished, and the stars looked pale. The prison, which had been a mere black mass with little shape or form, put on its usual aspect; and ever and anon a solitary watchman could be seen upon its roof, stopping to look down upon the preparations in the street. This man, from forming, as it were, a part of the jail, and knowing or being supposed to know all that was passing within, became an object of as much interest, and was as eagerly looked for, and as awfully pointed out, as if he had been a spirit.

By and bye, the feeble light grew stronger, and the houses with their signboards and inscriptions stood plainly out, in the dull grey morning. Heavy stage waggons crawled from the Inn-yard opposite; and travellers peeped out; and as they rolled sluggishly away, cast many a backward look towards the jail. And now the sun's first beams came glancing into the street; and the night's work, which, in its various stages and in the varied fancies of the lookers-on had taken a hundred shapes, wore its own proper form—a scaffold, and a gibbet.

As the warmth of cheerful day began to shed itself upon the scanty crowd, the murmur of tongues was heard, shutters were thrown open, and blinds drawn up, and those who had slept in rooms over against the prison, where places to see the execution were let at high prices, rose hastily from their beds. In some of the houses people were busy taking out the window sashes for the better accommodation of spectators; in others the spectators were already seated, and beguiling the time with cards, or drink, or jokes among themselves. Some had purchased seats upon the house-tops, and were already crawling to their stations from parapet and garret window. Some were yet bargaining for good places, and stood in them in a state of indecision: gazing at the slowly-swelling crowd, and at the workmen as they rested listlessly against the scaffold; and affecting to listen with indifference to the proprietor's eulogy of the commanding view his house afforded, and the surpassing cheapness of his terms.

A fairer morning never shone. From the roofs and upper stories of these buildings, the spires of city churches and the great cathedral dome were visible, rising up beyond the prison, into the blue sky: clad in the colour of light summer clouds, and showing in the clear atmosphere their every scrap of tracery and fretwork, and every niche and loophole. All was brightness and promise, excepting in the street below, into which (for it yet lay in shadow) the eye looked down as into a dark trench, where, in the midst of so much life, and hope, and renewal of existence, stood the terrible instrument of death. It seemed as if the very sun forbore to look upon it.

But it was better, grim and sombre in the shade, than when, the day being more advanced, it stood confessed in the full glare and glory of the sun, with its black paint blistering, and its nooses dangling in the light like loathsome garlands. It was better in the solitude and gloom of midnight with a few forms clustering about it, than in the freshness and the stir of morning: the centre of an eager crowd. It was better haunting the street like a spectre, when men were in their beds; and influencing perchance the city's dreams; than braving the broad day, and thrusting its obscene presence upon their waking senses.

Five o'clock had struck—six—seven—and eight. Along the two main streets at either end of the cross-way, a living stream had now set in: rolling towards the marts of gain and business. Carts, coaches, waggons, trucks, and barrows, forced a passage through the outskirts of the throng, and clattered onward in the same direction. Some of these which were public conveyances and had come from a short distance in the country, stopped; and the driver pointed to the gibbet with his whip, though he might have spared himself the pains, for the heads of all the passengers were turned that way without his help, and the coach windows were stuck full of staring eyes. In some of the carts and waggons, women might be seen glancing fearfully at the same unsightly thing; and even little children were held up above the people's heads to see what kind of toy a gallows was, and learn how men were hanged.

Two rioters were to die before the prison, who had been concerned in the attack upon it; and one directly afterwards in Bloomsbury Square.* At nine o'clock, a strong body of military marched into the street, and formed and lined a narrow passage into Holborn, which had been indifferently kept all night by constables. Through this, another cart was brought (the one already mentioned had been employed in the construction of the scaffold), and wheeled up to the prison gate. These preparations made, the soldiers stood at ease; the officers lounged to and fro, in the alley they had made, or talked together at the scaffold's foot; and the concourse, which had been rapidly augmenting for some hours, and still received additions every minute, waited with an impatience which increased with every chime of St. Sepulchre's clock, for twelve at noon.

Up to this time they had been very quiet, comparatively silent, save when the arrival of some new party at a window, hitherto unoccupied, gave them something new to look at or to talk of. But as the hour approached, a buzz and hum arose, which, deepening every moment, soon swelled into a roar, and seemed to fill the air. No words or even voices could be distinguished in this clamour, nor did they speak much to each other; though such as were better informed upon the topic than the rest, would tell their neighbours, perhaps, that they might know the hangman when he came out, by his being the shorter one: and that the man who was to suffer with him was named Hugh: and that it was Barnaby Rudge who would be hanged in Bloomsbury Square. As it is the nature of men in a great heat to perspire spontaneously, so this wild murmur, floating up and down, seemed born of their intense impatience, and quite beyond their restraint or control.

It grew, as the time drew near, so loud, that those who were at the windows could not hear the church-clock strike, though it was close at hand. Nor had they any need to hear it, either, for they could see it in the people's faces. So surely as another quarter chimed, there was a movement in the crowd—as if something had passed over it—as if the light upon them had been changed—in which the fact was readable as on a brazen dial, figured by a giant's hand.

Three quarters past eleven! The murmur now was deafening, yet every man seemed mute. Look where you would among the crowd, you saw strained eyes and lips compressed; it would have been difficult for the most vigilant observer to point this way or that, and say that yonder man had cried out: it were as easy to detect the motion of lips in a sea-shell.

Three quarters past eleven! Weary spectators who had retired from the windows, came back refreshed, as though their watch had just begun. Those who had fallen asleep roused themselves; and every person in the crowd made one last effort to better his position—which caused a press against the sturdy barriers that made them bend and yield like twigs. The officers, who until now had kept together, fell into their several positions, and gave the words of command. Swords were drawn, muskets shouldered, and the bright steel winding its way among the crowd, gleamed and glittered in the sun like a river. Along this shining path two men came hurrying on, leading a horse, which was speedily harnessed to the cart at the prison door. Then a profound silence replaced the tumult that had so long been gathering, and a breathless pause ensued. Every window was now choked up with heads; the house-tops teemed with people—clinging to chimneys, peering over gable-ends, and holding on where the sudden loosening of any brick or stone would dash them down into the street. The church tower, the church roof, the church yard, the prison leads, the very water-spouts and lamp-posts—every inch of room—swarmed with human life.

At the first stroke of twelve the prison bell began to toll. Then the roar—mingled now with cries of "Hats off!" and "Poor fellows!" and, from some specks in the great concourse, with a shriek or groan—burst forth again. It was terrible to see—if any one in that distraction of excitement could have seen—the world of eager eyes, all strained upon the scaffold and the beam.

The hollow murmuring was heard within the jail as plainly as without. The three were brought forth into the yard, together, as it resounded through the air: and knew its import well.

"D'ye hear?" cried Hugh, undaunted by the sound. "They expect us! I heard them gathering when I woke in the night, and turned over on t'other side and fell asleep again. We shall see how they welcome the hangman, now that it comes home to him. Ha, ha, ha!"

The ordinary coming up at this moment, reproved him for his indecent mirth, and advised him to alter his demeanour.

"And why, master?" said Hugh. "Can I do better than bear it easily? *You* bear it easily enough. Oh! never tell me," he cried, as the other would have spoken, "for all your sad look and your solemn air, you think little enough of it! They say you're the best maker of lobster salads in London. Ha, ha, ha! I've heard that, you see, before now. Is it a good one, this morning—is your hand in? How does the breakfast look? I hope there's enough, and to spare, for all this hungry company that'll sit down to it, when the sight's over."

"I fear," observed the clergyman, shaking his head, "that you are incorrigible."

"You're right. I am," rejoined Hugh sternly. "Be no hypocrite, master. You make a merry-making of this, every month; let me be merry, too. If you want a frightened fellow, there's one that'll suit you. Try your hand upon him."

He pointed, as he spoke, to Dennis, who, with his legs trailing on the ground, was held between two men; and who trembled so, that all his joints and limbs seemed racked by spasms. Turning from this wretched spectacle, he called to Barnaby, who stood apart.

"What cheer, Barnaby? Don't be downcast, lad. Leave that to *him*."

"Bless you," cried Barnaby, stepping lightly towards him, "I'm not frightened, Hugh. I'm quite happy. I wouldn't desire to live now, if they'd let me. Look at me! Am I afraid to die? Will they see *me* tremble?"

Hugh gazed for a moment at his face, on which there was a strange, unearthly smile; and at his eye, which sparkled brightly; and interposing between him and the ordinary, gruffly whispered to the latter:

"I wouldn't say much to him, master, if I was you. He may spoil your appetite for breakfast, though you *are* used to it."

He was the only one of the three, who had washed or trimmed himself that morning. Neither of the others had done so, since their doom was pronounced. He still wore the broken peacock's feathers in his hat; and all his usual scraps of finery were carefully disposed about his person. His kindling eye, his firm step, his proud and resolute bearing, might have graced some lofty act of heroism; some voluntary sacrifice, born of a noble cause and pure enthusiasm; rather than that felon's death.

But all these things increased his guilt. They were mere assumptions. The law had declared it so, and so it must be. The good minister had been greatly shocked, not a quarter of an hour before, at his parting with Grip. For one in his condition, to fondle a bird!—

The yard was filled with people; bluff civic functionaries, officers of justice, soldiers, the curious in such matters, and guests who had been bidden as to a wedding. Hugh looked about him, nodded gloomily to some person in authority, who indicated with his hand in what direction he was to proceed; and clapping Barnaby on the shoulder, passed out with the gait of a lion.

They entered a large room, so near to the scaffold that the voices of those who stood about it, could be plainly heard: some beseeching the javelin-men to take them out of the crowd: others crying to those behind to stand back, for they were pressed to death, and suffocating for want of air.

In the middle of this chamber, two smiths, with hammers, stood beside an anvil. Hugh walked straight up to them, and set his foot upon it with a sound as though it had been struck by a heavy weapon. Then, with folded arms, he stood to have his irons knocked off: scowling haughtily round, as those who were present eyed him narrowly and whispered to each other.

It took so much time to drag Dennis in, that this ceremony was over with Hugh, and nearly over with Barnaby, before he appeared. He no sooner came into the place he knew so well, however, and among faces with which he was so familiar, than he recovered strength and sense enough to clasp his hands, and make a last appeal.

"Gentlemen, good gentlemen," cried the abject creature, grovelling down upon his knees, and actually prostrating himself upon the stone floor: "Governor, dear governor—honourable sheriffs—worthy gentlemen—have mercy upon a wretched man that has served His Majesty, and the Law, and Parliament, for so many years, and don't—don't let me die—because of a mistake."

"Dennis," said the governor of the jail, "you know what the course is, and that the order came with the rest. You know that we could do nothing, even if we would."

"All I ask, sir,—all I want and beg, is time, to make it sure," cried the trembling wretch, looking wildly round for sympathy. "The King and Government can't know it's me; I'm sure they can't know it's me; or they never would bring me to this dreadful slaughter-house. They know my name, but they don't know it's the same man. Stop my execution—for charity's sake stop my execution, gentlemen—till they can be told that I've been hangman here, nigh thirty year. Will no one go and tell them?" he implored, clenching his hands and glaring round, and round, and round again—"will no charitable person go and tell them!"

"Mr. Akerman," said a gentleman who stood by, after a moment's pause; "since it may possibly produce in this unhappy man a better frame of mind, even at this last minute, let me assure him that he was well known to have been the hangman, when his sentence was considered."

"—But perhaps they think on that account that the punishment's not so great," cried the criminal, shuffling towards this speaker on his knees, and holding up his folded hands; "whereas it's worse, it's worse a hundred times, to me than any man. Let them know that, sir. Let them know that. They've made it worse to me by giving me so much to do. Stop my execution till they know that!"

The governor beckoned with his hand, and the two men, who had supported him before, approached. He uttered a piercing cry:

"Wait! Wait. Only a moment—only one moment more! Give me a last chance of reprieve. One of us three is to go to Bloomsbury Square. Let me be the one. It may come in that time; it's sure to come. In the Lord's name let me be sent to Bloomsbury Square. Don't hang me here. It's murder!"

They took him to the anvil: but even then he could be heard above the clinking of the smith's hammers, and the hoarse raging of the crowd, crying that he knew of Hugh's birth—that his father was living, and was a gentleman of influence and rank—that he had family secrets in his possession—that he could tell nothing unless they gave him time, but must die with them on his mind; and he continued to rave in this sort until his voice failed him, and he sank down a mere heap of clothes between the two attendants.

It was at this moment that the clock struck the first stroke of twelve, and the bell began to toll. The various officers, with the two sheriffs at their head, moved towards the door. All was ready when the last chime came upon the ear.

They told Hugh this, and asked if he had anything to say.

"To say!" he cried. "Not I. I'm ready.—Yes," he added, as his eye fell upon Barnaby, "I have a word to say, too. Come hither, lad."

There was, for the moment, something kind, and even tender, struggling in his fierce aspect, as he wrung his poor companion by the hand.

"I'll say this," he cried, looking firmly round, "that if I had ten lives to lose, and the loss of each would give me ten times the agony of the hardest death, I'd lay them all down—ay I would, though you gentlemen may not believe it—to save this one. This one," he added, wringing his hand again, "that will be lost through me."

"Not through you," said the idiot, mildly. "Don't say that. You were not to blame. You have been always very good to me.—Hugh, we shall know what makes the stars shine, *now!*"

"I took him from her in a reckless mood, and didn't think what harm would come of it," said Hugh, laying his hand upon his head, and speaking in a lower voice. "I ask her pardon, and his.—Look here," he added roughly, in his former tone. "You see this lad?"

They murmured "Yes," and seemed to wonder why he asked.

"That gentleman yonder—" pointing to the clergyman—"has often in the last few days spoken to me of faith, and strong belief. You see what I am—more brute than man, as I have been often told—but I had faith enough to believe, and did believe as strongly as any of you gentlemen can believe anything, that this one life would be spared. See what he is!—Look at him!"

Barnaby had moved towards the door, and stood beckoning him to follow.

"If this was not faith, and strong belief!" cried Hugh, raising his right arm aloft, and looking upward like a savage prophet whom the near approach of Death had filled with inspiration, "where are they! What else should teach me—me, born as I was born, and reared as I have been—to hope for any mercy in this hardened, cruel, unrelenting place! Upon these human shambles, I, who never raised this hand in prayer till now, call down the wrath of God! On that black tree, of which I am the ripened fruit, I do invoke the curse of all its victims, past, and present, and to come. On the head of that man, who, in his conscience, owns me for his son, I leave the wish that he may never sicken in his bed of down, but die a violent death as I do now, and have the night-wind for his only mourner. To this I say, Amen, amen!"

His arm fell downward by his side; he turned; and moved towards them with a steady step: the man he had been before.

"There is nothing more?" said the Governor.

Hugh motioned Barnaby not to come near him (though without looking in the direction where he stood) and answered, "There is nothing more."

"Move forward!"

"—Unless," said Hugh, glancing hurriedly back,—"unless some person has a fancy for a dog; and not then, unless he means to use him well. There's one, belongs to me, at the house I came from; and it wouldn't be easy to find a better. He'll whine at first, but he'll soon get over that.—You wonder that I think about a dog just now," he added, with a kind of laugh. "If any man deserved it of me half as well, I'd think of him."

He spoke no more, but moved onward in his place, with a careless air, though listening at the same time to the Service for the Dead, with something between sullen attention, and quickened curiosity. As soon as he had passed the door, his miserable associate was carried out; and the crowd beheld the rest.

Barnaby would have mounted the steps at the same time—indeed he would have gone before them, but in both attempts he was restrained, as he was to undergo the sentence elsewhere. In a few minutes the sheriffs reappeared, the same procession was again formed, and they passed through various rooms and passages to another door—that at which the cart was waiting. He held down his head to avoid seeing what he knew his eyes must otherwise encounter, and took his seat sorrowfully,—and yet with something of a childish pride and pleasure,—in the vehicle. The officers fell into their places at the sides, in front, and in the rear; the sheriffs' carriages rolled on; a guard of soldiers surrounded the whole; and they moved slowly forward through the throng and pressure toward Lord Mansfield's ruined house.

It was a sad sight—all that show, and strength, and glitter, assembled round one helpless creature: and sadder yet to note, as he rode along, how his wandering thoughts found strange encouragement in the crowded windows and the concourse in the streets; and how, even then, he felt the influence of the bright sky, and looked up smiling into its deep unfathomable blue. But there had been many such sights since the riots were over—some so moving in their nature, and so repulsive too, that they were far more calculated to awaken pity for the sufferers, than respect for that law whose strong arm seemed in more than one case to be as wantonly stretched forth now that all was safe, as it had been basely paralysed in time of danger.

Two cripples—both mere boys—one with a leg of wood, one who dragged his twisted limbs along by the help of a crutch, were hanged in this same Bloomsbury Square.* As the cart was about to glide from under them, it was observed that they stood with their faces from, not to, the house they had assisted to despoil; and their misery was protracted that this omission might be remedied. Another boy was hanged in Bow Street; other young lads in various quarters of the town. Four wretched women, too, were put to death. In a word, those who suffered as rioters were for the most part the weakest, meanest, and most miserable among them. It was an exquisite satire upon the false religious cry which led to so much misery, that some of these people owned themselves to be catholics, and begged to be attended by their own priests.

One young man was hanged in Bishopsgate Street,* whose aged grey-headed father waited for him at the gallows, kissed him at its foot when he arrived, and sat there, on the ground, until they took him down. They would have given him the body of his child; but he had no hearse, no coffin, nothing to remove it in, being too poor; and walked meekly away beside the cart that took it back to prison, trying, as he went, to touch its lifeless hand.

But the crowd had forgotten these matters, or cared little about them if they lived in their memory: and while one great multitude fought and hustled to get near the gibbet before Newgate, for a parting look, another followed in the train of poor lost Barnaby, to swell the throng that waited for him on the spot.

CHAPTER THE SEVENTY-EIGHTH.

ON this same day, and about this very hour, Mr. Willet, the elder, sat smoking his pipe in a chamber of the Black Lion. Although it was hot summer weather, Mr. Willet sat close to the fire. He was in a state of profound cogitation, with his own thoughts, and it was his custom at such times to stew himself slowly, under the impression that that process of cookery was favourable to the melting out of his ideas, which, when he began to simmer, sometimes oozed forth so copiously as to astonish even himself.

Mr. Willet had been several thousand times comforted by his friends and acquaintance, with the assurance that for the loss he had sustained in the damage done to the Maypole, he could "come upon the county." But as this phrase happened to bear an unfortunate resemblance to the popular expression of "coming on the parish,"* it suggested to Mr. Willet's mind no more consolatory visions than pauperism on an extensive scale, and ruin in its most capacious aspect. Consequently, he had never failed to receive the intelligence with a rueful shake of the head, or a dreary stare, and had been always observed to appear much more melancholy after a visit of condolence than at any other time in the whole four-and-twenty hours.

It chanced, however, that sitting over the fire on this particular occasion—perhaps because he was, as it were, done to a turn; perhaps because he was in an unusually bright state of mind; perhaps because he had considered the subject so long; or perhaps because of all these favouring circumstances, taken together—it chanced that, sitting over the fire on this particular occasion, Mr. Willet did, afar off and in the remotest depths of his intellect, perceive a kind of lurking hint or faint suggestion, that out of the public purse there might issue funds for the restoration of the Maypole to its former high place among the taverns of the earth. And this dim ray of light did so diffuse itself within him, and did so kindle up and shine, that at last he had it as plainly and visibly before him as the blaze by which he sat: and, fully persuaded that he was the first to make the discovery, and that he had started, hunted down, fallen upon, and knocked on the head, a perfectly original idea which had never presented itself to any other man, alive or dead, he laid down his pipe, rubbed his hands, and chuckled audibly.

"Why, father!" cried Joe, entering at the moment, "you're in spirits to-day!"

"It's nothing partickler," said Mr. Willet, chuckling again. "It's nothing at all partickler, Joseph. Tell me something about the Salwanners." Having preferred this request, Mr. Willet chuckled a third time; and after these unusual demonstrations of levity, he put his pipe in his mouth again.

"What shall I tell you, father?" asked Joe, laying his hand upon his sire's shoulder, and looking down into his face. "That I have come back, poorer than a church mouse? You know that. That I have come back, maimed and crippled? You know that."

"It was took off," muttered Mr. Willet, with his eyes upon the fire, "at the defence of the Salwanners, in America, where the war is."

"Quite right," returned Joe, smiling, and leaning with his remaining elbow on the back of his father's chair; "the very subject I came to speak to you about. A man with one arm, father, is not of much use in the busy world."

This was one of those vast propositions which Mr. Willet had never considered for an instant, and required time to "tackle." Wherefore he made no answer.

"At all events," said Joe, "he can't pick and choose his means of earning a livelihood, as another man may. He can't say 'I will turn my hand to this,' or 'I won't turn my hand to that,' but must take what he can do, and be thankful it's no worse.—What did you say?"

Mr. Willet had been softly repeating to himself, in a musing tone, the words "defence of the Salwanners:" but he seemed embarrassed at having been overheard, and answered "Nothing."

"Now look here, father.—Mr. Edward has come to England from the West Indies. When he was lost sight of (I ran away on the same day, father), he made a voyage to one of the islands, where a schoolfriend of his had settled; and finding him, wasn't too proud to be employed on his estate; and—and in short, got on well, and is prospering, and has come over here on business of his own, and is going back again speedily. Our returning nearly at the same time, and meeting in the course of the late troubles, has been a good thing every way; for it has not only enabled us to do old friends some service, but has opened a path in life for me which I may tread without being a burden upon you. To be plain, father, he can employ me; I have satisfied myself that I can be of real use to him; and I am going to carry my one arm away with him, and to make the most of it."

In the mind's eye of Mr. Willet, the West Indies, and indeed all foreign countries, were inhabited by savage nations, who were perpetually burying pipes of peace, flourishing tomahawks, and puncturing strange patterns in their bodies. He no sooner heard this announcement, therefore, than he leaned back in his chair, took his pipe from his lips, and stared at his son with as much dismay as if he already beheld him tied to a stake, and tortured for the entertainment of a lively population. In what form of expression his feelings would have found a vent, it is impossible to say. Nor is it necessary: for before a syllable occurred to him, Dolly Varden came running into the room, in tears; threw herself on Joe's breast without a word of explanation; and clasped her white arms round his neck.

"Dolly!" cried Joe. "Dolly!"

"Ay, call me that; call me that always," exclaimed the locksmith's little daughter; "never speak coldly to me, never be distant, never again reprove me for the follies I have long repented, or I shall die."

"*I* reprove you!" said Joe.

"Yes—for every kind and honest word you uttered, went to my heart. For you, who have borne so much from me—for you, who owe your sufferings and pain to my caprice—for you to be so kind—so noble to me, Joe—"

He could say nothing to her. Not a syllable. There was an odd sort of eloquence in his one arm, which had crept round her waist: but his lips were mute.

"If you had reminded me by a word—only by one short word," sobbed Dolly, clinging yet closer to him, "how little I deserved that you should treat me with so much forbearance; if you had exulted only for one moment in your triumph, I could have borne it better."

"Triumph!" repeated Joe, with a smile which seemed to say, "I am a pretty figure for that."

"Yes, triumph," she cried, with her whole heart and soul in her earnest voice, and gushing tears; "for it *is* one. I am glad to think and

know it is. I wouldn't be less humbled, dear; I wouldn't be without the recollection of that last time we spoke together in this place—no, not if I could recal the past, and make our parting, yesterday."

Did ever lover look as Joe looked now!

"Dear Joe," said Dolly, "I always loved you—in my own heart I always did, although I was so vain and giddy. I hoped you would come back that night. I made quite sure you would; I prayed for it on my knees. Through all these long, long years, I have never once forgotten you, or left off hoping that this happy time might come."

The eloquence of Joe's arm surpassed the most impassioned language; and so did that of his lips—yet he said nothing, either.

"And now, at last," cried Dolly, trembling with the fervour of her speech, "if you were sick, and shattered in your every limb; if you were ailing, weak, and sorrowful; if, instead of being what you are, you were in everybody's eyes but mine, the wreck and ruin of a man; I would be your wife, dear love, with greater pride and joy, than if you were the stateliest lord in England!"

"What have I done," cried Joe, "what have I done, to meet with this reward?"

"You have taught me," said Dolly, raising her pretty face to his, "to know myself, and your worth; to be something better than I was; to be more deserving of your true and manly nature. In years to come, dear Joe, you shall find that you have done so; for I will be, not only now, when we are young and full of hope, but when we have grown old and weary, your patient, gentle, never-tiring wife. I will never know a wish or care beyond our home and you, and always study how to please you with my best affection and my most devoted love. I will: indeed I will."

Joe could only repeat his former eloquence—but it was very much to the purpose.

"They know of this, at home," said Dolly. "For your sake, I would leave even them; but they know it, and are glad of it, and are proud of you, as I am, and full of gratitude.—You'll not come and see me as a poor friend who knew me when I was a girl, will you?"

Well, well! It don't matter what Joe said in answer, but he said a great deal; and Dolly said a great deal too: and he folded Dolly in his one arm pretty tight, considering that it was but one; and Dolly made no resistance: and if ever two people were happy in this world—which is not an utterly miserable one, with all its faults—we may, with some appearance of certainty, conclude that they were.

To say that during these proceedings Mr. Willet the elder underwent the greatest emotions of astonishment of which our common nature is susceptible—to say that he was in a perfect paralysis of surprise, and that he wandered into the most stupendous and theretofore unattainable heights of complicated amazement—would be to shadow forth his state of mind in the feeblest and lamest terms. If a roc, an eagle, a griffin, a flying elephant, or winged sea-horse, had suddenly appeared, and, taking him on its back, carried him bodily into the very heart of the "Salwanners," it would have been to him as an every-day occurrence, in comparison with what he now beheld. To be sitting quietly by, seeing and hearing these things; to be completely overlooked, unnoticed, and disregarded, while his son and a young lady were talking to each other in the most impassioned manner, kissing each other, and making themselves in all respects perfectly at home; was a position so tremendous, so inexplicable, so utterly beyond the widest range of his capacity of comprehension, that he fell into a lethargy of wonder, and could no more rouse himself than an enchanted sleeper in the first year of his fairy lease, a century long.

"Father," said Joe, presenting Dolly. "You know who this is?"

Mr. Willet looked first at her, then at his son, then back again at Dolly, and then made an ineffectual effort to extract a whiff from his pipe, which had gone out long ago.

"Say a word, father, if it's only 'how d'ye do,'" urged Joe.

"Certainly, Joseph," answered Mr. Willet. "Oh yes! Why not?"

"To be sure," said Joe. "Why not?"

"Ah!" replied his father. "Why not?" and with this remark, which he uttered in a low voice as though he were discussing some grave question with himself, he used the little finger—if any of his fingers can be said to have come under that denomination—of his right hand, as a tobacco-stopper, and was silent again.

And so he sat for half an hour at least, although Dolly, in the most endearing of manners, hoped, a dozen times, that he was not angry with her. So he sat for half an hour, quite motionless, and looking all the while like nothing so much as a great Dutch Pin or Skittle. At the expiration of that period, he suddenly, and without the least notice, burst, to the great consternation of the young people, into a very loud and very short laugh; and repeating "Certainly, Joseph. Oh yes! Why not?" went out for a walk.

CHAPTER THE SEVENTY-NINTH.

OLD John did not walk near the Golden Key, for between the Golden Key and the Black Lion there lay a wilderness of streets—as everybody knows who is acquainted with the relative bearings of Clerkenwell and Whitechapel—and he was by no means famous for pedestrian exercises. But the Golden Key lies in our way, though it was out of his; so to the Golden Key this chapter goes.

The Golden Key itself, fair emblem of the locksmith's trade, had been pulled down by the rioters, and roughly trampled under foot. But now it was hoisted up again in all the glory of a new coat of paint, and showed more bravely even than in days of yore. Indeed the whole house-front was spruce and trim, and so freshened up throughout, that if there yet remained at large any of the rioters who had been concerned in the attack upon it, the sight of the old, goodly, prosperous dwelling, so revived, must have been to them as gall and wormwood.

The shutters of the shop were closed, however, and the window-blinds above were all pulled down, and in place of its usual cheerful appearance, the house had a look of sadness and an air of mourning; which the neighbours who in old days had often seen poor Barnaby go in and out, were at no loss to understand. The door stood partly open; but the locksmith's hammer was unheard: the cat sat moping on the ashy forge; all was deserted, dark, and silent.

On the threshold of this door, Mr. Haredale and Edward Chester met. The younger man gave place; and both passing in with a familiar air, which seemed to denote that they were tarrying there, or were well-accustomed to go to and fro unquestioned, shut it behind them.

Entering the old back parlour, and ascending the flight of stairs, abrupt and steep, and quaintly fashioned as of old, they turned into the best room; the pride of Mrs. Varden's heart, and erst the scene of Miggs's household labours.

"Varden brought the mother here last evening, he told me?" said Mr. Haredale.

"She is above stairs now—in the room over here," Edward rejoined. "Her grief, they say, is past all telling. I needn't add—for that you know beforehand—that the care, humanity, and sympathy of these good people have no bounds."

"I am sure of that. Heaven repay them for it, and for much more! Varden is out?"

"He returned with your messenger, who arrived almost at the moment of his coming home himself. He was out the whole night—but that of course you know. He was with you the greater part of it?"

"He was. Without him, I should have lacked my right hand. He is an older man than I; but nothing can conquer him."

"The cheeriest, stoutest-hearted fellow in the world."

"He has a right to be. He has a right to be. A better creature never lived. He reaps what he has sown—no more."

"It is not all men," said Edward, after a moment's hesitation, "who have the happiness to do that."

"More than you imagine," returned Mr. Haredale. "We note the harvest more than the seed-time. You do so in me."

In truth his pale and haggard face, and gloomy bearing, had so far influenced the remark, that Edward was, for the moment, at a loss to answer him.

"Tut, tut," said Mr. Haredale, "'twas not very difficult to read a thought so natural. But you are mistaken nevertheless. I have had my share of sorrows—more than the common lot, perhaps—but I have borne them ill. I have broken where I should have bent; and have mused and brooded, when my spirit should have mixed with all God's great creation. The men who learn endurance, are they who call the whole world, brother. I have turned *from* the world, and I pay the penalty."

Edward would have interposed, but he went on without giving him time.

"It is too late to evade it now. I sometimes think, that if I had to live my life once more, I would amend this fault—not so much, I discover when I search my mind, for the love of what is right, as for my own sake. But even when I make these better resolutions, I instinctively recoil from the idea of suffering again what I have undergone; and in this circumstance I find the unwelcome assurance that I should still be the same man, though I could cancel the past, and begin anew, with its experience to guide me."

"Nay, you make too sure of that," said Edward.

"You think so," Mr. Haredale answered, "and I am glad you do. I know myself better, and therefore distrust myself more. Let us leave this subject for another—not so far removed from it as it might, at first sight, seem to be. Sir, you still love my niece, and she is still attached to you."

"I have that assurance from her own lips," said Edward, "and you know—I am sure you know—that I would not exchange it for any blessing life could yield me."

"You are frank, honourable, and disinterested," said Mr. Haredale; "you have forced the conviction that you are so, even on my once-jaundiced mind; and I believe you. Wait here till I come back."

He left the room as he spoke; but soon returned, with his niece.

"On that first and only time," he said, looking from the one to the other, "when we three stood together under her father's roof, I bade you quit it, and charged you never to return."

"It is the only circumstance arising out of our love," observed Edward, "that I have forgotten."

"You own a name," said Mr. Haredale, "I had deep reason to

remember. I was moved and goaded by recollections of personal wrong and injury, I know: but even now I cannot charge myself with having then, or ever, lost sight of a heartfelt desire for her true happiness; or with having acted—however much I was mistaken—with any other impulse than the one pure, single, earnest wish to be to her, as far as in my inferior nature lay, the father she had lost."

"Dear uncle," cried Emma, "I have known no parent but you. I have loved the memory of others, but I have loved you all my life. Never was father kinder to his child than you have been to me, without the interval of one harsh hour, since I can first remember."

"You speak too fondly," he answered, "and yet I cannot wish you were less partial; for I have a pleasure in hearing those words, and shall have in calling them to mind when we are far asunder, which nothing else could give me. Bear with me for a moment longer, sir, for she and I have been together many years; and although I believe that in resigning her to you I put the seal upon her future happiness, I find it needs an effort."

He pressed her tenderly to his bosom, and after a minute's pause, resumed:

"I have done you wrong, sir, and I ask your forgiveness—in no common phrase, or show of sorrow; but with earnestness and sincerity. In the same spirit, I acknowledge to you both that the time has been when I connived at treachery and falsehood—which if I did not perpetrate myself, I still permitted—to rend you two asunder."

"You judge yourself too harshly," said Edward. "Let these things rest."

"They rise up in judgment against me when I look back, and not now for the first time," he answered. "I cannot part from you without your full forgiveness; for busy life and I have little left in common now, and I have regrets enough to carry into solitude, without addition to the stock."

"You bear a blessing from us both," said Emma. "Never mingle thoughts of me—of me who owe you so much love and duty—with anything but undying affection and gratitude for the past, and bright hopes for the future."

"The future," returned her uncle, with a melancholy smile, "is a bright word for you, and its image should be wreathed with cheerful hopes. Mine is of another kind, but it will be one of peace; and free, I trust, from care or passion. When you quit England I shall leave it too. There are cloisters abroad; and now that the two great objects of my life are set at rest, I know no better home. You droop at that, forgetting I am growing old, and that my course is nearly run. Well, we will speak of it again—not once or twice, but many times; and you shall give me cheerful counsel, Emma."

"And you will take it?" asked his niece.

"I'll listen to it," he answered, kissing her fair brow, "and it will have its weight, be certain. What have I left to say? You have of late been much together. It is better and more fitting that the circumstances attendant on the past, which wrought your separation, and sowed between you suspicion and distrust, should not be entered on by me."

"Much, much better," whispered Emma. "Remember them no more!"

"I avow my share in them," said Mr. Haredale, "though I held it at the time in detestation. Let no man turn aside, ever so slightly, from the broad path of honour, on the plausible pretence that he is justified by the goodness of his end. All good ends can be worked out by good means. Those that cannot, are bad; and may be counted so at once, and left alone."

He looked from her to Edward, and said in a gentler tone:

"In goods and fortune you are now nearly equal; I have been her faithful steward, and to that remnant of a richer property which my brother left her, I desire to add, in token of my love, a poor pittance, scarcely worth the mention, for which I have no longer any need. I am glad you go abroad. Let our ill-fated house remain the ruin it is. When you return after a few thriving years, you will command a better, and more fortunate one. We are friends?"

Edward took his extended hand, and grasped it heartily.

"You are neither slow nor cold in your response," said Mr. Haredale, doing the like by him, "and when I look upon you now, and know you, I feel that I would choose you for her husband. Her father had a generous nature, and you would have pleased him well. I give her to you in his name, and with his blessing. If the world and I part in this act, we part on happier terms than we have lived for many a day."

He placed her in his arms, and would have left the room, but that he was stopped in his passage to the door by a great noise at a distance, which made them start and pause.

It was a loud shouting, mingled with boisterous acclamations, that

rent the very air. It drew nearer and nearer every moment, and approached so rapidly, that even while they listened, it burst into a deafening confusion of sounds at the street corner.

"This must be stopped—quieted," said Mr. Haredale, hastily. "We should have foreseen this, and provided against it. I will go out to them at once."

But before he could reach the door, and before Edward could catch up his hat and follow him, they were again arrested by a loud shriek from above stairs: and the locksmith's wife, bursting in, and fairly running into Mr. Haredale's arms, cried out:

"She knows it all, dear sir!—she knows it all! We broke it out to her by degrees, and she is quite prepared." Having made this communication, and furthermore thanked Heaven with great fervour and heartiness, the good lady, according to the custom of matrons on all occasions of excitement, fainted away directly.

They ran to the window, threw up the sash, and looked into the crowded street. Among a dense mob of persons, of whom not one was for an instant still, the locksmith's ruddy face and burly form could be descried, beating about as though he were struggling with a rough sea. Now he was carried back a score of yards, now onward nearly to the door, now back again, now forced against the opposite houses, now against those adjoining his own: now carried up a flight of steps, and greeted by the outstretched hands of half a hundred men, while the whole tumultuous concourse stretched their throats, and cheered with all their might. Though he was really in a fair way to be torn to pieces in the general enthusiasm, the locksmith, nothing discomposed, echoed their shouts till he was hoarse as they, and in a glow of joy and right good-humour, waved his hat until the daylight shone between its brim and crown.

But in all the bandyings from hand to hand, and strivings to and fro, and sweepings here and there, which—saving that he looked more jolly and more radiant after every struggle—troubled his peace of mind no more than if he had been a straw upon the water's surface, he never once released his firm grasp of an arm, drawn tight through his. He sometimes turned to clap this friend upon the back, or whisper in his ear a word of staunch encouragement, or cheer him with a smile; but his great care was to shield him from the pressure, and force a passage for him to the Golden Key. Passive and timid, scared, pale, and wondering, and gazing at the throng as if he were newly risen from the dead, and felt himself a ghost among the living, Barnaby—not Barnaby in the spirit, but in flesh and blood, with pulses, sinews, nerves, and beating heart, and strong affections— clung to his stout old friend, and followed where he led.

And thus, in course of time, they reached the door, held ready for their entrance by no unwilling hands. Then slipping in, and shutting out the crowd by main force, Gabriel stood between Mr. Haredale and Edward Chester, and Barnaby, rushing up the stairs, fell upon his knees beside his mother's bed.

"Such is the blessed end, sir," cried the panting locksmith, to Mr. Haredale, "of the best day's work we ever did. The rogues! it's been hard fighting to get away from 'em. I almost thought, once or twice, they'd have been too much for us with their kindness!"

They had striven all the previous day to rescue Barnaby from his impending fate. Failing in their attempts, in the first quarter to which they addressed themselves, they renewed them in another. Failing there, likewise, they began afresh at midnight; and made their way, not only to the judge and jury who had tried him, but to men of influence at court, to the young Prince of Wales,* and even to the antechamber of the king himself. Successful, at last, in awakening an interest in his favour, and an inclination to inquire more dispassionately into his case, they had had an interview with the minister, in his bed, so late as eight o'clock that morning. The result of a searching inquiry (in which they, who had known the poor fellow from his childhood, did other good service, besides bringing it about) was, that between eleven and twelve o'clock, a free pardon to Barnaby Rudge was made out and signed, and entrusted to a horse-soldier for instant conveyance to the place of execution. This courier reached the spot just as the cart appeared in sight; and Barnaby being carried back to jail, Mr. Haredale, assured that all was safe, had gone straight from Bloomsbury Square to the Golden Key, leaving to Gabriel the grateful task of bringing him home in triumph.

"I needn't say," observed the locksmith, when he had shaken hands with all the males in the house, and hugged all the females, five-and-forty times, at least, "that, except among ourselves, *I* didn't want to make a triumph of it. But directly we got into the streets we were known, and this hubbub began. Of the two," he added, as he wiped his crimson face, "and after experience of both, I think I'd rather be taken out of my house by a crowd of enemies, than escorted home by a mob of friends!"

It was plain enough, however, that this was mere talk on Gabriel's part, and that the whole proceeding afforded him the keenest delight; for the people continuing to make a great noise without, and to cheer as if their voices were in the freshest order, and good for a fortnight, he sent up stairs for Grip (who had come home at his master's back, and had acknowledged the favours of the multitude by drawing blood from every finger that came within his reach), and with the bird upon his arm, presented himself at the first-floor window, and waved his hat again until it dangled by a shred, between his fingers and thumb. This demonstration having been received with appropriate shouts, and silence being in some degree restored, he thanked them for their sympathy; and taking the liberty to inform them that there was a sick person in the house, proposed that they should give three cheers for King George, three more for Old England, and three more for nothing particular, as a closing ceremony. The crowd assenting, substituted Gabriel Varden for the nothing particular; and giving him one over, for good measure, dispersed in high good-humour.

What congratulations they exchanged when they were left alone; what an overflowing of joy and happiness there was among them; how incapable it was of expression in Barnaby's own person; and how he went wildly from one to another, until he became so far tranquillized as to stretch himself on the ground beside his mother's couch, and fall into a deep sleep; are matters that need not be told. And it is well they happen to be of this class, for they would be very hard to tell, were their narration ever so indispensable.

Before leaving this bright picture, it may be well to glance at a dark and very different one which was presented to only a few eyes, that same night.

The scene was a churchyard; the time, midnight; the persons, Edward Chester, a clergyman, a grave-digger, and the four bearers of a homely coffin. They stood about a grave which had been newly dug, and one of the bearers held up a dim lantern,—the only light there—which shed its feeble ray upon the book of prayer. He placed it for a moment on the coffin, when he and his companions were about to lower it down. There was no inscription on the lid.

The mould fell solemnly upon the last house of this nameless man; and the rattling dust left a dismal echo even in the accustomed ears of those who had borne it to its resting-place. The grave was filled in to the top, and trodden down. They all left the spot together.

"You never saw him, living?" asked the priest, of Edward.

"Often, years ago; not knowing him for my brother."

"Never since?"

"Never. Yesterday, he steadily refused to see me. It was urged upon him, many times, at my desire."

"Still he refused? That was hardened and unnatural."

"Do you think so?"

"I infer that you do not."

"You are right. We hear the world wonder every day at monsters of ingratitude. Did it never occur to you that it often looks for monsters of affection, as though they were things of course?"

They had reached the gate by this time, and bidding each other good night, departed on their separate ways.

CHAPTER THE EIGHTIETH.

THAT afternoon, when he had slept off his fatigue; had shaved, and washed, and dressed, and freshened himself from top to toe; when he had dined, comforted himself with a pipe, an extra Toby, a nap in the great arm-chair, and a quiet chat with Mrs. Varden on everything that had happened, was happening, or about to happen, within the sphere of their domestic concern; the locksmith sat himself down at the tea-table in the little back parlour: the rosiest, cosiest, merriest, heartiest, best-contented old buck, in Great Britain or out of it.

There he sat, with his beaming eye on Mrs. V., and his shining face suffused with gladness, and his capacious waistcoat smiling in every wrinkle, and his jovial humour peeping from under the table in the very plumpness of his legs: a sight to turn the vinegar of misanthropy into purest milk of human kindness. There he sat, watching his wife as she decorated the room with flowers for the greater honour of Dolly and Joseph Willet, who had gone out walking, and for whom the tea-kettle had been singing gaily on the hob full twenty minutes, chirping as never kettle chirped before; for whom the best service of real undoubted china, patterned with divers round-faced mandarins holding up broad umbrellas, was now displayed in all its glory; to tempt whose appetites a clear, transparent, juicy ham, garnished with cool green lettuce leaves and fragrant cucumber, reposed upon a shady table, covered with a snow white cloth; for whose delight, preserves and jams, crisp cakes and other pastry, short to eat, with cunning twists and cottage loaves, and rolls of bread both white and brown, were all set forth in rich profusion; in whose youth Mrs. V. herself had grown quite young, and stood there in a gown of red and white; symmetrical in figure, buxom in boddice, ruddy in cheek and lip, faultless in ankle, laughing in face and mood, in all respects delicious to behold—there sat the locksmith among all and every these delights, the sun that shone upon them all: the centre of the system: the source of light, heat, life, and frank enjoyment in the bright household world.

And when had Dolly ever been the Dolly of that afternoon? To see how she came in arm-in-arm with Joe; and how she made an effort not to blush or seem at all confused; and how she made believe she didn't care to sit on his side of the table; and how she coaxed the locksmith in a whisper not to joke; and how her colour came and went in a little restless flutter of happiness, which made her do everything wrong, and yet so charmingly wrong that it was much better than right!—why, the locksmith could have looked on at this (as he mentioned to Mrs. Varden when they retired for the night) for four-and-twenty hours at a stretch, and never wished it done.

The recollections, too, with which they made merry over that long protracted tea! The glee with which the locksmith asked Joe if he remembered that stormy night at the Maypole when he first asked after Dolly—the laugh they all had about that night when she was going out to the party in the sedan-chair—the unmerciful manner in which they rallied Mrs. Varden about putting those flowers outside that very window—the difficulty Mrs. Varden found in joining the laugh against herself at first, and the extraordinary perception she had of the joke when she overcame it—the confidential statements of Joe concerning the precise day and hour when he was first conscious of being fond of Dolly, and Dolly's blushing admissions, half volunteered, and half extorted, as to the time from which she dated the discovery that she "didn't mind" Joe—here was an exhaustless fund of mirth and conversation!

Then there was a great deal to be said regarding Mrs. Varden's doubts, and motherly alarms, and shrewd suspicions; and it appeared that from Mrs. Varden's penetration and extreme sagacity nothing had ever been hidden. She had known it all along. She had seen it from the first. She had always predicted it. She had been aware of it before the principals. She had said within herself (for she remembered the exact words) "that young Willet is certainly looking after our Dolly, and *I* must look after *him*." Accordingly she had looked after him, and had observed many little circumstances (all of which she named) so exceedingly minute that nobody else could make anything out of them even now; and had, it seemed from first to last, displayed the most unbounded tact and most consummate generalship.

Of course the night when Joe *would* ride homeward by the side of the chaise, and when Mrs. Varden *would* insist upon his going back again, was not forgotten—nor the night when Dolly fainted on his name being mentioned—nor the times upon times when Mrs. Varden, ever watchful and prudent, had found her pining in her own chamber. In short, nothing was forgotten; and everything by some means or other brought them back to the conclusion, that that was the happiest hour in all their lives; consequently, that everything must have occurred for the best, and nothing could be suggested which would have made it better.

While they were in the full glow of such discourse as this, there came a startling knock at the door, opening from the street into the workshop, which had been kept closed all day that the house might be more quiet. Joe, as in duty bound, would hear of nobody but himself going to open it; and accordingly left the room for that purpose.

It would have been odd enough, certainly, if Joe had forgotten the way to this door; and even if he had, as it was a pretty large one and stood straight before him, he could not easily have missed it. But Dolly, perhaps because she was in the flutter of spirits before mentioned, or perhaps because she thought he would not be able to open it with his one arm—she could have had no other reason—hurried out after him; and they stopped so long in the passage—no doubt owing to Joe's entreaties that she would not expose herself to the draught of July air which must infallibly come rushing in on this same door being opened—that the knock was repeated, in a yet more startling manner than before.

"Is anybody going to open that door?" cried the locksmith. "Or shall I come?"

Upon that, Dolly went running back into the parlour, all dimples and blushes; and Joe opened it with a mighty noise, and other superfluous demonstrations of being in a violent hurry.

"Well," said the locksmith, when he reappeared: "what is it? eh Joe? what are you laughing at?"

"Nothing sir. It's coming in."

"Who's coming in? what's coming in?" Mrs. Varden, as much at a loss as her husband, could only shake her head in answer to his inquiring look: so the locksmith wheeled his chair round to command a better view of the room door, and stared at it with his eyes wide open, and a mingled expression of curiosity and wonder shining in his jolly face.

Instead of some person or persons straightway appearing, divers remarkable sounds were heard, first in the workshop and afterwards in the little dark passage between it and the parlour, as though some unwieldy chest or heavy piece of furniture were being brought in, by an amount of human strength inadequate to the task. At length after much struggling and bumping, and bruising of the wall on both sides, the door was forced open as by a battering-ram; and the locksmith, steadily regarding what appeared beyond, smote his thigh, elevated his eyebrows, opened his mouth, and cried in a loud voice expressive of the utmost consternation:

"Damme, if it an't Miggs come back!"

The young damsel whom he named no sooner heard these words, than deserting a very small boy and a very large box by whom she was accompanied, and advancing with such precipitation that her bonnet flew off her head, burst into the room, clasped her hands (in which she held a pair of pattens, one in each), raised her eyes devotedly to the ceiling, and shed a flood of tears.

"The old story!" cried the locksmith, looking at her in inexpressible desperation. "She was born to be a damper, this young woman! nothing can prevent it!"

"Ho master, ho mim!" cried Miggs, "can I constrain my feelings in these here once agin united moments! Ho Mr. Warsen, here's blessedness among relations, Sir, here's forgivenesses of injuries, here's amicablenesses!"

The locksmith looked from his wife to Dolly, and from Dolly to Joe, and from Joe to Miggs, with his eyebrows still elevated and his mouth still open: when his eyes got back to Miggs, they rested on her; fascinated.

"To think," cried Miggs with hysterical joy, "that Mr. Joe, and dear Miss Dolly, has raly come together after all as has been said and done contrairy! To see them two a settin' along with him and her, so pleasant and in all respects so affable and mild; and me not knowing of it, and not being in the ways to make no preparations for their teas. Ho what a cutting thing it is, and yet what sweet sensations is awoke within me!"

Either in clasping her hands again, or in an ecstacy of pious joy, Miss Miggs clinked her pattens after the manner of a pair of cymbals, at this juncture; and then resumed in the softest accents:

"And did my missis think—ho goodness, did she think—as her own Miggs, which supported her under so many trials, and understood her natur' when them as intended well but acted rough, went so deep into her feelings—did she think as her own Miggs would ever leave her? Did she think as Miggs, though she was but a servant, and knowed that servitudes was no inheritances, would forgit that

she was the humble instruments as always made it comfortable between them two when they fell out, and always told master of the meekness and forgiveness of her blessed dispositions. Did she think as Miggs had no attachments? Did she think the wages was her only object?"

To none of these interrogatories, whereof every one was more pathetically delivered than the last, did Mrs. Varden answer one word: but Miggs, not at all abashed by this circumstance, turned to the small boy in attendance—her eldest nephew; son of her own married sister; born in Golden Lion Court, number twenty-sivin; and bred in the very shadow of the second bell handle on the right hand door post—and with a plentiful use of her pocket hand-kerchief, addressed herself to him: requesting that on his return home he would console his parents for the loss of her, his aunt, by delivering to them a faithful statement of his having left her in the bosom of that family, with which, as his aforesaid parents well knew, her best affections were incorporated; that he would remind them that nothing less than her imperious sense of duty, and devoted attachment to her old master and missis, likewise Miss Dolly and young Mr. Joe, should ever have induced her to decline that pressing invitation which they, his parents, had, as he could testify, given her, to lodge and board with them, free of all cost and charge, for ever-more; lastly, that he would help her with her box up stairs, and then repair straight home, bearing her blessing and her strong injunctions to mingle in his prayers a supplication that he might in course of time grow up a locksmith, or a Mr. Joe, and have Mrs. Vardens, and Miss Dollys for his relations and friends.

Having brought this admonition to an end, upon which, to say the truth, the young gentleman for whose benefit it was designed, bestowed little or no heed, having to all appearance his faculties absorbed in the contemplation of the sweetmeats,—Miss Miggs sig-nified to the company in general that they were not to be uneasy, for she would soon return; and, with her nephew's aid, prepared to bear her wardrobe up the staircase.

"My dear," said the locksmith to his wife. "Do you desire this?"

"I desire it!" she answered. "I am astonished—I am amazed—at her audacity. Let her leave the house this moment."

Miggs, hearing this, let her end of the box fall heavily to the floor, gave a very loud sniff, crossed her arms, screwed down the corners of her mouth, and cried, in an ascending scale, "Ho, good gracious!" three distinct times.

"You hear what your mistress says, my love," remarked the lock-smith. "You had better go, I think. Stay; take this with you, for the sake of old service."

Miss Miggs clutched the bank-note he took from his pocket-book and held out to her; deposited it in a small, red leather purse; put the purse in her pocket (displaying, as she did so, a considerable portion of some under-garment, made of flannel, and more black cotton stocking than is commonly seen in public); and, tossing her head, as she looked at Mrs. Varden, repeated—

"Ho good gracious!"

"I think you said that once before, my dear," observed the locksmith.

"Times is changed, is they, mim!" cried Miggs, bridling; "you can spare me now, can you? You can keep 'em down without me? You're not in wants of any one to scold, or throw the blame upon, no longer, an't you, mim? I'm glad to find you've grown so independent. I wish you joy, I'm sure!"

With that she dropped a curtsey, and keeping her head erect, her ear towards Mrs. Varden, and her eye on the rest of the company, as she alluded to them in her remarks, proceeded:

"I'm quite delighted, I'm sure, to find sich independency, feeling sorry though, at the same time mim, that you should have been forced into submissions when you couldn't help yourself—he he he! It must be great vexations, 'specially considering how ill you always spoke of Mr. Joe—to have him for a son-in-law at last; and I wonder Miss Dolly can put up with him, either, after being off and on for so many years with a coach-maker. But I *have* heerd say that the coachmaker thought twice about it—he he he!—and that he told a young man as was a frind of his, that he hoped he knowed better than to be drawed into that; though she and all the family *did* pull uncommon strong!"

Here she paused for a reply, and receiving none, went on as before.

"I *have* heerd say, mim, that the illnesses of some ladies was all pretensions, and that they could faint away stone dead whenever they had the inclinations so to do. Of course I never see sich cases with my own eyes—ho no! He he he! Nor master neither—ho no! He he he! I *have* heerd the neighbours make remark as some one as they was acquainted with, was a poor good-natur'd mean-spirited creetur, as went out fishing for a wife one day, and caught a Tartar.* Of course I never to my knowledge see the poor person himself. Nor did you neither, mim—ho no. I wonder who it can be—don't you, mim? No doubt you do, mim. Ho yes. He he he!"

Again Miggs paused for a reply; and none being offered, was so oppressed with teeming spite and spleen, that she seemed like to burst.

"I'm glad Miss Dolly can laugh," cried Miggs with a feeble titter. "I like to see folks a laughing—so do you, mim, don't you? You was always glad to see people in spirits, wasn't you, mim? And you always did your best to keep 'em cheerful, didn't you, mim? Though there an't such a great deal to laugh at now either; is there, mim? It an't so much of a catch after looking out so sharp ever since she was a little chit, and costing such a deal in dress and show, to get a poor, common soldier, with one arm, is it, mim? He he! I wouldn't have a husband with one arm, anyways. I would have two arms. I would have two arms, if it was me, though instead of hands they'd only got hooks at the end, like our dustman."

Miss Miggs was about to add, and had, indeed, begun to add, that, taking them in the abstract, dustmen were far more eligible matches than soldiers, though, to be sure, when people were past choosing they must take the best they could get, and think themselves well off too; but her vexation and chagrin being of that internally bitter sort which finds no relief in words, and is aggravated to madness by want of contradiction, she could hold out no longer, and burst into a storm of sobs and tears.

In this extremity she fell on the unlucky nephew, tooth and nail, and plucking a handful of hair from his head, demanded to know how long she was to stand there to be insulted, and whether or no he meant to help her to carry out the box again, and if he took a pleasure in hearing his family reviled, with other inquiries of that nature: at which disgrace and provocation, the small boy, who had been all this time gradually lashed into rebellion by the sight of unattainable pastry, walked off indignant, leaving his aunt and the box to follow at their leisure. Somehow or other, by dint of pushing and pulling, they did attain the street at last; where Miss Miggs, all blowzed with the exertion of getting there, and with her sobs and tears, sat down upon her property; to rest and grieve until she could ensnare some other youth to help her home.

"It's a thing to laugh at, Martha, not to care for," whispered the locksmith, as he followed his wife to the window, and good-humouredly dried her eyes. "What does it matter? You had seen your fault before. Come! Bring up Toby again, my dear; Dolly shall sing us a song; and we'll be all the merrier for this interruption."

CHAPTER THE EIGHTY-FIRST.

ANOTHER month had passed, and the end of August had nearly come, when Mr. Haredale stood alone in the mail-coach office at Bristol. Although but a few weeks had intervened since his conversation with Edward Chester and his niece, in the locksmith's house, and he had made no change, in the mean time, in his accustomed style of dress, his appearance was greatly altered. He looked much older, and more care-worn. Violent agitation and anxiety of mind scatter wrinkles and grey hairs with no unsparing hand; but deeper traces follow on the silent uprooting of old habits, and severing of dear, familiar ties. The affections are not so easily wounded as the passions, but their hurts are deeper, and more lasting. He was now a solitary man, and the heart within him was dreary and lonesome.

He was not the less alone for having spent so many years in seclusion and retirement. This was no better preparation than a round of social cheerfulness: perhaps it even increased the keenness of his sensibility. He had been so dependent upon her for companionship and love; she had come to be so much a part and parcel of his existence; they had had so many cares and thoughts in common, which no one else had shared; that losing her was beginning life anew, and being required to summon up the hope and elasticity of youth, amid the doubts, distrusts, and weakened energies of age.

The effort he had made to part from her with seeming cheerfulness and hope—and they had parted only yesterday—left him the more depressed. With these feelings, he was about to revisit London for the last time, and look once more upon the walls of their old home, before turning his back upon it, for ever.

The journey was a very different one in those days from what the present generation find it; but it came to an end, as the longest journey will, and he stood again in the streets of the metropolis. He lay at the inn where the coach stopped, and resolved, before he went to bed, that he would make his arrival known to no one; would spend but another night in London; and would spare himself the pang of parting even with the honest locksmith.

Such conditions of the mind as that to which he was a prey when he lay down to rest, are favourable to the growth of disordered fancies, and uneasy visions. He knew this, even in the horror with which he started from his first sleep, and threw up the window to dispel it by the presence of some object, beyond the room, which had not been, as it were, the witness of his dream. But it was not a new terror of the night; it had been present to him before, in many shapes; it had haunted him in bygone times; and visited his pillow again and again. If it had been but an ugly object, a childish spectre, haunting his sleep, its return, in its old form, might have awakened a momentary sensation of fear, which, almost in the act of waking, would have passed away. This disquiet, however, lingered about him, and would yield to nothing. When he closed his eyes again, he felt it hovering near; as he slowly sunk into a slumber, he was conscious of its gathering strength and purpose, and gradually assuming its recent shape; when he sprang up from his bed, the same phantom vanished from his heated brain, and left him filled with a dread against which reason and waking thought were powerless.

The sun was up before he could shake it off. He rose late, but not refreshed, and remained within doors all that day. He had a fancy for paying his last visit to the old spot in the evening, for he had been accustomed to walk there at that season, and desired to see it under the aspect that was most familiar to him. At such an hour as would afford him time to reach it a little before sunset, he left the inn, and turned into the busy street.

He had not gone far, and was thoughtfully making his way among the noisy crowd, when he felt a hand upon his shoulder, and, turning, recognised one of the waiters from the inn, who begged his pardon, but he had left his sword behind him.

"Why have you brought it to me?" he asked, stretching out his hand, and yet not taking it from the man, but looking at him in a disturbed and agitated manner.

The man was sorry to have disobliged him, and would carry it back again. The gentleman had said that he was going a little way into the country, and that he might not return till late. The roads were not very safe for single travellers after dark; and since the riots, gentlemen had been more careful than ever not to trust themselves unarmed in lonely places. "We thought you were a stranger, sir," he added, "and that you might believe our roads to be better than they are; but perhaps you know them well, and carry fire-arms—"

He took the sword, and putting it up at his side, thanked the man, and resumed his walk.

It was long remembered that he did this in a manner so strange, and with such a trembling hand, that the messenger stood looking after his retreating figure, doubtful whether he ought not to follow, and watch him. It was long remembered that he had been heard pacing his bed-room in the dead of the night; that the attendants had mentioned to each other in the morning, how fevered and how pale he looked; and that when this man went back to the inn, he told a fellow-servant that what he had observed in this short interview lay very heavy on his mind, and that he feared the gentleman intended to destroy himself, and would never come back alive.

With a half consciousness that his manner had attracted the man's attention (remembering the expression of his face when they parted), Mr. Haredale quickened his steps; and arriving at a stand of coaches, bargained with the driver of the best to carry him so far on his road as the point where the footway struck across the fields, and to await his return at a house of entertainment which was within a stone's-throw of that place. Arriving there in due course, he alighted and pursued his way on foot.

He passed so near the Maypole, that he could see its smoke rising from among the trees, while a flock of pigeons—some of its old inhabitants, doubtless—sailed gaily home to roost, between him and the unclouded sky. "The old house will brighten up now," he said, as he looked towards it, "and there will be a merry fireside beneath its ivied roof. It is some comfort to know that everything will not be blighted hereabouts. I shall be glad to have one picture of life and cheerfulness to turn to!"

He resumed his walk, and bent his steps towards the Warren. It was a clear, calm, silent evening, with hardly a breath of wind to stir the leaves, or any sound to break the stillness of the time, but drowsy sheep-bells tinkling in the distance, and at intervals the far-off low-ing of cattle, or bark of village dogs. The sky was radiant with the softened glory of sunset; and on the earth, and in the air, a deep repose prevailed. At such an hour, he arrived at the deserted man-sion which had been his home so long, and looked for the last time upon its blackened walls.

The ashes of the commonest fire are melancholy things, for in them there is an image of death and ruin,—of something that has been bright, and is but dull, cold, dreary dust,—with which our nature forces us to sympathise. How much more sad the crumbled embers of a home: the casting down of that great altar, where the worst among us sometimes perform the worship of the heart; and where the best have offered up such sacrifices, and done such deeds of heroism as, chronicled, would put the proudest temples of old Time, with all their vaunting annals, to the blush!

He roused himself from a long train of meditation, and walked slowly round the house. It was by this time almost dark.

He had nearly made the circuit of the building, when he uttered a half-suppressed exclamation, started, and stood still. Reclining, in an easy attitude, with his back against a tree, and contemplating the ruin with an expression of exquisite pleasure,—a pleasure so keen that it overcame his habitual indolence and command of feature, and displayed itself utterly free from all restraint or reserve,—before him, on his own ground, and triumphing over him then, as he had done in every misfortune and disappointment of his life, there stood the man whose presence, of all mankind, in any place, and least of all in that, he could the least endure.

Although his blood so rose against this man, and his wrath so stirred within him, that he could have struck him dead, he put such fierce constraint upon himself that he passed him without a word or look. Yes, and he would have gone on, and not turned, though to resist the Devil who poured such hot temptation in his brain, required an effort scarcely human, if this man had not himself summoned him to stop: and that, with an assumed compassion in his voice which drove him well-nigh mad, and in an instant routed all the self-command it had been anguish—acute, poignant anguish—to sustain.

All consideration, reflection, mercy, forbearance; everything by which a goaded man can curb his rage and passion; fled from him as he turned back. And yet he said, slowly and quite calmly—far more calmly than he had ever spoken to him before:

"Why have you called to me?"

"To remark," said Sir John Chester with his wonted composure, "what an odd chance it is, that we should meet here!"

"It *is* a strange chance."

"Strange! The most remarkable and singular thing in the world. I never ride in the evening; I have not done so for years. The whim seized me, quite unaccountably, in the middle of last night.— How very picturesque this is!"—He pointed, as he spoke, to the dismantled house, and raised his glass to his eye.

"You praise your own work very freely."

Sir John let fall his glass; inclined his face towards him with an air of the most courteous inquiry; and slightly shook his head as though he were remarking to himself, "I fear this animal is going mad!"

"I say you praise your own work very freely," repeated Mr. Haredale.

"Work!" echoed Sir John, looking smilingly round. "Mine!—I beg your pardon, I really beg your pardon—"

"Why you see" said Mr. Haredale, "those walls. You see those tottering gables. You see on every side where fire and smoke have raged. You see the destruction that has been wanton here. Do you not?"

"My good fellow," returned the knight, gently checking his impatience with his hand, "of course I do. I see everything you speak of, when you stand aside, and do not interpose yourself between the view and me. I am very sorry for you. If I had not had the pleasure to meet you here, I think I should have written to tell you so. But you don't bear it as well as I had expected—excuse me—no, you don't indeed."

He pulled out his snuff-box, and addressing him with the superior air of a man who by reason of his higher nature has a right to read a moral lesson to another, continued:

"For you are a philosopher, you know—one of that stern and rigid school who are far above the weaknesses of mankind in general. You are removed, a long way, from the frailties of the crowd. You contemplate them from a height, and rail at them with a most impressive bitterness. I have heard you."

—"And shall again," said Mr. Haredale.

"Thank you," returned the other. "Shall we walk as we talk? The damp falls rather heavily. Well,—as you please. But I grieve to say that I can spare you only a very few moments."

"I would," said Mr. Haredale, "you had spared me none. I would, with all my soul, you had been in Paradise (if such a monstrous lie could be enacted), rather than here to-night."

"Nay," returned the other—"really—you do yourself injustice. You are a rough companion, but I would not go so far to avoid you."

"Listen to me," said Mr. Haredale. "Listen to me."

"While you rail?" inquired Sir John.

"While I deliver your infamy. You urged and stimulated to do your work a fit agent, but one who in his nature—in the very essence of his being—is a traitor, and who has been false to you, despite the sympathy you two should have together, as he has been to all others. With hints, and looks, and crafty words, which told again are nothing, you set on Gashford to this work—this work before us now. With these same hints, and looks, and crafty words, which told again are nothing, you urged him on to gratify the deadly hate he owes me—I have earned it, I thank Heaven—by the abduction and dishonour of my niece. You did. I see denial in your looks"—he cried, abruptly pointing in his face, and stepping back. "Denial is a lie!"

He had his hand upon his sword; but the knight, with a contemptuous smile, replied to him as coldly as before.

"You will take notice sir—if you can discriminate sufficiently— that I have taken the trouble to deny nothing. Your discernment is hardly fine enough for the perusal of faces, not of a kind as coarse as your speech; nor has it ever been, that I remember; or, in one face that I could name, you would have read indifference, not to say disgust, somewhat sooner than you did. I speak of a long time ago,— but you understand me."

"Disguise it as you will, you mean denial. Denial explicit or reserved, expressed or left to be inferred, is still a lie. You say you don't deny. Do you admit?"

"You yourself," returned Sir John, suffering the current of his speech to flow as smoothly as if it had been stemmed by no one word of interruption, "publicly proclaimed the character of the gentleman in question (I think it was in Westminster Hall) in terms which relieve me from the necessity of making any further allusion to him. You may have been warranted; you may not have been; I can't say. Assuming the gentleman to be what you described, and to have made to you or any other person any statements that may have happened to suggest themselves to him, for the sake of his own security, or for the sake of money, or for his own amusement, or for any other consideration,—I have nothing to say of him, except that his extremely degrading situation appears to me to be shared with his employers. You are so very plain yourself, that you will excuse a little freedom in me, I am sure."

"Attend to me again Sir John—but once," cried Mr. Haredale; "in your every look, and word, and gesture, you tell me this was not your act. I tell you that it was, and that you tampered with the man I speak of, and with your wretched son (whom God forgive), to do this deed. You talk of degradation and character. You told me once that you had purchased the absence of the poor idiot and his mother, when (as I have discovered since, and then suspected) you had gone to tempt them, and had found them flown. To you I traced the insinuation that I alone reaped any harvest from my brother's death; and all the foul attacks and whispered calumnies that followed in its train. In every action of my life, from that first hope which you converted into grief and desolation, you have stood, like an adverse fate, between me and peace. In all, you have ever been the same cold-blooded, hollow, false, unworthy villain. For the second time, and for the last, I cast these charges in your teeth, and spurn you from me as I would a faithless dog!"

With that, he raised his arm, and struck him on the breast so that he staggered back. Sir John, the instant he recovered, drew his sword, threw away the scabbard and his hat, and rushing on his adversary made a desperate lunge at his heart, which, but that his guard was quick and true, would have stretched him dead upon the grass.

In the act of striking him, the torrent of his opponent's rage had reached a stop. He parried his rapid thrusts, without returning them, and called to him with a frantic kind of terror in his face to keep back.

"Not to-night! not to-night!" he cried. "In God's name, not to-night!"

Seeing that he lowered his weapon, and that he would not thrust in turn, Sir John lowered his.

"I warn you, not to-night!" his adversary cried. "Be warned in time!"

"You told me—it must have been in a sort of inspiration—" said Sir John, quite deliberately, though now he dropped his mask, and showed his bitter hatred in his face, "that this was the last time. Be assured it is! Did you believe our last meeting was forgotten? Did you believe that your every word and look was not to be accounted for, and was not well remembered? Do you believe that I have waited your time, or you mine? What kind of man is he who entered, with all his sickening cant of honesty and truth, into a bond with me to prevent a marriage he affected to dislike, and when I had redeemed my part to the spirit and the letter, skulked from his, and brought the match about in his own time, to rid himself of a burden he had grown tired of, and cast a spurious lustre on his house?"

"I have acted," cried Mr. Haredale, "with honour and in good faith. I do so now. Do not force me to renew this duel to-night!"

"You said my 'wretched' son, I think?" said Sir John, with a smile. "Poor fool! The dupe of such a shallow knave—trapped into marriage by such an uncle and by such a niece—he well deserves your pity. But he is no longer son of mine: you are welcome to the prize your craft has made, sir."

"Once more," cried his opponent, wildly stamping on the ground, "although you tear me from my better angel, I implore you not to come within the reach of my sword to-night. Oh! why were you here at all! Why have we met! To-morrow would have cast us far apart for ever!"

"That being the case," returned Sir John, without the least emotion, "it is very fortunate we have met to-night. Haredale, I have always despised you, as you know, but I have given you credit for a species of brute courage. For the honour of my judgment, which I had thought a good one, I am sorry to find you a coward."

Not another word was spoken on either side. They crossed swords, though it was now quite dusk, and attacked each other fiercely. They were well matched. Each was skilled in the management of his weapon. Mr. Haredale had the advantage in strength and height; on the other hand his adversary could boast superior address, and certainly a greater share of coolness.

After a few seconds they grew hotter and more furious, and pressing on each other inflicted and received several slight wounds. It was directly after receiving one of these in his arm, that Mr. Haredale,

making a keener thrust as he felt the warm blood spirting out, plunged his sword through his opponent's body to the hilt.

Their eyes met, and were on each other as he drew it out. He put his arm about the dying man, who repulsed him, feebly, and dropped upon the turf. Raising himself upon his hands, he gazed at him for an instant, with scorn and hatred in his look: but seeming to remember, even then, that this expression would distort his features after death, he tried to smile; and, faintly moving his right hand, as if to hide his bloody linen in his vest, fell back dead—the phantom of last night.

CHAPTER THE LAST.

A PARTING glance at such of the actors in this little history as it has not, in the course of its events, dismissed, will bring it to an end.

Mr. Haredale fled that night. Before pursuit could be begun, indeed before Sir John was traced or missed, he had left the kingdom. Repairing straight to a religious establishment, known throughout Europe for the rigour and severity of its discipline, and for the mournful penitence it exacted from those who sought its shelter as a refuge from the world, he took the vows which thenceforth shut him out from nature and his kind, and after a few remorseful years was buried in its gloomy cloisters.

Two days elapsed before the body of Sir John was found. As soon as it was recognised and carried home, the faithful valet, true to his master's creed, eloped with all the cash and moveables he could lay his hands on, and started as a finished gentleman upon his own account. In this career he met with great success, and would certainly have married an heiress in the end, but for an unlucky check which led to his premature decease. He sank under a contagious disorder, very prevalent at that time, and vulgarly termed the jail fever.

Lord George Gordon, remaining in his prison in the Tower until Monday the Fifth of February in the following year, was on that day solemnly tried at Westminster for High Treason. Of this crime he was, after a patient investigation, declared Not Guilty; upon the ground that there was no proof of his having called the multitude together with any traitorous or unlawful intentions. Yet so many people were there still, to whom those riots taught no lesson of reproof or moderation, that a public subscription was set on foot in Scotland to defray the cost of his defence.

For seven years afterwards he remained, at the strong intercession of his friends, comparatively quiet; saving that he every now and then took occasion to display his zeal for the Protestant faith in some extravagant proceeding which was the delight of its enemies; and saving, besides, that he was formally excommunicated by the Archbishop of Canterbury, for refusing to appear as a witness in the Ecclesiastical Court when cited for that purpose.* In the year 1788 he was stimulated by some new insanity to write and publish an injurious pamphlet, reflecting on the Queen of France, in very violent terms. Being indicted for the libel,* and (after various strange demonstrations in court) found guilty, he fled into Holland in place of appearing to receive sentence: from whence, as the quiet burgomasters of Amsterdam had no relish for his company, he was sent home again with all speed. Arriving in the month of July at Harwich, and going thence to Birmingham, he made in the latter place, in August, a public profession of the Jewish religion;* and figured there as a Jew until he was arrested, and brought back to London to receive the sentence he had evaded. By virtue of this sentence he was, in the month of December, cast into Newgate for five years and ten months, and required besides to pay a large fine, and to furnish heavy securities for his future good behaviour.*

After addressing, in the midsummer of the following year, an appeal to the commiseration of the National Assembly of France, which the English minister* refused to sanction, he composed himself to undergo his full term of punishment; and suffering his beard to grow nearly to his waist, and conforming in all respects to the ceremonies of his new religion, he applied himself to the study of history, and occasionally to the art of painting, in which, in his younger days, he had shown some skill. Deserted by his former friends, and treated in all respects like the worst criminal in the jail, he lingered on, quite cheerful and resigned, until the 1st of November 1793, when he died in his cell, being then only three-and-forty years of age.

Many men with fewer sympathies for the distressed and needy, with less abilities and harder hearts, have made a shining figure and left a brilliant fame. He had his mourners. The prisoners bemoaned his loss, and missed him; for though his means were not large his charity was great, and in bestowing alms among them he considered the necessities of all alike, and knew no distinction of sect or creed. There are wise men in the highways of the world who may learn something, even from this poor crazy Lord who died in Newgate.

To the last, he was truly served by bluff John Grueby. He was at his side before he had been four-and-twenty hours in the Tower, and he never left him until he died. He had one other constant attendant, in the person of a beautiful Jewish girl; who attached herself to him from feelings half religious, half romantic, but whose virtuous and disinterested character appears to have been beyond the censure even of the most censorious.

Gashford deserted him, of course. He subsisted for a time upon his traffic in his master's secrets; and, this trade failing when the stock was quite exhausted, procured an appointment in the honourable corps of spies and eaves-droppers employed by the government. As one of these wretched underlings, he did his drudgery, sometimes abroad, sometimes at home; and long endured the various miseries of such a station. Ten or a dozen years ago—not more—a meagre, wan old man, diseased and miserably poor, was found dead in his bed at an obscure inn in the Borough, where he was quite unknown. He had taken poison. There was no clue to his name; but it was discovered from certain entries in a pocket-book he carried, that he had been secretary to Lord George Gordon in the time of the famous riots.

Many months after the re-establishment of peace and order; and even when it had ceased to be the town talk, that every military officer, kept at free quarters by the city during the late alarms, had cost for his board and lodging four pounds four per day, and every private soldier two and twopence halfpenny; many months after even this engrossing topic was forgotten, and the United Bull-Dogs were to a man all killed, imprisoned or transported; Mr. Simon Tappertit, being removed from a hospital to prison, and thence to his place of trial, was discharged by proclamation, on two wooden legs. Shorn of his graceful limbs, and brought down from his high estate to circumstances of utter destitution, and the deepest misery, he made shift to stump back to his old master, and beg for some relief. By the locksmith's advice and aid, he was established in business as a shoe-black, and opened shop under an archway near the Horse Guards. This being a central quarter, he quickly made a very large connection; and on levee days, was sometimes known to have as many as twenty half-pay officers waiting their turn for polishing. Indeed his trade increased to that extent, that in course of time he entertained no less than two apprentices, besides taking for his wife the widow of an eminent bone and rag collector, formerly of Milbank. With this lady (who assisted in the business) he lived in great domestic happiness, only chequered by those little storms which serve to clear the atmosphere of wedlock, and brighten its horizon. In some of these gusts of bad weather, Mr. Tappertit would, in the assertion of his prerogative, so far forget himself, as to correct his lady with a brush, or boot, or shoe; while she (but only in extreme cases) would retaliate by taking off his legs, and leaving him exposed to the derision of those urchins who delight in mischief.

Miss Miggs, baffled in all her schemes, matrimonial and otherwise, and cast upon a thankless, undeserving world, turned very sharp and sour; and did at length become so acid, and did so pinch and slap and tweak the hair and noses of the youth of Golden Lion Court, that she was by one consent expelled that sanctuary, and desired to bless some other spot of earth, in preference. It chanced at that moment, that the justices of the peace for Middlesex proclaimed by public placard that they stood in need of a female turnkey for the County Bridewell, and appointed a day and hour for the inspection of candidates. Miss Miggs, attending at the time appointed, was instantly chosen and selected from one hundred and twenty-four competitors, and at once promoted to the office; which she held until her decease, more than thirty years afterwards, remaining single all that time. It was observed of this lady that while she was inflexible and grim to all her female flock, she was particularly so to those who could establish any claim to beauty: and it was often remarked as a proof of her indomitable virtue and severe chastity, that to such as had been frail she showed no mercy; always falling upon them on the slightest occasion, or on no occasion at all, with the fullest measure of her wrath. Among other useful inventions which she practised upon this class of offenders and bequeathed to posterity, was the art of inflicting an exquisitely vicious poke or dig with the wards of a key in the small of the back, near the spine. She likewise originated a mode of treading by accident (in pattens) on such as had small feet; also very remarkable for its ingenuity, and previously quite unknown.

It was not very long, you may be sure, before Joe Willet and Dolly

Varden were made husband and wife, and with a handsome sum in bank (for the locksmith could afford to give his daughter a good dowry), reopened the Maypole. It was not very long, you may be sure, before a red-faced little boy was seen staggering about the Maypole passage, and kicking up his heels on the green before the door. It was not very long, counting by years, before there was a red-faced little girl, another red-faced little boy, and a whole troop of girls and boys: so that, go to Chigwell when you would, there would surely be seen, either in the village street, or on the green, or frolicking in the farm-yard—for it was a farm now, as well as a tavern—more small Joes and small Dollys than could be easily counted. It was not a very long time before these appearances ensued; but it *was* a *very* long time before Joe looked five years older, or Dolly either, or the locksmith either, or his wife either: for cheerfulness and content are great beautifiers, and are famous preservers of youthful looks, depend upon it.

It was a long time, too, before there was such a country inn as the Maypole, in all England: indeed it is a great question whether there has ever been such another to this hour, or ever will be. It was a long time too—for Never, as the proverb says, is a long day—before they forgot to have an interest in wounded soldiers at the Maypole; or before Joe omitted to refresh them, for the sake of his old campaign; or before the serjeant left off looking in there, now and then; or before they fatigued themselves, or each other, by talking on these occasions of battles and sieges, and hard weather and hard service, and a thousand things belonging to a soldier's life. As to the great silver snuff-box which the King sent Joe with his own hand, because of his conduct in the Riots, what guest ever went to the Maypole without putting finger and thumb into that box, and taking a great pinch, though he had never taken a pinch of snuff before, and almost sneezed himself into convulsions even then? As to the purple-faced vintner, where is the man who lived in those times and never saw *him* at the Maypole: to all appearance as much at home in the best room, as if he lived there? And as to the feastings and christenings, and revellings at Christmas, and celebrations of birth-days, wedding-days, and all manner of days, both at the Maypole and the Golden Key,—if they are not notorious, what facts are?

Mr. Willet the elder, having been by some extraordinary means possessed with the idea that Joe wanted to be married, and that it would be well for him, his father, to retire into private life, and enable him to live in comfort, took up his abode in a small cottage at Chigwell; where they widened and enlarged the fire-place for him, hung up the boiler, and furthermore planted in the little garden outside the front-door, a fictitious Maypole: so that he was quite at home directly. To this, his new habitation, Tom Cobb, Phil Parkes, and Solomon Daisy went regularly every night: and in the chimney-corner, they all four quaffed, and smoked, and prosed, and dozed, as they had done of old. It being accidentally discovered after a short time that Mr. Willet still appeared to consider himself a landlord by profession, Joe provided him with a slate, upon which the old man regularly scored up vast accounts for meat, drink, and tobacco. As he grew older this passion increased upon him; and it became his delight to chalk against the name of each of his cronies a sum of enormous magnitude, and impossible to be paid: and such was his secret joy in these entries, that he would be perpetually seen going behind the door to look at them, and coming forth again, suffused with the liveliest satisfaction.

He never recovered the surprise the Rioters had given him, and remained in the same mental condition down to the last moment of his life. It was like to have been brought to a speedy termination by the first sight of his first grandchild, which appeared to fill him with the belief that a miracle had happened to Joe, and that something alarming had occurred. Being promptly blooded, however, by a skilful surgeon, he rallied; and although the doctors all agreed, on his being attacked with symptoms of apoplexy six months afterwards, that he ought to die, and took it very ill that he did not, he remained alive—possibly on account of his constitutional slowness—for nearly seven years more, when he was one morning found speechless in his bed. He lay in this state, free from all tokens of uneasiness, for a whole week, when he was suddenly restored to consciousness by hearing the nurse whisper in his son's ear that he was going. "I'm a-going, Joseph," said Mr. Willet, turning round upon the instant, "to the Salwanners"—and immediately gave up the ghost.

He left a large sum of money behind him; even more than he was supposed to have been worth, although the neighbours, according to the custom of mankind in calculating the wealth that other people ought to have saved, had estimated his property in good round numbers. Joe inherited the whole; so that he became a man of great consequence in those parts, and was perfectly independent.

Some time elapsed before Barnaby got the better of the shock he had sustained, or regained his old health and gaiety. But he recovered by degrees: and although he could never separate his condemnation and escape from the idea of a terrific dream, he became, in other respects, more rational. Dating from the time of his recovery, he had a better memory and greater steadiness of purpose; but a dark cloud overhung his whole previous existence, and never cleared away.

He was not the less happy for this; for his love of freedom and interest in all that moved or grew, or had its being in the elements, remained to him unimpaired. He lived with his mother on the Maypole farm, tending the poultry and the cattle, working in a garden of his own, and helping everywhere. He was known to every bird and beast about the place, and had a name for every one. Never was there a lighter-hearted husbandman, a creature more popular with young and old, a blither or more happy soul than Barnaby: and though he was free to ramble where he would, he never quitted Her, but was for evermore her stay and comfort.

It was remarkable that although he had that dim sense of the past, he sought out Hugh's dog, and took him under his care; and that he never could be tempted into London. When the Riots were many years old, and Edward and his wife came back to England with a family almost as numerous as Dolly's, and one day appeared at the Maypole porch, he knew them instantly, and wept and leaped for joy. But neither to visit them, nor on any other pretence, no matter how full of promise and enjoyment, could he be persuaded to set foot in the streets: nor did he ever conquer this repugnance or look upon the town again.

Grip soon recovered his looks, and became as glossy and sleek as ever. But he was profoundly silent. Whether he had forgotten the art of Polite Conversation in Newgate, or had made a vow in those troubled times to forego, for a period, the display of his accomplishments, is matter of uncertainty; but certain it is that for a whole year he never indulged in any other sound than a grave, decorous croak. At the expiration of that term the morning being very bright and sunny, he was heard to address himself to the horses in the stable upon the subject of the Kettle, so often mentioned in these pages;

and before the witness who overheard him could run into the house with the intelligence, and add to it upon his solemn affirmation the statement that he had heard him laugh, the bird himself advanced with fantastic steps to the very door of the bar, and there cried "I'm a devil, I'm a devil, *I*'m a devil!" with extraordinary rapture.

From that period (although he was supposed to be much affected by the death of Mr. Willet senior), he constantly practised and improved himself in the vulgar tongue; and as he was a mere infant for a raven, when Barnaby was grey, he has very probably gone on talking to the present time.

THE END.

APPENDIX A

The Gordon Riots

UNTIL the passing of Catholic Emancipation in 1829, only twelve years before Dickens wrote *Barnaby Rudge*, Catholics did not enjoy full political and civil liberties in Britain. Penal laws set terms of life imprisonment for Catholic school proprietors and priests carrying out their ministry, offering £100 rewards to informers.[1] It was the repeal of these laws in the Catholic Relief Act (18 Geo. II, c. 60) of 1778 that rallied anti-Catholic feeling in England into such organizations as the Protestant Association, founded in February 1779. Although Dickens gives the impression to his readers that Gordon was rallying support against the passing of the Act in the first place, two years elapsed between the Relief Act and the riots of 1780.

On Friday, 2 June 1780, the Protestant Association assembled at St George's Fields on the south side of the River Thames. They were demanding that the 1778 Relief Act be overturned. Public meetings, petitions, pamphlets, and riots had already proved successful in preventing similar legislation being enacted for Scotland.[2] Lord George Gordon, President of the Protestant Association and member of the House of Commons, let it be known that he would present the Association's monster petition for repeal of this Act to Parliament, but only if large numbers turned up.[3] Some 60,000 gathered in the fields, wearing blue cockades provided and paid for by the Association. Following an address by Gordon, the crowd marched to Parliament (in four divisions over the three bridges then existing, as Dickens describes), picking up bystanders along the routes. Outside Westminster, the crowd jostled peers and MPs as they arrived for the parliamentary day and many packed into the Lobby. Lord

[1] This Act did not grant freedom of worship—that came in 1791. However, it ratified the current practice of toleration and removed the livelihoods of professional informers such as William Payne. Catholics were able to take a new Oath of Allegiance that did not require them to set aside various doctrinal beliefs. See Colin Haydon, *Anti-Catholicism in Eighteenth-Century England, c.1714–1780: A Political and Social Study* (Manchester: Manchester University Press, 1993), 204.

[2] For a discussion of the views and membership of the Association, see Nicholas Rogers, *Crowds, Culture and Politics in Georgian Britain* (Oxford: Clarendon Press, 1998), 156–8. The Scottish context is discussed in Robert Kent Donovan, *No Popery and Radicalism: Opposition to Roman Catholic Relief in Scotland, 1778–1782* (New York: Garland, 1987), particularly ch. 1.

[3] The resolution of the Protestant Association of 29 May 1780 concerning the arrangements for the monster meeting is given in J. Paul de Castro, *The Gordon Riots* (London: Oxford University Press, 1926), 25.

George came out of the Chamber from time to time to let them know the progress of the debate on accepting the petition. Dickens's account of this and the exchange of words with the enraged General Conway and Lord George's kinsman Colonel Gordon are based on the historical sources. The parliamentarians were trapped in Westminster until the Horse and Foot Guards arrived to disperse the mob, and many found it a terrifying experience.

The crowd then moved on to destroy the chapels attached to the Bavarian and Sardinian embassies, where English Catholics often worshipped. It was outside the latter that Sampson Rainsforth, a Justice of the Peace, summoned the Guards and arrested several of the rioters with the help of a coach-maker called Maberly, one of the few instances of firm action by the magistracy during the riots. The next day, the Catholic chapel in Ropemakers' Alley, Moorfields, was threatened. At this stage, however, it was still possible for magistrates to disperse the crowd without the aid of troops. Not all magistrates were willing to act, for fear of reprisals. Efforts by two merchants to warn the Lord Mayor, Brackley Kennett, of the likely return of the rioters to the Moorfields chapel fell on deaf ears. They were concerned (with good cause) that their businesses in the locality were vulnerable. While Dickens used this episode in Chapter 61 to the point of repeating actual sentences from the historical record, he gave the words to another Catholic target, Thomas Langdale, the vintner, who appears several times in the novel.[4] Kennett was present the following day while the Moorfields chapel was pulled down and its contents burnt, but he did not order the troops to intervene. After the Riots, Kennett was examined by the Privy Council who concluded that he had acted 'with great timidity'. He was found guilty of criminal negligence and fined £1,000. So ambiguous was the law about the powers and responsibilities of magistrates and officers in riots that the military was unwilling to take the initiative without an explicit command from Kennett.

The riots escalated on 5 June and spread into other areas of London. The mass-house in Wapping was destroyed and Catholic houses were attacked. Also targeted were houses in Spitalfields where Irish weavers lived. Apart from threatening Catholic property, the crowd began to attack houses belonging to those associated with the Relief Act or with the civil authorities. Sir George Savile's house in Leicester Fields was burnt and plundered because he was the Member who had introduced the Bill in Parliament. Retribution was also taken against the houses of Rainsforth and Maberly, who had acted so promptly on the first day of the disturbances. By Tuesday, 6 June the civil authority had lost control of London. Even the Lord Mayor became alarmed when he received information that

---

[4] See p. 487 and de Castro, *Gordon Riots*, 52–3.

the Bank of England was about to be attacked. The Secretary of State ordered troops into London from outlying areas, but they were often more than a day's march away. Parties were sent to protect Parliament and the houses of notables considered likely targets, including Lambeth Palace, home of the Archbishop of Canterbury. Parliament reassembled that Tuesday, but the members were so much in fear of the crowd milling around Westminster that they adjourned until Thursday. Justice Hyde, one of the more active magistrates, read the Riot Act in Parliament Yard and ordered the Horse to disperse the crowd. As revenge, the crowd moved on to destroy Hyde's house at St Martin's Street, Leicester Fields. Although some troops were present, the crowd ignored the ensign's plea to desist, but when the house of Lord Mansfield, the Chief Justice, in Bloomsbury Square was attacked, a magistrate, Mr Durden, arrived with a platoon of Foot Guards. He read the Riot Act and, when the rioters continued to burn furniture and papers, he gave Colonel Woodford permission to fire. This was the first time in these Riots that the military fired into the crowd. The troops killed seven, wounded more, and dispersed the rioters.

Prisons were an important target for the rioters. Newgate Prison was breached and the Keeper's house burnt down on 7 June. Those rioters who had been arrested on 2 June and housed there were freed along with many other prisoners. The Fleet, King's Bench, and other prisons in the capital were also attacked and their prisoners freed. The Police Office of Sir John Fielding, magistrate at Bow Street, was destroyed. Although attempts were made on the Bank of England and the Royal Exchange, these institutions were successfully defended by troops, but so widespread was the violence, fire, and destruction on 7 June that it became known as 'Black Wednesday'. For protection, people hung blue flags and No Popery signs on their houses. Troops now converged on London, setting up military camps in the parks, and confronting the rioters at key points. There was more destruction of Catholic houses, shops and businesses in Westminster, the City, and Middlesex. Public houses in Golden Lane and Whitechapel were destroyed. When Thomas Langdale's distillery in Holborn burnt down, twenty-one neighbouring houses caught fire. Many people, inebriated and possibly poisoned by the contents of Langdale's vats, were burnt alive in this conflagration. The fascinating horror of this scene in Chapter 68 (reinforced by the illustration by Browne, 'The rioters drink from the gutters') is firmly based on a knowledge of the historical sources.

On the evening of 'Black Wednesday', the King summoned the Privy Council. A legal opinion obtained from the Attorney-General clarified the Riot Act and the relationship between the military and the civil power, making it clear that the former could fire on the crowd without a specific order from the latter. Clearer directions given in an Order in Council now enabled officers to use force if buildings were being destroyed and lives threatened by the rioting crowd. Thus, when the crowd captured Blackfriars Bridge and burnt down the loathed tollhouse, the troops opened fire leaving many dead. After the Privy Council met, the conduct of operations passed from the Secretary of State into the hands of the Commander-in-Chief, Lord Amherst. This move from civil to military control was underlined by the decision of the House of Commons on Thursday, 8 June to adjourn until 19 June. Although rioting continued in Southwark and Bermondsey and the crowd attacked more Catholic shops and pubs, the military began to reassert order. Fifty people were arrested in the ruins of Newgate. There were deaths in Fleet Street and St George's Fields, when the military fired upon the crowds. In all, over 200 people died in the Riots with another 75 dying later from their injuries. The troops, both regular and militia, augmented by Military Associations of citizens who took up arms to defend their localities, now numbered 10,000. The authorities regained control of London.

Lord George Gordon was arrested on Friday, 9 June and taken to the Tower. However, at his trial the following February the prosecution could not prove his intention to cause a riot when he called the monster meeting of 2 June. He was freed. Of the rioters, 450 were arrested of whom 160 appeared for trial. Of these, 62 were sentenced to death, 12 received varying terms of imprisonment and 85 were found not guilty and discharged.[5] Many of those sentenced to death were reprieved, including the two black men convicted.[6] The twenty-five public hangings took place over several days in July 1780, not only at Tyburn, but also near specific buildings destroyed in the riots and linked to the actions of the convicted felon.[7]

Almost immediately, contemporaries began to consider the implications of the Riots, coming as they did at a critical point in the American war and in the campaign for parliamentary reform. It put supporters of reform, religious toleration, and American liberty such as Edmund Burke in a difficult position. He thoroughly disapproved of the violence and destruction, but suggested in his 'Letters and Reflections on the Execution of the Rioters in 1780' that 'its cause is national', to be found in the

---

[5] George Rudé, 'The Gordon Riots: A Study of the Rioters and Their Victims' in his *Paris and London in the Eighteenth Century: Studies in Popular Protest* (New York: Viking Press, 1971), 275.

[6] See details of the three cases in Marika Sherwood, 'Blacks in the Gordon Riots', *History Today*, 47/12 (1997), 24–8.

[7] See e.g. the list given in V. A. C. Gatrell, *The Hanging Tree: Execution and the English People 1770–1868* (Oxford: Oxford University Press, 1994), 31–2.

parlous state of England, and he argued for clemency for the rioters.[8] The Gordon Riots soon passed into the national mythology and were frequently invoked during debates over public order and political reform in the decades that followed. Burke made frequent mention of them in condemning the effects of revolutionary change in his *Reflections on the Revolution in France* (1790). One of the earliest modern historians to work through the historical records (many of them available to Dickens—see Appendix B), was J. Paul de Castro, writing in 1926 within the context of the General Strike and contemporary issues of public order and popular protest. His focus was on the actions and decisions of government officials and a reconstruction of events through the eyes of contemporaries, many of whose testimonies he very usefully reproduces.[9] The classic analysis, however, remains George Rudé's study of the official trial records of those arrested and prosecuted.[10] Rudé came to the conclusion that economic grievances were as important as anti-popery as the motivation for the Riots. For some time the class-based approach to the study of the Georgian crowd and the Gordon Riots was axiomatic, but more recently the Gordon Riots have been placed by historians within the context of the American war, radical politics, and developments in English national identity.[11] These are contexts ignored by Dickens who, for example, makes only a brief mention of the war in relation to Joe, omits the xenophobic element in his account of the attack on the Sardinian and Bavarian chapels, and denies any role to the radicalism associated with John Wilkes and others in the city.

[8] Tom Middlebro', 'Burke, Dickens and the Gordon Riots', *Humanities Association Review*, 31 (Winter/Spring 1980), 88. Burke had himself been threatened and had defended his house with the help of friends.

[9] de Castro, *Gordon Riots*.

[10] Rudé, 'The Gordon Riots: A Study'.

[11] See, e.g. Rogers, *Crowds, Culture and Politics*; Donovan, *No Popery and Radicalism*; Gerald Newman, *The Rise of English Nationalism: A Cultural History 1740–1830* (New York: St Martin's Press, 1987); Haydon, *Anti-Catholicism*; Kathleen Wilson, *The Sense of the People: Politics, Culture and Imperialism in England, 1715–1785* (Cambridge: Cambridge University Press, 1995).

APPENDIX B

Historical Sources and Contemporary Contexts

CRITICS have argued that in *Barnaby Rudge* Charles Dickens showed an unusual, possibly unique, willingness to engage in political and historical analysis. Two types of explanation are advanced for this departure from the usual: first, Dickens was consciously trying to emulate Walter Scott as a historical novelist (see Appendix C); second, Dickens saw remarkable parallels between the turbulent popular politics of the late 1770s and those of the late 1830s when the novel was coming into being. There is force in both arguments. Dickens undoubtedly discovered in 'the Riots of 'Eighty' a series of apt symbols and analogies for analysing his own times. In letters to friends, advertisements for the forthcoming novel, and in the text itself, Dickens hinted that the Gordon Riots should serve as a warning for his contemporaries. Contemporaries, such as Thomas Hood, certainly read it in this way (see Introduction, p. x). Conditions that had produced the most fearsome mob eruption of the eighteenth century threatened to generate a comparable result half a century later. The riot that set London aflame in June 1780 had obvious echoes in popular disorders of his day.

First, there was the Anti-Poor Law movement of the mid-1830s—a series of northern working-class protests against the Poor Law Amendment Act of 1834 which had abandoned the traditional provision of 'outdoor relief' in the form of money payments or goods. By the new legislation, poor relief was to be administered in purpose-built workhouses, where husbands, wives, and children were separated and given monotonous or arduous tasks as a form of deterrence and cost recovery. Dickens made his own protest against the system in *Oliver Twist*, but on the national stage paternalist Tories made common cause with working-class radicals to agitate against the resulting dehumanization—an unusual alliance that seemed to present parallels with the associations between political reformers and anti-Catholic agitators at the time of the Gordon Riots.

The Chartist movement provided Dickens with a second possible source of analogy with the anti-Catholic riots of 1778–80. Chartism was an independent, loosely structured, mass political movement, originating in 1838, that sought political rights for the disenfranchised lower class of Britain. Its explicit political goals—the six-point charter of universal male suffrage, annual parliaments, secret ballot, payment of members, equal electoral districts, and abolition of property requirements for MPs—were certainly radical in the sense that they went much further than the limited reforms that had been inaugurated in the Great Reform Act of 1832.

During the time Dickens was writing *Barnaby Rudge*, the Chartist movement was developing a variety of protest tactics, which ranged from peaceable mass petitions to Parliament to a few small attempts at armed uprising. Specific examples of the latter that might have attracted Dickens's attention include the Birmingham 'Bull-Ring' Riots of 1839 and the attempted Chartist rising at Newport in Wales in November 1839. The latter was easily crushed and the ringleaders executed. The bloodthirsty speeches of Hugh, Dennis, Gashford, and the *Thunderer* newspaper could be equated, too, with the inflammatory physical-force rhetoric of Chartist leaders like Feargus O'Connor and his large-circulation newspaper, the *Northern Star*. Sim Tappertit's 'Brotherhood of United Bulldogs' also had its counterpart in 1830s trade society actions, particularly a violent strike of Glasgow cotton spinners in 1837–8. Trade combinations or unions were hedged around with restrictive legislation that made them effectually illegal, particularly if intimidation or oath-taking could be proved.[1]

At the same time, labour historians and literary scholars have wondered why Dickens so badly misread the Chartist movement. Neither the Anti-Poor Law movement, nor Chartism, nor the 1830s Union agitations could be seen as generically violent and anarchic. Moreover, the bulk of the early Victorian working class exhibited ideals that were generally close to Dickens's heart. Here was a massive, disciplined flowering of working-class aspirations, marked less by a thirst for violence than by moral earnestness and a desire for community education, recreation, health, sobriety, and self-respect.[2] True, some other popular movements in the 1830s were less amenable to being understood as moderate and enlightened. The anti-Catholic slogans of the Protestant Association of 1839 directly echoed the bigotry of Lord George Gordon's Protestant Association of 1778–80.[3] Dickens no doubt also noted that the strange alliance of 1780 between Gordon's anti-Catholic agitators and popular political reformers had its counterpart in the 1830s when militant Anti-Poor Law agitators like Revd Joseph Rayner Stephens took the same platform as Chartists like Feargus O'Connor. Inside Parliament, a similar alliance between Ultra-Tories and Radicals helped bring down Lord Melbourne's Whig-Liberal government

[1] Peter Scheckner, 'Chartism, Class and Social Struggle: A Study of Charles Dickens', *Midwest Quarterly*, 29/1 (1987), 93–112; Paul Stignant and Peter Widdowson, 'Barnaby Rudge—a Historical Novel?', *Literature and History*, 2 (1975), 2–42.

[2] James Epstein and Dorothy Thompson (eds.), *The Chartist Experience: Studies in Working-Class Radicalism and Culture, 1830–1860* (London: Macmillan, 1982).

[3] See Dennis Walder, *Dickens and Religion* (London: Allen and Unwin, 1981), ch. 4.

(which Dickens supported) in favour of Robert Peel's Tory government (which he disliked).[4]

There is no doubt that Dickens showed an unusual preoccupation with historical and contemporary politics when researching and writing *Barnaby Rudge*. This can be seen in the impressive array of historical sources he consulted.[5] The novel drew, for instance, on eyewitness descriptions of the Gordon Riots by Hester Thrale (via Boswell's *Life of Johnson*), Frederick Reynolds, and Samuel Romilly. Frequently, too, Dickens borrowed the names, actions and speeches of historical figures from favoured daily newspapers such as the *Morning Chronicle, St James's Chronicle* and *Daily Advertizer*, or from journalistic summaries in the *Annual Register* (1781) and *Gentleman's Magazine* (1780–1). He also combed through published accounts of trials and executions, mainly looking for colourful period detail. Significantly, Dickens owned most of the best analyses of the Gordon Riots produced by eighteenth-century observers: Edmund Burke's *Letters to Earl Bathurst, with Reflections on the Executions of the Rioters* (1826) and famous *Reflections on the Revolution in France* (1790); William Vincent's [Thomas Holcroft] *A Plain and Succinct Narrative of the Riots* (with an appendix by journalist James Perry); a shrewd anonymous tract called *Fanaticism and Treason* (1780); Nathaniel Wraxall's *Historical Memoirs of My Own Time* (1815); and Robert Watson's substantial *Life of Lord Gordon, with a Philosophical Review of his Political Conduct* (1795).

Yet Dickens's use of these key interpretative works was more interesting for its omissions than its inclusions. He excised their central premise— a compelling *political* explanation of the events of 1778–80. Irrespective of their political affiliation, all these contemporary observers depicted the Gordon Riots as a *révolution manqué*, a popular political revolution that only just failed to ignite. For the Irishman Edmund Burke, personally threatened by the mob for his pro-Catholic views, the Riots were a terrible regression to seventeenth-century Puritan fanaticism, combined with new and rootless doctrines of radical reform.[6] For the middle-class radical Thomas Holcroft, the rioters' plans to storm the Bank of England and Tower of London suggested a deep-seated political plot to overthrow the government, probably fomented by agents of the French monarchy.

[4] Thomas J. Rice, 'The Politics of *Barnaby Rudge*', in Robert Giddens (ed.), *The Changing World of Charles Dickens* (London: Vision, 1983), 51–73.

[5] Thomas J. Rice, *Barnaby Rudge: An Annotated Bibliography* (New York: Garland, 1987), 74–144; John Butt and Kathleen Tillotson, '*Barnaby Rudge*: The First Projected Novel', in their *Dickens at Work* (1957: 2nd edn., London: Methuen, 1988), 76–89.

[6] Iain McCalman, 'Mad Lord George and Madame La Motte: Riot and Sexuality in the Genesis of Burke's Reflections on the Revolution in France', *Journal of British Studies*, 35 (1996), 343–67.

Writing in 1815, the Whig politician Nathaniel Wraxall drew a subtle and compelling analogy between the Gordon Riots and France's recent Revolution, arguing that the same conditions were present for each. Only the firmer conduct of Britain's monarch averted the disaster that struck France.

Dr Robert Watson, a Scottish-born revolutionary who became an ardent supporter of Lord George Gordon during the late 1780s, presented the most sustained version of this *révolution manqué* thesis. He saw the Riots as a sweeping popular insurrection that went awry. Watson depicted Gordon as a Scottish patriot and a natural democrat who had repudiated his corrupt aristocratic family. The agitations of the Protestant Association were motivated, Watson claimed, not by religious bigotry but by a humane desire to end an unjust war against democratic Americans. Watson echoed Gordon's own claim that Lord North's government passed the Catholic Relief Act of 1778 not out of compassion for Catholics but for the sinister purpose of recruiting Irish and Highlander troops to fight the American colonists.

Far from adopting any of these contemporary political interpretations in *Barnaby Rudge*, Dickens went to considerable lengths to expunge any trace of them from the novel. Although inclined towards Watson's sympathetic depiction of Gordon's personal character, Dickens made no mention of the young lord's ardent political views. His Gordon is a dreamy, weak-headed idealist who is easily manipulated by the conspirator Gashford. In presenting him thus, Dickens also committed a historical injustice to Gashford's prototype Robert Watson. He knew Watson's story well enough to borrow details from the startling inquest reported in *The Times* of 22 November 1838, after Watson committed suicide in a London tavern. That account also revealed Watson's revolutionary past; he had fought for both the Americans and the French against the British, accumulating nineteen wounds in the process. Dickens may have been one of the distinguished literary men who apparently visited the body to view the scars. Even so, Dickens deliberately purged Gashford of any of the political commitments of his real-life prototype. The oily, self-serving conspirator of *Barnaby Rudge* is an embittered, sexually perverted ex-Catholic who seeks revenge against his own kind. He later becomes a government spy, and eventually kills himself with poison. The real-life Watson was so poor, sick, and isolated at the age of 88 that he killed himself by self-strangulation with a necktie.[7]

Purging the Gordon Riots of their revolutionary political dimensions was not simply a consequence of Dickens having conservative or reaction-

[7] Iain McCalman, 'Controlling the Riots: Dickens, *Barnaby Rudge* and Romantic Revolution', *History*, 84 (1999), 458–76.

ary views. Patrick Brantlinger has perceptively situated the novel within the political context of mid-Victorian populism.[8] Dickens always identified political legitimacy with the common people, but feared that their values and aspirations had been distorted or subverted through the influence of a corrupt, vicious and weak ruling class. Such populism tended to generate contradictory political tendencies: on the one hand, Dickens favoured liberal-radical activities designed to moralize the working classes and free them from oppressive social conditions; on the other hand, he was predisposed towards conspiratorial explanations of ruling-class power and paranoid fears of a corrupted populace. These opinions were not uncommon among writers and journalists of lower-middle-class origins, including contemporaries and friends of Dickens, such as Harrison Ainsworth, Douglas Jerrold, Henry Mayhew, and G. W. M. Reynolds.

For Dickens and many of his contemporaries in the press, the danger of both the 1780s and the 1840s lay not in any specific political programme, whether of the Protestant Association or the Chartists, but in social conditions that led to blind, anarchistic eruptions of popular fury. This was history's recurrent nightmare—a return of the repressed that might only be avoided by good rule and personal moral regulation. The ingredients of popular combustion were the same in both periods: a weak and corrupt ruling class, self-serving conspirators, and a populace devoid of moral responsibility. Dickens believed that the common people had been driven, literally, to the brink of madness by cruel laws, terrible living conditions, and an absence of all hope.

For this reason, *Barnaby Rudge* is primarily an exploration of conditions that conduce to individual and social pathologies of madness and crime. In his earliest conception of the book, Dickens intended to pivot the story around three lunatics who escape from Bedlam. And of course three lunatics drive much of the action of the Riots: Hugh, an *enfant sauvage* raised as an animal without the benefits of civil or moral education; Barnaby, whose mind has been cracked by the genetic and cultural stain of his murderous father; and Ned Dennis the hangman, whose personality has been perverted by the cruelty of his trade. All three have blighted 'souls', as do the random accumulation of people from the gutters and rookeries of London who join the mob. Although the three madmen have obvious literary referents (such as Wordsworth's 'Idiot Boy'), Dickens also went to considerable lengths to research historical and contemporary examples of socially induced madness. The figure of Barnaby, for example, owes his inspiration in part to Dickens's visits to Coldbath Fields and Tothill Fields prisons in 1840–1 to study inmates with 'light

[8] Patrick Brantlinger, 'Did Dickens Have a Philosophy of History? The Case of *Barnaby Rudge*', *Dickens Studies Annual*, 30 (2001), 59–74.

reason'. He was especially moved by the plight of 'Boy' Jones, a mentally impaired young man imprisoned for breaking into Buckingham Palace to speak to the Queen.[9]

The more sinister and darkly-comical figure of Sim Tappertit may owe some inspiration to a lad called Thomas Taplin, executed after the Gordon Riots despite a plea of insanity. But Tappertit's main model was the demented figure of Edward Oxford, who attempted to assassinate Queen Victoria with a pistol on 10 June 1840. Oxford was an unemployed barboy of 18; fatherless, small, full of conceit, and utterly delusional. Like Tappertit, he had concocted an imaginary secret society with elaborate rules and rituals, of which he was the towering leader. Dickens followed Oxford's trial closely and suggested privately to friends that the boy should have been smothered at birth. This uncharacteristically cruel observation, like the sad fate of Tappertit, was prompted by Dickens's conviction that lost and grotesque individuals like this were the natural leaders of mobs.[10]

During the Edward Oxford sensation, Dickens was also assiduously following another law case. This was the trial of François Benjamin Courvoisier, a valet who had brutally cut the throat of his master, Lord William Russell, in May 1840. As well as providing the inspiration for the crime of Barnaby's father, the Courvoisier affair engaged the compassionate side of Dickens's nature. He attended the valet's public execution in July 1840 and was revolted by the personal brutality of the spectacle and its degrading effects on the crowd. These sentiments triggered Dickens's journalistic campaign against capital punishment in the *Daily News* of 1846, and also help to explain his bouts of sympathy with the rioters in *Barnaby Rudge*, both when the mob burns down Newgate and when Hugh makes his passionate social prophecy at the foot of the gallows.

Just as the individual and social pathologies of five families at the beginning of the novel fed into the later eruption of the Riots, so the solution for this popular madness lay in the domestic example of Gabriel Varden. Despite rebellions within his own family and pressures placed on him by the mob, Varden holds firm because he has a disciplined moral centre arising from his healthy socialization and education. As a result, Varden has been inoculated against the temptations of mob contagion.[11] Dickens's most ardent hope was that the social reform of the ruling class and the moral education of the lower class would generate enough Gabriel Vardens to prevent a return to the madness of 'the Riots of 'Eighty'.

[9] Scott Dransfield, 'Reading the Gordon Riots in 1841: Social Violence and Moral Management in *Barnaby Rudge*', *Dickens Studies Annual*, 27 (1998), 69–96.

[10] F. B. Smith, 'Lights and Shadows in the Life of John Freeman', *Victorian Studies*, 30 (1997), 459–73.

[11] Dransfield, 'Reading the Gordon Riots', 82–9.

APPENDIX C

Dickens and Scott

MANY critics have pointed out that *Barnaby Rudge* seems to represent a bid by Dickens for literary respectability after the example of Scott's historical novels.[1] Sir Walter Scott (1771–1832), an international figure when he died in 1832, was widely perceived to have raised the novel into a serious art form dealing with national issues, but he had first come to literary notice as a collector of ballads with *Minstrelsy of the Scottish Border* (1802–3) and then as a poet in his own right with *The Lay of the Last Minstrel* (1805), *Marmion* (1808), *The Lady of the Lake* (1810), and a series of other verse narratives. Such was his success that he was able to enter into partnership in the bookselling business Ballantyne & Co. to sell his works, and in 1811 had a stately residence built for himself at Abbotsford on the Tweed. Only the emergence of Lord Byron a few years later eclipsed his success as a poet, but by this stage he was turning his attention to the novel as a means of treating important historical and national themes. The first of these, *Waverley; or 'Tis Sixty Years Since* was published anonymously in 1814. There followed a highly successful series dealing with Scottish history that have become known as the 'Waverley novels': the earliest of these were *Guy Mannering* (1815), *The Antiquary* (1816), *Rob Roy* (1817), and, perhaps the greatest, *The Heart of Midlothian* (1818). This last centred around the dramatic storming of the Tolbooth gaol in Edinburgh in 1736 that provided Dickens with an obvious source of inspiration for writing a novel on the Gordon Riots. Scott only revealed his identity as the author of the novels in 1827, although the secret had been known almost from the beginning. The previous year Ballantyne & Co. had been caught by a widespread economic crash, and as a partner in the firm Scott found himself liable for a huge debt. He took on a heavy workload of writing until his death to pay off the creditors of the firm. John Gibson Lockhart's *Memoirs of the Life of Sir Walter Scott* (1837–8) represented him as a martyr to the financial mismanagement (and perhaps worse) of others, as well as a great hero of British literature.

There is no doubt as to the admiration Dickens felt for Scott at this time. Dickens had married Catherine Hogarth in 1836. She was the daughter of his senior colleague on the *Morning Chronicle*, George Hogarth, and part of the attraction may have been the fact that the latter

---

[1] For a summary account of these responses, see John Bowen, *Other Dickens: Pickwick to Chuzzlewit* (Oxford: Oxford University Press, 2000), 162–3 n.

had been an associate of Scott's in Edinburgh. Dickens certainly boasted of and perhaps even exaggerated the connection at the time.[2] Soon after his marriage, Dickens was avidly reading each volume of Lockhart's *Life of Scott* as it came out. He wrote three anonymous letters to the *Examiner* over 1838–9 taking the side of Scott against his former publishers in the controversy that sprang up in the wake of Lockhart's biography. To Dickens, Scott was a 'giant' who worked himself to death saving 'pygmies' from the consequences of their own folly and error.[3] Even the various contractual negotiations Dickens fought through in the 1830s may have been intensified by his sense of the injustice of Scott's final years. Scott gave Dickens a deeper sense of the worth of a literary career, and the need for writers to have their rights of property in their writing protected. On his American journey of 1842, he reverted again and again to the example of Scott as evidence of the need for proper copyright legislation to protect authors. During the composition of *Barnaby Rudge*, he visited Scotland and was to his delight hailed as Scott's successor. He also played an active part in the campaign (1840–4) to have a monument to Scott erected in Edinburgh.

The influence of Scott is felt not just in the decision to write a historical novel, or in Dickens's idea of the literary career, but in the structure and themes of *Barnaby Rudge*. Dickens opens his novel with a precise reference to time and place 'sixty-six years ago' that recalls the 'sixty years since' of *Waverley*'s subtitle. Significant parts of the action recall *The Heart of Midlothian* (1818). The conception of Barnaby himself may owe something to Madge Wildfire, the madwoman in Scott's story. More generally, the handling of the transition from domestic matters to the larger national context of the Gordon Riots in *Barnaby Rudge* parallels similar transitions in the treatment of the Jacobite cause in *Waverley* and *Rob Roy* (1817).[4] Often in Scott's fiction larger national conflicts, especially those between Scotland and England, find resolution in a romance plot centred on a virtuous daughter whose love overcomes cultural and social differences. The role of Emma Haredale and Dolly Varden in *Barnaby Rudge* shows Dickens learning from novels such as *The Heart of Midlothian* in this respect. Plenty of other local factors in *Barnaby Rudge* can be traced back

[2] 'To T. C. Barrow, 31 March 1836' in *The Letters of Charles Dickens*, 12 vols. ed. Madeline House, Graham Storey, *et al.* (Oxford: Clarendon Press 1965–2002), i. 144.

[3] Quoted in Peter Ackroyd, *Dickens* (London: Sinclair-Stevenson, 1990), 272. The letters were originally published in the *Examiner*, 2 Sept. 1838, 31 March 1839, and 29 Sept. 1839.

[4] See Ian Duncan, *Modern Romance and Transformations of the Novel: The Gothic, Scott, Dickens* (Cambridge: Cambridge University Press, 1992), 229–35, for these and other parallels between characters, themes, and structure in Scott's novels and *Barnaby Rudge*.

to specific incidents or characters in Scott's novels. More fundamental, perhaps, is the question of whether they shared the same perception of the historical novel as a genre.

Critics such as Jack Lindsay have argued that Dickens 'was building on the ground that Scott had cleared with his strong sense of the dialectical interrelation of individual and society at a specific crisis-moment of national growth'.[5] More recent critics have pointed out deep dissimilarities beneath their conceptions of the historical novel and history itself, often returning to Georg Lukács's criticism that Dickens failed to convey 'the totality of social life, be it present or past'.[6] For all its reference to a specific era in the past, the positioning of Dickens's plot in terms of time and space is much vaguer than it is in Scott's novels. Nor does Dickens have the same interest as Scott in the detail of the social and political background to the public events he describes (see Appendix B). Scott is justly famous for his ability to represent historical process through details, character, and plot. Compared to the fanatical actions of Dickens's rioters, the attack on the Tolbooth in *The Heart of Midlothian* is represented by Scott as the result of a grievance with specific origins in the historical situation. Behind that grievance is the response of an entire people to a perceived injustice and the broader question of English power in Scotland. Whereas the grievances of the Scottish populace are taken seriously in Scott's novel, even if subsumed by larger historical developments, Sim's appeals to ancient custom are mocked as the products of ignorance and vanity in *Barnaby Rudge*. His interest in the ancient constitution is, like Ned Dennis's, more an occasion for comedy than the expression of socio-political disaffection. There is no attempt to explain, as Dickens might have done, Sim's nostalgia in terms of the constitutionalist language of radicalism at the time, nor trace its causes to the social situation of apprentices. Although Dickens blames various aspects of eighteenth-century English society for the Riots, he also represents them as manifestations of a universal propensity within the people that is exploited by the machinations of private individuals (such as Sir John Chester and Gashford). Of course, *Waverley* and *Barnaby Rudge* deal with events that were historically different in nature: the former was a more targeted and deliberate action, whereas the latter was an unstable and multi-faceted expression of popular rage.[7] Even so, the choice of events would seem to be significant. Scott chose incidents that allowed him to range broadly over

[5] Jack Lindsay, 'Barnaby Rudge', in John Gross and Gabriel Pearson (eds.), *Dickens and the Twentieth Century* (London: Routledge and Kegan Paul, 1962), 105.

[6] Georg Lukács, *The Historical Novel*, translated from the German by Hannah and Stanley Mitchell (Harmondsworth: Penguin, 1981), 290.

[7] See Alison Case, 'Against Scott: The Antihistory of Dickens's *Barnaby Rudge*', *Clio*, 19/2 (1990), 134.

issues of historical development informed by the theories of the Scottish Enlightenment on the relationship between historical change and socio-economic conditions. Dickens chose what looked in some respects more like a historical dead end. The Gordon Riots were widely regarded as proof of a tendency towards anarchy in the people that was always in danger of sparking to life. Of course, these differences do not necessarily mean that Dickens failed as a historical novelist. Rather, they illuminate the different perspectives Dickens and Scott had on history and the novel. Indeed, one might say that Dickens's attempt to affiliate himself to the memory of Scott had aspects of an oedipal struggle for literary authority.

Carlyle's accounts both of Chartism and the French Revolution contained their own version of the idea of an anarchic strain within the popular unconscious (see Introduction, p. x). In many ways the form of the historical novel that emerges in *Barnaby Rudge* is the result of a conflict between the influence of Carlyle – who wrote a critical review of Lockhart's *Life of Scott* – and Scott on Dickens, although neither exactly wins out.[8] The emphasis in Dickens on the private and domestic as a kind of sanctuary from history belongs to neither Carlyle nor Scott, and he shares little of the sense of historical process of either. The parallel between rebellion in the family and the rioters rebelling against the authority of the state is not a sustained one. Joe's leaving home is represented as a healthy natural development in a way that the novel suggests the Riots are not, although the domestic space is not quite so idealized in *Barnaby Rudge* as some critics suggest (see Introduction, p. xii). What is more certain is that 'the world of *Barnaby Rudge* totally lacks Scott's spacious solidity' and even the detail of Carlyle's *The French Revolution*.[9] Instead, it offers a vision of the relationship between the past and the future characterized more by haunting repetitions than by anything as coherent as either Scott's idea of development or Carlyle's more apocalyptic vision of history. Critics impressed by Lukács's praise of Scott are apt to see Dickens as a failed historical novelist in this refusal to deal with historical process, but it might be more accurate to say that the strain of Gothic in Dickens, while far from absent in Scott's writing, speaks of a conception of the relationship between the past and present as less predictable and more unstable than the latter's Enlightenment historicism could allow.[10]

[8] See Duncan, *Modern Romance*, 235.

[9] See S. J. Newman, '*Barnaby Rudge*: Dickens and Scott', in R. T. Davies and B. G. Beatty (eds.), *Literature of the Romantic Period, 1750–1850* (Liverpool: Liverpool University Press, 1976), 174.

[10] On the Gothic in Scott, see Duncan, *Modern Romance* and Fiona Robertson, *Legitimate Histories: Scott, Gothic, and the Authorities of Fiction* (Oxford: Oxford University Press, 1994).

EXPLANATORY NOTES

Written for the publication of *Barnaby Rudge* as a single volume in 1841. It was first published in the final number of *Master Humphrey's Clock*, 4 December 1841. For the dates of the original publication of the sequence of chapters in *Master Humphrey's Clock*, see Appendix C in the Oxford World Classics edition of *The Old Curiosity Shop*.

3 *Mr. Dennis's allusions to the flourishing condition of his trade*: Edward Dennis was the public hangman at the time of the events described by Dickens. The hangman was kept busy in England. Although not all those convicted of capital offences were actually hanged, around 190 capital offences had been added to the statute book between 1660 and 1820, making it a 'Bloody Code' indeed. During the 1840s Dickens became involved in the debate about the abolition of capital punishment. To an extent, *Barnaby Rudge* represents one of his contributions, but by the end of the decade his position had changed from one of outright opposition to one more concerned with the effects of public executions of the sort described in *Barnaby*. By the end of his life, he had dropped his opposition to hanging entirely. See 'Capital Punishment' in Paul Schlicke (ed.), *Oxford Reader's Companion to Dickens* (Oxford: Oxford University Press, 1999), 66–7.

the case of Mary Jones: Dennis discusses Mary Jones's case at p. 301. Dickens also elaborated on it in his Preface of 1849; see pp. 7–8.

4 *Sir Samuel Romilly*: (1757–1818), the son of a Huguenot refugee, politician and legal reformer who campaigned for the reduction of the number of capital offences. He published his *Thoughts on Executive Justice* in 1786 and on becoming Solicitor-General and an MP in 1806 took up his campaign in Parliament. In 1808 Parliament passed his Bill (48 Geo. III, c. 129) repealing the Elizabethan statute which had made pickpocketing a capital offence. Other successes followed.

Dickens revised the 1841 Preface for a new single volume edition published in 1849. See the 'Note on the Text' of the present volume for further details of the publishing history.

5 *Mr Waterton's opinion*: Dickens is referring to the essay on 'The Raven' in Charles Waterton's *Essays on Natural History* (1838).

as Sir Hugh Evans says of Anne Page: a reference to characters from Shakespeare's *The Merry Wives of Windsor*, I, i: 'I know the young gentlewoman; she has good gifts.'

7 *Sir William Meredith*: (died 1790), MP from 1754 to 1780 and Lord of the Admiralty in Rockingham's ministry in 1765; he was not only an advocate for the reduction of capital offences but also argued for religious toleration.

Shop-lifting Act: an Act of 1699 (10 and 11 Wm III, c. 23) which made it a capital offence to steal goods from a shop worth five shillings or more.

the alarm about Falkland Islands: on 10 June 1770 the Spanish had seized the British fort of Port Egmont, garrisoned since 1765.

pressed: as a means of providing sufficient men, the Admiralty employed press-gangs, whose task was to 'press' men into the navy. Separated from their families and dependants for years at sea, they often experienced difficulties in sending sufficient portions of their wages home. The Falklands crisis had resulted in a new Act—the Comprehending or Impressing Act (18 Geo. III, c. 53). The impress lasted from 22 September 1770 to 22 February 1771 by which time fifty-five ships were two-thirds filled. The impressment caused a flurry of pamphlets opposing its use. See J. S. Bromley (ed.), *The Manning of the Royal Navy* (London: Naval Records Society, 1974).

8 *Tyburn*: notorious site for public executions in London until 1783. Prisoners were led through the streets from Newgate prison to the gallows, also known as the 'Tyburn Tree' (see Map). The gallows consisted of a triangle supported on three legs, enabling the simultaneous execution of three convicts. On the eight annual hanging days, public stands were erected. Apprentices were given the day off. See discussion in Peter Linebaugh, 'The Tyburn Riot against the Surgeons', in Douglas Hay *et al.*, *Albion's Fatal Tree* (Harmondsworth: Penguin, 1975).

BARNABY RUDGE

9 *the Standard in Cornhill*: an old water conduit on Cornhill at the junction with Leadenhall Street in central London. Built in 1582 to bring water from the Thames, it had four spouts operating every tide. No longer operating by the eighteenth century, it had become the point from which distances were measured in London and the surrounding counties.

12 *Life Guardsmen*: a bodyguard of soldiers in the British Army, who, with the Horse Guards, form the household cavalry. The Guards were the only regiments explicitly detailed for riot duty in London.

13 *Chigwell*: a village approximately 12 miles north-east of London in Epping Forest. Dating from primeval times, it had many hornbeams, bogs of sphagnum and rarely used grassy tracks.

15 *the Warren*: also the name of the Blacking Factory, where, traumatically for him, Dickens was sent to work as a 12-year-old, due to the financial problems faced by his parents. See 'Warren's Blacking', in Schlicke, *Oxford Reader's Companion*, 585.

23 *corpse candles*: 'a lambent flame seen in a churchyard or over a grave, and superstitiously believed to appear as an omen of death, or to indicate the route of a coming funeral' (*OED*).

27 *ride the whirlwind and direct the storm*: a quotation from Joseph Addison's *The Campaign*. (1705): 'And, pleased th' Almighty's orders to perform, | Rides in the whirl-wind, and directs the storm.'

28 *bob-wig*: a wig with its ends turned up into bobs or curls.

33 *mumchance*: silent or tongue-tied (*OED*).

36 *the Great Mogul*: common name in England for the emperor of Delhi, who ruled over most of Hindustan until dethroned by the British in 1857.

38 *light guinea*: the guinea was a gold coin minted between 1663 and 1813. Its value of 21 shillings (£1.05) was fixed in 1717. A 'light' guinea weighed less than the legal weight, probably from friction applied deliberately. For an account of 'Yorkshire guineas' and their recall for reminting in the 1770s, see John Styles, 'Our Traitorous Moneymakers', in John Brewer and John Styles (eds.), *An Ungovernable People* (London: Hutchinson, 1980).

39 *Clerkenwell*: a suburb of London (see Map) populated by craftsmen and merchants *c.*1775, especially notable for its jewellers and clockmakers. Slums, however, engulfed the area. By 1841 it was no longer genteel and respectable.

Charter House: located on a site to the north of the City of London close to Clerkenwell, its origins lie in Carthusian monastic foundations of the fourteenth century. By the eighteenth century the Charterhouse had become a school noted for its literary education; its former pupils included Addison, Blackstone, Steele, and Thackeray.

40 *six-and-sixty years ago*: writing in 1841, Dickens is describing events *c.*1775.

streets connecting Highgate with Whitechapel: Dickens here shows his extensive knowledge of London and its growth in the period between the 1770s and the 1830s. He is specifically referring to the streets and sub-urbs which sprang up to connect Whitechapel, an area to the east of the City, and Highgate, a suburb which used to be a village on the northern heights of London.

New River: a channel created by the New River Company in the seven-teenth century, which brought water (38 miles) from Hertfordshire to reservoirs in North London. It became a key water supply, and the New River Head at Islington became a target for the rioters because of its importance in quenching the fires they had started. See p. 533.

44 *Prometheus*: in Greek mythology a demigod, who, for stealing fire from Olympus and teaching men how to use it, was chained by Zeus to a rock in the Caucasus. His liver was preyed upon daily by a vulture.

44 *George Barnwell*: an allusion to George Lillo's play *The History of George Barnwell, or The London Merchant* (1731). The play is a tragedy centred upon George Barnwell, a young apprentice who is seduced and then betrayed by a wily courtesan, Millwood. She convinces him to steal money from his employer, and then murder his wealthy uncle. She eventually betrays him, and just as he is to be executed, the daughter of Barnwell's employer visits him, revealing that she has loved him all along. Dickens saw this play as a child.

a certain Lion Heart: an (ironic) allusion to the strength and courage attributed to a well-known icon of English history, Richard I.

46 *Carlisle House*: a popular venue for balls, masquerades, and concerts in this period. Run by the Austrian opera singer and courtesan, Theresa Cornelys, until she was declared bankrupt in 1772.

domino: a loose cloak, chiefly worn at masquerades, 'with a small mask covering the upper part of the face, by persons not personating a character' (*OED*).

Toby: a jug in the form of a rotund little man wearing a three-cornered hat.

48 *Protestant Manual . . . post octavo*: its full title was *The Protestant Manual of Christian Devotions, composed of instructions, offices, and forms of prayer, in a plain, rational and scriptural method, etc.* Published in London in 1750 in two parts, it was the official organ of the Protestant Association. Post-octavo refers to the size of the paper. It was octavo as each sheet had been folded and bound into the book to make eight leaves. Hablot K. Browne depicted it in his illustration (see Illus. 27 'Mr. Chester with Mrs. Varden'). As Dennis Walder points out in his *Dickens and Religion* (London: Allen and Unwin, 1981, 97), Browne has, with a touch of irony, portrayed Chester pointing it towards a picture of the Holy Family.

50 *a by-street in Southwark, not far from London Bridge*: Southwark (see Map) was a locality on the south bank of the Thames, a mixture of respectable households, 'criminal' dens, and industries including tanneries and breweries as well as being home to weavers, printers, soap- and candle-makers. The Rudges' lodgings, though humble, were respectable.

64 *Macbeth*: an allusion to Macbeth's question in *Macbeth*, ii. iii: 'Who can be wise, amaz'd, temperate, and furious, | Loyal, and neutral, in a moment?'

triple bob major: one of the changes in bell-ringing. A change consists of a set of bells rung in a fixed sequence. A bob minor is rung on six bells, a bob major on eight bells. The treble bob is a method in which the bells have a dodging course. Dickens uses this as a metaphor for Mrs Varden's changeable temper.

65 *pattens*: overshoes or sandals designed to raise ordinary shoes out of the mud or wet. Also a figurative term for making a great clatter, especially of the tongue.

69 *smalls*: small clothes, knee breeches (*OED*).

70 *Barbican*: a street running east between Aldersgate Street and Red Cross Street. An easy walk from Varden's house in Clerkenwell.

72 *usquebaugh*: the Irish Gaelic word for whiskey (*uisge beatha*), from which the English is derived.

73 *Atlas-wise*: in Greek mythology, Atlas was the brother of Prometheus. When he rebelled against Zeus, he was condemned to bear the world on his back. In sculpture, he is depicted on one knee with the globe on his shoulders.

74 *bag-wig*: a kind of wig fashionable in the eighteenth century, 'the back-hair of which was enclosed in an ornamental bag' (*OED*).

75 *marry her at the Fleet*: until the passage of Hardwicke's Marriage Act in 1753, clergymen in the Fleet Prison performed clandestine marriages for a fee. The term had notorious associations with the seduction or abduction of young heiresses. Thereafter, Gretna Green became the destination for couples who wished to marry without their parents' consent.

76 *the court of aldermen*: the court of aldermen was one constituent part of the governance of the City of London, and was drawn largely from the merchant classes.

Temple Bar: a well-known gate of the City of London, marking the City of London's western boundary on Fleet Street. It was decorated with statues of James I, Charles I, and Charles II—a tempting trio for disfigurement.

79 *Fleet Market*: a food market located on the site of the former Fleet Ditch between Fleet Street and Holborn, which was bridged for the purpose of this market in the 1730s. The whole Fleet Ditch area was notorious for its criminal associations.

81 *henbane*: a drug extracted from a plant of the same name. Dickens used this to treat pain.

86 *fire-dogs*: a pair of iron or brass fittings on either side of the fireplace to support the logs of wood for the fire or to rest the fire-irons upon.

splatterdashes: long gaiters or leggings to prevent trousers or stockings from being splattered (*OED*).

89 *standish*: a stand containing ink, pens, and other writing materials (*OED*).

96 *flip*: a mixture of beer and spirit sweetened with sugar and heated with a hot iron (*OED*).

98 *passing bad Notes*: as credit facilities expanded in the eighteenth century, so too did the number of statutes dealing with counterfeiting coins and notes. Counterfeiting was seen as treason as it attacked the royal monopoly over currency.

110 *quarter-days*: customary days for payment of rents to landlords and for settling accounts. Quarter-days in England are Lady Day (25 March),

Midsummer Day (24 June), Michaelmas (29 September), and Christmas (25 December).

117 *the chair that was ordered for her*: a mode of hired transport; a sedan chair carried on poles by two men.

119 *poussetting*: to dance as a couple with hands joined (*OED*). This meant more intimacy than was customary in dances at the time.

120 *travelling post*: travelling post-haste, travelling with all possible speed, the speed of the post.

125 *dun-haunted*: haunted by debt and creditors (*OED*).

the Temple ... the Strand or Fleet Street ... Fountain Court ... Paper Buildings ... Temple Gardens: the Temple consists of the Inner and Middle Temples, two of the four Inns of Court. Inside the confines of the Inner Temple are the Temple Gardens and the Paper Buildings, while Fountain Court is located within Middle Temple.

128 *Valentine and Orson*: heroes of an early French romance. The twin sons of Bellisant, sister of King Pepin and wife of Alexander, emperor of Constantinople, they were separated at birth, one being raised as a wild animal (Orson), and the other as a knight (Valentine). The two met in later life.

centaurs: mythical creatures from classical mythology that were half-human and half-horse and thus opposed to the values of social order. See Iain Crawford, 'Dickens, Classical Myth and the Representation of Social Order in *Barnaby Rudge*', *Dickensian*, 93/3 (1997), 185–97.

134 *fee a link-boy*: pay a boy to carry a link or a torch to light the way for pedestrians along the dark streets.

136 *hooped and furbelowed*: wearing a skirt expanded with hoops and often somewhat ostentatiously ornamented with flounces or trimming (*OED*).

drums: fashionable and noisy evening parties, often with several tables for cards.

quadrille: a card game played by four people with forty cards (*OED*), not to be confused with the early nineteenth-century dance formation.

Public Progress ... to Tyburn: the route to Tyburn (see n. to p. 8) went from Newgate through the densely populated parishes of St. Giles and St. Andrew's, Holborn, along Oxford Street to Tyburn (see Map). See V. A. C. Gatrell, *The Hanging Tree: Execution and the English People 1770–1868* (Oxford: Oxford University Press, 1994), 32–3 for an account of the Progress.

the ordinary: the chaplain of Newgate prison. He prepared condemned prisoners for death. From 1774 until he died in office in 1799, the incumbent was John Villette. He wrote a considerable number of the accounts of the convicted felons' last thoughts as well as editing a four-volume collection entitled *The Malefactors' Register: Or the Annals of Newgate* published in 1776. For the financial rewards of this post, see Peter

Linebaugh, 'The Ordinary of Newgate and his Account' in J. S. Cockburn (ed.), *Crime in England, 1550–1800* (London: Methuen, 1977).

137 *they who dealt in bodies with the surgeons*: with the creation of more medical schools in the eighteenth century and the changed methods of teaching anatomy, there was an increased demand for bodies to dissect. Following the Murder Act of 1752, agents such as sheriff's officers and the hangman were permitted to take the bodies from the gallows for this purpose. See Linebaugh, 'The Tyburn Riot', 70–6.

155 *like love among the roses*: according to T. W. Hill, 'Notes on *Barnaby Rudge*', in *Dickensian*, 51 (1955), 139, this is from a ballad by J. C. Doyle; the author of the words is unknown: 'Young Love flew to the Paphian bower . . . | The Graces there were cutting posies, | And found young Love among the roses.'

159 *hartshorning*: offering smelling salts. Hartshorn is a solution of ammonia.

161 *Gretna Green*: a town just over the border in Scotland, where couples fled to marry in order to avoid the English Marriage Act of 1753. This act required that a marriage had to be performed by a clergyman in a building licensed for the purpose, and contracted by licence or by the reading of banns. In Scotland, marriage merely required a mutual declaration of consent and two witnesses.

164 *whose foster-sister she was*: possibly Dolly's mother had looked after Emma after her mother's death, perhaps even acting as wet-nurse, making the girls stepsisters in a loose sense, and accounting for their closeness throughout the novel.

165 *crossed afterwards*: letter-writers were in the habit of writing horizontally across the paper and then vertically, to save money before the Penny Post (for letters under 4 ounces) was extended to all of the United Kingdom in 1840. Until then, the recipient of a letter paid postage according to its weight, unless resident within a 10-mile radius of the City of London.

176 *Mussulman*: obsolete form of Muslim.

wild Islander: published accounts of the newly explored areas of the Pacific were very popular in England at this time. These journals included illustrations of the flora and fauna as well as the indigenous inhabitants. Islanders were even brought to London to be fêted, such as Omai who arrived in England in 1774, the year before the events in the first part of *Barnaby Rudge*. See National Library of Australia, *Cook & Omai: The Cult of the South Seas* (Parkes, Australia: National Library of Australia, 2001; exhibition catalogue).

178 *missionaries in foreign parts*: the evangelical revival of the late eighteenth century in Britain coupled with British maritime expansion enabled the expansion of missionary activities in the newly explored areas.

179 *over the Monument and the top of Saint Paul's in love*: two of the highest features of London's Georgian skyline. The Monument, designed by Sir Christopher Wren, was erected in 1671–7 to mark the site of the outbreak

of the Great Fire of London, 'begun and carried on by ye popish factors' according to the inscription. St Paul's Cathedral was a well-known landmark with a magnificent dome towering over the city.

187 *Lord Chesterfield*: the 4th Earl of Chesterfield (1694–1773) was the author of the book being read by Chester, *Letters written by the late Right Honourable Philip Dormer Stanhope, Earl of Chesterfield to his Son, Philip Stanhope, Esq.; late Envoy Extraordinary at the Court of Dresden*. Chesterfield had begun writing letters to his illegitimate son (then aged 5) from 1737 until his son's death in 1768. Published posthumously in 1774 (the year before these events), they contained advice on manners and behaviour in elegant society. So popular were they that the book reached its fifth edition within a year, but by Dickens's time the book had become a byword for the hypocrisy and sterility of eighteenth-century aristocratic culture. Chester's name invokes these nineteenth-century associations.

197 *Gunpowder Plot*: a plot to blow up the Houses of Parliament by a group of Roman Catholic conspirators on 5 November 1605. The plot was discovered on 4 November, and the conspirators, including Guy Fawkes, were executed.

198 *E.C.*: as Chester's name was John, this is either a mistake on the part of Tappertit or Dickens. Possibly he is meant to be wearing his son's cap.

213 *hackney-coach*: a four-wheeled coach for hire, drawn by two horses, and able to seat six people.

215 *hipped*: to be affected with hypochondria, depressed or low-spirited (*OED*).

219 *we never know the full value of some wines and fig-trees till we lose 'em*: a reference to Zechariah 3: 10, 'shall ye call every man his neighbour under the vine and under the fig-tree.'

   she were Hope and that her Anchor: a reference to Hebrews 6: 19, '[W]hich *hope* we have as an anchor of the soul, both sure and steadfast, and which entereth into that within the veil.'

238 *apostrophising the air*: a rhetorical flourish. He addresses the air in an exclamatory manner.

242 *having an inch . . . take an ell*: a proverb using measurements now obsolete. An English ell was 45 inches.

   Flemish ell: a Flemish ell was shorter than an English one, being 27 inches.

   Yards, furlongs, miles: imperial measurements used before metrification. There were 1,760 yards to the mile and 8 furlongs to the mile.

250 *very little wool*: a variation on the proverb, 'Much cry, little wool' according to Hill, 'Notes on *Barnaby Rudge*', 136.

253 *since the time of noble Whittington*: a popular legend concerning the merchant Richard Whittington (d. 1423) recounted that when in Highgate on his departure from London voices in the bells entreated him to

return to seek his fortune. He later held the London mayoralty three times. The place commemorating this legend has been marked by a stone for many centuries.

Fortunatus: hero of a medieval legend who has an inexhaustible purse which constantly contained the same amount despite money being drawn from it. The story, which appeared in a German *Volksbuch* of 1509, was dramatised by Sachs in 1553 and by Dekker in *Pleasant Comedy of Old Fortunatus* (1599).

266 *indited*: to compose, to put into words, especially as in a literary composition (*OED*).

275 *swing it like a censer*: a censer is a vessel that dispenses incense at Mass. The word is a reminder to the reader of Haredale's Catholic religion.

279 *tagrag and bobtail*: the common herd or the rabble (*OED*).

280 *John Grueby*: this character is based on the historical figure of John M'Queen, manservant to Lord George Gordon.

Lord George Gordon: born in 1751, he was the third son of the 3rd Duke of Gordon. As President of the London Protestant Association, he led the campaign against the Catholic Relief Act (1778). See Robert Kent Donovan, *No Popery and Radicalism: Opposition to Roman Catholic Relief in Scotland, 1778–1782* (New York: Garland, 1987), 241–8 and Appendix A of the present volume.

Bloody Mary: Mary Tudor, Queen of England (1553–8), daughter of Henry VIII (d. 1547) and successor to her brother, Edward VI, during whose reign the Protestant Reformation had become entrenched in England. Mary re-introduced Catholicism, burning heretics at the stake. This made her the bogey-woman of the Protestant Association. See Colin Haydon, *Anti-Catholicism in Eighteenth-Century England, c.1714–80: A Political and Social Study* (Manchester: Manchester University Press, 1993), 210.

281 *Gashford*: see the Introduction and Appendix B for a discussion of the extent to which Gashford is based on the historical figure Robert Watson, biographer of Lord George, who claimed to have been his secretary during the time of the Riots.

282 *single-stick*: 'fighting, fencing, or exercise with a stick provided with a guard or basket and requiring only one hand' (*OED*).

285 *blue cockade*: cockades were worn in the hat as an indicator of party affiliation. Blue had been adopted by the Scottish Presbyterian Covenanters in the seventeenth century, a group with whom Gordon identified. Blue was also the colour of conservatism, conserving the Protestant religion. Provided by the Protestant Association, the cockades were made by Washington & Wharton, milliners, of 100 Salisbury Court, Fleet Street. By Wednesday, 7 June, those still wearing them were liable to arrest as an enemy of the peace.

286 *men across the Scottish border*: the English Catholic Relief Bill of 1778 was

to be followed by similar bills for Scotland and Ireland. However, Scots hostility to this was such that riots broke out in Glasgow and Edinburgh. Gordon's speech in support for the Protestant position in the House of Commons in May 1779 resulted in his election to the presidency of the Scottish Protestant Association.

286 *shall never be repealed*: Dickens altered the historical situation to suit his own ends. The Catholic Relief Bill actually came into effect on 3 June 1778, and the Gordon Riots were aimed at securing its repeal. Roman Catholics in England suffered various civil disabilities as a result of Acts of 1699 and 1700 (11 and 12 William III, c. 4) which among other prohibitions prevented them from inheriting or purchasing land, and receiving a Catholic education.

287 *refused a minister's bribe*: Lord North had offered a sinecure worth £1,000 p.a. to the Duke of Gordon if he could persuade his brother to resign his seat in Parliament. This was revealed by Lord George in the Commons on 13 April 1778.

Called and chosen and faithful: an allusion to Revelation 17: 14: 'These shall make war with the Lamb, and the Lamb shall overcome them: for he is Lord of lords, and King of kings: and they that are with him *are* called, and chosen, and faithful.' However, this is not the Gordon hereditary family motto; that is *animo non astutia* (by courage not craft).

Puritan's demeanour: Gordon looked to the tradition of the seventeenth-century Puritans who abhorred any suggestion of Catholic ritual or theology in the practices and beliefs of the Established Churches of both England and Scotland. This included wearing plain, even severe, clothing as opposed to the flamboyance associated with the Royalist costume in the Civil War period.

288 *Protestant associations*: the Association in London was founded in February 1779 to procure the repeal of the 1778 Catholic Relief Act. On 12 November, Lord George was offered the presidency to add to his presidency of the Scottish Association. The Association was revived as a consequence of the furore surrounding Catholic Emancipation in 1829. For details, see Walder, *Dickens and Religion*, 94–6.

290 *manna in the wilderness*: an allusion to Exodus 16, where God promises bread ('manna') to the children of Israel after their departure from Egypt.

Bedlam: the popular abbreviation of the Hospital of St Mary of Bethlehem, an asylum for the insane in London. Located in Moorfields between 1676 and 1814 (or 15), to the north of the Bank of England and the Mansion House, it occupied a curious place in the life of eighteenth-century London as an attraction for sightseers, who came to gaze at the inmates.

Dennis the hangman: an historical figure, Edward Dennis was the hangman at Newgate prison. He took part in the Gordon Riots and was found guilty for his role in the attack on the Ship Alehouse in Turnstile, Gate Street. He was saved from hanging two days after his sentencing, as his professional services were needed to hang the other condemned prisoners. See Horace Bleackley, *The Hangmen of England* (London: Chapman and Hall, 1929).

291 *A malignant*: the term attached to supporters of Charles I by parliamentarians during the English Civil War.

292 *dangerous confederacy of Popish powers*: the traditional enemies of England —France (in 1778) and Spain (in 1780)—had entered the American War of Independence on the American side. Since these countries were Catholic, English Catholics were suspected of divided loyalties.

294 *Smithfield market*: an ancient horse, cattle, and meat market, also used as a site for public executions. It was especially notorious for the execution of heretics during Queen Mary's reign.

295 *successful disturbances . . . in Scotland*: riots in Edinburgh and Glasgow in February 1779 had destroyed much Catholic property and had succeeded in preventing the extension of the 1778 Catholic Relief Act to Scotland. See n. to p. 286.

299 *Whitechapel, Leadenhall Street, and Cheapside, and into St Paul's Churchyard . . . the Strand . . . Oxford-road . . . to his house in Welbeck-street, near Cavendish-square*: Gordon and his entourage traversed the greater part of central London from the eastern end, across the centre of the City, to the west. Gordon's house in Welbeck Street was in a fashionable upper-class residential area, reflecting his aristocratic background.

pitch and toss . . . other Protestant recreations: as these are all betting games and therefore abhorrent to the Puritan tradition, the use of the word 'Protestant' is ironical.

301 *half for myself*: one way to meet the enlistment shortfall for the American War was to recruit criminals. Upon enlistment, many criminals were pardoned.

Mary Jones: see note to Preface, p. 3. Mary Jones was hanged by Dennis on 16 October 1771.

we've been going down hill ever since: by the time Dickens wrote *Barnaby Rudge*, there were only 8 capital offences left on the statute books, whereas in 1800 there had been over 200 offences. Growing opposition to the death penalty for minor property crimes and concern about the arbitrary operation of pardons had resulted in new approaches to punishment, for example, solitary confinement with hard labour in long-term prisons (the Penitentiary Act of 1779). For a discussion of the new approaches, see J. M. Beattie, *Crime and the Courts in England 1660–1800* (Oxford: Oxford University Press, 1986). Dickens was deeply involved in continuing debates about crime and punishment from the 1830s. The fullest discussion is to be found in Philip Collins, *Dickens and Crime* 3rd edn. (Basingstoke and London: Macmillan, 1994).

308 *the Boot*: this was an actual inn in Lamb's Conduit Fields.

the Foundling Hospital: granted a Royal Charter in 1739, it was set up by the childless Captain Thomas Coram for the care of abandoned babies. Artists such as Hogarth and musicians such as Handel contributed to its upkeep through benefit exhibitions and concerts.

311 *the Lobby*: the large room or entrance hall to the House of Commons where Members of Parliament mix, meet with their constituents, and receive petitions from the public.

312 *seven-shilling piece*: a coin worth one-third of a guinea (21 shillings) but as it was not issued until 1797, Dickens is anachronistic. For guinea, see note to p. 38.

315 *Chronicle*: Dickens had worked as a parliamentary and political reporter for the *Morning Chronicle*.

The Thunderer: this was an actual pamphlet, the printer of which was arrested. According to Rice, Dickens is having a joke against *The Times*. The latter, known as the Thunderer, only began publishing in 1785, but was well known for its campaign against radicals. See Thomas J. Rice, *Barnaby Rudge: An Annotated Bibliography* (New York: Garland, 1987), 91–2.

318 *Old Bailey*: a Court of Sessions that had exercised criminal jurisdiction over London for centuries. It was located near Newgate Prison.

319 *Saint Dunstan's giants*: two giant figures that struck the hours and quarters on the clock at the church of St Dunstan (demolished 1829).

321 *close borough*: a pocket borough; an electorate controlled by a local land-owner through scrutiny of voting at the public ballot. Secret voting was not introduced until 1872. Once Chester became an MP, he could not be pursued for debt.

Insolvent Act: in the 1770s Parliament had passed a series of Temporary Relief or Insolvency Acts. As an alternative to prison, debtors made themselves temporarily insolvent, provided a schedule of their assets (apart from land or future earnings) which the creditors proceeded against in payment of the debt. This is how John Dickens obtained his release from the Marshalsea Debtors' Prison in 1824. For an account of a debtors' prison, see Joanna Innes, 'The King's Bench Prison in the Late Eighteenth Century' in Brewer and Styles, *An Ungovernable People*, 353–4.

322 *Bruin*: a generic term for bear, drawn from the bear in the medieval epic, *Reynard the Fox*; also an oblique allusion to Butler's *Hudibras* (1663, 1664, and 1678), a burlesque poem satirizing the excesses and hypocrisies of Puritanism in the Civil War period. In the bear-baiting scene of Part I, Bruin is one of the leaders arrayed against the hero Sir Hudibras, a Puritan knight.

324 *Saville, who introduces their bill*: Sir George Savile (1726–84) introduced the Catholic Relief Bill (18 Geo. II, c. 60) in the House of Commons on

15 May 1778; that is, before the events described here. It passed through all three readings in the two Houses in a fortnight without a single division. The Royal Consent was given on 3 June. See Robert Kent Donovan, 'The Military Origins of the Catholic Relief Programme of 1778', *Historical Journal*, 28/1 (1985), 87, for a discussion of his motivation.

327 *Royal East-London Volunteers*: perhaps based on one of the volunteer units which emerged in Westminster and Middlesex as a response to the American emergency in 1779, but this unit seems to be an invention. The London Military Association offered assistance on 7 June and was on duty by the evening. See Stephen Conway, *The British Isles and the War of American Independence* (Oxford: Oxford University Press, 2000), 22–3.

330 *Blue Beard*: a popular fairy-tale, retold in Charles Perrault's *Histoires et Contes du Temps Passé* (1697). In an oriental setting, Blue Beard has had several wives who have all disappeared mysteriously. His newest wife, when entrusted with the key to a room which she is told never to enter, is overcome by curiosity. In the room she finds the bodies of his previous wives. After she drops the key in fright, it is stained with blood, revealing her act to Blue Beard on his return. She is narrowly saved from death by her brothers.

331 *counterfeit presentment*: from *Hamlet*, III. iv: 'Look here upon this picture, and on this, | The counterfeit presentment of two brothers.'

336 *Chelsea Bun-house*: located on Jew's Road, Pimlico, the Chelsea Bun House was renowned during the eighteenth century for its fine buns, counting several members of the royal family among its customers.

342 *Vauxhall*: at this time a relatively quiet precinct of London on the south bank of the Thames. Haredale travelled by water (north and east) along the Thames to London Bridge from Westminster, to avoid the danger of recognition.

Westminster Hall into Palace Yard: Westminster Hall was part of the Palace of Westminster, the location of the Houses of Parliament. George Cattermole has captured the gothic arches of the entrance porch to the medieval hall in his illustration 'The Greeting' (Illus. 41) New Palace Yard lay next to it, allowing Haredale access to the Westminster Stairs, from where he could be ferried along the river by the boatmen.

346 *seminary at St. Omer's*: the Jesuits had established a seminary in 1593 at Saint-Omer in France to provide an education for English Catholic boys forbidden to them by the Penal Laws.

349 *must hold my property . . . by a trick at which the state connives*: a provision of the Catholic Relief Act (1778) allowed Catholics who took the new oath of allegiance to inherit or legally purchase land. Before then, Catholics had to find ways round this Penal Law in order to keep hold of their land.

352 *Life Guards*: see n. to p. 12.

353 *Parliament Street, past Saint Martin's church ... Saint Giles's to Tottenham Court Road ... the Green Lanes*: this journey took them north from the Houses of Parliament to Green Lanes, through areas such as St Giles's that were notorious for their 'criminal' or underclass inhabitants (see Map).

355 *No, by the Lord Harry*: an eighteenth-century expletive. The Lord Harry or Old Harry was the Devil.

374 *whipping-post*: under the Vagrant Act of 1744 (17 Geo. II, c. 5, s. 6) rogues and vagabonds were liable to whipping as well as six months' detention. The whippings were carried out at a post in a public place.

375 *county institutions*: the poor were deemed the responsibility of the parish and supported out of the rates. Those who did not receive outdoor relief (abolished in 1834 by the Poor Law Amendment Act) were put into the parish workhouse. This also housed the insane and feeble-minded.

380 *second of June*: although this does not tally with other indications in the text about the length of their journey, Dickens has Mrs Rudge and Barnaby arriving on the actual day of the beginning of the historical sequence of events.

381 *gave them the wall*: to leave the wall side of the pavement free where it was safer and less liable to mud-splattering.

382 *forty thousand good and true men*: the Protestant Association met on 29 May and decided to assemble in St George's Fields on 2 June. Lord George resolved not to present the Petition to Parliament unless 20,000 turned up. He also moved that 'they should arrange themselves in four divisions' and 'to know their friends from their enemies each real Protestant and friend of the Petition should come with a blue cockade in his hat'. See J. Paul de Castro, *The Gordon Riots* (London: Oxford University Press, 1926), 25 for the text of the resolution and public announcement of the meeting.

383 *Saint George's Fields*: a large open area on the south side of the Thames, often used for large meetings and gatherings in the eighteenth century. The fields largely disappeared as urban development spread in the nineteenth century. Ironically, the area where Gordon addressed the crowd is now the site of the Roman Catholic St George's Cathedral.

389 *The mob had been divided ... the London, the Westminster, the Southwark and the Scotch*: see note to p. 382 above. These four divisions were specified in the announcement of the meeting in the *Public Advertiser* on 31 May, 1 June, and 2 June.

390 *Westminster Bridge*: one of three bridges across the Thames in central London built by 1780, the Westminster Bridge joined Westminster with Lambeth and was the most direct route to the Houses of Parliament from St George's Fields.

Blackfriars: Blackfriars Bridge was London's third bridge across the

Thames, completed in 1769. It joined the area surrounding the Fleet Ditch in the City of London to Southwark.

London Bridge: the oldest bridge was London Bridge. The third group had the longest route to the Houses of Parliament and therefore picked up stragglers and ne'er-do-wells along the way. It was led by Alderman Frederick Bull, a tea merchant hostile to the American War. A former Lord Mayor, he was also MP for the City. In the House of Commons later that day he seconded Gordon's motion to present the Petition. Also at its head was the informer, William Paine or Payne, who had lost his income when the Catholic Relief Act of 1778 abolished the £100 reward for prosecution of priests. That this had been quite lucrative is shown by figures given for 1767 by E. R. Norman, *Roman Catholics in England* (Oxford: Oxford University Press, 1985), 54, who says Payne initiated cases against fifteen priests and four Catholic schoolteachers.

393 *worst conceivable police*: the London Metropolitan Police was not established until 1829. Until then, unpaid, untrained parish constables, chosen annually by the parish vestry, policed each parish. The Fielding brothers, successive magistrates at Bow Street from 1749 to 1780, pioneered the establishment of a public office manned by paid constables. This was extended to seven other districts in London with the passing of the Middlesex Justices Act in 1792 (32 Geo. III, c. 53). See David Phillips, 'A New Engine of Power and Authority: The Institutionalization of Law-Enforcement in England, 1780–1830', in V. A. C. Gatrell *et al.* (eds.), *Crime and the Law: The Social History of Crime in Western Europe since 1500* (1980), 155–90. Dickens was critical of the older forms of policing, including the Bow Street Runners, and retained an enthusiasm for the Metropolitan Police and their new methods throughout his life, lauding them both in his journalism and novels, and even accompanying the detective police on patrol in the 1850s. For details see Collins, *Dickens and Crime*, ch. IX.

a porter's knot: a kind of shoulder-pad used by London market-porters for carrying burdens (*OED*).

394 *before the Speaker went to prayers*: every sitting of the House of Commons begins with the Speaker's chaplain reciting prayers. Gordon had obviously taken his seat prior to the beginning of the session. The Speaker from 1770 to October 1780 was Sir Fletcher Norton (1716–89).

stranger's gallery: the strangers' gallery, open to the public, allowed interested parties to watch the business of the House.

fugleman: one who serves or leads as an example, or who provides signals to followers.

395 *General Conway*: Henry Seymour Conway (1721–95) had a dual political and military career. His post as governor and captain of Jersey required his frequent absence from Parliament to defend the island against French invasion. However, he was present in May to introduce a bill for the

pacification of the American colonies and for these June events. Dickens
has based this exchange on Conway's actual words.

396 *Colonel Gordon*: Lord Adam Gordon (1726–1801) and fourth son of the
2nd Duke of Gordon (who was Catholic), was a kinsman of Lord George,
son of the 3rd Duke. He and his siblings had been reared as Protestants
by their mother. Joining the army after Culloden, he had a successful
military career culminating in his command of the forces in Scotland in
1782. He was also Member for Aberdeenshire and then Kincardineshire
over a period of thirty-four years.

397 *The Riot Act was read*: the Riot Act of 1714 (1 Geo. I, c. 5. s. 2) made it a
capital offence for a rioting crowd of people (twelve or more) to remain in
the area within one hour of being read the relevant statutory proclama-
tion by a magistrate or JP. See Tony Hayter, *The Army and the Crowd in
Mid-Georgian England* (London: Macmillan, 1978) for a discussion of the
problems faced by the magistrates and the soldiers.

401 *the petition is rejected by a hundred and ninety-two, to six*: according to John
Aikin's *Annals of George III* (1816), 261: 'Lord G. Gordon having
brought up the petition, moved to have it taken into immediate considera-
tion . . . His motion was negatived by 192 votes to 6.' For the wording of
the petition and the identification of Gordon's supporters, see *Parlia-
mentary History of England*, 21 (1780–1), 654.

402 *Duke Street Lincoln's-Inn Fields, and in Warwick Street Golden Square*: the
site of the Sardinian and Bavarian chapels respectively. The Sardinian
chapel of St Anselm and St Cecilia, built in 1648, was reached through
the house of the Ambassador. The Bavarian chapel (formerly the Portu-
guese chapel) backed on to the house of the Portuguese Ambassador.
English Catholics attended these chapels.

403 *Holborn*: a major thoroughfare through and into central London along
which Gashford certainly would have travelled many times.

405 *uses of the block, the rack, the gibbet, and the stake, in cruel Mary's reign*:
instruments of torture and execution for heretics used during the Tudor
period. See note on p. 280. A new edition of Foxe's *Book of Martyrs* was
published in 1776 giving full details of the modes of punishment used.

406 *basilisk*: a mythical reptile; 'ancient authors stated that its hissing drove
away all other serpents, and that its breath, and even its look, was fatal'
(*OED*)

408 *Tower Stairs, and away by the Gravesend tide-boat*: Tower Stairs was a
landing place for boats, below Tower Hill. One could probably catch the
boat to Gravesend.

409 *read as follows*: this wording comes from an actual document granting
safety to a Richard Pond, signed by Lord George on 7 June. See de
Castro, *Gordon Riots*, 118 for the wording of the historical document
produced at the treason trial of Lord George.

418 *Moorfields*: an area on the northern edges of the City of London, close to

Bedlam, it was one of the poorest districts of London near the slums of St Giles. A colony of Irish and Catholic weavers had lodgings and employment there. See C. Hibbert, *King Mob: The Story of Lord George Gordon and the London Riots of 1780* (New York: World Publishing, 1958), 86, on the employment in the silk business by a Mr. Malo of his co-religionists at cheaper rates—a dual reason for the hostility of the mob.

a rich chapel: this was in Ropemakers' Alley, Moorfields. See note to p. 487. Hablot K. Browne ('Phiz'), in his illustration 'The rendezvous of the mob' (Illus. 49) has reinforced the suggestion of a mindless mob as the rioters plunder the chapel of vestments and statues. They swirl into a vortex.

421 *King's evidence*: when an accomplice in crime offers himself as a witness for the prosecution against the others implicated, usually in return for a lighter sentence.

437 *winding-sheets*: a mass of solidified drippings on a candle (*OED*). As they resembled the creased cloth that wrapped a corpse before burial, they were widely regarded as omens of death.

445 *Clare Market*: a food market located immediately to the south of Lincoln's Inn Fields. A report by Lieutenant Fanshawe, 1st Guards, refers to the routing of a mob here on 5 June.

458 *the solemn league*: the Scots agreed a Solemn League and Covenant in 1643 with the Parliamentarians. The Scots provided military aid against King Charles I in return for the recognition of Presbyterianism as the religion of Scotland.

464 *what's the officer to do?*: following the legal opinion of the Attorney-General in 1732, it was believed that troops could act against a mob only under the direction of the Civil Authority. Since some magistrates were refusing to read the Riot Act (see note to p. 397), the officers felt unable to act as happened at the destruction of the chapel in Moorfields. See note to p. 418.

Sir John Fielding: reformer of the police and the magistracy and blind from birth, he succeeded his half-brother, Henry Fielding, as presiding magistrate at the Magistrates' Court, Bow Street (1754–80). The Court had been established in 1740. Apart from pioneering the use of paid police (the Bow Street thief-takers; see note to p. 489), he also introduced the keeping of records on criminals and their past crimes. He died later in 1780.

482 *hot purl*: 'a mixture of hot beer with gin . . . sometimes also with ginger and sugar' (*OED*).

485 *scapegrace*: a scamp, or a man of reckless habits (*OED*).

486 *Mile-end*: a largely industrial area on the north-eastern approach to central London, at this time populated by many poorer artisans and immigrants.

486 *the Mansion House*: from 1752 this was the official residence of the Lord Mayor of London. Located close to the Bank of England between Poultry and Cornhill, its windows were broken during the Gordon Riots.

487 *The Lord Mayor*: the incumbent at the time of the riots was Alderman Brackley Kennett. By this time he was a wine and spirit merchant, but he had worked his way up from waiting in a brothel to owning one himself. Apart from refusing to act when the chapel in Moorfields was attacked (see note to p. 418 above), he and his City Council agreed on the fifth day of the riots (7 June) to petition Parliament for the repeal of the Catholic Relief Act. The Privy Council questioned him when the Riots were over and found he had acted with 'great timidity in the whole affair'. He was found guilty of criminal negligence and fined £1,000.

488 *There are great people at the bottom of these riots*: Kennett in fact said this on 3 June to a silk-merchant called Malo from Moorfields who came to warn of the proposed attack on the chapel in Ropemakers' Alley. Malo's business was nearby, employing 1,000 on 200 looms. He repeatedly asked the Lord Mayor for protection. See also note to p. 418.

javelin-man: a sheriff's man who carries pikes and spears (*OED*).

489 *Langdale*: Thomas Langdale (1714–90) was a vintner and distiller from Holborn Hill. He had a large stock of spirits. The distillery was actually burnt on 7 June along with his other houses on Holborn Hill. The fire destroyed eight houses back from the Holborn frontage. An estimated 120,000 gallons worth £38,000 were lost and rioters probably died there from alcohol poisoning.

a body of thief-takers: the precursors of the Bow Street Runners and the later Metropolitan Police, this was a mobile group of paid men set up by the Fielding brothers. John Fielding published his *Plan for preventing robberies within twenty miles of London with an account of the rise and establishment of thieftakers* in 1755 to spread his idea to other parts of metropolitan London but it took until 1829 for his plan to come to fruition. See also note to p. 393.

Newgate, then a new building: rebuilt 1770–80 to a design by architect George Dance only to be destroyed again in the riots. Dickens took a life-long interest in prisons and visited them whenever he could (both in Britain and abroad). For details, see Collins, *Dickens and Crime*, chs. I–VII. He first visited Newgate in 1835 for an article entitled 'A Visit to Newgate' published in *Sketches by Boz* (1836). He went again in 1837. For a history of Newgate, see Anthony Babington, *The English Bastille: A History of Newgate Gaol and Prison Conditions in Britain 1188–1902* (London: Macdonald and Co., 1971).

490 *another bead in the long rosary of his regrets*: a Catholic allusion. A rosary is a Catholic devotion in which a set of rosary beads is used to count the specified number of prayers.

499 *commander-in-chief*: this was Jeffrey Amherst (1717–97), later 1st Baron Amherst. He had been in command of the 1758 expedition to North

America. Following the surrender of Montreal, he became Governor-General of British North America. He held the position of Commander-in-Chief of the forces from 1778 to 1782. Normally the Secretary at War dealt with the deployment of troops in riots, but the scale of the Gordon Riots prompted the Privy Council to transfer this power to Amherst on the night of 7 June.

500 *even the Jews in Houndsditch, Whitechapel, and those quarters*: the poorer Jewish population of London was concentrated around Whitechapel, Houndsditch, Petticoat Lane and Mile End.

501 *tow smeared with pitch, and tar, and brimstone*: tar and brimstone both possess inflammable qualities. Pitch is a dark-coloured resinous substance, a by-product of the boiling or distillation of tar. Tow is a rope, sometimes specifically used to refer to a hangman's rope.

503 *lath and plasture*: a lath is a thin narrow strip of wood, which forms the groundwork for a coat of plaster, or plasture, in a building's structure. Also rhyming slang for master (*OED*).

to prenounce the Pope of Babylon: Miggs cannot bring herself to utter 'whore' of Babylon, instead indirectly alluding in this way to Revelation 17.

508 *Mr Akerman*: the Keeper of Newgate from 1754 to his death in 1792, he had a good reputation as an humane man who even contributed to the relief of poor prisoners. See Babington, *English Bastille*, 119–20. He refused the demands of the crowd to release rioters committed from Bow Street.

512 *church clock of St Sepulchre's*: between Snow Hill and Giltspur Street, near Newgate.

523 *Sessions House*: this was the Old Bailey Sessions House, next to Newgate.

526 *Secretary of State*: the incumbent was David Murray (1727–96), 7th Viscount Stormont, nephew of Lord Mansfield (whom he succeeded as 2nd Earl) who held this office from 1779 to 1782. He had been 'bepelted with mud' on his way into parliament on 2 June when the Petition was being presented. That evening, he had asked the Bow Street and Lichfield Street magistrates to take every legal method to keep the peace and to guard the houses of foreign ministers. He wrote to the Secretary of War for troops (but he was away). By 6 June he had urgently requested the Commander-in-Chief to bring in Light Horse to supplement the Horse Guards. He admitted later that he had misinterpreted the law about the Riot Act and the relationship of the military to the civil authority. See Hayter, *The Army and the Crowd*, 47–8, on the responsibilities of a Secretary of State and a Secretary of War during riots.

myrmidons of justice: a term usually applied contemptuously to inferior administrative officers of the law. The word 'myrmidon' derives from the name of the warlike Thessalian people who went with Achilles to Troy.

529 *Lord Mansfield's house in Bloomsbury square*: William Murray (1705–93),

1st Earl of Mansfield, was Chief Justice between 1756 and 1788. Although nearly 300 soldiers were in the square, no magistrate could be found at first until Mr. Burden (Lichfield Street) arrived and read the Riot Act. When the crowd began destroying the contents of the house, he ordered Col. Woodford to fire. One motive for the attack could have been Mansfield's reputation as a judge. He showed so little mercy that the spikes on the wall of King's Bench prison were known as 'Mansfield's teeth'. It is possible that among his 200 notebooks destroyed by the fire were items to be introduced into court. See Peter Linebaugh, *The London Hanged: Crime and Civil Society in the Eighteenth Century* (Cambridge: Cambridge University Press, 1992), 360 for statistics on his conviction rates. He had also recently questioned the motives of Paine, the informer (see note to p. 390, *London Bridge*) at a trial of a priest who faced a life sentence under the Penal Laws (11 and 12 William III, c. 4). All these reasons contributed to his house becoming a target on the night of 6/7 June.

530 *Lord Mansfield's country seat at Caen Wood*: the rioters were prevented from destroying Lord Mansfield's country house, Kenwood (between Highgate and Hampstead), by a group of Dragoons and Horse Grenadiers who were sent by Lord Amherst, the Commander-in-Chief, at Lord Stormont's request.

including those of Sir John Fielding and two other justices: for Fielding, see the note to p. 464. The burning of his house in Bow Street near Covent Garden was described by Susan Burney. See de Castro, *Gordon Riots*, 84. One of the others was Justice Hyde. Earlier on 6 June, he had read the Riot Act in Palace Yard and then ordered the Horse to ride into the crowd to disperse it. Hibbert in *King Mob* describes Hyde as riding on a white horse up and down the lines of the soldiers. As a punishment the mob went to his house in St Martin's Street, Leicester Square.

532 *New Jail at Clerkenwell*: the New Jail or Prison at Clerkenwell had been built to house the overflow of prisoners from Newgate, and was located immediately to the south of another prison, the Clerkenwell Bridewell. Neither the New Prison nor the Clerkenwell Bridewell were destroyed in the riots. The Bridewell's gates had been forced open, rather than fired. The prisoners in the New Prison were released during the attacks on the building in order to avert its destruction.

all enacted before midnight: in fact, the rioting in Bloomsbury Square occurred in the early hours after midnight

533 *Lord President's in Piccadilly . . . at the Lord Chancellor's in Great Ormond Street*: the Lord President (of the Privy Council) at the time was Henry Bathurst (1714–94), 2nd Earl Bathurst. He had been de-wigged on his way to Parliament on 2 June. The Lord Chancellor was Edward Thurlow (1731–1806), 1st Baron Thurlow. His brother, the Bishop of Lincoln, had had his carriage wheels wrenched off and his throat seized on the way to Parliament on 2 June. Thurlow himself had supported Savile's Catholic Relief Act. Lambeth Palace was the residence of the Archbishop of

Canterbury, the most senior of the bishops of England. The incumbent at the time was Frederick Cornwallis (1713–83), identical twin brother of General Cornwallis. His palace was surrounded by over 500 rioters crying 'No Popery' but a large military presence prevented an attack. All three offices were very important within the Establishment as indicated in an Act dating from Tudor times (31 Hen.VIII, c. 10 'For Placing of Lords' added as an Appendix to the Standing Orders of the House of Lords, 9 February 1825). An attack on these office-bearers could be seen as an attack on the government itself.

the Royal Exchange . . . the Guildhall: the Royal Exchange served as a meeting place for merchants, and was located between Cornhill and Threadneedle Street, near the Bank of England and the Mansion House. The Guildhall was the administrative centre of the City of London.

Militia: under the 1757 Militia Act, county-based forces could be raised by ballot in emergencies, under the command of the lord-lieutenant of a county who was responsible to the Home Secretary. The militias were able to assist so quickly since they had been 'embodied' for the American War emergency in March 1778.

Inns of Court . . . Westminster Hall . . . Palace-yard . . . New-River Head: for Westminster Hall and Palace Yard see note to p. 342; for New River Head see note to p. 40; for Inns of Court, see note on the Temple, p. 125.

the Poultry, and on Cornhill: main thoroughfares close to the Royal Exchange, the Bank and the Mansion House. The Poultry is a continuation of Cheapside.

Lord Rockingham's in Grosvenor Square: Charles Watson-Wentworth (1730–82), 2nd Marquis of Rockingham, had spoken in support of the Catholic Relief Bill during the Lords' debate on 25 May 1778.

King's Bench and Fleet Prisons: the King's Bench was a debtors' prison on Newington Causeway, south of the Thames and close to St George's Fields. The Fleet was also a debtors' prison, located on the Fleet Ditch. These prisons were burnt on 7 June. For a description of life in the former prison, see Joanna Innes, 'The King's Bench Prison in the Late Eighteenth Century', in Brewer and Styles (eds.), *An Ungovernable People*, 250–98.

534 *the Mint, the Arsenal at Woolwich*: the Royal Mint in this period was located within the Tower of London. The Arsenal developed at the Woolwich Warren from 1671 (it became Royal Woolwich in 1805). Amherst, the Commander-in-Chief, was understandably concerned about the security of its store of powder and arms. General Belford, the Commandant at Woolwich, assuring Amherst of his defence plans, became so stressed that he burst a blood vessel, and died on 1 July 1780.

535 *privy council*: a council of advisers to the Monarch, existing since Tudor times. At a meeting of the Council on 7 June, Alexander Wedderburn (1733–1805), Attorney-General since 1778, advised the King that he believed that the military had the power to disperse rioters without

needing to wait for the reading of the Riot Act. The wording of the consequent order from Lord Amherst to all military officers in London to act on their own initiative can be found in Hibbert, *King Mob*, 130.

535 *The city authorities . . . held a common council*: the City of London was administered by the Lord Mayor and aldermen who met in the Court of Common Council (held in Guildhall). Just before they received Lord Amherst's order, they had passed unanimously a resolution to petition parliament for a repeal of the Catholic Relief Bill. See also note on aldermen at p. 76 and note on police at p. 393.

the queen's palace: located in St James' Park, this palace was bought by George III for Queen Charlotte in 1762. On 6 June there had been a determined effort to get through the Park, but the officer of the Guards said he would fire even without an order from a magistrate.

536 *In Lincoln's Inn . . . the Northumberland militia*: on 7 June this particular militia had been ordered by Lord Amherst into London as one of seven militias and 2.5 regular regiments of foot and 4 of cavalry to supplement the Horse and Foot Guards. A return of 8 June estimated there were 500 Northumberland Militia at Lincoln's Inn Fields. See Hayter, *The Army and the Crowd*, 151–2, for a list of the troops deployed. The contemporary concern about the use of the militia for civil control is discussed by Conway, *British Isles*, 158.

Lord Algernon Percy: second son of Hugh Smithson Percy, Duke of Northumberland. After arriving too late to defend Langdale's distillery, Percy had marched his Militia to protect the Bank of England, which was attacked just before midnight on 7 June. His technique of twice ordering his men to present arms at the mob without firing was praised at the time for its restraint as well as its effectiveness.

the burgesses . . . halls of the different companies: burgesses or citizens of the borough, often merchants and craftsmen, belonged to occupational associations that from the time of the medieval guilds had their own halls as meeting-places.

Borough Clink in Tooley-street: this was the Episcopal prison, near Bankside, fired by the mob on 7 June after they attacked the Fleet prison.

the New Bridewell: a bridewell was a house of correction for prisoners, a place of forced labour (*OED*). The New Bridewell is not to be confused with the Bridewell at Clerkenwell on the other side of the river (see p. 532). This was the Surrey Bridewell, near St George's Fields, south of the river. Lord Amherst had sent warning on 7 June that it and the King's Bench were going to be burnt.

537 *St. Mildred's church*: nearly opposite the Mansion House, it was located on the Poultry, to be distinguished from St Mildred's church on Bread Street. It was rebuilt by Christopher Wren after the Great Fire between 1670 and 1676 and was demolished in 1872.

Holborn Bridge: at the foot of Holborn Hill; it crossed the Fleet River.

a charmed life: *Macbeth*, V. vii.

Toll-houses on Blackfriars Bridge: a toll of a halfpenny charged for each crossing was a great source of grievance for the very poor. On 7 June flames were carried from the Fleet prison to the houses of the toll-gatherers. The houses burnt well, being built mainly of wood. Large stocks of halfpennies were collected by the mob as the houses burnt. Many were killed there when the troops opened fire.

554 *tipstaff, or a bailiff's follower*: an official, often attached to a bailiff, who carried a tipped staff (*OED*).

560 *bradawl or gimlet*: a kind of small boring tool (*OED*).

564 *St. James's Square*: the square originally had a central pool of water when it was laid out in 1727. This is quite clear on contemporary maps.

568 *potter's vessel*: Miggs alludes to Psalm 2: 9: 'Thou shalt break them with a rod of iron; thou shalt dash them in pieces like a potter's vessel.' Also, to Isaiah 30: 14: 'And he shall break it as the breaking of the potter's vessel that is broken in pieces.' See also Jeremiah 19: 11.

whitening and suppulchres: Miggs again jumbles her biblical verses. Matthew 23: 27: 'Woe unto you, scribes and Pharisees, hypocrites! for ye are like unto whited sepulchres which indeed appear beautiful outward, but are within full of dead men's bones, and of all uncleanness.'

569 *pomatums*: scented ointment used for the skin of the head and for dressing the hair (*OED*).

577 *defence of the Savannah*: during the American War, Savannah, Georgia, was held by British troops. It was besieged by French and American troops in 1779. When an assault on 9 October was unsuccessful, the siege was abandoned. This is the only reference in the novel to the war—its cost and lack of success contributing to the unrest.

580 *Upwards of two hundred had been shot dead*: George Rudé, in 'The Gordon Riots: A Study of the Rioters and their Victims' in his *Paris and London in the Eighteenth Century: Studies in Popular Protest* (New York: Viking Press, 1970), 275, says 210 were killed outright by the troops firing into the crowd. A further 75 died in hospital from their wounds and another 173 were treated. However, Hibbert in his *King Mob*, 179 n. believes that the Government figures of 285 are an underestimate. He estimates the number as not less than 850.

581 *Seventy-two private houses and four strong jails*: Rudé lists 58 private houses in six parishes of the metropolis ('The Gordon Riots', 285). See also Hayter's list of embassies, institutions, businesses, and private houses attacked or threatened sufficiently to request troops (*The Army and the Crowd*, 160–1).

exceeded one hundred and twenty-five thousand pounds: on 6 June, one of four resolutions passed by the House of Commons, was that compensation should be paid. Eighty-one people were paid compensation for the damage done to private property in the City of London and the County

of Middlesex, totalling £63,269, 6s. 1d. Damage to public buildings was
assessed at over £30,000. See Rudé, 'The Gordon Riots', 276.

581   *Mr. Herbert*: Henry Herbert (1741–1811), later 1st Earl of Carnarvon.
According to the *Parliamentary History of England*, 21 (1779–80), 6 June,
col. 663, Herbert threatened to cross the House and take the blue cockade
off Lord George's clothing.

Monday se'ennight: the House of Commons resolved to adjourn on
Thursday, 8 June until the following Monday week (19 June); that is,
seven nights from the following Monday.

589   *on a charge of High Treason*: following the cabinet meeting of 9 June, a
warrant was issued for the arrest of Lord George on the charge of trea-
son. After questioning by Privy Councillors at the War Office, Gordon
was escorted to the Tower under heavy guard. He was tried at the court
of King's Bench on 5 February 1781, but was acquitted.

590   *round-house*: a lock-up or place of detention for arrested persons (*OED*).

594   *there's all the chances of the law*: 135 rioters were arraigned of whom 59
were convicted and given capital sentences but only 21 of these actually
hanged. This rate of executions to capital sentences was normal. See, for
example, the figures for 1776–82 in Surrey given in Beattie, *Crime and the
Courts in England*, 502–3. Only some were actually hanged 'to make
public examples'. The choice suggested by Sir John Fielding should fall
on 'the most abandoned, dangerous, and incorrigible offenders.' Dennis
had reason to feel hopeful he would be lucky in this lottery because a
former hangman, Thomas Turlis, convicted for stealing coal, was
reprieved in order to hang those sentenced during a coal strike in 1768.
Dennis appeared at the Old Bailey on 3 July.

599   *Surgeons' Hall*: the Murder Act of 1752 (25 Geo II, c. 37) aimed to add
'further Terror and peculiar Mark of Infamy' to the punishment by death
for committing this crime. This was achieved by holding the execution
within two days of conviction and by having the body dissected and
anatomized by the Surgeons in their hall at Old Bailey around the corner
from Newgate. This also met the growing need for bodies to dissect in
anatomy classes for the progress of medicine. The dissection was held in
public and became notorious for its encouragement of morbid, voyeur-
istic excitements. The delivery of the body from Tyburn also became the
focus for riot and public disorder as friends and family attempted to
prevent this final indignity. The practice continued until 1832. See
Gatrell, *The Hanging Tree*, 255–6 and Linebaugh, 'The Tyburn Riot'.

615   *Two rioters were to die before the prison . . . and one directly afterwards in
Bloomsbury Square*: to make an example of the convicted rioters, the King
in Council ordered their executions to be as near as possible to the loca-
tions of their crimes. For example, Bloomsbury Square was chosen as it
was the scene of the destruction of the house of the Chief Justice, Lord
Mansfield. For a list of places of execution for eleven of the twenty-five
hanged, see Gatrell, *The Hanging Tree*, 31–2.

623 *Two cripples . . . hanged in this same Bloomsbury Square*: the case of *Royce* (1767) had extended the death penalty under the Riot Act (1714) to include those present at a riot and shouting encouragement to those pulling down buildings. They were considered principals in the second degree, aiding and abetting the rioters. Linebaugh names *three* people who were hanged at Bloomsbury Square (on 22 June 1780)—Charles Kent, Laetitia Holland and John Gray—in his *The London Hanged*, 364.

Bishopsgate Street: this street runs north from Cornhill. Gatrell (*The Hanging Tree*, 31) names the felon as William Brown who was hanged there on Tuesday, 11 July as near as possible to the house of Charles Daking.

624 *coming on the parish*: Willet is alive to the stigma associated with being a pauper and either being sent to the Workhouse or being dependent on outdoor relief. See note to p. 375.

635 *the young Prince of Wales*: Prince George, b. 1762, later Prince Regent and then George IV (1820–30)

644 *caught a Tartar*: became burdened with a person who cannot be controlled.

655 *excommunicated by the Archbishop of Canterbury . . . when cited for that purpose*: John Moore (1730–1805) was Archbishop of Canterbury from 1783. Thus he was the most important cleric in the Church of England. He had the power to summon citizens to the Ecclesiastical Court and was able to excommunicate (expel) people from the Church. Lord George was excommunicated in May 1786 at a ceremony at the church of St Mary La Bonne. It should be noted that Lord George was not an Anglican but a Presbyterian until he converted to Judaism (see note below). He had refused to accept the competency of the Ecclesiastical Court to deal with the deceased estate of a dissenting minister; he believed it should be dealt with by a civil magistrate so he had refused to turn up.

Being indicted for the libel: Lord George was sued for libel in 1787 when he published allegations about Marie Antoinette, Queen of France. This was one of two libel cases against him at the time. See Iain McCalman, 'Mad Lord George and Madame la Motte', *Journal of British Studies*, 35 (July 1996), 363 ff.

a public profession of the Jewish religion: Lord George converted to Judaism in 1787 making him the butt of satirists, but his strand of Scottish Presbyterianism identified strongly with the sufferings of the people of Israel and the apocalyptic coming of the new Jerusalem.

future good behaviour: on 8 January 1788 he was sentenced to three years in Newgate for the Botany Bay libel to be followed by two further years for the libel on the Queen of France. On his release he was to pay a fine of £500 and find securities for his own good behaviour for fourteen more years. He was to pledge £10,000 on his own security and find two people to offer securities of £2,500 each. He died in prison, singing the 'Ça ira' (according to *DNB*).

655 *English minister*: in current terminology this means the Home Secretary, responsible for domestic justice and the prison system. William Wydham Grenville (1759–1834), later 1st Baron Grenville, was Secretary of State for the Home Department from 1789 to 1791 at the time of Lord George's petition to the French Assembly.